HOUGHTON MIFFLIN

SOCIAL STUDIES

Bringing the World to Your Classroom!

Our easy-to-use program is sure to make history with a whole new way to teach, learn, and explore social studies!

HOUGHTON MIFFLIN

Designed for the Way You Want to Teach Social Studies

Whether you're teaching just the **Core Lesson** for complete content coverage or adding more with a dynamic **Extend Lesson**, your students are sure to gain a thorough understanding of the content.

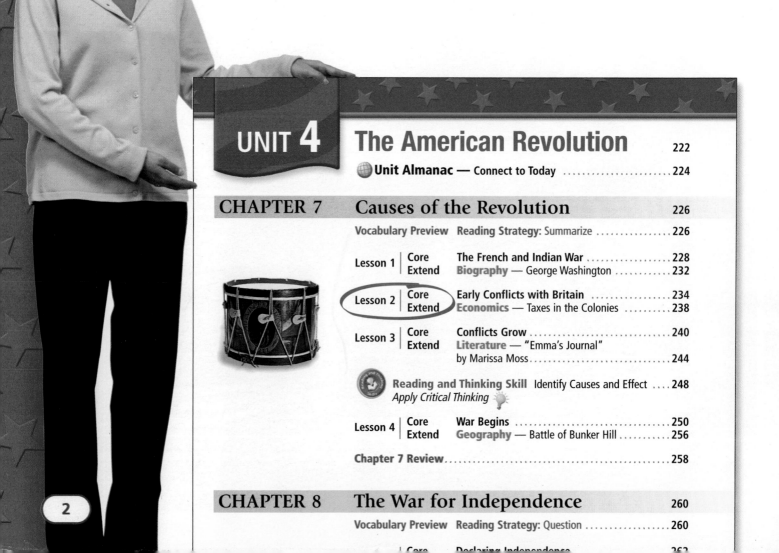

Begin with the Core

Teach critical social studies concepts and topics to meet your state standards. Helpful reading skills and strategies make the text easily accessible for students.

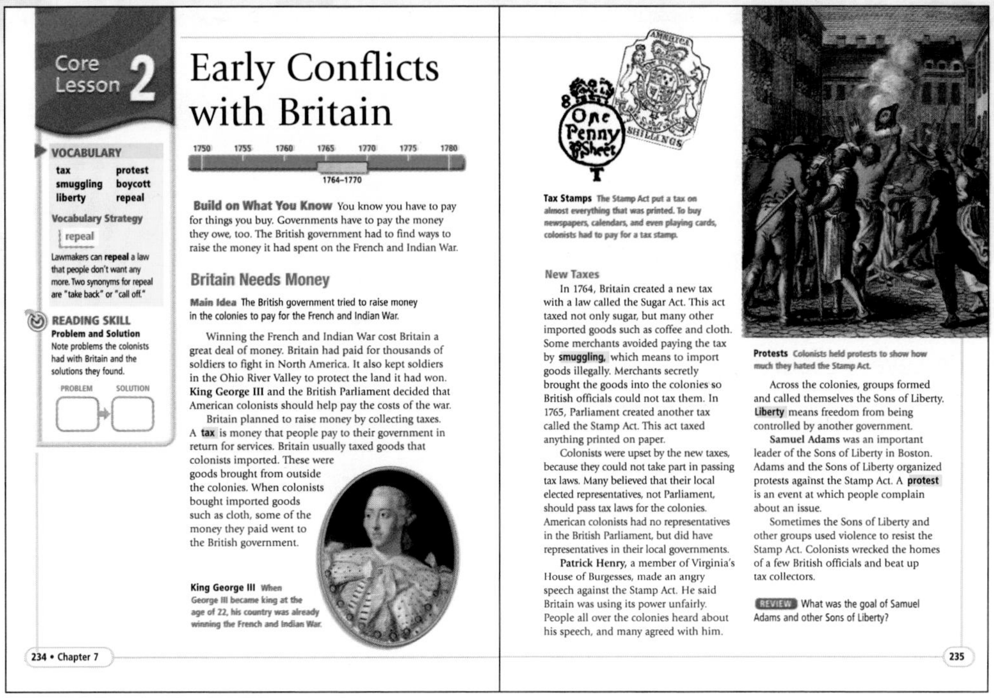

Core Lesson 2

Early Conflicts with Britain

1750 1755 1760 1765 1770 1775 1780

1764–1770

VOCABULARY

tax, protest, smuggling, boycott, liberty, repeal

Vocabulary Strategy

repeal

Lawmakers can **repeal** a law that people don't want any more. Two synonyms for repeal are "take back" or "call off."

READING SKILL

Problem and Solution

Note problems the colonists had with Britain and the solutions they found.

PROBLEM → SOLUTION

Build on What You Know You know you have to pay for things you buy. Governments have to pay the money they owe, too. The British government had to find ways to raise the money it had spent on the French and Indian War.

Britain Needs Money

Main Idea The British government tried to raise money in the colonies to pay for the French and Indian War.

Winning the French and Indian War cost Britain a great deal of money. Britain had paid for thousands of soldiers to fight in North America. It also kept soldiers in the Ohio River Valley to protect the land it had won. **King George III** and the British Parliament decided that American colonists should help pay the costs of the war.

Britain planned to raise money by collecting taxes. A **tax** is money that people pay to their government in return for services. Britain usually taxed goods that colonists imported. These were goods brought from outside the colonies. When colonists bought imported goods such as cloth, some of the money they paid went to the British government.

King George III When George III became king at the age of 22, his country was already winning the French and Indian War.

Tax Stamps The Stamp Act put a tax on almost everything that was printed. To buy newspapers, calendars, and even playing cards, colonists had to pay for a tax stamp.

New Taxes

In 1764, Britain created a new tax with a law called the Sugar Act. This act taxed not only sugar, but many other imported goods such as coffee and cloth. Some merchants avoided paying the tax by **smuggling**, which means to import goods illegally. Merchants secretly brought the goods into the colonies so British officials could not tax them. In 1765, Parliament created another tax called the Stamp Act. This act taxed anything printed on paper.

Colonists were upset by the new taxes, because they could not take part in passing tax laws. Many believed that their local elected representatives, not Parliament, should pass tax laws for the colonies. American colonists had no representatives in the British Parliament, but did have representatives in their local governments.

Patrick Henry, a member of Virginia's House of Burgesses, made an angry speech against the Stamp Act. He said Britain was using its power unfairly. People all over the colonies heard about his speech, and many agreed with him.

Protests Colonists held protests to show how much they hated the Stamp Act.

Across the colonies, groups formed and called themselves the Sons of Liberty. **Liberty** means freedom from being controlled by another government.

Samuel Adams was an important leader of the Sons of Liberty in Boston. Adams and the Sons of Liberty organized protests against the Stamp Act. A **protest** is an event at which people complain about an issue.

Sometimes the Sons of Liberty and other groups used violence to resist the Stamp Act. Colonists wrecked the homes of a few British officials and beat up tax collectors.

REVIEW What was the goal of Samuel Adams and other Sons of Liberty?

234 • Chapter 7

235

Extend for More

Meet your students' diverse learning needs with motivating Extend Lessons that emphasize Core Lesson concepts in a different way, including

- Biography
- Citizenship
- Economics
- Geography
- History
- Literature
- Primary Source
- Readers' Theater

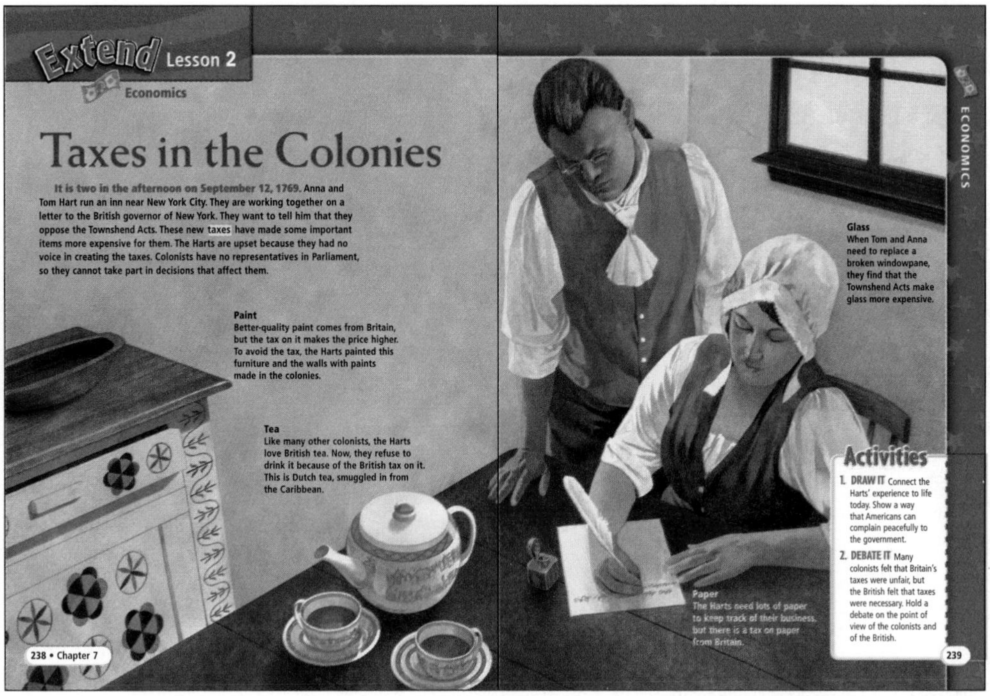

Extend Lesson 2

Economics

Taxes in the Colonies

It is two in the afternoon on September 12, 1769. Anna and Tom Hart run an inn near New York City. They are working together on a letter to the British governor of New York. They want to tell him that they oppose the Townshend Acts. These new taxes have made some important items more expensive for them. The Harts are upset because they had no voice in creating the taxes. Colonists have no representatives in Parliament, so they cannot take part in decisions that affect them.

Paint
Better-quality paint comes from Britain, but the tax on it makes the price higher. To avoid the tax, the Harts painted this furniture and the walls with paints made in the colonies.

Tea
Like many other colonists, the Harts love British tea. Now, they refuse to drink it because of the British tax on it. This is Dutch tea, smuggled in from the Caribbean.

Glass
When Tom and Anna need to replace a broken windowpane, they find that the Townshend Acts make glass more expensive.

Paper
The Harts need lots of paper to keep track of their business, but there is a tax on paper from Britain.

ECONOMICS

Activities

1. **DRAW IT** Connect the Harts' experience to life today. Show a way that Americans can complain peacefully to the government.
2. **DEBATE IT** Many colonists felt that Britain's taxes were unfair, but the British felt that taxes were necessary. Hold a debate on the point of view of the colonists and of the British.

238 • Chapter 7

239

Teaching Is Manageable with Our Complete Teaching Tools

Teacher's Resource Kit

With support for teaching, this rich collection of resources saves valuable time. It includes:

- Unit Resources
- Grade-Level Resources
- Assessment Options
- Resources for Reaching All Learners
- Bringing Social Studies Alive
- Primary Source Plus
- Research and Writing Projects
- Skillbuilder Transparencies
- Unit Big Idea/Key Concepts Transparencies
- Audio Student Book with Primary Sources and Songs MP3 CD

Teacher's Resource Kit

Primary Source Plus

Resources for Reaching All Learners

Bringing Social Studies Alive

Multimedia Solutions

A variety of technology tools support students in their learning and help teachers with planning:

- Unit Videos
- eSocial Studies Book
- Lesson Planner and Teacher Resource CD-ROM
- Test Generator CD-ROM
- eTeacher's Edition
- Education Place® featuring *Weekly Reader*®

Plus, our comprehensive **Teacher's Edition** and unique **Student Book** format ensure success.

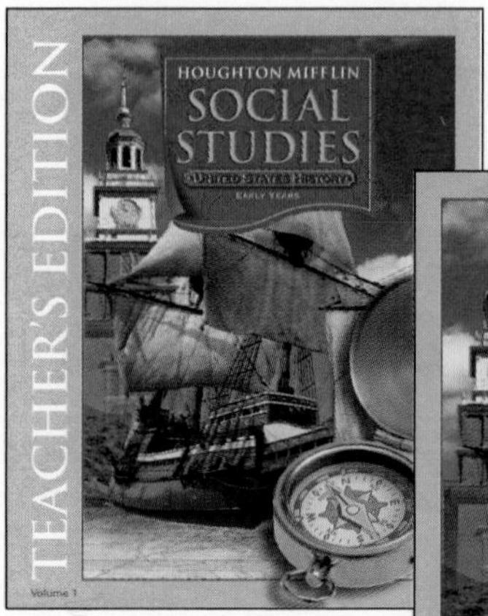

Teacher's Edition

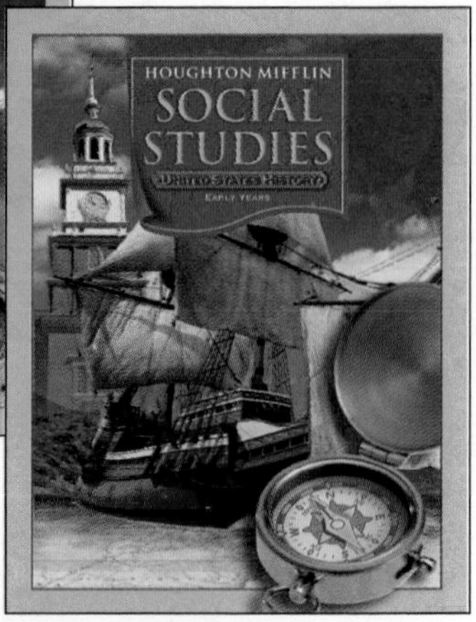

Student Book

For a complete list of the program components, see page 8.

Reaching All Learners with Compelling Leveled Nonfiction

Social Studies Independent Books

With three books for each unit plus accompanying teaching plans in the Teacher's Edition, these leveled books:

- Support unit content
- Reinforce vocabulary and reading skills
- Meet the needs of diverse learners

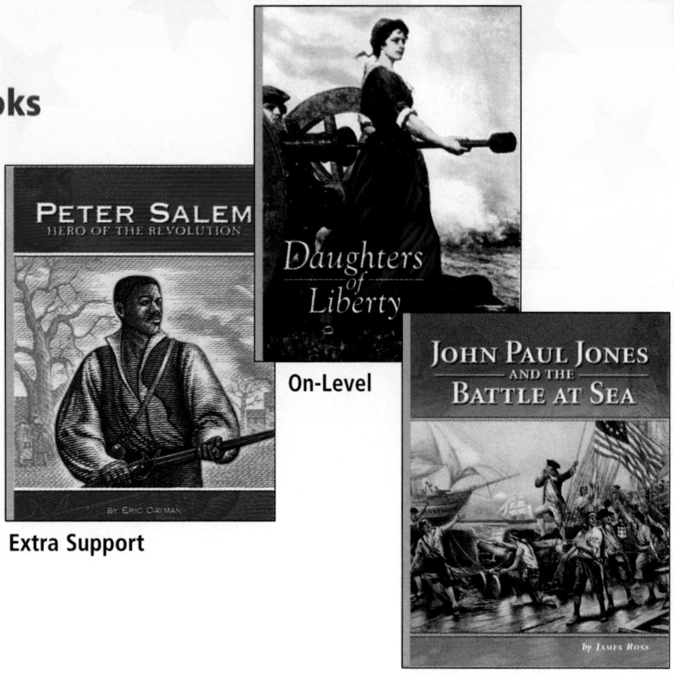

Extra Support
On-Level
Challenge

Social Studies Leveled Readers

Brand new for our program and developed with consulting author **Irene C. Fountas**, these leveled readers add flexibility to your curriculum while helping you to meet state standards. With an accompanying Teacher's Guide, the text on audio CDs, plus activity cards. These readers can be used:

- As a supplement to your basal social studies program
- As the main materials in your social studies program
- As an extension to your daily reading instruction

Putting Powerful Experience to Work for You and Your Students

FOCUS ON HISTORY
Herman Viola, Lead Author
Curator Emeritus
The Smithsonian Institution

"As the son of Italian immigrants, I got to tell my parents the stories about American history that I was learning in school. I've never stopped telling these stories."

FOCUS ON GEOGRAPHY
Sarah Bednarz
Associate Professor of Geography
Texas A&M University

"Maps, of course they're important, but geography is so much more than maps."

FOCUS ON WORLD AND CULTURAL STUDIES
Carlos Cortés
Professor Emeritus of History
University of California at Riverside

"Recognizing that not all people share the same personal experiences or perspectives is a necessary early step toward intercultural understanding."

FOCUS ON ECONOMICS AND TEACHER EDUCATION
Cheryl Jennings
Project Director
Florida Institute of Education
University of North Florida at Jacksonville

"Watching children's thinking develop as they take part in an economic simulation makes it clear that the experience is much more than a game."

FOCUS ON ECONOMICS
Mark Schug
Professor and Director of the
Center for Economic Education
University of Wisconsin at Milwaukee

"If you think economics is too hard for elementary students, you should see the third graders at Kilbourn Elementary School."

FOCUS ON CIVICS
Charles White
Associate Professor
Boston University School of Education

"Nothing makes you appreciate our democracy more than teaching civics to children of the former Soviet Union."

Program Consultants
MaryEllen Vogt, Codirector of the Center for the Advancement of Reading, California State University

Dolores Beltran, Assistant Professor, Charter College of Education, California State University at Los Angeles

Teacher Reviewers for Grade 5
Skip Bayliss
Surfside Elementary
Satellite Beach, Florida

Annette Bomba
Schenevus Central School
Schenevus, New York

Amy Clark
Gateway Elementary
Travelers Rest, South Carolina

Melissa Cook
Machado Elementary
Lake Elsinore, California

Kelli Dunn
Lindop School
Broadview, Illinois

Peggy Greene
Upson-Lee North Elementary
Thomaston, Georgia

Elyce Kaplan
Kumeyaay Elementary
San Diego, California

Julia McNeal
Webster Elementary
Dayton, Ohio

Theresa Powell
Harbor View School
Charleston, South Carolina

Lesa Roberts
Hampton Cove
Middle School
Huntsville, Alabama

Lynn Schew
Leila G. Davis Elementary
Clearwater, Florida

Linda Whitford
Manning Oaks Elementary
Alpharetta, Georgia

Lisa Yingling
Round Hills Elementary
Williamsport, Pennsylvania

Program Components

Components Chart	PRE K	K	1	2	3	4	5	6
Student Book			●	●	●	●	●	●
Big Books	●	●	●	●				
The Holidays Book		●						
Teacher's Edition	●	●	●	●	●	●	●	●
Social Studies Independent Books 5 copies of		●	●	●	●	●	●	●
Social Studies Leveled Readers		●	●	●	●	●	●	●
Let's Read Biographies			●	●				
Practice Book (Consumable)		●	●	●	●	●	●	●
Unit Resources and TAE* (Blackline Masters) blue folder								
Vocabulary and Study Guide		●	●	●	●	●	●	●
Reading Skills and Strategies		●	●	●	●	●	●	●
Skillbuilder		●	●	●	●	●	●	●
Almanac Map Practice					●	●	●	●
Almanac Graph Practice					●	●	●	●
Grade-Level Resources red folder								
Family Newsletter		●	●	●	●	●	●	●
Outline Maps		●	●	●	●	●	●	●
Generic Graphic Organizers		●	●	●	●	●	●	●
Vocabulary Cards			●	●	●	●	●	●
My Community Handbook (Blackline Masters)					●			
My State Handbook (Blackline Masters)						●		
Assessment Options* (Blackline Masters) booklet								
Lesson Test					●	●	●	●
Chapter Test					●	●	●	●
Unit Test		●	●	●	●	●	●	●
Unit Performance Assessment		●	●	●	●	●	●	●
Multiple-Use Masters		●	●	●	●	●	●	●
Resources for Reaching All Learners (includes ELL)* (Blackline Masters) Challenge, ELL, inter			●	●	●	●	●	●
Bringing Social Studies Alive* (Blackline Masters)		●	●	●	●	●	●	●
Primary Source Plus* (Blackline Masters)			●	●	●	●	●	●
Research and Writing Projects* (Blackline Masters)			●	●	●	●	●	●
Floor and Desk Maps	●	●	●	●	●	●	●	●
Multimedia Solutions								
Audio Student's Book with Primary Sources and Songs MP3 CD*		●	●	●	●	●	●	●
GeoNet CD-ROM					●	●	●	●
Unit Videos		●	●	●	●	●	●	●
eSocial Studies Book (includes audio and interactive maps)			●	●	●	●	●	●
Lesson Planner and Teacher Resource CD-ROM		●	●	●	●	●	●	●
Test Generator CD-ROM		●	●	●	●	●	●	●
eTeacher's Edition		●	●	●	●	●	●	●
Unit Big Idea/Skillbuilder Transparencies*			●	●	●	●	●	●
Interactive Transparencies*			●	●	●	●	●	●
Education Place® featuring *Weekly Reader®*		●	●	●	●	●	●	●

*** Teacher's Resource Kit**

HOUGHTON MIFFLIN

SOCIAL STUDIES

UNITED STATES HISTORY

EARLY YEARS

TEACHER'S EDITION

VOLUME 1

Visit Education Place®
www.eduplace.com/kids

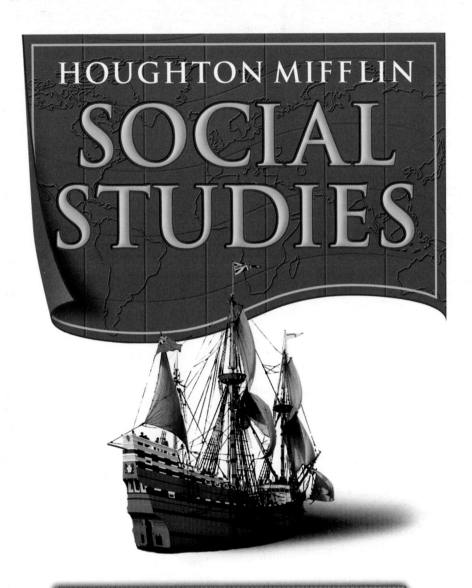

HOUGHTON MIFFLIN BOSTON

Authors and Reviewers

Lead Author
Dr. Herman J. Viola
Smithsonian Institution

Authors
Dr. Sarah Witham Bednarz
Texas A&M University

Dr. Carlos E. Cortés
University of California, Riverside

Dr. Cheryl Jennings
Institute of Education
University of North Florida

Dr. Mark C. Schug
University of Wisconsin, Milwaukee

Dr. Charles S. White
Boston University

Consulting Authors
Dr. Dolores Beltran
California State University — Los Angeles
(Support for English Language Learners)

Dr. MaryEllen Vogt
California State University Center for the Advancement of Reading
(Reading in the Content Area)

Teacher Reviewers

Grade 3

Stacy Acker
Columbia Station, OH

Kerrie Bandyk
Grand Rapids, MI

Julie Bauer
East St. Louis, IL

Rosie Becerra-Davies
Montebello, CA

Cris Ferguson
Chula Vista, CA

Nancy Hassard
Ringwood, NJ

Lynda Lemon-Rush
Covina, CA

Karen Pratt
North Miami Beach, FL

Stephanie Raker
Rochester, NY

Lorrie Soria
Oakland, CA

Sandra Stroud-Pennington
Decatur, GA

Peggy Yelverton
Palm Bay, FL

Grade 4

Kristy Bouck
Port Orchard, WA

Martha Eckhoff
St. Louis, MO

Melanie Gates
Long Beach, CA

Jo Ann Gillespie
Saratoga, CA

Sharon Hawthrone
Medford, NJ

Martha Lewis
Oviedo, FL

Tammy Morici
Piñon Hills, CA

Andrea Orndorff
Ellicott City, MD

Kay Renshaw
Clearwater, FL

Kristin Roemhildt
Moundsview, MN

Cathy Stubbs
Ft. Lauderdale, FL

Tonya Torres
North Miami Beach, FL

Kristen Werk
Pittsburg, CA

Grade 5

Skip Bayliss
Satellite Beach, FL

Annette Bomba
Schenevus, NY

Amy Clark
Travelers Rest, SC

Melissa Cook
Lake Elsinore, CA

Kelli Dunn
Broadview, IL

Peggy Greene
Thomaston, GA

Elyce Kaplan
San Diego, CA

Julia McNeal
Dayton, OH

Theresa Powell
Charleston, SC

Lesa Roberts
Huntsville, AL

Lynn Schew
Clearwater, FL

Linda Whitford
Alpharetta, GA

Lisa Yingling
Williamsport, PA

Credits
Illustration: Timothy Johnson

Photography:
Library of Congress ID # LC-USZ62-77160, p. 534

Printed in the U.S.A.

ISBN: 0-618-50266-1

123456789 — WC — 13 12 11 10 09 08 07 06 05 04

Contents

United States History: Early Years

Volume 1

AUTHORS

Senior Author
Dr. Herman J. Viola
Curator Emeritus
Smithsonian Institution

Dr. Cheryl Jennings
Project Director
Florida Institute of Education
University of North Florida

Dr. Sarah Witham Bednarz
Associate Professor, Geography
Texas A&M University

Dr. Mark C. Schug
Professor and Director
Center for Economic Education
University of Wisconsin, Milwaukee

Dr. Carlos E. Cortés
Professor Emeritus, History
University of California, Riverside

Dr. Charles S. White
Associate Professor
School of Education
Boston University

Consulting Authors
Dr. Dolores Beltran
Assistant Professor
Curriculum Instruction
California State University, Los Angeles
(Support for English Language Learners)

Dr. MaryEllen Vogt
Co-Director
California State University Center for the Advancement of Reading
(Reading in the Content Area)

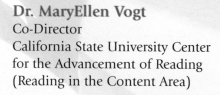

The United States Mint honors the Louisiana Purchase and the Lewis and Clark expedition in a new nickel series. The first nickel of the series features a rendition of the Jefferson Peace Medal. Thomas Jefferson commissioned this medal for Lewis and Clark's historic trip, which began in 1804.

Louisiana Purchase/Peace Medal nickel circulating coin images courtesy United States Mint. Used with Permission.

HOUGHTON MIFFLIN

SOCIAL STUDIES

UNITED STATES HISTORY

EARLY YEARS

Visit Education Place®
www.eduplace.com/kids

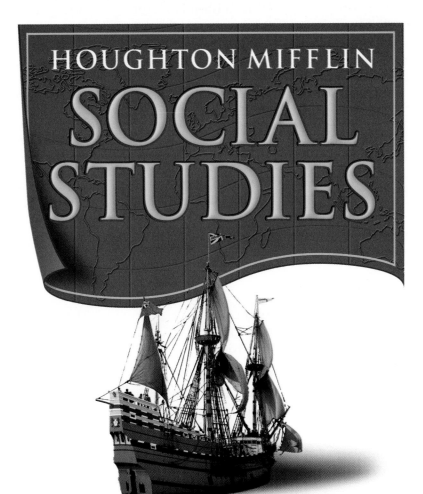

HOUGHTON MIFFLIN BOSTON

Consultants

Philip J. Deloria
Associate Professor
Department of History and Program in American Studies
University of Michigan

Lucien Ellington
UC Professor of Education and Asia Program Co-Director
University of Tennessee, Chattanooga

Thelma Wills Foote
Associate Professor
University of California

Stephen J. Fugita
Distinguished Professor
Psychology and Ethnic Studies
Santa Clara University

Charles C. Haynes
Senior Scholar
First Amendment Center

Ted Hemmingway
Professor of History
The Florida Agricultural & Mechanical University

Douglas Monroy
Professor of History
The Colorado College

Lynette K. Oshima
Assistant Professor
Department of Language, Literacy and Sociocultural Studies and Social Studies Program Coordinator
University of New Mexico

Jeffrey Strickland
Assistant Professor, History
University of Texas Pan American

Clifford E. Trafzer
Professor of History and American Indian Studies
University of California

Teacher Reviewers

Skip Bayliss
Surfside Elementary
Satellite Beach, FL

Annette Bomba
Schenevus Central School
Schenevus, NY

Amy Clark
Gateway Elementary
Travelers Rest, SC

Melissa Cook
Machado Elementary
Lake Elsinore, CA

Kelli Dunn
Lindop School
Broadview, IL

Peggy Greene
Upson-Lee North Elementary
Thomaston, GA

Elyce Kaplan
Kumeyaay Elementary
San Diego, CA

Julia McNeal
Webster Elementary
Dayton, OH

Theresa Powell
Harbor View School
Charleston, SC

Lesa Roberts
Hampton Cove Middle School
Huntsville, AL

Lynn Schew
Leila G. Davis Elementary
Clearwater, FL

Linda Whitford
Manning Oaks Elementary
Alpharetta, GA

Lisa Yingling
Round Hills Elementary
Williamsport, PA

Printed in the U.S.A.

ISBN: 0-618-42885-2

123456789-DW-13 12 11 10 09 08 07 06 05 04

Contents

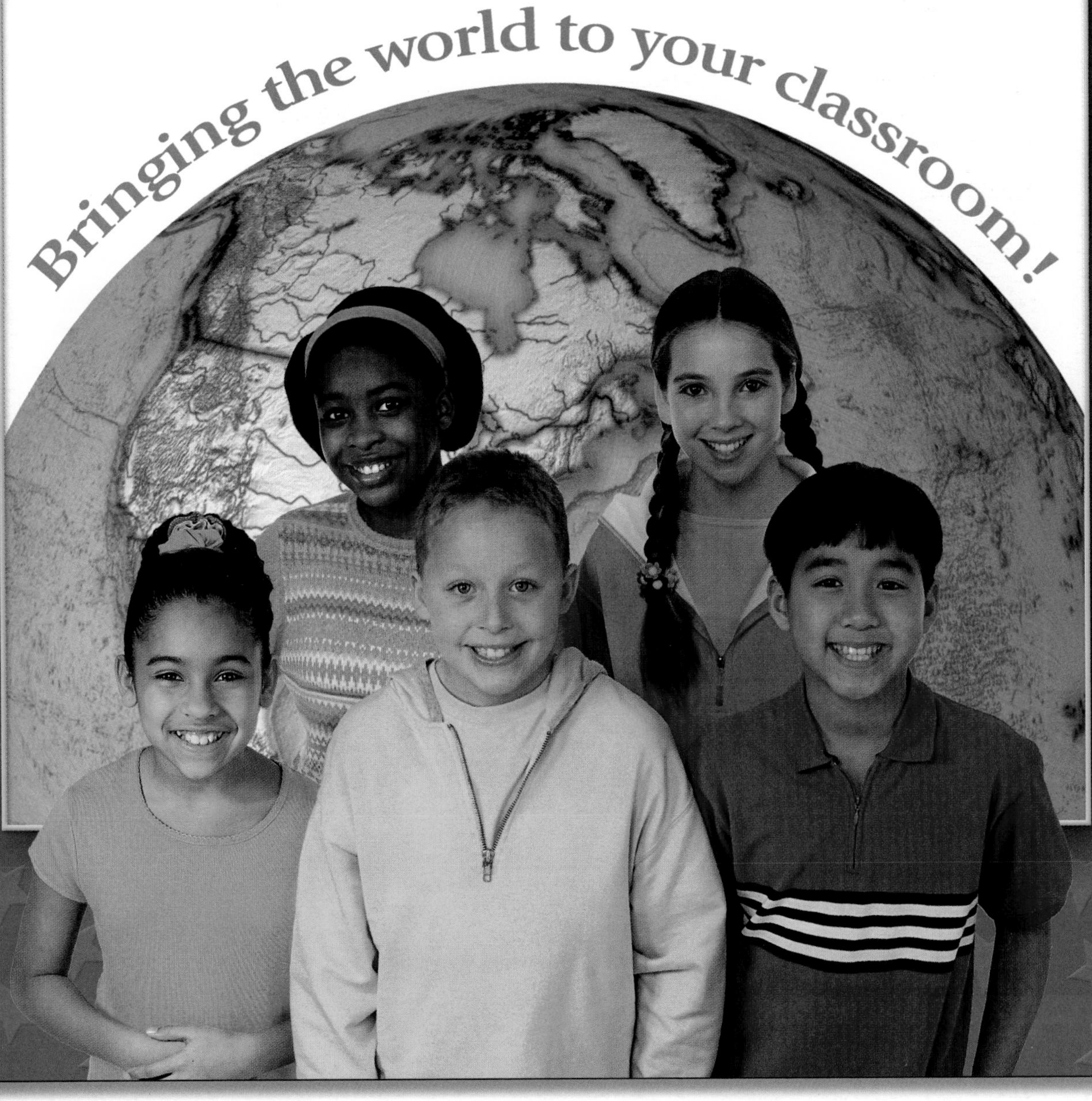
Bringing the world to your classroom!

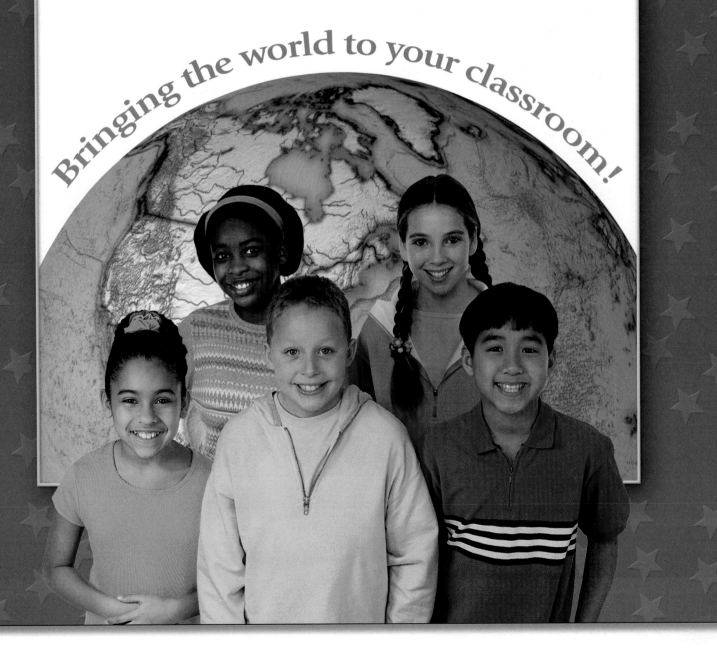

UNIT 1 Our Land and First People

CHAPTER 2 The First Americans 36

UNIT 2 Exploration and Settlement 78

CHAPTER 3 Age of Exploration 82

CHAPTER 4 European Settlements 120

viii

UNIT 3 The English Colonies 154

CHAPTER 5 New England Colonies 158

CHAPTER 6 Middle and Southern Colonies 186

ix

CHAPTER 7 Causes of the Revolution 226

xi

UNIT 5 The New Nation

CHAPTER 10 The Early Republic

CHAPTER 11 A Growing Country

xii

UNIT 6 The Civil War

xiii

UNIT 7

Linking to Today

CHAPTER 14 Immigration

CHAPTER 15 The Promise of America

xiv

References

Extend Lessons

Connect the core lesson to an important concept and dig into it. Extend your social studies knowledge!

Readers' Theater

Geography

Citizenship

Technology

Biography

Economics

Primary Sources

History

Literature

Skill Lessons

Take a step-by-step approach to learning and practicing key social studies skills.

Map and Globe Skills

Chart and Graph Skills

Study Skills

Citizenship Skills

Reading and Thinking Skills

Reading Skills/Graphic Organizer

xviii

Visual Learning

Become skilled at reading visuals. Graphs, maps, and fine art help you put all the information together.

Maps

xix

Charts and Graphs

Interpreting Fine Art

xx

Diagrams and Infographics

Timelines

About Your Textbook

❶ How It's Organized

Units The major sections of your book are units. Each starts with a big idea.

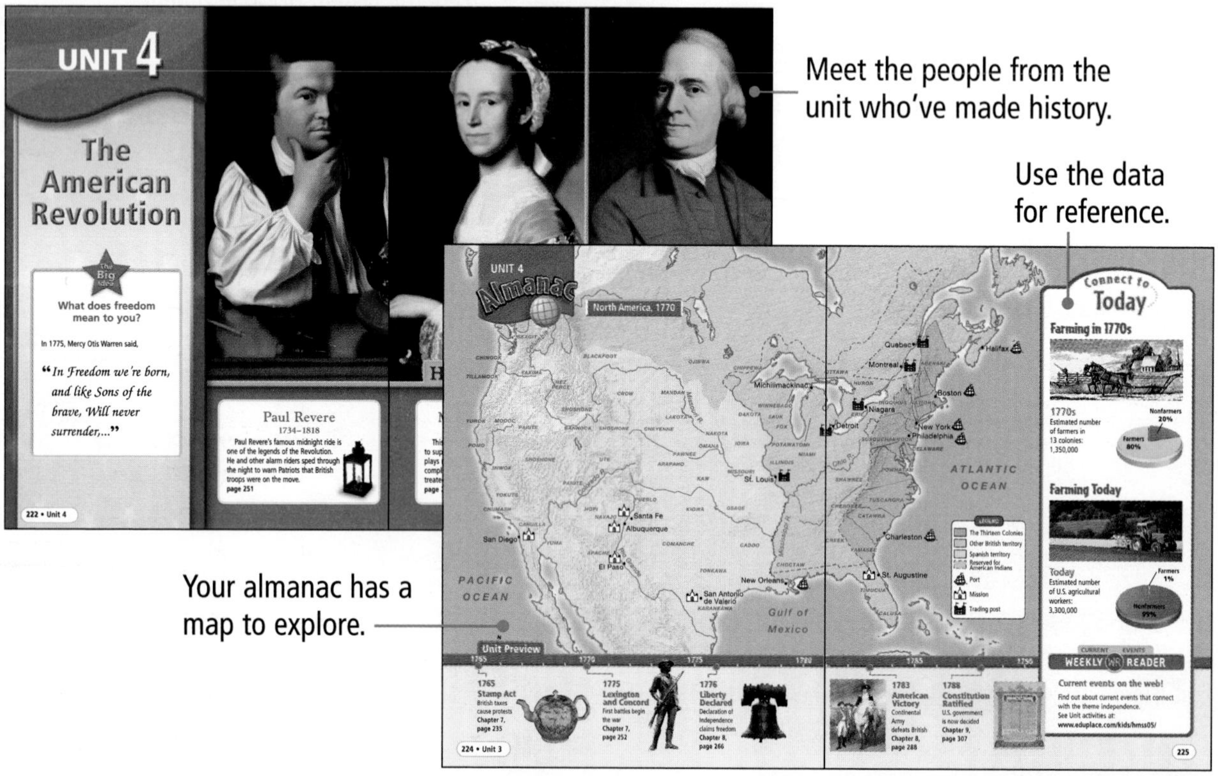

Meet the people from the unit who've made history.

Use the data for reference.

Your almanac has a map to explore.

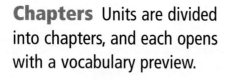

Get ready for reading.

Chapters Units are divided into chapters, and each opens with a vocabulary preview.

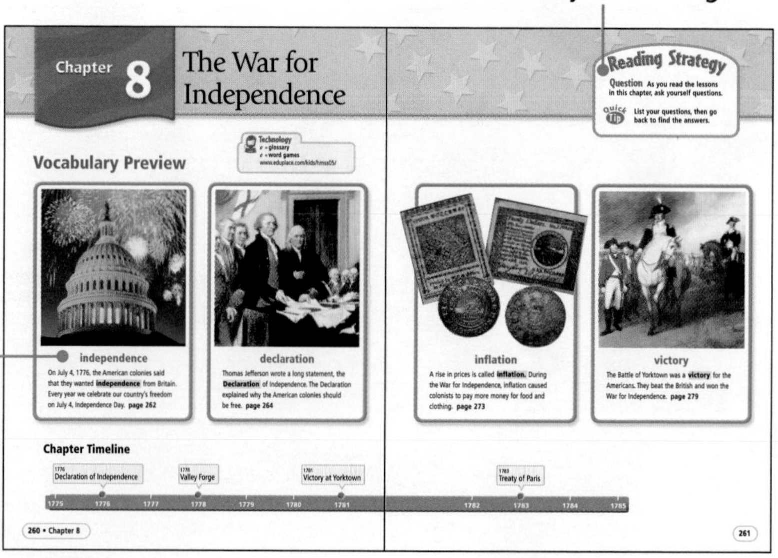

Four important concepts get you started.

xxii

2 Core and Extend

Lessons The lessons in your book have two parts: core and extend.

Core Lessons

Lessons bring the events of history to life and help you meet your state's standards.

Extend Lessons

Go deeper into an important topic.

Core Lesson

Vocabulary strategies help with word meanings.

Before you read, use your prior knowledge.

Reading skills support your understanding of the text.

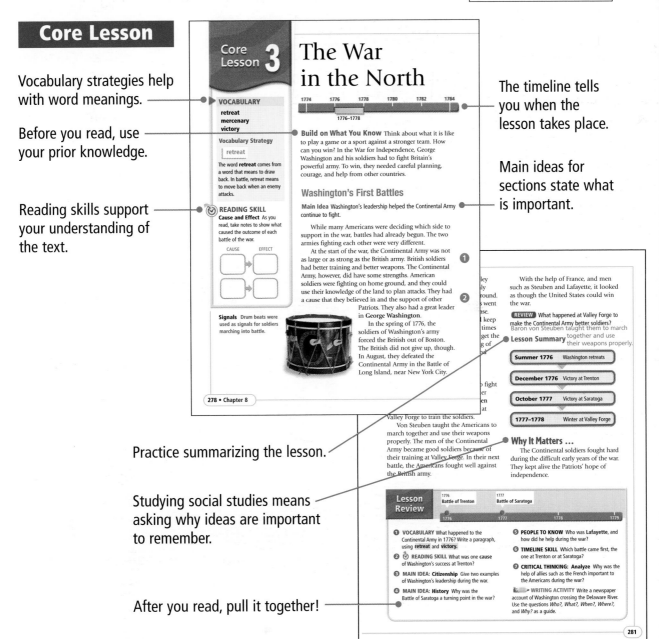

The timeline tells you when the lesson takes place.

Main ideas for sections state what is important.

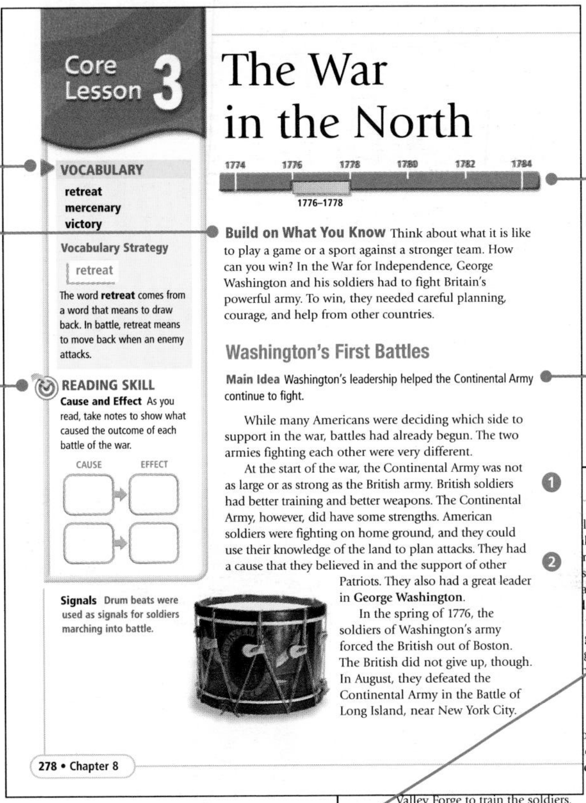

Core Lesson 3

The War in the North

1774 1776 1778 1780 1782 1784

1776–1778

VOCABULARY
retreat
mercenary
victory

Vocabulary Strategy

retreat

The word **retreat** comes from a word that means to draw back. In battle, retreat means to move back when an enemy attacks.

READING SKILL
Cause and Effect As you read, take notes to show what caused the outcome of each battle of the war.

CAUSE EFFECT

Build on What You Know Think about what it is like to play a game or a sport against a stronger team. How can you win? In the War for Independence, George Washington and his soldiers had to fight Britain's powerful army. To win, they needed careful planning, courage, and help from other countries.

Washington's First Battles

Main Idea Washington's leadership helped the Continental Army continue to fight.

While many Americans were deciding which side to support in the war, battles had already begun. The two armies fighting each other were very different.

At the start of the war, the Continental Army was not as large or as strong as the British army. British soldiers had better training and better weapons. The Continental Army, however, did have some strengths. American soldiers were fighting on home ground, and they could use their knowledge of the land to plan attacks. They had a cause that they believed in and the support of other Patriots. They also had a great leader in George Washington.

In the spring of 1776, the soldiers of Washington's army forced the British out of Boston. The British did not give up, though. In August, they defeated the Continental Army in the Battle of Long Island, near New York City.

Signals Drum beats were used as signals for soldiers marching into battle.

278 • Chapter 8

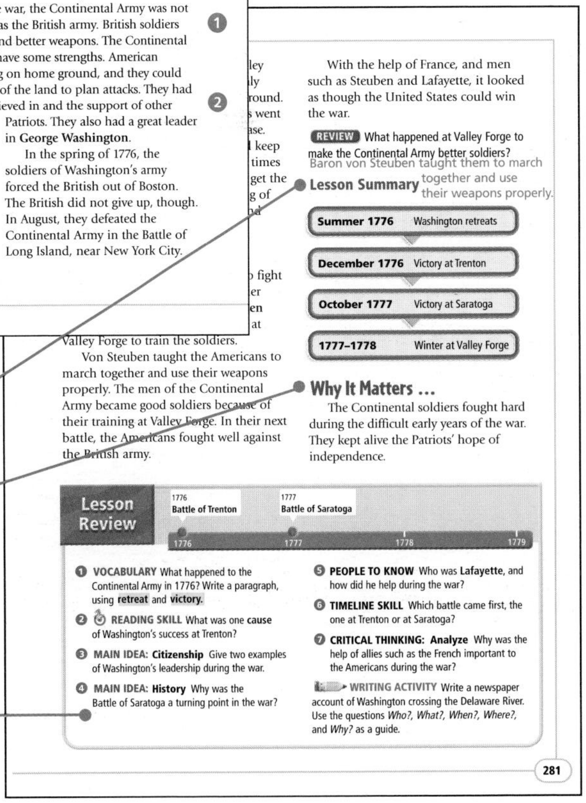

Valley Forge to train the soldiers.

Von Steuben taught the Americans to march together and use their weapons properly. The men of the Continental Army became good soldiers because of their training at Valley Forge. In their next battle, the Americans fought well against the British army.

With the help of France, and men such as Steuben and Lafayette, it looked as though the United States could win the war.

REVIEW What happened at Valley Forge to make the Continental Army better soldiers? Baron von Steuben taught them to march together and use their weapons properly.

Lesson Summary

Summer 1776	Washington retreats
December 1776	Victory at Trenton
October 1777	Victory at Saratoga
1777–1778	Winter at Valley Forge

Why It Matters ...

The Continental soldiers fought hard during the difficult early years of the war. They kept alive the Patriots' hope of independence.

Lesson Review

1776 Battle of Trenton; 1777 Battle of Saratoga

1776 1777 1778 1779

1. **VOCABULARY** What happened to the Continental Army in 1776? Write a paragraph, using **retreat** and **victory**.
2. **READING SKILL** What was one **cause** of Washington's success at Trenton?
3. **MAIN IDEA: Citizenship** Give two examples of Washington's leadership during the war.
4. **MAIN IDEA: History** Why was the Battle of Saratoga a turning point in the war?
5. **PEOPLE TO KNOW** Who was Lafayette, and how did he help during the war?
6. **TIMELINE SKILL** Which battle came first, the one at Trenton or at Saratoga?
7. **CRITICAL THINKING: Analyze** Why was the help of allies such as the French important to the Americans during the war?

WRITING ACTIVITY Write a newspaper account of Washington crossing the Delaware River. Use the questions *Who?, What?, When?, Where?,* and *Why?* as a guide.

281

Practice summarizing the lesson.

Studying social studies means asking why ideas are important to remember.

After you read, pull it together!

xxiii

Extend Lesson

Learn more about an important topic from each core lesson.

Dig in and extend your knowledge.

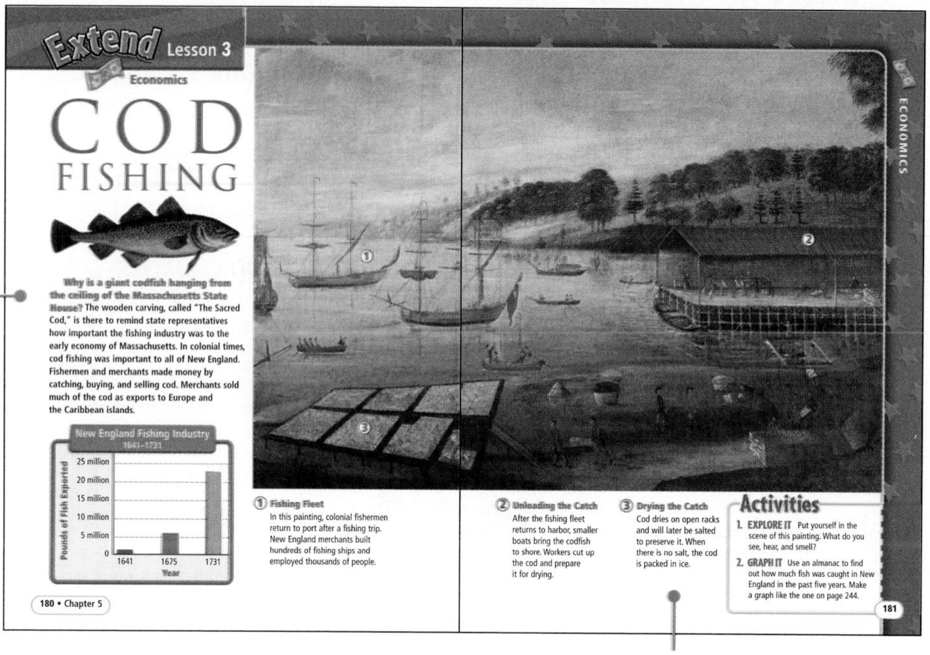

Extend Lesson 3

Economics

COD FISHING

Why is a giant codfish hanging from the ceiling of the Massachusetts State House? The wooden carving, called "The Sacred Cod," is there to remind state representatives how important the fishing industry was to the early economy of Massachusetts. In colonial times, cod fishing was important to all of New England. Fishermen and merchants made money by catching, buying, and selling cod. Merchants sold much of the cod as exports to Europe and the Caribbean islands.

New England Fishing Industry
1641–1731
Pounds of Fish Exported
25 million
20 million
15 million
10 million
5 million
0
1641
1675
1731
Year
ECONOMICS

① **Fishing Fleet**
In this painting, colonial fishermen return to port after a fishing trip. New England merchants built hundreds of fishing ships and employed thousands of people.

② **Unloading the Catch**
After the fishing fleet returns to harbor, smaller boats bring the codfish to shore. Workers cut up the cod and prepare it for drying.

③ **Drying the Catch**
Cod dries on open racks and will later be salted to preserve it. When there is no salt, the cod is packed in ice.

Activities

1. **EXPLORE IT** Put yourself in the scene of this painting. What do you see, hear, and smell?
2. **GRAPH IT** Use an almanac to find out how much fish was caught in New England in the past five years. Make a graph like the one on page 244.

180 • Chapter 5

181

Look closely. Connect the past to the present.

Look for literature, readers' theater, geography, economics—and more.

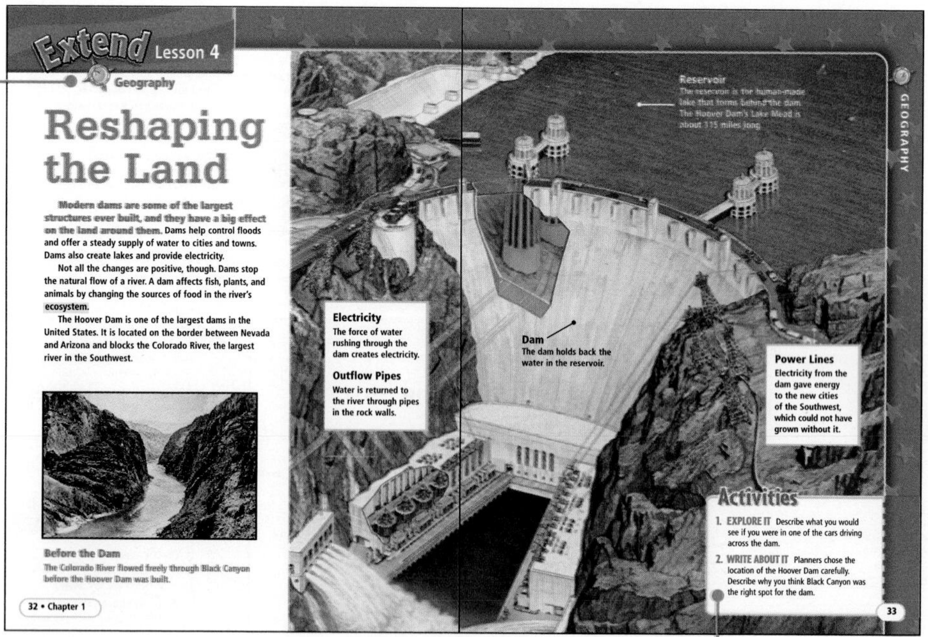

Extend Lesson 4

Geography

Reshaping the Land

Modern dams are some of the largest structures ever built, and they have a big effect on the land around them. Dams help control floods and offer a steady supply of water to cities and towns. Dams also create lakes and provide electricity.

Not all the changes are positive, though. Dams stop the natural flow of a river. A dam affects fish, plants, and animals by changing the sources of food in the river's ecosystem.

The Hoover Dam is one of the largest dams in the United States. It is located on the border between Nevada and Arizona and blocks the Colorado River, the largest river in the Southwest.

Before the Dam
The Colorado River flowed freely through Black Canyon before the Hoover Dam was built.

Reservoir
The reservoir is the human-made lake that forms behind the dam. The Hoover Dam's Lake Mead is about 115 miles long.
Electricity
The force of water rushing through the dam creates electricity.
Outflow Pipes
Water is returned to the river through pipes in the rock walls.
Dam
The dam holds back the water in the reservoir.
Power Lines
Electricity from the dam gave energy to the new cities of the Southwest, which could not have grown without it.
GEOGRAPHY

Activities

1. **EXPLORE IT** Describe what you would see if you were in one of the cars driving across the dam.
2. **WRITE ABOUT IT** Planners chose the location of the Hoover Dam carefully. Describe why you think Black Canyon was the right spot for the dam.

32 • Chapter 1

33

Write, talk, draw, and debate!

xxiv

3 Skills

Skill Building Learn map, graph, and study skills, as well as citizenship skills for life.

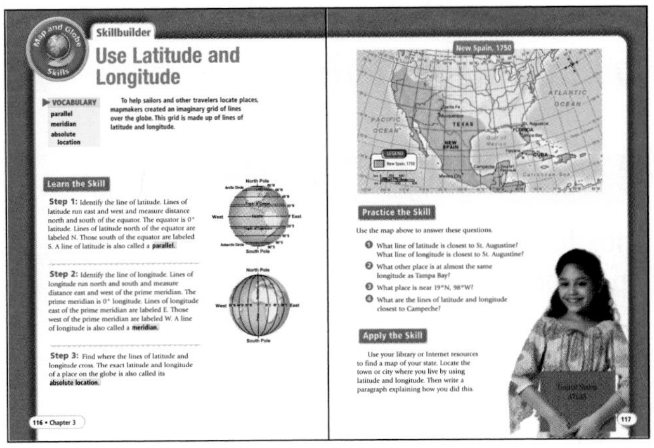

Each Skill lesson steps it out.

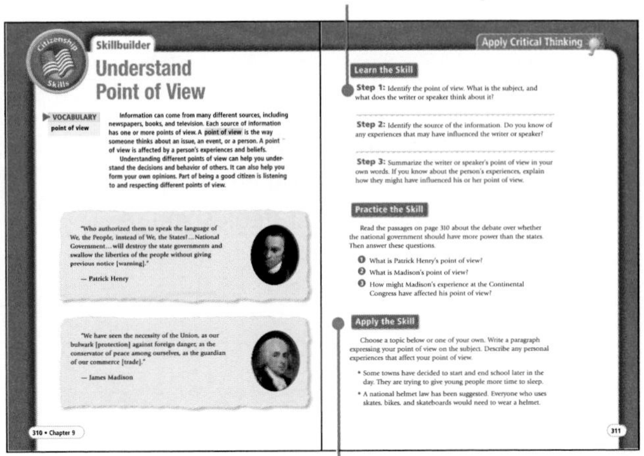

Practice and apply social studies skills.

4 References

Citizenship Handbook

The back of your book includes sections you'll refer to again and again.

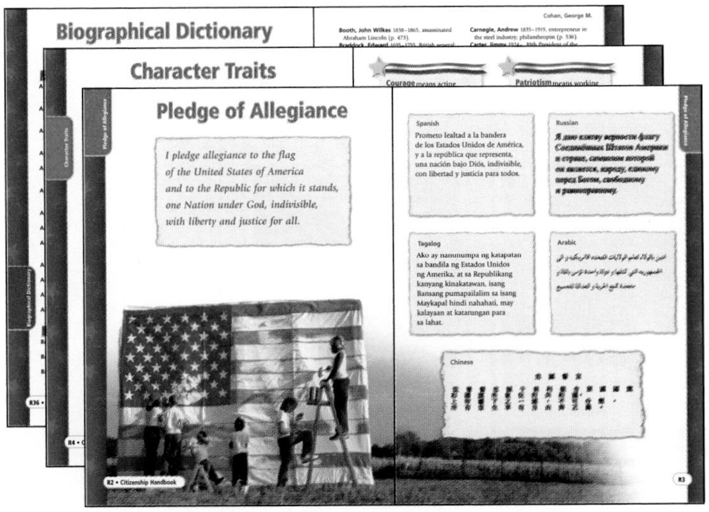

Resources

Look for atlas maps, a glossary of social studies terms, and an index.

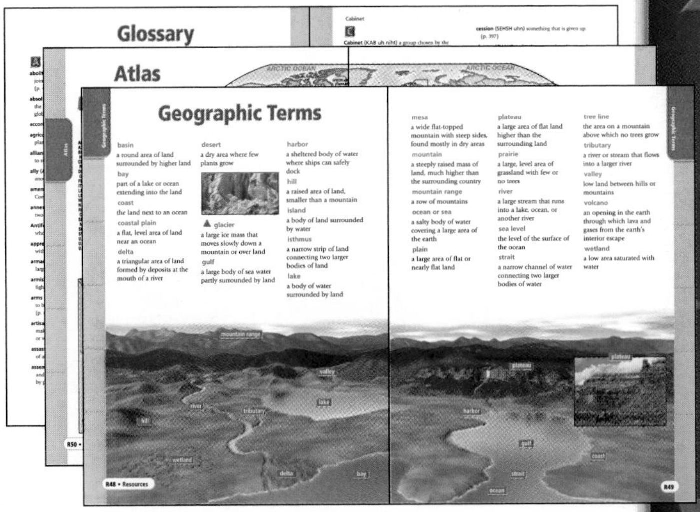

XXV

Reading Social Studies

Your book includes many features to help you be a successful reader. Here's what you will find:

VOCABULARY SUPPORT

Every chapter and lesson helps you with social studies terms. You'll build your vocabulary through strategies you're learning in language arts.

Preview
Get a jump start on four important words from the chapter.

Vocabulary Strategies
Focus on word roots, prefixes, suffixes, or compound words, for example.

Vocabulary Practice
Reuse words in the reviews, skills, and extends. Show that you know your vocabulary.

READING STRATEGIES

Look for the reading strategy and quick tip at the beginning of each chapter.

Predict and Infer
Before you read, think about what you'll learn.

Monitor and Clarify
Check your understanding. Could you explain what you just read to someone else?

Question
Stop and ask yourself a question. Did you understand what you read?

Summarize
After you read, think about the most important ideas of the lesson.

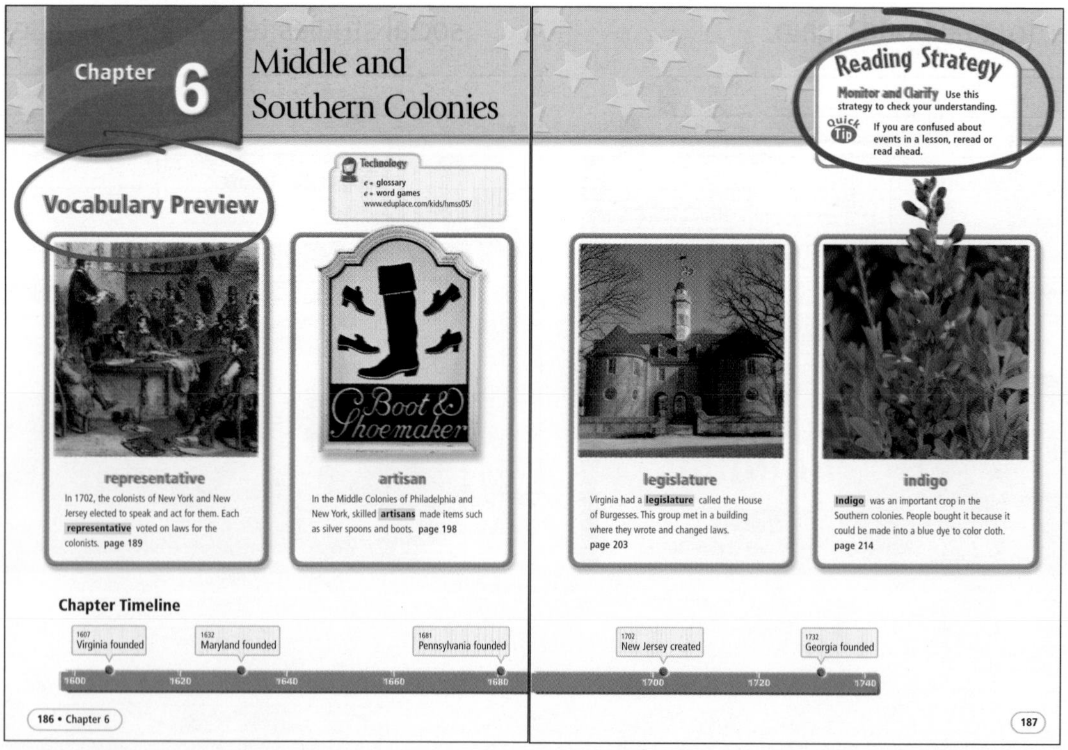
Chapter 6 Middle and Southern Colonies

Vocabulary Preview

Technology
e • glossary
e • word games
www.eduplace.com/kids/hmss05/

representative
In 1702, the colonists of New York and New Jersey elected to speak and act for them. Each **representative** voted on laws for the colonists. page 189

artisan
In the Middle Colonies of Philadelphia and New York, skilled **artisans** made items such as silver spoons and boots. page 198

Chapter Timeline
1607 Virginia founded
1632 Maryland founded
1681 Pennsylvania founded
1600 1620 1640 1660 1680

186 • Chapter 6

Reading Strategy
Monitor and Clarify Use this strategy to check your understanding.
Quick Tip If you are confused about events in a lesson, reread or read ahead.

legislature
Virginia had a **legislature** called the House of Burgesses. This group met in a building where they wrote and changed laws. page 203

indigo
Indigo was an important crop in the Southern colonies. People bought it because it could be made into a blue dye to color cloth. page 214

1702 New Jersey created
1732 Georgia founded
1700 1720 1740

187

xxvi

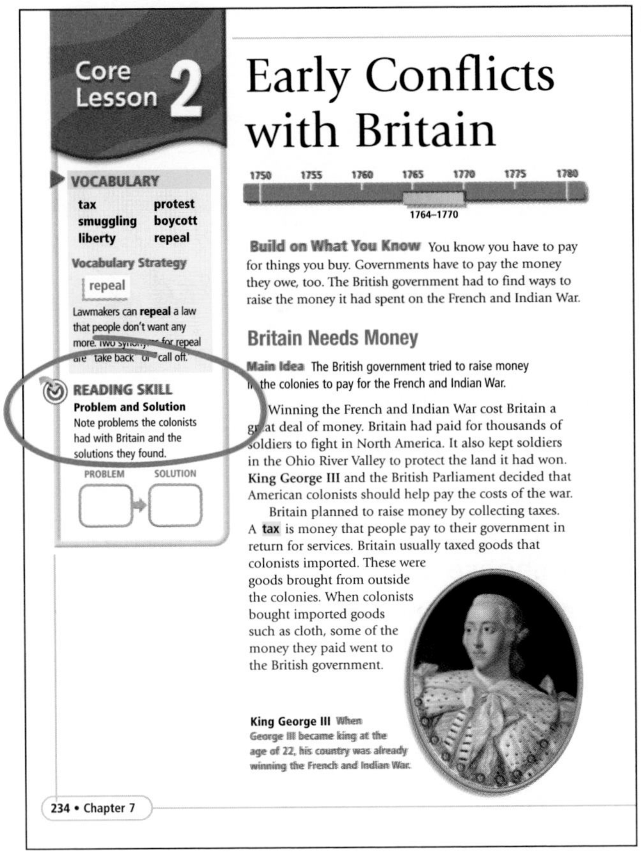

Core Lesson 2

Early Conflicts with Britain

1750 1755 1760 1765 1770 1775 1780

1764–1770

VOCABULARY

tax	**protest**
smuggling	**boycott**
liberty	**repeal**

Vocabulary Strategy

repeal

Lawmakers can **repeal** a law that people don't want any more. Two synonyms for repeal are "take back" or "call off."

READING SKILL

Problem and Solution

Note problems the colonists had with Britain and the solutions they found.

PROBLEM → SOLUTION

Build on What You Know You know you have to pay for things you buy. Governments have to pay the money they owe, too. The British government had to find ways to raise the money it had spent on the French and Indian War.

Britain Needs Money

Main Idea The British government tried to raise money in the colonies to pay for the French and Indian War.

Winning the French and Indian War cost Britain a great deal of money. Britain had paid for thousands of soldiers to fight in North America. It also kept soldiers in the Ohio River Valley to protect the land it had won. **King George III** and the British Parliament decided that American colonists should help pay the costs of the war.

Britain planned to raise money by collecting taxes. A **tax** is money that people pay to their government in return for services. Britain usually taxed goods that colonists imported. These were goods brought from outside the colonies. When colonists bought imported goods such as cloth, some of the money they paid went to the British government.

King George III When George III became king at the age of 22, his country was already winning the French and Indian War.

234 • Chapter 7

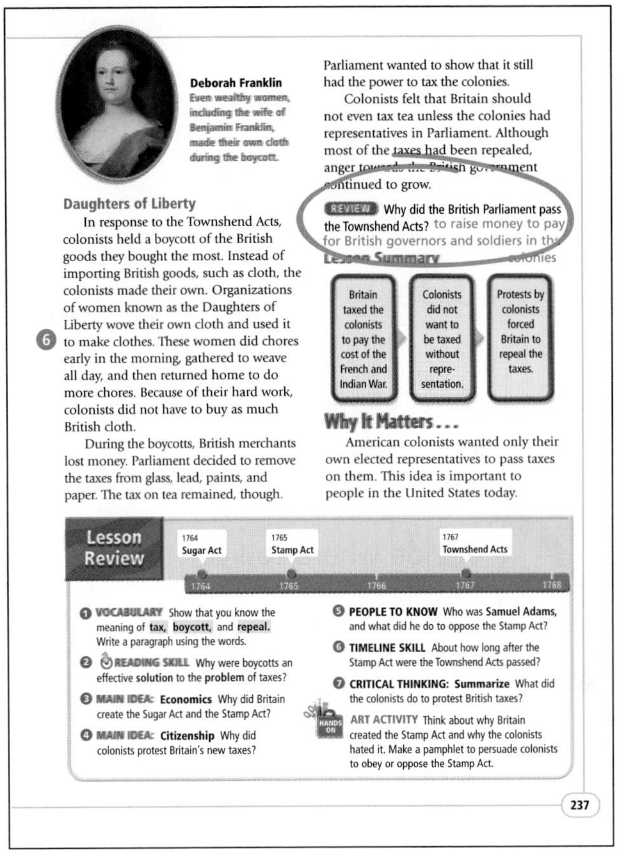

Deborah Franklin Even wealthy women, including the wife of Benjamin Franklin, made their own cloth during the boycott.

Daughters of Liberty

In response to the Townshend Acts, colonists held a boycott of the British goods they bought the most. Instead of importing British goods, such as cloth, the colonists made their own. Organizations of women known as the Daughters of Liberty wove their own cloth and used it

6 to make clothes. These women did chores early in the morning, gathered to weave all day, and then returned home to do more chores. Because of their hard work, colonists did not have to buy as much British cloth.

During the boycotts, British merchants lost money. Parliament decided to remove the taxes from glass, lead, paints, and paper. The tax on tea remained, though. Parliament wanted to show that it still had the power to tax the colonies.

Colonists felt that Britain should not even tax tea unless the colonies had representatives in Parliament. Although most of the taxes had been repealed, anger towards the British government continued to grow.

REVIEW Why did the British Parliament pass the Townshend Acts? to raise money to pay for British governors and soldiers in the colonies

Lesson Summary

Britain taxed the colonists to pay the cost of the French and Indian War. → Colonists did not want to be taxed without representation. → Protests by colonists forced Britain to repeal the taxes.

Why It Matters . . .

American colonists wanted only their own elected representatives to pass taxes on them. This idea is important to people in the United States today.

Lesson Review

1764 Sugar Act — 1765 Stamp Act — 1767 Townshend Acts

1764 1765 1766 1767 1768

1. **VOCABULARY** Show that you know the meaning of **tax, boycott,** and **repeal.** Write a paragraph using the words.
2. **READING SKILL** Why were boycotts an effective **solution** to the **problem** of taxes?
3. **MAIN IDEA: Economics** Why did Britain create the Sugar Act and the Stamp Act?
4. **MAIN IDEA: Citizenship** Why did colonists protest Britain's new taxes?
5. **PEOPLE TO KNOW** Who was **Samuel Adams,** and what did he do to oppose the Stamp Act?
6. **TIMELINE SKILL** About how long after the Stamp Act were the Townshend Acts passed?
7. **CRITICAL THINKING: Summarize** What did the colonists do to protest British taxes?

HANDS ON **ART ACTIVITY** Think about why Britain created the Stamp Act and why the colonists hated it. Make a pamphlet to persuade colonists to obey or oppose the Stamp Act.

237

READING SKILLS

As you read, organize the information. These reading skills will help you:

Sequence

Cause and Effect

Compare and Contrast

Problem and Solution

Draw Conclusions

Predict Outcomes

Categorize (or) Classify

Main Idea and Details

COMPREHENSION SUPPORT

Build on What You Know

Check your prior knowledge. You may already know a lot!

Review Questions

Connect with the text. Did you understand what you just read?

Summaries

Look for three ways to summarize–a list, an organizer, or a paragraph.

xxvii

Social Studies: Why It Matters

Learning social studies will help you know how to get along better in your everyday life, and it will give you confidence when you make important choices in your future.

WHEN I
▸ decide where to live
▸ travel
▸ look for places on a map—
I'll use the geography information I've learned in social studies.
WHEN I
▸ choose a job
▸ make a budget
▸ decide which product to buy—
I'll use economic information.

xxviii

WHEN I
▶ hear the story of a person from the past
▶ read books and visit museums
▶ look closely at the world around me—
I'll use what I've learned about history.
WHEN I
▶ go to a neighborhood meeting
▶ decide who to vote for
▶ get a driver's license—
I can use what I've learned about citizenship.
MUSEUM
HALL
Town Meeting Tonight
Meeting Tonight
xxix

Unit 1

Unit Planner

Begin with Core. Extend for more.

Our Land and Its First People

Chapter 1 Pages 4–35

America's Land

Core Lesson 1 pp. 6–9
Land and Climate

Extend Lesson 1 pp. 10–11
Geography Trouble from the Tropics

Skillbuilder
Review Map Skills pp. 12–13

Core Lesson 2 pp. 14–19
Our Nation's Resources

Extend Lesson 2 pp. 20–21
Technology The Race for Solar Power

Core Lesson 3 pp. 22–25
Regions of the United States

Extend Lesson 3 pp. 26–27
Biographies Caretakers of the Earth

Core Lesson 4 pp. 28–31
People and the Land

Extend Lesson 4 pp. 32–33
Geography Reshaping the Land

Chapter Review pp. 34–35

Chapter 2 Pages 36–75

The First Americans

Core Lesson 1 pp. 38–43
Ancient Americans

Extend Lesson 1 pp. 44–45
History Tenochtitlán

Core Lesson 2 pp. 46–49
Peoples of the West

Extend Lesson 2 pp. 50–53
Literature "Chinook Wind Wrestles Cold Wind," from *They Dance in the Sky: Native American Star Myths* by Ray A. Williamson

Core Lesson 3 pp. 54–57
Peoples of the Southwest

Extend Lesson 3 pp. 58–59
Biographies Keepers of Tradition

Core Lesson 4 pp. 60–63
Peoples of the Plains

Extend Lesson 4 pp. 64–65
Primary Sources Art of the Plains Indians

Skillbuilder
Summarize pp. 66–67

Core Lesson 5 pp. 68–71
Peoples of the East

Extend Lesson 5 pp. 72–73
History American Indian Shelters

Chapter Review pp. 74–75

Unit Review
pp. 76–77

LEVELED BOOKS

The following Social Studies Independent Books are available for extending and supporting students' social studies experience as they read the unit.

Differentiated Instruction

Extra Support

Tracing the Anasazi

By Alison Wells

Summary: Scientists and historians have studied the sites of Anasazi cliff dwellings to learn about their way of life and culture. There are many theories about what happened to them.

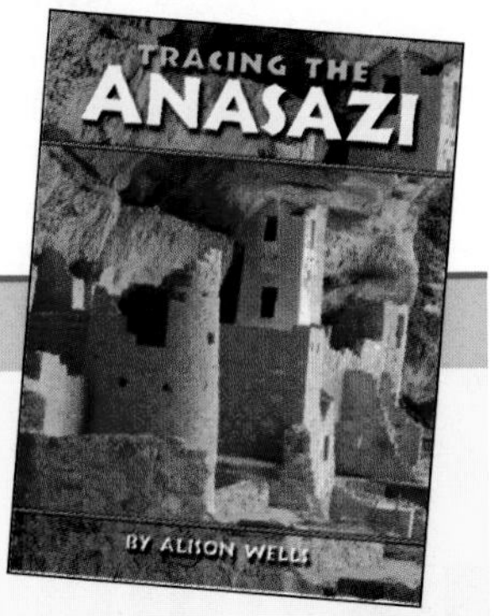

TRACING THE ANASAZI
BY ALISON WELLS

Vocabulary

theory
agriculture
staple
ceremony

Extending Understanding

Oral Language: Narration Ask students to serve as narrators of a documentary on the Anasazi. You may suggestion that they present the narration as though walking through an Anasazi settlement.

Independent Writing: Historical fiction Have students write a short story about life for an Anasazi child.

Graphic Organizer: Have students use a word web to record words related to the Anasazi.

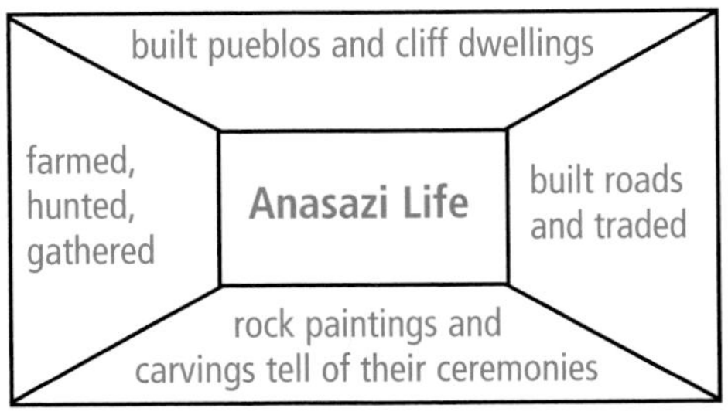

built pueblos and cliff dwellings
farmed, hunted, gathered
Anasazi Life
built roads and traded
rock paintings and carvings tell of their ceremonies

On Level

A Walk with John Muir

By Carl W. Grody

Summary: John Muir's writings and actions inspired environmentalists and helped to create many U.S. National Parks.

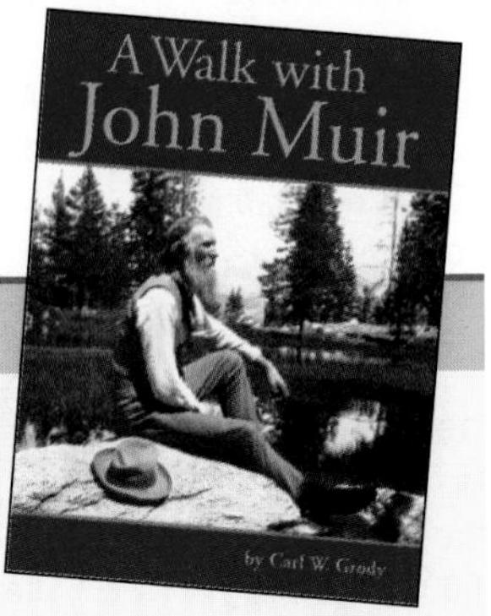

A Walk with John Muir
by Carl W. Grody

Vocabulary

environment
plateau
landform

Extending Understanding

Oral Language: Speech Have partners be John Muir and his grandchild. John Muir should tell about how he feels about nature and the grandchild can ask questions. Then have them reverse roles.

Independent Writing: Poster Have students create a fact poster about John Muir. Have them include the quote they like best and number the facts. Encourage them to illustrate their posters.

Graphic Organizer: Students can use a cause-and-effect chart to show Muir's influence on conservation.

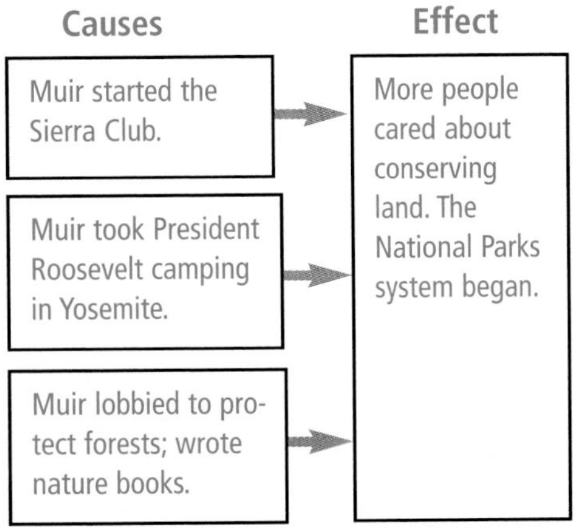

Causes
Effect
Muir started the Sierra Club.
Muir took President Roosevelt camping in Yosemite.
Muir lobbied to protect forests; wrote nature books.
More people cared about conserving land. The National Parks system began.

Challenge

Wind and Water: Two Great Powers

By Susan Ring

Summary: Where does electricity come from? The advantages and disadvantages of tapping the great energy forces of wind and water to make electricity are explored.

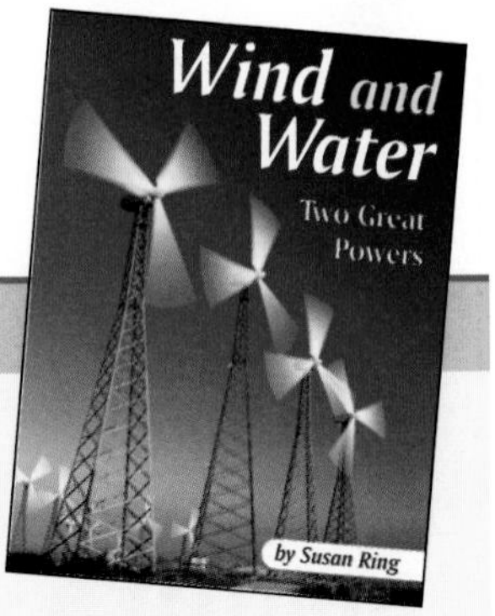

Wind and Water
Two Great Powers
by Susan Ring

Vocabulary

climate
erosion
pollution

Extending Understanding

Oral Language: Presentation Have one group prepare an oral presentation on water power and the other group on wind power. Have them prepare and use visuals in their talks.

Independent Writing: Description Have students pretend they are visiting the Hoover Dam or the Desert Sky Wind Project. Have them write a description of what they see and tell how electricity is made.

Graphic Organizer: Students can use a two-column chart to compare water and wind power.

Water Power	Wind Power
• building dams can cause land to flood • changes the habitat of fish and animals downstream	• wind farms need lots of land and are expensive to build • can be used only when wind blows at good speed • no plants

Choices for Reading

- **Extra Support/ELL** Read the selection aloud as students follow along in their books. Pause frequently and help students monitor understanding.
- **On Level** Have partners take turns reading aloud. Students can pause at the end of each page to ask each other questions and check understanding.
- **Challenge** Students can read the selection and write down any questions they have. Then they can work in small groups to answer their questions.

Go to www.eduplace.com/ss/hmss05/ for answers to Responding questions found at the back of the books.

Bibliography

Books for Independent Reading

Social Studies Key

- Biography
- Citizenship
- Cultures
- Economics
- Geography
- History

Social Studies Leveled Readers with lesson plans by Irene Fountas support the content of this unit.

Extra Support

United States of America
by Christine and David Petersen
Children's Press, 2001
This book provides an accessible overview of United States geography, history, people, and culture.

Across America, I Love You
by Christine Loomis
Hyperion, 2000
This is a lyrical ode to the American landscape, from Alaska's wildlands to the Florida Everglades.

Mystic Horse
by Paul Goble
Harper, 2003
After caring for an old abandoned horse, a poor young Pawnee boy is rewarded by the horse's mystic powers.

The Sioux
by Petra Press
Compass Point, 2001
Readers learn about this diverse group of Native American people who once widely populated the northern plains and woodlands. See others in series.

Southeast Indians
by Mir Tamim Ansary
Heinemann, 2000
A glossary and maps help readers to understand the culture and history of Southeastern Native Americans.

On Level

The Midwest: Its History and People
National Geographic, 2003
A guide takes readers back in time to discover how each region of the United States came to be. See others in series.

The Ancient Cliff Dwellers of Mesa Verde
by Caroline Arnold
Clarion, 2000
Readers explore the culture and history of the Anasazi people who mysteriously vanished from the American Southwest.

The Wave of the Sea Wolf
by David Wisniewski
Clarion, 1998
This Native American legend is followed by an informative explanation of the northwestern culture and natural phenomena that inspired it.

The Wigwam and the Longhouse
by Charlotte and David Yue
Houghton, 2000
Text and illustrations describe how Native Americans of the East lived both before and after the arrival of European settlers.

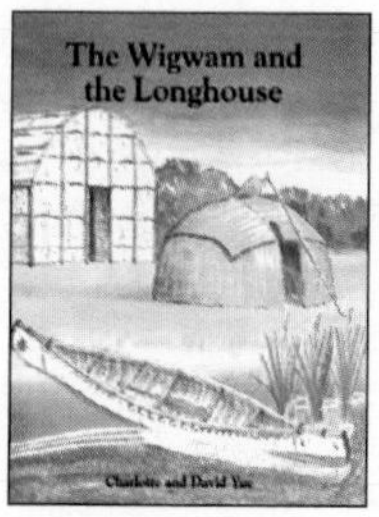

We Are the Many
by Doreen Rappaport
Harper, 2002
The author chronicles the lives of remarkable Native Americans from the 1500s to the present day.

Challenge

Places in Time: A New Atlas of American History
by E. Leacock and S. Buckley
Houghton, 2003
The authors put a geographical spin on United States history. See also *Journeys in Time.*

The Great Mystery: Myths of Native America
by Neil Philip
Clarion, 2001
The author provides extensive retellings and explanations of Native American myths and legends.

Great Spirit Horse
by Linda Little Wolf
Pelican, 2003
This is the legend of Sunka Waken, the blue-eyed horse of the Great Plains who possessed great powers.

Minik's Story
by Jennifer O. Dewey
Cavendish, 2003
A 12-year-old Inuit girl comes of age at a time when her community is on the verge of change.

The Cherokee
by Raymond Bial
Benchmark, 1999
A history of one of the largest Native American groups is supplemented with extensive resources. See others in series.

With the Program

Your State Specific Materials

at www.eduplace.com/ss/hmss05

Read Aloud and Reference

Read Aloud Books

My America: A Poetry Atlas of the United States
by Lee Bennett Hopkins
Simon, 2000
Seven regions plus Washington, D.C., are explored through 51 poems by 40 different poets.

Sweet Land of Story
by Pleasant DeSpain
August House, 2000
Thirty-six regional tales are gathered from the six major regions of the United States.

A Braid of Lives
edited by Neil Philip
Houghton, 2000
Personal remembrances of 33 individuals from 22 different Native American nations are told here.

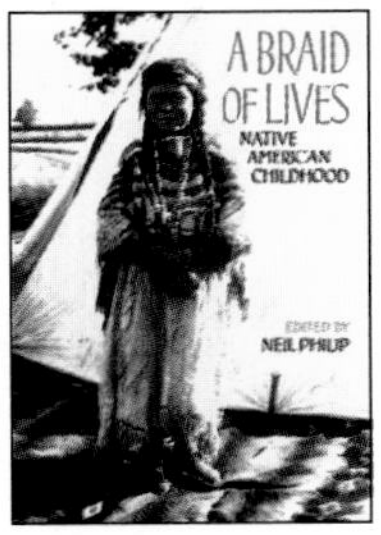

The Earth Under Sky Bear's Feet
by Joseph Bruchac
Puffin, 1998
Abenaki storyteller Joseph Bruchac writes poems about an American landscape as diverse as the Native American cultures that populate it.

Weather Legends
by Carole Vogel
Millbrook, 2001
Tales from Native American groups across the United States reflect how weather in different regions affects the people.

Reference Books

The Young People's Atlas of the United States
by James Harrison
Kingfisher, 1996
United States regions and states are profiled, including state symbols and statistics.

Wood
by Christin Ditchfield
Children's Press, 2003
The author explains how this North American natural resource is formed, used, and preserved. See others in series.

The Earliest Americans
by Helen Roney Sattler
Clarion, 2001
Readers discover how ancient artifacts can tell us who the earliest Americans were, where they might have come from, and how they adapted to this new land.

Free and Inexpensive Materials

Smithsonian Institute Information
PO Box 37012
SI Building, Room 153, MRC 010
Washington, DC 20013-7012

The website (www.si.gov) allows you to rummage about in the "Nation's Attic" and read selected articles from the ***Smithsonian*** *magazine.*

MULTIMEDIA RESOURCES

PROGRAM RESOURCES

Unit Video
Audio Student's Book with Primary Sources and Songs MP3/CD
Lesson Planner and Teacher Resource CD-ROM
Test Generator CD-ROM
eBook
eBook, Teacher's Edition
Transparencies: Big Idea & Skillbuilder, Interactive
Almanac Map & Graph Practice
Primary Sources Plus: Document-Based Questions
Research and Writing Projects
Bringing Social Studies Alive
Family Newsletter
GeoNet

CD-ROM

U.S. Regional Geography series. National Geographic

Native Americans 1 & 2 Picture Show. National Geographic

VIDEOCASSETTES

Physical Geography of North America series. National Geographic

American Indians: A Brief History. National Geographic

Native American Life. Schlessinger Media

Really Wild Animals: Amazing North America. National Geographic

AUDIOCASSETTES

Sees Behind Trees, *Michael Dorris.* Listening Library

The Love Flute, *Paul Goble.* Spoken Arts

Assessment Options

TEST PREP

You are the best evaluator of your students' progress and attainments. To help you in this task, Houghton Mifflin Social Studies provides you with a variety of assessment tools.

Classroom-Based Assessment

Written and Oral Assessment

In the student book:
- **Lesson Reviews** appear at the end of each lesson.
- **Chapter Reviews** appear on pp. 34–35, 74–75.
- **Unit Reviews** appear on pp. 76–77.

In the *Assessment Options* ancillary:
- **Lesson Tests** appear for all lessons.
- **Chapter Tests** appear for all chapters.
- **Unit Tests** appear for all units.

Technology:
- **Test Generator** provides even more assessment options.

Informal, Continuous Assessment

Comprehension

In the student book:
- **Review** questions appear at the end of each section.

In the teacher's edition:
- **"Talk About It" questions** monitor student comprehension.
- **Tested Objectives** appear at the beginning and end of each lesson.

In the student practice book:
- **Study Guide** pages aid student comprehension.

Reading

In the teacher's edition:
- **Reading Strategy** is featured in every chapter.

Thinking

In the student book:
- **Critical Thinking** questions teach higher-order thinking skills.

In the teacher's edition:
- **"Think Alouds"** let you model thinking critically for your students.

In the *Assessment Options* ancillary:
- **Observation Checklists** give you another option for assessment.

HANDS ON Rubric for Unit 1 Performance Assessment

4	Tour clearly articulates regional differences; describes landforms found in each region; gives several examples of how geography affects people.
3	Tour states that the regions differ, but does not tell how; describes landforms of several regions; gives one example of how geography affects people.
2	Tour describes regions, but does not tell how they differ; describes landforms of one region; mentions that geography affects people, but gives no examples.
1	Tour shows little to no understanding of regions; describes no landforms; does not discuss how a region's geography affects its people.

In *Assessment Options*, p. 23

Standardized Test Practice

In the student book:
- **Lesson Review/Test Prep** appears at the end of each lesson.
- **Chapter Review/Test Prep** appears at the end of each chapter.
- **Unit Review/Test Prep** appears at the end of each unit.

In the *Assessment Options* ancillary:
- **Lesson Tests for all lessons.**
- **Chapter Tests for all chapters.**
- **Unit Test for all units.**

Technology:
- **Test Generator** provides even more assessment options.

Student Self-Assessment

In the student book:
- **Hands-On Activities** appear in each chapter.
- **Writing Activities** appear in each chapter.

In the Unit Resources:
- **Reading Skill/Strategy** pages give students the chance to practice the skills and strategies of each lesson and chapter.
- **Vocabulary Review/Study Guide** pages provide an opportunity for self-challenge or review.

In the *Assessment Options* ancillary:
- **Self-Assessment Checklists**

Unit 1 Test

Standard Test

TEST PREP

Unit 1 Test

Test Your Knowledge

Circle the letter of the best answer.

1. By what means do many scientists think humans first came to the Americas? Obj. U1–12
   A. They rowed wooden canoes.
   (B.) They walked across a land bridge.
   C. They sailed across the Atlantic Ocean.
   D. They followed a long river.

2. Which of the following are capital resources that can be used in the production of goods? Obj. U1–6
   F. wind and sunshine
   G. trees and plants
   H. oil and coal
   (J.) tools and machines

3. Why did horses change the lives of the Plains Indians? Obj. U1–19
   A. because horses made farming easier
   B. because horses helped promote peace between Indian groups
   (C.) because horses made it easier to hunt and travel
   D. because they started hunting horses instead of buffalo

4. Which of the following is a long, deep gap cut into the land? Obj. U1–1
   F. plateau
   (G.) canyon
   H. mountain
   J. plain

5. Why did American Indians living in the Southwest use irrigation? Obj. U1–16
   (A.) They needed to water their crops.
   B. They used it to protect their homes.
   C. It helped them hunt for food.
   D. They carried their belongings with it.

6. Why are resources important for the growth of a region's economy? Obj. U1–9
   F. they determine what language people speak in the region.
   G. they keep consumers from buying products from other regions.
   H. they help reduce trade between regions.
   (J.) they help people decide which products or services they should specialize in.

Standard Test

TEST PREP

Test the Skills: Review Map Skills; Summarize

Use the map to answer the questions below.

7. Is the Atlantic Ocean north, south, east, or west of the Mississippi River? East Obj. U1–3

8. What countries share a border with the United States? Obj. U1–3
   Canada and Mexico

> The Haudenosaunee lived in clans. The clan mother was the oldest woman in the clan. She played an important part in Haudenosaunee government. Clan mothers chose the chiefs who led the nations. They chose a chief for life, but they could replace him with someone else if they felt he was not doing a good job.

9. What is the topic of the passage? Obj. U1–20 clan mothers

10. Write a short summary of the passage. Obj. U1–20
    Sample answer: The Haudenosaunee lived in clans. The clan mothers chose the chiefs for the nations for life. However, the mothers could also replace any chief who was not doing a good job.

Standard Test

TEST PREP

Apply Your Knowledge and Skills

> The Adena, Hopewell, and Mississippians were all called Mound Builders. They built giant mounds out of the earth. They often used these mounds to bury their dead. Some of these mounds still exist today. The town of Cahokia in Illinois is one of the most famous sites, with over 85 mounds.

11. Which group lived west of the Mississippi River? Obj. U1–3
    A. Iroquois
    (B.) Caddo
    C. Adena
    D. Hopewell

12. Which statement best summarizes the map and passage? Obj. U1–20
    (F.) The Adena, Hopewell, and Mississippians built mounds, some of which exist today.
    G. Most early American Indian groups built large burial mounds.
    H. All Mound Builders lived west of the Mississippi River.
    J. No mounds built by the Adena, Hopewell or Mississippians remain today.

13. Write a brief essay about one of the groups of American Indians you learned about in this unit. Where did they live? How did they use their natural resources? Write your essay on a separate sheet of paper. Obj. U1–13 **Essays may refer to the American Indians in the unit, where they lived as shown on the map, and their careful use of land, water, plants, and animals.**

Standard Test

TEST PREP

Apply the Reading Skills and Strategies

> Most Woodland Indians were farmers. They made fields in the forest by cutting down the larger trees and then burning the area. They planted crops between the tree stumps. Corn, beans, and squash were the staple for most groups and were known as "the three sisters."
>
> Some Woodland Indians grew these three plants together. When the cornstalks grew, they supported the vines of the bean plants. The farmers reduced the weeds in their fields by planting squash. The shade from the large squash leaves kept the weeds from growing and spreading.

Reading Skills

Use the passage above to answer each question.

14. **Main Idea and Details** Which details support the main idea that the Woodland Indians were farmers? Obj. U1–21
    Sample answer: The Woodland Indians made fields in the forest and planted corn, beans, and squash.

15. **Problem and Solution** What is one problem that the Woodland Indians needed to solve when growing crops? How did they solve it? Obj. U1–21
    Sample answer: Problem: The bean vines needed support. Solution: The Woodland Indians planted corn next to the beans so that the vines could grow up the cornstalks.

Reading Strategy: Predict and Infer

16. Think about what the author does not say directly in the passage above. What can you infer about the farming skills of the Woodland Indians?
    Sample answer: I can tell that the Woodland Indians were excellent farmers because they thought of good solutions for their problems when growing crops.

Reaching All Learners

Extra Support

Link Resources and Their Use

Groups	25 minutes
Objective	To create a word web
Materials	poster paper, crayons or markers

- Have students brainstorm to create word webs about the use of natural resources.
- Assign each group one of the following types of resources as its central topic: land, water, vegetation.
- Students use the surrounding cells of the web to describe broadly the ways the resource is used.
- Each group can post its findings for the class. Ask students to look around the classroom and find further examples of how these basic resources are used.

Visual-spatial; verbal-linguistic

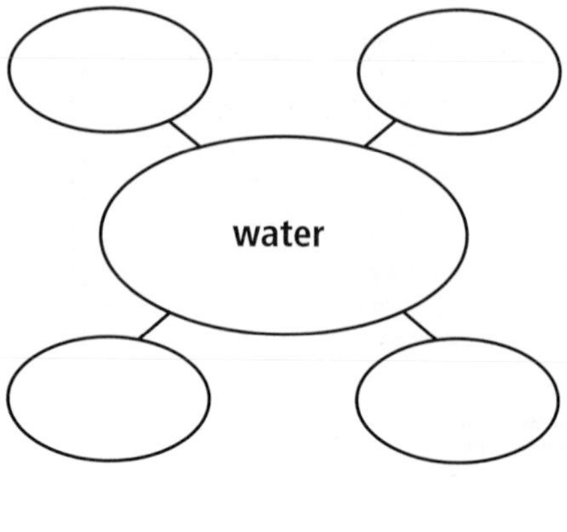

Challenge

Draw a Native American Dwelling

Pairs	30 minutes
Objective	To illustrate a link between resources and their use
Materials	paper, markers or crayons

- Explain that Native Americans built their dwellings from the natural resources readily available to them.
- Have each pair of students select one Native American group to demonstrate this relationship. The pair makes a drawing or diagram of a dwelling from that group and the landscape in which the dwelling would have been set.
- Students label the materials used to build the home and the resources in the landscape—stones, trees, and so forth—from which the materials came.

Visual-spatial; verbal-linguistic

ELL

Picture Geographic Terms

Groups	25 minutes
Objective	To picture geographic terms
Materials	paper, pencils, crayons

Beginning
Help students find pictures of geographic features such as *plain, mountain, mountain range, plateau, river,* and *woods* or *woodland* or *forest.* Individually, students can then enter the terms in a geographic section of their personal word study books, making a sketch to illustrate each term.

Visual-spatial; verbal-linguistic

Intermediate
After students have placed the geographic terms in their personal word study books along with illustrations and definitions, give them cloze sentences to complete by choosing descriptive terms from a list. Example: *The cowboys rode their horses across the plain, which looked ___.* (flat)

Visual-spatial; verbal-linguistic

Advanced
Students include geographic terms and definitions in their word study books. Have students form a conversation group to discuss the question, *If you visited the plains and the mountains, what would you find in each place?*

Verbal-linguistic

Cross-Curricular Activities

Language Arts

Write a Persuasive Letter

Singles	25 minutes
Objective	To write a persuasive letter
Materials	pens or pencils, paper

- Have each student choose a geographical region other than his or her own and write a letter to persuade a friend to vacation there.
- Tell students to begin their letters by saying that their chosen region is a good place to visit, followed by three convincing reasons why.
- Students can use information from the unit to think of recreational activities based on landforms and climate.

Verbal-linguistic

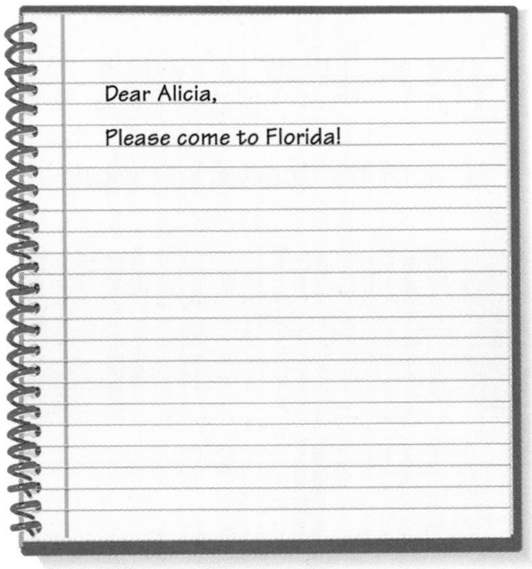

Math

Create a Climate Table

Singles	25 minutes
Objective	To make a table
Materials	pencils, paper

- Have students locate these cities within the regions discussed in the unit.
- Give each city's average daily high temperature in degrees Fahrenheit for January and July.

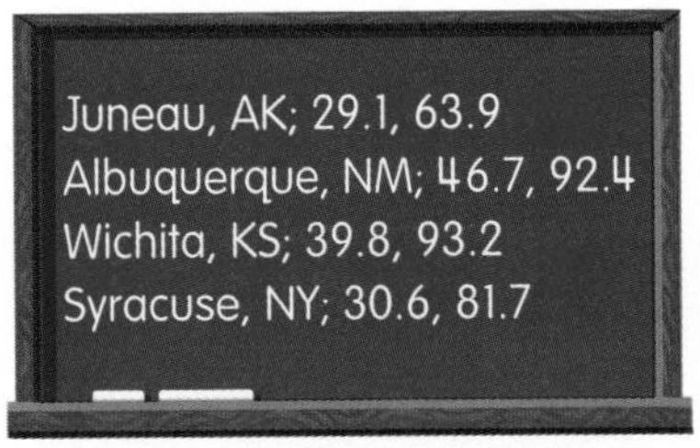

- Have students display the information in a four-column table.
- For the fourth column, students calculate the difference between January and July highs.
- Students label the columns and title the table with a sentence that expresses what the table tells them.

Logical-mathematical

Music

Sing a Song of Home

Pairs	30 minutes
Objective	To write a song
Materials	flip pad, marker, paper, pencils

- Challenge students to name as many songs about American places as they can—songs about states, cities, regions, mountains, rivers, and valleys. Students can prepare ahead of time by brainstorming with family members.
- List their suggestions on the board or large sheets of paper.
- Ask, why do people write songs about places?
- Have pairs of students work together to write a song about their community or state.

> **"My Hometown"**
>
> There's a place that I know
> With houses and roads . . .

Musical; verbal-linguistic

Begin the Unit

Unit Quick Look

Chapter 1 describes landforms, natural resources, and regions of the United States, as well as how people interact with the land and its resources.

Chapter 2 discusses Ancient Americans, and describes American Indians of the West, the Southwest, the Plains, and the East.

Introduce the Big Idea

Geography The appearance of the United States varies throughout the nation, as do the resources and ways that land is used. As students discuss the land around them, ask how it is different and similar to land in other parts of the country. Encourage students to go beyond the appearance of the land, and to talk about how geography affects the way that people live.

Primary Sources

Ask a student to read the line from the song, "This Land is Your Land" by Woody Guthrie. Ask students what it means for the land to be "your land" as well as "my land."

You might point out that the song was written in 1940. Ask students if they think that the meaning of this line might have changed in the past 60 years. Do students feel that the land around them is "their" land today?

UNIT 1

Our Land and First People

The Big Idea

What does the land around you look like?

"This land is your land, this land is my land."

a song by Woody Guthrie

Technology

Motivate and Build Background

You may wish to show the Unit Video after students have discussed the Big Idea question on this page.

After viewing, ask students to **summarize** what they already know about the exploration and settlement of the Americas. Ask volunteers to **predict** what else they think they will learn.

You can find more video teaching suggestions on pages TR1 and TR2 in the Resources Section in the back of the Teacher's Edition.

Correcting Misconceptions

Ask students what they know about the geography of the United States and about American Indians before Europeans arrived. List student responses on the board.

As students read the unit, return to the list periodically to see if any of their responses have been shown to be misconceptions.

Discuss why students may have thought as they did, and what they have learned.

Visual Learning

Explain to students that the photograph on these pages shows part of Wyoming's Grand Teton National Park. Ask students to identify the physical features that they see in the photograph. mountains, trees, grass, river Ask them how they think people might use or interact with these features. Possible answers include that since the environment does not look settled, this might be an area that people use for recreation. Or students might suggest that in a different location, the river is used as a source of fresh water or for water power.

Web Link

E-Biographies

To learn more about the primary sources and people mentioned in this unit, visit www.eduplace.com/kids/hmss05/

Designed to be accessed by your students, this information can be used for

- Research Projects
- Character Education
- Developing students' technology skills

Map and Graph Skills

Interpreting Maps

Talk About It

1. **Q Geography** What type of information about the world can you learn from this map?
   A where mountains, rivers, and plains are throughout the world
2. **Q Geography** On which continent would you find Mt. Kilimanjaro?
   A Africa
3. **Q Geography** What types of landforms can you see in eastern South America
   A interior plains and low mountains
4. **Q Geography** Name a landform and a body of water in Asia.
   A Mt. Everest and the Chang Jiang River

Interpreting Timelines

Ask students if they can identify any of the images shown on the timeline. Ancient Pueblo pictographs; painting of Hiawatha; Aztec stone calendar; painting of Comanche village

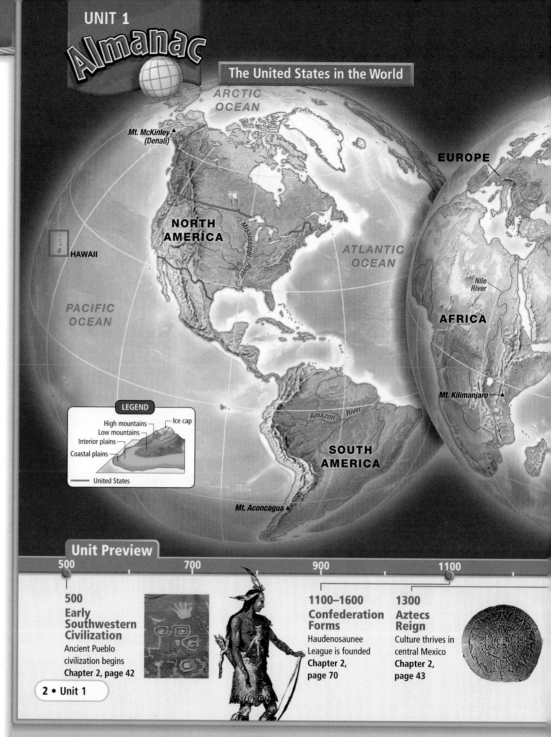

UNIT 1 Almanac

The United States in the World

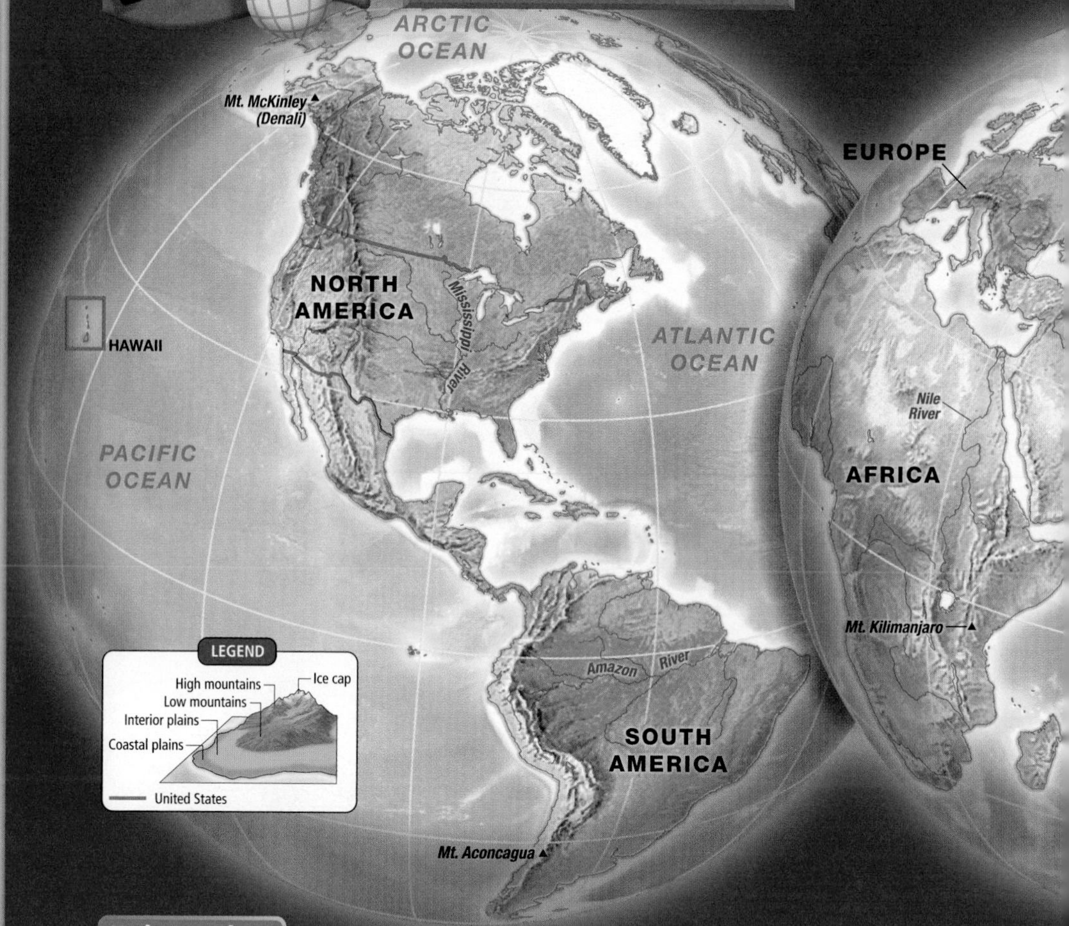

Unit Preview

500 | 700 | 900 | 1100

500
Early Southwestern Civilization
Ancient Pueblo civilization begins
Chapter 2, page 42

1100–1600
Confederation Forms
Haudenosaunee League is founded
Chapter 2, page 70

1300
Aztecs Reign
Culture thrives in central Mexico
Chapter 2, page 43

2 • Unit 1

Technology

GeoNet

To support student geography skills, you may wish to have them go to www.eduplace.com/kids/hmss05/ to play GeoNet.

Math

How Much Longer?

Have students use the pictograph of mountains to estimate how much longer the Nile is than the Mississippi.

4,150 − 2,350 = 1,800 mi.

Connect to...

The World

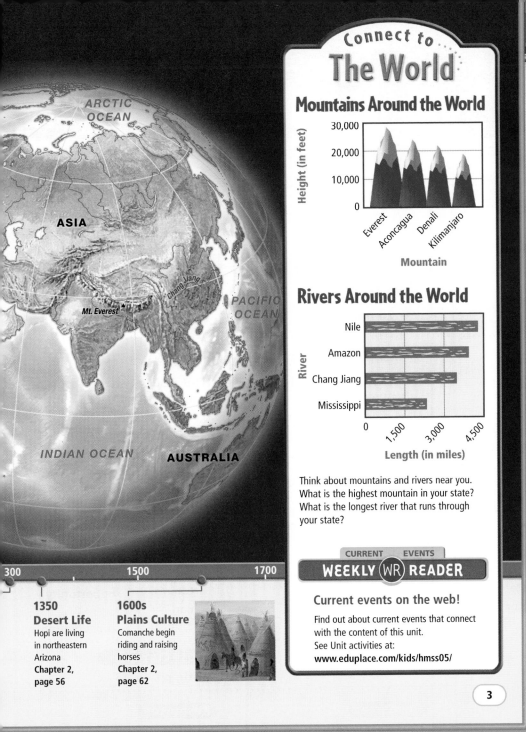

Mountains Around the World

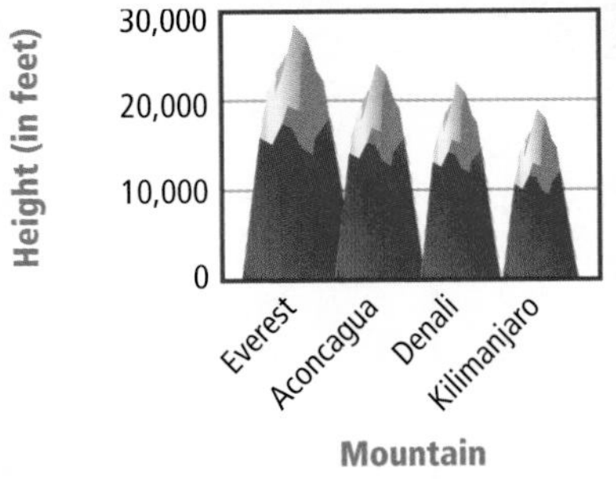

Rivers Around the World

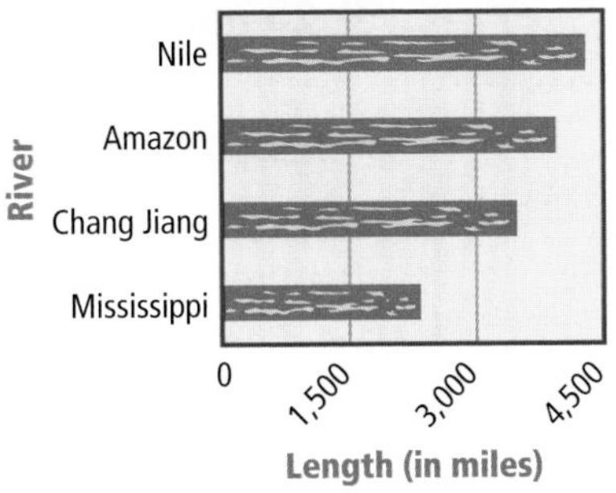

Think about mountains and rivers near you. What is the highest mountain in your state? What is the longest river that runs through your state?

CURRENT EVENTS
WEEKLY WR READER

Current events on the web!

Find out about current events that connect with the content of this unit.
See Unit activities at:
www.eduplace.com/kids/hmss05/

300 | 1500 | 1700

1350
Desert Life
Hopi are living in northeastern Arizona
Chapter 2, page 56

1600s
Plains Culture
Comanche begin riding and raising horses
Chapter 2, page 62

Current Events

For information about current events related to this unit, visit www.eduplace.com/ss/hmss05/.

Web links to Weekly Reader will help students work on the Unit Current Events Project. The Unit 1 Current Events Project will involve creating a notebook about American Indians today.

As you go through the unit, encourage students to use the web to find information for their notebooks.

Interpreting Graphs

Talk About It

5 **Q Geography** On what continent is the highest mountain on Earth? On what continent is the longest river?

A The highest mountain is in Asia. The longest river is in Africa.

6 **Q Geography** Major civilizations have grown up around the major rivers of the world. Do you think the same is true for the mountains? Why?

A No. Rivers provide a source for fishing, irrigation, and transportation, but mountains are often colder than surrounding land or do not have good farmland, so it is more difficult to live on or right near mountains.

Find Out More

Living on the Edge Ask students to investigate cultures in extreme climate regions such as the Amazon, the Himalayas, and the Andes. What specific challenges might one encounter in such regions?

Create Your Own Ask students to do research to find the five highest mountains or the five longest rivers in the United States. Have them create a bar graph to show their findings.

Chapter 1 Planning Guide

America's Land

Chapter Opener

Pages 4–5

30 minutes

Reading/Vocabulary

Chapter Reading Strategy:
Predict and Infer, p. 3F

Resources

Grade Level Resources
- Vocabulary Cards, pp. 1–10

Reaching All Learners
- Challenge Activities, p. 79

Primary Sources Plus, p. 1

Big Idea Transparency 1

Interactive Transparency 1

Text & Music Audio CD

Lesson Planner & TR CD-ROM

eBook

eTE

Core Lesson 1

Land and Climate

Pages 6–9

40 minutes

Tested Objectives

U1-1 Describe landforms and other physical features of the United States.

U1-2 Explain how and why climate varies throughout the United States.

Reading/Vocabulary

Reading Skill: Categorize geography

landform, climate, plateau, equator

Cross-Curricular

Art, p. 8

Resources

Unit Resources:
- Reading Skill/Strategy, p. 3
- Vocabulary/Study Guide, p. 4

Reaching All Learners:
- Lesson Summary, p. 1
- Support for Lang. Dev./ELL, p. 98

Assessment Options:
- Lesson Test, p. 1

Extend Lesson 1

Geography

Trouble from the Tropics

20–30 minutes

Pages 10–11

Focus: Students learn more about climate.

Skillbuilder

Map and Globe Skills

Review Map Skills

Pages 12–13

20 minutes

Tested Objectives

U1-3 Review standard features of a map.

U1-4 Compare political and physical maps.

Reading/Vocabulary

physical map, political map

Resources

Unit Resources:
- Skill Practice, p. 5

Skill Transparency 1

Core Lesson 2

Our Nation's Resources

Pages 14–19

50 minutes

Tested Objectives

U1-5 Define natural resources and conservation.

U1-6 Summarize use of resources in the production of goods and services.

U1-7 Define scarcity.

Reading/Vocabulary

Reading Skill: Draw Conclusions

capital resource, scarcity, human resource, opportunity cost, conservation

Cross-Curricular

Math, pp. 16, 18

Resources

Unit Resources:
- Reading Skill/Strategy, p. 6
- Vocabulary/Study Guide, p. 7

Reaching All Learners:
- Lesson Summary, p. 2
- Support for Lang. Dev./ELL, p. 99

Assessment Options:
- Lesson Test, p. 2

Extend Lesson 2

Technology

The Race for Solar Power

20–30 minutes

Pages 20–21

Focus: What can solar power do for you?

National Standards

III a Mental maps
III b Representations of the earth
III c Resources, data sources, and geographic tools
III e Varying landforms and geographic features
III f Physical system changes
III h Interaction of human beings and their physical environment
III i Change of earth's physical features
III k Uses of resources and land
VII a Scarcity and choice
VII c Private and public goods and services
VII d Institutions that make up economic systems
VII e Workers with specialized jobs
IX e Tensions between personal wants and needs and various global concerns

With the Program

CURRENT EVENTS from **WEEKLY WR READER** at www.eduplace.com

Core Lesson 3

Regions of the United States

Pages 22–25

40 minutes

Tested Objectives

U1-8 Explain what regions are and describe different types of regions.

U1-9 Describe how regions specialize and trade with each other.

Reading/Vocabulary

Reading Skill: Problem/Solution

region, consumer, economy, trade, specialization

Cross-Curricular

Music, p. 24

Resources

Unit Resources:
- Reading Skill/Strategy, p. 7
- Vocabulary/Study Guide, p. 9

Reaching All Learners:
- Lesson Summary, p. 3
- Support for Lang. Dev./ELL, p. 100

Assessment Options:
- Lesson Test, p. 3

www.eduplace.com/ss/hmss05/

Extend Lesson 3

Biographies

Caretakers of the Earth

20–30 minutes

Pages 26–27

Focus: Meet the people behind maps, and more.

Core Lesson 4

People and the Land

Pages 28–31

40 minutes

Tested Objectives

U1-10 Explain how geography affects settlement and other human activities.

U1-11 Describe natural forces and human activities that can change the environment.

Reading/Vocabulary

Reading Skill: Classify

environment, pollution, erosion, ecosystem

Cross-Curricular

Science, p. 30

Resources

Unit Resources:
- Reading Skill/Strategy, p. 10
- Vocabulary/Study Guide, p. 11

Reaching All Learners:
- Lesson Summary, p. 4
- Support for Lang. Dev./ELL, p. 101

Assessment Options:
- Lesson Test, p. 4

Extend Lesson 4

Geography

Reshaping the Land

20–30 minutes

Pages 32–33

Focus: How can a dam alter the land?

Chapter Review

Pages 34–35

30 minutes

Resources

Assessment Options:
- Chapter 1 Test
- Test Generator

Chapter 1 Practice Options

Lesson 1 Skill and Strategy

TEST PREP

Reading Skill and Strategy

Reading Skill: Categorize

This skill helps you understand and remember what you have read by organizing facts into groups or categories.

Read "A Varied Land." Then fill in the category chart below. What are some landforms of Canada, Mexico, and the United States?

Canada	Mexico	United States
1. Sample answer: Arctic Coastal Plain, Canadian Shield	2. Sample answer: Basin and Range	3. Sample answer: Ozark Plateau, Rocky Mountains

Reading Strategy: Predict and Infer

4. Read "Climate." Then check the best inference.
   - ✓ Landforms and closeness to the equator determine a region's climate.
   - ___ Western states have a cooler climate than eastern states.
   - ___ States in the southern United States get less precipitation.

5. Read "Landforms." Then check the best inference.
   - ___ The landforms in the United States are unique to this nation.
   - ___ All parts of the United States have the same kind of climate.
   - ✓ The United States has a variety of landforms and climates.

Lesson 1 Vocabulary/Study Guide

TEST PREP

Vocabulary and Study Guide

Vocabulary

After you read the section, fill in the word web.

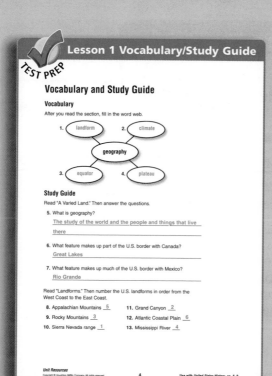

geography: 1. landform 2. climate 3. equator 4. plateau

Study Guide

Read "A Varied Land." Then answer the questions.

5. What is geography?
   The study of the world and the people and things that live there
6. What feature makes up part of the U.S. border with Canada?
   Great Lakes
7. What feature makes up much of the U.S. border with Mexico?
   Rio Grande

Read "Landforms." Then number the U.S. landforms in order from the West Coast to the East Coast.

8. Appalachian Mountains 5
9. Rocky Mountains 3
10. Sierra Nevada range 1
11. Grand Canyon 2
12. Atlantic Coastal Plain 6
13. Mississippi River 4

also in *Practice Book*, p. 3

Skillbuilder Practice

TEST PREP

Skillbuilder: Review Map Skills

Practice

1. Circle the legend on the map. What symbols does the legend show?
   National capital, state capital, national border, state border
2. To get from Austin, Texas, to Albany, New York, which direction would you travel? You would have to travel northeast.
3. Which states share borders with Mexico? Texas, New Mexico, Arizona, and California

Apply

Look at the natural resources map in Lesson 2. Find the region where you live. Write the name of your state and two resources that come from your region.

Sample answer: Washington; forests and a source of water power

also in *Practice Book*, p. 4

Lesson 2 Skill and Strategy

TEST PREP

Reading Skill and Strategy

Reading Skill: Draw Conclusions

Sometimes when you read, you have to figure out things that the writer doesn't tell you. This skill is called drawing conclusions.

Read "Our Nation's Resources." How are goods and services provided to people?

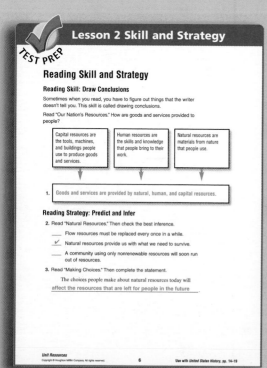

- Capital resources are the tools, machines, and buildings people use to produce goods and services.
- Human resources are the skills and knowledge that people bring to their work.
- Natural resources are materials from nature that people use.

1. Goods and services are provided by natural, human, and capital resources.

Reading Strategy: Predict and Infer

2. Read "Natural Resources." Then check the best inference.
   - ___ Flow resources must be replaced every once in a while.
   - ✓ Natural resources provide us with what we need to survive.
   - ___ A community using only nonrenewable resources will soon run out of resources.
3. Read "Making Choices." Then complete the statement.
   The choices people make about natural resources today will affect the resources that are left for people in the future.

Lesson 2 Vocabulary/Study Guide

TEST PREP

Vocabulary and Study Guide

Vocabulary

Write the definition of each vocabulary word below.

1. capital resource A tool, machine, or building used to produce goods
2. human resources A person and the skills and knowledge he or she brings to a job
3. conservation The protection of natural resources
4. scarcity Not having as much of something as people would like
5. opportunity cost What you give up in order to have something else
6. Use two of the words in a sentence.
   Sample answer: Because of scarcity, a person's decision to buy something has an opportunity cost.

Study Guide

Read "Natural Resources." Then fill in the barrels below with examples of resources for each category.

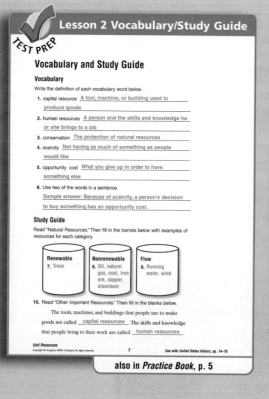

Renewable	Nonrenewable	Flow
7. Trees	8. Oil, natural gas, coal, iron ore, copper, aluminum	9. Running water, wind

10. Read "Other Important Resources." Then fill in the blanks below.
    The tools, machines, and buildings that people use to make goods are called capital resources. The skills and knowledge that people bring to their work are called human resources.

also in *Practice Book*, p. 5

Lesson 3 Skill and Strategy

TEST PREP

Reading Skill and Strategy

Reading Skill: Problem and Solution

This skill helps you see what problems some people faced and how they resolved them.

Read "Regions and Resources." How do people in all regions get everything they want?

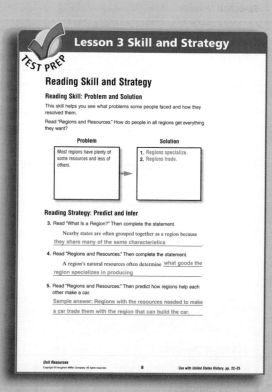

Problem	Solution
Most regions have plenty of some resources and less of others.	1. Regions specialize. 2. Regions trade.

Reading Strategy: Predict and Infer

3. Read "What Is a Region?" Then complete the statement.
   Nearby states are often grouped together as a region because they share many of the same characteristics.
4. Read "Regions and Resources." Then complete the statement.
   A region's natural resources often determine what goods the region specializes in producing.
5. Read "Regions and Resources." Then predict how regions help each other make a car.
   Sample answer: Regions with the resources needed to make a car trade them with the region that can build the car.

Lesson 3 Vocabulary/Study Guide

TEST PREP

Vocabulary and Study Guide

Vocabulary

Solve the clue and write the answer in the blank. Then find the word in the puzzle. Look up, down, forward, and backward. Look for a bonus word!

1. An area that has one or more features in common __region__
2. The buying and selling of goods __trade__
3. A person who buys goods and services __consumer__
4. Specialization helps each region make more of this __money__

Bonus Word: Economy

A	D	O	K	P	T	S	G
E	Y	J	E	D	A	R	T
C	H	E	C	N	E	E	K
O	F	U	N	G	U	M	O
N	X	B	I	O	H	U	C
O	W	O	P	Q	M	S	T
M	N	C	M	V	K	N	H
Y	F	Z	Y	U	B	O	P
I	L	O	S	M	A	C	Q

Study Guide

Read "What Is a Region?" Then answer the questions.

5. Why do geographers divide areas into regions?

   Because it helps them learn more about different places

6. What are some ways to divide an area into regions?

   By location, geographically, politically, by population, by climate, by shared activities

7. Read "Regions and Resources." Then fill in the blanks below.

   A region's resources are important for the growth of that region's __economy__. The type of __soil__ a region has helps that region's farmers decide which __crops__ to grow. Certain regions specialize in certain crops, such as __cotton__ in the South and __wheat__ in the northern plains states. To increase the variety of available products, __trade__ exists among regions.

Unit Resources 9 Use with *United States History*, pp. 22–25

also in *Practice Book*, p. 6

Lesson 4 Skill and Strategy

TEST PREP

Reading Skill and Strategy

Reading Skill: Classify

This skill helps you understand and remember what you have read by organizing, or classifying, facts into groups.

Read "Changing the Land." Then fill in the classification chart below. How does the land change?

Natural Changes	Human Changes
1. Wind and moving water change the shape of the land.	2. Building highways and digging mines change the land.

Reading Strategy: Predict/Infer

3. Look over "People and the Land." Read the headings and scan the photographs. Then make a prediction about what each section will be about.

   Heading 1: How Land Affects People

   Prediction: Sample answer: People live and work differently depending on the resources near their homes.

   Heading 2: Changing the Land

   Prediction: Sample answer: The ways that people use natural resources affect how the land changes.

Unit Resources 10 Use with *United States History*, pp. 28–31

Lesson 4 Vocabulary/Study Guide

TEST PREP

Vocabulary and Study Guide

Vocabulary

Write each vocabulary word or phrase in the correct column.

harms the environment erosion pollution ecosystem

Natural force	Human activity
1. erosion ecosystem	2. pollution harms the environment

Study Guide

3. Read "How Land Affects People." Then fill in the blanks below.

   People settle in places where they are able to __earn a living__. A city's resources and its __location__ help its economy and __population__ grow. People also choose where they want to live based on geography or the __environment__. Some people live close to mountains or lakes because they enjoy certain __activities__.

Read "Changing the Land." Then fill in the chart below to show how human activities can affect ecosystems.

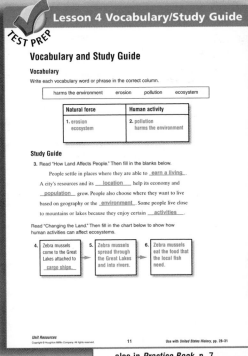

4. Zebra mussels come to the Great Lakes attached to __cargo ships.__ →
5. Zebra mussels spread through the Great Lakes and into rivers. →
6. Zebra mussels eat the food that the local fish need.

Unit Resources 11 Use with *United States History*, pp. 28–31

also in *Practice Book*, p. 7

Chapter 1

Assessment Options

Chapter 1 Test

TEST PREP

Chapter 1 Test

Test Your Knowledge

climate	scarcity	specialization	erosion

Fill in the blank with the correct word from the box.

1. When regions use __specialization__, they can produce goods at a lower cost. Obj. U1–9
2. Water and wind wear away the land in the process of __erosion__. Obj. U1–11
3. Mountains, trees, and distance from the equator all affect __climate__. Obj. U1–2
4. One condition that forces people to make decisions about what they want is __scarcity__. Obj. U1–7

Circle the letter of the best answer.

5. What landforms are found in the western United States? Obj. U1–1
   - A. low, rounded mountains and coastal plains
   - (B.) sharp mountain peaks and deep canyons
   - C. river plains and low, rounded mountains
   - D. plateaus and low, rounded mountains
6. Which of the following are all nonrenewable natural resources? Obj. U1–5
   - (F.) coal, natural gas, and oil
   - G. water, oil, and natural gas
   - H. corn, oil, and iron ore
   - J. coal, wood, and oil
7. What type of resources are farm tractors and computers? Obj. U1–6
   - A. flow resources
   - B. renewable resources
   - C. human resources
   - (D.) capital resources
8. How did the geography and resources of San Diego, California, help it grow? Obj. U1–10
   - (F.) Its good harbor helped shipping and trade grow.
   - G. Its gold and silver mines helped businesses grow.
   - H. Its mountains helped businesses grow.
   - J. Its fishing industry helped trade grow.

Chapter 1 Test

TEST PREP

Apply Your Knowledge

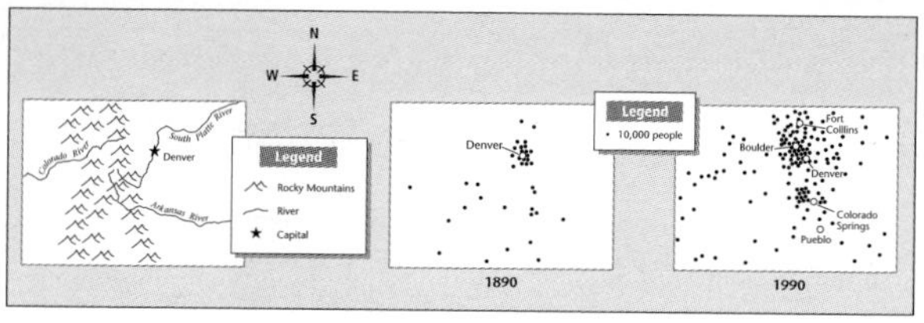

Use the map to answer the following questions.

9. On what river is Denver, Colorado, located? Obj. U1–10
   - A. Arkansas River
   - B. Colorado River
   - (C.) South Platte River
   - D. Rocky Mountain River
10. Which of the following helped Denver's population grow from 1890 to 1990? Obj. U1–10
    - F. its location in the mountains and on the Colorado River
    - G. its location in the mountains and on the South Platte River
    - H. its location in the mountains
    - (J.) the discovery of gold and silver

Apply the Reading Skill: Draw Conclusions

Read the passage below. Then answer the question. Obj. U1–11

> Human activities affect the environment. Mining may make nearby rivers unsafe for fish, wildlife, and people. Humans use ships to carry important cargo. Sometimes, plants and animals travel with the ships and affect the local ecosystems.

11. Write two details that support the following conclusion: Human activities can affect the environment.
    __Mining may make rivers unsafe. Shipping can affect ecosystems.__

Chapter 1 Test

TEST PREP

Test the Skill: Review Map Skills

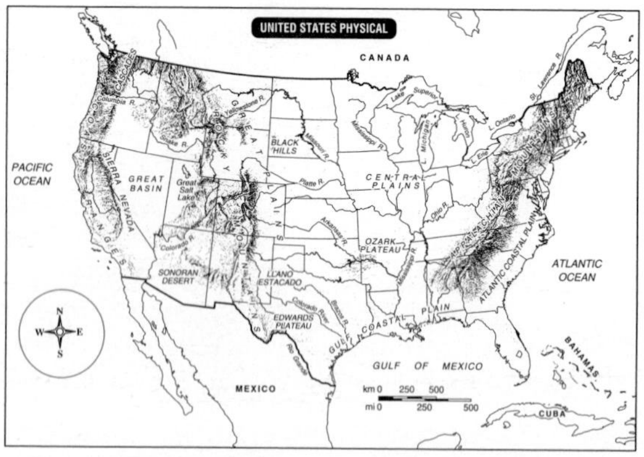

12. Circle the compass rose on the map. Obj. U1–3
13. What landform lies along the Gulf Coast and the Atlantic Coast? Obj. U1–3
    __the Atlantic Coastal Plain and the Gulf Coastal Plain__
14. What is the largest mountain range in the eastern United States? Obj. U1–3
    __The Appalachian Mountains__

Apply the Skill

15. What are two ways in which the physical map above is different from a political map of the United States? Obj. U1–4 __Sample answer: A physical map would not show the names of states. A political map would not show landforms.__

Chapter 1 Test

TEST PREP

Think and Write

16. **Short Response:** Explain what a region is, and describe two types of regions in the United States. Obj. U1–8
    __Sample answer: A region is an area that has one or more features in common. One way to divide the United States is by political region, such as states, and another way is to group states that are close to each other, such as the West and Midwest.__
17. **Critical Thinking: Infer** Why would the climate in the Appalachian Mountains be warmer than in the Rocky Mountains? Obj. U1–2
    __Sample answer: The Appalachian Mountains are lower than the Rockies. As you climb higher into the mountains, the air gets cooler. Since the Rockies are taller, the climate there is cooler.__
18. **Extended Response:** If you wanted to start a business to produce peanut butter, what resources would you need? On a separate sheet of paper, write a list of natural, capital, and human resources for your business. Obj. U1–6 **List may include the following: Natural resources: soil, water, and sunshine to grow the peanuts, oil to run the farm machines, coal to run factory machines; Capital resources: tractors, factory buildings, ovens, grinding machines; Human resources: farmers, machine inventors, factory workers, label artists.**

Self-Assessment

What is the most important thing I learned about the land and natural resources in the United States? Why is it important to me?

Teacher Read Aloud
A Story in History

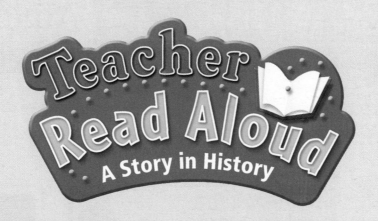

You can share the following fiction selection with students before beginning the chapter.

Activate Prior Knowledge
Ask students to talk about any times they may have seen trash or garbage left in public places in their community, such as parks, ponds, rivers, or even the schoolyard. Explain that the Read-Aloud selection describes one class's response to pollution in their community.

Preview the Chapter
Have students skim the section Changing the Land on pages 30–31 of their books. Ask them how the Read-Aloud selection reflects the information in this section.

Read-Aloud Vocabulary
Explain that an **ecosystem** is a community of plants, animals, and the surrounding water, soil, and air. Ask volunteers to define **pollution** in their own words.

Preview the Reading Strategy
Predict/Infer Explain to students that the reading strategy they will use in this chapter is predicting, or guessing what will happen next based on information they already have. You may wish to use the Read Aloud to model the strategy.

Think Aloud *The teacher and student in the first paragraph are pulling an old rusty shopping cart out of a river. The title is "Cleanup Day," so they must be spending the day cleaning. I think I'm going to hear about a teacher and students cleaning up trash from a river.*

Cleanup Day

"Here, let me help," Cassius said to his teacher, Ms. Thorne. Together, they were able to wrestle the rusty shopping cart out of the shallow river. "Yuck!" he said, picking up a slimy broken wheel that had fallen off.

Ms. Thorne nodded. "You're right there, Cassius. Major yuck!" She turned to look at the piles of trash the fifth-graders had spent the day removing from the slow-moving water. "There's been a lot of **pollution** in this river for years. Some of it you can see, like all this junk that you've collected here."

"But there's a lot you can't see, right?" Jem asked, as she dropped grimy soda cans into the cart. "Like runoff from roads?"

"Right. But thanks to all of you, and other volunteers, this river's **ecosystem** might one day be restored, and the water will be clear and clean again."

"Then maybe we can see fish here instead of garbage," Cassius said.

"And ducks instead of shopping carts," Jem added.

Ms. Thorne smiled. "That's what we're hoping for," she said.

Begin the Chapter

Chapter Quick Look

Core Lesson 1 describes the different landforms and climates of the United States.

Core Lesson 2 focuses on the natural, capital, and human resources available in the United States.

Core Lesson 3 discusses the various regions of the United States and how they provide specific goods and services.

Core Lesson 4 shows how the land affects people and how people affect the land.

Vocabulary Preview

Use the vocabulary cards to preview the key vocabulary words before starting the lessons and to prepare students to understand the content of the chapter.

Vocabulary Strategy

Vocabulary strategies for this chapter:

- Structural analysis, p. 24
- Synonyms/antonyms, p. 8, 18
- Root words, p. 8, 17, 24
- Prefixes and suffixes, p. 7
- Word origins, p. 8, 23, 30

Vocabulary Help

Vocabulary card for landform Mountains are often formed by the folding of rock layers as the plates of the earth's crust come together.

Vocabulary card for specialization *Specialization* is not limited to farming; manufacturers and service providers also specialize.

Chapter 1 America's Land

Technology
e • glossary
e • word games
www.eduplace.com/kids/hmss05/

Vocabulary Preview

landform

The landscape of the United States takes many forms. Mountains are a type of **landform.** **page 8**

conservation

When people save natural resources, they are working for **conservation.** Water is an important natural resource. **page 18**

Background

Geographical Terms

Tell students that as they read this chapter, they will find the following terms:

- *borders,* p. 6
- *physical features,* p. 6
- *mountain range,* p. 8
- *canyons,* p. 8
- *plains,* p. 8
- *valley,* p. 8

Explain that geographers use these terms to describe the physical world.

Vocabulary

Forming Related Words

Use a simple equation (base + suffix = word) to show how related words are formed by adding different suffixes to the same base.

Base	+ Suffix	= Word
special	+ ity	= speciality
special	+ ize	= specialize
special	+ ization	= specialization

Reading Strategy

Predict and Infer

As you read each lesson, use this strategy.

Quick Tip Look at the pictures in a lesson to predict what it will be about. What will you read about?

specialization

Warm weather is a resource that Florida farmers use to grow oranges. Each region has certain resources that lead to **specialization.** **page 24**

ecosystem

The soil, air, and plant and animal communities of a wetland area make up an **ecosystem.** Every part of this ecosystem needs the other parts. **page 31**

5

Reading Strategy: Predict and Infer

To predict or infer, the reader uses information that he or she has. When predicting, the reader uses that information to make an informed guess about what will happen next. When inferring, the readers use information to "read between the lines," and draw out information that the author has not explicitly stated.

Explain to students that predict and infer are different, but related. Both are based on using knowledge at hand to determine what is not known. Tell students that they can make predictions and inferences using information from the title of the chapter or lesson, the headings, illustrations and captions, graphic organizers, and what they have read so far.

To predict, a reader should ask the question, "What will happen next?"

To infer, a reader should ask the question, "Based on what I know, what can I figure out about this?"

Students can practice this reading strategy throughout the chapter, including on their Skill and Strategy pages.

Leveled Practice

Extra Support

Students can **play an association game** with each vocabulary card. Display a vocabulary card and say the word. Ask students to write down all the things they think of when they see and hear the word. Verbal-linguistic

Challenge

Have students **write two more sentences** for each vocabulary card. Encourage them to use strong context clues in their sentences. Verbal-linguistic

ELL

Beginning

- Generate simple sentences using each of the four vocabulary words. For example: *A mountain is a landform. The opposite of scarcity is plenty.*
- As you say each sentence, hold up the appropriate vocabulary card, pointing to the picture and word. Have students recite each sentence after you. Repeat several times until students are proficient with pronunciation.

Musical-auditory

Tested Objectives

U1-1 Geography Describe landforms and other physical features of the United States.

U1-2 Geography Explain how and why climate varies throughout the United States.

Lesson Quick Look

This lesson describes the United States's location, physical features, landforms, and climates.

Teaching Option: Extend Lesson 1 teaches students about climate.

1 Get Set to Read

Preview Have students look at the lesson's pictures and say what they think the lesson is about.

Reading Skill: Categorize Landforms should include mountains, plains, and plateaus.

Build on What You Know Ask students to describe the land where they live. Then ask them to describe a place they know about or have visited that has very different land. Explain that our country is made up of land that varies a lot from place to place.

Vocabulary

geography *noun,* the study of the world and its features

landform *noun,* a physical feature of the earth's surface, such as a mountain

plateau *noun,* a high, steep-sided area that rises above the nearby land

climate *noun,* the type of weather in a place over a long period of time

equator *noun,* the imaginary line dividing the Northern and Southern Hemispheres

Core Lesson 1

Land and Climate

VOCABULARY

geography
landform
plateau
climate
equator

Vocabulary Strategy

equator

To remember **equator,** think of the word "equal." The equator divides the world into two equal parts.

READING SKILL

Categorize As you read, list the names of landforms in the two categories below.

MOUNTAINS	PLAINS

Build on What You Know Is it easy to walk to your school or do you have to huff and puff to get up a hill? Take a look at the land near your school and where you live. It affects what you do every day.

A Varied Land

Main Idea The United States has many different landforms.

What would you call a land with sandy beaches, high mountains, wide-open plains, thick forests, and strong rivers? You might call it home. The United States, one of the three countries in North America, includes all these places.

In this book, you will learn about the people who have lived in the United States. As you read, you will see how important the land has been in their lives.

To understand the United States, we must learn geography. **Geography** is the study of the world and the people and things that live there. Geographers think about the Earth and the way people make it their home. They ask questions about where a place is, and what it is like. They also ask how the land affects people and how people affect the land. Their answers help us better understand our past, present, and future. 1

REVIEW What questions do geographers ask?

where a place is, what it's like, and how people and the land affect each other

Skill and Strategy

Reading Skill and Strategy

Reading Skill: Categorize

This skill helps you understand and remember what you have read by organizing facts into groups or categories.

Read "A Varied Land." Then fill in the category chart below. What are some landforms of Canada, Mexico, and the United States?

Canada	Mexico	United States
1. Sample answer: Arctic Coastal Plain, Canadian Shield	2. Sample answer: Basin and Range	3. Sample answer: Ozark Plateau, Rocky Mountains

Reading Strategy: Predict and Infer

4. Read "Climate." Then check the best inference.
   - ✓ Landforms and closeness to the equator determine a region's climate.
   - ___ Western states have a cooler climate than eastern states.
   - ___ States in the southern United States get less precipitation.
5. Read "Landforms." Then check the best inference.
   - ___ The landforms in the United States are unique to this nation.
   - ___ All parts of the United States have the same kind of climate.
   - ✓ The United States has a variety of landforms and climates.

Unit Resources 3 Use with United States History, pp. 6–9

Unit Resources, p. 3

Background

Earth's Four Systems

Scientists consider Earth to be made up of four interacting systems:

- The lithosphere, which is all the rocks of the earth;
- The atmosphere, which is the layer of gases that surround the planet;
- The hydrosphere, which is all the water on Earth, whether liquid, solid, or vapor; and
- The biosphere, which is all living things on Earth.

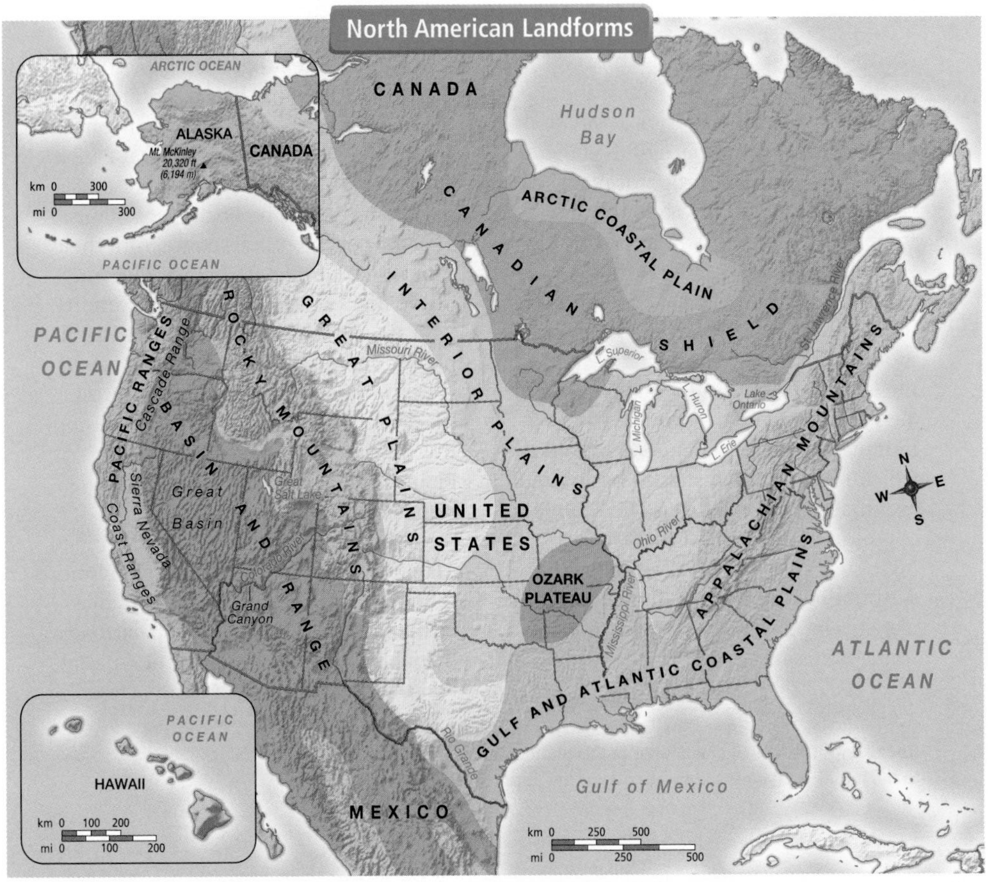

Landform Areas North America is covered with large areas of mountains and plains. The Rocky Mountains run from northern Canada through the United States and into Mexico. SKILL **Reading Maps** Which plains are along the Gulf of Mexico?
the Gulf and Atlantic Coastal Plains

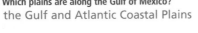

2
3

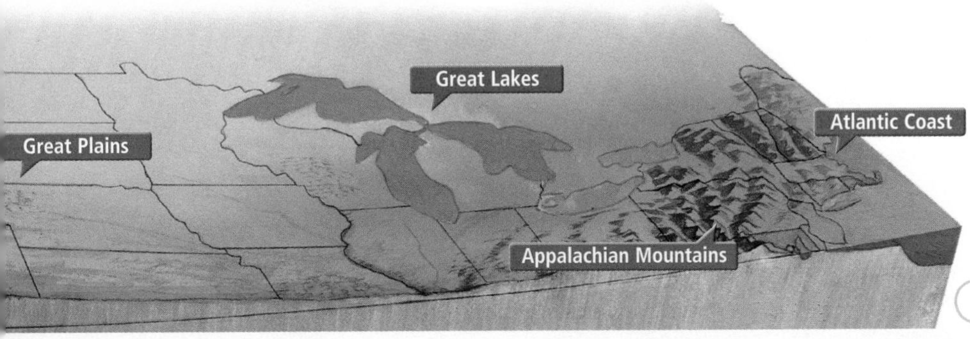

7

2 Teach

A Varied Land

Talk About It

1 **Q Geography** What do geographers ask questions about?
A the physical world and the life in it

2 **Q Visual Learning** What physical feature runs from Maine to Georgia and Alabama?
A the Appalachian mountains

3 **Q Visual Learning** In what state is the Sierra Nevada?
A California

Vocabulary Strategy

geography Tell students that the prefix *geo-* refers to the earth.

Reading Strategy: Predict/Infer Explain to students they can use what they have just read to predict what might happen next. You may wish to model the strategy.

Think Aloud *The first page of the lesson introduces the geography of North America. I predict that I will need to look back at the map on page 7 as I read, because the rest of the lesson will probably go into detail about different kinds of geography.*

REACHING ALL LEARNERS

Leveled Practice

Extra Support

On an outline map of North America, have students **locate and label** the geographic features that are mentioned in the text, including bodies of water, countries, lakes, rivers, mountains, deserts, and plains. Visual-spatial

Challenge

Have students **make a relief map** of the North American continent that includes mountains, deserts, plains, and major bodies of water. Bodily-kinesthetic

REACHING ALL LEARNERS

ELL

Beginning

Have students **make a picture dictionary** of landforms, including an island, a lake, a mountain, a desert, and a plain. Tell students to label each picture with the word it illustrates.

Visual-spatial

A Varied Land *continued*

Talk About It

4 **Q Geography** By what process are canyons formed?

A They are formed when rivers flowing over plateaus wear away the rock and cut long, deep gaps into the earth.

5 **Q Geography** In what way is climate different in the northern and southern states? Why?

A Southern states tend to be warmer because they are closer to the equator.

Vocabulary Strategy

landform *Form* is a synonym for *shape.*

plateau Tell students that *plateau* comes from a Middle French word for "platter."

climate Explain to students that *climate* and *weather* do not mean the same thing. *Weather* describes daily changing conditions, while *climate* describes the conditions in a place over time.

equator Remind students of the related word *equal.* The equator divides the globe into two equal parts.

Critical Thinking

Synthesize Where is the climate likely to be colder, in the Rocky Mountains or in the Grand Canyon?

Landforms

Landforms give each part of the country its special character. A **landform** is a feature on the surface of the land, such as a mountain, valley, or plain. If you traveled across the United States from the Pacific to the Atlantic coast, you would see a variety of landforms.

Starting on the Pacific coast and moving east, you quickly climb up into mountains. These mountains are part of the Coast Ranges and the higher, rugged Sierra Nevada range. Beyond these mountains is the Basin and Range area, which includes bowl-shaped basins and mountain ranges. Plateaus (PLA tohz) are common in this area. A **plateau** is a high, steep-sided area rising above the surrounding land. Rivers flowing over the plateaus have worn away the rock in
4 some places and carved out canyons.

Canyons are long, deep gaps cut into the earth. Rivers in Utah have carved the famous canyons at Bryce Canyon National Park and Zion National Park.

Moving east, you come to another mountain range, the Rocky Mountains. The "Rockies" get their name from their sharp, rocky peaks. They include some of the highest mountains in the country.

East of the Rockies you find wide, flat plains. The plains slope toward a broad valley in the middle of the country. At the center of this valley is the Mississippi River. Beyond the river, the Interior Plains rise again until they meet the Appalachian Mountains.

The Appalachians run from Maine to Alabama. They are older, lower, and more rounded than the Sierra Nevada range or the Rockies. East of the Appalachians, the land drops into the Atlantic Coastal Plain, which meets the Atlantic Ocean.

Rocky Mountains The mountains in this photograph are the Grand Tetons in Wyoming. They are part of the Rocky Mountains.

Art

Make a Poster

- Have students create a poster for one of the 50 United States.
- Tell students to include descriptions and drawings of the state's major landforms and its climate.

Visual-spatial

Language Arts

Write a Story

- Have students write a story about someone traveling in a specific climate.
- They might choose to write about someone who gets lost in the Arizona desert or someone who decides to climb a mountain in the Canadian Rockies.
- Encourage them to use the climate of the region to create drama in the story.

Verbal-linguistic

Climate

Main Idea The equator, landforms, and plants and trees affect a location's climate.

The climate in the United States is as varied as its landforms. **Climate** is the type of weather a place has over a long period of time. The climate of a place includes its temperature and the amount of precipitation it gets. Precipitation is rain, snow, sleet, and other moisture that falls to earth.

5 States in the southern half of the country usually have a warmer climate than northern states. One reason southern states are warmer is that they are closer to the equator. The **equator** is the imaginary line around the middle of the Earth. As the Earth moves around the sun, sunlight strikes it most directly at the equator. The more direct sunlight a place receives, the warmer it is.

Landforms, especially mountains, can affect climate, too. Lower places are warmed by the Earth's surface. As you climb higher into the mountains, you get farther from the Earth's surface and the air becomes cooler. Plants and trees also affect climate. Their leaves release water and create shade. By doing this, trees can make an area cooler.

REVIEW What is climate? the type of weather a place has over time

Lesson Summary

- The United States has many kinds of landforms, including mountains, canyons, and plateaus.
- Climate in the United States differs from place to place.
- Climate is affected by distance from the equator, landforms, and plants.

Why It Matters . . .

The land and climate of the United States affect every person in this country.

Lesson Review

1. **VOCABULARY** Choose the correct word to complete each sentence.

   climate **plateau** **equator**

   Florida has a warm ______.

   A ______ is a high area that rises above the surrounding land.

2. **READING SKILL** Would you put the Sierra Nevada in the **category** of mountains or plains?
3. **MAIN IDEA: Geography** What are three landforms you might see if you took a trip across the United States?
4. **MAIN IDEA: Geography** Why are places closer to the equator warmer than places farther from the equator?
5. **CRITICAL THINKING: Compare and Contrast** Compare the Rocky Mountains with the Appalachian Mountains. How are they similar? How are they different?

HANDS ON **MAP ACTIVITY** Use library resources to find out about the geography of your state. Then make a map showing the state's major landforms.

9

Study Guide/Homework

Vocabulary and Study Guide

Vocabulary

After you read the section, fill in the word web.

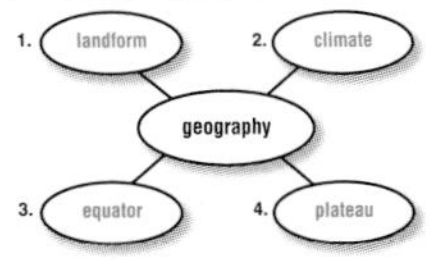

Study Guide

Read "A Varied Land." Then answer the questions.

5. What is geography?
   The study of the world and the people and things that live there
6. What feature makes up part of the U.S. border with Canada?
   Great Lakes
7. What feature makes up much of the U.S. border with Mexico?
   Rio Grande

Read "Landforms." Then number the U.S. landforms in order from the West Coast to the East Coast.

8. Appalachian Mountains 5
9. Rocky Mountains 3
10. Sierra Nevada range 1
11. Grand Canyon 2
12. Atlantic Coastal Plain 6
13. Mississippi River 4

Unit Resources 4 Use with *United States History*, pp. 6–9

Unit Resources, p. 4

Reteach Minilesson

Use a description wheel to reteach the lesson.

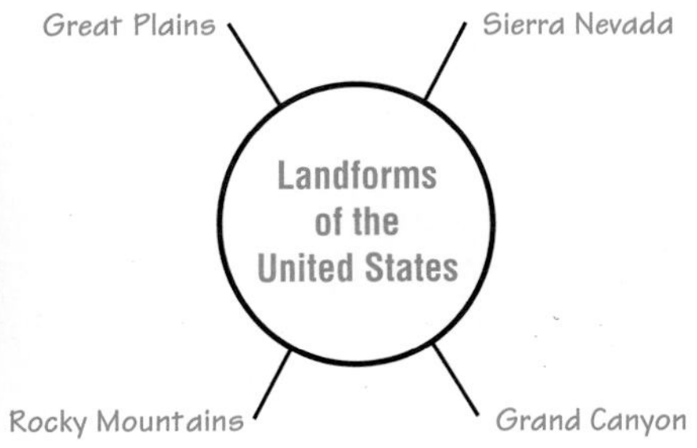

Graphic Organizer 7

3 Review/Assess

Review Tested Objectives

U1-1 Landforms include the Grand Canyon and the Rocky Mountains.

U1-2 Climate is influenced by landforms and by distance from the equator.

Lesson Review Answers

1. climate; plateau
2. mountains
3. Sample answer: mountains, canyons, plains
4. Places closer to the equator receive more direct sunlight.
5. Similarities: they are both mountain landforms; differences: the Rockies are higher and more rugged than the Appalachians.

HANDS ON Performance Task Rubric

4	Map is accurate; all major landforms are located and labeled correctly.
3	Map is generally accurate; most major landforms are located and labeled correctly.
2	Map contains some errors; few major landforms are located and labeled correctly.
1	Map is inaccurate; major landforms are not located and labeled.

Quick Look

Connect to the Core Lesson Students have learned about landforms in the United States. In Extend Lesson 1, students will learn why hurricanes are a part of North America's climate and which landforms of the United States are most threatened by them.

1 Teach the Extend Lesson

Connect to the Big Idea

The World in Spatial Terms Weather forecasters know where and when hurricanes usually form. They track the paths of hurricanes, and this helps them to pinpoint where in the United States the hurricanes may hit land. This also gives them time to warn people who live in the path of the hurricane to prepare for a big storm.

Geography

TROUBLE FROM THE TROPICS

A hot sun over tropical waters can sometimes stir up trouble. When the sun beats down on the sea, the water warms and evaporates. The evaporated water forms clouds when it rises. In tropical seas where the sun is at its hottest, huge amounts of water evaporate. All that rising moisture can feed giant storms called hurricanes. Hurricanes are tropical storms with winds over 74 miles per hour.

During hurricane season, when tropical seas are warmest, weather forecasters are on the alert. They follow hurricanes as they form and move toward land. With strong winds and heavy rains, hurricanes are sometimes a dangerous part of the climate in North America.

The storm in the large picture formed over the Pacific Ocean. It is viewed from above, using satellite technology. You can see Mexico's Baja (BAH hah) Peninsula just above the storm and San Diego just above Baja.

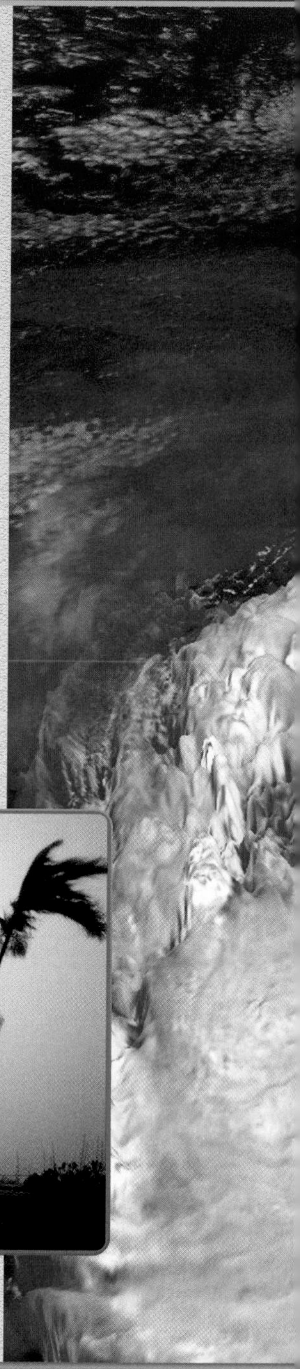

Hurricanes often strike the East Coast. In 1992, Hurricane Andrew in Florida had winds up to 165 miles per hour.

Reaching All Learners

Extra Support

Make a Storyboard

Have students make a storyboard that illustrates how hurricanes form.

- In the first frame or panel, tell students to show the sun beating down on the sea and the water evaporating.
- The second frame should show the evaporated water forming clouds as it rises.
- The last frame should show the moisture changing into a hurricane.

Visual-spatial

On Level

Create a Venn Diagram

- Ask students to compare and contrast the climate of their community with the climate of a community located near a tropical coast.
- Have students create a Venn diagram showing the similarities and differences between their community and a tropical, coastal community.

Visual-spatial

Challenge

Name Hurricanes

- Have students use library or Internet sources to find out how hurricanes get their names.
- Invite students to create a system for naming hurricanes.
- Ask students to use their system to name three hurricanes.
- Have students present their naming systems and hurricane names to the class.

Verbal-linguistic

San Diego
GEOGRAPHY

Activities

1. **DESCRIBE IT** In most parts of the country, weather changes from season to season. Which season is stormiest where you live, and what are those storms like?
2. **CREATE IT** If you knew a hurricane was coming, what would you do? Create a list of steps to prepare for a big storm.

11

2 Leveled Activities

❶ **Describe It** *For Extra Support*

Answers will vary but should show an understanding that the climate where students live is the result of weather patterns that have been observed over long periods of time.

❷ **Create It** *For Challenge*

Writing Rubric

4	List is creative, thorough, and reflects a thoughtful understanding of hurricanes and their effects on communities.
3	List is thorough and reflects an understanding of hurricanes and their effects.
2	Some tasks are listed; list reflects a partial understanding of hurricanes and their effects.
1	Tasks not listed; list does not reflect an understanding of hurricanes and their effects.

ELL

Beginning

Have students **make a picture dictionary** of the different types of weather mentioned in the lesson, including sun, clouds, wind, rain, and hurricane. Tell students to label each picture with the English word it illustrates.

Visual-spatial; verbal-linguistic

Science

Track Hurricanes

- Have students use library or Internet resources to track the course of three of the worst hurricanes in recent American history: Hurricane Andrew, Hurricane Camille, and Hurricane Hugo.
- When students are finished, have them make a list of things these hurricanes had in common and things that were different about them.

Verbal-linguistic

Graphic Organizer

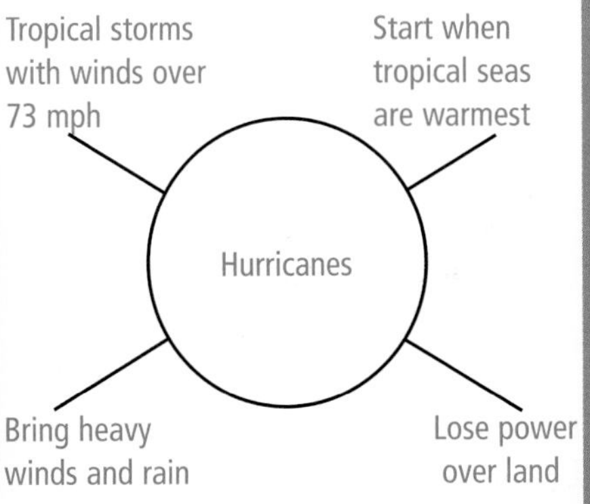
Tropical storms with winds over 73 mph
Start when tropical seas are warmest
Hurricanes
Bring heavy winds and rain
Lose power over land

Graphic Organizer 7

Tested Objectives

U1-3 Review standard features of a map, including map title, map scale, compass rose, map legend, and inset map.

U1-4 Compare information on political and physical maps.

1 Teach the Skill

- Have students read aloud the introductory paragraph on page 12.
- Discuss the elements of a political map. Which are the same as those on other maps? (title, legend, compass rose, inset map, map scale)
- Ask students what is shown on a political map that may not be shown on other kinds of maps. (cities, states, and countries)
- Go through the steps under "Learn the Skill" on page 13. Answer any questions students have about reading maps.

Map and Globe Skills

Skillbuilder

Review Map Skills

VOCABULARY
physical map
political map

Maps tell you many things about the world you live in. For example, the map on page 7 is a physical map. A **physical map** shows the location of physical features, such as landforms, bodies of water, or resources. The map on this page is a political map. A **political map** shows cities, states, and countries. Although different types of maps show different types of information, most maps share certain elements.

Leveled Practice

Extra Support

Assign partners a map element, such as the compass rose. Have them explain the purpose of their element to the group, using the map on page 12. Visual-spatial

Challenge

Have students make a political map of a state. They may choose a state where they have traveled or one they would like to visit. Ask them to show several cities or landmarks and the common map elements, such as a compass rose and map title. Visual-spatial

ELL

Beginning

Use the names of cities on the map on page 12 to practice pronunciation. Then have students work in pairs to figure out what the state name abbreviations on the map stand for. Compare answers as a class.

Verbal-linguistic

Learn the Skill

Step 1: Read the title and labels to find the subject of the map. Look at the area that is shown on the map. Check if there is an inset map. An inset map may show a close-up of an area or bring a distant area onto the map.

Step 2: Study the map legend. What symbols are used on the map?

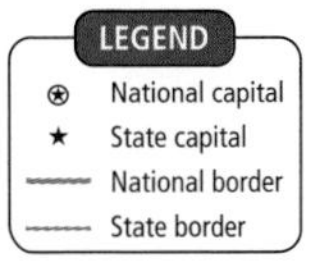

Step 3: Check directions and distances. The compass rose shows the cardinal and intermediate directions. The map scale compares distance on a map to the distance in the real world.

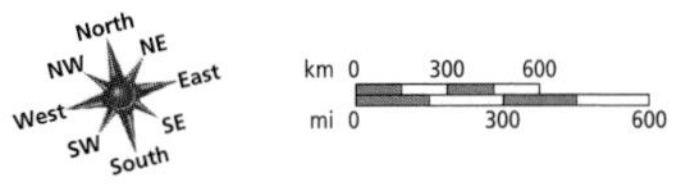

Practice the Skill

Use the map on page 12 to answer the following questions.

1. What is the distance between Santa Fe, New Mexico, and Phoenix, Arizona?
2. In what direction would you travel to go from Columbia, South Carolina, to Frankfort, Kentucky?

Apply the Skill

Use the maps on pages 7 and 12 to answer these questions.

1. Name three landforms in the United States.
2. Which of the two maps would you use to compare the size of different states?
3. Which mountains would you cross to travel from Denver, Colorado, to Salt Lake City, Utah? Use both maps.

13

Skill Practice

Skillbuilder: Review Map Skills

Practice

1. Circle the legend on the map. What symbols does the legend show? National capital, state capital, national border, state border
2. To get from Austin, Texas, to Albany, New York, which direction would you travel? You would have to travel northeast.
3. Which states share borders with Mexico? Texas, New Mexico, Arizona, and California

Apply

Look at the natural resources map in Lesson 2. Find the region where you live. Write the name of your state and two resources that come from your region.

Sample answer: Washington; forests and a source of water power

Unit Resources

5
Use with *United States History*, pp. 12–13

Unit Resources, p. 5

Skill Transparency

Skillbuilder Transparency 1
Review Map Skills

1 Political Map of the United States

Step 1 Read the map's title and labels to find its subject. Then study any inset maps for more information.

Step 2 Look at the map legend and find the symbols used on the map.

Step 3 Check the directions and distances of the map. Use the compass rose and the map scale to match the map to the real world.

Skillbuilder Transparency

Use with *United States History*, pp. 12–13

Transparency 1

2 Practice the Skill

1. around 400 miles
2. northwest

3 Apply the Skill

1. Sample answer: mountains, valleys, plains
2. the political map
3. the Rocky Mountains

Tested Objectives

U1-5 Economics Define different types of natural resources and the need to conserve them.

U1-6 Economics Summarize how natural, capital, and human resources are used in the production of goods and services.

U1-7 Economics Define scarcity and explain how it affects economic choices.

Lesson Quick Look

This lesson explains what natural, capital, and human resources are.

Teaching Option: **Extend Lesson 2** teaches students about the uses of solar power.

1 Get Set to Read

Preview Have students read the headings and say what they think they are going to read.

Reading Skill: Draw Conclusions Students should use facts from the lesson to help them.

Build on What You Know Ask students if they know what material their clothes are made of. Then ask them where this material comes from.

Vocabulary

capital resource *noun,* a tool, machine, or building people use to produce goods and services

human resource *noun,* a person and the skills and knowledge he or she brings to the job

scarcity *noun,* a lack of something

opportunity cost *noun,* the most important thing that people give up so they can have or do something else

conservation *noun,* the protection and careful use of natural resources

Core Lesson 2

Our Nation's Resources

VOCABULARY

capital resource
human resource
scarcity
opportunity cost
conservation

Vocabulary Strategy

conservation

A synonym for **conservation** is "saving." Conservation saves resources for the future.

READING SKILL

Draw Conclusions Use details from the lesson to decide whether protecting resources is important.

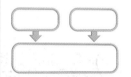

Build on What You Know You know that you need to eat food, wear clothes, and live in some sort of shelter. Do you know where all of these things come from? Almost everything we use starts with nature, but that is just the beginning.

Natural Resources

Main Idea Natural resources in the United States include renewable, nonrenewable, and flow resources.

Many of the things we use every day come from nature. The water you drink may come from rivers or lakes. The gasoline to run your school bus may have come from oil wells in Alaska. The bus itself began as iron ore that may have come from Minnesota.

Water, oil, and iron ore are natural resources, which are useful materials from nature. Nature also gives us air to breathe, and soil and sunshine for growing crops. Without natural resources, human beings would not be able to survive. 1

Corn Fields Natural resources such as soil, sun, and water are needed to raise corn and other crops.

Skill and Strategy

Reading Skill and Strategy

Reading Skill: Draw Conclusions

Sometimes when you read, you have to figure out things that the writer doesn't tell you. This skill is called drawing conclusions.

Read "Our Nation's Resources." How are goods and services provided to people?

Capital resources are the tools, machines, and buildings people use to produce goods and services.	Human resources are the skills and knowledge that people bring to their work.	Natural resources are materials from nature that people use.

1. Goods and services are provided by natural, human, and capital resources.

Reading Strategy: Predict and Infer

2. Read "Natural Resources." Then check the best inference.

___ Flow resources must be replaced every once in a while.

_✓_ Natural resources provide us with what we need to survive.

___ A community using only nonrenewable resources will soon run out of resources.

3. Read "Making Choices." Then complete the statement.

The choices people make about natural resources today will affect the resources that are left for people in the future.

Unit Resources 6 Use with *United States History*, pp. 14–19

Unit Resources, p. 6

Background

Economic Systems

- Every economic system must answer three questions: What goods will be produced? How will goods be produced? Who will receive the goods?
- In the United States' free market economy, individuals—not the government—decide the answers to these questions.

Renewable Resources

One important natural resource is wood. People use wood to make paper, pencils, furniture, and hundreds of other
(2) products. Wood comes from trees, which are a renewable resource. Renewable resources are resources that can be replaced, or renewed.

In Georgia, for example, farmers grow trees just like other crops. When farmers cut down the trees after many years, they plant new ones in their place.

Fisheries are another renewable resource. A fishery is a place where many fish are caught. If people limit the number of fish they catch at one time, new fish will be able to hatch and grow.

Nonrenewable Resources

Some of the resources in nature are nonrenewable. Nonrenewable resources cannot be replaced once they are used up. Oil is one of the United States' nonrenewable resources. After oil is removed from the ground, no new oil will take its place. (3)

Oil, iron ore, and copper are mineral resources. They are mined, or taken from the ground. Some mineral resources, such as oil and coal, give us energy to heat our homes, run our cars, and cook our food. Other mineral resources include metals, such as nickel, gold, and silver. All of these mineral resources are nonrenewable.

REVIEW What is the difference between renewable and nonrenewable resources?

Renewable resources can be replaced, nonrenewable resources cannot.

Resources Across the Land Resources such as coal and oil are found underground. Other resources, such as forests, are above ground. **SKILL Reading Maps** Where are most of the country's forests found? in the West

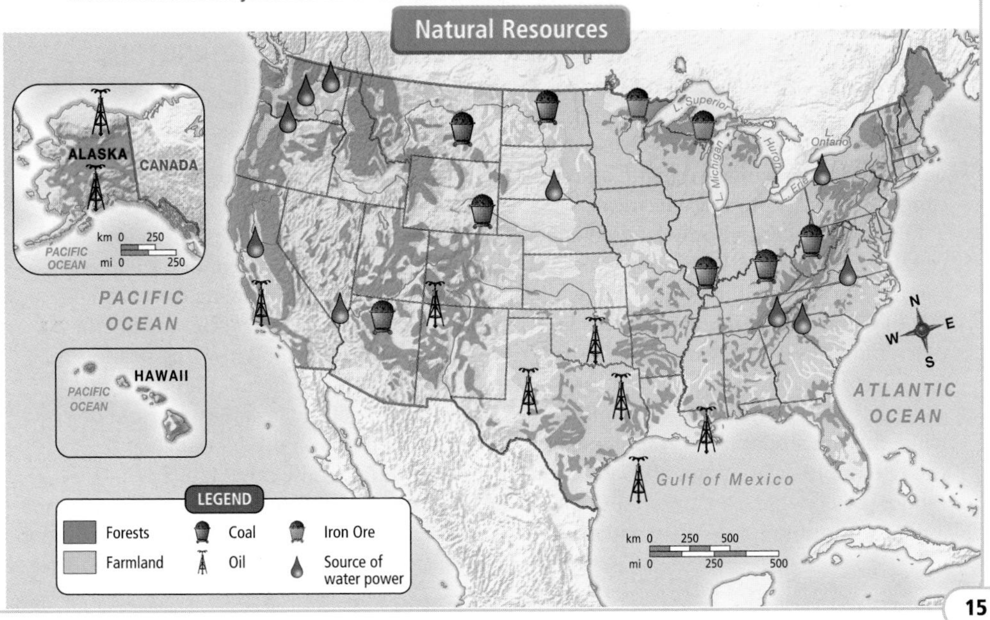

15

2 Teach

Natural Resources

Talk About It

1 **Q Geography** What are some examples of natural resources?

A air; water; soil

2 **Q Geography** What type of resource are trees an example of?

A a renewable resource

3 **Q Geography** What are some examples of nonrenewable resources?

A oil and other minerals

Reading Strategy: Predict/Infer Have students read the first page of the lesson. Work with them to apply the predict/infer strategy to understand how people use and conserve resources. Ask them to make inferences about why it might be difficult to conserve some resources.

The United States is a land of varied terrains and climate regions, as shown in this photograph.

Leveled Practice

Extra Support

Have students **make a bulletin-board display** of renewable, non-renewable, and flow resources by drawing pictures of each type of resource. Challenge them to think of examples that are not discussed in the text. Visual-spatial

Challenge

Have students **make dioramas** that display the products made from the natural resources mentioned in the text. Display completed dioramas in the classroom.
Visual-spatial

ELL

Beginning

Assemble pictures of examples of the three types of natural resources discussed in the text. Ask students to **place the pictures** into three different piles, one for renewable, one for nonrenewable, and one for flow resources.

Visual-spatial

Natural Resources

continued

Talk About It

4 **Q Geography** What are some examples of flow resources?

A wind and water

Critical Thinking

Synthesize What can a nation do to make sure that its human resources are the best they can be? You may want to model the process of thinking through the question.

Think Aloud *"Human resources" means the skills and knowledge that people bring to their work. What can a nation do to improve its citizens' skills and knowledge? It can provide free public education. It can also pay for people to teach each other skills.*

Producing Peanut Butter

1 Growing Peanuts The peanuts you eat are the seeds of peanut plants. The nuts grow in underground pods.

2 Harvesting Peanuts This farmer's knowledge and hard work move the process along.

Flow Resources

4 Flow resources are the third type of natural resource. Wind, sunlight, and water are flow resources. People use the energy of strong winds, sunlight, and running water to produce electricity.

Flow resources can only be used at a certain time or place. For example, people can use the power of the wind only while it is blowing. The wind turns the blades of a windmill, which changes that power into electricity. Special panels can turn sunlight into electricity, too, but only when the sun shines. Flow resources are not renewable or nonrenewable. People cannot use up wind, sun, or running water, and they cannot replace them, either.

Other Important Resources

Main Idea People use capital resources and human resources to produce goods and services.

Natural resources are important to us, but they are not enough. It takes many steps to turn these resources into products. For example, peanut butter starts out as peanuts growing on a farm. Natural resources such as soil, water, and sunshine are needed to grow the peanuts.

People depend on other kinds of resources to get the peanuts to a store or to turn them into a product, such as peanut butter. These other kinds of resources are not found in nature. They are created or supplied by people.

Language Arts

An Important Resource

- Have students write a first-person statement based upon a resource. For example, a statement about oil might begin: "I live deep in the ground. I was formed many years ago from plant remains."
- Have students share their statements and guess each other's resources.
- Encourage them to write about capital and flow resources as well as natural resources.

Verbal-linguistic

Math

The Price of Gasoline

Have students make a line graph of U.S. gasoline prices using the information in the table that follows. Discuss with them what might have caused the changes in price.

Date	Average Price per Gallon
8/28/02	$1.41
11/13/02	$1.48
2/21/03	$1.65
5/22/03	$1.46
8/30/03	$1.74

Logical-mathematical

4 Finished Product Natural, human, and capital resources go into every single product you eat, wear, and use, including this book.

3 Supplies and Equipment The machines that grind the peanuts and fill the jars are capital resources.

Capital Resources

People use capital resources to turn the peanuts into peanut butter. A **capital resource** is a tool, machine, or building people use to produce goods and services. To raise peanuts, farmers use tractors to plant and harvest the crop. The tractor is a capital resource. Later, factory workers roast the peanuts in ovens and use machines to grind the peanuts into peanut butter. The ovens and grinding machines are also capital resources. 5

The computer in your classroom or school library is a capital resource. The computer is a tool that helps students learn. Think of other capital resources found at your home or school.

Human Resources

All the natural resources and capital resources in the world would be useless without one other kind of resource: human resources. A **human resource** is a person and the skills and knowledge he or she brings to a job. The farmers who plant the peanuts, the people who invent the grinding machines, and the people who design the labels on the jars are all human resources. At every stage of making peanut butter or any other product, human resources make the process work. Your teacher and school principal are also good examples of human resources. 6

REVIEW What is the difference between capital resources and human resources?
capital resources: tools, machines, and buildings; human resources: people and their knowledge and skills

Other Important Resources

Talk About It

5 Q Economics Why are capital resources needed to produce goods and services?

A They are the tools, machines, and buildings that turn the natural resources into something people want.

6 Q Economics What are human resources?

A people and their skills and knowledge

Vocabulary Strategy

capital resources Tell students that *capital* has more than one meaning. Discuss the terms *capital city* and *capital letter.*

human resources Explain that *human resources* is an example of a compound word. Ask students to think of other compound words that use *human (human being, human nature, human rights)* and *resources (capital resources, natural resources).*

Reading Strategy: Predict/Infer Have students continue to read the lesson. Ask them to make inferences about some resources the lesson does not mention that may be limited. Have students share their inferences and compare thoughts.

Reaching All Learners — Extra Support

Resource Web

- Have partners make a word web called "Other Important Resources."
- Tell them to complete the web with main ideas and details from the text.
- Ask students to display their word webs on the board.

Verbal-linguistic

Reaching All Learners — Challenge

Conservation Posters

- Have students make posters to persuade people to preserve natural resources.
- Before students begin, have them brainstorm a list of natural resources and think of ways each can be preserved.
- Put their ideas on the chalkboard so they can refer to the list as they design their posters.

Visual-spatial

Other Important Resources *continued*

Talk About It

7 **Q Economics** Why does scarcity make people think carefully before spending their money?

A They must choose between different goods and services based on need or desire for each item and the amount of money they have to spend.

8 **Q Economics** Why is conservation a wise economic choice?

A It helps conserve resources for future use.

Vocabulary Strategy

scarcity Tell students that an antonym for *scarcity* is *plenty.*

opportunity cost Point out the word *opportunity* to students. Tell them that when people have the opportunity to buy an item, it costs them something in return.

conservation Explain that conservation comes from *conserve,* "to save."

Critical Thinking

Decision Making Why might someone who never thinks about opportunity costs have trouble saving money?

Making Choices

Peanut butter is just one of many goods that a person might buy. Most people have a long list of things they want. However, there are not enough resources to provide all that people want. This problem is called scarcity. **Scarcity** means not having as much of something as people would like.

7 The problem of scarcity means that people have to make decisions about what they want most. For example, your teacher might want to buy a wall map and a video. The school may not have enough money to buy both. If your teacher chooses to buy the video, he or she gives up the opportunity to buy the map. The map is called an opportunity cost. An **opportunity cost** is the thing you give up when you decide to do or have something else. Every choice people make about how to spend their money or their time has an opportunity cost.

Conservation

Another choice that people make is how to use resources. People will always need natural resources. They have to find ways to make sure those resources are here for people in the future. One way to balance the needs of today with care for the future is to practice conservation. **Conservation** is the protection and wise use of natural resources. 8

There are many ways to conserve resources. Some people work to save soil from being washed or blown away. Others find ways to mine resources without harming the land.

The United States government supports conservation by creating national parks to protect plants and animals from human activities. Businesses can practice conservation by using containers that can be recycled, such as metal and cardboard.

Flow Resources Wind power can provide electricity while saving nonrenewable resources, such as coal. These windmills are in California.

18 • Chapter 1

Math

Opportunity Costs

Ask students to decide how they would spend their Saturday afternoon (from 1 p.m. to 5 p.m.) if given the following choices:

- Walking dog, takes 1 hour, pays $3
- Going to the movies, takes 2-3 hours, costs $5
- Babysitting, takes 2 hours, pays $6
- Going to the arcade, takes 2 hours, costs $6
- Cleaning room, takes 1 hour, pays $3
- Going for a bike ride, takes 1 hour, no cost

Have students share these answers and explain why they made their choices.

Logical-mathematical

Language Arts

Letter to the Editor

Tell students that some people believe Americans should be required to recycle items in their garbage, such as glass, metal, and plastics. Other people think recycling should be optional. Ask students to write a letter to the editor of a local newspaper explaining their point of view on this issue.

Verbal-linguistic

People can practice conservation at home and in school, too. Everyone can use fewer resources by not wasting water, gas, or electricity. They can also make the resources they use last much longer.

Conserving Resources Through everyday actions, people can help conserve natural resources. Riding a bike instead of driving a car saves gas and oil.

When students write on both sides of a piece of paper instead of just one side, they use less paper. Everyone can also recycle paper, cans, and bottles, so that they can be used again. In all these ways, people help conserve natural resources for the future.

REVIEW Why do people practice conservation? so that natural resources will be here for people in the future

Lesson Summary

- Natural resources, human resources, and capital resources are used to provide goods and services.
- Because of scarcity, people make decisions about what they want most and what they can do without.
- Conservation is one important way to preserve natural resources and use them wisely.

Why It Matters . . .

Today and in the future, Americans will face many important decisions about how to use and protect natural resources.

Lesson Review

1. **VOCABULARY** Write a short paragraph about resources, using **scarcity** and **conservation.**
2. **READING SKILL** Why do nonrenewable resources need to be used wisely?
3. **MAIN IDEA: Economics** Why does scarcity force people to make choices?
4. **MAIN IDEA: Geography** What are two examples of each kind of resource: renewable, nonrenewable, and flow?
5. **CRITICAL THINKING: Decision Making** Describe the opportunity cost if you decide to check out a mystery book instead of a science video from the library.
6. **CRITICAL THINKING: Synthesize** What are some ways you could conserve resources such as paper and electricity in your classroom?

HANDS ON **ART ACTIVITY** Resources are necessary for businesses. Create a poster for a T-shirt company, showing the different types of resources the business uses to make its product.

3 Review/Assess

Review Tested Objectives

U1-5 Resource types include renewable, nonrenewable, and flow resources; conservation allows use of these resources for future generations.

U1-6 Natural resources are modified using capital and human resources to become useful for people and economies.

U1-7 Scarcity refers to limits on what someone can afford to buy; economic limits force people to make choices as to how to spend their money.

Lesson Review Answers

1. Answers should demonstrate understanding of the meaning of these terms as defined in the lesson.
2. Sample answer: because once they are used up, they cannot be replaced.
3. There are not enough resources to provide all that people want.
4. Sample answers: renewable: wood; nonrenewable: oil; flow: wind
5. Answers will vary; should show understanding of opportunity costs.
6. Sample answer: use both sides of a piece of paper; turn off lights when no one is in the classroom

HANDS ON Performance Task Rubric

4	Poster is very persuasive and interesting; lists several well-chosen resources.
3	Poster is persuasive and interesting; lists several resources.
2	Poster is somewhat persuasive and interesting; lists one or two resources.
1	Poster is not persuasive or interesting; resources are poorly chosen or not listed.

Study Guide/Homework

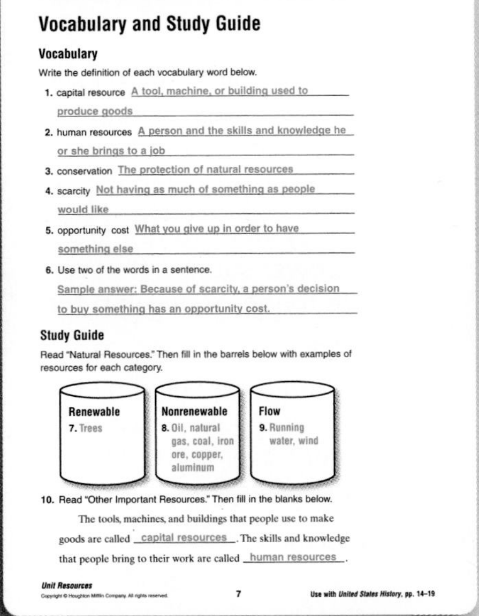

Vocabulary and Study Guide

Vocabulary

Write the definition of each vocabulary word below.

1. capital resource A tool, machine, or building used to produce goods
2. human resources A person and the skills and knowledge he or she brings to a job
3. conservation The protection of natural resources
4. scarcity Not having as much of something as people would like
5. opportunity cost What you give up in order to have something else
6. Use two of the words in a sentence. Sample answer: Because of scarcity, a person's decision to buy something has an opportunity cost.

Study Guide

Read "Natural Resources." Then fill in the barrels below with examples of resources for each category.

Renewable	Nonrenewable	Flow
7. Trees	8. Oil, natural gas, coal, iron ore, copper, aluminum	9. Running water, wind

10. Read "Other Important Resources." Then fill in the blanks below.

The tools, machines, and buildings that people use to make goods are called capital resources. The skills and knowledge that people bring to their work are called human resources.

Unit Resources 7 Use with *United States History*, pp. 14–19

Unit Resources, p. 7

Reteach Minilesson

Use a summary chart to reteach conservation.

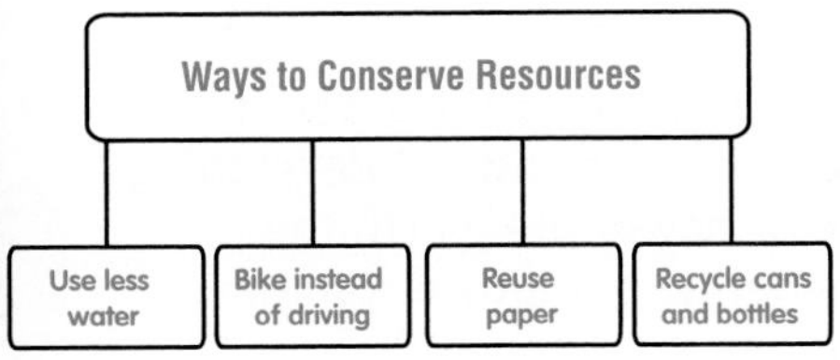
Ways to Conserve Resources
Use less water
Bike instead of driving
Reuse paper
Recycle cans and bottles

www.eduplace.com/ss/hmss05/

Quick Look

Connect to the Core Lesson In Extend Lesson 2, students will learn more about efforts to conserve our environment by developing and improving solar technologies.

1 Teach the Extend Lesson

Connect to the Big Idea

Scarcity If people continue to rely on gasoline to power their cars, clean air will become scarce. Polluted air can harm the health of people and animals. Finding other sources of power, such as solar power, involves spending money. People must make choices about what they are willing to pay for this new energy source.

Technology

The Race for SOLAR POWER

What fuel or power will the cars of the future run on? Most cars today run on gasoline. But gas-powered cars pollute the air and may add to overall warming of the Earth. Researchers want to find better, cleaner ways to power cars. Some think that solar power may replace gas as the energy source of the future.

To make solar power useful, solar technologies must be less expensive. Solar technology is better now than ever before, and scientists continue to look for new ways to improve it.

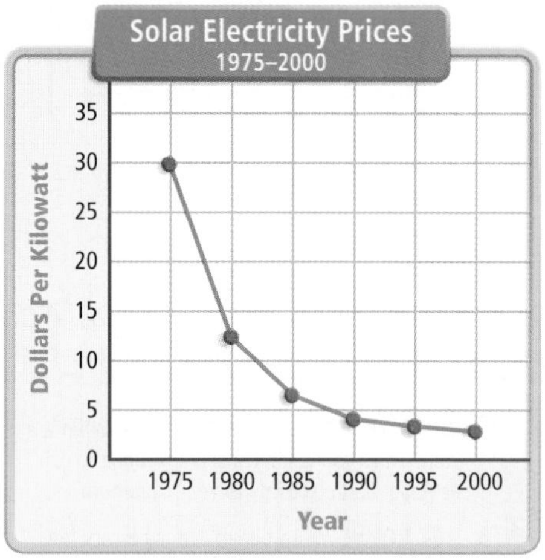

How much did the price of solar electricity decrease between 1975 and 2000?

The Solar Challenge
Every year, teams of university students compete in solar-powered car races. Their discoveries may be useful in building future cars.

Reaching All Learners

Extra Support

Draw a Poster

- Have students make a poster that shows the effect of gasoline-powered cars on the environment.
- Tell students to create a caption or slogan for their posters.

Visual-spatial

On Level

Write a Letter

- Have students write letters to the editor of the local newspaper explaining their views on solar power.
- Tell students to think about whether the costs of developing solar power are worth the benefits solar power can have on our environment.

Verbal-linguistic

Challenge

Invent Future Fuel

Invite students to write an answer to the question, "What fuel or power will the cars of the future run on?"

- Students may want to research fuel and power sources that scientists are trying to develop for future use.
- Answers should explain why the fuel or power would be an improvement over current fuel or power sources.

Verbal-linguistic

Power from the Sun

Solar-powered cars are covered with special panels that turn sunlight into electric energy. The electricity can either turn the car's wheels or be stored in the battery.

TECHNOLOGY

Activities

1. **TALK ABOUT IT** Look closely at the photo. Describe how the design of this car can help it collect energy from the sun.
2. **DRAW IT** Draw your own design for a solar-powered car that will make good use of the sun's rays.

21

2 Leveled Activities

❶ **Talk About It** *For Extra Support*
Sample answer: The top of the car is covered with special panels that turn sunlight into electric energy.

❷ **Draw It** *For Challenge*

HANDS ON Performance Task Rubric

4	Design is creative, thoughtful, and reflects an understanding of solar power; drawing is detailed and clear.
3	Design is thoughtful and reflects an understanding of solar power; drawing shows some detail, is mostly clear.
2	Design reflects a partial understanding of solar power; drawing lacks detail and clarity.
1	Design does not reflect an understanding of solar power; drawing is incomplete or illegible.

ELL

Beginning

Have students make vocabulary cards for any unfamiliar words they find in the lesson.

- Ask students to write each word on one side of an index card. Then, have them look up the meaning of the word and write it on the other side of the card.
- Students can use the cards to practice their vocabulary.

Verbal-linguistic

Math

Use a Line Graph

Ask students to use the line graph on page 20 to answer the following questions.

- What five-year period shows the largest decrease in solar electricity prices? 1975–1980
- Based on the graph, do you think the price of solar electricity will probably increase or decrease in the future? decrease

Logical-mathematical

Graphic Organizer

Solar Power

Disadvantages	Advantages
Not yet cheap enough or efficient enough to replace gasoline power	Cleaner way to power cars

Graphic Organizer 1

Core Lesson 3 Pages 22–23

Tested Objectives

U1-8 Geography Explain what regions are and describe different types of regions.

U1-9 Economics Describe how regions specialize and trade with each other.

Lesson Quick Look

This lesson identifies different regions of the United States and describes some of the features that set regions apart.

Teaching Option: Extend Lesson 3 introduces students to geographers in different fields.

1 Get Set to Read

Preview Have students look at the map and say what the lesson will be about.

Reading Skill: Problem and Solution A solution is trade.

Build on What You Know Explain that each slice would be different, yet each is pizza. This is also true of the states and regions of the United States.

Vocabulary

region *noun,* an area with certain characteristics that set it apart from surrounding areas

economy *noun,* the system people use to produce goods and services

specialization *noun,* the result of people making the goods they are best able to produce with the resources they have

consumer *noun,* a person who spends money on goods and services

trade *noun,* buying and selling goods

Core Lesson 3

VOCABULARY

- region
- economy
- specialization
- consumer
- trade

Vocabulary Strategy

consumer

Consumer includes the word **consume.** Consumers are people who buy, or consume, goods and services.

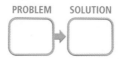

READING SKILL

Problem and Solution As you read, note how regions have solved the problem of lack of resources.

PROBLEM → SOLUTION

Regions of the United States

Build on What You Know Imagine a pizza with different toppings on each slice. Each slice is different from the others, but together they make a whole. The United States can be divided into sections, too.

What Is a Region?

Main Idea Geographers divide the United States into many types of regions.

To learn more about the world around us, geographers divide it into regions. A **region** is an area that has one or more features in common. Those physical or human features make the region different from other regions.

One way to divide the United States into regions is to group together states that are close to each other. The feature the states have in common is their location. The United States can be divided into four regions this way: Northeast, South, Midwest, and West. 1

Deserts These regions are hot and dry. This desert is in Arizona.

These four regions have features that make each one special. For example, states in a region may share physical features, such as landforms. 2 The Midwestern states have wide plains and few mountains. The West has many mountains.

The United States can be divided into political regions, such as states and counties. The country can be divided into climate regions, too. Look at the map on the next page to locate deserts and other climate regions.

Skill and Strategy

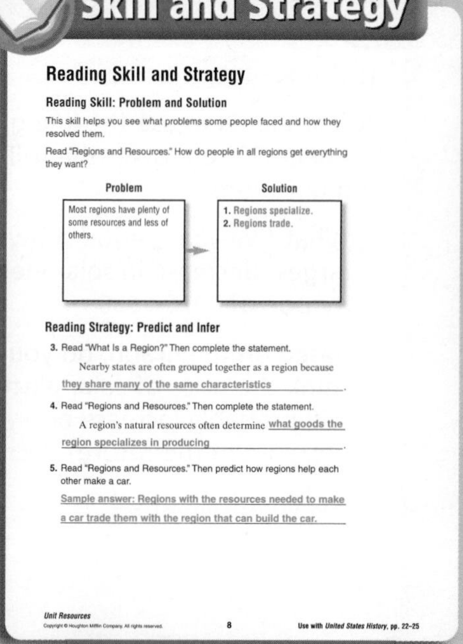

Reading Skill and Strategy

Reading Skill: Problem and Solution

This skill helps you see what problems some people faced and how they resolved them.

Read "Regions and Resources." How do people in all regions get everything they want?

Problem	Solution
Most regions have plenty of some resources and less of others.	1. Regions specialize. 2. Regions trade.

Reading Strategy: Predict and Infer

3. Read "What Is a Region?" Then complete the statement.
   Nearby states are often grouped together as a region because they share many of the same characteristics.
4. Read "Regions and Resources." Then complete the statement.
   A region's natural resources often determine what goods the region specializes in producing.
5. Read "Regions and Resources." Then predict how regions help each other make a car.
   Sample answer: Regions with the resources needed to make a car trade them with the region that can build the car.

Unit Resources

8 Use with *United States History,* pp. 22–25

Unit Resources, p. 8

Background

Growing Fast

- According to the U.S. Census Bureau, the fastest growing region of the country during the 1990s was the West (20 percent), followed by the South (17 percent).
- The population of the Midwest grew 8 percent, while the Northeast grew by 6 percent.

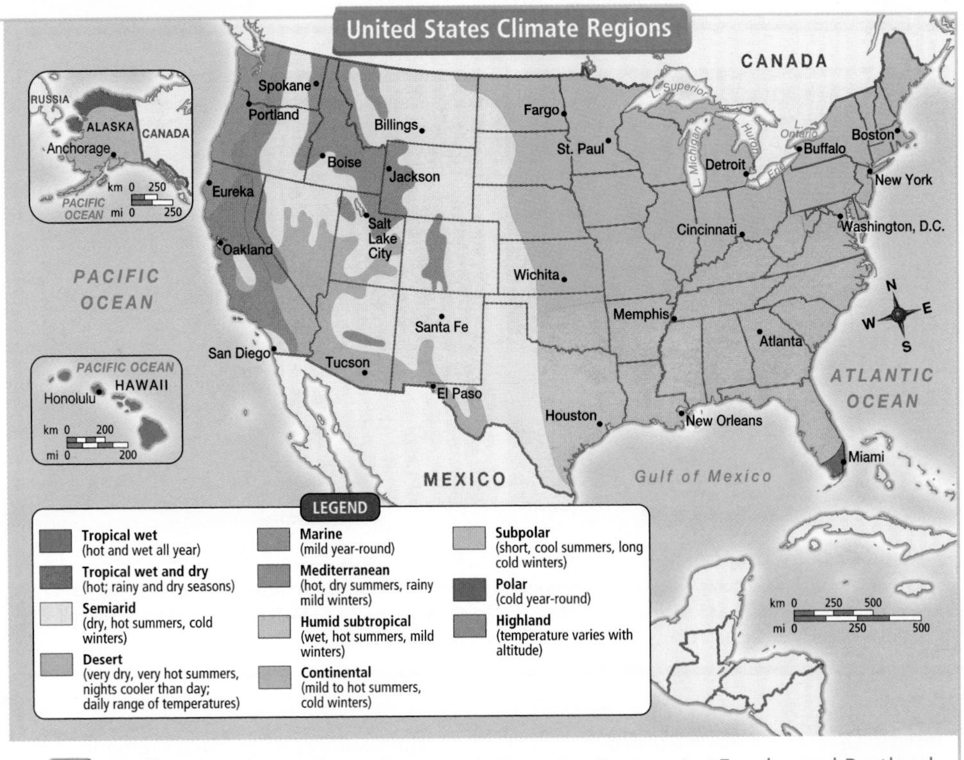

SKILL **Reading Maps** Which cities on the map are in the marine climate region? Eureka and Portland

Regions and Human Activities

Regions can be defined by the activities people in the area share. For example, the United States can be divided into regions based on the kinds of work people do. The Dairy Belt region is good for dairy farming and produces a lot of milk. It includes parts of the Midwest and the Northeast. Other regions might be places where most people speak the same language or share the same customs.

People often have ideas about what regions are like, but those ideas can change over time. For example, people used to call the Great Plains the "Great American Desert." It looked too empty and dry to be good for farming.

When people developed better farming methods, the area blossomed with fields of crops. Today, it is called the "breadbasket" of the country, because so much food is grown there. The region produces much of the nation's wheat.

People's ideas about regions are also affected by their own experiences. If you have never been to the Great Plains you might guess that most people there are farmers. If you visit the region, you will see that people on the Great Plains have all kinds of jobs, and many live in cities. 3

REVIEW What are the different ways the United States can be divided into regions? by location, landforms, climate, economic activities, customs, and language

23

2 Teach

What Is a Region?

Talk About It

1 **Q Geography** What are the four major regions of the United States?
A Northeast, South, Midwest, and West

2 **Q Geography** What do the states in a geographic region have in common?
A location and physical features

3 **Q Geography** What is an example of people's ideas about a region changing over time?
A the perception of the Great Plains

Vocabulary Strategy

region Tell students that synonyms for *region* are *district, area* and *section.*

Reading Strategy: Predict/Infer Ask students how a region's features can affect the people who live there. What might the next section be about?

Leveled Practice

REACHING ALL LEARNERS

Extra Support

Have students **plan a quiz game** about regions. Tell students that their answers should describe features of the four regions in the United States. When students are done writing questions, divide them into groups of four and play the game. Verbal-linguistic

Challenge

Have students **find five facts** about one of the four regions. Ask students to write down the facts on an outline map of the region. Verbal-linguistic

ELL

REACHING ALL LEARNERS

Beginning

Have students **draw pictures of landforms** that are found in each of the regions of the United States. Then have them place the drawings on an outline map of the United States.

Visual-spatial

Regions and Resources

Talk About It

4 Q Geography Why is cotton an important resource in the South but not in other regions?

A The South has an ideal climate for growing cotton. Other regions do not.

5 Q Economics When a region specializes in certain products, what effect does this have on the region's economy?

A The region must trade with other regions to get all the goods that its people may want or need.

Vocabulary Strategy

specialization Explain to students that the root word of *specialization* is *special,* which means particular.

consumers Tell students that the verb *consume* means to eat or to use up.

trade Tell students that *trade* may refer to a swap, or to buying and selling.

Critical Thinking

Cause and Effect Why might it hurt or help a region's economy to specialize in making only one product?

Specialization

Wisconsin Dairy

Florida Citrus

Wisconsin Dairy Dairy farming is an important part of Wisconsin's economy. The state specializes in products such as milk and cheese, which are shipped to many other states.

Florida Citrus Because of its warm climate, Florida specializes in citrus fruit, such as oranges. Orange juice made from Florida oranges is sold all over the country.

Regions and Resources

Main Idea Each region uses its resources to focus on producing certain goods and services.

Another way to define a region is by its resources. Most regions have plenty of some resources and less of others. For example, the Appalachian Mountain region has many coal mines. The region lacks other resources, though, such as oil and deep soil.

Resources are important for the growth of a region's economy. An **economy** is the system people use to produce goods and services. These goods and services include the things people buy and sell and the work that people do for others. Through the economy, people get the food, clothing, shelter, and other things they need or want.

The resources of each region help people decide which crops to grow and which goods to produce for the economy. Farmers in the South use the resources of good soil and a warm climate to raise the cotton that is made into clothing, towels, and other goods. Cotton grows well in some places, such as the South, but not in others. In North and South Dakota, the climate and soil are good for producing large amounts of wheat, but not cotton. 4

When a region makes a lot of one product it is called specialization. **Specialization** happens when people make the goods they are best able to produce with the resources they have. By specializing, people can usually produce more goods and services at a lower cost and earn more money.

Music

Regions in Song

Distribute the lyrics to Woody Guthrie's "This Land Is Your Land" and teach the song to the class. Ask which regions of the nation are referred to in the song. Then have students make up a new verse to the song about the region they live in.

Musical-auditory

Language Arts

Changing Home Regions

Have students write a letter, journal entry, short story, or other creative piece in the voice of someone who moves from one region of the United States to a new home in another region. Remind them to include details about both regions.

Verbal-linguistic

Specialization and Trade

When regions specialize in certain products, they do not produce all the goods and services that consumers may want. A **consumer** is someone who buys goods and services.

People and businesses in different regions trade with each other to make more goods available to consumers.

5 **Trade** is the buying and selling of goods. For example, oil and natural gas from the Gulf of Mexico are sold beyond that region. People in the Gulf area use money from the oil and other products they sell to buy goods from other regions.

Countries such as the United States and Mexico also specialize in producing goods. They then trade with each other for products that their people want. For example, people in the United States buy oil from Mexico, which produces large amounts of oil.

The United States has many car makers. Mexicans, like people all over the world, buy American-designed cars. Businesses in countries around the world are connected through trading.

REVIEW Why do people in regions trade with each other? to get goods and services produced in other regions

Lesson Summary

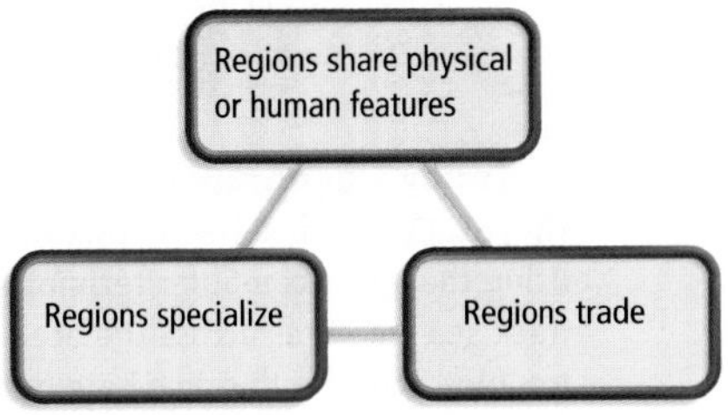

Why It Matters . . .

Specialization and trade increase the amount of goods and services people produce.

Lesson Review

1. **VOCABULARY** Write a short paragraph about where you live, using **region, specialization,** and **trade.**
2. **READING SKILL** If a region doesn't have resources that it needs, what is one **solution** to the **problem?**
3. **MAIN IDEA: Culture** Why did people's ideas about the Great Plains change?
4. **MAIN IDEA: Economics** How do the natural resources in a region affect which products people make?
5. **PLACES TO KNOW:** Where is the Dairy Belt region and what products is it known for?
6. **CRITICAL THINKING: Cause and Effect** What effect does trade have on consumers?

WRITING ACTIVITY Write a poem that describes the natural resources, climate, landforms, foods, customs, or other features that make your region of the United States different from the rest of the country.

3 Review/Assess

Review Tested Objectives

U1-8 Regions are areas connected by geographic or other similarities; examples include political regions and climate regions.

U1-9 Regions tend to produce certain goods in abundance and trade with other regions for other goods.

Lesson Review Answers

1. Paragraphs should show understanding of the meaning of the terms as used in the lesson.
2. to trade with another region that does have these things
3. At first, the area seemed too difficult to farm, but as people developed better farming techniques it turned out to be a rich source of farmland.
4. People make resources based partly on the natural features and climate of their region.
5. It includes parts of the Midwest and the Northeast; milk and cheese
6. Trade allows consumers to buy things that are not produced in their region.

Writing Rubric

4	Poem is clearly written and shows considerable creative effort; descriptions are accurate; mechanics are correct.
3	Poem is adequately written and shows creative effort; descriptions are generally accurate; few errors in mechanics are present.
2	Poem is written in a confused or disorganized way and shows some creative effort; descriptions are partly accurate; some errors in mechanics are present.
1	Poem is disorganized and shows little effort; descriptions are inaccurate; many errors in mechanics are present.

Study Guide/Homework

Vocabulary and Study Guide

Vocabulary

Solve the clue and write the answer in the blank. Then find the word in the puzzle. Look up, down, forward, and backward. Look for a bonus word!

1. An area that has one or more features in common region
2. The buying and selling of goods trade
3. A person who buys goods and services consumer
4. Specialization helps each region make more of this money

Bonus Word: Economy

A	D	O	K	P	T	S	G
E	Y	J	E	D	A	R	T
C	H	E	C	N	E	E	K
O	F	U	N	G	U	M	O
N	X	B	I	O	H	U	C
O	W	O	P	Q	M	S	T
M	N	C	M	V	K	N	H
Y	F	Z	Y	U	B	O	P
I	L	O	S	M	A	C	Q

Study Guide

Read "What Is a Region?" Then answer the questions.

5. Why do geographers divide areas into regions?
Because it helps them learn more about different places
6. What are some ways to divide an area into regions?
By location, geographically, politically, by population, by climate, by shared activities
7. Read "Regions and Resources." Then fill in the blanks below.

A region's resources are important for the growth of that region's economy. The type of soil a region has helps that region's farmers decide which crops to grow. Certain regions specialize in certain crops, such as cotton in the South and wheat in the northern plains states. To increase the variety of available products, trade exists among regions.

Unit Resources

9 Use with *United States History*, pp. 22–25

Unit Resources, p. 9

Reteach Minilesson

Use a graphic organizer to reteach regional divisions.

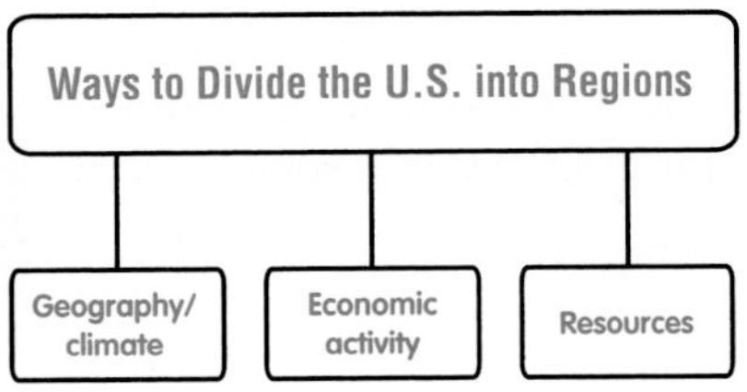

Graphic Organizer 8

Extend

Quick Look

Connect to the Core Lesson In Extend Lesson 3, students will learn more about the work that geographers do today and how their work affects our everyday lives.

1 Teach the Extend Lesson

Connect to the Big Idea

Human/Environment Interaction In addition to studying the earth, geographers also study the ways in which humans use and change the earth. For example, human events, such as wars, can force people to have to find new lands and new ways of making a living from it.

Extend Lesson 3

Biographies

Caretakers of the Earth

Today's geographers do much more than map the earth. They study how people interact with the land and the world around them. Using the latest computer technology, they can forecast earthquakes and track sea creatures across the ocean floor. They study regions with political troubles and help decide where boundaries should be drawn. Geographers today are problem solvers, helping to show how the physical world affects the lives of everyone.

Dawn Wright

An oceanographer is a geographer who studies the ocean. Dawn Wright knew that was what she wanted to do since she was a child in Hawaii, surrounded by the sea.

Wright is now a professor at Oregon State University. She uses computers to study underwater volcanoes and fissures, or cracks, along the sea floor. She is an expert in Geographic Information Systems (GIS), a computer program that can map the ocean floor in three dimensions. It can show how ocean temperatures affect sea creatures.

To future oceanographers, Wright says, "Get as much experience as you can on computers. That is a big part of oceanography today."

26 • Chapter 1

Reaching All Learners

Extra Support

Summarize

- Ask students to select one of the three geographers featured in the lesson, and have them summarize the work their geographer does.
- Tell students to write a statement that explains why the work done by this geographer is important.

Verbal-linguistic

On Level

Make a List

Ask students to consider the type of work each of the three geographers does and the skills that they have. Have students make a list of the reasons why they would or would not want to be a geographer.

Verbal-linguistic

Challenge

Give a Presentation

- Ask students to find out about other types of work that geographers do today and how their work helps humanity.
- Have students write thank you notes to geographers for the work they do. Notes should clearly describe the benefits of the geographers' work.

Verbal-linguistic

Mei-Po Kwan

Mei-Po Kwan likes being a geographer because she can travel and learn about different cultures. A professor at Ohio State University, Kwan uses new computer systems to learn about the behaviors of groups of people around the world. Kwan is interested in seeing whether women in different places have the same opportunities as men. She also studies how people in different nations use their resources. With this information she can find out whether they have enough medical care.

She says, "Geography provides us with training to see connections and understand the world better."

William Wood

As the geographer for the Department of State, William Wood works on issues that are on the front pages of newspapers around the world. Wood helps world leaders solve disagreements over land and water. He also works with countries recovering from war by showing them where to find resources, such as food and shelter.

Wood says, "Geography can help people better use natural resources, such as clean water and productive farmland, so that future generations in these countries can benefit."

Activities

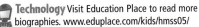

1. **TALK ABOUT IT** Choose one geographer and tell what would be interesting about his or her work.
2. **WRITE ABOUT IT** Write about what a geographer might want to study in your community.

Technology Visit Education Place to read more biographies. www.eduplace.com/kids/hmss05/

27

2 Leveled Activities

1 Talk About It *For Extra Support*
Answers may vary, but should reflect an understanding of the geographer's work.

2 Write About It *For Challenge*

Writing Rubric

4	Statement is creative, clear, and accurate; supports main ideas with relevant details; mechanics are correct.
3	Statement is mostly clear and accurate; most main ideas supported with details; most mechanics are correct.
2	Statement is somewhat unclear and inaccurate; main ideas are supported with few details; several mechanical errors present.
1	Statement is incomplete, inaccurate, or unclear; main ideas are not supported with details; many mechanical errors present.

ELL

Intermediate/Advanced

- Ask pairs of students to read one of the biographies together.
- Have each pair list three facts about the geographer profiled in the biography. Ask each pair to swap their list with another pair and read each other's list.

Verbal-linguistic

Art

Design a Homepage

Have students design the homepage of a Web site about careers for today's geographers.

- Remind students that they want their homepage to attract and interest viewers.
- They will also want to have icons on the homepage that will take viewers to pages that will have additional information about careers in geography.

Visual-spatial

Graphic Organizer

Modern geographers do much more than map the earth.

- Study changes in the ocean
- Make sure people have enough health and medical care
- Help countries recover from war

Graphic Organizer 8

Tested Objectives

U1-10 Geography Explain how geography affects settlement and other human activities.

U1-11 Geography Describe natural forces and human activities that can change the environment.

Lesson Quick Look

This lesson describes how the land and its resources influence where people live and how people and nature can alter the land.

Teaching Option: Extend Lesson 4 teaches students about the Hoover Dam.

1 Get Set to Read

Preview Have students look at the photo on page 28. Ask students how the land and climate are affecting the way people in the picture live.

Reading Skill: Classify Erosion is an example of a natural process.

Build on What You Know Have students name jobs that people in your area do. Ask them what the list of jobs tells them about your state's resources.

Vocabulary

environment *noun,* the things that surround someone, including water and land

erosion *noun,* the process by which water and wind wear away the land

pollution *noun,* harmful materials that damage or contaminate air, water, or soil

ecosystem *noun,* a community of animals and plants interacting with their environment

Core Lesson 4

People and the Land

VOCABULARY

environment
erosion
pollution
ecosystem

Vocabulary Strategy

pollution

The suffix **-ion** turns a word into a noun. When people **pollute,** the result is **pollution.**

READING SKILL

Classify As you read, note how nature and humans have brought changes to the land.

NATURE	HUMANS

Build on What You Know What makes the area where you live a good place for people? Maybe it is the geography. Geography always affects where people live and the work they do.

How Land Affects People

Main Idea The land and its resources affect where and how people live.

More than one million people live in San Diego, California. It is one of the largest cities in the United States. Why is San Diego so big? Geography is part of the reason. Like many large cities, San Diego has the resources and location that allow many people to live there.

San Diego is located on the Pacific coast. The city has a fine harbor, one of its most important resources. A harbor is a body of water where ships can load and unload goods. Shipping and trade have helped San Diego grow and are still important to the city's economy. Today, San Diego's economy provides many kinds of jobs for the people who live there.

San Diego, California Many business owners choose to start companies in San Diego because of its pleasant climate.

Skill and Strategy

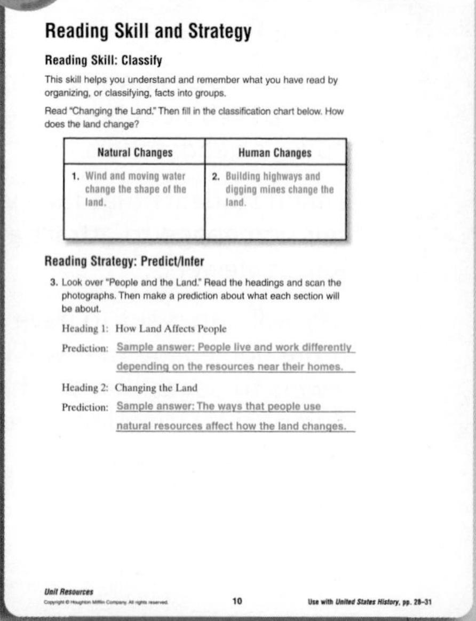

Reading Skill and Strategy

Reading Skill: Classify

This skill helps you understand and remember what you have read by organizing, or classifying, facts into groups.

Read "Changing the Land." Then fill in the classification chart below. How does the land change?

Natural Changes	Human Changes
1. Wind and moving water change the shape of the land.	2. Building highways and digging mines change the land.

Reading Strategy: Predict/Infer

3. Look over "People and the Land." Read the headings and scan the photographs. Then make a prediction about what each section will be about.

Heading 1: How Land Affects People

Prediction: Sample answer: People live and work differently depending on the resources near their homes.

Heading 2: Changing the Land

Prediction: Sample answer: The ways that people use natural resources affect how the land changes.

Unit Resources

10 Use with *United States History,* pp. 28–31

Unit Resources, p. 10

Background

Where People Live Today

- Port cities like San Diego are important centers of population. Other important port cities in the United States are New York City, New York, New Orleans, Louisiana, Mobile, Alabama, and San Francisco, California.
- The five fastest-growing U.S. cities with populations of 100,000 or more in 2002 were Gilbert, Arizona; North Las Vegas, Nevada; Henderson, Nevada; Chandler, Arizona; and Peoria, Arizona.

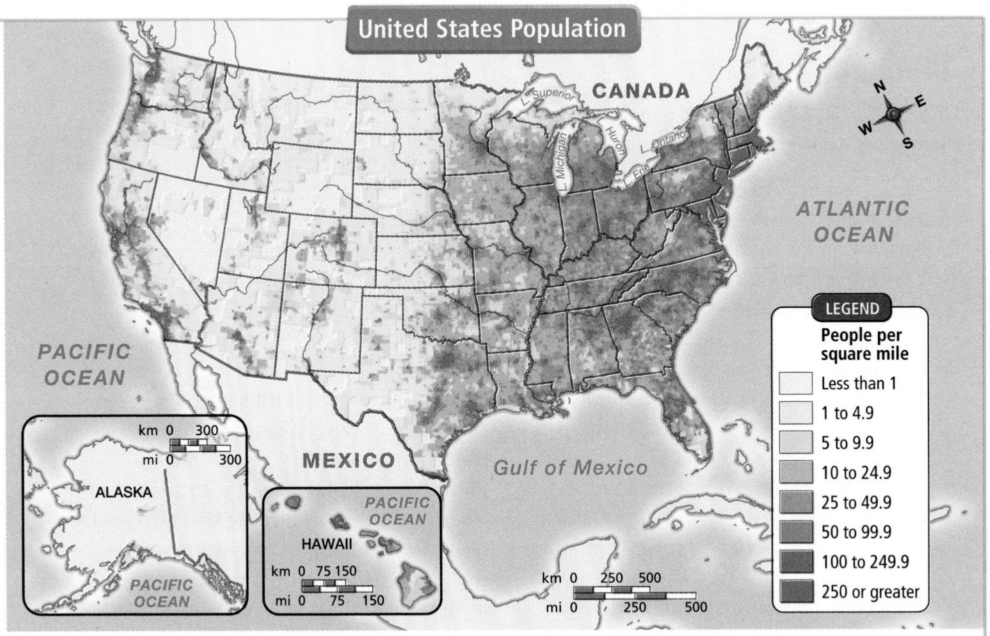

Where People Live This map shows that some areas have many people and other areas have very few. SKILL **Reading Maps** Do more people live in the eastern half or in the western half of the United States? in the eastern half

Where People Live

People often live near resources such as water, transportation routes, or jobs.
1 Denver, Colorado, grew partly because gold and silver were discovered near there. Mining became a way for many people to earn a living. As the number of miners grew, so did the number of stores, restaurants, and other businesses that served the miners. Denver's population grew as its economy grew.

People settle in places where they are able to earn a living, but they also choose to settle in places they enjoy. Geography affects those choices, too. Many people live in Florida and Arizona because they like the environments there. The **environment** is the surroundings in which people, plants, and animals live.

A warm, sunny climate is part of the environment in the South and Southwest. These regions are the fastest growing in the United States. Millions of people have moved there from the Northeast, where winters can be long and cold.

Geography also affects the activities people do for fun. The mountains in Vermont make downhill skiing a popular winter activity and hiking a popular summer activity. People can't ski on snow in Florida, but many people like to waterski in that state's lakes and rivers. 2

REVIEW Why does San Diego's location attract businesses and people? The harbor is good for shipping and trade; businesses moved there for the climate. This creates jobs and attracts new residents.

2 Teach

How Land Affects People

Talk About It

1 **Q Geography** Explain how the presence of gold and silver helped Denver grow.

A The discovery of the metals drew miners to the area. As the number of miners grew, so did the number of businesses that served them.

2 **Q Geography** How does geography influence what people do for fun?

A People choose activities such as skiing or fishing based on geography.

Vocabulary Strategy

environment Tell students that a school may be called a "learning environment."

Reading Strategy: Predict/Infer Ask students to make inferences as they read about the effects of humans on their environment.

Reaching All Learners — Leveled Practice

Extra Support

Ask students to **write a paragraph** telling where they might like to live when they are adults. Have them explain their choices by describing what attracts them to a place. Verbal-linguistic

Challenge

Have students **infer** why so many people live in the five largest U.S. cities. Ask them to find out what the land, climate, and resources of these cities are like. Students can make a chart and discuss it as a class. Visual-spatial

Reaching All Learners — ELL

Intermediate

Have students **interview** someone to find out why they settled where they live now. Have students write a paragraph about what they have learned.

Verbal-linguistic

Changing the Land

Talk About It

3 **Q Geography** What kinds of natural forces can change the land?

A Water and wind can change the land.

4 **Q Geography** What are some human activities that can change the land?

A building highways; mining; using chemicals; introducing new life forms into ecosystems

Vocabulary Strategy

erosion *Erosion* comes from a Latin word that means "to eat away."

pollution Tell students that the verb related to *pollution* is *pollute*.

ecosystem Explain that *system* comes from a Greek verb that means "to combine." An ecosystem is a combination of living and nonliving things.

Critical Thinking

Draw Conclusions What are some possible ways to lower our dependence on nonrenewable resources such as oil? You may want to model the process of thinking through the question.

Think Aloud *We might develop human-made products that serve the same needs as oil. We could also use solar power more often to do things such as heat our homes and power our cars.*

Changing the Land

Main Idea Natural forces and human activities both affect the land.

3 The land is always changing. Natural forces, such as wind and moving water, constantly shape and reshape the land. For example, the Colorado River has carved the Grand Canyon through erosion. **Erosion** is the process by which water and wind wear away the land. Erosion has been shaping the Grand Canyon for several million years, and it is still cutting the canyon deeper and wider.

Wind and water change the land in other ways, too. Strong wind and rushing water can carry bits of soil for miles. Soil that is blown or washed away collects in other places. Over time it can build up and form whole new areas of land. Much of Louisiana was formed from soil that was carried there by the Mississippi River.

Human Activities

Human activities, such as building highways and digging mines, also change the land. These activities can bring many benefits, but they often have costs too. Big projects can hurt the environment or change how the land may be used in the future. Building highways provides a way for people to travel, but the land cannot be used for other purposes, such as farming. 4

Mining provides jobs and resources that people want. When people dig mines, however, they often destroy plant life and places where animals live. Chemicals used in mining can also create pollution. **Pollution** is anything that makes the soil, air, or water dirty and unhealthy. Pollution from mines may make nearby rivers unsafe for fish, wildlife, and people.

Strip Mining Erosion from strip mining can carry pollution away from the site. An employee from a mining company (right) tests the quality of water in this lake to make sure it is safe for fish and wildlife.

Science

Human-animal Interaction

- As humans change the land, wildlife adapts, even to the point of living among us.
- Have students research the animal species that live with people in your area.
- A good starting point is *Animals Among Us*, by Fran Hodgkins, and your state wildlife department.

Visual-spatial

Language Arts

Write a Newspaper Article

- Have students write a newspaper article explaining what your community does to practice conservation.
- Remind students to answer the questions *who, what, when, where,* and *how.*

Verbal-linguistic

Effects on the Environment

Humans sometimes make small changes to the environment that have big effects. The environment is made up of many ecosystems. An **ecosystem** is a community of plants and animals along with the surrounding soil, air, and water. Each part of an ecosystem affects the health of all the other parts. A lake is an ecosystem that contains water, plants, fish, and birds. If the water becomes polluted, the lake's plants and animals will suffer.

Human activity can affect an ecosystem in ways people never expected. Ships have accidentally carried plants and animals from one ecosystem to another. In their new ecosystems, these plants and animals sometimes spread quickly. This happened in the Great Lakes. The zebra mussel, a type of shellfish, came to the Great Lakes attached to ships. The mussels have spread throughout the Great Lakes and many of the country's rivers.

Zebra mussels can cause big problems. They form groups that clog pipes, and they eat the food that local fish depend on. Today, people are aware that what they do always has an effect on the environment.

REVIEW What is one example of how natural forces can change the land? Sample answer: The Colorado River has eroded the land and carved the Grand Canyon.

Lesson Summary

Landforms, natural resources, environment, and other features of the land affect where and how people live. People change the environment to meet their needs. Building highways and digging mines are two of the many ways humans have changed their environment. When people change the environment, the effects can be surprising.

Why It Matters . . .

People's lives are always connected to the land, so learning about the environment is important.

Lesson Review

1. **VOCABULARY** Write a sample e-mail to the editor of your local newspaper, using **environment** and **pollution.**
2. **READING SKILL** What is erosion's effect on the land?
3. **MAIN IDEA: Economics** Give an example from the lesson of how resources affect the work people do.
4. **MAIN IDEA: Geography** How does climate influence where people live?
5. **CRITICAL THINKING: Draw Conclusions** What is the relationship between the geography in your region and the activities people there do for fun?
6. **CRITICAL THINKING: Cause and Effect** What effect did the spread of zebra mussels have on the Great Lakes?

WRITING ACTIVITY Find out about an ecosystem near where you live. Prepare a short talk on the parts of that ecosystem and the impact people have on it.

Study Guide/Homework

Vocabulary and Study Guide

Vocabulary

Write each vocabulary word or phrase in the correct column.

harms the environment erosion pollution ecosystem

Natural force	Human activity
1. erosion ecosystem	2. pollution harms the environment

Study Guide

3. Read "How Land Affects People." Then fill in the blanks below.

People settle in places where they are able to earn a living. A city's resources and its location help its economy and population grow. People also choose where they want to live based on geography or the environment. Some people live close to mountains or lakes because they enjoy certain activities.

Read "Changing the Land." Then fill in the chart below to show how human activities can affect ecosystems.

4. Zebra mussels come to the Great Lakes attached to cargo ships. → 5. Zebra mussels spread through the Great Lakes and into rivers. → 6. Zebra mussels eat the food that the local fish need.

Unit Resources 11 Use with *United States History*, pp. 28–31

Unit Resources, p. 11

Reteach Minilesson

Use a cause-and-effect chart to reteach natural and human effects on the land.

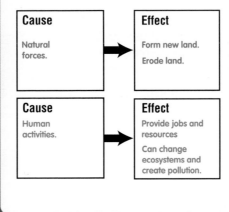

Cause		Effect
Natural forces.	→	Form new land. Erode land.
Cause		**Effect**
Human activities.	→	Provide jobs and resources Can change ecosystems and create pollution.

Graphic Organizer 4

3 Review/Assess

Review Tested Objectives

U1-10 Geographic features such as harbors encourage settlement and commerce.

U1-11 The environment may be affected by natural processes, such as erosion, and by human activities such as building and mining.

Lesson Review Answers

1. Answers will vary; should use e-mail format and show understanding of terms as defined in the lesson.
2. Erosion wears away the land.
3. Resources help people decide where they will live and what work they will do; examples will vary.
4. People often choose to live in places where they like the climate.
5. Answers will vary; should show understanding of the relationship between geography and human activities.
6. Zebra mussels clogged pipes and ate the food of local fish.

Writing Rubric

4	Talk is well organized; lists several effects of people on ecosystem; mechanics are correct.
3	Talk is mostly well organized; lists effects of people on ecosystem; mechanics are mostly correct.
2	Talk is somewhat organized; attempts to list effects of people on ecosystem; some errors in mechanics.
1	Talk lacks organization; does not list effects of people on ecosystem; many errors in mechanics.

Quick Look

Connect to the Core Lesson In Extend Lesson 4, students will learn more about how natural forces and human activities both affect the land by examining the effects of the construction of the Hoover Dam.

1 Teach the Extend Lesson

Connect to the Big Idea

Human Systems By constructing the Hoover Dam, humans have changed the environment and the economy around parts of the Southwest. The dam contributed to the growth of cities in the Southwest because it brought electricity to them. The dam also caused nearby wetlands to dry up because it changed the course of the river.

Geography

Reshaping the Land

Modern dams are some of the largest structures ever built, and they have a big effect on the land around them. Dams help control floods and offer a steady supply of water to cities and towns. Dams also create lakes and provide electricity.

Not all the changes are positive, though. Dams stop the natural flow of a river. A dam affects fish, plants, and animals by changing the sources of food in the river's ecosystem.

The Hoover Dam is one of the largest dams in the United States. It is located on the border between Nevada and Arizona and blocks the Colorado River, the largest river in the Southwest.

Before the Dam
The Colorado River flowed freely through Black Canyon before the Hoover Dam was built.

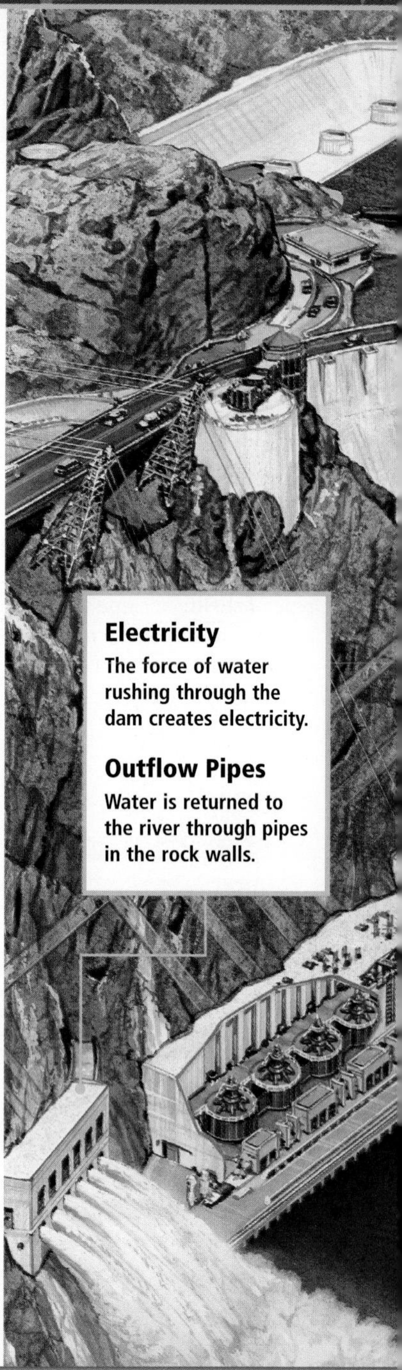

Electricity
The force of water rushing through the dam creates electricity.

Outflow Pipes
Water is returned to the river through pipes in the rock walls.

Reaching All Learners

Extra Support

Draw a Picture

Have students make a list on the chalkboard of the ways that dams affect the land around them. Then ask students to choose one of these ways and illustrate it in a drawing.

Visual-spatial

On Level

Brainstorm Questions

Have students brainstorm a list of questions about the history and construction of the Hoover Dam.

- Tell students to select three questions and use library or Internet resources to locate the answers to these questions.
- Post the questions and answers on the board.

Verbal-linguistic

Challenge

Hold a Debate

Divide students into two groups to debate whether dams do more harm than good for people and the environment.

- Tell students to use Internet and library resources to help them find information to support their arguments.
- After the debate, ask the rest of the class to identify which side was most persuasive. Have students explain their choices.

Verbal-linguistic

GEOGRAPHY
Reservoir
The reservoir is the human-made lake that forms behind the dam. The Hoover Dam's Lake Mead is about 115 miles long.
Dam
The dam holds back the water in the reservoir.
Power Lines
Electricity from the dam gave energy to the new cities of the Southwest, which could not have grown without it.

Activities

1. **EXPLORE IT** Describe what you would see if you were in one of the cars driving across the dam.
2. **WRITE ABOUT IT** Planners chose the location of the Hoover Dam carefully. Describe why you think Black Canyon was the right spot for the dam.

33

2 Leveled Activities

1 Explore It *For Extra Support*

Answers may vary, but should reflect student's understanding of visuals in the lesson.

2 Write About It *For Challenge*

Writing Rubric

4	Explanation is creative, accurate, logical, and clear; reasons supported with details; mechanics are correct.
3	Explanation is mostly logical, accurate, and clear; most reasons supported with details; most mechanics are correct.
2	Explanation contains some illogical, inaccurate, or unclear statements; some reasons supported with details; has some mechanical errors.
1	Explanation is illogical, inaccurate, unclear or incomplete; reasons are not supported with details; has many mechanical errors.

ELL

REACHING ALL LEARNERS

Intermediate

Have students use the visuals and captions on pages 32 and 33 to make an outline of the different parts of the Hoover Dam.

Verbal-linguistic; visual-spatial

Math

Multiplication

Put the following table of wages of various Hoover Dam workers in the 1930s on the chalkboard. Tell students that these were hourly wages. Have students figure out how much each worker would make in an 8-hour day and in a 40-hour week.

Job	Wage
Electrician	$0.75 $6; $30
Shovel Operator	$1.25 $10; $50
Miner	$0.70 $5.60; $28
Boat Operator	$0.625 $5; $25

Graphic Organizer

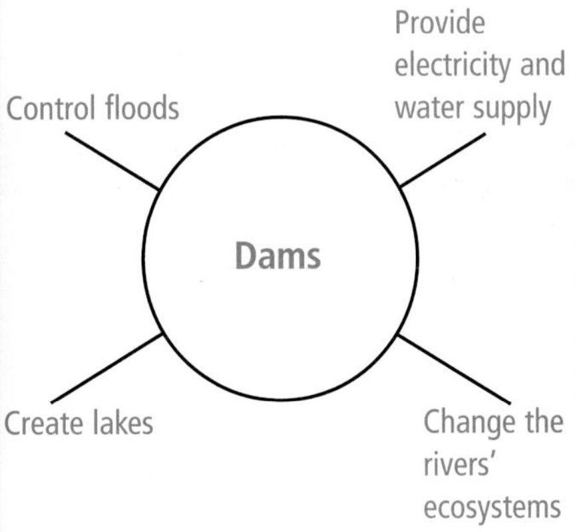
Control floods
Provide electricity and water supply
Dams
Create lakes
Change the rivers' ecosystems

Graphic Organizer 7

Chapter Review

Tested Objectives

The lesson objective assessed by each question is shown in parentheses after the answer.

Visual Summary

1. materials that come from nature, such as water, air, soil, and sunshine *(Obj. U1-5)*
2. areas that have features in common, such as landforms, climate, or location *(Obj. U1-8)*
3. Natural forces and human activities change the land. *(Obj. U1-11)*

Facts and Main Ideas

4. Sunlight strikes the Earth most directly at the equator. Places close to the equator get more direct sunlight and are warmer than places farther away. *(Obj. U1-2)*
5. recycle paper, cans, bottles; not waste water, gas, electricity; ride bikes instead of driving cars *(Obj. U1-5)*
6. Specialization increases trade between regions. *(Obj. U1-9)*
7. People moved to the area to look for gold and silver. The city grew as the number of stores, restaurants, and other businesses increased to serve the miners. The population grew as the economy grew. *(Obj. U1-10)*
8. landform and climate *(Obj. U1-8)*

Vocabulary

9. **erosion** *(Obj. U1-11)*
10. **scarcity** *(Obj. U1-7)*
11. **consumer** *(Obj. U1-7)*
12. **plateau** *(Obj. U1-1)*

Chapter 1

Review and Test Prep

Visual Summary

1.–3. Describe what you learned about each item named below.

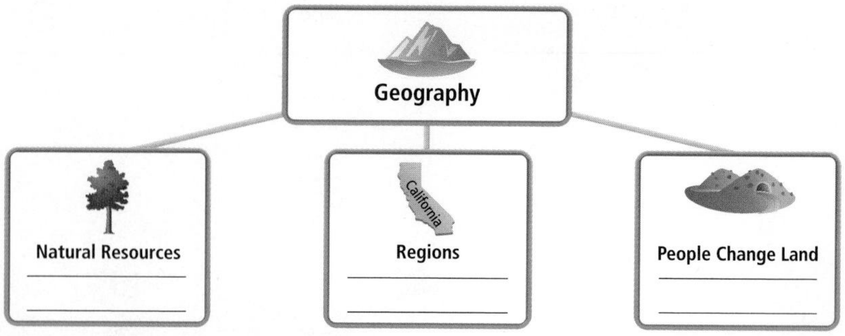

Facts and Main Ideas

TEST PREP Answer each question with information from the chapter.

4. **Geography** In what way does the equator affect the climate of a place?
5. **Citizenship** Name three ways people can conserve resources.
6. **Economics** How does specialization affect trade between regions?
7. **History** Why did the discovery of gold and silver help the city of Denver grow?
8. **Geography** Name two kinds of regions.

Vocabulary

TEST PREP Choose the correct word from the list below to complete each sentence.

plateau, p. 8
scarcity, p. 18
consumer, p. 25
erosion, p. 30

9. Mountains wear down over time because of _____.
10. _____ exists when people cannot get everything they would like.
11. A _____ buys goods and services.
12. A _____ is a high, steep-sided area that rises above the surrounding land.

Reading/Language Arts Wrap-Up

Reading Strategy: Predict/Infer

Review with students the process of evaluating information in order to make a prediction.

Based on what students have read in the chapter, you may wish to involve the class in making predictions about what they will read next.

Writing Strategy

As students write, they can apply what they know about predicting and inferring to how their readers will react to their text.

Have students review their written work and look for places where the reader has to infer or predict. Have students do a self-check: "Have I given the reader enough information to predict or infer correctly?"

Apply Skills

TEST PREP **Map Skill** Study the climate map below. Then use your map skills to answer each question.

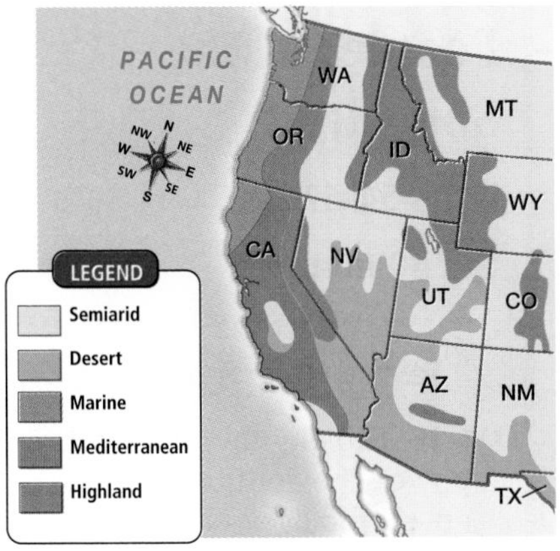

13. Which state shown here has the most climate regions?
    A. Nevada
    B. Oregon
    C. California
    D. Washington
14. In which direction would you travel to get from the marine climate region to the desert climate region?
    A. northeast
    B. southeast
    C. northwest
    D. southwest

Critical Thinking

TEST PREP Write a short paragraph to answer each question.

15. **Classify** Place the resources named below in one of these categories: Renewable Resources, Nonrenewable Resources, or Flow Resources.

trees	oil	sunlight
wind	iron	coal

16. **Summarize** What geographic and economic features can influence where people choose to live?

Activities

HANDS ON **Research Activity** Use library or Internet resources to locate two states that have nicknames based on their landforms. Illustrate your discoveries with pictures or drawings.

Writing Activity If you had a choice, where in the United States would you live? Write a personal essay explaining your answer based on landforms, climate, and resources.

Technology
Writing Process Tips
Get help with your essay at
www.eduplace.com/kids/hmss05/

Technology

Test Generator

You can generate your own version of the chapter review by using the **Test Generator CD-ROM**.

Web Link

For more ideas, visit
www.eduplace.com/ss/hmss05/

Standards

National Standards

III a Mental maps **III b** Representations of the earth **III c** Resources, data sources, and geographic tools **III e** Varying landforms and geographic features **III f** Physical system changes **III h** Interaction of human beings and their physical environment **III i** Change of earth's physical features **III k** Uses of resources and land **VII a** Scarcity and choice **VII c** Private and public goods and services **VII d** Institutions that make up economic systems **VII e** Workers with specialized jobs **IX e** Tensions between personal wants and needs and various global concerns

Apply Skills

13. C *(Obj. U1-4)*
14. B *(Obj. U1-4)*

Critical Thinking

15. Renewable Resources: trees; Nonrenewable Resources: oil, coal, iron; Flow Resources: wind, sunlight *(Obj. U1-5)*

16. geography, climate, environment, location, resources, jobs *(Obj. U1-10)*

Leveled Activities

HANDS ON Performance Task Rubric

4	Information clearly depicted; poster is very creative; mechanics are correct.
3	Information adequately depicted; poster is creative; few errors in mechanics.
2	Information is depicted; poster is fairly creative; some errors in mechanics.
1	Information not depicted; creativity lacking; many errors in mechanics.

Writing Rubric

4	Position clearly stated; reasons supported by information from the text; mechanics are correct.
3	Position adequately stated; most reasons supported by information from the text; few errors in mechanics.
2	Position is stated; reasons confused or poorly supported by text information; some errors in mechanics.
1	Position not stated; reasons not supported; many errors in mechanics.

Chapter 2 Planning Guide

The First Americans

	Core Lesson 1	Core Lesson 2	Core Lesson 3
Chapter Opener pp. 36–37 30 minutes	**Ancient Americans** Pages 38–43 50 minutes	**Peoples of the Northwest** Pages 46–49 40 minutes	**Peoples of the Southwest** Pages 54–57 40 minutes
	Tested Objectives **U1-12** Summarize how people first came to the Americas. **U1-13** Describe two important civilizations that developed in North America.	**Tested Objectives** **U1-14** Explain how the geography of the Northwest influenced the lives of American Indians. **U1-15** Describe the way of life and culture of the Tlingit.	**Tested Objectives** **U1-16** Explain how the geography of the Southwest influenced the lives American Indians. **U1-17** Describe the way of life and culture of the Hopi.
Reading/Vocabulary **Chapter Reading Strategy:** Question, p. 35F	**Reading/Vocabulary** **Reading Skill:** Sequence glacier, civilization, migration, pueblo, agriculture	**Reading/Vocabulary** **Reading Skill:** Main Idea/Details surplus, clan, potlatch	**Reading/Vocabulary** **Reading Skill:** Cause and Effect irrigation, ceremony, staple
	Cross-Curricular **Science,** p. 40 **Art,** p. 42	**Cross-Curricular** **Art,** p. 48	**Cross-Curricular** **Math,** p. 56
Resources **Grade Level Resources** Vocabulary Cards, pp. 1–10 **Reaching All Learners** Challenge Activities, p. 80 **Primary Sources Plus,** p. 2 **Big Idea Transparency 1** **Interactive Transparency 1** **Text & Music Audio CD** **Lesson Planner & TR CD-ROM** **eBook** **eTE**	**Resources** **Unit Resources:** Reading Skill/Strategy, p. 12 Vocabulary/Study Guide, p. 13 **Reaching All Learners:** Lesson Summary, p. 5 Support for Lang. Dev./ELL, p. 102 **Assessment Options:** Lesson Test, p. 9	**Resources** **Unit Resources:** Reading Skill/Strategy, p. 14 Vocabulary/Study Guide, p. 15 **Reaching All Learners:** Lesson Summary, p. 6 Support for Lang. Dev./ELL, p. 103 **Assessment Options:** Lesson Test, p. 10	**Resources** **Unit Resources:** Reading Skill/Strategy, p. 16 Vocabulary/Study Guide, p. 17 **Reaching All Learners:** Lesson Summary, p. 7 Support for Lang. Dev./ELL, p. 104 **Assessment Options:** Lesson Test, p. 11 www.eduplace.com/ss/hmss05/
	Extend Lesson 1 **History** Tenochtitlán **20–30 minutes** Pages 44–45 **Focus:** Diego Rivera's mural shows students Aztec life.	**Extend Lesson 2** **Literature** "Chinook Wind Wrestles Cold Wind" **40–50 minutes** Pages 50–53 **Focus:** Students read a legend of the Wasco people.	**Extend Lesson 3** **Biographies** Keepers of Tradition **20–30 minutes** Pages 58–59 **Focus:** Students learn about three notable people of today.

National Standards

I a Similarities and differences in addressing human needs
I d Different cultures related to their physical environment
II c Compare and contrast stories or accounts
III g How people create places
III h Interaction of human beings and their physical environment

CURRENT EVENTS
With the Program
from WEEKLY WR READER
at www.eduplace.com

Core Lesson 4

Peoples of the Plains

Pages 60–63
40 minutes

Tested Objectives

U1-18 Explain how the geography of the Plains influenced the lives of American Indians.
U1-19 Describe the culture of the Comanche.

Reading/Vocabulary

Reading Skill: Draw Conclusions

lodge, summary, nomad, travois

Cross-Curricular

Physical Education, p. 62

Resources

Unit Resources:
- **Reading Skill/Strategy,** p. 18
- **Vocabulary/Study Guide,** p. 19

Reaching All Learners:
- **Lesson Summary,** p. 8
- **Support for Lang. Dev./ELL,** p. 105

Assessment Options:
- **Lesson Test,** p. 12

Extend Lesson 4

Primary Sources
Art of the Plains Indians
20–30 minutes
Pages 64–65
Focus: Students get a closer look at Plains Indians artifacts.

Skillbuilder

Reading and Thinking Skill

Summarize

Pages 66–67
20 minutes

Tested Objective

U1-20 Organize important information in a summary.

Reading/Vocabulary

summary

Resources

Unit Resources:
- Skill Practice, p. 20

Skill Transparency 2

Core Lesson 5

Peoples of the East

Pages 68–71
40 minutes

Tested Objectives

U1-21 Explain how the geography of the Eastern Woodlands influenced the lives of American Indians.
U1-22 Describe the culture of the Haudenosaunee.

Reading/Vocabulary

Reading Skill: Compare and Contrast

longhouse, wampum, confederation, barter

Cross-Curricular

Math, p. 70

Resources

Unit Resources:
- **Reading Skill/Strategy,** p. 21
- **Vocabulary/Study Guide,** p. 22

Reaching All Learners:
- **Lesson Summary,** p. 9
- **Support for Lang. Dev./ELL,** p. 106

Assessment Options:
- **Lesson Test,** p. 13

Extend Lesson 5

Geography
American Indian Shelters
20–30 minutes
Pages 72–73
Focus: Students learn how the environment's demands affect human housing.

Chapter Review

Pages 74–75
30 minutes

Resources

Assessment Options:
- Chapter 2 Test
- Test Generator

Chapter 2 Practice Options

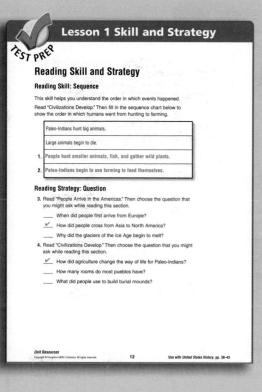

Lesson 1 Skill and Strategy

TEST PREP

Reading Skill and Strategy

Reading Skill: Sequence

This skill helps you understand the order in which events happened.

Read "Civilizations Develop." Then fill in the sequence chart below to show the order in which humans went from hunting to farming.

Paleo-Indians hunt big animals.
Large animals begin to die.
1. People hunt smaller animals, fish, and gather wild plants.
2. Paleo-Indians begin to use farming to feed themselves.

Reading Strategy: Question

3. Read "People Arrive in the Americas." Then choose the question that you might ask while reading this section.
   - ___ When did people first arrive from Europe?
   - ✓ How did people cross from Asia to North America?
   - ___ Why did the glaciers of the Ice Age begin to melt?
4. Read "Civilizations Develop." Then choose the question that you might ask while reading this section.
   - ✓ How did agriculture change the way of life for Paleo-Indians?
   - ___ How many rooms do most pueblos have?
   - ___ What did people use to build burial mounds?

Unit Resources

12 Use with *United States History*, pp. 38–43

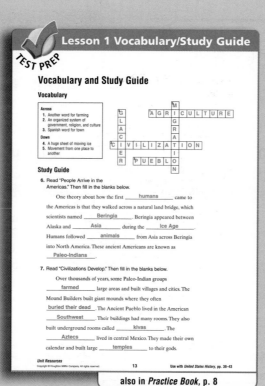

Lesson 1 Vocabulary/Study Guide

TEST PREP

Vocabulary and Study Guide

Vocabulary

Across
1. Another word for farming
2. An organized system of government, religion, and culture
3. Spanish word for town

Down
4. A huge sheet of moving ice
5. Movement from one place to another

Study Guide

6. Read "People Arrive in the Americas." Then fill in the blanks below.

One theory about how the first __humans__ came to the Americas is that they walked across a natural land bridge, which scientists named __Beringia__. Beringia appeared between Alaska and __Asia__ during the __Ice Age__. Humans followed __animals__ from Asia across Beringia into North America. These ancient Americans are known as __Paleo-Indians__.

7. Read "Civilizations Develop." Then fill in the blanks below.

Over thousands of years, some Paleo-Indian groups __farmed__ large areas and built villages and cities. The Mound Builders built giant mounds where they often __buried their dead__. The Ancient Pueblo lived in the American __Southwest__. Their buildings had many rooms. They also built underground rooms called __kivas__. The __Aztecs__ lived in central Mexico. They made their own calendar and built large __temples__ to their gods.

Unit Resources

13 Use with *United States History*, pp. 38–43

also in *Practice Book*, p. 8

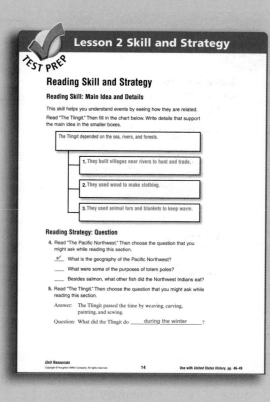

Lesson 2 Skill and Strategy

TEST PREP

Reading Skill and Strategy

Reading Skill: Main Idea and Details

This skill helps you understand events by seeing how they are related.

Read "The Tlingit." Then fill in the chart below. Write details that support the main idea in the smaller boxes.

The Tlingit depended on the sea, rivers, and forests.
1. They built villages near rivers to hunt and trade.
2. They used wood to make clothing.
3. They used animal furs and blankets to keep warm.

Reading Strategy: Question

4. Read "The Pacific Northwest." Then choose the question that you might ask while reading this section.
   - ✓ What is the geography of the Pacific Northwest?
   - ___ What were some of the purposes of totem poles?
   - ___ Besides salmon, what other fish did the Northwest Indians eat?
5. Read "The Tlingit." Then choose the question that you might ask while reading this section.

   Answer: The Tlingit passed the time by weaving, carving, painting, and sewing.

   Question: What did the Tlingit do __during the winter__?

Unit Resources

14 Use with *United States History*, pp. 46–49

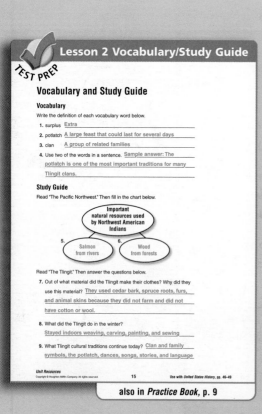

Lesson 2 Vocabulary/Study Guide

TEST PREP

Vocabulary and Study Guide

Vocabulary

Write the definition of each vocabulary word below.

1. surplus __Extra__
2. potlatch __A large feast that could last for several days__
3. clan __A group of related families__
4. Use two of the words in a sentence. __Sample answer: The potlatch is one of the most important traditions for many Tlingit clans.__

Study Guide

Read "The Pacific Northwest." Then fill in the chart below.

Important natural resources used by Northwest American Indians
5. Salmon from rivers
6. Wood from forests

Read "The Tlingit." Then answer the questions below.

7. Out of what material did the Tlingit make their clothes? Why did they use this material? __They used cedar bark, spruce roots, furs, and animal skins because they did not farm and did not have cotton or wool.__
8. What did the Tlingit do in the winter? __Stayed indoors weaving, carving, painting, and sewing__
9. What Tlingit cultural traditions continue today? __Clan and family symbols, the potlatch, dances, songs, stories, and language__

Unit Resources

15 Use with *United States History*, pp. 46–49

also in *Practice Book*, p. 9

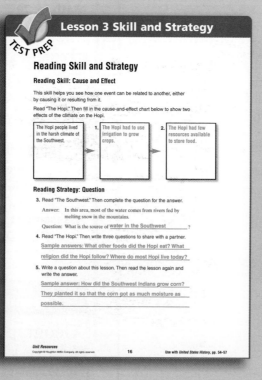

Lesson 3 Skill and Strategy

TEST PREP

Reading Skill and Strategy

Reading Skill: Cause and Effect

This skill helps you see how one event can be related to another, either by causing it or resulting from it.

Read "The Hopi." Then fill in the cause-and-effect chart below to show the effects of the climate on the Hopi.

The Hopi people lived in the harsh climate of the Southwest. → 1. The Hopi had to use irrigation to grow crops. → 2. The Hopi had few resources available to store food.

Reading Strategy: Question

3. Read "The Southwest." Then complete the question for the answer.

   Answer: In this area, most of the water comes from rivers fed by melting snow in the mountains.

   Question: What is the source of __water in the Southwest__?
4. Read "The Hopi." Then write three questions to share with a partner.
   __Sample answers: What other foods did the Hopi eat? What religion did the Hopi follow? Where do most Hopi live today?__
5. Write a question about this lesson. Then read the lesson again and write the answer.
   __Sample answer: How did the Southwest Indians grow corn? They planted it so that the corn got as much moisture as possible.__

Unit Resources

16 Use with *United States History*, pp. 54–57

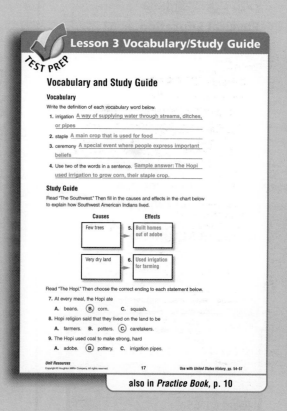

Lesson 3 Vocabulary/Study Guide

TEST PREP

Vocabulary and Study Guide

Vocabulary

Write the definition of each vocabulary word below.

1. irrigation __A way of supplying water through streams, ditches, or pipes__
2. staple __A main crop that is used for food__
3. ceremony __A special event where people express important beliefs__
4. Use two of the words in a sentence. __Sample answer: The Hopi used irrigation to grow corn, their staple crop.__

Study Guide

Read "The Southwest." Then fill in the causes and effects in the chart below to explain how Southwest American Indians lived.

Causes	Effects
Few trees	5. Built homes out of adobe
Very dry land	6. Used irrigation for farming

Read "The Hopi." Then choose the correct ending to each statement below.

7. At every meal, the Hopi ate
   A. beans. (B.) corn. C. squash.
8. Hopi religion said that they lived on the land to be
   A. farmers. B. potters. (C.) caretakers.
9. The Hopi used coal to make strong, hard
   A. adobe. (B.) pottery. C. irrigation pipes.

Unit Resources

17 Use with *United States History*, pp. 54–57

also in *Practice Book*, p. 10

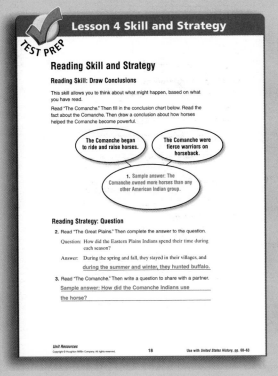

Lesson 4 Skill and Strategy

TEST PREP

Reading Skill and Strategy

Reading Skill: Draw Conclusions

This skill allows you to think about what might happen, based on what you have read.

Read "The Comanche." Then fill in the conclusion chart below. Read the fact about the Comanche. Then draw a conclusion about how horses helped the Comanche become powerful.

The Comanche began to ride and raise horses.

The Comanche were fierce warriors on horseback.

1. Sample answer: The Comanche owned more horses than any other American Indian group.

Reading Strategy: Question

2. Read "The Great Plains." Then complete the answer to the question.

Question: How did the Eastern Plains Indians spend their time during each season?

Answer: During the spring and fall, they stayed in their villages, and during the summer and winter, they hunted buffalo.

3. Read "The Comanche." Then write a question to share with a partner.

Sample answer: How did the Comanche Indians use the horse?

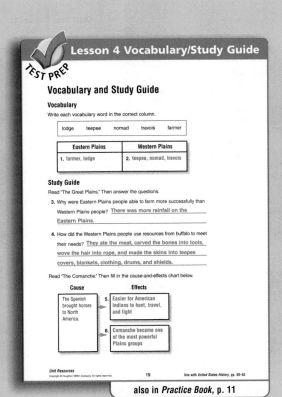

Lesson 4 Vocabulary/Study Guide

TEST PREP

Vocabulary and Study Guide

Vocabulary

Write each vocabulary word in the correct column.

lodge teepee nomad travois farmer

Eastern Plains	Western Plains
1. farmer, lodge	2. teepee, nomad, travois

Study Guide

Read "The Great Plains." Then answer the questions.

3. Why were Eastern Plains people able to farm more successfully than Western Plains people? There was more rainfall on the Eastern Plains.

4. How did the Western Plains people use resources from buffalo to meet their needs? They ate the meat, carved the bones into tools, wove the hair into rope, and made the skins into teepee covers, blankets, clothing, drums, and shields.

Read "The Comanche." Then fill in the cause-and-effects chart below.

Cause	Effects
The Spanish brought horses to North America.	5. Easier for American Indians to hunt, travel, and fight
	6. Comanche became one of the most powerful Plains groups

also in *Practice Book*, p. 11

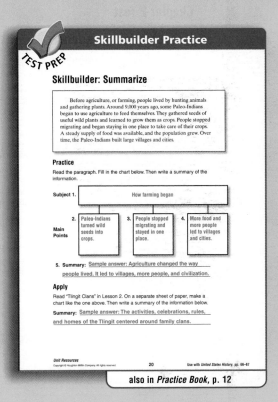

Skillbuilder Practice

TEST PREP

Skillbuilder: Summarize

Before agriculture, or farming, people lived by hunting animals and gathering plants. Around 9,000 years ago, some Paleo-Indians began to use agriculture to feed themselves. They gathered seeds of useful wild plants and learned to grow them as crops. People stopped migrating and began staying in one place to take care of their crops. A steady supply of food was available, and the population grew. Over time, the Paleo-Indians built large villages and cities.

Practice

Read the paragraph. Fill in the chart below. Then write a summary of the information.

Subject 1. How farming began

Main Points

2. Paleo-Indians turned wild seeds into crops.

3. People stopped migrating and stayed in one place.

4. More food and more people led to villages and cities.

5. **Summary:** Sample answer: Agriculture changed the way people lived. It led to villages, more people, and civilization.

Apply

Read "Tlingit Clans" in Lesson 2. On a separate sheet of paper, make a chart like the one above. Then write a summary of the information below.

Summary: Sample answer: The activities, celebrations, rules, and homes of the Tlingit centered around family clans.

also in *Practice Book*, p. 12

Lesson 5 Skill and Strategy

TEST PREP

Reading Skill and Strategy

Reading Skill: Compare and Contrast

This skill helps you understand how historical events or people are similar and different.

Read "The Eastern Woodlands." Then fill in the diagram below to contrast Woodland Indians of the north and south.

Woodland Indians of the North	Woodland Indians of the South
1. Colder climate; Longhouses for shelter; Clothing from deerskin	2. Warmer climate; Houses without walls; Light clothing

Reading Strategy: Question

3. Read "Peoples of the East." Read the headings. Then turn each heading into a question. As you read, look for the answers to those questions.

Heading 1: The Eastern Woodlands

Question: Sample answer: How did the American Indians of the Eastern Woodlands live?

Answer: Sample answer: They lived by farming, hunting, and gathering.

Heading 2: The Haudenosaunee

Question: Sample answer: For what act are the Haudenosaunee most remembered?

Answer: Sample answer: Different groups of Haudenosaunee made a peace treaty and helped each other.

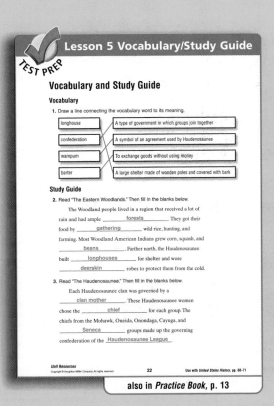

Lesson 5 Vocabulary/Study Guide

TEST PREP

Vocabulary and Study Guide

Vocabulary

1. Draw a line connecting the vocabulary word to its meaning.

longhouse	A type of government in which groups join together
confederation	A symbol of an agreement used by Haudenosaunee
wampum	To exchange goods without using money
barter	A large shelter made of wooden poles and covered with bark

Study Guide

2. Read "The Eastern Woodlands." Then fill in the blanks below.

The Woodland people lived in a region that received a lot of rain and had ample forests. They got their food by gathering wild rice, hunting, and farming. Most Woodland American Indians grew corn, squash, and beans. Farther north, the Haudenosaunee built longhouses for shelter and wore deerskin robes to protect them from the cold.

3. Read "The Haudenosaunee." Then fill in the blanks below.

Each Haudenosaunee clan was governed by a clan mother. These Haudenosaunee women chose the chief for each group. The chiefs from the Mohawk, Oneida, Onondaga, Cayuga, and Seneca groups made up the governing confederation of the Haudenosaunee League.

also in *Practice Book*, p. 13

Chapter 2 Assessment Options

Chapter 2 Test

TEST PREP

Chapter 2 Test

Test Your Knowledge

migration	potlatch	nomad	longhouse

Fill in the blank with the correct word from the box.

1. Over many years, hunters followed the **migration** of animals across Beringia. Obj. U1–12
2. Many Haudenosaunee families lived together in a **longhouse**. Obj. U1–22
3. The hosts of the **potlatch** ceremony served a large amount of food and gave valuable gifts to the guests. Obj. U1–15
4. The **nomad** groups on the Western Plains relied on buffalo for food, shelter, and clothing. Obj. U1–18

Circle the letter of the best answer.

5. What is true about the Adena and Hopewell civilizations? Obj. U1–13
   - (A.) They were Mound Builders and lived in the Ohio Valley.
   - B. They were Mound Builders and lived in the lower Mississippi Valley.
   - C. They were nomads and lived on the Great Plains.
   - D. They were nomads and lived in present-day Mexico.
6. Why did the Southwest Indians have to rely on irrigation to grow their crops? Obj. U1–16
   - F. because they planted in areas that flooded
   - G. because they planted corn deep in the ground
   - H. because few trees grew in the area
   - (J.) because of the lack of rain in the region
7. Which American Indian group had skilled horse riders and warriors? Obj. U1–19
   - A. Tlingit
   - (B.) Comanche
   - C. Hopi
   - D. Mohawk
8. How did geography help the Northwest Indians survive? Obj. U1–14
   - F. The Northwest Indians depended on cotton for their way of life.
   - (G.) The Northwest Indians depended on the sea, rivers, and forests for their way of life.
   - H. The Northwest Indians depended on traps for their way of life.
   - J. The Northwest Indians depended on farming and clans for their way of life.

Chapter 2 Test

TEST PREP

Apply Your Knowledge

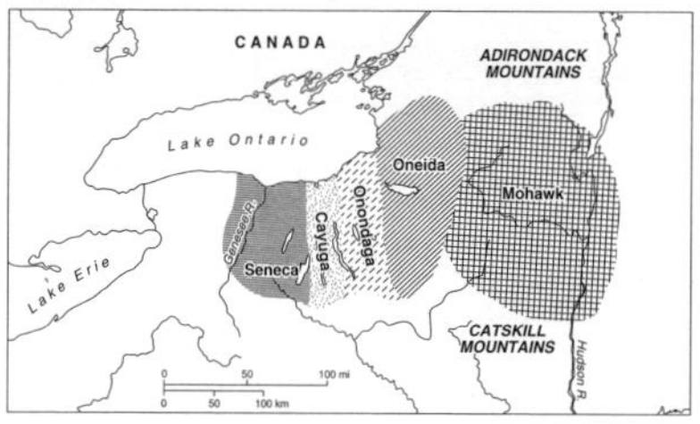

Use the map to answer the following questions.

9. Which Haudenosaunee groups lived on Lake Ontario? Obj. U1–21
   - A. Seneca, Cayuga, and Onondaga
   - B. Cayuga, Onondaga, Oneida, and Mohawk
   - C. Cayuga, Onondaga, and Oneida
   - (D.) Seneca, Cayuga, Onondaga, and Oneida
10. What did the Haudenosaunee do to make their nation stronger? Obj. U1–22
    - F. They hunted large animals.
    - (G.) They created a confederation and formed a league.
    - H. They replaced the chiefs with clan mothers.
    - J. They stopped trading with other American Indian nations.

Apply the Reading Skill: Sequence

Read the passage below. Then answer the question. Obj. U1–12

> During the Ice Age, part of the ocean floor became a grassland. This grassland formed a land bridge called Beringia. Animals and people migrated from Asia to North America over Beringia. As the Ice Age ended, the glaciers slowly melted. The oceans filled with more water and covered Beringia.

11. Name two events that happened after Beringia formed. Write the events in their correct sequence.
    Sample answer: First, people and animals crossed into North America from Asia. Then, the ocean filled and covered Beringia.

Chapter 2 Test

TEST PREP

Test the Skill: Summarize

> The land that early colonists found harsh and dangerous had been the home of American Indians for countless years. The American Indians had respect for nature and its renewal. American Indians also looked to nature for healing. For example, the Apache made paintings out of sand to help cure illness because of the connection they felt with the earth.

12. What is the subject of the passage? Obj. U1–20
    The American Indians' relationship with nature and the land
13. List three details from the passage. Obj. U1–20
    Sample answer: American Indians lived on the land for many years; they respected nature; they believed the land could be used to heal people.
14. Write a one- or two-sentence summary of the information. Obj. U1–20
    Sample answer: American Indians had a deep respect for and connection to nature.

Apply the Skill

15. Write a short summary of the passage below. Obj. U1–20

> The Ancient Pueblo people, or Anasazi, lived in the American Southwest from around the years 500 to 1300. The Ancient Pueblo built large buildings with many rooms. They also built underground rooms, called *kivas,* to use for religious ceremonies. No one knows why the Ancient Pueblo left their villages and moved south. Today, their descendants live in Arizona, New Mexico, and northern Mexico.

Summary: **Sample answer: The Ancient Pueblo created a long, successful civilization in the Southwest. Their descendants still live in North America.**

Chapter 2 Test

TEST PREP

Think and Write

16. **Short Response:** Describe the way of life and culture of the Hopi. Obj. U1–17
    Sample answer: The Hopi used irrigation to grow corn in the dry climate. They built large buildings known as pueblos. Religion was at the center of their customs. They lived as caretakers of the land.
17. **Critical Thinking: Infer** Why did having horses make hunting easier for Western Plains people? Obj. U1–19
    Sample answer: Buffalo was their main source of food and resources. The buffalo were huge animals that roamed the Plains in herds, so horses made hunting buffalo easier.
18. **Extended Response:** Write a paragraph describing a day in the life of a Tlingit boy. Explain what he might eat, what he might wear, and what he might celebrate in his home. Write your paragraph on a separate sheet of paper. Obj. U1–15 **Paragraphs may explain that the Tlingit ate salmon, wore clothes made of cedar bark, made totem poles, lived in clans, and had potlatches.**

Self-Assessment

What is one important thing I learned about the American Indian groups from this chapter? Why do I think it is important?

Teacher Read Aloud

A Story in History

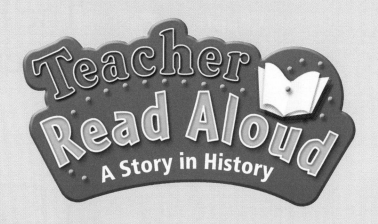

You can read the following fiction selection to your students before beginning the chapter. Before you read, ask students to look at the Southwest Indians map on page 55 of their books.

Activate Prior Knowledge

Ask students to share what they know about the American Indians of the Southwest. Tell students that the Read-Aloud selection presents a picture of how the Southwest Indians farm the land today, as they have always done. As they read the chapter, they will learn more about the Southwest Indians.

Preview the Chapter

Have students skim the section The People and the Land on page 55. Ask them how the Read-Aloud selection reflects the information in this section.

Read-Aloud Vocabulary

Explain that **irrigation** is a method of moving water through ditches or pipes in order to grow crops on dry land. A **staple** is a main food crop.

Preview the Reading Strategy

Question Explain to students that the reading strategy they will use in this chapter is questioning, or asking about what is happening. You may wish to use the Read Aloud to model the strategy.

Think Aloud *The main character in the first three paragraphs wants to work in the garden, but the father says "you are not old enough." I wonder why the character wants to work in the garden, and if he or she will accept the father's opinion.*

Our Desert Garden

"I would like to help with the planting," I told my father.

We stood outside, just the two of us, looking at the garden bed. It was still covered with short corn stubble from last year.

"Little one," my father said kindly, "you are not old enough yet."

"I am not so little anymore. I am strong, and good at growing things."

He rubbed his chin thoughtfully. "That is very true. You have been taking care of the animals for some time now."

"And look how big they are!" I said.

He laughed, then, but he let me start helping him that very day. We set to work turning the soil and mixing in fertilizer. Then my father showed me how our **irrigation** system worked. Without it, we would not have enough water to farm.

I watched the water trickle around the roots of the plants, soaking the dry earth and turning it from light brown to dark brown. The wonderful smell of damp soil tickled my nostrils. It is a smell that always makes me happy.

"Dad," I said, "have you always planted corn?"

"Yes. Our people have planted corn since the beginning of time. It is a **staple** for us." He turned and smiled at me. "You will make a good farmer, little one."

Begin the Chapter

Chapter Quick Look

Core Lesson 1 focuses on the development of early civilizations in the Americas.

Core Lesson 2 details how Native Americans of the Northwest coast used the abundant natural resources of the region.

Core Lesson 3 discusses how the Indians of the Southwest created a rich culture in a dry land with few natural resources.

Core Lesson 4 focuses on the Native Americans who lived as farmers and migrating hunters on the Great Plains.

Core Lesson 5 discusses how the many different Indian peoples of the Eastern Woodlands lived by farming, hunting, and gathering.

Vocabulary Preview

Use the vocabulary cards to preview the key vocabulary words before starting the lessons.

Vocabulary Strategy

Vocabulary strategies for this chapter:

- Structural analysis, p. 69
- Synonyms/antonyms, p. 39, 56, 70
- Root words, p. 40
- Word origins, p. 42, 47, 48, 55

Vocabulary Help

Vocabulary card for irrigation The photograph showing irrigation methods in the Southwest is called an aerial photograph.

Vocabulary card for nomad The illustration showing nomadic people of the Western Plains was drawn by George C. Catlin (1796-1872). Catlin sketched and painted thousands of Native Americans before photography was invented.

Chapter 2

The First Americans

Technology
e • glossary
e • word games
www.eduplace.com/kids/hmss05/

Vocabulary Preview

agriculture

Aztecs used a special type of farming, or **agriculture.** They grew their crops on floating islands. **page 40**

clan

People who are part of the same **clan** share a common ancestor. The Tlingit people organize themselves into clans. **page 48**

Chapter Timeline

about 1100 Earliest Ancient Pueblo stone buildings

about 1300 Aztecs rule Central Mexico

1100 — 1200 — 1300 — 1400

Background

Anthropological Terms

Tell students that as they read this chapter, they will find the following terms:

- *Paleo-Indians,* p. 40
- *cultural traditions,* p. 49
- *customs,* p. 56
- *adapted,* p. 61
- *common language,* p. 68

Explain that terms like these are used by social scientists called anthropologists to describe the development of human civilization.

Vocabulary

Compound Words

Use a graphic organizer to help students list compound words in the chapter.

Lesson 1: grassland, p. 39, etc.
Lesson 2: Northwest, p. 46, etc.
Lesson 3: Southwest, p. 54, etc.
Lesson 4: rainfall, p. 60, etc.
Lesson 5: Woodland, p. 66, etc.

Reading Strategy

Question As you read, ask questions to check your understanding.

Quick Tip Write down your questions. Go back to them once you finish reading.

irrigation

Farmers in the dry Southwest bring water from rivers and streams to their crops. This method of watering crops is **irrigation.** page 55

nomad

A **nomad** does not live in only one place. Nomads move when they need to find food or water. page 61

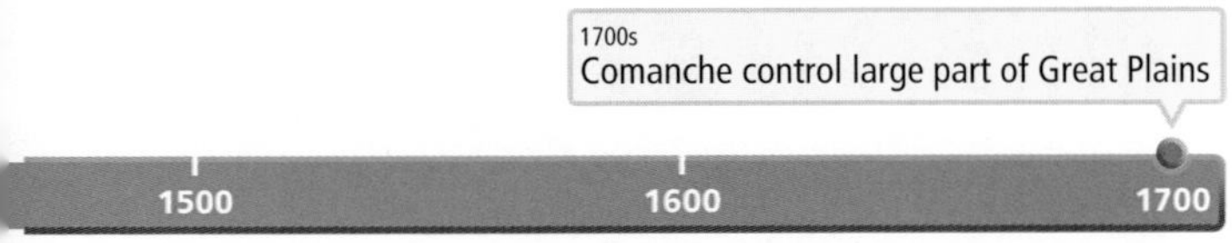

Leveled Practice

Extra Support

Ask students to **write a short poem** using the four vocabulary words. Collect the poems and read them aloud. Ask students to listen for a different vocabulary word each time you read a poem. Have them stand or clap when they hear the word. Bodily-kinesthetic

Challenge

Have students use the dictionary to **identify related words** for *agriculture, irrigation,* and *nomad.* (For example, *agricultural* and *agronomy* for *agriculture.*) Verbal-linguistic

ELL

All Proficiency Levels

- Write the following words on the board: *crops, water, move,* and *home.* Draw or show a picture that depicts each word.
- Show each vocabulary card one at a time, reading aloud the text and emphasizing key words with your voice and body.
- Ask students to tell which word on the board goes with each vocabulary card. Have them explain their answers.

Verbal-linguistic; visual-spatial

Using the Timeline

- Direct students to look at the timeline on pages 36 and 37. Point out the segments of the timeline. Explain that the timeline covers vast periods of time.
- It may be difficult for students to grasp the great span of time represented on the timeline. You may wish to use a KWL chart to access students' prior knowledge of the animals and people who lived during the periods presented on the timeline.

Reading Strategy: Question

To question, the reader asks questions to himself or herself about the material, in order to better understand it. The reader then attempts to answer these questions as he or she reads on or finishes a section.

Explain to students that to question successfully, they should follow these steps:

- Read the passage.
- Think about what the passage says.
- Ask yourself: Is there anything I don't understand or find confusing?
- Write a question about what you don't understand on a self-stick note. Place the note in the margin near the passage.
- Read on.
- If you find the answer to your question, go back to the note and either orally or in writing answer your question.
- If you can't find the answer to your question by reading on, then reread the passage. Then try answering the question.

Students can practice this reading strategy throughout the chapter, including on their Skill and Strategy pages.

Tested Objectives

U1-12 Geography Summarize how people first came to the American continents.

U1-13 History Describe some important civilizations that developed in North America.

Lesson Quick Look

This lesson tells how the first people came to the Americas, where they settled, and how they lived.

Teaching Option: Extend Lesson 1 presents a Diego Rivera mural about the Aztec city of Tenochtitlán.

1 Get Set to Read

Preview Ask students to look at the images on pages 38–39. What do the images tell them about the chapter they are going to read?

Reading Skill: Sequence Students should check that they have put the main events in order.

Build on What You Know Ask students to discuss what a land bridge between two continents might look like. What reasons might people have to go from one continent to the other?

Vocabulary

glacier *noun,* a mass of ice that moves slowly over land

migration *noun,* movement of people or animals from one region to another

agriculture *noun,* growing plants for food; farming

civilization *noun,* a culture with cities, a government, and many different jobs for people to do

pueblo *noun,* a town

Core Lesson 1

Ancient Americans

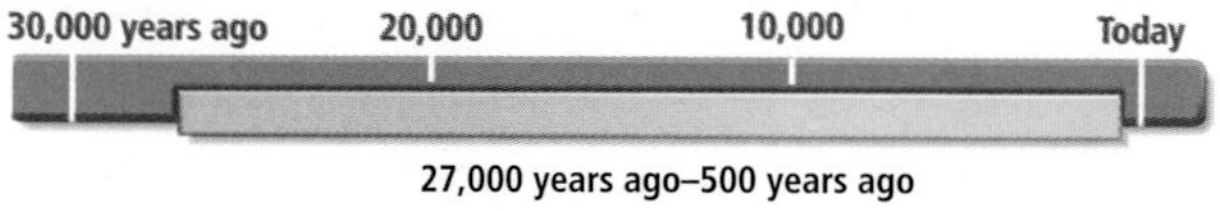

VOCABULARY

glacier
migration
agriculture
civilization
pueblo

Vocabulary Strategy

migration

The word **migrate** means "to move." When the suffix **-ion** is added, the word becomes **migration**, or movement.

READING SKILL

Sequence As you read, use an organizer to put important events in order.

1	
2	
3	
4	

Build on What You Know We have built thousands of bridges in this country, but humans didn't build the earliest ones. The bridges formed naturally. Scientists think people first came to the Americas by walking across a land bridge that linked Asia and North America.

People Arrive in the Americas

Main Idea People began arriving in the Americas around 27,000 years ago.

Scientists are not sure how the first humans came to North America. They have more than one theory. A theory is an explanation or belief about how things happen or will happen. The most common theory is that hunters first came to the Americas by walking across a natural land bridge that linked Asia and North America. Another theory is that some people may have traveled by boat along the coast or across the oceans.

Glaciers Today, glaciers can still be found in the coldest parts of the world, such as Alaska (below) and Antarctica.

38 • Chapter 2

Skill and Strategy

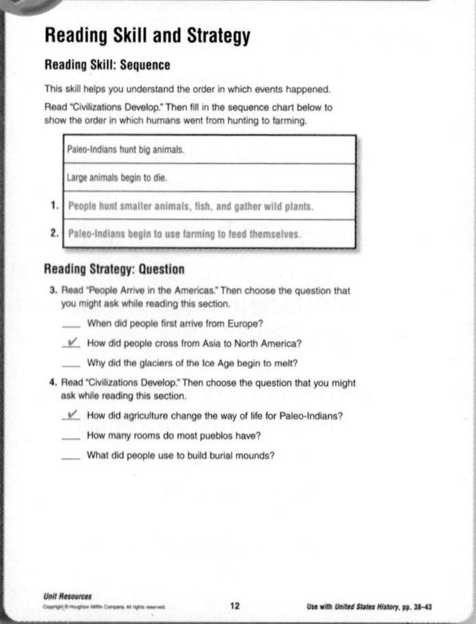

Reading Skill and Strategy

Reading Skill: Sequence

This skill helps you understand the order in which events happened.

Read "Civilizations Develop." Then fill in the sequence chart below to show the order in which humans went from hunting to farming.

	Paleo-Indians hunt big animals.
	Large animals begin to die.
1.	People hunt smaller animals, fish, and gather wild plants.
2.	Paleo-Indians begin to use farming to feed themselves.

Reading Strategy: Question

3. Read "People Arrive in the Americas." Then choose the question that you might ask while reading this section.
   ___ When did people first arrive from Europe?
   ✓ How did people cross from Asia to North America?
   ___ Why did the glaciers of the Ice Age begin to melt?
4. Read "Civilizations Develop." Then choose the question that you might ask while reading this section.
   ✓ How did agriculture change the way of life for Paleo-Indians?
   ___ How many rooms do most pueblos have?
   ___ What did people use to build burial mounds?

Unit Resources

12
Use with *United States History*, pp. 38–43

Unit Resources, p. 12

Background

American Indians

- This book uses the term "American Indian," rather than "Native American." Explain to students that both terms are commonly used today.

Beringia

Thousands of years ago, the Earth was much colder than it is today. This time in history is called the Ice Age because glaciers covered almost half of the world. A **glacier** is a huge, thick sheet of slowly moving ice.

During the Ice Age, much of the Earth's water was frozen in glaciers. In some areas, the ocean floor was no longer covered by water. At the Bering Strait, between Alaska and Asia, the ocean floor became grassland and formed a bridge
1 that scientists call Beringia.

Beringia was a cool, wet land where many kinds of animals lived. Humans hunted the biggest animals. Over many years, hunters followed these animals from Asia across Beringia into North America. Movement like this, from one region to another, is called **migration.**

Scientists know that the migration
2 over Beringia stopped about 10,000 years ago. Around that time, the Ice Age began to end. The glaciers slowly melted, filling the oceans with water. Water covered the land bridge between Asia and North America. It is still covered by water today.

The people who crossed into North America followed the migrating
3 animal herds south. The hunters spread across North and South America. These ancient Americans are known as Paleo-Indians. Paleo (PAY lee oh) means past. They were the ancestors of modern American Indians. Ancestors are relatives who lived before you.

REVIEW According to scientists, how did people first come to North America? by crossing a land bridge that linked Asia and North America

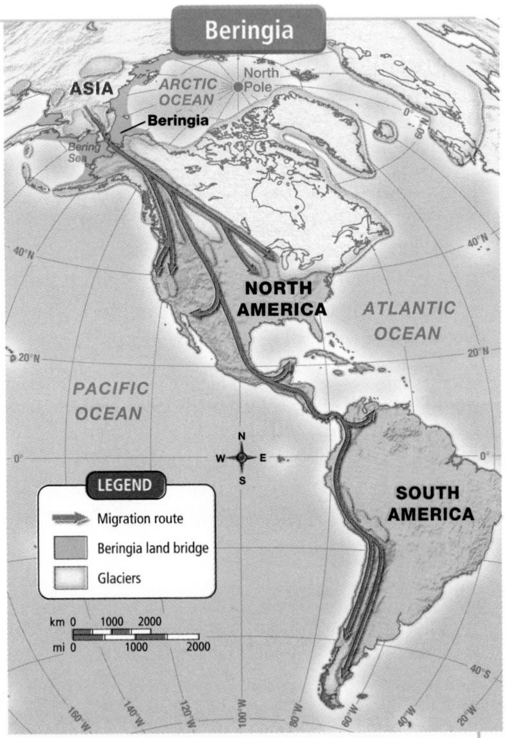

Land Bridge Over many years, Paleo-Indians crossed the Beringia land bridge and moved throughout the Americas.

SKILL Reading Maps How far south did Paleo-Indians migrate? to the tip of South America

Woolly Mammoth This large animal was hunted by Paleo-Indians.

39

Leveled Practice

Extra Support

Have partners **write simple questions** based on material in the lesson, for example, "What was Beringia?" Have students answer each other's questions. Verbal-linguistic

Challenge

Ask small groups to **create a song** that might have been sung by people who migrated across Beringia. The song should include details about what they saw and did on their journey. Musical-auditory

ELL

Intermediate

Remind students that many people today move from one region to another. Using the map on page 39 as a model, have students **draw a map** of a route that someone they know may have taken to move. Have students form small groups and share their maps.

Visual-spatial

2 Teach

People Arrive in the Americas

Talk About It

1 **Q Geography** Which two continents did the Beringia land bridge link?
A It linked Asia and North America.

2 **Q History** When did migration over the land bridge stop?
A It stopped around 10,000 years ago when the Ice Age ended and the glaciers began to melt.

3 **Q Geography** Why did the people who crossed over to North America move south?
A They followed the large animals that were migrating south.

Vocabulary Strategy

glacier Point out that the first part of *glacier* looks like *glass,* and that glass is smooth like ice.

migration Tell students that *journey* and *trek* are synonyms for *migration*.

Reading Strategy: Question Explain to students that asking questions helps them focus on what they want to find out while reading a lesson. You may wish to model the strategy for students.

Think Aloud *These first two pages talk about people who may have crossed a land bridge from Asia into North America. I wonder why they decided to migrate.*

Civilizations Develop

Talk About It

4 **Q History** When did the Paleo-Indians begin using agriculture?

A They began using agriculture about 9,000 years ago.

5 **Q Culture** What is a civilization?

A a group of people living together with systems of government, religion, and culture

Vocabulary Strategy

agriculture Point out that *culture* is related to *cultivate*. A farmer cultivates crops, or makes them grow.

civilization Point out to students that *civilization* contains the word *civil*, which means "having to do with citizens."

Critical Thinking

Synthesize Why were civilizations like the Mound Builders able to develop in North America?

Think Aloud *A civilization is a group of people living together with organized systems of government, religion, and culture. People started to live together in one place once they practiced agriculture. Perhaps agriculture is one reason civilizations like the Mound Builders were able to develop.*

Civilizations Develop

Main Idea Farming led to villages, more people, and civilizations.

For thousands of years Paleo-Indians lived by hunting big animals. About 11,000 years ago, many of these animals began to die. Over time, people adapted by finding other ways of getting food. To adapt is to change a way of life to fit an environment. As the large animals died, people hunted smaller animals, fished, and gathered wild plants.

4 Around 9,000 years ago, some Paleo-Indians began to use agriculture to feed themselves. **Agriculture** is farming, or growing plants.

Scientists think that people in present-day Mexico were the first people in the Americas to practice agriculture. They gathered the seeds of useful wild plants and learned to grow them as crops. These crops included corn, beans, and squash.

Agriculture not only changed the food people ate, it changed the way they lived. It takes months to raise crops, so many Paleo-Indians began staying in one place to care for the plants. With a steady supply of food, more families could survive. Populations grew and people built villages and cities. These changes were all part of the growth of civilizations. A **civilization** is a group of people living together who have systems of government, religion, and culture. 5

Mississippian Village Mississippians made the tops of some of their mounds flat so they could build temples there.

40 • Chapter 2

Science

Geology

Glaciers play a big part in shaping the Earth's surface. Ask students to research the effect of glaciers on geology, such as the formation of mountains and valleys. Have them illustrate their findings.

Visual-spatial

Language Arts

Mound Animals

Have students read the section about the Mound Builders on page 41. Have partners list several animals or symbols that the Adena might have chosen to model a mound after. Discuss possibilities as a group.

Visual-spatial

The Mound Builders

6 The Adena (Uh DEE nuh), Hopewell, and Mississippians were among the earliest people to create large, complex villages in North America. These three civilizations are all called Mound Builders. They built giant mounds, or hills, out of the earth, which they often used to bury their dead. Both the Adena and the Hopewell buried jewelry, tools, and pottery inside their mounds. Some of these mounds still exist today. The town of Cahokia (Kah HOE kee uh) in Illinois is one of the most famous sites, with over 85 mounds.

The mound building civilizations began about 3,000 years ago and lasted for about 2,500 years. The Adena and Hopewell lived in what is now the Ohio River Valley.

The Adena made some of their mounds in the shape of animals or symbols. The Great Serpent Mound in Ohio is shaped like a snake.

The Mississippian civilization was similar to the Adena and Hopewell civilizations. It spread along the lower Mississippi Valley, over most of the Southeast, and as far north as Wisconsin. Some experts believe that the Mississippians are the ancestors of Creek Indians. 7

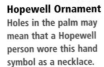

REVIEW Where did the mound building civilizations live? in the Ohio River Valley, the lower Mississippi Valley, over most of the Southeast, and as far north as Wisconsin

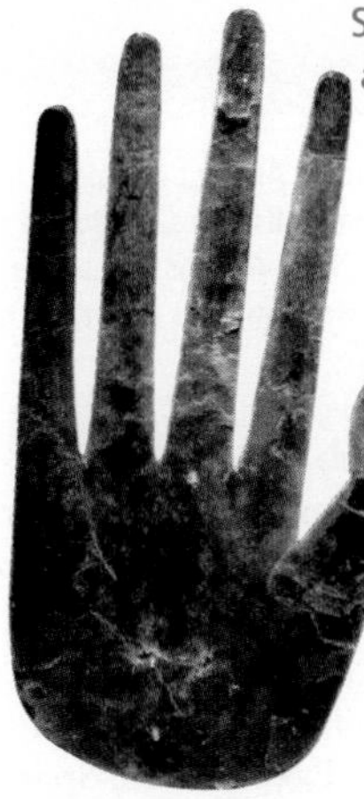

Hopewell Ornament Holes in the palm may mean that a Hopewell person wore this hand symbol as a necklace.

Adena Figure The Adena made this figure out of red and yellow clay about 2,000 years ago.

41

Civilizations Develop

continued

Talk About It

6 **Q History** What name was given to the Adena, Hopewell, and Mississippian people?

A They are called Mound Builders.

7 **Q Geography** Where was the Mississippian civilization located?

A in the lower Mississippi Valley, over most of the Southeast, and as far north as Wisconsin

Reading Strategy: Question Explain to students that asking questions can help them focus on what they want to find out when they look at pictures that go with the text they are reading. Ask students to look at the pictures on pages 40 and 41. What questions do they have about the people and objects shown?

Extra Support

Agriculture Today

Point out that many people in North America still make a living through agriculture. Have partners make a chart of items that a farmer in various parts of the United States might grow. Compare charts as a group.

Visual-spatial

Challenge

Locate Regions

Have students use a United States map to find the approximate locations of the Ohio Valley, the lower Mississippi Valley, Illinois, and Wisconsin. On a copy of the map, have them shade in the regions where mound building civilizations were. Compare maps as a group.

Visual-spatial

Civilizations Develop

continued

Talk About It

8 **Q History** How long did the Ancient Pueblo civilization last?

A It lasted about 800 years.

9 **Q History** When did the ancient Pueblo leave their villages? Where did they go?

A about 1300; south

10 **Q History** What were some of the accomplishments of the Aztec civilization?

A The Aztecs made their own calendar, built large temples, and made hundreds of buildings and roads.

Critical Thinking

Synthesize Describe three reasons why people today choose to migrate from one place to another.

Vocabulary Strategy

pueblo The word *pueblo* can also mean "people" or "nation." *Pueblo* and *people* both come from the Latin word *populus,* meaning "the people."

Cliff Palace Some Ancient Pueblo villages were built into canyon walls. The Cliff Palace in Mesa Verde, Colorado, (above) was like a small city. The Ancient Pueblo drew images (right) on their walls.

Ancient Pueblo Peoples

Another American Indian civilization lived in what is now the Southwest, from about the year 500 to about 1300. They
8 were the Ancient Pueblo (PWEH bloh) peoples, also known as the Anasazi (Ahn uh SAH zee). **Pueblo** is the Spanish word for town. The Ancient Pueblo lived in large buildings with many rooms. The buildings looked like towns to the Spanish who arrived in North America many years later.

By constructing their houses out of stone, the Ancient Pueblo could group homes on top of one another. Around the year 1100, the Ancient Pueblo were building structures as large as modern apartment buildings. They built Pueblo Bonito in New Mexico, which was five stories high with hundreds of rooms.

The Ancient Pueblo also built underground rooms called kivas (KEE vahs). The kivas were used for religious ceremonies. Each village had a number of kivas. Pueblo Bonito had two huge kivas, where hundreds of people could gather.

Around 1300, the Ancient Pueblo left 9
their villages. No one knows why. It is possible that lack of rain or wood and warfare with other people caused them to move. Many went south and settled along the Rio Grande and Little Colorado rivers. Today, the descendants of the Ancient Pueblo live in Arizona, New Mexico, and northern Mexico.

42 • Chapter 2

Art

Illustrate a Dwelling

Ask students to create illustrations of an inhabited Ancient Pueblo dwelling, using information from this chapter as well as from library and Internet resources.

Visual-spatial

Language Arts

Write a Story

- Have students write a story about why the Ancient Pueblo left their villages.
- Share stories as a group.

Aztec Coyote
Aztecs carved this coyote figure out of stone.

The Aztecs

The Aztec civilization ruled in Central Mexico for about 200 years, beginning around the year 1300. Their capital city was Tenochtitlán (teh NOHCH tee TLAN).

Tenochtitlán had hundreds of buildings, roads, and a population of
10 250,000 people. The Aztecs made their own calendar, and built large temples as part of their religion. Some temples had a playing court for a game that was like modern-day basketball.

At the time the Aztec civilization lived in Central Mexico, groups of American Indians had settled in almost every region of North America. These groups adapted to different environments and developed their own cultures.

REVIEW What were kivas? underground rooms that the Ancient Pueblo used for religious ceremonies

Lesson Summary

- During the Ice Age, Asian hunters followed large animals across Beringia to North America.
- Around 9,000 years ago, people in the Americas began farming.
- Important early civilizations of the Americas included the Mound Builders, the Ancient Pueblo, and the Aztecs.

Why It Matters ...

The history of the people of North America began with the American Indians. They practiced agriculture and built civilizations.

Lesson Review

3,000 years ago	About 1,500 years ago	About 700 years ago
Mound Builders civilizations	**Ancient Pueblo civilization grows**	**Aztecs rule in Central Mexico**

3,500 years ago — 2,500 — 1,500 — 500 — Today

1. **VOCABULARY** Write an explanation of the Beringia land bridge using the words **glacier** and **migration.**
2. **READING SKILL** Review your chart. Who were some of the earliest people to build large villages in North America?
3. **MAIN IDEA: History** Why do scientists think the migration over Beringia stopped 10,000 years ago?
4. **MAIN IDEA: Culture** In what ways did agriculture change life for Paleo-Indians?
5. **TIMELINE SKILL** Which civilization is older, the Ancient Pueblo or the Mound Builders?
6. **CRITICAL THINKING: Synthesize** Describe the ways the Aztec culture fits the definition of a civilization.

HANDS ON **ART ACTIVITY** Find out more about the Great Serpent Mound by using library resources. Use clay to make a model of the mound or draw a picture of it.

43

3 Review/Assess

Review Tested Objectives

U1-12 Many scientists think that during the Ice Age, Asian hunters followed large animals across a land bridge to North America.

U1-13 Some important North American civilizations include the Mound Builders (Adena, Hopewell, Mississippian), the Ancient Pueblo peoples (Anasazi), and the Aztecs.

Lesson Review Answers

1. Explanations should show an understanding of *glacier* and *migration.*
2. the Adena, the Hopewell, and the Mississippians
3. They think that Beringia was covered with water from melting glaciers as the Ice Age ended.
4. Some began to stay in one place to care for the plants. With a steady diet, more people survived; populations grew; people built villages and cities.
5. Mound Builders
6. The Aztecs lived together and had organized systems of government, religion, and culture. Their capital city, Tenochtitlán, had buildings, roads, and a population of 250,000 people. They had their own calendar and built large temples as part of their religion.

HANDS ON Performance Task Rubric

4	Model or picture is accurate; mound details are all present.
3	Model or picture is generally accurate; most mound details are present.
2	Model or picture contains some errors; few mound details are present.
1	Model or picture is inaccurate; mound details are absent.

Study Guide/Homework

Vocabulary and Study Guide

Vocabulary

Across
1. Another word for farming
2. An organized system of government, religion, and culture
3. Spanish word for town

Down
4. A huge sheet of moving ice
5. Movement from one place to another

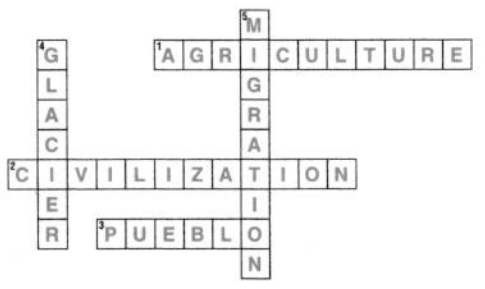

Study Guide

6. Read "People Arrive in the Americas." Then fill in the blanks below.

One theory about how the first ___humans___ came to the Americas is that they walked across a natural land bridge, which scientists named ___Beringia___. Beringia appeared between Alaska and ___Asia___ during the ___Ice Age___. Humans followed ___animals___ from Asia across Beringia into North America. These ancient Americans are known as ___Paleo-Indians___.

7. Read "Civilizations Develop." Then fill in the blanks below.

Over thousands of years, some Paleo-Indian groups ___farmed___ large areas and built villages and cities. The Mound Builders built giant mounds where they often ___buried their dead___. The Ancient Pueblo lived in the American ___Southwest___. Their buildings had many rooms. They also built underground rooms called ___kivas___. The ___Aztecs___ lived in central Mexico. They made their own calendar and built large ___temples___ to their gods.

Unit Resources

13
Use with *United States History*, pp. 38–43

Unit Resources, p. 13

Reteach Minilesson

Use a KWL chart to reteach the lesson.

K	W	L
I know that the Ancient Pueblo... 1) 2)	I want to know... 1) 2)	I learned that the Ancient Pueblo... 1) 2)

Graphic Organizer 2

Quick Look

Connect to Core Lesson In Extend Lesson 1, students will use a primary source to find out more about the Aztecs and life in their ancient home, the city of Tenochtitlán.

1 Teach the Extend Lesson

Connect to Primary Sources

Through primary sources, we can gain a sense of what the past was like. As students examine the painting, they can learn more about community life in the Aztec capital.

More About the Artist

Diego Rivera was born in 1886, in Guanajuato, Mexico. At the age of 10, Rivera won a scholarship to study art at the Academy of San Carlos in Mexico City. Later, he studied in Europe. In 1921, Rivera returned to Mexico, where he began to paint murals of Mexican agriculture, industry, and culture on public buildings. He painted *The Great City of Tenochtitlán* for the National Palace in Mexico City.

History

Tenochtitlán

Caged geese honk, shopkeepers shout, cacao beans rattle out of sacks. These are some of the sounds the Aztecs heard 500 years ago in the busy markets of the city of Tenochtitlán. Aztec culture centered around Tenochtitlán, which was their capital city. The Aztecs ruled about 12 million people in the surrounding region.

The scene of Aztec life shown here comes from a mural called *The Great City of Tenochtitlán*, painted by Mexican artist Diego Rivera in 1945. He researched Aztec civilization so his painting would be accurate. This mural is now in Mexico City. Mexico City was built on the ruins of Tenochtitlán. Look closely at this portion of Rivera's mural. Find the details described below.

1 **Island City** The Aztecs built Tenochtitlán on an island in the middle of a lake. Their city included temples, palaces, paved roads, and a huge marketplace.

2 **Moctezuma** The ruler of the Aztecs is shown being carried through the streets of the city. Moctezuma holds a fan made of bird feathers. The feathers of tropical birds were a valuable trade item.

3 **Marketplace** Sellers brought rare goods such as jaguar skin and jade from distant lands to the marketplace.

4 **Corn** Rivera shows the different kinds of corn—red, blue, and yellow—the Aztecs grew and sold. They built artificial "floating gardens" on which they also grew onions, peppers, avocados, tomatoes, and other crops.

5 **Cacao Money** Aztecs used cacao beans as money. They also ground the beans into a powder to make chocolate.

Reaching All Learners

Extra Support

Write a Narrative

- Have students write a paragraph describing the activity in the market, as if they were visitors there.
- Ask students to describe the sounds, smells, and sights that they might find.

Verbal-linguistic

On Level

Research Aztec Money

- Ask students to use library resources or the Internet to find out more about the way the Aztecs used cacao beans as money. How were the beans valued?
- Have them write a short dialogue between two Aztecs in which cacao beans are traded for goods.

Verbal-linguistic

Challenge

Paint a Mural

- Have students study Rivera's visual style and subject matter.
- Then, have them use what they have learned to create a Rivera-style mural showing some aspect of life in their own community.
- This activity pairs well with the Connect It activity.

Visual-spatial

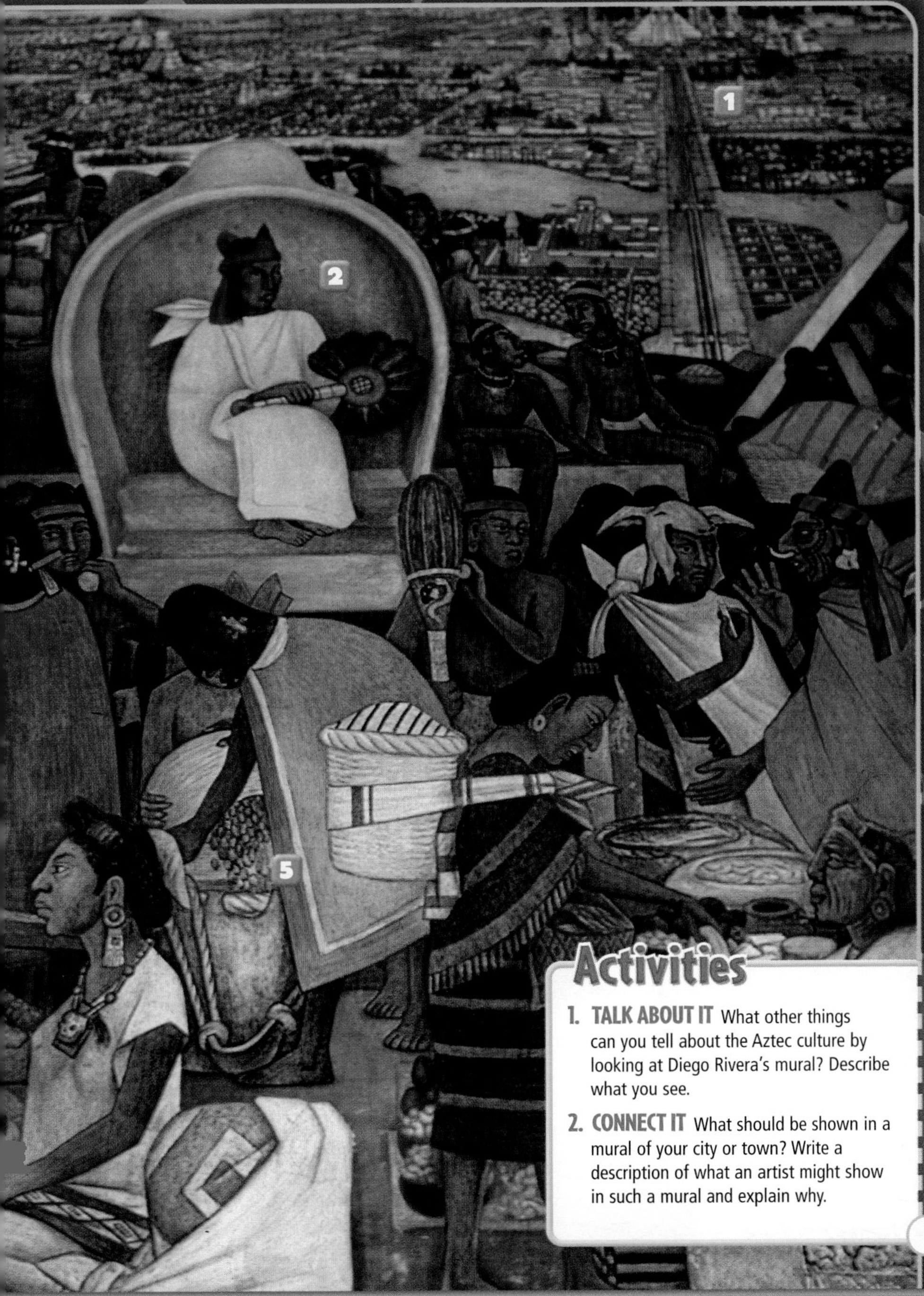

HISTORY

Activities

1. **TALK ABOUT IT** What other things can you tell about the Aztec culture by looking at Diego Rivera's mural? Describe what you see.
2. **CONNECT IT** What should be shown in a mural of your city or town? Write a description of what an artist might show in such a mural and explain why.

45

2 Leveled Activities

1 Talk About It *For Extra Support*
Answers will vary, but may include descriptions of buildings, the landscape, bridges, transportation, goods, baskets, workers, sellers, or clothing.

2 Connect It *For Challenge*

Writing Rubric

4	Description is well organized; facts are accurate; mechanics are correct.
3	Description is adequately organized; facts are mostly accurate; mechanics are correct.
2	Description is somewhat organized; some factual errors; some errors in mechanics.
1	Description is disorganized; many factual errors; many errors in mechanics.

ELL

REACHING ALL LEARNERS

Advanced

- Ask students to reread the caption about Moctezuma.
- Ask them to make a list of five questions that they would have liked to ask the Aztec ruler.

Verbal-linguistic

Science

Discuss Agriculture

- The Aztecs built artificial islands called *chinampas,* or floating gardens. They packed mud on top of twigs. The *chinampas* floated along until the roots grew down far enough to anchor the island to the lake floor.
- Ask students to think about why the Aztecs might have made the *chinampas* to grow crops.
- What might be the advantages of planting their crops on islands?

Logical-mathematical

Graphic Organizer

What do I know about Tenochtitlán?

K	W	L
I know that…	I want to learn…	I have learned…

Graphic Organizer 2

✔ Tested Objectives

U1-14 Geography Explain how the geography of the Northwest influenced the lives of the native peoples of the region.

U1-15 History Describe the way of life and culture of the Tlingit.

Lesson Quick Look

This lesson tells how the Indians of the Pacific Northwest lived and adapted to their coastal environment.

Teaching Option: Extend Lesson 2 provides students with a legend told by the Wasco.

1 Get Set to Read

Preview Have students look at the map on page 47. Ask what region it shows.

Reading Skill: Main Idea and Details Students may list details such as the use of salmon, cedar trees, and spruce trees.

Build on What You Know Ask students to name items that are made out of plastic. Explain that, just as we have many uses for plastic, the Northwest Indians made many items out of wood. As students read, have them list these items.

Vocabulary

surplus *adjective*, extra

potlatch *noun*, a traditional feast of Northwest Indians

clan *noun*, a group of related families

Core Lesson 2

Peoples of the Northwest

VOCABULARY

surplus
potlatch
clan

Vocabulary Strategy

sur|plus

To remember that **surplus** means an extra amount, think of the **plus** sign from arithmetic.

READING SKILL
Main Idea and Details
What details support the first main idea in the lesson?

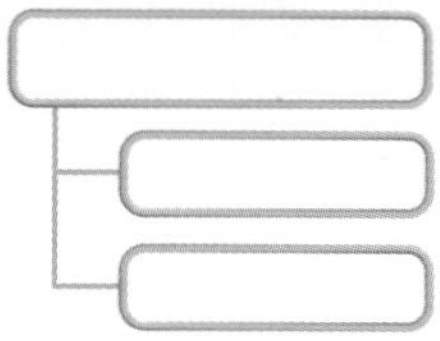

Build on What You Know Can you think of a material that you use in different ways? Plastic is one such material. It can be made into a bag or part of a computer or a drinking cup. In a similar way, the Northwest Indians found many uses for wood.

The Pacific Northwest

Main Idea American Indians of the Northwest coast learned to make use of the natural resources around them.

The Pacific Northwest is a coastal area that stretches from Alaska to northern California. The region is bordered by mountains to the east and ocean to the west. The coastline has thousands of islands and bays. Thick forests cover much of the land. 1

Several American Indian groups lived in this region when Europeans first came to North America. Many still live there today.

Pacific Northwest Warm winds coming off the ocean keep the climate rainy and mild.

Skill and Strategy

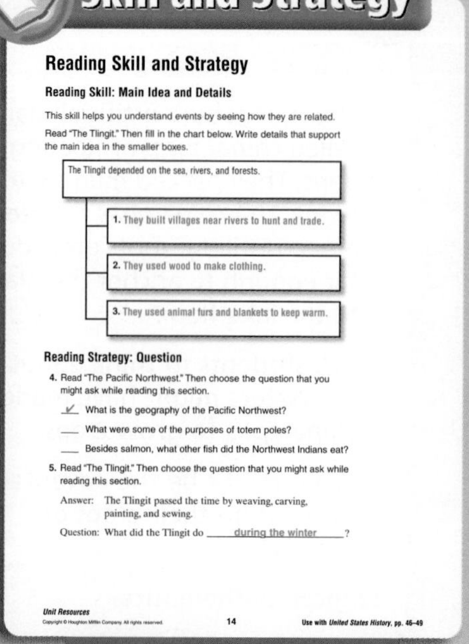

Reading Skill and Strategy

Reading Skill: Main Idea and Details

This skill helps you understand events by seeing how they are related.

Read "The Tlingit." Then fill in the chart below. Write details that support the main idea in the smaller boxes.

The Tlingit depended on the sea, rivers, and forests.

1. They built villages near rivers to hunt and trade.
2. They used wood to make clothing.
3. They used animal furs and blankets to keep warm.

Reading Strategy: Question

4. Read "The Pacific Northwest." Then choose the question that you might ask while reading this section.
   - ✓ What is the geography of the Pacific Northwest?
   - ___ What were some of the purposes of totem poles?
   - ___ Besides salmon, what other fish did the Northwest Indians eat?
5. Read "The Tlingit." Then choose the question that you might ask while reading this section.

   Answer: The Tlingit passed the time by weaving, carving, painting, and sewing.

   Question: What did the Tlingit do ___during the winter___?

Unit Resources

14
Use with *United States History*, pp. 46–49

Unit Resources, p. 14

Background

Potlatches

- Potlatches are an important part of Tlingit history and modern life.
- The most common Tlingit potlatches today are given for funerals, memorials, adoptions, totem-pole raisings, and the building of houses or lodges.

The People and the Land

American Indians who lived in the Northwest around the year 1500 hunted and gathered everything they needed from the land and waters near them. Salmon from the rivers was an important
2 resource.

In spring and summer, thousands of these fish filled the streams. During these months, the Indians caught so much **surplus,** or extra, salmon that they dried and ate it all year. Dried salmon was part of everyone's diet, but it was not their only food. Northwest Indians also ate shellfish, whales, and seals. In the forests, they gathered berries and fern roots and hunted geese, deer, elks, and bears.

Wood was another important resource for the Northwest peoples. They carved cedar logs into canoes called dugouts. Dugouts were used to carry goods on trading trips along the seacoast and rivers. Some groups paddled out to sea in dugouts to hunt for whales.

The Northwest Indians built large houses using boards cut from cedar or spruce trees. They decorated the houses
3 with carvings and paint.

Skilled craftspeople also used cedar logs to make totem poles. Totem poles are tall poles that are carved and painted with human and animal figures. Northwest peoples often used totem poles to mark the entrance to their houses. The figures on a totem pole told the history of the families who lived there.

Families held potlatches to celebrate important events, such as a marriage or the building of a house. A **potlatch** was a large feast that could last for several days.

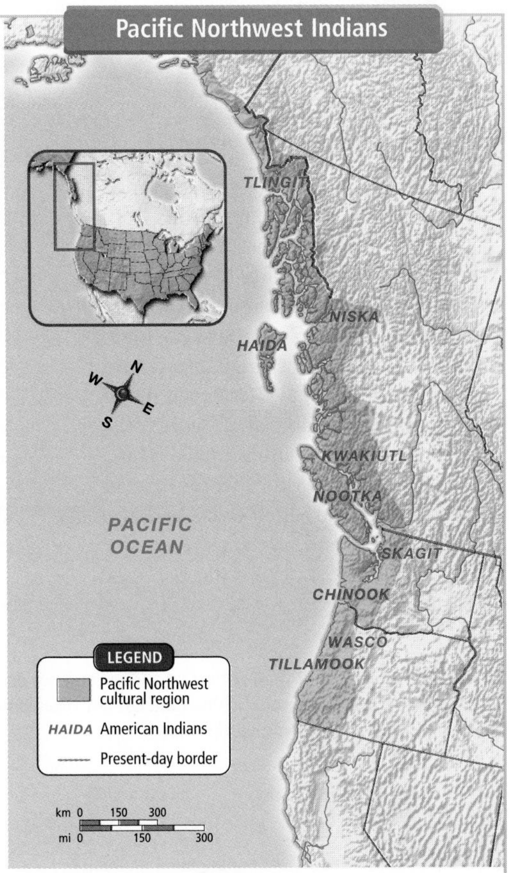

On the Coast The Pacific Northwest Indians settled in an area that was rich in natural resources.

SKILL **Reading Maps** Which American Indian group lived the farthest north in the Pacific Northwest region? the Tlingit

At a potlatch, the hosts served huge amounts of food and gave valuable gifts to the guests. At times, potlatches were like competitions. Families would try to give the largest and most expensive potlatch to show their wealth.

REVIEW Which two important resources helped the Northwest Indians live? salmon and wood

47

2 Teach

The Pacific Northwest

Talk About It

1 **Q Geography** What part of North America is considered the Pacific Northwest?

A the coastal area that reaches from Alaska to Northern California

2 **Q Economics** What important resource did the Northwest Indians catch in rivers?

A They caught salmon.

3 **Q Culture** What kind of houses did the Northwest Indians build?

A They built large houses using cedar or spruce boards. They decorated their houses with carvings and paint.

Vocabulary Strategy

surplus Tell students that this word may be used as an adjective or a noun.

potlatch Tell students that *potlatch* comes from the Nootka word *p'achitl,* "to make a gift." The Nootka are another Pacific Northwest Indian group.

Reading Strategy: Question Have students read the first two pages of the lesson. As they read, they should ask themselves, "What natural resources did the Northwest American Indians use?"

REACHING ALL LEARNERS

Leveled Practice

Extra Support

Ask students to make a description wheel **graphic organizer** about the potlatch. Verbal-linguistic; visual-spatial

Challenge

Have students look at the map on page 47 and **calculate the size** of the Pacific Northwest cultural region. They can use the scale of miles and kilometers shown on the map. Encourage them to estimate. Logical-mathematical

REACHING ALL LEARNERS

ELL

Advanced

Have partners **write** down three ways that the Northwest Indians interacted with their environment. Encourage them to illustrate their ideas.

Visual-spatial

The Tlingit

Talk About It

4 Q History What resources did the Tlingit use to make clothes?

A cedar bark and spruce roots

5 Q History What did the inside of a Tlingit house look like?

A It was divided to give each family its own area. A fire for cooking burned in the center of the house.

6 Q Technology How did a salmon trap work?

A It stopped the salmon. Some fish were speared and others were swept into the traps on either side.

Vocabulary Strategy

clan Tell students that other cultures also use a clan system. The word *clan* comes from an old Scottish word for "family."

Critical Thinking

Infer If the Tlingit had been farmers long ago, do you think they would still be?

The Tlingit

Main Idea The Tlingit depended on the sea, rivers, and forests for their way of life.

The Tlingit (KLINK-it) were one of the largest American Indian groups in the Pacific Northwest. Their way of life was similar to that of other Northwest peoples. They built their villages near the coast or rivers to make hunting and trading easier. The Tlingit also found many uses for trees. They even made clothing from bark. Because the Tlingit did not farm or herd animals, they did not have cotton or wool. Instead,
4 people used shredded cedar bark to make skirts, capes, and raincoats. They also made rain hats out of cedar bark and spruce roots.

Tlingit Clans

During the winter, the Tlingit wore fur and animal skins to keep warm and stayed indoors. They passed the time weaving, carving, painting, and sewing. People also gathered for dances, ceremonies, potlatches, and other feasts.

The Tlingit divided themselves into clans. A **clan** is a group of related families. The Tlingit had strict rules about how clans should treat one another. For example, a clan might pay a fine if one of its members insulted someone from another clan.

Several families from the same clan lived together. They put dividers in the 5
houses so that each family had its own area. People gathered around a fire in the center of the house to cook and talk.

Trapping Salmon The Tlingit set up a wooden fence across the stream to stop the salmon. Fish that did not get speared were swept by the current into traps on either side. 6

48 • Chapter 2

Art

Diagrams of a Tlingit House

Have students draw a sketch of what the inside of a Tlingit house might look like, based on the information in the lesson. They may choose to draw a floorplan or an illustration.

Visual-spatial

Language Arts

Write a Questionnaire

Ask students to write a list of questions about the way Pacific Northwest Indians used wood. Questions may be about the way they built canoes or what their clothing looked like.

Verbal-linguistic

The Tlingit Today

Today, about 17,000 Tlingit live in southeastern Alaska. Most live in cities, but some stay in villages. Many Tlingit have jobs fishing or working in the forests cutting wood. Others are business owners, teachers, doctors, and lawyers.

Tlingit Fishing Boat The Tlingit still fish the rivers and waters of the Alaskan coast.

The Tlingit carry on many cultural traditions. They have kept their dances, songs, and stories. Their clans are still strong, and people often wear clan or family symbols on their jewelry or clothes. The potlatch remains one of their most important traditions. It connects the modern Tlingit to their past.

REVIEW What role did clans have in Tlingit culture? People lived with their clans and had strict rules about how clans should treat one another.

Lesson Summary

- Salmon and wood were two important resources for Northwest Indians.
- The potlatch is a giant feast given to celebrate important events.
- The Tlingit today have a modern way of life but keep many of their traditions.

Why It Matters ...

The Northwest Indians were the first to make use of the natural resources, such as wood, which are important to the Pacific Northwest today.

Lesson Review

1. **VOCABULARY** Choose the correct word to complete the sentence:

   potlatch surplus clan

   The Tlingit lived in large houses with members of their ________.
2. **READING SKILL** Which **details** explain how the Northwest Indians used salmon?
3. **MAIN IDEA: Economics** List three ways the Northwest Indians used wood.
4. **MAIN IDEA: Culture** What were totem poles used for and what did they look like?
5. **PLACES TO KNOW** In what state do many Tlingit live today?
6. **CRITICAL THINKING: Infer** How might the lives of Pacific Northwest Indians have been different if they had not had resources from the ocean?

WRITING ACTIVITY Use the information from this lesson to write a brief Table of Contents for the chapters of a nonfiction book on the Tlingit. Include chapters about their culture and the way they adapted to their environment.

3 Review/Assess

Review Tested Objectives

U1-14 American Indians of the Northwest coast learned to make use of the natural resources around them.

U1-15 The Tlingit depended on the sea, rivers, and forests for their way of life.

Lesson Review Answers

1. clan
2. Possible details: Northwest Indians caught salmon. They dried the surplus salmon and ate it all year.
3. to make canoes, build houses, and carve totem poles
4. Totem poles marked the entrance of houses and told the history of the families who lived there. They were tall cedar poles carved and painted with human and animal figures.
5. Alaska
6. Possible answers: The climate might have been different; they might have had different resources for food, clothing, shelter, and tools; they might have farmed or herded animals.

Writing Rubric

4	Table of Contents format is used correctly; main points are correct and supported by details; mechanics are correct.
3	Table of Contents format is used; most main points are correct and supported by details; mechanics are generally correct.
2	Table of Contents format is attempted; main points/details contain errors or omissions; some errors in mechanics are present.
1	Table of Contents format is not used; main points/details contain errors or omissions; many errors in mechanics are present.

Study Guide/Homework

Vocabulary and Study Guide

Vocabulary

Write the definition of each vocabulary word below.

1. surplus Extra
2. potlatch A large feast that could last for several days
3. clan A group of related families
4. Use two of the words in a sentence. Sample answer: The potlatch is one of the most important traditions for many Tlingit clans.

Study Guide

Read "The Pacific Northwest." Then fill in the chart below.

Important natural resources used by Northwest American Indians

5. Salmon from rivers
6. Wood from forests

Read "The Tlingit." Then answer the questions below.

7. Out of what material did the Tlingit make their clothes? Why did they use this material? They used cedar bark, spruce roots, furs, and animal skins because they did not farm and did not have cotton or wool.
8. What did the Tlingit do in the winter? Stayed indoors weaving, carving, painting, and sewing
9. What Tlingit cultural traditions continue today? Clan and family symbols, the potlatch, dances, songs, stories, and language

Unit Resources 15 Use with *United States History*, pp. 46–49

Practice Book, p. 15

Reteach Minilesson

Use a main-idea-and-details chart to reteach the lesson.

Peoples of the Northwest

got their food from the sea, rivers, and forests	used wood to build houses, canoes, and totem poles	held potlatches

Graphic Organizer 8

Extend Quick Look

Connect to Core Lesson In the lesson they have just read, students learned about the peoples of the Pacific Northwest. In Extend Lesson 2, students will read a legend told by one of these peoples, the Wasco.

1 Preview the Extend Lesson

Connect to the Big Idea

Transmission Wasco culture is passed along from generation to generation through legends such as the legend of Chinook Wind and Cold Wind.

Connect to Prior Knowledge

Ask students to discuss what they know about legends. How does a legend differ from other types of stories, such as a myth or a tall tale?

Literature

Chinook Wind Wrestles Cold Wind

American Indians passed down what they learned about the world of nature through special stories called legends. Some stories gave human characteristics to objects in nature, such as stars and wind. The legend of Chinook Wind and Cold Wind was passed down from the Wasco people of the Northwest. The first paragraphs below tell about the wind along the Columbia River where the Wasco lived.

The grand Columbia River was a major passageway from the plateau region east of the Cascade Mountains to the Pacific Ocean, first for the Native Americans of the region and later for the white settlers who moved into the area. Living upriver of the long series of rapids and steep channels that cut through the Cascades, on a region of the river called the Dalles, the Wasco Indians and their neighbors on the north banks of the Columbia, the Wishram, established themselves as traders with the many visitors who passed their way each year. From the Plateau region came buffalo robes, dried roots, and camas bulbs. From the coast and along the Columbia came salmon, canoes, marine shells, and shell beads.

In the winter months, the wind brings with it the warmth of the Japanese current to the west, and it frees the snow-laden lower slopes of their winter burden. Because it comes from the direction of the Chinook tribe on the coast, the early traders called it the Chinook wind. The Cold Wind comes from the direction of Walla Walla to the east. The struggle between Cold Wind and Chinook Wind is a theme that appears in several Wasco stories.

Reaching All Learners

Background

Wasco Language

- Lewis and Clark encountered the Wasco Indians in 1805. The Wasco sold fish, dogs, acorns, and roots to members of the expedition.
- Today, only a handful of Wasco Indian elders still speak their native language, so the language is in danger of dying out.

Extra Support

Write a Report

- Ask students to reread the Extend Lesson. What connections can they find between the legend of Chinook Wind and Cold Wind, and the natural world?
- Have students write their opinions in a one-page report.

Verbal-linguistic; logical-mathematical

On Level

Write a Book Jacket

- Have students write the description for a book jacket for this story.

Verbal-linguistic

As they looked up at the star pattern symbolizing the wrestling match during the nights when Cold Wind blew, the Wasco could take comfort that Chinook Wind would soon appear to overpower Cold Wind and unlock the ice-choked streams again. According to legend, this struggle began a long time ago when all stars were human beings.

Once there was an old grandfather who always caught many salmon in Big River. His grandson Chinook Wind was very proud of him. They always had plenty to eat and some to give away to more unfortunate fishermen's families. This began to change, however, when Chinook Wind left to visit relatives in a faraway camp. That was when Cold Wind decided he should take over.

Cold Wind wanted salmon too. But because he was lazy, he always came to Big River too late for good fishing. He would go down to the river to fish and see Chinook Wind's grandfather going home with plenty of salmon. Cold Wind usually caught nothing and this made him angry. He decided simply to take a salmon from Old Grandfather.

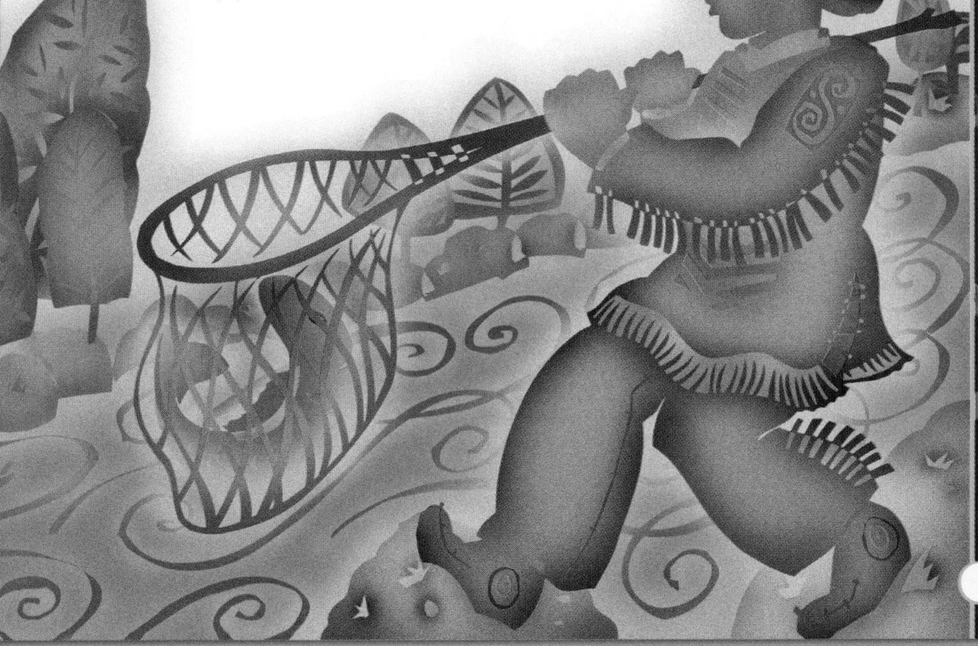

2 Teach the Extend Lesson

Learning Through Legends

You may want to read the legend in Extend Lesson 2 aloud to your class. Afterward, discuss with students what the legend is about. How does the legend relate to what students know about the lives of the Wasco and other Pacific Northwest Indians?

Challenge

Rewrite the Ending

Have students rewrite the legend of Chinook Wind and Cold Wind with a different ending, in which Cold Wind defeats Chinook Wind.

Verbal-linguistic

ELL

Intermediate

- Ask students to draw a picture illustrating the legend of Chinook Wind and Cold Wind.
- Have them write a caption that describes the picture.

Visual-spatial; verbal-linguistic

Literature

Legends

Indian Legends of the Pacific Northwest by Ella E. Clark. Place this book in your reading center for students who want to find out more about the stories of Pacific Northwest Indians.

Critical Thinking

Cause and Effect What did Chinook Wind's anger at Cold Wind cause him to do, and what was the result?

Analyze Ask students what the legend tells them about family relationships among the Wasco. Do they think that families were close, or not? What makes them think so?

Of course, if he had been less impatient, he would not have had to steal the salmon. Old Grandfather was such a generous soul that he would gladly have given Cold Wind a share. But greedy people are seldom patient or courteous.

Every day, Cold Wind got up later and later. Every day he went down to fish too late to catch anything. Every day he stole a salmon from Old Grandfather. Oh, how bold he got!

One day, Chinook Wind returned from his journey. When he heard how Cold Wind had been taking salmon from Old Grandfather, he grew angry and decided to teach him a lesson.

Chinook Wind hid in Old Grandfather's tipi and waited patiently until he came home from fishing. That day Old Grandfather returned whistling merrily, for he had caught more fish than usual. Everyone in the village would feast that night.

52 • Chapter 2

Reaching All Learners

Language Arts

Write a Legend

- Ask students to write a legend that explains a natural phenomenon, such as the sun rising and setting.
- Have them illustrate their legend.

Verbal-linguistic; visual-spatial

Math

Calculate: Multiplication

- If a Wasco family had twelve people in it, and each person needed to eat one salmon per day, how many salmon would the family have to catch over the course of the year to feed itself? 4380 salmon
- If each person needed to eat one and a half salmon per day, how many salmon would the family need to catch over the course of one year? 6570 salmon

Logical-mathematical

Science

Experiment with Evaporation

All large bodies of water, such as the "Big River"—the Columbia River—described in the legend, are affected by evaporation. Here is a simple experiment that will help students understand this process:

- Have students fill a plastic container with water and place it in a warm place, such as in a sunny window. Ask them to take notes on what happens to the water after one hour, one day, and one week. They can chart their results using a **bar graph**.

Logical-mathematical

LITERATURE

As usual, Cold Wind came roaring up to the tipi demanding salmon. This time, however, Chinook Wind boldly stepped out. "You cannot take any more of my grandfather's salmon!" he exclaimed.

"You cannot stop me, you scrawny boy," said Cold Wind. "I will wrestle you for Old Grandfather's salmon."

All right," said Chinook Wind. "That is why I am come—to do whatever I have to do to protect the tribe and my grandfather."

And so the two wrestled. Chinook Wind fought hard and won the match. Because Chinook Wind won, Cold Wind can never again take salmon away from Old Grandfather. To this day, Chinook Wind is stronger than Cold Wind.

If you look closely at the sky, you can see Chinook Wind and his brothers in their canoe close to Old Grandfather's salmon. Cold Wind and his brothers are in a canoe far behind. Cold Wind can never get Old Grandfather's last salmon.

Activities

1. **THINK ABOUT IT** The story says "greedy people are seldom patient or courteous." Do you agree? Why or why not?
2. **WRITE ABOUT IT** What kind of weather is powerful where you live? Write a legend that explains why it is so powerful.

53

3 Leveled Activities

1 Think About It *For Extra Support*
You may want to have students sit in a circle to discuss the question.

2 Write About It *For Challenge*

Writing Rubric

4	Legend is well told; has a clear beginning, middle, and end; shows considerable creativity.
3	Legend is fairly well told; has a beginning, middle, and end; shows creativity.
2	Legend is told in a fairly disorganized way; beginning, middle, and end are unclear; shows little creativity.
1	Legend is very disorganized; no beginning, middle, or end; shows no creativity.

Drama

Write a Play

Ask students to work in small groups to adapt the legend of Chinook Wind and Cold Wind as a play to present for the class.

Verbal-linguistic; bodily-kinesthetic

Graphic Organizer

Compare Chinook Wind and Cold Wind

Chinook Wind	Cold Wind
Helpful	Selfish
Generous	Greedy
Strong	Weak
Patient	Impatient

Graphic Organizer 1

Core Lesson 3 Pages 54–55

Tested Objectives

U1-16 Geography Explain how the geography of the Southwest influenced the lives of the native peoples of the region.

U1-17 History Describe the way of life and culture of the Hopi.

Lesson Quick Look

This lesson tells how the Southwest Indians were able to live successfully in a region with little water.

Teaching Options: Extend Lesson 3 presents the biographies of three notable Southwest Indians.

1 Get Set to Read

Preview Have students look at the map of the Southwest on page 55. What does it tell them about what they are going to read?

Reading Skill: Cause and Effect Students may note ways in which scarcity of water affected Southwest Indians.

Build on What You Know Ask students how they use water every day. Discuss what life would be like if they did not have enough water to use. What are some things they could do to cope with this shortage?

Vocabulary

irrigation *noun,* a method of channeling water in order to grow crops in dry land

staple *noun,* a main crop and food

ceremony *noun,* a formal act determined by ritual or custom

Core Lesson 3

Peoples of the Southwest

VOCABULARY

irrigation
staple
ceremony

Vocabulary Strategy

staple

You may be familiar with a staple as something that goes in a stapler. However, in this lesson, the word **staple** means a major crop or food.

READING SKILL

Cause and Effect As you read, take notes to show how climate affected the lives of Southwest Indians.

CAUSE	EFFECT

Build on What You Know Water is necessary for life. After all, two-thirds of the human body is made of water! In the Southwest, water is scarce. The American Indians who lived there learned to use water carefully.

The Southwest

Main Idea In different ways, the Southwest Indians solved the problem of having little water.

The Southwest is a region that includes all of present-day Arizona and New Mexico. It also stretches across sections of what are now Utah, Colorado, Nevada, Texas, southern California, and northern Mexico. Parts of the Rocky Mountains are in the Southwest.

A large part of the region is low, flat desert, but in places the desert rises to high plateaus. The land of the Southwest receives only a small amount of rain and is very dry. Most of the water in the area flows in rivers fed by melting snow in the mountains. 1

Canyons and Plateaus Thousands of years ago, rivers cut canyons through the high plateaus of the region.

Skill and Strategy

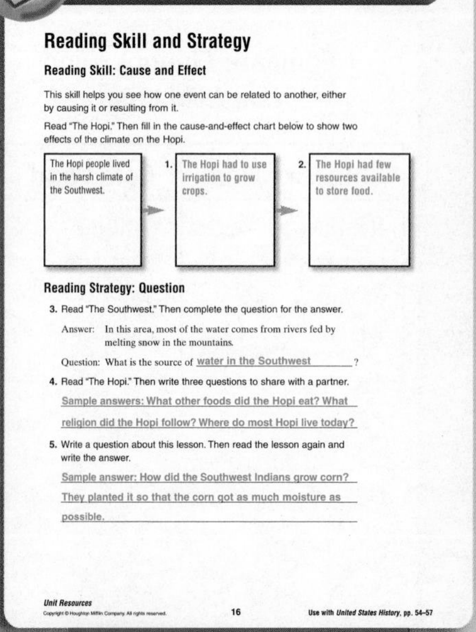

Reading Skill and Strategy

Reading Skill: Cause and Effect

This skill helps you see how one event can be related to another, either by causing it or resulting from it.

Read "The Hopi." Then fill in the cause-and-effect chart below to show two effects of the climate on the Hopi.

	1.	2.
The Hopi people lived in the harsh climate of the Southwest.	The Hopi had to use irrigation to grow crops.	The Hopi had few resources available to store food.

Reading Strategy: Question

3. Read "The Southwest." Then complete the question for the answer.

Answer: In this area, most of the water comes from rivers fed by melting snow in the mountains.

Question: What is the source of water in the Southwest?

4. Read "The Hopi." Then write three questions to share with a partner.

Sample answers: What other foods did the Hopi eat? What religion did the Hopi follow? Where do most Hopi live today?

5. Write a question about this lesson. Then read the lesson again and write the answer.

Sample answer: How did the Southwest Indians grow corn? They planted it so that the corn got as much moisture as possible.

Unit Resources

16
Use with *United States History*, pp. 54–57

Unit Resources, p. 16

Background

Hopi Culture

- Hopi society is divided into clans.
- Hopi children belong to their mother's clan.

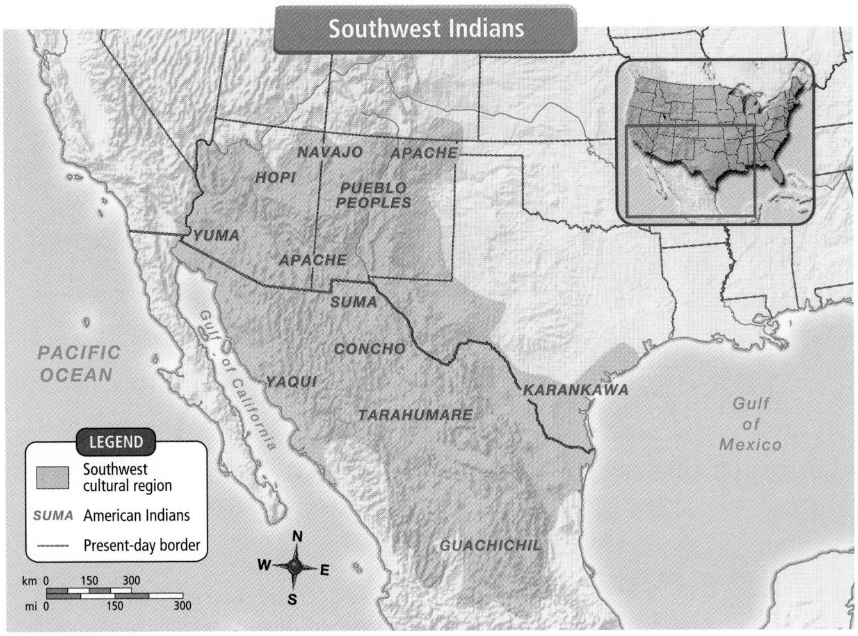

A Dry Land The dry Southwest region spreads across parts of the United States and Mexico. SKILL **Reading Maps** The Hopi live in present-day Arizona. Which other Southwest Indians live in Arizona? Yuma, Navajo, Apache

The People and the Land

Throughout history, the climate of the Southwest has influenced the way American Indians of the region lived. Much of the area was so dry that few
2 trees grew there. To build their homes, Southwest Indians used sticks, stones, and a clay called adobe (uh DOH bee). They often built their homes on top of steep mesas to protect them from attack. Mesas are like small plateaus with steep sides and flat tops.

The climate of the Southwest affected life in another way. Many Southwest peoples were farmers. The lack of rain made agriculture difficult. They could never be sure that crops would survive.

Southwest Indians had to find ways to get water to their crops in order to have a successful harvest. Many used irrigation. **Irrigation** is a way of supplying water to crops with streams, ditches, or pipes. Some groups dug long, narrow ditches from the rivers to their fields. Water from the rivers flowed through the ditches to the crops.

Southwest Indians planted corn deep in the ground so that the roots of the plant could get moisture from the earth. They also planted crops in areas that flooded during the spring rains.

REVIEW Why was irrigation necessary for the Southwest Indians? the Southwest has little rainfall

55

2 Teach

The Southwest

Talk About It

1 **Q Geography** What is the land like in the Southwest?

A Much of it is low, flat desert, with high plateaus in some places.

2 **Q History** Why couldn't the Southwest Indians use wood to build their houses?

A The Southwest was so dry that few trees grew there.

Vocabulary Strategy

irrigation This word comes from the Latin word *rigare,* meaning "water."

Reading Strategy: Question As students read, suggest that they keep in mind the question, "What were some of the different ways Southwest Indians solved the problem of living in a dry land?"

REACHING ALL LEARNERS

Leveled Practice

Extra Support

Working in groups, have students use library or Internet resources to research how the Southwest Indians built adobe houses. Have them **create a mural** showing the building of an adobe home.
Visual-spatial

Challenge

Ask students to **write and illustrate** directions on how to build and use irrigation to water fields.
Verbal-linguistic

REACHING ALL LEARNERS

ELL

Beginning

Have students **list unfamiliar or difficult words** from this lesson, for example, *irrigation* and *plateau.* Have them work with a partner to write sentences using these words that illustrate the words' meanings.

Verbal-linguistic

The Hopi

Talk About It

3 **Q History** What larger group are the Hopis part of?

A the Pueblo Indians

4 **Q Culture** Why did the Hopi try to keep their land healthy?

A to have good harvests and enough rainfall

5 **Q Economics** What kinds of work do modern-day Hopi do?

A Many are skilled at making traditional pots, weavings, baskets, and silver jewelry. Some are farmers. Others hold jobs in local companies, are teachers, or run their own businesses.

Vocabulary Strategy

staple Point out that having a *staple* helps a culture be *stable.*

ceremony A synonym for *ceremony* is *ritual.*

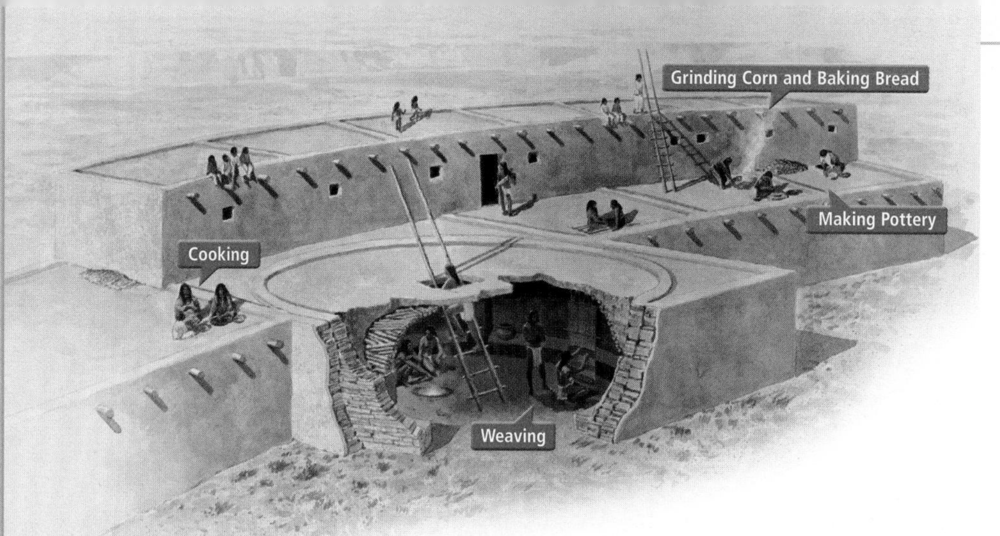

Hopi Pueblo The Hopi built their pueblos with many rooms and used ladders to connect the stories.

The Hopi

Main Idea The Hopi found natural resources in a dry land.

The Hopi are among the oldest Indian groups in the Southwest. They began living in the northeastern part of present-day Arizona before 1350. They
3 are one of several groups known as Pueblo Indians because of their large buildings. One of their villages is about a thousand years old.

Living in a Dry Land

The early Hopi used irrigation to grow beans, squash, and corn, their most important crop. Corn was the staple for the Hopi and part of every meal. A **staple** is a main crop that is used for food. The Hopi grew yellow, blue, red, white, and purple corn. They grew enough to last for the whole year and kept it in storage rooms in their pueblos.

Hopi people used the resources available to them to make containers to store their food and water. They dug clay and shaped it into large and small pots. The Hopi were some of the first people in the world to fire their pottery with coal. Firing pottery makes it strong and hard.

Religion was at the center of many Hopi customs. They believed that their creator had led them to the Southwest. The Hopi felt that they were meant to be caretakers of the land.

As caretakers, the Hopi tried to keep their land healthy. If the land was healthy, 4
they would have good harvests and enough rainfall. For the Hopi, caretaking included prayer and a yearlong calendar of ceremonies. A **ceremony** is a special event at which people gather to express important beliefs. For example, at a ceremony called the Bean Dance, the Hopi danced and prayed for a good harvest.

56 • Chapter 2

Math

Calculating Time Spans

- If a Hopi village was built around the year 1700, and still survives, about how old would that village be today? about three hundred years old
- About how long ago did the Hopi begin living in present-day northeastern Arizona? over 650 years, or more than six centuries

Logical-mathematical

Language Arts

Write a Poem

Have students write a poem that reflects what they have read about Southwest Indians. Ask them to include details about food, farming, shelters, and the environment.

Verbal-linguistic

Hopi Farmer
People still farm the Southwest. This Hopi farmer grows squash.

The Hopi Today

Modern-day Hopi still follow many of their cultural traditions. Most Hopi live in their villages in the Southwest and continue to take part in dances and ceremonies.

5 Many Hopi are skilled at making traditional pots, weavings, baskets, and silver jewelry. Others hold jobs in local companies, are teachers, or run their own businesses.

REVIEW What is the importance of the Bean Dance? Through the ceremony of the Bean Dance, the Hopi prayed for a good harvest.

Lesson Summary

The Hopi and other American Indians built pueblos in the Southwest. They used irrigation and other methods to grow beans, squash, and corn in a dry climate. Hopi culture included religious ceremonies throughout the year. Many Hopi people today still take part in their cultural traditions.

Why It Matters ...

Lack of water is part of life in the Southwest, even today. The Southwest Indians showed how to adapt to this dry climate.

Lesson Review

1. **VOCABULARY** Write a paragraph describing the way Southwest Indians used **irrigation.**
2. **READING SKILL** What **effect** did the climate have on Hopi shelters?
3. **MAIN IDEA: Technology** What were two methods the Southwest peoples used to water their crops?
4. **MAIN IDEA: Culture** For what purpose did the Hopi make pots?
5. **FACTS TO KNOW** What was the staple crop of the early Hopi Indians?
6. **CRITICAL THINKING: Infer** Why did the Southwest Indians grow crops instead of relying on hunting and gathering?

HANDS ON **SCIENCE ACTIVITY** Southwest Indians had to think carefully about the water they used. Make a chart of the ways you use water in one week. Then, identify one or two ways you could use less water.

3 Review/Assess

Review Tested Objectives

U1-16 In different ways, the American Indians of the Southwest solved the problem of having little water.

U1-17 The Hopi created a rich culture in a dry land with few natural resources.

Lesson Review Answers

1. Paragraph should reflect student's understanding of the meaning of irrigation and that the Southwest Indians used it to solve the problem of having little water.
2. The dry climate meant that few trees were available as a resource. Instead, the Hopi used sticks, stones, and adobe to build their homes.
3. Sample answers: used irrigation; planted corn deep in the ground; planted crops in areas that flooded during spring rains
4. to store food and water
5. corn
6. The dry climate probably limited the amount and variety of plants and animals they could have hunted or gathered for food.

HANDS ON Performance Task Rubric

4	Chart is well organized; shows important information; mechanics are correct.
3	Chart is adequately organized; shows some key information; few errors in mechanics.
2	Chart is somewhat organized; some important information is missing; several errors in mechanics.
1	Chart is disorganized; important information is not shown; many errors in mechanics.

Study Guide/Homework

Vocabulary and Study Guide

Vocabulary

Write the definition of each vocabulary word below.

1. irrigation A way of supplying water through streams, ditches, or pipes
2. staple A main crop that is used for food
3. ceremony A special event where people express important beliefs
4. Use two of the words in a sentence. Sample answer: The Hopi used irrigation to grow corn, their staple crop.

Study Guide

Read "The Southwest." Then fill in the causes and effects in the chart below to explain how Southwest American Indians lived.

Causes	Effects
Few trees	5. Built homes out of adobe
Very dry land	6. Used irrigation for farming

Read "The Hopi." Then choose the correct ending to each statement below.

7. At every meal, the Hopi ate
   A. beans. (B.) corn. C. squash.
8. Hopi religion said that they lived on the land to be
   A. farmers. B. potters. (C.) caretakers.
9. The Hopi used coal to make strong, hard
   A. adobe. (B.) pottery. C. irrigation pipes.

Unit Resources

17
Use with *United States History*, pp. 54–57

Unit Resources, p. 17

Reteach Minilesson

Use a word web to reteach the lesson.

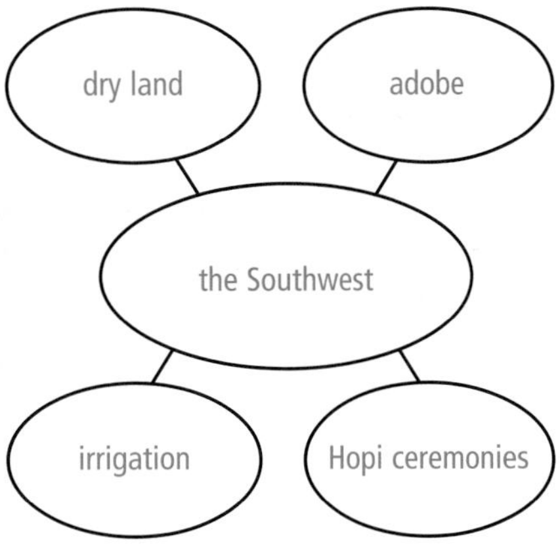

Graphic Organizer 13

Extend Quick Look

Connect to Core Lesson Students have read about American Indians of the Southwest. In Extend Lesson 3, students will learn more about how Southwest Indians today keep their traditions alive.

1 Teach the Extend Lesson

Connect to the Big Idea

Transmission The people featured in Extend Lesson 3 pass on their culture and share their heritage through their knowledge, beliefs, values, and traditions. Cultural learning begins at birth and continues throughout life.

Biographies

Keepers of Tradition

Many American Indians of the Southwest stay connected to their heritage. They want to keep alive the values and traditions of the past. Read about how a Laguna writer, a Navajo scientist, and a Hopi filmmaker share their traditions with others.

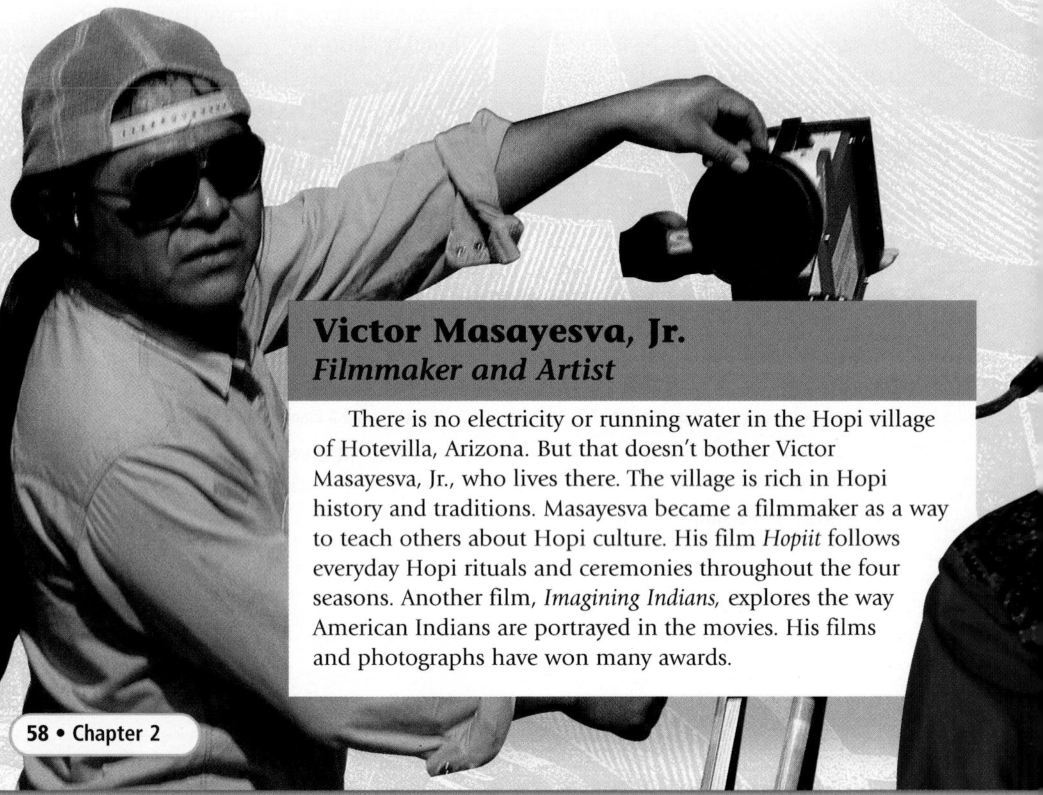

Victor Masayesva, Jr.

Filmmaker and Artist

There is no electricity or running water in the Hopi village of Hotevilla, Arizona. But that doesn't bother Victor Masayesva, Jr., who lives there. The village is rich in Hopi history and traditions. Masayesva became a filmmaker as a way to teach others about Hopi culture. His film *Hopiit* follows everyday Hopi rituals and ceremonies throughout the four seasons. Another film, *Imagining Indians,* explores the way American Indians are portrayed in the movies. His films and photographs have won many awards.

Reaching All Learners

Extra Support

Summarize a Biography

- Have students select one of the Southwest Indians whose biography appears in this Extend Lesson.
- Ask them to write a sentence that summarizes the person's biography.

Verbal-linguistic

On Level

Write a List of Questions

- Ask students to write a list of questions they would like to ask one of the Southwest people profiled here if they could interview them.

Challenge

Make a Storyboard

- Explain to students that a storyboard shows each image in a movie.
- Have them draw a storyboard for the first five images of a movie about their community.

Visual-spatial

Fred Begay
Nuclear Physicist

Fred Begay believes that the Navajo traditions he learned as a boy helped prepare him for his career as a scientist. Begay's parents taught him Navajo prayers and songs that explain the origin of the natural world. As a young man, Begay trained to be a farmer, but after serving in the Army, he enrolled at the University of New Mexico and earned a degree in nuclear physics. Now he works at the Los Alamos National Laboratory and teaches science to middle school students on a Navajo reservation.

BIOGRAPHIES

Leslie Marmon Silko
Writer

Author Leslie Marmon Silko was raised in the Laguna Pueblo in New Mexico. As a child, she spent many hours listening to her great-grandmother tell stories about the earth and sky. Silko planned to become a lawyer, but she felt an even stronger pull toward the Laguna tradition of storytelling. So she became a writer and teacher instead, publishing her first story in 1969. Silko says, "What I know is the Laguna. This place I am from is everything I am as a writer and a human being."

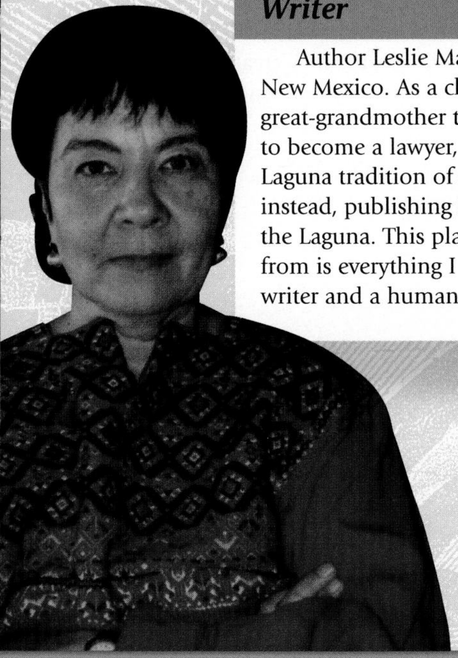

Activities

1. **TALK ABOUT IT** What questions would you like to ask each of these people about their traditions?
2. **SHOW IT** Research information about Southwest Indian traditions. Present the information in a bulletin board display.

Technology Visit Education Place for more biographies. www.eduplace.com/kids/hmss05/

59

2 Leveled Activities

1 Talk About It *For Extra Support*

Questions should demonstrate students' understanding of what traditions are. Questions should also reflect material from the Extend Lesson biographies.

2 Show It *For Challenge*

Performance Task Rubric	
4	Research is thorough; information is clear and accurate; presentation is creative; mechanics are correct.
3	Research is adequate; most information is clear and accurate; presentation is fairly creative; most mechanics are correct.
2	Research is somewhat incomplete; information is somewhat unclear or inaccurate; presentation is slightly creative; some errors in mechanics.
1	Research is incomplete; information is unclear or inaccurate; presentation is not creative; many errors in mechanics.

ELL

REACHING ALL LEARNERS

Intermediate

- Have pairs of students find three facts about one of the individuals profiled in Extend Lesson 3.
- Then have students create questions that could be answered by each of these facts.
- Have pairs ask the class their questions and share answers with one another.

Verbal-linguistic

Language Arts

Write a Biography

Ask students to write a short biography of someone they admire.

Verbal-linguistic

Graphic Organizer

Graphic Organizer 13

Tested Objectives

U1-18 Geography Explain how the geography of the Great Plains influenced the lives of the American Indians of the region.

U1-19 History Describe the way of life and culture of the Comanche.

Lesson Quick Look

This lesson discusses the American Indians who lived on the Eastern and Western Plains, and the different ways they interacted with their environments.

Teaching Option: Extend Lesson 4 features the art of Plains Indians.

1 Get Set to Read

Preview Have students look at the picture on page 60. What animal is shown?

Reading Skill: Draw Conclusions Students may conclude that buffalo were extremely important to Plains Indians.

Build on What You Know Ask students if they have ever been in a big field. What was it like? Did it seem empty or full of life? Ask them to imagine what it might be like to make their homes on an enormous field of grass.

Vocabulary

lodge *noun,* an American Indian dwelling that several families lived in

nomad *noun,* a person who moves around and does not live in one place

travois *noun,* a sled-like carrier pulled by a dog or horse

Core Lesson 4

Peoples of the Plains

VOCABULARY

lodge
nomad
travois

Vocabulary Strategy

nomad

The word **nomad** comes from a word meaning "to wander in search of land." Nomads wandered the Great Plains in search of buffalo.

READING SKILL

Draw Conclusions Use details from the lesson to draw a conclusion about the importance of the buffalo to Plains Indians.

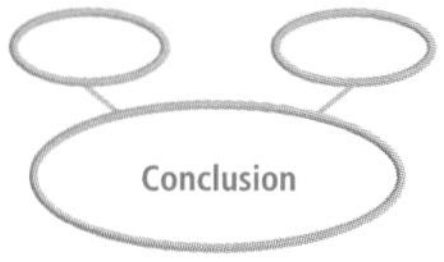

Build on What You Know When you see a large grassy field, do you think of it as empty? The Plains Indians lived on huge plains of grass that stretched for hundreds of miles in every direction. But those grasslands were far from empty.

The Great Plains

Main Idea American Indians lived as farmers and as migrating hunters on the Great Plains.

The Great Plains lie in the center of North America. The Plains stretch from the Mississippi River to the Rocky Mountains and from Texas into Canada. Much of the Plains used to be grassland. In the Eastern Plains, rainfall could cause the grasses to grow eight feet high. In the dry Western Plains, the grass was shorter. Although they might have seemed empty, the grasslands were a rich environment. American Indians have lived on the Plains for thousands of years. Over time they created two different ways of life from the two different environments where they lived.

The Great Plains Millions of buffalo used to roam over the Plains, eating the endless supply of grass.

60 • Chapter 2

Skill and Strategy

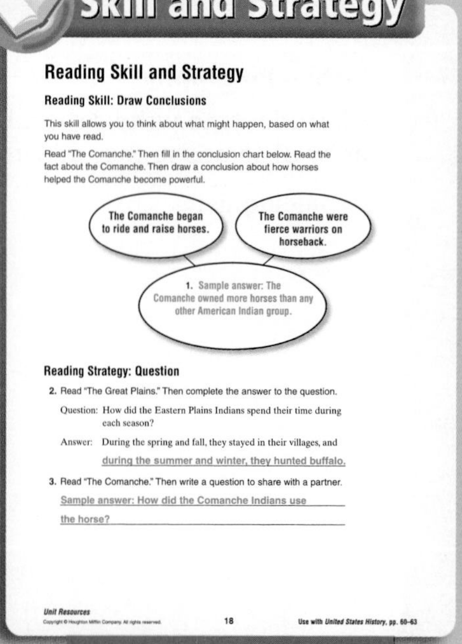

Reading Skill and Strategy

Reading Skill: Draw Conclusions

This skill allows you to think about what might happen, based on what you have read.

Read "The Comanche." Then fill in the conclusion chart below. Read the fact about the Comanche. Then draw a conclusion about how horses helped the Comanche become powerful.

The Comanche began to ride and raise horses.

The Comanche were fierce warriors on horseback.

1. Sample answer: The Comanche owned more horses than any other American Indian group.

Reading Strategy: Question

2. Read "The Great Plains." Then complete the answer to the question.

Question: How did the Eastern Plains Indians spend their time during each season?

Answer: During the spring and fall, they stayed in their villages, and during the summer and winter, they hunted buffalo.

3. Read "The Comanche." Then write a question to share with a partner.

Sample answer: How did the Comanche Indians use the horse?

Unit Resources

18
Use with *United States History*, pp. 60–63

Unit Resources, p. 18

Background

Teepees

- People of the Great Plains sometimes painted designs on the outsides of their teepees.
- In warm weather, the buffalo hides on the outside of a teepee could be rolled up to let in fresh air.

Life on the Eastern Plains

Rainfall on the Eastern Plains made it possible for American Indians such as the Pawnee and
1 the Omaha to farm successfully. They settled in villages near rivers and built earth lodges to live in. A **lodge** is a home that Plains Indians made using bark, earth, and grass. Lodges protected people from cold and stormy weather.

Each year, the Eastern Plains Indians spent spring and fall farming in their villages. Every summer and winter, they left their villages to hunt buffalo.

Life on the Western Plains

The dry land of the Western Plains made farming difficult. But the area had important resources,
2 such as the buffalo. These huge woolly animals gave the Western Plains Indians everything they needed to live. Western Plains people ate buffalo meat. They carved the bones into tools and wove the hair into rope. They even turned the tail into a fly swatter! The buffalo skin had different uses. Plains people made it into covers for their shelters, blankets, clothing, drums, and shields. They decorated these everyday items with painted designs, porcupine quills, and other materials.

The Western Plains Indians were nomads who followed the buffalo herds. A **nomad** is a person who moves around and does not live in one place. These nomads used a travois (truh VOY) to carry their belongings. A **travois** was similar to a sled. It was made from two poles and usually pulled by a dog.

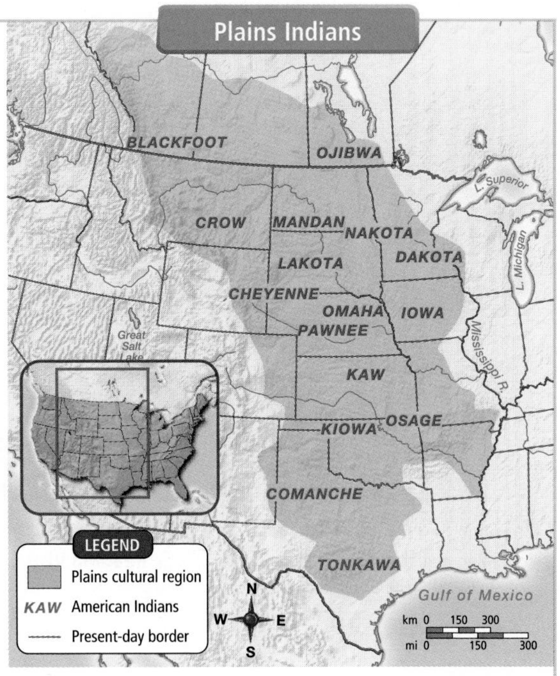

Eastern and Western Plains In the vast area of the Plains, some American Indian groups controlled large sections of land.

Travois poles were also used to set up teepees. A teepee was a cone-shaped tent covered with buffalo skins. Teepees were easy to set up and take down.

Plains Indian groups could move between the Eastern and Western Plains. The Lakota, for example, used to farm the land along the Mississippi River on the Eastern Plains. Then they fought with another group, the Ojibwa (oh JEEB wah) and were forced to migrate to the Western Plains. There, they adapted to life in the west. They became nomads who used horses to hunt buffalo.

REVIEW In what ways were the lives of the Eastern and Western Plains Indians different?
Eastern Plains Indians had villages and practiced agriculture; Western Plains Indians did not farm and lived as nomads.

61

Leveled Practice

Extra Support

Ask students to imagine they are creating a website about the Plains Indians. In groups, have them **make a list** of the topics they would include and the research they need to do. Verbal-linguistic

Challenge

Ask students to find out more about the prairie (grassland) habitat, including the plants and animals that lived there around 1500. Have them write and illustrate a **short report** about their findings. Verbal-linguistic

ELL

Intermediate

Have students create a **word web** for the word "buffalo" that shows why this animal was important to the Plains Indians.

Visual-spatial

2 Teach

The Great Plains

Talk About It

1 **Q Geography** What was the land of the Eastern Plains like?
A It had tall grasses and received enough rainfall for farming.

2 **Q Economics** How did the people of the Western Plains get food?
A They hunted buffalo.

3 **Q Visual Learning** What Plains Indians groups lived in Texas?
A the Comanche and the Tonkawa

Vocabulary Strategy

lodge Tell students that another meaning of this word is "to give shelter to."

nomad Tell students that this word comes from the Latin word *nomas,* meaning "a wandering person."

travois Use this mnemonic to help students remember *travois:* "The *travois* *tr*ailed behind a dog during *tr*avel."

Reading Strategy: Question As students read, suggest that they develop their own questions and seek the answers. You may wish to use any unanswered questions as a jumping-off point for class discussion.

The Comanche

Talk About It

4 **Q History** When did the Comanche start riding and raising horses?
A in the 1600s

5 **Q Economics** Why were the Comanche thought to be rich and powerful?
A They owned more horses than any other American Indian nation and controlled a large area of the Plains.

6 **Q Citizenship** In what ways do modern Comanche maintain their culture?
A They value their traditions, such as pow-wows, and have their own government.

Critical Thinking

Compare and Contrast What are some of the similarities and differences between the Comanche and other groups who lived on the Plains? You may want to model for students the process of thinking through the question. For example:

Think Aloud *I read that the Comanche became one of the most powerful Plains groups. They also owned more horses than any other American Indian group. Like other groups who lived on the Plains, they were nomads. They valued horses because they made hunting, traveling, and fighting easier.*

Comanche Life This painting by artist George Catlin shows the Comanche scraping and stretching buffalo skins. SKILL **Reading Visuals** What kind of shelter did the Comanche live in? teepees

The Comanche

Main Idea The Comanche Indians were skilled horse riders, hunters, and warriors.

Spanish explorers brought horses to North America in the 1500s. These animals changed the lives of the Plains Indians. By the mid-1700s, almost all the American Indians on the Great Plains had horses, which made it easier for the nomad groups to hunt and travel. Plains Indians valued horses so highly that wealth was measured by how many horses a person owned.

3 The Comanche (kuh MAN chee) Indians started riding and raising horses in the 1600s. They migrated from what is now Wyoming to the Great Plains. By the 1700s, they had spread across large parts of what are now Oklahoma and Texas, living as nomads. At times, the Comanche were at war with other American Indian groups.

The Comanche were fierce warriors on horseback. They could bend down and shoot an arrow from under a horse's chin, while riding at a full gallop.

The Comanche became one of the most powerful Plains groups, or nations. They owned more horses than any other American Indian nation and controlled a 4 large area of the Plains. In the early 1800s, people called the Comanche "the lords of the Southern Plains" because of their wealth and strength.

Comanche Government

The Comanche had a system of government that fit their lives as nomads. They divided themselves into groups. Each group hunted and traveled freely. Members of the group chose leaders, called chiefs. They had different chiefs for war and for peace. At times, the chiefs of all the Comanche met to talk about and decide issues that affected the groups.

62 • Chapter 2

Physical Education

Play a Plains Indian Game

Tell students that Plains Indians children may have played games like this one to help them hone their skills of observation. Have students sit in a wide circle. One student should sit in the middle, eyes closed. Choose another student to try to tap the sitter's shoulder without being heard. When the sitter senses the approacher, the sitter shouts "There!" and points to the approacher's location.

Bodily-kinesthetic

Language Arts

Write an Essay

Ask students to write a personal opinion essay about the advantages of living as either a nomad or in a village. Have students share their essay with a partner.

Verbal-linguistic

The Comanche Today

About 8,500 Comanche live in the United States today. Most of them live in Oklahoma, working as farmers or ranchers. Some work in the oil fields or cities of Oklahoma and Texas.

5 Though their way of life has changed greatly in the past 400 years, modern Comanche value their traditions.

Comanche Girl This Comanche girl is wearing traditional clothing at a pow-wow.

The Comanche still have their own government. Attending pow-wows, or dance gatherings, has been important in maintaining their culture.

REVIEW Why were horses important to Western Plains Indians? Horses made it easier for Western Plains Indians to hunt and travel.

Lesson Summary

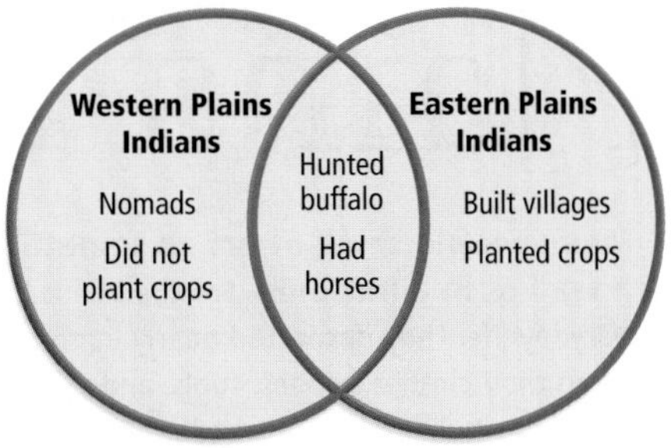

Why It Matters ...

Great Plains Indians, such as the Comanche, built some of the most powerful nations of all the American Indian groups.

Lesson Review

1. **VOCABULARY** Write a description of the life of the Western Plains Indians, using the words **travois** and **nomad.**
2. **READING SKILL** What did you **conclude** about the buffalo's importance? What details support it?
3. **MAIN IDEA: Geography** Why were the Eastern Plains Indians able to farm their land and live in villages?
4. **MAIN IDEA: Economics** Why was the horse so valuable to Western Plains Indians?
5. **CRITICAL THINKING: Summarize** What did the Comanche chiefs do as leaders?
6. **CRITICAL THINKING: Evaluate** Which animal was more important to the Western Plains Indians, the buffalo or the horse? Explain your answer.

HANDS ON **ART ACTIVITY** Make a fact file on the life of Western Plains Indians. Illustrate their food, shelter, and way of traveling.

Study Guide/Homework

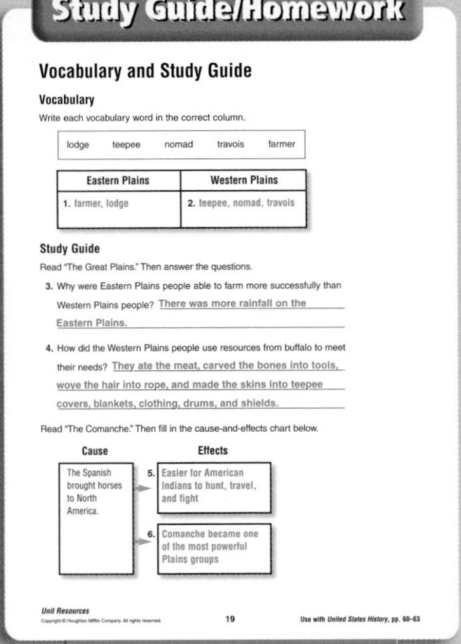

Vocabulary and Study Guide

Vocabulary

Write each vocabulary word in the correct column.

lodge teepee nomad travois farmer

Eastern Plains	Western Plains
1. farmer, lodge	2. teepee, nomad, travois

Study Guide

Read "The Great Plains." Then answer the questions.

3. Why were Eastern Plains people able to farm more successfully than Western Plains people? There was more rainfall on the Eastern Plains.
4. How did the Western Plains people use resources from buffalo to meet their needs? They ate the meat, carved the bones into tools, wove the hair into rope, and made the skins into teepee covers, blankets, clothing, drums, and shields.

Read "The Comanche." Then fill in the cause-and-effects chart below.

Cause	Effects
The Spanish brought horses to North America.	5. Easier for American Indians to hunt, travel, and fight
	6. Comanche became one of the most powerful Plains groups

Unit Resources

19
Use with *United States History*, pp. 60–63

Unit Resources, p. 19

Reteach Minilesson

Use a compare-and-contrast chart to reteach what it was like to live on the Eastern and Western Plains.

People of Eastern Plains	People of Western Plains
lived in villages built lodges raised corn, beans, and squash hunted buffalo in the summer and winter	nomads used teepees for shelter hunted buffalo all year

Graphic Organizer 1

3 Review/Assess

Review Tested Objectives

U1-18 American Indians lived as farmers and migrating hunters on the Great Plains.

U1-19 The Comanche Indians were skilled horseback riders, hunters, and warriors who controlled a large area of the Plains.

Lesson Review Answers

1. Descriptions should demonstrate students' understanding of *travois* and *nomad.*
2. Sample answer: The buffalo was extremely important to Plains Indians. They hunted it for food. Western Plains Indians also used buffalo skin for shelter and clothing and bones for tools.
3. the Eastern Plains received more rain
4. Horses made it easier for them to hunt and travel.
5. The Comanche chiefs led the Comanche groups and met to talk about issues that affected all groups.
6. Western Plains Indians relied on the buffalo for all of their needs. They didn't rely on the horse in the same way, but having horses made hunting buffalo and traveling across the Plains easier.

Writing Rubric

4	Fact file shows evidence of excellent research; illustrations are accurate.
3	Fact file shows evidence of good research; illustrations are mostly accurate.
2	Fact file shows evidence of some research; illustrations are somewhat accurate.
1	Fact file shows lack of research; illustrations are inaccurate or unclear.

Quick Look

Connect to Core Lesson Students have learned about Native Americans who lived on the Great Plains. In Extend Lesson 4, students will learn more about the art and artifacts of the Plains Indians.

1 Teach the Extend Lesson

Connect to the Big Idea

Cultural Images The Plains Indians project an image of themselves through their customs, beliefs, and arts, such as the items featured here.

Primary Sources

Art of the Plains Indians

Many people think of art as something that belongs on a wall or in a museum. For the Plains Indians, art was part of everyday life. They decorated nearly everything they made, including their clothes, tepees, tools, and weapons.

The Plains Indians' designs and patterns were inspired by the natural world—by plants, animals, the sky, and the land. These designs often had spiritual meaning for the Plains people, who expressed some of their most important ideas in their art.

Nakota Warrior's Shield
Plains Indian warriors rode into battle carrying shields made from thick buffalo hide. The shield was sturdy enough to protect a warrior from arrows or tomahawk blows.

Painted Designs
The owner of a shield believed its protection came from the painted designs, the eagle feathers, and blessings given the shield during a special ceremony.

Reaching All Learners

Extra Support

Make a Model

- Ask students to make a three-dimensional replica using available materials of one of the artifacts shown in this lesson.
- Display student work in a classroom gallery.

Visual-spatial

On Level

Create a Chart

- Have students use library resources or the Internet to find out more about the materials the Plains people used to make their art.
- Ask students to create a chart that shows the materials and the way they were used.

Logical-mathematical

Challenge

Write a Speech

- Ask groups of students to study the artifacts shown in this Extend Lesson.
- Then, using library resources or the Internet, have students find out what the symbols on these artifacts meant to the Plains Indians.
- Students should write a short speech based on their findings to present to the class.

Verbal-linguistic

Crow Warrior's Shirt
This shirt is made of buffalo skin. A shirt like this was usually sewn and decorated by a warrior's wife or mother. She might add locks of hair from family members, who believed that their prayers would protect the warrior.

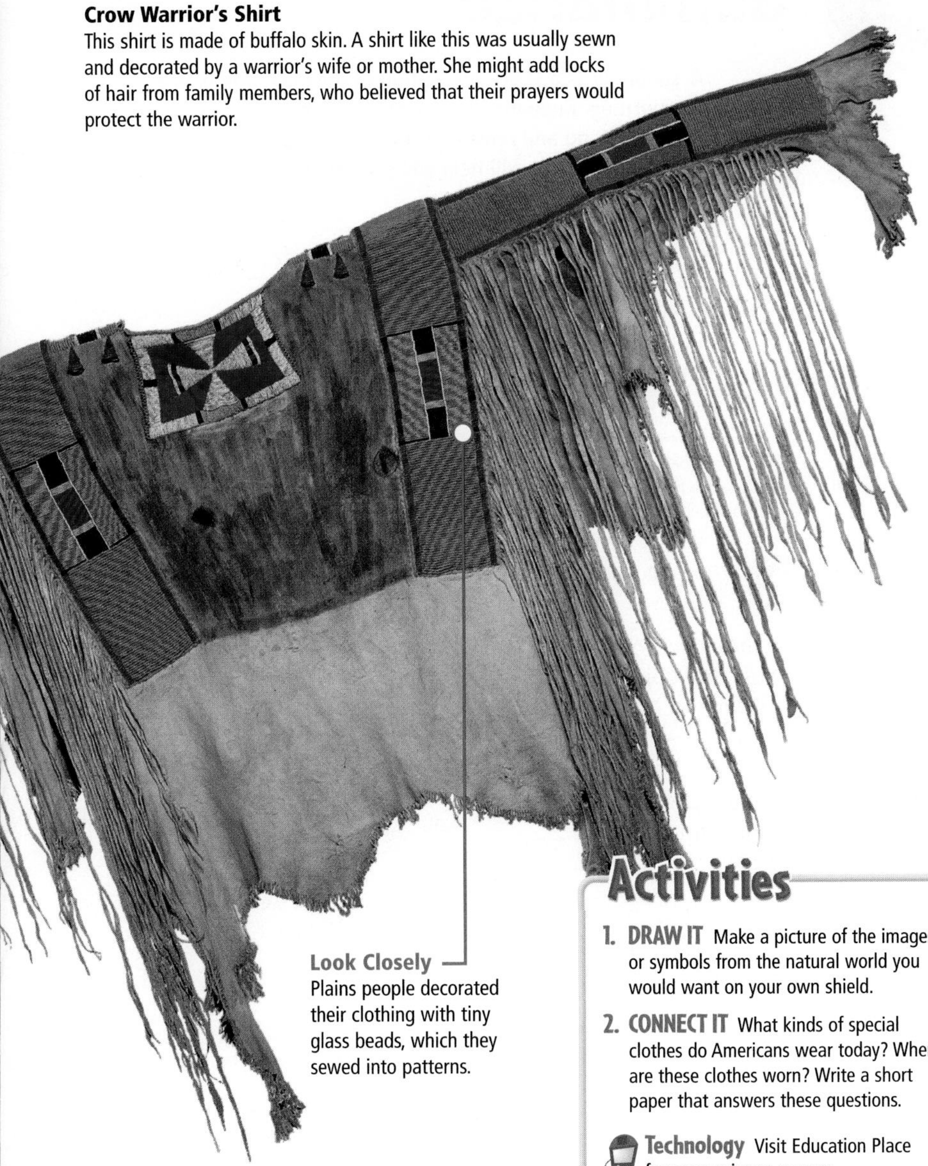

Look Closely
Plains people decorated their clothing with tiny glass beads, which they sewed into patterns.

PRIMARY SOURCES

Activities

1. **DRAW IT** Make a picture of the images or symbols from the natural world you would want on your own shield.
2. **CONNECT IT** What kinds of special clothes do Americans wear today? When are these clothes worn? Write a short paper that answers these questions.

Technology Visit Education Place for more primary sources. www.eduplace.com/kids/hmss05/

65

2 Leveled Activities

❶ **Draw It** *For Extra Support*
Drawings will vary, but should reflect students' understanding of the Extend Lesson.

❷ **Connect It** *For Challenge*

Writing Rubric

4	Report is well organized; answers questions clearly; mechanics are correct.
3	Report is adequately organized; answers questions adequately; few errors in mechanics.
2	Report is organized; answers some questions; some errors in mechanics.
1	Report is disorganized; does not answer questions; many errors in mechanics.

ELL

REACHING ALL LEARNERS

Intermediate/Advanced

- Have students work in pairs.
- Ask one student in the pair to take the role of the artist who made one of the artifacts shown in this lesson.
- Ask the other student to take the role of interviewer, and to write five questions about the artifact to ask the artist.
- After the interview is completed, students should switch roles.

Verbal-linguistic

Language Arts

Write a Description

- Ask students to think of a common tool or an object that they use every day.
- Have students consider the object as if they are finding it for the first time and know nothing about who made it, the uses of the object, or how it is used.
- Then have them write a description of what the object looks like and what purpose it might serve.

Verbal-linguistic

Graphic Organizer

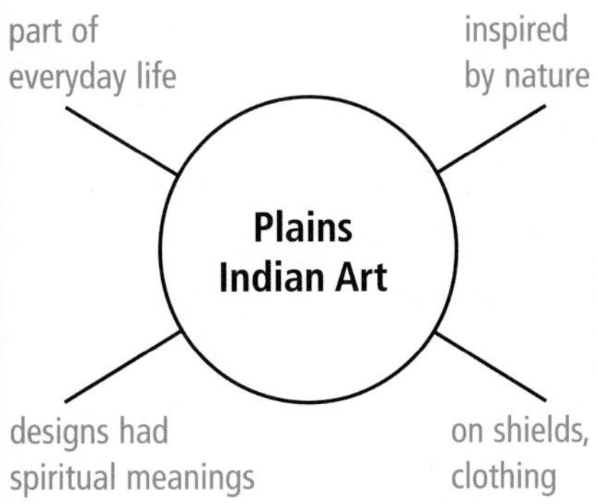

Graphic Organizer 7

Tested Objective

U1-20 Organize important information in a summary.

1 Teach the Skill

- Have students read aloud the definition of *summary* at the top of page 66. Then ask them to cover up the "Learn the Skill" section of the page and to read the paragraph about Western Plains people.
- After they read the paragraph, have students uncover one by one the three steps under "Learn the Skill."
- Discuss each step. Make sure students understand the subject of the paragraph (Step 1), the main points of the paragraph (Step 2), and the summary (Step 3).
- Ask volunteers to explain why the summary in Step 3 fits the definition of *summary* at the top of the page.

Reading and Thinking Skills

Skillbuilder

Summarize

VOCABULARY
summary

A summary is a short description of the main points in a piece of writing. Knowing how to write a summary can help you to understand and remember the main ideas of what you read. The steps below will help you summarize this paragraph from Lesson 4.

> Western Plains people ate the buffalo meat. They made buffalo skin into tepee covers, blankets, clothing, drums, and shields. They carved the bones into tools and wove the hair into rope. They even turned the tail into a fly swatter!

Learn the Skill

Step 1: Identify the subject of the piece of writing. Write the subject in the top box of the diagram.

Step 2: Identify the main points of the piece of writing. Write each main point in a box.

Step 3: Use your own words to write a summary of the information. Combine the important ideas into one or two sentences.

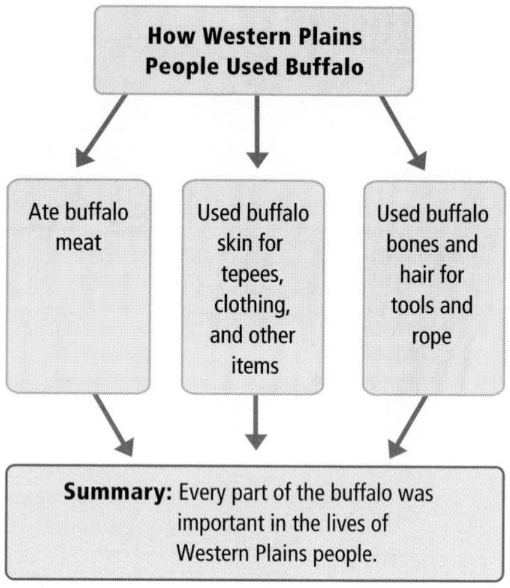

Leveled Practice

Extra Support

Have partners read the paragraph under "Practice the Skill" on page 67. Have them write on the board important phrases that will help them write their summaries. Remind them that they cannot include all the details in their summary. Verbal-linguistic

Challenge

Have students write a summary of a story or book they have read. Discuss how they chose what information to put in and what to leave out when writing their summary. Verbal-linguistic

ELL

Beginning

Have small groups make a poster showing Western Plains people using the buffalo. Have them write a sentence summarizing what is shown in their picture. Then have them trade posters with another group and write a sentence summarizing what they see in the other group's picture.

Visual-spatial; verbal-linguistic

Practice the Skill

Write a summary of the following paragraph. Make a diagram like the one on page 66 to help you identify the main points.

The Lakota once lived along the Mississippi River. Fighting with the Ojibwa forced the Lakota to move west, onto the Great Plains. They met other American Indian nations already living there, such as the Cheyenne, Arapaho, and Crow. Later, settlers from the eastern United States arrived. Competition for land and resources increased. The Lakota felt they were being pushed off the land. They went to war against the settlers and other Plains Indians.

Apply the Skill

Read the four paragraphs on page 55 in Lesson 3 about how climate affected Southwest Indians. Fill out a diagram like the one on page 66. Then write a summary of the information.

67

2 Practice the Skill

1. Subject: how competition for land affected the Lakota
2. Main Points: Fighting with Ojibwa forced Lakota west. Settlers moved onto Great Plains. Lakota fought settlers and other Plains Indians.
3. Summary: After moving to the Great Plains, the Lakota fought European settlers and other American Indian nations for land.

3 Apply the Skill

Ask students to turn to page 55 in their books and read the paragraphs. Have them fill out a diagram like the one on the opposite page and use it to write a summary of the information. When evaluating students' summaries, consider:

- Did the student correctly identify the subject of the passage?
- Did the student correctly identify the main points?
- Did the student use his or her own words?
- Did the student create a brief and accurate summary?

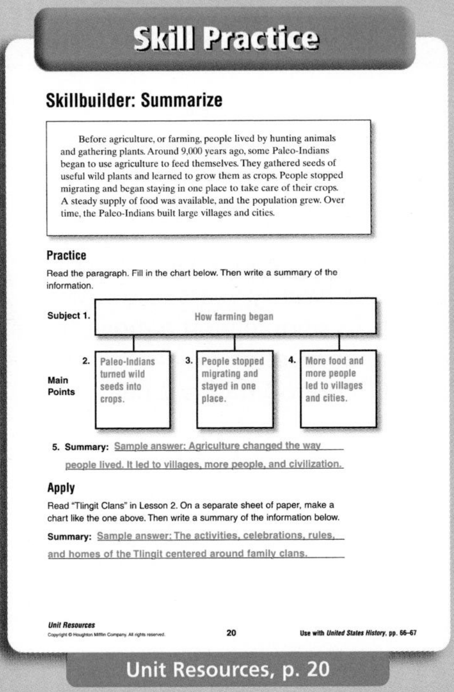

Skill Practice

Skillbuilder: Summarize

Before agriculture, or farming, people lived by hunting animals and gathering plants. Around 9,000 years ago, some Paleo-Indians began to use agriculture to feed themselves. They gathered seeds of useful wild plants and learned to grow them as crops. People stopped migrating and began staying in one place to take care of their crops. A steady supply of food was available, and the population grew. Over time, the Paleo-Indians built large villages and cities.

Practice

Read the paragraph. Fill in the chart below. Then write a summary of the information.

Subject 1. How farming began

Main Points
2. Paleo-Indians turned wild seeds into crops.
3. People stopped migrating and stayed in one place.
4. More food and more people led to villages and cities.

5. Summary: Sample answer: Agriculture changed the way people lived. It led to villages, more people, and civilization.

Apply

Read "Tlingit Clans" in Lesson 2. On a separate sheet of paper, make a chart like the one above. Then write a summary of the information below.

Summary: Sample answer: The activities, celebrations, rules, and homes of the Tlingit centered around family clans.

Unit Resources

20
Use with *United States History*, pp. 66–67

Unit Resources, p. 20

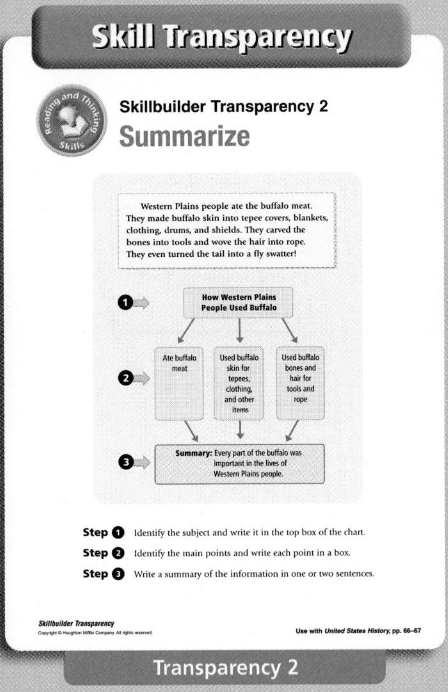

Skill Transparency

Skillbuilder Transparency 2
Summarize

Western Plains people ate the buffalo meat. They made buffalo skin into tepee covers, blankets, clothing, drums, and shields. They carved the bones into tools and wove the hair into rope. They even turned the tail into a fly swatter!

1. How Western Plains People Used Buffalo
2. Ate buffalo meat | Used buffalo skin for tepees, clothing, and other items | Used buffalo bones and hair for tools and rope
3. Summary: Every part of the buffalo was important in the lives of Western Plains people.

Step 1 Identify the subject and write it in the top box of the chart.
Step 2 Identify the main points and write each point in a box.
Step 3 Write a summary of the information in one or two sentences.

Skillbuilder Transparency

Use with *United States History*, pp. 66–67

Transparency 2

✔ Tested Objectives

U1-21 Geography Explain how the geography of the Eastern Woodlands influenced the lives of the American Indians of the region.

U1-22 History Describe the way of life and culture of the Haudenosaunee.

Lesson Quick Look

This lesson describes the lives of the American Indians in the Eastern Woodlands, and how some of their nations united and worked together.

Teaching Option: Extend Lesson 5 examines American Indian shelters in different regions.

1 Get Set to Read

Preview Ask students to look at the map on page 69. What does it tell them about the chapter they are about to read?

Reading Skill: Compare and Contrast Students may list differences in climate and shelter.

Build on What You Know Ask students to describe a time when they have worked in a team to get something done. What was this experience like? Do they think they could have gotten as much done if they worked on their own?

Vocabulary

longhouse *noun,* a large house made with wood poles and bark

confederation *noun,* an organization of groups that band together to form a type of government

wampum *noun,* a shaped and cut seashell used to symbolize agreements and show important events

barter *verb,* to exchange goods without using money

Core Lesson 5

Peoples of the East

VOCABULARY

longhouse
confederation
wampum
barter

Vocabulary Strategy

confederation

The prefix **con-** in **confederation** means "with." When groups join with one another, they form a confederation.

READING SKILL

Compare and Contrast

Note the ways that the Woodland Indians in the North and in the South were alike and different.

ALIKE	DIFFERENT

Build on What You Know When you team up with other people, you can do more than when you work alone. In this lesson, you will learn how five Eastern Woodland Indian nations decided to work together as a group.

The Eastern Woodlands

Main Idea Eastern Woodland Indians lived by farming, hunting, and gathering.

The eastern third of the United States is a large varied region. It has hills, mountains, plains, and valleys. Yet the whole area has one thing in common. It receives plenty of rain, enough to support a forest. This forest, known as the Eastern Woodlands, once stretched from 1 the Atlantic Ocean to the Mississippi River, and from the Gulf of Mexico to the Great Lakes. Many different American Indian nations lived in these woodlands.

Eastern Woodlands The Woodlands are made up of different kinds of trees, such as cedar, oak, maple, pine, and birch.

Skill and Strategy

Reading Skill and Strategy

Reading Skill: Compare and Contrast

This skill helps you understand how historical events or people are similar and different.

Read "The Eastern Woodlands." Then fill in the diagram below to contrast Woodland Indians of the north and south.

Woodland Indians of the North	Woodland Indians of the South
1. Colder climate; Longhouses for shelter; Clothing from deerskin	2. Warmer climate; Houses without walls; Light clothing

Reading Strategy: Question

3. Read "Peoples of the East." Read the headings. Then turn each heading into a question. As you read, look for the answers to those questions.

Heading 1: The Eastern Woodlands

Question: Sample answer: How did the American Indians of the Eastern Woodlands live?

Answer: Sample answer: They lived by farming, hunting, and gathering.

Heading 2: The Haudenosaunee

Question: Sample answer: For what act are the Haudenosaunee most remembered?

Answer: Sample answer: Different groups of Haudenosaunee made a peace treaty and helped each other.

Unit Resources

 21 Use with *United States History*, pp. 68–71

Unit Resources, p. 21

Background

Longhouses and Villages

- A longhouse might measure 50 to 150 feet. Its length depended on how many families lived in it.
- A Haudenosaunee village might last for twenty years or so. After that, its people would move to another location where the land and firewood had not been depleted.

The People and the Land

The natural resources of the Eastern Woodlands shaped the lives of the American Indians who lived there. The Woodland peoples 2 hunted deer, bears, and rabbits for food. They also got food from the region's plants. In the north, they made syrup from the sap of maple trees. Near the Great Lakes, people gathered the wild rice that grew there. Unlike the Plains Indians, Woodland Indians did not rely on a single source of food, such as the buffalo, for their needs.

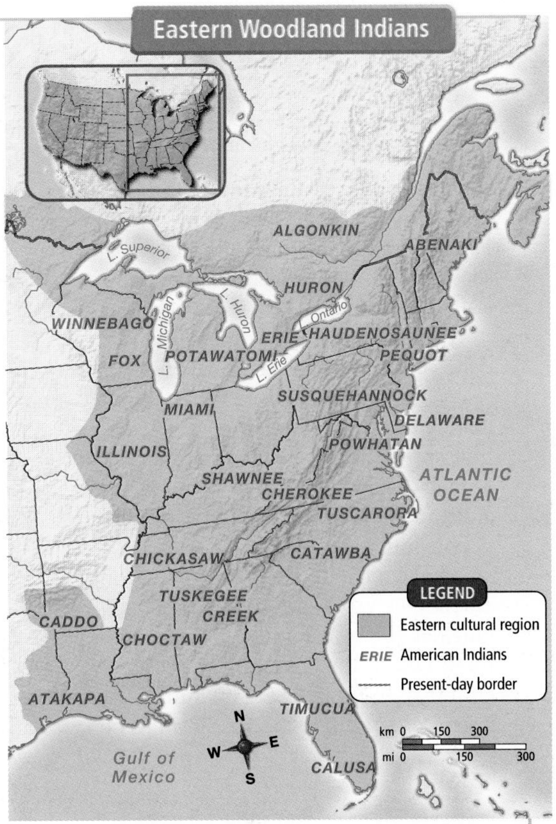

Land of Many Peoples The Great Lakes made traveling and trading easy for the Woodland Indians.

SKILL **Reading Maps** Which American Indians lived near the Great Lakes? Winnebago, Fox, Miami, Potawatomi, Haudenosaunee, Erie, and Huron

Farming and Building

Most Woodland Indians were farmers. They cleared fields in the forests by cutting down the larger trees and then burning the area. They planted crops between the tree stumps. Corn, beans, and squash were the staple for most groups and were known as "the three sisters."

Some Woodland Indians grew these three plants together. When the cornstalks grew, they supported the vines of the bean plants. The shade from the squash leaves kept the weeds from spreading.

Woodland Indians made different kinds of homes and clothing to fit the climate where they lived. In warm 3 southern climates, people built houses without walls. These homes had just a roof for shade and protection from rain. People made light clothing, woven from grass and other materials, to wear in the hot weather.

Farther north, American Indians needed protection from the cold. They wore clothing made from deerskin.

The Haudenosaunee (haw dah noh SAW nee), also known as the Iroquois (IHR uh kwoi), built longhouses for shelter. A **longhouse** was a large house made with wood poles and bark. Families lived in them and lit fires for cooking and warmth. These houses were so important to the Haudenosaunee that their name means "people of the longhouse."

REVIEW What were the three sisters? the staple crops of Woodland Indians—corn, beans, and squash

69

2 Teach

The Eastern Woodlands

Talk About It

1 **Q Geography** Where were the Eastern Woodlands?

A They stretched from the Atlantic Ocean to the Mississippi River and from the Gulf of Mexico to the Great Lakes.

2 **Q History** What types of resources were found in the Eastern Woodlands?

A many varieties of trees, plants, and animals such as maple trees, wild rice, deer, bears, and rabbits

3 **Q History** In what way did homes in the Southern Woodlands differ from homes in the Northern Woodlands?

A The Southern Woodland Indians had some houses without walls. The Northern Woodland Indians lived in enclosed longhouses.

Vocabulary Strategy

longhouse Tell students that a compound word is made up of two different words. Ask them to name the two words found in *longhouse.* long, house

Reading Strategy: Question As students read, suggest that they develop their own questions and seek the answers. You may wish to use any unanswered questions as a jumping-off point for class discussion.

REACHING ALL LEARNERS

Leveled Practice

Extra Support

Have students **write an encyclopedia entry** about the geography of the Eastern Woodlands.
Verbal-linguistic; bodily-kinesthetic

Challenge

Have students look at a detailed map of New York state to find place names related to the nations of the Haudenosaunee League.
Visual-spatial

REACHING ALL LEARNERS

ELL

Intermediate

- Have students **make flashcards** showing pictures and names of natural resources that were important to the Woodland Indians. Examples might include the three sisters, deer, and maple trees. Have them quiz each other on the resources and what they were used for.

Verbal-linguistic; visual-spatial

The Haudenosaunee

Talk About It

4 Q History What type of government did the Haudenosaunee form?
A They formed a confederation.

5 Q Citizenship How were decisions reached at League meetings?
A The chiefs talked until they all agreed.

6 Q Geography Where do some Haudenosaunee live today?
A New York and Canada

Vocabulary Strategy

confederation Tell students that a synonym for *confederation* is *league.*

wampum Explain to students that *wampum* is an abbreviation of a longer word: *wampumpeag.*

barter A synonym of *barter* is *swap.*

Critical Thinking

Decision Making The Haudenosaunee tribes shared a common language. Why would this make it easier for their confederacy to make decisions?

The Haudenosaunee

Main Idea Five Haudenosaunee nations joined together to form a powerful union.

The Haudenosaunee lived in what is now New York State. There were several Haudenosaunee nations. Although they shared a common language, they often fought each other.

Fighting one another made the Haudenosaunee weak. Sometime between the years 1100 and 1600, five of the nations made peace. They joined in a confedera-
4 tion known as the Haudenosaunee League. A **confederation** is a type of government in which separate groups of people join together, but local leaders still make most decisions for their group. The League was a union of Mohawks, Oneidas (oh NY duhz), Onondagas (aw nuhn DAG uhz), Cayugas (ky YOO guhz), and Senecas (SEN uh kuhz). Later, a sixth group called the Tuscarora joined.

Hiawatha According to Haudenosaunee history, Hiawatha helped the five nations unite. The wampum belt (below) was made to celebrate the formation of the Haudenosaunee League.

Haudenosaunee Government

The League was governed by chiefs from each Haudenosaunee nation. The chiefs from each nation had a voice at League meetings. All five nations had to agree before the League would take any 5
action. The chiefs talked together until they reached agreement.

The Haudenosaunee lived in clans. Clan mothers, who were the oldest women in the clan, played an important part in Haudenosaunee government. They chose the chiefs who led the nations. The clan mothers chose a chief for life, but they could replace him with someone else if he was not doing a good job.

Haudenosaunee Trading

The nations traded with other Woodland Indians. They sometimes used wampum to symbolize agreements. **Wampum** were pieces of carefully shaped and cut seashell. American Indians strung wampum like beads. The Haudenosaunee valued wampum highly and so did other Woodland Indians.

The Haudenosaunee bartered for goods. When people **barter,** they trade goods without using money. After Europeans arrived in the 1600s, the Haudenosaunee bartered fur for blankets and knives.

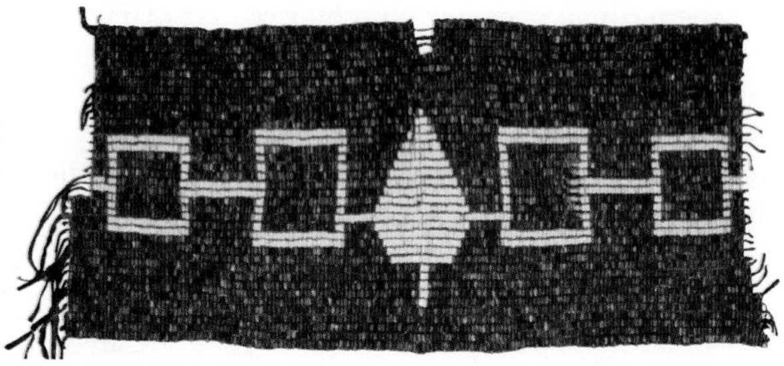

70 • Chapter 2

Math

Calculate Fractions

Remind students that the League was initially made up of five nations. Ask these questions:

- If two nations in the League agreed about something, and the others disagreed, what fraction of the League disagreed? three out of five nations = three-fifths
- If one tribe disagreed with the others, what fraction of the League agreed with each other? four-fifths

Logical-mathematical

Language Arts

Discuss and Decide

- Working in small groups, ask students to each take the role of a Haudenosaunee chief at a meeting of the League.
- Have the chiefs come up with a problem they need to solve.
- Ask them to discuss the problem and try to decide on a solution they all agree on.

Verbal-linguistic

The Haudenosaunee Today

More than 50,000 Haudenosaunee live in North America. Some live in their
6 homelands in New York and Canada. Many still follow their traditional customs and ceremonies.

More Haudenosaunee live in big cities and towns, however. They hold jobs in factory work, health care, and teaching. Mohawk ironworkers are famous for their skills in building skyscrapers. They helped build landmarks such as the Empire State Building and the Golden Gate Bridge.

REVIEW Why did the Haudenosaunee use wampum? to symbolize agreements and show important events

Mohawk Ironworkers For more than 100 years, Mohawk ironworkers have built skyscrapers and bridges throughout the world.

Lesson Summary

- The Eastern Woodlands was an area of forests and rich resources that spread across much of eastern North America.
- Most Eastern Woodland peoples used farming, hunting, and gathering to get food.
- The Mohawk, Oneida, Onondaga, Cayuga, and Seneca nations formed the Haudenosaunee League.
- The Haudenosaunee lived in longhouses and traded goods with other American Indian groups.

Why It Matters ...

The Haudenosaunee nations created a strong union when they stopped fighting each other and worked together.

Lesson Review

1. **VOCABULARY** Choose the correct words to complete the sentence.

   confederation **longhouses** **wampum**

   The Haudenosaunee strung ______ to symbolize agreements, such as the formation of their ______.

2. **READING SKILL** **Contrast** the differences in clothing for Woodland Indians in the North and in the South.

3. **MAIN IDEA: History** Why did Woodland Indians grow corn, beans, and squash together?

4. **MAIN IDEA: Geography** What did the Woodland Indians in the south do to adapt to a warm climate?

5. **CRITICAL THINKING: Analyze** What role did clan mothers play in Haudenosaunee government?

6. **CRITICAL THINKING: Decision Making** What were the effects of the Haudenosaunee groups' decision to form a confederation?

HANDS ON **DRAMA ACTIVITY** Prepare a skit in which two people barter food. What foods do they barter? Do they each end up getting what they want?

3 Review/Assess

Review Tested Objectives

U1-21 Eastern Woodland Indians lived by farming, hunting, and gathering.

U1-22 Haudenosaunee, also called the Iroquois, lived in longhouses in villages and traded goods. Five different Haudenosaunee groups joined together to form a powerful union, the Iroquois League.

Lesson Review Answers

1. barter, wampum
2. north: wore warm clothing made from deerskin; south: made light clothing woven from grass and other materials
3. Growing cornstalks supported bean vines; planting squash created shade that helped to reduce weeds in the fields.
4. They built some homes with just a roof for shade and shelter from rain. They made light clothing to wear in the hot weather.
5. They chose chiefs who led the nations and could replace a chief with someone else if they felt he was not doing a good job.
6. It made the Haudenosaunee more powerful and helped them maintain peace,

HANDS ON Performance Task Rubric

4	Skit shows understanding of barter concept; conveys concept effectively; skit is performed well.
3	Skit shows some understanding of barter concept; conveys concept; skit is performed adequately.
2	Skit shows little understanding of barter concept; conveys part of the concept; skit is performed poorly.
1	Skit does not show understanding of barter concept; skit is not about barter; skit is not performed.

Study Guide/Homework

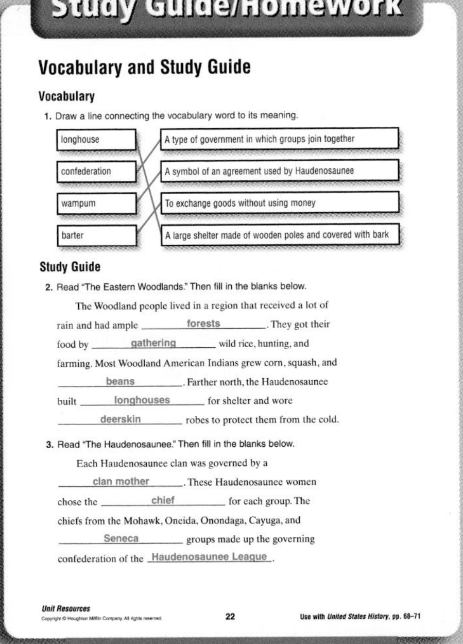

Vocabulary and Study Guide

Vocabulary

1. Draw a line connecting the vocabulary word to its meaning.

longhouse	A type of government in which groups join together
confederation	A symbol of an agreement used by Haudenosaunee
wampum	To exchange goods without using money
barter	A large shelter made of wooden poles and covered with bark

Study Guide

2. Read "The Eastern Woodlands." Then fill in the blanks below.

   The Woodland people lived in a region that received a lot of rain and had ample __forests__. They got their food by __gathering__ wild rice, hunting, and farming. Most Woodland American Indians grew corn, squash, and __beans__. Farther north, the Haudenosaunee built __longhouses__ for shelter and wore __deerskin__ robes to protect them from the cold.

3. Read "The Haudenosaunee." Then fill in the blanks below.

   Each Haudenosaunee clan was governed by a __clan mother__. These Haudenosaunee women chose the __chief__ for each group. The chiefs from the Mohawk, Oneida, Onondaga, Cayuga, and __Seneca__ groups made up the governing confederation of the __Haudenosaunee League__.

Unit Resources 22 Use with *United States History*, pp. 68–71

Unit Resources, p. 22

Reteach Minilesson

Use a word web to reteach the Haudenosaunee.

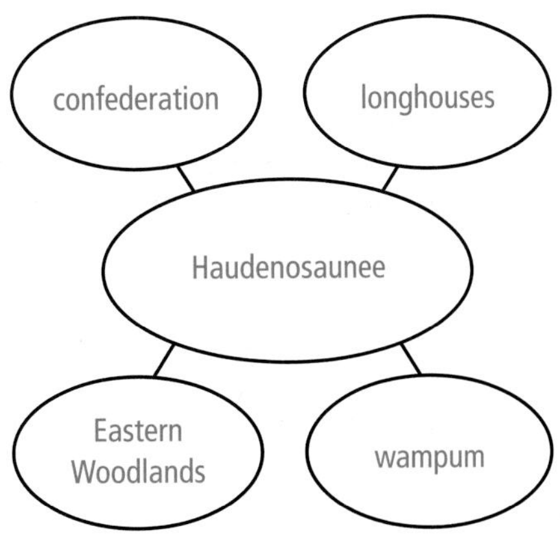

Graphic Organizer 13

Extend Quick Look

Connect to Core Lesson In the lessons they have just read, students have learned about American Indians from all over the United States. In this Extend Lesson, they will find out more about the types of shelters that people in each region built.

1 Teach the Extend Lesson

Connect to the Big Idea

Places and Regions In each region of North America, American Indians used local resources to build shelters appropriate to the climate and other physical characteristics of their environment.

Geography

AMERICAN INDIAN SHELTERS

In a harsh climate, good shelter can mean survival. American Indians across the continent faced severe weather at times. Blizzards swept the Plains, hurricanes and rainstorms pounded the coasts, and long winters froze the Northeast.

In every region, American Indians built shelters for protection and comfort. Using local resources, they created homes that suited their needs and their environment.

Pacific Northwest

Type of Shelter
Large house

Materials Used
Boards cut from cedar trees

Unique Features
Totem poles were placed at entrances or used to support a roof. House heated by central open fireplaces.

Southwest

Type of Shelter
Pueblo

Materials Used
Stone and adobe bricks

Unique Features
Ladders connected several stories. Rooms heated by coal fires instead of wood.

Reaching All Learners

Extra Support

Create a Postage Stamp

Ask students to create a postage stamp showing one of the structures mentioned in the chart.

Visual-spatial

On Level

Write an Editorial

Have students write an editorial about which structure they would want to live in and why.

Verbal-linguistic

Challenge

Write a List of Instructions

- Have students use library resources and the Internet to find out more about the way that one of the structures named above was made.
- Then have them write a list of instructions that describes how to make this structure.

Verbal-linguistic

GEOGRAPHY

Western Great Plains	**Northeastern Woodlands**	**Southeastern Woodlands**
Type of Shelter Teepee	**Type of Shelter** Longhouse	**Type of Shelter** Roundhouse
Materials Used Buffalo skins and wooden poles	**Materials Used** Bark and wooden poles	**Materials Used** Wooden poles covered with clay and bark
Unique Features Easy to pack up and move. Flaps on teepee acted as vents to let out smoke or let in fresh air.	**Unique Features** Long enough to hold several families and keep several fires going.	**Unique Features** Used for dances and ceremonies. Sometimes used as shelter for the elderly.

Activities

1. **TALK ABOUT IT** In what ways were the shelters of American Indian groups the same? How were they different?
2. **RESEARCH IT** Research information about the shelters of a group of American Indians from the region where you live. Write and illustrate a one-page report.

73

2 Leveled Activities

1 Talk About It *For Extra Support*
Sample answer: Alike: They all used materials from nature; Different: Some housed one family, some housed several families; they used different natural materials depending on what was available; they were different shapes; some were movable and some were not.

2 Research It *For Challenge*

Writing Rubric

4	Report is thoroughly researched and accurate; writing is clear and creative; mechanics are correct.
3	Report is researched and mostly accurate; writing is adequately clear and shows some creativity; most mechanics are correct.
2	Report is poorly researched and somewhat inaccurate; writing is somewhat unclear; some errors in mechanics.
1	Report is incomplete and lacks research and accuracy; writing is unclear; many errors in mechanics.

ELL

REACHING ALL LEARNERS

Beginning

Ask students to draw or create a model of one of the houses mentioned in the chart, using such materials as wooden sticks, clay, or paper.

Visual-spatial

Math

Make a Bar Graph

- Have students make a bar graph of the building materials used, as shown in the chart.
- Tell students that one bar should represent wood, a second bar, clay and stone, and a third, buffalo skins.
- The numbers on the graph's left axis correspond to the number of times each material is mentioned in the chart.

Logical-mathematical

Graphic Organizer

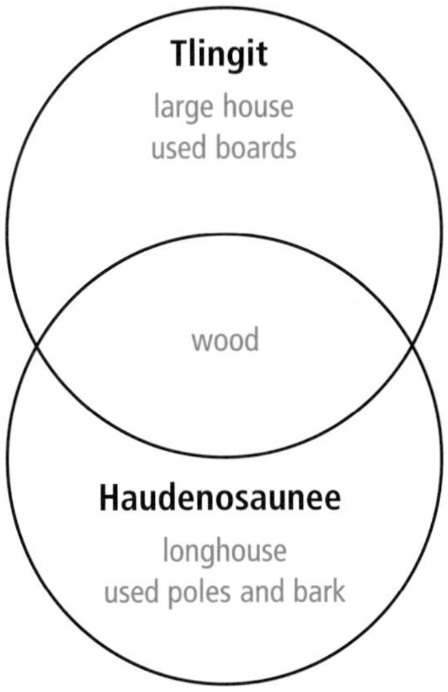

Graphic Organizer 11

Chapter Review

Tested Objectives

The lesson objective assessed by each question is shown in parentheses after the answer.

Visual Summary

1. The Tlingit used canoes to transport goods on trading trips along the seacoast and rivers. *(Obj. U1-15)*
2. Corn was the staple of the Hopi. They kept the corn in storage rooms in their pueblos. *(Obj. U1-17)*
3. The Comanche made buffalo skin into covers for their shelters, blankets, clothing, drums, and shields. *(Obj. U1-19)*
4. The Haudenosaunee built longhouses with wood poles and bark. Families shared them. *(Obj. U1-22)*

Facts and Main Ideas

5. Beringia was a land bridge that once connected Asia and North America. *(Obj. U1-12)*
6. The Hopi built shelters using stones and clay, and irrigated their crops. *(Obj. U1-16)*
7. Horses made it easier for the Comanche to hunt and travel, and became a measure of wealth. *(Obj. U1-19)*
8. a form of trade in which items are exchanged without money *(Obj. U1-22)*
9. chiefs of the five nations in the confederation *(Obj. U1-22)*

Vocabulary

10. **confederation** *(Obj. U1-22)*
11. **staple** *(Obj. U1-17)*
12. **civilization** *(Obj. U1-13)*
13. **lodge** *(Obj. U1-18)*

Review and Test Prep

Visual Summary

1–4. Write a description of how American Indians used the items pictured below: canoe, corn, buffalo skin, and longhouse.

Tlingit	Hopi	Comanche	Haudenosaunee

Facts and Main Ideas

TEST PREP Answer each question with information from the chapter.

5. **Geography** What was Beringia, and where was it located?
6. **History** Name three ways the Hopi adapted to the dry climate of the Southwest.
7. **History** In what ways did horses change life for the Comanche?
8. **Economics** What is barter?
9. **Government** Who governed the Haudenosaunee League?

Vocabulary

TEST PREP Choose the correct word to complete each sentence.

civilization, p. 40
staple, p. 56
lodge, p. 61
confederation, p. 70

10. The Haudenosaunee government was a ______.
11. Corn was a ______ for the Hopi and a part of every meal.
12. The Hopewell ______ was one of the first to create large villages in North America.
13. A Pawnee ______ was made of bark, earth, and grass.

Reading/Language Arts Wrap-Up

Reading Strategy: Question

Review with students the steps involved when they develop questions about a passage of text.

In pairs, have students take turns modeling the process of questioning as they read.

Ask students to do a self-check: "How well did I practice questioning as I read?"

Writing Strategy

Explain to students that the process they use in questioning as they read can be used when they have to write questions.

You may wish to review questions that students wrote for the chapter. Guide students who want to revise their questions based on the discussion.

CHAPTER SUMMARY TIMELINE

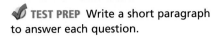

about 1100	about 1300	1700s
Earliest Ancient Pueblo stone buildings	Aztecs rule Central Mexico	Comanche control large part of Great Plains

1100 — 1200 — 1300 — 1400 — 1500 — 1600 — 1700

TEST PREP

TEST PREP Study Skill Read the paragraph below. Then use what you have learned about summarizing to answer each question.

> Totem poles are carved out of red cedar and painted in bright colors. They show images of human beings, birds, and animals. The images tell a story about the family or clan who had the pole made. Totem poles are sacred to Northwest Indian peoples because the poles represent a tie to their ancestors. Potlatches are held to celebrate the raising of a totem pole.

14. What is the subject of the paragraph?
- **A.** American Indian ancestors
- **B.** potlatches
- **C.** totem poles
- **D.** bird carvings

15. Which statement best summarizes the paragraph?
- **A.** Totem poles are important because they show images that tell family or clan stories.
- **B.** Being connected to ancestors is important to the Northwest Indian peoples.
- **C.** Totem poles are carved from red cedar.
- **D.** It takes a long time to carve the images on totem poles.

Critical Thinking

TEST PREP Write a short paragraph to answer each question.

16. Cause and Effect In what ways did agriculture change the lives of people in the Americas?

17. Draw Conclusions Were the Western Plains Indians or the Pacific Northwest Indians more dependent on one natural resource? Explain your answer.

Timeline

Use the Chapter Summary Timeline above to answer the question.

18. At what time did the Comanche control a large part of the Great Plains?

Activities

HANDS ON **Speaking Activity** Find an American Indian legend or folktale in your school or local library. Prepare a retelling of the story in your own words.

Writing Activity Write a description comparing a Mound Builder village with an Ancient Pueblo village.

Technology
Writing Process Tips
Get help with your description at **www.eduplace.com/kids/hmss05/**

75

Apply Skills

14. C *(Obj. U1-20)*

15. A *(Obj. U1-20)*

Critical Thinking

16. Agriculture changed the kind of food people ate and the way they lived. It led to the creation of civilizations because people could stop migrating. *(Obj. U1-13)*

17. The Western Plains Indians were dependent on one natural resource—the buffalo—for food, clothing, and tools. The Pacific Northwest Indians had more varied natural resources. They could fish, hunt animals, gather plants, and use wood. *(Obj. U2-18)*

Timeline

18. 1700s *(Obj. U1-19)*

Leveled Activities

HANDS ON Performance Task Rubric

4	Story is well organized and shows considerable creative effort; mechanics are correct; written in present tense.
3	Story is adequately organized and shows creative effort; few errors; written in present tense.
2	Story is somewhat organized and shows some creative effort; some errors, including shifts in tense.
1	Story is disorganized and shows little effort; many errors in mechanics; present tense is absent.

Writing Rubric

4	Description is accurate; spelling, grammar, and punctuation are correct.
3	Description is generally accurate; spelling, grammar, and punctuation are mostly correct.
2	Description is partly accurate; some errors of spelling, grammar and punctuation.
1	Description is incomplete; many errors in spelling, grammar and punctuation.

Technology

Test Generator

You can generate your own version of the chapter review by using the **Test Generator CD-ROM**.

Web Link

For more ideas, visit
www.eduplace.com/ss/hmss05/

Standards

National Standards

I a Similarities and differences in addressing human needs
I d Different cultures related to their physical environment
II c Compare and contrast stories or accounts
III g How people create places
III h Interaction of human beings and their physical environment

Unit Review

Vocabulary and Main Ideas

1. People need capital resources, such as tools and machines, to make products. Human resources, which are people and their skills, make the process work. *(Obj. U1-6)*
2. People produce goods from available resources and then trade the goods they make so they can have goods they can't produce themselves. *(Obj. U1-9)*
3. People live in places that have resources and a location that allows them to earn a living. *(Obj. U1-10)*
4. During the Ice Age, Asian hunters followed the animals across a land bridge into North America. *(Obj. U1-12)*
5. The extra salmon could be dried and eaten all year. *(Obj. U1-14)*
6. Southwest Indians used materials such as stone instead of wood to build their homes. They irrigated their crops, too. *(Obj. U1-16)*

Critical Thinking

7. Answers will vary. *(Obj. U1-8)*
8. Sample answer: The Haudenosaunee understood that cooperating would be better than fighting. Five nations joined the confederation, so the idea had strong support. *(Obj. U1-22)*

Apply Skills

9. C *(Obj. U1-20)*
10. D *(Obj. U1-20)*

Vocabulary and Main Ideas

TEST PREP Write a sentence to answer each question.

1. Why are **capital resources** and **human resources** important for producing goods and services?
2. In what way does **specialization** affect **trade?**
3. In what ways does **geography** influence where people live?
4. What is one theory about early **migration** to North America?
5. Why was a **surplus** of salmon important for the Northwest Indians' survival?
6. In what ways did the **climate** of the Southwest influence the way American Indians lived there?

Critical Thinking

TEST PREP Write a short paragraph to answer each question.

7. **Infer** Silicon Valley and the Corn Belt are names for regions in the United States. What name would you give your region and why?
8. **Draw Conclusions** The Haudenosaunee made peace with each other and formed a confederation. Write a short paragraph giving a conclusion you might draw from their example.

Apply Skills

TEST PREP Reading and Thinking Skill Use the paragraph below to answer each question.

> Agriculture changed the way people lived. The Paleo-Indians had to stay in one place to care for plants. Some people stopped migrating. With a steady supply of food, more families could survive. Populations grew. Over thousands of years, groups of Paleo-Indians farmed large areas and built villages and cities.

9. What is the subject of the paragraph?
   - **A.** the migration of Paleo-Indians
   - **B.** the villages and cities that Paleo-Indians built
   - **C.** the way agriculture changed the lives of Paleo-Indians
   - **D.** the methods Paleo-Indians used to raise crops
10. Which of the following statements best summarizes the paragraph?
    - **A.** The Paleo-Indians ate different kinds of foods after they started farming.
    - **B.** It took months to raise crops, so the Paleo-Indians did not migrate anymore.
    - **C.** The population grew because farming provided a steady supply of food.
    - **D.** Farming changed the way Paleo-Indians lived in many ways.

Technology

Test Generator

- Use the **Test Generator CD-ROM** to create tests customized to your class.
- Access hundreds of test questions and make lesson, chapter, and unit quizzes and tests.

Web Updates

Curious about new trade book titles that you can use with the program? Visit www.eduplace.com/ss/hmss05/ to update your Unit Bibliography.

Extra Support

REACHING ALL LEARNERS

Use a Word Web

Have students use a word web graphic organizer to review vocabulary words or concepts.

Unit Activity

The Big Idea

Play a Place Card Game

- Choose a place in the United States that you have lived in, visited, or would like to visit.
- Write four fact cards about your place. Each card should identify the place and tell one fact about it.
- Mix up the cards. With a group of four, take turns picking a card from the pile.
- The first person to pick two cards about the same place wins.

At the Library

You may find these books at your library.

United States of America by Christine and David Petersen

This book gives an overview of United States geography, history, people, and culture.

The Wigwam and the Longhouse by Charlotte and David Yue

American Indian life in the East changed after European settlers arrived.

CURRENT EVENTS

WEEKLY WR READER

Connect to Today

Create a notebook about American Indians who are in the news today.

- Find articles about American Indians and issues affecting them today.
- Write or draw a short summary of each article.
- Place the articles and your summaries in a notebook for the class to share.

Technology

Get information about American Indians in the news from the Weekly Reader at **www.eduplace.com/kids/hmss05/**

Read About It

Look for these Social Studies Independent Books in your classroom.

77

Language Arts

Test Taking Tip

Tell students that when they read a passage, they should look for the main idea and underline it (if appropriate). This will help them understand what the passage is about before they start answering questions.

Standards

National Standards

I d Different cultures related to their physical environment
III c Resources, data sources, and geographic tools
III e Varying landforms and geographic features
III f Physical system changes
III h Interaction of human beings and their physical environment
III k Uses of resources and land

Unit Activity

HANDS ON Performance Task Rubric

4	Place is identified correctly; facts are accurate.
3	Place is identified adequately; most facts cited are accurate.
2	Place is identified in a somewhat disorganized way; some factual errors.
1	No place is identified or is off topic; many factual errors.

WEEKLY WR READER

Unit Project

- Have students exchange and discuss their notebooks. Have volunteers present their research to the class.

At the Library

- You may wish to wrap up the unit by reading aloud from one of these suggested titles or from one of the Read-Aloud selections included in the Unit Bibliography.

Read About It

- You may wish to provide students with the appropriate Leveled Social Studies Books for this unit. Turn to page B for teaching options.
- If students have written summaries or reviews of the Leveled Books or the books in the Unit Bibliography, you may wish to post them in the classroom.

Unit 2

Unit Planner

Begin with Core. Extend for more.

Exploration and Settlement

LEVELED BOOKS

The following Social Studies Independent Books are available for extending and supporting students' social studies experience as they read the unit.

Differentiated Instruction

Extra Support

Pocahontas
By Carl W. Grody
Summary: The true story of Pocahontas, young daughter of Algonquin chief Powhatan, who welcomed the first permanent English settlement in America and later married colonist John Rolfe.

Vocabulary

settlement
colony

Extending Understanding

Oral Language: Interview Ask students to work in pairs, one taking the role of Pocahontas and the other that of a reporter interviewing Pocahontas about her life in America and England.

Independent Writing: Newpaper article Have students write an article for an English newspaper covering the arrival of Pocahontas in England. Encourage them to include background information for the English public.

Graphic Organizer: Students can use a sequence chart to keep track of the events.

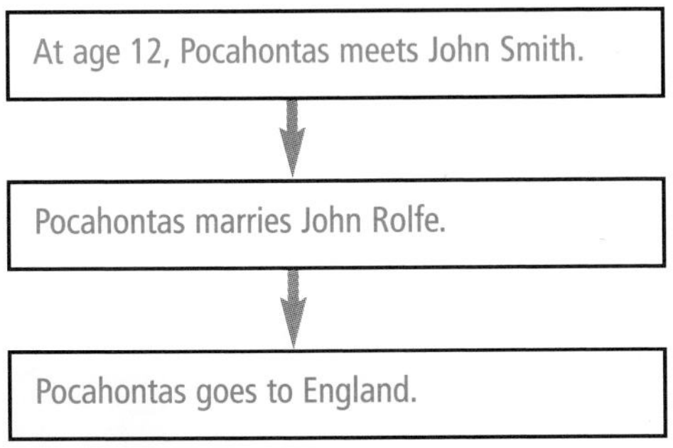

At age 12, Pocahontas meets John Smith.
Pocahontas marries John Rolfe.
Pocahontas goes to England.

On Level

On Board the *Santa María*
By Becky Cheston
Summary: Columbus's fateful voyage to the Americas, including the experiences of his crew. The book also focuses on the technology that built his famous ship.

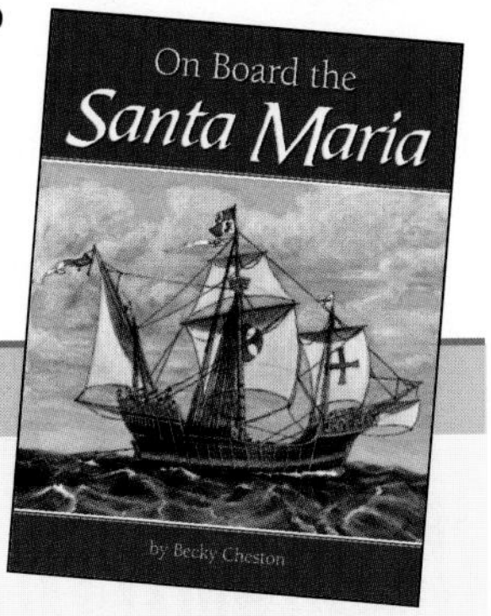

Vocabulary

compass
navigation
technology

Extending Understanding

Oral Language: Job Interview Have students work in pairs, one taking the role of Columbus and the other taking the role of someone who wants to join his crew. Columbus should question the job seeker's abilities and attitudes while the job seeker asks questions about what the journey will be like.

Independent Writing: Friendly Letter Have students pretend they are sailing with Columbus to the Americas and are writing a letter home to their families describing their life during the voyage.

Graphic Organizer: Students can use a word web to illustrate Columbus's many roles.

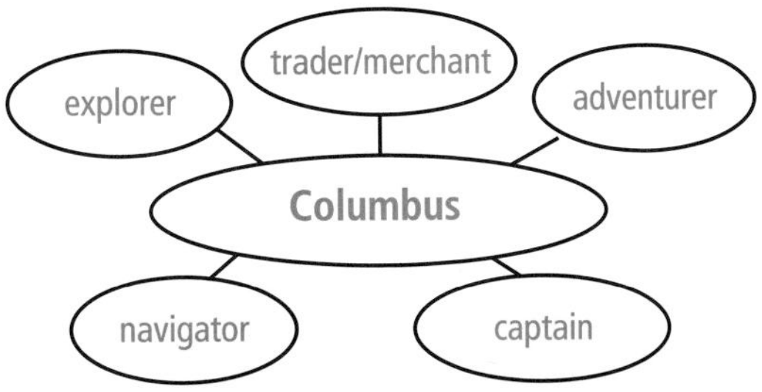

Challenge

Fur Traders of New France
By Lisa Moore
Summary: The first permanent settlers in what is now Canada traded furs between Native Americans and European merchants.

Vocabulary

profit
pelt
diverse

Extending Understanding

Oral Language: Monologue Have students take on the role of a French trader and explain the excitement and dangers of their life in New France.

Independent Writing: Want ads Have students create advertisements for job openings for trappers in New France describing the land, Native Americans, working conditions, and potential profits.

Graphic Organizer: Students can use a cause-and-effect diagram as they read.

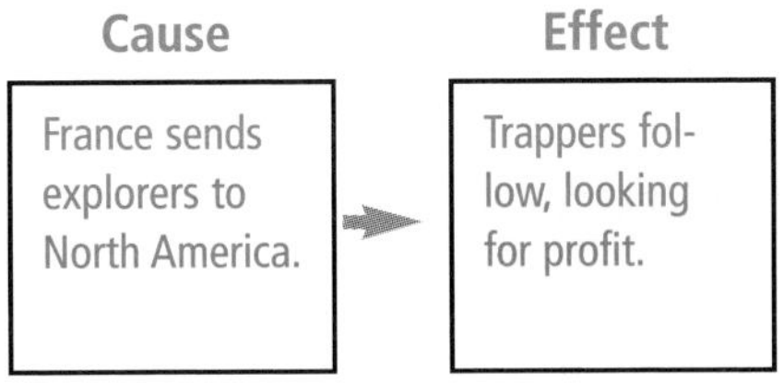

Choices for Reading

- **Extra Support/ELL** Read the selection aloud as students follow along in their books. Pause frequently and help students monitor understanding.
- **On Level** Have partners take turns reading aloud. Students can pause at the end of each page to ask each other questions and check understanding.
- **Challenge** Students can read the selection and write down any questions they have. Then they can work in small groups to answer their questions.

Go to www.eduplace.com/ss/hmss05/ for answers to Responding questions found at the back of the books.

Bibliography

Books for Independent Reading

Social Studies Key

- Biography
- Citizenship
- Cultures
- Economics
- Geography
- History

Extra Support

Land Ho! Fifty Glorious Years in the Age of Exploration
by Nancy Winslow Parker
Harper, 2001
From Columbus to Cabrillo, this book follows the adventures of 12 European explorers who found their way to the New World.

Roanoke: The Lost Colony
by Jane Yolen and Heidi Stemple
Simon, 2003
Readers are presented with five theories that might explain what happened to the people who vanished from Roanoke Island.

A Season of Promise: Elizabeth's Jamestown Colony Diary
by Patricia Hermes
Scholastic, 2002
In 1611 Jamestown, Elizabeth must face the reality of her mother's death and strict new laws imposed by the governor.

James Towne: Struggle for Survival
by Marcia Sewall
Atheneum, 2001
Readers learn about the 1606 voyage from England to Jamestown, the colony's early struggles, and the roles of Captain John Smith and Pocahontas.

Hard Labor: The First African-Americans, 1619
by P.C. McKissack and F.L. McKissack, Jr.
Simon, 2004
In 1619 twenty Africans came to Alexandria, Virginia, as indentured servants, ready to begin life anew in this new land.

On Level

Magellan and the First Voyage Around the World
by Nancy Smiler Levinson
Clarion, 2001
This biography vividly portrays Magellan's history-making circumnavigation.

We Asked for Nothing: The Remarkable Journey of Cabeza de Vaca
by Stuart Waldman
Mikaya Press, 2003
In 1528 the conquistador de Vaca is shipwrecked off the Texas coast and begins a journey that changes his attitude about the New World people.

Despite All Obstacles: La Salle and the Conquest of the Mississippi
by Joan E. Goodman
Mikaya Press, 2001
Primary source documents and engaging text recount La Salle's Mississippi River expedition. See others in series.

A Journey to the New World
by Kathryn Lasky
Scholastic, 1996
This fictional diary of a Pilgrim girl chronicles the Mayflower voyage and Plymouth settlement.

Mayflower 1620: A New Look at a Pilgrim Voyage
by C.O. Grace, P. Arenstam, J. Kemp
National Geographic, 2003
This photo essay uses historical reenactment to bring new perspective to the *Mayflower* voyage.

Challenge

Sir Walter Ralegh and the Quest for El Dorado
by Marc Aronson
Houghton, 2000
This biography chronicles the triumphs and failures of Ralegh, who sent a band of English settlers to Roanoke Island in 1587.

Around the World in a Hundred Years
by Jean Fritz
Puffin, 1998
Renowned author Jean Fritz provides a humorous and insightful look at 10 explorers who ventured into the unknown between 1421 and 1522.

Pocahontas
by Joseph Bruchac
Silver Whistle, 2003
The story of Jamestown is told in alternating chapters from Pocahontas's and John Smith's point of view.

Virginia Bound
by Amy Butler
Clarion, 2003
Rob Bracket, a boy kidnapped off the streets of London, is shipped to Virginia to be an indentured servant at Jamestown.

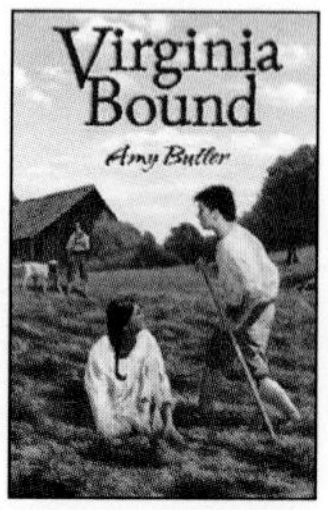

The Ransom of Mercy Carter
by Caroline B. Cooney
Delacorte, 2001
Based on actual events, a Massachusetts Puritan girl is kidnapped by Kahnawake Mohawks.

Houghton Mifflin Leveled Readers Social Studies

Social Studies Leveled Readers with lesson plans by Irene Fountas support the content of this unit.

With the Program

Your State Specific Materials

at www.eduplace.com/ss/hmss05

Read Aloud and Reference

Read Aloud Books

Morning Girl
by Michael Dorris
Hyperion, 1992

This classic narrative portrays the daily life of the Taino people up until the moment of Columbus's arrival on their island.

Stowaway
by Karen Hesse
Aladdin, 2002

Hesse creates a fictional journal of the real boy, Nicholas Young, who stowed away on explorer James Cook's ship, the *Endeavour.*

The Serpent Never Sleeps: A Novel of Jamestown and Pocahontas
by Scott O'Dell
Houghton, 1987

English castle maid, Serena Lynn, survives a shipwreck on her way to Jamestown, but that is only the beginning of the hardships she will face.

The Mississippi and the Making of a Nation
by Stephen Ambrose and Douglas Brinkley
National Geographic, 2003

Readers follow the authors as they follow the Mississippi and discover its rich history.

Reference Books

Early American Civilization and Exploration, 1607
by Helen Cothran and Brenda Stalcup
Greenhaven Press, 2003

Writings by contemporary historians and primary source information chronicle the exploration of the Americas from prehistory to 1607.

The Mayflower Compact
by E.J. Carter
Heinemann, 2004

Readers learn how the Mayflower Compact was written, what it means, and its historical impact.

Free and Inexpensive Materials

Library of Congress
101 Independence Ave. SE
Washington, DC 20540

The library's website (www.loc.gov) is a great place to start exploring.

MULTIMEDIA RESOURCES

PROGRAM RESOURCES

Unit Video
Audio Student's Book with Primary Sources and Songs MP3/CD
Lesson Planner and Teacher Resource CD-ROM
Test Generator CD-ROM
eBook
eBook, Teacher's Edition
Transparencies: Big Idea & Skillbuilder, Interactive
Almanac Map & Graph Practice
Primary Sources Plus: Document-Based Questions
Research and Writing Projects
Bringing Social Studies Alive
Family Newsletter
GeoNet

CD-ROM

The Age of Exploration 1 Picture Show. National Geographic

Explorers of the New World. Library Video

VIDEOCASSETTES

The Four Seasons in Lenape Indian Life. Spoken Arts

Explorers of the World series. Schlessinger Media

Journey to the New World. Weston Woods

Colonial Life for Children series. Schlessinger

America's Beginning. TMW Media

AUDIOCASSETTES

Stowaway, *Karen Hesse.* Listening Library

The Pilgrims of Plimoth, *Marcia Sewall.* Weston Woods

Assessment Options

TEST PREP

You are the best evaluator of your students' progress and attainments. To help you in this task, Houghton Mifflin Social Studies provides you with a variety of assessment tools.

Classroom-Based Assessment

Written and Oral Assessment

In the student book:
- **Lesson Reviews** appear at the end of each lesson.
- **Chapter Reviews** appear on pp. 118–119, 150–151.
- **Unit Reviews** appear on pp. 152–153.

In the *Assessment Options* ancillary:
- **Lesson Tests** appear for all lessons.
- **Chapter Tests** appear for all chapters.
- **Unit Tests** appear for all units.

Technology:
- **Test Generator** provides even more assessment options.

Informal, Continuous Assessment

Comprehension

In the student book:
- **Review** questions appear at the end of each section.

In the teacher's edition:
- **"Talk About It" questions** monitor student comprehension.
- **Tested Objectives** appear at the beginning and end of each lesson.

In the student practice book:
- **Study Guide** pages aid student comprehension.

Reading

In the teacher's edition:
- **Reading Strategy** is featured in every chapter.

Thinking

In the student book:
- **Critical Thinking** questions teach higher-order thinking skills.

In the teacher's edition:
- **"Think Alouds"** let you model thinking critically for your students.

In the *Assessment Options* ancillary:
- **Observation Checklists** give you another option for assessment.

HANDS ON Rubric for Unit 2 Performance Assessment

4	Journal entry shows excellent understanding; includes at least two descriptions, which are accurate and detailed; uses first person.
3	Journal entry shows clear understanding; includes one description, which is accurate; detail somewhat lacking; uses first person with lapses into third.
2	Journal entry shows partial understanding; mentions but does not describe one experience; detail lacking; written half in first person and half in third.
1	Journal entry shows little or no understanding; offers no experiences or details; not written in first person.

In *Assessment Options*, p. 46

Standardized Test Practice

In the student book:
- **Lesson Review/Test Prep** appears at the end of each lesson.
- **Chapter Review/Test Prep** appears at the end of each chapter.
- **Unit Review/Test Prep** appears at the end of each unit.

In the *Assessment Options* ancillary:
- **Lesson Tests for all lessons.**
- **Chapter Tests for all chapters.**
- **Unit Test for all units.**

Technology:
- **Test Generator** provides even more assessment options.

Student Self-Assessment

In the student book:
- **Hands-On Activities** appear in each chapter.
- **Writing Activities** appear in each chapter.

In the Unit Resources:
- **Reading Skill/Strategy** pages give students the chance to practice the skills and strategies of each lesson and chapter.
- **Vocabulary Review/Study Guide** pages provide an opportunity for self-challenge or review.

In the *Assessment Options* ancillary:
- **Self-Assessment Checklists**

Unit 2 Test

Standard Test

TEST PREP

Unit 2 Test

Test Your Knowledge

Circle the letter of the best answer.

1. What was the opinion of the people of New Netherland about Peter Stuyvesant? Obj. U2–19
   - A. They thought he was a fair ruler.
   - B. They did not have a strong opinion about him either way.
   - (C.) They were angry with him because of the laws he made.
   - D. They were very pleased with the job he did.

2. What was the main reason that Spanish rulers sent explorers to the Americas? Obj. U2–8
   - F. They wanted to become famous.
   - (G.) They wanted to find gold and spices.
   - H. They wanted to conquer the Aztecs.
   - J. They wanted the explorers to become conquistadors.

3. In what way did the discovery of gunpowder help European explorers? Obj. U2–3
   - A. It made it easier for them to navigate.
   - B. It helped them sail their ships faster.
   - (C.) It gave them confidence to travel because they could protect themselves.
   - D. It allowed them to build small, light caravels.

4. Who formed the Massachusetts Bay Colony? Obj. U2–18
   - F. Massasoit
   - G. the Pilgrims
   - H. the Dutch
   - (J.) the Puritans

5. Where did Columbus think he was when he landed in San Salvador? Obj. U2–5
   - A. in Portugal
   - (B.) off the coast of Asia
   - C. on the Caribbean Sea
   - D. in North America

6. What happened as a result of the Spanish Armada's defeat? Obj. U2–13
   - F. The Dutch searched for a Northwest Passage.
   - G. Spain began to explore the Americas.
   - (H.) England claimed more land in the Americas.
   - J. Spain became a Roman Catholic nation.

Standard Test

TEST PREP

Test the Skills: Use Latitude and Longitude; Use Parallel Timelines

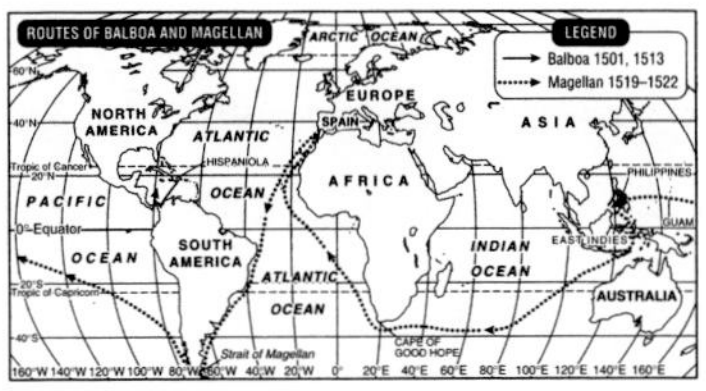

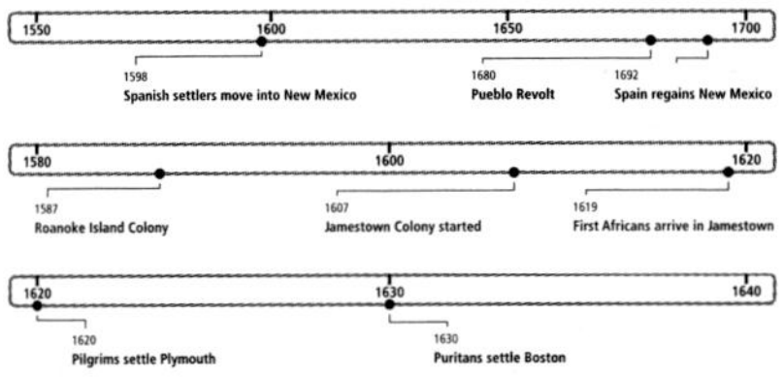

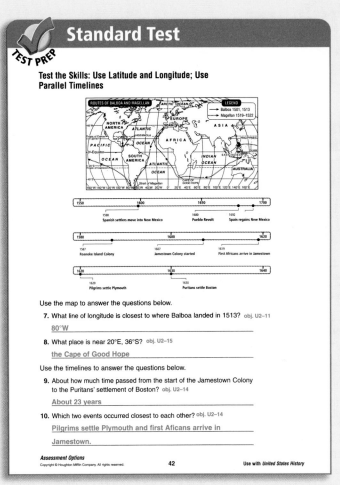

Use the map to answer the questions below.

7. What line of longitude is closest to where Balboa landed in 1513? obj. U2–11

   80°W

8. What place is near 20°E, 36°S? obj. U2–15

   the Cape of Good Hope

Use the timelines to answer the questions below.

9. About how much time passed from the start of the Jamestown Colony to the Puritans' settlement of Boston? obj. U2–14

   About 23 years

10. Which two events occurred closest to each other? obj. U2–14

    Pilgrims settle Plymouth and first Aficans arrive in Jamestown.

Standard Test

TEST PREP

Apply Your Knowledge and Skills

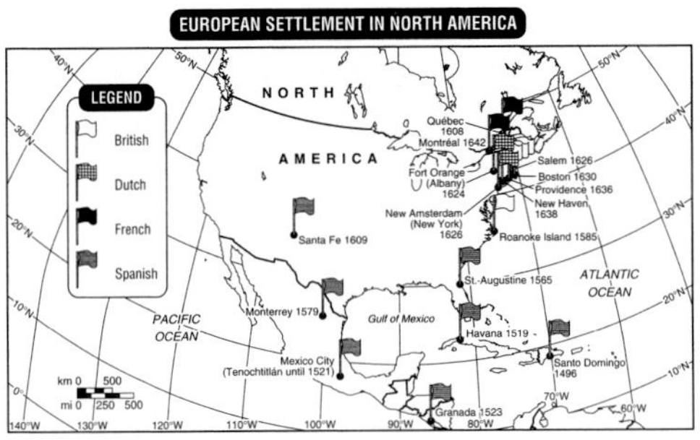

After the Jamestown Colony was founded in 1607, the English settlers fought with the Powhatan over the control of land around Jamestown. The two groups made peace in 1614. However, when the English tried to take more land, the Powhatan fought back. After many Powhatan were killed in 1646, the English took control of most of the land.

11. Which settlement was located close to 30°N, 80°W? obj. U2–11
    - A. Havana
    - B. Roanoke Island
    - C. Santo Domingo
    - (D.) St. Augustine

12. Which settlement was founded after the Powhatan and Jamestown settlers made peace? obj. U2–14
    - (F.) Salem
    - G. Havana
    - H. Santo Domingo
    - J. Roanoke Island

13. Write a brief essay about what may have happened to the Roanoke Island Colony. Write your essay on a separate sheet of paper. obj. U2–15

    Essays may refer to Roanoke as one of the first colonies and discuss the struggles its people faced with weather, food, or American Indians, much like in the Jamestown Colony.

Standard Test

TEST PREP

Apply the Reading Skills and Strategies

Many animals with thick fur, including beaver, mink, fox, and otter, lived in the cold forests of North America. Beaver hats and fur clothing were popular in Europe. French merchants made money selling these furs to Europeans. Fur traders traveled throughout New France searching for American Indians with whom they could trade. The American Indian nations gave the French pelts from animals they had trapped. A pelt is the skin of an animal with the fur still on. In exchange, the French traded goods, such as beads, iron tools, copper pots, knives, and cloth, with the American Indians.

Reading Skills

Use the passage above to answer each question.

14. **Cause and Effect** What effect did the fur trade have on relations between French settlers and American Indians? Obj. U2–20

    The French settlers and American Indians formed a partnership because of the fur trade.

15. **Main Idea and Details** What is the main idea of the passage? What details support the main idea? Obj. U2–20

    Sample answer: Main idea: French traders established a fur trade with American Indians. Details: Traders looked for American Indians to trade with. American Indians traded furs for goods, such as beads, iron tools and cloth.

Reading Strategy: Summarize

16. Write a short summary of the passage. Obj. U2–20

    Sample answer: French traders established a fur trade with American Indians. The French traded goods to the American Indians for their animal furs, which French merchants then sold to Europeans.

Reaching All Learners

Extra Support

Make a Who, Where, When, and Why Chart

Singles	30 minutes
Objective	To chart exploration and settlement
Materials	Paper, pencils, markers

- As students read the unit, they can maintain a chart of exploration and settlement, including each explorer and group of settlers. Have students allot a column for each of the following: who came, from where, to where, when, and why.
- At the end of the unit, each student selects one explorer or group of settlers and prints a newspaper headline summarizing the reason that person or group came to the Americas. Headlines can be posted in the classroom.

Explorers and Settlers

Who Came?	From Where?	To Where?	When?	Why?

Visual-spatial

Challenge

Make a Language Map

Groups	25 minutes
Objective	To make a language map
Materials	Political outline maps of North and South America, colored pencils

- Groups can do research to discover the official language of each North and South American country. You might want to have students include Quebec as a special case. An ambitious group might also add the Caribbean countries.
- Groups can display their results on a map, filling in each country with a color keyed to a legend representing the various languages. Ask: *What do languages spoken in North and South America today tell about the paths of early explorers and settlers?*

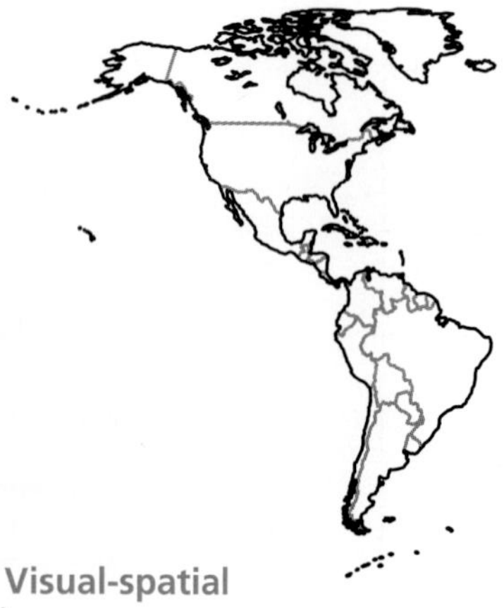

Visual-spatial

ELL

Understanding Directions on a Map

Groups	25 minutes
Objective	To understand directions on a map
Materials	Compass, paper, pencil, blank world maps

Beginning
As students study the unit, they can maintain a list of place names—continents, oceans, nations, regions explored and settled. Have students letter these names on a world map and add a direction indicator. Assist students in using a magnetic compass to orient their classroom in terms of the four cardinal directions. Have students then place their maps on a flat surface with the north arrow pointing north as indicated by the compass.

Intermediate
Have students complete the map activity. Each student describes to the group one explorer's route in terms of direction, e.g., Columbus sailed west from Spain toward North America.

Advanced
Each student uses the map to describe to the group the explorer's route in terms of direction. In addition, the student explains the reason for the voyage.

Visual-spatial; verbal-linguistic

Cross-Curricular Activities

Language Arts

Improvise a Conversation on the Trail

Class	25 minutes
Objective	To role-play historical figures
Materials	Index cards, pencils

- On index cards, write names or brief identifiers for explorers and settlers encountered in Unit 2. Students form groups and each student draws a name. One group can include characters from different times and places.
- Groups prepare for a conversation as if participants had just met and asked, *What have you been doing lately?* Conversations should include where the characters came from, where they went, and their reasons for going.
- Groups perform their conversations for the class. Other students try to identify the participants.

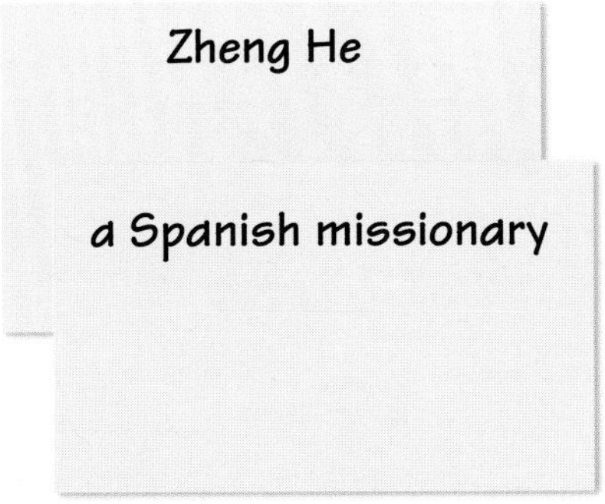

Verbal-linguistic

Math

Make a Pictograph

Singles	25 minutes
Objective	To make a pictograph
Materials	Graph paper, pencils, colored pencils

- Using a scale of a quarter inch for each ten feet, students create a horizontal graph comparing a number of historic ships. The graph can be made up of ships drawn to the correct length.
  Santa Maria, 75 feet (est.); *Nina,* 66 feet; *Victoria* (Magellan), 75.5 feet; *Golden Hind* (Drake), 120 feet; *Half Moon* (Hudson): 85 feet; *Mayflower,* 106 feet
- Ask, How many more inches of paper would you need to add these modern ships to your graph? *Titanic,* 852.5 feet; *Queen Mary,* 1,020 feet; *USS Ronald Reagan,* 1,092 feet.

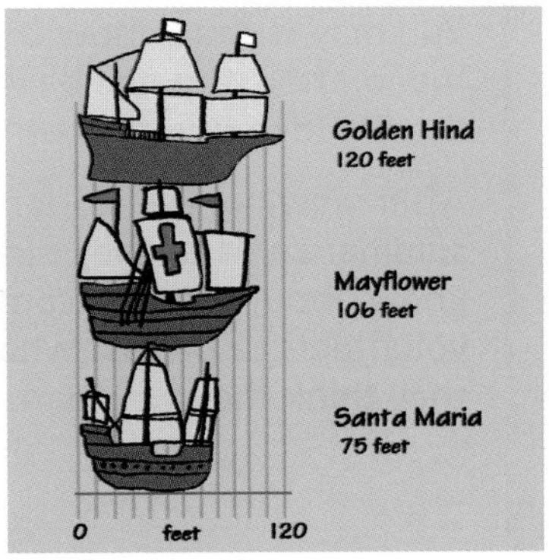

Logical-mathematical

Art

Make a Compass Rose

Singles	20 minutes
Objective	To make a compass rose
Materials	Mason jar lids or large paper cups, paper, crayons

- Provide examples of the traditional compass rose. Explain that its main points signify north, east, south, and west, while other points may mark the directions in between. North often has its own special design.
- Have students make decorated compass roses. Students can use Mason jar lids or paper cups to trace a circle, then cut out the circle and fold it in half. Fold that figure in half, then fold yet again. Students unfold their circles and follow the creases to make eight points, giving north a special design.

Visual-spatial

Begin the Unit

Unit Quick Look

Chapter 3 discusses the expansion of travel, technology, and trade between Europe, Asia, Africa, and the Americas from the 1200s to the 1700s.

Chapter 4 describes European exploration and settlement of North America, from the search for a Northwest Passage through the New England settlements, to later French and Dutch settlements of the early 1600s.

Introduce the Big Idea

History Exploration has affected not only what people know, but where different groups of people have settled. As students discuss where they would like to explore, have them consider how exploration has affected what they know about the world today.

Explain that this unit describes how the exploration of Asia and Africa led to European settlement in the Americas.

Primary Sources

Invite a volunteer to read the quote by a Spanish explorer on page 78. Ask students how they think he might have felt. List student responses on the board.

Ask students to think about what such an explorer might have been looking at. What kinds of things might an explorer of today have the same reaction to? Why or why not?

UNIT 2

Exploration and Settlement

The Big Idea

Where would you like to explore?

"Gazing on such wonderful sights we did not know what to say."

A Spanish explorer, on arriving in the Aztec capital in 1519

Christopher Columbus
1451–1506

This explorer had a bold plan to sail west to Asia. Although he never reached his goal, his journeys to the Americas changed history for millions of people.
page 96

Technology

Motivate and Build Background

You may wish to show the Unit Video after students have discussed the Big Idea question on this page.

After viewing, ask students to **summarize** what they already know about the unit content. Ask volunteers to **predict** what else they think they will learn.

You can find more video teaching suggestions on pages R1 and R2 in the Resources Section in the back of the Teacher's Edition.

Queen Isabella
1451–1504

Why did Queen Isabella take a chance on Columbus? She agreed to pay for his voyages because she thought they would bring power and wealth to Spain.

page 96

Moctezuma
1480?–1520

Moctezuma ruled the great Aztec empire in the 1500s. When Spanish explorers arrived in the Aztec capital, he welcomed them and treated them like honored guests.

page 105

79

Web Link

E-Biographies

To learn more about the History Makers on these pages and in this unit, visit www.eduplace.com/kids/hmss05/

Designed to be accessed by your students, these biographies can be used for

- research projects
- Character Education
- developing students' technology skills

Correcting Misconceptions

Ask students what they know about exploration and settlement. Write their responses as a list on the board.

As students read the unit, return to the list periodically to see if any of their responses have been shown to be misconceptions.

Discuss why students may have thought as they did, and what they have learned.

History Makers

Christopher Columbus Even though Columbus spent part of his life in Portugal, and got money for his voyages from the rulers of Spain, Christopher Columbus was actually from Genoa, Italy. He sailed in ships similar to the one shown.

Queen Isabella Under the rule of Isabella and her husband Ferdinand, large parts of Spain were unified. Isabella helped scholars and artists by starting schools and collecting art. She made sure both her sons and daughters got an education.

Moctezuma The emperor known as Moctezuma was actually Moctezuma II. He had his own zoo in his palace, and wore sandals made of gold. A piece of Aztec pottery is shown.

Map and Graph Skills

Interpreting Maps

Talk About It

1 **Q Geography** What can you learn about North American exploration from this map?

A The routes of explorers and the dates of their voyages

2 **Q Geography** Which explorer crossed the Appalachian Mountains and explored the Southeast?

A De Soto

3 **Q Geography** Find five American Indian tribes whose names have been used for U.S. states.

A Possible answers include: Massachuset, Delaware, Illinois, Missouri, Iowa, Dakota, Ute.

Critical Thinking

Infer Look at the four land routes shown. Based on what you know about the geography and history of the United States, what might be some obstacles that these explorers faced? Possible obstacles include geographic features such as the deserts of the Southwest, the cold climate of the Northeast, mountain ranges such as the Appalachians. Indians already living in North America could also have been considered obstacles.

Interpreting Timelines

Ask students if they can identify any of the images shown on the timeline. painting of Columbus; astrolabe; conquistador's helmet; image of John Smith; painting of the *Mayflower*

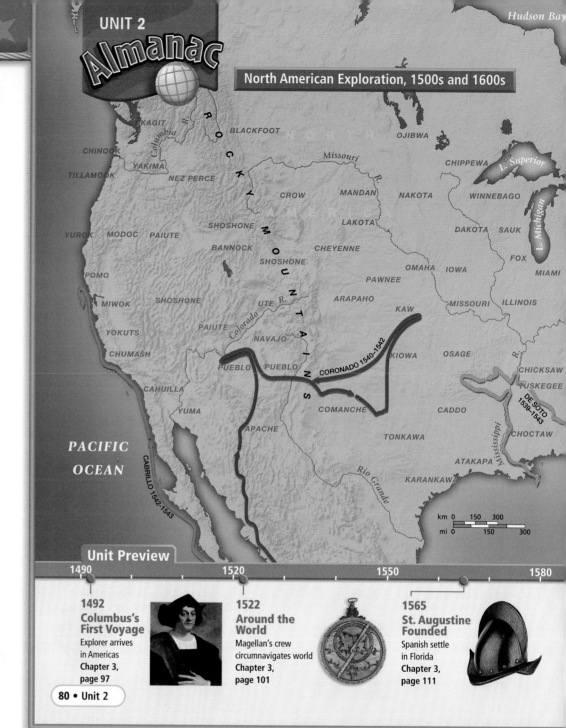

UNIT 2 Almanac

North American Exploration, 1500s and 1600s

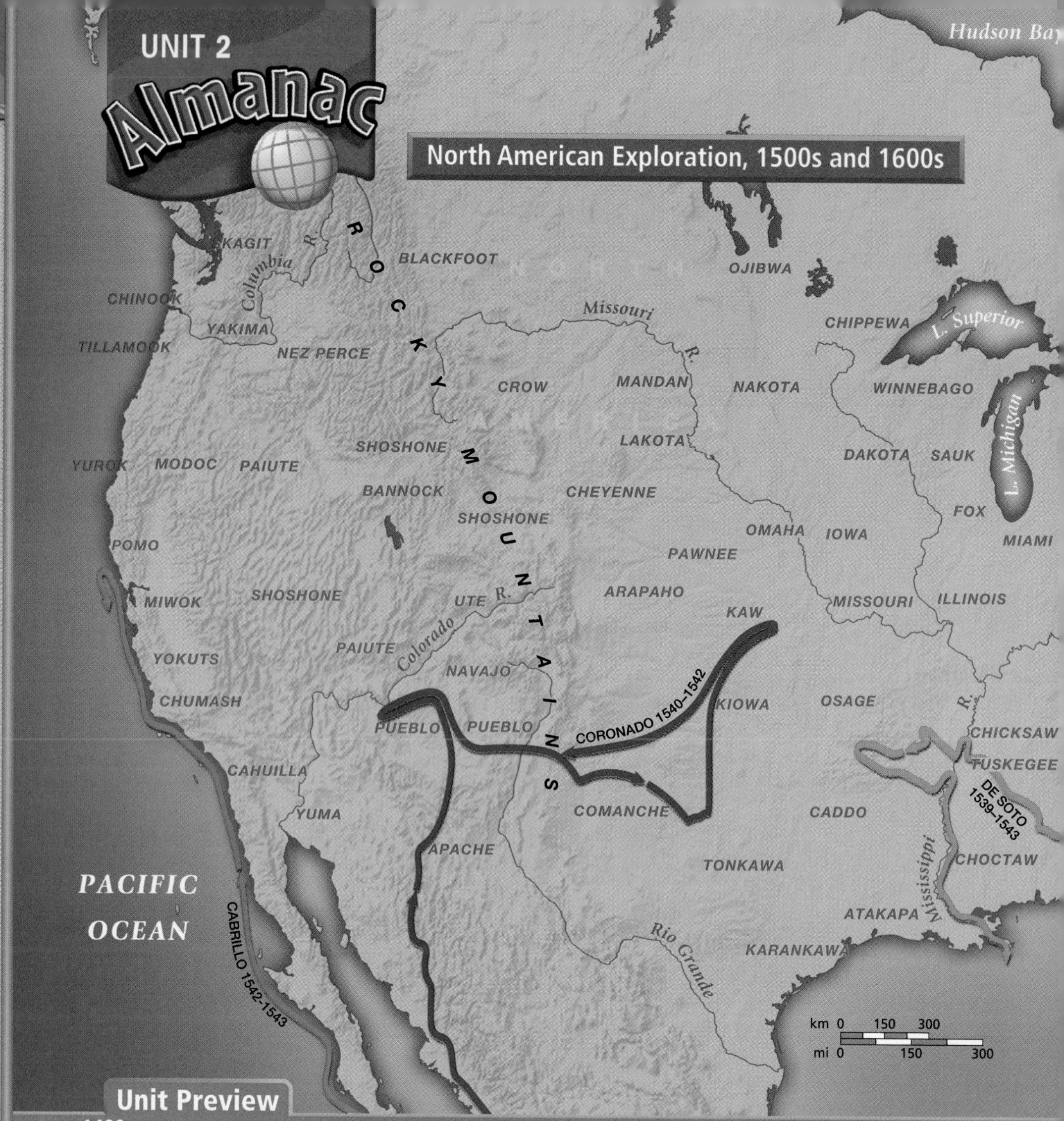

Unit Preview

1490 1520 1550 1580

1492 Columbus's First Voyage Explorer arrives in Americas **Chapter 3, page 97**

1522 Around the World Magellan's crew circumnavigates world **Chapter 3, page 101**

1565 St. Augustine Founded Spanish settle in Florida **Chapter 3, page 111**

Technology

GeoNet

To support student geography skills, you may wish to have them go to www.eduplace.com/kids/hmss05/ to play GeoNet.

Math

Hudson on the Hudson

Have students use the map scale to estimate about how far up the Hudson River Henry Hudson traveled.

1 in. = about 300 mi.

$\frac{1}{2}$ in. = about 300 ÷ 2

$\frac{1}{2}$ in. = about 150 miles

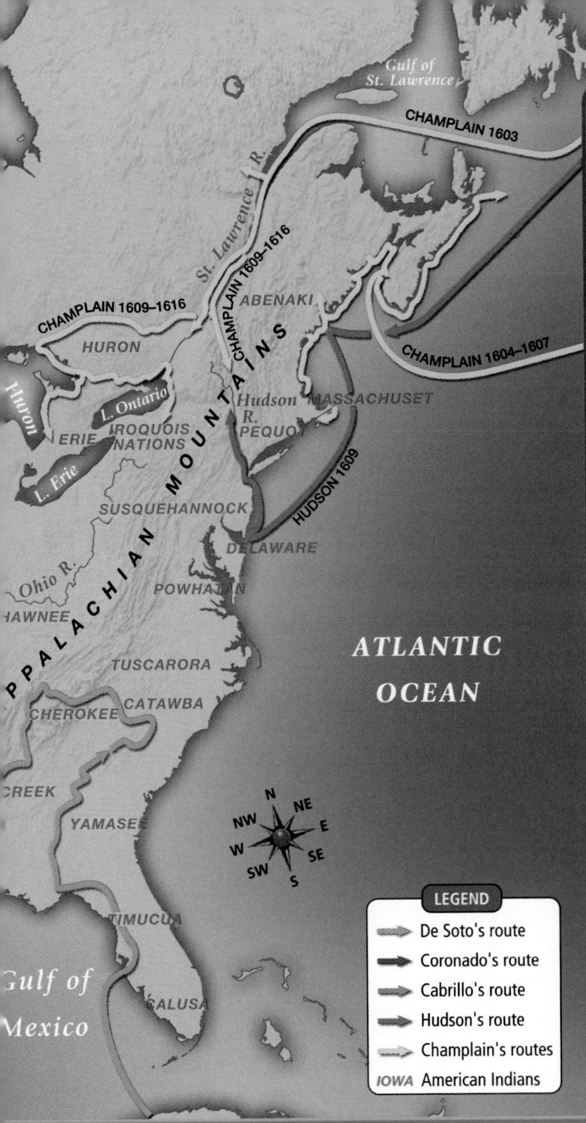

1610 | 1640

1607 Jamestown Founded
First successful English colony in Americas
Chapter 4, page 131

1620 Mayflower Voyage
Pilgrims land at Plymouth
Chapter 4, page 137

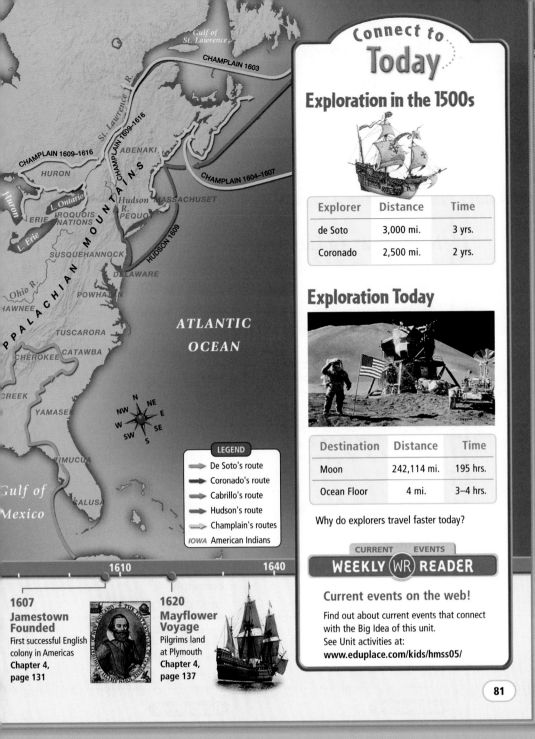

Connect to Today

Exploration in the 1500s

Explorer	Distance	Time
de Soto	3,000 mi.	3 yrs.
Coronado	2,500 mi.	2 yrs.

Exploration Today

Destination	Distance	Time
Moon	242,114 mi.	195 hrs.
Ocean Floor	4 mi.	3–4 hrs.

Why do explorers travel faster today?

CURRENT EVENTS
WEEKLY WR READER

Current events on the web!
Find out about current events that connect with the Big Idea of this unit.
See Unit activities at:
www.eduplace.com/kids/hmss05/

81

Current Events

For information about current events related to this unit, visit www.eduplace.com/ss/hmss05/.

Web links to Weekly Reader will help students work on the Current Events Unit Project. The Unit 2 Project will involve creating a class book about contemporary exploration around the world.

As you go through the unit, encourage students to use the web to find information for the class book.

Interpreting Graphs

Talk About It

4 Q Economics In what ways might the explorers' long journeys have created a financial risk for the countries that paid for them?

A Expeditions needed supplies for long voyages, but the countries financing the voyages didn't know for years what was happening on the expedition or if the expedition would even return.

5 Q Culture How might people's attitudes about exploration in the 1500s compare to attitudes about exploration today?

A Possible answers include that people might be more open to exploration today because they have seen benefits from past expeditions.

Find Out More

Exploration Then and Now Ask students to suggest reasons why explorers' journeys took so long in the 1500s. Encourage students to do research to check their ideas or to check them as they read the unit.

Under the Sea Ask students to consider why explorers might have been unable to explore the ocean floor until recently. List the students' ideas on the board. Encourage students to do Internet or library research to see which ideas are correct.

Chapter 3

Planning Guide

Age of Exploration

Chapter Opener

Pages 82–83

30 minutes

Reading/Vocabulary

Chapter Reading Strategy:
Monitor and Clarify, p. 81F

Resources

Grade Level Resources
Vocabulary Cards, pp. 11–20

Reaching All Learners
Challenge Activities, p. 81

Primary Sources Plus, p. 5

Big Idea Transparency 2

Interactive Transparency 2

Text & Music Audio CD

Lesson Planner & TR CD-ROM

eBook

eTE

Core Lesson 1

World Travel and Trade

Pages 84–87

40 minutes

Tested Objectives

U2-1 Describe Chinese trade, inventions, and exploration from the 1200s—1400s.

U2-2 Identify West African kingdoms and trade routes.

Reading/Vocabulary

Reading Skill: Cause and Effect

merchant
caravan
kingdom

Cross-Curricular

Art, p. 86

Resources

Unit Resources:
Reading Skill/Strategy, p. 25
Vocabulary/Study Guide, p. 26

Reaching All Learners:
Lesson Summary, p. 10
Support for Lang. Dev./ELL, p. 107

Assessment Options:
Lesson Test, p. 24

Extend Lesson 1

Geography
The Silk Road
20–30 minutes
Pages 88–89
Focus: Students see the route of the Silk Road and learn about a musical project.

Core Lesson 2

New Ideas in Europe

Pages 90–93

40 minutes

Tested Objectives

U2-3 Describe new ideas in Europe and their effects exploration.

U2-4 Summarize the achievements of early Portuguese exploration around Africa.

Reading/Vocabulary

Reading Skill: Problem and Solution

technology
astrolabe
navigation

Cross-Curricular

Music, p. 92

Resources

Unit Resources:
Reading Skill/Strategy, p. 27
Vocabulary/Study Guide, p. 28

Reaching All Learners:
Lesson Summary, p. 11
Support for Lang. Dev./ELL, p. 108

Assessment Options:
Lesson Test, p. 25

Extend Lesson 2

Technology
Tools for Discovery
20–30 minutes
Pages 94–95
Focus: Students learn about technological advances that changed exploration.

Core Lesson 3

Europeans Arrive in the Americas

Pages 96–101

50 minutes

Tested Objectives

U2-5 Describe and evaluate the significance of Columbus's voyages to the Americas.

U2-6 Identify early European explorations, including Magellan's voyage.

Reading/Vocabulary

Reading Skill: Compare and Contrast

settlement
epidemic
circumnavigate

Cross-Curricular

Math, p. 100
Science, p. 98

Resources

Unit Resources:
Reading Skill/Strategy, p. 29
Vocabulary/Study Guide, p. 30

Reaching All Learners:
Lesson Summary, p. 12
Support for Lang. Dev./ELL, p. 109

Assessment Options:
Lesson Test, p. 26

www.eduplace.com/ss/hmss05/

Extend Lesson 3

Primary Source
Mapping New Lands
20–30 minutes
Pages 102–103
Focus: A 1507 map lets students see the world as European explorers saw it.

National Standards

I a Similarities and differences in addressing human needs and concerns **II b** Cause and effect relationships **II e** People in different times and places view the world differently **III c** Resources, data sources, and geographic tools **V b** Group and institutional influences **VI f** Factors that contribute to cooperation and cause disputes **VII d** Institutions that make up economic systems **VII f** Influence of incentives, values, traditions, and habits **VIII a** How science and technology have changed lives **VIII b** How science and technology have changed the physical environment **IX b** Conflict, cooperation, and interdependence **IX c** Effects of changing technologies on the global community

With the Program

CURRENT EVENTS from WEEKLY WR READER at www.eduplace.com

Core Lesson 4

Conquest of the Americas

Pages 104–107

40 minutes

Tested Objectives

U2-7 Describe and evaluate the significance of Spain's conquest of the Aztec Empire.

U2-8 Identify achievements of Spanish explorers.

Reading/Vocabulary

Reading Skill: Compare and Contrast

expedition **empire** **conquistador**

Cross-Curricular

Drama, p. 106

Resources

Unit Resources:
- **Reading Skill/Strategy,** p. 31
- **Vocabulary/Study Guide,** p. 32

Reaching All Learners:
- **Lesson Summary,** p. 13
- **Support for Lang. Dev./ELL,** p. 110

Assessment Options:
- **Lesson Test,** p. 27

www.eduplace.com/ss/hmss05/

Extend Lesson 4

Biographies

Spanish Explorers

20–30 minutes

Pages 108–109

Focus: Five Spanish explorers are profiled.

Core Lesson 5

New Spain

Pages 110–113

40 minutes

Tested Objectives

U2-9 Describe Spain's colonial system in the Americas.

U2-10 Evaluate the impact of Spanish colonization.

Reading/Vocabulary

Reading Skill: Draw Conclusions

colony **hacienda** **mission** **revolt** **convert**

Cross-Curricular

Math, p. 112

Resources

Unit Resources:
- **Reading Skill/Strategy,** p. 33
- **Vocabulary/Study Guide,** p. 34

Reaching All Learners:
- **Lesson Summary,** p. 14
- **Support for Lang. Dev./ELL,** p. 111

Assessment Options:
- **Lesson Test,** p. 28

www.eduplace.com/ss/hmss05/

Extend Lesson 5

Biographies

Leadership in New Spain

20–30 minutes

Pages 114–115

Focus: Students learn more about De las Casas, Popé, and Serra.

Skillbuilder

Map and Globe Skill

Use Latitude and Longitude

Pages 116–117

20 minutes

Tested Objectives

U2-11 Use latitude and longitude to determine absolute locations.

Reading/Vocabulary

parallel **absolute location** **meridian**

Resources

Practice Book:
- **Skill Practice,** p. 35

Skill Transparency 3

Chapter Review

Pages 118–119

30 minutes

Resources

Assessment Options:
- Chapter 3 Test
- Test Generator

Chapter 3 Practice Options

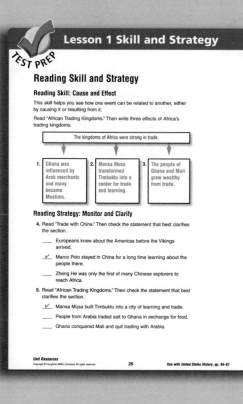

Lesson 1 Skill and Strategy

TEST PREP

Reading Skill and Strategy

Reading Skill: Cause and Effect

This skill helps you see how one event can be related to another, either by causing it or resulting from it.

Read "African Trading Kingdoms." Then write three effects of Africa's trading kingdoms.

The kingdoms of Africa were strong in trade.

1. Ghana was influenced by Arab merchants and many became Muslims.
2. Mansa Musa transformed Timbuktu into a center for trade and learning.
3. The people of Ghana and Mali grew wealthy from trade.

Reading Strategy: Monitor and Clarify

4. Read "Trade with China." Then check the statement that best clarifies the section.

____ Europeans knew about the Americas before the Vikings arrived.

✓ Marco Polo stayed in China for a long time learning about the people there.

____ Zheng He was only the first of many Chinese explorers to reach Africa.

5. Read "African Trading Kingdoms." Then check the statement that best clarifies the section.

✓ Mansa Musa built Timbuktu into a city of learning and trade.

____ People from Arabia traded salt to Ghana in exchange for food.

____ Ghana conquered Mali and quit trading with Arabia.

Unit Resources

25
Use with *United States History*, pp. 84–87

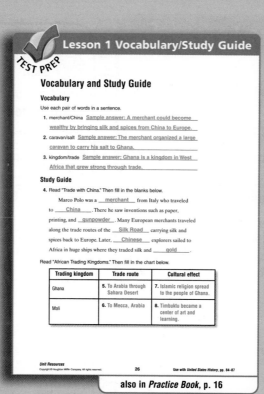

Lesson 1 Vocabulary/Study Guide

TEST PREP

Vocabulary and Study Guide

Vocabulary

Use each pair of words in a sentence.

1. merchant/China Sample answer: A merchant could become wealthy by bringing silk and spices from China to Europe.
2. caravan/salt Sample answer: The merchant organized a large caravan to carry his salt to Ghana.
3. kingdom/trade Sample answer: Ghana is a kingdom in West Africa that grew strong through trade.

Study Guide

4. Read "Trade with China." Then fill in the blanks below.

Marco Polo was a merchant from Italy who traveled to China. There he saw inventions such as paper, printing, and gunpowder. Many European merchants traveled along the trade routes of the Silk Road carrying silk and spices back to Europe. Later, Chinese explorers sailed to Africa in huge ships where they traded silk and gold.

Read "African Trading Kingdoms." Then fill in the chart below.

Trading kingdom	Trade route	Cultural effect
Ghana	5. To Arabia through Sahara Desert	7. Islamic religion spread to the people of Ghana.
Mali	6. To Mecca, Arabia	8. Timbuktu became a center of art and learning.

Unit Resources

26
Use with *United States History*, pp. 84–87

also in *Practice Book*, p. 16

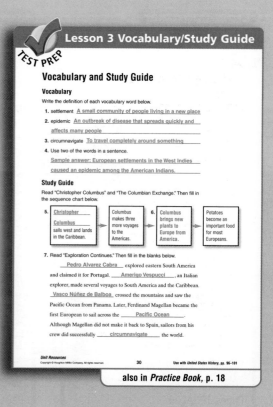

Lesson 2 Skill and Strategy

TEST PREP

Reading Skill and Strategy

Reading Skill: Problem and Solution

This skill helps you see what problems some people faced and how they resolved them.

Read "The Renaissance." Then write two solutions to the problem of navigating a ship at sea.

Problem	Solutions
Sailors found it difficult and dangerous to navigate the seas.	1. North Africans taught sailors to use the astrolabe. 2. The Chinese showed sailors the compass, which made navigation easier.

Reading Strategy: Monitor and Clarify

3. Read "The Renaissance." Then check the statement that best clarifies the section.

✓ After the printing press, more books were available to people.

____ Sailors navigated by watching the direction in which fish were swimming.

____ European sailors introduced the compass to Chinese sailors.

4. Read "A Sea Route to Asia." Then complete the statement.

The first European sailors to discover a water route to Asia were Portuguese.

Unit Resources

27
Use with *United States History*, pp. 90–93

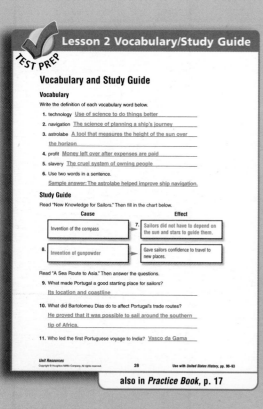

Lesson 2 Vocabulary/Study Guide

TEST PREP

Vocabulary and Study Guide

Vocabulary

Write the definition of each vocabulary word below.

1. technology Use of science to do things better
2. navigation The science of planning a ship's journey
3. astrolabe A tool that measures the height of the sun over the horizon
4. profit Money left over after expenses are paid
5. slavery The cruel system of owning people
6. Use two words in a sentence.

Sample answer: The astrolabe helped improve ship navigation.

Study Guide

Read "New Knowledge for Sailors." Then fill in the chart below.

Cause	Effect
Invention of the compass	7. Sailors did not have to depend on the sun and stars to guide them.
8. Invention of gunpowder	Gave sailors confidence to travel to new places.

Read "A Sea Route to Asia." Then answer the questions.

9. What made Portugal a good starting place for sailors?

Its location and coastline

10. What did Bartolomeu Dias do to affect Portugal's trade routes?

He proved that it was possible to sail around the southern tip of Africa.

11. Who led the first Portuguese voyage to India? Vasco da Gama

Unit Resources

28
Use with *United States History*, pp. 90–93

also in *Practice Book*, p. 17

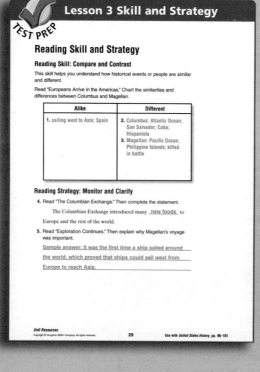

Lesson 3 Skill and Strategy

TEST PREP

Reading Skill and Strategy

Reading Skill: Compare and Contrast

This skill helps you understand how historical events or people are similar and different.

Read "Europeans Arrive in the Americas." Chart the similarities and differences between Columbus and Magellan.

Alike	Different
1. sailing west to Asia; Spain	2. Columbus: Atlantic Ocean; San Salvador; Cuba; Hispaniola 3. Magellan: Pacific Ocean; Philippine Islands; killed in battle

Reading Strategy: Monitor and Clarify

4. Read "The Columbian Exchange." Then complete the statement.

The Columbian Exchange introduced many new foods to Europe and the rest of the world.

5. Read "Exploration Continues." Then explain why Magellan's voyage was important.

Sample answer: It was the first time a ship sailed around the world, which proved that ships could sail west from Europe to reach Asia.

Unit Resources

29
Use with *United States History*, pp. 96–101

Lesson 3 Vocabulary/Study Guide

TEST PREP

Vocabulary and Study Guide

Vocabulary

Write the definition of each vocabulary word below.

1. settlement A small community of people living in a new place
2. epidemic An outbreak of disease that spreads quickly and affects many people
3. circumnavigate To travel completely around something
4. Use two of the words in a sentence.

Sample answer: European settlements in the West Indies caused an epidemic among the American Indians.

Study Guide

Read "Christopher Columbus" and "The Columbian Exchange." Then fill in the sequence chart below.

5. Christopher Columbus sails west and lands in the Caribbean. → Columbus makes three more voyages to the Americas. → 6. Columbus brings new plants to Europe from America. → Potatoes become an important food for most Europeans.

7. Read "Exploration Continues." Then fill in the blanks below.

Pedro Alvarez Cabra explored eastern South America and claimed it for Portugal. Amerigo Vespucci, an Italian explorer, made several voyages to South America and the Caribbean. Vasco Núñez de Balboa crossed the mountains and saw the Pacific Ocean from Panama. Later, Ferdinand Magellan became the first European to sail across the Pacific Ocean. Although Magellan did not make it back to Spain, sailors from his crew did successfully circumnavigate the world.

Unit Resources

30
Use with *United States History*, pp. 96–101

also in *Practice Book*, p. 18

Lesson 4 Skill and Strategy

TEST PREP

Reading Skill and Strategy

Reading Skill: Compare and Contrast

This skill helps you understand how historical events or people are similar and different.

Read "Cortés Conquers the Aztecs." Chart the similarities and differences between how the Aztecs felt about the Spanish when they first met and later on.

First Meeting	Later On
1. Moctezuma welcomed Cortés.	2. The Aztecs drove the Spanish from Tenochtitlán.

Reading Strategy: Monitor and Clarify

3. Read "Cortés Conquers the Aztecs." Then complete the statement.

   Indian nations that had been conquered by the Aztecs helped Cortés, and he used guns, steel armor, and horses to defeat the Aztec army.

4. Read "Exploring North America." Then explain what the conquistadors accomplished.

   Sample answer: The Spanish conquistadors explored much of North America while searching for gold.

Lesson 4 Vocabulary/Study Guide

TEST PREP

Vocabulary and Study Guide

Vocabulary

Write each vocabulary word in the correct column.

conquistador empire expedition person thing event

Aztec civilization	Francisco Pizzaro	Cortés's journey to Mexico
1. thing, empire	2. person, conquistador	3. event, expedition

Study Guide

Read "Cortés Conquers the Aztecs." Then answer the questions.

4. What were three things that helped Spain defeat the Aztecs?

   Neighboring American Indian nations helped the Spanish; Malinche helped Cortés communicate and plan; The Aztec army was weakened by a smallpox infection.

5. What happened after Cortés conquered the Aztecs?

   Spain claimed all of Mexico and renamed it New Spain; Other conquistadors explored Central and South America.

Read "Exploring North America." Then fill in the chart below.

Explorer	Goal	Achievement
Hernando de Soto	6. Conquer and settle Florida	7. Became the first European to reach the Mississippi River
Francisco Vázquez de Coronado	8. Find cities of gold	9. Led the first group of Europeans to see the Grand Canyon

also in *Practice Book*, p. 19

Lesson 5 Skill and Strategy

TEST PREP

Reading Skill and Strategy

Reading Skill: Draw Conclusions

Sometimes when you read, you have to figure out things that the writer doesn't tell you. This skill is called drawing conclusions.

Read "New Spain Grows." Then fill in the draw conclusions chart below. Draw a conclusion from the statement. Then draw a final conclusion from the first conclusion.

Spain's rulers sent priests with the explorers to spread Christianity.

↓

1. Sample answer: Many American Indians and explorers converted to Catholicism.

↓

2. Sample answer: The people living in New Spain were almost all Christians.

Reading Strategy: Monitor and Clarify

3. Read "New Spain Grows." Then explain how Spain spread religion in North America.

   Sample answer: Priests traveled with explorers and started missions in or near the settlements.

4. Read "Life in New Spain." Then explain how hacienda owners became rich.

   Sample answer: Farmers forced American Indians and enslaved Africans to work on their haciendas for little or no money.

Lesson 5 Vocabulary/Study Guide

TEST PREP

Vocabulary and Study Guide

Vocabulary

Solve the clue and write the answer in the blank. Then find the word in the puzzle. Look up, down, forward, and backward.

1. A territory ruled by another country colony
2. A violent uprising against a ruler revolt
3. A large farm or ranch hacienda
4. A community where priests taught Christianity mission
5. To change a religion or belief convert

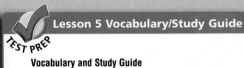

A	N	T	L	O	V	E	R
D	Y	R	B	S	A	D	A
E	N	E	R	V	J	D	N
C	O	V	T	X	N	O	T
I	L	N	S	E	I	S	G
H	O	O	I	S	K	R	H
M	C	C	S	F	N	V	E
Q	A	I	G	E	P	A	M
H	M	T	U	I	R	W	I

Study Guide

6. Read "New Spain Grows." Then fill in the blanks below.

   After settling the colony of New Spain, explorers and priests went north. They started missions where they worked to convert American Indians to Roman Catholicism. Spanish settlers built forts called presidios to protect Spanish land claims. The Spanish were the first Europeans to settle the Southwest, Florida, and California.

7. Read "Life in New Spain." Then fill in the blanks below.

   The Spanish found good soil in North America. To make money, they built haciendas and forced American Indians to farm the land. Thousands of American Indians died from overwork. To replace these workers, Spain imported enslaved Africans. Some American Indians converted to Catholicism, but others kept their own religions.

also in *Practice Book*, p. 20

Skillbuilder Practice

TEST PREP

Skillbuilder: Use Latitude and Longitude

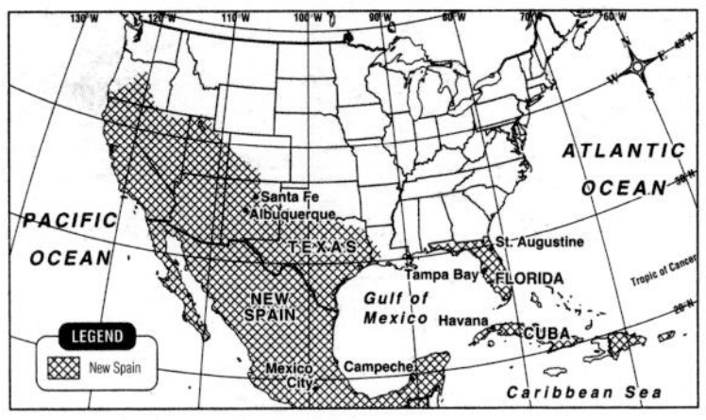

Practice

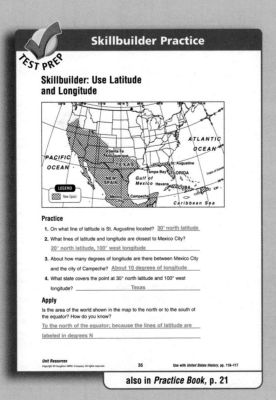

1. On what line of latitude is St. Augustine located? 30° north latitude
2. What lines of latitude and longitude are closest to Mexico City?

   20° north latitude, 100° west longitude

3. About how many degrees of longitude are there between Mexico City and the city of Campeche? About 10 degrees of longitude
4. What state covers the point at 30° north latitude and 100° west longitude? Texas

Apply

Is the area of the world shown in the map to the north or to the south of the equator? How do you know?

To the north of the equator; because the lines of latitude are labeled in degrees N

also in *Practice Book*, p. 21

Chapter 3 Assessment Options

Chapter 3 Test

TEST PREP

Chapter 3 Test

Test Your Knowledge

caravan	astrolabe	conquistador	hacienda

Write *T* if the statement is true or *F* if it is false.

1. T Merchants traveled in a large caravan to bring salt to Ghana. Obj. U2–2
2. F European navigators used an astrolabe to measure the size of continents. Obj. U2–3
3. F The conquistador, Hernando de Soto, was sent to build missions in Florida. Obj. U2–8
4. T Spanish hacienda owners relied on American Indians to farm the land. Obj. U2–10

Circle the letter of the best answer.

5. What effect did Marco Polo's book have on Europeans? Obj. U2–1
   - A. Admiral Zheng He sailed to Africa's east coast.
   - B. They did not find Marco Polo's book interesting.
   - (C.) They became more interested in travel to Asia.
   - D. Mansa Musa traveled to Mecca.
6. What important contribution did Portuguese explorers make to European trade? Obj. U2–4
   - (F.) They found a sea route to Asia.
   - G. They discovered the Silk Road.
   - H. They brought the first Asian spices to Europe.
   - J. They founded colonies along the coast of Africa.
7. What was Ferdinand Magellan's purpose when he set sail from Spain in 1519? Obj. U2–6
   - A. to explore the Americas and create maps
   - (B.) to cross the Pacific Ocean and return to Spain
   - C. to explore South America and claim it for Portugal
   - D. to reach the Philippine Islands and bring back spices
8. Which of the following did Spanish colonists build in the Americas? Obj. U2–9
   - (F.) religious settlements called missions
   - G. cities of gold
   - H. the city of Tenochtitlán
   - J. towns called pueblos

Chapter 3 Test

TEST PREP

Apply Your Knowledge

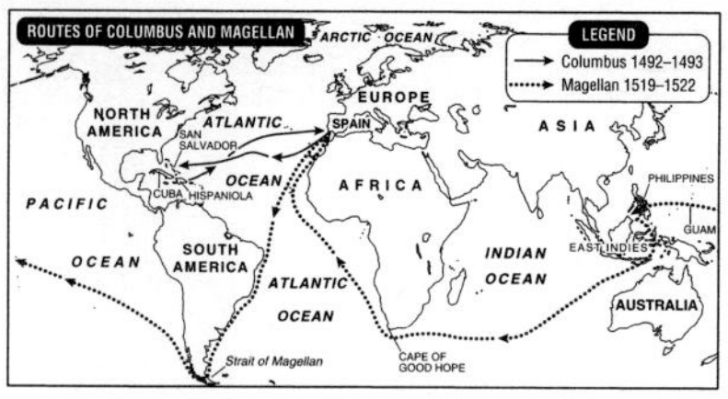

Use the map to answer the following questions.

9. When did Magellan begin his voyage? Obj. U2–6
   - A. in 1522
   - B. the same year as Columbus
   - C. before Columbus
   - (D.) in 1519
10. Where did Columbus first land? Obj. U2–5
    - F. at Cape Horn
    - G. in Asia
    - (H.) on an island in the Caribbean Sea
    - J. in South America

Apply the Reading Skill: Cause and Effect

Read the passage below. Then answer the question. Obj. U2–3

> During the Renaissance, new technology encouraged exploration. European sailors learned how to navigate using a compass. With this instrument, used by the Chinese long before, they could check whether they were heading north, south, east, or west. The improved sailing technology of the caravel ship also helped sailors. The caravel's triangular sails allowed the ship to sail directly into the wind.

11. What new technologies caused exploration to change during the Renaissance?

    The compass and the caravel.

Chapter 3 Test

TEST PREP

Test the Skill: Use Latitude and Longitude

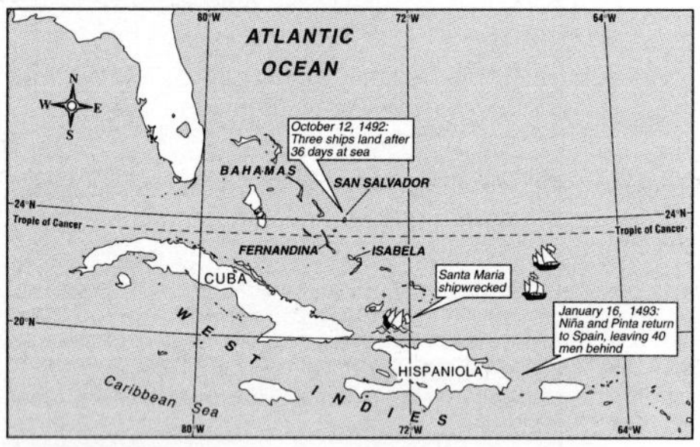

12. What line of longitude shown on the map runs through Hispaniola? Obj. U2–11

    72°W runs through Hispaniola.
13. Which line of latitude is closest to the island of San Salvador? Obj. U2–11

    24°N
14. At approximately what lines of longitude and latitude was the Santa Maria shipwrecked? Obj. U2–11 72°W, 20°N

Apply the Skill

15. When Christopher Columbus made his return voyage to Spain from the West Indies, he sailed toward the east. Was he sailing toward the prime meridian or away from it? How does the information on the map help you figure this out? Obj. U2–11

    He was sailing toward the prime meridian; the map shows this because the prime meridian is at 0° longitude, and the degrees of each west meridian line get smaller as you travel east from the West Indies.

Chapter 3 Test

TEST PREP

Think and Write

16. **Short Response:** Describe the trade routes and the trade products of one of the West African trading kingdoms. Obj. U2–2

    Sample answer: Merchants from Arabia traveled in caravans to bring salt across the Sahara on a trade route to Ghana. Ghana traded gold for salt.
17. **Critical Thinking: Evaluate** What were two important results of European exploration in the 1400s and the 1500s? Obj. U2–5

    Sample answers: The discovery of new lands; the opening of trade routes; the expansion of awareness of other cultures
18. **Extended Response:** In 1519, Hernán Cortés made an expedition to Mexico to conquer the Aztecs. Write a description of the journey, of what Cortés did, and of what happened to the Aztecs. Write your description on a separate sheet of paper. Obj. U2–7

    Descriptions may describe how Hernán Cortés carried an army to present-day Mexico and got help from an Aztec woman named Malinche; the Aztec army was weakened by a smallpox infection; Cortés convinced neighboring American Indian nations to join his army and used guns, horses, and armor to defeat the Aztecs.

Self-Assessment

What have I learned about the cost of European exploration on native inhabitants in the Americas? What do I think about this?

Teacher Read Aloud
A Story in History

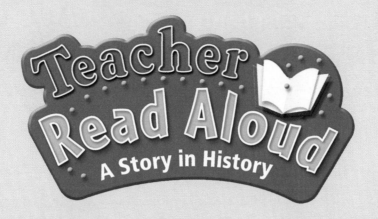

You may want to read the following fiction selection to your students before beginning the chapter.

Activate Prior Knowledge
Ask students what they know about Columbus's exploration of the West Indies. Explain that this Read Aloud helps them imagine the reactions of two members of Columbus's crew soon after they arrived on the island of Hispaniola.

Preview the Chapter
Ask students to look at the map on page 97 of their books and trace the route Columbus's ships took to reach Hispaniola.

Read-Aloud Vocabulary
Explain that an **expedition** is a journey with a specific goal, such as Columbus's voyage to find a new route to Asia. A **settlement** is a small community of people in a new area.

Preview the Reading Strategy
Monitor/Clarify Explain to students that the reading strategy they will use in this chapter is monitor/clarify. When they use this strategy, students pause during their reading and check their understanding. You may wish to use the Read Aloud to model the strategy.

Think Aloud *I've read the first two paragraphs, and I want to make sure I understand what's going on. There are two main characters, and they both seem nervous. I don't understand why, though. I'll keep reading to clarify this.*

Expedition to a New Land

"I'll never get used to this place," Giovanni said. "Do you really think we can start a **settlement** here?"

Giovanni and I had entered the forest to look for firewood. "I don't know. Are you afraid?" I asked.

He didn't reply. I had to admit I was nervous, too. The trees were so lush, hung with huge vines, and the birds and frogs made such strange noises.

I had never in my whole life imagined that such a place could exist. I had grown up in a great city, filled with buildings and streets and—most of all—people.

"This place is so different," I said to my shipmate. "Have you ever seen so many plants in one place?"

Giovanni grunted. "The only plants I ever liked were the ones in the vineyard where my family worked. There are too many here. They are too close together. Too—wild."

"But Giovanni," I began.

He waved his hand impatiently. "Enough talk. Let's just get the wood and get out of here. I don't like it here. I don't like it here at all."

We hadn't gone far when Giovanni stopped in his tracks. I looked where he was looking. A large pair of eyes stared at us from one of the trees.

"What should we do?" he whispered.

I hesitated. Then I remembered why we were there—to get firewood.

"Let's return to the edge of the forest," I said. "We can cut down some trees there."

Begin the Chapter

Chapter Quick Look

Core Lesson 1 describes world travel and trade between 1271 and 1465.

Core Lesson 2 discusses how new knowledge and inventions led to further world exploration between 1454 and 1498.

Core Lesson 3 describes the period of European arrival and exploration in the Americas between 1400 and 1550.

Core Lesson 4 focuses on the Spanish conquest of the Americas between 1519 to 1540.

Core Lesson 5 explores the development of "New Spain" in North America.

Vocabulary Preview

Use the vocabulary cards to preview the key vocabulary words before starting the lessons and to prepare students to understand the content of the chapter.

Vocabulary Strategy

Vocabulary strategies for this chapter:

- Structural analysis, p. 90
- Synonyms/antonyms, p. 84
- Prefixes and suffixes, pp. 96, 104
- Word origins, p. 110

Vocabulary Help

Vocabulary card for navigation Finding your way on the sea is different from finding your way on land. Sailors need special tools for navigation, to figure out how to guide a ship between one place and another.

Vocabulary card for expedition The word *expedition* can describe both an organized trip to a place, and the group of people who went on the trip. The painting on page 83 shows Coronado leading an expedition.

Chapter 3 Age of Exploration

Vocabulary Preview

Technology
e • glossary
e • word games
www.eduplace.com/kids/hmss05/

navigation

In the 1400s, Europeans studied ways to improve **navigation.** They wanted to plan and control the direction in which they sailed on long voyages. **page 91**

circumnavigate

In 1522, explorers sailed around the world. Magellan led this first successful effort to **circumnavigate** the earth. **page 101**

Chapter Timeline

1271
Marco Polo goes to China

1270 | 1320 | 1370 | 1420

Background

Nautical Terms

Tell students that as they read this chapter, they will find nautical terms:

- *voyage,* p. 85
- *navigation, astrolabe, compass,* p. 91
- *caravel,* p. 92
- *fleet,* p. 93
- *crew,* p. 91
- *circumnavigate,* p. 101

Explain that nautical terms are words having to do with sailors, ships, or navigation.

Vocabulary

Use the frame game to help students understand vocabulary.

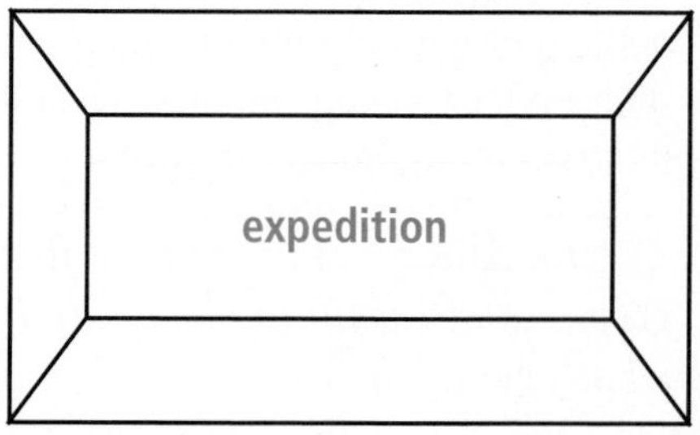

Reading Strategy

Monitor and Clarify Use this strategy to check your understanding of the events in this chapter.

Quick Tip If you are confused about events in a lesson, reread or read ahead.

expedition

Francisco Vazquez de Coronado led an **expedition** into present-day Arizona and New Mexico. He hoped to find wealth for Spain and for himself. **page 104**

colony

Spanish explorers took land in present-day Mexico for Spain. Settlers built towns and farmed in this **colony.** **page 112**

1492 Columbus reaches West Indies

1540 Coronado's explorations

1470 — 1520 — 1570

83

Using the Timeline

- Direct students to look at the timeline on pages 82 and 83. Point out that more than two centuries passed after Marco Polo's journey before Columbus reached the West Indies.
- Ask if any of the words on the timeline sound familiar; you may wish to make a list of familiar words to access students' prior knowledge of the events.

Reading Strategy: Monitor and Clarify

To monitor and clarify, the reader reviews the material after reading and draws out important information. The reader also asks questions about the material, to determine what he or she understands or needs clarification on.

Explain to students that to monitor and clarify successfully, they should follow these steps:

- Read the passage.
- Think about what the passage says.
- Ask yourself: What is important about this passage?
- Review the passage.
- Ask yourself: Does this passage make sense? Am I learning what I think I should be learning?
- If you don't understand something, reread, read ahead, or use the headings, graphic organizers, illustrations, and captions.

Students can practice this reading strategy throughout this chapter, including on their Skill and Strategy pages in their Practice Book.

Reaching All Learners: Leveled Practice

Extra Support

Help students find the words being defined in the sentences on each of the four cards. Discuss what each word means; then ask students to write a definition in their own words. **Verbal-linguistic**

Challenge

Ask students to write a journal entry from the point of view of a sailor whose ship is on a long voyage of exploration. Students can share their writing with small groups or with the class. **Verbal-linguistic**

Reaching All Learners: ELL

All Proficiency Levels

- Have students work in pairs to create an illustrated story about an expedition.
- One student may write the text, and the other draw the pictures.
- Place the illustrated stories in the class reading center for others to enjoy.

Visual-spatial

Tested Objectives

U2-1 History Describe Chinese trade, inventions, and exploration from the 1200s through the 1400s.

U2-2 Geography Identify West African trading kingdoms and trade routes.

Lesson Quick Look

This lesson talks about early trade between countries of Europe, Asia, and Africa, and how the exchange of goods and ideas changed the cultures of these countries.

Teaching Option: Extend Lesson 1 tells students more about the Silk Road and the Silk Road Project directed by cellist Yo-Yo Ma.

1 Get Set to Read

Preview Ask students to read the headings in this lesson. What do they think the lesson is about?

Reading Skill: Cause and Effect Students may note the availability of new goods and religious and cultural exchange.

Build on What You Know Ask students if they have ever traded something to get something else they wanted. How did they go about it?

Vocabulary

merchant *noun,* a person who makes money by buying and selling goods

kingdom *noun,* a country ruled by a king or queen

caravan *noun,* a group of travelers journeying together

Core Lesson 1

World Travel and Trade

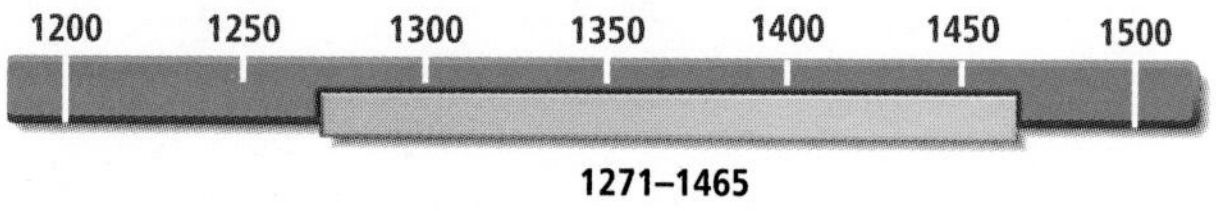

VOCABULARY

merchant
kingdom
caravan

Vocabulary Strategy

merchant

Trader is a synonym for **merchant.** To earn money, merchants trade goods that people want.

READING SKILL

Cause and Effect Note the effects that trade had on people in Europe, Asia, and Africa.

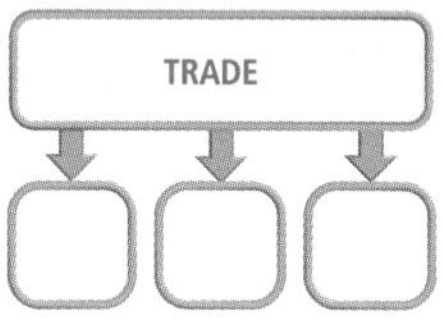

Build on What You Know Have you ever traded one thing for something you wanted more? Hundreds of years ago, people made long journeys to trade the goods they had for other goods they wanted.

Trade with China

Main Idea Trade between Europe and Asia spread new ideas.

Before 1500, there were few connections between the Eastern and the Western hemispheres. Most Europeans, Africans, and Asians did not know that the Americas existed. The Vikings, a group of people from northern Europe, had sailed to what is now eastern Canada and started a settlement there. The settlement did not last, however, and other Europeans didn't follow them. Some historians believe that African or Asian sailors may have also traveled to the Americas, but if they did, few people learned of the journeys.

Marco Polo Travels to China

The travelers to distant places were often merchants. A **merchant** is someone who buys and sells goods to earn money. In 1271, three merchants from Venice, Italy, began a trading journey to China. One of them was **Marco Polo**. He was only about 17 years old when he left Italy with his father and uncle. The journey to China took three years. 1

Marco Polo stayed in China for 16 years. He worked for China's ruler, **Kublai Khan** (KOO bly KAHN). While traveling in China, Marco Polo saw many inventions, such as paper, printing, and gunpowder. 2

Skill and Strategy

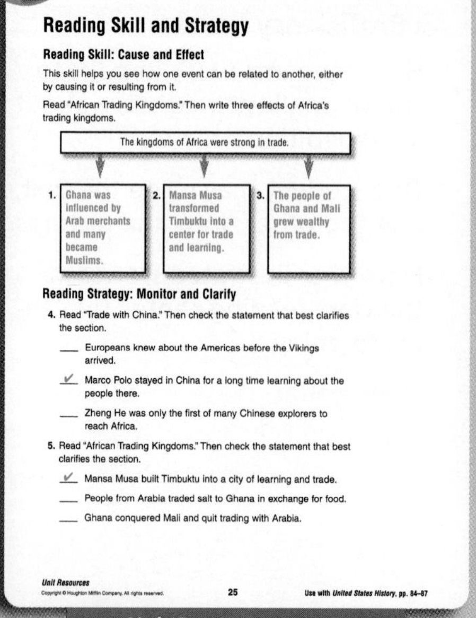

Reading Skill and Strategy

Reading Skill: Cause and Effect

This skill helps you see how one event can be related to another, either by causing it or resulting from it.

Read "African Trading Kingdoms." Then write three effects of Africa's trading kingdoms.

The kingdoms of Africa were strong in trade.

1. Ghana was influenced by Arab merchants and many became Muslims.
2. Mansa Musa transformed Timbuktu into a center for trade and learning.
3. The people of Ghana and Mali grew wealthy from trade.

Reading Strategy: Monitor and Clarify

4. Read "Trade with China." Then check the statement that best clarifies the section.

___ Europeans knew about the Americas before the Vikings arrived.

_✓_ Marco Polo stayed in China for a long time learning about the people there.

___ Zheng He was only the first of many Chinese explorers to reach Africa.

5. Read "African Trading Kingdoms." Then check the statement that best clarifies the section.

_✓_ Mansa Musa built Timbuktu into a city of learning and trade.

___ People from Arabia traded salt to Ghana in exchange for food.

___ Ghana conquered Mali and quit trading with Arabia.

Unit Resources

25

Use with *United States History*, pp. 84–87

Unit Resources, p. 25

Background

Marco Polo

- Marco Polo's accounts of what he saw in China inspired Europeans to travel to Asia.
- Marco Polo's stories are still widely read today, though people debate about whether the details in them are really accurate.

Traveling Merchants This illustration, made in the 1300s, shows Marco Polo and his family traveling by camel and horse on the Silk Road.

When Polo returned to Venice, he told about his travels in a book. His stories of China and the journey on the Silk Road fascinated Europeans. They became more interested in traveling to Asia.

3 The Silk Road was not one road, but several trade routes connecting China and Europe. Merchants traveled the routes to China to buy silk, spices, and other goods. The Chinese made silk, which is a very finely woven cloth. Wealthy Europeans were willing to pay high prices for silk. Merchants became rich by bringing goods from Asia to Europe on the Silk Road.

Chinese Sailors Explore

More than 100 years after Marco Polo visited China, the Chinese explored the world. The ruler of China wanted to impress other countries with China's power. He sent Admiral **Zheng He** (jung HUH) on a series of voyages. In 1405, Zheng He set sail with hundreds of ships and thousands of sailors. Some of the ships were longer than a football field.

Zheng He sailed throughout Southeast Asia and all the way to Africa's east coast. Zheng He traded goods, such as gold and silk, with the people he met. He once brought a giraffe from Africa back to China. 4

In 1434, a new ruler stopped Chinese exploration. He believed that China did not need to have contact with other countries. Zheng He's amazing voyages came to an end.

REVIEW What was the importance of the Silk Road? It connected China and Europe.

Zheng He The Chinese explorer sits on one of his boats.

Leveled Practice

Extra Support

Have students locate Eastern and Western hemispheres on a globe. Have them locate the continents mentioned in this lesson. Verbal-linguistic

Challenge

Have students look at a physical map of Europe and Asia. Ask them to **explain** what route they would take to travel from Venice to China, and why. Discuss possible challenges that merchants might have faced in the late 1200s. Visual-spatial

ELL

Beginning

Have students **illustrate** and label inventions, goods, and animals that Marco Polo and Admiral Zheng He saw on their voyages.

Visual-spatial

2 Teach

Trade with China

Talk About It

1 **Q History** Who was Marco Polo?

A He was a merchant from Venice who traveled to China in 1271.

2 **Q Technology** What inventions did Marco Polo see in China?

A He saw many inventions, such as paper, printing, and gunpowder.

3 **Q Economics** What was the Silk Road?

A It was the name for several trade routes connecting China and Europe.

4 **Q Geography** Where did Admiral Zheng He and his crew sail?

A throughout Southeast Asia and all the way to Africa's east coast

Vocabulary Strategy

merchant Discuss the related word *merchandise.* Explain that merchandise is goods bought or sold for a profit. A merchant buys or sells merchandise.

Reading Strategy: Monitor/Clarify

Explain to students that monitoring their reading helps them make sure that they understand the information before they move on to other material.

Think Aloud *The first section of this lesson talks about trade with China. I will monitor who the trading partners were, when they began to trade, what they traded, and why they wanted to trade.*

African Trading Kingdoms

Talk About It

5 **Q Economics** Why did people in Ghana trade gold for salt?

A They did not have enough salt, which was used to keep food from spoiling.

6 **Q Geography** In what kingdom was the city of Timbuktu located?

A Mali

7 **Q History** Who was Mansa Musa?

A He was a Muslim ruler who was Mali's greatest king.

Vocabulary Strategy

kingdom Tell students they can remember the meaning of this word by remembering that *-dom* is short for "domain," or "king's domain."

caravan Students may wish to remember that a caravan is a group of people who keep moving, like a car or a van.

Critical Thinking

Synthesis Why did the voyages of Marco Polo, Zheng He, and Mansa Musa spread learning among countries?

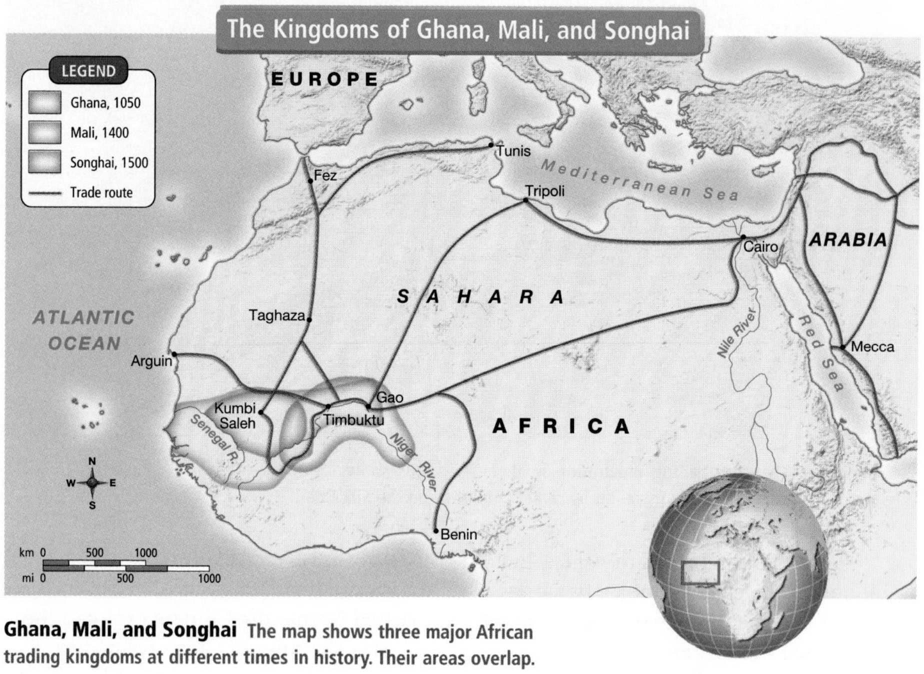

Ghana, Mali, and Songhai The map shows three major African trading kingdoms at different times in history. Their areas overlap.

SKILL **Reading Maps** Which kingdom covered the largest area? Mali

African Trading Kingdoms

Main Idea People in West Africa gained wealth and knowledge through trade.

Trade took place in Africa as well as in Europe and Asia. Several kingdoms in West Africa grew strong through trade. A **kingdom** is a place ruled by a king or queen.

The first West African trading kingdom was Ghana, which grew powerful in the 700s. Ghana was rich in gold, but did not
5 have enough salt. Salt was used to keep food from spoiling. Merchants from Arabia brought salt to Ghana by crossing the Sahara, the largest desert in the world.

This desert crossing was dangerous. For safety, merchants traveled in large caravans, using camels to carry their goods and supplies. A **caravan** is a group of people and animals who travel together. After reaching Ghana, the Arab merchants traded their salt for gold.

Arab merchants taught people in Ghana about their religion, Islam. Many people in Ghana became Muslims, or followers of Islam.

In 1234, the nearby kingdom of Mali conquered Ghana. Mali's cities became new centers for trade. One of its largest 6
and most important cities was Timbuktu (TIHM buhk TOO).

Art

Make a Stamp

- Ask students to make a postage stamp that depicts a journey taken by Marco Polo, Zheng He, or Mansa Musa.
- Stamps should reflect students' understanding of information from the lesson.
- Have students write paragraphs, explaining what their stamps show.

Visual-spatial

Language Arts

Write a Report

- Ask students to research one of the inventions Marco Polo saw in China or one of the scholars or artists that Mansa Musa brought back to Timbuktu.
- Have them write a report about the invention or person, including how the invention or person changed peoples' lives.

Verbal-linguistic

Mansa Musa

7 Mali's greatest king was the Muslim ruler, **Mansa Musa** (MAHN sah MOO sah). One person said that Mansa Musa was

> "the most powerful, the richest, the most fortunate, the most feared by his enemies, and the most able to do good to those around him."

In 1324, Mansa Musa traveled to Mecca, the most holy Muslim city in Arabia. He set up trade agreements with the cities he visited. When he returned to Mali, he brought scholars and artists from Arabia with him. They made Timbuktu a center for learning and art as well as trade.

Mali grew weaker after Mansa Musa's rule. A new kingdom called Songhai (SONG hy) took over much of Mali in 1468. For over one hundred years, Songhai continued the trade begun by the earlier kingdoms.

REVIEW What effect did trade with North Africa have on Ghana's culture? Many people in Ghana became Muslims.

Lesson Summary

Trade connected people in Europe, Asia, and Africa. Marco Polo, Zheng He, and Mansa Musa spread new ideas as well as goods. Their travels inspired others to explore even farther, seeking new trade routes and new knowledge.

Why It Matters . . .

Trade and travel brought the people of Asia, Europe, and Africa in contact with each other. Ideas and goods began to flow freely between them.

Mansa Musa
He brought hundreds of pounds of gold with him to Mecca to give away as gifts.

Lesson Review

1271 Marco Polo goes to China — 1324 Mansa Musa visits Mecca — 1405 Zheng He explores

1260 · 1290 · 1320 · 1350 · 1380 · 1410

1. **VOCABULARY** choose the correct words to complete this sentence.

   merchant **caravan** **kingdom**

   A ______ traveled in a ______ for safety and protection.

2. **READING SKILL** What **effect** did Mansa Musa's trip to Mecca have on Mali?
3. **MAIN IDEA: Culture** What did Europeans learn from Marco Polo's trip to China?
4. **MAIN IDEA: Economics** What did Ghana and Arabia trade with each other?
5. **PEOPLE TO KNOW** Why do you think **Marco Polo** is remembered today?
6. **TIMELINE SKILL** In what year did Mansa Musa visit Mecca?
7. **CRITICAL THINKING: Synthesize** Explain how trade increased connections among Europe, Asia, and Africa.

WRITING ACTIVITY What were some of the reasons that people traded with each other in Marco Polo's time and Mansa Musa's time? Write two paragraphs explaining your answer.

3 Review/Assess

Review Tested Objectives

U2-1 European merchants traveled to China to buy silk, spices, and other goods. Marco Polo saw Chinese inventions such as paper, printing, and gunpowder. Chinese explorer Zheng He sailed throughout Southeast Asia and all the way to Africa's east coast.

U2-2 Ghana, Mali, and Songhai traded with Arabian merchants. Their trade routes crossed the Sahara to Fez, Tunis, Tripoli, Cairo, and Mecca.

Lesson Review Answers

1. merchant; caravan
2. The scholars and artists who returned to Mali with Mansa Musa helped make Timbuktu a center of learning and art, as well as trade.
3. They learned about paper, printing, and gunpowder. They also learned about different trade routes to China, and about silk.
4. Ghana's gold for Arabian salt
5. He is remembered because he wrote a book about his travels to China, his 16-year stay there, and things he saw.
6. 1324
7. Trade between Europe and Asia and in Africa spread ideas and goods. More people became interested in traveling to the places they heard about from merchants.

Writing Rubric

4	Reasons are clearly stated and supported by information from the text; mechanics are correct.
3	Reasons are adequately stated; most reasons are supported by information from the text; few errors in mechanics.
2	Reasons are stated; reasons are confused or poorly supported by text information; some errors in mechanics.
1	Reasons are not stated; reasons are not supported; many errors in mechanics.

Study Guide/Homework

Vocabulary and Study Guide

Vocabulary

Use each pair of words in a sentence.

1. merchant/China Sample answer: A merchant could become wealthy by bringing silk and spices from China to Europe.
2. caravan/salt Sample answer: The merchant organized a large caravan to carry his salt to Ghana.
3. kingdom/trade Sample answer: Ghana is a kingdom in West Africa that grew strong through trade.

Study Guide

4. Read "Trade with China." Then fill in the blanks below.

   Marco Polo was a merchant from Italy who traveled to China. There he saw inventions such as paper, printing, and gunpowder. Many European merchants traveled along the trade routes of the Silk Road carrying silk and spices back to Europe. Later, Chinese explorers sailed to Africa in huge ships where they traded silk and gold.

Read "African Trading Kingdoms." Then fill in the chart below.

Trading kingdom	Trade route	Cultural effect
Ghana	5. To Arabia through Sahara Desert	7. Islamic religion spread to the people of Ghana.
Mali	6. To Mecca, Arabia	8. Timbuktu became a center of art and learning.

Unit Resources 26 Use with *United States History*, pp. 84–87

Unit Resources, p. 26

Reteach Minilesson

Compare the voyages of Marco Polo and Mansa Musa.

Marco Polo	Mansa Musa
Merchant	King of Mali
Traveled from Venice to China	Traveled from Mali to Mecca
Wrote a book about his journey	Brought scholars and artists back to Mali

Graphic Organizer 1

Extend

Quick Look

Connect to Core Lesson In the Core Lesson, students read about the exchange of goods and ideas between East and West during the 1400s. In Extend Lesson 1, students will learn more about one of the most important trade routes, the Silk Road.

1 Teach the Extend Lesson

Connect to the Big Idea

Trade and Money/Location People and nations gained through trade along the Silk Road. Travelers on the Silk Road helped to spread culture, diseases, ideas, plants, and animals between locations in Asia and Europe.

Extend Lesson 1

Geography

The Silk Road

Eight hundred years ago, silk and spices from China traveled by caravan on the Silk Road. The Silk Road was a series of trade routes between Europe and Asia. Merchants traded goods, especially Chinese silks, in hopes of earning a profit. European traders often paid for silks with gold, because they had no goods the Chinese wanted.

The Silk Road was dangerous. It ran beside the hot, dry Taklamakan Desert and crossed high mountains. Merchants risked thirst, hunger, and attacks by bandits.

Reaching All Learners

Extra Support

Use the Map

Instruct students to use the map on pages 88–89 to answer the following questions:

- Where did the Silk Road begin and end? Antioch or Tyre on the Mediterranean Sea and Luoyang, China.
- What rivers does the Silk Road cross? Tigris, Euphrates, Huang He
- Approximately how many miles was the journey between Merv and Baghdad? about 1250 miles

Visual-spatial; logical-mathematical

On Level

Create a Map

- Have students create a large map (mural style) showing a portion of the Silk Road.
- Ask them to show relative distances between the towns, as well as the terrain (desert, mountains, etc.).
- They may need to do research in the library or on the Internet before beginning this project.

Visual-spatial; logical-mathematical

Challenge

Write a Report

- Have students use library resources or the Internet to find out more about the Silk Road, especially the scientific ideas or inventions that were exchanged between East and West.
- Ask them to write a one- or two-page report describing their findings.

Verbal-linguistic; logical-mathematical

GEOGRAPHY

Yo-Yo Ma and the Silk Road Project

Today, the Silk Road continues to inspire new discoveries. Yo-Yo Ma, a Chinese American cellist, directs the Silk Road Project. The project builds cultural understanding by performing the music that is still played along the Silk Road. He says, "We live in a world where we can no longer afford not to know our neighbors. The Silk Road Project is a musical way to get to know our neighbors."

Activities

1. **LOCATE IT** Look closely at the map. Trace a route from Beijing to Antioch. Find the distance in miles and kilometers between the two cities.
2. **WRITE IT** Write a dialogue between two merchants who have just arrived in Rome. Have them describe where they traveled on the Silk Road.

89

2 Leveled Activities

1 Locate It *For Extra Support*
Answers will vary based on route taken.

2 Write It *For Challenge*

Writing Rubric

4	Dialogue is well organized and shows considerable creative effort; mechanics are correct; facts are accurate.
3	Dialogue is adequately organized and shows creative effort; few errors in mechanics; facts are mostly accurate.
2	Dialogue is somewhat organized and shows some creative effort; some errors in mechanics; some factual errors.
1	Dialogue is disorganized and shows little effort; many errors in mechanics; many factual errors.

ELL

REACHING ALL LEARNERS

Intermediate/Advanced

- Ask students to choose one city along the Silk Road. Have them use the library or Internet resources to find out more about that city.
- Ask them to illustrate a scene in that city, showing the people who lived there. They should also include a caption describing their illustration.

Visual-spatial; verbal-linguistic

Math

Calculate Distances

- Ask students to research the distances in miles between the cities on the Silk Road. Have them write down their findings.
- Have students calculate the entire length of the Silk Road.
- If they were to travel one-third the length of the Silk Road, where would they be? Where would they be if they traveled two-thirds the distance?

Logical-mathematical

Graphic Organizer

Cause

The Silk Road spanned the width of Asia.

Effect	Effect	Effect
Goods were traded more than once from one end of the Silk Road to the other.	Merchants learned about Asian peoples, lands, religions, and scientific inventions.	The terrain along the Silk Road changed often.

Graphic Organizer 8

Core Lesson 2 **Pages 90–91**

Tested Objectives

U2-3 Technology Describe new ideas and technology in Europe and their effects on overseas exploration.

U2-4 History Summarize the achievements of early Portuguese exploration around Africa.

Lesson Quick Look

This lesson talks about changes in technology during the Renaissance, and the Portuguese discovery of a sea route around Africa to Asia.

Teaching Option: Extend Lesson 2 tells students more about the caravel, the astrolabe, and the compass.

1 Get Set to Read

Preview Ask students what countries and cities appear on the map on page 92.

Reading Skill: Problem and Solution Problems might include inaccurate navigation and fear of new places; solutions might include the astrolabe and gunpowder.

Build on What You Know Have students share their ideas about how recent inventions have changed their lives. Explain that in the 1400s, some new inventions helped Europeans find ways to reach Asia by sea.

Vocabulary

technology *noun,* the use of scientific knowledge and tools to solve problems

navigation *noun,* the science of planning and controlling the direction of a ship

astrolabe *noun,* an instrument once used by sailors for navigation

profit *noun,* money left over after all expenses have been paid

slavery *noun,* a system in which people could be bought and sold and were forced to work with no pay

Core Lesson 2

New Ideas in Europe

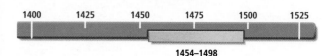

1400 1425 1450 1475 1500 1525

1454–1498

VOCABULARY

technology
navigation
astrolabe
profit
slavery

Vocabulary Strategy

navigation

To remember **navigation,** think of the word "navy." A navy uses navigation to know where to sail.

READING SKILL

Problem and Solution

Portuguese explorers faced a problem in trying to get to Asia. Find their solution.

PROBLEM	SOLUTION

Build on What You Know Are there any recent inventions that are important in your life? How do you use them? Europeans in the 1400s used new inventions to find sea routes to Asia.

The Renaissance

Main Idea New learning spread through Europe, leading to better tools for sailors and explorers.

Important changes took place in Europe during the 1300s and 1400s. This period of time was called the Renaissance (REN nuh sahnce), which means rebirth. 1 The Renaissance was a rebirth in learning and knowledge. Europeans took new interest in the writing, art, science, and ideas of the ancient Greeks and Romans. They also learned from people in Africa and Asia.

During the Renaissance, technology in Europe changed. **Technology** is the use of scientific knowledge and tools to do things better and more rapidly. The printing press was an example of new technology. Developed in 1454 by **Johannes Gutenberg,** the printing 2 press made it possible to print many copies of a page of type quickly. Before the printing press, people had to copy books by hand. The printing press allowed books and ideas to spread across Europe.

Printing Press Books were printed by pressing one page at a time.

Skill and Strategy

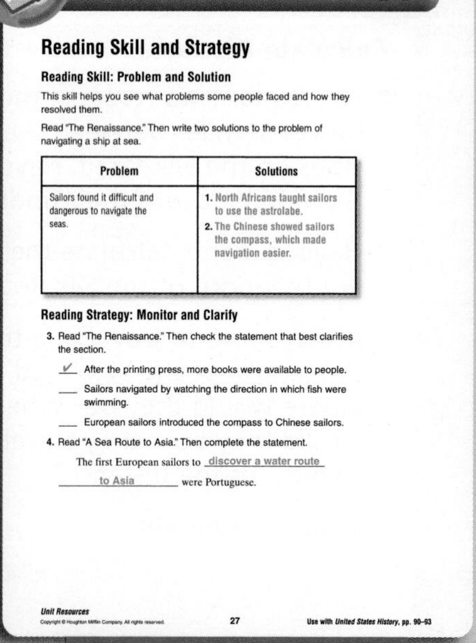

Reading Skill and Strategy

Reading Skill: Problem and Solution

This skill helps you see what problems some people faced and how they resolved them.

Read "The Renaissance." Then write two solutions to the problem of navigating a ship at sea.

Problem	Solutions
Sailors found it difficult and dangerous to navigate the seas.	1. North Africans taught sailors to use the astrolabe. 2. The Chinese showed sailors the compass, which made navigation easier.

Reading Strategy: Monitor and Clarify

3. Read "The Renaissance." Then check the statement that best clarifies the section.

✓ After the printing press, more books were available to people.

___ Sailors navigated by watching the direction in which fish were swimming.

___ European sailors introduced the compass to Chinese sailors.

4. Read "A Sea Route to Asia." Then complete the statement.

The first European sailors to discover a water route to Asia were Portuguese.

Unit Resources

27 Use with *United States History*, pp. 90–93

Unit Resources, p. 27

Background

Leonardo da Vinci

- Leonardo da Vinci was one of the most famous people of the Renaissance. He was a painter and inventor who kept notebooks filled with sketches of people, animals, and machines.

Sea Exploration New technologies helped European explorers travel farther than ever before. Find the sailor who is using an astrolabe. (left)

New Knowledge for Sailors

New technology also helped European exploration by making navigation easier and more accurate. **Navigation** is the science of planning and controlling the direction of a ship.

3 Europeans learned about a navigation tool called the astrolabe from North Africans. An **astrolabe** is a tool that measures the height of the sun or a star above the horizon. Using an astrolabe, sailors could tell how far north or south of home they were.

European sailors learned about the compass from the Chinese. A compass is an instrument with a magnetic needle that always points to the north.

Chinese sailors did not have to depend on the sun or the stars to tell them which direction they were traveling. They could use a compass to check whether they were heading north, south, east, or west.

Another Chinese invention that helped European sailors was gunpowder. Sailors used gunpowder in weapons such as guns and cannons. Cannons defended their ships. Guns gave sailors confidence that they could protect themselves if they were attacked or in danger on land.

REVIEW What did new technology do to make exploration easier?
New tools made it easier for sailors to find their way on the sea.

91

2 Teach

The Renaissance

Talk About It

1 **Q History** What was the Renaissance?
A It was a period during the 1300s and 1400s when a rebirth of learning took place in Europe.

2 **Q Technology** What invention did Johannes Gutenberg develop?
A He developed a printing press that could print many copies of a page quickly.

3 **Q Technology** From whom did Europeans learn about the astrolabe?
A North Africans

Vocabulary Strategy

technology Have students think of other words ending in *-logy,* such as *biology* and *anthropology.* Explain that this suffix often refers to the study of a subject.

navigation Point out the related words *navigate* and *navigator.*

astrolabe Tell students that the prefix *astro-* means "star or heavenly body."

Reading Strategy: Monitor/Clarify After students read the first section of the lesson, ask them if anything they read did not make sense to them. Help them look back in the text and find the answers.

Pronunciation Help

Astrolabe: AS tro LABE

Leveled Practice

Reaching All Learners

Extra Support

Have students make a Renaissance technology **word web.** Their webs might include *printing press, astrolabe, compass,* and *gunpowder.* Ask students to discuss what each invention helped people do.
Visual-spatial; verbal-linguistic

Challenge

Ask students to learn more about a painter or sculptor from the Renaissance. Then have them **write a profile** of that artist's life and accomplishments. Encourage them to illustrate their reports.
Verbal-linguistic; visual-spatial

ELL

Reaching All Learners

Beginning

- Introduce the word *technology* by showing students a pair of binoculars. Explain how science of magnification makes binoculars a useful tool—a kind of technology.
- Have students find words from the lesson that could be considered tools of technology in the Renaissance.

Bodily-kinesthetic

A Sea Route to Asia

Talk About It

4 Q Economics Why did European countries want to find a sea route to Asia?

A Merchants believed that they would make larger profits if they found a sea route because it would be faster and they could trade more goods.

5 Q Technology Why did the caravel improve sailing technology?

A The small, light ship had triangular sails and could sail into the wind, unlike other European ships.

6 Q History Who were Bartolomeu Dias and Vasco da Gama?

A They were Portuguese explorers. Dias proved it was possible to sail around Africa and reach its east coast. Da Gama led the first Portuguese voyage to reach India.

Vocabulary Strategy

profit Tell students they can remember the meaning of this word by thinking that a *profit* keeps a business "fit." The extra money from a profit can be used to improve the business.

slavery Point out the related word *enslaved.*

Critical Thinking

Compare and Contrast What were the similarities and differences in traveling by caravan and caravel?

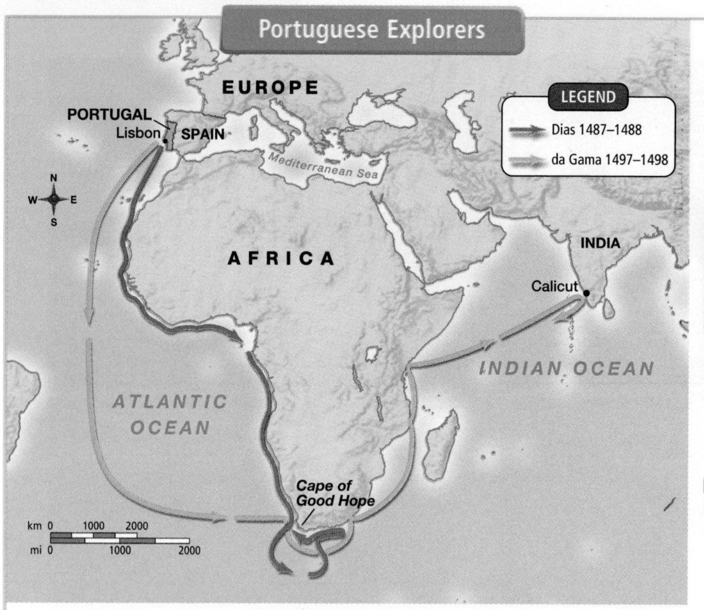

A New Route to Asia Vasco da Gama (above) used the knowledge gained by Bartolomeu Dias.

SKILL Reading Maps Which explorer sailed the farthest? da Gama

A Sea Route to Asia

Main Idea Portuguese explorers were the first Europeans to find a sea route to Asia.

4 Merchants believed that they would make more money if they found a sea route to Asia. In Asia, merchants bought spices such as pepper, and earned a profit by selling them for a higher price in Europe. A **profit** is the money a business has left over after all of its expenses have been paid.

A sea route to Asia was thousands of miles longer than the Silk Road, but the sea trip would be faster. The country that found a sea route to Asia could trade more goods than countries that used the slow-moving caravans of the Silk Road.

Portugal was the first European country to find a sea route to Asia. Portugal is a small European country. Portugal's location and coastline made it a good starting place for sailors. The Portuguese thought they could reach Asia by sailing around the southern tip of Africa. From there, they hoped to sail up Africa's east coast and find a route to India and China.

Prince Henry of Portugal created a school for navigation. He brought shipbuilders, mapmakers, and sea captains to Sagres (SAH grehsh), Portugal. They shared their knowledge of navigation and sailing. People at Sagres improved sailing 5
technology by creating the caravel. This small, light ship had triangular sails. Caravels were good for exploring. They could sail into the wind, unlike other European ships. Because he encouraged exploration, Prince Henry became known as "the Navigator," even though he didn't go on any voyages.

Music

Write Renaissance Lyrics

Music, like all art forms, changed during the Renaissance. Ask students to use information from the text to write lyrics for a song about the Renaissance.

Musical-auditory

Language Arts

Write a Scene

Have students work in small groups to write a scene set during the Renaissance. The piece should show a group of Europeans talking about a new invention or trade route. Have students choose a cast of characters, create a setting, and write down dialogue.

Verbal-linguistic

Dias and da Gama

Portuguese sailors' early voyages went south along Africa's west coast. In 1448, Portugal set up a trading post in West Africa. Portuguese traders forced Africans there into slavery and sold them in Europe. **Slavery** is a cruel system in which people are bought and sold and made to work without pay. Slavery had existed before the Portuguese arrived, but the Portuguese increased the number of enslaved people brought to Europe.

In 1487, **Bartolomeu Dias** (bart OH lo MEH oo DEE ahs) was exploring the coast of West Africa when a fierce storm blew his ships off course. When the storm ended, Dias realized he had actually sailed around the southern tip of Africa. The Portuguese named the tip of Africa the Cape of Good Hope. Dias proved that it was possible to sail around Africa and reach its east coast. From Africa's east coast, ships could then sail east to India.

Vasco da Gama led the first Portuguese voyage to reach India. In 1497, his fleet reached the Indian port of Calicut. Other Portuguese sailors soon followed da Gama's route to India and used it for spice trading. 6

REVIEW Why was sailing around the Cape of Good Hope important? Dias proved it was possible to sail from Portugal to India.

Lesson Summary

During the Renaissance, Europeans used new navigation tools. This technology helped them find faster ways to trade goods with Asia. Portuguese sailors, such as Vasco da Gama, sailed around Africa to reach Asia.

Why It Matters . . .

The search for a sea route to Asia led to important discoveries in navigation and geography.

Lesson Review

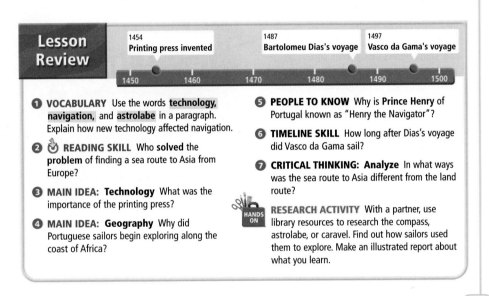

1454 Printing press invented
1487 Bartolomeu Dias's voyage
1497 Vasco da Gama's voyage

1450 | 1460 | 1470 | 1480 | 1490 | 1500

1. **VOCABULARY** Use the words **technology, navigation,** and **astrolabe** in a paragraph. Explain how new technology affected navigation.
2. **READING SKILL** Who **solved** the **problem** of finding a sea route to Asia from Europe?
3. **MAIN IDEA: Technology** What was the importance of the printing press?
4. **MAIN IDEA: Geography** Why did Portuguese sailors begin exploring along the coast of Africa?
5. **PEOPLE TO KNOW** Why is **Prince Henry** of Portugal known as "Henry the Navigator"?
6. **TIMELINE SKILL** How long after Dias's voyage did Vasco da Gama sail?
7. **CRITICAL THINKING: Analyze** In what ways was the sea route to Asia different from the land route?

HANDS ON **RESEARCH ACTIVITY** With a partner, use library resources to research the compass, astrolabe, or caravel. Find out how sailors used them to explore. Make an illustrated report about what you learn.

3 Review/Assess

Review Tested Objectives

U2-3 The printing press helped spread learning throughout Europe. New inventions made sea exploration easier, faster, and safer.

U2-4 Portuguese explorers were the first Europeans to prove that it was possible to sail around Africa to Asia.

Lesson Review Answers

1. Paragraphs should show an understanding that the astrolabe was new technology that aided navigation.
2. Bartolomeu Dias and Vasco de Gama
3. It allowed books and the ideas within them to spread across Europe.
4. They wanted to find a sea route to Asia by sailing around the southern tip of Africa.
5. He created a school for navigation and encouraged exploration.
6. 10 years
7. The sea route was thousands of miles longer but also faster than the land route.

HANDS ON Performance Task Rubric

4	Report is clearly written and informative; mechanics are correct.
3	Report is adequately written and informative; most mechanics are correct.
2	Report is somewhat unclear or disorganized; some errors in mechanics are present.
1	Report does not reflect any research; many errors in mechanics are present.

Study Guide/Homework

Vocabulary and Study Guide

Vocabulary

Write the definition of each vocabulary word below.

1. technology Use of science to do things better
2. navigation The science of planning a ship's journey
3. astrolabe A tool that measures the height of the sun over the horizon
4. profit Money left over after expenses are paid
5. slavery The cruel system of owning people
6. Use two words in a sentence.
Sample answer: The astrolabe helped improve ship navigation.

Study Guide

Read "New Knowledge for Sailors." Then fill in the chart below.

Cause	Effect
Invention of the compass	7. Sailors did not have to depend on the sun and stars to guide them.
8. Invention of gunpowder	Gave sailors confidence to travel to new places.

Read "A Sea Route to Asia." Then answer the questions.

9. What made Portugal a good starting place for sailors?
Its location and coastline
10. What did Bartolomeu Dias do to affect Portugal's trade routes?
He proved that it was possible to sail around the southern tip of Africa.
11. Who led the first Portuguese voyage to India? Vasco da Gama

Unit Resources

28
Use with *United States History*, pp. 90–93

Unit Resources, p. 28

Reteach Minilesson

Use a cause-and-effect chart to reteach Renaissance technology and exploration.

New inventions created
↓
Exploration and trade become easier, faster, safer.
↓
New trade routes discovered; new goods imported; slave trade increases.

www.eduplace.com/ss/hmss05/

Extend

Quick Look

Connect to Core Lesson In the Core Lesson, students read about new technology that helped European explorers in the 1400s. In Extend Lesson 2, students will find out more about three of these inventions—the caravel, the astrolabe, and the compass.

1 Teach the Extend Lesson

Connect to the Big Idea

Human Systems Human systems and activities, such as technological innovation, cause places to change over time. The caravel, astrolabe, and the compass were innovations that helped people travel around the world.

Technology

Tools for Discovery

In 1420, the oceans of the world were a mystery to most Europeans. Sailors told stories of monsters and boiling seas. Portuguese explorers soon showed that those stories were false. They used new inventions and new ship designs and traveled farther than before.

Ship captains sailed with the latest maps and with new navigations tools, including the compass and astrolabe. Later inventions, such as the sextant and the chronometer, made navigation even better.

Also, shipbuilders designed a ship that was small, light, and easy to control. Because it could sail in shallow water, explorers could travel near coastlines and up rivers. Improvements also made it possible for explorers to sail over long distances. This ship, the *Santa Maria*, could cross the Atlantic Ocean.

Crew
Most of the space on a ship was used for equipment and supplies. In good weather, the crew could sleep on the deck, but if the weather was bad they slept in the storage rooms.

Reaching All Learners

Extra Support

Make a Chart

Have students use a two-column chart to note each invention and its purposes.

- Ask them to list inventions in the left column.
- For each invention, have students list its purpose in the right column.
- Ask students to share their charts with the class.

Verbal-linguistic; visual-spatial

On Level

Make a Model

- Ask students to make a three-dimensional model of one of the inventions described in this Extend Lesson. They may use cardboard, paper, wood, or other materials as available.
- Students may want to use library resources or the Internet to find more images of the inventions before they begin work on their model.

Visual-spatial; bodily-kinesthetic

Challenge

Write a Scene

- Have students find out more about the stories Europeans of the early 1400s told about the dangers of traveling on the ocean.
- Then, ask students to write a dramatic scene showing sailors telling some of these stories to others.
- Have small groups of students choose parts and act their scene aloud for the class.

Verbal-linguistic; bodily-kinesthetic

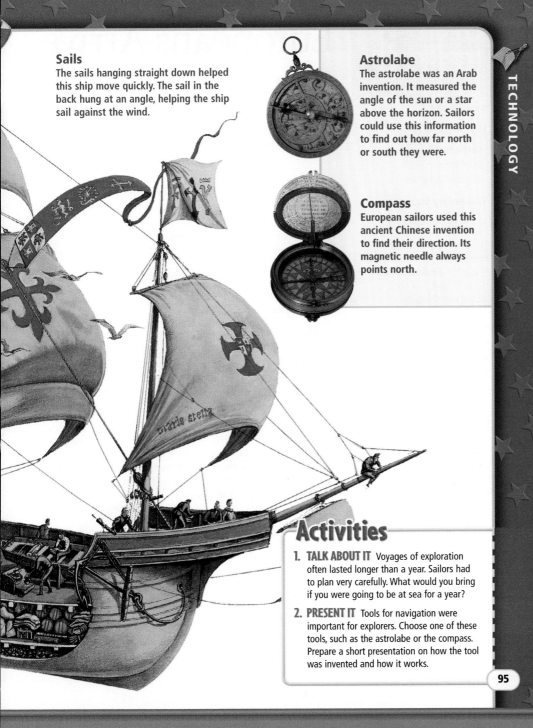

Sails
The sails hanging straight down helped this ship move quickly. The sail in the back hung at an angle, helping the ship sail against the wind.

Astrolabe
The astrolabe was an Arab invention. It measured the angle of the sun or a star above the horizon. Sailors could use this information to find out how far north or south they were.

Compass
European sailors used this ancient Chinese invention to find their direction. Its magnetic needle always points north.

TECHNOLOGY

Activities

1. **TALK ABOUT IT** Voyages of exploration often lasted longer than a year. Sailors had to plan very carefully. What would you bring if you were going to be at sea for a year?
2. **PRESENT IT** Tools for navigation were important for explorers. Choose one of these tools, such as the astrolabe or the compass. Prepare a short presentation on how the tool was invented and how it works.

95

2 Leveled Activities

❶ **Talk About It** *For Extra Support*
I would bring plenty of food that did not spoil easily. I would bring a lot of fresh water, and clothing.

❷ **Present It** *For Challenge*

HANDS ON Performance Task Rubric

4	Presentation is well organized; conveys ideas clearly; facts are accurate.
3	Presentation is adequately organized; conveys ideas adequately; most facts cited are accurate.
2	Presentation is somewhat organized; conveys ideas adequately; some factual errors.
1	Presentation is disorganized; conveys ideas in a very general or incomprehensible way; many errors.

ELL

Intermediate

- Have students make vocabulary cards for unfamiliar or difficult words in the lesson.
- Ask them to write each word down on an index card.
- On the back of each card, have students write down the dictionary definition of the word. Students may also wish to draw a picture to help them remember what the word means.
- Students can use their cards as study aids.

Verbal-linguistic; visual-spatial

Science

Report on Navigation

- Before the Europeans started using the astrolabe and compass, sailors had to rely on the sun, stars, and other celestial bodies to find direction at sea.
- Ask students to use library resources or the Internet to learn more about how sailors navigated using celestial bodies.
- Have students write a short report about their findings.

Logical-mathematical; verbal-linguistic

Graphic Organizer

K	W	L
I know that . . .	I want to learn . . .	I have learned . . .

Graphic Organizer 2

Tested Objectives

U2-5 History Describe and evaluate the significance of Columbus's voyages to the Americas.

U2-6 History Identify early European explorations, including Magellan's voyage to circumnavigate the earth.

Lesson Quick Look

This lesson discusses European exploration of the Americas and the effect these explorations had on the peoples of both continents.

Teaching Option: **Extend Lesson 3** tells students more about world maps created during the 1500s.

1 Get Set to Read

Preview Ask students to look at the map on page 97. What does it show?

Reading Skill: Compare and Contrast Similarities might include wealth as motivator; differences might include route taken.

Build on What You Know Ask students how they would feel if they had to eat bland food all the time. Explain that in the 1400s, most Europeans did not have spices such as pepper to flavor food.

Vocabulary

epidemic *noun,* an outbreak of disease that makes many people sick at once

settlement *noun,* a small community of people in a frontier region

circumnavigate *noun,* to sail all the way around something

Core Lesson 3

Europeans Arrive in the Americas

VOCABULARY

settlement
epidemic
circumnavigate

Vocabulary Strategy

circumnavigate

The prefix **circum-** comes from a word that means "circle." To **circumnavigate** means to travel in a circle around something.

READING SKILL

Compare and Contrast
List ways in which the voyages of the explorers in this lesson were alike and different.

ALIKE	DIFFERENT

Build on What You Know Many people today like spicy food. In the 1400s, European countries had very few spices. Europeans traveled far to bring spices and other riches back to Europe from distant lands.

Christopher Columbus

Main Idea Christopher Columbus sailed to the islands of the West Indies trying to reach Asia.

Christopher Columbus was born in 1451 near Genoa, in Italy. Columbus studied navigation and believed he could reach Asia by a new route. He wanted to sail west across the Atlantic Ocean, instead of south around Africa. He did not know that North and South America were between Europe and Asia. 1

In 1486, Columbus asked **King Ferdinand** and **Queen Isabella** of Spain to pay for a westward voyage to Asia. Ferdinand and Isabella didn't have money for exploration at that time. They were fighting to take back southern Spain from North African Muslims, who had ruled the region for 700 years. Spain's attempt to push the Muslims out was called the Spanish Reconquista (reh con KEY sta).

Christopher Columbus This explorer wanted to find a new route to India.

Skill and Strategy

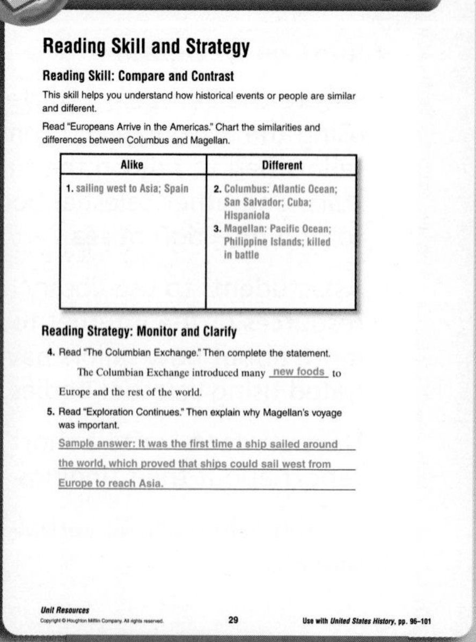

Reading Skill and Strategy

Reading Skill: Compare and Contrast

This skill helps you understand how historical events or people are similar and different.

Read "Europeans Arrive in the Americas." Chart the similarities and differences between Columbus and Magellan.

Alike	Different
1. sailing west to Asia; Spain	2. Columbus: Atlantic Ocean; San Salvador; Cuba; Hispaniola 3. Magellan: Pacific Ocean; Philippine Islands; killed in battle

Reading Strategy: Monitor and Clarify

4. Read "The Columbian Exchange." Then complete the statement.

The Columbian Exchange introduced many new foods to Europe and the rest of the world.

5. Read "Exploration Continues." Then explain why Magellan's voyage was important.

Sample answer: It was the first time a ship sailed around the world, which proved that ships could sail west from Europe to reach Asia.

Unit Resources

29
Use with *United States History*, pp. 96–101

Unit Resources, p. 29

Background

Columbus and the Taíno

- Some words that English speakers use today, such as *hammock*, originally came from the Taíno language.
- Columbus Day is a national holiday in the United States. The holiday falls in the second week of October.

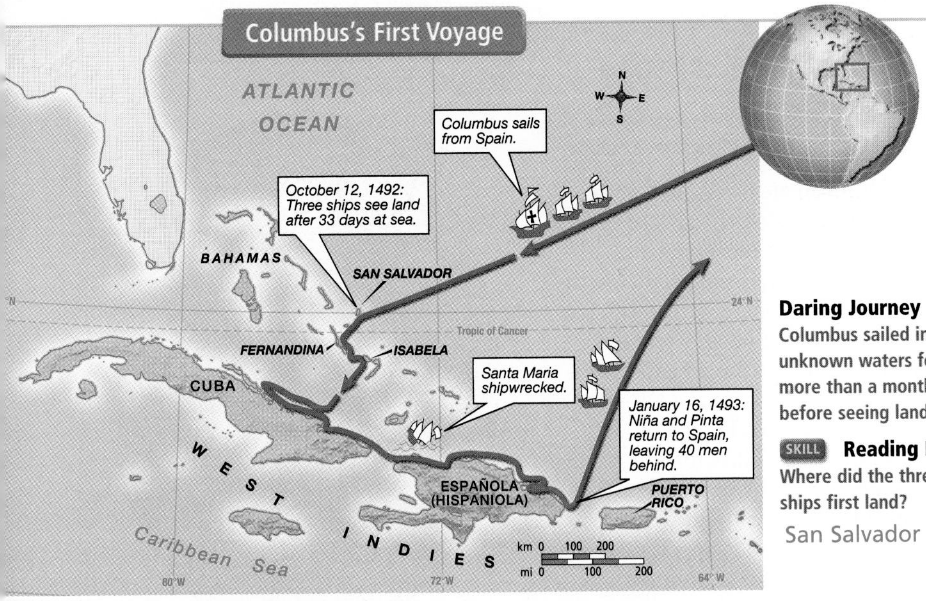

Daring Journey
Columbus sailed into unknown waters for more than a month before seeing land.

SKILL **Reading Maps** Where did the three ships first land?
San Salvador

Columbus Sails West

Six years later, in 1492, Columbus again asked Ferdinand and Isabella for money. This time they agreed. Spain had
2 won the Reconquista and needed to pay for it. Ferdinand and Isabella hoped to make money from the gold and spices they believed Columbus would find in Asia. They also wanted to teach others about their religion, Roman Catholicism.

Columbus set sail from Palos, Spain, on August 3, 1492. He carried enough supplies for a year. Close to 90 men traveled in three ships named the Niña, the Pinta, and the Santa María. The sailors did not know how long the trip would take or where they would land. Shortly after midnight on October 12, 1492, a sailor aboard the Pinta saw land.

The ships had arrived at an island in the Caribbean Sea that Columbus named San Salvador. This island is part of the present-day Bahamas, east of Mexico.

Columbus mistakenly believed he had reached land off the coast of Asia, near India. He named the islands the West Indies and the people living on them Indians.

The sailors on this expedition were the first Europeans to meet people of the Caribbean. These people called themselves the Taíno (TY noh), which means "good." The Taíno were peaceful and fought only to defend their villages from attacks. More than 600,000 Taíno lived in the Caribbean at the time of Columbus's visit. 3

After meeting the Taíno and trading with them, Columbus sailed on with his crew. They visited two other large islands, Cuba and Hispaniola, before returning home.

REVIEW Why did Ferdinand and Isabella finally agree to give Columbus money for his voyage in 1492?
They needed money to pay for the Spanish Reconquista.

97

2 Teach

Christopher Columbus

Talk About It

1 **Q Geography** How did Columbus plan to reach Asia?
A by sailing west across the Atlantic Ocean instead of south around Africa

2 **Q History** What did King Ferdinand and Queen Isabella hope to gain from Columbus's journey?
A They wanted to make money from the Asian gold and spices they hoped he would find; they also wanted to spread Roman Catholicism.

3 **Q History** Who did Columbus and his crew meet in the Caribbean?
A the Taíno

Reading Strategy: Monitor/Clarify Have students read the first page, stopping at the end of each paragraph. Ask them to explain what the paragraph was about. If they do not understand something, review the paragraph. If their question is not answered, show them how to read on to find the answer.

REACHING ALL LEARNERS

Leveled Practice

Extra Support

Have students use the dates mentioned on pages 96 and 97 to **create a timeline** of Christopher Columbus's life. Students may wish to illustrate their timelines.
Visual-spatial

Challenge

Columbus had to persuade King Ferdinand and Queen Isabella to give him the money for his journey in 1492. Ask students to **write a persuasive essay** asking for money to accomplish something that they badly want to do.
Verbal-linguistic

REACHING ALL LEARNERS

ELL

Advanced

- Working in small groups, have students retell the story of Columbus's first voyage.
- Students should establish the setting of their story and try to use dialogue. Encourage them to tell their story to the class.

Verbal-linguistic; bodily-kinesthetic

The Columbian Exchange

Talk About It

4 Q Geography Which parts of the Americas did Columbus reach?

A the coasts of Central and South America, and islands in the West Indies, including Hispaniola

5 Q History In what ways was the arrival of Europeans in the West harmful?

A Europeans cut down rain forests on Caribbean islands; many American plants and animals were destroyed; many Taíno died from diseases that the Europeans brought over.

6 Q History What was the Columbian Exchange?

A the movement of plants, animals, and people between the Eastern and Western Hemispheres

Vocabulary Strategy

settlement Discuss the related words *settle* and *settler*. Explain that a *settler* can *settle*, or decide to live, in a new *settlement*.

epidemic Tell students that a synonym for this word is *outbreak*.

Critical Thinking

Cause and Effect How did the Columbian Exchange affect Europeans? You may wish to model for your students the process of thinking through this question.

Think Aloud *Europeans got new foods from America. This probably made them healthier. Some Europeans must have made money selling American goods. In general, I think Europeans benefited from the Columbian Exchange.*

The Columbian Exchange

Main Idea Columbus carried new plants and animals to and from the Americas and Europe.

4 Columbus made three more voyages to the Caribbean and the coasts of Central and South America. Ferdinand and Isabella wanted him to start settlements and to search for gold. A **settlement** is a small community of people living in a new place. Columbus sailed a fleet of 17 ships back to the island of Hispaniola. He also explored and claimed more islands in the West Indies for Spain.

Columbus and the settlers with him brought ships filled with horses, cows, pigs, wheat, barley, and sugar cane plants to the Western Hemisphere. These animals and plants did not live in the Americas before Columbus brought them there. Some European crops were able to grow in places

5 where local crops could not.

The arrival of Europeans in the West Indies had many harmful effects. Europeans cut down rain forests on Caribbean islands and built sugar plantations. Many American plants and animals were destroyed. The Europeans also brought diseases that the Taíno had never had before. Many Taíno died from epidemics. An **epidemic** is an outbreak of disease that spreads quickly and affects many people. Within 50 years of Columbus's arrival, almost no Taíno people were left.

Columbus returned to Spain with plants no one in Europe had seen. These included maize (corn), peanuts, potatoes, tomatoes, cacao (chocolate), and certain peppers, beans, and squashes.

Columbus Lands This woodcut from the 1500s shows Columbus meeting the Taíno people in the Caribbean.

This movement of plants, animals, and people between the Eastern and Western Hemispheres is known as the Columbian Exchange. 6

The Columbian Exchange benefited people all over the world. Potatoes from the Americas became an important food for most Europeans. Corn became an important crop in Africa. Sweet potatoes were grown as far away as China. Today, tomatoes, peanuts, and American beans and peppers are grown in many lands.

REVIEW How did the Columbian Exchange change the diet of Europeans?
Potatoes became an important food in Europe.

98 • Chapter 3

Science

What Plants Need for Growth

Have students choose one plant that was part of the Columbian Exchange and research what the plant needs to grow well.
Hint: climate and soil conditions

Logical-mathematical; bodily-kinesthetic

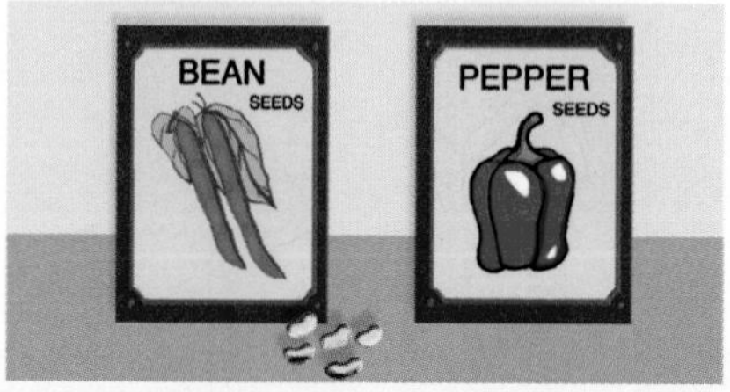

Language Arts

Create Menus

- Ask students to name the plants that were part of the Columbian Exchange. List these plants on the board.
- Have students write a menu for a meal made from these foods.
- Ask students to share their menus with the class. Students may wish to bring in a dish from their menu to share.

Visual-spatial

7 8

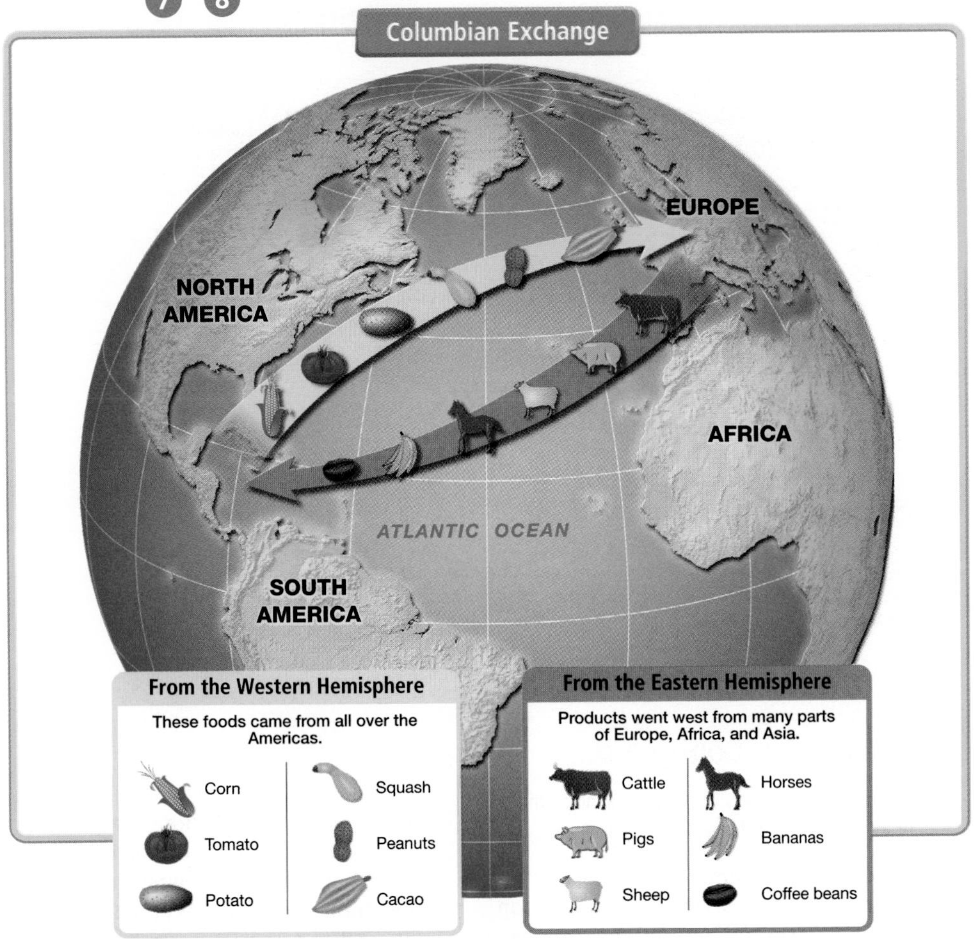

Mustangs These wild horses, called mustangs, were brought to the Americas by Spanish explorers.

The Columbian Exchange *continued*

Talk About It

7 Q Visual Learning What foods came from Europe to the Americas?

A bananas, coffee beans

8 Q Visual Learning What animals came to the Americas from Europe?

A horses, cattle, pigs, and sheep

Reading Strategy: Monitor/Clarify Have students look at the map, photograph, and captions on page 99. Ask them to explain what these images show. If they do not understand something, have students re-examine the page. If their question is not answered, have them read on to find the answer.

Extra Support

Illustrate Foods and Animals

Have students read the section titled "The Columbian Exchange." What foods and animals did Columbus and his crew take to the West Indies? Ask students to create a short illustrated book showing each of these foods and animals, with a caption for each illustration.

Visual-spatial; bodily-kinesthetic

Challenge

Write a Poem

- Have students write a poem about the event pictured on page 98 or about either of the visuals on page 99.
- Ask them to include information from the lesson in their poems.
- Have students share completed poems with the class.

Verbal-linguistic

Exploration Continues

Talk About It

9 **Q History** Which explorer claimed eastern South America for Portugal in 1500?

A Pedro Alvarez Cabral

10 **Q History** Who was Amerigo Vespucci?

A He was an Italian who made several voyages to the Caribbean and South America.

11 **Q Geography** How did Balboa reach the Pacific Ocean?

A He crossed mountains and jungles in present-day Panama.

12 **Q Geography** When Magellan's crew circumnavigated the world, what did they prove?

A They proved that Columbus's theory about sailing west to Asia was correct.

Vocabulary Strategy

circumnavigate Ask students to find the word *navigate* in this word, and to explain that it means directing or setting the course of something such as a ship or car.

Critical Thinking

Compare and Contrast Compare the voyages of Columbus and Magellan.

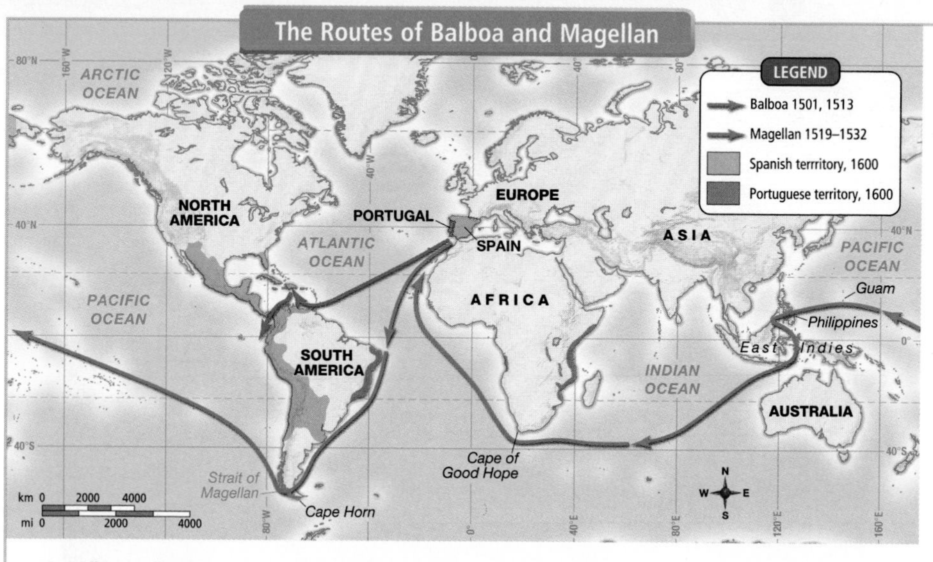

Magellan Sails Around the World This map shows the route of Magellan and his crew during the first round-the-world trip. SKILL **Reading Maps** How long did Magellan's voyage take? about 13 years

Exploration Continues

Main Idea Explorers continued to sail to the Americas to search for new routes to Asia.

Word of Columbus's voyage spread throughout Europe. European rulers soon sent their own explorers to the Americas.

Pedro Alvarez Cabral (ka BRAHL)
9 explored eastern South America in 1500
and claimed it for Portugal. An Italian
named **Amerigo Vespucci** (vehs POO
10 chee) made several voyages to South
America and the Caribbean. A Spanish
explorer, **Vasco Núñez de Balboa**, (VAS
11 coh NOON yez deh bal BOH ah) sailed to
present-day Panama in Central America. In
1513, he crossed the mountains and
jungles of Panama and reached the
Pacific Ocean.

Magellan

Ferdinand Magellan was a Portuguese soldier and sailor who sailed for Spain. Magellan had a daring idea. He believed that he could sail west, go around South America, cross the Pacific Ocean, and end up back in Spain.

Magellan left Spain in September 1519, with five ships and about 250 men. They crossed the Atlantic Ocean and arrived on the coast of present-day Brazil, where the crew waited for winter to pass. Magellan then sailed south down the east coast of South America. In November 1520, his ships entered the Pacific Ocean. He named it Pacific, which means "peaceful," because it looked so calm. Magellan and his crew had no idea how large the Pacific was.

Math

Calculate Distances

- Using calculators and globes, have students find out the distance that Magellan and his crew traveled around the world. How much of this journey was across the Atlantic Ocean? the Pacific Ocean? How does the length of Columbus's first journey compare with that of Magellan's?
- Ask students to write down their findings and to present them to the class.

Logical-mathematical

Language Arts

An Explorer Report

- Guide students to choose an explorer mentioned in the text. Encourage them to choose one they find interesting.
- Then have students write a one-page report about this explorer and his achievements, based on information from an encyclopedia article.
- Remind children to summarize facts and information from the article.

Verbal-linguistic

Ferdinand Magellan
His voyage proved people could sail around the world.

Sailing west, Magellan and his crew did not see land for more than three months. Many sailors died of disease and starvation along the way. When they reached the Philippine Islands off the coast of Asia, Magellan was killed in a battle with people on the islands.

Only one ship of the original five survived the trip. It arrived back in Spain in September 1522. It was loaded with valuable spices. Of the 250 men who began the journey, about 18 remained.
12 Magellan's crew became the first explorers to circumnavigate the world.

To **circumnavigate** is to sail completely around something. Although Magellan did not survive the voyage, he proved that Columbus's theory about sailing west to Asia was correct.

REVIEW Who named the Pacific Ocean and why? Magellan; he thought it looked peaceful.

Lesson Summary

- Columbus first landed in the Caribbean in 1492.
- Other explorers, including Vespucci and Balboa, traveled to the Americas.
- Magellan's crew was the first to circumnavigate the world.

Why It Matters . . .

The search for a route to Asia gave Europeans new knowledge of the world's size and geography.

Lesson Review

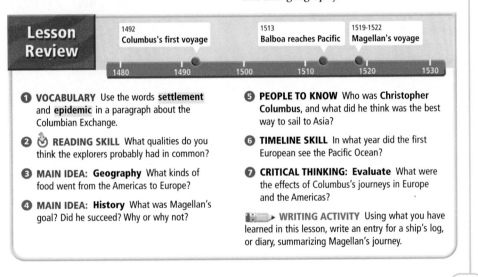

1492 Columbus's first voyage
1513 Balboa reaches Pacific
1519-1522 Magellan's voyage

1480 1490 1500 1510 1520 1530

1. **VOCABULARY** Use the words **settlement** and **epidemic** in a paragraph about the Columbian Exchange.
2. **READING SKILL** What qualities do you think the explorers probably had in common?
3. **MAIN IDEA: Geography** What kinds of food went from the Americas to Europe?
4. **MAIN IDEA: History** What was Magellan's goal? Did he succeed? Why or why not?
5. **PEOPLE TO KNOW** Who was **Christopher Columbus**, and what did he think was the best way to sail to Asia?
6. **TIMELINE SKILL** In what year did the first European see the Pacific Ocean?
7. **CRITICAL THINKING: Evaluate** What were the effects of Columbus's journeys in Europe and the Americas?

WRITING ACTIVITY Using what you have learned in this lesson, write an entry for a ship's log, or diary, summarizing Magellan's journey.

3 Review/Assess

Review Tested Objectives

U2-5 Columbus's voyages resulted in increased exploration and started the Columbian Exchange, the exchange of animals, plants, and people between hemispheres.

U2-6 Cabral, Vespucci, Balboa, and Magellan traveled to the Americas and beyond. Magellan's crew was the first to circumnavigate the world.

Lesson Review Answers

1. Paragraph should mention Taíno epidemics and European settlements.
2. Answers will vary.
3. maize (corn), potatoes, tomatoes, cacao (chocolate), and certain peppers, beans, and squashes
4. Magellan's goal was to sail west, go around South America, cross the Pacific Ocean, and end up back in Spain. He did not succeed himself, but his crew brought his ship back to Spain.
5. He was an explorer for Spain who wanted to reach Asia by sailing west across the Atlantic Ocean.
6. 1513
7. Columbian Exchange of animals and plants; world exploration and trade increased; Europeans destroyed rain forests in the Americas; epidemics killed most of the Taíno.

Writing Rubric

4	Ship's log format is used correctly; summary is complete and accurate; mechanics are correct.
3	Ship's log format is used; summary is mostly complete and accurate; most mechanics are correct.
2	Ship's log format is attempted; summary contains errors or omissions; some errors in mechanics.
1	Ship's log format is not used; summary contains many errors or omissions; many errors in mechanics are present.

Study Guide/Homework

Vocabulary and Study Guide

Vocabulary

Write the definition of each vocabulary word below.

1. settlement A small community of people living in a new place
2. epidemic An outbreak of disease that spreads quickly and affects many people
3. circumnavigate To travel completely around something
4. Use two of the words in a sentence.
Sample answer: European settlements in the West Indies caused an epidemic among the American Indians.

Study Guide

Read "Christopher Columbus" and "The Columbian Exchange." Then fill in the sequence chart below.

5. Christopher Columbus sails west and lands in the Caribbean. → Columbus makes three more voyages to the Americas. → 6. Columbus brings new plants to Europe from America. → Potatoes become an important food for most Europeans.

7. Read "Exploration Continues." Then fill in the blanks below.
Pedro Alvarez Cabra explored eastern South America and claimed it for Portugal. Amerigo Vespucci, an Italian explorer, made several voyages to South America and the Caribbean. Vasco Núñez de Balboa crossed the mountains and saw the Pacific Ocean from Panama. Later, Ferdinand Magellan became the first European to sail across the Pacific Ocean. Although Magellan did not make it back to Spain, sailors from his crew did successfully circumnavigate the world.

Unit Resources 30 Use with *United States History*, pp. 96–101

Unit Resources, p. 30

Reteach Minilesson

Use a KWL chart to reteach the lesson.

K	W	L
I know that Columbus… 1) 2)	I want to know… 1) 2)	I learned that… 1) 2)

www.eduplace.com/ss/hmss05/

Extend Quick Look

Connect to Core Lesson In the Core Lesson, students read about the arrival of European explorers in the Americas. In Extend Lesson 3, students will learn more about the world maps created as a result of these explorations.

1 Teach the Extend Lesson

Connect to the Big Idea

The World in Spatial Terms European explorers helped to expand people's perception of the world in spatial terms. The information they brought back helped to pinpoint locations and analyze characteristics and patterns among those locations.

Primary Source

Mapping New Lands

European explorers faced an interesting problem: There were no maps to show the new land they had seen. In the 1500s, new maps had to be created to show people's expanding understanding of the world.

Early world maps look very different from today's maps. Whole continents are missing because Europeans didn't know about them yet. The land and oceans are the wrong size or oddly shaped. The locations and distances recorded by explorers on their voyages were often not exact, so mapmakers did the best they could with the information they had.

The new maps created a lot of excitement in Europe. They sparked interest in more exploration and changed Europeans' picture of the world.

New View of the World
In 1507, Martin Waldseemüller (VAHLT zay mool uhr) published the first map to use the word "America." It was also the first map to show North and South America as continents separate from Asia.

Reaching All Learners

Extra Support

Identify Problem and Solution
Ask students:

- What problem did European explorers face in the 1500s? There were no maps to show the new lands they had seen.
- How did they solve this problem? They brought back information that was used to make new maps.
- What were some of the problems with the new maps? Continents were missing; land and oceans were the wrong size or oddly shaped.

Verbal-linguistic

On Level

Compare Maps

- Working in small groups, ask students to compare how much water and how much land are shown on this world map.
- Then have them look at a current world map and make the same comparison.
- In both cases, they should express their comparison as a ratio. Have students explain their thinking.

Logical-mathematical

Challenge

Write an Essay

- Have students examine the way North and South America are represented on this map.
- Ask them to write an essay stating why they think these continents may have been represented this way.

Verbal-linguistic

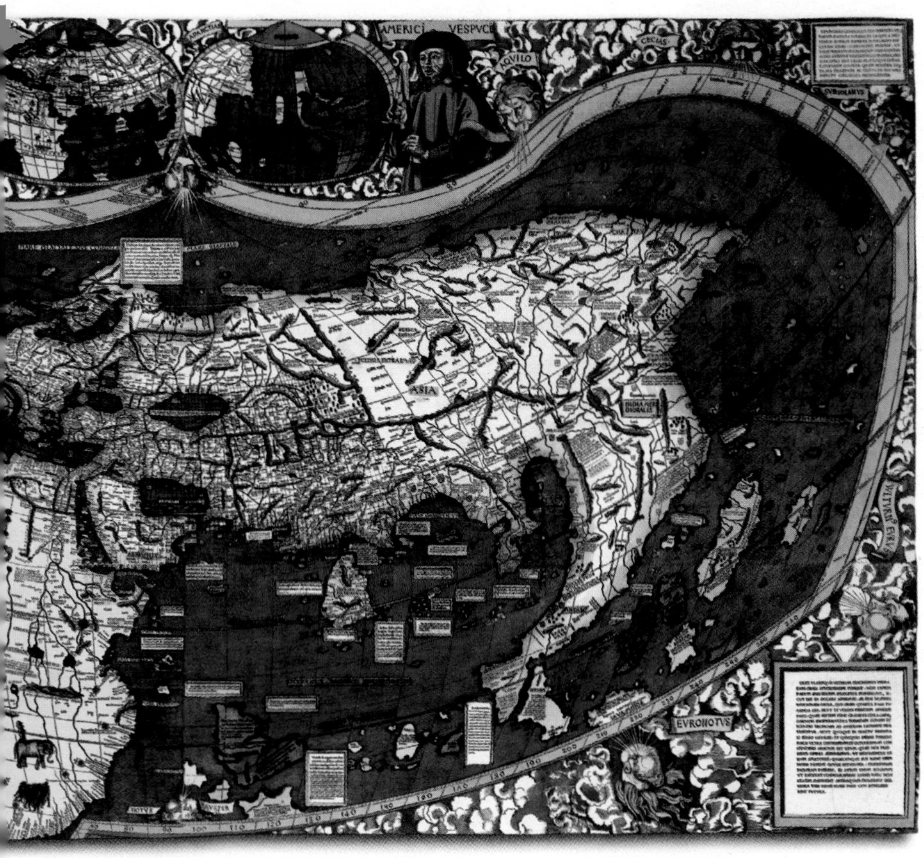

PRIMARY SOURCE

Amerigo Vespucci (1454–1512)

Vespucci is shown above on the border of the map. He realized that he and Columbus had not reached Asia but a continent unknown to Europeans. The land was named America, after Amerigo's first name.

Activities

1. **CONNECT TO TODAY** Compare this map with a modern world map. What parts of the old map do you recognize? What parts of the world are hard to recognize? Discuss the reasons for the differences.
2. **MAP IT** Make a map of your school playground or classroom. Discuss how to measure distances. Use your measurements to draw a map on graph paper.

2 Leveled Activities

1 Connect to Today *For Extra Support*

Sample answer: Europe, Africa, and parts of Asia are more or less correct because European map makers had more information about these areas. North and South America are not shown correctly, because there was very little information available to European mapmakers about these continents.

2 Map It *For Challenge*

HANDS ON Performance Task Rubric

4	Map is clearly drawn; details are correct; measurements are correct.
3	Map is adequately drawn; details are mostly correct; measurements are mostly correct.
2	Map is drawn; most details are correct; some errors in measurements.
1	Map is inadequately drawn; details are missing or incorrect; measurements are incorrect.

ELL

REACHING ALL LEARNERS

Intermediate

- Ask students to read the definitions for *latitude* and *longitude* in a dictionary or encyclopedia.
- Have them point out where latitude and longitude are shown on a current world map.
- Guide them to give an oral explanation of latitude and longitude, saying why they are important.

Verbal-linguistic

Drama

Perform a Monologue

- Invite students to write and perform a monologue from the point of view of a European mapmaker from the 1500s.
- Ask students to think about the challenges that mapmakers faced when they tried to create new maps.

Bodily-kinesthetic; verbal-linguistic

Graphic Organizer

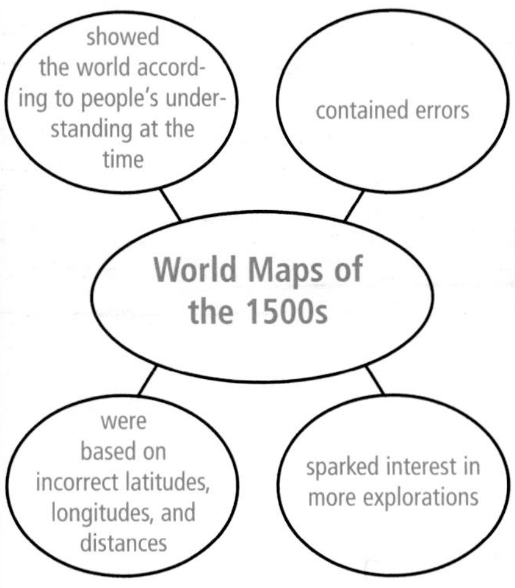
World Maps of the 1500s
showed the world according to people's understanding at the time
contained errors
were based on incorrect latitudes, longitudes, and distances
sparked interest in more explorations

Graphic Organizer 13

Tested Objectives

U2-7 History Describe and evaluate the significance of Spain's conquest of the Aztec Empire.

U2-8 History Identify motives and achievements of Spanish explorers in the Americas.

Lesson Quick Look

This lesson discusses Spanish explorations and conquests in the Americas during the 1500s.

Teaching Option: Extend Lesson 4 tells students more about Spanish explorers.

1 Get Set to Read

Preview Ask students to look at the pictures in this lesson before they read. What do they think the lesson is about?

Reading Skill: Compare and Contrast Students may refer to the sought-after cities of gold.

Build on What You Know Have students give an example of people traveling to other worlds from books they've read.

Vocabulary

expedition *noun,* a journey taken by a group for a definite purpose

conquistador *noun,* a Spanish soldier who helped conquer the native civilizations of Central and South America

empire *noun,* territories and groups of people controlled by one government

Core Lesson 4

Conquest of the Americas

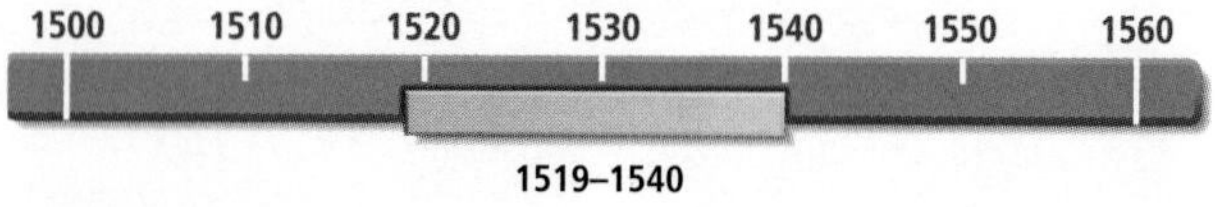

VOCABULARY

expedition
conquistador
empire

Vocabulary Strategy

expedition

The word **expedition** begins with the prefix **ex-**, meaning "out." An expedition goes out to explore.

READING SKILL

Compare and Contrast

Contrast what Spanish explorers were looking for with what they found.

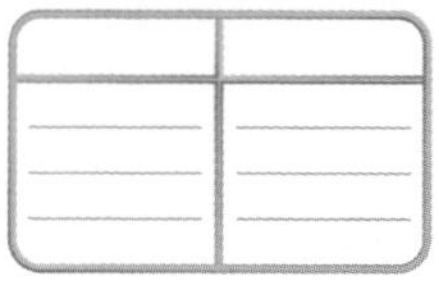

Build on What You Know Many books and movies today tell stories about people traveling to other worlds. In 1519, when the Spanish and the Aztecs first met, it was like a meeting of people from two different worlds.

Cortés Conquers the Aztecs

Main Idea Spanish soldiers conquered the Aztecs in present-day Mexico.

The travels of **Columbus** and **Balboa** were exciting news in Europe. Sending ships and soldiers across an ocean was expensive, but Spain's rulers believed the explorers would bring back gold.

One of these explorers was **Hernán Cortés** (er NAN kohr TEHS). In 1519, Cortés led an expedition to Mexico. An **expedition** is a journey to achieve a goal. Cortés' ships carried horses, weapons, and an army of 600 conquistadors (kohn KEY stah doors). **Conquistador** is Spanish for conqueror. The conquistadors were eager to find wealth and fame for themselves and their families. 1

Cortés had heard stories about the Aztec Indians in present-day Mexico. The Aztecs had built an empire by conquering other Indian nations. An **empire** is many nations or territories ruled by a single group or leader. 2

Aztec Sun Stone
The Aztec civilization had its own calendar. This carved stone is 13 feet across.

Skill and Strategy

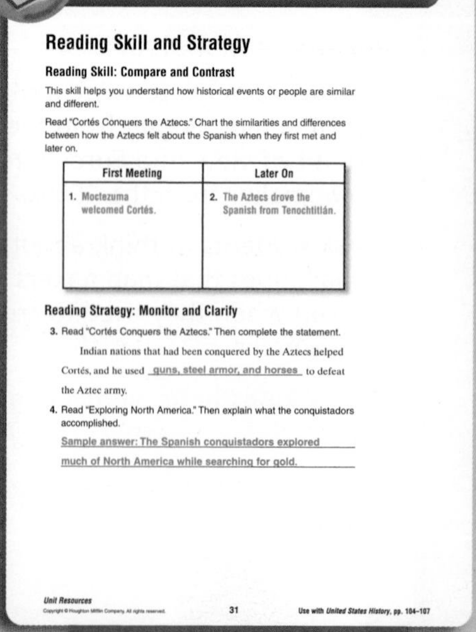

Reading Skill and Strategy

Reading Skill: Compare and Contrast

This skill helps you understand how historical events or people are similar and different.

Read "Cortés Conquers the Aztecs." Chart the similarities and differences between how the Aztecs felt about the Spanish when they first met and later on.

First Meeting	Later On
1. Moctezuma welcomed Cortés.	2. The Aztecs drove the Spanish from Tenochtitlán.

Reading Strategy: Monitor and Clarify

3. Read "Cortés Conquers the Aztecs." Then complete the statement.

Indian nations that had been conquered by the Aztecs helped Cortés, and he used guns, steel armor, and horses to defeat the Aztec army.

4. Read "Exploring North America." Then explain what the conquistadors accomplished.

Sample answer: The Spanish conquistadors explored much of North America while searching for gold.

Unit Resources

31
Use with *United States History*, pp. 104–107

Unit Resources, p. 31

Background

Moctezuma

- This Aztec leader's name may be seen with different spellings in various textbooks and articles. It is sometimes seen as *Montezuma,* which is what the Spanish called him.
- This book uses the spelling *Moctezuma.*

Cortés and Moctezuma A Spanish artist in the 1500s made this drawing of Cortés and Moctezuma at the gates of Tenochtitlán.

After landing in Mexico, Cortés met people who were enemies of the Aztec empire. Cortés convinced them to come with him to defeat the Aztecs. An Indian woman named **Malinche** (Mah LEEN chay) joined Cortés. She helped him to communicate with the Aztecs and gave advice about how to conquer them.

3 When the conquistadors arrived at the Aztec capital Tenochtitlán (tay nohch tee TLAHN), they were amazed by its size and beauty. One conquistador wrote,

> **“Indeed, some of our soldiers asked whether it was not all a dream.”**

Tenochtitlán was twice as big as any European city and was built in the middle of a large lake. Long causeways, or land bridges, stretched across the lake to the city.

At first, the Aztec ruler **Moctezuma** welcomed Cortés, but the conquistador's greed for gold soon angered the Aztecs. The Aztecs attacked the Spanish and drove them from Tenochtitlán. Cortés went to neighboring Indian nations that had been conquered by the Aztecs and persuaded them to join his army.

Contact with the Spanish had infected the Aztec army with disease. When Cortés returned to Tenochtitlán, he used guns, horses, and steel armor to defeat the weakened Aztec army. Cortés soon controlled the entire Aztec empire. By 1535, Spain had claimed all of Mexico and renamed it New Spain. 4

After Cortés, other conquistadors explored Central and South America to find more gold and treasures. In the 1530s, a conquistador named **Francisco Pizarro** defeated the powerful Inca empire in South America.

REVIEW Why did people inside the Aztec empire help Cortés defeat the Aztecs?
because the Aztecs had conquered them

105

2 Teach

Cortés Conquers the Aztecs

Talk About It

1 **Q History** Who was Hernán Cortés?
A a Spanish explorer and conquistador who led an expedition to Mexico in 1519

2 **Q Geography** Where was the Aztec empire?
A in present-day Mexico

3 **Q Geography** What made Tenochtitlán different from European cities?
A The Aztec capital was twice as big as any European city and was built in the middle of a lake.

4 **Q Geography** When the Spanish claimed all of Mexico in 1535, what did they call it?
A New Spain

Vocabulary Strategy

expedition Tell students that the root *ped* is based on the Latin word for foot.

conquistador The first part of this word sounds like *conqu*est. Explain that conquistadors conquered, or took control of, other peoples.

empire *Empire* is based on the Latin word *imperare,* meaning "emperor." An *emperor* rules an *empire*.

Reading Strategy: Monitor/Clarify As students read, suggest they pause after each paragraph and reflect on what they have read. After that, they should consider if anything is unclear.

Leveled Practice

Extra Support

Have students **make flow charts** to help them note the sequence of events that led to Cortés claiming the Aztec empire for Spain. Visual-spatial; verbal-linguistic

Challenge

Ask students to pick one aspect of Aztec culture, such as religion, art, or the calendar. Ask students to **write a report** describing it. Encourage them to illustrate their reports. Verbal-linguistic; visual-spatial

ELL

Beginning

After reading or listening to pages 104 and 105, have students **examine the art** on page 105. Have them discuss the following:

- What historical event does the picture show?
- Who are people in the picture?
- What are they doing?
- What will happen next?
- What does the caption tell of this event?

Exploring North America

Talk About It

5 Q History Who was the first Spanish conquistador to reach the present-day United States?

A Juan Ponce de León

6 Q Geography Where did Hernando de Soto go on his search for gold?

A present-day Florida, Georgia, and throughout the American Southeast, including the Mississippi River

7 Q History What did Coronado and his soldiers hope to find?

A the cities of gold he and other explorers had heard about

Critical Thinking

Fact and Opinion "The Spanish were more powerful than the Aztecs." Is this statement a fact or an opinion?

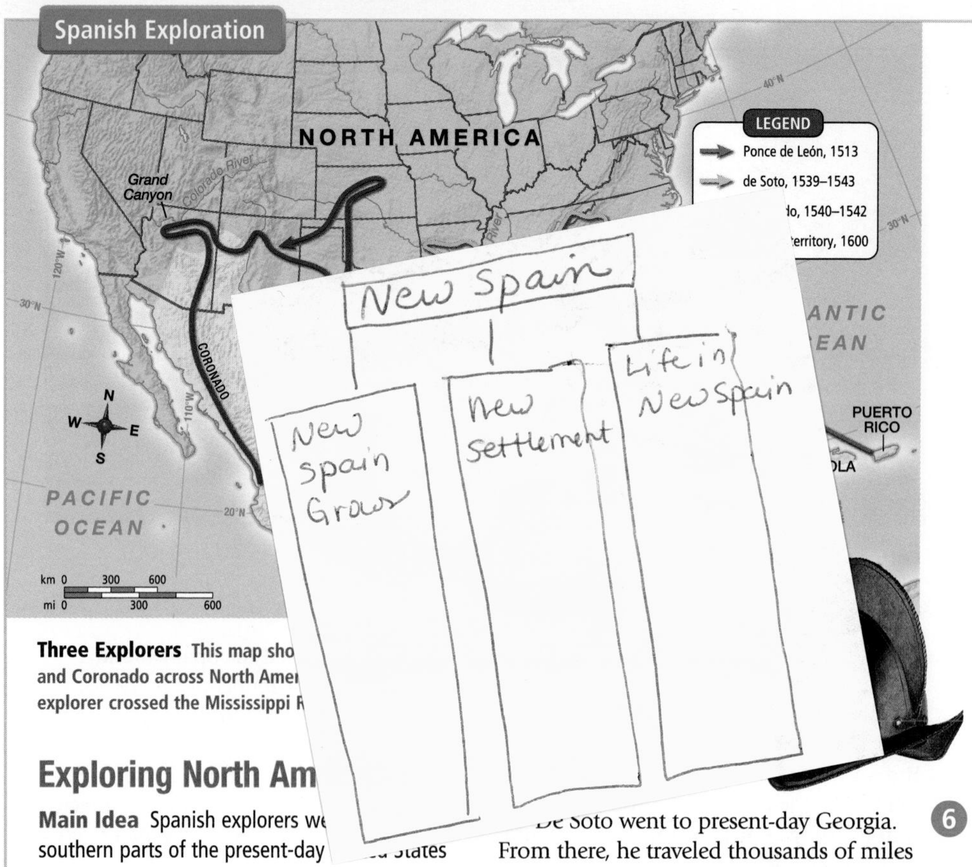

Three Explorers This map sho... and Coronado across North Ame... explorer crossed the Mississippi R...

Exploring North Am...

Main Idea Spanish explorers we... southern parts of the present-day ... States looking for gold.

Conquistadors also explored North America in their search for gold. The first conquistador to reach the land that is now the United States was **Juan Ponce de León** (pon seh deh leh OHN). In 1513, he led an expedition to present-day Florida. Ponce de León claimed Florida for Spain. He was looking for a "fountain of youth" that legend said could make old people young again. A legend is a story handed down from earlier times. 5

In 1539, Spain sent a conquistador named **Hernando de Soto** to conquer and settle Florida and the lands beyond. De Soto went to present-day Georgia. From there, he traveled thousands of miles through the American Southeast. De Soto was the first European explorer to reach the Mississippi River. 6

Along the way, De Soto found many American Indians but no riches. The conquistadors fought and enslaved American Indians they met. Many Spanish died in battles as well. De Soto died in 1542, without starting any settlements in North America.

In 1540, a conquistador named **Francisco Vásquez de Coronado** led an expedition into North America. Coronado was looking for cities of gold that he had heard about in legends.

106 • Chapter 3

Drama

Dramatic Reading

- Ask small groups to write and perform a dramatic reading about the journey of Ponce de León, de Soto, or Coronado.
- The text might include references to what each explorer wanted to find and what they found instead.
- Have students assign parts for each member of the group to read.

Bodily-kinesthetic

Language Arts

Write a Poem

- Have students discuss Ponce de León's search for a fountain of youth and Coronado's desire to find cities made of gold. Did these explorers find what they were looking for?
- Have each student write a poem about a real or imaginary explorer's quest. You might post the completed poems or have them share them in small groups.

Verbal-linguistic

The Grand Canyon Coronado's soldiers were the first Europeans to see the Grand Canyon in Arizona.

Cities of Gold

American Indians had told two earlier explorers named **Álvar Núñez Cabeza de Vaca** (AHL vah rehs NOON yez ca BEH sa deh VAH ca) and **Estevanico** (es STEH vahn EE KO) of rich cities to the north. Coronado and other explorers thought 7 these cities might be the cities of gold. During the search for them, Coronado's soldiers traveled over 3,500 miles.

Spanish conquistadors faced many obstacles, including long distances, bad weather, and starvation as they explored the continent. They also learned much about the geography and peoples of North America.

REVIEW What did the Spanish hope to find in the lands north of Mexico?
gold; cities made of gold; a fountain of youth

Lesson Summary

- The Aztecs ruled a large empire in present-day Mexico. Hernán Cortés conquered the Aztecs in 1521.
- Spanish conquistadors explored much of the southern United States.

Why It Matters . . .

What the Spanish learned about the American Southwest helped future explorers for hundreds of years.

Lesson Review

1513	1521	1535
Ponce de León reaches Florida	Cortés defeats Aztecs	New Spain becomes a colony

1500 · 1510 · 1520 · 1530 · 1540 · 1550

1. **VOCABULARY** Write a paragraph about Hernán Cortez using **conquistador** and **expedition.**
2. **READING SKILL** What did the explorers find that was **different** from what they were looking for?
3. **MAIN IDEA: History** Why was Cortés able to defeat the powerful Aztec Empire?
4. **MAIN IDEA: Geography** What areas of the present-day United States did Coronado and De Soto explore?
5. **PEOPLE TO KNOW** Who was **Moctezuma?**
6. **TIMELINE SKILL** How long after Cortés conquered the Aztecs did New Spain become a colony?
7. **CRITICAL THINKING: Fact and Opinion** Write one fact about the Spanish conquest of the Americas. Then write an opinion about that fact.

ECONOMICS ACTIVITY Choose an explorer in the lesson. Think about his goals and the risks he took. Make a list of the risks.

3 Review/Assess

Review Tested Objectives

U2-7 Spanish conquistadors led by Hernán Cortés conquered the Aztecs in what is now Mexico. Spain soon claimed all of Mexico.

U2-8 In their search for gold and other treasures, Juan Ponce de León, Hernando de Soto, and Francisco Vásquez de Coronado explored much of what is now the southern United States.

Lesson Review Answers

1. Paragraphs should mention that Cortés led conquistadors on an expedition to find gold in present-day Mexico.
2. They found many obstacles, including long distances, bad weather, and starvation.
3. After the Aztec army had been weakened by disease, Cortés used guns, horses, and steel armor to defeat them.
4. Coronado explored what is now the southwestern United States. De Soto explored what is now the southeastern United States.
5. He was the ruler of the Aztec empire.
6. about 14 years
7. Answers will vary, but facts and opinions should reflect information from the lesson.

Writing Rubric

4	List format is used effectively; list focuses on an explorer from the lesson; risks are assessed accurately.
3	List format is used; list focuses on an explorer from the lesson; risks are assessed.
2	List format is attempted; list focuses on an explorer from outside the lesson; risks are assessed in a confusing or inaccurate manner.
1	List format is not used; list does not focus on an explorer; risks are not assessed.

Study Guide/Homework

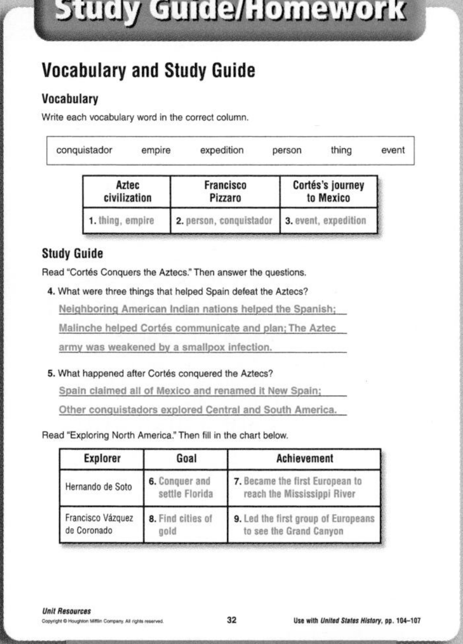

Vocabulary and Study Guide

Vocabulary

Write each vocabulary word in the correct column.

conquistador empire expedition person thing event

Aztec civilization	Francisco Pizzaro	Cortés's journey to Mexico
1. thing, empire	2. person, conquistador	3. event, expedition

Study Guide

Read "Cortés Conquers the Aztecs." Then answer the questions.

4. What were three things that helped Spain defeat the Aztecs?
Neighboring American Indian nations helped the Spanish; Malinche helped Cortés communicate and plan; The Aztec army was weakened by a smallpox infection.

5. What happened after Cortés conquered the Aztecs?
Spain claimed all of Mexico and renamed it New Spain; Other conquistadors explored Central and South America.

Read "Exploring North America." Then fill in the chart below.

Explorer	Goal	Achievement
Hernando de Soto	6. Conquer and settle Florida	7. Became the first European to reach the Mississippi River
Francisco Vázquez de Coronado	8. Find cities of gold	9. Led the first group of Europeans to see the Grand Canyon

Unit Resources

32
Use with *United States History*, pp. 104–107

Unit Resources, p. 32

Reteach Minilesson

Use a main-idea-and-details chart to reteach the lesson.

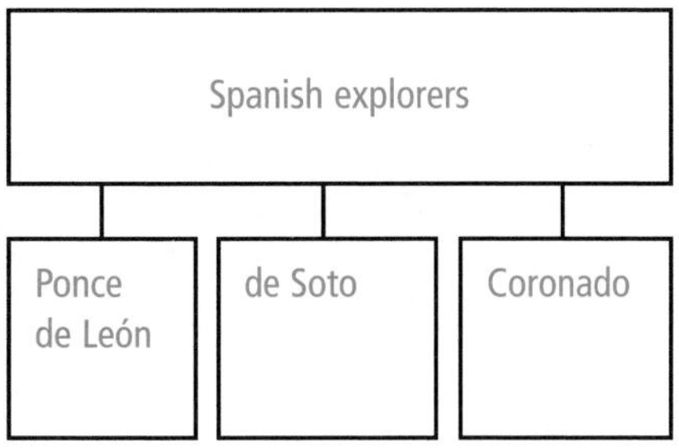

Graphic Organizer 8

Extend

Quick Look

Connect to Core Lesson In the Core Lesson, students read about the Spanish conquistadors who explored North America. In Extend Lesson 4, they will learn more about what these explorers were looking for.

1 Teach the Extend Lesson

Connect to the Big Idea

Influences on History/Settlement and Exploration Spanish explorers influenced the course of history as they explored the North American continent.

Biographies

SPANISH EXPLORERS

What were explorers looking for? What drove them to take great risks? Spanish explorers came to North America looking for treasures and for places they had heard stories about. They hoped their discoveries would make them rich and famous.

None of the expeditions of the Spanish explorers was easy. They didn't always find what they were looking for.

Juan Ponce de León 1460–1521

Goal: Wanted to find gold and a legendary "fountain of youth."

Explorations: Was the first European to set foot in Florida in 1513. Explored the Florida coast.

Interesting fact: Named Florida after the Spanish words for Easter, "Pascua de Florida" (Feast of Flowers), because it was the Easter season when he landed there.

Hernando de Soto 1500–1542

Goal: Wanted wealth and power.

Explorations: Led a large army through the American Southeast, from present-day Florida to Arkansas. Planned to conquer and colonize the region.

Interesting fact: He and his all-volunteer army were the first Europeans to see the Mississippi River.

Francisco Vásquez de Coronado 1510–1554

Goal: Wanted to find gold.

Explorations: An adventurer, Coronado assembled a large expedition and traveled throughout the Great Plains and the Southeast. He hoped to find some legendary cities of gold.

Interesting fact: Some of his men were the first Europeans to be in California, to see the Grand Canyon, and to live among the Pueblo Indians.

Reaching All Learners

Extra Support

Make a Model

Have students create a three-dimensional scene that shows one of the explorers in an important moment of their journey.

Visual-spatial; bodily-kinesthetic

On Level

Hold a Panel Discussion

Have small groups of students select on explorer and do additional research to participate in a panel discussion.

- Appoint one student to be a moderator. The moderator should think of two topics the "explorer specialists" will discuss.
- Ask the panelists to discuss their explorer's experiences exploring North America.

Verbal-linguistic; bodily-kinesthetic

Challenge

Create a Map

Ask students to choose one of the places named in this lesson, such as Arkansas, the Mississippi River, or the Grand Canyon.

- Using library resources or the Internet, have students find out more about the early history of that place.
- Have them create a map of that place based on the information they have.

Visual-spatial; logical-mathematical

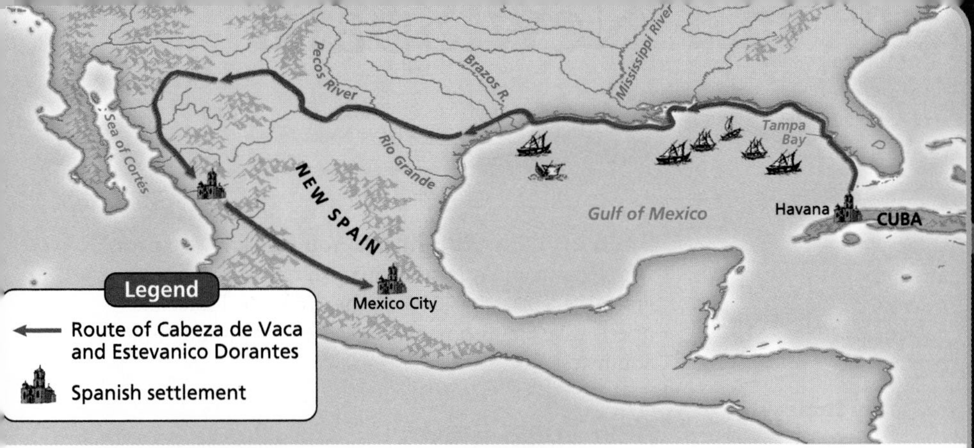

BIOGRAPHIES

Alvar Nuñez Cabeza de Vaca
1490–1557

Goal: Wanted travel and adventures.

Explorations: Was shipwrecked by a hurricane near present-day Texas. He and three other members of the expedition survived. They traveled across the Southwest, eventually reaching Mexico City.

Interesting fact: Published an account of his experiences, urging better treatment of American Indians.

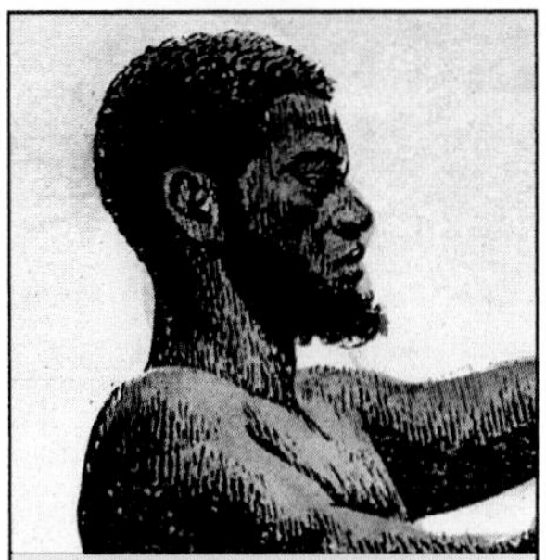

Estevanico Dorantes
1500–1528

Goal: Wanted travel and adventures.

Explorations: Sold into slavery in Spain, he traveled as a servant to one of the officers on the same voyage as Cabeza de Vaca. He was one of only four survivors of the shipwreck.

Interesting fact: Was part of the first overland expedition to explore the American Southwest.

Cabeza de Vaca and Estevanico Dorantes spent eight years traveling on the route shown above.

Activities

1. **THINK ABOUT IT** What were these Spanish explorers looking for? What did they find?
2. **REPORT IT** Write a letter to the king of Spain from the point of view of one of these explorers. Describe what you have found on your expedition, or what you hope to find.

2 Leveled Activities

1 Think About It *For Extra Support*
Sample answer: They were looking for riches, and mythical places such as the fountain of youth and the cities of gold. They found places in North America like the Grand Canyon and the Mississippi River.

2 Report It *For Challenge*

Writing Rubric

4	Report/letter is well organized; conveys ideas clearly; facts are accurate.
3	Report/letter is adequately organized; conveys ideas adequately; most facts cited are accurate.
2	Report/letter is somewhat organized; conveys ideas adequately; some factual errors.
1	Report/letter is disorganized; conveys ideas in a very general or incomprehensible way; many errors.

ELL

REACHING ALL LEARNERS

Intermediate

- Have pairs of students read the biographies.
- For each explorer, ask pairs to **write down one fact.**
- Have pairs **write down a question** that can be answered with the fact.
- Invite pairs to share their questions with the class. Have the class try to answer the questions.

Verbal-linguistic

Math

Calculate

- Have students use information from the biographies to answer the following questions:
- About how old was Ponce de León when he set foot in Florida? about 53 years-old
- Who was the youngest of the five explorers? Coronado
- Who lived to be the oldest? Cabeza de Vaca

Logical-mathematical

Graphic Organizer

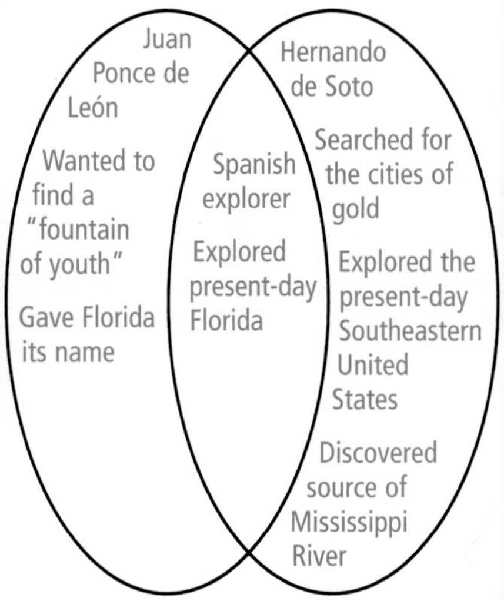

Graphic Organizer 11

Tested Objectives

U2-9 History Describe the features of Spain's colonial system in the Americas.

U2-10 History Evaluate the impact of Spanish colonization on Native Americans.

Lesson Quick Look

This lesson discusses the growth of Spanish settlements in what is now the southeastern and southwestern United states.

Teaching Options: In **Extend Lesson 5,** students will learn more about religious leaders in New Spain.

1 Get Set to Read

Preview Ask students to look at the map on page 111. Where was New Spain?

Reading Skill: Draw Conclusions Details may include missions, haciendas, and enforced labor.

Build on What You Know Ask students to think of cities or towns in the United States with Spanish names.

Vocabulary

colony *noun,* a settlement ruled by a distant country

mission *noun,* a Christian settlement and religious community

convert *verb,* to force or convince someone to change to another religion

hacienda *noun,* a plantation or large ranch owned by Spanish colonists

revolt *noun,* a rebellion against a ruler

Core Lesson 5

New Spain

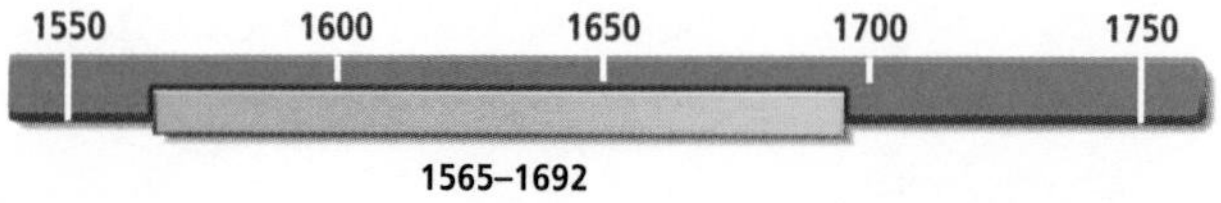

VOCABULARY

colony
mission
convert
hacienda
revolt

Vocabulary Strategy

convert

The verb **convert** comes from a word meaning "to turn around." Someone who converts turns around, or changes, to a new religion.

READING SKILL

Draw Conclusions Note details that will help you draw a conclusion about life in New Spain for American Indians.

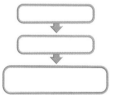

Build on What You Know You may know someone who lives in a place with a Spanish name, such as San Francisco. From the 1500s to the 1700s, explorers and priests gave Spanish names to settlements throughout the Southwest and Florida.

New Spain Grows

Main Idea The Spanish increased the size of New Spain and spread their rule in North America.

By 1535, the Spanish government controlled the former Aztec empire in Mexico. They made it a colony called New Spain. A **colony** is an area of land ruled by another country. In New Spain, Spanish settlers started towns and farmed the land. They built mines wherever they found valuable minerals, such as gold or silver. The colony of New Spain grew larger as government officials, settlers, soldiers, and priests arrived. 1

Spain's rulers sent priests with the explorers to spread Christianity. Over the next 200 years, Spanish explorers and priests traveled farther north and started settlements called missions. A **mission** was a religious community where priests taught Christianity.

Juana Inés de la Cruz
She was a well-known poet in Mexico City, the capital of New Spain.

Skill and Strategy

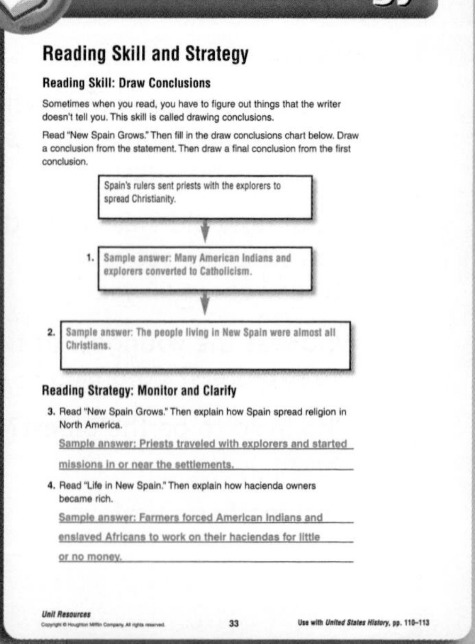

Reading Skill and Strategy

Reading Skill: Draw Conclusions

Sometimes when you read, you have to figure out things that the writer doesn't tell you. This skill is called drawing conclusions.

Read "New Spain Grows." Then fill in the draw conclusions chart below. Draw a conclusion from the statement. Then draw a final conclusion from the first conclusion.

Spain's rulers sent priests with the explorers to spread Christianity.

1. Sample answer: Many American Indians and explorers converted to Catholicism.

2. Sample answer: The people living in New Spain were almost all Christians.

Reading Strategy: Monitor and Clarify

3. Read "New Spain Grows." Then explain how Spain spread religion in North America.
Sample answer: Priests traveled with explorers and started missions in or near the settlements.

4. Read "Life in New Spain." Then explain how hacienda owners became rich.
Sample answer: Farmers forced American Indians and enslaved Africans to work on their haciendas for little or no money.

Unit Resources

33
Use with *United States History*, pp. 110–113

Unit Resources, p. 33

Background

St. Augustine

- St. Augustine, Florida, was part of the Spanish colonial empire.
- Pedro Menéndez de Aviles, St. Augustine's founder, became Florida's first governor.

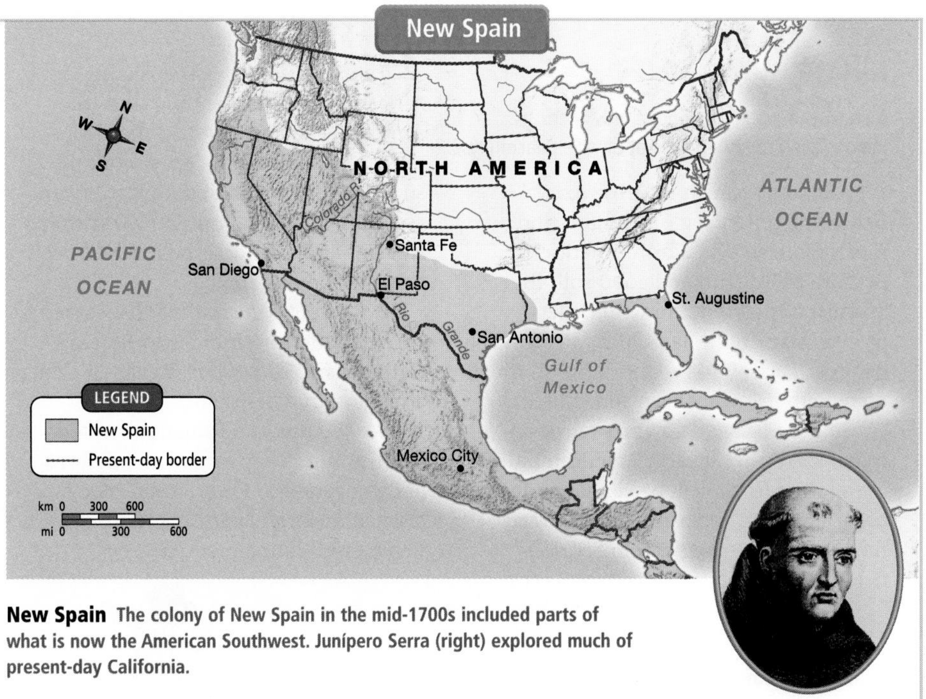

New Spain The colony of New Spain in the mid-1700s included parts of what is now the American Southwest. Junípero Serra (right) explored much of present-day California.

New Settlements

Spain was not the only nation trying to claim North American lands. The English,
2 French, Dutch, and later the Russians, were also exploring North America. The Spanish hoped to prevent other countries from claiming land. They built forts called presidios to protect Spanish claims and guard themselves against attack.

In 1565, **Pedro Menéndez de Aviles**
3 (AH vee lehs) started the settlement of St. Augustine in Florida. St. Augustine is the oldest city in the United States built by Europeans. The conquistador went north up the Gulf coast and started settlements all the way into present-day Georgia. Spanish settlers in Georgia tried to convert the Guale (WAH li) Indians to Roman Catholicism. The settlers forced them to work building roads and growing crops.

The Spanish also built settlements in what is now the southwestern United States. In 1598, the conquistador **Juan de Oñate** (ohn YAH teh) led settlers, soldiers, and priests to present-day New Mexico. In 1610, the city of Santa Fe became the capital of that part of New Spain.

Later, Spanish soldiers and priests also settled and explored present-day Texas and California. In 1769, a priest
named **Junípero Serra** (hoo NEE peh roh 4
SEH ra) led an expedition up the coast of California. After helping to build the settlement of San Diego, Serra continued north, building more presidios and missions along the way.

REVIEW Why did the Spanish build presidios in New Spain? to protect Spanish claims and guard themselves from attack

111

2 Teach

New Spain Grows

Talk About It

1. **Q History** What did Spanish settlers do in New Spain?
   A They started towns, farmed land, and built gold and silver mines.

2. **Q Geography** Which nations tried to claim North American lands?
   A Spain, England, France, Holland, and Russia

3. **Q History** What settlement did Pedro Menéndez de Aviles start in 1565?
   A St. Augustine

4. **Q History** What settlement did Junípero Serra help build?
   A San Diego

Vocabulary Strategy

colony Tell students that *colony* is related to the Latin *colōnia,* meaning "settler."

mission Tell students that one meaning of *mission* is "an important task."

convert Explain to students that the prefix *con-* means "together" or "with."

Reading Strategy: Monitor/Clarify As students read, suggest they pause after each paragraph and reflect on what they have read. After that, they should consider if anything is unclear.

Leveled Practice

Extra Support

Have students **make a chart** noting the names of Spanish settlers, the settlements they helped to build, and the locations of the settlements. Verbal-linguistic

Challenge

Ask students to find out when the English, French, Dutch, and Russians began to explore North America. Have students **create a map** that shows their findings. Visual-spatial

ELL

Intermediate

- Have students **look at the map** of New Spain.
- Ask them what the map shows about New Spain.
- Have students compare the boundaries of present-day Mexico and the United States to the map of New Spain and describe the differences in land area.

Visual-spatial

Life in New Spain

Talk About It

5 **Q Economics** What did the Spanish do to make money when they did not find much gold in North America?

A They farmed.

6 **Q History** Where were many American Indians and enslaved Africans forced to work?

A at Spanish haciendas and mines; at sugar plantations in the Caribbean

7 **Q History** Who led the 1680 revolt against the Spanish in New Mexico?

A Popé, a Pueblo Indian leader

Vocabulary Strategy

hacienda Explain that synonyms for this Spanish word include *estate* and *plantation.*

revolt Tell students that this word may be used as a noun or a verb.

Critical Thinking

Decision Making Why do you think some American Indians decided to accept Spanish rule, while others refused?

Life in New Spain

Main Idea Spanish settlers and American Indians lived together, but not always peacefully.

5 After the Spanish took the Aztecs' riches, the conquistadors did not find much more gold in North America. Because New Spain had good soil, the Spanish turned to farming to make money. Many built haciendas (ah see YEN dahs). A **hacienda** is a large farm or ranch, often with its own village and church.

6 Spanish hacienda owners relied on Indians to farm the land. American Indians were forced to work at haciendas and were often cheated out of their pay. Many of them died from overwork in Spanish fields and mines.

The Spanish brought enslaved Africans to replace the thousands of American Indians who had died. Most of these Africans were forced to work on sugar plantations in Spain's Caribbean colonies. By 1650, about 130,000 enslaved Africans and their descendants had been brought to New Spain.

Priests at Spanish missions wanted to convert American Indians to Roman Catholicism. To **convert** means to change a religion or a belief.

Some American Indians accepted Spanish rule. They moved to missions and converted to Catholicism. They learned to speak Spanish and to use European farming methods.

Spanish Missions This photo shows a mission in Carmel, California. The main church building is on the left. The bell at right is from a mission in Pala, California.

Math

Determine Distance

- Have students use the map on page 111 to answer the following questions:

  Which settlement in New Spain was farthest from Mexico City? San Diego

  Which settlement in New Spain was closest to El Paso? Santa Fe

  How many miles would you travel if you went from St. Augustine to Santa Fe by way of San Antonio? about 1600

Visual-spatial; logical-mathematical

Language Arts

Write a Letter

- Have students use information from the lesson to write a letter from the point of view of a priest who has just arrived at a mission in New Spain to a fellow priest back home in Spain.
- Remind them to write in the first person.

Verbal-linguistic

A Spanish priest named **Bartolomé de las Casas** wanted to protect all American Indians. He spoke out against their mistreatment in the Spanish colonies. He convinced the Spanish king to make laws to help protect them. Most settlers, however, ignored these laws and continued to mistreat them.

American Indians who did not live at missions continued to practice their own traditions and religions. In 1680, a Pueblo Indian leader named **Popé** (poh PEH) led a revolt against the Spanish in New Mexico. A **revolt** is a violent uprising against a ruler. The Pueblo kept the Spanish out of New Mexico until 1692, when the Spanish returned and conquered them again.

7

REVIEW What did some American Indians learn when they moved to Spanish missions?

They learned to speak Spanish and use European farming methods.

Lesson Summary

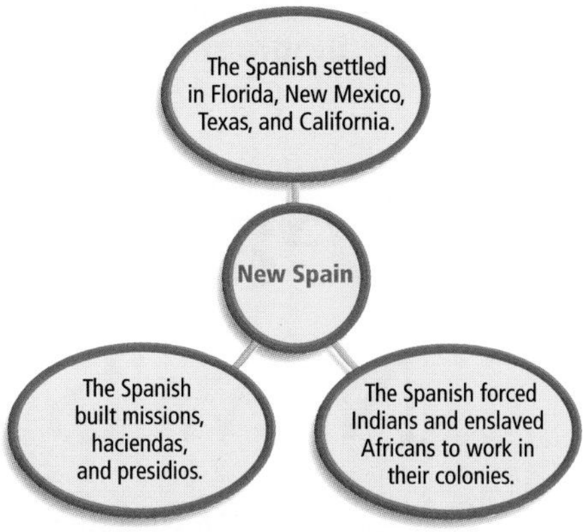

The Spanish settled in Florida, New Mexico, Texas, and California.
New Spain
The Spanish built missions, haciendas, and presidios.
The Spanish forced Indians and enslaved Africans to work in their colonies.

Why It Matters . . .

The growth of New Spain spread Spanish language and customs in the southern United States.

Lesson Review

1565 Avilés founds St. Augustine

1598 Oñate arrives in New Mexico

1680 Popé leads Pueblo Revolt

1550 | 1575 | 1600 | 1625 | 1650 | 1675 | 1700

1. **VOCABULARY** Match the definitions with the words below.
   mission **hacienda** **revolt**
   a. a Spanish farm **b.** a place where religion was taught **c.** an uprising
2. **READING SKILL** In what ways did life change for American Indians who lived at missions?
3. **MAIN IDEA History** Why did the Spanish build haciendas?
4. **MAIN IDEA Culture** What was the main goal of the Spanish missions?
5. **PLACES TO KNOW** Why is St. Augustine an important place in American history?
6. **TIMELINE SKILL** How long after Oñate arrived in New Mexico did the Pueblo Revolt occur?
7. **CRITICAL THINKING: Analyze** How was Menéndez de Aviles's exploration of Florida and Georgia similar to Serra's exploration of California?

HANDS ON **ART ACTIVITY** Find out more about the fort that was built at St. Augustine. Make a drawing or model of it.

113

Study Guide/Homework

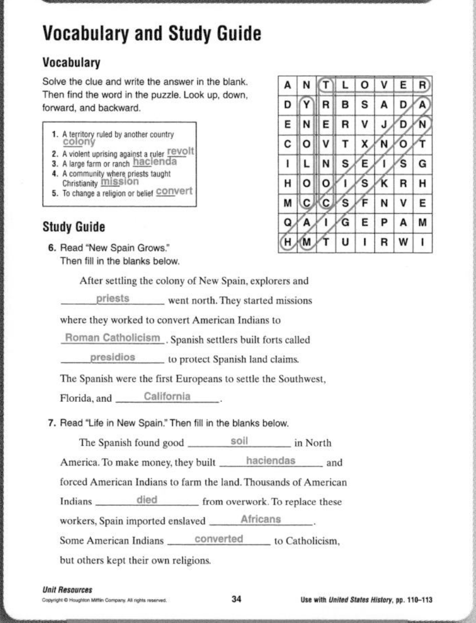

Vocabulary and Study Guide

Vocabulary

Solve the clue and write the answer in the blank. Then find the word in the puzzle. Look up, down, forward, and backward.

1. A territory ruled by another country colony
2. A violent uprising against a ruler revolt
3. A large farm or ranch hacienda
4. A community where priests taught Christianity mission
5. To change a religion or belief convert

A	N	T	L	O	V	E	R
D	Y	R	B	S	A	D	A
E	N	E	R	V	J	D	N
C	O	V	T	X	N	O	T
I	L	N	S	E	I	S	G
H	O	O	I	S	K	R	H
M	C	C	S	F	N	V	E
Q	A	I	G	E	P	A	M
H	M	T	U	I	R	W	I

Study Guide

6. Read "New Spain Grows." Then fill in the blanks below.

   After settling the colony of New Spain, explorers and ___priests___ went north. They started missions where they worked to convert American Indians to ___Roman Catholicism___. Spanish settlers built forts called ___presidios___ to protect Spanish land claims. The Spanish were the first Europeans to settle the Southwest, Florida, and ___California___.

7. Read "Life in New Spain." Then fill in the blanks below.

   The Spanish found good ___soil___ in North America. To make money, they built ___haciendas___ and forced American Indians to farm the land. Thousands of American Indians ___died___ from overwork. To replace these workers, Spain imported enslaved ___Africans___. Some American Indians ___converted___ to Catholicism, but others kept their own religions.

Unit Resources

34 Use with *United States History*, pp. 110–113

Unit Resources, p. 34

Reteach Minilesson

Use a sequence chart to reteach the lesson.

Spanish priests and explorers begin to travel north to start missions.

↓

Menéndez de Aviles starts St. Augustine.

↓

De Oñate settles present-day New Mexico.

↓

Serra helps build San Diego.

www.eduplace.com/ss/hmss05/

3 Review/Assess

Review Tested Objectives

U2-9 The Spanish built missions to help spread Roman Catholicism. They built presidios to protect Spanish claims and guard settlements from attack.

U2-10 American Indians were forced to work on Spanish missions and haciendas where they were often mistreated. Some American Indians accepted Spanish rule, converted to Catholicism, learned to speak Spanish, and used European farming methods. Others refused Spanish traditions and religions and practiced their own; some revolted against Spanish rule.

Lesson Review Answers

1. a) hacienda; b) mission; c) revolt
2. Many were forced to work for the Spanish and were mistreated. Some converted to Catholicism, learned to speak Spanish, and used European farming methods.
3. They did not find much gold in North America, so many turned to farming.
4. to convert American Indians to Roman Catholicism
5. It is the oldest city in the United States built by Europeans.
6. about 82 years
7. Answers will vary.

HANDS ON Performance Task Rubric

4	Model or picture is accurate and shows evidence of thorough research.
3	Model or picture is accurate and shows evidence of research.
2	Model or picture is somewhat accurate and shows evidence of some research.
1	Model or picture is not attempted.

Quick Look

Connect to Core Lesson In Core Lesson 5, students learned about the Spanish colonists who came to New Spain. In Extend Lesson 5, students will learn more about some of New Spain's religious leaders.

1 Teach the Extend Lesson

Connect to the Big Idea

Influences on History Individuals such as Bartolomé de las Casas, Junípero Serra, and Popé influenced the course of New Spain's history.

Biographies

Leadership in New Spain

Leaders in New Spain were not always conquistadors. Religious leaders also played an important role in the way Spanish colonists and Indians lived together. Here are three who left a lasting mark on the history of New Spain.

BARTOLOMÉ DE LAS CASAS
(1474–1566)

Bartolomé de las Casas was a priest who believed that colonists and Indians should live as equals. He devoted his life to improving the lives of Indian workers. In 1542, he wrote a book to tell people about the brutal treatment of Indians. He persuaded the king of Spain to issue laws that protected their rights. Although the laws were not fully enforced, de las Casas's ideas influenced the views of many Europeans.

Las Casas's most famous book, *A Brief Report on the Destruction of the Indies*, was read by people all over Europe.

Reaching All Learners

Extra Support

Use a Venn Diagram

- Instruct students to use a Venn diagram to **compare and contrast** two of the religious leaders featured on pages 114–115.
- Have students share their diagrams with the class.

Visual-spatial; verbal-linguistic

On Level

Make a List

- Ask students to list the facts about the work of each of the leaders in this Extend lesson.
- Have pairs quiz each other about the facts from their cards.

Verbal-linguistic

Challenge

Compare Leaders Then and Now

Have students think of a community, state, or national leader and make a compare contrast chart, comparing the present-day leader to one of the leaders in this lesson.

Verbal-linguistic

(1713–1784)

Junípero Serra was a priest and tireless explorer who helped found 21 missions along the coast of California. He believed he was serving his God by converting thousands of Indians to the Christian faith. However, many Indians suffered at the missions. They were overworked and some starved or died of diseases. Their work included building churches, canals, and mills for the Spanish.

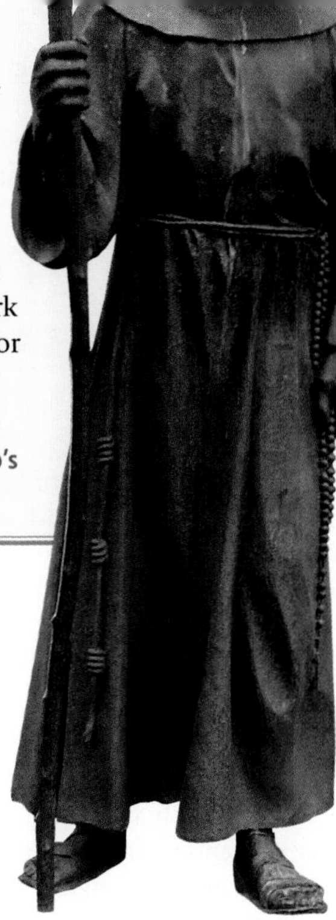

Junípero Serra's statue stands in San Francisco's Golden Gate Park.

Popé

(1630–1690)

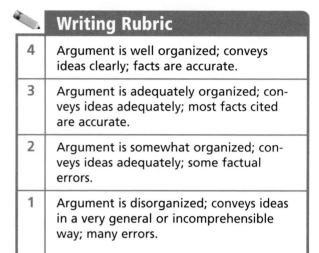

Popé was a religious leader of the Pueblo Indians. He thought the time had come to drive out the Spanish colonists who had been forcing the Pueblo to give up their religious beliefs. Popé planned a revolt against the Spanish and persuaded others to join him. In 1680, his followers burned churches and attacked haciendas and missions. After the Spanish fled to Mexico, Popé ordered the destruction of all Spanish buildings and artifacts. The Pueblo people's revolt was the most successful Indian uprising in the history of New Spain.

Activities

1. **TALK ABOUT IT** Why do you think the laws protecting Indians were not enforced?
2. **WRITE ABOUT IT** Choose one of the three religious leaders. Describe what you think were that leader's most important accomplishments.

❶ **Talk About It** *For Extra Support*
The colonists did not think that the Indians deserved equal treatment. They wanted the Indians to do their hard work for them.

❷ **Write About It** *For Challenge*

Writing Rubric

4	Argument is well organized; conveys ideas clearly; facts are accurate.
3	Argument is adequately organized; conveys ideas adequately; most facts cited are accurate.
2	Argument is somewhat organized; conveys ideas adequately; some factual errors.
1	Argument is disorganized; conveys ideas in a very general or incomprehensible way; many errors.

ELL

Intermediate

Ask students to choose an important scene from the life of one of the leaders discussed in this Extend lesson. Have them **create an illustration** showing the scene.

Visual-spatial

Drama

Write a Scene

- Divide class into groups of three or four. Ask students to write a dramatic scene based on the life of one of the leaders discussed.
- Have students act out their scene for the class.

Verbal-linguistic; bodily-kinesthetic

Graphic Organizer

de las Casas	Popé	Serra
Spanish	Pueblo Indian	Spanish
Tried to create settlements where colonists and Indians could live as equals	Thought Pueblo Indians should be able to practice their traditions	Converted many Indians to Christianity
Wrote a book about the brutal treatment of the Indians	Led Pueblo Indians in a successful uprising against the Spanish	Created missions where many Indians suffered

Graphic Organizer 2

Skillbuilder Pages 116–117

Tested Objective

U2-11 Use latitude and longitude to determine absolute locations.

1 Teach the Skill

- Discuss the words *latitude* and *longitude* with students. Point out these lines on the globes on page 116.
- Have students look at the map on page 117. Point out that the latitude and longitude lines on this map form a grid.
- Have several students read aloud the steps under "Learn the Skill." Answer any questions they have.
- Discuss with students reasons that latitude and longitude lines are useful.

Map and Globe Skills

Skillbuilder

Use Latitude and Longitude

VOCABULARY
parallel
meridian
absolute location

To help sailors and other travelers locate places, mapmakers created an imaginary grid of lines over the globe. This grid is made up of lines of latitude and longitude.

Learn the Skill

Step 1: Identify the line of latitude. Lines of latitude run east and west and measure distance north and south of the equator. The equator is 0° latitude. Lines of latitude north of the equator are labeled N. Those south of the equator are labeled S. A line of latitude is also called a **parallel.**

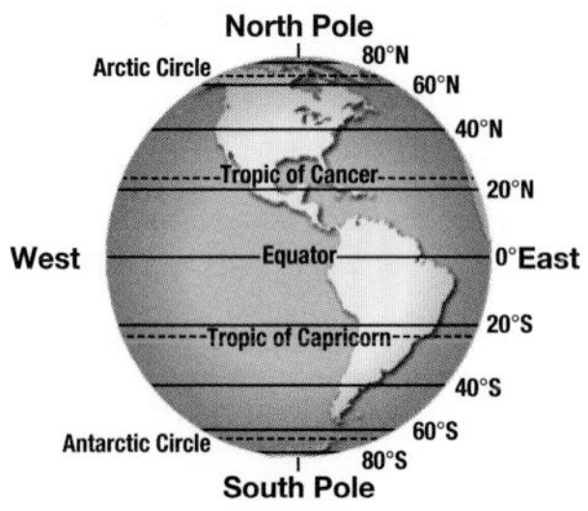

Step 2: Identify the line of longitude. Lines of longitude run north and south and measure distance east and west of the prime meridian. The prime meridian is 0° longitude. Lines of longitude east of the prime meridian are labeled E. Those west of the prime meridian are labeled W. A line of longitude is also called a **meridian.**

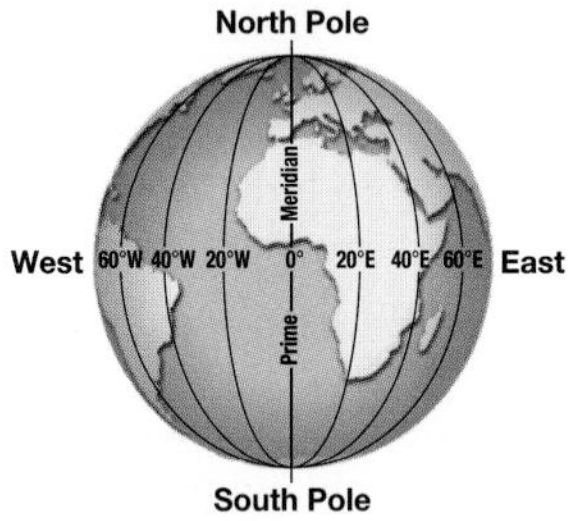

Step 3: Find where the lines of latitude and longitude cross. The exact latitude and longitude of a place on the globe is also called its **absolute location.**

Leveled Practice

Extra Support

Have students indicate the prime meridian and the equator on a world map or globe. Clarify the meanings of *parallel* and *meridian.* Visual-spatial

Challenge

Ask students to use an atlas to pinpoint the absolute location of their places of birth or other places of interest. Have them compile this information in a chart. Visual-spatial

ELL

Intermediate

Have students use an atlas to find the location of their places of birth or of their families' places of origin. Have students point out these locations on the globe and tell the approximate latitude and longitude of each place.

Verbal-linguistic; visual-spatial

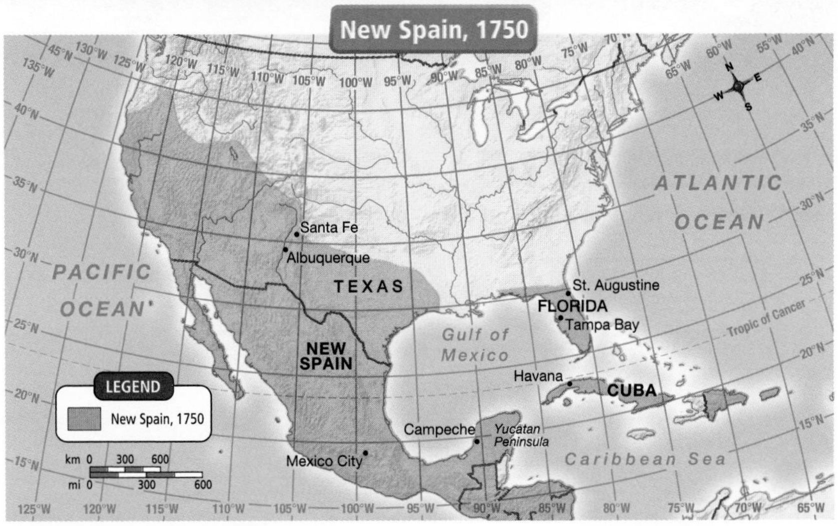

Practice the Skill

Use the map above to answer these questions.

1. What line of latitude is closest to St. Augustine? What line of longitude is closest to St. Augustine?
2. What other place is at almost the same longitude as Tampa Bay?
3. What place is near 19°N, 98°W?
4. What are the lines of latitude and longitude closest to Campeche?

Apply the Skill

Use your library or Internet resources to find a map of your state. Locate the town or city where you live by using latitude and longitude. Then write a paragraph explaining how you did this.

2 Practice the Skill

1. 30°N; 80°W
2. Havana, Cuba
3. Mexico City
4. 20°N; 90°W

3 Apply the Skill

Ask students to locate their town or city on a state map and write a paragraph explaining how they did this. When evaluating students' paragraphs, consider:

- Did the student use longitude and latitude to locate the town or city?
- Did the student clearly explain the process by which he or she located the town or city?
- Did the student use correct mechanics?

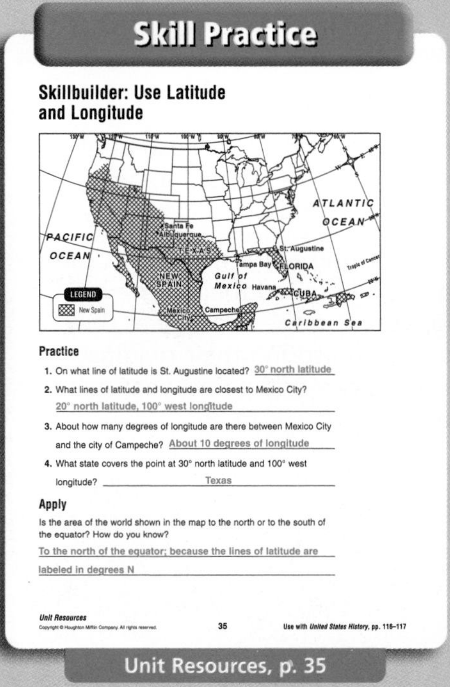

Skill Practice

Skillbuilder: Use Latitude and Longitude

Practice

1. On what line of latitude is St. Augustine located? 30° north latitude
2. What lines of latitude and longitude are closest to Mexico City? 20° north latitude, 100° west longitude
3. About how many degrees of longitude are there between Mexico City and the city of Campeche? About 10 degrees of longitude
4. What state covers the point at 30° north latitude and 100° west longitude? Texas

Apply

Is the area of the world shown in the map to the north or to the south of the equator? How do you know?
To the north of the equator; because the lines of latitude are labeled in degrees N

Unit Resources 35 Use with *United States History*, pp. 116–117

Unit Resources, p. 35

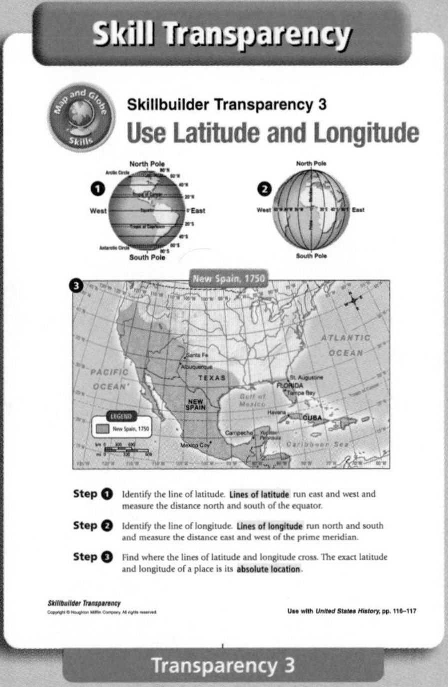

Skill Transparency

Skillbuilder Transparency 3

Use Latitude and Longitude

Step 1 Identify the line of latitude. **Lines of latitude** run east and west and measure the distance north and south of the equator.

Step 2 Identify the line of longitude. **Lines of longitude** run north and south and measure the distance east and west of the prime meridian.

Step 3 Find where the lines of latitude and longitude cross. The exact latitude and longitude of a place is its **absolute location**.

Skillbuilder Transparency Use with *United States History*, pp. 116–117

Transparency 3

Chapter Review

Tested Objectives

The lesson objective assessed by each question is shown in parentheses after the answer.

Visual Summary

1. Italian merchant who led a trading journey to China in 1271 *(Obj. U2-1)*
2. king of Mali who traveled to Mecca; set up trade with the cities he visited *(Obj. U2-2)*
3. the first European to sail across the Pacific Ocean; *(Obj. U2-6)*
4. Spanish explorer who conquered the Aztec Empire *(Obj. U2-7)*

Facts and Main Ideas

5. several trade routes connecting China and Europe *(Obj. U2-3)*
6. astrolabe and compass *(Obj. U2-3)*
7. Columbus wanted to sail west across the Atlantic Ocean instead of south around Africa. *(Obj. U2-5)*
8. Aztecs were people living in a powerful empire in present-day Mexico; Cortés wanted to capture their wealth. *(Obj. U2-7, U2-8)*
9. Spanish priests set up missions to spread Christianity. *(Obj. U2-9)*

Vocabulary

10. **colony** *(Obj. U2-9)*
11. **merchant** *(Obj. U2-1)*
12. **circumnavigate** *(Obj. U2-6)*
13. **slavery** *(Obj. U2-10)*

Visual Summary

1.–4. Describe what you learned about each person named below.

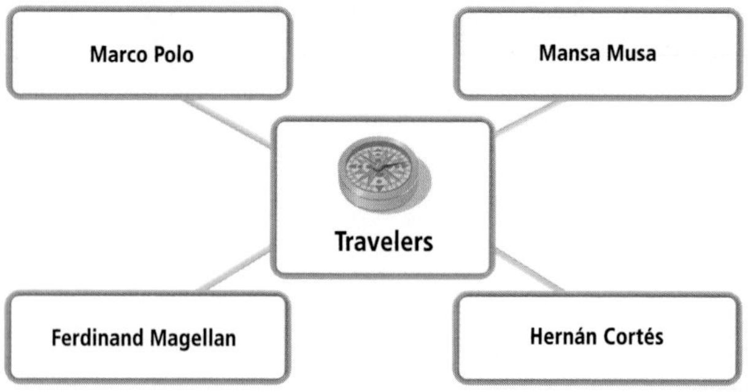

Facts and Main Ideas

TEST PREP Answer each question with information from the chapter.

5. **Economics** What was the Silk Road?
6. **History** What were two inventions that improved navigation?
7. **Geography** How was Christopher Columbus's route to Asia different from those of earlier explorers?
8. **History** Who were the Aztecs and why did Hernán Cortés want to conquer them?
9. **History** Why did priests travel to New Spain and what did they do there?

Vocabulary

TEST PREP Choose the correct word from the list below to complete each sentence.

merchant, p. 85
slavery, p. 92
circumnavigate, p. 101
colony, p. 112

10. The _____ of New Spain was started in present-day Mexico.
11. Marco Polo was a _____ who traveled to China to find spices and silk.
12. Members of Ferdinand Magellan's crew were the first people to _____ the world.
13. Many Portuguese traders forced Africans into _____ and sold them in Europe.

Reading/Language Arts Wrap-Up

Reading Strategy: Monitor/Clarify

Review with students the process of monitoring their understanding and clarifying anything they do not understand.

Have students work in pairs, taking turns to model the process as they read.

Partners can help each other clarify important points.

Writing Strategy

As students write, they can apply what they have learned about monitoring and clarifying text.

After writing a draft, students can go back and read their own writing, applying the strategy as they do. By monitoring their reading, students can find points that need clarification.

Apply Skills

TEST PREP **Map Skill** Study the map of explorers in Florida. Then use what you have learned about latitude and longitude to answer each question.

14. Which explorer or explorers started voyages at about 23°N, 83°W?

A. Juan Ponce de León

B. Juan Ponce de León and Hernando de Soto

C. Hernando de Soto

D. Francisco Vásquez de Coronado

15. What was the most northern line of latitude that Ponce de León reached?

A. about 30°S.

B. about 87°W

C. about 30°N

D. about 87°E

Critical Thinking

TEST PREP Write a short paragraph to answer each question.

16. **Cause and Effect** What were four lasting effects of the Columbian Exchange?

17. **Fact and Opinion** Bartolomé de las Casas wanted to convince the king of Spain to protect American Indians. Write one fact and one opinion that he might have included in his argument.

Timeline

Use the Chapter Summary Timeline above to answer the question.

18. In what year did Europeans first arrive in the Americas?

Activities

HANDS ON **Art Activity** The Spanish built different kinds of buildings in New Spain. Find pictures of a presidio, a mission, or a hacienda, and make your own drawing of it.

Writing Activity Write a personal essay telling what you think of Marco Polo's adventures. Include information about his journey to China on the Silk Road and the things he saw in China.

Technology
Writing Process Tips
Get help with your essay at www.eduplace.com/kids/hmss05/

119

Technology

Test Generator

You can generate your own version of the chapter review by using the **Test Generator CD-ROM**.

Web Link

For more ideas, visit
www.eduplace.com/ss/hmss05/

Standards

National Standards

I a Addressing human needs **II b** Cause and effect relationships **II e** People in different times and places view the world differently **III c** Resources, data sources, and geographic tools **V b** Group and institutional influences **VI f** Cooperation and disputes **VII d** Institutions that make up economic systems **VII f** Influence of incentives, values, traditions, and habits **VIII a** How science and technology have changed lives **VIII b** How science and technology have changed the physical environment **IX b** Conflict, cooperation, and interdependence **IX c** Effects of changing technologies on the global community

Apply Skills

14. C *(Obj. U2-11)*

15. C *(Obj. U2-11)*

Critical Thinking

16. Sample answer: Trade; exchange of ideas and inventions; enslavement of Africans and American Indians; disease *(Obj. U2-10)*

17. Sample answer: Facts: American Indians forced to work, often for no pay; many died from overwork; Opinions: wrong to treat people this way; against Catholic religion; American Indians should be able to live freely. *(Obj. U2-10)*

Timeline

18. 1492 *(Obj. U2-5)*

Leveled Activities

HANDS ON Performance Task Rubric

4	Drawing is creative, accurate, and complete; mechanics correct.
3	Drawing is complete and mostly accurate; mechanics correct.
2	Drawing is somewhat accurate; problems with mechanics.
1	Drawing is inaccurate and incomplete; many errors.

Writing Rubric

4	Essay is creative, well organized, accurate, and includes opinion and relevant details; mechanics are correct.
3	Essay is organized, accurate, and includes opinion and relevant details; mechanics are mostly correct.
2	Essay is fairly accurate, and includes some opinion and details; some errors.
1	Essay is incomplete or inaccurate; opinion and details absent; many errors.

Chapter Opener

Pages 120–121

30 minutes

Reading/Vocabulary

Chapter Reading Strategy: Summarize, p. 119F

Resources

Grade Level Resources
- Vocabulary Cards, pp. 11–20

Reaching All Learners
- Challenge Activities, p. 82

Primary Sources Plus, p. 6

Big Idea Transparency 2

Interactive Transparency 2

Text & Music Audio CD

Lesson Planner & TR CD-ROM

eBook

eTE

Core Lesson 1

A Northwest Passage

Pages 122–125

40 minutes

Tested Objectives

U2-12 Describe the motives and achievements of early English, French, and Dutch explorers.

U2-13 Explain the significance of the Spanish Armada.

Reading/Vocabulary

Reading Skill: Main Idea and Details

claim, invasion, armada

Cross-Curricular

Science, p. 124

Resources

Unit Resources:
- **Reading Skill/Strategy,** p. 36
- **Vocabulary/Study Guide,** p. 37

Reaching All Learners:
- **Lesson Summary,** p. 15
- **Support for Lang. Dev./ELL,** p. 112

Assessment Options:
- **Lesson Test,** p. 33

www.eduplace.com/ss/hmss05/

Extend Lesson 1

Biographies

Rulers of Land and Sea

20–30 minutes

Pages 126–127

Focus: Students learn more about King Philip II and Queen Elizabeth I.

Skillbuilder

Chart and Graph Skill

Use Parallel Timelines

Pages 128–129

30 minutes

Tested Objective

U2-14 Interpret information from multiple timelines.

Reading/Vocabulary

parallel timelines

Resources

Unit Resources:
- **Skill Practice,** p. 38

Skill Transparency 4

Core Lesson 2

Roanoke and Jamestown

Pages 130–133

40 minutes

Tested Objectives

U2-15 Explain the reasons for the establishment of early English settlements.

U2-16 Describe the experiences of settlers in Jamestown.

Reading/Vocabulary

Reading Skill: Draw Conclusions

charter, cash crop, invest, indentured servant, stock

Cross-Curricular

Math, p. 132

Resources

Unit Resources:
- **Reading Skill/Strategy,** p. 39
- **Vocabulary/Study Guide,** p. 40

Reaching All Learners:
- **Lesson Summary,** p. 16
- **Support for Lang. Dev./ELL,** p. 113

Assessment Options:
- **Lesson Test,** p. 34

Extend Lesson 2

Geography

Jamestown 1607

20–30 Minutes

Pages 134–135

Focus: Students get a bird's-eye view of the settlement.

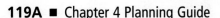

National Standards

II b Read and construct simple timelines
III g How people create places
III h Interaction of human beings and their physical environment
VI f Factors that contribute to cooperation and cause disputes
VII a Scarcity and choice
VII f Influence of incentives, values, traditions, and habits
IX b Conflict, cooperation, and interdependence
IX f Concerns, issues, standards, and conflicts related to human rights

With the Program — CURRENT EVENTS from WEEKLY WR READER at www.eduplace.com

Core Lesson 3

New England Settlements

Pages 136–139
40 minutes

Tested Objectives

U2-17 Explain why and how the Pilgrims and Puritans settled in America.
U2-18 Describe the Plymouth and Massachusetts Bay settlements.

Reading/Vocabulary

Reading Skill: Cause and Effect
pilgrim **cape**
compact

Cross-Curricular

Drama, p. 138

Resources

Unit Resources:
- **Reading Skill/Strategy,** p. 41
- **Vocabulary/Study Guide,** p. 42

Reaching All Learners:
- **Lesson Summary,** p. 17
- **Support for Lang. Dev./ELL,** p. 114

Assessment Options:
- **Lesson Test,** p. 35

Extend Lesson 3

Literature
This New Land
40–50 minutes
Pages 140–143
Focus: This selection tells how Squanto helped European settlers.

Core Lesson 4

Dutch and French Colonies

Pages 144–147
40 minutes

Tested Objectives

U2-19 Describe the Dutch settlement of New Netherland.
U2-20 Summarize the experiences of settlers, missionaries, and explorers in New France.

Reading/Vocabulary

Reading Skill: Compare and Contrast
diversity **missionary**
tolerance

Cross-Curricular

Music, p. 146

Resources

Unit Resources:
- **Reading Skill/Strategy,** p. 43
- **Vocabulary/Study Guide,** p. 44

Reaching All Learners:
- **Lesson Summary,** p. 18
- **Support for Lang. Dev./ELL,** p. 115

Assessment Options:
- **Lesson Test,** p. 36

Extend Lesson 4

Economics
French Fur Trading
20–30 minutes
Pages 148–149
Focus: Students learn more about the people of the fur trade.

Chapter Review

Pages 150–151
30 minutes

Resources

Assessment Options:
- **Chapter 4 Test**
- **Test Generator**

Practice Options

Lesson 1 Skill and Strategy

TEST PREP

Reading Skill and Strategy

Reading Skill: Main Idea and Details

This skill helps you understand events by seeing how they are related.

Read "France Explores North America." Then fill in the chart below. Write details that support the main idea in the smaller boxes.

French explorers searched for the Northwest Passage, but were unsuccessful.

1. Verrazano explored the east coast of North America.
2. Cartier sailed up the St. Lawrence River in Canada.
3. Champlain founded Quebec.

Reading Strategy: Summarize

4. Read "Searching for a Passage to Asia." Then check the best summary.
   - ✓ Explorers searched for a water route through North America to Asia.
   - ___ John Cabot found excellent fishing waters off the coast of present-day Canada.
   - ___ The Hudson River and Hudson Bay were named for the explorer Henry Hudson.
5. Read "The Spanish Armada." Then check the best summary.
   - ___ The English sea captain Francis Drake attacked and robbed many Spanish ships.
   - ___ Most English people were Protestants, and most Spanish people were Catholics.
   - ✓ The fighting between England and Spain ended after the English navy defeated the Spanish Armada.

Unit Resources

36
Use with *United States History*, pp. 122–125

Lesson 1 Vocabulary/Study Guide

TEST PREP

Vocabulary and Study Guide

Vocabulary

Write the definition of each vocabulary word below.

1. armada The Spanish word for a large fleet of ships
2. claim Something declared as one's own, especially a piece of land
3. invasion An attack by an armed force to conquer another country
4. Choose two words. Use each word in a sentence about the lesson.
   Sample answers: England prepared its navy for Spain's invasion. Many countries began making claims to land in North America.

Study Guide

Read "Searching for a Passage to Asia." Then fill in the chart below.

Explorer	Explored North America for this nation	What this explorer did
John Cabot	5. England	6. Reached present-day Canada
Giovanni da Verrazano	7. France	8. Explored the area now known as New York City
9. Samuel de Champlain	10. France	Founded Quebec
Henry Hudson	11. The Netherlands and England	12. Sailed up the river now called the Hudson River and found the body of water now called the Hudson Bay

Unit Resources

37
Use with *United States History*, pp. 122–125

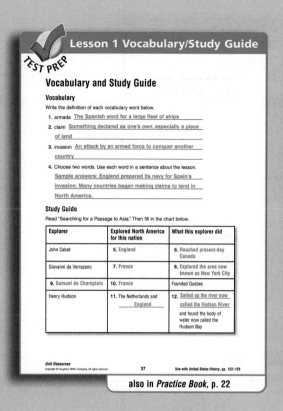

also in *Practice Book*, p. 22

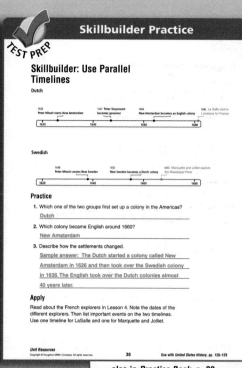

Skillbuilder Practice

TEST PREP

Skillbuilder: Use Parallel Timelines

Dutch

1620 – 1640 – 1660 – 1680

- 1626 Peter Minuit starts New Amsterdam
- 1647 Peter Stuyvesant becomes governor
- 1664 New Amsterdam becomes an English colony
- 1682 La Salle claims Louisiana for France

Swedish

1620 – 1640 – 1660 – 1680

- 1638 Peter Minuit creates New Sweden
- 1655 New Sweden becomes a Dutch colony
- 1673 Marquette and Jolliet explore the Mississippi River

Practice

1. Which one of the two groups first set up a colony in the Americas?
   Dutch
2. Which colony became English around 1660?
   New Amsterdam
3. Describe how the settlements changed.
   Sample answer: The Dutch started a colony called New Amsterdam in 1626 and then took over the Swedish colony in 1638. The English took over the Dutch colonies almost 40 years later.

Apply

Read about the French explorers in Lesson 4. Note the dates of the different explorers. Then list important events on the two timelines. Use one timeline for LaSalle and one for Marquette and Jolliet.

Unit Resources

38
Use with *United States History*, pp. 128–129

also in *Practice Book*, p. 23

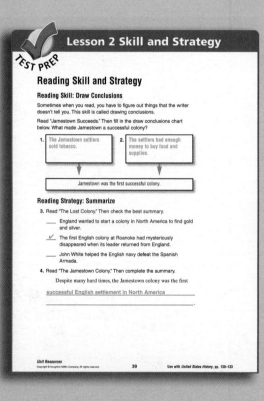

Lesson 2 Skill and Strategy

TEST PREP

Reading Skill and Strategy

Reading Skill: Draw Conclusions

Sometimes when you read, you have to figure out things that the writer doesn't tell you. This skill is called drawing conclusions.

Read "Jamestown Succeeds." Then fill in the draw conclusions chart below. What made Jamestown a successful colony?

1. The Jamestown settlers sold tobacco.
2. The settlers had enough money to buy food and supplies.

Jamestown was the first successful colony.

Reading Strategy: Summarize

3. Read "The Lost Colony." Then check the best summary.
   - ___ England wanted to start a colony in North America to find gold and silver.
   - ✓ The first English colony at Roanoke had mysteriously disappeared when its leader returned from England.
   - ___ John White helped the English navy defeat the Spanish Armada.
4. Read "The Jamestown Colony." Then complete the summary.
   Despite many hard times, the Jamestown colony was the first successful English settlement in North America

Unit Resources

39
Use with *United States History*, pp. 130–133

Lesson 2 Vocabulary/Study Guide

TEST PREP

Vocabulary and Study Guide

Vocabulary

Solve the clue and write the answer in the blank. Then find the word in the puzzle. Look up, down, forward, and backward.

1. A crop that people grow and sell to earn money cash crop
2. A piece of ownership of a company stock
3. To put money into something to try to make more money invest
4. A document that gives certain freedoms to a person or group charter

A	I	X	D	K	G	S	C
M	S	V	F	D	G	T	N
C	A	S	H	C	R	O	P
H	P	B	L	T	N	C	D
A	R	M	E	U	Y	K	Q
R	E	Q	O	K	O	I	J
T	H	I	N	V	E	S	T
E	S	Z	R	C	T	A	C
R	H	U	W	L	F	J	B

Study Guide

5. Read "The Lost Colony." Then fill in the blanks below.
   In 1585, about 100 men from England settled on Roanoke Island. Most of them returned to England because they could not grow crops. In 1587, the English tried again to settle there. When John White returned from a trip to England to get more supplies, the colonists had disappeared.
6. Read "The Jamestown Colony." Then fill in the blanks below.
   A group of English merchants started the Virginia Company of London in 1606. They wanted to build a settlement in North America. The company sent men and boys there to build a fort. The settlers named their colony Jamestown.

Unit Resources

40
Use with *United States History*, pp. 130–133

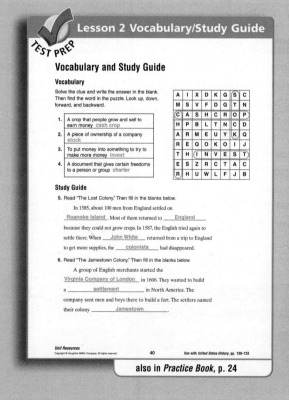

also in *Practice Book*, p. 24

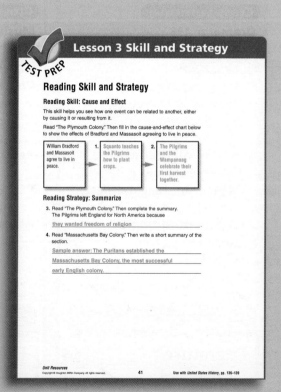

Lesson 3 Skill and Strategy

TEST PREP

Reading Skill and Strategy

Reading Skill: Cause and Effect

This skill helps you see how one event can be related to another, either by causing it or resulting from it.

Read "The Plymouth Colony." Then fill in the cause-and-effect chart below to show the effects of Bradford and Massasoit agreeing to live in peace.

William Bradford and Massasoit agree to live in peace. → 1. Squanto teaches the Pilgrims how to plant crops. → 2. The Pilgrims and the Wampanoag celebrate their first harvest together.

Reading Strategy: Summarize

3. Read "The Plymouth Colony." Then complete the summary.
   The Pilgrims left England for North America because they wanted freedom of religion.
4. Read "Massachusetts Bay Colony." Then write a short summary of the section.
   Sample answer: The Puritans established the Massachusetts Bay Colony, the most successful early English colony.

Unit Resources

41
Use with *United States History*, pp. 136–139

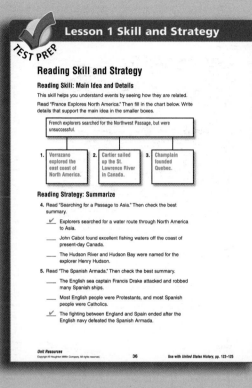

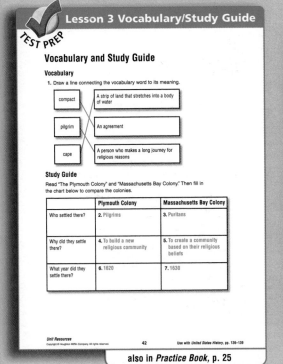

Lesson 3 Vocabulary/Study Guide

TEST PREP

Vocabulary and Study Guide

Vocabulary

1. Draw a line connecting the vocabulary word to its meaning.

compact	A strip of land that stretches into a body of water
pilgrim	An agreement
cape	A person who makes a long journey for religious reasons

Study Guide

Read "The Plymouth Colony" and "Massachusetts Bay Colony." Then fill in the chart below to compare the colonies.

	Plymouth Colony	Massachusetts Bay Colony
Who settled there?	2. Pilgrims	3. Puritans
Why did they settle there?	4. To build a new religious community	5. To create a community based on their religious beliefs
What year did they settle there?	6. 1620	7. 1630

also in *Practice Book*, p. 25

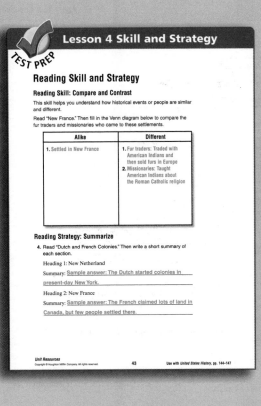

Lesson 4 Skill and Strategy

TEST PREP

Reading Skill and Strategy

Reading Skill: Compare and Contrast

This skill helps you understand how historical events or people are similar and different.

Read "New France." Then fill in the Venn diagram below to compare the fur traders and missionaries who came to these settlements.

Alike	Different
1. Settled in New France	1. Fur traders: Traded with American Indians and then sold furs in Europe 2. Missionaries: Taught American Indians about the Roman Catholic religion

Reading Strategy: Summarize

4. Read "Dutch and French Colonies." Then write a short summary of each section.

Heading 1: New Netherland

Summary: Sample answer: The Dutch started colonies in present-day New York.

Heading 2: New France

Summary: Sample answer: The French claimed lots of land in Canada, but few people settled there.

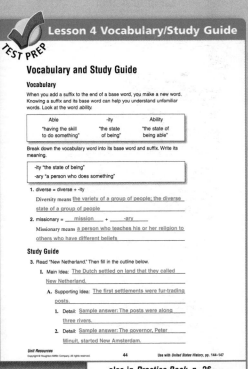

Lesson 4 Vocabulary/Study Guide

TEST PREP

Vocabulary and Study Guide

Vocabulary

When you add a suffix to the end of a base word, you make a new word. Knowing a suffix and its base word can help you understand unfamiliar words. Look at the word *ability*.

Able	-ity	Ability
"having the skill to do something"	"the state of being"	"the state of being able"

Break down the vocabulary word into its base word and suffix. Write its meaning.

-ity "the state of being"
-ary "a person who does something"

1. diverse = diverse + -ity

Diversity means the variety of a group of people; the diverse state of a group of people

2. missionary = mission + -ary

Missionary means a person who teaches his or her religion to others who have different beliefs

Study Guide

3. Read "New Netherland." Then fill in the outline below.

I. Main Idea: The Dutch settled on land that they called New Netherland.

A. Supporting Idea: The first settlements were fur-trading posts.

1. Detail: Sample answer: The posts were along three rivers.

2. Detail: Sample answer: The governor, Peter Minuit, started New Amsterdam.

also in *Practice Book*, p. 26

Chapter 4 Assessment Options

Chapter 4 Test

TEST PREP

Chapter 4 Test

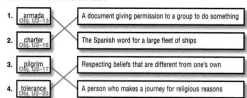

Test Your Knowledge

Match each word to its definition.

1. armada Obj. U2–13 — A document giving permission to a group to do something
2. charter Obj. U2–16 — The Spanish word for a large fleet of ships
3. pilgrim Obj. U2–17 — Respecting beliefs that are different from one's own
4. tolerance Obj. U2–20 — A person who makes a journey for religious reasons

Circle the letter of the best answer.

5. What was life like for settlers in Jamestown? Obj. U2–16
   - A. The settlers built large homes and lived comfortably.
   - (B.) The settlers did not have enough food, and many died.
   - C. The settlers farmed and had plenty of food.
   - D. The settlers found gold and bought large pieces of land.
6. Why did the Pilgrims settle in North America? Obj. U2–17
   - F. They wanted to bring silks and spices to Europe.
   - G. They wanted to find a Northwest Passage.
   - H. They wanted to teach American Indians how to farm.
   - (J.) They wanted to practice their religion freely.
7. How were the settlements at the Plymouth colony and the Massachusetts Bay colony similar? Obj. U2–18
   - A. The settlers in both colonies learned to plant corn from the Wampanoag.
   - B. The settlers arrived at a good time to plant crops in each colony.
   - (C.) Each group of settlers created a community based on religious beliefs.
   - D. The settlers named each colony after American Indians living there.
8. Why did John Cabot and Jacques Cartier travel to North America? Obj. U2–12
   - (F.) They were looking for a water route through North America to Asia.
   - G. They were looking for the Dutch West India Company.
   - H. They were looking for a shorter route to the Netherlands.
   - J. They were looking for a faster route from France to Quebec.

Chapter 4 Test

TEST PREP

Apply Your Knowledge

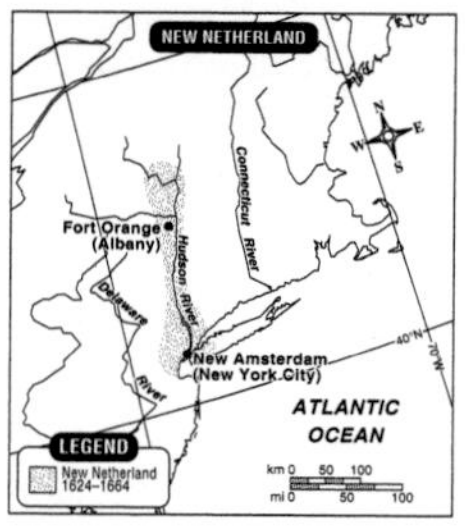

Use the map to answer the following questions.

9. What is New Amsterdam now called? Obj. U2–19
   - (A.) New York City
   - B. Fort Orange
   - C. Albany
   - D. Connecticut
10. What natural feature made it easy for the English to attack New Amsterdam? Obj. U2–19
   - F. the Connecticut River
   - G. the Delaware River
   - (H.) the Atlantic Ocean
   - J. the Pacific Ocean

Apply the Reading Skill: Compare and Contrast

Read the passage below. Then answer the question. Obj. U2–15

> In 1587, the English started a colony called Roanoke, which was led by John White. Roanoke did not survive. In 1606, English merchants started a colony called Jamestown. John Smith, its leader, told people to farm. Jamestown became a successful colony.

11. How were Jamestown and Roanoke similar? How were they different?
    Both were started by the English. Roanoke did not survive, but Jamestown did.

Chapter 4 Test

TEST PREP

Test the Skill: Use Parallel Timelines

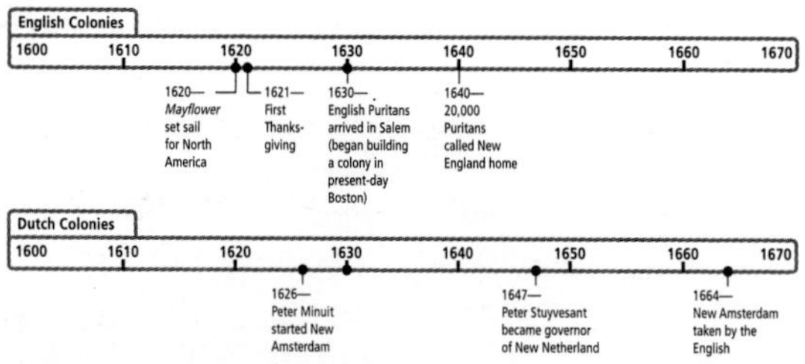

12. About how much time passed from the time the *Mayflower* set sail for North America to the time New Amsterdam was started? 6 years Obj. U2–14
13. About how much time passed from the first Thanksgiving to the English takeover of New Amsterdam? 43 years Obj. U2–14
14. Based on the information in the timelines, what can you say about the English and the Dutch between 1620 and 1630?
    Sample answer: Both the English and the Dutch started new colonies between 1620 and 1630. Obj. U2–14

Apply the Skill

15. Create parallel timelines. Draw and label two timelines on a separate sheet of paper. Mark each day for one week, starting with Sunday and ending with Saturday. List activities taking place in your life this week. Place these on one timeline. Then switch lists with a classmate, and place his or her activities on the other timeline. Compare the timelines to see how they are related and different. Obj. U2–14
    Two timelines should be labeled Sunday through Saturday. Activities for each student should be on separate timelines.

Chapter 4 Test

TEST PREP

Think and Write

16. **Short Response:** Describe the relationship the French missionaries and fur traders had with the American Indians in New France. Obj. U2–20
    Traders had strong partnerships with the Huron and Algonquin and traded furs for metal goods and beads. Missionaries built missions to teach American Indians Roman Catholicism.
17. **Critical Thinking: Draw Conclusions** Why do you think the defeat of the Spanish Armada by the English was important?
    Sample answer: Defeating the Spanish made it possible for the English to set up more colonies in America. Obj. U2–13
18. **Extended Response:** Write a journal entry that John Rolfe might have written about Jamestown. Include comments about the relationship between the Powhatans and the Jamestown colonists. Write your journal entry on a separate sheet of paper. Obj. U2–16 Journal entries may refer to the struggles over land, the colonists' lack of food, what Rolfe learned from the Powhatans about growing tobacco, and Rolfe's marriage to Pocahontas.

Self-Assessment

Who do I think was an important leader in the early colonies? Why do I think so?

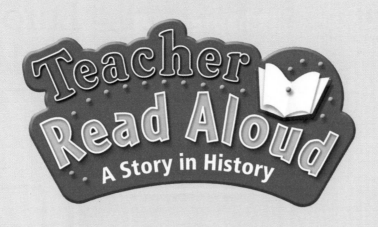

Teacher Read Aloud
A Story in History

You can share the following fiction selection with students before beginning the chapter. Ask students to look at the picture and map on page 145 of their books as you read.

Activate Prior Knowledge
Tell students that the city of New York was originally called New Amsterdam. Explain that the Read-Aloud selection describes the arrival of a settler in New Amsterdam in the 1600s.

Preview the Chapter
Have students skim the section Settlers in New Netherland on page 145. Ask them to find similarities and differences between the information in this section and the details mentioned in the Read-Aloud selection.

Read-Aloud Vocabulary
Tell students that **diversity** is variety within a group of people. Explain that people who respect others' beliefs are showing **tolerance.**

Preview the Reading Strategy
Summarize Explain to students that the reading strategy they will use in this chapter is summarizing, or putting something in their own words. You may wish to use the Read Aloud to model summarizing.

Think Aloud *Josef is arriving by ship in a new place, New Amsterdam. The captain tells him that it is a land of opportunity. People from many different countries are welcome. He tells Josef that some people may recognize his family's name. Josef hopes to make a new start as a sculptor in New Amsterdam.*

A New Beginning

The journey was nearly over, and for that, Josef was thankful. The weeks aboard the ship had been nothing but misery. How, he wondered, was it possible to be constantly seasick?

A slap on the back jolted him from his thoughts. "There 'tis, young man, just as I told you," said the captain. "New Amsterdam. Land of opportunity."

" **Diversity** was the word you used, Captain," Josef said.

"Aye, a land of diversity as well. You'll hear a dozen languages before you even get to the center of town. All people are welcome, no matter where they hail from." The captain's jovial face turned serious. "Yes, it's rare to find a place of **tolerance** in the world today, even if it is the 1600s." Then he looked at Josef with a twinkle in his eye. "There's plenty of good chances here. I'm sure that some will recognize your family's name."

Josef grinned back. "I hope they don't hold that against me. A Breyerhof who doesn't cut stone, but carves it—no one knew what to think of me back home."

"Well, laddie, stonecutter or sculptor, you'll make a new start here."

Begin the Chapter

Quick Look

Core Lesson 1 focuses on how explorers sought a Northwest Passage and how their countries claimed land.

Core Lesson 2 describes the first English settlements in North America.

Core Lesson 3 discusses Pilgrim and Puritan settlements in New England.

Core Lesson 4 explores the first Dutch and French colonies in North America.

Vocabulary Preview

Use the vocabulary cards to preview the key vocabulary words before starting the lessons and to prepare students to understand the content of the chapter.

Vocabulary Strategy

Vocabulary strategies for this chapter:

- Structural analysis, p. 132, 145
- Synonyms/antonyms, p. 131, 132, 137, 145
- Root words, p. 132
- Prefixes and suffixes, p. 124
- Word origins, p. 131, 137

Vocabulary Help

Vocabulary card for charter Explain to students that a *charter* is an official document creating or making rules for a colony, city, or government.

Vocabulary card for tolerance *Tolerance* means accepting people's different beliefs and practices.

Chapter 4 European Settlements

Technology
e • glossary
e • word games
www.eduplace.com/kids/hmss05/

Vocabulary Preview

armada

King Philip of Spain sent an **armada** to fight against England. This large fleet of ships sailed in 1588.
page 125

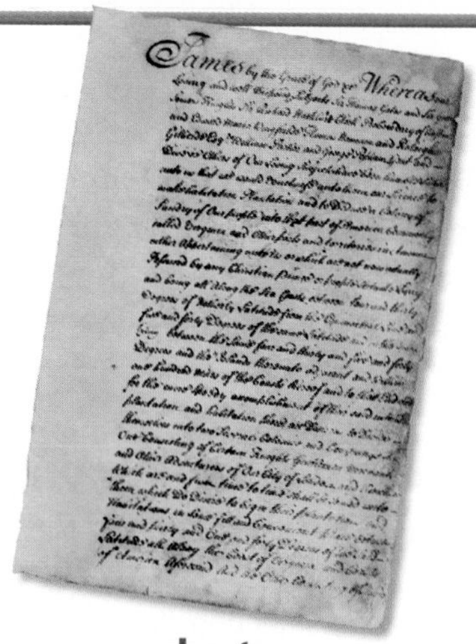

charter

King James of England gave merchants a **charter.** This document gave them permission to start a settlement, which they named Jamestown. **page 131**

Chapter Timeline

Background

Explain that these words are used to discuss how groups of people lived together in particular areas during the period when Europeans explored and settled North America.

Vocabulary

Use the following graphic organizer to discuss the word *claim* and how its meaning changes with the addition of prefixes and suffixes.

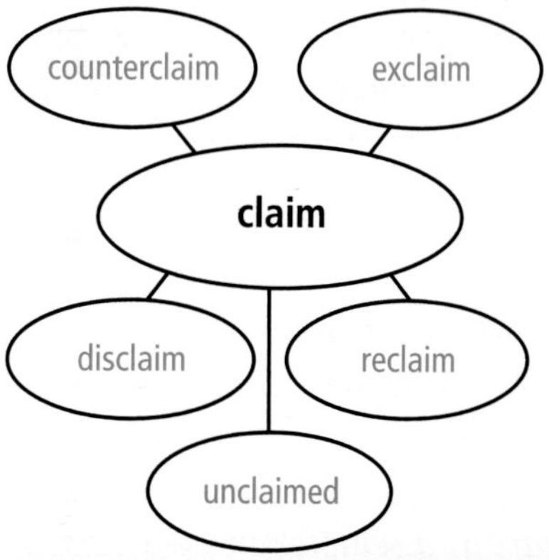

Reading Strategy

Summarize Use this strategy to focus on important ideas.

Quick Tip Review the main ideas. Then look for important details that support the main idea.

compact

The Pilgrims wrote a **compact** before they started their settlement. The Mayflower Compact was an agreement about the laws that would govern them. **page 137**

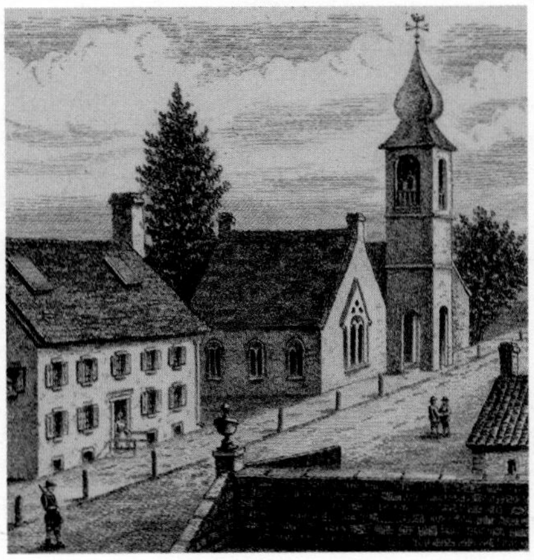

tolerance

Settlers in New Netherland practiced **tolerance.** People with different ideas and beliefs came to live in the colony.
page 145

1620 Plymouth founded

1682 La Salle claims Louisiana territory

1650 | 1690

Leveled Practice

Extra Support

Ask students if they have heard any of the vocabulary terms, and in what context the words appeared. If necessary, explain the difference between the word they heard and the meaning as it is used in the chapter (for example, a makeup compact). Verbal-linguistic

Challenge

Have students make a synonym/antonym chart using the four words shown. (For example, *claim: demand/refuse)*

Logical-mathematical

ELL

All Proficiency Levels

- Have students prepare entries for the four vocabulary words in their word-study notebooks.
- Some students may wish to draw pictures to illustrate the words' meanings; others may wish to write definitions in their own words.
- Encourage students to write down and share any questions they have about the words.

Using the Timeline

- Direct students to look at the timeline on pages 120 and 121. Point out the segments of the timeline. Ask them how many years this chapter will cover.
- You may wish to use a KWL chart to access students' prior knowledge of the events on the timeline. This is also an excellent opportunity to determine what, if any, misconceptions students may hold about the material.

Reading Strategy: Summarize

To summarize, a reader identifies and pulls together the essential information in a longer text passage and restates that information in a condensed fashion.

Explain to students that to summarize successfully, they should follow these steps:

- Read the passage twice.
- Think about what the passage says.
- Ask yourself: What is the main topic this passage is describing?
- Find the main point of the passage. Jot it down (or underline it.)
- Use your own words to tell what the passage means.
- Look back at the passage to check if your summary is accurate.

Students can practice this reading strategy throughout this chapter, including on their Skill and Strategy pages.

Tested Objectives

U2-12 History Describe the motives and achievements of early English, French, and Dutch explorers.

U2-13 History Explain the significance of the defeat of the Spanish Armada.

Lesson Quick Look

In the 1500s and 1600s, European explorers came to North America seeking a Northwest Passage, or sea route, to Asia.

Teaching Option: Extend Lesson 1 provides biographies of Queen Elizabeth and King Philip.

1 Get Set to Read

Preview After students look at the map on page 123, ask them what they think the lesson will be about.

Reading Skill: Main Idea and Details Details should include the explorer's nation of origin.

Build on What You Know Ask students about shortcuts they take. Explain that European countries wanted to find a shortcut from the Atlantic to the Pacific Ocean.

Vocabulary

claim *noun,* something declared to belong to someone, especially land

armada *noun,* a fleet of warships

invasion *noun,* the entry of an armed force into another country to conquer it

---

Core Lesson 1

A Northwest Passage

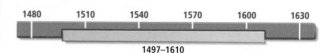

1480 | 1510 | 1540 | 1570 | 1600 | 1630

1497–1610

VOCABULARY

claim
armada
invasion

Vocabulary Strategy

invasion

The suffix **-ion** changes a verb to a noun. The verb invade, to attack, becomes the noun **invasion**, an attack, when this suffix is added.

READING SKILL

Main Idea and Details As you read, make a list of details about each explorer.

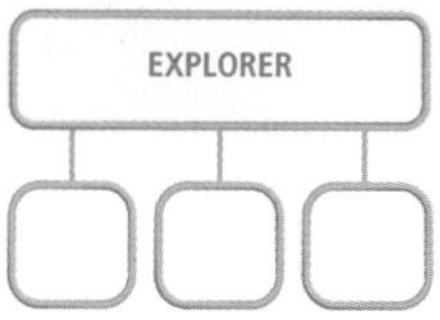

Build on What You Know Have you ever taken a shortcut? In the 1500s and 1600s, European explorers wanted a shortcut to Asia. They looked for a water route through North America.

Searching for a Passage to Asia

Main Idea In the 1500s and 1600s, explorers looked for a water route through North America to Asia.

Christopher Columbus first landed in the Americas while looking for a route to Asia. Over the next 125 years, European explorers looked for a sea route to Asia that would be faster than sailing around South America. Europeans wanted to bring back silk and spices from Asia.

Leaving England John Cabot prepares to sail across the Atlantic Ocean in 1497, five years after Columbus's first voyage.

Skill and Strategy

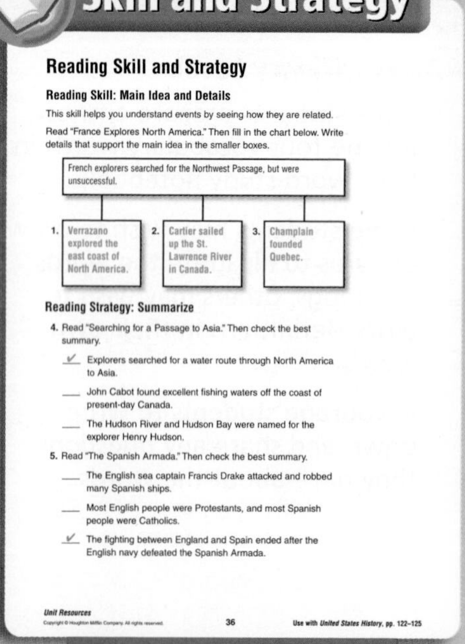

Reading Skill and Strategy

Reading Skill: Main Idea and Details

This skill helps you understand events by seeing how they are related.

Read "France Explores North America." Then fill in the chart below. Write details that support the main idea in the smaller boxes.

French explorers searched for the Northwest Passage, but were unsuccessful.

1. Verrazano explored the east coast of North America.
2. Cartier sailed up the St. Lawrence River in Canada.
3. Champlain founded Quebec.

Reading Strategy: Summarize

4. Read "Searching for a Passage to Asia." Then check the best summary.

✓ Explorers searched for a water route through North America to Asia.

___ John Cabot found excellent fishing waters off the coast of present-day Canada.

___ The Hudson River and Hudson Bay were named for the explorer Henry Hudson.

5. Read "The Spanish Armada." Then check the best summary.

___ The English sea captain Francis Drake attacked and robbed many Spanish ships.

___ Most English people were Protestants, and most Spanish people were Catholics.

✓ The fighting between England and Spain ended after the English navy defeated the Spanish Armada.

Unit Resources

36

Use with *United States History*, pp. 122–125

Unit Resources, p. 36

Background

Samuel de Champlain

- Champlain, the founder of Quebec, was an explorer, navigator, and geographer.
- The excellent maps he drew of the lands he explored helped people understand North American geography.

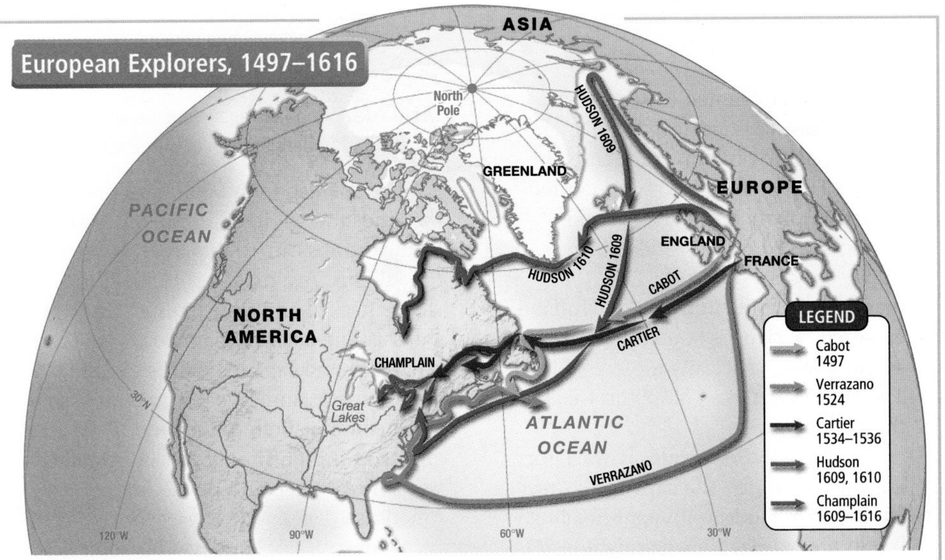

European Exploration Europeans explored the northeast coast of North America as they searched for a westward passage to Asia. SKILL **Reading Maps** Which explorer sailed the farthest south? Verrazano

John Cabot

John Cabot, an Italian explorer, thought he could reach Asia by sailing across the Atlantic Ocean. The king of England agreed to pay for his voyage. Cabot left England in 1497. After a
1 month at sea, he reached present-day Canada, which he thought was Asia. He explored the land and waters, but he found no people, silks, or spices. Cabot did find a rich fishing area off the coast of Canada. After he returned to England and told about what he had found, European fishing boats began sailing to these waters.

Once people knew that the land Cabot had found was not part of Asia, explorers continued their search for a water passage through the North American continent. The sea route that explorers looked for became known as the Northwest Passage.

France Explores North America

In 1524, France sent an Italian sea captain, **Giovanni da Verrazano** (VEHR uh ZAH noh), to look for a Northwest Passage. Verrazano explored much of the east coast of North America, including the area where New York City is now.

About 10 years later, **Jacques Cartier** (kahr TYAY) continued France's search for a water route to Asia. He sailed far up the St. Lawrence River in Canada.

In 1608, **Samuel de Champlain** (sham PLAYN) founded a fur-trading post on the St. Lawrence River. He called it Quebec 2
(kwih BEHK), from the Indian word kebec, which means "the place where the river narrows." Quebec was the first permanent French settlement in North America.

REVIEW What did John Cabot find during his exploration of Canada? He found a rich fishing area off the coast of Canada.

123

2 Teach

Searching for a Passage to Asia

Talk About It

1 **Q History** What land did John Cabot think he had reached in 1497? What land had he really reached?

A He thought he had reached Asia, but it was present-day Canada.

2 **Q Geography** Where was the settlement of Quebec founded?

A on the St. Lawrence River

Reading Strategy: Summarize Tell students that summarizing a passage is a good way to make sure they understand the important points. You may wish to model the strategy with the first paragraph of the lesson.

Think Aloud *This paragraph mentions Christopher Columbus, Europeans, Asia, and South America. I'll reread it to understand the main idea. I can summarize like this: European explorers had looked for many years for a westward sea route to Asia. They wanted to bring back goods from Asia without sailing all the way around South America.*

Leveled Practice

REACHING ALL LEARNERS

Extra Support

Have partners **create a conversation** between John Cabot and the king of England. Students may read their conversations aloud or role-play them for the class. **Verbal-linguistic**

Challenge

Ask students to make a timeline showing all of the explorers discussed in this lesson. Have them color-code the events on the timeline to show which country paid for each voyage. **Visual-spatial**

ELL

REACHING ALL LEARNERS

Intermediate

- Have partners **make a list** of supplies and equipment an explorer from the 1600s would need to sail across the Atlantic Ocean.
- Encourage them to draw and label pictures of three or four important things to bring on such a voyage.
- Then have partners explain their choices to the class.

Verbal-linguistic; visual-spatial

Searching for a Passage to Asia *continued*

Talk About It

3 **Q Geography** What body of water did Hudson find in 1610, and where did he think it might lead?

A Hudson found the Hudson Bay, which he thought might lead to the Pacific.

Spain and England

Talk About It

4 **Q History** In what way were religious differences a problem between Spain and England?

A King Philip, who was Catholic, wanted to make the English, who were Protestant, practice his religion.

5 **Q History** What happened when Spain tried to invade England?

A The English fleet chased the Spanish ships away from England and sank many of them.

Vocabulary Strategy

claim *Claim* can be a verb or a noun.

armada To remember an armada is made up of warships, students can recall *army.*

invasion Explain to students that in this word, the prefix *in-* means "toward."

Critical Thinking

Compare and Contrast In what ways were the expeditions of Henry Hudson and Samuel de Champlain similar? In what ways were they different?

Think Aloud *They both explored rivers and helped their countries make land claims. However, they were working for different countries in different areas of northeastern North America.*

Henry Hudson

The Dutch wanted to search for a Northwest Passage, too. The Dutch are the people of the Netherlands. In 1609, a Dutch trading company hired **Henry Hudson**, an English captain. Hudson sailed up the Hudson River in present-day New York. The Dutch made land claims in the areas Hudson explored. A **claim** is something declared as one's own, especially a piece of land. The Dutch started a colony on this land the following year.

3 In 1610, Hudson made a voyage for England. He found the bay now known as Hudson Bay. Hudson thought this huge bay in present-day Canada might lead to the Pacific Ocean, but it did not. England later claimed the land around Hudson Bay.

Neither Henry Hudson nor any other explorer ever found a Northwest Passage. Instead, they found more forests, fish, and wildlife than they had seen in Europe.

Spain and England

Main Idea Conflicts over treasure and religion led to fighting between Spain and England.

The Spanish found gold and silver in the lands they claimed in the Americas. Spanish ships carried this treasure across the Atlantic. Again and again, English ships attacked and stole treasure from ships sailing back to Spain. **Francis Drake,** an English sea captain, attacked many Spanish ships and gave the gold and silver to **Queen Elizabeth** of England. This angered **King Philip** of Spain. England was a threat to Spain's power in the Americas.

Spain and England also had conflicts about religion. 4 Spain was a Roman Catholic country. England broke away from the Catholic Church and formed its own church during the Protestant Reformation.

England Fights Spain English ships led by Drake battle the Spanish Armada off the southern coast of England.

Science

Ocean Currents

- The explorers who sailed across the Atlantic understood ocean currents.
- Ask students to research what currents are, and to list the main currents in the Atlantic Ocean.
- Then they may create a map showing these currents.

Visual-spatial

Language Arts

Write an Eyewitness Account

- Ask students to think of the experiences a settler in the new Hudson River Valley colony might have had.
- Have them write a letter home to a friend or family member in the Netherlands from the viewpoint of such a person, describing what life in the settlement is like.

Verbal-linguistic

The Spanish Armada

King Philip was part of a movement called the Counter Reformation that tried to spread the Catholic religion. He wanted England to be a Catholic nation again. He also wanted to stop English attacks on his ships.

Philip built an armada of 130 warships. An **armada** is the Spanish word for a large fleet of ships. In 1588, the Spanish Armada sailed to England to attack.

England was prepared for Spain's invasion. An **invasion** is an attack by an armed force to conquer another country. When the Spanish Armada appeared off the coast of England, Francis Drake led the English into battle.

5 The English fleet chased the Spanish ships away from the coastline and sank many of them. The rest of the Armada returned to Spain. On the way, some ships were wrecked in bad weather.

After the defeat of the Spanish Armada, England used its new power to claim more land in the Americas.

REVIEW Why did the king of Spain attack England? He wanted England to be a Catholic nation and to stop attacking Spanish ships.

Lesson Summary

- Explorers searched for a Northwest Passage to Asia in the 1500s and 1600s.
- England, France, and the Netherlands made land claims in North America as they searched for a Northwest Passage.
- England and Spain went to war over religion and English attacks on Spanish ships.

Why It Matters ...

Spain was no longer the only European power exploring North America. England, France, and the Netherlands began to claim land on the eastern part of the continent during the 1500s and 1600s.

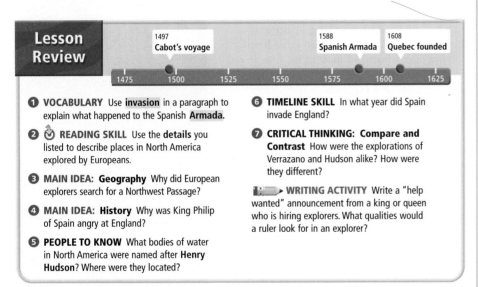

Lesson Review

1497
Cabot's voyage
1588
Spanish Armada
1608
Quebec founded
1475
1500
1525
1550
1575
1600
1625

1. **VOCABULARY** Use **invasion** in a paragraph to explain what happened to the Spanish **Armada.**
2. **READING SKILL** Use the **details** you listed to describe places in North America explored by Europeans.
3. **MAIN IDEA: Geography** Why did European explorers search for a Northwest Passage?
4. **MAIN IDEA: History** Why was King Philip of Spain angry at England?
5. **PEOPLE TO KNOW** What bodies of water in North America were named after **Henry Hudson**? Where were they located?
6. **TIMELINE SKILL** In what year did Spain invade England?
7. **CRITICAL THINKING: Compare and Contrast** How were the explorations of Verrazano and Hudson alike? How were they different?

WRITING ACTIVITY Write a "help wanted" announcement from a king or queen who is hiring explorers. What qualities would a ruler look for in an explorer?

3 Review/Assess

Review Tested Objectives

U2-12 Motives included the search for a Northwest Passage and new land claims.

U2-13 The defeat of the Spanish Armada made England the more dominant colonial power in the Americas.

Lesson Review Answers

1. Sentence should reflect understanding of vocabulary.
2. Description should include information from the lesson.
3. They wanted to find a faster route to Asia, where they could get silk and spices.
4. He was angry that English ships were attacking Spanish ships, and he wanted England to be a Catholic nation.
5. Hudson River in present-day New York, Hudson Bay in present-day Canada
6. 1588
7. Alike: They both explored present-day New York; different: Verrazano explored for France, Hudson for the Netherlands and England.

Writing Rubric

4	Announcement clearly stated; several qualities listed; mechanics are correct.
3	Announcement is adequately stated; two qualities listed; few errors in mechanics.
2	Announcement is stated in a confused or disorganized way; one quality listed; some errors in mechanics.
1	No announcement given; no qualities listed; many errors in mechanics.

Study Guide/Homework

Vocabulary and Study Guide

Vocabulary

Write the definition of each vocabulary word below.

1. armada The Spanish word for a large fleet of ships
2. claim Something declared as one's own, especially a piece of land
3. invasion An attack by an armed force to conquer another country
4. Choose two words. Use each word in a sentence about the lesson.
Sample answers: England prepared its navy for Spain's invasion. Many countries began making claims to land in North America.

Study Guide

Read "Searching for a Passage to Asia." Then fill in the chart below.

Explorer	Explored North America for this nation	What this explorer did
John Cabot	5. England	6. Reached present-day Canada
Giovanni da Verrazano	7. France	8. Explored the area now known as New York City
9. Samuel de Champlain	10. France	Founded Quebec
Henry Hudson	11. The Netherlands and England	12. Sailed up the river now called the Hudson River and found the body of water now called the Hudson Bay

Unit Resources 37 Use with *United States History*, pp. 122–125

Unit Resources, p. 37

Reteach Minilesson

Use a graphic organizer to reteach the Spanish Armada.

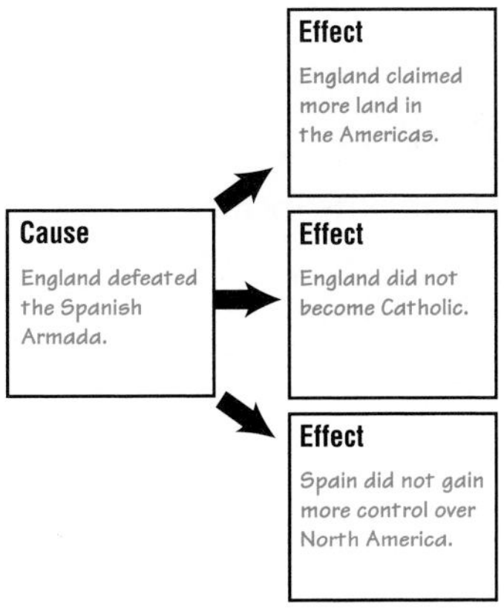

Cause
England defeated the Spanish Armada.
Effect
England claimed more land in the Americas.
Effect
England did not become Catholic.
Effect
Spain did not gain more control over North America.

www.eduplace.com/ss/hmss05/

Quick Look

Connect to the Core Lesson Students have just learned about the rivalry between Spain and England during the 1500s. In Extend Lesson 1, they will learn more about the rulers of these countries and their responsibilities.

1 Teach the Extend Lesson

Connect to the Big Idea

Influences on History As powerful rulers, both Elizabeth of England and Philip of Spain wielded great influence over their countries' histories. Their rivalry influenced the history of Europe and the Americas during the 1500s.

Biographies

Rulers of Land and Sea

In the 1500s, Elizabeth of England and Philip of Spain were the most powerful leaders in the world. Both wanted to rule the world's oceans and build colonies in the Americas. Yet they had different ways of ruling.

King Philip II
1527–1598

When Philip II became king, Spain was already a powerful nation. Philip was a hard-working ruler who spent most of his time in an office in Madrid, writing letters and managing his empire. He sent explorers to start colonies in the Americas and enlarged the army and the navy.

Philip was deeply religious, and wanted to strengthen Roman Catholicism throughout Europe and the Americas. He tried to conquer England and other countries. Spain was still a great power when Philip died in 1598.

A lover of books and paintings, Philip supported Spanish writers and artists during his reign.

Reaching All Learners

Extra Support

Make a Venn Diagram

- Have pairs of students work together to make Venn diagrams that compare and contrast Queen Elizabeth I and King Philip II.
- Ask pairs to share their diagrams with the class. As a class, discuss what the rulers shared in common and the ways in which they differed.

Verbal-linguistic; visual-spatial

On Level

Write a Skit

- Ask students to write a one-page skit, using dialogue, about a meeting between Queen Elizabeth of England and King Philip of Spain.
- Suggest that skits include a discussion of the conflicts between the two countries.

Verbal-linguistic

Challenge

Perform a Readers' Theater

- Ask students to present a readers' theater set in either Spain or England in the 1500s.
- Have the characters discuss the decision of their rulers (either King Philip or Queen Elizabeth) to expand their empires to the Americas. Do they think this is a good idea? Why? Why not?
- Have students read their pieces aloud to the class.

Verbal-linguistic; bodily-kinesthetic

Queen Elizabeth I

1533–1603

Here Elizabeth appears with her hand on a globe to show that England is a world power.

When Elizabeth Tudor became Queen of England in 1558, England was not as strong as Spain. Elizabeth reorganized the government so that it would run better. She surrounded herself with trustworthy advisors, and attended nearly every one of their meetings. She often appeared in public, making speeches and shaking hands with as many people as she could.

Elizabeth sent explorers on costly expeditions to find new trade routes. She built up the English navy, but was careful about money. By the end of her reign, England was one of the world's most powerful nations.

BIOGRAPHIES

Activities

1. **THINK ABOUT IT** In what ways did Queen Elizabeth show her sense of **responsibility** for England and its people?
2. **MAP IT** How large was the Spanish Empire at the end of King Philip's reign? Find out. Color in the Spanish Empire on a world map.

Technology Visit Education Place for more biographies. www.eduplace.com/kids/hmss05/

127

2 Leveled Activities

1 Think About It *For Extra Support*
Sample answer: Queen Elizabeth reorganized the government so it ran better; surrounded herself with trustworthy advisors and attended almost every advisors' meeting; spent money wisely.

2 Map It *For Challenge*

HANDS ON **Performance Task Rubric**

4	Map clearly drawn; size of empire shown accurately; map details are all present.
3	Map clearly drawn; size of empire is generally accurate; most map details are present.
2	Map is drawn; size of empire is somewhat accurate; few map details are present.
1	Map is not clearly drawn; size of empire is not shown; map details are absent.

Character Trait: Responsibility

Ask students to compare and contrast King Philip's responsibilities as a ruler with Queen Elizabeth's responsibilities.

For more on character traits, turn to pages R4–R5.

ELL

Intermediate/Advanced

- Have students look at the portraits of King Philip and Queen Elizabeth on pages 126 and 127.
- Ask students what they can **infer** about each ruler based on these portraits.
- Have students **discuss similarities and differences** between the two rulers, based on the portraits.

Visual-spatial

Math

Use a Timeline

- Have students make a timeline showing the dates that Queen Elizabeth and King Philip lived.
- Ask them to use different colors to show the lifetime of each ruler.
- Which ruler was older? Which had a longer life?

Logical-mathematical

Graphic Organizer

Queen Elizabeth	King Philip
Turned England from a weak to a powerful nation	Spain already powerful when he became king
Trusted her advisors	Did not trust anyone, even his advisors
Sent explorers on costly expeditions	Tried to conquer England, France
Avoided religious conflicts	Wanted to spread Catholic religion

Graphic Organizer 1

Tested Objective

U2-14 Interpret information from multiple timelines.

1 Teach the Skill

- Discuss with students the subjects of different timelines they have seen. Explain that timelines can depict information on a wide variety of subjects.
- Discuss the definition of parallel timelines on page 128. Students should understand that these timelines are grouped together to show events that happened during the same time period in different places.
- Have students study the timelines on these pages using the steps under "Learn the Skill." Have volunteers read aloud events on the timelines.
- Encourage students to discuss possible connections between events on the different countries' timelines.

Use Parallel Timelines

VOCABULARY
parallel timelines

A timeline shows events in the order that they happened. Parallel timelines are two or more timelines grouped together. They show events happening in different places during the same period of time. Comparing timelines can help you see connections between events.

Learn the Skill

Step 1: Find the subject of each timeline.

Step 2: Identify the time period between the first and last dates. Look at how each timeline is divided. Some timelines are divided into single years. Others are divided into decades, which are periods of 10 years, or centuries, which are periods of 100 years.

Step 3: Study the timelines to see how events might be related. Events that happen in one place may affect events in another place.

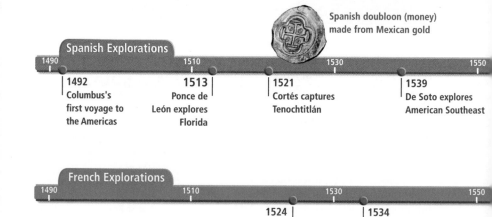

Spanish doubloon (money) made from Mexican gold

Spanish Explorations (1490 – 1510 – 1530 – 1550)

- **1492** Columbus's first voyage to the Americas
- **1513** Ponce de León explores Florida
- **1521** Cortés captures Tenochtitlán
- **1539** De Soto explores American Southeast

French Explorations (1490 – 1510 – 1530 – 1550)

- **1524** Verrazano's voyages to east coast of North America
- **1534** Cartier's voyage in Canada

Leveled Practice

Extra Support

Invite students to combine the events from the parallel timelines onto one "Exploring the Americas" timeline. Students can use different color ink for events from the different timelines. Visual-spatial

Challenge

Have students write a paragraph describing the connections they see between the events on the parallel timelines. Encourage them to make inferences. Verbal-linguistic

ELL

Intermediate

Explain that the word *parallel* is used in mathematics to describe two straight lines that run in the same direction but do not intersect. Remind students that they saw the word in the latitude and longitude lesson. Discuss the meaning in that context. Have students list objects that consist of parallel lines, for example, train tracks or the sides of a skyscraper. Have them draw examples on the board.

Visual-spatial; verbal-linguistic

Practice the Skill

Answer the following questions using the parallel timelines below.

1. Which country sent more explorers to the Americas?
2. Which explorers came to the Americas during the decade of the 1520s?
3. How long after Columbus's voyage did France send an explorer to the Americas? Why might France have sent him at that time?

Apply the Skill

Create your own parallel timelines. Use a calendar to list the events taking place in your life this week. Then draw and label two timelines. Mark each day, starting with Sunday and ending with Saturday. Place the events at home on one timeline, and the events at school on the other. Then compare the timelines to see how they may be related.

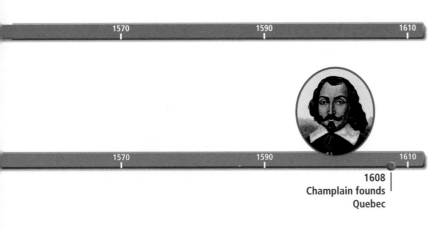

2 Practice the Skill

1. Spain
2. Cortés and Verrazano
3. 32 years; Sample answer: Spain had sent several explorers to the Americas by then. France wanted to get part of the riches in the Americas, too.

3 Apply the Skill

Ask students to create their own parallel timelines showing events from their lives over the course of a week. When evaluating students' timelines, consider:

- Did the student create two separate timelines, one for events at home and one for events at school?
- Did the student mark each day on the timelines?
- Did the student start with Sunday and end with Saturday when labeling the timelines?
- Did the student make connections between the timelines?

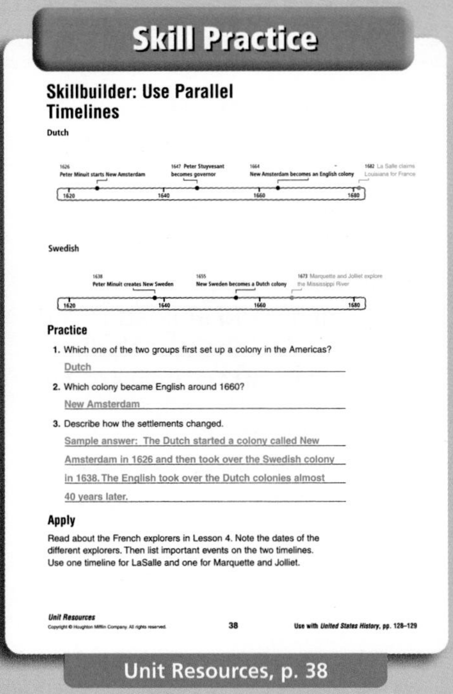

Skill Practice

Skillbuilder: Use Parallel Timelines

Dutch

1626 Peter Minuit starts New Amsterdam; 1647 Peter Stuyvesant becomes governor; 1664 New Amsterdam becomes an English colony; 1682 La Salle claims Louisiana for France (1620, 1640, 1660, 1680)

Swedish

1638 Peter Minuit creates New Sweden; 1655 New Sweden becomes a Dutch colony; 1673 Marquette and Jolliet explore the Mississippi River (1620, 1640, 1660, 1680)

Practice

1. Which one of the two groups first set up a colony in the Americas?
   Dutch
2. Which colony became English around 1660?
   New Amsterdam
3. Describe how the settlements changed.
   Sample answer: The Dutch started a colony called New Amsterdam in 1626 and then took over the Swedish colony in 1638. The English took over the Dutch colonies almost 40 years later.

Apply

Read about the French explorers in Lesson 4. Note the dates of the different explorers. Then list important events on the two timelines. Use one timeline for LaSalle and one for Marquette and Jolliet.

Unit Resources
Copyright © Houghton Mifflin Company. All rights reserved. 38 Use with *United States History*, pp. 128–129

Unit Resources, p. 38

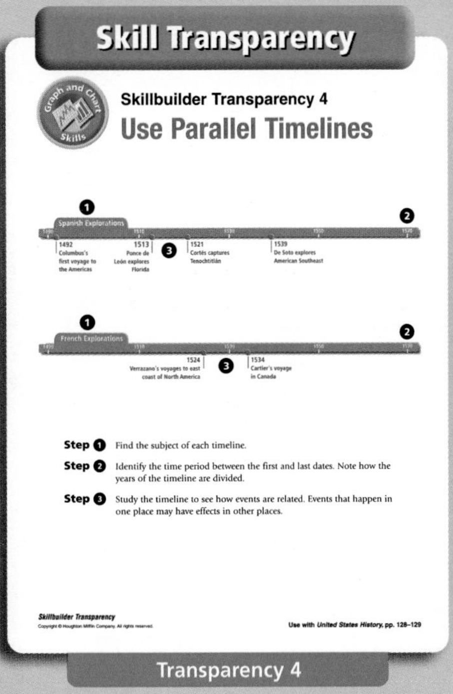

Skill Transparency

Skillbuilder Transparency 4
Use Parallel Timelines

Spanish Explorations: 1492 Columbus's first voyage to the Americas; 1513 Ponce de León explores Florida; 1521 Cortés captures Tenochtitlán; 1539 De Soto explores American Southeast

French Explorations: 1524 Verrazano's voyages to east coast of North America; 1534 Cartier's voyage in Canada

Step 1 Find the subject of each timeline.
Step 2 Identify the time period between the first and last dates. Note how the years of the timeline are divided.
Step 3 Study the timeline to see how events are related. Events that happen in one place may have effects in other places.

Skillbuilder Transparency
Copyright © Houghton Mifflin Company. All rights reserved. Use with *United States History*, pp. 128–129

Transparency 4

✔ Tested Objectives

U2-15 History Explain the reasons for the establishment of early English settlements in America.

U2-16 History Describe the experiences of settlers in Jamestown.

Lesson Quick Look

North America's first English settlers had great difficulties until they learned how to farm the land.

Teaching Option: Extend Lesson 2 shows students a bird's-eye view of Jamestown.

1 Get Set to Read

Preview Ask students what the pictures tell them about the lesson.

Reading Skill: Draw Conclusions Have students use the graphic organizer to draw conclusions about the failure of Roanoke and the success of Jamestown.

Build on What You Know Ask students how they felt about an unexpected change of plans. How might settlers have felt?

Vocabulary

charter *noun,* a written agreement giving someone the right to establish a colony

invest *verb,* to put money into a business in the hope of earning a profit

stock *noun,* a share or part of a company

cash crop *noun,* a crop that a farmer grows only to sell

indentured servant *noun,* a person who agreed to work for a certain number of years in return for passage to America, food, clothing, and shelter

Core Lesson 2

Roanoke and Jamestown

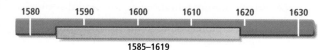

1580 1590 1600 1610 1620 1630

1585–1619

VOCABULARY

- charter
- invest
- stock
- cash crop
- indentured servant

Vocabulary Strategy

cash **crop**

A **cash** crop is raised so that farmers can sell it for money, or cash.

READING SKILL

Draw Conclusions Use facts and details from the lesson to draw a conclusion about why Roanoke failed and Jamestown succeeded.

DETAIL → CONCLUSION
DETAIL → CONCLUSION

Build on What You Know Think of a time when you had to change your plans. When English colonists traveled to North America, they planned to look for treasure. They had to change their plans after they arrived.

The Lost Colony

Main Idea The first English settlements in North America failed.

England's rulers and merchants wanted a colony in North America. They hoped to find gold and silver, just as the Spanish had in their colonies. In 1585, about 100 English men settled on Roanoke Island, off the coast of present-day North Carolina. The colonists barely survived. They could not grow crops in the sandy soil. Most of them went back to England.

In 1587, the English tried again to settle Roanoke. **John White** was the leader of the colony. Shortly after landing in America, White returned to England for supplies. When he returned nearly three years later, the colonists had disappeared. White thought they had gone to live with nearby American Indians, but he never found them. The "Lost Colony" of Roanoke is still a mystery today. 1

The Lost Colony John White found a mysterious message when he returned to Roanoke. The Croatoan were American Indians who lived nearby.

Skill and Strategy

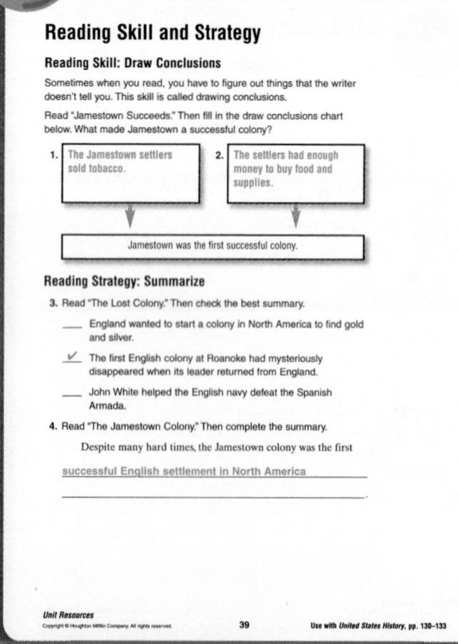

Reading Skill and Strategy

Reading Skill: Draw Conclusions

Sometimes when you read, you have to figure out things that the writer doesn't tell you. This skill is called drawing conclusions.

Read "Jamestown Succeeds." Then fill in the draw conclusions chart below. What made Jamestown a successful colony?

1. The Jamestown settlers sold tobacco.
2. The settlers had enough money to buy food and supplies.

Jamestown was the first successful colony.

Reading Strategy: Summarize

3. Read "The Lost Colony." Then check the best summary.
   - ___ England wanted to start a colony in North America to find gold and silver.
   - ✓ The first English colony at Roanoke had mysteriously disappeared when its leader returned from England.
   - ___ John White helped the English navy defeat the Spanish Armada.
4. Read "The Jamestown Colony." Then complete the summary.

   Despite many hard times, the Jamestown colony was the first successful English settlement in North America.

Unit Resources

39
Use with *United States History*, pp. 130–133

Unit Resources, p. 39

Background

- One hundred fifty people, including men, women, and children, settled in Roanoke in 1587. They depended on the Croatoan Indians to help them plant crops.
- Settlers in the Jamestown colony found many wild animals in the woods around them, including bears, foxes, otters, beavers, and muskrats.

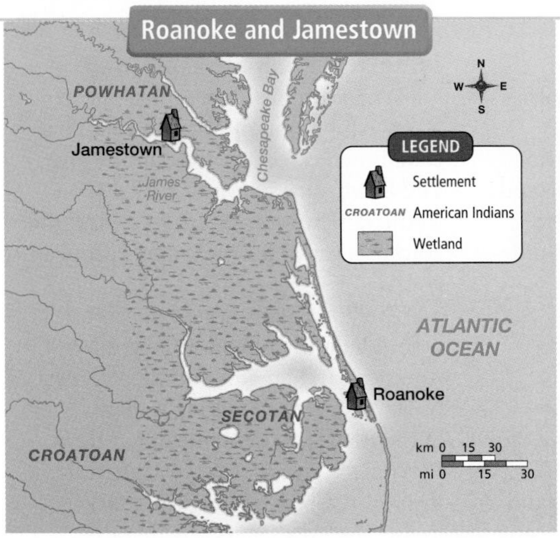

English Settlements Roanoke and Jamestown were about 140 miles from each other. The photograph above shows the way land in Jamestown probably looked when settlers arrived.

The Jamestown Colony

Main Idea Jamestown was the first successful English settlement in America.

In 1606, English merchants started the Virginia Company of London. Their goal was to build a settlement in North America. The king of England gave the Virginia Company a charter to start their settlement. A **charter** is a document giving permission to a person or group to do something.

The owners of the Virginia Company needed money to buy ships and supplies. They raised money by asking people to invest in their company. To **invest** means to put money into something to try to earn more money. If colonists found treasure, people who invested in the company would earn money.

2 People invested in the Virginia Company by buying stocks. A **stock** is a piece of ownership in a company. The amount of money an investor earns or loses depends on how much stock the investor owns and the value of the stock.

In 1607, about 100 men and boys traveled to present-day Virginia. The settlers built a fort on the banks of a river. They named their colony Jamestown after **King James I.**

The land in Jamestown was damp and swampy. The water wasn't good for drinking, and insects carried diseases. 3 Most of the settlers were gentlemen who had never worked hard. They did not know how to farm. Instead, they searched for gold. The settlers ran out of food, and within a few months, almost half of them had died from hunger and disease.

Then **John Smith** took command of Jamestown. He ordered people to plant crops. He said:

> **"He who does not work, will not eat."**

Life in Jamestown was still hard. Smith went back to England in 1609. During the following winter, known as the "starving time," most of the colonists died.

REVIEW Why did the Jamestown colonists run out of food? Most colonists didn't know how to farm, and they looked for gold instead of growing food.

131

2 Teach

The Lost Colony

Talk About It

1 **Q History** Where did John White think the Roanoke settlers had gone?

A He thought they had gone to live with nearby American Indians.

The Jamestown Colony

Talk About It

2 **Q Economics** What did the Virginia Company sell to its investors?

A The company sold stocks to its investors.

3 **Q Geography** What kind of land did the settlers find in Jamestown?

A They found damp, swampy land.

Vocabulary Strategy

charter *Deed* is a synonym for *charter.*

invest The word *invest* comes from the Latin word *vestire,* meaning "to clothe."

stock Another meaning of the word *stock* is *to supply with goods.*

Reading Strategy: Summarize Write the first paragraph on the board. Work with students to edit it into a summary.

Reaching All Learners: Leveled Practice

Extra Support

Have students **look at images** in this lesson and write down at least three details about each one. Have them compare answers with a partner. Verbal-linguistic

Challenge

Ask students to **write a persuasive paragraph** encouraging investors to buy stock in the Virginia Company. Have them trade paragraphs with a partner and compare their ideas. Verbal-linguistic

Reaching All Learners: ELL

Beginning

Have students **illustrate scenes** from life in Jamestown. They should label their illustrations to show what people in their drawings are doing.

Visual-spatial

The Jamestown Colony *continued*

Talk About It

4 **Q Economics** What cash crop brought money to Jamestown?
A tobacco

5 **Q History** Why did the English settlers and the Powhatans briefly make peace?
A John Rolfe, a Jamestown settler, married Pocahontas, a Powhatan woman.

Vocabulary Strategy

cash crop The word *crop* also means "to cut."

indentured servant Have students find part of the word *serve* in this term.

Critical Thinking

Cause and Effect What caused the Virginia Company to sell stocks? You may wish to model how to think through the question.

Think Aloud *The Virginia Company needed a lot of money to start their settlement in North America, to buy ships and supplies, and to send settlers there. Selling stocks in their company was a way for them to raise money for this venture.*

Jamestown Succeeds

In 1612, a settler named **John Rolfe** learned from local American Indians that tobacco grew well in Virginia's hot, humid weather. Many people in England smoked tobacco. They were willing to pay a high price for the crop, which did not grow well in England.

4 Jamestown merchants grew and sold thousands of pounds of tobacco to England. Tobacco was a cash crop. A **cash crop** is a crop that people grow and sell to earn money. Tobacco gave the colony enough income to buy much-needed food and supplies from England.

In 1619, the first women and Africans arrived in Jamestown. The first Africans were probably indentured servants. An **indentured servant** was someone who agreed to work for a number of years in exchange for the cost of a voyage to North America. Later, enslaved Africans were forced to work in Jamestown.

Jamestown and the Powhatans

When colonists first settled Jamestown, a powerful group of American Indians called the Powhatans lived in the area. The Powhatans gave and traded food to the Jamestown settlers. In return, the colonists gave the Powhatans European goods.

The Powhatans hoped the colonists would help them fight against other American Indian groups. The colonists, however, were not willing to help. Sometimes they demanded that the Powhatans give them food. When the Indians refused, the English attacked them. The Powhatans saw that the English were trying to take over their land, and they fought back. The two sides made peace after John Rolfe married a Powhatan woman, **Pocahontas**, in 1614. 5 Pocahontas was a daughter of the Powhatans' leader.

The Powhatans This Indian nation lived in domed houses. The chief of the Powhatans wore this deerskin cloak (right). SKILL **Primary Source** Look at the figures on the cloak. What do you think they represent? deer, people, hunting

Math

Make a Timeline

- Have students make a simple timeline using the events mentioned in the lesson.
- Have them create subtraction questions for each other about the amount of time between events.
- Have students trade questions and quiz one another.

Logical-mathematical

Language Arts

Write a Charter

The Virginia Company had a document called a charter that granted them the right to settle in North America. Have students write a charter of their own granting rights to a person or group to do something of importance.

Verbal-linguistic

Peace did not last, however. The English tried to take more land. The Powhatans fought back until 1646, when the English killed many of them. The English then took control of most of the land around Jamestown.

REVIEW Why did colonists in Jamestown fight the Powhatans? The Powhatans sometimes refused to give the colonists food, and the colonists wanted the Powhatans' land.

Pocahontas After Pocahontas married colonist John Rolfe, she went to England where her portrait was painted.

Lesson Summary

- The Roanoake settlers disappeared mysteriously.
- In 1607, Jamestown was founded in the colony of Virginia.
- After John Rolfe began growing tobacco, the Jamestown settlement grew.
- The Powhatan and the English colonists fought over land for decades.

Why It Matters ...

Jamestown was the first successful English settlement in North America. The Jamestown settlers led the way for other English settlements in North America.

Lesson Review

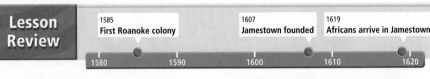

Timeline: 1580 – 1590 – 1600 – 1610 – 1620
- 1585 First Roanoke colony
- 1607 Jamestown founded
- 1619 Africans arrive in Jamestown

1. **VOCABULARY** Use the words **charter, invest,** and **stock** in a paragraph explaining how Jamestown began.
2. **READING SKILL** Which fact or detail best explains why Roanoke failed? How did you **draw** this **conclusion**?
3. **MAIN IDEA: History** Why did England's rulers and merchants want to start a colony in North America?
4. **MAIN IDEA: Geography** How did the land in Jamestown affect the settlers?
5. **CRITICAL THINKING: Decision Making** What might have been the opportunity cost for someone who went to Jamestown as an indentured servant? Remember that an opportunity cost is the thing you give up when you decide to do or have something else.
6. **TIMELINE SKILL** Which colony was settled first, Jamestown or Roanoke?

HANDS ON **INTERVIEW ACTIVITY** What questions might a reporter have asked John Smith about the Jamestown colony? Interview a partner who can answer as John Smith might have.

3 Review/Assess

Review Tested Objectives

U2-15 Reasons included the search for gold and silver and the desire for colonial expansion.

U2-16 Settlers in Jamestown struggled with hunger and disease until they developed tobacco as a cash crop. They received food aid from the Powhatan Indians and fought with them over the land.

Lesson Review Answers

1. Paragraph should explain that a charter from the king of England allowed people to settle in Jamestown and that the Virginia Company raised money by asking people to invest in stocks.
2. Conclusion should be based on information from the lesson.
3. They hoped to find gold and silver in North America.
4. Because the land was swampy, had many insects, and had poor drinking water, many settlers died.
5. Possible answer: The opportunity cost might have been that the indentured servant had to move away from his or her home and leave family and friends.
6. Roanoke

HANDS ON Performance Task Rubric

4	Interview format is used; several questions are asked and answered.
3	Interview format is attempted; two questions are asked and answered.
2	Interview format is attempted; one question is asked and answered.
1	Interview format is not used; no questions are asked or answered.

Study Guide/Homework

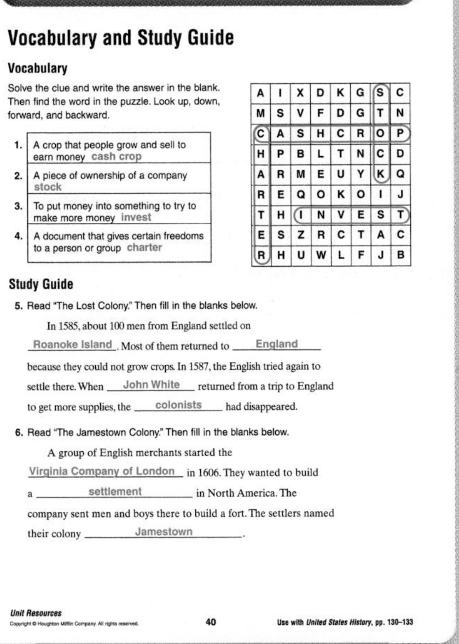

Vocabulary and Study Guide

Vocabulary

Solve the clue and write the answer in the blank. Then find the word in the puzzle. Look up, down, forward, and backward.

1. A crop that people grow and sell to earn money cash crop
2. A piece of ownership of a company stock
3. To put money into something to try to make more money invest
4. A document that gives certain freedoms to a person or group charter

A	I	X	D	K	G	S	C
M	S	V	F	D	G	T	N
C	A	S	H	C	R	O	P
H	P	B	L	T	N	C	D
A	R	M	E	U	Y	K	Q
R	E	Q	O	K	O	I	J
T	H	I	N	V	E	S	T
E	S	Z	R	C	T	A	C
R	H	U	W	L	F	J	B

Study Guide

5. Read "The Lost Colony." Then fill in the blanks below.

In 1585, about 100 men from England settled on Roanoke Island. Most of them returned to England because they could not grow crops. In 1587, the English tried again to settle there. When John White returned from a trip to England to get more supplies, the colonists had disappeared.

6. Read "The Jamestown Colony." Then fill in the blanks below.

A group of English merchants started the Virginia Company of London in 1606. They wanted to build a settlement in North America. The company sent men and boys there to build a fort. The settlers named their colony Jamestown.

Unit Resources

40
Use with *United States History*, pp. 130–133

Unit Resources, p. 40

Reteach Minilesson

Use a Venn diagram to reteach the lesson.

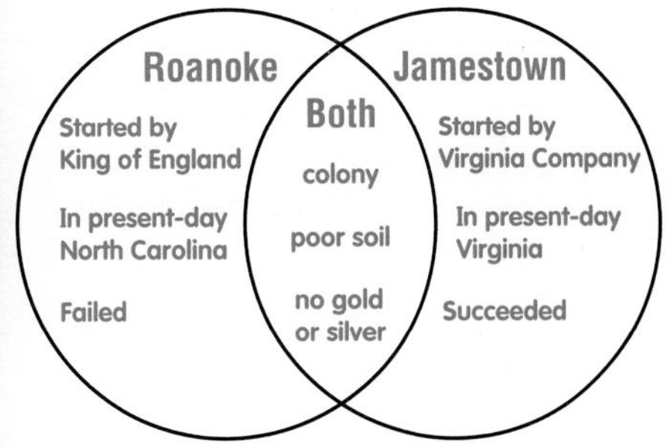

Graphic Organizer 11

Extend

Quick Look

Connect to the the Core Lesson Students have just read about the settlement of Jamestown. In Extend Lesson 2, they will learn more about the challenges the settlers faced because of the geographic location of Jamestown.

1 Teach the Extend Lesson

Connect to the Big Idea

Human/Environment Interaction In Jamestown the settlers interacted with and changed the environment. Jamestown's environment affected the settlers' health and economy.

Extend Lesson 2

Geography

Jamestown · 1607

The welfare of the settlers in the Jamestown colony depended on the environment. Settlers chose a place that they thought had many geographic advantages. It lay sixty miles up the James River, out of sight of Spanish ships on the Chesapeake Bay. Forests provided lumber for buildings. Winters were not as harsh as in more northern locations.

The geography of the Jamestown settlement had major drawbacks. The area had wetlands full of mosquitos. The soil was not good for growing food crops, and the drinking water was unhealthy. However, tobacco could grow there, and it became an important cash crop.

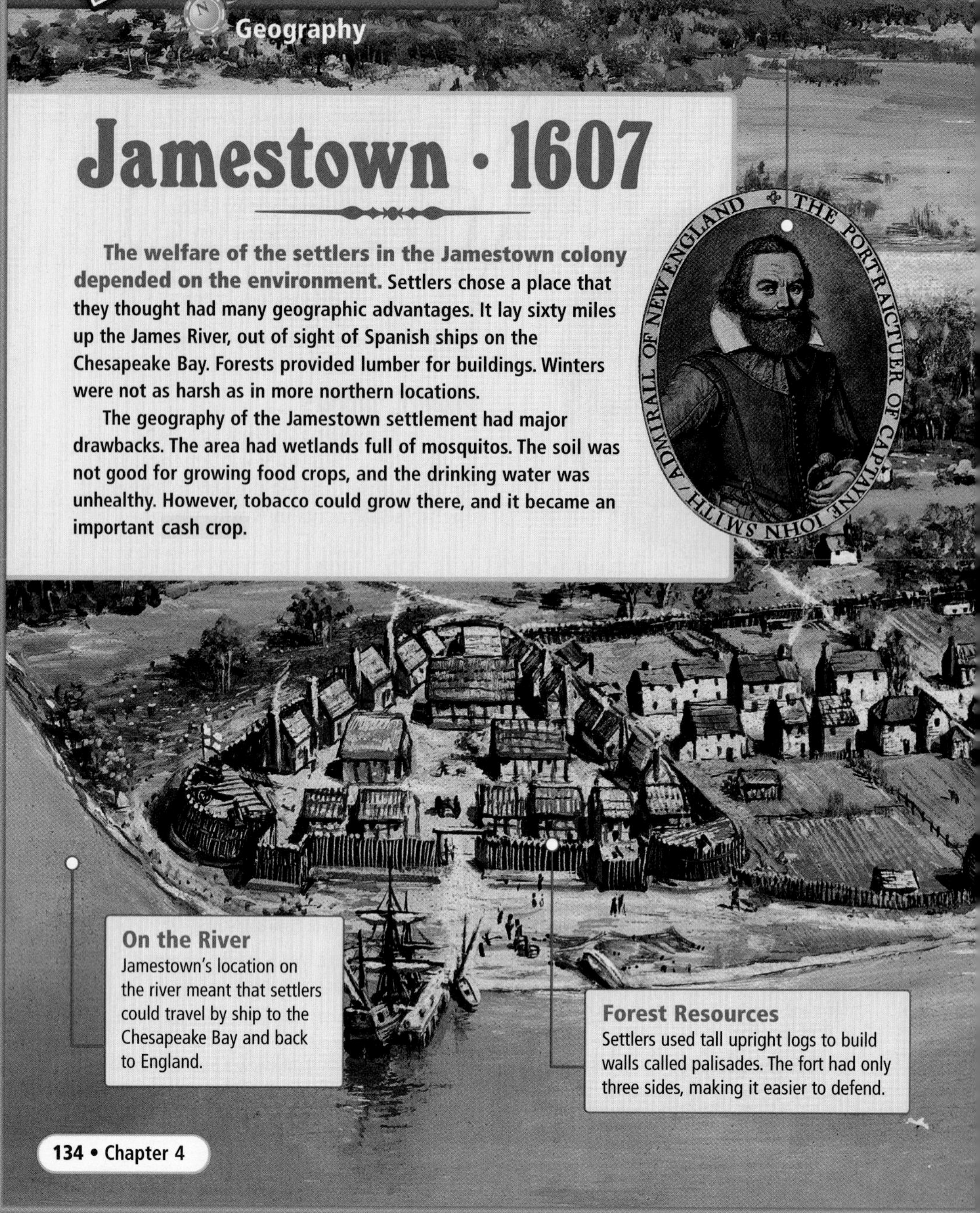

On the River
Jamestown's location on the river meant that settlers could travel by ship to the Chesapeake Bay and back to England.

Forest Resources
Settlers used tall upright logs to build walls called palisades. The fort had only three sides, making it easier to defend.

134 • Chapter 4

Reaching All Learners

Extra Support

Make a Cause-and-Effect Chart

Ask students to make a cause-and-effect chart about events in Jamestown. Items on the chart might include effects of the environment on the settlers' lives, causes of laying out the settlement as they did, and effects of tobacco on Jamestown's economy.

On Level

Chart Crops

Ask students to make a chart listing crops that were successful, and crops that were not successful, and why.

Verbal-linguistic; logical-mathematical

Challenge

Make a Map

Have students use library resources or the Internet to find John Smith's map of the Jamestown area. Then have them make their own map of the Jamestown colony from a bird's-eye perspective.

Visual-spatial; bodily-kinesthetic

John Smith
Smith saw that the Powhatans did not drink the river water. He ordered settlers to dig wells for clean water.
Climate and Soil
The growing season was long and humid. Tobacco plants grew well in these conditions.

GEOGRAPHY

Activities

1. **EXPLORE IT** Step into the picture and imagine walking through the settlement or through the fields near the wetlands. Describe the environment around you.
2. **WRITE ABOUT IT** Write a first-person narrative that tells what Jamestown was like for one settler. Include the role of natural resources in his or her daily life.

2 Leveled Activities

❶ **Explore It** *For Extra Support*
Students' descriptions of the settlement or wetlands should include details from the Extend Lesson.

❷ **Write About It** *For Challenge*

Writing Rubric

4	Narrative is well organized and shows considerable creative effort; uses many details from lesson; mechanics are correct.
3	Narrative is adequately organized and shows creative effort; uses some details from lesson; few errors in mechanics.
2	Narrative is somewhat organized and shows some creative effort; uses few details from lesson; some errors in mechanics.
1	Narrative is disorganized and shows little effort; uses no details from lesson; many errors in mechanics.

ELL

REACHING ALL LEARNERS

Beginning

- Have pairs of students make vocabulary cards for unfamiliar or difficult words from the lesson.
- Ask pairs to write each word on an index card. Then have them look up the definition and write it on the other side. If they wish, they can draw a picture for the word on the front of the card.
- Pairs can use the cards to review the lesson and practice vocabulary skills.

Verbal-linguistic

Physical Education

Role-Play Work

- Have students think about the physical work that settlers in Jamestown would have had to do. What made this work difficult?
- Ask them to role-play one of these activities for the class.

Bodily-kinesthetic

Graphic Organizer

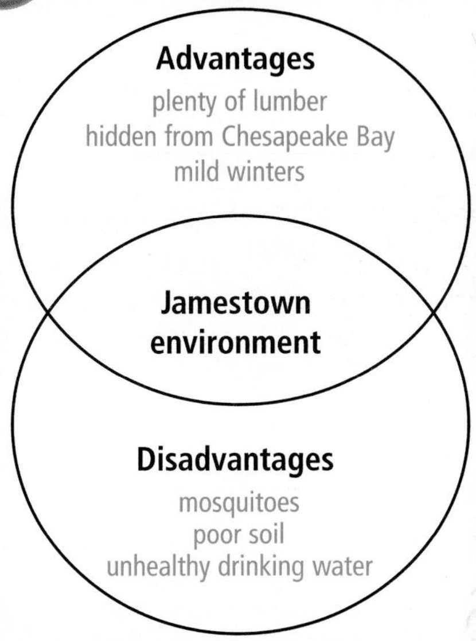

Graphic Organizer 11

Tested Objectives

U2-17 History Explain why and how the Pilgrims and Puritans settled in America.

U2-18 History Describe the settlements at Plymouth and Massachusetts Bay.

Quick Look

This lesson tells how the Pilgrims and the Puritans came to North America to find religious freedom.

Teaching Option: Extend Lesson 3 gives students insight through literature into the world of the Pilgrims.

1 Get Set to Read

Preview Have students read the headings and suggest the topic of the lesson.

Reading Skill: Cause and Effect Students should note both groups' experiences in Europe.

Build on What You Know Ask students to discuss the role religion plays in many people's lives. Explain the importance of religion to many of the first English settlers.

Vocabulary

pilgrim *noun,* a person who makes a long journey for religious reasons

compact *noun,* an agreement

cape *noun,* a strip of land that stretches into a body of water

Core Lesson 3

New England Settlements

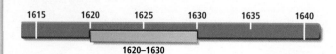

1615 | 1620 | 1625 | 1630 | 1635 | 1640

1620–1630

VOCABULARY

pilgrim
compact
cape

Vocabulary Strategy

compact

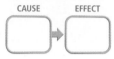

The prefix **com-** means together. People make a **compact,** or agreement, together with others.

READING SKILL

Cause and Effect As you read, list causes that led to the Pilgrims' and Puritans' settlements in North America.

CAUSE → EFFECT

Build on What You Know You know that religion is important to many people. It can affect the choices they make and what they think is right or wrong. Religion was very important to many of the first English settlers in North America.

The Plymouth Colony

Main Idea The Pilgrims came to America for religious freedom.

By law, everyone in England was supposed to belong to the Church of England. Some people, however, were not happy with that church. They had different beliefs. These people decided to break away, or separate, from the Church of England and set up their own churches. They became known as Separatists.

One small group of Separatists went to the Netherlands in the early 1600s to find religious freedom. These Separatists called themselves Pilgrims. A **pilgrim** is a person who makes a long journey for religious reasons.

The Mayflower This ship is an exact model of the original *Mayflower* that the Pilgrims sailed on in 1620.

136 • Chapter 4

Skill and Strategy

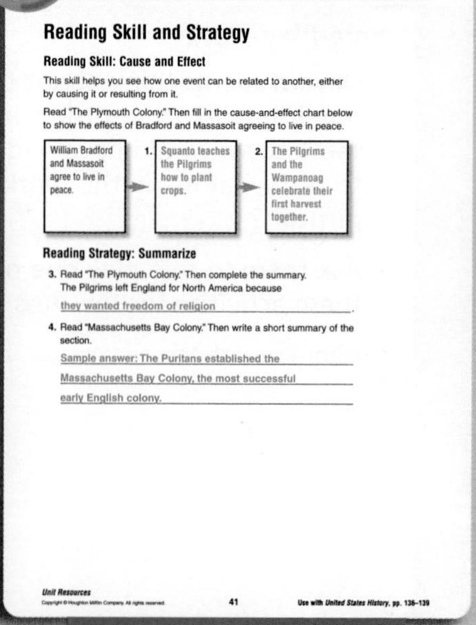

Reading Skill and Strategy

Reading Skill: Cause and Effect

This skill helps you see how one event can be related to another, either by causing it or resulting from it.

Read "The Plymouth Colony." Then fill in the cause-and-effect chart below to show the effects of Bradford and Massasoit agreeing to live in peace.

William Bradford and Massasoit agree to live in peace. → 1. Squanto teaches the Pilgrims how to plant crops. → 2. The Pilgrims and the Wampanoag celebrate their first harvest together.

Reading Strategy: Summarize

3. Read "The Plymouth Colony." Then complete the summary.
The Pilgrims left England for North America because
they wanted freedom of religion.

4. Read "Massachusetts Bay Colony." Then write a short summary of the section.
Sample answer: The Puritans established the Massachusetts Bay Colony, the most successful early English colony.

Unit Resources
Copyright © Houghton Mifflin Company. All rights reserved. 41 Use with *United States History,* pp. 136–139

Unit Resources, p. 41

Background

Thanksgiving's Menu

- Accounts of the feast shared between the Pilgrims and the Wampanoags show that wildfowl, such as duck or goose, and venison (deer meat) were eaten.
- We are not sure that turkey was part of the meal.

Mayflower Compact
Pilgrims write the compact aboard the *Mayflower.* It was the first written plan for government in North America.

SKILL **Reading Visuals**
What are the two groups of people in this painting doing?
men: writing compact; women: reading, caring for baby

Pilgrims Sail to North America

The Pilgrims could practice their religious beliefs in the Netherlands, but they wanted to live apart from people of other beliefs. The Pilgrims were also bothered that their children were learning Dutch customs. They decided to build a new religious community in North America. The Virginia Company of London agreed to let the Pilgrims start a settlement in the colony of Virginia.

In 1620, about 100 men, women, and children set sail across the Atlantic Ocean in the English ship *Mayflower*. Fierce storms pushed the ship off course, however. Instead of landing in Virginia, the *Mayflower* anchored off the coast of present-day Massachusetts.

Because the Pilgrims landed in Massachusetts, they would not be governed by the Virginia Company. The passengers created their own plan for government.

The Pilgrims called their plan the Mayflower Compact. A **compact** is an agreement. In this compact, the passengers agreed to make laws for the "general good" of the colony, and to obey them. 1

The Pilgrims landed briefly at the tip of Cape Cod. A **cape** is a strip of land that stretches into a body of water. They chose a site on the other side of Cape Cod Bay to build a settlement. The colony was named Plymouth after a town in England.

The Plymouth settlers had a hard time at first. They had arrived in November when it was too late to plant crops. They did not have enough food. During this first harsh winter, about half of the Pilgrims died. 2

REVIEW Why did the Pilgrims leave the Netherlands for North America?
They wanted to live apart from people with other religious beliefs.

137

2 Teach

The Plymouth Colony

Talk About It

1 **Q Citizenship** What did the Pilgrims agree to in the Mayflower Compact?
A They agreed to make laws for the good of the colony, and to obey them.

2 **Q History** What difficulty did the Pilgrims face after they landed at Plymouth?
A It was November and too late to plant crops, so food ran out.

Vocabulary Strategy

pilgrim A synonym for the word *pilgrim* is *traveler.*

compact This word comes from the Latin word *compacisci,* meaning "to make an agreement."

cape Another meaning for the word *cape* is a short, sleeveless cloak.

Reading Strategy: Summarize With students, summarize the first section of the lesson, "The Plymouth Colony."

REACHING ALL LEARNERS

Leveled Practice

Extra Support

Have students **find a detailed illustration** of the *Mayflower.* Ask them to describe the ship in three paragraphs. Verbal-linguistic

Challenge

Have students work in small groups to write a poem for the first Thanksgiving celebration. Encourage them to read their poems to the class. Bodily-kinesthetic

REACHING ALL LEARNERS

ELL

Advanced

- Have students **research an actual person** who lived in the Plymouth colony.
- Then ask them to imagine they are a newspaper reporter and write an interview with that person.
- Invite them to share their work with the class.

Verbal-linguistic

The Plymouth Colony

continued

Talk About It

3 Q History How did Squanto help the Pilgrims after their first winter?

A He taught them how to plant crops such as maize, pumpkins, and beans.

Massachusetts Bay Colony

Talk About It

4 Q History Did the Puritans want to separate from the Church of England? Why or why not?

A No; they wanted to remain part of the church and to make it more pure.

5 Q History What helped make the Puritans more successful than the Jamestown colonists?

A The Puritans came better prepared; they arrived in time to plant crops.

Critical Thinking

Predict What might have happened if the Puritans had not been so well prepared for starting a settlement in North America?

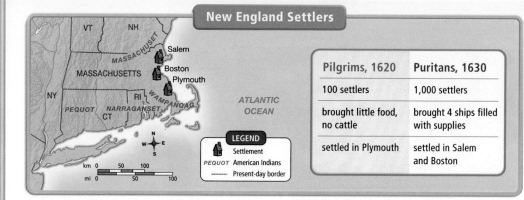

New England Settlers

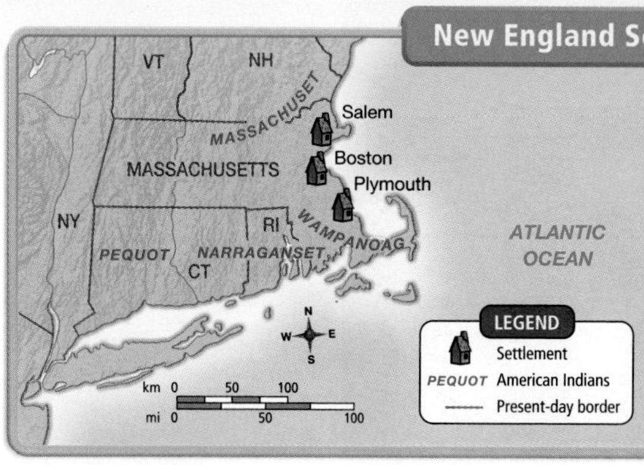

Pilgrims, 1620	Puritans, 1630
100 settlers	1,000 settlers
brought little food, no cattle	brought 4 ships filled with supplies
settled in Plymouth	settled in Salem and Boston

Pilgrims and Puritans This map shows settlements founded by the Pilgrims and the Puritans. SKILL **Reading Charts** How many Puritans first settled in New England? 1,000

Pilgrims Give Thanks

The following spring, an American Indian named **Squanto** (SKWAHN toh) visited the Pilgrims. Squanto had been to Europe and spoke English. He introduced the Pilgrims to **Massasoit** (MAS uh SOYT), the leader of the nearby Wampanoag (WAHM puh NOH ag). **William Bradford,** the governor of Plymouth, and Massasoit agreed to live in peace.

3 Squanto taught the Pilgrims how to plant crops such as maize (corn), pumpkins, and beans. He guided the Pilgrims in hunting and fishing. By the fall of 1621, the colony had become more successful. The Pilgrims had plenty of food, and new settlers and supplies had recently arrived from England.

The Pilgrims held a feast to thank their God for their first harvest. About 50 Pilgrims and 90 Wampanoags celebrated together for three days. People in the United States remember this feast during Thanksgiving, a national holiday celebrated every November.

Massachusetts Bay Colony

Main Idea English Puritans settled the Massachusetts Bay Colony.

The Puritans were another religious group who disagreed with the Church of England. Puritans, however, did not want to separate from the church. They wanted to make themselves and their church pure, or free from fault. 4

The Puritans decided to start a colony in North America. Unlike the colonists in Jamestown, the Puritans did not come to America to earn money. Like the Pilgrims, they wanted to create a community based on their religious beliefs.

John Winthrop, a lawyer, was the first governor of the new colony. He told his followers,

> “**We shall be as a city upon a hill. The eyes of all people are upon us.**”

He meant that they should set a good example for others to follow. Puritans believed that if they lived by their religious beliefs, their community would succeed.

138 • Chapter 4

Drama

Write a Scene

- Have pairs of students write a one-page scene showing the first meeting between William Bradford, the governor of Plymouth, and Massasoit, the Wampanoag chief.
- They should use dialogue and include a description of the setting.
- Invite pairs to perform their scenes.

Verbal-linguistic; bodily-kinesthetic

Language Arts

Write Historical Fiction

Have students write a piece of historical fiction set in the New England settlements during this time period. They may choose to write a journal entry, a letter, or a short story. Remind them to include historical details and to think about what it might have been like to live in this place at that time.

Verbal-linguistic

The Colony Grows

5 The Puritans were better prepared to settle in North America than the Pilgrims had been 10 years earlier. They had a large group of people with many different skills. The Puritans set sail in March, allowing enough time to plant crops once they came to America.

Winthrop and his followers arrived in the town of Salem, north of Plymouth, in June 1630. They soon moved a few miles south where they began building their colony in present-day Boston. They named their settlement the Massachusetts Bay Colony after the Massachuset Indians. The colony was so successful that many more Puritans left England to move there.

John Winthrop

By the 1640s, as many as 20,000 English Puritans had moved to what is now the northeastern part of the United States. This region became known as New England because so many people from England lived there.

REVIEW How did Squanto help the Plymouth colony succeed? He taught the Pilgrims how to plant crops, hunt, and fish.

Lesson Summary

The Pilgrims sailed to North America to find religious freedom in 1620. They wrote the Mayflower Compact, the first written plan for government in North America. Ten years later, the Puritans, led by John Winthrop, settled the successful Massachusetts Bay Colony.

Why It Matters ...

The Massachusetts Bay Colony brought large numbers of English people to what would become the United States.

Lesson Review

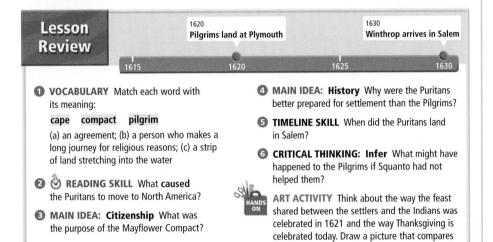

Timeline: 1615 — 1620 (1620 Pilgrims land at Plymouth) — 1625 — 1630 (1630 Winthrop arrives in Salem)

1. **VOCABULARY** Match each word with its meaning:
   cape **compact** **pilgrim**
   (a) an agreement; (b) a person who makes a long journey for religious reasons; (c) a strip of land stretching into the water
2. **READING SKILL** What caused the Puritans to move to North America?
3. **MAIN IDEA: Citizenship** What was the purpose of the Mayflower Compact?
4. **MAIN IDEA: History** Why were the Puritans better prepared for settlement than the Pilgrims?
5. **TIMELINE SKILL** When did the Puritans land in Salem?
6. **CRITICAL THINKING: Infer** What might have happened to the Pilgrims if Squanto had not helped them?

HANDS ON **ART ACTIVITY** Think about the way the feast shared between the settlers and the Indians was celebrated in 1621 and the way Thanksgiving is celebrated today. Draw a picture that compares the two celebrations.

139

3 Review/Assess

Review Tested Objectives

U2-17 Pilgrims came searching for religious freedom, intending to establish their own church. The Puritans wanted to reform the existing church.

U2-18 Plymouth Pilgrims struggled to survive before learning from local Indians how to plant, hunt, and fish. Massachusetts Bay Puritans created a larger and more successful colony, having come better prepared.

Lesson Review Answers

1. compact; pilgrim; cape
2. They wanted to create a community based on their religious beliefs.
3. to create a plan so that the Pilgrims could govern themselves
4. The Puritans had a large, skilled group of people, and they had enough time to plant crops in America.
5. 1630
6. Possible answer: The Pilgrims might not have survived in North America because they would have had a harder time farming and hunting.

HANDS ON Performance Task Rubric

4	Drawing depicts both first and modern Thanksgivings; differences between the two are clear and numerous.
3	Drawing depicts both first and modern Thanksgivings; several differences between the two are clear.
2	Drawing depicts both first and modern Thanksgivings; differences between the two are few or unclear.
1	Drawing depicts only one Thanksgiving; no comparison is made.

Study Guide/Homework

Vocabulary and Study Guide

Vocabulary

1. Draw a line connecting the vocabulary word to its meaning.

compact	A strip of land that stretches into a body of water
pilgrim	An agreement
cape	A person who makes a long journey for religious reasons

Study Guide

Read "The Plymouth Colony" and "Massachusetts Bay Colony." Then fill in the chart below to compare the colonies.

	Plymouth Colony	Massachusetts Bay Colony
Who settled there?	2. Pilgrims	3. Puritans
Why did they settle there?	4. To build a new religious community	5. To create a community based on their religious beliefs
What year did they settle there?	6. 1620	7. 1630

Unit Resources 42 Use with *United States History*, pp. 136–139

Unit Resources, p. 42

Reteach Minilesson

Use a graphic organizer to contrast the Pilgrims and the Puritans.

Pilgrims	Puritans
Separated from the Church of England	Remained part of the Church of England
Founded their colony in Plymouth, Massachusetts	Founded their colony in Salem and Boston, Massachusetts
Were not prepared to farm	Were well prepared to farm
Colony remained small	Colony grew quickly

Graphic Organizer 1

Extend

Quick Look

Connect to Core Lesson Students have just learned about life in the Plymouth Colony. In Extend Lesson 3, they will read a fictional narrative from the point of view of a Pilgrim boy.

1 Preview the Extend Lesson

Connect to the Big Idea

Individuals and Communities in American History Our national history is composed of individual and group stories of adjustment, adaptation, struggle, and survival. This fictional narrative tells the story of one young Pilgrim's adaptation and survival in Plymouth.

Connect to the Core Lesson

Ask students to think about what they learned about the first winter in the Plymouth Colony. What kinds of hardships did the Pilgrims face? How do they think the coming of springtime might have changed things?

Extend Lesson 3

Literature

This New Land

by G. Clifton Wisler

After living in Leyden, in the Netherlands, Richard Woodley, 12, and his family have sailed on the Mayflower to a new life in the settlement of Plymouth. Richard, his sister Mary, and brothers Thom and Edward have survived a brutal winter that took their mother's life. Spring has brought help from American Indian neighbors. The author, G. Clifton Wisler, tells this story from Richard Woodley's point of view.

Our great benefactor during this time was the Patuxet Indian, Squanto. Samoset, our earlier visitor, had returned to his home to the north, but Squanto had adopted our village as his own. Indeed, he had been born on this very ground and knew the wood and fields. He devoted himself to becoming our tutor in all matters of importance.

Our first lesson was in the catching of eels. In the Netherlands, they were most expensive, and I had never tasted one. Eels abounded in the muddy bottom of the brook. We had attempted to catch them earlier, but they did not bite our hooks.

Squanto brought us to the brook each morning. We would remove our boots and stockings and wade into the waters. With our feet we searched the mud for eels. It was strange at first, waiting for the unearthly sensation of the ropelike creatures. Once we located an eel, we would plunge our hands into the shallow stream and capture it. Often we would also fall into the brook, splashing and laughing as the water enveloped us. For a moment we were children, and I thank Squanto as much for the joy we shared as for eels caught.

In such a manner Edward and I caught three eels in a single morn. Mary cooked them in Mother's great iron kettle, adding such seasoning as she had. The meat proved fat and sweet.

140 • Chapter 4

Reaching All Learners

Background

Plymouth

The Pilgrims named their colony Plymouth after the port in Britain from which they sailed to America. The Plymouth colony became part of the Massachusetts Bay Colony in 1691. The town of Plymouth, Massachusetts, includes the site of the Pilgrims' original settlement.

Extra Support

Draw a Picture

Ask students to draw a picture of Richard Woodley and his family involved in one of the activities described in this narrative.

Visual-spatial

On Level

Make a Poster

In the narrative, Richard describes using salt to dry fish. Have students use the Internet or library resources to gather information about how salt is used to preserve food.

- Then ask them to make a poster showing their findings.

Verbal-linguistic; visual-spatial

A boy in the role of a Pilgrim at Plimoth Plantation

When berries appeared on the forest plants, Squanto taught us which ones should be taken. Some could be eaten. Others provided remedies for common ailments. We also dug certain roots near the brook and gathered wild onions and turnips in the wood.

The women recognized familiar simples and herbs among the plants. Mary removed some to her garden and placed them beside the rows planted with seeds Mother had brought from Leyden. Others were ground into powders to be added to our food or kept ready for illnesses.

We made salt from the sea. Great buckets of seawater were collected. As these dried in the sun or were boiled upon a fire, layers of salt collected, which was of much use in the drying of fish.

2 Teach the Extend Lesson

Learning Through Historical Fiction

Choose three students to take turns reading this fictional narrative aloud to the rest of the class. Discuss with students some of the characteristics of historical fiction. What have they learned from Richard's narrative that adds to their knowledge of Pilgrim life?

Challenge

Report on Herbs

- In the narrative, Richard talks about herbs that the Pilgrims used for common ailments.
- Ask students to research what kinds of herbs they used, and why. Then have them write a brief report about their findings.
- Encourage them to illustrate their reports and share them with the class.

Verbal-linguistic; visual-spatial

ELL

Intermediate

- Ask students to **create cartoon strips** showing part of Richard's narrative.
- Working in pairs, students can draw pictures and include captions or speech balloons.

Visual-spatial

Literature

Historical Fiction

Sarah Morton's Day: A Day in the Life of a Pilgrim Girl and *Samuel Eaton's Day: A Day in the Life of a Pilgrim Boy,* both by Kate Waters.

Place these works of historical fiction in your reading center for students who want to find out more about life for young Pilgrims in Plymouth Colony.

Critical Thinking

Predict Have students reread the dialogue between Richard and Master Clarke. How do they think the dialogue would have been different if Richard wanted to leave with the *Mayflower*?

Compare and Contrast What plants and other foods were familiar to Richard from Europe? Which were unfamiliar?

While we rejoiced of the plentiful food and renewed warmth which visited us, the new season brought another anguish. I was in the wood with Edward when he suddenly became pale as death. I took his hand to lead him homeward, but we had not reached the brook before his breathing became heavy.

"Richard?" he gasped.

I thought for a moment that he would join Mother, but although his breathing was much labored, and he shivered as with a winter chill, I was able to help him to the fields. There Master Winslow took Edward in his arms and carried him to our dwelling.

We were fearful of a new plague, but Mary would hear nonesuch. She located two dried leaves of rosemary and rolled them in her fingers. She next drew the leaves close to Edward's nose. As he inhaled, his breathing eased, and his face grew bright.

As the trees regained their leaves, we began our preparations for the planting. Already the fields had been made ready for what wheat and barley we had seed to plant. A few acres of peas were to be set out. From Squanto we learned it was yet early to plant the corn.

In late March Master Carver was reelected our governor. Much work was carried out in the village, and Father planned a cottage to replace the small hut we now inhabited. Great barrels were brought ashore from Mayflower to be filled with fresh water for the ship's voyage back to England.

I found my heart growing heavy as the final preparations were made for Mayflower's departure. I had come to look upon the ship as both my friend and protector, as our home for so long a time. On the eve of her sailing, I found myself walking with Master Clarke on the beach.

"You will be asea once again on the morrow," I said, staring out past the horizon, imagining it was possible to see the distant coast of England.

"Aye, by sundown we will be out to sea," he said.

"It is a long way to Southampton."

" 'Tis but another ocean to cross. To a sailor, it is as green a pasture as yon field."

"You can't plant seed in an ocean," I told him.

"Aye, but a sailor's no planter. He is a reaper at times, for he harvests fish from the sea. Nay, more often he's a wanderer with no home port, cast upon a wind."

"I fear it would be a life I would grow weary of."

Reaching All Learners

Language Arts

Write a Personal Narrative

- Ask students to write their own personal narrative from the point of view of a Pilgrim.
- Have them describe the experience of one day in the Plymouth Colony.

Math

Make a Bar Graph

- Have students make a bar graph showing the foods that Richard mentions in his narrative.
- Have students label the bars. Each bar should represent one of the foods.
- The numbers along the left side of the chart should represent how many times each food is mentioned in the narrative.

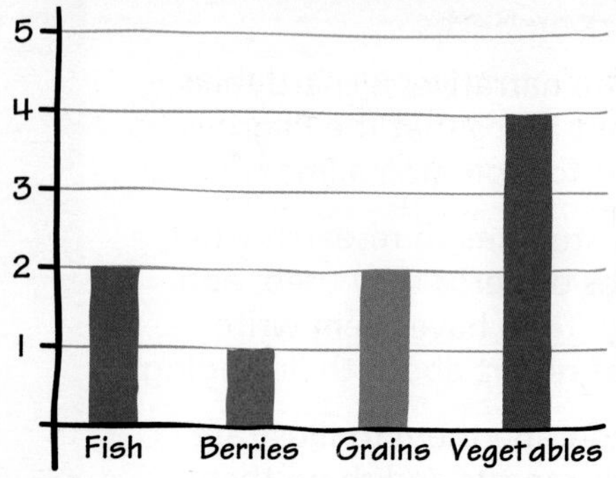

Logical-mathematical

"There is a weariness, Richard Woodley, but there is a joy of discoveries, fair harbors, and new lands."

"Like this one?"

"Aye."

"Have you ever found a place you wished to make your home?"

"I have a home: the sea."

"And a family?"

"Aye, my mates. Upon occasion I acquire others."

"Boys who listen to tales?"

"Aye, and those who steer a ship or caulk a boat."

I found myself smiling, and I wish my tongue had been able to give him my thanks.

"Ye would have made a fine sailor," he told me. "But I see the heart of a farmer. Ye wish to grow things."

"Perhaps I shall grow myself," I said, hoping to lighten the mood.

"I never knew a boy to stand so tall," Master Clarke said. "If the winds were to blow me to the Americas years hence, I would find you a great man, Lord of the Manor or the like."

"There's a greater likelihood I'll be a poor farmer, but you will be welcome to share my table."

"Men who weather the storm are bound by it," he said, setting his great rough hand upon my head. "I bid ye a fair harvest and a better winter."

"May you find the winds fair to England," I replied. Reluctantly I watched him walk to the ship's boat.

A reconstruction of the original Mayflower

LITERATURE

Activities

1. **THINK ABOUT IT** What events and people in this story are real? Which are not real, but were made up by the author? How can you tell the difference?
2. **CHART IT** Make a chart that lists the foods mentioned in the story. Describe how the foods were gathered or prepared. Add pictures to illustrate your chart.

143

3 Leveled Activities

1 Think About It *For Extra Support*

Sample answer: Real: Squanto, using herbs, making salt from the sea, Master Carver; Made up: Woodley family, Edward's illness, the conversations and events of the story. You can tell the difference because historical fiction uses details from the historical background to tell a fictional story.

2 Chart It *For Challenge*

HANDS ON Performance Task Rubric

4	Chart is well organized; information is complete and accurate; mechanics are correct.
3	Chart is adequately organized; information is mostly complete and accurate; mechanics are mostly correct.
2	Chart is somewhat organized; information is incomplete; some inaccuracies; some errors in mechanics.
1	Chart is disorganized; information is incomplete and inaccurate; many errors in mechanics.

Drama

Write a Scene

Ask students to write, in dialogue, the scene in which Richard's brother Edward becomes ill in the woods, and their sister Mary treats him.

Verbal-linguistic

Graphic Organizer

What do I know about the Pilgrims' first spring?

K	W	L
I know that . . .	I want to learn . . .	I have learned . . .

Graphic Organizer 2

✔ Tested Objectives

U2-19 History Describe the Dutch settlement of New Netherland.

U2-20 History Summarize the experiences of settlers, missionaries, and explorers in New France.

Lesson Quick Look

This lesson describes the growth of Dutch and French colonies in North America.

Teaching Option: **Extend Lesson 4** teaches students about the fur trade.

1 Get Set to Read

Preview Have students describe what they see in the illustration on page 145.

Reading Skill: Compare and Contrast Students should include the relations of the settlers with other people.

Build on What You Know Have students think about how trade affected settlers and native peoples.

Vocabulary

diversity *noun,* the variety of backgrounds found in a group of people

tolerance *noun,* acceptance of different beliefs or behavior

missionary *noun,* someone who travels to do religious work

Core Lesson 4

Dutch and French Colonies

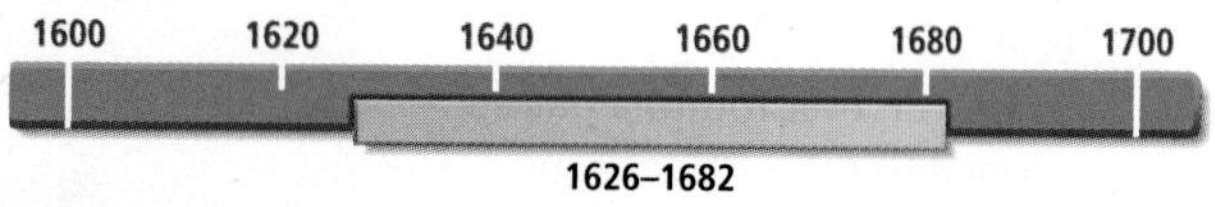

VOCABULARY

diversity
tolerance
missionary

Vocabulary Strategy

missionary

Look for the word **mission** in **missionary**. Missionaries have a mission, or goal, to teach others about their religion.

READING SKILL

Compare and Contrast

As you read, make a list of similarities and differences between the Dutch and French settlements.

ALIKE	DIFFERENT

Build on What You Know Have you ever traded books or toys? People usually trade when they want something that someone else has. In the 1600s, American Indians and European settlers traded with each other.

what did they trade?

New Netherland

Main Idea The Dutch settled in what is now the northeastern United States.

Remember that in the 1500s and 1600s, European explorers claimed land in North America. Henry Hudson made land claims for the Netherlands on one of his voyages. The Dutch called this land New Netherland.

The first settlements in New Netherland were fur-trading posts. In 1626, the governor of New Netherland, **Peter Minuit** (MIHN yoo IHT), bought Manhattan Island 1
in present-day New York from the Manhates Indians. He started a settlement there called New Amsterdam, the capital of New Netherland. Minuit also set up a colony for Sweden on the Delaware River. New Sweden lasted for 17 years before it was taken over by New Netherland in 1655.

Peter Minuit He was the first leader of New Netherland.

Skill and Strategy

Reading Skill and Strategy

Reading Skill: Compare and Contrast

This skill helps you understand how historical events or people are similar and different.

Read "New France." Then fill in the Venn diagram below to compare the fur traders and missionaries who came to these settlements.

Alike	Different
1. Settled in New France	1. Fur traders: Traded with American Indians and then sold furs in Europe 2. Missionaries: Taught American Indians about the Roman Catholic religion

Reading Strategy: Summarize

4. Read "Dutch and French Colonies." Then write a short summary of each section.

Heading 1: New Netherland

Summary: Sample answer: The Dutch started colonies in present-day New York.

Heading 2: New France

Summary: Sample answer: The French claimed lots of land in Canada, but few people settled there.

Unit Resources

43
Use with *United States History*, pp. 144–147

Unit Resources, p. 43

Background

Names from Other Languages

- Names of many places in New York City come from the Dutch language, including Lang Eylant (Long Island), Breuckelen (Brooklyn), Haarlem (Harlem), and Staten Eylant (Staten Island).
- Many towns that still exist on or near the Mississippi River have French names. These include Prairie du Chien, Wisconsin; Baton Rouge, Louisiana; Belleville, Illinois; and Des Moines, Iowa.

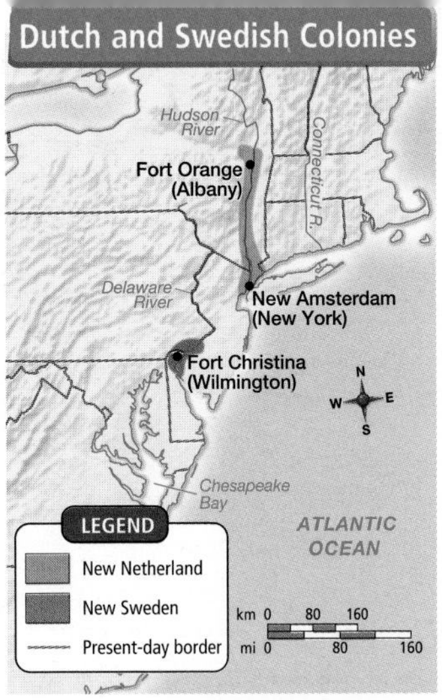

Dutch and Swedish Settlements Located at the mouth of the Hudson River, New Amsterdam (above) had one of the best harbors in North America. The map shows the location of the Dutch and Swedish colonies in 1650.

Settlers in New Netherland

The Dutch West India Company was an important trading company in the Netherlands. The owners of the company controlled the New Netherland settlements. The company brought some families to North America to farm, but few people from the Netherlands wanted to move across the Atlantic.

2 The company looked for settlers from other countries. They welcomed all people, no matter what country they came from or what religion they practiced. New settlers added to the diversity of New Netherland. **Diversity** is the variety of people in a group. In New Amsterdam alone, 18 languages were spoken. The population included German, English, Swedish, French, and free and enslaved African settlers.

Have you heard the term melting pot?

New York

In 1647, **Peter Stuyvesant** (STY vih suhnt) became governor of New Netherland. Stuyvesant was a harsh man. He made laws that angered colonists. Unlike most settlers in New Netherland, he did not practice tolerance. **Tolerance** is respecting beliefs that are different from one's own. Stuyvesant did not want settlers with different religious beliefs in the colony.

In 1664, English ships sailed into the harbor at New Amsterdam to attack. The settlers of New Amsterdam were so unhappy with Stuyvesant that they refused to fight the English. The Dutch colony of New Netherland became an English colony. The English renamed New Amsterdam to honor the Duke of York. They called it New York. 3 * test question

REVIEW Why was Stuyvesant an unpopular governor? He made laws that angered colonists and did not practice tolerance.

145

2 Teach

New Netherland

Talk About It

1 **Q History** Who were the original inhabitants of Manhattan Island?

A the Manhates Indians

2 **Q Economics** What kinds of settlers did the Dutch West India Company look for?

A They looked for settlers from different countries and different religions.

3 **Q History** Why did the New Amsterdam settlers refuse to fight the English?

A They were unhappy with their governor, Peter Stuyvesant.

Vocabulary Strategy

diversity A synonym for diversity is "variation."

tolerance Explain that this is the noun form of the verb *tolerate*. The adjective is *tolerant*.

Reading Strategy: Summarize Ask students to write their own summaries of the first page of this lesson and share them with the class.

Leveled Practice

REACHING ALL LEARNERS

Extra Support

Have partners **interview each other,** taking roles of settlers in New Amsterdam. Verbal-linguistic

Challenge

Have students research place names in your area. What languages are the names based in? Why? Verbal-linguistic

ELL

REACHING ALL LEARNERS

Intermediate

- Have partners make a sequence chart showing how New Amsterdam became New York.
- Ask partners to compare charts with another pair. They should work together to correct factual, grammatical, and spelling errors.
- Help students create a master sequence chart on the board.

Visual-spatial; verbal-linguistic

New France

Talk About It

4 Q History Who settled in New France, and what did they do?

A young men who worked the fur and fishing trades

5 Q History Who helped the Huron and Algonquin in fighting the Iroquois?

A the French fur traders, led by Champlain

6 Q Geography What region did Robert La Salle name after Louis XIV?

A Louisiana, the land around the Mississippi

Vocabulary Strategy

missionary The suffix *-ary* means "connected with"—in this case, someone connected with a mission.

Critical Thinking

Evaluate Why do you think few people wanted to move from the Netherlands to North America?

French Settlements, 1700

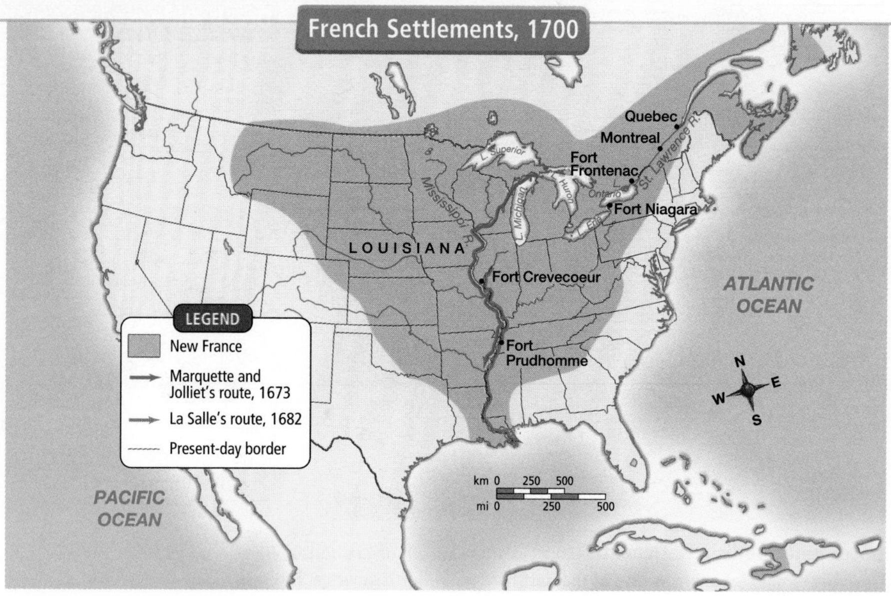

New France After 1682, France's land claims covered a large part of North America. SKILL **Reading Maps** Which river did Marquette, Jolliet, and La Salle explore? the Mississippi River

New France

Main Idea France claimed much of North America in the 1600s, but few settlers lived there.

In the early 1600s, the French claimed land in present-day Canada. This land was called New France. Few settlers lived there. Its cold climate made farming difficult. Most settlers were young men who worked
4 in the fur and fishing trades. They lived near the fur-trading post of Quebec.

Missionaries moved to New France as well. A **missionary** is a person who teaches his or her religion to others who have different beliefs. Missionaries from France taught people of present-day Canada about Catholicism. They built missions throughout New France.

The Fur Trade

Animals with thick fur, including beaver, fox, and otter, lived in the forests of North America. French merchants made money selling these furs in Europe.

Fur traders traveled throughout New France to trade with Indians. People of Indian nations gave the furs from animals they had trapped to the French. In exchange, the French traded goods such as beads, tools, pots, knives, and cloth.

The French formed a partnership with the Huron and Algonquin, who lived near Quebec. The Huron and Algonquin were at war with the powerful Iroquois, a group of five American Indian nations. French fur traders, led by **Samuel de Champlain**, 5
fought with the Huron and Algonquin against their enemies.

Music

Research Musical Styles

- Have students find out about one of the many kinds of music that developed along the Mississippi River (for example, the blues, gospel, and cajun music).
- Ask them to find a recording of a song in one of these styles.
- Invite them to play the recording and share what they learned with the class.

Musical-auditory

Language Arts

Write a Personal Essay

- Have students write a one-page personal essay about a trip they have recently taken.
- They may choose to describe a walk through their neighborhood, a trip to visit a relative, or any other recent journey.
- They should include as many details as possible.

Verbal-linguistic

Traveling by Canoe Marquette and Jolliet on the Mississippi River.

Exploring the Mississippi

Jacques Marquette (mahr KEHT) was a missionary in New France. In 1673, he traveled by canoe down the Mississippi River to set up missions. **Louis Jolliet** (JOH lee EHT), an explorer, joined him. Jolliet thought the Mississippi might lead to the Pacific Ocean.

Robert La Salle (luh SAL) also explored the region in 1682. He claimed the Mississippi River and all the land around it for France. La Salle named this vast area Louisiana after **King Louis XIV**. 14 6

REVIEW How did the traders of New France get fur to sell to Europeans? They traded for fur with Indian nations in present-day Canada.

Lesson Summary

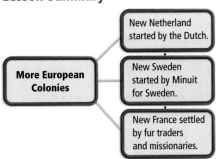

- More European Colonies
  - New Netherland started by the Dutch.
  - New Sweden started by Minuit for Sweden.
  - New France settled by fur traders and missionaries.

Why It Matters ...

New Netherland and New France included land that would one day become part of the United States.

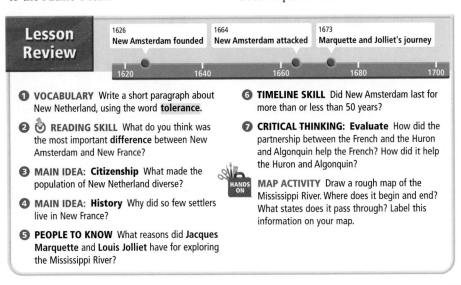

Lesson Review

1626	1664	1673
New Amsterdam founded	New Amsterdam attacked	Marquette and Jolliet's journey

Timeline: 1620 — 1640 — 1660 — 1680 — 1700

1. **VOCABULARY** Write a short paragraph about New Netherland, using the word **tolerance.**
2. **READING SKILL** What do you think was the most important **difference** between New Amsterdam and New France?
3. **MAIN IDEA: Citizenship** What made the population of New Netherland diverse?
4. **MAIN IDEA: History** Why did so few settlers live in New France?
5. **PEOPLE TO KNOW** What reasons did **Jacques Marquette** and **Louis Jolliet** have for exploring the Mississippi River?
6. **TIMELINE SKILL** Did New Amsterdam last for more than or less than 50 years?
7. **CRITICAL THINKING: Evaluate** How did the partnership between the French and the Huron and Algonquin help the French? How did it help the Huron and Algonquin?

HANDS ON **MAP ACTIVITY** Draw a rough map of the Mississippi River. Where does it begin and end? What states does it pass through? Label this information on your map.

Study Guide/Homework

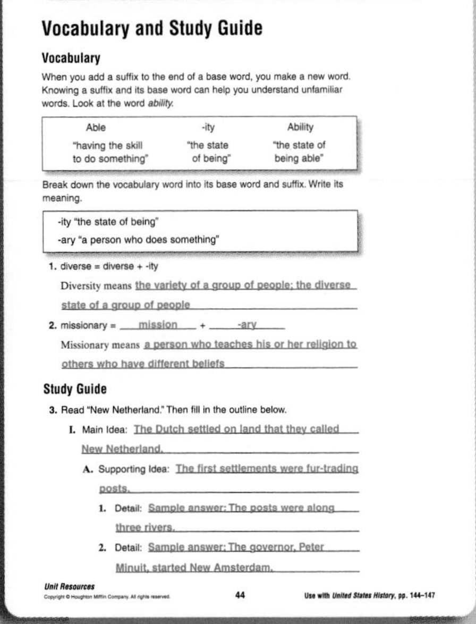

Vocabulary and Study Guide

Vocabulary

When you add a suffix to the end of a base word, you make a new word. Knowing a suffix and its base word can help you understand unfamiliar words. Look at the word *ability*.

Able	-ity	Ability
"having the skill to do something"	"the state of being"	"the state of being able"

Break down the vocabulary word into its base word and suffix. Write its meaning.

-ity "the state of being"
-ary "a person who does something"

1. diverse = diverse + -ity
   Diversity means the variety of a group of people; the diverse state of a group of people
2. missionary = mission + -ary
   Missionary means a person who teaches his or her religion to others who have different beliefs

Study Guide

3. Read "New Netherland." Then fill in the outline below.
   I. Main Idea: The Dutch settled on land that they called New Netherland.
      A. Supporting Idea: The first settlements were fur-trading posts.
         1. Detail: Sample answer: The posts were along three rivers.
         2. Detail: Sample answer: The governor, Peter Minuit, started New Amsterdam.

Unit Resources 44 Use with United States History, pp. 144–147

Unit Resources, p. 44

Reteach Minilesson

Use a Main Idea and Details chart to review the lesson.

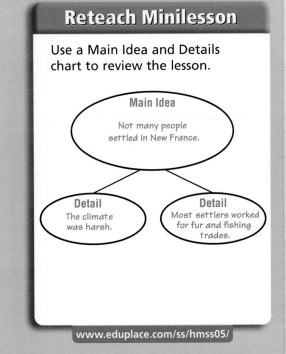

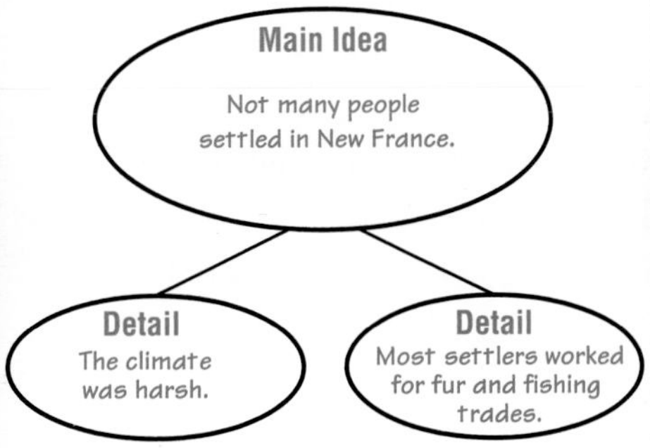
Main Idea
Not many people settled in New France.
Detail
The climate was harsh.
Detail
Most settlers worked for fur and fishing trades.

www.eduplace.com/ss/hmss05/

3 Review/Assess

Review Tested Objectives

U2-19 New Netherland was a diverse settlement made up of fur-trading posts. It was taken over by the English in 1664 and renamed New York.

U2-20 Many settlers in New France were fur-traders and fishermen. They formed partnerships with and fought against local Indians. Missionaries in this area were Roman Catholic. Explorers such as Jolliet traveled the Mississippi River. La Salle claimed lands for France along the river, naming the area Louisiana.

Lesson Review Answers

1. Paragraph should express how most settlers in New Netherland practiced tolerance, while Stuyvesant did not.
2. Answer should be based on information from the lesson.
3. The Dutch West India Company welcomed settlers from all countries and religions.
4. New France's cold climate made farming difficult.
5. Marquette wanted to set up missions along the Mississippi, and Jolliet thought the Mississippi might lead to the Pacific.
6. less
7. The partnership helped the French because they were able to get furs to sell in Europe. It helped the Huron and Algonquin because they received trade goods and help in fighting the Iroquois.

HANDS ON Performance Task Rubric

4	Map shows Mississippi River; includes three or more accurate details; labeling and other mechanics correct.
3	Map shows Mississippi River; includes two accurate details; labeling and other mechanics mostly correct.
2	Map attempts to show Mississippi River; includes one accurate detail; some errors in labeling and other mechanics.
1	Map does not show Mississippi River; includes no accurate details; many errors in labeling and other mechanics.

Extend Quick Look

Connect to the Core Lesson Students have just read about the fur trade in New France. In Extend Lesson 4, they will learn more about the people who took part in the fur trade, and the profits they made from it.

1 Teach the Extend Lesson

Connect to the Big Idea

Trade and Money/Market Economies

People and nations gained through the world fur trade during the 1600s. Market economies favor certain characteristics: freedom of enterprise, profit, competition, voluntary exchange, and limited government; depend on supply and demand to determine price; and rely on increased productivity to address scarcity. In New France, traders profited by supplying beaver pelts and other furs to meet Europe's demand for fur hats.

Extend Lesson 4

Economics

French Fur Trading

A lone fur trader travels remote lands of northern New France. Though he is far from Europe, he is part of world trade in the 1600s. The demand for fur hats in Europe has resulted in an active business for the trapping and shipping of beaver pelts and other furs.

This trader in North America meets with Huron and Ottawa people who trap beavers. He trades goods for their beaver pelts. Then he carries the pelts by canoe to sell to merchants in Quebec and other trading posts. French merchants pay ship owners to send the furs to Europe. In Europe, the furs are sold to hatmakers, and their fur hats are sold to buyers.

Deerskin Clothes
Traders wore deerskin clothes as did the Huron and Ottawa. These clothes were strong and did not wear out.

Canoes
Traders could not travel on swift rivers without canoes. They used canoes like those the Huron and Ottawa built.

148 • Chapter 4

Reaching All Learners

Extra Support

Illustrate a Trade

Have students make an illustration showing a trade between a French fur trader and a Huron or Ottawa fur trapper.

Visual-spatial

On Level

Write a Description

- Have students look at the illustration. What does it tell them about the life of a fur trader?
- Have them write a description of the illustration and their reactions to it.

Verbal-linguistic; visual-spatial

Challenge

Make a Model Canoe

- Ask students to use library resources or the Internet to research canoes used by the Huron and Ottawa Indians. How were these canoes made? What materials were used to make them?
- Have them make a model of such a canoe, using construction paper or cardboard.

Bodily-kinesthetic

ECONOMICS

Why Did They Trade?

New France

American Indians in New France wanted European goods, especially iron goods. Iron kettles could be placed directly over a fire for cooking, and iron blades were strong enough to chop and carve wood.

Europe

Merchants earned money by selling furs to European hatmakers. Hatmakers prepared the pelts for different styles of hats which were warm, waterproof, and long-lasting. The beaver hat below is soft like felt.

Furs and Supplies
A canoe could carry about 40 pelts. Traders also needed to carry trade goods, which were heavy, to supply the American Indians.

Activities

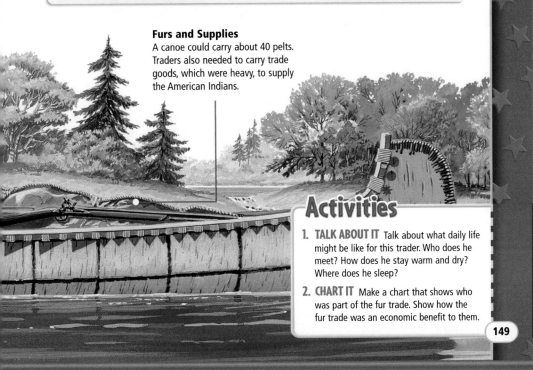

1. **TALK ABOUT IT** Talk about what daily life might be like for this trader. Who does he meet? How does he stay warm and dry? Where does he sleep?
2. **CHART IT** Make a chart that shows who was part of the fur trade. Show how the fur trade was an economic benefit to them.

149

2 Leveled Activities

1 Talk About It *For Extra Support*
Sample answers: He met with Huron and Ottawa beaver trappers, and merchants in Quebec and other trading posts. He wore deerskin clothes to keep warm and dry. He might have slept in the wool blankets he carried with him.

2 Chart It *For Challenge*

Writing Rubric

4	Chart is clear, accurate, and complete; shows who was part of the fur trade and the economic benefits they gained from it; no errors in mechanics.
3	Chart is mostly clear, accurate, and complete; adequately shows who was part of the fur trade and what they gained; few errors in mechanics.
2	Chart is somewhat unclear, inaccurate, or incomplete; partially shows who was part of the fur trade and what they gained; some errors in mechanics.
1	Chart is unclear, inaccurate, or incomplete; does not show who was part of the fur trade or what they gained; many errors in mechanics.

REACHING ALL LEARNERS

ELL

Beginning

Ask students to **illustrate** some of the trade items mentioned in the Extend Lesson. Have them **write captions** for their illustrations.

Visual-spatial; verbal-linguistic

Math

Calculate

Have students use information from the lesson to help them solve the following problem:

- If a trader could exchange one kettle for 10 pelts, how many kettles would a trader need to trade in order to fill his canoe with as many pelts as it could carry? 4

Logical-mathematical

Graphic Organizer

Steps in Fur Trade

1	Illinois, Miami, and Kickapoo trapped furs.
2	Furs were gathered by Huron and Ottawa canoeists.
3	Furs were brought to the French traders.
4	Furs were taken to France by ship.

Graphic Organizer 15

Chapter Review

Tested Objectives

The lesson objective assessed by each question is shown in parentheses after the answer.

Visual Summary

1. Jamestown was the first permanent English settlement in North America. *(Obj. U2-16)*
2. New France was settled by fur trappers and missionaries in present-day Canada. *(Obj. U2-20)*
3. New Netherland was a group of Dutch settlements in North America. *(Obj. U2-19)*

Facts and Main Ideas

4. to find a shorter trade route to Asia *(Obj. U2-12)*
5. by asking people to invest in the company by buying stocks *(Obj. U2-12)*
6. Both groups ran out of food in the first months, and about half of each group died. Both groups had to learn to farm and use resources. *(Obj. U2-16, U2-18)*
7. It was a plan for government that the Pilgrims created. *(Obj. U2-18)*
8. The colonists were so unhappy with their governor that they refused to fight the English. *(Obj. U2-19)*

Vocabulary

9. **tolerance** *(Obj. U2-19)*
10. **armada** *(Obj. U2-13)*
11. **charter** *(Obj. U2-12)*

Visual Summary

1–3. Write a description of each colony named below.

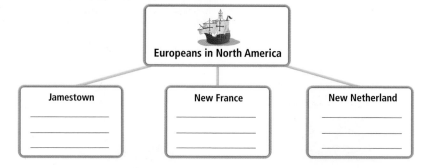

Europeans in North America

Jamestown	New France	New Netherland
______	______	______

Facts and Main Ideas

TEST PREP Answer each question with information from the chapter.

4. **Geography** Why did explorers look for a Northwest Passage?
5. **Economics** How did the Virginia Company raise money to buy ships and supplies to start a settlement in North America?
6. **History** What difficulties did settlers in Plymouth and Jamestown have in common?
7. **Government** What was the Mayflower Compact?
8. **History** Why was it easy for England to take control of New Amsterdam?

Vocabulary

TEST PREP Choose the correct word from the list below to complete each sentence.

armada, p. 125
charter, p. 131
tolerance, p. 145

9. A person who has respect for others' beliefs shows ______.
10. King Philip of Spain built an ______ to fight the English.
11. The King of England gave the Virginia Company a ______ to start a settlement.

Reading/Language Arts Wrap-Up

Reading Strategy: Summarize

Review with students the steps involved when they summarize a passage of text.

Have students work in small groups. Each member of the group should take a paragraph and summarize it for the rest of the group.

Ask students to do a self-check: "How well did I do in summarizing?"

Writing Strategy

Explain to students that summarizing will be a valuable tool when they need to write.

For example, if students are taking a test in which they must write short answers to questions, they can use the summarizing strategy as they review what they know and choose the details most pertinent to the answer.

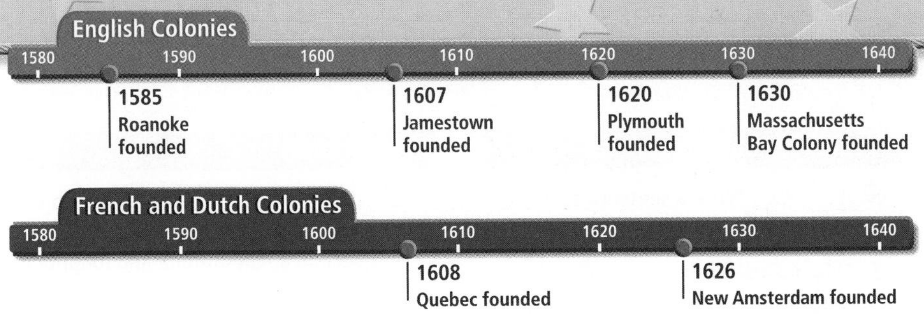

Apply Skills

TEST PREP Chart and Graph Skill Use the parallel timelines above to answer each question.

12. Which colony was founded first?
    - **A.** Jamestown
    - **B.** Quebec
    - **C.** Roanoke
    - **D.** Plymouth
13. Which colony was settled just one year after Jamestown?
    - **A.** Plymouth
    - **B.** Roanoke
    - **C.** New Amsterdam
    - **D.** Quebec
14. How many colonies were founded in the 1620s?
    - **A.** 0
    - **B.** 2
    - **C.** 4
    - **D.** 6

Critical Thinking

TEST PREP Write a short paragraph to answer each question.

15. **Compare and Contrast** How were the Pilgrims and the Puritans alike? How were they different?
16. **Classify** What three categories of information would you use for a report on the Jamestown colony?

Activities

HANDS ON **Debate Activity** Research one of the theories about why the Roanoke colonists disappeared. Prepare notes for a class debate on the lost colony.

Writing Activity Write a one-page short story about the celebration of the Pilgrims' first harvest. Write from the point of view of the Wampanoag Indians who were there.

Technology
Writing Process Tips
Get help with your story at
www.eduplace.com/kids/hmss05/

Apply Skills

12. C *(Obj. U2-14)*
13. D *(Obj. U2-14)*
14. B *(Obj. U2-14)*

Critical Thinking

15. Alike: Both wanted religious freedom, and to create a community based on their beliefs. Different: The Pilgrims wanted to separate from the Church of England. The Puritans wanted to change it to make it better. *(Obj. U2-17)*
16. Sample answer: Difficulties, Successes, Powhatans *(Obj. U2-16)*

Leveled Activities

HANDS ON Performance Task Rubric

4	Position clearly stated; reasons supported by research; mechanics correct.
3	Position adequately stated; most reasons supported by research; few errors in mechanics.
2	Position is stated; reasons confused or poorly supported by research; some errors in mechanics.
1	Position not stated; reasons not supported; many errors in mechanics.

Writing Rubric

4	Story is well organized and shows considerable creative effort; mechanics are correct; written in present tense.
3	Story is adequately organized and shows creative effort; few errors; written in present tense.
2	Story is somewhat organized and shows some creative effort; some errors, including shifts in tense.
1	Story is disorganized and shows little effort; many errors in mechanics; present tense is absent.

Technology

Test Generator

You can generate your own version of the chapter review by using the **Test Generator CD-ROM**.

Web Link

For more ideas, visit
www.eduplace.com/ss/hmss05/

Standards

National Standards

II b Read and construct simple timelines
III g How people create places
III h Interaction of human beings and their physical environment
VI f Factors that contribute to cooperation and cause disputes
VII a Scarcity and choice
VII f Influence of incentives, values, traditions, and habits
IX b Conflict, cooperation, and interdependence
IX f Concerns, issues, standards, and conflicts related to human rights

Unit Review

Vocabulary and Main Ideas

1. Caravans kept merchants safe during the journey. *(Obj. U2-2)*
2. astrolabe, compass, caravel *(Obj. U2-3)*
3. They were amazed because it was much bigger than European cities, and it was built in the middle of a lake. *(Obj. U2-7)*
4. because Henry Hudson explored the Hudson River and other areas of New York for the Dutch *(Obj. U2-12)*
5. Investors could make money if colonists found treasure in North America. *(Obj. U2-12)*
6. Missionaries moved to New France to teach people living there about the Roman Catholic religion. *(Obj. U2-20)*

Critical Thinking

7. Europeans brought new animals and plants to the Americas. *(Obj. U2-10)*
8. Settlers in New Spain, New England, and New France traveled to North America for religious reasons. Settlers in New Spain and New England were successful farmers. Most settlers in New France, fished and traded fur instead of farming. *(Obj. U2-15 through U2-20)*

Apply Skills

9. D *(Obj. U2-11)*
10. D *(Obj. U2-11)*

UNIT 2 Review and Test Prep

Vocabulary and Main Ideas

TEST PREP Write a sentence to answer each question.

1. Why did Arab merchants travel by **caravan** across the desert?
2. What are three examples of **technology** used by sailors in the 1400s?
3. What was the reaction of the **conquistadors** when they arrived at Tenochtitlán? Why?
4. Why did the Dutch make land **claims** in present-day New York State?
5. Why did people **invest** in the Virginia Company?
6. Why would a **missionary** move to New France?

Critical Thinking

TEST PREP Write a short paragraph to answer each question.

7. **Cause and Effect** How did European exploration affect the land and people of the Americas?
8. **Compare and Contrast** Write a short paragraph about the settlers of New Spain, New England, New France, and New Netherland. What did they have in common? What differences did they have?

Apply Skills

TEST PREP Map Skill Use the map of Balboa's journey to answer each question about latitude and longitude.

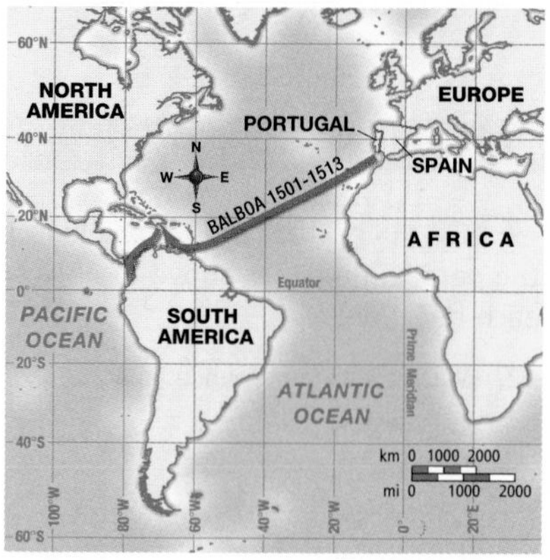

9. What lines of latitude and longitude are closest to Spain?
   - **A.** 20°N, 0°
   - **B.** 40°S, 0°
   - **C.** 40°N, 40°W
   - **D.** 40°N, 0°
10. At about what line of longitude did Balboa first enter the Pacific Ocean?
    - **A.** 0°
    - **B.** 20°W
    - **C.** 40°W
    - **D.** 80°W

Technology

Test Generator

- Use the **Test Generator CD-ROM** to create tests customized to your class.
- Access hundreds of test questions and make lesson, chapter, and unit quizzes and tests.

Web Updates

Curious about new trade book titles that you can use with the program? Visit **www.eduplace.com/ss/hmss05/** to update your Unit Bibliography.

Extra Support

REACHING ALL LEARNERS

Make Flash Cards

Have students create flash cards on material from the unit. They can work in pairs quizzing each other.

Unit Activity

The Big Idea

Create Explorer Postcards

- Choose any place in North America that you would like to have explored.
- Research information about the geography and early people of the place you chose.
- Create one or more postcards an explorer might have sent home.
- One side of your postcard might be an illustration of the place. The other side might be a written message about it.

At the Library

Check your school library for these books.

Hard Labor: The First African-Americans, 1619 by P. C. McKissack and F. L. McKissack Jr.

In 1619, twenty Africans came to Virginia as indentured servants, ready to begin life anew.

Sir Walter Raleigh and the Quest for El Dorado by Marc Aronson

This biography tells about successes and failures of Sir Walter Raleigh.

CURRENT EVENTS WEEKLY WR READER

Connect to Today

Create a class book about exploration today.

- Find articles that tell about the exploration of new frontiers, such as the ocean and space.
- Write a summary of each article. Draw a picture or map to illustrate each summary.
- Gather your illustrated summaries into a class book.

Technology

Get information for the class book from the Weekly Reader at **www.eduplace.com/kids/hmss05/**

Read About It

Look for these Social Studies Independent Books in your classroom.

153

Unit Activity

HANDS ON Performance Task Rubric

4	Postcard shows considerable creative effort; research is accurate and complete; spelling, grammar, and punctuation are correct.
3	Postcard shows creative effort; research is generally accurate and complete; spelling, grammar, and punctuation mostly correct.
2	Postcard shows some creative effort; research is partly accurate and partly complete; some errors in spelling, grammar and punctuation.
1	Postcard shows little effort; research is absent or incomplete; many errors in spelling, grammar and punctuation.

WEEKLY WR READER

Unit Project

- Have students present their contributions to the class exploration book.

At the Library

- You may wish to wrap up the unit by reading aloud from one of these suggested titles or from one of the Read-Aloud selections included in the Unit Bibliography.

Read About It

- You may wish to provide students with the appropriate Leveled Social Studies Books for this unit. Turn to page 77B for teaching options.
- If students have written summaries or reviews of the Leveled Books or the books in the Unit Bibliography, you may wish to have students read them aloud to the class.

Math

Test Taking Tip

Tell students that they should read all the parts of a chart, table, graph, or map, including the title, when they encounter one in a test. The title contains important information that will help them understand what they are seeing.

Standards

National Standards

II b Cause and effect relationships
II e People in different times and places view the world differently
III c Resources, data sources, and geographic tools
III g How people create places
VII f Influence of incentives, values, traditions, and habits
VIII a How science and technology have changed lives
IX b Conflict, cooperation, and interdependence

Unit 3

Unit Planner

Begin with Core.
Extend for more.

The English Colonies

LEVELED BOOKS

The following Social Studies Independent Books are available for extending and supporting students' social studies experience as they read the unit.

Differentiated Instruction

Extra Support

Schools Days in 1700
By Nancy Garhan Attebury

Summary: In the 1700s, before there were free public schools for everyone, your social level, sex, religion, geography, and race determined how—and whether—you went to school.

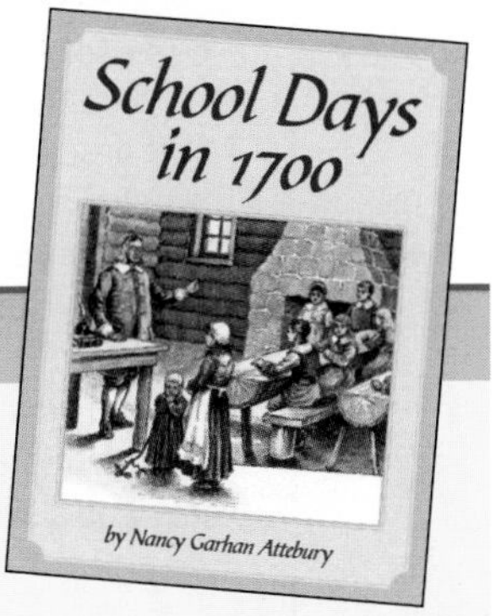

Vocabulary

apprentice
growing season

Extending Understanding

Oral Language: Speech Ask students to take the part of a colonial schoolmaster at a Boston boy's school as he tells students what they can expect to learn and how they are expected to behave.

Independent Writing: Journal Have students take on the role of schoolchildren in the 1700s and write a journal entry about a typical day at school, describing both the teacher and what they study.

Graphic Organizer: Students can use a compare-and-contrast chart to show the differences between school experiences for each group in the book.

	Location	Studies	Teacher
Boys	schoolhouse	Latin	schoolmaster
Girls	private home	dancing	tutor

On Level

Whale! Nantucket Whaling Days
By Susan Ring

Summary: Whaling was the backbone of industry in colonial New England, where whaling ships filled the harbors and whale-based products filled store shelves.

Vocabulary

naval stores
export
industry

Extending Understanding

Oral Language: Job Interview Have students work in pairs, one taking the role of a whaling captain and the other taking the role of someone who wants to join his crew and asks questions about what the journey will be like.

Independent Writing: Persuasive Letter Have students pretend they are Jacob Rodríguez Rivera writing a letter to convince Newport merchants to get involved in whaling, describing the many ways whaling will make money for them.

Graphic Organizer: Students can use a word web to illustrate the impact of whaling on colonial society.

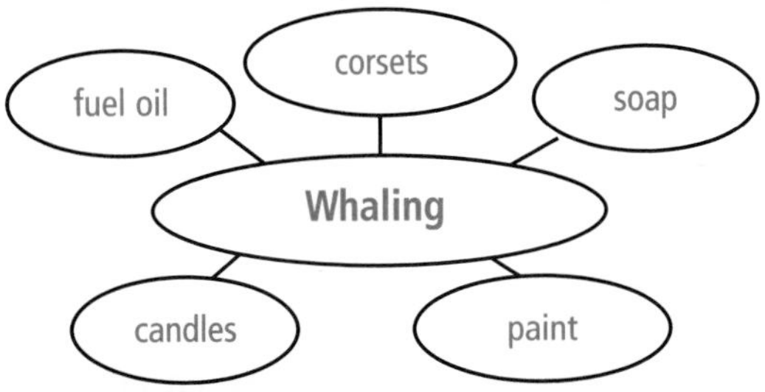

Challenge

Who was Poor Richard? Colonials to Remember
By Carl W. Grody

Summary: The remarkable and very different lives of Benjamin Franklin, Olaudah Equiano, Mary Musgrove, and Jonathan Edwards.

Vocabulary

middle passage
slave trade
artisan

Extending Understanding

Oral Language: Monologue Have students take on the role of one of the people profiled in the book and describe the most important event in their lives and why it had such a big effect on them.

Independent Writing: Persuasive Essay Have students write persuasive essays in which they choose one of the colonial Americans in the book and describe why that person is still important today.

Graphic Organizer: Students can use a sequence chart to keep track of events in each person's life as they read. For example:

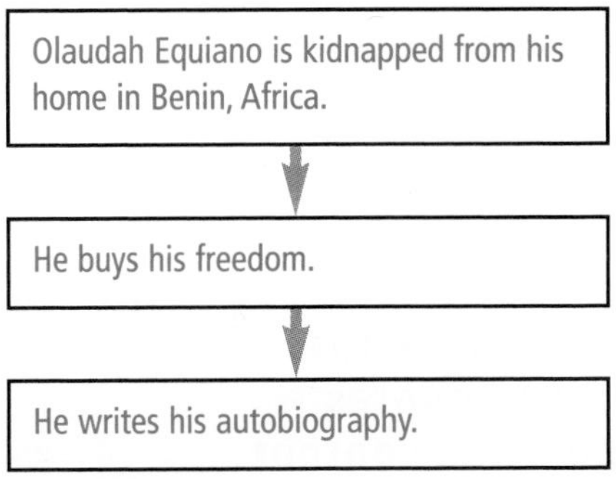

Olaudah Equiano is kidnapped from his home in Benin, Africa.
He buys his freedom.
He writes his autobiography.

Choices for Reading

- **Extra Support/ELL** Read the selection aloud as students follow along in their books. Pause frequently and help students monitor understanding.
- **On Level** Have partners take turns reading aloud. Students can pause at the end of each page to ask each other questions and check understanding.
- **Challenge** Students can read the selection and write down any questions they have. Then they can work in small groups to answer their questions.

Go to www.eduplace.com/ss/hmss05/ for answers to Responding questions found at the back of the books.

Bibliography

Books for Independent Reading

Social Studies Key

- Biography
- Citizenship
- Cultures
- Economics
- Geography
- History

Extra Support

Giants in the Land
by Diana Applebaum
Houghton, 2000
This is the story of how colonial New England's forests of giant white pine trees were cleared to build British warships.

A Voice of Her Own: The Story of Phillis Wheatly, Slave Poet
by Kathryn Lasky
Candlewick, 2003
Wheatly, an African slave, became a widely recognized poet published in the United States and Europe.

Who Was Ben Franklin?
by Dennis Brindell Fradin
Grosset, 2002
This lively biography shows Franklin in his roles as inventor, printer, writer, and statesman.

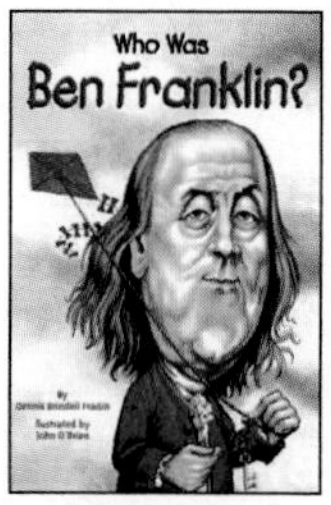

Life on a Southern Plantation
by Sally Senzell Isaacs
Heinemann, 2001
The many facets of daily life of both slaves and planters are explored.

Finding Providence
by Avi
Harper, 1997
This is the fictionalized story of Roger Williams's founding of Providence, as told by his daughter.

On Level

African-Americans in the Thirteen Colonies
by Deborah Kent
Children's Press, 1996
Kent discusses the contributions of notable African Americans and the reasons slavery was able to exist in the thirteen colonies.

The Printers
by Leonard E. Fisher
Benchmark, 2000
The history of printing in Colonial America is presented here. See others in the *Colonial Craftsmen* series.

William Penn: Founder of Pennsylvania
by Steven Kroll
Holiday House, 2000
This is the biography of Quaker reformer and Pennsylvania founder, William Penn.

Anne Hutchinson: Religious Reformer
by Melina Mangal
Capstone, 2004
This is the biography of Hutchinson, who was banished from Boston to Rhode Island for her religious beliefs. See other New Nation Biographies.

Weeatmoo: Heart of the Pocassets
by Patricia C. Smith
Scholastic, 2003
Weeatmoo, leader of the Pocasset tribe, faces the challenge of coexisting with growing numbers of English colonists.

Challenge

Good Women of a Well-Blessed Land
by Brandon Marie Miller
Lerner, 2003
Miller describes the Colonial life and vital roles of Native American women and European women, indentured servants, and slaves.

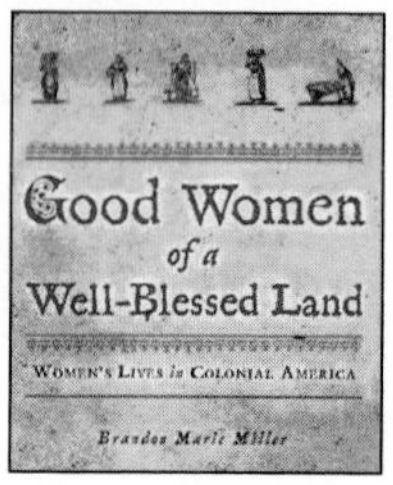

Leonard Calvert and the Maryland Adventure
by Ann Jensen
Tidewater, 1998
This biography focuses on the life of Leonard Calvert, founder of Maryland.

The Voyage of Patience Goodspeed
by Heather V. Frederick
Simon, 2002
Patience and her younger brother join their captain father aboard his Nantucket whaling ship for a three-year journey.

The Kidnapped Prince: The Life of Olaudah Equiano
by Ann Cameron, Olaudah Equiano
Random House, 2000
Cameron adapts the 1789 autobiography of Equiano, a boy who was kidnapped from Africa, sold into slavery, and eventually bought his own freedom.

Social Studies Leveled Readers with lesson plans by Irene Fountas support the content of this unit.

With the Program

Your State Specific Materials

at www.eduplace.com/ss/hmss05

Read Aloud and Reference

Read Aloud Books

The Witch of Blackbird Pond
by Elizabeth George Speare
Houghton, 1959
This Newbery Medal-winning classic tells the tale of a girl living in Puritan Connecticut who is falsely accused of being a witch.

The Sign of the Beaver
by Elizabeth George Speare
Houghton, 1983
In this classic story, a boy survives alone in his family's wilderness home in Maine by learning skills from local Native Americans.

Ben Franklin's Almanac
by Candace Fleming
Atheneum, 2003
This anecdotal biography imparts bits of Franklin's wisdom, advice, and his countless accomplishments.

Hasty Pudding, Johnny Cakes
by Loretta F. Ichord
Millbrook, 1999
The author takes readers on an engaging tour of colonial American culinary matters, from cuisine to cooking methods to customs.

Reference Books

Making Thirteen Colonies, 1600–1740
by Joy Hakim
Oxford University Press, 2002
Hakim chronicles the development of the colonies from Jamestown to the opening of the Appalachian Wilderness Road in 1775.

How We Lived in Colonial New England
by Deborah Kent
Benchmark, 2000
Extensive information about life in the early American colonies. See also *How We Lived in the Middle Colonies* and *How We Lived in the Southern Colonies.*

The New York Colony
by Barbara Somervill
Child's World, 2003
New York is explored from prehistory to Henry Hudson's exploration to its ratification as the eleventh state in 1788. See others in *Our Thirteen Colonies* series.

Growing Up in a New World 1607 to 1775
by Brandon Marie Miller
Lerner, 2003
Readers learn what life was like in America before the Revolution.

Free and Inexpensive Materials

National Park Service Headquarters
1849 C Street NW
Washington, DC 20240
Phone: (202) 208-6843
Through the National Park Service's website, www.nps.gov, you can find information about colonial-era places that have been preserved as national historic sites.

MULTIMEDIA RESOURCES

PROGRAM RESOURCES

Unit Video
Audio Student's Book with Primary Sources and Songs MP3/CD
Lesson Planner and Teacher Resource CD-ROM
Test Generator CD-ROM
eBook
eBook, Teacher's Edition
Transparencies: Big Idea & Skillbuilder, Interactive
Almanac Map & Graph Practice
Primary Sources Plus: Document-Based Questions
Research and Writing Projects
Bringing Social Studies Alive
Family Newsletter
GeoNet

CD-ROM

African-American History: Heroism, Struggle and Hope, Part 1. Library Video

Search for the Golden Dolphin. Library Video

Colonial America. Library Video

VIDEOCASSETTES

Roger Williams and Rhode Island. Schlessinger

William Penn and Pennsylvania. Schlessinger

The Sign of the Beaver, *Elizabeth George Speare.* Perma-Bound

Standing in the Light, *Mary Pope Osbourne.* Weston Woods

AUDIOCASSETTES

The Light in the Forest *Conrad Richter.* Audio Bookshelf

The Sign of the Beaver. *Elizabeth George Speare.* Library Video

The Witch of Blackbird Pond. *Elizabeth George Speare.* Library Video

Assessment Options

TEST PREP

You are the best evaluator of your students' progress and attainments. To help you in this task, Houghton Mifflin Social Studies provides you with a variety of assessment tools.

Classroom-Based Assessment

Written and Oral Assessment

In the student book:

Lesson Reviews appear at the end of each lesson.
Chapter Reviews appear on pp. 184–185, 218–219.
Unit Reviews appear on pp. 220–221.

In the *Assessment Options* ancillary:

Lesson Tests appear for all lessons.
Chapter Tests appear for all chapters.
Unit Tests appear for all units.

Technology:

Test Generator provides even more assessment options.

Informal, Continuous Assessment

Comprehension

In the student book:

Review questions appear at the end of each section.

In the teacher's edition:

"Talk About It" questions monitor student comprehension.
Tested Objectives appear at the beginning and end of each lesson.

In the student practice book:

Study Guide pages aid student comprehension.

Reading

In the teacher's edition:

Reading Strategy is featured in every chapter.

Thinking

In the student book:

Critical Thinking questions teach higher-order thinking skills.

In the teacher's edition:

"Think Alouds" let you model thinking critically for your students.

In the *Assessment Options* ancillary:

Observation Checklists give you another option for assessment.

HANDS ON Rubric for Unit 3 Performance Assessment

4	Letter shows clear understanding; includes interesting details; details difference between expectation and reality; letter format used; no errors in mechanics.
3	Letter shows some understanding; includes some details; states general dif-ference between expectation and reality; letter format used; few errors.
2	Letter shows some understanding; details and difference between expectation and reality not related to time; letter format used; several errors in mechanics.
1	Letter shows little or no understanding; details few or absent; does not state difference between expectation and reality; letter format not used; many errors.

In *Assessment Options*, p. 67

Standardized Test Practice

In the student book:

Lesson Review/Test Prep appears at the end of each lesson.
Chapter Review/Test Prep appears at the end of each chapter.
Unit Review/Test Prep appears at the end of each unit.

In the *Assessment Options* ancillary:

Lesson Tests for all lessons.
Chapter Tests for all chapters.
Unit Test for all units.

Technology:

Test Generator provides even more assessment options.

Student Self-Assessment

In the student book:

Hands-On Activities appear in each chapter.
Writing Activities appear in each chapter.

In the Unit Resources:

Reading Skill/Strategy pages give students the chance to practice the skills and strategies of each lesson and chapter.
Vocabulary Review/Study Guide pages provide an opportunity for self-challenge or review.

In the *Assessment Options* ancillary:

Self-Assessment Checklists

Unit 3 Test

Standard Test

TEST PREP

Unit 3 Test

Test Your Knowledge

Circle the letter of the best answer.

1. What did the proprietors of New York and New Jersey want? Obj. U3–8
   - (A.) They wanted to make money from the colonies.
   - B. They wanted religious freedom.
   - C. They wanted to send money to the king of England.
   - D. They wanted to build ships.

2. Which was a growing industry in New England? Obj. U3–5
   - F. farming wheat
   - G. making soap
   - H. farming tobacco
   - (J.) shipbuilding

3. Why did Roger Williams form the colony of Rhode Island? Obj. U3–3
   - A. He wanted to establish better relations with American Indians.
   - B. He wanted to hold more town meetings.
   - (C.) He wanted to keep government separate from the church.
   - D. He wanted to end slavery and give equal rights to all people.

4. Which of the following did William Penn accomplish? Obj. U3–1
   - F. He settled Charles Town.
   - G. He created a refuge for Catholics.
   - H. He published a newspaper and *Poor Richard's Almanack*.
   - (J.) He gave Pennsylvania colonists a representative government.

5. Why was Charles Town important to the Southern Colonies? Obj. U3–16
   - (A.) Tobacco, rice, and indigo were bought, sold, and exported at this port.
   - B. It was a plantation that grew tobacco.
   - C. It was located where two rivers met.
   - D. It was a shipbuilding center.

6. Which colony was started as a place where debtors could start new lives? Obj. U3–15
   - F. Maryland
   - (G.) Georgia
   - H. South Carolina
   - J. North Carolina

Standard Test

TEST PREP

Test the Skills: Make a Line Graph; Make a Decision

Delaware Colony 1710–1740

Year	Estimated Population (in thousands)
1710	3,645
1720	5,385
1730	9,170
1740	19,870

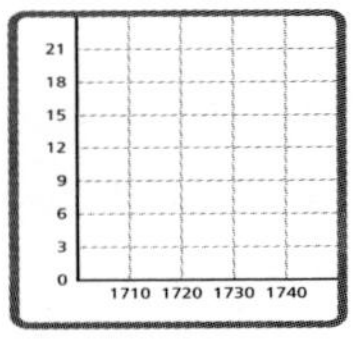

Use the data table to make a line graph and answer the questions.

7. Complete the line graph. Be sure to draw and label the axes. Obj. U3–7
8. Does the line on the graph slope upwards or downwards? Why? Obj. U3–7
   It slopes upwards because the population increased over time.

Suppose you are an adult living in Delaware Colony in 1730. You are thinking about opening a general store to supply items to new residents of the colony. Fill in the chart below to think about the costs and benefits of opening a store. Then tell whether or not you will open the store and why you made that decision. Obj. U3–10

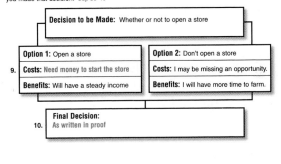

Decision to be Made: Whether or not to open a store

	Option 1: Open a store	Option 2: Don't open a store
9.	**Costs:** Need money to start the store	**Costs:** I may be missing an opportunity.
	Benefits: Will have a steady income	**Benefits:** I will have more time to farm.

10. **Final Decision:** As written in proof

Standard Test

TEST PREP

Apply Your Knowledge and Skills

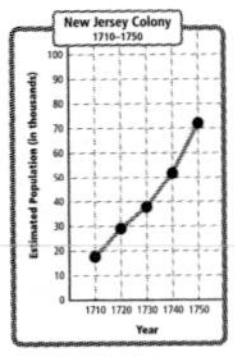

The proprietors, or owners, of New Jersey and New York lived in England. This made it difficult for them to control their faraway property. They decided to pick governors to rule their colonies. Each governor chose a small group of people called a *council* to help make important decisions.

11. What does the line graph tell you about New Jersey's population? Obj. U3–7
    - A. The population decreased over time.
    - B. The population sharply decreased after 1710.
    - C. The population stayed the same from 1710 to 1750.
    - (D.) The population increased steadily.

12. Based on the graph and the passage, why was it important for the proprietors to pick governors? Obj. U3–7
    - F. The proprietors needed governors to start new industries.
    - (G.) The proprietors lived in England and needed someone to rule the colony.
    - H. The governors could decrease the colonies' populations.
    - J. The proprietors need governors to farm.

13. Choose one of the colonies you learned about in the unit. Write a brief essay about why people started the colony. Explain the decisions the founding colonists had to make. Write your essay on a separate sheet of paper. Obj. U3–1
    Essays may refer to the money wanted by the proprietors of New York and New Jersey, the religious freedom wanted by the Puritans and Pilgrims of Massachusetts, or the fresh starts wanted by the people of Georgia.

Standard Test

TEST PREP

Apply the Reading Skills and Strategies

The land and climate of New England and the Middle Colonies affected farming there. As glaciers moved across New England during the Ice Age, they scraped up much of the topsoil and pushed it south, leaving behind only a thin, rocky layer of dirt, which was difficult to farm. Because the winters were long and bitterly cold, the growing season in New England was short. The glaciers later dropped fertile soil in the Middle Colonies, which made it easier to grow crops. The Middle Colonies also had a warmer climate and plenty of rain, so the growing season was longer.

Reading Skills

Use the passage above to answer each question.

13. **Cause and Effect** What effects did the glaciers have on the land in New England and the Middle Colonies? Obj. U3–2
    Sample answer: The glaciers scraped away the fertile soil in New England, making it hard to grow crops there. The glaciers dropped that soil in the Middle Colonies, so it was easier to farm in those colonies.

14. **Compare and Contrast** In what ways were the climates and growing seasons in New England and the Middle Colonies alike and different? Obj. U3–2
    Alike: In both, the climate affected farming. Different: New England had long, cold winters and, therefore, a short growing season. The Middle Colonies had a milder climate and plenty of rain, so the growing season was longer.

Reading Strategy: Monitor and Clarify

15. What words or phrases in the passage above help you better understand how the land and climate affected farming in New England? Obj. U3–2
    Sample answers: *scraped up topsoil, difficult to farm, glaciers, Ice Age, rocky, cold winters, short growing season*

Reaching All Learners

Extra Support

Make a Poster of Colonial Regions

Groups	25 minutes
Objective	To characterize colonial regions
Materials	poster paper, crayons or markers

- Students can make posters illustrating the characteristics of the three colonial regions. Each group focuses on one region — New England, Middle, or Southern. Students title their posters with the name of their region and identify its colonies, either with a list or on a map. Students print at least six terms that describe the region and distinguish it from the others, e.g., on a New England poster: "rocky soil," "town meetings." Students can add illustrations.

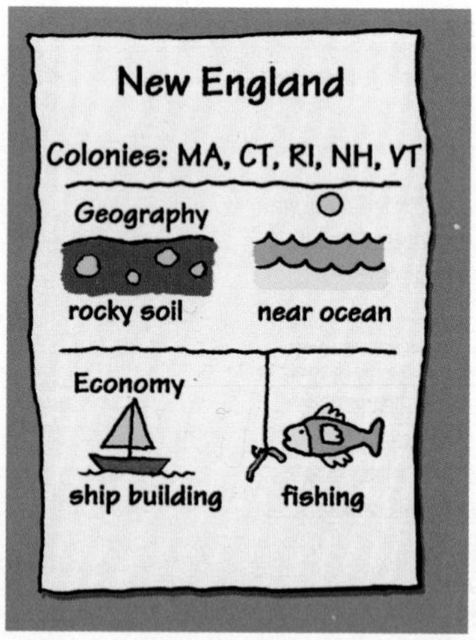

Challenge

Report on Colonial Childhood

Pairs	25 minutes
Objective	To compare colonial and modern childhood
Materials	pencils, paper

- Students can do research to learn what life was like for colonial children and compare it with their own. Each pair might choose one or two topics, such as attitudes toward children, chores, work away from home; play, clothing, school.
- Researchers might summarize their findings for the class. For example, each pair might tell the two most interesting facts they found about the lives of colonial children and explain one way colonial childrens' lives were different from and/or similar to their own.

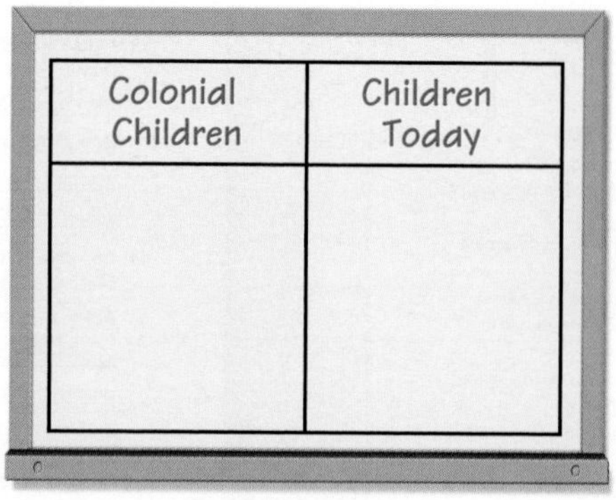

ELL

Compare Colonial Regions

Groups	25 minutes
Objective	To compare and contrast colonial regions
Materials	three small boxes, index cards, pencils, paper, colored pencils

Beginning
Ask students to point out the New England, Middle, and Southern colonies on a map. Assist students in pronouncing the names of colonies and cities. Provide three containers labeled by region. Students can sort into the containers index cards with names of individual colonies and major cities printed on them.

Intermediate
Ask students to take turns naming a region and one crop that grew there. Alternately, you might name the region and ask students to identify a crop that grew there. Students might also each draw a picture of one colonial crop.

Advanced
Students work together to create a brief, oral description of the physical features and climate of each of the colonial regions. Students might imagine themselves to be TV reporters and plan a program for a small group or the class describing landforms, climate, and crops of the different regions.

Cross-Curricular Activities

Language Arts

Interpret Poor Richard's Sayings

Singles	20 minutes
Objective	To interpret Benjamin Franklin's sayings
Materials	list of Franklin aphorisms, paper, pencils

- Students can select one Franklin aphorism, then write a composition addressing one or more of these questions: What did Franklin mean? What kind of person might say it? Can you say the same thing another way?

When the Well's dry, we know the Worth of Water.

A good Example is the best sermon.

Diligence is the mother of good luck.

Well done is better than well said.

People who are wrapped up in themselves make small packages.

Math

Scale a Recipe

Singles	20 minutes
Objective	To scale a recipe
Materials	pencils, paper

- English colonists would have followed a pound cake recipe much like this one. Have students scale the recipe to make the right amount to invite another class.

Pound Cake Recipe

2/3 cup butter

3/4 cup sugar

2 or 3 eggs

1 1/3 cups flour, preferably whole wheat

1/4 cup orange juice or apple juice

- Cream butter and sugar. Beat in eggs one at a time. Alternate flour and any liquid, beating well. Pour into a buttered 8-inch loaf pan. Bake at 350 degrees for 60 minutes. Serves 10.

Physical Education

Play Dutch Ninepins

Class	25 minutes
Objective	To simulate Dutch ninepins
Materials	plastic sheet, liter plastic drink bottles with caps, water or sand, 5-inch ball or bean bag, masking tape

- Dutch settlers introduced bowling to North America. They played with nine pins and a five-inch wooden ball. Tamped earth or planking became an alley.
- Lay out a plastic sheet, perhaps a waterslide. Weight plastic bottles with a little sand or water, set them up and tape a throw line.
- Students form teams. Each time up, every team member takes two tries. After each team has had four turns, the team with the highest total number of knock-downs wins.

Begin the Unit

Unit Quick Look

Chapter 5 introduces the thirteen colonies, and discusses the New England colonies.

Chapter 6 tells about the founding of the Middle and Southern colonies, and what life was like for the people who settled them.

Introduce the Big Idea

History The Puritans moved to a new place to find religious freedom. People from all over the world still come to the United States and other countries in search of a better life. As students discuss reasons why they might move to a new place, have them consider how their community has been affected by the movement of people.

Explain that this unit describes the settlement of the first English colonies.

Primary Sources

Invite a volunteer to read the quote by a Anne Bradstreet on page 154. Ask students how they think she felt about moving to a new place. List student responses on the board.

Ask students to think about what the new manners might have been. What kinds of reactions might a person of today have when moving to a new place? Why?

UNIT 3

The English Colonies

The Big Idea

Why do people move to new places?

"I found a new world and new manners, at which my heart rose."

Anne Bradstreet, colonial poet

Anne Hutchinson

1591–1643

This religious leader moved from England to Boston. She was not afraid to speak out about her beliefs. The things she said made Puritan leaders angry, but she did not back down.
page 167

Technology

Motivate and Build Background
You may wish to show the Unit Video after students have discussed the Big Idea question on this page.

After viewing, ask students to **summarize** what they already know about the unit content. Ask volunteers to **predict** what else they think they will learn.

You can find more video teaching suggestions on pages R1 and R2 in the Resources Section in the back of the Teacher's Edition.

History Makers

William Penn
1644–1718

William Penn created the first planned city in the colonies. He called it Philadelphia, "the city of brotherly love." He wanted people in the colony of Pennsylvania to live in peace. **page 189**

James Oglethorpe
1696–1785

This wealthy Englishman wanted to help people who owed money or were very poor. He started the colony of Georgia to give them a new beginning in North America. **page 204**

155

Correcting Misconceptions

Ask students what they know about the English colonies. Write their responses as a list on the board.

As students read the unit, return to the list periodically to see if any of their responses have been shown to be misconceptions.

Discuss why students may have thought as they did, and what they have learned.

History Makers

Anne Hutchinson Anne Hutchinson discussed her religious beliefs with both women and men. Puritan leaders thought it was wrong for women to teach men about religion. Candlesticks such as the one shown were valuable sources of light for the early colonists.

William Penn William Penn was a Quaker who believed in religious liberty. He was the governor of the Pennsylvania colony. The symbol on page 155 is the colony's official seal.

James Oglethorpe Oglethorpe was given a charter like the rolled parchment in the picture. This charter allowed him to found the colony of Georgia. He wanted it to be a place where poor people and people who owed money could live.

Web Link

E-Biographies

To learn more about the History Makers on these pages and in this unit, visit www.eduplace.com/kids/hmss05/

Designed to be accessed by your students, these biographies can be used for

- research projects
- Character Education
- developing students' technology skills

Map and Graph Skills

Interpreting Maps

Talk About It

1 **Q Geography** What can you learn about European land claims in North America from this map?
A Which areas were claimed by Britain, France, and Spain, and what types of settlements each nation established

2 **Q Geography** Which two nations claimed some of the same territory in eastern North America? How can you tell?
A France and Britain; the colors for the disputed territory match those for French and British territories.

3 **Q Geography** Along what river were several Spanish missions established?
A the Rio Grande

Critical Thinking

Analyze Ask students to consider why New Orleans would have been an excellent location for a French trading post. Goods could be sent down the Mississippi River (which was fed by the Ohio and the Missouri rivers), and sent by ship from New Orleans to Europe.

Interpreting Timelines

Ask students if they can identify any of the images shown on the timeline. The House of Burgesses; colonial settlers; Metacomet; William Penn

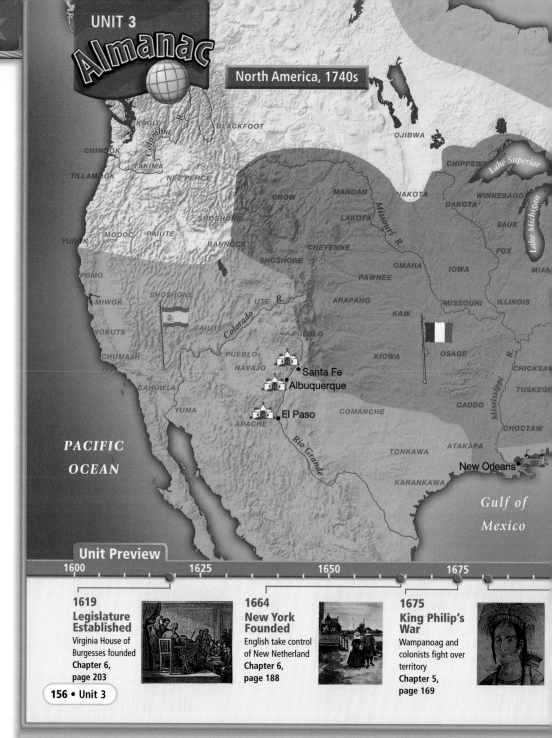

UNIT 3 Almanac

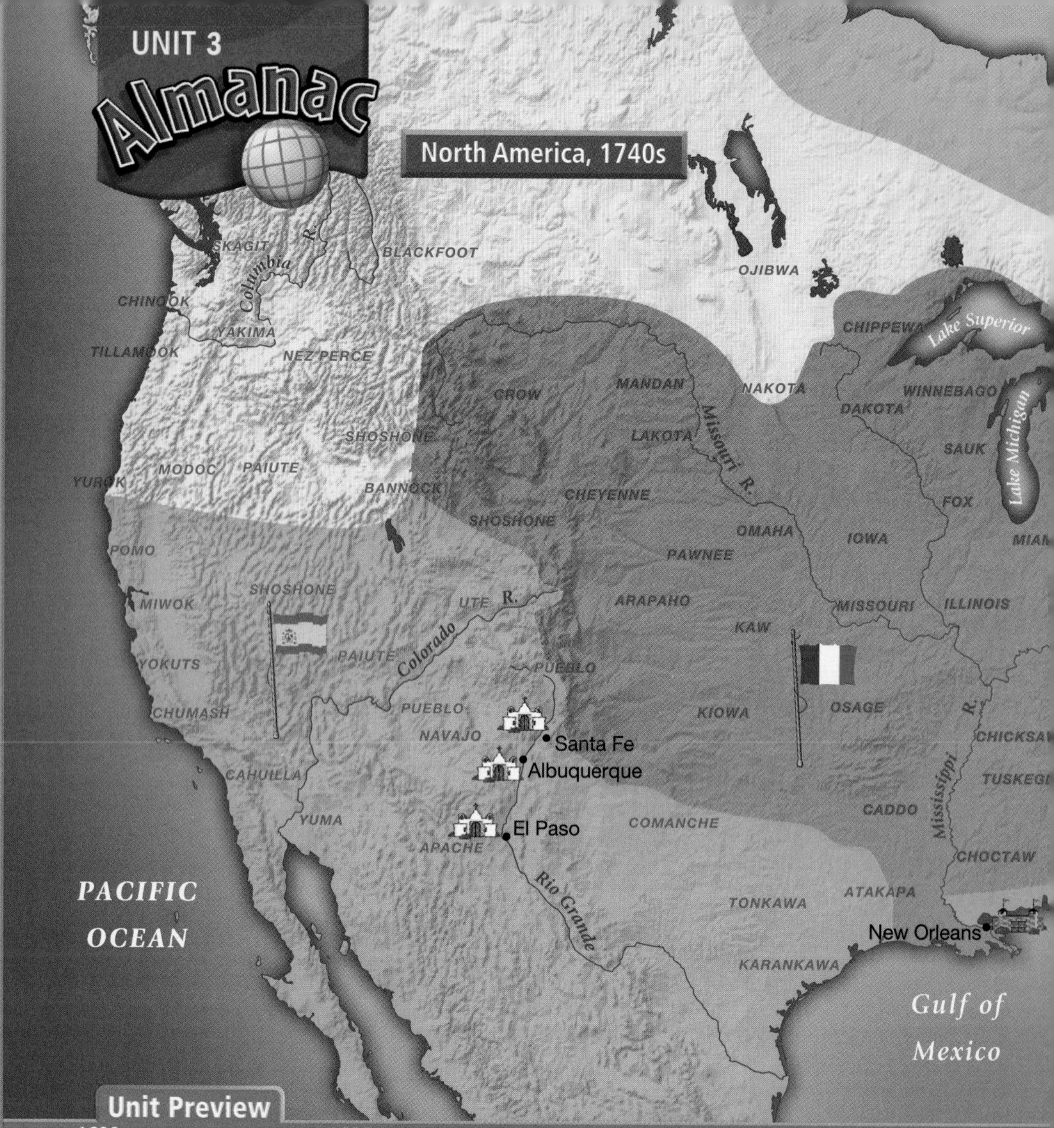

Unit Preview

1600 — 1625 — 1650 — 1675

1619
Legislature Established
Virginia House of Burgesses founded
Chapter 6, page 203

1664
New York Founded
English take control of New Netherland
Chapter 6, page 188

1675
King Philip's War
Wampanoag and colonists fight over territory
Chapter 5, page 169

156 • Unit 3

Technology

GeoNet

To support student geography skills, you may wish to have them go to <u>www.eduplace.com/kids/hmss05/</u> to play GeoNet.

Math

Head Count

Inform students that since 1740, Philadelphia has grown from 13,300 to 1,518,000 people. Ask students to calculate how many more people live in the city today than lived there in 1740.
1,518,000 − 13,300 = 1,504,700 more people today

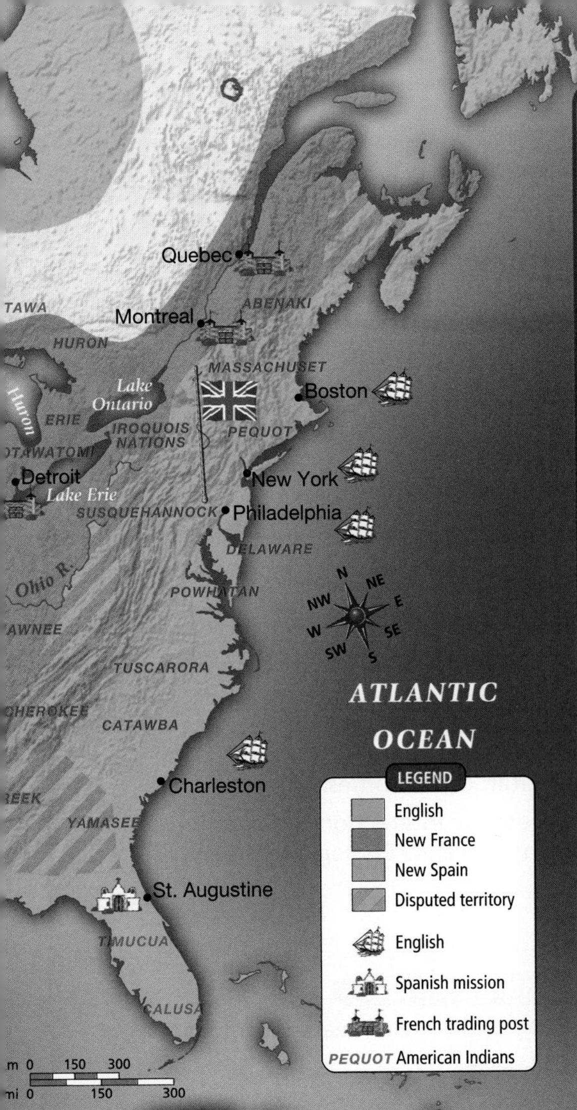

1700 — 1725 — 1750

1681
Pennsylvania Founded
Penn promotes freedom and tolerance
Chapter 6, page 189

1730
Great Awakening
Religion spreads throughout colonies
Chapter 5, page 178

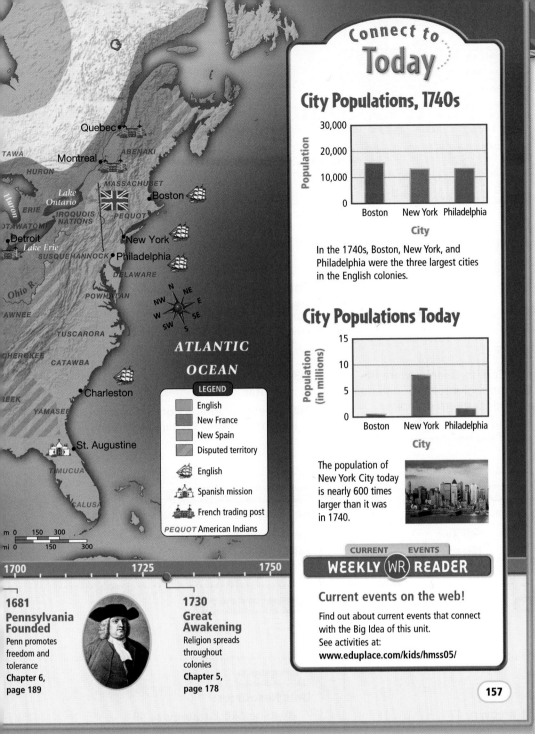

Connect to Today

City Populations, 1740s

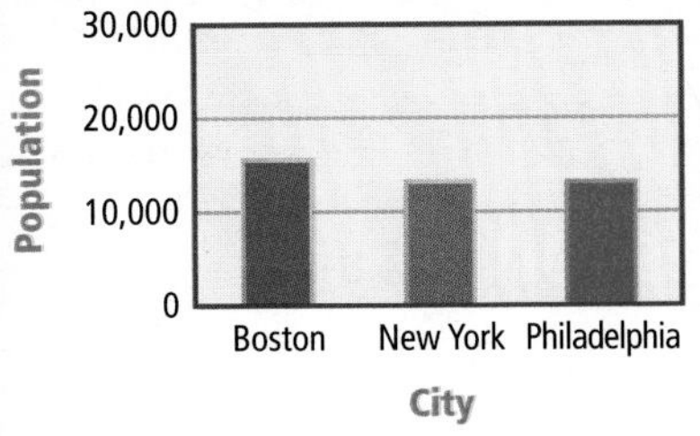

In the 1740s, Boston, New York, and Philadelphia were the three largest cities in the English colonies.

City Populations Today

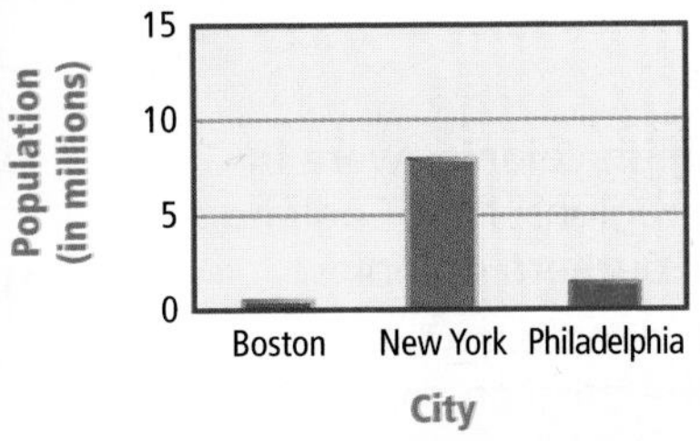

The population of New York City today is nearly 600 times larger than it was in 1740.

CURRENT EVENTS
WEEKLY WR READER

Current events on the web!

Find out about current events that connect with the Big Idea of this unit.
See activities at:
www.eduplace.com/kids/hmss05/

Current Events

For information about current events related to this unit, visit www.eduplace.com/ss/hmss05/.

Web links to Weekly Reader will help students work on the Current Events Unit Project. The Unit 3 Project will involve creating a bulletin board display about people migrating to new places today.

As you go through the unit, encourage students to use the web to find information for the bulletin board.

Interpreting Graphs

Talk About It

4 Q Economics What advantages might the British have had because their major cities were along the East coast?

A easier trade among colonies; easier transportation of goods and people between colonies and Britain

5 Q History What possible reasons are there for why New York has grown so much larger than Boston or Philadelphia? Look at the map for ideas.

A New York is not only along the coast, it is also located at the mouth of the wide Hudson River, which allows people and goods to move easily from the coast to much farther inland. Later in history, the Erie Canal would let ships travel from New York City all the way to the Great Lakes.

Find Out More

Hometown History Ask students to investigate what the region where they live was like in 1740. Who lived there and how did they earn their living?

Matching Up What would a bar graph look like for your community? Have students do research and create bar graphs comparing the population of their town or city to neighboring towns or cities.

Chapter 5
Planning Guide
New England Colonies

Chapter Opener
Pages 158–159
30 minutes

Reading/Vocabulary

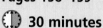

Chapter Reading Strategy: Predict and Infer, p. 157F

Resources

Grade Level Resources
- Vocabulary Cards, pp. 21–28

Reaching All Learners
- Challenge Activities, p. 83

Primary Sources Plus, p. 9

Big Idea Transparency 3

Interactive Transparency 3

Text & Music Audio CD

Lesson Planner & TR CD-ROM

eBook

eTE

Core Lesson 1
The Geography of the Colonies
Pages 160–163
40 minutes

Tested Objectives

U3-1 Identify which English colonies were in each of the following regions: New England, Middle Colonies, and Southern Colonies.

U3-2 Describe the land, climate, and natural resources of each of the thirteen colonies.

Reading/Vocabulary

Reading Skill: Compare and Contrast

growing season, fall line, tidewater, backcountry

Cross-Curricular

Science, p. 162

Resources

Unit Resources:
- Reading Skill/Strategy, p. 47
- Vocabulary/Study Guide, p. 48

Reaching All Learners:
- Lesson Summary, p. 19
- Support for Lang. Dev./ELL, p. 116

Assessment Options:
- Lesson Test, p. 47

Extend Lesson 1

Geography
The Appalachians

20–30 minutes

Pages 164–165

Focus: Students see how this mountain range blocked western settlement.

Core Lesson 2
New England
Pages 166–169
40 minutes

Tested Objectives

U3-3 Explain the impact of religion and dissent in Puritan communities.

U3-4 Describe interactions between American Indians and New England settlers.

Reading/Vocabulary

Reading Skill: Main Idea and Details

town meeting, dissenter, self-government, banish

Cross-Curricular

Art, p. 168

Resources

Unit Resources:
- Reading Skill/Strategy, p. 49
- Vocabulary/Study Guide, p. 50

Reaching All Learners:
- Lesson Summary, p. 20
- Support for Lang. Dev./ELL, p. 117

Assessment Options:
- Lesson Test, p. 48

Extend Lesson 2

Readers' Theater
Town Meeting, April 5, 1749

40–50 minutes

Pages 170–173

Focus: A town meeting discussion shows that each citizen has a voice.

National Standards

III b Representations of the earth
III f Physical system changes
III g How people create places
III h Interaction of human beings and their physical environment
IV e Influence of family, groups, and community
V e Tension between an individual's beliefs and government policies and laws
VI f Factors that contribute to cooperation and cause disputes
VII c Private and public goods and services
VII f Influence of incentives, values, traditions, and habits
IX b Conflict, cooperation, and interdependence

With the Program
CURRENT EVENTS from WEEKLY WR READER at www.eduplace.com

Core Lesson 3

Life in New England

Pages 174–179

50 minutes

Tested Objectives

U3-5 Describe major industries, especially those related to sea, in New England.

U3-6 Identify features of home and community life in New England.

Reading/Vocabulary

Reading Skill: Problem and Solution

industry
export
import
Middle Passage
slave trade

Cross-Curricular

Art, p. 176
Physical Education, p. 178

Resources

Unit Resources:
- **Reading Skill/Strategy,** p. 51
- **Vocabulary/Study Guide,** p. 52

Reaching All Learners:
- **Lesson Summary,** p. 21
- **Support for Lang. Dev./ELL,** p. 118

Assessment Options:
- **Lesson Test,** p. 49

Extend Lesson 3

Economics

Cod Fishing

20–30 minutes

Pages 180–181

Focus: Students learn why the fishing industry was so important in New England.

Skillbuilder

Chart and Graph Skill

Make a Line Graph

Pages 182–183

20 minutes

Tested Objective

U3-7 Organize and present historical data in a line graph.

Reading/Vocabulary

data
line graph

Resources

Unit Resources:
- **Skill Practice,** p. 53

Skill Transparency 5

Chapter Review

Pages 184–185

30 minutes

Resources

Assessment Options:
- **Chapter 5 Test**
- **Test Generator**

Practice Options

Lesson 1 Skill and Strategy

TEST PREP

Reading Skill and Strategy

Reading Skill: Compare and Contrast

This skill helps you understand how historical events or people are similar and different.

Read "Geography of the Colonies." Then fill in the chart below to compare and contrast the features of the regions listed.

New England	Middle Colonies	Southern Colonies
1. Poor soil and a cold climate	2. Fertile soil and a warm climate	A warmer climate and waterways for trade

Reading Strategy: Predict and Infer

3. Read the red and blue headings in "Geography of the Colonies." Then check the best prediction.

____ Most settlers in the thirteen colonies had moved south from Canada.

✓ Many factors affected how the settlers in all thirteen colonies lived and worked.

____ The colonists in New England built larger homes than the other colonists.

4. Read "Geography of the Colonies." Then check the best inference.

✓ The weather and soil made growing crops easier in the Middle Colonies than in New England.

____ The shipbuilding industry helped the Southern Colonies grow quickly.

____ Colonists living in New England took vacations to the Southern and Middle Colonies.

Unit Resources

47
Use with *United States History*, pp. 160–163

Lesson 1 Vocabulary/Study Guide

TEST PREP

Vocabulary and Study Guide

Vocabulary

If you do not know a word's meaning, try breaking it into smaller parts. It may contain a smaller word that you know.

Find the smaller words inside these words. Use what you know about the smaller word or words to write the meaning of the longer word.

	New word	Words in it that I know	Word meanings that I know	What I think the word means
1.	fall line	Sample answer: fall; line	Sample answer: from high to low	Sample answer: where rivers fall
2.	growing season	Sample answer: grow; season	Sample answer: crops get taller	Sample answer: time to grow crops
3.	tidewater	Sample answer: tide; water	Sample answer: water rises, falls	Sample answer: rivers, streams rise with tide
4.	backcountry	Sample answer: back; country	Sample answer: beyond, rural	Sample answer: country beyond settlers

Study Guide

Read "Geography of the Colonies." Then fill in the compare and contrast chart below.

	Land	Climate/growing season	Natural resources
New England	Mountains and deep valleys; Rocky, sandy soil	5. Warm summers and long, cold winters; Short growing season	6. Wood, fish, and whales
Middle Colonies	7. Rolling hills and valleys; Fertile soil	8. Plenty of rain and sunshine; Longer growing season	9. Soil, wildlife, and long, wide rivers
Southern Colonies	10. Rich, fertile soil; The tidewater	11. Warm weather and plenty of rain; Long growing season	12. Soil and waterways

Unit Resources

48
Use with *United States History*, pp. 160–163

also in *Practice Book*, p. 29

Lesson 2 Skill and Strategy

TEST PREP

Reading Skill and Strategy

Reading Skill: Main Idea and Details

This skill helps you understand events by seeing how they are related.

Read "Rhode Island." Then fill in the chart below. Write two details that support the main idea.

Some people disagreed with Puritan leaders and left Massachusetts.

1. They did not want to be told what to believe.

2. They did not want to be told how to act.

Reading Strategy: Predict and Infer

3. Read the headings in "Massachusetts." Then check the best prediction.

____ The colonies of Rhode Island, Connecticut, and New Hampshire all began as part of Massachusetts.

____ Colonists in Georgia did not like the rules of the Puritans in Massachusetts.

✓ The Puritan religion shaped the lives of people in the Massachusetts Bay Colony.

4. Read "Conflicts over Land." Then complete the statement that you can infer.

If the colonists had not fought the American Indians, Sample answer: the colonists would not have moved west as quickly.

Unit Resources

49
Use with *United States History*, pp. 166–169

Lesson 2 Vocabulary/Study Guide

TEST PREP

Vocabulary and Study Guide

Vocabulary

Write the definition of each vocabulary word below.

1. dissenter A person who does not agree with the beliefs of leaders
2. banish To force someone to leave a place
3. town meeting A gathering where colonists held elections and voted on laws
4. self-government A type of government in which the people who live in a place make laws for themselves

Study Guide

Read "Massachusetts." Then fill in the sequence chart below.

5. Roger Williams believes that government should not make laws about religion. → 6. Puritan leaders disagree and banish him from Massachusetts. → 7. Williams forms the colony of Rhode Island. → Williams keeps Rhode Island's government separate from the church.

Read "Conflicts over Land." Then choose the correct ending to each statement below.

8. Colonists and American Indians had conflicts because of different views about

A. farming. (B.) land ownership. C. war.

9. The Pequot War ended when most of the Pequot Indians had been

(A.) killed. B. forced to leave. C. enslaved.

10. The war between the colonists and the Wampanoag was called

A. Metacomet's War. B. the New England War. (C.) King Philip's War.

Unit Resources

50
Use with *United States History*, pp. 166–169

also in *Practice Book*, p. 30

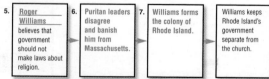

Lesson 3 Skill and Strategy

TEST PREP

Reading Skill and Strategy

Reading Skill: Problem and Solution

This skill helps you see what problem some people faced and how they resolved it.

Read "Work in the Home." Then fill in the problem and solutions chart below. How did colonial families get everything they needed at home?

Problem	Solution
Almost everything a colonial family needed had to be grown or made at home.	1. Men and boys worked in the fields and repaired buildings. 2. Women and girls prepared food. 3. Women and girls helped in the fields during the harvest.

Reading Strategy: Predict and Infer

4. Read the red and blue headings in "Life in New England." Based on the headings, make a prediction about what each section will be about.

Heading 1: Using the Sea

Sample answer: This section will be about how colonists used the sea for food and travel.

Heading 2: Home and Community Life

Sample answer: This section will be about how colonists in New England lived and what their communities believed.

Lesson 3 Vocabulary/Study Guide

TEST PREP

Vocabulary and Study Guide

Vocabulary

Across
1. A good brought into one country from another
2. Part of the triangular trade route from Africa to the West Indies
3. The business of buying and selling human beings

Down
1. All the businesses that make one type of product
4. Traders bought enslaved people from this continent
5. Ships from Europe carried spices, goods, and ____
6. A product sent to another country and sold

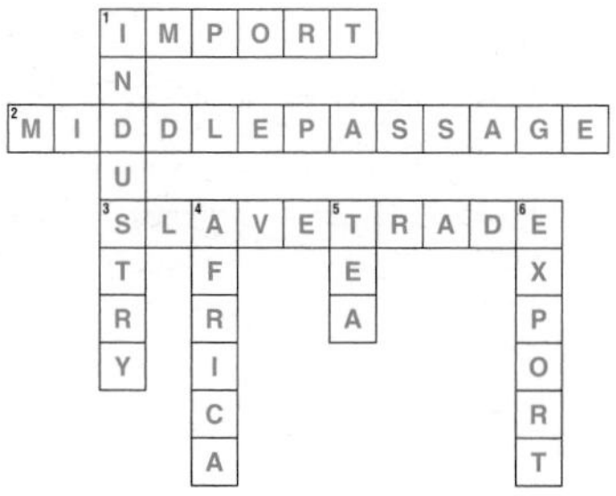

Study Guide

7. Read "Using the Sea." Then fill in the blanks below.

The geography of New England made the success of the shipbuilding, fishing, and whaling industries possible. New England merchants exported fish and lumber as part of the triangular trade route between North America, Europe, and Africa.

8. Read "Home and Community Life." Then fill in the blanks below.

New England families often had six or seven children and lived in a house with one main room. A table and sleeping mattresses might be the only furniture. Puritan families wanted everyone to be able to read the Bible. Massachusetts passed a law that said that towns with more than 50 people had to build a school.

also in *Practice Book*, p. 31

Skillbuilder Practice

TEST PREP

Skillbuilder: Make a Line Graph

Massachusetts Colony, 1680–1730

Year	Estimated Population (in thousands)
1680	39.8
1690	49.5
1700	55.9
1710	62.4
1720	91.0
1730	114.1

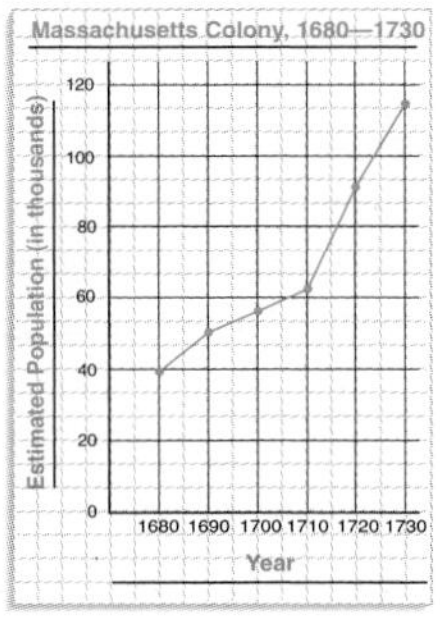

Practice

1. Label the horizontal axis on the graph.
   Students should write *Year* on the graph.
2. Label the vertical axis on the graph.
   Students should write *Estimated Population (in Thousands)* on the graph.
3. Draw dots on the graph to show the data in the table. Then draw a line to connect the dots.
   Students should draw the correct data points and line on the graph.
4. Give the graph a title.
   Title should be "Massachusetts Colony, 1680–1730"

Apply the Skill

Use your graph skills to draw your own line graph. Research and collect data that shows how the area where you live has changed over time. You can go to the library or call your town or county government. Arrange the data in a table, and then show it on a line graph. Draw your line graph on a seperate sheet of paper. Line graph and data table should be complete on separate sheet of paper.

also in *Practice Book*, p. 32

Chapter 5 Assessment Options

Chapter 5 Test

TEST PREP

Chapter 5 Test

Test Your Knowledge

growing season	fall line	dissenter	Middle Passage

Fill in the blank with the correct word from the box.

1. Roger Williams was a __dissenter__ who wanted more religious freedom. Obj. U3–3
2. Ships that carried enslaved people traveled the __Middle Passage__ from Africa to the West Indies. Obj. U3–5
3. The time of year when it is warm enough for plants to grow is called the __growing season__. Obj. U3–2
4. Rivers from higher land flow to lower lands at the __fall line__. Obj. U3–2

Circle the letter of the best answer.

5. Which colony was a part of the Southern Colonies? Obj. U3–1
   - A. Massachusetts Bay
   - B. Connecticut
   - C. Maine
   - (D.) Georgia
6. What happened after the Pequot War? Obj. U3–4
   - (F.) More colonists moved into American Indian lands in New England.
   - G. More American Indians moved to New England.
   - H. Colonists and American Indians lived peacefully together.
   - J. American Indians forced the colonists out of southern New England.
7. What three continents were part of the triangular trade route? Obj. U3–5
   - A. Europe, North America, and China
   - B. Europe, India, and Asia
   - (C.) North America, Europe, and Africa
   - D. North America, India, and Africa
8. What effect did the Great Awakening have on the colonies? Obj. U3–6
   - (F.) It led to new ways of thinking about religion among colonists.
   - G. It helped establish trade routes between the colonies.
   - H. It helped the colonies' fishing and whaling industries.
   - J. It helped establish the first college in the thirteen colonies.

Chapter 5 Test

TEST PREP

Apply Your Knowledge

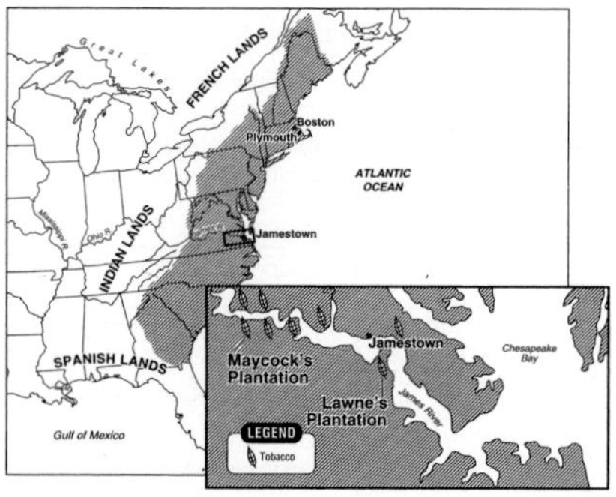

Use the map to answer the following questions.

9. Where were most of the James River tobacco farms? Obj. U3–2
   - (A.) near Maycock's Plantation
   - B. near Jamestown
   - C. near Lawne's Plantation
   - D. near Chesapeake Bay
10. What natural features made the Middle Colonies good for farming? Obj. U3–2
    - F. the rocky soil and ocean
    - (G.) the fertile soil and rivers
    - H. the sandy soil and ocean
    - J. the rugged mountains and sandy soil

Apply the Reading Skill: Compare and Contrast

Read the passage below. Then answer the question. Obj. U3–3

> The Puritans settled the Massachusetts Bay Colony. They formed a religious community with strict rules. Only male church members could vote. Thomas Hooker led colonists out of Massachusetts and formed the colony of Connecticut. In Connecticut, all men could vote.

11. How were the voting rules different in Connecticut and in Massachusetts Bay Colony?
    __In Massachusetts Bay Colony, only male church members could vote. In Connecticut, all men could vote.__

Chapter 5 Test

TEST PREP

Test the Skill: Make a Line Graph

Graduation Rate	
Year	Percentage of Students who Graduated
1930	20
1940	24
1950	35
1960	40
1970	55
1980	68
1990	76

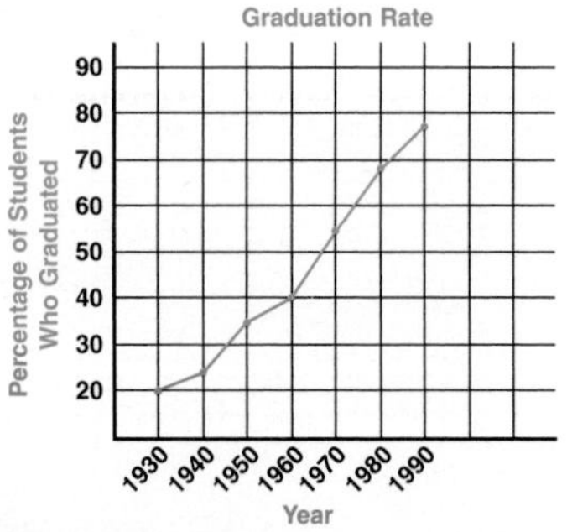

12. Provide a label for the horizontal axis on the graph. Obj. U3–7
    "Year" should be labeled on the graph.
13. Provide a label for the vertical axis on the graph. Obj. U3–7
    "Percentage of Students Who Graduated" should be labeled on the graph.
14. Draw dots on the graph to show the data in the table. Then draw a line to connect the dots. Obj. U3–7

Apply the Skill

15. Now use the data in the table below to make a line graph that shows Jamila's height over six years. Obj. U3–7

Jamila's Growth Record	
Year	Height in inches
1998	38
1999	40
2000	43
2001	46
2002	48
2003	50

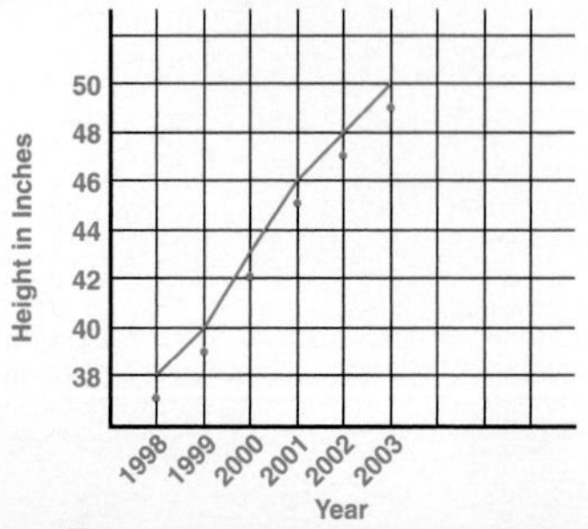

Chapter 5 Test

TEST PREP

Think and Write

16. **Short Response:** Describe two conflicts that the colonists had with the American Indians. Obj. U3–4
    __Pequot War: The colonists fought with the Pequot Indians in the 1630s. Most of the Pequots were killed.__
    __King Philip's War: In 1675, Metacomet led the Wampanoag in a war against the colonists. The Wampanoag lost and were enslaved or forced to leave.__
17. **Critical Thinking: Generalize** Why were the actions of Roger Williams, Ann Hutchinson, and Thomas Hooker important in the history of religious freedom in the United States? Obj. U3–3
    __Sample answer: They were the first people to take a stand against the government making laws about religion.__
18. **Extended Response:** Write a daily schedule that someone living in a colonial home in New England might have written. At the top of the schedule, note whether the colonist was male or female and the time of year. Give the details of tasks and other activities to be done from the morning until the night. Include a time for each activity. Write your schedule on a separate sheet of paper. Obj. U3–6 **Schedules may include working in the fields or building repair for males and weaving, preparing food, or cooking for females; at harvest time most everyone would be in the fields; in the evening, the family would move the table and prepare the beds.**

Self-Assessment

How well do I understand what life was like in New England in the 1600s? Why do I think so?

____
____
____
____

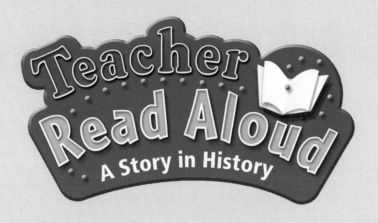

Teacher Read Aloud
A Story in History

You can share the following fiction selection with students before beginning the chapter.

Activate Prior Knowledge
Ask students if they can name any people in early American history who were dissenters—those who disagreed with the beliefs of their leaders. Explain that the Read-Aloud selection is a story about such a man. Students will read about real dissenters such as Roger Williams and Anne Hutchinson in this chapter.

Preview the Chapter
Have students skim the section Rhode Island on page 167 of their books. Ask them to talk about the similarities and differences between the dissenters discussed in this section and the man in the Read-Aloud story.

Read-Aloud Vocabulary
Explain that **backcountry** was land "in back of" the area where most colonists settled. A **dissenter** is someone who does not agree with his or her leaders' beliefs.

Preview the Reading Strategy
Predict/Infer Explain to students that the reading strategy they will use in this chapter is predicting, or guessing what will happen next based on information they already have. You may wish to use the Read Aloud to model this strategy.

Think Aloud *In the first paragraph, Michael is staring at a stranger who looks different. Michael is trying to memorize every detail about this stranger, so I think I'm going to hear more about him.*

Simon

Michael's eyes grew wide at the sight of the stranger. New people who wanted to start farms in the area often came into town, but this man was different. Michael was trying to memorize every detail.

The stranger towered over Mr. Cooper, who ran the shop, and a thick brown beard and moustache covered his face. A shapeless hat sat on his head, covering long hair. His clothes were dusty and well worn.

Mrs. Cooper noticed Michael's staring. "That's Simon," she whispered. "He comes in from the **backcountry** every few months, bringing us pelts of fox and beaver."

"He's a woodsman, then?" Michael asked. Ever since his family had come to this town, he'd hoped to see a woodsman—rough and brave. Yet something about this man didn't match Michael's imagination. Suddenly, he realized that the man's voice was soft, and as he spoke, he sounded like a teacher.

Michael said as much to Mr. Cooper once Simon had left. "You're very observant, young man," the shopkeeper said. "Simon is a well-educated man. Years ago, he disagreed with some colonial leaders and became a **dissenter.** He decided to live on his own, the way he thought was best."

Mrs. Cooper nodded. "There's more to bravery than hunting and shooting, Michael. Simon's living proof of that."

Begin the Chapter

Chapter Quick Look

Core Lesson 1 describes the geography of the colonies.

Core Lesson 2 tells more about the founding of the New England colonies.

Core Lesson 3 describes life in early New England.

Vocabulary Preview

Use the vocabulary cards to preview the key vocabulary words before starting the lessons and to prepare students to understand the content of the chapter.

Vocabulary Strategy

Vocabulary strategies for this chapter:

- Structural analysis, p. 161, 162, 176
- Synonyms/antonyms, p. 167, 175
- Root words, p. 167
- Prefixes and suffixes, p. 167, 175

Visual Learning

Vocabulary card for town meeting The town meeting is still alive and well in New England, although most communities have grown to large for every citizen to attend the gathering; instead, representatives are elected and go to town meetings today.

Vocabulary card for industry Fishing fleets today have technology on their side, making finding schools of fish easier than in the past.

Chapter 5 New England Colonies

Technology
e • glossary
e • word games
www.eduplace.com/kids/hmss05/

Vocabulary Preview

growing season

The New England **growing season** is short because winters are long and cold. New England farmers of the 1600s could grow only enough to feed their families. **page 161**

town meeting

In Massachusetts Bay, almost every community made decisions in a **town meeting.** The townspeople met in a large meetinghouse. **page 166**

Chapter Timeline

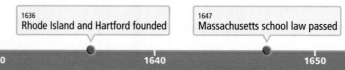

1636 Rhode Island and Hartford founded

1647 Massachusetts school law passed

1630 — 1640 — 1650

Background

New England

- Today, New England comprises six states: Maine, New Hampshire, Vermont, Massachusetts, Connecticut, and Rhode Island.
- During the time period students will be reading about, only four New England states existed; Maine was part of Massachusetts, and Vermont was claimed by both New Hampshire and New York.

Vocabulary

Students can use a description wheel graphic organizer to further their understanding of the vocabulary words.

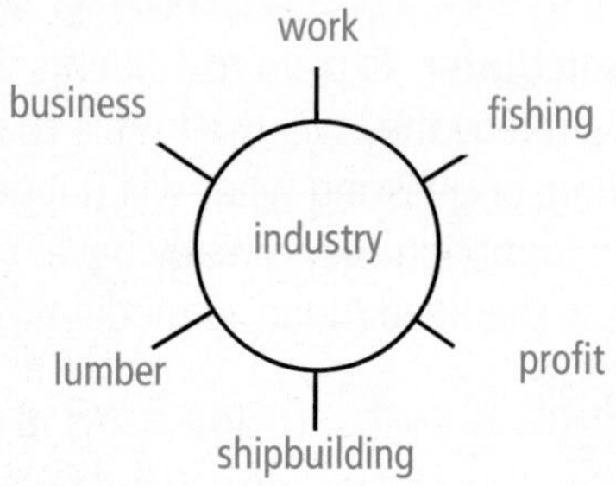

Reading Strategy

Predict and Infer Use this strategy before you read.

Quick Tip Look at the titles and pictures. What can you tell about the people and events in the lesson?

dissenter

Some colonists did not agree with the laws of their leaders. One **dissenter** was Roger Williams, who started his own settlement.

page 167

industry

Many New England colonists made a living from the sea. Some fished. Others worked in the shipbuilding **industry.**

page 174

1675
King Philip's War begins

1660 | 1670 | 1680

Leveled Practice

Extra Support

Have students make flash cards of the chapter's vocabulary words. On the front, they write the word, and on the back, the definition. They can work in pairs and quiz one another. Verbal-linguistic

Challenge

Have students create vocabulary games, such as crossword puzzles and acrostics, using the vocabulary from the chapter. Have them exchange games and quiz each other.

ELL

Intermediate/Advanced

- Have students complete the following sentences.

  Fishing was an important ____ in New England.

  Crops grow during the ____.

  Everyone in the town went to the ____.

  Roger Williams was a ____.

Using the Timeline

- Direct students to look at the timeline on pages 158 and 159. Point out the segments of the timeline. Ask them how many years this chapter will cover.
- You may wish to use a KWL chart to access students' prior knowledge of the events on the timeline. This is also an excellent opportunity to determine what, if any, misconceptions students may hold about the material.

Reading Strategy: Predict/Infer

To predict or infer, the reader uses information that he or she has. When predicting, the reader uses that information to make an informed guess about what will happen next. When inferring, the readers use information to "read between the lines," and draw out information that the author has not explicitly stated.

Explain to students that predict and infer are different, but related. Both are based on using knowledge at hand to determine what is not known.

To predict, a reader should ask the question, "What will happen next?"

To infer, a reader should ask the question, "Based on what I know, what can I figure out about this?"

Students can practice this reading strategy throughout this chapter, including on their Skill and Strategy pages.

Tested Objectives

U3-1 Geography Identify English colonies in each of the following regions: New England, Middle Colonies, and Southern Colonies.

U3-2 Geography Describe the land, climate, and natural resources of each region of the thirteen colonies.

Lesson Quick Look

This lesson describes the geography of the New England, Middle, and Southern Colonies.

Teaching Option: Extend Lesson 1 tells more about the Appalachian Mountains.

1 Get Set to Read

Preview Have students study the lesson's photographs and say what they think the lesson is about.

Reading Skill: Compare and Contrast Students should consider climate and geography.

Build on What You Know Have students describe the climate, weather, major landforms and water bodies, and most important natural resources of their community. How does their local geography affect the way people they know work and have fun?

Vocabulary

growing season *noun,* the time of year when it is warm enough to grow plants

tidewater *noun,* coastal area of the South with rivers that rise and fall with the tides

fall line *noun,* a line between the eastern edge of the Appalachian Mountains and the Atlantic coastal plain that connects waterfalls along the eastern coast of the United States and that marks the place where the height of the land drops

backcountry *noun,* the sparsely populated area on the western side of the fall line

Core Lesson 1

Geography of the Colonies

1550 1600 1650 1700 1750 1800

1600–1750

VOCABULARY

growing season
tidewater
fall line
backcountry

Vocabulary Strategy

tidewater

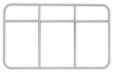

The word **tidewater** is a compound word. Break the word apart to help you remember its meaning.

READING SKILL

Compare and Contrast

As you read, take notes to compare and contrast the three regions of the English colonies.

Build on What You Know What is the geography like where you live? Are you close to mountains or is the land flat for miles around? Think about where you live and how it affects the way you live.

The Thirteen Colonies

Main Idea The geography and climate of the thirteen colonies affected how colonists lived and worked.

During the 1600s and 1700s, many English settlers moved to North America. People believed that they had a better chance to make a living in North America or to find freedoms that they didn't have at home. These settlers established thirteen English colonies.

The colonies were located along the Atlantic Ocean, with New France to the north and New Spain to the south. The Appalachian Mountains formed a natural boundary to the west.

The geography and climate of the thirteen colonies separated them into three different regions: New England, the Middle Colonies, and the Southern Colonies. 1

New England Coast
Rocky coasts are common in New England.

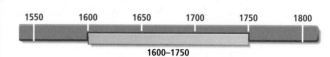

Skill and Strategy

Reading Skill and Strategy

Reading Skill: Compare and Contrast

This skill helps you understand how historical events or people are similar and different.

Read "Geography of the Colonies." Then fill in the chart below to compare and contrast the features of the regions listed.

New England	Middle Colonies	Southern Colonies
1. Poor soil and a cold climate	2. Fertile soil and a warm climate	A warmer climate and waterways for trade

Reading Strategy: Predict and Infer

3. Read the red and blue headings in "Geography of the Colonies." Then check the best prediction.
   - ___ Most settlers in the thirteen colonies had moved south from Canada.
   - ✓ Many factors affected how the settlers in all thirteen colonies lived and worked.
   - ___ The colonists in New England built larger homes than the other colonists.
4. Read "Geography of the Colonies." Then check the best inference.
   - ✓ The weather and soil made growing crops easier in the Middle Colonies than in New England.
   - ___ The shipbuilding industry helped the Southern Colonies grow quickly.
   - ___ Colonists living in New England took vacations to the Southern and Middle Colonies.

Unit Resources
 47 Use with *United States History*, pp. 160–163

Unit Resources, p. 47

Background

Early Colonial Life

- Life in the backcountry was difficult. In some areas, there was no well-established government, and conflicts with American Indians were common.
- One important cash crop grown in the tidewater region was tobacco. By the 1650s, Virginia and Maryland were exporting almost five million pounds of tobacco every year.

New England

New England's geography was shaped by glaciers. During the Ice Age, thick sheets of ice covered much of North America. As the glaciers moved slowly across New England, they carried rocks
2 trapped in the ice. The ice and rocks cut deep valleys through the mountains. They scraped up New England's rich soil and pushed it south, leaving a thin, rocky layer of dirt.

Farming was difficult in New England. Most of the land was filled with rocks or was too sandy to farm. The region's many forests and rugged mountains made it hard to find good farmland.

The climate also affected New England farming. Summers were warm, but winters were long and bitterly cold. The growing season was short. The **growing season** is the time of year when it is warm enough for plants to grow. In New England, the growing season lasted only from late May to early October. Most farmers could grow just enough food for their families, with a little left over to sell.

Farming in New England was hard, but the area had many natural resources. Colonists used these resources to make a
3 living. They took wood from the thick forests to make buildings and ships. They caught fish and whales from the Atlantic Ocean to use for food and other products.

REVIEW Why was farming difficult for New England colonists? soil too rocky and sandy; growing season too short.

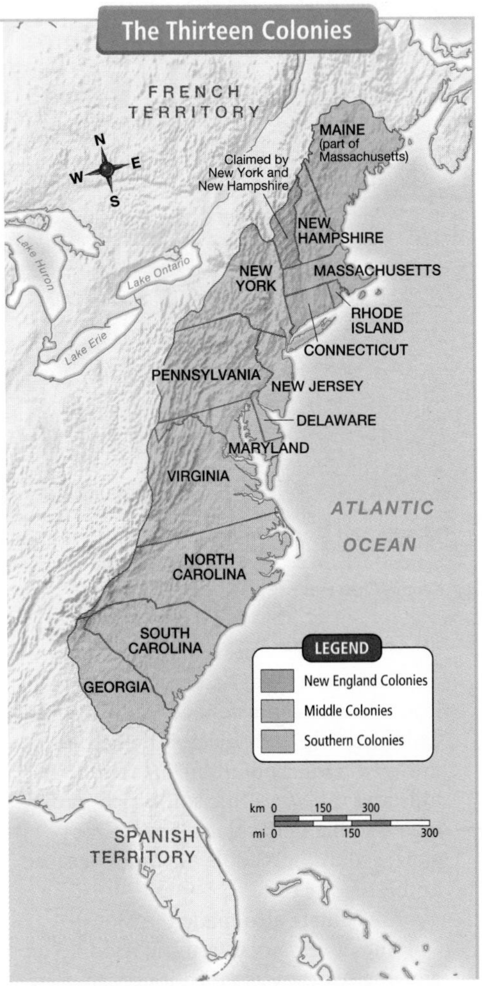

Three Regions This map divides the colonies into three regions. Each region has its own geography and climate. **SKILL Reading Maps** Which were the New England Colonies? MA; NH; RI; CT; ME

Leveled Practice

Extra Support

Have small groups **make fact cards** to compare the geography and climate of New England, Middle, and Southern Colonies. Visual-spatial

Challenge

Have students **create graphs** showing the average temperature for a city in each of the three different colonial areas. Have students explain why temperatures in the three cities are different. Visual-spatial

ELL

Beginning

- Write the names of the thirteen colonies on slips of paper.
- Have each student choose a slip and **find the chosen colony** on a United States map.
- Ask each student to give the class travel directions from that colony to one of the other original thirteen colonies.

Visual-spatial

2 Teach

The Thirteen Colonies

Talk About It

1 **Q Geography** What factors set the New England, Middle, and Southern colonial areas apart from each other?
A climate and geography

2 **Q Geography** In what ways did glaciers affect New England's geography?
A by cutting valleys and scraping up much of the rich soil, leaving only a thin layer of dirt

3 **Q Geography** What were New England's natural resources?
A forests, fish, and whales

Vocabulary Strategy

growing season Explain to students that the word *season* means "any special part of the year," such as winter or fall or the dry or rainy seasons.

Reading Strategy: Predict/Infer Tell students they can use what they have read to infer the effects of climate and geography on colonists in the Middle and Southern Colonies. You may wish to model the strategy for students.

Think Aloud *New England's climate and geography affected how colonists there lived. I can infer that people in other colonies were affected by their regions, too.*

The Thirteen Colonies

continued

Talk About It

4 Q Geography Why was the land in the Middle Colonies good for farming?

A Glaciers left behind fertile soil.

5 Q Geography Why were forests and rivers important resources for people in the Middle Colonies?

A Rivers were used for transportation and trade. Colonists hunted and trapped forest animals such as deer and beaver.

6 Q Geography How was the backcountry different from the tidewater?

A Land was steeper and covered with forests. Farms were smaller. Colonists hunted and fished for much of their food.

Vocabulary Strategy

tidewater Explain to students that ocean *tides* are the regular rise and fall of the oceans that occur about twice a day.

fall line A *fall line* is the *line* where many *waterfalls* meet.

backcountry Tell students that they can break apart the compound word *backcountry* to help them remember its meaning.

Critical Thinking

Draw Conclusions Does the geography and climate of an area have a greater influence on the way people live today or was it more important in colonial times?

Middle and Southern Colonies Gentle, rolling hills were a common feature of the Middle Colonies (left). The tidewater of the Southern Colonies had many rivers (right).

The Middle Colonies

The glaciers that had scooped up soil from New England stopped in the Middle Colonies. When the glaciers melted, they dropped fertile soil on the area's rolling hills and valleys. Fertile soil is rich in the
4 material that helps plants grow. Crops grew well in the Middle Colonies because of their fertile soil.

The climate also made the Middle Colonies a very good farming region. The growing season was much longer than in New England. The Middle Colonies had many sunny days and plenty of rain.

The Middle Colonies' wide rivers, such as the Delaware and the Hudson, were ideal for transportation. Farmers used riverboats to sell their crops in nearby
5 towns and to bring supplies to their farms. The woods near these farms were full of wildlife. Colonists hunted and trapped animals such as deer and beaver.

The Southern Colonies

The geography of the Southern Colonies was very different from that of the other colonies. The southern coast is a watery world of rivers, bays, and wetlands. This area is called the tidewater. In the **tidewater,** the water in rivers and streams rises and falls every day with the ocean's tides.

The climate and soil of the tidewater were excellent for farming. Many southern colonists grew cash crops. The weather was warm for much of the year, and crops could grow for seven or eight months. Soil in the tidewater was rich and fertile, and the area received plenty of rain.

Colonists used the waterways in the tidewater to ship crops to markets in other towns and countries. The tidewater ended at the fall line, about 150 miles inland. At the **fall line,** rivers from higher land flow to lower lands and often form waterfalls.

Science

Make a Report

The tidewater has many marshes and swamps. These are coastal wetland areas. Have students research and report to the class on why wetlands are important to the environment.

Verbal-linguistic

Language Arts

Write an Essay

Have students write a short essay in which they compare and contrast the climate and geography of the New England, Middle, and Southern Colonies.

Verbal-linguistic

The fall line followed the eastern edge of the Appalachian Mountains, from the Southern Colonies to New England. The higher land on the other side of the fall line was known as the **backcountry.** The
6 backcountry was "in back of" the area where most colonists settled. The land in the backcountry was steep and covered with forests. Farms there were small, and colonists hunted and fished for much of their food.

REVIEW Why was farming in the Middle and Southern colonies better than in New England?
fertile soil and longer growing season.

Fall Line Waterfalls are common along the area where the backcountry and the tidewater meet.

Lesson Summary

The thirteen English colonies in North America formed three unique regions. New England had poor soil and a cold climate, but plenty of forests and fish. The Middle Colonies had fertile soil, a warmer climate, and rivers for transportation. The Southern Colonies had an even warmer climate and many waterways in the tidewater.

Why It Matters...

For the thirteen colonies to grow, colonists had to learn how to adapt to the geography and climate of each of these three regions.

Lesson Review

1. **VOCABULARY** Complete the following sentence, using two of the words listed below.
   fall line **tidewater** **backcountry**
   The ______ was the higher land on the western side of the ______.
2. **READING SKILL** Write a short paragraph that **compares** and **contrasts** the growing season and soil in each region.
3. **MAIN IDEA: Geography** Why was the tidewater good for growing crops?
4. **MAIN IDEA: Economics** In what ways did the geography and climate of the Southern Colonies affect how colonists made a living?
5. **PLACES TO KNOW** What natural resources did colonists have in New England?
6. **CRITICAL THINKING: Draw Conclusions** Why would colonists want to settle near rivers and other waterways? Use facts and details to support your answer.
7. **CRITICAL THINKING: Analyze** Climate is one way to divide places into regions. What are some other ways?

HANDS ON **ART ACTIVITY** Use library resources to learn more about how glaciers changed New England's geography. Draw a picture to show what you learned.

3 Review/Assess

Review Tested Objectives

U3-1 New England: Connecticut, Massachusetts, New Hampshire, Rhode Island; Middle Colonies: Delaware, New Jersey, New York, Pennsylvania; Southern Colonies: Georgia, Maryland, North Carolina, South Carolina, Virginia

U3-2 New England: warm summers, long and cold winters; Middle Colonies: many sunny days, plenty of rain; Southern Colonies: warm weather most of the year, plenty of rain

Lesson Review Answers

1. backcountry; fall line
2. New England has the shortest growing season, the harshest weather, and the poorest soil. The Southern Colonies have the longest growing season, the best soil, and the mildest climate.
3. Soil in the tidewater was rich and fertile.
4. The climate and soil were excellent for farming, so many southern colonists grew cash crops.
5. forests and Atlantic Ocean for fishing and catching whales
6. It was easier for settlers to reach areas along rivers; colonists wanted to settle near transportation routes; colonial settlements needed a source of fresh water.
7. geography; population; how people earn a living

HANDS ON Performance Task Rubric

4	Picture is accurate, clear, informative, and well researched; mechanics are correct.
3	Picture is generally accurate, clear, informative, and well researched; mechanics are correct.
2	Picture is inaccurate, unclear, and difficult to understand; errors in mechanics.
1	Picture is inaccurate and lacks research; many errors in mechanics.

Study Guide/Homework

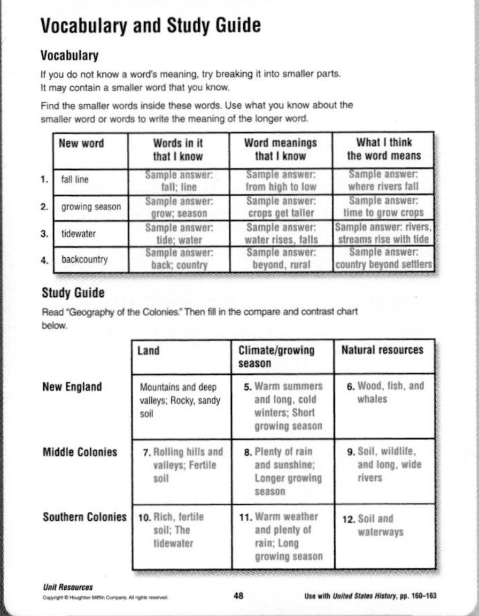

Vocabulary and Study Guide

Vocabulary

If you do not know a word's meaning, try breaking it into smaller parts. It may contain a smaller word that you know.

Find the smaller words inside these words. Use what you know about the smaller word or words to write the meaning of the longer word.

	New word	Words in it that I know	Word meanings that I know	What I think the word means
1.	fall line	Sample answer: fall; line	Sample answer: from high to low	Sample answer: where rivers fall
2.	growing season	Sample answer: grow; season	Sample answer: crops get taller	Sample answer: time to grow crops
3.	tidewater	Sample answer: tide; water	Sample answer: water rises, falls	Sample answer: rivers, streams rise with tide
4.	backcountry	Sample answer: back; country	Sample answer: beyond, rural	Sample answer: country beyond settlers

Study Guide

Read "Geography of the Colonies." Then fill in the compare and contrast chart below.

	Land	Climate/growing season	Natural resources
New England	Mountains and deep valleys; Rocky, sandy soil	5. Warm summers and long, cold winters; Short growing season	6. Wood, fish, and whales
Middle Colonies	7. Rolling hills and valleys; Fertile soil	8. Plenty of rain and sunshine; Longer growing season	9. Soil, wildlife, and long, wide rivers
Southern Colonies	10. Rich, fertile soil; The tidewater	11. Warm weather and plenty of rain; Long growing season	12. Soil and waterways

Unit Resources
Copyright © Houghton Mifflin Company. All rights reserved.
48
Use with *United States History*, pp. 160–163

Unit Resources, p. 48

Reteach Minilesson

Use a main idea chart to reteach the geography of New England.

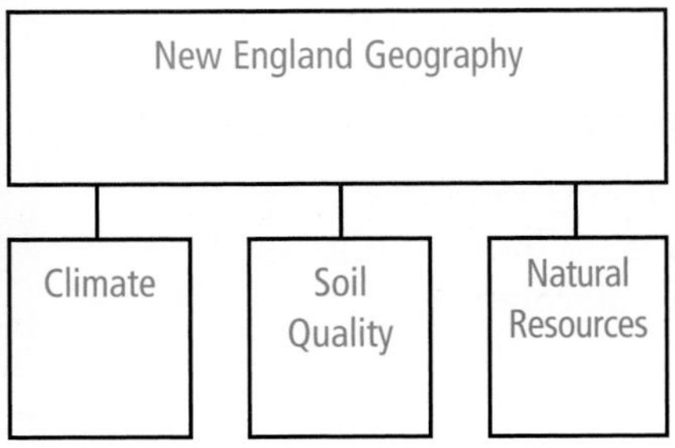

Graphic Organizer 6

Extend Quick Look

Connect to the Core Lesson Students have learned about the geography of the New England, Middle, and Southern Colonies. In Extend Lesson 1, they will learn about the Appalachian Mountains, a landform that had an impact on colonial life in all three regions.

1 Teach the Extend Lesson

Connect to the Big Idea

Places and Regions Places and regions have physical and human characteristics that result from the interaction between people and their environment. The Appalachian Mountains on the western border of the British colonies greatly influenced early settlement of North America, hindering the expansion of the British colonies.

Connect to Prior Knowledge

Remind students that during colonial times, the Appalachian Mountains formed a natural western boundary to the British colonies. Have students locate the mountains on the map on this page and name the colonies along their length.

Geography

THE APPALACHIANS

The Appalachian Mountains aren't the tallest mountains in the world, but they are some of the oldest, and they show it. For over 400 million years, wind, rain, and snow have worn them down. In the north, Ice Age glaciers ground and scraped them. This endless erosion created the rounded mountains and hills people know today.

Though the Appalachian Mountains are not very high, they were hard to cross in early colonial times. Settlers who tried to use rivers were usually stopped by waterfalls, rushing waters, and deep gorges.

Another challenge to travelers was the Appalachians' forests. The forests were so hard to pass through that few settlers lived west of the fall line at the edge of the Appalachians.

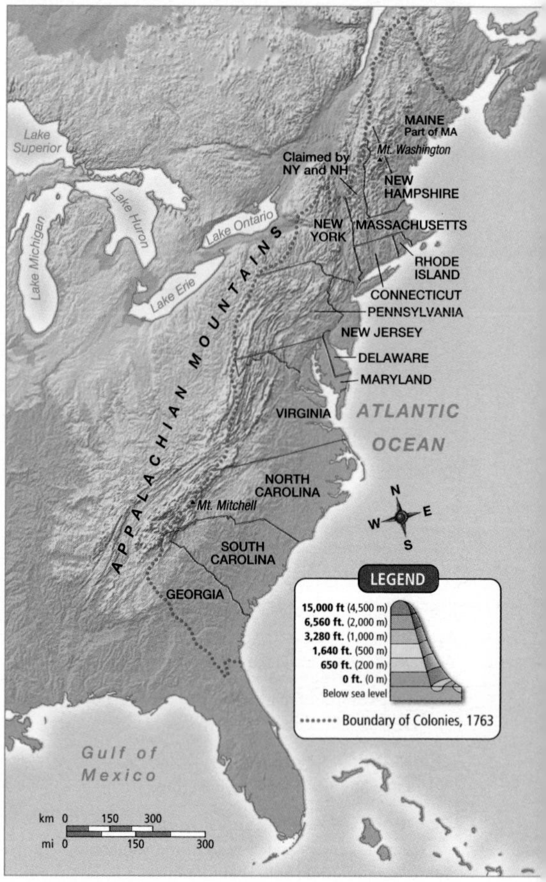

The Appalachian Mountains stretch 1,600 miles. In most places, the Appalachians are nearly 100 miles wide.

Reaching All Learners

Extra Support

Make Predictions

- Have students **make a list** of the challenges colonial settlers faced when they tried to cross the Appalachians.
- For each challenge listed, have students make predictions about how later settlers overcame these challenges.

Verbal-linguistic

On Level

Make a Poster

- Ask students to make posters showing some of the many ways people today use the Appalachians for recreation.
- Students can use the Internet to learn more about the Appalachian Trail or the national and state parks and parkways in or near these mountains.

Visual-spatial

Challenge

Write an Essay

- Have students write an essay comparing and contrasting the Atlantic Ocean and the Appalachian Mountains as the eastern and western natural borders of the British colonies.
- Students might consider how each was an obstacle to settlement as well as a natural resource.

Verbal-linguistic

Ridges and Valleys Some areas of the Appalachians are rugged and steep. A narrow ridge can be seen in this photograph, running along the top of the mountains.

GEOGRAPHY

Activities

1. **TALK ABOUT IT** What challenges did people face crossing the Appalachians in the 1600s?
2. **CHART IT** Use an atlas to find the five highest mountains in the Appalachians. Make a chart giving the name, location, and altitude of each peak.

165

2 Leveled Activities

❶ **Talk About It** *For Extra Support*

Waterfalls, rushing waters, and deep gorges made river travel difficult to impossible. Appalachian forests were so thick and dense, and some mountains in this range were so steep that overland travel was also difficult. Weather at higher altitudes was and still can be a problem.

❷ **Chart It** *For Challenge*

HANDS ON Performance Task Rubric

4	Chart format is used; information is well organized, accurate, clear, and complete; mechanics are correct.
3	Chart format is used: information is adequately organized, accurate, clear, and complete; few errors in mechanics.
2	Chart format is used; information is somewhat disorganized, unclear, inaccurate, or incomplete; some errors in mechanics.
1	Chart format is not used; information is incomplete, inaccurate, disorganized or confusing; many errors in mechanics.

ELL

Intermediate

- Direct students to the first sentence in the lesson. Ask them to look at the words *tallest* and *oldest.*
- Have students **explain** how the suffix *-est* changes the meaning of the root words.
- Then have students **give examples** of how the meaning of other adjectives such as *short, smart, high, long,* and so on change when this suffix is added.

Verbal-linguistic

Science

Prepare a Diagram

- Have students prepare a diagram illustrating how weathering and erosion have reshaped the Appalachians.
- Diagrams can show the effects of wind, rain, snow, and glaciers.
- Have students use their diagrams to explain this process to the class.

Visual-spatial; logical-mathematical

Graphic Organizer

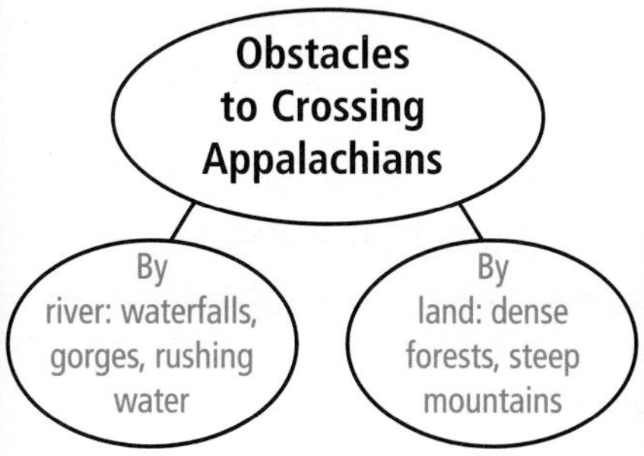

www.eduplace.com/ss/hmss05/

Core Lesson 2 **Pages 166–167**

✔ Tested Objectives

U3-3 Citizenship Explain the impact of religion and dissent in Puritan communities.

U3-4 History Describe interactions between American Indians and settlers in the New England Colonies.

Lesson Quick Look

This lesson describes the founding of the New England Colonies.

Teaching Option: **Extend Lesson 2** is a readers' theater about a New England town meeting.

1 Get Set to Read

Preview Have students read headings in this lesson. Ask them what they think this lesson is about.

Reading Skill: Main Idea and Details Details should include the different views of ownership.

Build on What You Know Discuss some of the ways that people students know try to set a good example for others. Ask students if people always agree on what a "good example" is.

Vocabulary

town meeting *noun,* an assembly of qualified local voters who hold elections and vote on laws for their communities

self-government *noun,* the government of a community, state, or nation by the people living in that place; a democracy

dissenter *noun,* a person who disagrees strongly or refuses to go along with what his or her leaders believe

banish *verb,* to drive someone out of their home as a punishment

Core Lesson 2

New England

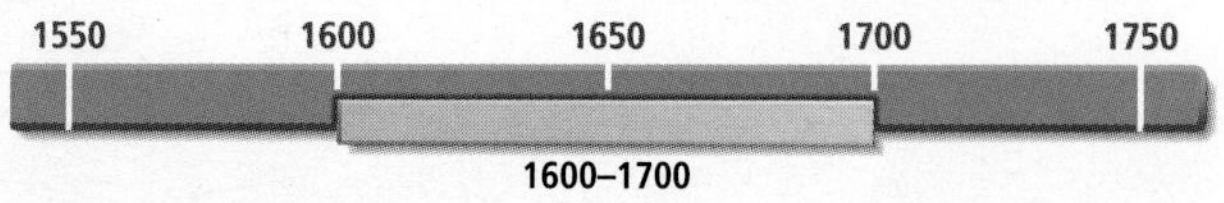

VOCABULARY

town meeting
self-government
dissenter
banish

Vocabulary Strategy

dissenter

Dissent means to disagree. The suffix **-er** changes the meaning to a person who disagrees.

READING SKILL

Main Idea and Details

As you read, note details that support the second main idea in this lesson.

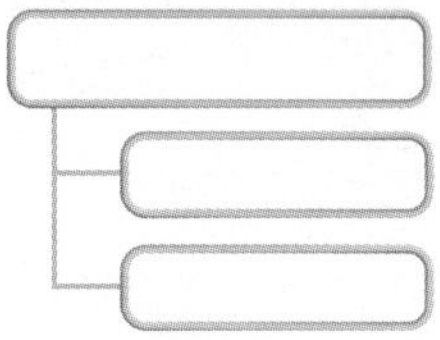

Build on What You Know Have you ever wanted to set a good example for others? Puritan colonists did. They believed that they should set a good example for other people by following laws based on the Bible.

Massachusetts

Main Idea Religion was at the center of Puritan government and community life.

The Puritans were English colonists who settled in New England in the 1600s. These settlers wanted to form communities where they could follow the rules of the Bible and serve their God.

Puritan religion shaped the government of the Massachusetts Bay Colony. Usually, only male church members could vote or serve in town government. Town leaders made laws to control how people worshipped. One law required all people to attend church services. 1

On Sundays, the town gathered at the meetinghouse for church. The meetinghouse was the most important building in a Puritan community and was often built in the middle of town.

Community members came to the meetinghouse at least once a year for a town meeting. A **town meeting** was a gathering where colonists held elections and voted on the laws for their towns.

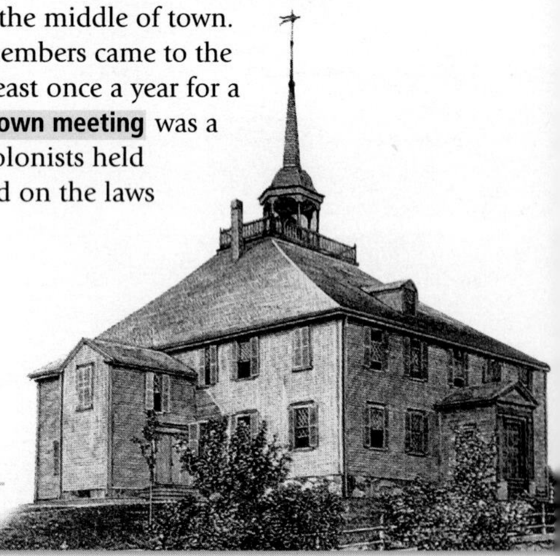

Puritan Meetinghouse This meetinghouse still stands in Hingham, Massachusetts.

Skill and Strategy

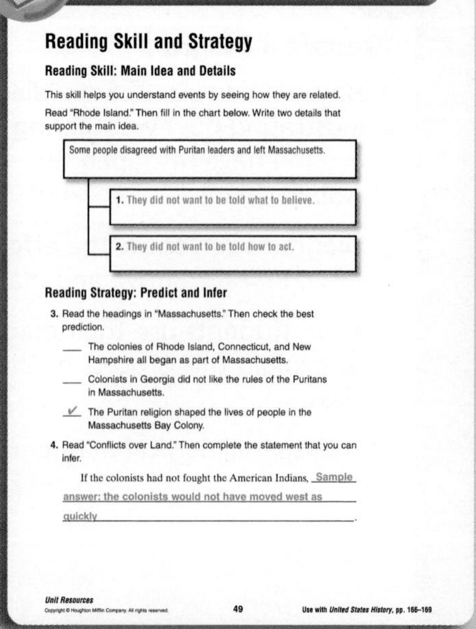

Reading Skill and Strategy

Reading Skill: Main Idea and Details

This skill helps you understand events by seeing how they are related.

Read "Rhode Island." Then fill in the chart below. Write two details that support the main idea.

Some people disagreed with Puritan leaders and left Massachusetts.

1. They did not want to be told what to believe.

2. They did not want to be told how to act.

Reading Strategy: Predict and Infer

3. Read the headings in "Massachusetts." Then check the best prediction.

___ The colonies of Rhode Island, Connecticut, and New Hampshire all began as part of Massachusetts.

___ Colonists in Georgia did not like the rules of the Puritans in Massachusetts.

✓ The Puritan religion shaped the lives of people in the Massachusetts Bay Colony.

4. Read "Conflicts over Land." Then complete the statement that you can infer.

If the colonists had not fought the American Indians, Sample answer: the colonists would not have moved west as quickly.

Unit Resources

49
Use with *United States History*, pp. 166–169

Unit Resources, p. 49

Background

Puritans

- Some American Indians came to live in Puritan communities, integrating into colonial culture.
- King Philip's War led to the deaths of many American Indians as well as colonists. At least thirteen colonial villages were completely destroyed by the time the war ended.

Dissenters Roger Williams (above) receives advice from Narragansett Indians in Rhode Island. Both Williams and Anne Hutchinson (right) challenged Puritan teachings.

In Massachusetts Bay, everyone could attend a town meeting, but only men who owned property could vote. Even so, Puritans still had more self-government than people in most other European colonies. When people make laws for themselves, they have **self-government.**

The Puritans had some experience with self-government in England. The law-making body in England was called Parliament. Some members of Parliament were elected by the people.

Rhode Island

Some colonists thought that Puritan leaders should not tell them what to believe or how to act. These colonists were called dissenters. A **dissenter** is a person who does not agree with the beliefs of his or her leaders.

Roger Williams was a dissenter who wanted more religious freedom. Puritan leaders, however, believed that everyone had to follow the same religious laws.

Williams believed that the government should not make laws about religion. Because of his views, Puritan leaders, banished him from Massachusetts. To **banish** means to force someone to leave.

In 1636, Williams founded a new colony that became known as Rhode (2) Island. There, people could worship freely. Williams also kept the government separate from the church. This was an (3) important event in the history of religious freedom in North America.

Another Puritan who challenged church leaders was **Anne Hutchinson.** Hutchinson criticized Puritan ministers. She also held meetings in her home where men and women talked about religion. Puritan leaders did not like this. They said her beliefs went against Puritan teachings and that women should not teach men about religion. Like Roger Williams, Hutchinson was banished and moved to Rhode Island.

REVIEW In what ways were Roger Williams and Anne Hutchinson alike? They were both banished because they spoke out against Puritan leaders.

167

2 Teach

Massachusetts

Talk About It

1 **Q Citizenship** How did religion influence the government of the Massachusetts Bay Colony?

A Often, only male church members could vote or serve in town governments. Laws controlled how people worshiped.

2 **Q History** When did Roger Williams form the colony of Rhode Island?

A 1636

3 **Q History** How was the government of Rhode Island different from that of Massachusetts?

A In Rhode Island, the government was separate from the church.

Vocabulary Strategy

town meeting Tell students that the *town meeting* is a form of local government that is still used in some of New England's small towns today.

self-government Tell students that *self-* is a prefix that means "by oneself."

dissenter Tell students that synonyms for *dissent* include *oppose* and *disagree.*

banish Point out that the word root *ban* means to "forbid or prohibit."

Reading Strategy: Predict/Infer Ask students whether they think religion and self-government were important to other colonists.

Reaching All Learners: Leveled Practice

Extra Support

Have small groups of students **make a fact file** about one of the New England Colonies. The file can include a **map** showing the colony's location, resources, settlements, and landforms. Visual-spatial

Challenge

Have students **research** the life of Anne Hutchinson or Roger Williams. Students can debate the pros and cons of the decision by Puritan leaders to banish Hutchinson and Williams from the colony. Verbal-linguistic

Reaching All Learners: ELL

Beginning/Intermediate

Have pairs of students **find details to support the main idea** that religion was central to Puritan communities and governments. Have students read their findings aloud to the class.

Verbal-linguistic

Massachusetts *continued*

Talk About It

4 Q History Why did Thomas Hooker decide to form a new colony?

A He wanted to form a community where all men could vote, even if they were not church members.

5 Q Geography In addition to Rhode Island, what other colonies were started by colonists from Massachusetts Bay?

A Connecticut, New Hampshire, and Maine

Conflicts over Land

Talk About It

6 Q History What was the Pequot War?

A a struggle in the 1630s over land in New England between the Pequots and the colonists

Critical Thinking

Decision Making If colonists had understood American Indian beliefs about land use, do you think the colonists would have made different decisions?

Think Aloud *If the colonists had understood, they might have decided to share the land instead of buying it or fighting over it. Or they might have decided to start fighting American Indians sooner.*

Connecticut, New Hampshire, Maine

4 A minister named **Thomas Hooker** also did not like some of the rules made by Puritan leaders. He wanted to form a new community where all men could vote, even if they were not church members.

In 1636, Hooker led about 100 colonists west to the Connecticut River. There they founded the town of Hartford. Colonists looking for good farmland started other towns in the area. These towns joined Hartford to create the colony of Connecticut. Other colonists from Massachusetts Bay moved north

5 and settled the area that became New Hampshire and Maine.

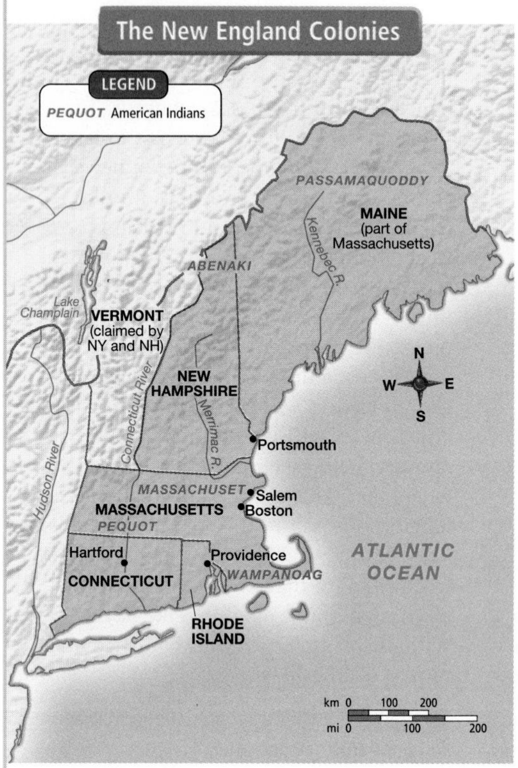

New England Settlement here began in Massachusetts. From there, colonies started new communities elsewhere in New England.

SKILL Reading Maps Where in New England did the Pequots live?
Massachusetts

Conflicts over Land

Main Idea Puritans and American Indians fought over land in New England.

The New England colonies were founded on lands where American Indians lived. Indians and colonists disagreed about who owned the land. American Indians believed that land was for everyone to use and that no one could truly own it. They thought that when they sold land to colonists they were only agreeing to share it. Colonists, however, expected the Indians to move from the land once they sold it. These different views of ownership often led to conflict.

In the 1630s, a war broke out between colonists and the Pequot (PEE kwawt) Indians. This struggle over land became known as the Pequot War, and ended when the 6
colonists killed most of the Pequots. The few surviving Pequots were enslaved or fled.

After the Pequot War, more colonists moved onto American Indian lands in New England. **Metacomet** (MEHT uh kah meht) was a leader of the Wampanoag (wahm pah NOH ahg) nation. He wanted to avoid war, but he believed that his people had to fight to stay on their lands.

168 • Chapter 5

Art

Make an Exhibit

- Have students work in groups to **research and make an exhibit** showing the way of life of the Wampanoag when the English colonists came and their life today.
- The exhibit might include profiles of Squanto, Massasoit, and Metacomet and a map showing where modern Wampanoag people live.

Visual-spatial

Language Arts

Write an Essay

- Ask students to **write a short essay** showing how Roger Williams, Anne Hutchinson, and Thomas Hooker were alike and different.

Verbal-linguistic

Metacomet The Leader of the Wampanoags feared that the growth of English settlements would destroy his people's way of life.

In 1675, Metacomet, who was known to colonists as King Philip, attacked Massachusetts villages. Fierce fighting spread across New England in a series of battles called King Philip's War. The colonists had more soldiers and better weapons than Metacomet's small army.

In 1676, Metacomet was defeated. After the war, colonists killed and enslaved some of the defeated Indians. They forced many others to leave. Few American Indians remained in southeastern New England after the war.

REVIEW What caused the Pequot War? Colonists and Pequots fought over land.

Lesson Summary

- Religion was an important part of the government in the Massachusetts Bay Colony.
- Some people disagreed with Puritan leaders and left Massachusetts Bay to form new colonies.
- The settlement of New England led to war with American Indians.

Why It Matters ...

Self-government and the actions of dissenters led to freedom of thought and religion in parts of New England.

Lesson Review

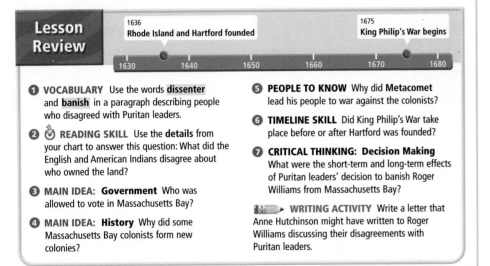

1636 Rhode Island and Hartford founded

1675 King Philip's War begins

1630 | 1640 | 1650 | 1660 | 1670 | 1680

1. **VOCABULARY** Use the words **dissenter** and **banish** in a paragraph describing people who disagreed with Puritan leaders.
2. **READING SKILL** Use the **details** from your chart to answer this question: What did the English and American Indians disagree about who owned the land?
3. **MAIN IDEA: Government** Who was allowed to vote in Massachusetts Bay?
4. **MAIN IDEA: History** Why did some Massachusetts Bay colonists form new colonies?
5. **PEOPLE TO KNOW** Why did Metacomet lead his people to war against the colonists?
6. **TIMELINE SKILL** Did King Philip's War take place before or after Hartford was founded?
7. **CRITICAL THINKING: Decision Making** What were the short-term and long-term effects of Puritan leaders' decision to banish Roger Williams from Massachusetts Bay?

WRITING ACTIVITY Write a letter that Anne Hutchinson might have written to Roger Williams discussing their disagreements with Puritan leaders.

Study Guide/Homework

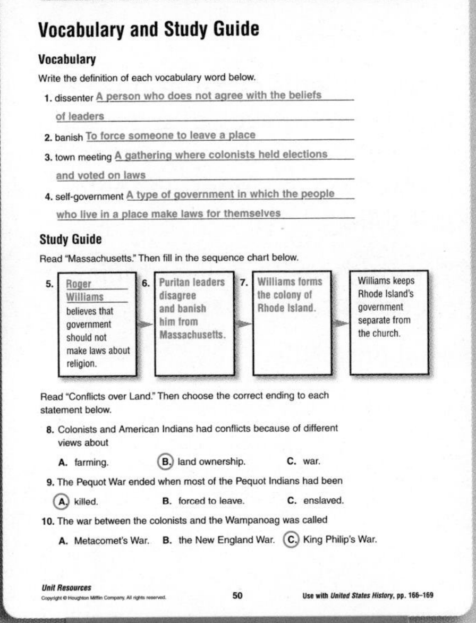

Vocabulary and Study Guide

Vocabulary

Write the definition of each vocabulary word below.

1. dissenter A person who does not agree with the beliefs of leaders
2. banish To force someone to leave a place
3. town meeting A gathering where colonists held elections and voted on laws
4. self-government A type of government in which the people who live in a place make laws for themselves

Study Guide

Read "Massachusetts." Then fill in the sequence chart below.

5. Roger Williams believes that government should not make laws about religion.
6. Puritan leaders disagree and banish him from Massachusetts.
7. Williams forms the colony of Rhode Island.

Williams keeps Rhode Island's government separate from the church.

Read "Conflicts over Land." Then choose the correct ending to each statement below.

8. Colonists and American Indians had conflicts because of different views about
   A. farming. (B.) land ownership. C. war.
9. The Pequot War ended when most of the Pequot Indians had been
   (A.) killed. B. forced to leave. C. enslaved.
10. The war between the colonists and the Wampanoag was called
   A. Metacomet's War. B. the New England War. (C.) King Philip's War.

Unit Resources

50

Use with *United States History*, pp. 166–169

Unit Resources, p. 50

Reteach Minilesson

Use a cause-and-effect chart to reteach the impact of religion and dissent on Puritan communities.

Cause

Dissenters disagree with Massachusetts Bay leaders about the role of religion in government.

Effects

Anne Hutchinson is banished and goes to Rhode Island colony.

Thomas Hooker starts town of Hartford, part of Connecticut colony.

Graphic Organizer

3 Review/Assess

Review Tested Objectives

U3-3 Religion shaped the government of Massachusetts Bay and led dissenters Roger Williams and Thomas Hooker to leave and start their own colonies. Dissent led to the banishment of Anne Hutchinson.

U3-4 Conflicts over land use led to two wars in New England between American Indians and colonists—the Pequot War and King Philip's War.

Lesson Review Answers

1. Answers will vary but should mention that dissenters were banished by Puritan leaders.
2. Answers should describe the different beliefs that the American Indians and English settlers had about land ownership.
3. Only male colonists who were property-owners could vote.
4. They disagreed with some of the rules and beliefs of the Puritan leaders. Some wanted greater religious freedom and favored separation of church and government.
5. Metacomet believed the Indians had to fight to stay on their lands.
6. after
7. Short-term: Williams formed the colony of Rhode Island. Long-term: His decision to keep government separate from the church was an important first step in establishing religious freedom in America.

HANDS ON Performance Task Rubric

4	Letter format is used correctly; main points are correct and supported by details; mechanics are correct.
3	Letter format is used; most main points are correct and supported by details; mechanics are generally correct.
2	Letter format is attempted; main points/details contain errors or omissions; some errors in mechanics are present.
1	Letter format is not used; main points/details contain errors or omissions; many errors in mechanics are present.

Extend

Quick Look

Students have learned about the political and religious life of colonists in New England. In this Readers' Theater, they will learn more about the role of town meetings in the government of New England's Puritan communities.

1 Preview the Extend Lesson

Connect to the Big Idea

Democratic Values One of the values that is central to American democracy is self-government. In the New England colonies, the town meeting was an important first step towards self-government.

Connect to Prior Knowledge

Remind students that although the Puritans had self-government, it was limited. Have students describe the restrictions on voting. Ask them to list similarities and differences between the Puritans' self-government and American self-government today.

Readers' Theater

Town Meeting

APRIL 5, 1749

The New England town of Linton has a problem to resolve. Colonists from the southern part of Linton want to form their own town, so they are meeting to try to reach an agreement. Today, many New England towns still hold town meetings. Listen to what the residents of Linton have to say to one another.

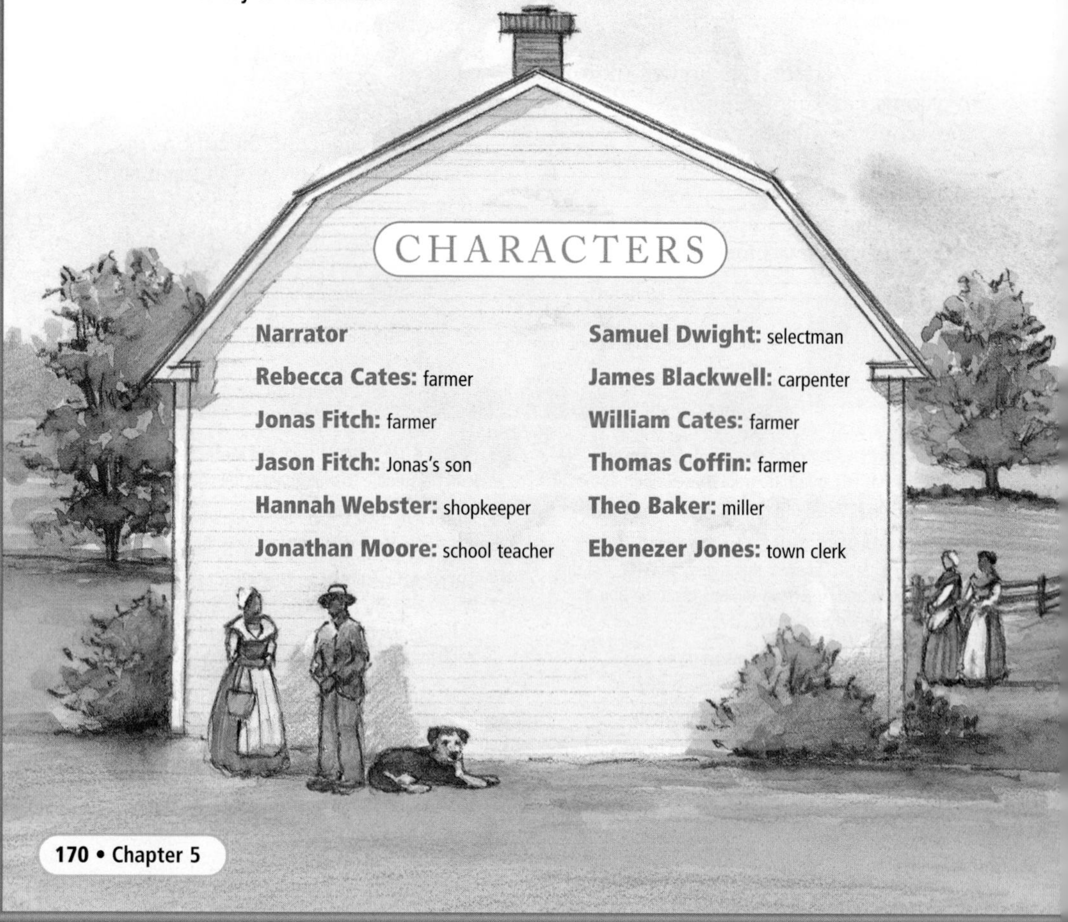

CHARACTERS

Narrator
Rebecca Cates: farmer
Jonas Fitch: farmer
Jason Fitch: Jonas's son
Hannah Webster: shopkeeper
Jonathan Moore: school teacher
Samuel Dwight: selectman
James Blackwell: carpenter
William Cates: farmer
Thomas Coffin: farmer
Theo Baker: miller
Ebenezer Jones: town clerk

Reaching All Learners

Background

Town Meeting

- At town meetings, voters elected local officials. Town officials also might call a special meeting to discuss an important issue, such as the building of a new road.
- In many New England communities, the tradition of open town meetings continues today.

Extra Support

Chart the Arguments

Have students make a two-column chart showing the arguments for and against allowing residents in the southern part of Linton to form their own town.

Verbal-linguistic; visual-spatial

On Level

Write a Speech

- Have students pick out one argument in favor of separating from Linton and write a speech supporting or opposing that position.
- Ask students to deliver their speeches to the class.

Verbal-linguistic

Narrator: People are arriving for today's town meeting in Linton. Some families have walked for miles to get here.

Rebecca Cates: You see? This is why we need our own town! Just getting here in the spring is exhausting—never mind making the trip during the winter!

Jonas Fitch: Spring's bad enough. The mud was almost up to my knees in places. I had to carry Jason on my shoulders, didn't I, son?

Jason Fitch: Yes, sir. Nearly took us all day to get here.

Hannah Webster: I know you have hardships. But I hate to think of so many families leaving us. Shopkeepers will lose customers. What will we do if you don't come into town?

Rebecca Cates: I wish no disrespect, Hannah, but Linton has changed. Our families no longer live close together as we once did.

Jonathan Moore: True. And if we had our own school south of the river, it would be better for our children—and I wouldn't have to spend four hours a day walking back and forth to teach them.

Hannah Webster

Farmer Jonas Fitch

2 Teach the Extend Lesson

Learning Through Drama

Assign each of the roles in the play to students and have them read the play aloud to the class. Discuss with students how the play shows the role of town meetings in establishing self-government in the New England colonies.

Challenge

Write a Scene

- Have students look through a local newspaper for issues such as traffic, garbage collection, or water quality that concern people in the community.
- Ask students to write a scene in which one such issue is discussed at a modern-day town meeting.

Bodily-kinesthetic; verbal-linguistic

ELL

Beginning

Have students suggest possible meanings for the word *selectman* on page 172. Then have them **use a dictionary** to find the word's exact meaning.

Verbal-linguistic

Literature

Historical Fiction

The Witch of Blackbird Pond by Elizabeth George Speare is about a girl from Barbados who moves to Connecticut at the end of the seventeenth century. Place this work of historical fiction in your Reading Center for students who want to find out what life was like in a Puritan town in New England.

Critical Thinking

Draw Conclusions Why would it be difficult to have town meetings as the main form of local government in a large town or city?

Compare and Contrast In what ways are the televised "town meetings" held by today's political candidates similar to and different from the New England town meetings held by the Puritans?

Narrator: The people have taken their seats inside the meetinghouse. Let's go in and listen. I see that Selectman Dwight has given Tom Coffin permission to speak.

Tom Coffin: I represent the families south of the Fox River. We want to split off from Linton and build our own meetinghouse and school. We need our own town now.

Samuel Dwight: How many families are you speaking for, Tom?

Tom Coffin: Eighty-two.

Samuel Dwight: That would be a heavy loss.

James Blackwell: A heavy loss to the town treasury! If taxpayers leave, we won't have enough money to keep the town going.

William Cates: May I speak, please?

Samuel Dwight: Yes, Mr. Cates.

William Cates: Why should we support a town we can't even reach easily? Remember how deep the snow was last winter?

Jason Fitch: It was over my head!

Theo Baker: We could hold a town meeting in the summer. Special meetings could be held near you.

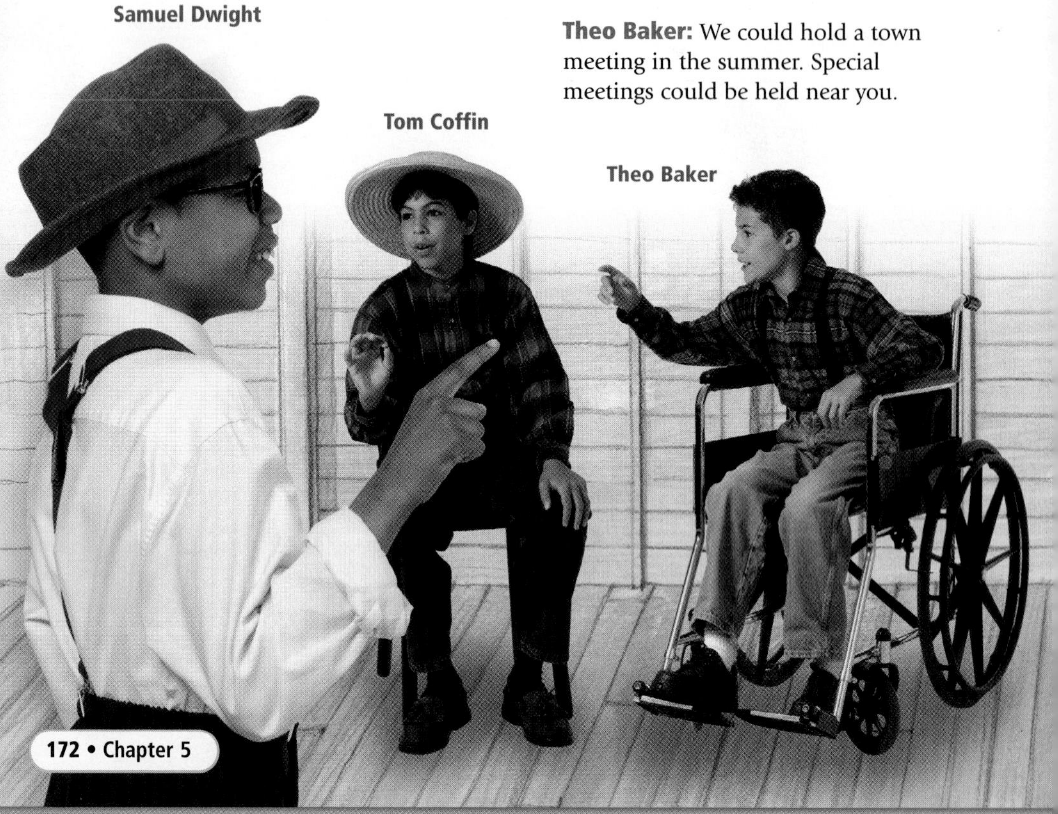

172 • Chapter 5

Reaching All Learners

Language Arts

Write a Newspaper Article

- Have students suppose that they are reporters for the "Linton Gazette." Ask them to write an article for the newspaper about the town meeting.
- Remind students to answer the questions *who, what, where, when,* and *why* in their articles.
- Encourage students to include quotes from characters in the readers' theater who favored and opposed the final decision.

Verbal-linguistic

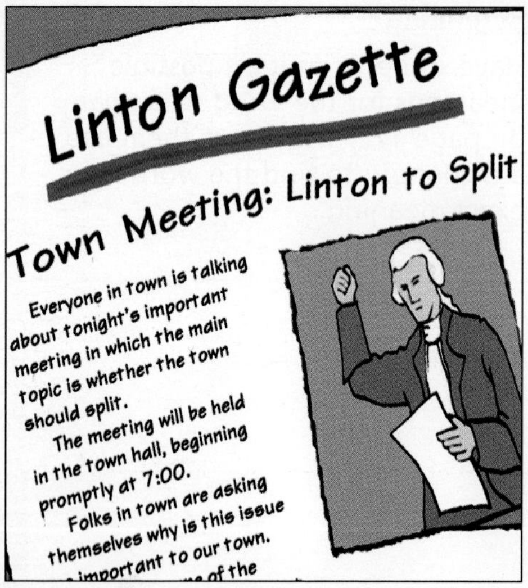
Linton Gazette

Town Meeting: Linton to Split

Everyone in town is talking about tonight's important meeting in which the main topic is whether the town should split.

The meeting will be held in the town hall, beginning promptly at 7:00.

Folks in town are asking themselves why is this issue important to our town.

Math

Multiplication and Fractions

- Have students suppose that Linton has about 900 inhabitants at the time of this meeting.
- If 82 families leave the town, with an average of four people per family, how many people will leave? about $82 \times 4 = 328$
- About what fraction of the town is that? a little more than one third

Logical-mathematical

William Cates: Summer is a bad time for farmers to leave their plows.

Rebecca Cates: It wouldn't matter where you hold the meeting. Just getting to town is hard. We are too far from you!

Samuel Dwight: Does anyone else wish to speak about that?

Theo Baker: Maybe we need to build a better road.

James Blackwell: Hold on there. The town does not have enough money for a new road. Perhaps in a year or so we could patch up the old one.

Samuel Dwight: Jonas Fitch, it's your turn to speak.

Jonas Fitch: For years, this meeting has been full of arguments about where money should go. You who live in the center of town are not farmers like us. Our problems are different from yours. I say it's time for us to part.

Theo Baker: Jonas, it makes me sad to say this, but I believe I must agree.

Narrator: All have had a chance to give their opinions, but only white men who are church members may vote. In many towns they must be property owners, as well. After the vote, the town clerk reads the decision aloud.

Ebenezer Jones: It is so decided in Linton Town Meeting on April 5, in the year of 1749: that part of the town of Linton which lies north of the Fox River shall remain Linton, and that part which lies south of the river shall be built into a town by the name of South Linton.

Rebecca Cates

Activities

1. **THINK ABOUT IT** In what ways did the townspeople show **civic virtue** in their discussion?
2. **DEBATE IT** With partners, decide on an issue to discuss and resolve in a class town meeting. Write reasons for and against the issue. Then hold a town meeting in your classroom.

3 Leveled Activities

❶ **Think About It** *For Extra Support*
Sample answer: They listened to one another's opinions and tried to make the best decision for the community.

❷ **Debate It** *For Challenge*

Writing Rubric

4	Speaker states position on issue clearly; gives reasons for position; facts are accurate.
3	Speaker states position well; gives reasons for position; facts are mostly accurate.
2	Speaker states position in a somewhat disorganized way; gives some reasons for position; some factual errors are present.
1	Speaker states no position or one that is off-topic; does not give reasons for position; many factual errors are present.

Character Trait: Civic Virtue

Ask students to infer what the townspeople's discussion might have sounded like if they did not show civic virtue.

For more on character traits, turn to pages R4–R5.

Art

Draw a Political Cartoon

- Remind students that newspapers sometimes include political cartoons. These cartoons often comment on or make fun of local or national politics.
- Have them draw a cartoon that might have appeared in Linton's newspaper about this town meeting or its outcome.
- Display completed cartoons in the classroom.

Visual-spatial

Graphic Organizer

Forming a New Town

Reasons in Favor	Reasons Opposed
• Too far to come for town meeting • Want children to have shorter walk to school • Want to address different problems and needs	• Shopkeepers will lose customers • Town treasury will lose tax funds • Town might not be able to function

Graphic Organizer 1

✓ Tested Objectives

U3-5 Economics Describe major industries, especially those related to the sea, in the New England Colonies.

U3-6 History Identify features of home and community life in New England.

Lesson Quick Look

This lesson describes economic and social life in colonial New England.

Teaching Option: Extend Lesson 3 shows students a New England cod-fishing operation.

1 Get Set to Read

Preview Ask students how the map and chart might relate to the lesson title.

Reading Skill: Problem and Solution Problems include the lack of good farmland in New England.

Build on What You Know As students read the lesson, encourage them to compare and contrast their daily lives to those of young people in colonial times.

Vocabulary

industry *noun,* a business that sells a product or a service to other people

export *noun,* a product that is sold or traded to another country

import *noun,* a product brought into one country from another for sale or use

Middle Passage *noun,* the voyage enslaved Africans made, against their will, from Africa across the Atlantic Ocean to the Americas

slave trade *noun,* buying and selling of human beings

Core Lesson 3

Life in New England

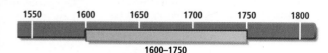

1550 1600 1650 1700 1750 1800

1600–1750

VOCABULARY

industry
export
import
Middle Passage
slave trade

Vocabulary Strategy

import; export

To remember the difference between **import** and **export,** think of into and exit. Imports come into a country. Exports exit, or leave, a country.

READING SKILL
Problem and Solution
What problem did colonists face in trying to earn a living by farming? Look for their solutions.

PROBLEM	SOLUTION

Build on What You Know Have you ever helped an adult do chores around your home? Children in New England spent much of their time doing hard work to help their families.

Using the Sea

Main Idea New England colonists made a living by using resources from the land and the sea.

Most people in New England were farmers. They worked on small plots of land growing crops such as wheat, oats, and peas. Farmers usually grew just enough to feed their families. Because farming in New England was difficult, some colonists looked for other ways to earn a living.

The geography of New England made it a good place to make a living from the sea. The rocky coast had many 1
good harbors, and thick forests provided wood to build ships. Boston soon became a center for New England's growing shipbuilding industry. An **industry** is all the businesses that make one kind of product or provide 2
one kind of service.

Shipbuilding Workers used oak trees to build the bodies of ships. Pine trees were used for ships' masts, the tall pole where sails are attached.

Skill and Strategy

Reading Skill and Strategy

Reading Skill: Problem and Solution

This skill helps you see what problem some people faced and how they resolved it.

Read "Work in the Home." Then fill in the problem and solutions chart below. How did colonial families get everything they needed at home?

Problem	Solution
Almost everything a colonial family needed had to be grown or made at home.	1. Men and boys worked in the fields and repaired buildings. 2. Women and girls prepared food. 3. Women and girls helped in the fields during the harvest.

Reading Strategy: Predict and Infer

4. Read the red and blue headings in "Life in New England." Based on the headings, make a prediction about what each section will be about.

Heading 1: Using the Sea

Sample answer: This section will be about how colonists used the sea for food and travel.

Heading 2: Home and Community Life

Sample answer: This section will be about how colonists in New England lived and what their communities believed.

Unit Resources

51
Use with *United States History,* pp. 174–179

Unit Resources, p. 51

Background

The Salem Witch Trials

- In 1692 and 1693, over 160 people in Massachusetts were accused of witchcraft. At least twenty-five of them were executed.
- After these trials ended, no more people in New England were convicted of witchcraft.

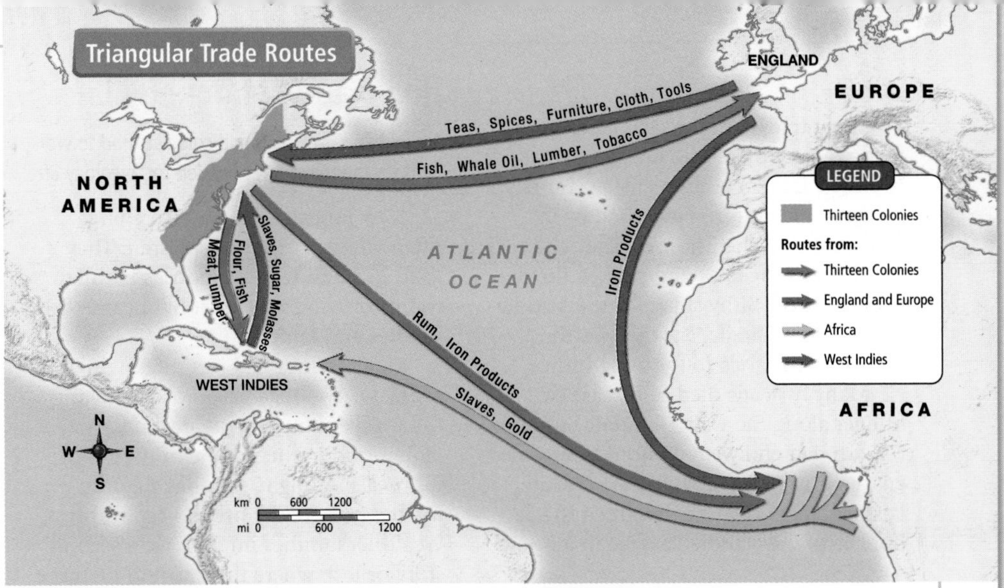

Triangular Trade This trade network exchanged imports and exports among three continents. SKILL **Reading Maps** What types of goods were traded from colonies in North America to countries in Europe? fish, whale oil, lumber, tobacco

Fishing and Whaling

The ocean waters off the New England coast were full of fish. Many people made their living by catching and selling fish, and the fishing industry grew quickly. New Englanders caught 600,000 pounds of fish in 1641. By 1675, their catch was
3 ten times as much—six million pounds!

The most common fish was cod, which became a key part of New England's economy. Merchants sold much of the cod as exports to Europe and the West Indies. An **export** is a product sent to another country and sold.

Sailors from New England also hunted whales. Colonists used whales to make products such as oil for lamps. By the 1700s, whaling was one of the most important industries in New England.

Triangular Trade

The products of New England were often traded to other places. New England merchants shipped fish and lumber to Europe, Africa, and the West Indies. They traded these goods for imports to bring back to the colonies. An **import** is a product brought into one country from another. Ships from Europe carried imports, such as tea and spices, to sell in the colonies.

The shipping routes between North America, Europe, and Africa formed an imaginary triangle across the Atlantic. These trade routes became known as the triangular trade. Many of New England's merchants and traders became rich from this trade.

REVIEW What was triangular trade? trade routes among Europe, Africa, North America, and the West Indies

175

2 Teach

Using the Sea

Talk About It

1 **Q Geography** Why was New England a good place to make a living from the sea?

A The New England coast had many good harbors. Thick forests provided wood for shipbuilding. The ocean waters off the coast were full of fish.

2 **Q Economics** What were three New England industries that depended on the sea?

A shipbuilding, fishing, whaling

3 **Q Economics** What fish became important to the economy of New England?

A cod

Vocabulary Strategy

industry *Business* is a synonym.

export Tell students that the prefix *ex-* means "out of." They can think of goods going *out of a port.*

import Explain that the prefix *im-* means "into." They can think of goods coming *into a port.*

Reading Strategy: Predict/Infer Ask students to infer why the triangular trade made many New Englanders rich.

REACHING ALL LEARNERS

Leveled Practice

Extra Support

Have students **use a map** of the world to show the triangular trade routes and identify the products going in each direction. Have students identify natural resources in each area that made trade possible. Visual-spatial

Challenge

Have students **make a diagram** and **give a report** to the class on the ships, tools, and techniques used by New England whalers to track and catch whales. Visual-spatial

REACHING ALL LEARNERS

ELL

Beginning

- Review the meaning of the words *triangle* and *triangular* with students.
- Have students explain why the early colonial trade routes have this name.
- Students can also take turns pointing out the three sides of the trade triangle on a world map using the map on page 175 as a guide.

Verbal-linguistic

Using the Sea *continued*

Talk About It

4 Q History What were conditions like aboard the slave ships?

A People were chained together and packed into crowded, filthy ships. Many died of disease and lack of food during the voyage.

5 Q History Who was Olaudah Equiano?

A Enslaved as a boy, he later gained his freedom and became a writer. He wrote about the horrors of the Middle Passage.

Home and Community Life

Talk About It

6 Q History What did colonists use to light their houses?

A candles and lamps

7 Q History What took place in the main room of a New England house?

A cooking, eating, sleeping, working

Vocabulary Strategy

Middle Passage Explain to students that *passage* here means "a journey, especially by boat."

slave trade Point out that the word *trade* in this context means "business."

Slavery

Some traders in the triangular trade made money by selling human beings. In Africa, traders bought enslaved men, women, and children who had been
4 captured from their homes. They chained the Africans together and packed them into crowded, filthy ships for the Middle Passage. The **Middle Passage** was the voyage from Africa to the West Indies.

Many Africans died of disease or hunger along the way. **Olaudah Equiano,**
5 (OL uh dah eh kwee AH noh) who was enslaved as a boy, survived the Middle Passage. Years later, he described the horrors of the Middle Passage in a book:

"I became so sick and low that I was not able to eat, nor had I the least desire to taste anything. I now wished for . . . death."

Olaudah Equiano

In North America, the Africans who survived the ocean voyage were sold to colonists who forced them to work. During the 1600s and 1700s, hundreds of thousands of Africans were brought to the colonies in the slave trade. The **slave trade** was the business of buying and selling human beings.

Home and Community Life

Main Idea New England colonists had to work hard for the things they needed for everyday life.

New England families were large, often with six or seven children. They lived in small wooden houses with few rooms or windows. Most light came from 6
candles and lamps.

Many homes had just one main room, with a huge fireplace. A cooking fire was kept burning at all times. A table stood in the middle of the room for meals. At night, families slept on 7
mattresses near the fire to keep warm. Wealthier families might have a second story or loft, where there would be more room for sleeping.

Language Arts

African Art

- Enslaved people from Africa were able to retain some of their cultures, despite efforts to strip them of their traditions.
- Have students research the visual arts of one African culture.
- Then have them write a report on what they found.

Visual-spatial

Music

Musical Traditions

Explain to students that many enslaved Africans sang songs about their trip to North America and their life there. Have students write and perform a song about Olaudah Equiano or the Middle Passage.

Musical-auditory; verbal-linguistic

Work in the Home

A colonial home was more than just a building where a family ate and slept. It was also a workshop. Almost everything a family needed had to be grown or made by hand at home.

8 Men and boys spent most of their time working in the fields. They planted crops such as wheat and corn in the spring and harvested them in the fall. They built and repaired buildings and tools and took care of the family's animals.

Colonial women and girls were just as busy. They spent much of their time preparing and preserving food for the family. Women and girls made household items such as clothing, soap, and candles. During planting and harvest seasons, they also helped in the fields.

REVIEW How did boys and girls help their families? See Daily Chores Chart

Colonial home Children were expected to help around the house. Below, a busy colonial family is gathered in their one-room home.

Daily Chores 9

Boys	Girls
Bring in wood for fireplace	Weave cloth for clothing
Care for farm animals	Preserve fruit and vegetables
Gather wild berries and vegetables	Cook food
Help plow fields and plant crops	Make soap and candles
Help build and repair buildings	Help with planting and harvesting

177

Home and Community Life *continued*

Talk About It

8 **Q History** What kind of work did colonial men, women, and children do?

A Men and boys planted and harvested crops, built and repaired buildings and tools, and took care of farm animals. Women and girls cooked and preserved food, and made household items such as soap, clothing, and candles. During planting and harvesting, they helped in the fields.

9 **Q Visual Learning** What natural resources are the table and cradle in the painting probably made of?

A wood

Reading Strategy: Predict/Infer Ask students what the advantages were of dividing up the tasks in a colonial household, and assigning different tasks to individual family members.

Reaching All Learners: Extra Support

Create a Diorama

Have students create a diorama showing the inside of a one-room New England home or a schoolhouse. Remind students to include cooking utensils, beds, or other furniture and show people at work.

Visual-spatial

Reaching All Learners: Challenge

Give a Demonstration

- Candle-making was one of the many chores women in colonial New England performed.
- Have students create an instruction sheet and demonstrate how candles were made in colonial times.

Bodily-kinesthetic; verbal-linguistic

Home and Community Life *continued*

Talk About It

10 Q History How did the leaders of the Massachusetts Bay Colony support education?

A By law, any town with 50 or more families had to build a school. Harvard College in Massachusetts was the first college in the thirteen colonies.

11 Q History Who were Jonathan Edwards and George Whitefield?

A two of the ministers whose sermons inspired the Great Awakening

12 Q History What was the Great Awakening?

A It was a popular movement that renewed interest in religion in the 1730s.

Critical Thinking

Cause and Effect In what ways did the Great Awakening influence life in the British colonies?

Colonial Schoolhouse Most early New England schoolhouses (above) were just one room. Students of all ages shared the same classroom. They used hand-held tablets called hornbooks (right) to learn how to read.

Education and Recreation

Puritans wanted everyone to be able to read the Bible. Some parents taught their children how to read and write at home, but many New England towns had schools.

10 In 1647, Massachusetts passed a law that said any town with 50 or more families had to build a school to teach reading and writing. Older boys could go on to study at colleges such as Harvard College in Massachusetts. Harvard was founded in 1636, and was the first college in the thirteen colonies.

Although New England colonists worked hard, they made time for play. Sports such as horseracing and bowling were common. People also played an early version of baseball called town ball. In winter, colonists went ice skating or sledding down hills.

The Great Awakening

Religion was a central part of New England life, but by the early 1700s, the church had become less powerful. Many colonists did not share the strong religious beliefs of their parents. Fewer people belonged to local churches.

This changed in the 1730s, when young, exciting ministers began speaking throughout the English colonies. The two most famous were **Jonathan Edwards** of 11 Massachusetts and **George Whitefield** of England. These and other ministers traveled around New England urging people to renew their faith.

Both ministers gave inspiring sermons and many New England colonists began to make religion a more important part of their lives. This renewed interest in religion became known as the Great 12 Awakening because people felt as if they were waking up with new faith.

Physical Education

Teach a Game

Colonial New England children played a variety of circle, counting, and ball games, such as town ball. Have groups of students pick a game, research it, and teach it to the class.

Bodily-kinesthetic

Language Arts

Write an Announcement

Have students write an announcement for a town meeting in New England. Have them include a date, time, place, and topic of the meeting.

Verbal-linguistic

George Whitefield The minister's fiery sermons inspired colonists to return to religion.

During the Great Awakening, new churches with new ideas developed throughout the colonies. Many people joined these new Protestant groups. Some of these churches accepted women, African Americans, and American Indians.

As the Great Awakening spread, people all over the colonies began to question their religious leaders and place more trust in their own beliefs.

REVIEW Why did many New England colonists return to religion in the 1730s?

Lesson Summary

- Most people in New England worked on family farms.
- Some New England colonists used the nearby ocean for fishing, shipbuilding, and trade.
- Thousands of Africans were enslaved and brought to the colonies.
- In the Great Awakening, exciting ministers inspired colonists to become more religious.

Why It Matters ...

The triangular trade made the New England economy strong. The growth of the slave trade, however, would later lead to a war between American states.

Lesson Review

1. **VOCABULARY** Use **industry** and **export** in a short paragraph describing the economy of New England.
2. **READING SKILL** Write a paragraph about how New England colonists **solved** the **problem** of poor farming conditions.
3. **MAIN IDEA: Economics** What kinds of products did the colonies import from England in the triangular trade?
4. **MAIN IDEA: History** What was the Middle Passage?
5. **EVENTS TO KNOW** What was the Great Awakening?
6. **CRITICAL THINKING: Compare and Contrast** How were the chores New England girls did different from the chores New England boys did? How were they similar?
7. **CRITICAL THINKING: Cause and Effect** What effect did triangular trade have on Africans?

WRITING ACTIVITY Write a diary entry describing a day in the life of a New England girl or boy. Use what you have learned in the lesson to write in your entry.

REVIEW: The ministers of the Great Awakening inspired colonists to join new churches with new ideas.

3 Review/Assess

Review Tested Objectives

U3-5 Major industries included shipbuilding, fishing, whaling, and trade.

U3-6 New England families generally grew or made most of the things they needed. They divided labor between genders. They valued education and showed renewed interest in religion.

Lesson Review Answers

1. Paragraphs might discuss shipbuilding, fishing, or whaling.
2. They turned to occupations that were better suited to the natural resources of the area.
3. Paragraphs should describe each leg of the trade route.
4. The Middle Passage was the trip by sea from Africa to the West Indies that enslaved Africans were forced to take.
5. It was the renewed interest in religion that occurred in the 1730s.
6. Answers should include details from the lesson.
7. It had a devastating effect on Africans. They were taken from their homes and families and shipped to North America where they were forced to work without pay. Many died on the journey.

Writing Rubric

4	Diary entry format is used correctly; entry is well organized and shows considerable creative effort; information on New England life is accurate and mechanics are correct.
3	Diary entry format is used correctly; entry is adequately organized and shows creative effort; few errors in information and mechanics.
2	Diary entry format is attempted; entry is somewhat organized and shows some creative effort; some errors in information and mechanics.
1	Diary entry format not used; entry is disorganized and shows little effort; many errors in information and mechanics.

Study Guide/Homework

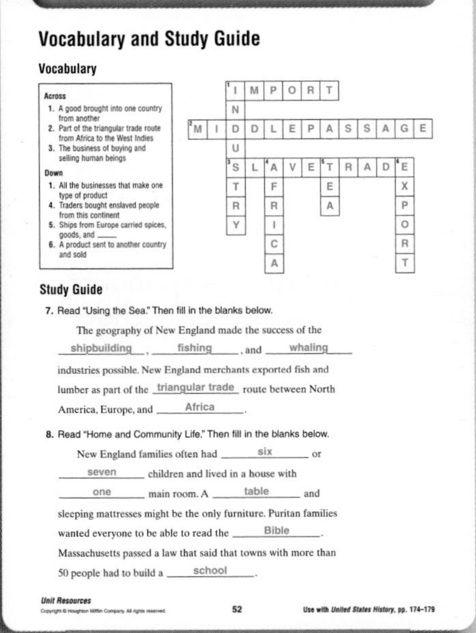

Vocabulary and Study Guide

Vocabulary

Across
1. A good brought into one country from another
2. Part of the triangular trade route from Africa to the West Indies
3. The business of buying and selling human beings

Down
1. All the businesses that make one type of product
4. Traders bought enslaved people from this continent
5. Ships from Europe carried spices, goods, and ____
6. A product sent to another country and sold

Across: 1 IMPORT; 2 MIDDLE PASSAGE; 3 SLAVE TRADE
Down: 1 INDUSTRY; 4 AFRICA; 5 TEA; 6 EXPORT

Study Guide

7. Read "Using the Sea." Then fill in the blanks below.

The geography of New England made the success of the shipbuilding, fishing, and whaling industries possible. New England merchants exported fish and lumber as part of the triangular trade route between North America, Europe, and Africa.

8. Read "Home and Community Life." Then fill in the blanks below.

New England families often had six or seven children and lived in a house with one main room. A table and sleeping mattresses might be the only furniture. Puritan families wanted everyone to be able to read the Bible. Massachusetts passed a law that said that towns with more than 50 people had to build a school.

Unit Resources

52
Use with *United States History*, pp. 174–179

Unit Resources, p. 52

Reteach Minilesson

Use a word web to reteach the economy of colonial New England.

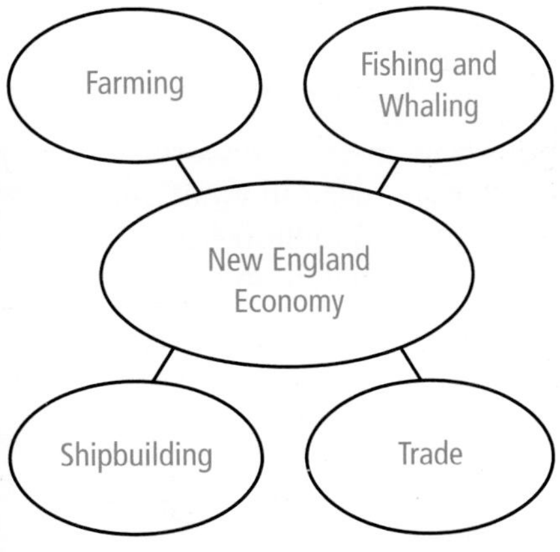

Graphic Organizer 13

Quick Look

Students have learned about the importance of the fisheries and other ocean resources to the New England colonies. In this Extend Lesson, students will learn why cod and other saltwater fish were central to the New England economy.

1 Teach the Extend Lesson

Connect to the Big Idea

Places and Regions The Atlantic Ocean provided many natural resources that helped New England grow and prosper. One of the ways New Englanders developed these resources was by creating a fishing industry.

Connect to Prior Knowledge

Remind students that many other industries developed in this region because of New England's location on the Atlantic coast. Have students name these industries.

Economics

COD FISHING

Why is a giant codfish hanging from the ceiling of the Massachusetts State House? The wooden carving, called "The Sacred Cod," is there to remind state representatives how important the fishing industry was to the early economy of Massachusetts. In colonial times, cod fishing was important to all of New England. Fishermen and merchants made money by catching, buying, and selling cod. Merchants sold much of the cod as exports to Europe and the Caribbean islands.

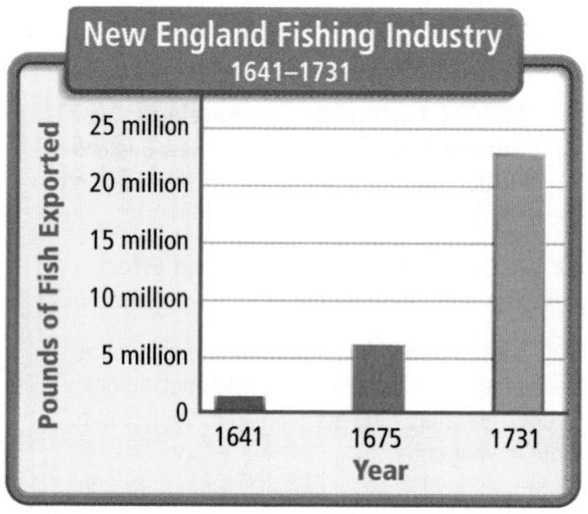

1 Fishing Fleet
In this painting, colonial fishermen return to port after a fishing trip. New England merchants built hundreds of fishing ships and employed thousands of people.

Reaching All Learners

Extra Support

Make a Poster

- Have students make a poster showing the many different kinds of workers whose jobs were connected with the fishing industry.
- Posters may show fishermen, shipbuilders, pilots, sail makers, net makers, port workers, merchants, and others involved in catching, preserving, and selling fish.

Visual-spatial

On Level

Understand the Chart

Have students answer these questions about the chart.

- In what year were the most fish exported? the least? 1731; 1641
- About how many fish were exported in 1641? In what year were around 6 million fish exported? 1 million pounds; 1675
- Approximately how many more fish were caught in 1731 than in 1675? about 17 million pounds more

Logical-mathematical

Challenge

Create a Symbol

- Ask students to use library or Internet resources to find out what industries were important to the early economy of their state, city, or town.
- Have them create a symbol of one of the industries to show its importance.

Visual-spatial

ECONOMICS

② **Unloading the Catch**
After the fishing fleet returns to harbor, smaller boats bring the codfish to shore. Workers cut up the cod and prepare it for drying.

③ **Drying the Catch**
Cod dries on open racks and will later be salted to preserve it. When there is no salt, the cod is packed in ice.

Activities

1. **EXPLORE IT** Put yourself in the scene of this painting. What do you see, hear, and smell?
2. **GRAPH IT** Use an almanac to find out how much fish was caught in New England in the past five years. Make a graph like the one on page 244.

181

2 Leveled Activities

❶ **Explore It** *For Extra Support*
Sample answer: I see boats on the water; I hear people shouting and speaking to each other; I smell fish drying and the salty ocean air.

❷ **Graph It** *For Challenge*

HANDS ON **Performance Task Rubric**

4	Graph format is used; information is accurate; mechanics are correct.
3	Graph format is used; information is mostly accurate; mechanics are mostly correct.
2	Graph format is used; information is somewhat accurate; some errors in mechanics are present.
1	Graph format is not used; information is inaccurate or off-topic; many errors in mechanics are present.

ELL

REACHING ALL LEARNERS

Beginning

- Explain to students that the word *catch* has one meaning as a verb and another meaning as a noun.
- Discuss with students other words that have different meanings when used as noun or verb, such as *plant, watch,* and *match.*
- Have students **write two sentences** that use each word correctly.

Science

Create Solutions

- Tell students that many fish that were once plentiful are becoming less common. Have students brainstorm causes for this, for example, overfishing and pollution.
- Have students work in small groups to create possible solutions to this problem.
- **Compare solutions** as a class. You may wish to have interested students find out more about what the fishing industry and other groups are doing about fish depletion.

Verbal-linguistic

Graphic Organizer

1	Unload the catch
2	Cut up the cod
3	Dry the cod
4	Preserve the cod with salt or ice

Graphic Organizer 15

Tested Objective

U3-7 Organize and present historical data in a line graph.

1 Teach the Skill

- Ask students to describe the kinds of line graphs they have seen. What information did they show?
- Explain that facts or numbers are often shown in a line graph to make them easier to understand.
- Discuss what information is shown on the horizontal axis of a line graph and what is shown on the vertical axis.
- Have students look at the graph shown on page 182 and discuss what it shows.
- Have students read aloud and discuss the steps under "Learn the Skill." Ask them why it is important that both axes on a line graph are divided into even increments.

Graph and Chart Skills

Skillbuilder

Make a Line Graph

▶ **VOCABULARY**
data
line graph

Sometimes information, especially data, is easier to understand when it is presented as a graph or a chart. Data are facts or numbers. A line graph shows changes in data over time. Read the steps below to learn how to make a line graph.

Learn the Skill

Step 1: Collect the data you will use. You can arrange the data in a table, such as the one here.

Year	Value of New England Exports to England (in British pounds)
1728	64,700
1729	52,500
1730	54,700
1731	49,000
1732	64,100
1733	62,000

Step 2: Draw and label the axes of your line graph.

Step 3: Create a grid for your line graph. Divide the axes into equal segments and label each grid line with a number.

Step 4: Draw dots on the graph to show the data. For each year, draw a dot where the grid line for that year and the correct value meet. You may have to estimate where to draw a dot.

Step 5: Draw a line to connect the dots.

Step 6: Give the line graph a title.

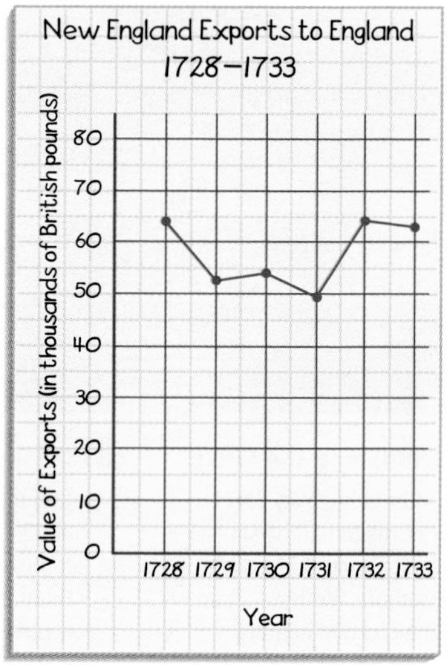

Leveled Practice

REACHING ALL LEARNERS

Extra Support

Explain to students that the line on a graph can show peaks (high points) and valleys (low points) as data changes over time. Have them identify the peaks and valleys shown on the line graph shown. **Visual-spatial**

Challenge

Have students draw sketches of one of the following as line graphs: the profits of a successful company; the U.S. population of trees being logged and replanted. **Visual-spatial**

ELL

REACHING ALL LEARNERS

Beginning

Have students make sketches of different kinds of graphs they have seen. Discuss ways in which each graph can be useful.

Visual-spatial; verbal-linguistic

Practice the Skill

Make a line graph using the data below. Show how the number of ships built in New England changed between 1700 and 1706. Label the horizontal axis *Year* and the vertical axis *Number of Ships Built.*

Year	Number of Ships
1700	68
1701	47
1702	48
1703	43
1704	63
1705	75
1706	77

Apply the Skill

Collect data that shows change over a period of time. For example, you might collect data showing the change in your height over several years. Or you could research the change in temperature outside every day for a week. Arrange the data in a table, and then show it on a line graph.

2 Practice the Skill

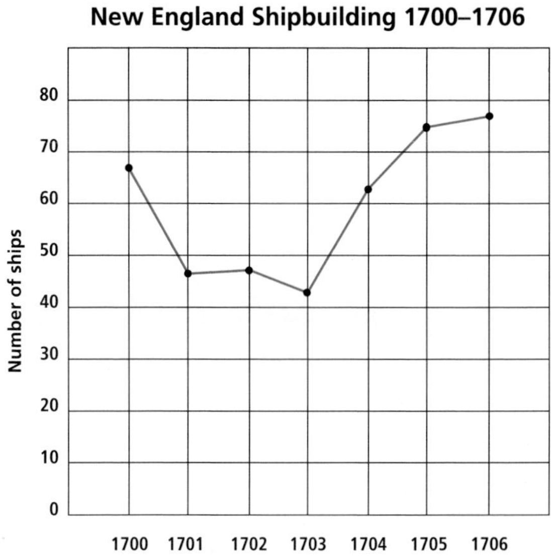

3 Apply the Skill

Ask students to make new line graphs with different data they collected. When evaluating students' line graphs, consider:

- Did the student use the axes correctly?
- Did the student plot the data correctly on the grid?
- Did the student show the changes in the data over time?

Skill Practice

Skillbuilder: Make a Line Graph

Massachusetts Colony, 1680–1730

Year	Estimated Population (in thousands)
1680	39.8
1690	49.5
1700	55.9
1710	62.4
1720	91.0
1730	114.1

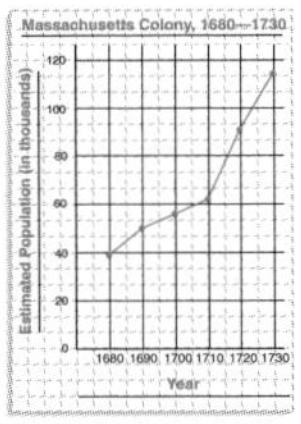

Practice

1. Label the horizontal axis on the graph.
   Students should write *Year* on the graph.
2. Label the vertical axis on the graph.
   Students should write *Estimated Population (in Thousands)* on the graph.
3. Draw dots on the graph to show the data in the table. Then draw a line to connect the dots.
   Students should draw the correct data points and line on the graph.
4. Give the graph a title.
   Title should be "Massachusetts Colony, 1680–1730"

Apply the Skill

Use your graph skills to draw your own line graph. Research and collect data that shows how the area where you live has changed over time. You can go to the library or call your town or county government. Arrange the data in a table, and then show it on a line graph. Draw your line graph on a seperate sheet of paper. Line graph and data table should be complete on separate sheet of paper.

Unit Resources

53 Use with *United States History*, pp. 182–183

Unit Resources, p. 53

Skill Transparency

Skillbuilder Transparency 5

Make a Line Graph

Year	Value of New England Exports to England (in British pounds)
1728	64,700
1729	52,500
1730	54,700
1731	49,000
1732	64,100
1733	62,000

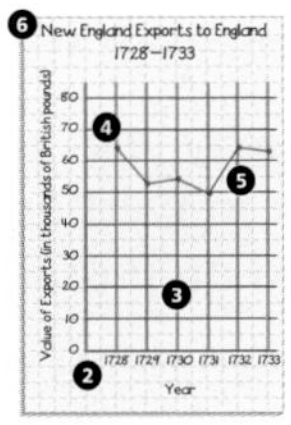

Step 1 Collect the data you will use. You can arrange the data in a table.

Step 2 Draw and label the axes of your line graph.

Step 3 Create a grid for your line graph. Divide the axes into equal segments and label each grid line with a number.

Step 4 Draw dots on the graph to show the data. Draw a dot where the grid line for each year and the correct value meet.

Step 5 Draw a line to connect the dots.

Step 6 Give the line graph a title.

Skillbuilder Transparency

Use with *United States History*, pp. 182–183

Transparency 5

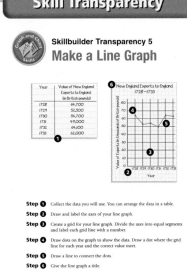

Chapter Review

Tested Objectives

The lesson objective assessed by each question is shown in parentheses after the answer.

Visual Summary

1–2. Land: shaped by glaciers; rocky, sandy soil; good harbors; thick forests; Climate: warm summers; long, cold winters; short growing season *(Obj. U3-2)*

3–4. Farming: difficult, but most people were farmers; Sea: shipbuilding, fishing, whaling, and trading *(Obj. U3-5)*

Facts and Main Ideas

5. The Southern Colonies had a much longer growing season and rich, fertile soil. *(Obj. U3-2)*
6. He believed that government should not make laws about religion. She criticized Puritan leaders and led meetings where women discussed religion. *(Obj. U3-3)*
7. to vote even if they were not church members. *(Obj. U3-3)*
8. It caused people to question religious leaders and trust more in their own beliefs. *(Obj. U3-3)*
9. because the routes formed an imaginary triangle across the ocean *(Obj. U3-5)*

Vocabulary

10. **dissenter** *(Obj. U3-3)*
11. **export** *(Obj. U3-5)*
12. **town meeting** *(Obj. U3-6)*
13. **fall line** *(Obj. U3-2)*

Chapter 5 Review and Test Prep

Visual Summary

1–4. Write a description of each item named below.

Geography of New England

Land ______________________

Climate ______________________

Work in New England

Farming ______________________

The Sea ______________________

Facts and Main Ideas

TEST PREP Answer each question with information from the chapter.

5. **Geography** Why were the Southern colonies better for growing crops than the New England colonies?
6. **Government** Why did Puritan leaders banish Roger Williams and Anne Hutchinson from the Massachusetts Bay Colony?
7. **Citizenship** What did Thomas Hooker give people in Connecticut the right to do?
8. **History** What changes did the Great Awakening bring?
9. **Economics** Why were the Atlantic trade routes called the Triangular Trade?

Vocabulary

TEST PREP Choose the correct word to complete each sentence.

fall line, p. 162
town meeting, p. 166
dissenter, p. 167
export, p. 175

10. Roger Williams was a _____ who wanted more religious freedom.
11. Cod was an important _____ for the New England colonies.
12. Colonists voted on laws at a _____.
13. Rivers flowing from higher to lower ground form waterfalls at the _____.

Reading/Language Arts Wrap-Up

Reading Strategy: Predict/Infer

Review with students what they need to do when they are inferring information from a passage.

You may wish to have students work in pairs and practice inferring based on passages from the chapter.

Have students discuss what they inferred, and why.

Writing Strategy

As students write, they can apply what they know about predicting and inferring to how their readers will react to their text.

Have students review their written work and look for places where the reader has to infer or predict. Have students do a self-check: "Have I given the reader enough information to predict or infer correctly?"

CHAPTER SUMMARY TIMELINE

1636	1647	1675
Rhode Island founded	Massachusetts school law passed	King Philip's War begins

1630 1640 1650 1660 1670 1680

Apply Skills

TEST PREP **Chart and Graph Skill** Read the data below. Then use what you have learned about making a line graph to answer each question.

Year	Population of Massachusetts
1650	14,000
1660	20,000
1670	30,000
1680	40,000
1690	50,000
1700	56,000

14. If you were making a line graph using the data above, what would you label the horizontal axis?
A. Year
B. 1650
C. Massachusetts
D. 1700

15. If you were making a line graph using the data above, what number would you place at the top of the vertical axis?
A. 14,000
B. 40,000
C. 50,000
D. 60,000

Critical Thinking

TEST PREP Write a short paragraph to answer each question.

16. Summarize Explain why colonists and American Indians fought over land.

17. Cause and Effect Why did the Massachusetts Bay Colony create a law that required communities to build schools?

Timeline

Use the Chapter Summary Timeline above to answer the question.

18. In what year did King Philip's War begin?

Activities

HANDS ON **Citizenship Activity** The Puritans in New England made laws for their communities. Create a list of rules for your classroom community. Explain the reasons behind each rule.

Writing Activity Think about life on a New England farm in the 1600s. Use what you learned to write a description of what one day might have been like for someone your age.

Technology
Writing Process Tips
Get help with your description at
www.eduplace.com/kids/hmss05/

185

Technology

Test Generator

You can generate your own version of the chapter review by using the **Test Generator CD-ROM**.

Web Link

For more ideas, visit
www.eduplace.com/ss/hmss05/

Standards

National Standards

III b Representations of the earth
III f Physical system changes
III g How people create places
III h Interaction of human beings and their physical environment
IV e Influence of family, groups, and community **V e** Tension between an individual's beliefs and government policies and laws **VI f** Factors that contribute to cooperation and cause disputes **VII c** Private and public goods and services **VII f** Influence of incentives, values, traditions, and habits **IX b** Conflict, cooperation, and interdependence

Apply Skills

14. A *(Obj. U3-7)*
15. D *(Obj. U3-7)*

Critical Thinking

16. American Indians believed that land belonged to everyone and that no one could own it. They were willing to share with the colonists, but the colonists expected them to move from the land. *(Obj. U3-4)*

17. The Puritans wanted children to be able to read the Bible; because of that, they wanted children to go to school. *(Obj. U3-6)*

Timeline

18. in 1675 *(Obj. U3-4)*

Leveled Activities

HANDS ON Performance Task Rubric

4	Rules clearly stated; reasons supported by information; mechanics are correct.
3	Rules adequately stated; most reasons supported by information; few errors in mechanics.
2	Rules are stated; reasons confused or poorly supported by information; some errors in mechanics.
1	Rules not stated; reasons not supported; many errors in mechanics.

Writing Rubric

4	Description supported by information from the text; mechanics are correct.
3	Most of description supported by information from the text; few errors in mechanics.
2	Description confused or poorly supported by text information; some errors in mechanics.
1	Description not supported; many errors in mechanics.

Chapter 6 Planning Guide

Middle and Southern Colonies

Chapter Opener

Pages 186–187

30 minutes

Reading/Vocabulary

Chapter Reading Strategy:
Monitor and Clarify, p. 185F

Resources

Grade Level Resources
- Vocabulary Cards, pp. 21–28

Reaching All Learners
- Challenge Activities, p. 84

Primary Sources Plus, p. 10

Big Idea Transparency 3

Interactive Transparency 3

Text & Music Audio CD

Lesson Planner & TR CD-ROM

eBook

eTE

Core Lesson 1

The Middle Colonies

Pages 188–191

40 minutes

Tested Objectives

U3-8 Describe the founding and government of New York and New Jersey.

U3-9 Explain the roles of William Penn and Benjamin Franklin in the early history of Pennsylvania and Philadelphia.

Reading/Vocabulary

Reading Skill: Problem and Solution

proprietor, treaty, representative

Cross-Curricular

Math, p. 190

Resources

Unit Resources:
- **Reading Skill/Strategy,** p. 54
- **Vocabulary/Study Guide,** p. 55

Reaching All Learners:
- **Lesson Summary,** p. 22
- **Support for Lang. Dev./ELL,** p. 119

Assessment Options:
- **Lesson Test,** p. 54

Extend Lesson 1

Technology

Ben Franklin: Inventor

20–30 minutes

Pages 192–193

Focus: Fascinating inventions from a founding father.

Skillbuilder

Citizenship Skill

Make a Decision

Pages 194–195

20 minutes

Tested Objectives

U3-10 Use cost and benefit analyses to make decisions.

U3-11 Understand how decisions can influence historical events.

Reading/Vocabulary

cost, benefit

Resources

Unit Resources:
- **Skill Practice,** p. 56

Skill Transparency 6

Core Lesson 2

Life in the Middle Colonies

Pages 196–199

40 minutes

Tested Objectives

U3-12 Describe and explain the diversity of the Middle Colonies.

U3-13 Compare life, including work and education, on farms and in cities in the Middle Colonies.

Reading/Vocabulary

Reading Skill: Cause and Effect

free market economy, free enterprise, artisan, laborer, apprentice

Cross-Curricular

Math, p. 198

Resources

Unit Resources:
- **Reading Skill/Strategy,** p. 57
- **Vocabulary/Study Guide,** p. 58

Reaching All Learners:
- **Lesson Summary,** p. 23
- **Support for Lang. Dev./ELL,** p. 120

Assessment Options:
- **Lesson Test,** p. 55

Extend Lesson 2

History

Colonial Apprentice, October 17, 1730

20–30 minutes

Pages 200–201

Focus: This moment in time shows life in a colonial printshop.

National Standards

I a Similarities and differences in addressing human needs
I e Importance of cultural unity and diversity
V e Tension between an individual's beliefs and government policies and laws
VI h Tensions between the wants and needs and fairness, equity, and justice
VII a Scarcity and choice
VI d Institutions that make up economic systems
VII f Influence of incentives, values, traditions, and habits on economic decisions
VII i Use economic concepts
X a Identify key ideals

With the Program

CURRENT EVENTS from WEEKLY WR READER at www.eduplace.com

Core Lesson 3

The Southern Colonies

Pages 202–205

50 minutes

Tested Objectives

U3-14 Explain the structure and importance of Virginia's colonial government.

U3-15 Summarize the founding of Maryland, North and South Carolina, and Georgia.

Reading/Vocabulary

Reading Skill: Sequence

plantation, refuge, legislature, debtor

Cross-Curricular

Drama, p. 204

Resources

Unit Resources:
- **Reading Skill/Strategy,** p. 59
- **Vocabulary/Study Guide,** p. 60

Reaching All Learners:
- **Lesson Summary,** p. 24
- **Support for Lang. Dev./ELL,** p. 121

Assessment Options:
- **Lesson Test,** p. 56

Extend Lesson 3

Literature

Ann's Story: 1747

40–50 minutes

Pages 206–209

Focus: A head-strong girl tells her parents of her hopes for an education.

Core Lesson 4

Life in the South

Pages 210–215

50 minutes

Tested Objectives

U3-16 Identify agriculture as the main economic activity of the Southern colonies.

U3-17 Compare life on a plantation to life on a small farm.

U3-18 Describe enslaved Africans' lives, work, and culture on southern plantations.

Reading/Vocabulary

Reading Skill: Compare and Contrast

indigo, spiritual, overseer

Cross-Curricular

Physical Education, p. 212

Resources

Unit Resources:
- **Reading Skill/Strategy,** p. 61
- **Vocabulary/Study Guide,** p. 62

Reaching All Learners:
- **Lesson Summary,** p. 25
- **Support for Lang. Dev./ELL,** p. 122

Assessment Options:
- **Lesson Test,** p. 57

Extend Lesson 4

History

Slavery's Past

20–30 minutes

Pages 216–217

Focus: Scientists are learning more about the daily lives of enslaved people.

Chapter Review

Pages 218–219

30 minutes

Resources

Assessment Options:
- Chapter 6 Test
- Test Generator

Chapter 6

Practice Options

Lesson 1 Skill and Strategy

TEST PREP

Reading Skill and Strategy

Reading Skill: Problem and Solution

This skill helps you see what problems some people faced and how they resolved them.

Read "New York and New Jersey." Then fill in the problem and solution chart below. How did the owners of New York and New Jersey deal with the colonists from England?

Problem	Solutions
Owners of New York and New Jersey lived in England.	1. Owners divided the land and sold pieces to the colonists. 2. Owners set up a council to help the governor make decisions.

Reading Strategy: Monitor and Clarify

3. Read "New York and New Jersey." Then check the statement that best clarifies the section.
   - ✓ The Duke of York changed the name of New Netherland to New York.
   - ___ After 1702, New Jersey split into East Jersey and West Jersey.
   - ___ The colonists were not represented in the government of New York and New Jersey.
4. Read "Pennsylvania and Delaware." Then check the statement that best clarifies the section.
   - ___ Benjamin Franklin wanted Pennsylvania to become part of Canada.
   - ___ American Indians disliked the Penn colony and waged war against its citizens.
   - ✓ Delaware was once part of William Penn's land.

Unit Resources

54 Use with *United States History*, pp. 188–191

Lesson 1 Vocabulary/Study Guide

TEST PREP

Vocabulary and Study Guide

Vocabulary

1. proprietor A person who owned and controlled all the land of a colony
2. representative Someone who is chosen to speak and act for others
3. treaty An official agreement between nations or groups
4. Use two of the words in a sentence.
   Sample answer: The proprietor of New Jersey allowed the colonists to elect a representative.

Study Guide

Read "New York and New Jersey." Then fill in the chart below to show how government worked in the colonies of New York and New Jersey.

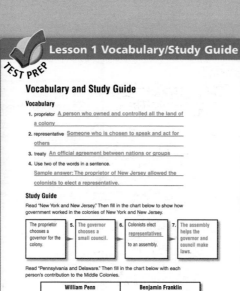

The proprietor chooses a governor for the colony. → 5. The governor chooses a small council. → 6. Colonists elect representatives to an assembly. → 7. The assembly helps the governor and council make laws.

Read "Pennsylvania and Delaware." Then fill in the chart below with each person's contribution to the Middle Colonies.

William Penn	Benjamin Franklin
8. Founded Pennsylvania; Allowed religious freedom; Treated American Indians with respect; Planned the city of Philadelphia	9. Helped start Philadelphia's first library, fire company, and hospital; Experimented with electricity; Invented wood stove and clock

Unit Resources

55 Use with *United States History*, pp. 188–191

also in *Practice Book*, p. 33

Skillbuilder Practice

TEST PREP

Skillbuilder: Make a Decision

> Many young people who lived in towns and cities became apprentices. An apprentice is someone who studies with a master to learn a skill or business. As a child, an apprentice often lived in the master's house. Apprentices usually worked with their masters for four to seven years. Boy apprentices learned shoemaking, printing, bookmaking, and other skills. Girl apprentices learned how to spin thread and weave cloth. By watching and helping, apprentices gained the skills they needed to enter the business as adults.

Practice

1. From reading the passage, what is an apprentice? Someone who studies with a master to learn a skill or business.
2. If a boy or girl decides to become an apprentice, what are the possible costs of this decision? Living away from parents and family for years; living with a stranger; having to grow up very quickly.
3. What are possible benefits of this decision? Learning a skill; becoming a master artisan; meeting new people.

Apply

Read about William Penn in "Pennsylvania and Delaware" in Lesson 1. Penn made many important decisions when he founded Pennsylvania. Choose one of his decisions and write the benefits and costs of it. What might have happened if Penn had made a different decision? Write a paragraph explaining how Penn might have acted differently. Paragraphs should accurately describe one of Penn's decisions and the costs and benefits of that decision.

Unit Resources

56 Use with *United States History*, pp. 194–195

also in *Practice Book*, p. 34

Lesson 2 Skill and Strategy

TEST PREP

Reading Skill and Strategy

Reading Skill: Cause and Effect

This skill helps you see how one event can be related to another, either by causing it or resulting from it.

Read "City Life." How were New York and Philadelphia affected by their population?

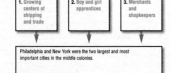

1. Growing centers of shipping and trade
2. Boy and girl apprentices
3. Merchants and shopkeepers

↓ Philadelphia and New York were the two largest and most important cities in the middle colonies.

Reading Strategy: Monitor and Clarify

4. Read "A Mix of People." Then check the statement that best clarifies the section.
   - ___ All of the people living in the Middle Colonies came from England.
   - ___ Many colonists moved back to Europe because of the expensive land in North America.
   - ✓ Religious tolerance attracted many people to the Middle Colonies.
5. Read "Making a Living." Then complete the statement.
   The Middle Colonies enjoyed a free market economy because the colonies' leaders did not tell the colonists how to run their businesses.

Unit Resources

57 Use with *United States History*, pp. 196–199

Lesson 2 Vocabulary/Study Guide

TEST PREP

Vocabulary and Study Guide

Vocabulary

Write the definition of each vocabulary word below.

1. free enterprise People can start any business they want
2. free market economy People decide what to produce
3. artisan A skilled maker of items
4. laborer A person who does hard physical work
5. apprentice Someone who studies with a master
6. Use two words in a sentence.
   Sample answer: An apprentice in silversmithing would live with and learn from a master artisan.

Study Guide

Read "A Mix of People." Then answer the questions.

7. Why did the Middle Colonies have a diverse population?
   Because colonial proprietors believed in religious tolerance and were willing to sell or rent land to anyone who could afford it

Read "Making a Living." Then fill in the chart below.

Workers in the country	Workers in the city
8. Worked long hours tending crops and caring for livestock; Gathered wood and furs to sell	9. Worked as merchants, shopkeepers, artisans, and laborers in busy shipping and trade centers; Some hired apprentices

Unit Resources

58 Use with *United States History*, pp. 196–199

also in *Practice Book*, p. 35

Lesson 3 Skill and Strategy

TEST PREP

Reading Skill and Strategy

Reading Skill: Sequence

This skill helps you understand the order in which events happened.

Read "The Southern Colonies." Then fill in the chart below to show the order in which new colonies were settled in the South.

1. Maryland began in 1632.
2. Carolina was formed in 1663.
3. Georgia began in 1732.

Reading Strategy: Monitor and Clarify

4. Read "Virginia." Then complete the statement.
   The House of Burgesses allowed the colonists to elect representatives to the colony's legislature.
5. Read "New Colonies in the South." Then explain how the colony of Georgia was founded.
   James Oglethorpe brought debtors from England to start new lives on farms in the colony.
6. Read "New Colonies in the South." Why did Lord Baltimore start the colony of Maryland?
   Lord Baltimore wanted to provide a refuge for Catholics who felt persecuted in England.

Unit Resources

59 Use with *United States History*, pp. 202–205

Lesson 3 Vocabulary/Study Guide

TEST PREP

Vocabulary and Study Guide

Vocabulary

Following the example below, break down the vocabulary word into its root and suffix. Then write its meaning.

-tion "the state of" or "the result of"
-ure "a group with a specific function"
-or "one who does a certain thing"

Example:

Conductor = conduct "to lead or to guide" + -or
Conductor means "one who leads or guides."

1. plantation = plant "farm" + -tion
   Plantation means "a large area of land that is used for farming."
2. legislature = legislate "to create laws" + -ure
   Legislature means "the group that creates laws."
3. debtor = debt "money owed" + -or
   Debtor means "one who owes money."

Study Guide

Read "New Colonies in the South." Then fill in the chart below.

Colony	Maryland	Carolinas	Georgia
Why it was founded	4. To be a refuge for Catholics; So all Christians could worship freely	5. Because the British king wanted to keep France and Spain out of the area	6. To be a place for debtors to start new lives

Unit Resources 60 Use with *United States History*, pp. 202–205

also in *Practice Book*, p. 36

Lesson 4 Skill and Strategy

TEST PREP

Reading Skill and Strategy

Reading Skill: Compare and Contrast

This skill helps you understand how historical events or people are similar and different.

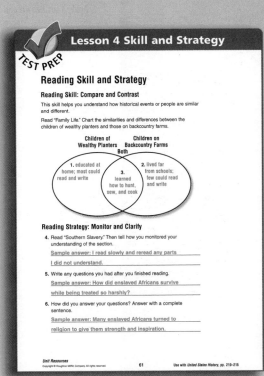

Read "Family Life." Chart the similarities and differences between the children of wealthy planters and those on backcountry farms.

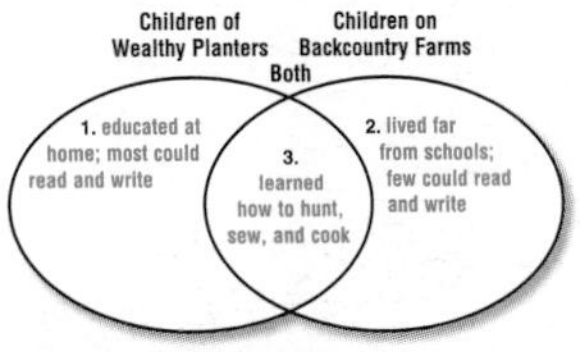

Reading Strategy: Monitor and Clarify

4. Read "Southern Slavery." Then tell how you monitored your understanding of the section.
   Sample answer: I read slowly and reread any parts I did not understand.
5. Write any questions you had after you finished reading.
   Sample answer: How did enslaved Africans survive while being treated so harshly?
6. How did you answer your questions? Answer with a complete sentence.
   Sample answer: Many enslaved Africans turned to religion to give them strength and inspiration.

Unit Resources 61 Use with *United States History*, pp. 210–215

Lesson 4 Vocabulary/Study Guide

TEST PREP

Vocabulary and Study Guide

Vocabulary

Solve the clue and write the answer in the blank. Then find the word in the puzzle. Look up, down, forward, and backward. Look for a bonus word!

1. An African American religious folk song spiritual
2. A plant used to color clothing blue indigo
3. An area where rivers rise and fall with ocean tides tidewater
4. A person who directs the work of other people overseer

Bonus Word: banjo

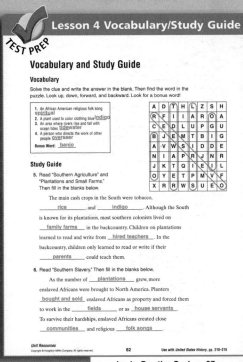

A	D	T	H	L	Z	S	H
R	F	I	I	A	R	O	A
C	E	D	L	U	P	G	U
B	J	E	M	T	B	I	G
A	V	W	S	I	D	D	E
N	I	A	P	R	J	N	R
J	K	T	Q	I	E	I	L
O	Y	E	T	P	M	V	F
X	R	R	W	S	U	E	O

Study Guide

5. Read "Southern Agriculture" and "Plantations and Small Farms." Then fill in the blanks below.

   The main cash crops in the South were tobacco, rice, and indigo. Although the South is known for its plantations, most southern colonists lived on family farms in the backcountry. Children on plantations learned to read and write from hired teachers. In the backcountry, children only learned to read or write if their parents could teach them.

6. Read "Southern Slavery." Then fill in the blanks below.

   As the number of plantations grew, more enslaved Africans were brought to North America. Planters bought and sold enslaved Africans as property and forced them to work in the fields or as house servants. To survive their hardships, enslaved Africans created close communities and religious folk songs.

Unit Resources 62 Use with *United States History*, pp. 210–215

also in *Practice Book*, p. 37

Chapter 6 Assessment Options

Chapter 6 Test

TEST PREP

Chapter 6 Test

Test Your Knowledge

proprietor	laborer	refuge	spiritual

Write *T* if the statement is true or *F* if it is false.

1. T James, the Duke of York, was once proprietor of present-day New York and New Jersey. Obj. U3–8
2. F A laborer is someone who studies to master a skill or business. Obj. U3–13
3. F Calvert hoped to make Georgia a refuge for Catholics. Obj. U3–15
4. T Enslaved Africans would combine Christian beliefs and musical traditions from Africa to create a spiritual. Obj. U3–18

Circle the letter of the best answer.

5. How did William Penn gain land to form a colony? Obj. U3–9
   - A. The Duke of York gave Penn a colony.
   - B. The Duke of York gave Penn a part of New Jersey.
   - C. King Charles gave the Quakers a part of England.
   - (D.) King Charles repaid a debt by giving Penn a piece of land.

6. Why did the Middle Colonies become a place where many different people lived? Obj. U3–12
   - F. The king of England wanted the colonies to be diverse.
   - (G.) The proprietors believed in religious tolerance.
   - H. New England was full, which caused many people to move south.
   - J. Many white colonists began moving south to start plantations.

7. Which of the following is true about life in the Middle Colonies? Obj. U3–13
   - A. Farmers did not grow enough food.
   - (B.) The government decided how colonists should do business.
   - C. Many young people who lived in cities became apprentices.
   - D. Artisans worked on docks and in laundries.

8. Why was Virginia's government important? Obj. U3–14
   - (F.) It had the first elected legislature in the colonies.
   - G. It was the first government to separate church and state.
   - H. It was the first government to make laws for religious tolerance.
   - J. It was the first colony to give every adult male the right to vote.

Chapter 6 Test

TEST PREP

Apply Your Knowledge

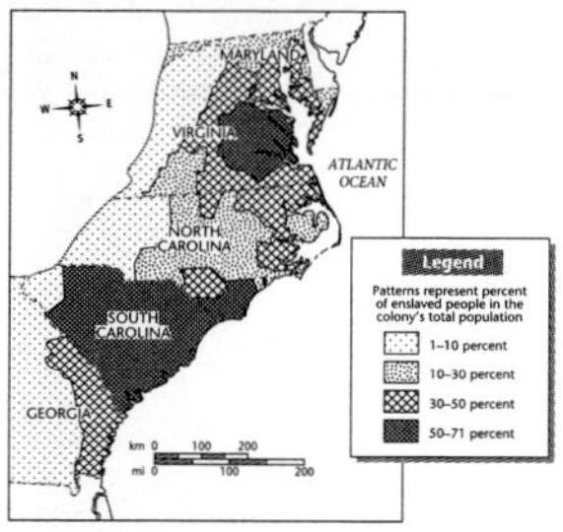

Use the map to answer the following questions.

9. Which of the following colonies had the largest population of enslaved people? Obj. U3–18
   - A. Maryland
   - B. North Carolina
   - C. Georgia
   - (D.) South Carolina

10. What knowledge did enslaved African people bring to South Carolina and Georgia? Obj. U3–17
    - F. methods of growing indigo
    - G. methods of trade
    - (H.) methods of growing rice
    - J. methods of growing tobacco

Apply the Reading Skill: Cause and Effect

Read the passage below. Then answer the question. Obj. U3–9

> For the location of Philadelphia, Penn chose the site where the Delaware and Schuylkill rivers meet. Ships bringing goods from other colonies and from Europe could land in the excellent harbor formed by these rivers. During the 1700s, Philadelphia became a center of trade. It was soon the largest city in all the colonies.

11. What caused Philadelphia to become the largest city in the colonies?
    Sample answer: It was built in an excellent location to become a center for trade.

Chapter 6 Test

TEST PREP

Test the Skill: Make a Decision

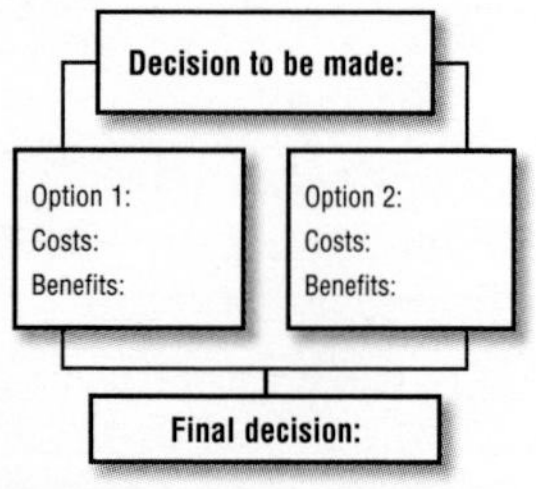

12. When William Penn founded Pennsylvania, he allowed colonists to speak and worship freely. Name another decision he made. Obj. U3–10
    Sample answer: He let colonists elect representatives.

13. What was one benefit of his decision to allow free speech? Obj. U3–10
    Sample answer: People would not have to go to jail for expressing their religious beliefs or opinions.

14. What was one cost of this decision? Obj. U3–10
    Sample answer: Penn and other colonists might have to live with and tolerate people whose beliefs they did not agree with.

Apply the Skill

15. How do you think the decisions William Penn made in Pennsylvania have influenced the history of the United States? Obj. U3–11
    Sample answer: Other colonies would follow his example. People today still enjoy religious freedoms.

Chapter 6 Test

TEST PREP

Think and Write

16. **Short Response:** Explain why agriculture became the main focus of the economy in the South. Obj. U3–16
    Sample answer: Agriculture became the main focus of the economy in the South because of the long growing season, warm climate, and fertile tidewater region. Crops such as rice, tobacco, and indigo grew well under these conditions.

17. **Critical Thinking: Draw Conclusions** What did Benjamin Franklin start in his community that you can find in your community today? Obj. U3–9
    Sample answer: He started a library, a fire company, and a hospital.

18. **Extended Response:** Write three paragraphs to compare and contrast a small farm and a plantation. Write your paragraphs on a separate sheet of paper. Obj. U3–17 Paragraphs may refer to the following: Plantation: many buildings, many enslaved Africans, huge cash crops, children had teachers, children learned to dance, ride, and sing; Family farm: whole family worked, few servants, food crops, small cash crops, children learned to plow and cook, children learned to read and write from parents; Similarities: Both grew crops.

Self-Assessment

Am I able to apply the skill Make a Decision to my own decision making? Why or why not?

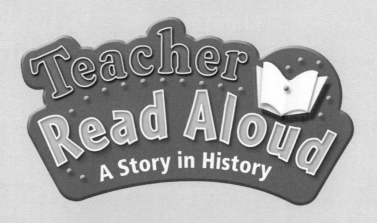

Teacher Read Aloud
A Story in History

You can read the following fiction selection to students before beginning the chapter.

Activate Prior Knowledge
Ask students to share what they know about apprentices. Explain that the Read-Aloud selection tells the story of a boy about to become an apprentice.

Preview the Chapter
Have students skim the first paragraph on page 199. Ask them how the selection reflects the information in this paragraph.

Read-Aloud Vocabulary
Explain that an **artisan** is skilled at making something by hand, such as wooden furniture or silverware. An **apprentice** learns a skill or business from an artisan or other master.

Preview the Reading Strategy
Monitor/Clarify Explain to students that the reading strategy they will use in this chapter is monitor/clarify. When they use this strategy, students pause during their reading and check their understanding. You may wish to use the Read Aloud to model the strategy.

Think Aloud *I've read the first paragraph, and I want to make sure I understand what's happening. Thomas is standing in front of a door, but he doesn't want to knock. He would like to run away. I can tell that he is afraid, but I don't know why, or whose door he is in front of. I'll keep reading to clarify these questions.*

Thomas, the New Apprentice

Thomas stood in front of the carved wooden door. He did not want to knock. *I'd run away, but I doubt my legs would carry me, so weak with fear they are,* he thought.

He leaped back as the door swung open suddenly. A girl of about his age, with bright green eyes and brown hair, seemed surprised to see someone just standing there on her doorstep. She tipped her head to one side.

"Pardon, miss," Thomas managed to say. "Is this where Master Nicholson lives? The **artisan**?"

"Yes, it is," the girl said. "But who are you?"

Thomas hurriedly removed his hat. "Thomas Fleming, miss. I'm to be Master Nicholson's **apprentice.**"

The girl smiled and Thomas felt the fear leave him. "Well, Thomas Fleming, welcome. I am Faith Nicholson." She turned and called over her shoulder. "Papa! The new apprentice is here!"

"Tell him to come in!" replied a voice from deep within the house.

Faith stood aside and said, "Come, I'll introduce you to Papa. He's cutting wood for a fine table for the governor. He'll be happy you're here."

Thomas stepped over the threshold into a new life.

Begin the Chapter

Quick Look

Core Lesson 1 describes the founding of the Middle Colonies.

Core Lesson 2 tells what life was like in the Middle Colonies.

Core Lesson 3 describes the founding of the Southern Colonies.

Core Lesson 4 describes life in the South, with a focus on its agricultural basis.

Vocabulary Preview

Use the vocabulary cards to preview the key vocabulary words before starting the lessons and to prepare students to understand the content of the chapter.

Vocabulary Strategy

Vocabulary strategies for this chapter:

- Structural analysis, p. 204
- Synonyms/antonyms, p. 189, 198
- Root words, p. 203, 214
- Prefixes and suffixes, p. 190, 198

Vocabulary Help

Vocabulary card for artisan Explain that an artisan is not technically an artist; rather, he or she is a skilled craftsperson who works in metal, fibers, wood (as shown) or other materials.

Vocabulary card for refuge Point out to students that a common use of refuge today is in the term wildlife refuge, a safe place for wild creatures to live.

Chapter 6 Middle and Southern Colonies

Vocabulary Preview

Technology
e • glossary
e • word games
www.eduplace.com/kids/hmss05/

representative

In 1702, the colonists of New York and New Jersey elected to speak and act for them. Each **representative** voted on laws for the colonists. **page 189**

artisan

In the Middle Colonies of Philadelphia and New York, skilled **artisans** made items such as silver spoons and boots. **page 198**

Chapter Timeline

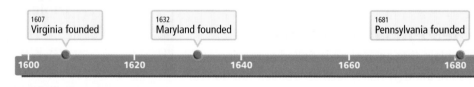

1607 Virginia founded

1632 Maryland founded

1681 Pennsylvania founded

1600 — 1620 — 1640 — 1660 — 1680

Background

Religious Toleration

- Unlike Puritan Massachusetts, the Middle Colonies were known for their tolerance of other religions.
- William Penn founded Pennsylvania in 1682, and called it a "holy experiment"—holy because it was governed according to Quaker beliefs, and an experiment because success was not guaranteed.

Vocabulary

Students can use a frame game graphic organizer to further their understanding of the vocabulary.

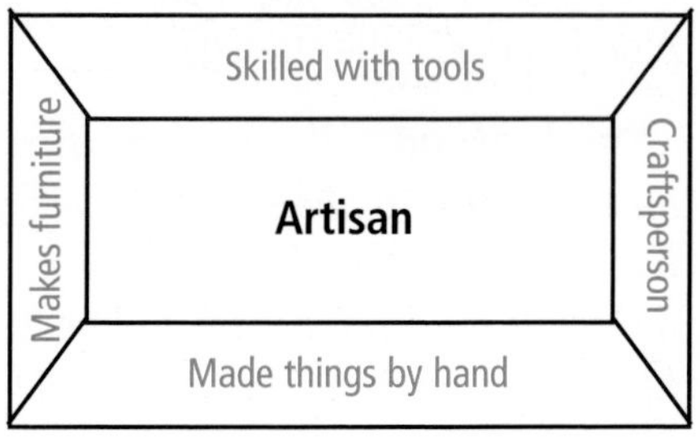

Reading Strategy

Monitor and Clarify Use this strategy to check your understanding.

Quick Tip If you are confused about events in a lesson, reread or read ahead.

legislature

Virginia had a **legislature** called the House of Burgesses. This group met in a building where they wrote and changed laws.
page 203

indigo

Indigo was an important crop in the Southern colonies. People bought it because it could be made into a blue dye to color cloth.
page 214

1702 New Jersey created

1732 Georgia founded

1700 1720 1740

Leveled Practice

Extra Support

Have students work in pairs to create word-search puzzles that include the vocabulary words. They can share their puzzles with other pairs and challenge them to find the words. Verbal-linguistic

Challenge

Encourage students to role-play immigrants from various countries who have arrived in the colonies. Have them introduce themselves and tell where they came from, and why. Bodily-kinesthetic

ELL

All Proficiency Levels

- Have students use a globe to find Germany, Scotland, Ireland, England, France, the Netherlands, Sweden, and Finland.
- Have them use a map of the U.S. to find the regions discussed in this chapter.

Visual-Spatial

Using the Timeline

- Have students study the timeline that appears on pages 186 and 187. With a partner, have them compare this timeline to the one on pages 158 and 159. Ask, What time periods do these timelines cover? What do they have in common?
- You may decide to have the students construct a timeline that encompasses the events from both Chapter 5 and Chapter 6.

Reading Strategy: Monitor/Clarify

To monitor and clarify, the reader reviews the material after reading and draws out important information. The reader also asks questions about the material, to determine what he or she understands or needs clarification on.

Students can practice this reading strategy throughout this chapter, including on their Skill and Strategy pages.

Tested Objectives

U3-8 History Describe the founding and government of New York and New Jersey.

U3-9 History Explain the roles of William Penn and Ben Franklin in the early history of Pennsylvania and Philadelphia.

Quick Look

This lesson describes the ways that proprietors solved the problem of governing their colonies.

Teaching Option: Students may read more about Benjamin Franklin in **Extend Lesson 1.**

1 Get Set to Read

Preview Have students look at the map on page 189 and name the Middle Colonies.

Reading Skill: Problem/Solution The solutions of proprietors included selling and renting land.

Build on What You Know Discuss with students how people look after houses, businesses, and land they own. Ask what responsibilities owners have when other people live on their land, and what problems can arise. Explain that proprietors of colonies had to deal with some of these problems.

Vocabulary

proprietor *noun,* a person in charge of a colony's land

representative *noun,* a person chosen by a group to speak or act for them

treaty *noun,* an official agreement between groups or nations

Core Lesson 1

The Middle Colonies

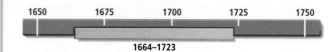

1650 | 1675 | 1700 | 1725 | 1750

1664–1723

VOCABULARY

proprietor
representative
treaty

Vocabulary Strategy

proprietor

To remember **proprietor,** think of the word "property." A proprietor owns property, often land.

READING SKILL
Problem and Solution
Note the **solutions** that English landowners found for the **problem** of governing their American colonies from far away.

PROBLEM	SOLUTIONS

Build on What You Know You know that people can own houses, businesses, or land. In the 1600s, a few wealthy people owned entire colonies.

New York and New Jersey

Main Idea The colonies of New York and New Jersey belonged to English landowners.

English settlement of the Middle Colonies began in 1664, when England captured the Dutch colony of New Netherland. The King of England gave this colony to his brother **James, the Duke of York**. James became the colony's proprietor. A **proprietor** was a person who owned and controlled all the land in a colony. 1

As proprietor of New Netherland, James could do what he liked with the land. He kept part of the large colony and changed its name to New York. He gave the rest to two friends, **John Berkeley** and **George Carteret.** Berkeley and Carteret divided their land into two colonies and named them East Jersey and West Jersey. In 1702, the colonies joined to form New Jersey.

New Amsterdam
After England captured New Amsterdam, it was renamed New York City. Many colonists there dressed and built in the Dutch style.

188 • Chapter 6

Skill and Strategy

Reading Skill and Strategy

Reading Skill: Problem and Solution

This skill helps you see what problems some people faced and how they resolved them.

Read "New York and New Jersey." Then fill in the problem and solution chart below. How did the owners of New York and New Jersey deal with the colonists from England?

Problem	Solutions
Owners of New York and New Jersey lived in England.	1. Owners divided the land and sold pieces to the colonists. 2. Owners set up a council to help the governor make decisions.

Reading Strategy: Monitor and Clarify

3. Read "New York and New Jersey." Then check the statement that best clarifies the section.
   - ✓ The Duke of York changed the name of New Netherland to New York.
   - ___ After 1702, New Jersey split into East Jersey and West Jersey.
   - ___ The colonists were not represented in the government of New York and New Jersey.
4. Read "Pennsylvania and Delaware." Then check the statement that best clarifies the section.
   - ___ Benjamin Franklin wanted Pennsylvania to become part of Canada.
   - ___ American Indians disliked the Penn colony and waged war against its citizens.
   - ✓ Delaware was once part of William Penn's land.

Unit Resources

54
Use with *United States History*, pp. 188–191

Unit Resources, p. 54

Background

Quakers in England

- Quakers faced great persecution in England. Between 1661 and 1685, at least 15,000 of them were imprisoned there.
- William Penn used his connections to the king and other government officials to fight laws that persecuted Quakers in England.

The proprietors of New York and New Jersey all wanted to make money from their colonies. They decided to divide the
2 fertile land into smaller pieces and sell or rent the pieces to colonists to farm.

Because proprietors lived in England, it was difficult for them to control their faraway property. Their solution was to pick governors in the colonies to rule them. Each governor chose a small group of people called a council to help make important decisions.

The proprietors also allowed colonists to elect representatives to an assembly. A **representative** is someone who is chosen to speak and act for others. The assembly helped the governor and council make laws, but it did not have much power. Even so, the assembly was an important step toward self-government.

Pennsylvania and Delaware

Main Idea William Penn founded Pennsylvania as a place where people could worship freely.

The colony of Pennsylvania was the idea of **William Penn.** In England, Penn was a member of a religious group called the Society of Friends, or Quakers. Quakers believed that all Christians should be free to worship in their own way. Penn and many Quakers were put in jail for their beliefs. Some were even killed. In England, everyone was supposed to belong to the Church of England.

Penn hoped to start a colony where all Christians could live together in peace. In North America, he thought, there might
be a place "for such a holy experiment." 3

In 1681, Penn's wish came true. King Charles II had owed money to Penn's family. The king repaid Penn by giving him a large piece of land in the Middle Colonies. The region was called Pennsylvania, which means "Penn's woods." The Duke of York later gave Penn even more land. For a time this land was part of Pennsylvania, but later it became the colony of Delaware.

REVIEW How did colonists in New York and New Jersey take part in government? Colonists elected representatives to assemblies.

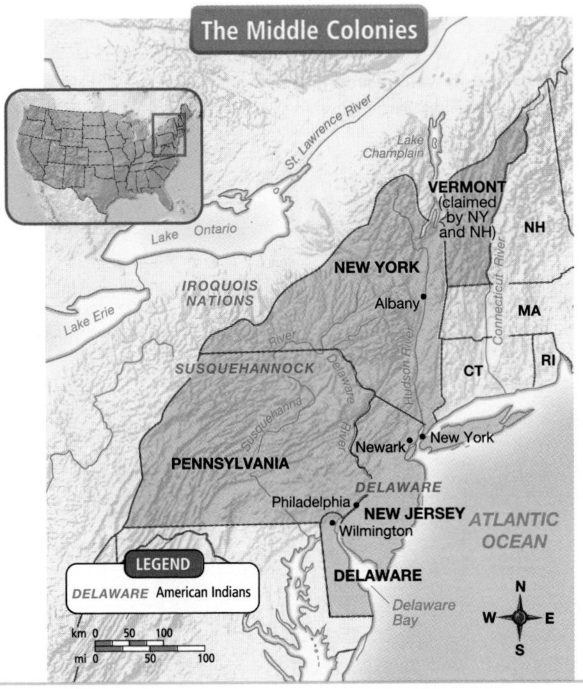

The Middle Colonies The Middle Colonies had good ports and lots of rich, rolling farmland.

SKILL Reading Maps Along which river was Philadelphia built? the Delaware River

2 Teach

New York and New Jersey

Talk About It

1 **Q History** How did the Duke of York become proprietor of New Netherland?

A He received the colony from his brother, the King of England.

2 **Q Economics** How did the Middle Colonies' proprietors hope to make money?

A by selling and renting the land to farmers

Pennsylvania and Delaware

Talk About It

3 **Q History** Why did Penn call his colony a "holy experiment"?

A He wanted to start a colony where all Christians could live together peacefully.

Vocabulary Strategy

proprietor Tell students that the proprietor of a store is the store's owner.

representative Remind students that we still elect people to *represent*, or speak and act, for us in government.

Reading Strategy: Monitor/Clarify
Explain to students that monitoring their reading helps them make sure that they understand information.

Think Aloud *The first page of this lesson says that proprietors controlled colonies' lands. It does not say how the colonists felt about this. I'll look for that information as I read.*

Leveled Practice

Extra Support

William Penn tried to understand the culture of the Lenni Lenape. Have students **research the culture** of these American Indians. Ask students to make a diorama depicting clothing, dwellings, and habitat. Visual-spatial

Challenge

Have students research Franklin's wise sayings. Ask students to **select three** and write a paragraph explaining each one. They may want to illustrate the sayings. Visual-spatial

ELL

Beginning

Place several small possessions on a desk, and model the meaning of *own* and *owner.* Explain that *proprietor* means almost the same as *owner.* Have students **create sentences** using *own, owner,* and *owns.*

Verbal-linguistic

Pennsylvania and Delaware *continued*

Talk About It

4 Q Citizenship In what way did Penn contribute to self-government?

A He gave the Pennsylvania Assembly the power to approve or reject laws.

5 Q Geography In what ways did geography contribute to the growth of Philadelphia as a center of trade?

A The city had an excellent harbor; roads were well designed and easy to travel.

6 Q History What was *Poor Richard's Almanack?*

A a popular book by Benjamin Franklin containing stories, jokes, and sayings

Vocabulary Strategy

treaty Explain that the plural form of a word ending in consonant + *y* is usually made by changing the *y* to *i* and adding *-es.* So, *treaty* becomes *treaties.*

Critical Thinking

Draw Conclusions Why do you think William Penn wanted to create a good relationship with the Lenni Lenape?

4 In Pennsylvania, Penn created laws that allowed colonists to voice their opinions and worship freely. Penn also let colonists elect representatives to an assembly, as colonists did in New York and New Jersey. The Pennsylvania Assembly, however, had more power. It could approve or reject laws that the governor and his council suggested.

Penn treated American Indians with respect. He tried to understand their culture and wanted colonists to live with them as equals. Penn made fair treaties with the Delaware, or Lenni Lenape (LEN ee LEN uh pee) Indians when he bought land from them. A **treaty** is an official agreement between nations or groups. Penn's fairness helped Pennsylvania's colonists and Indians live together peacefully for many years.

Philadelphia

William Penn did more than give Pennsylvania colonists a representative government. He also planned the colony's first large city, Philadelphia.

For the location of Philadelphia, Penn chose a site where the Delaware and Schuylkill (SKOO kill) rivers meet. Ships bringing goods from other colonies and from Europe could land in the excellent harbor formed by these rivers. Penn designed wide, straight roads that made it easy to travel throughout the city. 5 During the 1700s, Philadelphia became a center of trade. Soon it was the largest city in all the colonies.

Benjamin Franklin was Philadelphia's most famous citizen. He moved from Boston to Philadelphia in 1723. There, Franklin bought his own printing press.

Philadelphia William Penn (left) was the proprietor of Pennsylvania. He founded the city of Philadelphia shown below.

Math

A Colony Grows

- Ask students to suppose that a colony has a population of 10,000. If its population doubled, how many people would live there? (20,000)
- What if it then tripled its population? (60,000)
- If one-third of the colonists then moved away, how many would remain? (one-third of 60,000 = 20,000; 60,000 − 20,000 = 40,000)

Logical-mathematical

Language Arts

American Indian Legends

- Have students read traditional stories from Northeast American Indians.
- These may include trickster stories and creation myths.
- Then have students discuss the stories. Have them point out any lessons that could be learned from the characters' actions.

Verbal-linguistic

Franklin published a newspaper and a popular book of stories, jokes, and
6 sayings called *Poor Richard's Almanack*. One of his well-known sayings is,

> "Early to bed and early to rise, makes a man healthy, wealthy, and wise."

Franklin had many other interests, too. He helped start Philadelphia's first public library, fire company, and hospital. He was also a talented scientist and inventor. In a famous experiment, he flew a kite in a lightning storm to show that lightning was a form of electricity. He invented a wood stove, a clock, and many other useful things. Franklin became famous for his many achievements.

REVIEW How did the government of Pennsylvania differ from those of New York and New Jersey? The Pennsylvania assembly had more power.

Benjamin Franklin
He founded the Union Fire Company in 1736 to make Philadelphia a safer city.

Lesson Summary

- Proprietors owned the Middle Colonies.
- William Penn founded Pennsylvania as a place where colonists had religious freedom.
- Philadelphia became the biggest city in the British colonies, and Benjamin Franklin was its most famous citizen.

Why It Matters . . .

Today people still enjoy the religious freedoms that were practiced in Pennsylvania.

Lesson Review

1664 England takes New Netherland

1702 New Jersey formed

1723 Franklin moves to Philadelphia

1650 — 1675 — 1700 — 1725 — 1750

1. **VOCABULARY** Choose the correct words to complete each sentence.
   treaty **representative** **proprietor**
   William Penn was the _______ of Pennsylvania. He made a _______ with the Lenni Lenape.
2. **READING SKILL** Using your notes, write a paragraph telling how proprietors **solved** the **problem** of governing their faraway colonies.
3. **MAIN IDEA: History** What events led to the founding of New York as an English colony?
4. **MAIN IDEA: Citizenship** Why did William Penn start the colony of Pennsylvania?
5. **PEOPLE TO KNOW** Who was **Benjamin Franklin,** and what were three things that he did for Philadelphia?
6. **TIMELINE SKILL** Did New Jersey become a colony before or after England took control of New Netherland?
7. **CRITICAL THINKING: Draw Conclusions** The name Philadelphia comes from a Greek word that means "brotherly love." Use information from the lesson to tell why Penn might have chosen that name.

HANDS ON **ART ACTIVITY** Create a pamphlet to encourage people to move to Pennsylvania in the 1700s. Include drawings, maps, and persuasive reasons for moving.

3 Review/Assess

Review Tested Objectives

U3-8 Britain captured New Netherland and renamed part of it New York; the rest became New Jersey. Because their proprietors lived far away, the colonies were ruled by governors and small councils; an elected assembly of colonists advised them but had little real power.

U3-9 Penn founded Pennsylvania as a place where people of all religions could voice opinions and worship freely. He planned Philadelphia and worked for peace with local American Indians. Franklin was a publisher, scientist, and inventor.

Lesson Review Answers

1. proprietor; treaty
2. Paragraphs should include reference to governors, assemblies, and councils.
3. The English conquered the Dutch colony of New Netherland and renamed part of it New York.
4. to provide a place where all Christians could live in peace
5. Franklin was an inventor, scientist, and writer. He started the city's first public library, hospital, and fire department.
6. after
7. Answers should show awareness of Penn's belief in religious tolerance.

HANDS ON Performance Task Rubric

4	Pamphlet is very persuasive; includes many drawings, maps, and reasons for moving; mechanics are correct.
3	Pamphlet is persuasive; includes several drawings, maps, and reasons for moving; mechanics are mostly correct.
2	Pamphlet is somewhat persuasive; includes one or two drawings, maps, and reasons for moving; some errors in mechanics.
1	Pamphlet is not very persuasive; drawings, maps, and reasons for moving are absent; many errors in mechanics.

Study Guide/Homework

Vocabulary and Study Guide

Vocabulary

1. proprietor A person who owned and controlled all the land of a colony
2. representative Someone who is chosen to speak and act for others
3. treaty An official agreement between nations or groups
4. Use two of the words in a sentence.
   Sample answer: The proprietor of New Jersey allowed the colonists to elect a representative.

Study Guide

Read "New York and New Jersey." Then fill in the chart below to show how government worked in the colonies of New York and New Jersey.

The proprietor chooses a governor for the colony. → 5. The governor chooses a small council. → 6. Colonists elect representatives to an assembly. → 7. The assembly helps the governor and council make laws.

Read "Pennsylvania and Delaware." Then fill in the chart below with each person's contribution to the Middle Colonies.

William Penn	Benjamin Franklin
8. Founded Pennsylvania; Allowed religious freedom; Treated American Indians with respect; Planned the city of Philadelphia	9. Helped start Philadelphia's first library, fire company, and hospital; Experimented with electricity; Invented wood stove and clock

Unit Resources

55
Use with *United States History*, pp. 188–191

Unit Resources, p. 55

Reteach Minilesson

Use a chart to compare and contrast the Middle Colonies.

New York and New Jersey	Pennsylvania
Purpose: make money	Purpose: religious freedom
Colonists: not much political power	Colonists: more political power

Graphic Organizer 1

Quick Look

Connect to the Core Lesson Students have learned about the Middle Colonies, including Pennsylvania. In this Extend Lesson, students will learn more about the inventions of Philadelphia's most famous citizen and our nation's statesman, Ben Franklin.

1 Teach the Extend Lesson

Connect to the Big Idea

Influences on History Few people have had as strong an effect on the development of our nation as Ben Franklin, statesman, public servant, scientist, inventor, and printer. Typically, Franklin's scientific inventions sprang from necessity, improving the quality of life for him and for others. Many of them are still used today.

Technology

Benjamin Franklin: Inventor

Thunder rumbles overhead. A bolt of lightning brightens the night sky. Thanks to lightning rods, invented by Benjamin Franklin, the lightning will probably not damage any buildings.

Today, Ben Franklin is remembered for the important role he played in the struggle for independence. But did you know that he was also a famous scientist and inventor?

Franklin's inventions helped to improve people's lives. Five of them are shown here. Which ones are still used today?

Battery
Franklin's experiments with electricity led to the creation of the first battery. It could store electricity for later use.

Odometer
This machine measured how far people traveled by counting the revolutions of wagon wheels. It led to the modern car odometer.

Reaching All Learners

Extra Support

Draw Inventions

- Explain that Franklin was a keen problem solver. Many of his inventions improved people's lives.
- Use a **word web** to brainstorm with students devices that would help improve people's lives.
- Have students draw diagrams of their inventions, including a title, a description, and an explanation of how it improves living.

Visual-spatial

On Level

Create Safety Posters

- Explain that Franklin's experiment with the kite proved that lightning is electricity, and that electricity can be dangerous.
- Have students research safe behavior around electricity. Have them create posters describing electricity safety tips.
- Work with students to request permission to hang the posters in selected locations within the school.

Verbal-linguistic

Challenge

Compare Inventions

- Explain that many of Franklin's inventions are still used today, with present-day improvements and a modern appearance.
- Ask partners to research the contemporary use of one of Franklin's inventions.
- Have pairs use a Venn diagram to compare the original to the current version.

Verbal-linguistic; visual-spatial

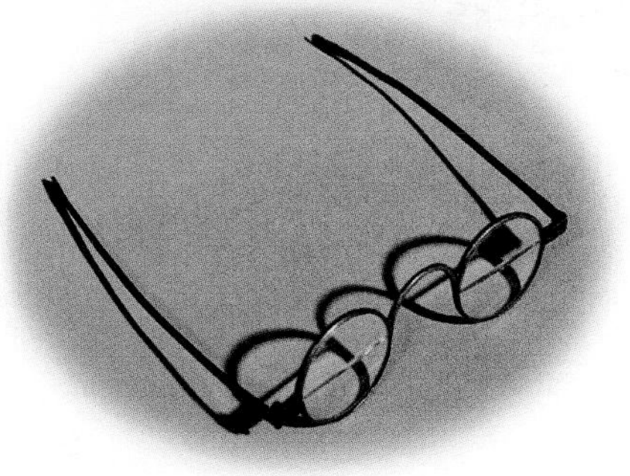

Bifocals
Some people need glasses to see both up close and far away. Franklin combined both types of glasses into a single pair called bifocals.

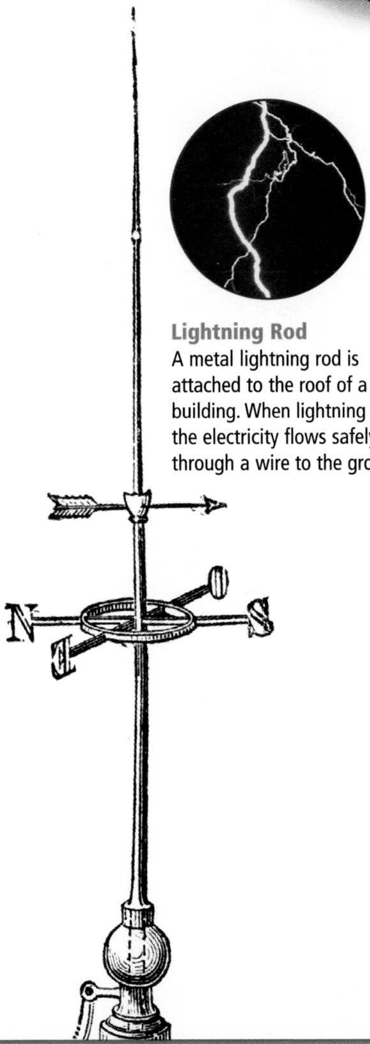

Lightning Rod
A metal lightning rod is attached to the roof of a building. When lightning hits, the electricity flows safely through a wire to the ground.

Pennsylvanian Fireplace
Franklin created an iron box with air chambers inside to spread heat more evenly.

Activities

1. **TALK ABOUT IT** Which of Benjamin Franklin's inventions do you think is the most useful? Why?
2. **REPORT IT** If you could interview Benjamin Franklin, what would you ask him about his inventions? Write your questions and his answers in the form of a radio or television interview.

2 Leveled Activities

1 Talk About It *For Extra Support*
Students' answers should name the invention that they consider to be the most useful. Students should note that all of the inventions pictured here are used today, although many have a modern form.

2 Report It *For Challenge*

Writing Rubric

4	Interview format includes thoughtful questions and answers; main points clearly stated, with supporting details; mechanics are correct.
3	Interview format includes questions and answers; main points adequately stated, with some supporting details; few errors in mechanics.
2	Interview format is attempted; main points stated, but with few supporting details; some errors in mechanics.
1	Interview format is not used; main points not stated; details contain errors; many errors in mechanics.

ELL

REACHING ALL LEARNERS

Intermediate/Advanced

- Have students learn more about Ben Franklin by **researching** his life and accomplishments.
- Have small groups use library and Internet resources to discover facts about Franklin and write them on 3" x 5" index cards.
- Then, have students **create a board game** using the information they have discovered.

Verbal-linguistic

Music

Play an Instrument

- Have students replicate the sound of the glass harmonica, a musical instrument that Franklin invented after he heard music performed on wine glasses in England.
- Assemble a set of glass bottles, and add water to varying levels. Demonstrate, and then have students lightly tap the bottles, blow across the tops, or gently rub a wet finger around the openings.

Musical-auditory

Graphic Organizer

Invention	Improved Technology
Tabletop Chair	Combines chair and desk, for comfort in writing activities
Odometer	Measures the distance a vehicle travels
Lightning Rod	Attracts lightning on a rooftop; carries the electricity, through a wire, into the ground
Bifocals	Lets people see up close and far away while using one pair of glasses
Pennsylvanian Fireplace	Spreads fireplace heat more evenly

www.eduplace.com/ss/hmss05/

✔ Tested Objective

U3-10 Use cost and benefit analyses to make decisions.

U3-11 Understand how decisions can influence historical events.

1 Teach the Skill

- Have volunteers discuss examples of challenging decisions they or people they know have faced. Encourage students to explain how they or the other people made these decisions.
- Note that making decisions requires clear thinking. Sometimes it may be difficult to think clearly about all the aspects of a decision.
- Explain that a chart or a diagram can help students organize their information and make the best decision.
- Have students discuss the steps under "Learn the Skill." You may wish to write the chart on the board with a sample decision and its costs and benefits.

Skills

Make a Decision

VOCABULARY
cost
benefit

Europeans had to think about many things before deciding to move to the Middle Colonies. They had to choose from several possible actions and consider the costs and benefits of each. A cost is a loss or sacrifice. A benefit is a gain or advantage. The steps below will help you understand one way to make a decision.

Learn the Skill

Step 1: Identify the decision to be made. Think about why it has to be made.

Step 2: Gather information. What do you need to know to make the decision? Can research or other people help you to decide?

Step 3: Think of the options that you have.

Step 4: Consider the costs and benefits of each option.

Step 5: Choose an option. Which one has the most benefits and the fewest costs? Important decisions may include some uncertainty about which option to choose.

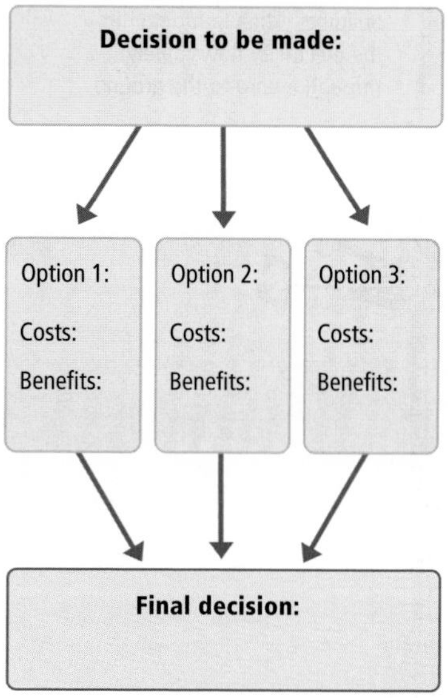

194 • Chapter 6

Leveled Practice

Extra Support

Have students think of a decision that would be difficult to make. Ask them to write a summary of the decision and to ask the class for advice about it. **Verbal-linguistic**

Challenge

Explain that sometimes several decisions must be made at the same time. Have partners think of situations when this could happen and discuss how multiple decisions could affect each other. **Verbal-linguistic**

ELL

Intermediate

Explain that *cost* and *benefit* have more than one meaning. *Cost* often refers to the price of an item or service. *Benefit* can mean a party that raises money for a charity. Companies also give special "benefits" such as paid health care to their employees. Help students write sentences using these words to show their different meanings.

Verbal-linguistic

Practice the Skill

What decisions do you think people had to make when coming to the Middle Colonies? Consider each person described below. Decide whether each one should leave Europe and move to the colony of Pennsylvania. Use a chart like the one on page 194 as you think about the costs and benefits of each person's options.

1. Quaker woman from England who is not allowed to practice her religious beliefs
2. Young German man who knows how to farm but has no land
3. Wealthy English man who will inherit a lot of land in a few years

Apply the Skill

Choose a current issue that people must make a decision about. You might choose a topic about the environment, your town's use of money, or some other important issue. Fill out a chart like the one on the page 194. Write a paragraph explaining your decision and how you made it.

2 Practice the Skill

Answers will vary. For each person, students should identify costs and benefits of each person staying in Europe and going to Pennsylvania. Students will likely decide that the Quaker woman and the German man should go to Pennsylvania and that the English man should stay in England.

3 Apply the Skill

Ask students to make a decision on a current issue facing the nation or your community. Students should create a chart listing options, costs, and benefits. Then have students write a paragraph explaining their decision. When evaluating students' charts and paragraphs, consider:

- Did the student clearly explain the issue?
- Did the student outline the possible options and the costs and benefits of each one?
- Did the student explain his or her decision and decision-making process?

Skill Practice

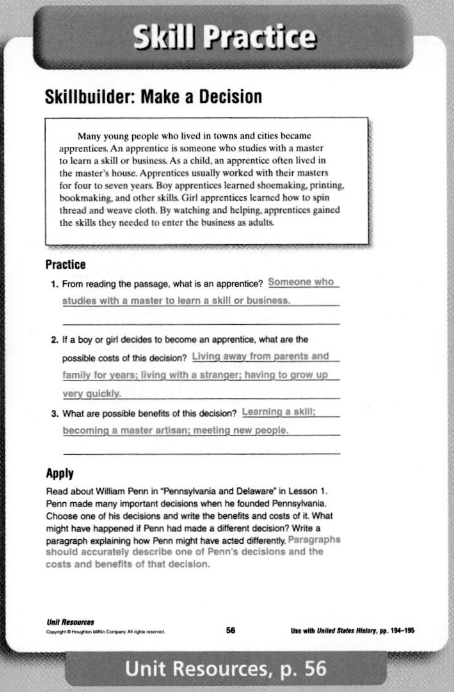

Skillbuilder: Make a Decision

Many young people who lived in towns and cities became apprentices. An apprentice is someone who studies with a master to learn a skill or business. As a child, an apprentice often lived in the master's house. Apprentices usually worked with their masters for four to seven years. Boy apprentices learned shoemaking, printing, bookmaking, and other skills. Girl apprentices learned how to spin thread and weave cloth. By watching and helping, apprentices gained the skills they needed to enter the business as adults.

Practice

1. From reading the passage, what is an apprentice? Someone who studies with a master to learn a skill or business.
2. If a boy or girl decides to become an apprentice, what are the possible costs of this decision? Living away from parents and family for years; living with a stranger; having to grow up very quickly.
3. What are possible benefits of this decision? Learning a skill; becoming a master artisan; meeting new people.

Apply

Read about William Penn in "Pennsylvania and Delaware" in Lesson 1. Penn made many important decisions when he founded Pennsylvania. Choose one of his decisions and write the benefits and costs of it. What might have happened if Penn had made a different decision? Write a paragraph explaining how Penn might have acted differently. Paragraphs should accurately describe one of Penn's decisions and the costs and benefits of that decision.

Unit Resources

56
Use with *United States History*, pp. 194–195

Unit Resources, p. 56

Skill Transparency

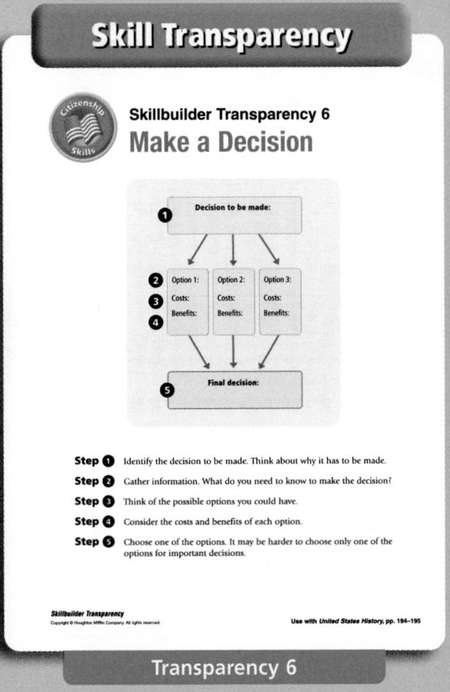

Skillbuilder Transparency 6

Make a Decision

Step 1 Identify the decision to be made. Think about why it has to be made.
Step 2 Gather information. What do you need to know to make the decision?
Step 3 Think of the possible options you could have.
Step 4 Consider the costs and benefits of each option.
Step 5 Choose one of the options. It may be harder to choose only one of the options for important decisions.

Skillbuilder Transparency

Use with *United States History*, pp. 194–195

Transparency 6

Tested Objectives

U3-12 Culture Describe and explain the diversity of the Middle Colonies.

U3-13 Culture Compare life, including work and education, on farms and in cities in the Middle Colonies.

Lesson Quick Look

This lesson describes the diverse population of the Middle Colonies and explores how people made a living.

Teaching Option: **Extend Lesson 2** shows students what life was like for a typical apprentice.

1 Get Set to Read

Preview Have students look at the chart on page 197. Ask what it shows about religion in the Middle Colonies.

Reading Skill: Cause and Effect Causes included religious tolerance and the availability of good farmland.

Build on What You Know Ask students to recall a time when they joined a group, such as a club or a sports team. Discuss how they felt about being "new" to the group. Ask them how people already in a group can make new people feel welcome.

Vocabulary

free market economy *noun,* economy in which citizens decide what will be produced, rather than the government

free enterprise *noun,* freedom of people or businesses to earn money by making their own economic decisions

artisan *noun,* someone who is skilled at making something by hand

laborer *noun,* a person whose job requires hard physical work

apprentice *noun,* someone who works for a more experienced person to learn a skill

Core Lesson 2

Life in the Middle Colonies

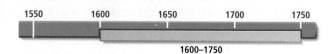

1550 1600 1650 1700 1750

1600–1750

VOCABULARY

free market economy
free enterprise
artisan
laborer
apprentice

Vocabulary Strategy

apprentice

An **apprentice** learns a skill from an expert. Apprentice comes from a word that means "to understand."

READING SKILL

Cause and Effect Take notes on what **caused** many people to come to the Middle Colonies.

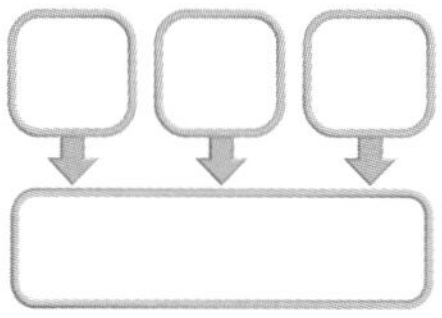

Build on What You Know If you and your family were moving to a new place, wouldn't you want to be accepted? In the 1600s, the Middle Colonies welcomed people of many different religions and countries.

A Mix of People

Main Idea People from many cultures and religions lived in the Middle Colonies.

The people of the Middle Colonies came from many lands. Colonists were German, Dutch, Scots-Irish, Scandinavian, and English. Some were enslaved Africans. Many colonists were Quakers or members of other Protestant churches. Others were Jews and Catholics.

Quaker Meetinghouse Quakers worshipped in meetinghouses. This New Jersey meetinghouse was built in 1683.

Skill and Strategy

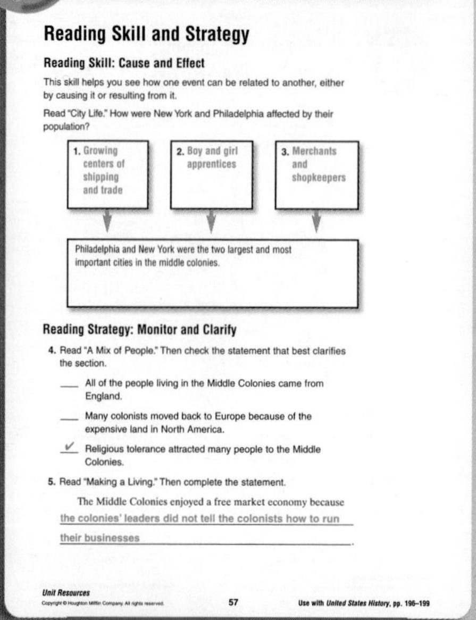

Reading Skill and Strategy

Reading Skill: Cause and Effect

This skill helps you see how one event can be related to another, either by causing it or resulting from it.

Read "City Life." How were New York and Philadelphia affected by their population?

1. Growing centers of shipping and trade
2. Boy and girl apprentices
3. Merchants and shopkeepers

Philadelphia and New York were the two largest and most important cities in the middle colonies.

Reading Strategy: Monitor and Clarify

4. Read "A Mix of People." Then check the statement that best clarifies the section.

___ All of the people living in the Middle Colonies came from England.

___ Many colonists moved back to Europe because of the expensive land in North America.

_✓_ Religious tolerance attracted many people to the Middle Colonies.

5. Read "Making a Living." Then complete the statement.

The Middle Colonies enjoyed a free market economy because the colonies' leaders did not tell the colonists how to run their businesses.

Unit Resources
Copyright © Houghton Mifflin Company. All rights reserved. 57 Use with *United States History*, pp. 196–199

Unit Resources, p. 57

Background

Daily Life

- Children learned to read using simple books called hornbooks or primers. These taught the alphabet, pronunciation of syllables, and simple prayers from the Bible.
- Between 1650 and 1750, the population of the Middle Colonies grew from about 4,000 to about 300,000.

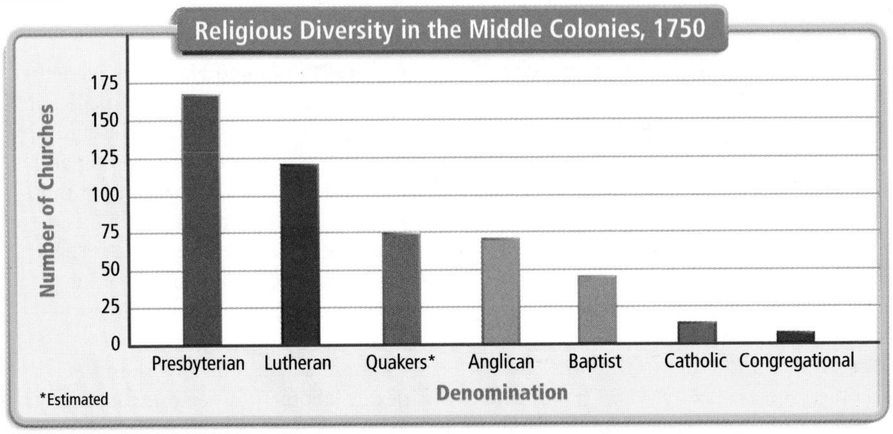

1 **Many People, Many Beliefs** The range of religious beliefs in the Middle Colonies was more diverse than those of New England and the Southern Colonies.

SKILL **Reading Charts** Which religious groups had about the same number of churches? Quakers and Anglican

The Middle Colonies had a diverse population because their proprietors believed in religious tolerance. Tolerance is respecting beliefs and practices that are different from one's own. **William Penn** supported tolerance. He believed that people of all religions should live together in peace. Other proprietors simply wanted colonists to buy or rent their land for farming. These proprietors did not care about colonists' religious beliefs as long as the colonists could pay for the land.

Religious tolerance and inexpensive land attracted people from many parts of Europe. Some came to escape punishment for their religious beliefs. Others came to farm their own land. All came to find a better way of life.

Newcomers to the Middle Colonies usually arrived at the ports of New York or Philadelphia. A few colonists stayed in the cities to find work, but most moved to the countryside to live and work on farms.

Making a Living

Main Idea Most people in the Middle Colonies farmed to earn a living, but cities were important centers of trade.

The climate and soil of the Middle Colonies were excellent for farming. Both men and women spent long hours working in the fields and in the home. As in New England, children helped out as soon as they were old enough. Boys helped plant and harvest crops. Girls cooked, sewed, and did housework. Children also cared for the family's animals and garden. 2 3

Farmers raised livestock such as cattle and pigs. They grew vegetables, fruits, and other crops in the fertile soil. Farmers grew many different grains, such as wheat, corn, and barley. In fact, they grew so much grain used to make bread that the Middle Colonies became known as the "breadbasket" of the thirteen colonies.

REVIEW Why did proprietors allow religious tolerance? It attracted Colonists to the area.

197

2 Teach

A Mix of People

Talk About It

1 **Q Visual Learning** About how many Presbyterian churches were there in the Middle Colonies?
A about 160

Making a Living

Talk About It

2 **Q Geography** What made the Middle Colonies a good place for farming?
A warm climate and fertile soil

3 **Q Economics** What did children do to help on farms?
A Children cared for the animals and the garden.

Reading Strategy: Monitor/Clarify After students read the first page of the lesson, ask them if anything they read did not make sense to them. Help them look back in the text and find answers.

REACHING ALL LEARNERS

Leveled Practice

Extra Support

Ask partners to read, orally or silently, the two main sections of this lesson. Have pairs **complete a graphic organizer** to keep track of the main idea and details in each section. Visual-spatial

Challenge

Have student pairs read the text that describes life in the country and the city. Then have partners **write an essay** that explains how colonists made a living in the country and the city. Verbal-linguistic

REACHING ALL LEARNERS

ELL

Intermediate

- Ask students to think about what it was like living in the Middle Colonies on a farm or in the city.
- Then have them tell three things to a friend, describing a typical day in the Middle Colonies.

Verbal-linguistic

Making a Living *continued*

Talk About It

4 **Q Economics** What could colonists do under the free enterprise system?

A Colonists were free to make their own business decisions.

5 **Q History** What did young people do as apprentices?

A Apprentices learned important work skills while they lived and worked with a master of a trade for four to seven years.

Vocabulary Strategy

free market economy Explain that *market* does not always mean a physical place.

free enterprise Tell students that *enterprise* can mean "a business organization" or "work for the purpose of profit."

artisan A synonym is *craftsperson.*

laborer Tell students that the suffix *-er* in *laborer* means "one who does."

apprentice A synonym is *trainee.*

Critical Thinking

Infer Why do you think the governors and proprietors encouraged free enterprise in their colonies?

Think Aloud *The governors and proprietors wanted their colonies to prosper and become wealthy. They probably thought that by letting people choose their own businesses they could bring more money into the colony.*

Agriculture in the Middle Colonies was so good that farmers usually grew enough to feed their families and still have a surplus. A surplus is more than what is needed. Farmers sold surplus goods to earn a living. Most farmers used the long, wide rivers of the Middle Colonies to ship grain and livestock to sell in Philadelphia or New York. Some colonists also sold wood or furs from their land. Merchants then sold the goods as exports to Europe, the West Indies, and cities in the other British colonies, such as Boston and Charles Town.

The Middle Colonies, like the other English colonies, had a free market economy. In a **free market economy,** the people, not the government, decide what will be produced. The Middle Colonies had a free market economy partly because the colonies' proprietors did not tell
4 colonists what to do. Colonists were free to make the decisions they believed would earn them the most money. The economic system in which people may start any business that they believe will succeed is called **free enterprise.** Enterprise is another word for business.

City Life

Philadelphia and New York were the two largest and most important cities in the Middle Colonies. Both cities had ports and were centers of shipping and trade. The free market economy of these successful cities attracted merchants, shopkeepers, and artisans. An **artisan** is a person who is skilled at making something by hand, such as silver spoons or wooden chairs.

Laborers also found work in the cities. A **laborer** is a person who does hard physical work. Some of the laborers in the Middle Colonies were enslaved Africans. They worked in laundries, as house servants, or on the docks loading and unloading ships.

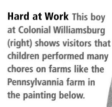

Hard at Work This boy at Colonial Williamsburg (right) shows visitors that children performed many chores on farms like the Pennsylvania farm in the painting below.

198 • Chapter 6

Math

Apprentice Years

- Suppose a ten-year-old girl begins an apprenticeship that will last five years. How old will she be when she finishes? fifteen
- What fraction of her life will she have spent in the apprenticeship? 5 out of 15 years = one-third

Logical-mathematical

Language Arts

Report on an Apprentice

- Have children create a book jacket for a story about the life of an apprentice.
- They should include a title, a summary of the story, and an illustration.

Verbal-linguistic

Colonial Shops Signs like these hung outside artisan workshops. The pictures show what artisans made or repaired, such as furniture and clothing.

5 Many young people who lived in towns and cities became apprentices. An **apprentice** is someone who studies with a master to learn a skill or business. As a child, an apprentice often lived in the master's house. Apprentices usually worked with their masters for four to seven years. Boy apprentices learned skills such as shoemaking, printing, and bookmaking. Girl apprentices learned how to spin thread and weave cloth. By watching and helping, apprentices gained the skills they needed to enter the business as adults.

colonists believed that it was most important for children to learn useful work skills. Parents expected their children to learn a business or run the family farm instead of going to college.

REVIEW Why did colonial children become apprentices? to learn the important work skills they would need as adults

Lesson Summary

The Middle Colonies were a place where people from many different countries could live together and earn a good living. Most colonists were farmers, but New York and Philadelphia were busy centers of shipping and trade. Children learned skills by helping on farms, at home, or as apprentices.

Why It Matters . . .

The diversity of the people in the Middle Colonies would help shape the kind of country the United States would later become.

Lesson Review

1. **VOCABULARY** Write a short paragraph about children's lives in the Middle Colonies, using **artisan** and **apprentice.**
2. **READING SKILL** What **caused** people with different religious beliefs to come to the Middle Colonies?
3. **MAIN IDEA: History** Why were the Middle Colonies known as the breadbasket?
4. **MAIN IDEA: Economics** How did most people in the Middle Colonies earn a living?
5. **PLACES TO KNOW** Why were Philadelphia and New York important cities?
6. **CRITICAL THINKING: Infer** How can a city's religious tolerance affect the growth and daily life of that city?
7. **CRITICAL THINKING: Evaluate** Do you think free enterprise was good for the Middle Colonies? Explain why or why not.

HANDS ON **DRAMA ACTIVITY** Create a dialogue between a 12-year-old colonist and his or her parents about becoming an apprentice. Use what you have learned in this lesson about an apprentice's work.

199

Study Guide/Homework

Vocabulary and Study Guide

Vocabulary

Write the definition of each vocabulary word below.

1. free enterprise People can start any business they want
2. free market economy People decide what to produce
3. artisan A skilled maker of items
4. laborer A person who does hard physical work
5. apprentice Someone who studies with a master
6. Use two words in a sentence.
Sample answer: An apprentice in silversmithing would live with and learn from a master artisan.

Study Guide

Read "A Mix of People." Then answer the questions.

7. Why did the Middle Colonies have a diverse population?
Because colonial proprietors believed in religious tolerance and were willing to sell or rent land to anyone who could afford it

Read "Making a Living." Then fill in the chart below.

Workers in the country	Workers in the city
8. Worked long hours tending crops and caring for livestock; Gathered wood and furs to sell	9. Worked as merchants, shopkeepers, artisans, and laborers in busy shipping and trade centers; Some hired apprentices

Unit Resources 58 Use with *United States History*, pp. 196–199

Unit Resources, p. 58

Reteach Minilesson

Use a compare/contrast chart to reteach life in the Middle Colonies.

Country	City
People lived and worked on farms.	People were involved in shipping and trade.
Children cared for animals and gardens.	Children often became apprentices.

Graphic Organizer 1

3 Review/Assess

Review Tested Objectives

U3-12 Colonists were German, Dutch, Scots-Irish, Scandinavian, English, and African; religious diversity was encouraged.

U3-13 Most people lived in the country and worked on farms; cities were important centers of trade; most children were taught to read and write, and most were expected to learn a business or work on the family farm.

Lesson Review Answers

1. Paragraphs should discuss children's apprenticeship experiences.
2. Answers should discuss tolerance and diversity in the Middle Colonies.
3. Food, especially grain, was grown there easily.
4. They became farmers, merchants, artisans, and laborers.
5. They were centers of shipping and trade.
6. Answers should discuss increased growth and cultural diversity.
7. Sample answer: Yes, because it allowed people to make money however they wished, and the Middle Colonies' economy grew.

HANDS ON Performance Task Rubric

4	Dialogue is well organized and shows considerable creative effort; historical details are accurate.
3	Dialogue is adequately organized and shows creative effort; historical details are mostly accurate.
2	Dialogue is somewhat organized and shows some creative effort; some historical details are absent or inaccurate.
1	Dialogue is disorganized and shows little effort; historical details are absent or inaccurate.

Extend

Quick Look

Connect to the Core Lesson Students have learned that cities were important centers of trade in the Middle Colonies. In Extend Lesson 2, students will learn more about how a boy apprentice gains the skills he will need to own and run a printing business as an adult.

1 Teach the Extend Lesson

Connect to the Big Idea

Individuals and the Economy In the Middle Colonies, people who lived in cities and towns made a living as merchants, shopkeepers, and artisans. Young people became apprentices and studied with a master tradesman to learn skills they would need in business as adults.

History

COLONIAL APPRENTICE

October 17, 1730

Today, 14-year-old Jacob Fielding will learn how to place type into the printing press at the print shop where he lives and works as an apprentice. He is excited and wants to do a good job so he can move up to the level of journeyman. One day he may even become a master at his own print shop. Until then, he will have to pay attention and work hard.

① Master
The master teaches the apprentice his trade, or work. Apprentices live and eat their meals with their masters.

② Apprentice
Apprentices live with their masters for as long as seven years. At first, a printer's apprentice does the messiest jobs, such as inking the press. Over time, an apprentice will learn to set type, or letters, which must be done skillfully.

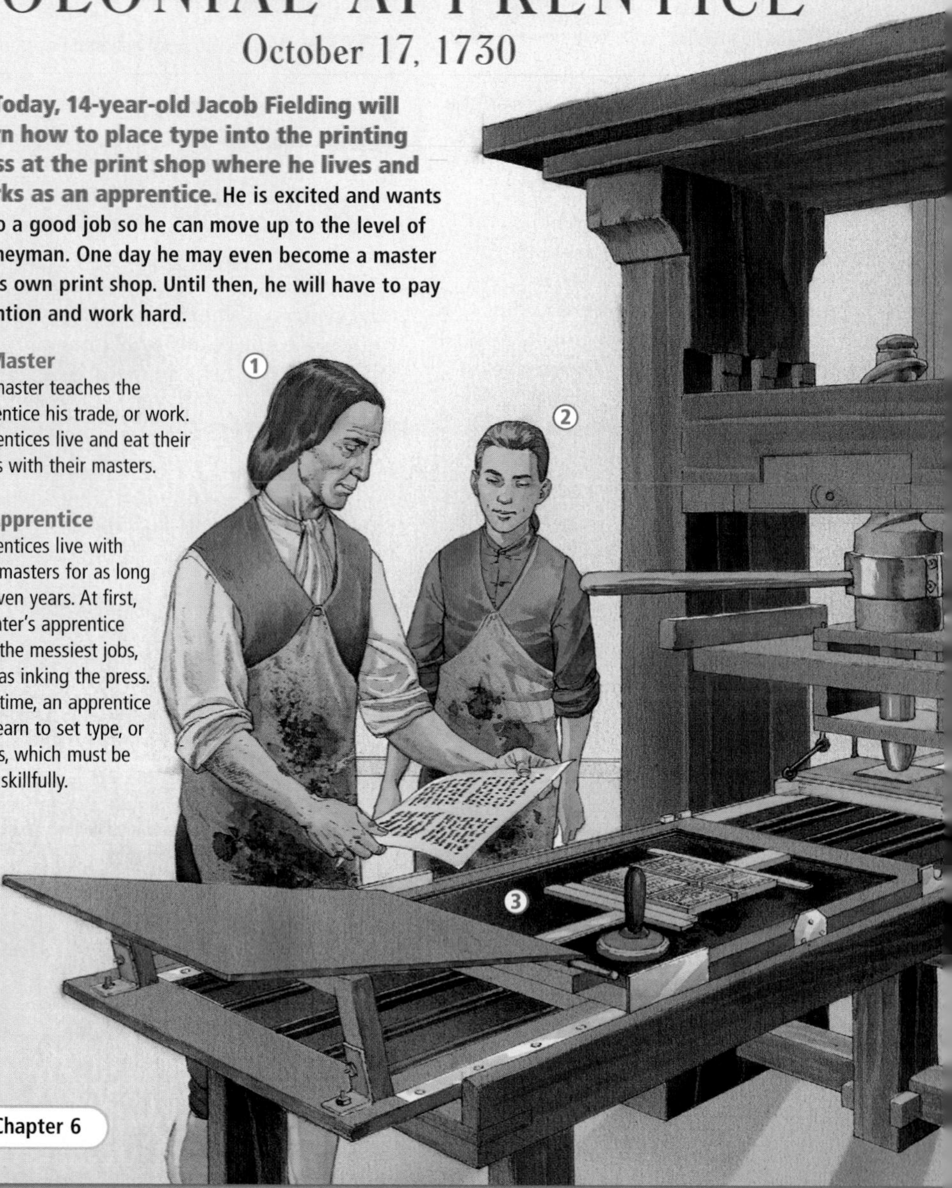

Reaching All Learners

Extra Support

Interview an Apprentice

- Ask partners to suppose that they are preparing a documentary about the role of an apprentice in a colonial print shop. Tell them to prepare a set of interview questions for a museum interpreter of the role. Have partners discuss and make notes about answers to the questions.
- Then, have students **role-play** the interview with the apprentice.
- Record students' presentation to the class on audio- or videotape.

Bodily-kinesthetic

On Level

Create a Word Wall

- Explain that apprentices studied trades such as apothecary, milliner, blacksmith, miller, cooper, printer, silversmith, and shoemaker.
- Brainstorm words related to the colonial print shop; list them on the board. Have pairs research a colonial trade, collecting relevant terms on blank 4" x 6" cards.
- Arrange the cards on a Word Wall. Have students use the terms for vocabulary and writing activities.

Verbal-linguistic

Challenge

Perform a Skit

- Explain that most colonial print shops set into type what customers brought in. Ask a small group of students to suppose that they work in a print shop in a colonial city. The shop publishes a weekly newspaper, sermons for churches, playbills and tickets, auction notices, and pamphlets for businesses.
- Have students write and perform a skit that tells the story of an apprentice in this print shop.

Verbal-linguistic

③ Setting the Type
Small, metal blocks of letters must be set in rows for each line on a printed page. All of the rows are held together in a wooden frame. The type is kept in the type case shown below.

④ Printing Press
The type is inked and paper is placed on it. The printer presses the paper onto the inked type to print a page. Colonial print shops printed newspapers, periodicals, pamphlets, and books.

⑤ Journeyman
After an apprentice learns his trade, he becomes a paid journeyman. Larger print shops had several experienced journeymen to work the presses. Often, a journeyman's wife would assist him.

HISTORY

Activities

1. **THINK ABOUT IT** If you were growing up in the colonies, what trade would you choose to learn? Why?
2. **WRITE ABOUT IT** Write a journal entry that Jacob Fielding might have written describing what he is learning about the printing trade.

2 Leveled Activities

❶ **Think About It** *For Extra Support*
Students' answers should name a trade, such as bookmaking or shoemaking, and give reasons why the trade was selected.

❷ **Write About It** *For Challenge*

Writing Rubric

4	Journal format is used correctly; main points are clearly stated; details support main points; no errors in mechanics.
3	Journal format is used; main points are adequately stated; details support most main points; few errors in mechanics.
2	Journal format is attempted; main points are stated; details are confused or vague; some errors in mechanics.
1	Journal format is not used; main points are not stated; details are incorrect; many errors in mechanics.

ELL

REACHING ALL LEARNERS

Beginning

- Discuss different meanings of *press,* including: (1) a machine that uses pressure to cut, shape, or stamp, (2) smoothing out creases by ironing, (3) a group of people who gather and report news. Use visual aids and props to reinforce understanding.
- Ask students to share their own experiences with the word *press.*
- Have students **illustrate and label** three meanings of *press*.

Visual-spatial

Math

Calculate

- If it takes one workday (14 hours) to set type for 2 newspaper pages, how many workdays are needed to set type for one 8-page issue? 4 workdays
- How many work hours would it take? 56 hours
- A good press team can print 220 sheets per hour. If there are 2 pages per sheet, how many hours are needed to print 110 copies of the 8-page issue? 2 hours

Logical-mathematical

Graphic Organizer

1	Set type
2	Ink type and place sheets of paper
3	Print sheets
4	After sheets dry, stack and deliver them

Graphic Organizer 15

✔ Tested Objectives

U3-14 Citizenship Explain the structure and importance of Virginia's colonial government.

U3-15 History Summarize the founding of Maryland, North and South Carolina, and Georgia.

Lesson Quick Look

This lesson describes the founding of the five Southern Colonies, which gave England control of the North American coast.

Teaching Option: **Extend Lesson 3** is a literature selection about a girl in colonial Williamsburg.

1 Get Set to Read

Preview Ask students to name Southern states. Explain that some of today's states were colonies.

Reading Skill: Sequence Events might include the creation of the House of Burgesses.

Build on What You Know Ask students why land near the coast may have been more desirable.

Vocabulary

plantation *noun,* a large farm on which crops are raised by workers who live on the land

legislature *noun,* a group of people with the power to make and change laws

refuge *noun,* a place protected from threat or harm

debtor *noun,* a person who owes money

Core Lesson 3

The Southern Colonies

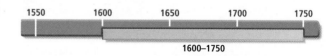

1550 | 1600 | 1650 | 1700 | 1750

1600–1750

VOCABULARY

plantation
legislature
refuge
debtor

Vocabulary Strategy

plantation

Think of the word **plant** to remember the meaning of **plantation.** A plantation is a very large farm on which crops are planted and grown.

READING SKILL

Sequence As you read, list the main events in the order in which they occur.

Build on What You Know You go into a movie theater, but all the good seats are taken! In the Southern Colonies, the first settlers claimed the best farmland near the ocean. Later colonists had to settle farther inland.

Virginia

Main Idea Virginia was the largest and wealthiest English colony and had the first elected government.

In 1607, Virginia became the first permanent English colony in North America. The first colonists came to Virginia to search for gold. When they realized that there was no gold there, many started plantations on the rich soil of the tidewater. A **plantation** is a large farm on which crops are raised by workers who live on the farm. 1

In the Southern Colonies, most plantation workers were indentured servants or enslaved Africans. Many plantation owners, or planters, became wealthy by growing and selling cash crops such as tobacco and rice.

As large plantations filled the tidewater, new colonists had to settle in the backcountry, farther from the ocean. To get more farmland, colonists often moved to areas where the Powhatan Indians lived. The Powhatans did not want colonists to take over this land, and they fought back. Many colonists and Indians were killed in these conflicts.

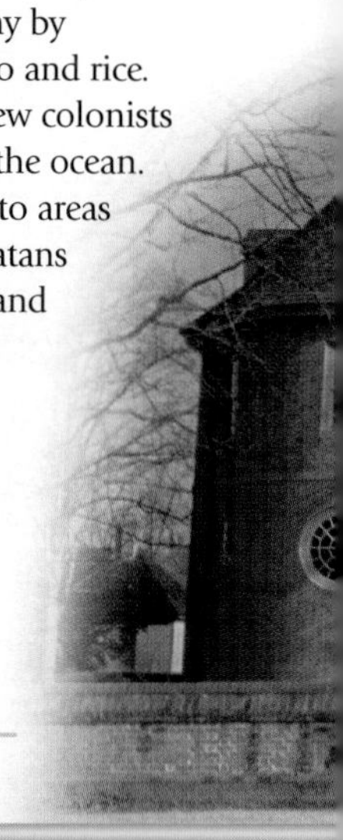

Skill and Strategy

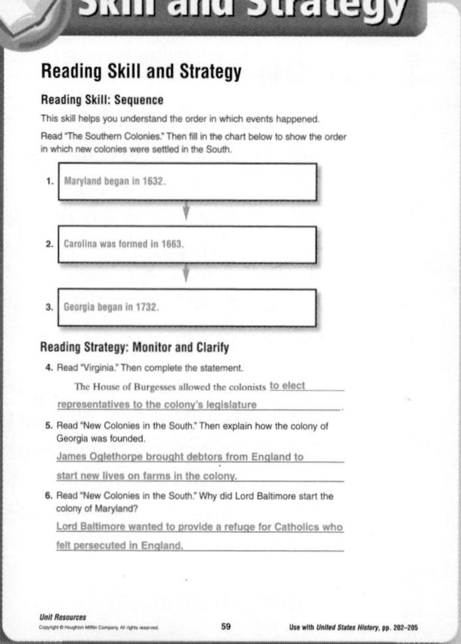

Reading Skill and Strategy

Reading Skill: Sequence

This skill helps you understand the order in which events happened.

Read "The Southern Colonies." Then fill in the chart below to show the order in which new colonies were settled in the South.

1. Maryland began in 1632.
2. Carolina was formed in 1663.
3. Georgia began in 1732.

Reading Strategy: Monitor and Clarify

4. Read "Virginia." Then complete the statement.
The House of Burgesses allowed the colonists to elect representatives to the colony's legislature.

5. Read "New Colonies in the South." Then explain how the colony of Georgia was founded.
James Oglethorpe brought debtors from England to start new lives on farms in the colony.

6. Read "New Colonies in the South." Why did Lord Baltimore start the colony of Maryland?
Lord Baltimore wanted to provide a refuge for Catholics who felt persecuted in England.

Unit Resources

59
Use with *United States History*, pp. 202–205

Unit Resources, p. 59

Background

Maryland and Georgia

- Maryland was named after England's queen, Henrietta Maria.
- James Oglethorpe, the proprietor of Georgia, became interested in prison reform when a friend of his, who was a debtor, died in prison.

Governing the Colony

As Virginia grew, colonists wanted to have a voice in the laws of the colony. In 1619, colonists created the first elected legislature in the colonies. A **legislature** is a group of people with the power to make and change laws. The legislature was called the House of Burgesses (BUR jihs iz) because the representatives in Virginia's legislature were known as burgesses. Colonists elected the burgesses, but only
2 planters and other white men who owned property were allowed to vote or be elected.

Nearly all of the members of the House of Burgesses were members of the Church of England, or the Anglican (ANG gli kun) Church. In 1632, the House of Burgesses made the Anglican Church the official church of Virginia. Puritans, Quakers, and others who were not Anglican had to leave the colony.

New Colonies in the South

Main Idea England founded four more colonies in the South during the 1600s and early 1700s.

Between 1632 and 1732, English colonists settled four more southern colonies. The colonies of Maryland, North Carolina, South Carolina, and Georgia were all created for different reasons.

Maryland

The colony of Maryland began in 1632, when **King Charles I** of England gave land in North America to **Cecilius Calvert.** Calvert, also known as **Lord Baltimore,** was a Catholic. Like Puritans and Quakers, Catholics in England were often punished for their religious beliefs.
Calvert hoped to make Maryland a refuge 3
for Catholics. A **refuge** is a safe place. In 1649, the Maryland government passed the Toleration Act. The Toleration Act was the first law in North America to promise that all Christians could worship freely.

REVIEW Who were burgesses? representatives elected by Virginia colonists

House of Burgesses The Virginia legislature first met in 1619. The burgesses later moved to this site (left).

2 Teach

Virginia

Talk About It

1 **Q Geography** Why did many plantations exist in Virginia?

A Virginia had rich soil suitable for growing crops like tobacco and rice.

2 **Q Citizenship** Who could be elected to the House of Burgesses?

A planters and other white men who owned property

New Colonies in the South

Talk About It

3 **Q History** What was Cecilius Calvert's purpose in founding Maryland?

A to provide a refuge for Catholics

Vocabulary Strategy

plantation Students can remember that a plantation is a farm by finding the word *plant* in *plantation.*

legislature Tell students that the word part *leg-* often has to do with laws.

refuge A "wildlife refuge" is a place that protects animals. Tell students that people sometimes also need a refuge.

Reading Strategy: Monitor/Clarify Have students read the first page, stopping at the end of each paragraph. Ask them to explain what the paragraph was about. If they do not understand something, have them review or read on to find the answer.

Leveled Practice

Extra Support

Have small groups **create a timeline** that shows when each English colony was founded. Have them include the New England, Middle, and Southern Colonies. Visual-spatial

Challenge

Have small groups read the sections of Lessons 1–3 that discuss the effect of religion on the Middle and Southern Colonies. Have students **create a chart** to organize the information. Verbal-linguistic

ELL

Intermediate/Advanced

- Have students work in pairs or small groups to research James Oglethorpe, founder of the colony of Georgia.
- Have students **write a short biography** that includes information about who he was, where and when he lived, and his major goals in establishing and governing the colony.

Verbal-linguistic

New Colonies in the South *continued*

Talk About It

4 Q Visual Learning Which American Indian groups lived in the area of the Southern Colonies?

A Powhatan, Tuscarora, Catawba, Cherokee, Waccamaw, and Guale

5 Q History In what ways did James Oglethorpe help debtors?

A He gave them free passage to Georgia and small farms.

6 Q History What were some of the first rules Oglethorpe made for the colony?

A They could not drink alcohol, own slaves, or elect their own legislature.

Vocabulary Strategy

debtor Explain that the phrase "to be in debt" means "to owe." Debtors are people who owe money.

Critical Thinking

Decision Making Did James Oglethorpe make a good decision by providing English debtors with free passage to Georgia? Explain.

The Carolinas

During the late 1600s, England, France, and Spain all claimed land that was south of Virginia. The new English king, **Charles II,** wanted to start another colony on this land. He hoped that a settlement would help keep France and Spain out of the area. In 1663, Charles II formed a new colony south of Virginia called Carolina.

Colonists first settled the southern part of Carolina. The southern area had good farmland and many excellent harbors. Planters built rice plantations in the tidewater. The city of Charles Town, later called Charleston, grew large and wealthy. The northern part of Carolina had few harbors and was not as good for farming. It grew more slowly than the south. In 1729, Carolina became two colonies, North Carolina and South Carolina.

Georgia

In 1732, England's King **George III** started another colony to keep the Spanish and French away from South Carolina. He gave this land to **James Oglethorpe,** an English lawmaker and army officer. The new colony was named Georgia to honor King George.

Oglethorpe wanted Georgia to be a place for poor people and debtors (DEHT ers). A **debtor** is a person who owes money. In England, debtors who could not pay the money they owed were put in prison. Oglethorpe thought it would be better to let debtors start new lives in
Georgia. He offered them a free trip to 5
Georgia and small farms of their own.

In 1733, Oglethorpe led the first group of settlers to Georgia. Soon, Oglethorpe developed friendly relations with nearby America Indians. He traded with Choctaws, Cherokees, and Creeks.

Oglethorpe made strict
rules for his colony. Georgian 6
colonists could not drink alcohol. They also could not own slaves or elect their own legislature.

4

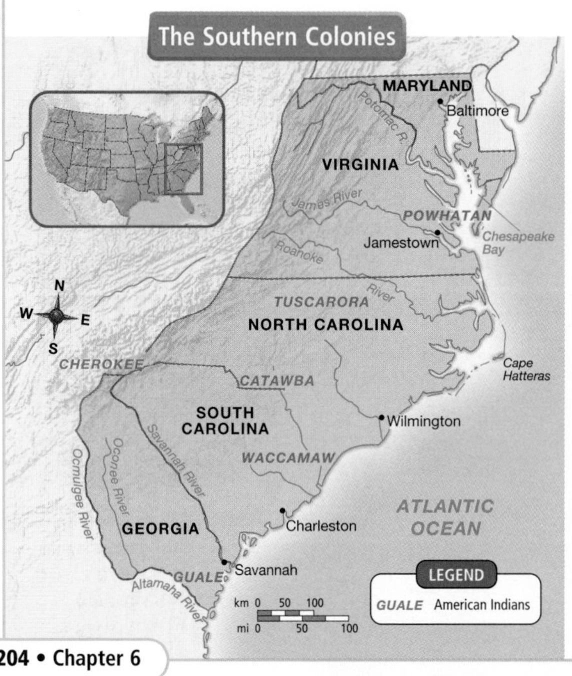

The Southern Colonies The region's fertile land and many waterways allowed most Southern colonists to make their living by farming.

SKILL **Reading Maps** Which places were named after people mentioned in this lesson?

Baltimore, Charleston, Georgia

204 • Chapter 6

Drama

A Meeting of Travelers

- Ask students to write and perform a scene about travelers from Virginia, North Carolina, South Carolina, Maryland, and Georgia who meet by chance at a country inn.
- The travelers will exchange information about life in the colony in which they live.

Verbal-linguistic; bodily-kinesthetic

Language Arts

Debtors' Debate

- Have partners create a conversation between two British debtors about James Oglethorpe and his new colony.
- In their scene, one of the debtors wants to go to Georgia, and the other does not.
- Remind students to include reasons for each person's choice. Have pairs perform their scenes for the class.

Bodily-kinesthetic; verbal-linguistic

Some colonists did not like these rules, and later many of the rules were changed. Slaves were brought to work on plantations as soon as slavery was allowed. Georgia quickly became a wealthy plantation colony like South Carolina.

REVIEW What were differences between North Carolina and South Carolina?

James Oglethorpe Under the leadership of this proprietor, the economy of Georgia succeeded.

Lesson Summary

Colony	Reason founded
Virginia	To find gold
Maryland	As a refuge for Catholics
Carolina	To help England control southeastern North America
Georgia	To help debtors and other poor people

Why It Matters ...

Establishing the Southern Colonies gave England control of the North American east coast, from New France in the north to Spanish Florida in the south.

Lesson Review

1619 House of Burgesses formed
1729 Carolinas created
1732 Georgia founded

1600 | 1630 | 1660 | 1690 | 1720 | 1750 | 1780

1. **VOCABULARY** Choose the correct words to fill in the blanks.

   refuge plantation legislature debtor

   To be a member of the Virginia _____, a person had to own a _____ or other piece of land.

2. **READING SKILL** In what **order** were the Southern Colonies founded?
3. **MAIN IDEA: Government** What was the House of Burgesses?
4. **MAIN IDEA: History** Why was Maryland founded?
5. **PEOPLE TO KNOW** Who was **James Oglethorpe,** and why did he found Georgia?
6. **TIMELINE SKILL** How many years after the House of Burgesses was formed was Georgia founded?
7. **CRITICAL THINKING: Decision Making** If you were a debtor in England in the 1700s, what could have been the costs and benefits of moving to Georgia?

WRITING ACTIVITY Learn more about the Powhatan Indians. Then write a short speech from a Powhatan Indian's point of view. Explain how he or she might feel about the conflicts with colonists over land.

REVIEW: South Carolina had better ports and farmland so it grew more quickly.

3 Review/Assess

Review Tested Objectives

U3-14 Virginia's House of Burgesses was the first elected legislature in the 13 colonies. Only planters and other white men who owned property could vote or be elected.

U3-15 Cecilius Calvert founded Maryland as a refuge for Catholics. King Charles II formed a colony called Carolina to keep Spain and France away; this colony was later divided into North and South Carolina. James Oglethorpe founded Georgia as a place where poor people and debtors could start new lives.

Lesson Review Answers

1. legislature; plantation
2. Virginia; Maryland; the Carolinas; Georgia
3. the first elected legislature in the colonies (in Virginia)
4. to provide a refuge for Catholics
5. Oglethorpe was a lawmaker and army officer; he founded Georgia as a refuge for debtors.
6. 113
7. Costs: taking the risk of leaving England and following strict rules in Georgia; benefits: free passage to North America, getting out of debt or prison, and the chance to start a new life.

Study Guide/Homework

Vocabulary and Study Guide

Vocabulary

Following the example below, break down the vocabulary word into its root and suffix. Then write its meaning.

-tion "the state of" or "the result of"
-ure "a group with a specific function"
-or "one who does a certain thing"

Example:

Conductor = conduct "to lead or to guide" + -or
Conductor means "one who leads or guides."

1. plantation = plant "farm" + -tion
   Plantation means "a large area of land that is used for farming."
2. legislature = legislate "to create laws" + -ure
   Legislature means "the group that creates laws."
3. debtor = debt "money owed" + -or
   Debtor means "one who owes money."

Study Guide

Read "New Colonies in the South." Then fill in the chart below.

Colony	Maryland	Carolinas	Georgia
Why it was founded	4. To be a refuge for Catholics; So all Christians could worship freely	5. Because the British king wanted to keep France and Spain out of the area	6. To be a place for debtors to start new lives

Unit Resources 60 Use with *United States History*, pp. 202–205

Unit Resources, p. 60

Reteach Minilesson

Use an idea web to reteach the founding of the Virginia colony.

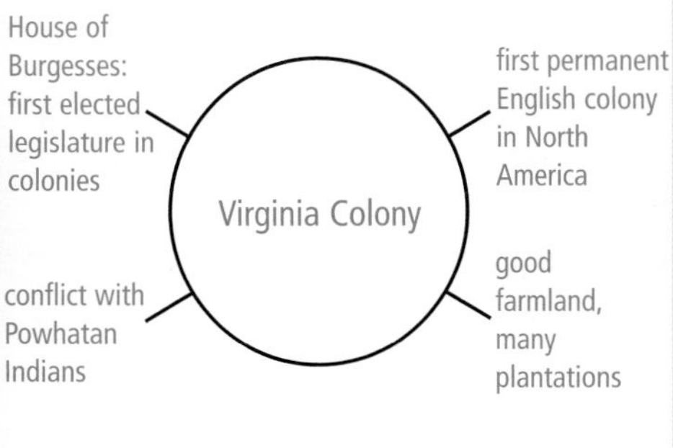

Graphic Organizer 7

Writing Rubric

4	Position is clearly stated; account of conflicts is supported by information from the text; mechanics are correct.
3	Position is adequately stated; account of conflicts is mostly supported by information from the text; few errors in mechanics are present.
2	Position is stated; account of conflicts is confused or poorly supported by text information; some errors in mechanics are present.
1	Position is not stated; account of conflicts is not supported or not present; many errors in mechanics are present.

Quick Look

Connect to the Core Lesson Students have just finished reading about the early history of the Southern Colonies. In Extend Lesson 3, they will read about a girl living in Williamsburg, Virginia.

1 Preview the Extend Lesson

Connect to the Big Idea

Change Beliefs in a society change over time, along with the society itself. In this selection, Ann expresses a desire to learn about mathematics, classical languages, and medicine. In the eighteenth century, these were not considered appropriate or necessary subjects for a girl. Today, most Americans consider these appropriate topics for anyone, male or female, to study.

Growing Up in Another Time Ask students to brainstorm ways in which the life of a young person was different in 1747 from today. They might consider topics such as education, home life, responsibilities, and family expectations.

Literature

Ann's Story: 1747

by Joan Lowery Nixon

Fire! On the morning of January 30, 1747, the residents of Williamsburg, Virginia, find their Capitol building in flames. Now a new town might have to serve as the colonial capital. Ann McKenzie, the nine-year-old daughter of a doctor, is worried that her family might have to move. She wonders what her future will be like.

That evening, after supper, Ann sat with her parents in the parlor and knitted on a stocking. She listened quietly as they talked about the Capitol fire and the effect it might have on Williamsburg. But as Dr. McKenzie spoke of problems involved in moving his practice and his apothecary, Ann forgot herself.

"Papa, we can't go to the Pamunkey River. There aren't even any houses built yet! We can't live in a hut with snakes!"

Her father's eyes widened in surprise. "Ann, I don't know where you got a strange idea like that," he said. "We will not live in a hut. And there will be no snakes allowed in our house."

"But Matthew said ..."

Mrs. McKenzie sighed and rolled her eyes. "We should have known. Matthew Davenport again. He seems to enjoy disturbing the younger children with wild tales." She kept her eyes on the small stocking she was knitting for William as she said, "I'm afraid the Davenport boys are not disciplined as carefully as they should be. Remember a number of years ago, when Matthew's older brother, Bedford, was reprimanded by the burgesses for writing indecent inscriptions on one of their chairs?"

Reaching All Learners

Background

Apothecary

- Explain that *apothecary* is used in the first paragraph to mean a pharmacy or doctor's office—the place where a doctor such as Ann's father would dispense medicine.
- *Apothecary* can also mean a person: "She went to get medicine from her cousin, who was an apothecary." This word is usually seen in stories or articles about earlier centuries; today, people generally use the terms *pharmacist* or *doctor.*

Extra Support

Compare Time Periods

- Have partners use a Venn diagram to compare boys' and girls' lives in America in 1747. Have them use details from the literature selection and their own knowledge.
- Then have them create another chart comparing and contrasting boys' and girls' lives in America today.
- Compare charts as a group.

Visual-spatial

On Level

Write About Ann's Future

- Have students write a paragraph describing what they think may happen to Ann in the future. Remind them to include evidence from the story.
- Share paragraphs as a group.

Verbal-linguistic

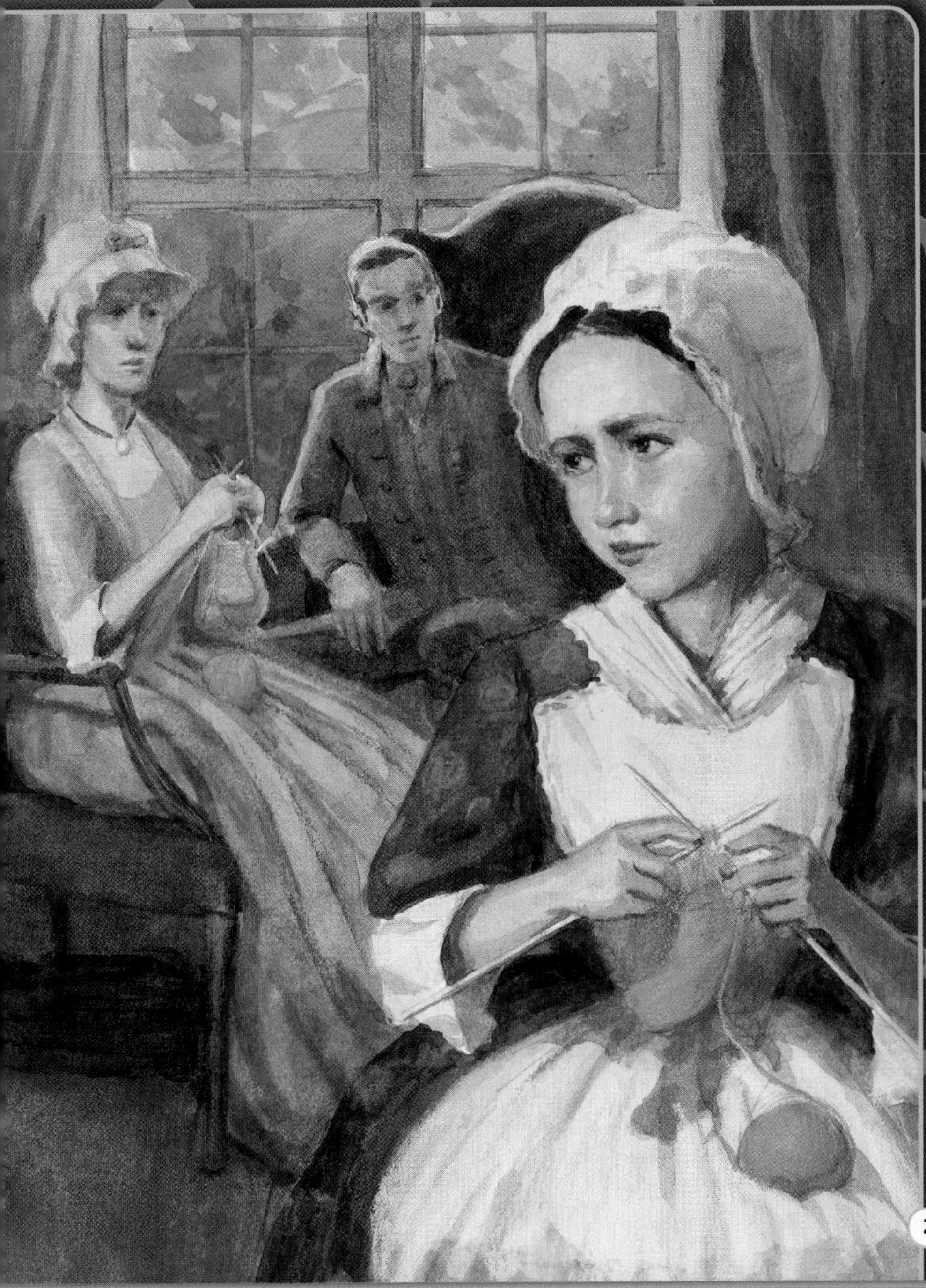

LITERATURE

207

2 Teach the Extend Lesson

Genre: Historical Fiction

Explain that historical fiction is fiction set in another time period. Point out that authors writing in this genre must include details to show what life was like in a certain time and place. As they read, students should list details that show the story is set in colonial America.

Challenge

Find Quotes

- Have students work in small groups. Assign each group member a character from the text.
- Ask each student to select several quotes that show something about their character's personality. Have them write these on index cards.
- Have students trade index cards within their group and discuss what the quotes show about the characters.

Verbal-linguistic

ELL

Beginning

- Have students list words or phrases from the text that they find difficult. Examples might include *reprimanded by the burgesses, only jesting,* and *greatly indulged you.*
- Have them work with a partner to **create flashcards** with illustrations or written definitions.
- Have pairs trade flashcards and quiz each other. Compare the definitions and illustrations students have chosen.

Verbal-linguistic; visual-spatial

Literature

Historical Fiction

Sign of the Beaver, by Elizabeth George Speare; *Johnny Tremain,* by Esther Forbes.

Add these works of historical fiction to your reading center for students who want to find out more about eighteenth-century colonial life.

Critical Thinking

Draw Conclusions Write the following statement on the board: "Ann's parents don't want her to study medicine because they think she is not smart enough." Have students explain why they agree or disagree with this statement.

Analyze Have students explain in their own words why Ann's parents discourage her from studying Latin and Greek and becoming a doctor. Remind them to use the characters' words to support their explanations.

"Really? What did he write?" Ann asked.

"I'm sure no one remembers now," Dr. McKenzie answered quickly. He smiled and added, "Trust me, Ann. I will do my best to take good care of you, your mother, and William for the rest of my life. Matthew was only jesting with you."

"It's not amusing," Ann grumbled. "And neither is Matthew."

"Pray don't think harshly of Matthew," Dr. McKenzie said. "He's a fine young man. He has shown an interest in my work, and it has been my pleasure to encourage him."

Before Ann could respond, Mrs. McKenzie leaned over to examine her knitting. "Dear," she said, "you dropped a stitch in this last row."

Ann groaned. "Will you tell me to pull them out and do them over?"

"It's all a part of learning," Mrs. McKenzie told her gently. "Someday you'll be grateful that you can knit well."

Ann let the stocking drop to the floor. "What good does it do to make neat stitches? Can't someone else make the stockings while I learn what I want to learn?"

"Exactly what is it that you want to learn?" her mother asked.

Even Ann's father looked up from his armchair in surprise.

"I want to learn Latin, and after that, Greek," she said. "The knowledge of Latin seems necessary to the study of medicine. I want to learn everything I'll need to know so that I can read all the books in Papa's library."

Mrs. McKenzie's expression showed that she had no patience with such a foolish wish. "Ann, you've learned to read well, and you find great pleasure in books, but the books in your father's library are beyond your abilities. They couldn't possibly interest you."

"But they do, Mama," Ann insisted. "Sometimes I take down one of Papa's medical books and read parts of it—the parts I can understand. I hope someday to know the meanings of all the words so that I can read entire books."

Mrs. McKenzie sighed. "Some of those books are not appropriate for you, daughter. There are many more useful things for you to learn. As you grow older, I hope there will be lessons for you in dancing and possibly the flute or harpsichord. And I'll continue to teach you how to manage a household."

208 • Chapter 6

Reaching All Learners

Language Arts

Write a Persuasive Letter

- Read aloud the last sentence of the selection: "How could she ever convince them that her life's work was to care for others?"
- Have students suppose that several years later, Ann still wants to be a doctor. Ask them to write a letter from Ann to her parents convincing them to let her study medicine.
- Share letters as a class.

Verbal-linguistic

Math

Calculate Ages

- Remind students that Ann is nine years old in this selection. Suppose that in four years she still wants to be a doctor. How old will she be then? 13 years old
- Suppose that Matthew Davenport is three years older than Ann. How old will Matthew be when Ann is twelve? 15 years old

Logical-mathematical

Art

Design a Shop Sign

- Explain that colonial shopkeepers and other professionals often hung a sign outside their place of business to show their trade, or job. If possible, show students pictures of typical colonial signs.
- Help students brainstorm a list of colonial trades. Ask partners to select a trade and design a sign for it.
- Compare designs as a class.

Visual-spatial

"I'll study whatever you wish, Mama, but I still hope to study Latin and mathematics, too," Ann said.

She saw her mother give a knowing look to her father.

"Your father has greatly indulged you in taking you beyond the fundamental rules of arithmetic, in teaching you mathematics," Mrs. McKenzie told her. "But all you need is enough knowledge of arithmetic to keep your household accounts. Forget this ridiculous desire to become a doctor."

Ann took a deep breath. "Mama, Papa came to the colonies from Scotland. He once told me it was because he was searching for opportunity. Should it surprise you that I am looking for opportunity, too? Here in Virginia I should have the opportunity to study the practice of medicine."

Dr. McKenzie sighed. "It's not that simple, daughter," he said. "A woman doctor would not be accepted. We must follow custom."

"But—"

"You're an eager student, but I'm afraid the study of Latin is suitable only to young gentlemen. I'd suggest you might try harder to please your mother with the neatness of your knitting."

Ann bent down to pick up her stocking. The lump in her throat hurt. No one—not even her parents or her best friends—understood. How could she ever convince them that her life's work was to care for others?

Activities

1. **TALK ABOUT IT** Which events and people in this story are real? Which ones were made up by the author? Explain how you can tell the difference.
2. **WRITE ABOUT IT** Do you think Ann should "follow custom," as her father says, or search for her opportunity? Write a paragraph explaining your ideas.

3 Leveled Activities

1 Talk About It *For Extra Support*

Sample answer: Real: Capitol fire, way of life, attitudes, family roles, reasons for immigrating; Made up: McKenzie family, Matthew Davenport, the conversation and events in the story. You can tell the difference because historical fiction uses details from the historical background to tell a fictional story.

2 Write About It *For Challenge*

Writing Rubric

4	Paragraph states position clearly; uses ideas and details from the literature selection to support position; mechanics are correct.
3	Paragraph states position; uses some ideas and details to support position; mechanics are mostly correct.
2	Paragraph states position in a confused or disorganized way; uses few ideas or details to support position; some errors in mechanics are present.
1	Paragraph does not state position or is off topic; uses no ideas or details to support position; many errors in mechanics are present.

Science

Write about Women in Science

- Have students choose a famous woman scientist, doctor, or mathematician. They may choose American women or women from other countries.
- Have them research and then write a short introduction to this person's achievements.
- Ask them to speak to the class about the woman they chose.

Verbal-linguistic

Graphic Organizer

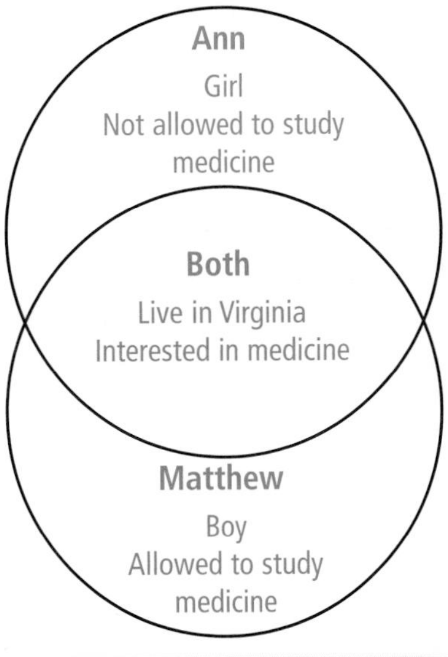

www.eduplace.com/ss/hmss05/

Tested Objectives

U3-16 Economics Identify agriculture as the main economic activity of the Southern Colonies.

U3-17 Culture Compare life on a plantation to life on a small farm.

U3-18 Culture Describe enslaved Africans' lives, work, and culture.

Lesson Quick Look

This lesson describes the economy and culture of the Southern Colonies, including plantations, backcountry farms, and cities.

Teaching Option: Extend Lesson 4 teaches students more about slave culture and daily life in the South in the 1700s. It also introduces archeologist Theresa Singleton.

1 Get Set to Read

Preview Have students look at the photographs on page 211. Ask why these plants were important.

Reading Skill: Compare and Contrast Students should note that plantations relied on enslaved workers.

Build on What You Know Ask students to share their gardening experiences or observations both indoors and outdoors. Explain that the location of the Southern Colonies made them suitable for growing cash crops.

Vocabulary

indigo *noun,* a plant that can be made into a dark blue dye

overseer *noun,* a person who watches and directs workers, especially laborers

spiritual *noun,* an African American religious folk song

Core Lesson 4

Life in the South

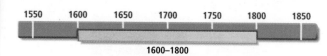

1550	1600	1650	1700	1750	1800	1850

1600–1800

VOCABULARY

indigo
overseer
spiritual

Vocabulary Strategy

overseer

The small two words in the compound word **overseer** show its meaning. An overseer watches over workers.

READING SKILL

Compare and Contrast Note the similarities and differences between plantations and backcountry farms.

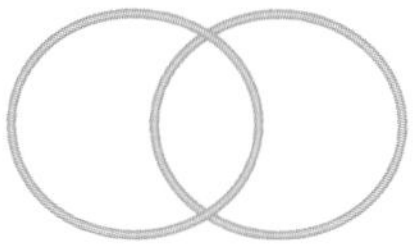

Build on What You Know Have you ever grown a plant from a seed or bulb? If you have, you know that plants need fertile soil, warm weather, and plenty of water. The Southern Colonies had all of these things.

Southern Agriculture

Main Idea Cash crops grew very well in the Southern Colonies.

The long growing season and warm, damp climate of the Southern Colonies made the region perfect for growing tobacco and rice. Many southern planters became very wealthy exporting these cash crops to other colonies and countries. Planters found, however, that tobacco and rice needed much more work and care than other crops. Planters used indentured servants and enslaved Africans to do this hard labor.

In Virginia and Maryland, the main cash crop was tobacco. Colonists grew tobacco on small farms as well as on large plantations. North Carolina had many small tobacco farms, but its greatest resource was its pine forests. Colonists took the sticky sap from pine trees and made it into a thick liquid called pitch. Pitch was used to seal the boards of ships and keep out water. 1

Tobacco Virginia farmers harvest tobacco leaves in the early 1600s.

Skill and Strategy

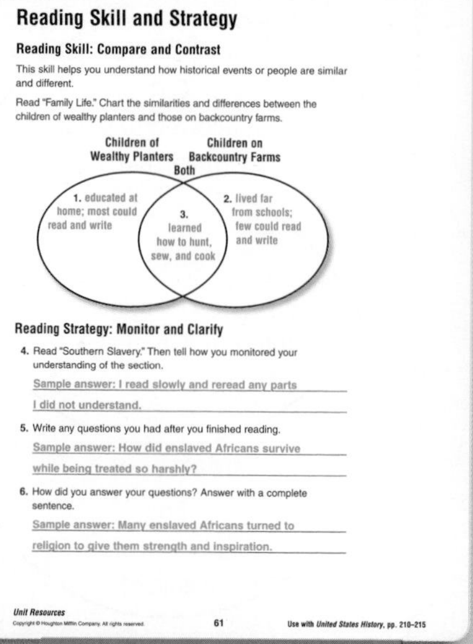

Reading Skill and Strategy

Reading Skill: Compare and Contrast

This skill helps you understand how historical events or people are similar and different.

Read "Family Life." Chart the similarities and differences between the children of wealthy planters and those on backcountry farms.

Reading Strategy: Monitor and Clarify

4. Read "Southern Slavery." Then tell how you monitored your understanding of the section.
Sample answer: I read slowly and reread any parts I did not understand.

5. Write any questions you had after you finished reading.
Sample answer: How did enslaved Africans survive while being treated so harshly?

6. How did you answer your questions? Answer with a complete sentence.
Sample answer: Many enslaved Africans turned to religion to give them strength and inspiration.

Unit Resources

61
Use with *United States History*, pp. 210–215

Unit Resources, p. 61

Background

African Influence

- Some plants, such as okra, were brought to North America from Africa.
- Skills enslaved people brought from Africa included metal- and wood-working, boat making, and navigation.

Cash Crops

Tobacco

Southern tobacco was exported all over the world.

Rice

Rice needs a steamy, hot climate to grow well.

Indigo

Without indigo, blue jeans wouldn't have their special color.

South Carolina and Georgia had two main cash crops. One was rice, which flourished in the hot, wet tidewater region. Planters learned methods for growing rice (2) from enslaved African workers. They brought their knowledge of rice growing from West Africa, where rice was an important food.

The other major cash crop in South Carolina and Georgia was indigo. **Indigo** is a plant that can be made into a dark blue dye. This dye is used to color clothing. Indigo was very difficult to grow, and planters had little success with it. Then 17-year-old **Eliza Lucas Pinckney** began to experiment with different kinds of indigo on her father's plantation.

In 1744, she developed a type of indigo that was much easier to grow. This indigo (3) was so successful that colonists in South Carolina soon sold more than 100,000 pounds of indigo each year.

Charles Town

The Southern Colonies had many farms and plantations but fewer towns and cities than New England or the Middle Colonies. By the mid-1700s, however, several ports in the South had grown into large cities. Charles Town, South Carolina, which became known as Charleston in 1783, was the biggest southern city. It was a busy center of trade and the capital of South Carolina.

In Charles Town, traders and planters bought, sold, and exported thousands of pounds of tobacco, rice, and indigo. Ships brought goods from Europe and the West Indies to sell in the colonies.

Charles Town had a diverse population. Its people were English, Scots-Irish, French, and West Indian. Free and enslaved Africans lived in the city as well. (4)

REVIEW Why was Charles Town an important city? It was the biggest southern city and a center of trade.

211

2 Teach

Southern Agriculture

Talk About It

1 **Q Economics** Where did pitch come from and what was it used for?

A Pitch came from pine sap, and was used to seal and waterproof ships.

2 **Q Economics** What were the main cash crops of South Carolina and Georgia?

A rice and indigo

3 **Q Economics** What was Eliza Lucas Pinckney's contribution to South Carolina's economy?

A She developed a type of indigo that was much easier to grow.

4 **Q Citizenship** Name some places of origin of the people who lived in Charles Town.

A England, Scotland, Ireland, France, West Indies, Africa

Vocabulary Strategy

indigo Explain that *indigo* is the name of a deep shade of blue. In this lesson, it refers to a plant that can be made into a dye of this color.

Reading Strategy: Monitor/Clarify As students read, suggest they pause after each paragraph and reflect on what they have read. After that, they should consider whether anything is unclear.

Leveled Practice

Reaching All Learners

Extra Support

Have partners **make a chart** showing the Southern Colonies and their cash crops. Display completed charts in the classroom. Visual-spatial

Challenge

Intermediate/Advanced

Have partners **write a letter** Eliza Lucas Pinckney might have written about her experiments with indigo. Letters can express how Eliza felt about her discoveries. Have students share their letters with the class. Verbal-linguistic

ELL

Reaching All Learners

- Have students **write a description** about life in the Southern Colonies.
- Provide a list of words that will help them focus their descriptions.
- Students can share descriptions with the class.

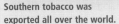

Visual-spatial

Plantations and Small Farms

Talk About It

5 **Q History** How was a plantation like a village?

A It might contain houses, workshops, horse stables, gardens, and fields. Many people lived and worked on plantations.

6 **Q Economics** In what ways was a small farm different from a plantation?

A Plantations were like small villages, with many workers, usually enslaved Africans, producing many cash crops. Planters lived in luxury. Small farms were run by families, often including a small number of servants or slaves. Backcountry farmers were poor and farmed mostly for their own survival.

Critical Thinking

Infer Why were small farms usually far away from the tidewater?

Think Aloud *It sounds like the tidewater had very good farmland. Probably this land was more expensive and got taken more quickly than land further out in the backcountry. A small farmer might not have had enough money to buy tidewater land, but could afford land in the backcountry.*

Plantations and Small Farms

Main Idea Southern plantations were large and needed many workers, but most southern colonists lived on small family farms.

The huge plantations in the South were more like small villages than farms. At the center of a plantation, often near a river or stream, was the planter's house.
5 The planter's house was surrounded by horse stables, workshops, gardens, fields, and workers' houses.

Many laborers were needed to keep a big plantation running. Plantation workers were usually enslaved Africans. Most spent long hours working in the plantation's fields. Other workers took care of the gardens or animals. Cooks and maids worked in the planter's house.

The South was known for its large plantations, but small farms were much 6
more common. Most southern colonists lived on small family farms in the backcountry, away from the tidewater. Backcountry colonists farmed with the help of family members and perhaps one or two servants or slaves. They grew their own food and sometimes small amounts of a cash crop, such as tobacco.

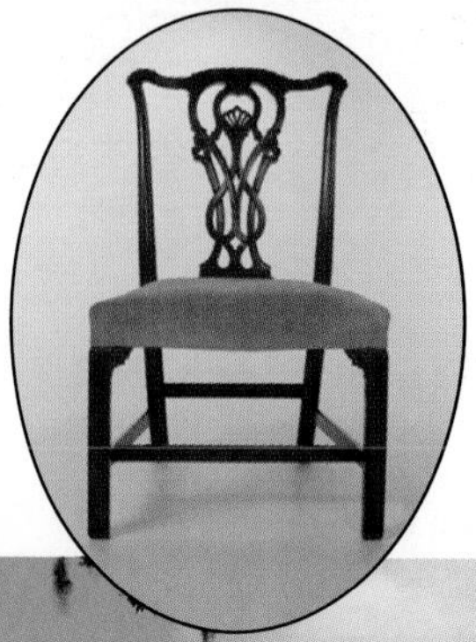

Plantation Life The planter's family usually lived in a grand mansion, such as this one in South Carolina (below). Mansions were often decorated with fine furniture like this chair (left). SKILL **Reading Visuals** Compare and contrast the chairs and houses shown on these two pages.

Physical Education

Hunt the Slipper

Teach students this colonial-style game. Players sit in a circle; one player (the hunter) leaves the room. One student in the circle is given a small object, such as a slipper, to hold. The hunter returns and stands in the middle of the circle; the others pass the "slipper" behind their backs, trying to avoid being detected. The hunter has three tries to find who is holding the slipper. When the hunter discovers the slipper, he or she changes places with the player holding it and play continues.

Bodily-kinesthetic

Math

Hours in a Day

- Have partners make a circle graph showing how many hours in each day a family on a small southern farm might spend doing various activities, such as working in the fields, cooking, cleaning, and sleeping.
- Compare partners' estimations.

Visual-spatial

Backcountry Life Simple wooden cabins (right) were home to most farming families who lived west of the tidewater. Most of their belongings, such as this chair (above), were either made by hand or traded from others.

Family Life

The children of wealthy planters lived fairly easy lives. Most were educated at home. Their parents hired teachers to instruct the children in reading, writing, dancing, and music. Boys spent their free time outdoors, learning how to ride horses and hunt. Girls learned how to sew and sing. As children got older, fathers taught boys how to run the plantation. Girls learned how to manage a large household with many servants.

Life was very different on backcountry farms. Backcountry farmers often lived far from schools and towns. Children learned how to read and write only if their parents could teach them. Backcountry children started helping around the house and farm at an early age. This was how they learned skills such as plowing, hunting, sewing, and cooking.

Southern Slavery

Main Idea Slavery was cruel, but enslaved people developed a culture that helped them survive.

The importance of slavery in the Southern Colonies changed over time. In the early 1600s, indentured servants did much of the hard work on plantations. As the number of plantations grew, however, southern planters began to use enslaved Africans as laborers. 7

More and more enslaved Africans were brought to North America during the 1600s and 1700s. By 1750, greater numbers of enslaved Africans lived in all thirteen colonies, but most slaves lived in the Southern Colonies.

REVIEW How did the children of planters and the children of backcountry farmers learn how to read and write?

213

REVIEW: plantation children: taught by private teachers; backcountry children: sometimes learned from their parents

Southern Slavery

Talk About It

7 **Q History** Why did the South begin to use more and more enslaved workers during the 1600s and 1700s?

A As the number of southern plantations grew, planters there began to use greater numbers of slaves.

Reading Strategy: Monitor/Clarify As students read, suggest they pause after each paragraph and reflect on what they have read. After that, they should consider whether anything is unclear.

Extra Support

Farm Life Poster

Have students create a poster depicting the life of a family on a small southern farm. Remind them to include historical details and to show the different family members doing various activities. Have children explain their posters.

Visual-spatial

Challenge

Helpful Tips

Have students write a list of tips a father might give his son about things he will need to know in order to run a farm. Other students may choose to write a list of tips a mother might give her daughter. Have students share their lists with the class.

Verbal-linguistic

Southern Slavery

continued

Talk About It

8 **Q History** Why did many enslaved Africans die at an early age?

A They had to work extremely hard and had poor food, clothing, and shelter.

9 **Q History** In what ways did enslaved Africans create a new culture?

A They blended African and American customs, religions, and music to form a unique culture.

Vocabulary Strategy

overseer Help students remember this word by telling them that many overseers rode horses while they worked. They were seeing "over" the people working.

spiritual Explain that enslaved people sang *spirituals* to "raise their spirits" as they worked under cruel conditions. Tell students that "the Holy Spirit" is a Christian term for God; this can remind them that spirituals are religious folk songs.

Critical Thinking

Infer Why did many enslaved Africans turn to Christianity?

Life Under Slavery

Enslaved Africans were not treated as human beings. They were bought and sold as property. Under slavery, husbands and wives were often separated from each other, and families were torn apart.

On a plantation, slaves usually worked as laborers in the fields or as house servants. Even young children were forced to work. Field work was exhausting. Workers labored from morning to night in the heat and the cold, nearly every day of the year. Overseers sometimes whipped and punished workers to keep them working hard. An **overseer** is a person who watches and directs the work of other people. Enslaved people had to work so hard and had such
8 poor food, clothing, and shelter that many died at an early age.

Planters used punishments and harsh laws to keep enslaved workers from resisting or running away. Many had to wear heavy iron chains. They could not leave the plantation without permission. They could be beaten or even killed by planters and overseers. Some slaves fought back by running away. Most resisted by working as slowly as they could without being punished.

African American Culture

To survive their harsh lives, enslaved Africans formed close ties with each other. They created a community that was like a large family. Enslaved Africans helped each other to survive the hardships of slavery.

Another source of strength was religion. Many enslaved people began to practice Christianity and looked to the Bible and its stories for inspiration. They combined Christian beliefs and musical traditions from Africa to create powerful spirituals. A **spiritual** is an African American religious folk song.

Over time, enslaved people created a new culture that blended African and American customs and religions. They 9
remembered their past by telling stories about their homelands in Africa. They made up work songs to help the time pass while working in the fields. They invented and played music on the banjo, a musical instrument based on African ones. In South Carolina, enslaved Africans created a new language, Gullah, out of African languages and English.

REVIEW What did slaves do to survive the hardships of slavery? built a close community; turned to Christianity; combined African and American customs, religions, and music

Slave Cabins This painting shows slave cabins on a South Carolina plantation. Slave houses were small and cramped.

214 • Chapter 6

Music

Spirituals

- Discuss spirituals with students.
- Explain that spirituals could be used to exchange secret information; for example, a worker could pass a message about an upcoming escape attempt by singing a certain verse or song.
- You may wish to play recorded spirituals for students and have them discuss the songs' lyrics and emotional content in a short paragraph.

Musical-auditory

Language Arts

African American Heritage

- Have students read books or stories about enslaved Africans and how they found the strength to survive.
- Encourage students to discuss what they read with their classmates or to write a response.

Verbal-linguistic

African Culture Enslaved Africans dance and make music in this painting called *The Old Plantation* (above). The banjo (right) became a popluar instrument in American folk music.

Lesson Summary

The Southern Colonies had an agricultural economy. Most colonists lived on small family farms, but some owned large plantations that produced cash crops such as tobacco and rice. Many slaves worked on plantations. Slavery was a cruel system. Enslaved Africans developed a culture that helped them survive.

Why It Matters . . .

Slavery would become a major source of conflict in the United States more than a hundred years later.

Lesson Review

1. **VOCABULARY** Write a short paragraph telling why **indigo** was important in the South.
2. **READING SKILL** What were some **differences** between plantations and backcountry farms?
3. **MAIN IDEA: Economics** What were the main cash crops in the Southern Colonies?
4. **MAIN IDEA: Culture** What new customs became part of the culture of enslaved Africans?
5. **PEOPLE TO KNOW** How did **Eliza Pinckney** affect the economy of the South?
6. **CRITICAL THINKING: Infer** Why did large plantations develop in the Southern Colonies?
7. **CRITICAL THINKING: Compare and Contrast** Compare and contrast the lives of children on plantations and on small farms.

WRITING ACTIVITY Do research and write a report about the many ways African American culture has affected American culture.

Study Guide/Homework

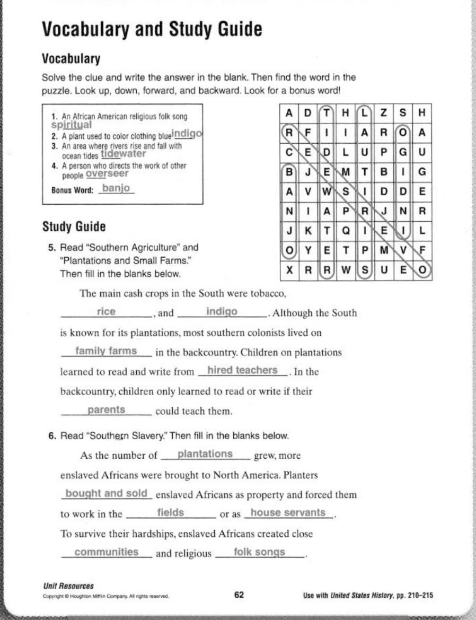

Vocabulary and Study Guide

Vocabulary

Solve the clue and write the answer in the blank. Then find the word in the puzzle. Look up, down, forward, and backward. Look for a bonus word!

1. An African American religious folk song spiritual
2. A plant used to color clothing blue indigo
3. An area where rivers rise and fall with ocean tides tidewater
4. A person who directs the work of other people overseer

Bonus Word: banjo

A	D	T	H	L	Z	S	H
R	F	I	I	A	R	O	A
C	E	D	L	U	P	G	U
B	J	E	M	T	B	I	G
A	V	W	S	I	D	D	E
N	I	A	P	R	J	N	R
J	K	T	Q	I	E	I	L
O	Y	E	T	P	M	V	F
X	R	R	W	S	U	E	O

Study Guide

5. Read "Southern Agriculture" and "Plantations and Small Farms." Then fill in the blanks below.

The main cash crops in the South were tobacco, rice, and indigo. Although the South is known for its plantations, most southern colonists lived on family farms in the backcountry. Children on plantations learned to read and write from hired teachers. In the backcountry, children only learned to read or write if their parents could teach them.

6. Read "Southern Slavery." Then fill in the blanks below.

As the number of plantations grew, more enslaved Africans were brought to North America. Planters bought and sold enslaved Africans as property and forced them to work in the fields or as house servants. To survive their hardships, enslaved Africans created close communities and religious folk songs.

Unit Resources 62 Use with *United States History*, pp. 210–215

Unit Resources, p. 62

Reteach Minilesson

Use an organizer to reteach the development of African American culture.

Enslaved Africans in America developed their own culture.

- strong community ties
- importance of religion
- blended customs, language, and music

Graphic Organizer 8

3 Review/Assess

Review Tested Objectives

U3-16 Most people lived on small family farms or plantations; cash crops grew well in the Southern Colonies.

U3-17 Plantations were like self-contained villages; workers were usually enslaved Africans; crops were grown to sell. Backcountry farms were much smaller, and farmed by families and small numbers of servants or slaves. Children on plantations learned reading, writing, dancing, and music. Backcountry farm children worked on the farm and also learned to hunt, sew, and cook.

U3-18 Enslaved Africans were bought and sold as property and lived harsh lives. They worked long hours in the fields or as house servants. Slaves created strong communities and a new culture by blending African and American customs, religion, and music.

Lesson Review Answers

1. Paragraphs should state indigo's economic importance.
2. Plantations grew cash crops, while backcountry farms grew food for personal use.
3. tobacco; indigo; rice
4. storytelling, music, religion, language
5. She developed a new kind of indigo that grew easily and sold well.
6. The climate allowed for crop growth; they became a center of southern economy.
7. Answers may compare education, daily activities, and skills learned.

Writing Rubric

4	Report is well organized and shows considerable effort; mechanics are correct.
3	Report is adequately organized and shows effort; few errors in mechanics.
2	Report is somewhat organized and shows some effort; some errors in mechanics.
1	Report is disorganized and shows little effort; many errors in mechanics.

Quick Look

Connect to the Core Lesson Students have learned about life in the Southern Colonies. In Extend Lesson 4, students will learn how artifacts found at archaeological digs help people living today understand more about the lives of enslaved people in the 1700s.

1 Teach the Extend Lesson

Connect to the Big Idea

Cultural Images At archaeological digs in Virginia, archaeologists have made many important discoveries about how enslaved people lived. Recovery of small, everyday items has offered clues to the customs, beliefs, arts, and activities of enslaved people in the Southern Colonies.

History

SLAVERY'S PAST

How did enslaved people live day by day? Narratives and clues dug up from historical sites are helping to answer this question.

In the 1700s, most slaves worked in the rice fields of South Carolina and the tobacco plantations of Virginia and Maryland. Researchers digging near Williamsburg, the colonial capital of Virginia, have found important information about the food that enslaved people ate, items they owned, and how they may have used the little free time they had.

Thousands of handmade objects and things bought in stores give clues to the past. Personal items such as hand-woven baskets, pencils, slates, and reading glasses show how people tried hard to keep part of their lives free from the burden of slavery.

Slave Quarters These cabins near Williamsburg, Virginia, have been restored to the way they looked in the 1700s.

Reaching All Learners

Extra Support

Today's Artifacts

- Have students get adult permission to collect "artifacts" from home.
- Have them display their artifacts and tell the story behind each.
- The class can discuss what people in the future might think the objects were used for.

Bodily-kinesthetic; verbal-linguistic

On Level

Time Capsule Items

Ask each student to select one item that they would include in a time capsule to be opened one hundred years from today. Have students draw a picture of the item they chose and write a brief explanation of why they would include it.

Visual-spatial; verbal-linguistic

Challenge

Identify Fragments

- Tell students that archaeologists often find only a fragment of an item. To identify the fragment, they compare it to artifacts that have already been found.
- Ask students to suppose that they are archaeologists living in the next century. Have each student prepare field notes describing a fragment that they have found at a twenty-first-century dig site. Ask the rest of the class to identify the fragment.

Verbal-linguistic; bodily-kinesthetic

Reading History's Clues

Dr. Theresa Singleton is a professor of archaeology at Syracuse University. She has a special interest in the lives of slaves. "To me," Singleton says, "the most important discoveries have been usable objects made from broken and discarded materials, such as fish-hooks from nails." Such findings prove that the people were not just victims, Singleton explains:

"They were thinkers and doers who improved their situations as best they could despite the odds against them."

— Dr. Theresa Singleton

HISTORY

① **Inside the Cabins** Fireplaces were made of clay and wood. As many as nine adults may have slept in one cabin on mattresses filled with corn husks.

② **Possessions** Furniture was simple: barrels, old tables, and chairs. This pewter plate may have been purchased through extra labor.

Activities

1. **TALK ABOUT IT** What questions would you like to ask Dr. Singleton about her discoveries?
2. **WRITE ABOUT IT** Why is it difficult for historians to find information about the daily lives of enslaved people? Write a one-page paper that answers this question.

217

2 Leveled Activities

❶ **Talk About It** *For Extra Support*
Sample response: What is the item found at the site that surprised you the most?

❷ **Write About It** *For Challenge*

Writing Rubric

4	Position clearly stated; reasons supported by examples; no errors in mechanics.
3	Position adequately stated; most reasons supported by examples; few errors in mechanics.
2	Position stated; reasons poorly supported by examples; some errors in mechanics.
1	Position not stated; reasons not supported by examples; many errors in mechanics.

ELL

Intermediate/Advanced

- Have students work in small groups. Place several tools on the table that an archaeologist might use at a dig, such as a trowel, measuring tape, small brush, and magnifying glass.
- Discuss with students the function of each tool. Use visual aids, props, and role-play to reinforce understanding.
- Have each student create an illustration showing how one of the tools is used at a dig.

Visual-spatial

Language Arts

Tell the Story of an Artifact

- Ask students to suppose that they are an artifact from the dig, such as a piece of pottery, a pair of reading glasses, an item of jewelry, or a fishhook made from a nail.
- Have students write a story from the point of view of that item. Explain that the story needs to give a glimpse of the life of the person who owned or used the artifact.

Verbal-linguistic

Graphic Organizer

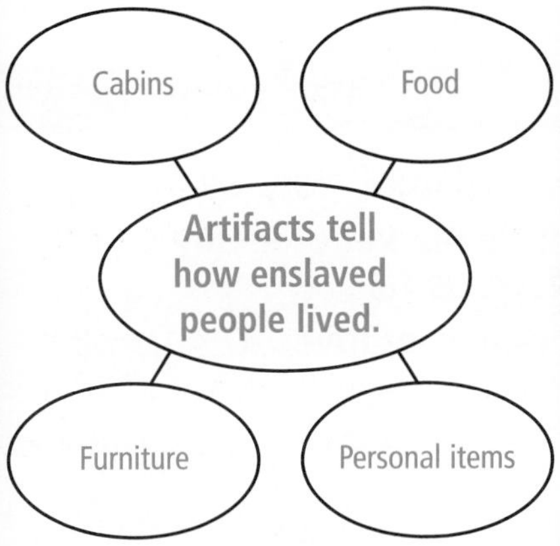

Graphic Organizer 13

Chapter Review

Tested Objectives

The lesson objective assessed by each question is shown in parentheses after the answer.

Visual Summary

1. William Penn; to create a colony where all Christians could live together in peace. *(Obj. U3-9)*
2. Cecilius Calvert (Lord Baltimore); to make a refuge for Catholics. *(Obj. U3-15)*
3. James Oglethorpe; to have a place for poor British people and debtors. *(Obj. U3-15)*

Facts and Main Ideas

4. England captured New Netherland; the king gave the land to the Duke of York; the duke gave part of it to the founders of New Jersey. *(Obj. U3-8)*
5. because the proprietors believed in religious tolerance and the land was inexpensive *(Obj. U3-12)*
6. planters and white men who owned property *(Obj. U3-14)*
7. the first law to promise that all Christians could worship freely *(Obj. U3-12)*
8. formed close ties, created a community adopted Christianity *(Obj. U3-18)*

Vocabulary

9. **legislature** *(Obj. U3-14)*
10. **free market economy** *(Obj. U3-16)*
11. **representative** *(Obj. U3-14)*

Review and Test Prep

Visual Summary

1–3. Complete the chart below with descriptions of each colony.

Colony	Founder	Reason for Settlement
Pennsylvania		
Maryland		
Georgia		

Facts and Main Ideas

TEST PREP Answer each question with information from the chapter.

4. **History** What events led to the founding of New York and New Jersey?
5. **History** Why did the Middle Colonies have such a diverse population?
6. **Citizenship** Who could vote and be elected to Virginia's House of Burgesses?
7. **Government** What was the Toleration Act in Maryland?
8. **History** Describe one thing that enslaved Africans did to survive life under slavery.

Vocabulary

TEST PREP Choose the correct word from the list below to complete each sentence.

representative, p. 189
free market economy, p. 198
legislature, p. 203

9. People in the Virginia ______ had the power to make and change laws.
10. Colonists were able to decide what crops and goods they wanted to produce in a ______.
11. A ______ was chosen by the colonists to speak and act for them in the House of Burgesses.

Reading/Language Arts Wrap-Up

Reading Strategy: Monitor/Clarify

Review with students the process of monitoring their understanding and clarifying anything they do not understand.

Have students work in pairs, taking turns to model the process as they read.

Partners can help each other clarify important points.

Writing Strategy

As students write, they can apply what they have learned about monitoring and clarifying text.

After writing a draft, students can go back and read their own writing, applying the strategy as they do. By monitoring their reading, students can find points that need clarification.

CHAPTER SUMMARY TIMELINE

1607 Virginia founded
1632 Maryland founded
1681 Pennsylvania founded
1702 New Jersey created
1732 Georgia founded

1600 1620 1640 1660 1680 1700 1720 1740

Apply Skills

TEST PREP **Citizenship Skill** Read the paragraph below. Then use what you have learned about making a decision to answer each question.

> In the 1600s, many Catholics in Britain were punished for their religious beliefs. John is a young Catholic man living in England. He is thinking about moving to the new colony of Maryland.

12. John needs to learn more about life in Maryland. Which of the following people could best help him make a decision?
- **A.** someone who heard about Maryland
- **B.** someone who visited Maryland
- **C.** someone who lived in Georgia
- **D.** a Catholic who lived in Germany

13. For John, what would be a benefit of moving to Maryland?
- **A.** There would be no slavery in Maryland.
- **B.** It would be very expensive to get to Maryland.
- **C.** He could be a member of the House of Burgesses in Virginia.
- **D.** Colonists in Maryland believe in religious tolerance.

Critical Thinking

TEST PREP Write a short paragraph to answer each question.

14. Compare and Contrast How was the Pennsylvania Assembly similar to and different from the New York and New Jersey assemblies?

15. Summarize What were the different ways people made a living in the Middle and Southern Colonies?

Timeline

Use the Chapter Summary Timeline above to answer the question.

16. Which of the colonies listed on the timeline were founded in the 1700s?

Activities

HANDS ON **Map Activity** Make a map of crops grown in the Middle and Southern Colonies. Use library resources and information from the chapter.

Writing Activity Write a short story about an apprentice. Describe his or her trade and life in the Middle Colonies.

Technology
Writing Process Tips
Get help with your story at
www.eduplace.com/kids/hmss05/

219

Apply Skills

12. B *(Obj. U3-10)*
13. D *(Obj. U3-10)*

Critical Thinking

14. Similar: All three assemblies were made up of representatives chosen by the colonists. Different: In Pennsylvania, the representatives could approve or reject laws that the governor and council suggested. In New York and New Jersey, the assembly helped the governor and council make laws, but it did not have much power.
(Obj. U3-8, U3-9)

15. Colonists were mainly farmers, but also merchants, shopkeepers, and artisans.
(Obj. U3-13, U3-16)

Timeline

16. Virginia, Maryland, and Pennsylvania
(Obj. U3-15)

Leveled Activities

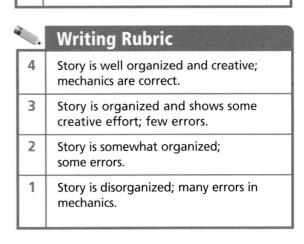

HANDS ON Performance Task Rubric

4	Information is accurate and very well presented; map details are all present.
3	Information is generally accurate and well presented; most details present.
2	Information contains some errors and fairly presented; few details present.
1	Information is inaccurate and poorly presented; map details are absent.

Writing Rubric

4	Story is well organized and creative; mechanics are correct.
3	Story is organized and shows some creative effort; few errors.
2	Story is somewhat organized; some errors.
1	Story is disorganized; many errors in mechanics.

Technology

Test Generator

You can generate your own version of the chapter review by using the **Test Generator CD-ROM**.

Web Link

For more ideas, visit
www.eduplace.com/ss/hmss05/

Standards

National Standards

I a Similarities and differences in addressing human needs
I e Importance of cultural unity and diversity
V e Tension between an individual's beliefs and government policies and laws
VI h Tensions between the wants and needs and fairness, equity, and justice
VII a Scarcity and choice
VI d Institutions that make up economic systems
VII f Influence of incentives, values, traditions, and habits on economic decisions
VII i Use economic concepts
X a Identify key ideals

Unit Review

Vocabulary and Main Ideas

1. A region's growing season will affect what crops a farmer plants. Longer growing seasons give crops more time to grow than shorter ones. *(Obj. U3-2)*
2. Colonists participated in town meetings. *(Obj. U3-6)*
3. They could not govern their colonies effectively from so far away so they sometimes allowed colonists to govern themselves. *(Obj. U3-8)*
4. The proprietors did not tell colonists how to earn their living, so they were free to earn money in whatever ways they thought were best. *(Obj. U3-13)*
5. Planters grew indigo, rice, and tobacco. *(Obj. U3-16)*
6. They needed to learn a trade or skill so that they could earn a living later in life. *(Obj. U3-6, U3-13)*

Critical Thinking

7. **Sample answer:** A region's rainfall, soil, and growing season all can affect farming. A forested area makes logging possible. A region with good harbors is good for shipping and fishing. *(Obj. U3-2)*
8. Answers should include a fact from the text and a statement of opinion. *(Obj. U3-3, U3-12, U3-16, U3-18)*

Apply Skills

9. C *(Obj. U3-7)*
10. A *(Obj. U3-7)*

UNIT 3 Review and Test Prep

Vocabulary and Main Ideas

TEST PREP Write a sentence to answer each question.

1. Why is a region's **growing season** important to farmers who live there?
2. What was one way in which New England colonists took part in **self-government?**
3. Why did some proprietors of the Middle Colonies allow colonists to elect **representatives** to assemblies?
4. In what ways did colonists in the Middle Colonies participate in a **free market economy?**
5. What cash crops were grown most commonly on southern **plantations?**
6. Why did some colonial children become **apprentices?**

Critical Thinking

TEST PREP Apply what you have learned about critical thinking to answer each question.

7. **Generalize** How can the geography and climate of a region affect how people earn a living there?
8. **Fact and Opinion** Write one fact and one opinion about life in each of the following regions: New England, the Middle Colonies, and the Southern Colonies.

Apply Skills

TEST PREP Chart and Graph Skill Use the unfinished line graph below and what you know about making a line graph to answer each question.

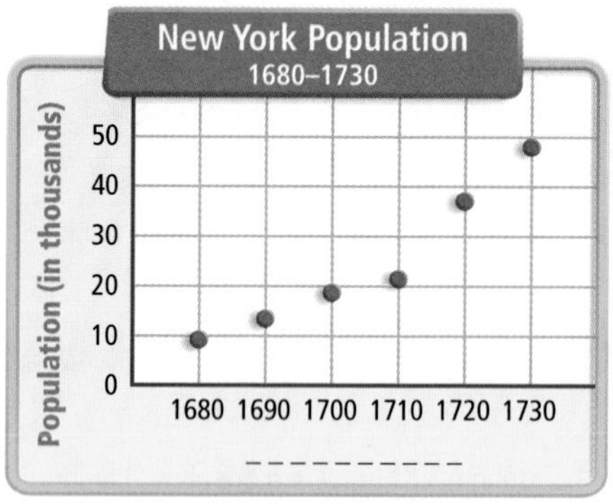

9. Which is the best label for the horizontal axis of this line graph?
   A. Number of People
   B. Time
   C. Year
   D. Population Growth
10. What should you do after you draw dots to show the data on the line graph?
   A. Connect the dots with a line.
   B. Draw a bar from the bottom of the graph to where the dot is.
   C. Choose a color for the dot.
   D. Connect each dot to the correct year.

Technology

Test Generator

- Use the **Test Generator CD-ROM** to create tests customized to your class.
- Access hundreds of test questions and make lesson, chapter, and unit quizzes and tests.

Web Updates

Curious about new trade book titles that you can use with the program? Visit www.eduplace.com/ss/hmss05/ to update your Unit Bibliography.

Extra Support

Write Cloze Sentences

Have students write cloze sentences about material in the unit and exchange sentences with another student. Challenge them to complete their partners' sentences.

Unit Activity

The Big Idea

Interview Different Colonists

- With three classmates, interview three people who have moved to different colonies.
- Ask which colony each person moved to and why he or she chose that colony.
- Ask the colonists how life in the colonies has differed from their expectations.
- Act out the interview for your class.

At the Library

You may find these books at your school or public library.

The Voyage of Patience Goodspeed by Heather V. Frederick
After their mother dies, Patience and her brother sail with their father aboard his Nantucket whaler.

Giants in the Land by Diana Applebaum
Colonial New England's forests of giant white pine trees were cleared to build British war ships.

CURRENT EVENTS
WEEKLY WR READER

Connect to Today

Create a bulletin board about people moving to new places.

- Find articles about people moving to new places.
- Write a summary of each article, explaining why people are moving. Draw a picture or map to show where or how they are traveling.
- Display your summaries and pictures on a bulletin board in your classroom.

Technology
Get information for your bulletin board from the Weekly Reader at **www.eduplace.com/kids/hmss05/**

Read About It

Look for these Social Studies Independent Books in your classroom.

Math

Test Taking Tip

Remind students that when a line graph starts low at the left and ends high on the right, the graph is showing an increase. When the line starts high at the left and ends low at the right, the graph is showing a decrease.

Standards

National Standards

I a Similarities and differences in addressing human needs; **I e** Importance of cultural unity and diversity; **III g** How people create places; **III h** Interaction of human beings and their physical environment; **IV e** Influence of family, groups, and community; **V e** Tension between an individual's beliefs and government policies and laws; **VII f** Influence of incentives, values, traditions, and habits on economic decisions; **VII i** Use economic concepts; **IX b** Conflict, cooperation, and interdependence

Unit Activity

HANDS ON Performance Task Rubric

4	Questions and answers clearly stated; reasons supported by information from the text; shows considerable creative effort; mechanics are correct.
3	Questions and answers adequately stated; most reasons supported by information from the text; shows creative effort; few errors in mechanics.
2	Questions and answers stated; reasons confused or poorly supported by text information; shows some creative effort; some errors in mechanics.
1	Questions and answers not stated; reasons not supported; shows no creative effort; many errors in mechanics.

WEEKLY WR READER

Unit Project

- Have volunteers present their bulletin board displays to the class. Have students discuss what they have learned about migration.

At the Library

- You may wish to wrap up the unit by reading aloud from one of these suggested titles or from one of the Read-Aloud selections included in the Unit Bibliography.

Read About It

- You may wish to provide students with the appropriate Leveled Social Studies Books for this unit. Turn to page 153B for teaching options.
- If students have written summaries or reviews of the Leveled Books or the books in the Unit Bibliography, you may wish to compile them in a class notebook.

Unit 4 Unit Planner

Begin with Core. Extend for more.

Revolution and Independence

Chapter 7 Pages 226–259

Causes of the American Revolution

Core Lesson 1 pp. 228–231
French and Indian War

Extend Lesson 1 pp. 232–233
Biography George Washington

Core Lesson 2 pp. 234–237
Early Conflicts with Britain

Extend Lesson 2 pp. 238–239
Economics Taxes in the Colonies

Core Lesson 3 pp. 240–243
Conflicts Grow

Extend Lesson 3 pp. 244–247
Literature *Emma's Journal* by Marissa Moss

Skillbuilder
Identify Causes and Effects pp. 248–249

Core Lesson 4 pp. 250–255
War Begins

Extend Lesson 4 pp. 256–257
Geography Battle of Bunker Hill

Chapter Review pp. 258–259

Chapter 8 Pages 260–293

The War for Independence

Core Lesson 1 pp. 262–267
Declaring Independence

Extend Lesson 1 pp. 268–269
Biography Thomas Jefferson

Core Lesson 2 pp. 270–273
Life During the War

Extend Lesson 2 pp. 274–277
Readers' Theater Patriot or Loyalist

Core Lesson 3 pp. 278–281
The War in the North

Extend Lesson 3 pp. 282–283
Primary Source Valley Forge

Skillbuilder
Read a Battle Map pp. 284–285

Core Lesson 4 pp. 286–289
Winning the War

Extend Lesson 4 pp. 290–291
Geography A Global View

Chapter Review pp. 292–293

Chapter 9 Pages 294–327

Creating a Nation

Core Lesson 1 pp. 296–299
A New Nation

Extend Lesson 1 pp. 300–301
Economics Chain of Debt

Core Lesson 2 pp. 302–307
Constitutional Convention

Extend Lesson 2 pp. 308–309
Citizenship World Constitutions

Skillbuilder
Understand Point of View pp. 310–311

Core Lesson 3 pp. 312–317
The Constitution

Extend Lesson 3 pp. 318–319
History The Liberty Bell

Core Lesson 4 pp. 320–323
President Washington

Extend Lesson 4 pp. 324–325
Citizenship Washington, D.C.

Chapter Review pp. 326–327

Special Section: Government pp. 328–335

Unit Review
pp. 336–337

LEVELED BOOKS

The following Social Studies Independent Books are available for extending and supporting students' social studies experience as they read the unit.

Differentiated Instruction

Extra Support

Peter Salem, Hero of the Revolution
By Eric Oatman

Summary: Peter Salem, a brave African American Patriot, fights many battles for his country's freedom from the British.

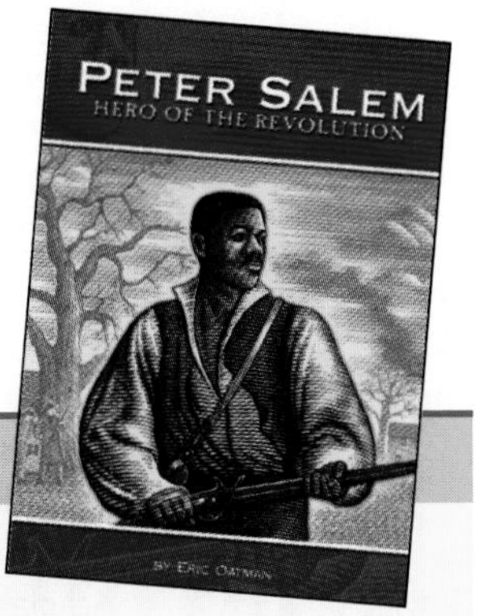

Vocabulary

militia
ammunition
stumbled

Extending Understanding

Oral Language: Interview Ask students to work in pairs, one taking the role of Peter Salem and the other, that of a reporter who interviews the hero about his life.

Independent Writing: Journal Have students pretend to be one of the Regulars who survived the charge up Breed's Hill. Ask them to write a journal entry describing the battle from a Regular's point of view.

Graphic Organizer Students can use a cause-and-effect diagram as they read.

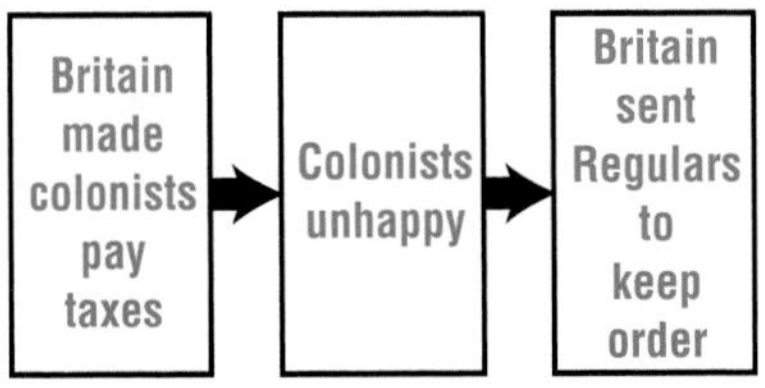

On Level

Daughters of Liberty
By Joan Kane Nichols

Summary: The inspiring stories of three young women who, each in her own way, came to be known as heroes of the American Revolution.

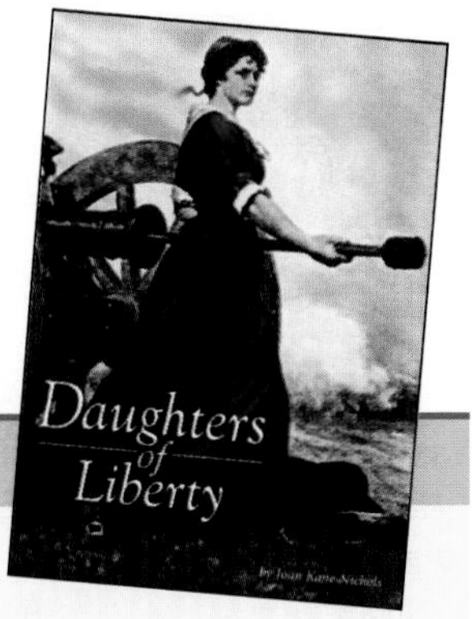

Vocabulary

compositor
Tories
enslaved

Extending Understanding

Oral Language: Dialogue Have students improvise a dialogue that Theodore Sedgewick and Elizabeth Freeman might have had as they discussed her right to freedom.

Independent Writing: Posters Have students create posters that advertise the sale of the first printed copies of the Declaration of Independence.

Graphic Organizer Students can use a word web to record words related to printing.

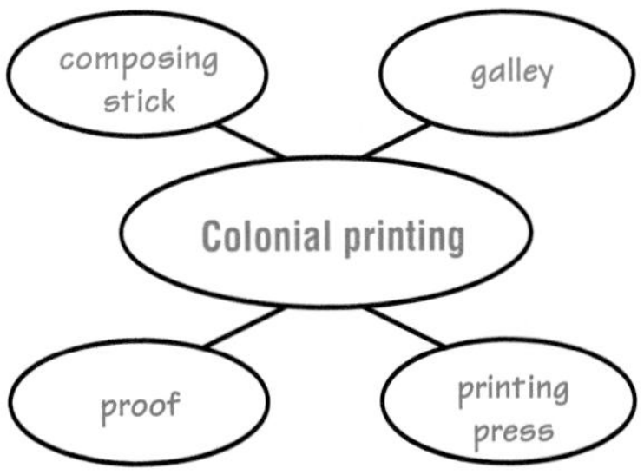

Challenge

John Paul Jones and the Battle at Sea
By James Ross

Summary: John Paul Jones, an ambitious and courageous sailor who fought the British at sea during the American Revolution.

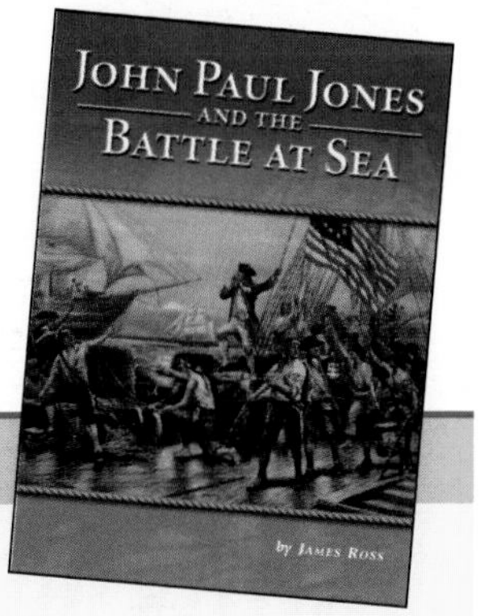

Vocabulary

apprentice
sloop-of-war
grappling hook

Extending Understanding

Oral Language: Speech Have students take the part of John Paul Jones as he tells sailors aboard the *Bonhomme Richard* of his adventures on previous warships and prepares them for the battle ahead.

Independent Writing: Interview Have students write three questions that they might ask John Paul Jones if they had the chance to interview him.

Graphic Organizer Students can use a sequence chart to keep track of the sequence of events.

1.	At age 13, Jones became an apprentice.
2.	Later, Jones became first mate on a slave ship.
3.	Jones joined a cargo ship of which he eventually became captain.

Choices for Reading

- **Extra Support/ELL** Read the selection aloud as students follow along in their books. Pause frequently and help students monitor understanding.
- **On Level** Have partners take turns reading aloud. Students can pause at the end of each page to ask each other questions and check understanding.
- **Challenge** Students can read the selection and write down any questions they have. Then they can work in small groups to answer their questions.

Go to www.eduplace.com/ss/hmss05/ for answers to Responding questions found at the back of the books.

Bibliography

Books for Independent Reading

Social Studies Key

- Biography
- Citizenship
- Cultures
- Economics
- Geography
- History

Social Studies Leveled Readers with lesson plans by Irene Fountas support the content of this unit.

Extra Support

The Declaration of Independence
by Sam Fink
Scholastic 2002

Each phrase of the Declaration of Independence is presented and accompanied by illustrations that help to explicate the meaning of the words.

George Washington
by Cheryl Harness
National Geographic 2000
This picture book biography of Washington focuses on the Revolutionary War years and his presidency.

The Boston Massacre
by Dee Ready
Bridgestone 2002
Reproductions of engravings, paintings, and documents supplement this brief introduction to the events of the Boston Massacre. See others in series.

Nathan Hale: Patriot Spy
by Shannon Zemlicka
Lerner 2002

Hale risked his honor and his life to become a spy for General Washington.

They Called Her Molly Pitcher
by Anne F. Rockwell
Knopf 2002

Molly Hays became a legend by carrying water to wounded soldiers and firing a canon during the Battle of Monmouth.

On Level

Growing Up in Revolution and the New Nation 1775 to 1800
by Brandon M. Miller
Lerner 2003
Primary source material reveals the lives of young people during the Revolution and through 1800.

Love Thy Neighbor: The Tory Diary of Prudence Emerson
by Ann Turner
Scholastic 2003
A girl chronicles the hardships British Loyalists face in western Massachusetts in 1774.

The Secret Soldier
by Ann McGovern
Scholastic 1999
Deborah Sampson became a soldier in the Continental Army by dressing as a man in this true story.

The Fighting Ground
by Avi
Harper 1987
Thirteen-year-old Jonathan, eager to fight the British, discovers that war is not all fame and glory.

Challenge

The Winter People
by Joseph Bruchac
Dial 2002

An Abenaki boy sets off to rescue his mother and sisters who have been kidnapped by the English during the French and Indian War.

Come All You Brave Soldiers: Blacks in the Revolutionary War
by Clinton Cox
Scholastic 1999

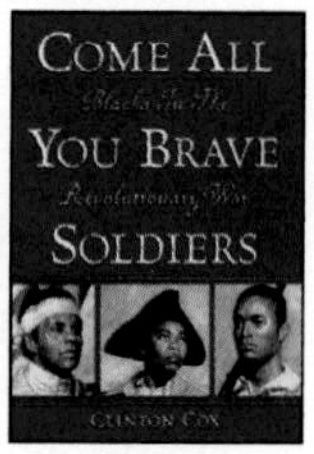

A survey of African American participation in the Revolution tells of soldiers who fought at Lexington, Concord, Yorktown, and elsewhere.

Yankee Doodle and the Redcoats
by Susan Beller Provost
Twenty-First Century 2003
Based on documents written by soldiers and others on both sides of the Revolutionary War, this books describes daily routines in the context of historical events.

Sarah Bishop
by Scott O'Dell
Houghton Mifflin 1980
Sarah struggles to make a new life for herself after the deaths of her father and brother in the Revolutionary War.

Your State Specific Materials

With the Program

at www.eduplace.com/ss/hmss05

Read Aloud and Reference

Read Aloud Books

Johnny Tremain
by Esther Forbes
Houghton 1943
Forbes's classic tells the story of a young silversmith's apprentice in Boston at the time of the American Revolution.

The Signers: The 56 Stories Behind the Declaration of Independence
by Dennis Fradin
Walker 2002
This collective biography introduces the signers of the Declaration of Independence and offers a short history of the thirteen colonies.

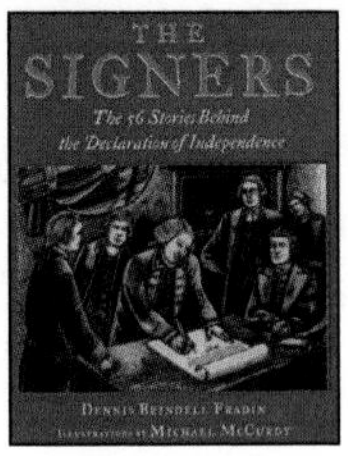

Hour of Freedom
by Milton Meltzer
Boyds Mills 2003
This collection of poems about America's history includes a section on the country's struggle for independence.

Reference Books

The French and Indian War: 1660-1763
by Christopher Collier and James L. Collier
Benchmark 1998
This comprehensive look at the French and Indian War explains why it became a key stepping stone to the American Revolution.

Countdown to Independence
by Natalie S. Bober
Atheneum 2001
Thirty-five brief chapters alternate between Britain and the colonies from George III's 1760 ascension to the throne to the Declaration of Independence on July 2, 1776.

The United States Constitution
by Karen Price Hossell
Heinemann 2004
This important document is clearly expounded for readers.

Free and Inexpensive Materials

The National Archives
700 Pennsylvania Ave. NW
Washington, DC 20408
Phone: (866) 272-6272

The National Archives website (www.archives.gov) allows you to virtually visit the archives and see important documents from our nation's history.

MULTIMEDIA RESOURCES

PROGRAM RESOURCES

Unit Video
Audio Student's Book with Primary Sources and Songs MP3/CD
Lesson Planner and Teacher Resource CD-ROM
Test Generator CD-ROM
eBook
eBook, Teacher's Edition
Transparencies: Big Idea & Skillbuilder, Interactive
Almanac Map & Graph Practice
Primary Sources Plus: Document-Based Questions
Research and Writing Projects
Bringing Social Studies Alive
Family Newsletter
GeoNet

CD-ROM

The American Revolution PictureShow. National Geographic

Shh! We're Writing the Constitution, *Jean Fritz.* Weston Woods

The Constitution. Tom Snyder Productions

VIDEOCASSETTES

The American Revolution 1770-1790. Media Basics

Minutemen of the American Revolution. Media Basics

Seeds of Liberty: Causes of the American Revolution. Rainbow Educational Media

Valley Forge. Media Basics

AUDIOCASSETTES

The Fighting Ground, *Avi.* Listening Library

Where Was Patrick Henry on the 29th of May? *Jean Fritz.* Weston Woods

Assessment Options

TEST PREP

You are the best evaluator of your students' progress and attainments. To help you in this task, Houghton Mifflin Social Studies provides you with a variety of assessment tools.

Classroom-Based Assessment

Written and Oral Assessment

In the student book:
- **Lesson Reviews** appear at the end of each lesson.
- **Chapter Reviews** appear on pp. 258–259, 292–293, and 326–327.
- **Unit Reviews** appear on pp. 336–337.

In the *Assessment Options* ancillary:
- **Lesson Quizzes** appear for all lessons.
- **Chapter Tests** appear for all chapters.
- **Unit Tests** appear for all units.

Technology:
- **Test Generator** provides even more assessment options.

Informal, Continuous Assessment

Comprehension

In the student book:
- **"Review"** questions appear at the end of each section.

In the teacher's edition:
- **"Talk About It" questions** monitor student comprehension.
- **Tested Objectives** appear at the beginning and end of each lesson.

In the student practice book:
- **Study Guide** pages aid student comprehension.

Reading

In the teacher's edition:
- **Reading Strategy** is featured in every chapter.

Thinking

In the student book:
- **Critical Thinking** questions teach higher-order thinking skills.

In the teacher's edition:
- **"Think Alouds"** let you model thinking critically for your students.

In the *Assessment Options* ancillary:
- **Observation Checklists** give you another option for assessment.

HANDS ON Rubric for Unit 4 Performance Assessment

4	Dialogue shows excellent understanding of events and gives details; events mentioned are in correct order; sounds like a real conversation.
3	Dialogue shows adequate understanding of events but does not give details; most events mentioned are in correct order; sounds mostly real.
2	Dialogue shows some understanding of events but does not give details; some events mentioned are in correct order; sounds mostly like expository text.
1	Dialogue shows little or no understanding of events, details absent; most events mentioned are in correct order; is expository text, not a conversation.

In *Assessment Options*, p. 97

Standardized Test Practice

In the student book:
- **Lesson Review/Test Prep** appears at the end of each lesson.
- **Chapter Review/Test Prep** appears at the end of each chapter.
- **Unit Review/Test Prep** appears at the end of each unit.

In the *Assessment Options* ancillary:
- **Lesson Tests for all lessons.**
- **Chapter Tests for all chapters.**
- **Unit Test for all units.**

Technology:
- **Test Generator** provides even more assessment options.

Student Self-Assessment

In the student book:
- **Hands-On Activities** appear in each chapter.
- **Writing Activities** appear in each chapter.

In the Unit Resources:
- **Reading Skill/Strategy** pages give students the chance to practice the skills and strategies of each lesson and chapter.
- **Vocabulary Review/Study Guide** pages provide an opportunity for self-challenge or review.

In the *Assessment Options* ancillary:
- **Self-Assessment Checklists**

Unit 4 Test

Standard Test

TEST PREP

Unit 4 Test

Test Your Knowledge

Circle the letter of the best answer.

1. What were the Articles of Confederation? Obj. U4–19
   - A. a plan to resolve the slavery conflict
   - (B.) a plan for central government
   - C. a plan for state government
   - D. a plan for the government of the Northwest Territory

2. What did Thomas Paine's *Common Sense* say? Obj. U4–10
   - (F.) The colonies should fight for independence from Britain.
   - G. The Declaration of Independence is a mistake.
   - H. The colonists should support the king.
   - J. All people have rights that cannot be taken away.

3. Why did the Antifederalists think the Constitution was dangerous? Obj. U4–23
   - A. It was not ratified by all of the colonies.
   - B. It eliminated the federal government.
   - (C.) It did not contain a Bill of Rights.
   - D. It set up courts to settle cases.

4. Why did the British start the French and Indian War? Obj. U4–1
   - F. They wanted to unite the American Indians.
   - (G.) They wanted to drive the French from the Ohio River Valley.
   - H. They wanted to stop the French from taking over their colonies.
   - J. They wanted to make American Indians end the fur trade.

5. In what way does the Constitution keep any one branch of government from becoming too powerful? Obj. U4–25
   - A. through the Senate and the House of Representatives
   - B. with amendments and bills
   - C. through the Bill of Rights
   - (D.) with a system of checks and balances

6. What problem faced the United States Congress after the Revolutionary War? Obj. U4–20
   - (F.) what to do with the Northwest Territory
   - G. which states to tax
   - H. who to put in charge of the army
   - J. how to spend money raised from taxes

Standard Test

TEST PREP

Test the Skills: Read a Battle Map; Identify Causes and Effects

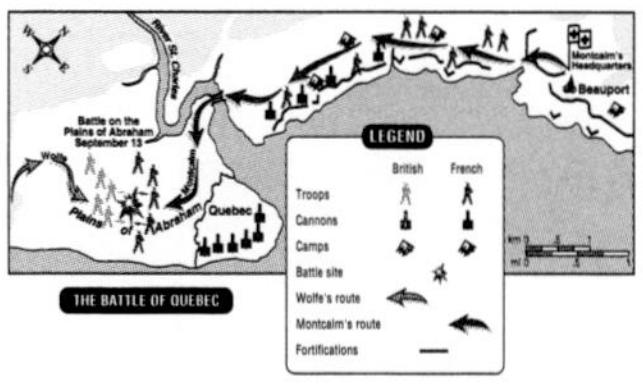

Use the battle map to answer the questions below.

7. Which group had cannons in Quebec? The French Obj. U4–16

8. Where were Montcalm's Headquarters located? Where did he and his troops march to fight? Obj. U4–16
   The headquarters were located at Beauport: Montcalm and his troops marched to the Plains of Abraham.

> Britain and France both had colonies in North America. The two nations fought over land in the Ohio River Valley. The French traded furs with the American Indians who lived there. The British began moving into the area. They wanted to trade furs, too, and farm the land. This conflict was one factor leading to the French and Indian War.

Write the causes for the French and British battle over the Ohio River Valley. Obj. U4–7

9. Both countries wanted to control the fur trade with the American Indians.

10. Britain wanted to farm the land.

The French and British fought over the Ohio River Valley.

Standard Test

TEST PREP

Apply Your Knowledge and Skills

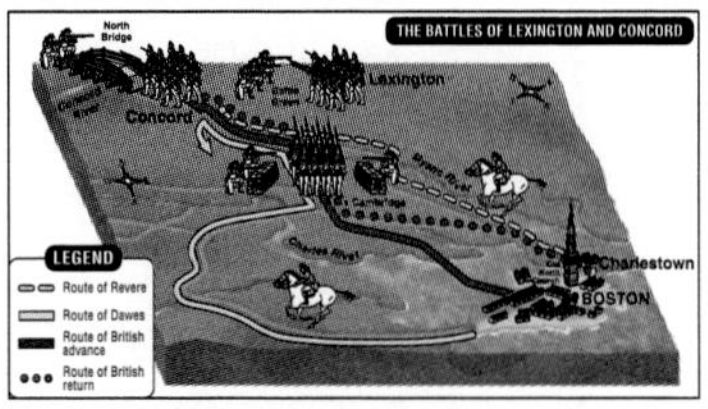

> In the spring of 1775, British spies sent word to General Gage that the Minutemen were collecting weapons and storing them in Concord, a town 17 miles northwest of Boston. On April 18, Gage prepared to send about 800 soldiers to seize the weapons. Patriot spies learned of Gage's plan. Paul Revere and William Dawes rode on horseback to warn the Patriots that the British were coming.

11. Based on the battle map, where did the British troops and the Minutemen battle? Obj. U4–16
    - A. Old North Church
    - B. Boston
    - (C.) Concord
    - D. Charlestown

12. Who wanted to seize the Patriots' weapons stored in Concord? Obj. U4–16
    - (F.) General Gage
    - G. Paul Revere
    - H. the Minutemen
    - J. William Dawes

13. Write a brief essay that describes how Patriot women helped support the American army. Explain what caused some women to become soldiers themselves. Write your essay on a separate sheet of paper. Obj. U4–12
    Essays may refer to the fact that some women worked as spies or messengers; some helped spread the message of freedom by writing letters, plays, and poems; some cooked for and brought water to soldiers on the battlefields; and some even fought in battles when their husbands were killed.

Standard Test

TEST PREP

Apply the Reading Skills and Strategies

> In response to the Townshend Acts, colonists held a boycott of the British goods they bought the most. Instead of importing cloth, for example, organizations of women, called the Daughters of Liberty, wove their own cloth and used it to make clothes. Because of the hard work of these organizations, colonists did not have to buy as much cloth from Britain. When colonists did not buy British goods, British merchants lost money. Once again, Parliament gave in to the colonists. In 1770, taxes were removed from glass, lead, paints, and paper.

Reading Skills

Use the passage above to answer each question.

13. **Sequence** What was the first response of the colonists to the Townshend Acts? Obj. U4–6
    The colonists boycotted the British goods they bought the most.

14. **Cause and Effect** Why did the British remove the tax on glass, lead, paints, and paper in 1770? Obj. U4–6
    The British removed the tax because the colonists boycotted British goods. As a result, British merchants lost money.

Reading Strategy: Question

15. Write two questions that you have that can be answered by the passage above. Obj. U4–6
    Sample answer: What did the Daughters of Liberty do?
    Why did British merchants lose money?

Reaching All Learners

Extra Support

Make a Cause-and-Effect Chart

Pairs	25 minutes
Objective	To track causes and effects
Materials	poster paper, crayons or markers, paper, pencils

- Students can work together on a graphic organizer that shows how various events are interrelated, and how several causes (such as the Stamp Act and the Intolerable Acts) contributed to a single effect.
- You might ask students to conduct an oral presentation to show the class what they have discovered.

Visual-spatial

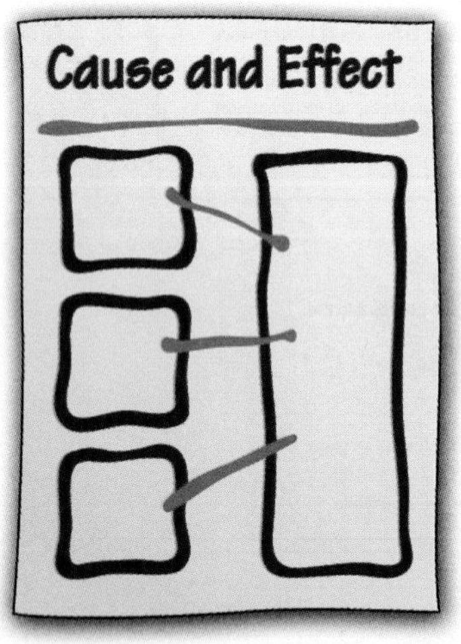

Challenge

Track Changes in Government

Singles	20 minutes
Objective	To observe changes in government over time
Materials	paper, pencils

- As they read this unit, ask students to find out how America's government changed between the time of the French and Indian War and the time George Washington became president.
- Students can create a chart that summarizes what they have learned.

Visual-spatial

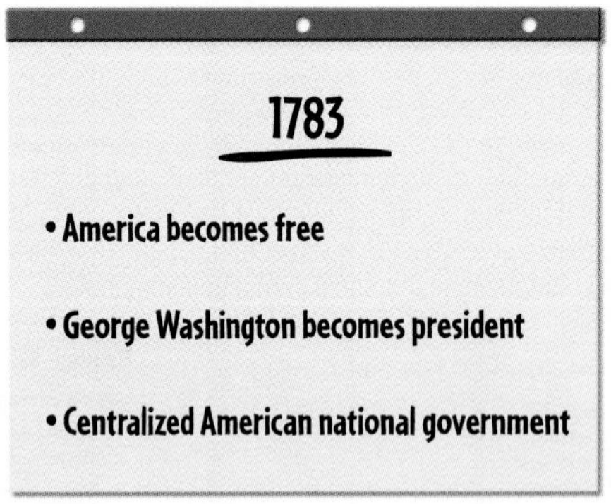

1783
• America becomes free
• George Washington becomes president
• Centralized American national government

ELL

Understanding Timelines

Groups	25 minutes
Objective	To create a timeline
Materials	paper, markers or crayons

Beginning
Explain that a timeline shows the order of events. Draw a timeline of the school year on the board: *September 5: first day of classes; December 22–January 3: winter vacation; June 10: last day.* Help students name other school events and add these to the timeline. Review the meanings of *before, after, first, next,* and other time-order words.

Intermediate
Ask, *What does a timeline help us to understand?* If students need support, explain that a timeline shows the order in which events happened. At the end of each chapter, list some important events on the board. Have partners put the events on a timeline in the correct order.

Advanced
As students read, have them list important dates and events. At the end of each chapter, have partners create a chapter timeline. Compare timelines as a class.

Visual-spatial

Cross-Curricular Activities

Language Arts

Write Historical Fiction

Groups	20 minutes
Objective	To write a story about a Revolutionary character
Materials	paper, pencils, markers or crayons

- Tell students to work together to make up a character who lived at the time of the American Revolution. Ask them to create a story about that character.
- As they read the chapters in this unit, they can add to the character's story, explaining the effect of the events on the character.
- At the end of the unit, students may illustrate their book, bind it, and place it in the Reading Center for all to share.

Verbal-linguistic

Math

Make a Population Graph

Singles	25 minutes
Objective	To make bar graphs of population
Materials	paper, pencil, ruler

- Explain to students that during the time period covered in this unit, the population of the United States changed, particularly in the cities. You may wish to write the following figures on the board:

New York City (1760) 13,500
New York City (1775) 22,000
New York City (1790) 33,000

Philadelphia (1760) 19,000
Philadelphia (1775) 24,000
Philadelphia (1790) 42,000

Charleston (1760) 8,000
Charleston (1775) 13,500
Charleston (1790) 17,000

- Ask students to use the data given to create bar graphs that show each city's changes in population.

Logical-mathematical

Science

Do a Colonial-Era Experiment

Class	25 minutes
Objective	To do a colonial-era experiment
Materials	3 coffee can lids; green, white, and black paper; pan of crushed ice; light source

- Benjamin Franklin was a noted scientist. The following experiment is based on one he did when he was 23.
- Cover one lid with black paper, one with white paper, and one with green.
- Place the lids on the ice in a pan. Put the pan in a sunny window. Which lid sinks most?
- With this experiment, Franklin showed that dark colors absorb heat energy better than light colors do. He used panes of glass and pieces of cloth.

Logical-mathematical

Begin the Unit

Quick Look

Chapter 7 discusses the many causes of the American Revolution, including conflicts with Britain and the French and Indian War.

Chapter 8 discusses the Revolutionary War, from its beginnings in the pages of *Common Sense* to the war-ending Treaty of Paris.

Chapter 9 describes the struggle to form a new nation as outlined in the Constitution of the United States.

Introduce the Big Idea

Citizenship One of the key democratic values of the United States is the importance of freedom, both as a nation and as individuals. As students discuss what freedom means to them personally, have them consider how they are affected by the fact that they live in a free society.

Explain that this unit is about the struggle to set up this free society.

Primary Sources

Invite a volunteer to read the quote by Mercy Otis Warren on page 222. Ask students what they think she means. List student responses on the board.

UNIT 4

The American Revolution

The Big Idea

What does freedom mean to you?

In 1775, Mercy Otis Warren said,

"In Freedom we're born, and like Sons of the brave, Will never surrender,..."

Paul Revere
1734–1818

Paul Revere's famous midnight ride is one of the legends of the Revolution. He and other alarm riders sped through the night to warn Patriots that British troops were on the move.
page 251

Unit Video

Motivate and Build Background

You may wish to show the Unit Video after students have discussed the Big Idea question on this page.

After viewing, ask students to **summarize** what they already know about the content covered in this unit. Ask volunteers to **predict** what else they think they will learn.

You can find more video teaching suggestions on pages TR1 and TR2 in the Resource Section in the back of the Teacher's Edition.

History Makers

Mercy Otis Warren
1728–1814

This playwright used her skills as a writer to support the cause of freedom. Her plays made fun of British leaders and complained about how the British treated the colonies.

page 250

Samuel Adams
1722–1803

What weapon did this famous Patriot use against the British? His sharp mind. Adams got Patriots together and secretly planned the Boston Tea Party, which enraged the British.

page 235

Technology

E-Biographies

To learn more about the History Makers on these pages and in this unit, visit **www.eduplace.com/kids/hmss05/**

Designed to be accessed by your students, these biographies can be used for

- research projects
- Character Education
- developing students' technology skills

Correcting Misconceptions

Ask students what they know about the American Revolution. Write their responses as a list on the board. As students read this unit, periodically check the list to see if any of their responses have been shown to be misconceptions. Discuss why students may have thought as they did, and what they have learned.

History Makers

Paul Revere Paul Revere was one of the men who spread the alarm when the British marched on Lexington. Lanterns similar to the one shown here were placed in a church tower to alert him as he waited across the river.

Mercy Otis Warren The pen, even when it is made from a feather such as the one shown, can be mightier than the sword. Mercy Otis Warren wielded her pen well as she wrote poems and plays that poked fun at the British and led many Americans to support the Patriot cause.

Samuel Adams Samuel Adams wrote and spoke in strong support for the Patriots. That's not all he did: he was a brilliant planner, and came up with the idea behind the Boston Tea Party, during which tea chests similar to the one shown were thrown into Boston Harbor in protest.

Map and Graph Skills

Interpreting Maps

Talk About It

1. **Q Geography** What type of information can you learn from this map?
   A what countries had land claims in North America in the 1760s
2. **Q Geography** Which nation—Spain or Britain—claimed the largest part of what is now the United States?
   A Spain
3. **Q Geography** Which European settlements fell within territory reserved for American Indians?
   A Niagara, Detroit, Michilimackinac

Critical Thinking

Infer Ask students to find St. Augustine on the map. According to the map legend, what type of settlement is it? a Spanish mission From that fact, what can they infer about the previous history of St. Augustine, which in the 1760s was located in a British-claimed area? The area must have once been claimed by Spain.

Interpreting Timelines

Ask students if they can identify any of the images shown on the timeline. Anti-Stamp Act teapot; Minuteman Statue; Liberty Bell; painting of the surrender at Yorktown (which appears in full on page 261); a copy of the Constitution of the United States

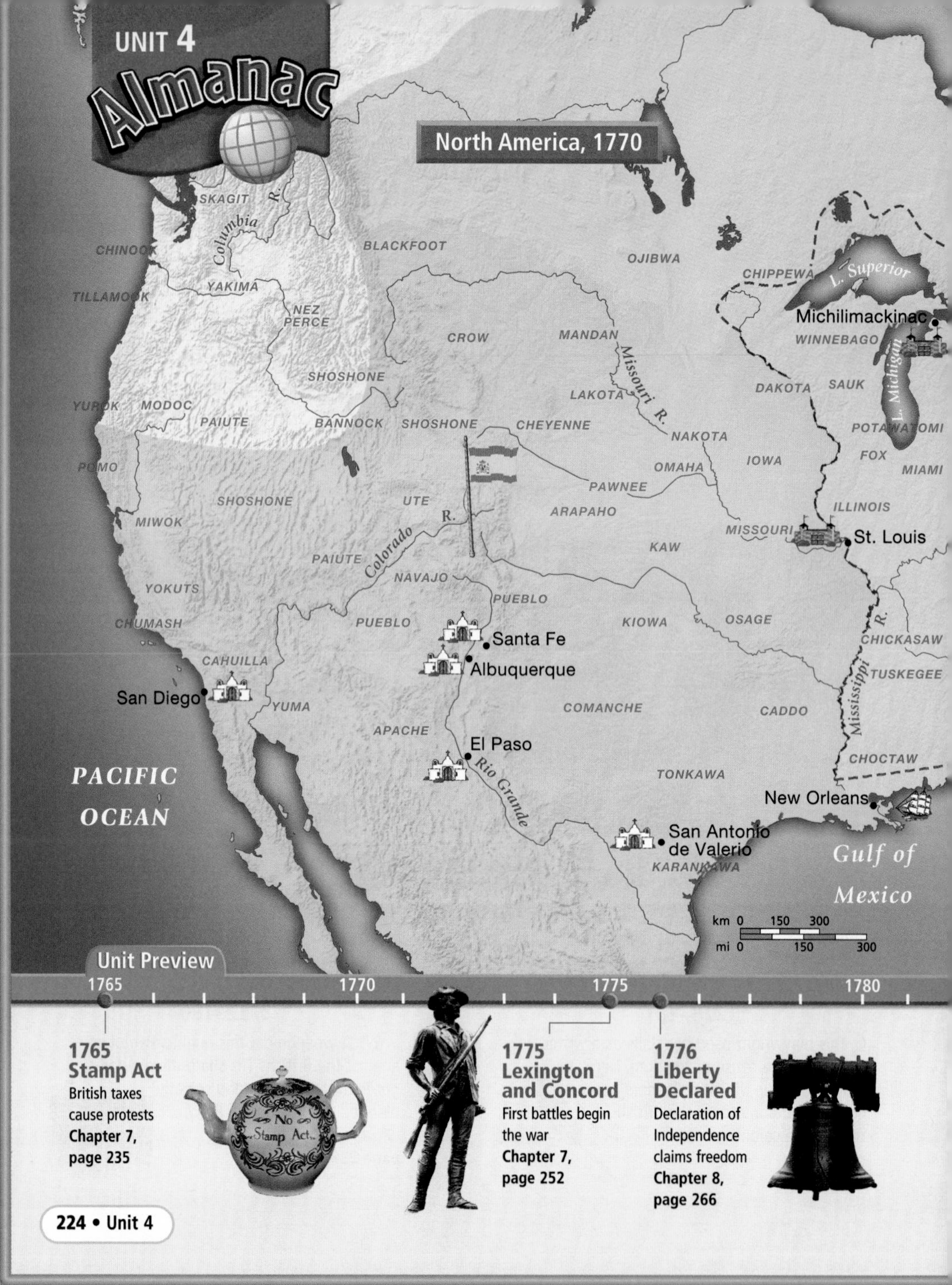

Technology

GeoNet

To support student geography skills, you may wish to have them go to www.eduplace.com/kids/hmss05/ to play GeoNet.

Math

How Many People?

Have students calculate the total population of the 13 colonies in the 1760s, with the understanding that 80 percent of the population equals 1,350,000 people.

$$80\% \text{ of } x = 1.35 \text{ million}$$
$$\frac{0.8x}{0.8} = \frac{1.35 \text{ million}}{0.8}$$
$$x = 1.6875 \text{ million}$$
or about 1,690,000

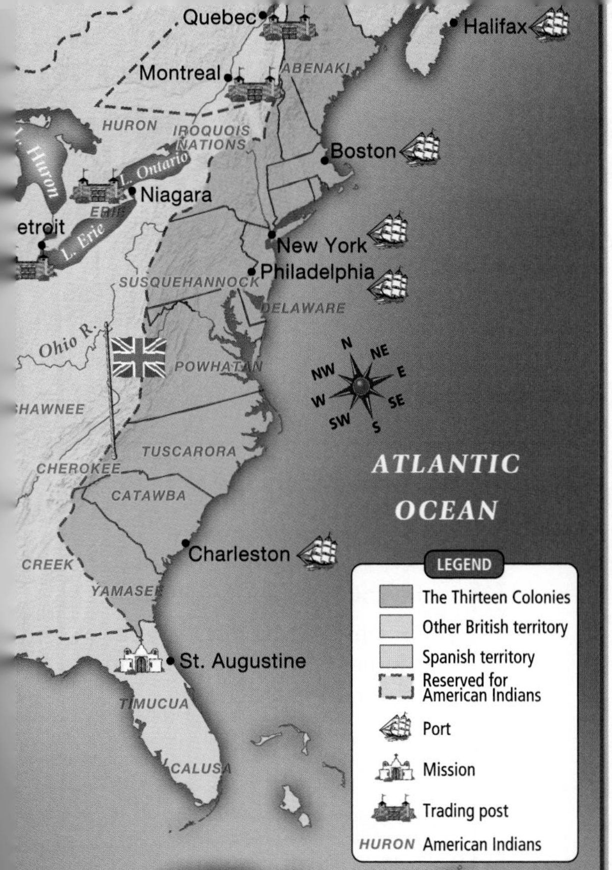

1785 1790

1783 American Victory
Continental Army defeats British
Chapter 8, page 288

1788 Constitution Ratified
U.S. government is now decided
Chapter 9, page 307

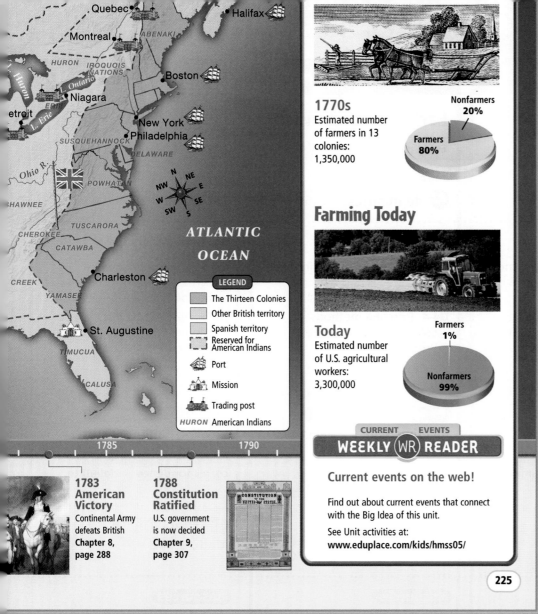

1770s
Estimated number of farmers in 13 colonies: 1,350,000

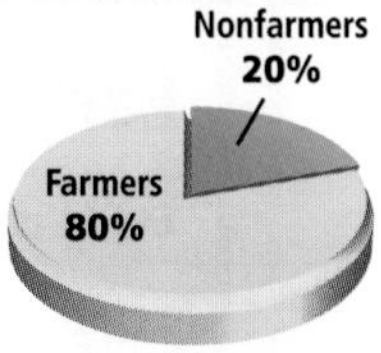

Farming Today

Today
Estimated number of U.S. agricultural workers: 3,300,000

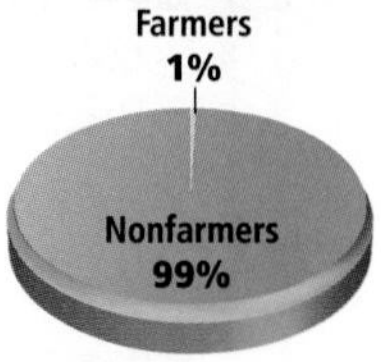

CURRENT EVENTS
WEEKLY WR READER

Current events on the web!

Find out about current events that connect with the Big Idea of this unit.

See Unit activities at:
www.eduplace.com/kids/hmss05/

225

Talk About It

4 Q Culture If eight out of every 10 workers were farmers in the 1770s, how do you think life was different than it is today?

A Possible answers include: not as many big cities; people did not live as close to each other; more open space.

5 Q Economics If eight out of every 10 workers were farmers in the 1770s, what other occupations might have been common?

A Occupations that supported agriculture, such as millers and goods merchants.

Find Out More

Jobs Today, Jobs Yesterday Ask students why so few Americans work as farmers today, as compared to the 1760s. List their ideas on the board. Challenge students to do research in the library or online to find out which ideas are correct.

A New Circle What would the circle graph look like for your state? Ask students to research the occupation statistics of their state and create a circle graph of the state's occupations.

Current Events

For information about current events related to this unit, visit www.eduplace.com/ss/hmss05/.

Web links to Weekly Reader will help students work on the Unit Current Events Project.

As you go through the unit, encourage students to use the web to find information for their bulletin board.

Chapter Opener

Pages 226–227

30 minutes

Reading/Vocabulary

Chapter Reading Strategy: Summarize, p. 225F

Resources

Grade Level Resources
- Vocabulary Cards, pp. 29–42

Reaching All Learners
- Challenge Activities, p. 85

Primary Sources Plus, p. 13

Big Idea Transparency 4

Interactive Transparency 4

Text & Music Audio CD

Lesson Planner & TR CD-ROM

eBook

eTE

Core Lesson 1

The French and Indian War

Pages 228–231

40 minutes

Tested Objectives

U4-1 Explain why France and Britain fought for control of North American lands.

U4-2 Summarize the impact of the French and Indian War on Britain, France, colonists, and Native Americans.

Reading/Vocabulary

Reading Skill: Sequence

ally **rebellion**
congress **proclamation**

Cross-Curricular

Art, p. 230

Resources

Unit Resources:
- **Reading Skill/Strategy,** p. 65
- **Vocabulary/Study Guide,** p. 66

Reaching All Learners:
- **Lesson Summary,** p. 26
- **Support for Lang. Dev./ELL,** p. 123

Assessment Options:
- **Lesson Test,** p. 68

www.eduplace.com/ss/hmss05/

Extend Lesson 1

Biography

George Washington

20–30 minutes

Pages 232–233

Focus: Was Washington always a great general? Students will find out.

Core Lesson 2

Early Conflicts with Britain

Pages 234–237

40 minutes

Tested Objectives

U4-3 Explain why Britain taxed the colonies and why colonists opposed this.

U4-4 Describe methods colonists used to protest British policies.

Reading/Vocabulary

Reading Skill: Problem and Solution

tax **liberty**
smuggling **protest**

Cross-Curricular

Drama, p. 236

Resources

Unit Resources:
- **Reading Skill/Strategy,** p. 67
- **Vocabulary/Study Guide,** p. 68

Reaching All Learners:
- **Lesson Summary,** p. 27
- **Support for Lang. Dev./ELL,** p. 124

Assessment Options:
- **Lesson Test,** p. 69

Extend Lesson 2

Economics

Taxes in the Colonies

20–30 minutes

Pages 238–239

Focus: Two innkeepers illustrate why colonists objected to the Townshend Acts.

Core Lesson 3

Conflicts Grow

Pages 240–243

40 minutes

Tested Objectives

U4-5 Analyze how events increased tensions between the colonists and the British.

U4-6 Describe how different colonies worked together to oppose British actions.

Reading/Vocabulary

Reading Skill: Predict

massacre **quarter**
correspondence **delegate**

Cross-Curricular

Math, p. 242

Resources

Unit Resources:
- **Reading Skill/Strategy,** p. 69
- **Vocabulary/Study Guide,** p. 70

Reaching All Learners:
- **Lesson Summary,** p. 28
- **Support for Lang. Dev./ELL,** p. 125

Assessment Options:
- **Lesson Test,** p. 70

Extend Lesson 3

Literature

Emma's Journal

40–50 minutes

Pages 244–247

Focus: A girl's journal shows life in Boston during the British blockade.

National Standards

V e Tension between an individual's beliefs and government policies and laws
VI c How government does/does not provide for needs and wants of people, establish order and security, and manage conflict
VI f Factors that contribute to cooperation and cause disputes
VI h Tensions between the wants and needs and fairness, equity, and justice
VII f Influence of incentives, values, traditions, and habits on economic decisions
VII i Use economic concepts
IX b Conflict, cooperation, and interdependence

CURRENT EVENTS from WEEKLY WR READER at www.eduplace.com — With the Program

Skillbuilder

Reading and Thinking Skill

Identify Causes and Effects

Pages 248–249

20 minutes

Tested Objectives

U4-7 Identify and interpret multiple causes and effects of events.

Reading/Vocabulary

cause
effect

Resources

Unit Resources:
Skill Practice, p. 71
Skill Transparency 7

Core Lesson 4

War Begins

Pages 250–255

50 minutes

Tested Objectives

U4-8 Describe the first battles of the Revolutionary War.

U4-9 Explain how the fighting spread and colonists prepared for war in 1775.

Reading/Vocabulary

Reading Skill: Cause and Effect

Patriot
militia
minutemen
commander
petition

Cross-Curricular

Math, p. 252 **Art,** p. 254
Music, p. 252

Resources

Unit Resources:
Reading Skill/Strategy, p. 72
Vocabulary/Study Guide, p. 73
Reaching All Learners:
Lesson Summary, p. 29
Support for Lang. Dev./ELL, p. 126
Assessment Options:
Lesson Test, p. 71

Extend Lesson 4

Geography

Battle of Bunker Hill

20–30 minutes

Pages 256–257

Focus: Find out why a hill was an important factor in the battles.

Chapter Review

Pages 258–259

30 minutes

Resources

Assessment Options:
Chapter 7 Test
Test Generator

Practice Options

Lesson 1 Skill and Strategy

TEST PREP

Reading Skill and Strategy

Reading Skill: Sequence

This skill helps you understand the order in which events happened.

Read "War Between France and Britain." Then fill in the chart to show the order in which the events took place.

The British and French began fighting in the Ohio River Valley.

1. Sample answer: George Washington led an army into the valley.
2. Sample answer: George Washington's army was defeated.

Reading Strategy: Summarize

3. Read "War Between France and Britain." Then check the sentence that best summarizes this section.

___ France and Britain fought over how much land was worth in North America.

___ The American Indians sided with the French in the war.

✓ Britain and France went to war to control the Ohio River Valley.

4. Read "Victory for Britain." Then check the sentence that best summarizes this section.

___ Most American Indians moved to Canada after Britain's victory.

✓ After the war, Britain controlled more land but had problems governing it.

___ The British declared that colonists could not move farther west than the Mississippi River.

Unit Resources 65 Use with *United States History*, pp. 228–231

Lesson 1 Vocabulary/Study Guide

TEST PREP

Vocabulary and Study Guide

Vocabulary

Solve the clue and write the answer in the blank. Then find the word in the puzzle. Look up, down, forward, and backward. Look for a bonus word!

1. A fight against a government rebellion
2. A group of representatives who meet to discuss a subject congress
3. An official public statement proclamation
4. A person or group that joins with another to work toward a goal ally

Bonus Word: government

H	A	F	D	Z	B	T	U	J	W	G	M
P	R	O	C	L	A	M	A	T	I	O	N
L	E	H	S	C	X	L	A	M	W	V	U
B	B	O	K	O	E	W	P	Q	C	E	O
F	E	V	Y	N	C	A	K	J	H	R	L
A	L	L	Y	G	T	D	L	N	S	N	P
R	L	I	N	R	N	E	M	K	G	M	S
O	I	B	U	E	F	O	X	P	D	E	R
G	O	J	Z	S	R	Q	P	Y	I	N	B
A	N	C	M	S	P	E	G	I	K	T	F

Study Guide

5. Read "War Between France and Britain." Then fill in the outline below.

I. Main Idea: France and Britain fought for control of the eastern part of North America.

A. Supporting Idea: France had colonies and trade in the region.

1. Detail: France built forts to keep the British out.
2. Detail: American Indian nations were allies of France.

B. Supporting Idea: Britain had colonies in the region.

1. Detail: Britain wanted to trade fur and farm.
2. Detail: Benjamin Franklin wanted the colonies to fight together.

Unit Resources 66 Use with *United States History*, pp. 228–231

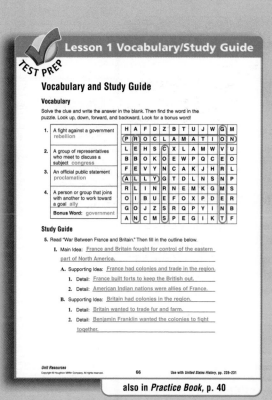

also in *Practice Book*, p. 40

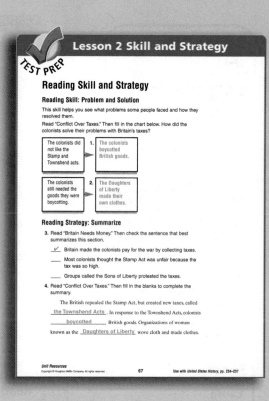

Lesson 2 Skill and Strategy

TEST PREP

Reading Skill and Strategy

Reading Skill: Problem and Solution

This skill helps you see what problems some people faced and how they resolved them.

Read "Conflict Over Taxes." Then fill in the chart below. How did the colonists solve their problems with Britain's taxes?

Problem	Solution
The colonists did not like the Stamp and Townshend acts.	1. The colonists boycotted British goods.
The colonists still needed the goods they were boycotting.	2. The Daughters of Liberty made their own clothes.

Reading Strategy: Summarize

3. Read "Britain Needs Money." Then check the sentence that best summarizes this section.

✓ Britain made the colonists pay for the war by collecting taxes.

___ Most colonists thought the Stamp Act was unfair because the tax was so high.

___ Groups called the Sons of Liberty protested the taxes.

4. Read "Conflict Over Taxes." Then fill in the blanks to complete the summary.

The British repealed the Stamp Act, but created new taxes, called the Townshend Acts. In response to the Townshend Acts, colonists boycotted British goods. Organizations of women known as the Daughters of Liberty wove cloth and made clothes.

Unit Resources 67 Use with *United States History*, pp. 234–237

Lesson 2 Vocabulary/Study Guide

TEST PREP

Vocabulary and Study Guide

Vocabulary

Write the definition of each vocabulary word below.

1. boycott To refuse to buy, sell, or use goods
2. tax Money that people pay to their government in return for services
3. protest An activity at which people complain about an issue
4. repeal To cancel a law
5. liberty Freedom from being controlled by another government
6. smuggling To import goods illegally
7. Choose two words. Use each word in a sentence about the lesson.
Sample answer: Merchants started a boycott against British goods. Britain put a tax on tea.

Study Guide

Read "Early Conflicts with Britain." Then fill in the comparison chart below.

What the British government wanted	What the colonists wanted
8. Sample answer: To raise money by collecting taxes; To tax sugar, coffee, and cloth; To tax anything printed on paper; To tax tea, glass, lead, and paints	9. Sample answer: To avoid paying taxes; British soldiers to leave Boston; To have representatives in Parliament

Unit Resources 68 Use with *United States History*, pp. 234–237

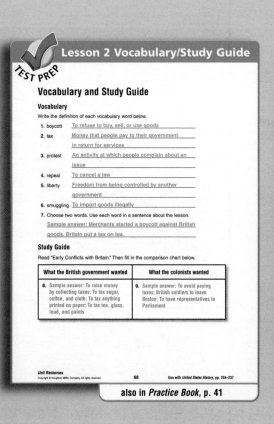

also in *Practice Book*, p. 41

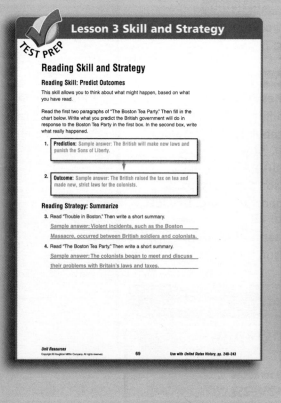

Lesson 3 Skill and Strategy

TEST PREP

Reading Skill and Strategy

Reading Skill: Predict Outcomes

This skill allows you to think about what might happen, based on what you have read.

Read the first two paragraphs of "The Boston Tea Party." Then fill in the chart below. Write what you predict the British government will do in response to the Boston Tea Party in the first box. In the second box, write what really happened.

1. **Prediction:** Sample answer: The British will make new laws and punish the Sons of Liberty.
2. **Outcome:** Sample answer: The British raised the tax on tea and made new, strict laws for the colonists.

Reading Strategy: Summarize

3. Read "Trouble in Boston." Then write a short summary.
Sample answer: Violent incidents, such as the Boston Massacre, occurred between British soldiers and colonists.
4. Read "The Boston Tea Party." Then write a short summary.
Sample answer: The colonists began to meet and discuss their problems with Britain's laws and taxes.

Unit Resources 69 Use with *United States History*, pp. 240–243

Lesson 3 Vocabulary/Study Guide

TEST PREP

Vocabulary and Study Guide

Vocabulary

1. Draw a line connecting the vocabulary word to its meaning.

correspondence	To provide people with food and shelter
massacre	Someone chosen to speak and act for others
delegate	The killing of many people
quarter	Written communication

Study Guide

2. Read "Trouble in Boston." Then fill in the blanks below.

The people of Boston were angry with the British government. The colonists did not want soldiers in their city. A fight started on March 5, 1770. Crispus Attucks, an African American sailor, was killed in the fight. This event came to be known as the Boston Massacre. When the British soldiers were put on trial, John Adams defended them. In 1772, Samuel Adams set up Committees of Correspondence to help colonists share news about the British.

Unit Resources 70 Use with *United States History*, pp. 240–243

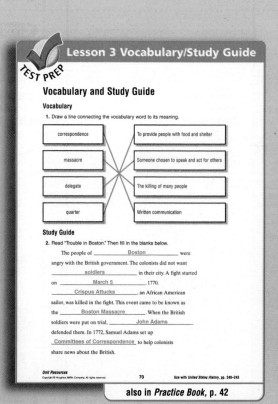

also in *Practice Book*, p. 42

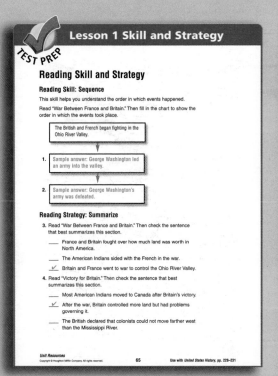

Skillbuilder Practice

TEST PREP

Skillbuilder: Identify Causes and Effects

Cause	Effects
Britain needs money	Britain passes Stamp Act
	Britain passes Townshend Acts

Practice

1. What is the first effect of Britain needing money? Stamp Act
2. What is the second effect of Britain needing money? Townshend Acts
3. Why are the Stamp Act and Townshend Acts effects of Britain needing money? Britain created these acts so that it could tax the colonists and make money.

Apply

Now you can use your cause and effect skills to show another version of events. Many times an effect can cause another event or action. Read "The Boston Tea Party." Fill in the chart with the cause and effect of the Boston Tea Party.

4. Tea Act → Boston Tea Party → 5. Intolerable Acts

Unit Resources

71
Use with *United States History*, pp. 248–249

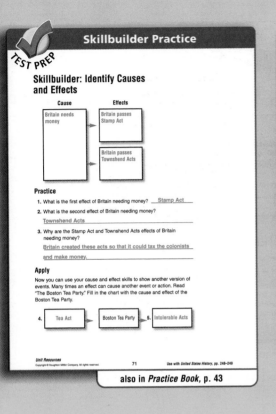

also in *Practice Book*, p. 43

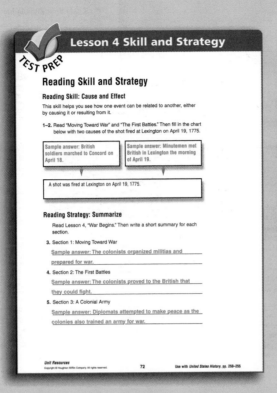

Lesson 4 Skill and Strategy

TEST PREP

Reading Skill and Strategy

Reading Skill: Cause and Effect

This skill helps you see how one event can be related to another, either by causing it or resulting from it.

1–2. Read "Moving Toward War" and "The First Battles." Then fill in the chart below with two causes of the shot fired at Lexington on April 19, 1775.

- Sample answer: British soldiers marched to Concord on April 18.
- Sample answer: Minutemen met British in Lexington the morning of April 19.

→ A shot was fired at Lexington on April 19, 1775.

Reading Strategy: Summarize

Read Lesson 4, "War Begins." Then write a short summary for each section.

3. Section 1: Moving Toward War
Sample answer: The colonists organized militias and prepared for war.
4. Section 2: The First Battles
Sample answer: The colonists proved to the British that they could fight.
5. Section 3: A Colonial Army
Sample answer: Diplomats attempted to make peace as the colonies also trained an army for war.

Unit Resources

72
Use with *United States History*, pp. 250–255

Lesson 4 Vocabulary/Study Guide

TEST PREP

Vocabulary and Study Guide

Vocabulary

Write the word for each definition below.

1. commander — The officer in charge of an army
2. minutemen — Militia with special training
3. Patriot — A colonist who opposed British rule
4. petition — A written request from a number of people
5. militia — A group of ordinary people who train for battle

Study Guide

Read "Moving Toward War." Then fill in the sequence chart below.

Militia prepare for war. → 6. General Gage sends soldiers to destroy militia supplies. → Patriots warn the militia. → 7. An army of 700 British soldiers goes to Concord.

Read "The First Battles." Then fill in the sequence chart below.

The British reach Lexington and fight with minutemen. → 8. The British march to Concord and fight with minutemen. → Militia build a fort at Bunker Hill. → 9. After much fighting, the British win the Battle of Bunker Hill.

Read "A Colonial Army." Then fill in the sequence chart below.

The Second Continental Congress meets in 1775. → 10. Congress decides to build a new army called the Continental Army. → 11. Congress chooses George Washington as the commander of the Continental Army. → Congress sends a petition to King George.

Unit Resources

73
Use with *United States History*, pp. 250–255

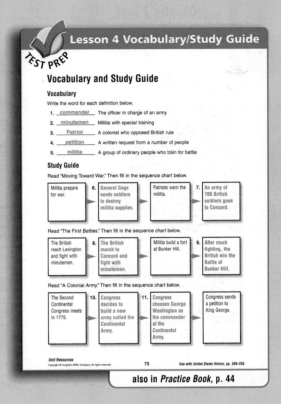

also in *Practice Book*, p. 44

Assessment Options

Chapter 7 Test

TEST PREP

Chapter 7 Test

Test Your Knowledge

ally	protest	massacre	militia

Fill in the blank with the correct word from the box.

1. When soldiers killed five people during a fight in Boston, angry colonists called it a __massacre__. Obj. U4–5
2. Samuel Adams and the Sons of Liberty organized a __protest__ against the Stamp Act. Obj. U4–4
3. In the French and Indian War, France relied on American Indians as an important __ally__. Obj. U4–1
4. In 1775, many colonists joined a __militia__ to help the colonies prepare for war. Obj. U4–9

Circle the letter of the best answer.

5. Why did the British Parliament need to tax the colonies? Obj. U4–3
   - A. The British owed money to the American Indians.
   - (B.) The French and Indian War had cost them a lot of money.
   - C. The British owed money to the French.
   - D. The British owed money to the Spanish.
6. Why did Parliament create the Townshend Acts? Obj. U4–3
   - F. to raise money for the Sons of Liberty
   - G. to raise money for the Patriots
   - H. to raise money for the Continental Congress
   - (J.) to pay for services in the colonies
7. How did the colonists work together to oppose British actions? Obj. U4–6
   - (A.) They created the Committees of Correspondence.
   - B. They met with British officials to discuss the taxes.
   - C. They met with the American Indians to oppose the taxes.
   - D. They met with the king of England.
8. Why were the colonists upset about the new taxes? Obj. U4–3
   - F. The merchants wanted to tax their own goods.
   - G. The colonists were not members of the East India Company.
   - (H.) The colonists believed only their representatives could tax them.
   - J. The tax money went to the French.

Chapter 7 Test

TEST PREP

Apply Your Knowledge

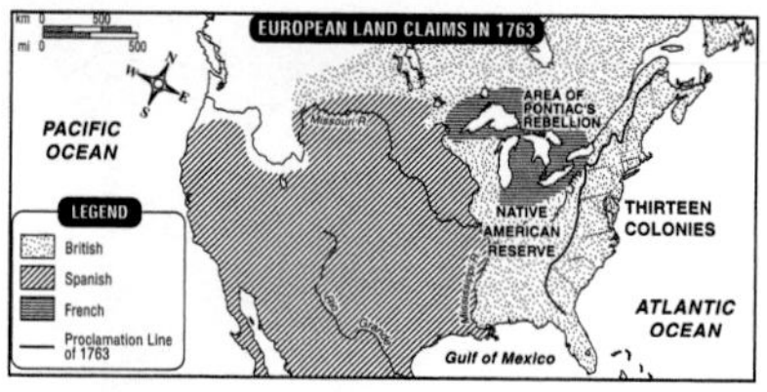

Use the map to answer the following questions.

9. What two groups were separated by the Proclamation Line of 1763? Obj. U4–2
   - (A.) the colonists and the American Indians
   - B. the British and the French
   - C. the French and the American Indians
   - D. the French and the Spanish
10. Which is a true statement about the effect of the French and Indian War? Obj. U4–2
   - F. The French gained more land from the Proclamation of 1763.
   - G. The colonists could only move west of the Appalachian Mountains.
   - (H.) Britain gained a large amount of land.
   - J. American Indians continued to live east of the Appalachian Mountains.

Apply the Reading Skill: Problem and Solution

Read the passage below. Then answer the question. Obj. U4–4

> Many colonists were upset by the British taxes. As a result, merchants started a boycott. When the British Parliament demanded a tea tax, the merchants refused to sell tea. In 1774, the First Continental Congress wrote a letter to the British government asking Parliament to stop taxing the colonists.

11. How did the First Continental Congress try to solve the conflict over the tea tax?

    by writing a letter to the British government

Chapter 7 Test

TEST PREP

Test the Skill: Identify Causes and Effects

Cause	Effect
British soldiers stayed in the Ohio River Valley.	Pontiac's Rebellion occurred.
The Proclamation of 1763 by Britain recognized American Indians' land rights.	Colonists began to disagree openly with Britain.

Practice

12. What was an effect of British soldiers staying in the Ohio River Valley?

    Pontiac's Rebellion Obj. U4–7
13. Why were colonists openly disagreeing with the British?

    British recognition of American Indians' land rights meant colonists could not settle the Ohio River Valley. Obj. U4–7
14. In what way would one of the effects above become a cause?

    Sample answer: Pontiac's Rebellion would lead to Britain's recognition of American Indians' land rights. Obj. U4–7

Apply the Skill

15. Think about how an effect can become a cause of another event. Then think about the effect of the Proclamation of 1763. How was this part of the cause of the Revolutionary War? Obj. U4–7

    Sample answer: The colonists were tired of the British soldiers living among them and began to grow angry with them. The disagreement with the British drew the colonists together to oppose Britain.

Chapter 7 Test

TEST PREP

Think and Write

16. **Short Response:** Describe the Battles of Lexington and Concord. Obj. U4–8

    Lexington: Sample answer: These were the first battles of the Revolutionary War. British soldiers arrived in Lexington on April 19. They ordered the Minutemen to leave, but then someone fired a shot. Both sides then fired many shots, and eight colonists died.

    Concord: Sample answer: British soldiers searched for hidden weapons in Concord. The Minutemen forced the British to go back to Boston.
17. **Critical Thinking: Draw Conclusions** Why do you think the actions of the British caused the people in different colonies to work together as one nation? Obj. U4–9

    Sample answers: The actions of the British affected all of the colonies; they had a common goal to be free from British rule.
18. **Extended Response:** Write an article for a colonial Boston newspaper, as a reporter might have. Write your article about the taxes. Tell your readers why colonists are upset about the taxes. Explain what colonists can do about it. Write your article on a separate sheet of paper. Obj. U4–5 **Articles may refer to the high costs of buying food and clothes; the colonists could protest the taxes; they could refuse to buy British goods; they could write a letter to the British government.**

Self-Assessment

What do I think is the most important reason that the colonists opposed the British government? Why do I think so?

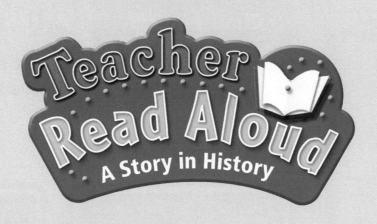

Teacher Read Aloud
A Story in History

You can read the following fiction selection to students before beginning the chapter.

Activate Prior Knowledge
Ask students to share what they know about the Battles of Lexington and Concord. Explain that the Read-Aloud selection captures the experience of one young rider, who, along with Paul Revere and Samuel Prescott, warned the minutemen that the British were coming.

Preview the Chapter
Ask students to look at the map on page 251 of their books and trace the route Henry Alder might have taken.

Read-Aloud Vocabulary
Explain that the **minutemen** were militia who were trained to be ready for battle at a moment's notice. Tell students that colonists against British rule were called **Patriots.**

Preview the Reading Strategy
Summarize Explain to students that the reading strategy they will use in this chapter is summarizing, or putting something in their own words. You may wish to use the Read Aloud to model summarizing for your students.

Think Aloud *Henry Alder is riding his horse Mercy to warn the minutemen that the British are marching to Concord. Henry and Mercy ride all night. Finally, a minuteman orders a fresh horse and rider and tells Henry to rest. Henry wants to take care of Mercy first because she did all the work.*

Mercy Brings a Message

"Just a few miles more, Mercy," Henry Alder whispered. The little mare turned her ears to listen, and then pointed them forward again. He felt her gather herself and put on yet another burst of speed.

He patted Mercy's neck and marveled at his brave little horse. They had run nonstop all night.

Mercy shied suddenly as a man appeared from out of the trees on the side of the road. "Halt, rider!"

"Easy, Mercy!" Henry said, drawing her to a halt. She trembled with the effort of her run. More men appeared from among the trees, and to Henry's relief, he realized they were **minutemen.** "The British!" he called out. "They march for Concord. Your help is needed!"

The first man nodded and ordered, "Send a fresh horse and rider on ahead!" Then he turned to Henry. "Come, you young **Patriot.** You need to rest after bringing such important news."

"If you please, sir," Henry said politely, "first, I'll tend to Mercy's comfort. She is the one who brought you the news. I just came along for the ride."

Begin the Chapter

Chapter Quick Look

Core Lesson 1 discusses the French and Indian War.

Core Lesson 2 describes the early conflicts between the colonists and Britain.

Core Lesson 3 focuses on the resistance in Boston and how the British reacted.

Core Lesson 4 tells about the start of the war.

Vocabulary Preview

Use the vocabulary cards to preview the key vocabulary words before starting the lessons and to prepare students to understand the content of the chapter.

Vocabulary Strategy

Vocabulary strategies for this chapter:

- Structural analysis, p. 241, 251
- Synonyms/antonyms, p. 229, 230, 235, 236
- Prefixes and suffixes, p. 229
- Word origins, p. 230, 235, 236, 242

Vocabulary Help

Vocabulary card for congress Students may think of the Capitol Building in Washington, D.C. when they hear the word *congress*. Explain that a congress (with a small c) is a group of people who gather to discuss problems.

Vocabulary card for quarter Students may not be familiar with the verb *quarter*, but they may have heard *quarters*, meaning a place where soldiers live.

Chapter 7 Causes of the Revolution

Vocabulary Preview

Technology
e • glossary
e • word games
www.eduplace.com/kids/hmss05/

congress

In 1757, representatives from the colonies met in a **congress** at Albany to discuss how to fight France. The members of a congress gather to discuss important issues. **page 229**

boycott

Colonists refused to buy or use British goods. Protesters who joined the **boycott** of British tea dumped crates of it into Boston Harbor. **page 236**

Chapter Timeline

Background

- In 1707, England, Scotland, and Wales joined together to form the United Kingdom of Great Britain. Colonies and colonist that had been called "English" were now called "British."
- Beginning with this unit, this book will now use the terms "Britain" and "British" rather than "England" and "English."

Vocabulary

Use the following graphic organizer to discuss the word *petition.*

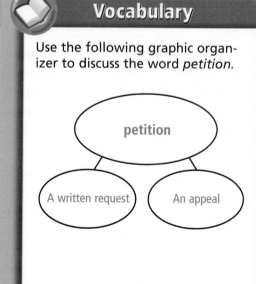

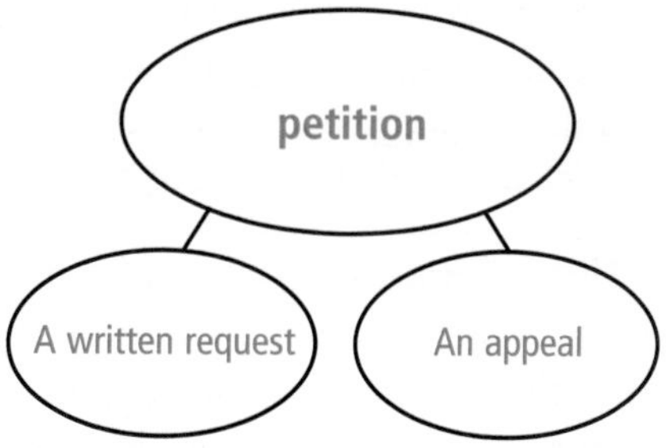

Monday March 6 Seatwork: Connex- Madlyn, Aaron	**8:50-10:50; 11:36-1:42 Integrated Language Arts / Social Studies** 1. Read aloud – <u>True Confessions of Charlotte Doyle</u> 2. Reading – **Reading Achievement Tests 8:50-11:33** 3. Writing – 4. SS – see separate plans – Open Wall – Math Prep HW- read 20 min. **Lunch Recess 12:18-12:58**
Tuesday March 7 Seatwork: Connex – Aaron	**8:50-10:50; 11:36-1:42 Integrated Language Arts / Social Studies** 1. Read aloud – <u>True Confessions of Charlotte Doyle</u> 2. Reading – intro. <u>GW Socks,</u> create character log and a folder; read Ch. 1-2 3 Writing – write Early Life paragraph on Fritz person 4. SS – see separate plans – begin American Revolution Unit **DARE 9:00-9:45 Roberts, 10:05-10:50 Pado** HW- read 20 min.
Wednesday March 8 Seatwork: Connex- Maggie, Donnie	**8:50-10:50; 11:36-1:42 Integrated Language Arts / Social Studies** 1. Read aloud – <u>True Confessions of Charlotte Doyle</u> 2. Reading – **Math Achievement Test 8:50-11:33** 3. Writing – 4. SS – see separate plans – Group Colonial Posters – Open Wall – SS posters **Lunch Recess 12:18-12:58** HW- read 20 min.; SS read pgs. 228-233 notes on important events
Thursday March 9 Seatwork: Connex- Donnie	**8:50-10:50; 11:36-1:42 Integrated Language Arts / Social Studies** 1. Read aloud – <u>True Confessions of Charlotte Doyle</u> 2. Reading – SSR <u>GW Socks</u> Ch. 3-4; add to character log; create Chapter Title list 3. Writing – write Adult life paragraph 4. SS- see separate plans – French/Indian War – begin timelines HW- read 20 min.; SS read pgs. 234-239 add events to timeline
Friday March 10 Seatwork:	**8:50-10:50; 11:36-1:42 Integrated Language Arts / Social Studies** 1. Read aloud- <u>True Confessions of Charlotte Doyle</u> 2. Reading- SSR <u>GW Socks</u> Ch. 5 as a group, making predictions 3. Writing- write Major Accomplishments paragraph 4. Social Studies- see separate plans- Conflicts Grow – Tax simulation **Library 9:00-9:15; 11:45-12:00**

10:54-11:34 Lunch / Recess   Exploratory 1:45-2:25   Connections 2:28-3;07   Closing 3:05-3:15

Topic: Winning the War **Objective:** explain how the United States became independent from Great Britain; construct a timeline for the American Revolution and use it to identify the relationships between the events, such as cause and effect **Procedure:** read aloud History of US; discuss pgs. 286-289; song "World Turned Upside Down" **HW/Assess: Study Guides**	Allow 2 days for study guide Go over in class Unit Assessment April Morning movie
Language Arts Activity **Topic:** Boston Tea Party **Objective:** give a persuasive speech **Procedure:** write persuasive speech as Sam Adams convincing us to take part in Boston Tea Party **HW/Assess:** present speech to class in language arts	

Reading Strategy

Summarize Use this strategy to better understand information in the text.

Quick Tip A summary includes only the most important information. Use main ideas to help you.

commander

George Washington was in charge of all the colonial soldiers. He was the **commander** of the Continental Army.
page 254

petition

Congress sent the Olive Branch Petition to King George. This **petition** asked for peace.
page 254

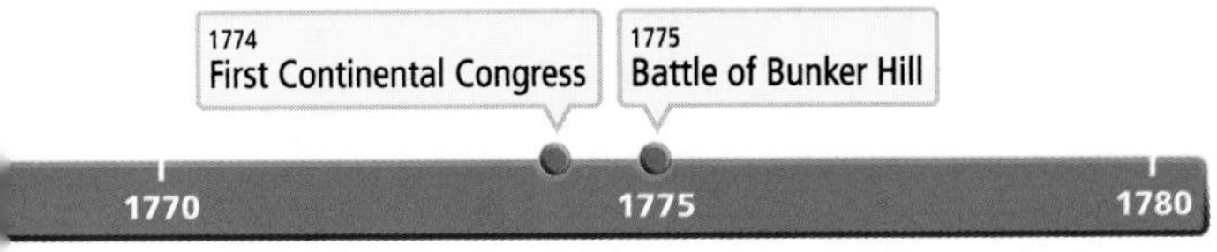

Leveled Practice

Extra Support

Have students make their own word cards for chapter vocabulary words not pictured here. They can draw the pictures, or look for pictures in magazines to use as illustrations. Visual-spatial

Challenge

Have students choose an event from the chapter and write two newspaper articles about it, one from the point of view of a reporter for a colonial newspaper, and the other from the point of view of a correspondent for the *London Times*. Verbal-linguistic

ELL

All Proficiency Levels

- Have students work together to prepare a dramatization of one of the vocabulary words.
- If they wish, they can include dialog that includes additional vocabulary words.
- Encourage students to share their dramatizations with the class.

Bodily-kinesthetic

Using the Timeline

- Direct students to look at the timeline on pages 226 and 227. Point out the segments of the timeline. Ask them how many years this chapter will cover.
- You may wish to use a KWL chart to access students' prior knowledge of the events on the timeline. This is also an excellent opportunity to determine what, if any, misconceptions students may hold about the material.

Reading Strategy: Summarize

To summarize, a reader identifies and pulls together the essential information in a longer text passage and restates that information in a condensed fashion.

Explain to students that to summarize successfully, they should follow these steps:

- Read the passage twice.
- Think about what the passage says.
- Ask yourself: What is the main topic this passage is describing?
- Find the main point of the passage. Jot it down (or underline it).
- Use your own words to tell what the passage means.
- Look back at the passage to check if your summary is accurate.

Students can practice this reading strategy throughout the chapter, including on their Skill and Strategy pages.

Tested Objectives

U4-1 History Explain why France and Britain fought for control of North American lands.

U4-2 History Summarize the impact of the French and Indian War on Britain, France, colonists, and Native Americans.

Lesson Quick Look

This lesson describes the causes, battles, outcome, and effects of the French and Indian War.

Teaching Option: Extend Lesson 1 tells students more about George Washington.

1 Get Set to Read

Preview Direct students to look at the maps on page 230. Ask students to describe what they show.

Reading Skill: Sequence Students should double-check their work to be sure events are in chronological order.

Build on What You Know Discuss with students the advantages of working in a group. Explain that the colonies worked together to solve their problems.

Vocabulary

ally *noun,* a person or group that has joined with another to accomplish a specific goal

congress *noun,* a meeting of representatives to discuss plans for the future

rebellion *noun,* an attempt to overthrow a government or authority by force

proclamation *noun,* an official announcement

Core Lesson 1

The French and Indian War

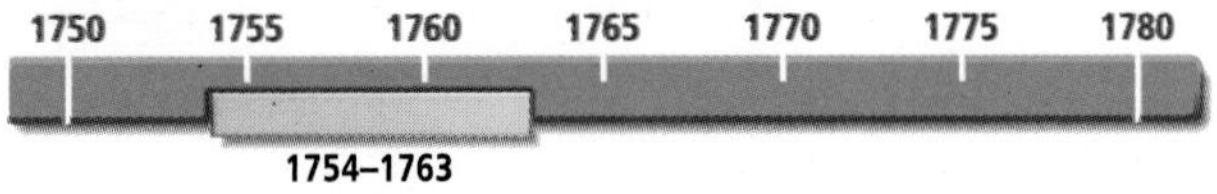

VOCABULARY

ally
congress
rebellion
proclamation

Vocabulary Strategy

congress

A **congress** is a meeting of representatives. The word part **con-** means together. At a congress, representatives gather together.

READING SKILL

Sequence Note the events of the French and Indian War in order.

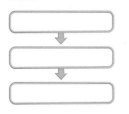

Build on What You Know Do you often work as part of a group? Sometimes you can get more done that way. When Britain and its colonies went to war with France, some people felt that the colonies would be stronger if they worked together.

War Between France and Britain

Main Idea Great Britain and France fought for control of eastern North America.

Britain and France both had colonies in North America. (In the 1700s, Britain became another name for England.) The two countries had been enemies for hundreds of years and had fought many wars. In the 1750s, they went to war again. This time, they fought over the Ohio River Valley.

The Ohio River Valley is the land around the Ohio River. This river flows 1,000 miles from the Appalachian Mountains to the Mississippi River. Many American Indians lived in the valley. They traded furs with the French in exchange for guns and other goods. The French wanted to have this trade all to themselves. They built forts to keep out the British.

British colonists wanted to trade furs and farm 1
the land around the Ohio River. In 1754, the governor of Virginia ordered a young officer named **George Washington** to lead an army into the valley. A larger French army met them and defeated Washington's soldiers. After this defeat, the British government sent a stronger army to North America, and Britain went to war against France.

228 • Chapter 7

Skill and Strategy

Reading Skill and Strategy

Reading Skill: Sequence

This skill helps you understand the order in which events happened.

Read "War Between France and Britain." Then fill in the chart to show the order in which the events took place.

The British and French began fighting in the Ohio River Valley.

1. Sample answer: George Washington led an army into the valley.

2. Sample answer: George Washington's army was defeated.

Reading Strategy: Summarize

3. Read "War Between France and Britain." Then check the sentence that best summarizes this section.

___ France and Britain fought over how much land was worth in North America.

___ The American Indians sided with the French in the war.

_✓_ Britain and France went to war to control the Ohio River Valley.

4. Read "Victory for Britain." Then check the sentence that best summarizes this section.

___ Most American Indians moved to Canada after Britain's victory.

_✓_ After the war, Britain controlled more land but had problems governing it.

___ The British declared that colonists could not move farther west than the Mississippi River.

Unit Resources

65
Use with *United States History*, pp. 228–231

Unit Resources, p. 65

Background

Great Britain

- In 1707, England, Scotland, and Wales joined together to form the United Kingdom of Great Britain. Colonies and colonists that had been called "English" were now called "British."
- Beginning with this unit, this book will now use the terms *Britain* and *British* rather than *England* and *English*.

Choosing Sides

The war that began in the Ohio River Valley was called the French and Indian War. It spread through eastern North America. Britain and its colonists fought against France and its American Indian allies. An **ally** is a person or group that joins with another to work toward a goal.

Most American Indian nations were allies of the French. They included the Delaware, Ottawa, and Shawnee. France was their trading partner. To the French, trade was more important than settlement. 2 Unlike the British, the French did not send many settlers to North America.

Some American Indian nations, such as the Mohawk, were allies of the British. The Mohawk had traded with the British for many years and had formed close ties.

George Washington The French and Indian War was his first experience in battle. This picture shows him at the capture of a French fort.

Albany Plan Benjamin Franklin used this cartoon to tell colonists that working together was the only way to defeat the French.

SKILL **Reading Visuals** What do the initials stand for in the cartoon?

the names of the colonies

Benjamin Franklin's Albany Plan

In 1754, representatives from the colonies held a meeting to discuss how to fight France. Because they met in Albany, New York, the meeting was called the Albany Congress. A **congress** is a group of representatives who meet to discuss a subject. Representatives to a congress often vote on important issues. 3

Benjamin Franklin was at the Albany Congress. He had a plan to unite the colonies, known as the Albany Plan of Union. Franklin believed the colonies could fight better if they worked together. In his plan, each colony would keep its own government. The colonies would also have an overall government to solve problems that affected them all, such as wars. The colonies did not accept the plan. They were not ready to join together under one government.

REVIEW What was the Albany Plan?

a plan for the colonies to unite under an overall government to solve common problems, such as wars

2 Teach

War Between France and Britain

Talk About It

1 **Q History** What did George Washington do in 1754?

A He led soldiers into the Ohio River Valley.

2 **Q History** What were the French more interested in, settlement or trade?

A trade

3 **Q Citizenship** What was the Albany Congress?

A a meeting of colonial representatives to discuss how to fight France

Vocabulary Strategy

ally Tell students that *helper, partner,* and *supporter* are other words for *ally.*

congress Explain to students that the prefix *con-* means "with," "together," or "jointly."

Reading Strategy: Summarize Explain to students that a summary is always shorter than the original text. Summarize the first two paragraphs of the lesson.

Think Aloud *Britain and France had competed for land in North America for many years. In the 1750s, they fought for control of the Ohio River Valley. The French wanted to protect their fur trading with American Indians, so they built forts to keep the British out.*

REACHING ALL LEARNERS

Leveled Practice

Extra Support

Write terms from the lesson on the board, including the Albany Congress, trading furs, and victory at Quebec. Have partners **choose a term to illustrate.** Then have them explain what they drew. Visual-spatial; verbal-linguistic

Challenge

Have students **prepare a short speech** from the viewpoint of an American Indian in the Ohio River Valley to persuade others to choose a side in the French and Indian War. Verbal-linguistic

REACHING ALL LEARNERS

ELL

Intermediate

- Ask students to **complete** the following sentences:
  My friend is my ____. ally
  The king made a ____. proclamation
  She represented our school at a state student ____. congress
  The leader's wise action prevented a ____. rebellion

Verbal-linguistic

Victory for Britain

Talk About It

4 Q Geography Why was the Battle of Quebec an important victory for the British?

A Quebec was a center of French power in Canada.

5 Q History Why did Britain make the Proclamation of 1763?

A to prevent more fighting with American Indians

6 Q Economics Why did colonists oppose the Proclamation of 1763?

A It prevented them from moving into the Ohio Valley to farm and trade furs.

Vocabulary Strategy

rebellion Explain that another word for *rebellion* is *revolt.*

proclamation Tell students that *proclaim* and *proclamation* come from the Latin word *clamare,* meaning "to cry out."

Critical Thinking

Cause and Effect What effect did the Proclamation of 1763 have on the colonists?

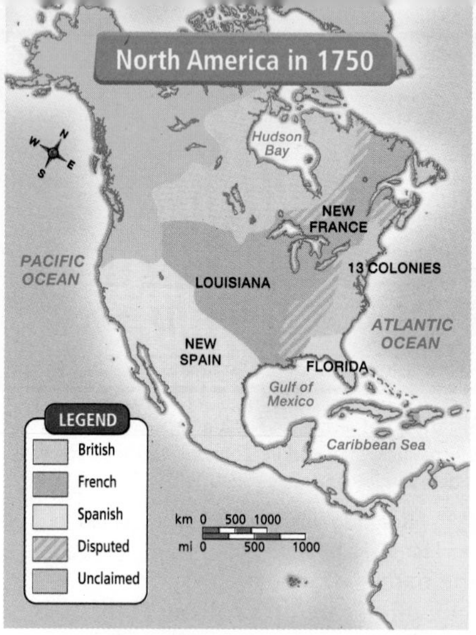

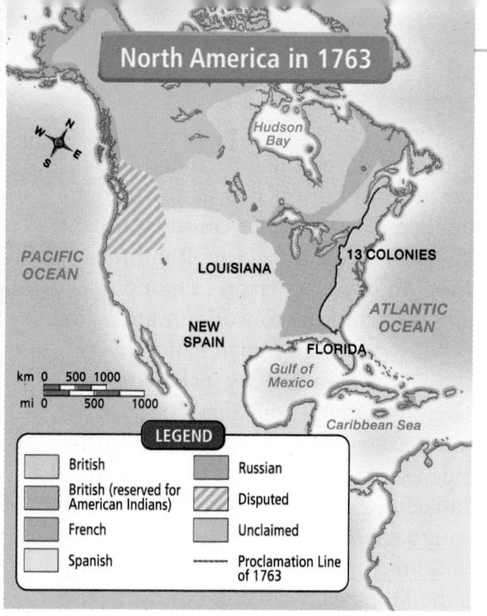

New Lands By 1763, Britain gained control of French lands in North America. SKILL **Reading Maps** Describe how the map of North America changed between 1750 and 1763. In 1763, Spain and Britain control the land that France controlled in 1750. Also, in 1763 Russia controlled some land.

Victory for Britain

Main Idea Britain gained new land in the French and Indian War, but it also had new problems.

Britain was losing the French and Indian War until 1757, when **William Pitt** became the leader of Britain's Parliament, or government. Pitt was determined to win the war. He sent many ships and soldiers to North America, where they helped capture French forts. In 1759, a British army defeated the French near
4 Quebec, which was a center of French power in Canada. The next year, Britain captured Montreal, another French city.

By 1763, France was ready to make peace with Britain. The two countries signed an agreement called the Treaty of Paris. As the map above shows, the treaty gave Britain control of Canada and most of the land east of the Mississippi River.

Troubles After the War

After the Treaty of Paris, British soldiers stayed in the Ohio River Valley. The American Indians who lived there wanted the British to leave. **Pontiac** (PAHN tee ak), an Ottawa chief, led American Indians in a war against the British, which was known as Pontiac's Rebellion. A **rebellion** is a fight against a government. Pontiac's warriors attacked British forts around the Great Lakes. Britain quickly defeated Pontiac's army. The rebellion lasted less than a year.

To prevent any more fighting with 5
American Indians, Britain made a **proclamation,** or an official public statement. The Proclamation of 1763, as it was called, said that colonists could not settle west of the Appalachian Mountains. Britain recognized the Indian nations' rights to their land.

Art

Create a Cartoon

- Have students look at Benjamin Franklin's cartoon on page 229. Discuss the purpose of the cartoon.
- Have students create their own cartoon illustrating an event or issue described in this lesson.
- Have students work in small groups to explain their cartoons.

Visual-spatial

Language Arts

Write an Editorial

- Remind students that editors of newspapers often write editorials or short essays that express their positions on issues.
- Have them write an editorial that might have appeared in a colonial newspaper following the Proclamation of 1763.
- Encourage students to include facts and evidence to back up their positions.

Verbal-linguistic

Many colonists were upset by the Proclamation of 1763. Now that the French were gone, colonists wanted to farm and settle in the Ohio River Valley. Colonists were also tired of British soldiers living among them. They no longer wanted the soldiers for protection.

6

As disagreements grew, colonists were willing to speak out. During the Great Awakening, 20 years before, colonists had challenged some of their church leaders. The colonists disagreed with them about religious ideas. After 1763, colonists began working together to oppose the decisions of their government as well.

REVIEW Why were colonists upset with Britain after the French and Indian War? Britain would not allow them to settle beyond the Appalachians and kept soldiers in place.

Lesson Summary

Britain won control of the Ohio River Valley in the French and Indian War. Afterward, Pontiac's Rebellion caused Britain to make the Proclamation of 1763 to stop colonists from settling west of the Appalachian Mountains.

Why It Matters ...

After the French and Indian War, colonists began to disagree with Britain's rule of the colonies.

Pontiac This Ottawa chief was determined to drive out the British. But without French support, he could not win.

Lesson Review

1754 French and Indian War
1758 Battle of Quebec
1763 Pontiac's Rebellion

1753 | 1755 | 1757 | 1759 | 1761 | 1763 | 1765

1. **VOCABULARY** Choose the correct word to complete each sentence.

   ally **congress** **proclamation**

   In Albany, the colonies held a _____ to discuss how to fight France.

   The Mohawk nation was an _____ of Britain.

2. **READING SKILL** Look at the **sequence** of events of the French and Indian War. What events were most important for Britain's success?

3. **MAIN IDEA: Economics** Why did British colonists want to control the Ohio River Valley?

4. **MAIN IDEA: Geography** Where did the Proclamation of 1763 divide British territory?

5. **PEOPLE TO KNOW** What role did **George Washington** play in the French and Indian War?

6. **TIMELINE SKILL** Which happened first, the Battle of Quebec or Pontiac's Rebellion?

7. **CRITICAL THINKING: Cause and Effect** What problems did Pontiac's Rebellion cause?

SPEAKING ACTIVITY Think about the advantages and disadvantages of the colonies joining together. Prepare a short speech to argue for or against the Albany Plan of Union.

3 Review/Assess

Review Tested Objectives

U4-1 Reasons included protection of trade and farming interests.

U4-2 The war ended with British victory. Because of tensions with American Indians in the area, the British government issued a proclamation forbidding settlement in the Ohio River Valley.

Lesson Review Answers

1. congress; ally
2. Answer should reflect information from the lesson.
3. It had rich farmland and many animals for the fur trade.
4. at the Appalachian Mountains
5. He led an army into the Ohio River Valley to fight the French.
6. Battle of Quebec
7. It led to the Proclamation of 1763, which said that colonists could not settle west of the Appalachians. This upset many colonists and strengthened their resentment of the British soldiers living among them.

HANDS ON Performance Task Rubric

4	Speech states position clearly; conveys ideas effectively; facts are accurate.
3	Speech states position well, conveys ideas adequately; most facts are accurate.
2	Speech states position in a somewhat disorganized way; conveys ideas adequately; some factual errors are present.
1	Speech states no position or one that is off topic; conveys ideas in a very general or incomprehensible way; many factual errors are present.

Study Guide/Homework

Vocabulary and Study Guide

Vocabulary

Solve the clue and write the answer in the blank. Then find the word in the puzzle. Look up, down, forward, and backward. Look for a bonus word!

1. A fight against a government rebellion
2. A group of representatives who meet to discuss a subject congress
3. An official public statement proclamation
4. A person or group that joins with another to work toward a goal ally

Bonus Word: government

H	A	F	D	Z	B	T	U	J	W	G	M
P	R	O	C	L	A	M	A	T	I	O	N
L	E	H	S	C	X	L	A	M	W	V	U
B	B	O	K	O	E	W	P	Q	C	E	O
F	E	V	Y	N	C	A	K	J	H	R	L
A	L	L	Y	G	T	D	L	N	S	N	P
R	L	I	N	R	N	E	M	K	G	M	S
O	I	B	U	E	F	O	X	P	D	E	R
G	O	J	Z	S	R	Q	P	Y	I	N	B
A	N	C	M	S	P	E	G	I	K	T	F

Study Guide

5. Read "War Between France and Britain." Then fill in the outline below.

   I. Main Idea: France and Britain fought for control of the eastern part of North America.
      A. Supporting Idea: France had colonies and trade in the region.
         1. Detail: France built forts to keep the British out.
         2. Detail: American Indian nations were allies of France.
      B. Supporting Idea: Britain had colonies in the region.
         1. Detail: Britain wanted to trade fur and farm.
         2. Detail: Benjamin Franklin wanted the colonies to fight together.

Unit Resources

66 Use with *United States History*, pp. 228–231

Unit Resources, p. 66

Reteach Minilesson

Use a cause-effect chart to reteach the French and Indian War.

Cause	Effect
Ohio River Valley has rich farmland.	France and Britain fight for control of the valley.
Proclamation of 1763 forbids settlement in Ohio River Valley.	Colonists become angry with Britain.

Graphic Organizer 11

Extend Quick Look

Connect to the Core Lesson In Extend Lesson 1, students will learn more about some of George Washington's earliest military experiences at the start of the French and Indian War.

1 Teach the Extend Lesson

Connect to the Big Idea

Influences on History People who have played important roles in our nation's history were not born with the skills and knowledge to make them heroes. They had to learn these things through experience and through education. George Washington gained valuable military experience during the French and Indian War.

Washington's Successes

Using the timeline and biographical information on these pages, discuss Washington's successes. Make sure students understand how Washington learned from his early fighting experiences. Ask them to discuss what the lesson means by saying, ". . . he learned some valuable lessons—the hard way."

Extend Lesson 1

Biography

George Washington

1732–1799

George Washington didn't know much about war. In 1755, he had been an army officer for only a year. He was 23 years old and hadn't had much success. Now he and British soldiers, led by General Braddock, were heading toward Fort Duquesne (doo KAYN), located on the Ohio River. General Braddock planned to seize the fort from the French.

Suddenly, shots rang out. A surprise attack! French soldiers and their American Indian allies had been waiting for the British. A tough battle followed. Washington helped lead injured soldiers to safety. After the battle, he found that his jacket was marked by bullet holes.

Three years later, Washington joined another British army. This time, the British soldiers weren't beaten, and they captured Fort Duquesne. Washington had learned from his experiences, and his bravery made him a hero in Virginia. Years later, he would apply his experience to a great challenge. He would lead an army against the British and create a new nation.

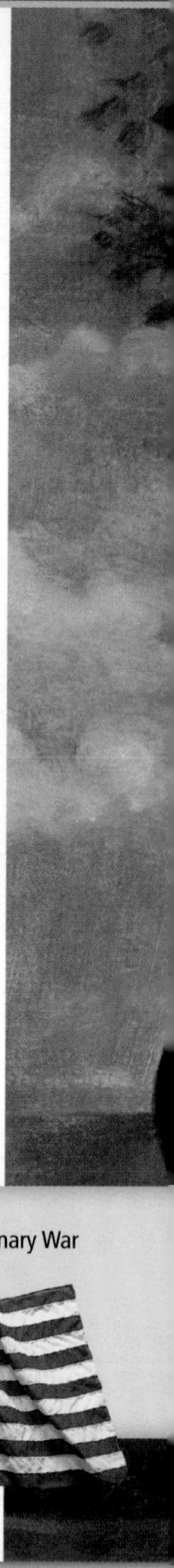

Major Achievements

1754–1763 Fights in French and Indian War

1775 Leads colonial army against British

1783 Wins Revolutionary War

Reaching All Learners

Extra Support

Illustrate a Battle

- Have students reread the paragraphs that describe what happened at the first battle at Fort Duquesne.
- Then ask them to draw a picture of what happened to George Washington and the British soldiers.
- Have students share and discuss their work.

Visual-spatial

On Level

Write a Poem

Have students write a poem about the life of George Washington that includes information about his background and his experiences. Ask volunteers to share their poems with the class.

Verbal-linguistic

Challenge

Hold a Debate

- Tell students that Americans elected George Washington to be the nation's first President because he had been such a successful military leader.
- Ask students to form two groups to debate whether military leadership and experience are important to becoming a successful national leader.

Verbal-linguistic

BIOGRAPHY

1789 Elected United States President

Activities

1. **TALK ABOUT IT** How did Washington show **courage** during the French and Indian War?
2. **RESEARCH IT** Find out more about Washington's early career. Then write a journal account of one day in the life of young George Washington.

Technology Read other biographies of people in this unit. www.eduplace.com/kids/hmss05/

233

2 Leveled Activities

❶ **Talk About It** *For Extra Support*
Sample answer: by leading injured soldiers to safety

❷ **Research It** *For Challenge*

Writing Rubric

4	Journal format is used correctly; account includes accurate information from research sources; mechanics are correct.
3	Journal format is used; account includes mostly accurate information from research sources; mechanics are generally correct.
2	Journal format is attempted; account contains errors; some errors in mechanics are present.
1	Journal format is not used; account contains many errors; many errors in mechanics are present.

Character Trait: Courage

Ask students how Washington used his experience and bravery after the French and Indian War. For more on character traits, see pages R4–R5.

ELL

Intermediate

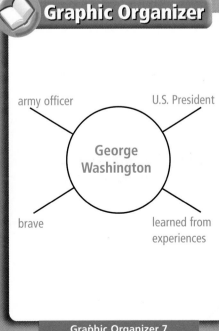

- Show students a U.S. quarter. Point out George Washington's profile on the front of the coin.
- Ask them to design a new image for the back of the coin, using the information in Extend Lesson 1.
- Students may draw their designs on posters or on the board.

Visual-spatial

Math

Use a Timeline

- Ask students how much time passed between the end of the French and Indian War and the end of the Revolutionary War. about 20 years
- Ask how long Washington fought in the French and Indian War. about nine years
- Have students create and solve other math problems using the information in the timeline and in the lesson.

Logical-mathematical

Graphic Organizer

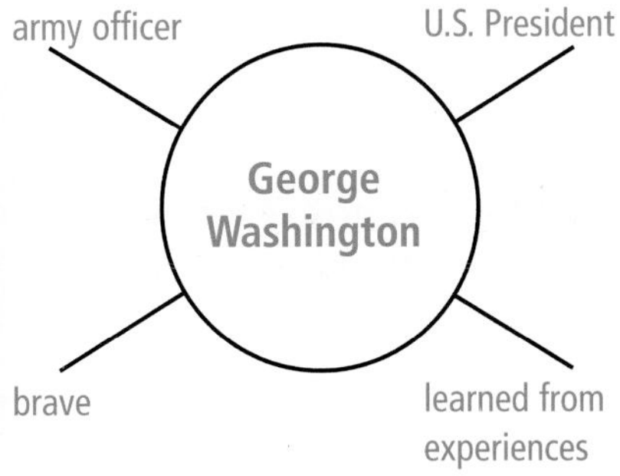

Graphic Organizer 7

✔ Tested Objectives

U4-3 History Explain why Britain imposed taxes on the American colonies and why colonists opposed them.

U4-4 History Describe the different methods colonists used to protest British policies.

Lesson Quick Look

This lesson focuses on the tensions that developed between Britain and the colonies as a result of Britain's attempts to tax the colonies.

Teaching Option: Extend Lesson 2 shows students examples of taxable goods in a colonial home.

1 Get Set to Read

Preview Have students read the captions in this lesson. Ask them why the colonists were upset with Britain.

Reading Skill: Problem and Solution You may wish to have students consider alternative, unused solutions.

Build on What You Know Discuss with students how governments get the money they need. Explain that governments use money to provide services to or protect their citizens.

Vocabulary

tax *noun,* money people give their government to pay for services it provides

smuggling *noun,* the secret import or export of illegal goods

liberty *noun,* freedom

protest *noun,* a gathering of people to show disapproval of something

boycott *verb,* to refuse to buy, sell, or use certain products as a way of protesting

repeal *verb,* to take a law out of effect

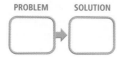

Core Lesson 2

Early Conflicts with Britain

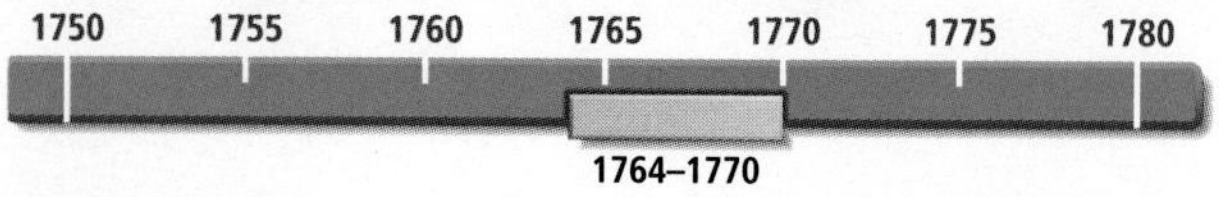

VOCABULARY

tax **protest**
smuggling **boycott**
liberty **repeal**

Vocabulary Strategy

repeal

Lawmakers can **repeal** a law that people don't want any more. Two synonyms for repeal are "take back" or "call off."

READING SKILL

Problem and Solution

Note problems the colonists had with Britain and the solutions they found.

PROBLEM → SOLUTION

Build on What You Know You know you have to pay for things you buy. Governments have to pay the money they owe, too. The British government had to find ways to raise the money it had spent on the French and Indian War.

Britain Needs Money

Main Idea The British government tried to raise money in the colonies to pay for the French and Indian War.

Winning the French and Indian War cost Britain a great deal of money. Britain had paid for thousands of soldiers to fight in North America. It also kept soldiers in the Ohio River Valley to protect the land it had won. **King George III** and the British Parliament decided that American colonists should help pay the costs of the war.

Britain planned to raise money by collecting taxes. A **tax** is money that people pay to their government in return for services. Britain usually taxed goods that colonists imported. These were goods brought from outside the colonies. When colonists bought imported goods such as cloth, some of the money they paid went to the British government.

King George III When George III became king at the age of 22, his country was already winning the French and Indian War.

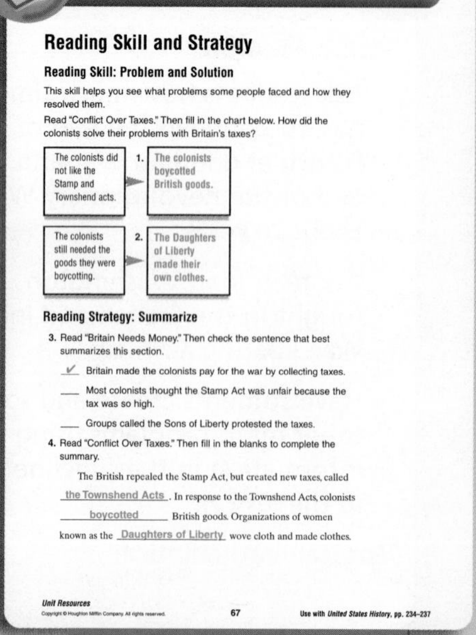

Skill and Strategy

Reading Skill and Strategy

Reading Skill: Problem and Solution

This skill helps you see what problems some people faced and how they resolved them.

Read "Conflict Over Taxes." Then fill in the chart below. How did the colonists solve their problems with Britain's taxes?

Problem		Solution
The colonists did not like the Stamp and Townshend acts.	1.	The colonists boycotted British goods.
The colonists still needed the goods they were boycotting.	2.	The Daughters of Liberty made their own clothes.

Reading Strategy: Summarize

3. Read "Britain Needs Money." Then check the sentence that best summarizes this section.

✓ Britain made the colonists pay for the war by collecting taxes.

___ Most colonists thought the Stamp Act was unfair because the tax was so high.

___ Groups called the Sons of Liberty protested the taxes.

4. Read "Conflict Over Taxes." Then fill in the blanks to complete the summary.

The British repealed the Stamp Act, but created new taxes, called the Townshend Acts. In response to the Townshend Acts, colonists boycotted British goods. Organizations of women known as the Daughters of Liberty wove cloth and made clothes.

Unit Resources 67 Use with *United States History*, pp. 234–237

Unit Resources, p. 67

Background

The Stamp Act

- Items to be stamped and taxed under the Stamp Act included newspapers, legal documents, pamphlets, playing cards, and dice.
- Americans from all walks of life were affected by this tax, including wealthy and powerful people. This made opposition to the Stamp Act unified and strong.

Tax Stamps The Stamp Act put a tax on almost everything that was printed. To buy newspapers, calendars, and even playing cards, colonists had to pay for a tax stamp.

New Taxes

In 1764, Britain created a new tax with a law called the Sugar Act. This act taxed not only sugar, but many other imported goods such as coffee and cloth. Some merchants avoided paying the tax
1 by **smuggling,** which means to import goods illegally. Merchants secretly brought the goods into the colonies so British officials could not tax them. In 1765, Parliament created another tax called the Stamp Act. This act taxed anything printed on paper.

Colonists were upset by the new taxes, because they could not take part in passing tax laws. Many believed that their local
2 elected representatives, not Parliament, should pass tax laws for the colonies. American colonists had no representatives in the British Parliament, but did have representatives in their local governments.

Patrick Henry, a member of Virginia's House of Burgesses, made an angry speech against the Stamp Act. He said Britain was using its power unfairly. People all over the colonies heard about his speech, and many agreed with him.

Protests Colonists held protests to show how much they hated the Stamp Act.

Across the colonies, groups formed and called themselves the Sons of Liberty. **Liberty** means freedom from being controlled by another government.

Samuel Adams was an important leader of the Sons of Liberty in Boston. Adams and the Sons of Liberty organized protests against the Stamp Act. A **protest** 3
is an event at which people complain about an issue.

Sometimes the Sons of Liberty and other groups used violence to resist the Stamp Act. Colonists wrecked the homes of a few British officials and beat up tax collectors.

REVIEW What was the goal of Samuel Adams and other Sons of Liberty?
to resist the Stamp Act

2 Teach

Britain Needs Money

Talk About It

1 **Q Economics** How did some merchants avoid paying the new taxes on sugar and other items?
A by smuggling

2 **Q Citizenship** Why did the colonists object to these new taxes?
A They had no say in the decision to tax because Americans had no representatives in the British Parliament.

3 **Q History** How did the Sons of Liberty protest the new taxes?
A They organized protests and used violence to resist.

Vocabulary Strategy

tax *Toll* and *fee* are other words for *tax.*

smuggling Explain that *smuggling* means bringing goods into a country illegally.

liberty Explain to students that *liberty* comes from *liber,* a Latin word for "free."

protest *Protest* can be used as a verb as well as a noun.

Reading Strategy: Summarize Ask a student to read the topic sentence of the lesson's first paragraph. Write the topic sentence on the board. With student help, edit the sentence to make it shorter but keep its essence. Explain that a summary of text is always shorter than the original text.

Reaching All Learners: Leveled Practice

Extra Support

Begin a **three-column chart.** Title the columns "Tax Laws Passed by Britain," "Items Taxed by These Laws," and "Colonists' Reactions." Have students come to the board and add to all three columns.
Verbal-linguistic

Challenge

Have partners **debate** whether the colonies should have paid part of Britain's war debt following the French and Indian War. Discuss as a class. Verbal-linguistic

Reaching All Learners: ELL

Intermediate/Advanced

Have students work in small groups to **role-play** the colonists' reactions to the Stamp Act. Encourage them to discuss how the colonists responded and to use lesson vocabulary words in their scene.

Verbal-linguistic

Conflict Over Taxes

Talk About It

4 Q Economics Why did Britain repeal the Stamp Act?

A The colonial boycott of British goods hurt British trade.

5 Q Visual Learning In what year did imports reach their lowest point?

A 1766

6 Q History Who were the Daughters of Liberty?

A women who protested the Townshend Acts by weaving their own cloth so they would not have to buy cloth from Britain

Vocabulary Strategy

boycott Tell students that Charles Boycott was a land manager in Ireland in the 1880s. Because of his high rents and unfair evictions, local people refused to work for Boycott, serve him in restaurants, or even deliver his mail.

repeal Tell students that another word for *repeal* is *revoke*.

Critical Thinking

Analyze Why were boycotts more effective than violence against British tax officials in getting the British to repeal taxes?

Think Aloud *Violence made Britain send more soldiers to the colonies. Boycotts hurt many British industries and had a big impact on the British economy.*

Conflict Over Taxes

Main Idea Britain canceled the Stamp Act but then tried to pass new taxes.

In October 1765, nine colonies sent representatives to a meeting in New York City called the Stamp Act Congress. This congress decided that only the colonial governments could tax the colonists.

Merchants in large port cities such as New York and Philadelphia agreed to hold a boycott of British goods. In a **boycott,** a group of people refuses to buy, sell, or use certain goods. Colonists stopped buying British cloth and other goods. The boycott was a way of hurting British trade. The merchants hoped that the boycott would force the British government to cancel the Stamp Act.

4 The boycotts and protests worked. Parliament agreed to repeal the Stamp Act in 1766. To **repeal** a law means to cancel it.

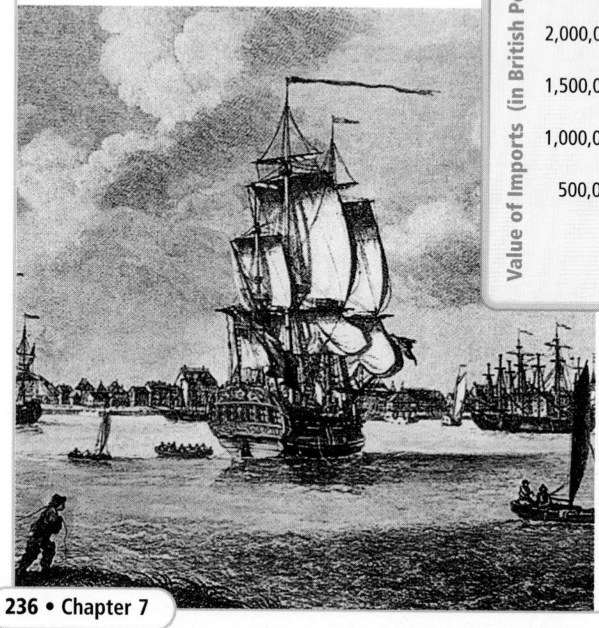

The Townshend Acts

Although the British government repealed the Stamp Act, it still needed money. In 1767, Parliament created new taxes to pay for the services of British governors and soldiers in the colonies.

The new taxes, called the Townshend Acts, put a tax on the tea, glass, lead, paints, and paper that the colonies imported. Colonists were just as angry about the Townshend Acts as they had been about the Stamp Act.

Colonists in Boston threatened to use violence against British tax officials. After an angry mob injured several people, the British government sent soldiers to protect its tax officials. Many people in Boston did not want British soldiers in their city.

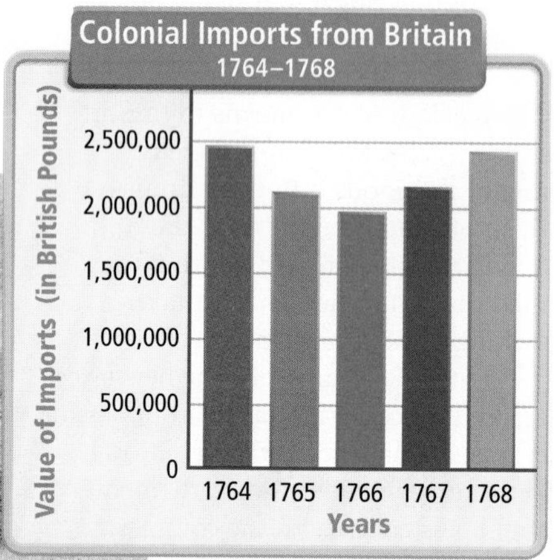

5

Boycott Colonial merchants in port cities refused to buy or sell goods brought from Britain by ship.

SKILL **Reading Graphs** Pounds are British money. How much did the value of imports decrease between 1764 and 1766?

about 500,000 pounds

236 • Chapter 7

Drama

Stamp Act Congress

- Have students role-play a meeting of the Stamp Act Congress.
- Divide the class into nine groups, representing the nine colonies that attended the meeting.
- Have each group discuss its colony's view of the Stamp Act and write a proposal for a course of action.
- After each colony presents its proposal, have the congress vote on the best proposal.

Bodily-kinesthetic; verbal-linguistic

Language Arts

Write About Rebellion

- Ask students to think about how a British official might have felt working in the colonies during this time.
- Have them write a journal entry from the point of view of a British tax official living in Boston.

Verbal-linguistic

Deborah Franklin
Even wealthy women, including the wife of Benjamin Franklin, made their own cloth during the boycott.

Daughters of Liberty

In response to the Townshend Acts, colonists held a boycott of the British goods they bought the most. Instead of importing British goods, such as cloth, the colonists made their own. Organizations of women known as the Daughters of Liberty wove their own cloth and used it
6 to make clothes. These women did chores early in the morning, gathered to weave all day, and then returned home to do more chores. Because of their hard work, colonists did not have to buy as much British cloth.

During the boycotts, British merchants lost money. Parliament decided to remove the taxes from glass, lead, paints, and paper. The tax on tea remained, though. Parliament wanted to show that it still had the power to tax the colonies.

Colonists felt that Britain should not even tax tea unless the colonies had representatives in Parliament. Although most of the taxes had been repealed, anger towards the British government continued to grow.

REVIEW Why did the British Parliament pass the Townshend Acts? to raise money to pay for British governors and soldiers in the colonies

Lesson Summary

Britain taxed the colonists to pay the cost of the French and Indian War. → Colonists did not want to be taxed without repre-sentation. → Protests by colonists forced Britain to repeal the taxes.

Why It Matters . . .

American colonists wanted only their own elected representatives to pass taxes on them. This idea is important to people in the United States today.

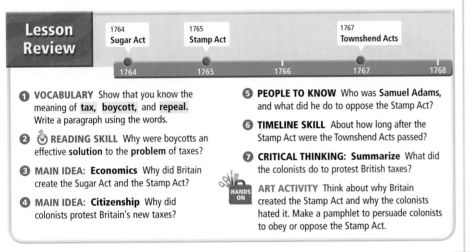

Lesson Review

1. **VOCABULARY** Show that you know the meaning of **tax, boycott,** and **repeal.** Write a paragraph using the words.
2. **READING SKILL** Why were boycotts an effective **solution** to the **problem** of taxes?
3. **MAIN IDEA: Economics** Why did Britain create the Sugar Act and the Stamp Act?
4. **MAIN IDEA: Citizenship** Why did colonists protest Britain's new taxes?
5. **PEOPLE TO KNOW** Who was **Samuel Adams,** and what did he do to oppose the Stamp Act?
6. **TIMELINE SKILL** About how long after the Stamp Act were the Townshend Acts passed?
7. **CRITICAL THINKING: Summarize** What did the colonists do to protest British taxes?

HANDS ON **ART ACTIVITY** Think about why Britain created the Stamp Act and why the colonists hated it. Make a pamphlet to persuade colonists to obey or oppose the Stamp Act.

237

3 Review/Assess

Review Tested Objectives

U4-3 Britain imposed taxes to pay its war costs; colonists opposed taxes because they were not represented in the British Parliament.

U4-4 Methods of objection included speeches, violence, smuggling, and boycotts.

Lesson Review Answers

1. Paragraphs should demonstrate understanding of these words.
2. Boycotts were effective because they cost the British lots of money, leading to the repeal of laws the colonists were protesting.
3. to help pay for the French and Indian War
4. American colonists were not represented in British Parliament and believed they should not be taxed by laws they had not agreed to.
5. Samuel Adams was a leader of the Sons of Liberty. He organized protests against the Stamp Act.
6. 2 years
7. Colonists gave speeches, smuggled, boycotted, and used violence to protest.

HANDS ON Performance Task Rubric

4	Position clearly stated; pamphlet is persuasive; mechanics are correct.
3	Position adequately stated; pamphlet is persuasive; few errors in mechanics are present.
2	Position is stated; pamphlet is fairly persuasive; some errors in mechanics are present.
1	Position not stated; pamphlet is not persuasive; many errors in mechanics are present.

Study Guide/Homework

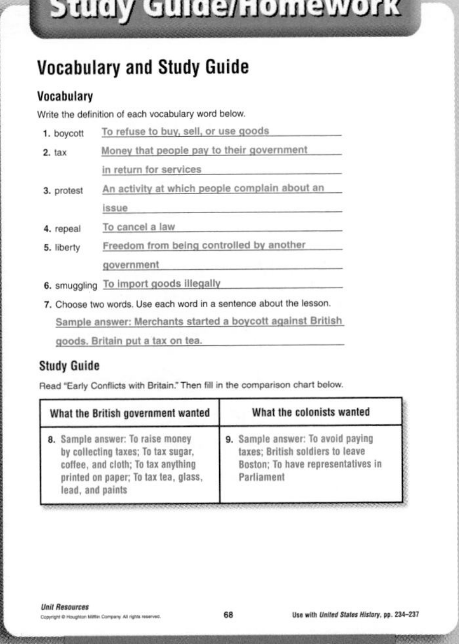

Vocabulary and Study Guide

Vocabulary
Write the definition of each vocabulary word below.

1. boycott To refuse to buy, sell, or use goods
2. tax Money that people pay to their government in return for services
3. protest An activity at which people complain about an issue
4. repeal To cancel a law
5. liberty Freedom from being controlled by another government
6. smuggling To import goods illegally
7. Choose two words. Use each word in a sentence about the lesson. Sample answer: Merchants started a boycott against British goods. Britain put a tax on tea.

Study Guide
Read "Early Conflicts with Britain." Then fill in the comparison chart below.

What the British government wanted	What the colonists wanted
8. Sample answer: To raise money by collecting taxes; To tax sugar, coffee, and cloth; To tax anything printed on paper; To tax tea, glass, lead, and paints	9. Sample answer: To avoid paying taxes; British soldiers to leave Boston; To have representatives in Parliament

Unit Resources 68 Use with United States History, pp. 234–237

Unit Resources, p. 68

Reteach Minilesson

Use a graphic organizer to reteach early conflicts with Britain.

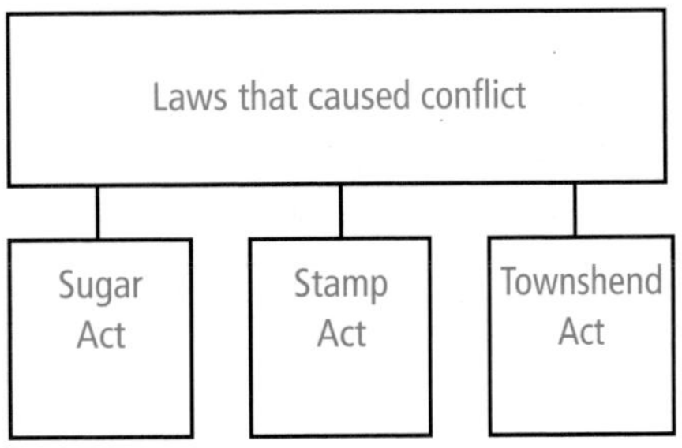

Graphic Organizer 8

Extend

Quick Look

Connect to the Core Lesson Students have learned about early conflicts between Britain and the colonies. In Extend Lesson 2, students will learn how British taxes affected the daily lives of American colonists.

1 Teach the Extend Lesson

Connect to the Big Idea

Democratic Principles British taxes made life hard and many goods expensive for American colonists like the Harts. The Harts joined with other colonists to protest the taxes because they believed that taxation without representation was undemocratic.

Connect to Prior Knowledge

Have students discuss what they know about taxes. Why do many people complain about paying them? What kinds of things do they pay for? Make sure students understand the difference between the taxes Americans pay today and the "taxation without representation" of the colonial era.

Extend Lesson 2

Economics

Taxes in the Colonies

It is two in the afternoon on September 12, 1769. Anna and Tom Hart run an inn near New York City. They are working together on a letter to the British governor of New York. They want to tell him that they oppose the Townshend Acts. These new taxes have made some important items more expensive for them. The Harts are upset because they had no voice in creating the taxes. Colonists have no representatives in Parliament, so they cannot take part in decisions that affect them.

Paint
Better-quality paint comes from Britain, but the tax on it makes the price higher. To avoid the tax, the Harts painted this furniture and the walls with paints made in the colonies.

Tea
Like many other colonists, the Harts love British tea. Now, they refuse to drink it because of the British tax on it. This is Dutch tea, smuggled in from the Caribbean.

238 • Chapter 7

Reaching All Learners

Extra Support

Draw a Cartoon

- Have students draw a cartoon to show what life was like for the Harts before and after the new British taxes.
- Ask students to write a caption or some call-outs to describe what is happening in the cartoon. The illustration on these pages can serve as a model.

Visual-spatial; verbal-linguistic

On Level

Write a Play

- Have students use the information in Extend Lesson 2 to write a play about how the Harts' life was changing in 1765 and what they thought about it.
- Ask students to perform the play for the class.

Verbal-linguistic; bodily-kinesthetic

Challenge

Write a Letter

- Divide the class into two groups.
- Have one group write a letter to the British governor from the Harts' point of view. Ask students to read their letters to the class or exchange them with students in the second group.
- Ask the second group to write a letter back to the Harts from the governor. Ask students to read their response letters aloud.

Verbal-linguistic

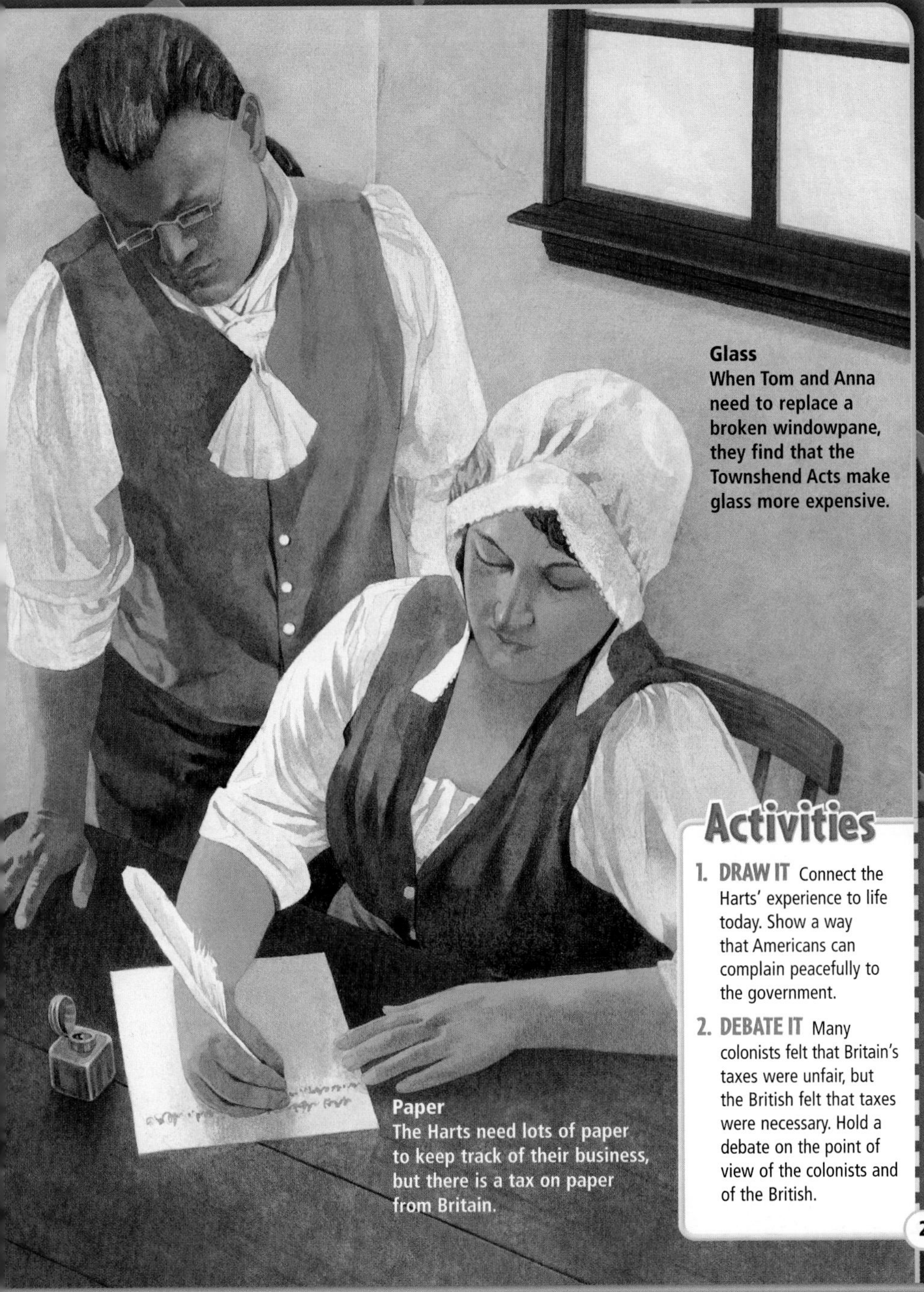

Glass
When Tom and Anna need to replace a broken windowpane, they find that the Townshend Acts make glass more expensive.

Paper
The Harts need lots of paper to keep track of their business, but there is a tax on paper from Britain.

Activities

1. **DRAW IT** Connect the Harts' experience to life today. Show a way that Americans can complain peacefully to the government.
2. **DEBATE IT** Many colonists felt that Britain's taxes were unfair, but the British felt that taxes were necessary. Hold a debate on the point of view of the colonists and of the British.

239

2 Leveled Activities

❶ **Draw It** *For Extra Support*
Drawings might show people demonstrating peacefully, writing letters, or signing a petition.

❷ **Debate It** *For Challenge*

HANDS ON Performance Task Rubric

4	Debate shows both points of view clearly; information cited is accurate and persuasive; students consistently listen and respond to one another.
3	Debate shows both points of view; information cited is mostly accurate and persuasive; students often listen and respond to one another.
2	Debate attempts to show points of view; some information cited is accurate and persuasive; students sometimes listen and respond to one another.
1	Debate does not show points of view; information cited is not accurate or persuasive; students do not listen or respond to one another.

REACHING ALL LEARNERS ELL

Intermediate

- Have partners or small groups role-play a conversation that the Harts might have had with each other, with neighbors, or with visitors to their inn.
- Topics might include the Townshend Acts or Stamp Act, the smuggling of tea, or business at the inn.

Bodily-kinesthetic; verbal-linguistic

Science

Making Paper

- Have students research how paper is made now and how it was made in colonial times. They might also choose to research glass, tea, or paint.
- Have students share their findings with the class. They may present them on a poster or orally.

Verbal-linguistic; visual-spatial

Graphic Organizer

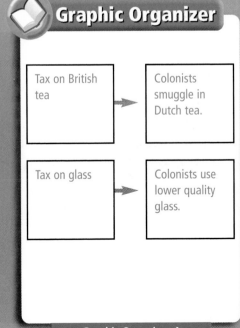

Cause		Effect
Tax on British tea	→	Colonists smuggle in Dutch tea.
Tax on glass	→	Colonists use lower quality glass.

Graphic Organizer 4

Core Lesson 3 Pages 240–241

Tested Objectives

U4-5 History Analyze how events in Boston increased tensions between the colonists and the British government.

U4-6 History Describe how people from different colonies began working together to oppose British actions.

Lesson Quick Look

This lesson describes the events that heightened the conflict between the colonies and Britain.

Teaching Option: Extend Lesson 3 details life in Boston during this time.

1 Get Set to Read

Preview Have students look at the image on page 241. What does it show them about conflict in the colonies?

Reading Skill: Predict Outcomes Students should consider the effects of events on both sides.

Build on What You Know: Ask students how long it takes to learn about current events today. Explain that in colonial times, people had to wait days, or even months, for news.

Vocabulary

massacre *noun,* the killing of many people, particularly defenseless people

correspondence *noun,* letters or other documents used to exchange information

quarter *verb,* to give food and shelter

delegate *noun,* one person chosen to speak or act for a number of people

3-5-1770
Crispus Attucks

Core Lesson 3

Conflicts Grow

1750 1755 1760 1765 1770 1775 1780
1770–1774

VOCABULARY
massacre
correspondence
quarter
delegate

Vocabulary Strategy

delegate

Delegate comes from a word meaning "to send." A delegate is someone you send in your place.

READING SKILL
Predict Outcomes As you read, predict what the colonists will do to complain to George III about taxes.

PREDICTION:

OUTCOME:

Build on What You Know Today, you can find out what is happening in the world from radio, television, newspapers, or the Internet. In colonial America, however, it was harder to learn about the news. Colonial leaders decided they needed better ways to share news.

Trouble in Boston

Main Idea Events in Boston created more trouble between the colonists and the British government.

Remember that Britain had sent soldiers to protect its officials in Boston. The people of Boston did not want British soldiers in their city. Frustrated colonists often fought with the soldiers.

On March 5, 1770, a fight began when a crowd of people in Boston argued with a British soldier. The crowd 1
yelled insults and threw snowballs. More soldiers arrived, and suddenly one of them fired a shot. Then several other soldiers fired their guns. Five colonists were killed. One of them was **Crispus Attucks,** an African American sailor who is remembered today as a hero. Afterward, angry colonists called the fight a massacre. A **massacre** is the killing of many people.

Crispus Attucks One of the five men killed during the Boston Massacre was Crispus Attucks. He was a sailor who had escaped from slavery.

Skill and Strategy

Reading Skill and Strategy

Reading Skill: Predict Outcomes

This skill allows you to think about what might happen, based on what you have read.

Read the first two paragraphs of "The Boston Tea Party." Then fill in the chart below. Write what you predict the British government will do in response to the Boston Tea Party in the first box. In the second box, write what really happened.

1. **Prediction:** Sample answer: The British will make new laws and punish the Sons of Liberty.

2. **Outcome:** Sample answer: The British raised the tax on tea and made new, strict laws for the colonists.

Reading Strategy: Summarize

3. Read "Trouble in Boston." Then write a short summary.
Sample answer: Violent incidents, such as the Boston Massacre, occurred between British soldiers and colonists.

4. Read "The Boston Tea Party." Then write a short summary.
Sample answer: The colonists began to meet and discuss their problems with Britain's laws and taxes.

Unit Resources 69 Use with United States History, pp. 240–243

Unit Resources, p. 69

Background

The Boston Massacre

- Nine British soldiers faced a mob of angry colonists. The crowd threw snowballs and stones.
- Clashes between Boston colonists and British soldiers were not unusual. Boston people referred to the soldiers as "lobsterbacks" because of their red coats.

The Boston Massacre Paul Revere made this image of the Boston Massacre.

SKILL **Primary Sources** How close is this picture to the truth? not very

❶ **Title** Revere's title begins with the words "The Bloody Massacre."

❷ **Soldiers** British soldiers are shown taking aim and firing as a group.

❸ **Colonists** Colonists are not shown attacking the soldiers. They do not look like an angry crowd.

Colonists Take Action

Paul Revere, a Son of Liberty and a Boston silversmith, created a picture of the Boston Massacre. It showed British soldiers shooting at colonists who are peaceful, not angry. The Sons of Liberty used the picture to convince colonists that British soldiers were dangerous.

The soldiers at the Boston Massacre were put on trial. **John Adams,** an important Boston lawyer, defended the soldiers at their trial. He wanted to show Britain that colonial courts were fair. Adams tried to prove that the soldiers had been protecting themselves from the crowd. Six soldiers were found innocent, and two were lightly punished.

At the time of the Boston Massacre, news traveled slowly. **Samuel Adams** wanted more colonists to know what was happening around the colonies. In 1772, Adams and other colonial leaders in Boston set up Committees of Correspondence to share news with the other colonies. **Correspondence** is written communication. 2

Soon every colony had Committees of Correspondence. They sent each other letters about what the British were doing and what actions colonists could take.

REVIEW What was the importance of the Committees of Correspondence? They kept people informed about British actions and discussed what the colonists could do.

② Teach

Trouble in Boston

Talk About It

1 Q History What was the cause of the Boston Massacre?

A Colonists who did not like having British soldiers in their city got into an argument with a British soldier, and the conflict escalated into a fight with gunfire.

2 Q History Why did colonists set up Committees of Correspondence?

A They wanted to be able to share news more easily.

Vocabulary Strategy

massacre Tell students that *slaughter* has a similar meaning to *massacre.*

correspondence Have students find the word *respond* in *correspondence*. Remind them that they may respond to a letter by writing back.

Reading Strategy: Summarize Have students read the second paragraph under "Trouble in Boston." Work with them to find the topic sentence. With student suggestions, write a summary of the paragraph on the board.

Leveled Practice

Extra Support

Have students **draw a picture** of the Boston Massacre. Then have them write a caption that explains why the event should or should not be called a massacre. Visual-spatial; verbal-linguistic

Challenge

Have students **research the trial** of the British soldiers who were involved in the Boston Massacre. Then ask them to write a skit about the trial, assign roles, and perform the play for the class. Verbal-linguistic

ELL

Intermediate

Have small groups work together to write a list of the people they read about in this lesson. Have them write a sentence describing what each person did. Then ask them to compare their sentences with another group's.

Verbal-linguistic

The Boston Tea Party

Talk About It

3 **Q History** What did Britain do in response to the Boston Tea Party?

A Britain passed laws that stopped town meetings, restricted trade, and required colonists to house British soldiers.

4 **Q History** For what did the First Continental Congress ask George III?

A to stop taxing the colonists and to repeal the Intolerable Acts

5 **Q History** How did George III respond to the letter?

A He declared that the colonists had begun a rebellion.

Vocabulary Strategy

quarter Tell students that another word for *quarter* is *shelter.*

delegate Explain to students that *legate* is a Latin word for *deputy.*

Critical Thinking

Evaluate Would some people have seen the Boston Tea Party as wrong? Why? You may wish to discuss with students how some actions can be seen as right and ethical by some people, and as unethical by others.

Boston Tea Party
A crowd of colonists watched as Sons of Liberty, dressed up to look like Mohawk Indians, emptied 342 chests of tea into Boston Harbor.

The Boston Tea Party

Main Idea Colonists worked together to oppose British taxes and laws.

In 1773, Parliament passed the Tea Act. This law allowed the East India Company of Britain to sell tea in America at a very low price. For years, merchants had avoided paying taxes by smuggling tea into the colonies from other countries. The Tea Act made taxed tea even cheaper than smuggled tea.

If colonists bought the inexpensive tea, they would be paying a British tax at the same time. They did not believe that Parliament should tax them without their agreement. They also did not want only one company to control the tea trade.

Boston merchants would not sell the East India Tea. It sat unloaded on the ships in Boston Harbor. British officials refused to allow the tea to go back to Britain. Colonists decided to get rid of the unwanted tea.

On the night of December 16, 1773, several dozen Sons of Liberty boarded the ships illegally. They threw the tea into the harbor. This event is known as the Boston Tea Party.

The Boston Tea Party shocked the British. Parliament, led by Lord **Frederick North,** passed laws called the Coercive Acts to punish colonists in Massachusetts. To coerce means to force. The colonists called these laws the Intolerable Acts. Intolerable means unbearable.

The laws stopped trade between Boston and Britain, ended most town meetings, and gave Britain more control over the colony's government. British soldiers returned to Boston. Bostonians had to quarter the soldiers. To **quarter** people is to give them food and shelter. 3

Committees of Correspondence spread news of the Intolerable Acts. People throughout the colonies were furious with Britain. They felt the laws were too harsh.

242 • Chapter 7

Math

Make a Line Graph

- Have students use the figures below to make a line graph about tea imports.

Year	Pounds of Tea Imported from England
1770	110,386
1771	363,257
1772	264,882
1773	739,221
1774	73,274

Logical-mathematical

Language Arts

Write a Poem

- Have students write a comical poem about one of the taxes the colonists opposed.
- They may use rhythm and rhyme to make their poems funny.
- Have some students read their poems to the class.

Verbal-linguistic

The First Continental Congress

Colonists agreed to hold a meeting to discuss the Intolerable Acts. They sent delegates to meet in Philadelphia. A **delegate** is someone chosen to speak and act for others. On September 5, 1774, delegates from every colony except Georgia met. The meeting became known as the First Continental Congress.

The congress wrote a letter to the British government and the American colonists. The letter said that colonists should have the same freedoms as other
4 British citizens. It asked **King George III** and Parliament to stop taxing colonists without their agreement and to repeal the Intolerable Acts.

The delegates decided to meet again in May if the king refused their demands. In the meantime, the colonists stopped trade with Britain. They began to train for battle in case war with Britain broke out.

The king made plans to send more soldiers to Boston. He declared that the colonists had begun a rebellion. 5

REVIEW Why did the First Continental Congress meet? to discuss what to do about the Intolerable Acts

Lesson Summary

- British soldiers killed several colonists in the Boston Massacre.
- Committees of Correspondence helped different colonies stay in touch.
- In 1773, colonists dumped tea into Boston Harbor to protest the Tea Act.
- Britain passed the Intolerable Acts in response to the Boston Tea Party.

Why It Matters . . .

Disagreement over taxes increased conflict between colonists and the British government.

Lesson Review

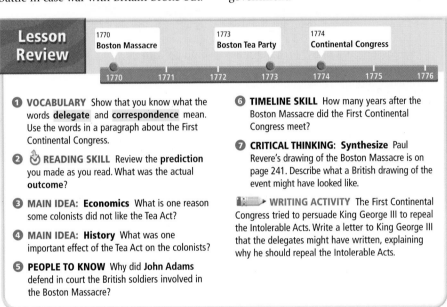

1770	1771	1772	1773	1774	1775	1776
1770 Boston Massacre			1773 Boston Tea Party	1774 Continental Congress		

1. **VOCABULARY** Show that you know what the words **delegate** and **correspondence** mean. Use the words in a paragraph about the First Continental Congress.
2. **READING SKILL** Review the **prediction** you made as you read. What was the actual **outcome**?
3. **MAIN IDEA: Economics** What is one reason some colonists did not like the Tea Act?
4. **MAIN IDEA: History** What was one important effect of the Tea Act on the colonists?
5. **PEOPLE TO KNOW** Why did **John Adams** defend in court the British soldiers involved in the Boston Massacre?
6. **TIMELINE SKILL** How many years after the Boston Massacre did the First Continental Congress meet?
7. **CRITICAL THINKING: Synthesize** Paul Revere's drawing of the Boston Massacre is on page 241. Describe what a British drawing of the event might have looked like.

WRITING ACTIVITY The First Continental Congress tried to persuade King George III to repeal the Intolerable Acts. Write a letter to King George III that the delegates might have written, explaining why he should repeal the Intolerable Acts.

3 Review/Assess

Review Tested Objectives

U4-5 Events such as the Boston Massacre and the Boston Tea Party increased tensions by showing the colonists' increasing anger about British taxation.

U4-6 The colonies created Committees of Correspondence and sent delegates to the First Continental Congress.

Lesson Review Answers

1. Paragraphs should demonstrate understanding of vocabulary.
2. Answers will vary.
3. They did not want Parliament to tax them, and they did not want just one company to control the tea trade.
4. It led to the Boston Tea Party, which in turn led to the Intolerable Acts.
5. Adams wanted the soldiers to have a fair trial to demonstrate to Britain that the colonial legal system was just.
6. four and a half years
7. The drawing might show a group of angry colonists threatening a soldier.

Study Guide/Homework

Vocabulary and Study Guide

Vocabulary

1. Draw a line connecting the vocabulary word to its meaning.

correspondence	To provide people with food and shelter
massacre	Someone chosen to speak and act for others
delegate	The killing of many people
quarter	Written communication

Study Guide

2. Read "Trouble in Boston." Then fill in the blanks below.

The people of Boston were angry with the British government. The colonists did not want soldiers in their city. A fight started on March 5, 1770. Crispus Attucks, an African American sailor, was killed in the fight. This event came to be known as the Boston Massacre. When the British soldiers were put on trial, John Adams defended them. In 1772, Samuel Adams set up Committees of Correspondence to help colonists share news about the British.

Unit Resources 70 Use with *United States History*, pp. 240–243

Unit Resources, p. 70

Reteach Minilesson

Use a cause-effect chart to reteach the growing conflict with Britain.

Cause	Effect
Colonists angry at British soldiers in Boston.	Boston Massacre takes place.
Boston Tea Party shocks British Government.	Parliament passes Intolerable Acts.

Graphic Organizer 11

Writing Rubric

4	Letter format is used correctly; main ideas are accurate and supported by details; mechanics are correct.
3	Letter format is used; many main ideas are accurate and supported by details; mechanics are generally correct.
2	Letter format is attempted; main ideas are sometimes inaccurate and not well supported; some errors in mechanics.
1	Letter format is not used; main ideas are mostly inaccurate and unsupported; many errors in mechanics.

Extend Quick Look

Connect to the Core Lesson Students have learned about the Boston Massacre and the Boston Tea Party. In Extend Lesson 3, students will learn what life was like for colonists in Boston after the Boston Tea Party.

1 Preview the Extend Lesson

Connect to the Big Idea

Individuals and Communities in American History Our national history is composed of individual and group stories of adjustment, adaptation/struggle, and survival. After the Boston Tea Party, colonists such as Emma had to adjust, adapt, struggle, and survive the British blockade of Boston Harbor.

Connect to Prior Knowledge

Ask students to look at the illustrations in Emma's journal. What events were on her mind? What kinds of things captured her interest and attention in Boston?

Extend Lesson 3

Literature

Emma's Journal

by Marissa Moss

When ten-year-old Emma Millar is sent to Boston to help her Aunt Harmony, she decides to write and illustrate a journal. The year is 1774, and British troops have blockaded Boston Harbor.

July 18, 1774

The house is hush and still. I should be asleep, like everyone else, but I am too excited, so I have taken my journal to the windowsill and write by the light of the full moon. Tomorrow I leave our farm in Menetomy and go to Boston, such a big, bustling city. I have never been there, but Daddy says 'tis a fine, fancy city, with cobbled streets, stores heaped with rich goods, and not one church but nine! I would go with all my heart if Daddy, Mamma, or even my little sister, Mercy, should stay with me, but I will be alone. Except, of course, for Aunt Harmony — 'tis for her sake I go. She has no serving girl since the British blockaded Boston. (This past winter Americans dumped British tea into the harbor to protest the new tea tax. Daddy called it a "tea party," but with the blockade as punishment, no one feels festive now.)

Emma Millar – 10 years old

The Boston "Tea Party"

244 • Chapter 7

Reaching All Learners

Background

Colonial Education

- Some girls in colonial New England were sent to school to learn to read and write.
- Girls' education focused on music, religion, dance, and mastering household tasks, such as needlework.

Extra Support

Illustrate the Narrative

Have students divide a sheet of drawing paper in half. On the left side, ask them to illustrate what Emma's life was like before she moved to Boston. On the right side, have them illustrate what Emma's life was like after she moved to Boston.

Visual-spatial

On Level

Make a Poster

- Have students use library and Internet resources to learn about the businesses and work that Emma would have seen Bostonians engaged in after she moved to the city.
- Ask students to select one of these jobs and illustrate and label it in a poster.

Verbal-linguistic; visual-spatial

LITERATURE

All of Aunt's boarders but one, Thankful Bliss, have left as well, fearful of the British troops that have taken over the city. I should think I should be fearful, too, but Daddy says we are good subjects of the King and have no cause to fret, especially not 10-year-old girls.

The city is as lively and fashionable as Daddy said. People dressed in London styles stroll the clean streets, and vendors hawk pies, eggs, and butter despite the blockade.

July 23, 1774

I woke in a strange room in a strange house to the sounds of fife and drum as the regulars drilled on the common. How I long for birdsong and the peaceful chirping of crickets! I miss the fresh country air and my dear Mamma and Daddy, Mercy, and my brothers, John, Paul, and Duncan. I feel out of place in this big, strange city, and out of sorts in this house.

I got this engraving from Mr. Revere when I took a spoon to his shop to be repaired. Boston, once full of merchantships, is now empty except for British warships.

245

2 Teach the Extend Lesson

Learning Through Historical Fiction

Assign four students to read the entries in *Emma's Journal* aloud to the class. Explain to students that this is an example of a fictional personal narrative. Tell them that historians use nonfiction personal narratives to find out how events affected people's daily lives. Ask students to give examples from the journal that show how Emma's life and the lives of people she knew were affected after the Boston Tea Party.

REACHING ALL LEARNERS — Challenge

Create a Timeline

- Have students use library or Internet resources to create a timeline of important events in the life of Paul Revere.
- Tell students that the events should include his achievements as an artist as well as an American patriot.

Verbal-linguistic

REACHING ALL LEARNERS — ELL

Beginning

- Have students use the information in Emma's journal to make a family tree of all the family members mentioned on these two pages.
- To help them correctly place Aunt Harmony on the family tree, tell students that she is Emma's father's sister.

Verbal-linguistic

Literature

Historical Fiction

Sleds on the Boston Common: A Story from the American Revolution by Louise Borden tells the story of a nine-year-old's attempt to sled on a hill in Boston Common where British soldiers are encamped in December 1774. The story is told in free verse.

Place this work of historical fiction in your Reading Center for students who want to find out what life was like for young people in Boston after the Boston Tea Party.

Critical Thinking

Infer Ask students why Emma needed a document in order to travel to see her family.

Draw Conclusions Ask students whether Emma's experience with Major Small was more likely to make her support the views of the colonists or the British. Have students explain their answers.

July 28, 1774

Dr. Joseph Warren came to tea today. Aunt is very proud of her tea service as 'twas made by Paul Revere, a fine silversmith, and, like Dr. Warren, a noted Son of Liberty. I call it tea, but we drink coffee or chocolate — Aunt is a staunch Whig and boycotts all British goods.

Dr. Warren

Dr. Warren is a fine, handsome gentleman, elegantly dressed and wearing a brown tie wig (which I much prefer to powdered hair — how it makes me sneeze!). Aunt dotes on him, but Thankful distrusts him as she is a fierce Tory while he thinks the colonies should govern themselves without England's interference. Thankful says the patriots are "low rabble" who want mob rule, but Dr. Warren is no ruffian. He is charming and interesting. Talking with him I feel I understand the world better. (And elsewhere it seems such a muddle. Are we British or American? What does it mean to be a Whig or a Tory? Dr. Warren says we can support the King but must first stand up for ourselves.)

Hairstyles of the illustrious and wealthy

September 15, 1774

I have found a friend in Amos, our neighbor. He fishes in the harbor (but the regulars allow it only so long as he sells most of his catch to them). He is so cheery and full of news, I relish his visits. It has been near 3 months since I left home and I miss my family terribly, so I asked Amos if he could take me for a short visit. (Aunt said 'twas fine with her.)

246 • Chapter 7

Reaching All Learners

Language Arts

Write a Personal Narrative

- Have students write a personal narrative like Emma's where they describe recent events in their lives that have personal importance.
- Remind students that an effective personal narrative puts the reader right in the middle of events.

Verbal-linguistic

Math

Calculate

Tell students that Menotomy, which is the present-day town of Arlington, was six miles northwest of Boston.

- Have students figure out how many feet Menotomy was from Boston. 31,680 feet
- Have students figure out how long it would take Emma to walk home if she walks at a pace of two miles per hour. 3 hours

Logical-mathematical

Art

Draw Colonial Fashions

- Have students use library or Internet resources to find out about colonial fashions.
- You may wish to divide the class into groups and have each group focus on different topics, such as men's clothing, women's clothing, children's clothing, hats, shoes, and uniforms.
- Ask students to draw pictures of the fashions they have found. Have them include descriptions of the items shown.

Visual-spatial

But when we came to the city gates, the sentries refused to let us pass without a permit. Off we went to military headquarters to procure the needed document, but all I procured was a stiff back from sitting on a hard bench, waiting, waiting, waiting. Finally Major Small deigned to see me and I begged to leave to see my family. He did not even glance my way but said, "No."

After waiting so long, I could not leave it at that. "But why, sir?" I protested. "I am a mere child. What danger can I be to His Majesty's army?"

"I said no," he repeated, and this time he did look at me, glaring, "because you are saucy and do not know your place. Is it the air you breathe that makes you colonists so impertinent? Even a young maid dares to sass an officer? Out with you — you have wasted enough of my time!"

I dared not murmur a word. I ran out, crying. Would I never see Mamma and Daddy again? Was Boston a city or a prison?

Amos said 'twas our timing that was bad — the regulars just seized some fieldpieces from the militia in Cambridge and in response guns were stolen from the British battery in Boston (right under the sentries' noses!). The officers now suspect everyone of preparing for an armed rebellion. Will arms really be taken up?

The soldiers are called lobsterbacks because of their red uniforms.

Activities

1. **THINK ABOUT IT** What things does Emma find strange about living in Boston?
2. **WRITE IT** After Emma meets Major Small, she wonders if Boston is a city or a prison. Write a letter from Emma to a Boston newspaper that expresses her feelings about the British occupation.

3 Leveled Activities

1 Think About It *For Extra Support*

Boston is noisier and bigger than Menotomy. Soldiers are everywhere. Her daily activities and chores are very different. She is the only child in the house.

2 Write It *For Challenge*

Writing Rubric

4	Letter states points of view clearly; conveys ideas effectively; facts are accurate; mechanics are correct.
3	Letter states points of view well; conveys ideas adequately; most facts cited are accurate; most mechanics are correct.
2	Letter states points of view in a somewhat disorganized way; conveys ideas adequately; some errors in facts or mechanics.
1	Letter is incomplete or states no points of view; conveys ideas in a very general or incomprehensible way; many errors in facts or mechanics.

Music

Listen to Fife and Drum Music

- Tell students that the British and colonial troops used the fife and drum as more than musical instruments.
- Have the class use library or Internet resources to find out what these instruments looked like and their uses.
- Locate a recording of fife and drum music and play it for the class. Ask students to describe the music and how it makes them feel.

Musical-auditory

Graphic Organizer

British troops take over Boston. Soldiers are everywhere.
Colonists boycott British goods.
After the Boston Tea Party
Colonists cannot travel in and out of Boston freely.
Suspicions and tensions increase.

Graphic Organizer 7

Skillbuilder Pages 248–249

Tested Objective

U4-7 Identify and interpret multiple causes and effects of events.

1 Teach the Skill

- Have students turn to pages 235–236 in their books. Ask them to reread these pages to remind themselves what Parliament did that angered colonists. created new taxes, including the Stamp Act and Townshend Acts
- Direct students' attention to the first diagram. Point out that the answers to the question that you asked are the effects shown in the diagram. Have students identify the cause shown in the chart. Britain needs money.
- Have students use the second diagram to explain how an effect became a cause. The colonists' boycott of British goods led to the repeal of the Townshend Acts.
- Go over the three steps for identifying causes and effects. Tell students to use these steps as they practice the skill.

Reading and Thinking Skills

Skillbuilder

Identify Causes and Effects

VOCABULARY
cause
effect

Historians want to know what happened in the past. They also want to know why it happened. They look for the causes and effects of events. A **cause** is an event or action that makes something else happen. An **effect** is another event or action that is a result of the cause.

Some events have more than one cause. Some have more than one effect.

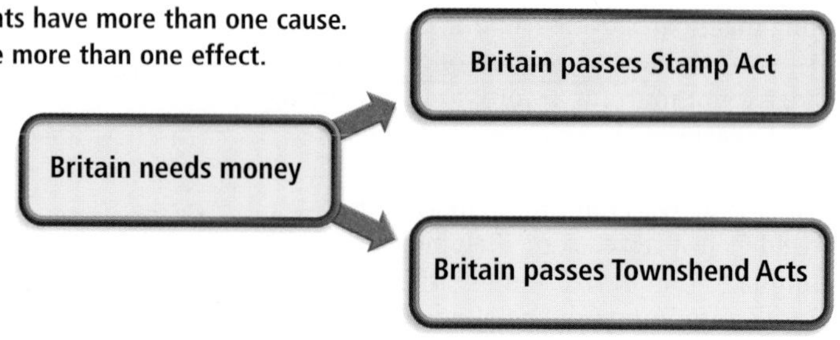

Many times, an effect can cause another event or action.

Leveled Practice

Extra Support

Demonstrate cause and effect by setting a row of dominos on end. Have a volunteer push the first domino. Have students identify the effect and the cause. Then ask other students to explain what happened using the signal word *because.* **Bodily-kinesthetic**

Challenge

Invite students to draw political cartoons showing one effect of an event from the chapter. Display completed cartoons in the classroom. **Visual-spatial**

ELL

Beginning

Have students create simple sentences using the key words listed in Step 1 on page 249. (Sample answers: "I fell because I tripped"; "Since she was ill, she stayed home.") Have students say each sentence twice. The second time, have them raise one hand when they hear a cause and both hands when they hear an effect.

Bodily-kinesthetic

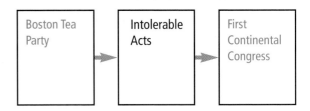

Apply Critical Thinking

Learn the Skill

Step 1: Look for clue words that signal causes and effects. Words such as *because, since, led to,* and *the reason why* signal causes. Words such as *so, therefore, after this,* and *as a result* signal effects.

Step 2: Identify the cause of an event. Check to see if there is more than one cause.

Step 3: Identify the effect. Check to see if there is more than one effect. Think about whether any of the effects then become causes.

Practice the Skill

Reread pages 242-243 of Lesson 3. Copy and fill out a diagram like the one below. Then answer the following questions.

[ ] ⇨ [Intolerable Acts] ⇨ [ ]

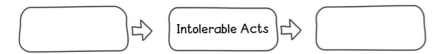

1. What was one cause of the Intolerable Acts?
2. What was one effect of the Intolerable Acts?
3. Explain in a few sentences how you identified the causes and effects.

Apply the Skill

Organize the major events on pages 228-231 of Lesson 1. Place the Proclamation of 1763 at the center of the chart. Then fill in the causes and effects. Make sure you have at least one cause and one effect.

249

2 Practice the Skill

Boston Tea Party → Intolerable Acts → First Continental Congress

1. the Boston Tea Party
2. Sample answers: the First Continental Congress; colonists became angry; other colonies supported Massachusetts.
3. Sample answer: I looked for the reason why Parliament passed the Intolerable Acts. Then I looked for the colonies' response.

3 Apply the Skill

Ask students to skim Lesson 1 (pages 228–231). Have them use a chart to organize the major events in the lesson. When evaluating students' charts, consider:

- Did the student place the Proclamation of 1763 at the center of the chart?
- Did the student correctly identify at least one cause?
- Did the student correctly identify at least one effect?

Skill Practice

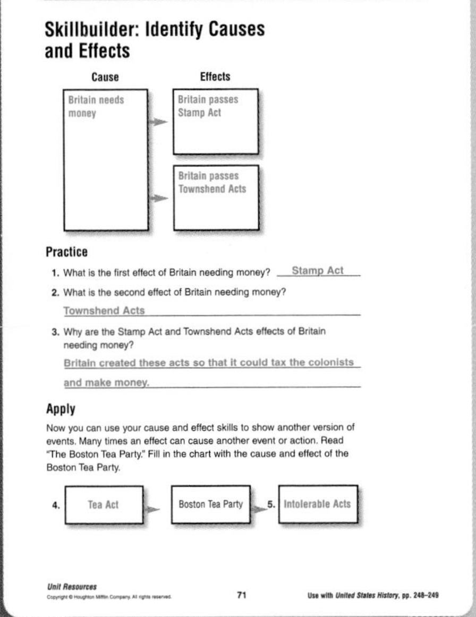
Skillbuilder: Identify Causes and Effects

Cause: Britain needs money
Effects: Britain passes Stamp Act; Britain passes Townshend Acts

Practice

1. What is the first effect of Britain needing money? Stamp Act
2. What is the second effect of Britain needing money? Townshend Acts
3. Why are the Stamp Act and Townshend Acts effects of Britain needing money? Britain created these acts so that it could tax the colonists and make money.

Apply

Now you can use your cause and effect skills to show another version of events. Many times an effect can cause another event or action. Read "The Boston Tea Party." Fill in the chart with the cause and effect of the Boston Tea Party.

4. Tea Act → Boston Tea Party → 5. Intolerable Acts

Unit Resources

71
Use with *United States History*, pp. 248–249

Unit Resources, p. 71

Skill Transparency

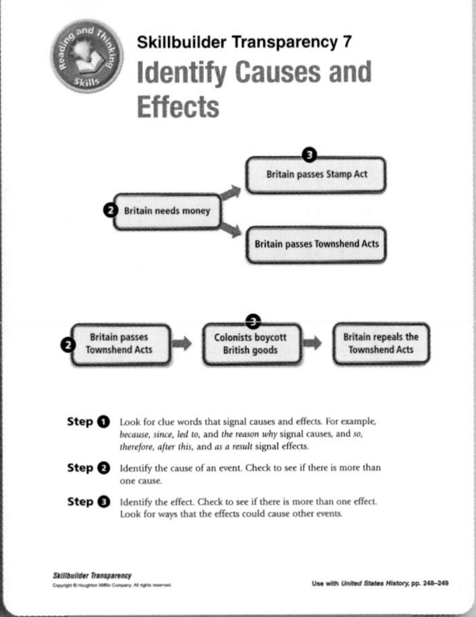
Skillbuilder Transparency 7

Identify Causes and Effects

2 Britain needs money → 3 Britain passes Stamp Act; Britain passes Townshend Acts

2 Britain passes Townshend Acts → 3 Colonists boycott British goods → Britain repeals the Townshend Acts

Step 1 Look for clue words that signal causes and effects. For example, *because, since, led to,* and *the reason why* signal causes, and *so, therefore, after this,* and *as a result* signal effects.

Step 2 Identify the cause of an event. Check to see if there is more than one cause.

Step 3 Identify the effect. Check to see if there is more than one effect. Look for ways that the effects could cause other events.

Skillbuilder Transparency

Use with *United States History*, pp. 248–249

Transparency 7

✔ Tested Objectives

U4-8 History Describe the first battles of the Revolutionary War.

U4-9 History Explain how the fighting spread and colonists prepared for war in 1775.

Lesson Quick Look

This lesson describes the outbreak of hostilities in the War for Independence and colonial efforts to prepare for war.

Teaching Option: Extend Lesson 4 provides a bird's-eye view the Battle of Bunker Hill.

1 Get Set to Read

Preview Direct students to read the title of the lesson. What does the title tell them about what they will read?

Reading Skill: Cause and Effect Students should include the blockade of Boston.

Build on What You Know Discuss with students times when they have disagreed with friends. Explain that disagreements can be settled peacefully through discussion or violently through fighting.

Vocabulary

Patriot *noun,* an American colonist who opposed the British

militia *noun,* an army made up of ordinary citizens, not professional soldiers

minutemen *noun,* members of the American colonial militia who were prepared to fight at a minute's notice

commander *noun,* the officer in charge of an army

petition *noun,* a written request to the government signed by many people

Core Lesson 4

War Begins

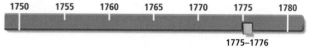

1750 1755 1760 1765 1770 1775 1780

1775–1776

VOCABULARY

Patriot
militia
minutemen
commander
petition

Vocabulary Strategy

militia

A **militia** is an army of ordinary people. It comes from the same word as military.

READING SKILL

Cause and Effect Note causes of the war between Britain and the colonies.

War with Britain

Build on What You Know When Britain and France could not agree on control of the Ohio River Valley, they went to war. What do you think happened when Britain and the colonists disagreed and could not get along anymore?

Moving Toward War

Main Idea Conflict between the colonists and Britain led to the Battles of Lexington and Concord.

In 1775, many colonists felt that the Intolerable Acts were too harsh. There were more than 3,000 British soldiers in Boston. The British navy blocked Boston Harbor to keep ships from entering or leaving Boston.

Patriots spoke out against the British government. Colonists who opposed British rule called themselves **Patriots.** **Mercy Otis Warren** was a Patriot writer. 1
She wrote plays criticizing British officials in Boston. In Virginia, **Patrick Henry,** another Patriot, said that he was eager for a war with Britain. Many colonists shared his views.

Throughout the colonies, militias prepared for war. A **militia** is a group of ordinary people who train for battle. Most of the men in the militia were farmers.

Militia The men in militias did not have much training, but they were willing to fight to defend their homes.

250 • Chapter 7

Skill and Strategy

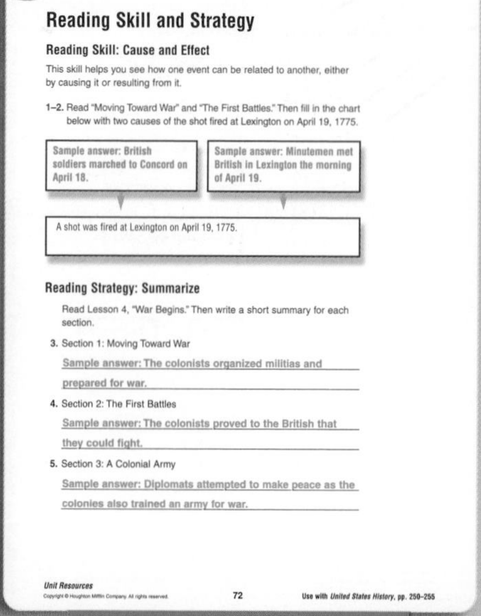

Reading Skill and Strategy

Reading Skill: Cause and Effect

This skill helps you see how one event can be related to another, either by causing it or resulting from it.

1–2. Read "Moving Toward War" and "The First Battles." Then fill in the chart below with two causes of the shot fired at Lexington on April 19, 1775.

Sample answer: British soldiers marched to Concord on April 18.

Sample answer: Minutemen met British in Lexington the morning of April 19.

A shot was fired at Lexington on April 19, 1775.

Reading Strategy: Summarize

Read Lesson 4, "War Begins." Then write a short summary for each section.

3. Section 1: Moving Toward War

Sample answer: The colonists organized militias and prepared for war.

4. Section 2: The First Battles

Sample answer: The colonists proved to the British that they could fight.

5. Section 3: A Colonial Army

Sample answer: Diplomats attempted to make peace as the colonies also trained an army for war.

Unit Resources 72 Use with *United States History,* pp. 250–255

Unit Resources, p. 72

Background

Willing to Fight

- Patrick Henry made a famous speech in 1775 in which he said, "Give me liberty or give me death!"
- Some members of the Patriot militia already had fighting experience from the French and Indian War.

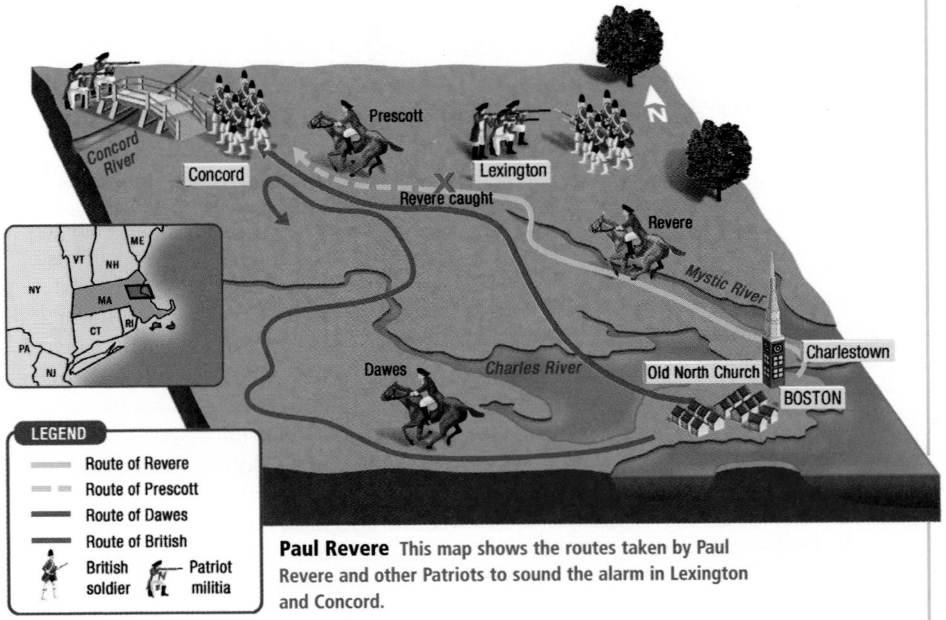

Paul Revere This map shows the routes taken by Paul Revere and other Patriots to sound the alarm in Lexington and Concord.

Paul Revere's Ride

British leaders were worried about the
2 militias. General **Thomas Gage,** the new British governor of Massachusetts, had orders to stop any possible rebellion. He learned that Patriots were storing gunpowder and cannons in Concord, about 20 miles from Boston. Gage decided to send soldiers to destroy the supplies. The soldiers would march at night to take the Patriots by surprise.

General Gage could not keep his plan secret. Patriots in Boston soon knew what was planned. They used lanterns in the tower of Boston's Old North Church to warn Patriots outside the city that British soldiers were coming. Two Patriots also rode out to warn the militia. One rider was **Paul Revere,** the silversmith. The other was **William Dawes.**

On the night of April 18, 1775, an army of 700 British soldiers set off for Concord. Revere and Dawes galloped ahead, alerting sleeping minutemen
along the way. **Minutemen** were militia 3
with special training. They had to be ready for battle at a minute's notice.

Racing through the night, Revere told the minutemen, "The Regulars are coming out!" Regulars was a word for British soldiers. Other riders, such as **Samuel Prescott,** helped Revere and Dawes spread the alarm.

British soldiers captured Revere in Lexington, but Dawes and Prescott escaped. Prescott rode on to Concord. The soldiers later released Revere.

REVIEW Why did General Gage send British soldiers to Concord?

to destroy the Patriots' stores of military supplies

2 Teach

Moving Toward War

Talk About It

1 **Q History** How did Mercy Otis Warren oppose the British?
A She wrote plays criticizing British officials.

2 **Q History** Who was Thomas Gage?
A the new British governor of Massachusetts

3 **Q History** Who were the minutemen?
A Patriot militia who were trained to fight on very short notice

Vocabulary Strategy

Patriot Explain that when the word *patriot* is not capitalized it means a person who loves and supports his or her country.

militia Remind students of the related word *military.*

minutemen Point out to students that *minutemen* is a compound word made up of the words *minute* and *men.*

Reading Strategy: Summarize As students read the first section, ask them to use what they know about summarizing to produce a summary of the section. Ask students to share their summaries with the class.

Leveled Practice

Extra Support

Distribute Henry Wadsworth Longfellow's poem "Paul Revere's Ride." Divide students up into small groups. Have each group **read one verse** aloud to the class and explain what it means. Verbal-linguistic

Challenge

Have students **write a story** about Paul Revere's ride or the Battles of Lexington and Concord. Remind them to start with a dramatic moment and to use accurate details. Verbal-linguistic

ELL

Beginning

Have students **draw pictures** of the important people and places involved in the events leading up to the Battle of Lexington and Concord. Ask students to explain what their picture shows.

Visual-spatial; verbal-linguistic

The First Battles

Talk About It

4 **Q History** Which side had more casualties at Lexington?

A the colonists

5 **Q Citizenship** What was the "shot heard 'round the world"?

A It was the first shot fired at the Battles of Lexington and Concord.

6 **Q History** What did colonists do to respond to the news of the Battles of Lexington and Concord?

A Thousands of armed colonists rushed to Boston to trap the British.

Critical Thinking

Infer Why do you think a Patriot leader at the Battle of Bunker Hill told his soldiers not to fire at the British until they saw "the whites of their eyes"?

Think Aloud *If you can see someone's eyes, they are very close. The militia was waiting for the British to come close before shooting at them. I know the Patriots had limited resources. They needed to make the best use of their gunpowder by waiting until the British were in close range. Otherwise they might have wasted ammunition and suffered a much worse defeat.*

The First Battles

Main Idea Colonists and British soldiers fought two battles in Massachusetts.

The British soldiers reached Lexington just before sunrise on April 19. A small group of minutemen were waiting there. A British officer told the minutemen to leave. As the minutemen turned to go, someone fired a shot. No one knows whether the shot came from a British soldier or a colonist. Both sides began shooting. When they stopped, eight
4 colonists were dead and nine were wounded. Only one British soldier had been hurt. The British marched on to Concord.

As the British searched Concord for hidden weapons, more minutemen gathered nearby. Fighting soon started.

The minutemen forced the British to turn back toward Boston. Many years later, the poet **Ralph Waldo Emerson** called this event 5

"the shot heard 'round the world."

The British soldiers were in a dangerous situation on the way back. Patriots from the towns between Concord and Boston, as well as towns farther north and south, were ready. As the British marched back to Boston, colonists shot at them from behind trees and stone walls. More than 250 British soldiers were wounded or killed before the British reached Boston.

News of the Battles of Lexington and Concord spread quickly. More and more militias arrived in Boston. Soon thousands of armed colonists surrounded the city. The British in Boston were trapped. 6

April 19, 1775

Battles of Lexington and Concord

1 A.M. Paul Revere and others warn the minutemen that British soldiers are marching to Concord.

5 A.M. Minutemen clash with the British at Lexington. The minutemen are forced to flee. The drum on the left was used by the minutemen at Lexington.

252 • Chapter 7

Music

Yankee Doodle

Have students familiar with the song "Yankee Doodle" sing it for the class. Explain that this song was originally sung by British soldiers to make fun of the Patriots. Have partners make up alternative lyrics to the song. They may choose to write lyrics that British soldiers or American Patriots might have sung.

Musical-auditory

Math

Bunker Hill

- Tell students that Bunker Hill is about 100 feet high, and Breed's Hill is about 80 feet high. The Washington Monument is 550 feet tall.
- Have students make a bar graph showing the heights.

Logical-mathematical

Bunker Hill

After the Patriot militia surrounded Boston, they had time to plan. Militia leaders decided to build a fort on Bunker Hill, across the Charles River from Boston. From there, they could fire cannons at the British soldiers in Boston.

When the militia reached Bunker Hill, they chose to build their fort on
7 Breed's Hill instead. It was closer to Boston. They worked through the night of June 16, building a fort with dirt walls six feet high. The next morning, the surprised British attacked the fort.

More than 2,000 British soldiers began to march up Breed's Hill. **William Prescott,** a Patriot leader, told the militia,

> **"Don't fire until you see the whites of their eyes."**

When the British were close enough, the militia in the fort began shooting. Many soldiers fell, and the British were forced back. Minutes later, the British attacked again and were turned back. The third time the British attacked, the Patriots ran out of gunpowder. The British finally captured the fort, but more than
half of their soldiers were hurt or killed. 8

The battle was called the Battle of Bunker Hill, although it was fought on Breed's Hill. The British won, but the Patriots had proved that they could fight well. One British general said that winning another battle like it "would have ruined us." They could not afford to lose so many soldiers.

REVIEW Why was the Battle of Bunker Hill important for the colonists?
They showed their militia could fight well.

8 A.M. Colonists and British soldiers begin shooting at each other at the Old North Bridge in Concord. The British turn back after several of their soldiers are killed.

NOON The British begin to march back to Boston. During their long march, thousands of minutemen shoot at them from behind trees and stone walls. The British soldiers finally reach safety in Charlestown at 7 P.M.

253

The First Battles *continued*

Talk About It

7 Q Geography Why did the Patriot militia decide to build a fort on Breed's Hill?

A It was closer to Boston.

8 Q History How many of the British soldiers were killed or wounded at the battle?

A more than half

Reading Strategy: Summarize As students read the second and third sections, ask them to use what they know about summarizing to produce a summary of each section. Ask students to share their summaries with the class.

Visual Learning

Discuss with students the four paintings on pages 252 and 253. Ask them what each tells about the event it depicts.

British soldiers charge up Breed's Hill.

Extra Support

REACHING ALL LEARNERS

Draw Uniforms

- Have students use Internet or library resources to find out about British and Patriot uniforms during the Revolution.
- Ask students to make drawings that illustrate the different uniforms.
- Have students discuss the differences in the uniforms in small groups.

Visual-spatial

Challenge

REACHING ALL LEARNERS

Battle Leaders

- Have students research the British and Patriot leaders who played important roles in the battle of Bunker Hill.
- Ask students to report their findings to the class.

Verbal-linguistic

A Colonial Army

Talk About It

9 Q History Why did Congress decide it needed to create an army?

A Soldiers would be trained to fight, and would fight until the war was over.

10 Q History Why did the Second Continental Congress send the Olive Branch Petition to King George III?

A They did not want to go to war with Britain and thought they should try one more time to make peace.

Vocabulary Strategy

commander Tell students that synonyms for *commander* include *leader* and *captain.*

petition Explain to students that *petition* comes from a Latin verb, *petere,* that means to request.

Critical Thinking

Analyze Could war between the colonies and Britain have been avoided? Why or why not?

A Colonial Army

Main Idea The Second Continental Congress prepared for a war against Britain.

Remember that the First Continental Congress had sent a list of demands to the British government. When Britain refused to meet their demands, the colonial delegates gathered again in Philadelphia in the spring of 1775. This meeting became known as the Second Continental Congress.

The delegates knew that they might soon be at war with Britain. They needed
9 more than an untrained militia to win a war against the British. They needed an army. The militia only fought for a few months at a time. Soldiers in an army fight until a war is over.

Congress decided to create a new army called the Continental Army. The members of the Continental Army would be trained soldiers, like the British.

Congress looked for a commander for the new Continental Army. A **commander** is the officer in charge of an army. In June of 1775, they chose **George Washington.** Washington had fought in the French and Indian War. People knew he was a brave and skilled soldier. Washington rode to Boston to organize the Continental Army.

The Olive Branch Petition

Many delegates to the Second Continental Congress did not want war with Britain. They only wanted to be treated
fairly. Congress made one more try at peace 10
with Britain. In July of 1775, the delegates sent **King George III** the Olive Branch Petition. A **petition** is a written request from a number of people. The olive branch is a symbol of peace. The petition asked the king to help end the conflict. King George did not even read the Olive Branch Petition. Instead, he sent more soldiers to the colonies.

Washington in Command
Washington became commander of the Continental Army in 1775. He used the writing case below while he was leading the army.

Art

Peace Symbols

Tell students that the olive branch is one of many symbols of peace. Have students research other peace symbols. Then ask them to make drawings of the peace symbols they find. Students should also find out how each of these symbols came to stand for peace. Display the drawings and information on the origin of the symbols on a bulletin board.

Visual-spatial

Language Arts

Write a Petition

The delegates to the Second Continental Congress made one last try at making peace with Britain by sending a formal request supported by many people to the king. Ask students to think of something that they would like to improve at their school. Have them work together to prepare a petition describing the improvement and its benefits. You can display the completed petition in the classroom.

Verbal-linguistic

Ticonderoga This important fort was captured from the British by Patriot militia in 1775. Its cannons were hauled to Boston to help the Continental Army.

For the next nine months, the British army stayed in Boston. Washington spent that time turning the colonial militia into a real army. He also sent a trusted officer, Colonel **Henry Knox,** to Fort Ticonderoga in New York. Americans had captured the fort and its cannons earlier that year.

Knox and his soldiers dragged the cannons to Boston. When the cannons arrived, the British decided to leave Boston. On March 17, 1776, they sailed out of Boston Harbor. Forcing the British to leave Boston was a success for the Patriots, but the war was just beginning.

REVIEW What was the Olive Branch Petition? It was a request sent to the king by the second Continental Congress seeking peace.

Lesson Summary

British soldiers and colonists fought at Lexington and Concord, and again on Breed's Hill. The Second Continental Congress made George Washington commander of the new Continental Army. Congress also sent King George III the Olive Branch Petition in an attempt to make peace, but he ignored it.

Why It Matters . . .

Battles in Massachusetts were the beginning of the war to free colonists from British rule.

Lesson Review

APRIL 1775 — Battles of Lexington and Concord
JUNE 1775 — Battle of Bunker Hill
1775 — 1776

1. **VOCABULARY** Write a news report about the Battles of Lexington and Concord using the words **Patriot, minutemen,** and **militia.**
2. **READING SKILL** Why were the Battles of Lexington and Concord a **cause** of war with Britain?
3. **MAIN IDEA: History** What prepared the militia for the arrival of the British soldiers at Lexington?
4. **MAIN IDEA: Government** Why did the Second Continental Congress send the Olive Branch Petition to King George III?
5. **PEOPLE TO KNOW** What did **Paul Revere** do to help the Patriot cause?
6. **TIMELINE SKILL** When did the battles of Lexington and Concord happen?
7. **CRITICAL THINKING: Compare and Contrast** In what ways are a militia and an army alike? In what ways are they different?

WRITING ACTIVITY The Battles of Lexington and Concord were the first fights between colonists and British soldiers. Write a description what happened on April 19 from the point of view of a minuteman or a British soldier.

3 Review/Assess

Review Tested Objectives

U4-8 The Battle of Lexington and Concord began the fighting; the Battle of Bunker Hill resulted in many British casualties.

U4-9 More and more militias got involved in the fighting. The Second Continental Congress decided to create a colonial army to prepare for war. They also chose General Washington to command the army.

Lesson Review Answers

1. Answers should include information from the lesson.
2. These were the first battles of the Revolution and resulted in the deaths of many British soldiers.
3. Paul Revere, William Dawes, and Samuel Prescott had alerted the minutemen.
4. They hoped to end the conflict without further fighting.
5. He warned the minutemen and other Patriots that British soldiers were on their way.
6. April 1775
7. A militia is a group of ordinary people who train to become fighters. An army is made of professional soldiers.

Writing Rubric

4	Account is clearly stated; point of view is clearly presented; mechanics are correct.
3	Account is adequately stated; point of view is mostly clear; few errors in mechanics are present.
2	Account is stated in a confused or disorganized way; point of view is confused or poorly presented; some errors in mechanics are present.
1	No account is given; point of view is not presented; many errors in mechanics are present.

Study Guide/Homework

Vocabulary and Study Guide

Vocabulary

Write the word for each definition below.

1. commander — The officer in charge of an army
2. minutemen — Militia with special training
3. Patriot — A colonist who opposed British rule
4. petition — A written request from a number of people
5. militia — A group of ordinary people who train for battle

Study Guide

Read "Moving Toward War." Then fill in the sequence chart below.

Militia prepare for war. → 6. General Gage sends soldiers to destroy militia supplies. → Patriots warn the militia. → 7. An army of 700 British soldiers goes to Concord.

Read "The First Battles." Then fill in the sequence chart below.

The British reach Lexington and fight with minutemen. → 8. The British march to Concord and fight with minutemen. → Militia build a fort at Bunker Hill. → 9. After much fighting, the British win the Battle of Bunker Hill.

Read "A Colonial Army." Then fill in the sequence chart below.

The Second Continental Congress meets in 1775. → 10. Congress decides to build a new army called the Continental Army. → 11. Congress chooses George Washington as the commander of the Continental Army. → Congress sends a petition to King George.

Unit Resources 73 Use with *United States History*, pp. 250–255

Unit Resources, p. 73

Reteach Minilesson

Use a sequence chart to reteach the beginning of the war.

1.	Battles of Lexington and Concord and the Battle of Bunker Hill take place.
2.	Congress creates Continental Army with George Washington in command.
3.	Congress sends Britain the Olive Branch Petition, and Britain sends more soldiers.
4.	British withdraw from Boston as American army around the city grows.

Graphic Organizer 15

Extend Quick Look

Connect to the Core Lesson Students have learned about the start of the War for Independence. In Extend Lesson 4, students will learn more about the Battle of Bunker Hill by examining a drawing of the battlefield.

1 Teach the Extend Lesson

Connect to the Big Idea

The World in Spatial Terms The location of the Patriots' fort on a hill made the attack by the British more difficult. It helped the Patriots to hold off the British attack.

Connect to Prior Knowledge

Discuss with students whether they find it easier to walk on a flat piece of ground or to climb a hill. Ask if they have ever walked carrying a lot of weight.

Make sure students understand that the Patriots did not win this battle—the British did capture the fort. However, there were so many British casualties that the battle helped encourage the Patriots in their efforts.

Extend Lesson 4

Geography

Battle of Bunker Hill

"Don't fire until you see the whites of their eyes!" A Patriot officer is said to have given this famous order as 2,000 British soldiers marched closer and closer up the hill. It was June 17, 1775. The Battle of Bunker Hill in Charlestown was the first major clash between large numbers of British soldiers and Patriot militia. The geography of Charlestown forced the British attackers to march uphill. Why did this make a difference?

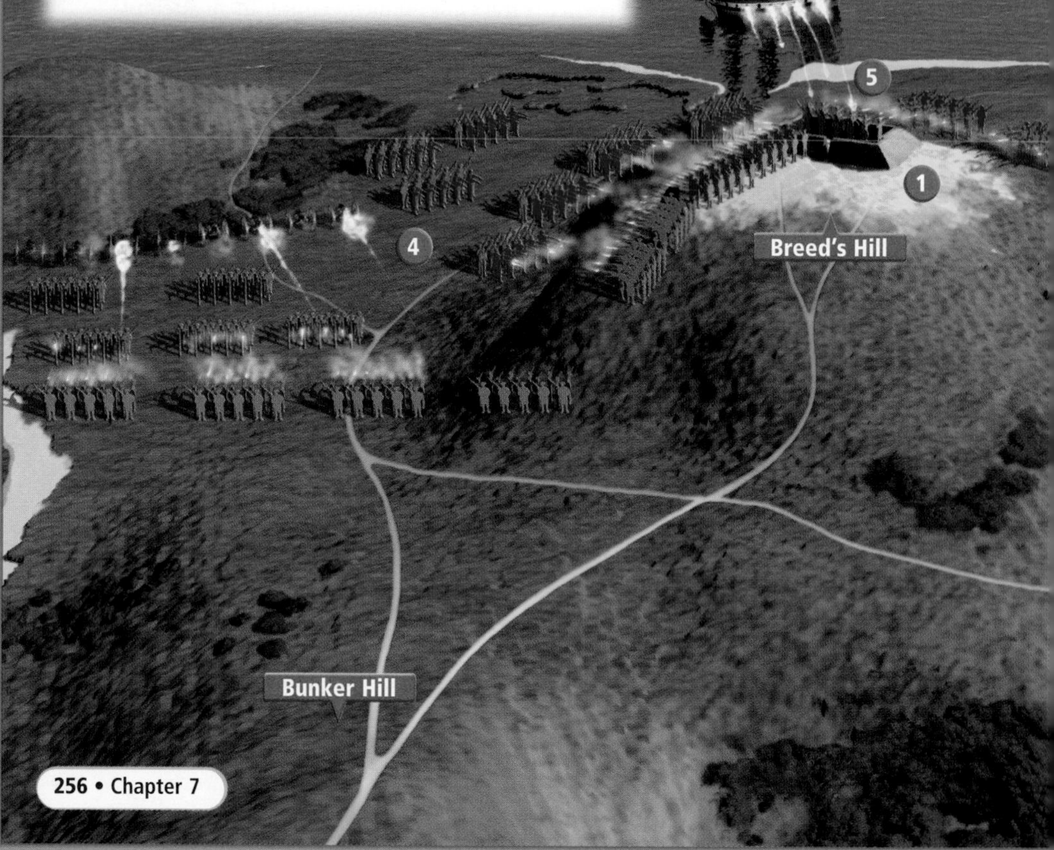

256 • Chapter 7

Reaching All Learners

Extra Support

Draw Conclusions

- Have students **make a chart** that compares and contrasts American troops and British troops at the time of this battle.
- Ask students to draw conclusions about which side was better prepared and how each side felt afterwards.

Verbal-linguistic

On Level

Write an Account

- Divide students into two groups. One group will act as reporters for a Boston newspaper, and the other as reporters for a British newspaper.
- Direct the students in each group to write an account of the Battle of Bunker Hill.
- Then compare accounts as a class.

Verbal-linguistic

Challenge

Infer

- Have students **make a list** of ways in which the battle would have been different if the colonists had chosen Bunker Hill as the location of their fort.
- Have students compare answers.

Verbal-linguistic

GEOGRAPHY

Events of June 17th, 1775

1. Patriot militia built a fort on Breed's Hill to fire on British ships and soldiers in Boston. They first planned to build their fort on Bunker Hill, but it was too far from Boston.
2. Cannons on British ships could not destroy the Patriots' fort.
3. The British in Boston fired red-hot cannonballs and set Charlestown on fire.
4. Three times, British soldiers marched slowly uphill toward the fort. Hot, tired, weighed down by 125 pounds of gear, the British soldiers were easy targets for Patriot gunfire.
5. To save ammunition, the Patriots waited to shoot until the British soldiers were almost on top of them. The British only captured the fort when the Patriots ran out of bullets.

Activities

1. **EXPLORE IT** Step into the picture and tell what you think the Patriot fort looked like to British soldiers on their march.
2. **WRITE YOUR OWN** Write directions for a Patriot battle plan at Breed's Hill. Explain what your fort's position would be. Use compasss directions.

257

2 Leveled Activities

1 Explore It *For Extra Support*
Answers should reflect information from the Extend Lesson.

2 Write Your Own *For Challenge*

Writing Rubric

4	Plans are clearly stated; fort's position is well chosen; compass directions are correct.
3	Plans are adequately stated; fort's position is fairly well chosen; directions are generally correct.
2	Plans are stated in a confused or disorganized way; fort's position is illogical or unclear; errors in directions are present.
1	Plans are not given; fort's position is not shown; many errors in directions are present.

ELL

REACHING ALL LEARNERS

Beginning

- Have students draw a series of pictures to illustrate the Battle of Bunker Hill.
- The pictures should show events before, during, and after the battle.
- Ask volunteers to explain their illustrations.

Visual-spatial

Language Arts

Write a Poem

- Ask students to use details from Extend Lesson 4 to write a poem about the Battle of Bunker Hill.
- You may wish to collect the poems in a class anthology and place it in the Reading Corner.

Verbal-linguistic

Graphic Organizer

1	Patriots build fort on Breed's Hill to attack the British.
2	British burn Charlestown.
3	British march up Breed's Hill but are forced back.
4	Patriots run out of ammunition; British capture Breed's Hill.

Graphic Organizer 15

Chapter Review

Visual Summary

1. It was a war between the British and French over control of the Ohio River Valley. *(Obj. U4-2)*
2. new taxes for paint, paper, tea, lead, and glass. *(Obj. U4-3)*
3. To protest the Tea Act, colonists dumped tea into Boston Harbor. *(Obj. U4-4)*
4. These were the first battles of the American Revolution. *(Obj. U4-8)*

Facts and Main Ideas

5. to keep settlers off of American Indian lands west of the Appalachians *(Obj. U4-1)*
6. a tax on printed items *(Obj. U4-3)*
7. to pay for the French and Indian War and keep soldiers in the Ohio River Valley *(Obj. U4-3)*
8. They were being taxed without consent or representation in Parliament. *(Obj. U4-3)*
9. a Patriot who rode to Lexington and Concord to warn the Minutemen that the British were coming *(Obj. U4-5)*
10. Delegates thought they would soon be at war with Britain. *(Obj. U4-6)*

Vocabulary

11. **liberty** *(Obj. U4-6)*
12. **ally** *(Obj. U4-1)*
13. **petition** *(Obj. U4-4)*

Visual Summary

1–4. Write a description of each event named below.

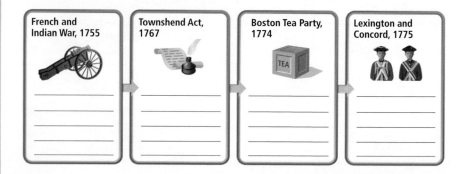

French and Indian War, 1755

Townshend Act, 1767

Boston Tea Party, 1774

Lexington and Concord, 1775

Facts and Main Ideas

TEST PREP Answer each question with information from the chapter.

5. **Geography** What was the purpose of the Proclamation of 1763?
6. **Economics** What was the Stamp Act?
7. **Economics** Why did the British government need to tax the colonists?
8. **Government** Why were colonists angry about British taxes?
9. **History** Who was Paul Revere?
10. **History** Why did the Second Continental Congress decide to form a colonial army?

Vocabulary

TEST PREP Choose the correct word from the list below to complete each sentence.

ally, p. 229
liberty, p. 235
petition, p. 254

11. Colonists opposed to the Stamp Act became members of the Sons of ______.
12. The Mohawk nation was an ______ of the British, not the French.
13. Colonists at the Second Continental Congress sent one final ______ to King George III.

Reading/Language Arts Wrap-Up

Reading Strategy: Summarize

Review with students the steps involved when they summarize a passage of text.

Have students work in small groups. Each member of the group should take a paragraph and summarize it for the rest of the group.

Ask students to do a self-check: "How well did I do in summarizing?"

Writing Strategy

Explain to students that summarizing will be a valuable tool when they need to write.

For example, if students are taking a test in which they must write short answers to questions, they can use the summarizing strategy as they review what they know and choose the details most pertinent to the answer.

CHAPTER SUMMARY TIMELINE

1754 Albany Congress — 1763 Proclamation of 1763 — 1765 Stamp Act — 1774 First Continental Congress — 1775 Battle of Bunker Hill

1750 | 1755 | 1760 | 1765 | 1770 | 1775 | 1780

Apply Skill

TEST PREP Reading and Thinking Skill Use the organizer below and what you have learned about causes and effects to answer each question.

The British went to find military supplies in Concord.
↓
The Battles of Lexington and Concord were fought.
↓
The Continental Army was formed.
↓
The British were forced out of Boston.

14. What was a cause of the Battles of Lexington and Concord?

- **A.** Committees of Correspondence formed.
- **B.** The British went to find military supplies in Concord.
- **C.** The British were forced out of Boston.
- **D.** The Continental Army was formed.

15. What was a result of the Battles of Lexington and Concord?

- **A.** Committees of Correspondence formed.
- **B.** The British went to find military supplies in Concord.
- **C.** British troops were sent to Boston.
- **D.** The Continental Army was formed.

Critical Thinking

TEST PREP Write a short paragraph to answer each question.

16. Infer Why do you think King George III did not accept the Olive Branch Petition?

17. Compare and Contrast List ways in which the First and Second Continental Congresses were alike and different.

Timeline

Use the Chapter Summary Timeline above to answer the question.

18. How long after the Albany Congress did the First Continental Congress meet?

Activities

HANDS ON **Art Activity** Create a poster that would encourage colonists to join the Sons or Daughters of Liberty. Describe the group and why new members are needed.

Writing Activity Colonists learned about events through the Committees of Correspondence. Write a short story about a committee member informing others about Paul Revere's ride.

Technology
Writing Process Tips
Get help with your short story at
www.eduplace.com/kids/hmss05/

259

Technology

Test Generator

- The questions in this review are part of the bank of questions that can be found on the **Test Generator CD-ROM.**
- You can generate your own version of the chapter review by using the Test Generator.

Web Link

For more ideas, visit
www.eduplace.com/ss/hmss05/

Standards

National Standards

V e Tension between an individual's beliefs and government policies and laws **VI c** How government does/does not provide for needs and wants of people, establish order and security, and manage conflict **VI f** Factors that contribute to cooperation and cause disputes **VI h** Tensions between the wants and needs and fairness, equity, and justice **VII f** Influence of incentives, values, traditions, and habits on economic decisions **VII i** Use economic concepts **IX b** Conflict, cooperation, and interdependence

Apply Skills

14. B *(Obj. U4-7)*
15. D *(Obj. U4-7)*

Critical Thinking

16. Sample answer: He was too angry at the colonists and he wanted to teach them a lesson. *(Obj. U4-4)*

17. Alike: both discussed ways to solve problems; tried to avoid war; sent documents to the British king; Different: First tried to make peace with Britain; Second, discussed breaking away and planning for war *(Obj. U4-6)*

Timeline

18. 20 years *(Obj. U4-6)*

Leveled Activities

HANDS ON Performance Task Rubric

4	Position clearly stated; poster is persuasive and accurate; mechanics correct.
3	Position adequately stated; poster is persuasive and accurate; few errors.
2	Position is stated; poster is fairly persuasive and somewhat accurate; some errors in mechanics.
1	Position not stated; persuasion lacking; inaccurate; many errors.

Writing Rubric

4	Story is well organized, accurate, and shows considerable creative effort; mechanics are correct.
3	Story is adequately organized, mostly accurate, and shows creative effort; few errors.
2	Story is somewhat organized, fairly accurate, and shows some creative effort; some errors.
1	Story is disorganized, inaccurate, and shows little effort; many errors in mechanics.

Chapter 8 Planning Guide

The War for Independence

Chapter Opener	Core Lesson 1	Core Lesson 2	Core Lesson 3
Chapter Opener Pages 260–261 30 minutes	**Declaring Independence** Pages 262–267 50 minutes	**Life During the War** Pages 270–273 40 minutes	**The War in the North** Pages 278–281 40 minutes
Tested Objectives	**Tested Objectives** **U4-9** Describe the events that led to the writing of the Declaration of Independence. **U4-10** State the main ideas in the Declaration and explain their significance.	**Tested Objectives** **U4-11** Explain why different groups of people chose to become Patriots or Loyalists. **U4-12** Describe some of the hardships Americans faced during the war.	**Tested Objectives** **U4-13** Describe the results of the major Revolutionary War battles that were fought in the North. **U4-14** Analyze how aid from Europe affected the war.
Reading/Vocabulary **Chapter Reading Strategy:** Question, p. 259	**Reading/Vocabulary** **Reading Skill:** Predict Outcomes independence, rights, declaration, treason	**Reading/Vocabulary** **Reading Skill:** Compare/Contrast Loyalist, inflation, neutral	**Reading/Vocabulary** **Reading Skill:** Cause/Effect retreat, victory, mercenary
Cross-Curricular	**Cross-Curricular** **Science,** p. 264 **Math,** p. 266	**Cross-Curricular** **Math,** p. 272 **Art,** p. 272	**Cross-Curricular** **Math,** p. 280
Resources **Grade Level Resources** Vocabulary Cards, pp. 29–42 **Reaching All Learners** Challenge Activities, p. 86 **Primary Sources Plus,** p. 14 **Big Idea Transparency 4** **Interactive Transparency 4** **Text & Music Audio CD** **Lesson Planner & TR CD-ROM** **eBook** **eTE**	**Resources** **Unit Resources:** Reading Skill/Strategy, p. 74 Vocabulary/Study Guide, p. 75 **Reaching All Learners:** Lesson Summary, p. 30 Support for Lang. Dev./ELL, p. 127 **Assessment:** Lesson Test, p. 76 www.eduplace.com/ss/hmss05/	**Resources** **Unit Resources:** Reading Skill/Strategy, p. 76 Vocabulary/Study Guide, p. 77 **Reaching All Learners:** Lesson Summary, p. 31 Support for Lang. Dev./ELL, p. 128 **Assessment:** Lesson Test, p. 77	**Resources** **Unit Resources:** Reading Skill/Strategy, p. 78 Vocabulary/Study Guide, p. 79 **Reaching All Learners:** Lesson Summary, p. 32 Support for Lang. Dev./ELL, p. 129 **Assessment:** Lesson Test, p. 78 www.eduplace.com/ss/hmss05/
	Extend Lesson 1 **Biography** Thomas Jefferson **20–30 minutes** Pages 268–269 **Focus** Learn more about Jefferson, the man behind the Declaration of Independence.	**Extend Lesson 2** **Readers' Theater** Patriot or Loyalist **40–50 minutes** Pages 274–277 **Focus** Who's a Patriot, and who's a Loyalist? Characters speak for themselves.	**Extend Lesson 3** **Primary Source** Valley Forge **20–30 minutes** Pages 282–283 **Focus** Find out what life was like for Continental soldiers at Valley Forge.

National Standards

II b Identify key concepts such as conflict
II f Develop historical empathy
VI b Purpose of government
VI f Conditions that contribute to conflict
VII b Describe supply and demand
X a Origins of key ideals

With the Program

CURRENT EVENTS from WEEKLY WR READER at www.eduplace.com

Skillbuilder

Map and Globe Skill

Read a Battle Map

Pages 284–285

30 minutes

Tested Objective

U4-15 Use a map to interpret the sequence of events during a battle.

Resources

Unit Resources:
- **Skillbuilder,** p. 80
- **Skillbuilder Transparency 8**

Core Lesson 4

Winning the War

Pages 286–289

50 minutes

Tested Objectives

U4-16 Describe the results of the major Revolutionary War battles that were fought in the South and the West.

U4-17 Explain how the Americans won the war.

Reading/Vocabulary

Reading Skill: Sequence

strategy
surrender
traitor

Cross-Curricular

Art, p. 288

Resources

Unit Resources:
- **Reading Skill/Strategy,** p. 81
- **Vocabulary/Study Guide,** p. 82

Reaching All Learners:
- **Lesson Summary,** p. 33
- **Support for Lang. Dev./ELL,** p. 130

Assessment:
- **Lesson Test,** p. 79

Extend Lesson 4

Geography

A Global View, 1783

20–30 minutes

Pages 290–291

Focus Learn what else was happening in the world during the Revolutionary War.

Chapter Review

Pages 292–293

30 minutes

Resources

Assessment Options:
- **Chapter 8 Test,** pp. 80–83
- **Test Generator**

Chapter 8

Practice Options

Lesson 1 Skill and Strategy

TEST PREP

Reading Skill and Strategy

Reading Skill: Predict Outcomes

This skill allows you to think about what might happen, based on what you have read.

Read the first paragraph of "Importance of the Declaration." Then fill in the prediction and outcome chart below. Write what you think happened after the signing of the Declaration of Independence in the first box. Then read the second paragraph. Write how the colonists reacted to the Declaration in the second box.

1. **Prediction:** Sample answer: The colonists were happy to be free from Britain.
2. **Outcome:** The colonists celebrated by tearing down pictures of King George, ringing bells, and firing cannons.

Reading Strategy: Question

3. Read "The Steps to Independence." Then check the question that you might ask while reading this section.
   - ___ What was the Patriots' plan for fighting the British army?
   - ✓ How did Thomas Paine's *Common Sense* change some people's minds about independence?
   - ___ Which colonies were most likely to stay loyal to King George III?
4. Read "Declaration of Independence." Then check the question that you might ask while reading this section.
   - ___ When did the delegate from Ohio sign the Declaration of Independence?
   - ✓ Who did the Congress choose to write the Declaration?
   - ___ How many delegates to the Congress did not support the Declaration?

Unit Resources

74
Use with *United States History*, pp. 262–267

Lesson 1 Vocabulary/Study Guide

TEST PREP

Vocabulary and Study Guide

Vocabulary

Across
1. A statement that announces an idea
2. Freedom from being ruled by someone else

Down
3. Freedoms protected by law
4. The crime of fighting against one's own government

	1 D	E	C	L	A	R	A	4 T	I	O	N
3 R								R			
2 I	N	D	E	P	E	N	D	E	N	C	E
G								A			
H								S			
T								O			
S								N			

Study Guide

5. Read "The Steps to Independence." Then fill in the blanks below.

   Thomas Paine wrote a small, inexpensive booklet called Common Sense. In the booklet, he explained that King George treated the colonies unfairly. He said the only way to stop this unfair treatment was for the colonies to become independent. After reading Paine's booklet, many people who had not wanted to separate from Britain changed their minds.

6. Read "Declaration of Independence." Then fill in the blanks below.

   Among the readers of Paine's booklet were the delegates of the Continental Congress. This group asked five delegates, including Thomas Jefferson to write a declaration to tell other countries and colonists why a break with Britain was needed. Jefferson said that people have certain rights that no one can take away. The delegates signed the document on July 4, 1776.

Unit Resources

75
Use with *United States History*, pp. 262–267

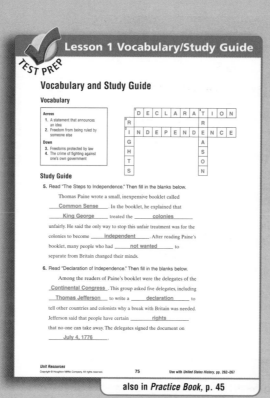

also in *Practice Book*, p. 45

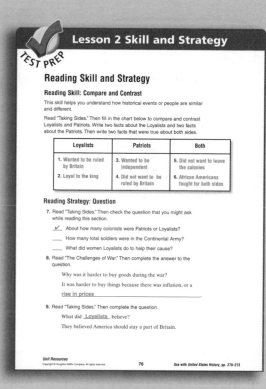

Lesson 2 Skill and Strategy

TEST PREP

Reading Skill and Strategy

Reading Skill: Compare and Contrast

This skill helps you understand how historical events or people are similar and different.

Read "Taking Sides." Then fill in the chart below to compare and contrast Loyalists and Patriots. Write two facts about the Loyalists and two facts about the Patriots. Then write two facts that were true about both sides.

Loyalists	Patriots	Both
1. Wanted to be ruled by Britain 2. Loyal to the king	3. Wanted to be independent 4. Did not want to be ruled by Britain	5. Did not want to leave the colonies 6. African Americans fought for both sides

Reading Strategy: Question

7. Read "Taking Sides." Then check the question that you might ask while reading this section.
   - ✓ About how many colonists were Patriots or Loyalists?
   - ___ How many total soldiers were in the Continental Army?
   - ___ What did women Loyalists do to help their cause?
8. Read "The Challenges of War." Then complete the answer to the question.

   Why was it harder to buy goods during the war?

   It was harder to buy things because there was inflation, or a rise in prices.
9. Read "Taking Sides." Then complete the question.

   What did Loyalists believe?

   They believed America should stay a part of Britain.

Unit Resources

76
Use with *United States History*, pp. 270–273

Lesson 2 Vocabulary/Study Guide

TEST PREP

Vocabulary and Study Guide

Vocabulary

Write the definition of each vocabulary word below.

1. neutral To avoid taking sides
2. inflation A rise in the prices of most goods
3. Loyalist Someone who was still loyal to the king
4. Use two words in a sentence.

   Sample answer: Though some Americans were Loyalists, others were neutral.

Study Guide

5. Read "Life During the War." Then draw a line connecting each person to what that person did.

Joseph Brant	Stayed at camp to help the soldiers
Peter Salem	Dressed in men's clothes and joined the American army
Deborah Sampson	Urged the Mohawk people to side with the British
Martha Washington	Fought in the Battle of Bunker Hill after being freed
Mary Ludwig Hays	Fought in her husband's place

Unit Resources

77
Use with *United States History*, pp. 270–273

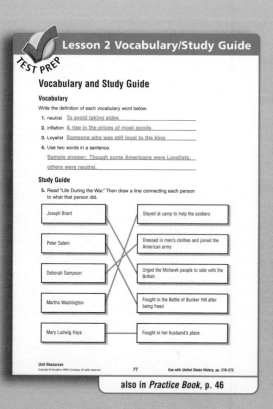

also in *Practice Book*, p. 46

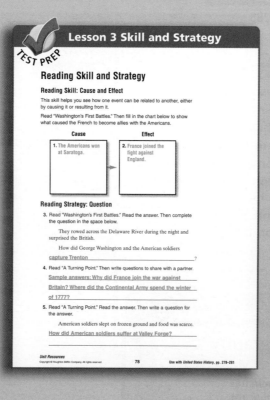

Lesson 3 Skill and Strategy

TEST PREP

Reading Skill and Strategy

Reading Skill: Cause and Effect

This skill helps you see how one event can be related to another, either by causing it or resulting from it.

Read "Washington's First Battles." Then fill in the chart below to show what caused the French to become allies with the Americans.

Cause	Effect
1. The Americans won at Saratoga.	2. France joined the fight against England.

Reading Strategy: Question

3. Read "Washington's First Battles." Read the answer. Then complete the question in the space below.

   They rowed across the Delaware River during the night and surprised the British.

   How did George Washington and the American soldiers capture Trenton?
4. Read "A Turning Point." Then write questions to share with a partner.

   Sample answers: Why did France join the war against Britain? Where did the Continental Army spend the winter of 1777?
5. Read "A Turning Point." Read the answer. Then write a question for the answer.

   American soldiers slept on frozen ground and food was scarce.

   How did American soldiers suffer at Valley Forge?

Unit Resources

78
Use with *United States History*, pp. 278–281

Lesson 3 Vocabulary/Study Guide

TEST PREP

Vocabulary and Study Guide

Vocabulary

As you read the chapter, fill in the word webs.

battle: 1. retreat, 2. victory

soldier: 3. mercenary, enemy

Study Guide

Read "Washington's First Battles." Then fill in the sequence chart below.

The Continental Army forces the British out of Boston.	4. The British defeat the Continental Army in the Battle of Long Island.	The Continental Army retreats.	5. The Continental Army surprises the enemy and wins a battle in Trenton.

Read "A Turning Point." Then fill in the sequence chart below.

6. The British attack from Canada.	The Continental Army wins the Battle of Saratoga.	7. The French government sends help to the Americans.	The Continental Army becomes stronger at Valley Forge.

Unit Resources

79
Use with *United States History*, pp. 278–281

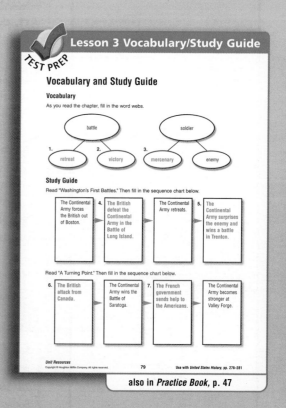

also in *Practice Book*, p. 47

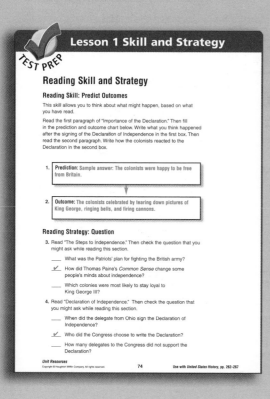

Skillbuilder Practice

TEST PREP

Skillbuilder: Read a Battle Map

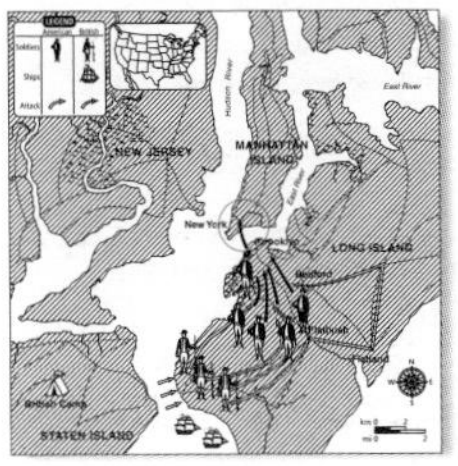

Practice

1. Who had ships in this battle? The British
2. Near what body of water is there a line of British soldiers?
   The Hudson River
3. Where did the American soldiers end up when they retreated? Circle the name of the place where the American soldiers retreated.
4. Did all of the British soldiers attack by moving in the same direction? What direction or directions did they travel? No. Some British soldiers moved north, some moved east, and some moved west.

Apply

Now you can use your map skills to show another version of this map. Show what might have happened if American soldiers standing on the coast of Long Island met the British ships. Using the same symbols as on this map, draw how the American soldiers and the British soldiers might have moved. Show which side might have retreated. Answers will vary.

Unit Resources

80
Use with *United States History*, pp. 284–285

also in *Practice Book*, p. 48

Lesson 4 Skill and Strategy

TEST PREP

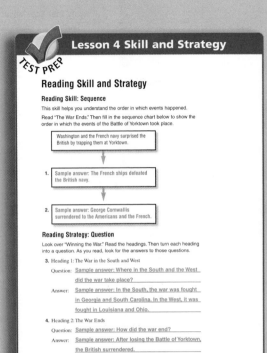

Reading Skill and Strategy

Reading Skill: Sequence

This skill helps you understand the order in which events happened.

Read "The War Ends." Then fill in the sequence chart below to show the order in which the events of the Battle of Yorktown took place.

Washington and the French navy surprised the British by trapping them at Yorktown.

↓

1. Sample answer: The French ships defeated the British navy.

↓

2. Sample answer: George Cornwallis surrendered to the Americans and the French.

Reading Strategy: Question

Look over "Winning the War." Read the headings. Then turn each heading into a question. As you read, look for the answers to those questions.

3. Heading 1: The War in the South and West
   Question: Sample answer: Where in the South and the West did the war take place?
   Answer: Sample answer: In the South, the war was fought in Georgia and South Carolina. In the West, it was fought in Louisiana and Ohio.
4. Heading 2: The War Ends
   Question: Sample answer: How did the war end?
   Answer: Sample answer: After losing the Battle of Yorktown, the British surrendered.

Unit Resources

81
Use with *United States History*, pp. 286–289

Lesson 4 Vocabulary/Study Guide

TEST PREP

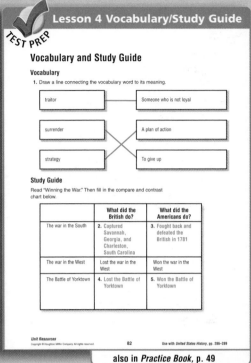

Vocabulary and Study Guide

Vocabulary

1. Draw a line connecting the vocabulary word to its meaning.

traitor	Someone who is not loyal
surrender	A plan of action
strategy	To give up

Study Guide

Read "Winning the War." Then fill in the compare and contrast chart below.

	What did the British do?	What did the Americans do?
The war in the South	2. Captured Savannah, Georgia, and Charleston, South Carolina	3. Fought back and defeated the British in 1781
The war in the West	Lost the war in the West	Won the war in the West
The Battle of Yorktown	4. Lost the Battle of Yorktown	5. Won the Battle of Yorktown

Unit Resources

82
Use with *United States History*, pp. 286–289

also in *Practice Book*, p. 49

Chapter 8 Assessment Options

Chapter 8 Test

TEST PREP

Chapter 8 Test

Test Your Knowledge

declaration	Loyalist	victory	strategy

Fill in the blank with the correct word from the box.

1. The British were able to capture Georgia and South Carolina by changing their war strategy. Obj. U4–17
2. A Loyalist was someone who supported Britain. Obj. U4–12
3. The colonists created a declaration to explain why the colonies should be free from British rule. Obj. U4–11
4. Americans won the War of Independence with the victory at the Battle of Yorktown. Obj. U4–18

Circle the letter of the best answer.

5. What was the main idea of Thomas Paine's *Common Sense*? Obj. U4–10
   - A. Patriots and Loyalists should learn to get along with each other.
   - B. Patriots should understand the power of the British military.
   - (C.) The American colonies should become independent.
   - D. Women deserve equal rights in the American colonies.
6. Why did some enslaved African Americans become Loyalists? Obj. U4–12
   - (F.) The British government promised them freedom.
   - G. They were born in Britain.
   - H. They believed that the king was doing a good job.
   - J. They believed the Patriots would never win the war.
7. What was the strategy of the American army in the South? Obj. U4–17
   - A. to overwhelm the British army with their fighting power
   - (B.) to keep the British army on the move until they were worn out
   - C. to buy superior weapons from the French and the Dutch
   - D. to hire the best mercenaries from several other countries
8. What did the Treaty of Paris do for the United States? Obj. U4–16
   - F. It pardoned the colonies for their treason against Britain.
   - G. It gave America international power.
   - H. It gave America control over the western part of Britain.
   - (J.) It gave the American colonies independence and land.

Chapter 8 Test

TEST PREP

Apply Your Knowledge

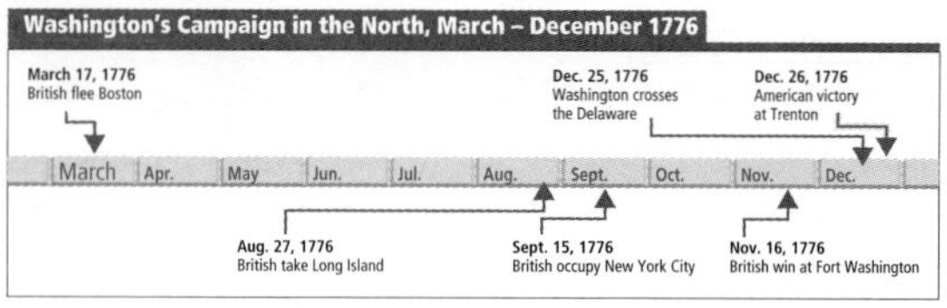

Use the timeline to answer the following questions.

9. When did the British flee Boston? Obj. U4–14
   - A. January 1776
   - B. February 1776
   - (C.) March 1776
   - D. April 1776
10. Why was it important for the Continental Army to cross the Delaware the night before attacking Trenton? Obj. U4–14
    - (F.) It was part of Washington's surprise attack.
    - G. It helped prepare the army for other battles.
    - H. It helped the army find new routes.
    - J. It helped Washington find mercenaries.

Apply the Reading Skill: Compare and Contrast

Read the passage below. Then answer the question. Obj. U4–13

> Women and men had to be brave during the American Revolution. Men had to leave their families to join the militia. Many women continued to care for their families while their husbands and brothers went to war. Some women went to the battlefields to care for soldiers. Others fought in battle when their husbands became hurt or killed. Everyone had to show courage in order to win freedom from Britain.

11. Compare the experience of men and women during the Revolution. How was it the same? How was it different?

    Both had to show courage. Men had to leave their families.

    Women had to care for their families alone and care for soldiers.

Chapter 8 Test

TEST PREP

Test the Skill: Read a Battle Map

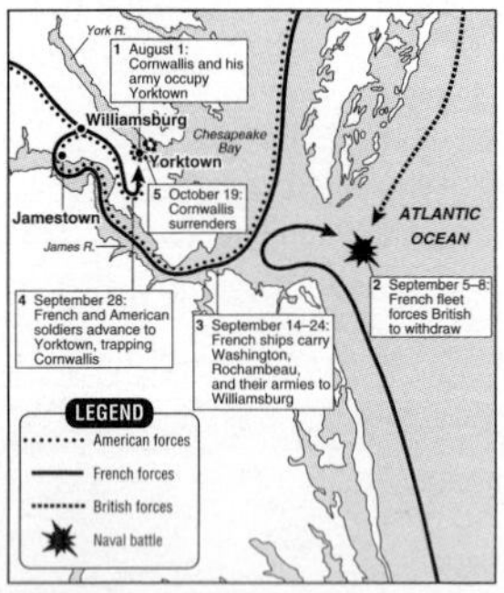

12. Where did the French and British naval battle occur? In the Atlantic Ocean Obj. U4–16
13. What natural feature did the French and American troops use to travel to Williamsburg? The James River Obj. U4–16
14. What event happened directly before Cornwallis surrendered?

    French and American soldiers trapped him in Yorktown. Obj. U4–16

Apply the Skill

15. What do you think was the most important contribution the French made to the victory at Yorktown? Use information from the map to support your answer. Obj. U4–16

    Sample answer: Blocking the British ships before they reached Yorktown and rescued Cornwallis was the most important contribution. Without this help, the British might have been able to keep Washington and Rochambeau from sailing up the James River and reaching Cornwallis. The British Navy might have been able to rescue Cornwallis.

Chapter 8 Test

TEST PREP

Think and Write

16. **Short Response:** Describe two strengths and two weaknesses of the Continental Army. Obj. U4–14

    Weaknesses: The Continental Army was smaller than the British army. The Continental Army was poorly trained and armed.

    Strengths: The Continental Army knew the land well, fought for a cause, and had a strong leader, George Washington.

17. **Critical Thinking: Infer** Why would nations other than Britain care about the outcome of the American Revolution? Obj. U4–15

    Sample answer: They saw the United States as a valuable trading partner.

18. **Extended Response:** Many colonists chose to side with either the Loyalists or the Patriots. Write a letter to a colonial newspaper explaining which side you chose and why. Write your letter on a separate sheet of paper. Obj. U4–12 **Letters from Loyalists may refer to not wanting to lose their job, or lose business, or that the British were right in their cause; Patriot letters may refer to having much to lose by staying loyal to an unjust king.**

Self-Assessment

What is the most important thing I learned about the American Revolution from this chapter? Why is it important to me?

Teacher Read Aloud
A Story in History

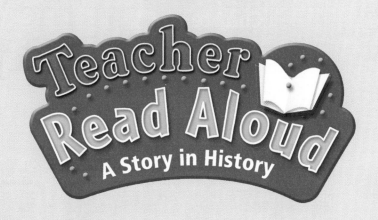

You can share the following fiction selection with students before beginning the chapter. Ask them to look at the painting on page 279 of their books as you read.

Activate Prior Knowledge
Ask students to discuss what they know about Washington's crossing of the Delaware River. Explain that the Read-Aloud selection helps them imagine the feelings of one soldier on the way to an important battle. Students will read about the real events of the battle in this chapter.

Preview the Chapter
Ask students to find similarities and differences between the painting on page 279 and the details mentioned in the Read Aloud.

Read-Aloud Vocabulary
Explain that a **strategy** is a plan for action. Ask students to define **victory** in their own words.

Preview the Reading Strategy
Question Explain to students that the reading strategy they will use in this chapter is questioning, or asking about what is happening. You may wish to use the Read Aloud to model this strategy.

Think Aloud *The main character in the first paragraph is in a rowboat in icy waters. It is dawn on the Delaware River. There are other boats, and all the oars have been muffled with cloth. I wonder where the boats are going and why the people in them are trying to be quiet.*

Dawn on the River

The icy river water ripples around your feet. Biting your lip against the cold, you shove the loaded rowboat away from shore, climb inside, and take up an oar. The sky shows the first pink of dawn as the boats make their way slowly across the Delaware River. The oars are wrapped with cloth to muffle their *plunk, plunk* in the water.

Another boat pulls alongside and your heart skips a beat. General Washington! The leader of the entire army looks over at you. You start to say, "Sir . . ." but the great man puts a finger against his lips. *Of course,* you think—*sound carries over water!* Silence is essential if Washington's **strategy**—a surprise attack at Trenton—is to lead to **victory** and the defeat of the British forces there.

Seeing your stricken look, Washington smiles to reassure you. You relax a little and smile back. Although you're nervous about what's coming next, you know you would follow George Washington anywhere.

Begin the Chapter

Quick Look

Core Lesson 1 focuses on the Declaration of Independence.

Core Lesson 2 details how life changed as people chose sides during the war.

Core Lesson 3 discusses the first part of the war and George Washington's efforts to lead the Continental Army to victory.

Core Lesson 4 describes the last years of the war and the Treaty of Paris.

Vocabulary Preview

Use the vocabulary cards to preview the key vocabulary words before starting the lessons and to prepare students to understand the content of the chapter.

Vocabulary Strategy

Vocabulary strategies for this chapter:

- Multiple meanings, p. 285
- Synonyms/antonyms, pp. 264, 271, 285
- Root words, p. 272
- Prefixes and suffixes, pp. 263, 271, 279
- Word origins, pp. 264, 266, 271, 286

Vocabulary Help

Vocabulary card for declaration Help students think of other words that end with the *-tion* or *-ion* suffix. Remind them that this suffix has the power to turn a verb such as declare into a noun.

Vocabulary card for victory Point out the word *victor* in *victory*. Explain that a victor is the winner of a fight, contest or struggle. By knowing what *victor* means, what can they predict about the meaning of *victory?*

Chapter 8 The War for Independence

Technology
e • glossary
e • word games
www.eduplace.com/kids/hmss05/

Vocabulary Preview

independence

On July 4, 1776, the American colonies said that they wanted **independence** from Britain. Every year we celebrate our country's freedom on July 4, Independence Day. **page 262**

declaration

Thomas Jefferson wrote a long statement, the **Declaration** of Independence. The Declaration explained why the American colonies should be free. **page 264**

Chapter Timeline

1776 Declaration of Independence
1778 Valley Forge
1781 Victory at Yorktown

1775 1776 1777 1778 1779 1780 1781

Background

A War of Many Names

Tell students that as they read this chapter, they will find the following terms:

- American Revolution
- Revolutionary War
- War for Independence

Explain that all three of these names refer to the war the American colonies fought against Britain for independence between 1776 and 1783.

Vocabulary

Use the word web graphic organizer to help students with vocabulary.

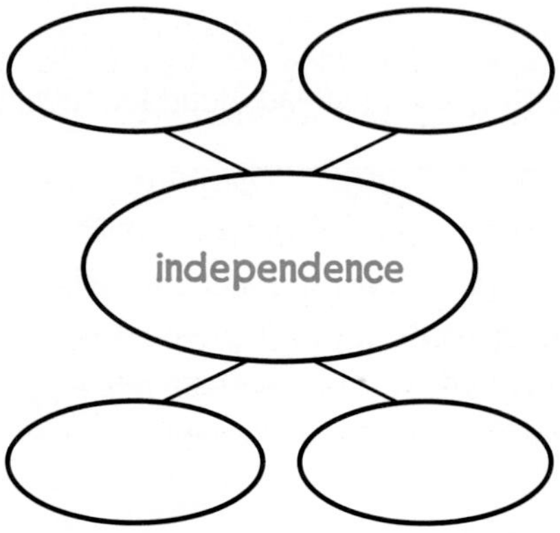

Reading Strategy

Question As you read the lessons in this chapter, ask yourself questions.

Quick Tip List your questions, then go back to find the answers.

inflation

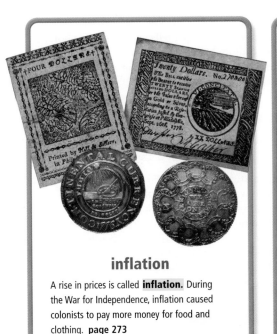

A rise in prices is called **inflation.** During the War for Independence, inflation caused colonists to pay more money for food and clothing. **page 273**

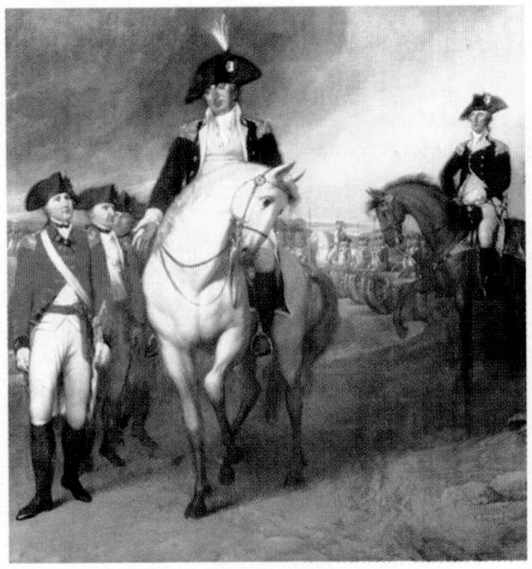

victory

The Battle of Yorktown was a **victory** for the Americans. They beat the British and won the War for Independence. **page 279**

261

Using the Timeline

- Direct students to look at the timeline on pages 260 and 261. Point out the segments of the timeline. Ask them how many years this chapter will cover. seven
- Ask if any events on the timeline sound familiar; you may wish to use a KWL chart to access students' prior knowledge of the events on the timeline.

Reading Strategy: Question

Using the question strategy, students can monitor their understanding as they read social studies. Some readers may find it useful to stop after each paragraph and ask themselves:

- What did I just read about?
- Was there anything I didn't understand?

Other readers may have to stop less frequently, but at the end of each section you may with to have students stop and write down any questions they have about the material in their notebooks. They can share these questions in small groups or with the class, which is an excellent opportunity for you to monitor student understanding. Students can practice this reading strategy throughout this chapter, including on the Skill and Strategy pages from the unit resources.

Reaching All Learners: Leveled Practice

Extra Support

Have students work in pairs to create their own version of one of the **vocabulary cards.** Have them write a definition in their own words on one side and illustrate the word on the other side.
Logical-mathematical

Challenge

Have students use the dictionary to **identify a related word** for each of the four words shown here. (For example, *inflate* for *inflation.*) Verbal-linguistic

Reaching All Learners: ELL

All Proficiency Levels

- **Dramatize** the word *independence.* For example, you might hold a sign saying "America" while the volunteer holds a sign saying "Britain," and then say, "Goodbye, I want to be free!" and walk away.
- Encourage other students to dramatize *independence, declaration, inflation,* or *victory.*

Bodily-kinesthetic

✓ Tested Objectives

U4-10 History Describe the events that led to the writing of the Declaration of Independence.

U4-11 Citizenship State the main ideas in the Declaration of Independence and explain their significance.

Lesson Quick Look

This lesson focuses on the Declaration of Independence.

Teaching Option: Extend Lesson 1 tells students more about Thomas Jefferson and provides leveled activities.

1 Get Set to Read

Preview Have students look at the pictures and ask them what they think the chapter will be about.

Reading Skill: Predict Outcomes Students should check their predictions after reading the lesson.

Build on What You Know Explain that the Declaration is like a birth certificate because its signing date was the day the United States declared itself an independent country.

Vocabulary

independence *noun,* freedom from being ruled by someone else

declaration *noun,* a statement that declares, or announces, an idea

rights *plural noun,* freedoms that are protected by law

treason *noun,* the crime of fighting against one's own government; a betrayal

---

Core Lesson 1

Declaring Independence

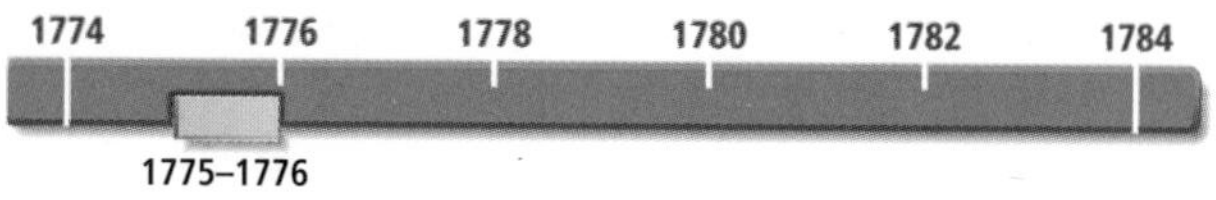

VOCABULARY

independence
declaration
rights
treason

Vocabulary Strategy

independence

Look for the word **depend** in **independence.** Independence means not depending on others.

READING SKILL

Predict Outcomes

As you read, predict the outcome of the arguments over independence.

PREDICTION

OUTCOME

Build on What You Know You may have a birth certificate at home. This paper tells when you were born. In a way, our country has a birth certificate. It's called the Declaration of Independence. The Declaration marks the beginning of the United States.

The Steps to Independence

Main Idea *Common Sense* and debates in Congress changed people's minds about being ruled by Britain.

After the battles of 1775, the American colonies and Britain were at war. However, not all colonists felt this was right. Many still thought of **King George III** as their ruler. They did not want a war with Britain. Other colonists were Patriots. They wanted independence. **Independence** means freedom from being ruled by someone else. Some Patriots felt that independence was worth fighting for. **Patrick Henry,** a Patriot from Virginia, said in a thrilling speech to a group of Virginia delegates,

"Give me liberty or give me death!" 1

Another Patriot, **Thomas Paine,** used the written word to argue for independence.

Patrick Henry Bold, persuasive speeches by Patrick Henry moved colonists toward independence.

262 • Chapter 8

Skill and Strategy

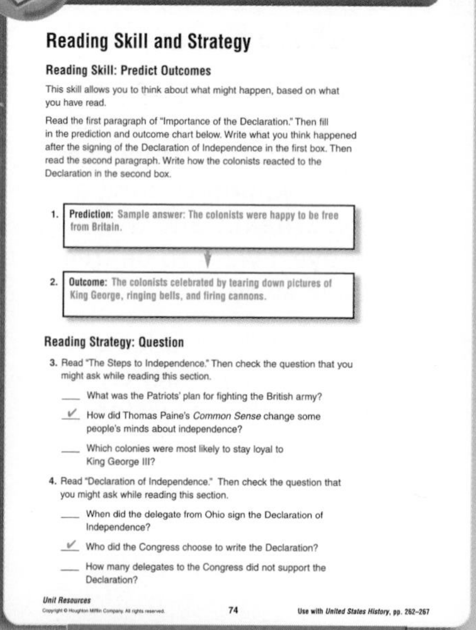

Reading Skill and Strategy

Reading Skill: Predict Outcomes

This skill allows you to think about what might happen, based on what you have read.

Read the first paragraph of "Importance of the Declaration." Then fill in the prediction and outcome chart below. Write what you think happened after the signing of the Declaration of Independence in the first box. Then read the second paragraph. Write how the colonists reacted to the Declaration in the second box.

1. **Prediction:** Sample answer: The colonists were happy to be free from Britain.
2. **Outcome:** The colonists celebrated by tearing down pictures of King George, ringing bells, and firing cannons.

Reading Strategy: Question

3. Read "The Steps to Independence." Then check the question that you might ask while reading this section.
   - ___ What was the Patriots' plan for fighting the British army?
   - _✓_ How did Thomas Paine's *Common Sense* change some people's minds about independence?
   - ___ Which colonies were most likely to stay loyal to King George III?
4. Read "Declaration of Independence." Then check the question that you might ask while reading this section.
   - ___ When did the delegate from Ohio sign the Declaration of Independence?
   - _✓_ Who did the Congress choose to write the Declaration?
   - ___ How many delegates to the Congress did not support the Declaration?

Unit Resources
Copyright © Houghton Mifflin Company. All rights reserved. 74 Use with *United States History*, pp. 262–267

Unit Resources, p. 74

Background

Essential Documents

- *Common Sense* was printed in Philadelphia on January 10, 1776. It was advertised as "Common Sense for eighteen pence."
- The Declaration of Independence was first read in public on July 8, 1776. Washington read it to his troops the next day.

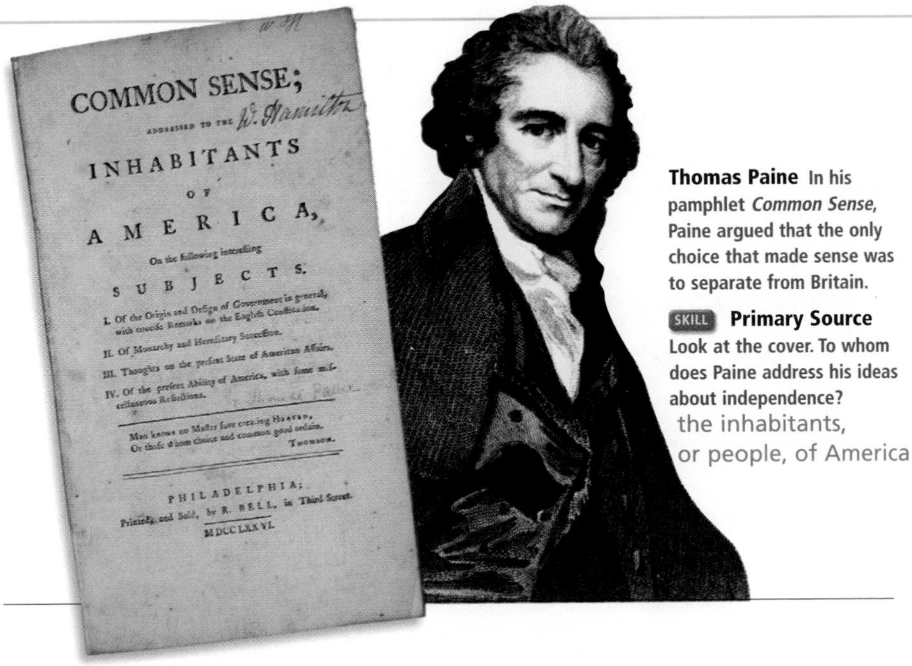

Thomas Paine In his pamphlet *Common Sense*, Paine argued that the only choice that made sense was to separate from Britain.

SKILL **Primary Source** Look at the cover. To whom does Paine address his ideas about independence? the inhabitants, or people, of America

Thomas Paine's *Common Sense*

Thomas Paine wrote a pamphlet called *Common Sense* in January 1776. *Common Sense* pushed for independence. The pamphlet was brief, inexpensive, and easy to understand. Paine wrote that King George treated the colonies unfairly. He
2 claimed that the only way to stop this was to become independent from Britain.

Colonists bought over 100,000 copies of *Common Sense* within a few months. **George Washington** said, "I find *Common Sense* is working a powerful change in the minds of many."

Thomas Paine put into writing what many of the boldest Patriots were already saying. He wrote that colonists had nothing to gain and much to lose by staying tied to an unjust king.

Debate in Congress

Delegates to the Second Continental Congress had read *Common Sense*. Many agreed that independence from Britain was necessary, but they also knew it was risky. Britain was a powerful country. King George III was already gathering
soldiers to attack the colonies. Could 3
the colonies stand up to Britain? Some delegates also worried that not enough colonists wanted independence. However, support for independence was growing all across the colonies.

John Adams argued strongly for independence. More and more of the delegates agreed with his point of view. At last, on June 7, 1776, a Virginia delegate named **Richard Henry Lee** asked Congress to officially declare independence.

REVIEW What were Thomas Paine's arguments for independence? He said Britain treated the colonies unfairly, and independence was the only solution.

263

2 Teach

The Steps to Independence

Talk About It

1 **Q Primary Source** What did Patrick Henry mean when he said, "Give me liberty or give me death"?

A He meant he would rather die than remain a British subject.

2 **Q History** What did Thomas Paine say was the only solution to unfair treatment by Britain?

A The colonies had to become independent.

3 **Q History** What were the delegates concerned about regarding independence?

A They worried that Britain was too strong to fight against and that not enough colonists wanted independence.

Vocabulary Strategy

independence Explain to students that the prefix *in-* in *independence* means *not.*

Reading Strategy: Question Explain to students that asking questions helps them focus on what they want to find out while reading a lesson. You may wish to model the strategy for the students.

Think Aloud *These first two pages talk about how the colonists were unhappy with British rule and how the Congress decided that it was time to declare independence. I wonder how the colonies will declare independence and how Britain will react.*

Leveled Practice

REACHING ALL LEARNERS

Extra Support

Have students **use visuals** by looking at the images and captions in the lesson and listing the names of the people and documents shown. Ask students to describe each entry on the list. Visual-spatial

Challenge

Have students use library or Internet resources **to research five facts** about one of the people or documents mentioned in the lesson. Ask them to share what they have learned with the class. Verbal-linguistic

ELL

REACHING ALL LEARNERS

Intermediate/Advanced

Working in pairs, have students **write down one big idea** from *Common Sense* and one from the Declaration of Independence. Encourage students to illustrate their ideas.

Visual-spatial

Declaration of Independence

Talk About It

4 Q History Why did Congress need a document like the Declaration of Independence?

A Congress needed to tell colonists, Britain, and the world why the break with Britain was necessary.

5 Q Citizenship What did Thomas Jefferson say about rights in the Declaration of Independence?

A Jefferson argued that all people have rights that no one can take away. These rights include the right to live, the right to be free, and the right to seek happiness.

Vocabulary Strategy

declaration *Declaration* builds on the smaller word *declare*, which means to say clearly.

rights Tell students that a synonym for *rights* is *freedoms.*

Critical Thinking

Compare and Contrast Think about the different parts of the Declaration and what they say. Why do you think some parts are longer than others?

Writing the Declaration
It took Thomas Jefferson two weeks to write the Declaration. When he finished his draft, four other delegates helped edit it. Shown here are Benjamin Franklin (left), John Adams (center), and Jefferson, who is standing.

Declaration of Independence

Main Idea The Declaration of Independence explains why the colonies should be free.

Congress asked **Thomas Jefferson** and four others to write a declaration of independence. A **declaration** is a statement that declares, or announces, an idea.
4 Congress needed a document to declare why the colonies had to become independent of Britain. In the Declaration of Independence, Jefferson wrote what many Americans believed about their rights. **Rights** are freedoms that are protected by a government's laws. Jefferson argued that all people are born with rights that no one can take away. He wrote that people have
5 the right to live, the right to be free, and the right to seek happiness.

> **"We hold these truths to be self-evident, that all men are created equal, that they are endowed by their Creator with certain unalienable Rights, that among these are Life, Liberty, and the Pursuit of Happiness . . ."**

Jefferson argued that a government should protect these rights. If it does not, then the people have the right to start a new government.

The ideas in the Declaration were not new. Jefferson used ideas that **John Locke** and other English thinkers had written about. Locke had said that governments should serve their people.

Jefferson listed many ways that Britain did not serve the colonists. For instance, King George had tried to take away rights. He had forced taxes on the colonists and sent soldiers to control them. Jefferson showed that the colonists had many reasons to separate from the king. They had the right to create their own government.

Mary Katherine Goddard
Congress hired Mary Katherine Goddard, a printer, to print an official copy of the Declaration.

264 • Chapter 8

Science

Letterpress Printing

Students can make their own letterpress stamps in the following way. (with a potato and sharp knife)

- Draw a design on the flat part of a cut potato.
- Carefully cut away around the design so it is raised about 1/4 inch.
- Ink the raised design on a stamp pad.
- Press the inked design onto paper to make an image.

Bodily-kinesthetic

Language Arts

Write a Persuasive Essay

Jefferson carefully planned the structure of the Declaration. Ask students to use a similar structure to write a persuasive essay of five paragraphs about an issue that they feel is important.

Verbal-linguistic

Parts of the Declaration

You can read the full text of the Declaration on pages 581 and 582 of this book. The Declaration begins by promising to explain why the colonies must break away from Britain (see ❶). The next section explains that people have rights that cannot be taken away. It says that

6 "all men are created equal" (see ❷). The longest section is a list of complaints against the king (see ❸).

The last section argues that the colonies have to be free to protect the colonists' rights. It declares that the colonies are independent (see ❹).

At the bottom of the document, delegates to Congress signed their names (see ❺). **John Hancock,** president of Congress, signed his name in large letters. 7

REVIEW According to the Declaration, why did the colonies have the right to their own government? because everyone has certain rights, and Britain had tried to take them away

Connect to Today
Notice the date of the Declaration. What do you do every year to celebrate that day?
Answers will vary.

Extra Support

Create a Mural

- Divide the class into small groups of mixed abilities.
- Have each group choose and illustrate one of the quotes from the Declaration.
- Attach each group's illustrations to a larger sheet to make a mural.

Visual-spatial

Challenge

Research a Signer

- Refer students to the list of signers of the Declaration of Independence on page 676.
- Have students use encyclopedias, the library, and the Internet to find out more about one signer of their choice.
- Students can make a poster with four important facts about the signer.

Verbal-linguistic

Declaration of Independence *continued*

Talk About It

6 **Q Primary Source** What does Jefferson mean when he writes, "All men are created equal"?

A that all people are the same, and no one is better than anyone else

7 **Q Primary Source** Why did the delegates sign the declaration?

A They believed in what it said, and to show their support signed their names.

Reading Strategy: Question Ask students to share the questions they formulated as they read these pages of the lesson.

Importance of the Declaration

Talk About It

8 **Q Citizenship** The signers knew they could be put to death because they signed the Declaration. Why do you think they signed anyway?

A They believed strongly that what they were doing was right.

9 **Q Citizenship** Why was it so remarkable that the colonies decided to "rule themselves"?

A They were no longer relying on a king to lead them.

10 **Q History** What did Abigail Adams want Congress to do?

A She wanted Congress to give women more rights.

11 **Q Citizenship** What are some ways we uphold equal rights for all?

A Laws have been passed to make discrimination illegal.

Vocabulary Strategy

treason Explain to students that people who do things that threaten a government are charged with treason. Spies who give secrets to an enemy government are committing treason.

Critical Thinking

Compare and Contrast How do you think women's lives at the time of Abigail Adams were like they are today? How do you think they are different?

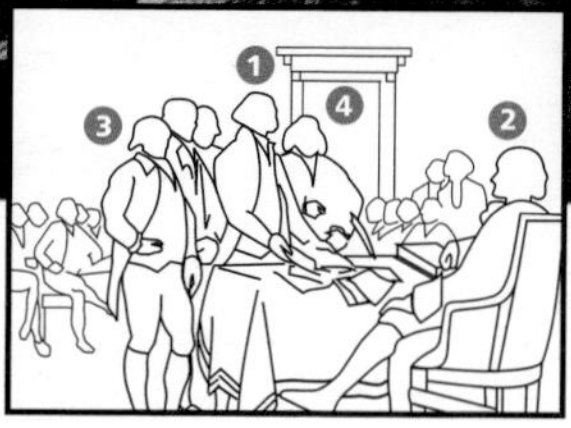

Signers of the Declaration Thomas Jefferson (1) presents the document to John Hancock (2) and the Continental Congress. Find John Adams (3) and Benjamin Franklin (4).

Importance of the Declaration

Main Idea The Declaration sets forth basic ideas of freedom and equality.

On July 4, 1776, the Second Continental Congress voted to accept the Declaration. The delegates knew that signing the Declaration was dangerous. Britain would call it treason. **Treason** is the crime of fighting against one's own government. Anyone who signed the
8 Declaration could be charged with treason and hanged. Yet delegates signed.

The Declaration was read aloud to excited crowds across the new nation. People tore down pictures and statues of King George. They celebrated by ringing bells and firing cannons. The Declaration of Independence marked the moment
9 when Americans chose to rule themselves.

Equality Then and Now

The Declaration is important today because it states that the people of the United States believe in equal rights for all. Today we know that Jefferson's words, "all men are created equal," include everyone: women as well as men, every race, every group, every ability. Is that what the words meant when the Declaration was written? Probably not.

In 1776, all Americans could not exercise the same rights. Only white men who owned property could vote. Many believed this was unfair. **Abigail Adams**
wanted Congress to recognize the equal 10
rights of women. She wrote to her husband, John Adams,

> **"... in the new Code of Laws ... Remember the Ladies ..."**

266 • Chapter 8

Math

Calculation: Division

Tell students that in January 1776, the American colonies still used British currency. A British pound was worth 20 shillings or 240 pence.

- If one copy of *Common Sense* sold for eighteen pence, how many shillings was each copy worth? one and a half shillings
- How many copies could a colonist buy for a pound? thirteen copies

Logical-mathematical

Language Arts

Award a Certificate

- Ask students to create a certificate that a group of journalists might have given Thomas Paine as an award for his pamphlet *Common Sense.*
- Ask them to write a short speech to be given when the certificate was awarded.

Verbal-linguistic

11 It took many years, but women, African Americans, American Indians, and other groups have gained equal rights. In later lessons, you'll read about important laws that guarantee these rights. The Declaration has inspired people, past and present, to work for liberty and equal rights.

REVIEW Why is the Declaration so important to Americans? It says everyone has the same rights.

Lesson Summary

- The colonies decided to declare their independence from Britain.
- Congress asked Thomas Jefferson to write the Declaration of Independence.
- The Declaration states that everyone has certain rights that no government can take away.

Why It Matters ...

The ideas in the Declaration of Independence have meaning today. The rights of freedom and equality that Jefferson wrote about are important American values and principles.

Martin Luther King Jr. In the 1960s, Martin Luther King Jr. was a great leader in the struggle for African Americans' equal rights. He and his wife, Coretta Scott King, led many marches to protest unjust treatment.

Lesson Review

January 1776
Common Sense printed

July 4,1776
Declaration of Independence signed

1776 — 1777

1. **VOCABULARY** Write a paragraph explaining why Americans needed **independence** to protect their **rights.** Use these words in your paragraph.
2. **READING SKILL** Look at your **prediction.** Does it agree with what actually happened?
3. **MAIN IDEA: History** How did *Common Sense* help lead to independence?
4. **MAIN IDEA: Citizenship** Why did delegates need courage to sign the Declaration?
5. **PEOPLE TO KNOW** Who was **Patrick Henry,** and what did he believe about independence?
6. **TIMELINE SKILL** How many months before the signing of the Declaration was *Common Sense* printed?
7. **CRITICAL THINKING: Compare and Contrast** How are *Common Sense* and the Declaration of Independence alike? How are they different?

HANDS ON **SPEAKING ACTIVITY** Would you have taken the risk of signing the Declaration? Prepare a short speech to explain your answer.

267

3 Review/Assess

Review Tested Objectives

U4-10 Thomas Paine wrote *Common Sense;* many colonists began to support independence; Congress asked Jefferson and others to write a declaration.

U4-11 All people are equal and have certain rights that no government can take away.

Lesson Review Answers

1. Paragraph should make a clear connection between independence and rights.
2. Students should evaluate their predictions with the events they have read about.
3. Answers should connect *Common Sense* with increased American support for independence.
4. To sign the Declaration was treason, a crime punishable by death under British law.
5. Patrick Henry was a Virginia Patriot who believed that life without independence was worthless.
6. six months
7. Alike: Both supported independence, stated why British rule was unfair and why the American colonies should separate. Different: *Common Sense* was a personal opinion addressed to colonists; the Declaration was an official document addressed to the world.

Study Guide/Homework

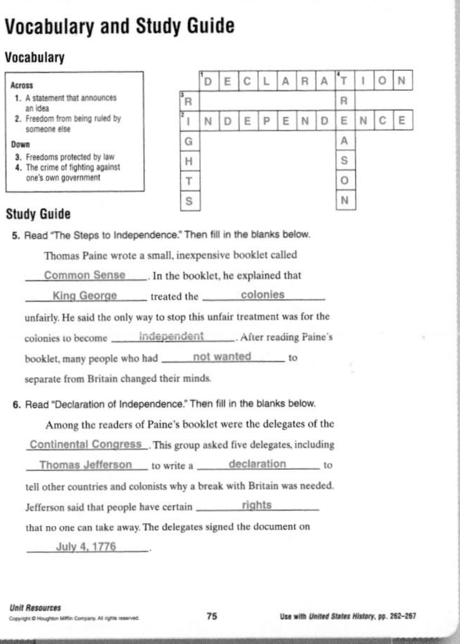

Vocabulary and Study Guide

Vocabulary

Across
1. A statement that announces an idea
2. Freedom from being ruled by someone else

Down
3. Freedoms protected by law
4. The crime of fighting against one's own government

Study Guide

5. Read "The Steps to Independence." Then fill in the blanks below.

Thomas Paine wrote a small, inexpensive booklet called Common Sense. In the booklet, he explained that King George treated the colonies unfairly. He said the only way to stop this unfair treatment was for the colonies to become independent. After reading Paine's booklet, many people who had not wanted to separate from Britain changed their minds.

6. Read "Declaration of Independence." Then fill in the blanks below.

Among the readers of Paine's booklet were the delegates of the Continental Congress. This group asked five delegates, including Thomas Jefferson to write a declaration to tell other countries and colonists why a break with Britain was needed. Jefferson said that people have certain rights that no one can take away. The delegates signed the document on July 4, 1776.

Unit Resources 75 Use with *United States History*, pp. 262–267

Unit Resources, p. 75

Reteach Minilesson

Use a spider map to reteach the Declaration.

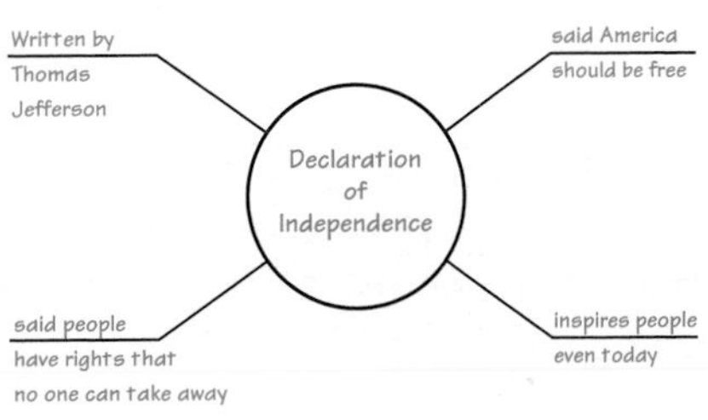

Graphic Organizer 14

HANDS ON Performance Task Rubric

4	Position is clearly stated; reasons are supported by information from the text; delivery is clear and easy to understand.
3	Position is adequately stated; most reasons are supported by information from the text; delivery is generally clear.
2	Position is stated, but reasons are confused or poorly supported by information from the text; delivery is adequate.
1	Position is not stated; reasons are absent; delivery is poor.

Extend

Quick Look

Connect to Core Lesson This Extend Lesson provides biographical information about Thomas Jefferson and adds to students' understanding of his historical importance.

1 Teach the Extend Lesson

Connect to the Big Idea

Foundations of Democracy Make sure students understand that the Declaration of Independence is one of the most important documents in the formation of the democratic government of the United States.

A Man of Many Talents

Using the timeline and biography on these pages as a guide, discuss Jefferson's qualifications for writing the Declaration of Independence.

Make sure students understand Jefferson's wide range of knowledge and accomplishments.

Biography

Thomas Jefferson

1743–1826

Thomas Jefferson is deep in thought. He must find the right words. Congress has chosen Jefferson to tell the king why the American colonies no longer belong to Britain. These are dangerous words, and they could cost Jefferson his life. Yet he loves his country and is writing the words that will create a new nation.

He dips his quill pen into the inkwell and rewrites a sentence in his draft. At this amazing moment in his life, he applies to his writing what he has learned and what he cares so much about.

All his life, Jefferson wanted to know the why and how of everything. He played the violin, studied the stars, invented things, and designed buildings.

He had read about government, history, and science as a young man. In his draft of the **Declaration,** he used ideas he had learned. The result was one of the most important documents in history.

Major Achievements

1768 Designs Monticello, a U.S. landmark

1776 Writes the Declaration

1801 Elected U.S. President

Reaching All Learners

Extra Support

Writing Drafts

- Point out to students the corrections Jefferson made in his draft of the Declaration.
- Encourage them to write a paragraph about someone in the chapter.
- Have them save each draft as they work.
- Have them review their drafts and note corrections that improved their paragraph.

Verbal-linguistic

On Level

Role-Play an Interview

- Have students make up questions they would like to ask Thomas Jefferson.
- Have small groups role-play an interview, with two or three students taking the parts of reporters and another playing Jefferson.

Verbal-linguistic

Challenge

Jefferson's Home

- Ask students to research information about Monticello.
- They can present their findings in the form of an oral presentation or they may build a model with informative labels.

Verbal-linguistic; bodily-kinesthetic

CHARACTER TRAIT: Patriotism

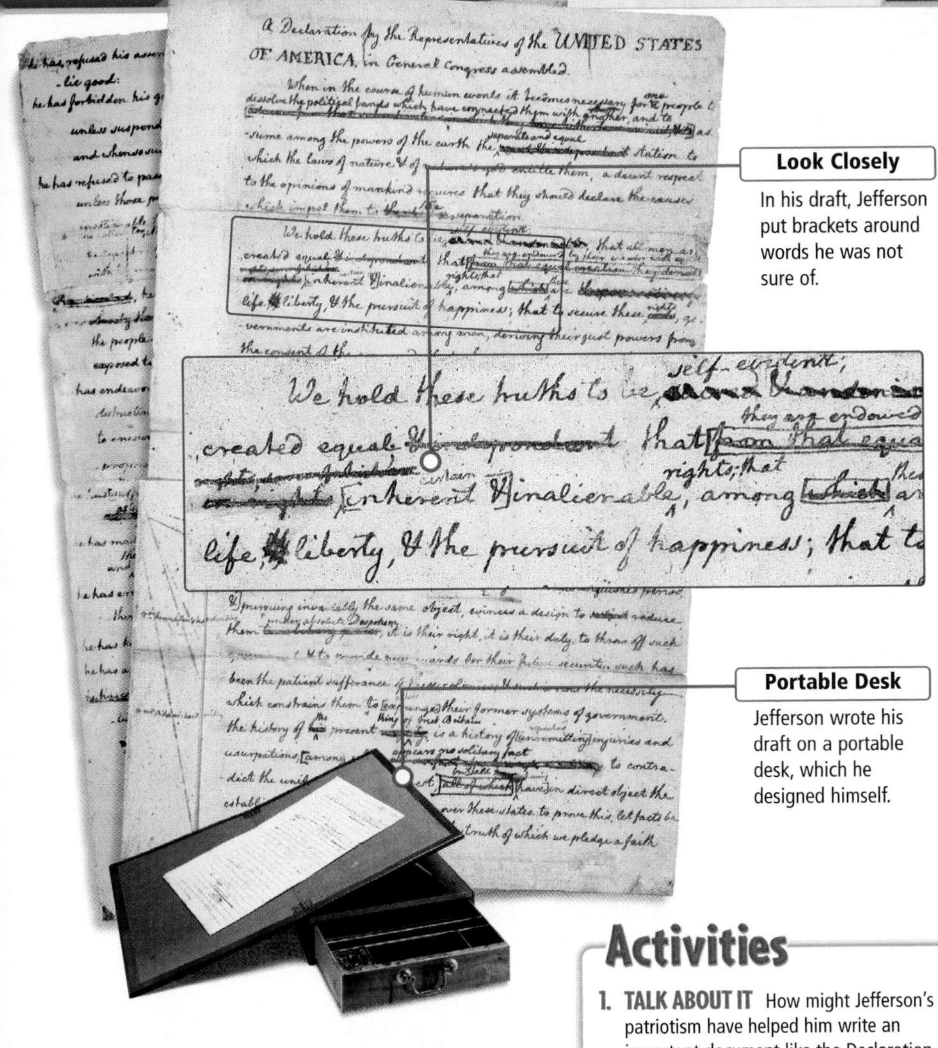

Look Closely
In his draft, Jefferson put brackets around words he was not sure of.

Portable Desk
Jefferson wrote his draft on a portable desk, which he designed himself.

BIOGRAPHY

1803
Doubles size of United States with the Louisiana Purchase

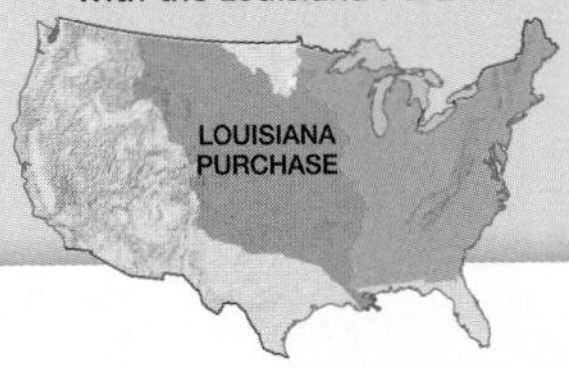

1804
Sends Lewis and Clark to explore the West

Activities

1. **TALK ABOUT IT** How might Jefferson's patriotism have helped him write an important document like the Declaration of Independence?
2. **WRITE ABOUT IT** What happens on June 28, 1776, when delegates in Congress hear the Declaration draft for the first time? Write a one-page story in the present tense.

Technology Visit Education Place at www.eduplace.com/kids/hmss05/ for more biographies of people in this unit.

269

2 Leveled Activities

1 **Talk About It** *For Extra Support*
Sample answer: It might have inspired him to write the best document he could.

2 **Write About It** *For Challenge*

Writing Rubric

4	Story is well organized and shows considerable creative effort; mechanics are correct; written in present tense.
3	Story is adequately organized and shows creative effort; few errors; written in present tense.
2	Story is somewhat organized and shows some creative effort; some errors, including shifts in tense.
1	Story is disorganized and shows little effort; many errors in mechanics; present tense is absent.

ELL

REACHING ALL LEARNERS

Intermediate/Advanced

- Ask students to name some important things Jefferson did. Have students refer to the timeline for the information.
- Have partners each write a question based on the timeline about events in Jefferson's life.
- Have them trade papers and answer their partner's question.

Visual-spatial

Science

Inventing

Thomas Jefferson was an architect and inventor as well as a leader. Challenge students to invent objects, like Jefferson's portable desk, that will make everyday life easier. Have students sketch and explain their ideas.

Logical-mathematical

Graphic Organizer

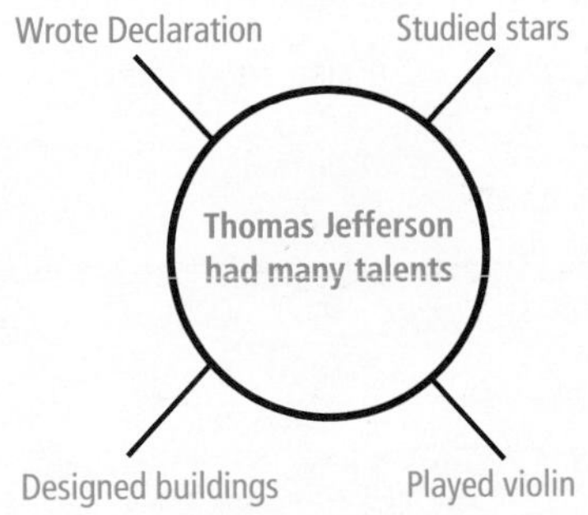

Graphic Organizer 7

Tested Objectives

U4-12 Citizenship Explain why different groups of people chose to become Patriots or Loyalists.

U4-13 History Describe life on the home front during the war.

Lesson Quick Look

Lesson 2 is about life during the war and the differences between Patriots and Loyalists.

Teaching Option: **Extend Lesson 2,** a readers' theater, brings Patriots, Loyalists, and neutrals to life for your class.

1 Get Set to Read

Preview After students read the headings, ask them what they think the lesson will be about.

Reading Skill: Compare and Contrast Students should consider why people held different views.

Build on What You Know Explain that when people make decisions, their choices affect their lives. Ask students to recall choices they have made that had a positive effect on their lives.

Vocabulary

Loyalist *noun,* someone who was still loyal to the King

neutral *adjective,* not taking sides

inflation *noun,* a rise in prices

Core Lesson 2

Life During the War

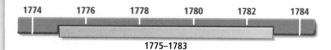

1774 1776 1778 1780 1782 1784

1775–1783

VOCABULARY

Loyalist
neutral
inflation

Vocabulary Strategy

Loyalist

A **Loyalist** is a person who is loyal to someone. Think of other words ending in the suffix **-ist** that describe a person, such as **artist.**

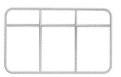

READING SKILL
Compare and Contrast
Take notes on the different views Americans had about war with Britain.

Build on What You Know Have you had to make a difficult decision? During the American Revolution, people had to make the hard decision whether to fight against Britain. How would a war affect their day-to-day lives?

Taking Sides

Main Idea Americans made difficult choices about whether to support Britain or the United States, or not to take sides at all.

On July 4, 1776, the Second Continental Congress declared independence. Not all Americans agreed that this was the right thing to do. Many felt that Britain should rule the colonies. Others believed that America should be independent. As the Revolutionary War began, people had to decide whether to support Britain, America, or neither side.

Almost half of all Americans were Patriots. Remember that a Patriot was someone who wanted independence for the colonies. About one-fifth of Americans were Loyalists. A **Loyalist** was someone who was still loyal to the king. Many Loyalists disagreed with how **King George III** governed the colonies, but they still wanted America to be part of Britain. The rest of Americans were neutral. To be **neutral** means not to take sides. 1

Skill and Strategy

Reading Skill and Strategy

Reading Skill: Compare and Contrast

This skill helps you understand how historical events or people are similar and different.

Read "Taking Sides." Then fill in the chart below to compare and contrast Loyalists and Patriots. Write two facts about the Loyalists and two facts about the Patriots. Then write two facts that were true about both sides.

Loyalists	Patriots	Both
1. Wanted to be ruled by Britain	3. Wanted to be independent	5. Did not want to leave the colonies
2. Loyal to the king	4. Did not want to be ruled by Britain	6. African Americans fought for both sides

Reading Strategy: Question

7. Read "Taking Sides." Then check the question that you might ask while reading this section.
   - ✓ About how many colonists were Patriots or Loyalists?
   - ___ How many total soldiers were in the Continental Army?
   - ___ What did women Loyalists do to help their cause?
8. Read "The Challenges of War." Then complete the answer to the question.
   Why was it harder to buy goods during the war?
   It was harder to buy things because there was inflation, or a rise in prices.
9. Read "Taking Sides." Then complete the question.
   What did Loyalists believe?
   They believed America should stay a part of Britain.

Unit Resources

76
Use with *United States History*, pp. 270–273

Unit Resources, p. 76

Background

Loyalists and Patriots

- The largest number of Loyalists lived in New York City and the surrounding area. New England had the fewest Loyalists.
- Some African Americans who joined the British army gained their freedom when the war ended. Several thousand left with the British and set up settlements in Nova Scotia, Canada.

Loyalists in America

Loyalists had different reasons for supporting Britain. Most Americans who worked for the British government were Loyalists because they would lose their
2 jobs if the Patriots won the war. Many wealthy merchants feared that war would hurt their businesses, so they supported Britain. Other Loyalists simply believed that the British cause was right.

Some enslaved African Americans became Loyalists. They were offered freedom if they helped the British. A few fought in the British army. Others built forts or drove carts.

More American Indians agreed to help the British than to help the Patriots. The Cherokee hoped that the British
3 would win the war and stop settlers from taking land. Mohawk leader **Joseph Brant** also urged his people to side with the British. Most American Indians stayed neutral during the war. Two Iroquois nations, the Oneida (oh NYE duh) and the Tuscarora (tus kuh ROAR uh), fought for the Patriots.

Joseph Brant In 1775, Brant went to Britain and met King George III. Later, Brant and the Mohawk nation sided with the British.

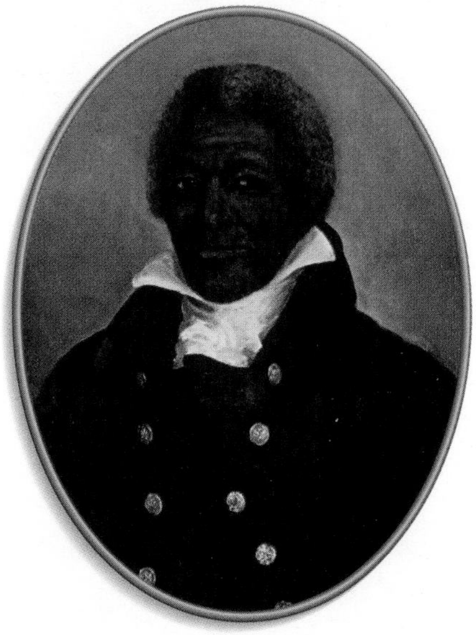

James Armistead A Patriot hero, Armistead spied on the British army. He provided information that helped Patriots win an important battle.

Patriots

Patriots found many ways to support the cause of independence. Some joined the Continental Army and fought the British. Patriots who did not fight gave support in other ways. **Haym Salomon** (HI em SAHL uh mun), a banker from Philadelphia, helped the United States get loans. He also lent his own money.

Many African Americans were Patriots. Some enslaved African Americans were offered freedom if they became Patriot soldiers. **Peter Salem,** a Patriot hero of the Battle of Bunker Hill, was one of them. Free African Americans also became soldiers. About 5,000 African Americans fought in the Continental Army, and another 2,500 served in the navy. 4

REVIEW Why did enslaved African Americans fight on both sides in the war? because both sides offered them their freedom if they fought

2 Teach

Taking Sides

Talk About It

1. **Q History** Which side did the largest number of Americans support during the Revolutionary War?
   A Almost half of all Americans were Patriots.

2. **Q History** Which groups of people became Loyalists?
   A Americans who worked for Britain, many wealthy American merchants, some enslaved African Americans, and many American Indians became Loyalists.

3. **Q History** Why did the Cherokee support the British?
   A They hoped if the British won, they would stop American settlers from taking Cherokee land.

4. **Q Citizenship** Why did some enslaved African Americans become Patriots?
   A They were offered freedom if they became Patriot soldiers.

Vocabulary Strategy

Loyalist The suffix *-ist* means "one who does." To be a *Loyalist* means to be one who is *loyal.*

neutral Neutral comes from the Latin word *ne,* meaning "not" and *uter* for "one or the other." Combine these meanings to define *neutral.*

Reading Strategy: Question Have students read the first two pages of the lesson. As they read, they should ask themselves, "Why did some people want to stay loyal to the king, while others didn't?"

Leveled Practice

REACHING ALL LEARNERS

Extra Support

Encourage students to use a **cause-and-effect** graphic organizer to better understand why life on the home front was difficult; for example, why prices went up.
Visual-spatial

Challenge

Have students **write and perform an announcement** that will persuade listeners to side with the Patriots, Loyalists, or neutrals.
Bodily-kinesthetic, verbal-linguistic

ELL

REACHING ALL LEARNERS

Beginning

Working in pairs, have students **design two T-shirts,** one for the Loyalists and one for the Patriots. Students show their understanding of the terms by the design of each shirt.
Visual-spatial

Taking Sides *continued*

Talk About It

5 **Q Visual Learning** What does the painting at the top of the page tell you about women Patriots during the Revolutionary War?

A Some were willing to fight for their country.

6 **Q History** What did women do to support soldiers?

A They cooked meals and carried water; some fought in their husbands' places.

The Challenges of War

Talk About It

7 **Q History** How were people affected when battles broke out?

A They had to leave their homes; both armies destroyed houses and robbed farms.

8 **Q Economics** Why did some merchants and farmers refuse to sell their goods during the Revolutionary War?

A They hoped that while they waited, prices would rise and they could sell their goods for more money.

Vocabulary Strategy

inflation Tell students that *inflation* is the noun form of the verb *inflate*.

Critical Thinking

Decision Making Ask students if they agree or disagree with the following statement: Merchants and farmers who wouldn't sell their goods to their fellow Americans were traitors. Ask students to explain their views.

5

Women Patriots Mary Ludwig Hays (above) took over her husband's cannon after he was hurt. Deborah Sampson (right) disguised herself as a man and fought as a soldier in the Continental Army. She was wounded twice.

Women and the War

6 Some women Patriots worked as spies and messengers. A few women, such as **Deborah Sampson,** dressed in men's clothes and joined the Continental Army. Others spread the message of freedom in letters, plays, and poems. African American poet **Phillis Wheatley** wrote a poem for **George Washington,** praising him and the cause of freedom.

Phillis Wheatley Her poems praised Washington and were popular in the colonies.

Many women, including General Washington's wife, followed their husbands who were in the army. Each winter during the eight years of the war, **Martha Washington** stayed at the general's camp. She did all she could to help the soldiers.

Some women cooked at camp or brought water to soldiers on the battlefield. They were nicknamed Molly Pitcher because of the pitchers of water they carried. A few of these women fought when their husbands were hurt or killed. One Molly Pitcher, **Mary Ludwig Hays,** was honored by General Washington for fighting in her husband's place after he was injured.

Another famous Patriot was **Nancy Morgan Hart** of Georgia. She once had to defend her home against a group of Loyalist fighters.

Math

Calculation: Multiplication and Division

Tell students that in 1777 a bushel of corn sold for about $1 in Massachusetts. By 1779, the price had increased to $80 per bushel.

- If flour cost 15 cents per pound in 1777, how much might you have had to pay in 1779? $12 per pound
- If a dozen eggs sold for 23 cents in 1777, how much would a dozen cost in 1779? $18.40

Logical-mathematical

Art

Continentals

- Have students look at the Continentals pictured on page 273. Tell them they were America's first printed currency.
- Ask students to design Continentals that represent the Patriots.

Visual-spatial

The Challenges of War

Main Idea Life was hard for many Americans during the war.

The War for Independence created many problems for Americans. When the British and American armies met in battle, people who lived nearby had to leave their
7 homes. Both armies destroyed houses and robbed farms. Everyone was affected, whether a Patriot, a Loyalist, or neutral.

During the war, the prices of food, clothing, and supplies increased. Inflation caused hardship in the colonies. A rise in the prices of goods is called **inflation.** Higher prices made it difficult for people to buy the goods they needed.

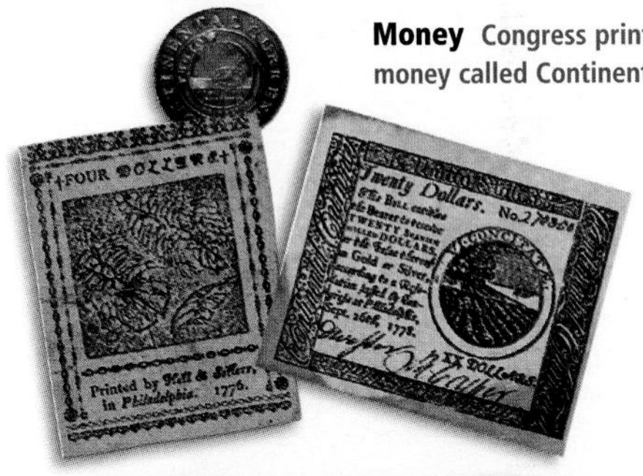

Money Congress printed money called Continentals.

Some merchants and farmers would not sell their goods. They waited for prices to go even higher so that they could sell their goods for more money. 8
Holding back goods lowered supplies of necessary items, which hurt people and made it difficult to feed and supply the army. Congress made it illegal to hold on to goods.

Life was hard because of the problems caused by war, but many Americans still wanted independence.

REVIEW Why was inflation a problem for Americans? It made prices rise, and goods harder to afford.

Lesson Summary

Americans were divided about which side to support during the American Revolution. Patriots found many ways to support the cause of independence. Whatever their choice, for most Americans, the war brought many hardships.

Why It Matters ...

Patriots believed strongly in their cause. They were determined not to give up the fight against British rule.

Lesson Review

1. **VOCABULARY** Use the words **Loyalist** and **neutral** in a paragraph about taking sides during the war.
2. **READING SKILL Compare** and **contrast** the different views of African Americans toward the war.
3. **MAIN IDEA: History** What is one reason some American Indians helped the British?
4. **MAIN IDEA: Economics** In what way did prices change during the Revolutionary War?
5. **PEOPLE TO KNOW** What did **Phillis Wheatley** become known for during the war?
6. **CRITICAL THINKING: Decision Making** For colonists in 1776, what were the costs and benefits of deciding to support the Patriots' fight for independence?

HANDS ON **ART ACTIVITY** Create a poster to persuade people to side with the Patriots or the Loyalists, or to remain neutral. Think about the persuasive words and pictures you can use.

273

Study Guide/Homework

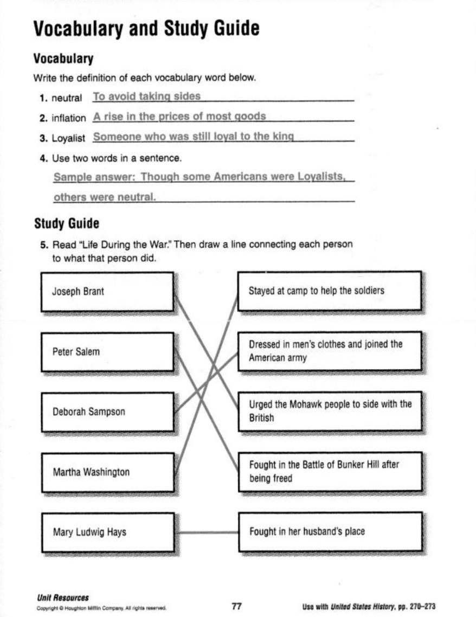

Vocabulary and Study Guide

Vocabulary

Write the definition of each vocabulary word below.

1. neutral To avoid taking sides
2. inflation A rise in the prices of most goods
3. Loyalist Someone who was still loyal to the king
4. Use two words in a sentence. Sample answer: Though some Americans were Loyalists, others were neutral.

Study Guide

5. Read "Life During the War." Then draw a line connecting each person to what that person did.

Joseph Brant	Stayed at camp to help the soldiers
Peter Salem	Dressed in men's clothes and joined the American army
Deborah Sampson	Urged the Mohawk people to side with the British
Martha Washington	Fought in the Battle of Bunker Hill after being freed
Mary Ludwig Hays	Fought in her husband's place

Unit Resources Copyright © Houghton Mifflin Company. All rights reserved. 77 Use with United States History, pp. 270–273

Unit Resources, p. 77

Reteach Minilesson

Use a Venn diagram to reteach the differences between Patriots and Loyalists.

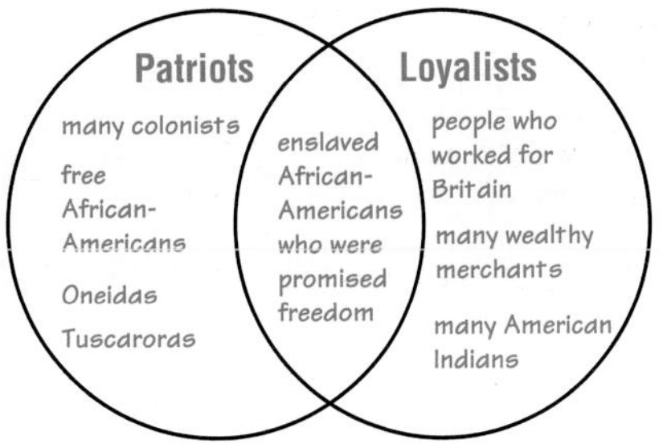

Graphic Organizer 11

3 Review/Assess

Review Tested Objectives

U4-12 Loyalists: Merchants: feared losing money; other people: felt loyal to king; Cherokee and Mohawk: wanted to keep land; enslaved African Americans: offered freedom if they fought. Patriots: some colonists, free African Americans, Oneidas, Tuscaroras: wanted independence; enslaved African Americans: offered freedom if they fought

U4-13 Many Americans lost their homes and farms; inflation and lack of supply drove up cost of necessities.

Lesson Review Answers

1. Paragraphs should show that *Loyalists* were loyal to the British king, and that *neutral* means not taking sides in a conflict.
2. Answer should give reasons for difference.
3. Some thought a British victory might stop the American colonists from taking their land.
4. Prices rose during the war.
5. Phillis Wheatley was an African American poet whose poems praised George Washington and were popular in the colonies.
6. Costs: Patriots could be arrested for treason; they stood to lose their homes, farms, their health, or even their lives. Benefits: If the Patriots won, they would win their freedom from British rule. For African American Patriots, they might win their personal freedom.

HANDS ON Performance Task Rubric

4	Position clearly stated; poster is persuasive; mechanics are correct.
3	Position adequately stated; poster is persuasive; few errors in mechanics.
2	Position is stated; poster is fairly persuasive; some errors in mechanics.
1	Position not stated; persuasion lacking; many errors in mechanics.

Quick Look

Teaching Option: Connect to Core Lesson
Students have just learned about the stands people held regarding the War of Independence. In this Extend Lesson, they will hear from characters who explain why they feel as they do.

1 Preview the Extend Lesson

Connect to the Big Idea

Foundations of Democracy When it came time to choose sides during the Revolution, the debate Americans engaged in was a true exercise in liberty. Having the power and freedom to join one side or the other, or neither, lies at the very heart of our democratic system.

Connect to Prior Knowledge

Ask students to look at the list of characters. Even if the roles were not labeled with the character's stance (Patriot, Loyalist, or neutral), what might students be able to predict about each character's feelings toward independence?

Readers' Theater

Patriot or Loyalist

Why were there so many different points of view? People from Georgia to New Hampshire talked and argued about the Revolution. The question of war was important to their lives. Listen to what these characters say.

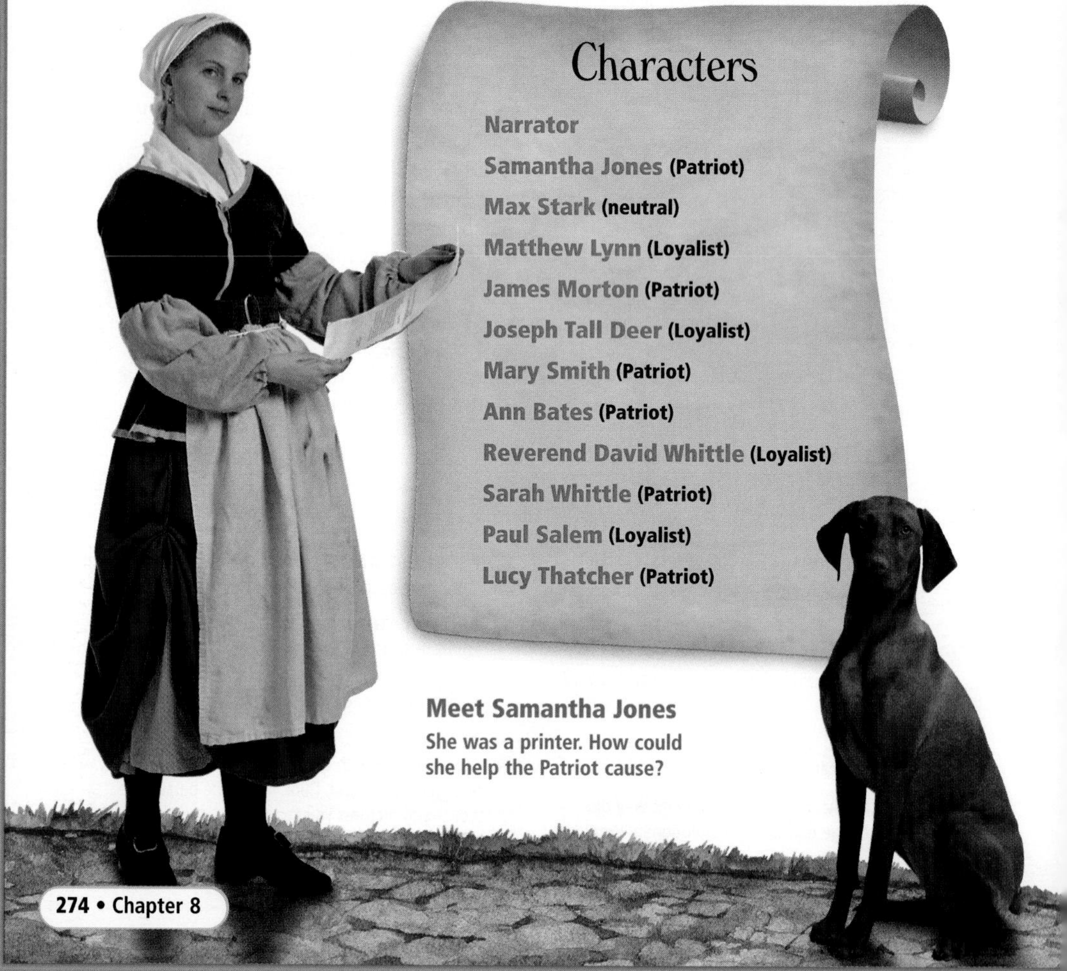

Characters

- Narrator
- Samantha Jones (Patriot)
- Max Stark (neutral)
- Matthew Lynn (Loyalist)
- James Morton (Patriot)
- Joseph Tall Deer (Loyalist)
- Mary Smith (Patriot)
- Ann Bates (Patriot)
- Reverend David Whittle (Loyalist)
- Sarah Whittle (Patriot)
- Paul Salem (Loyalist)
- Lucy Thatcher (Patriot)

Meet Samantha Jones
She was a printer. How could she help the Patriot cause?

Reaching All Learners

Background

A House Divided

- Deciding which side to support divided the people and tore families apart.
- It is estimated that one-fifth of the American men who took up arms during the war fought for the British.

Extra Support

Conduct an Interview

- Have students choose a character to interview.
- Before the interview, students should prepare at least three questions for the character.
- After the interview, invite them to share what they have learned with the class.

Verbal-linguistic

On Level

What Lies Ahead?

- Ask students to choose one character and think about what that character might do or say after the war ended.
- Students can present their ideas as an oral report, a dramatic presentation, or a letter the character might write.

Bodily-kinesthetic

Narrator: Samantha Jones, you are a printer. Max Stark, you are a farmer who has come here from Germany. I'm told that the two of you don't agree about the war.

Samantha Jones (Patriot): I like what Tom Paine wrote in *Common Sense.* He understands that people who work very hard are tired of being pushed around by King George. We want our own government so we can make our own laws.

Max Stark (neutral): I don't feel that way, Samantha. I moved to this country to make a better life for my family, not to make war. You may want more freedom, but I just want peace.

Matthew Lynn (Loyalist): Let me say something! There's another side to this.

Narrator: Matthew Lynn. You collect taxes in the community. What is your view?

Matthew Lynn: I don't understand why the Patriots are complaining. Britain protects the colonies, doesn't it? That protection costs a lot of money. I think it's only fair that the colonists pay taxes for it. Besides, I'd lose my job if the Patriots won.

James Morton (Patriot): The taxes aren't fair, Matthew!

Narrator: James Morton? You are a tea merchant, correct?

James Morton: I'm sorry I interrupted. I get very upset.

Narrator: We can all talk politely. Tell us. What isn't fair?

James Morton: When the British taxed the tea I bought from them, many of my customers refused to buy it. The British hurt my business. That's why I turned against them.

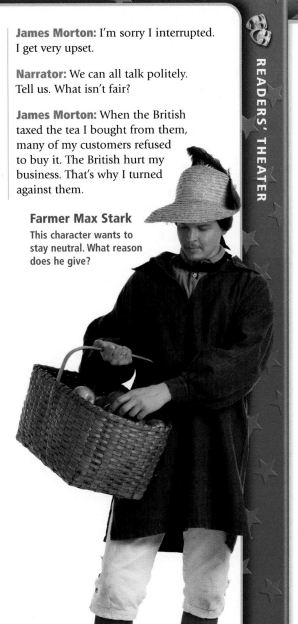

Farmer Max Stark
This character wants to stay neutral. What reason does he give?

2 Teach the Extend Lesson

Learning through Drama

Assign each of the roles in the play to students and have them read the play aloud to the class. Discuss with students how the play helps explain why Americans were so divided about declaring their independence from Britain. Ask students if they agree with their character's point of view and have them explain why.

Challenge

REACHING ALL LEARNERS

Hold a Debate

- Tell students that some Americans of 1776 lived well. Some merchants were earning the equivalent of $500,000 a year.
- Ask students to form two groups, Loyalist and Patriot, and debate whether independence was a good or bad idea financially.

Verbal-linguistic

ELL

REACHING ALL LEARNERS

Intermediate/Advanced

- Ask students to make cartoon frames with characters who are Patriots or Loyalists.
- They may use characters and phrases from Readers' Theater.
- Working in pairs, students can draw the pictures and dictate captions or speech balloons.

Visual-spatial

Literature

Historical Fiction

The Fighting Ground by Avi and *My Brother Sam Is Dead* by Christopher Collier and James Collier.

Place these works of historical fiction in your Reading Center for students who want to find out what it was like for young Americans during the Revolution.

Critical Thinking

Analyzing Information Have students reread the position of Ann Bates. Ask students if they agree that she is really neutral. Students should support their answers with information from her statement.

Synthesize After the reading, ask students to review James Morton's comments on page 275. Ask them if they are surprised by Morton's words, and if so, why. Morton, a merchant, was a Patriot, while many other merchants were on the side of the British.

Narrator: Each of you has a good reason for your opinion. There are many others here who have something to say. Joseph Tall Deer, you are of the Mohawk people. And Mary Smith, you are Oneida. Both of you are Iroquois. The Iroquois Nations have tried to stay neutral and united, but the war divides them. Do the Oneida support the Patriot cause?

Mary Smith (Patriot): We didn't take sides at first. Then a missionary came to live with us. He talked about reasons to fight the British. We had many discussions. I believe he is right.

Joseph Tall Deer (Loyalist): The British have been good to us, so we're on their side. The king told our leader, Joseph Brant, that no one will take away the land we live on. The colonists just want the land for themselves. We don't trust them.

Narrator: Ann Bates, what do you think?

Ann Bates (Patriot): We Quakers are against the whole idea of war. Some of us are determined to stay neutral, but I believe in the Patriot cause. Although I can't fight, I can do other things to support the Patriots. For example, I can refuse to buy British goods.

Opposing Views
All over the colonies, Americans shared their views. These people are dressed as characters. Who is a Patriot, a Loyalist, or neutral?

Reaching All Learners

Language Arts

Write a Play

- Ask students to write their own Readers' Theater.
- In it, Thomas Jefferson, author of the Declaration of Independence, has dinner with Reverend David Whittle, a Loyalist, and Sarah Whittle, a Patriot.

Verbal-linguistic

Math

Make a Bar Graph

- Have students make a bar graph of the views of the characters in the play.
- Tell students that one bar should represent the Loyalists, a second bar, Patriots, and a third, the neutrals.
- Have students label the bars, or color-code them, and include a key that explains what each color stands for.

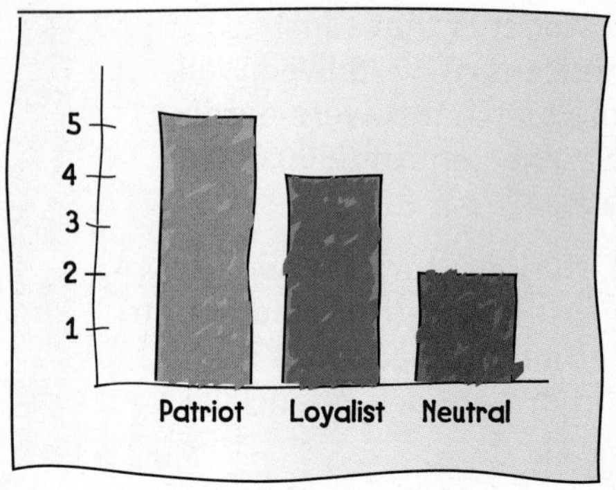

Logical-mathematical

Reverend David Whittle (Loyalist): I do not have Ann Bates's problem. I belong to Britain's official church. The king is the head of it. I believe I have a duty to be loyal to my church and my king.

Sarah Whittle (Patriot): Excuse me, please. I am Reverend Whittle's wife. I respectfully disagree with my husband. I feel the king does not take good care of us. Britain's laws and taxes are too harsh. Also, I like the idea of freedom. Maybe women will have more freedom in a country that says it believes in liberty and equal rights.

Narrator: The wish for personal freedom is very important to many. Lucy Thatcher, you are a free African American. Paul Salem, you are an enslaved African American. Both of you want freedom for all, yet you support different sides in the war. Please explain.

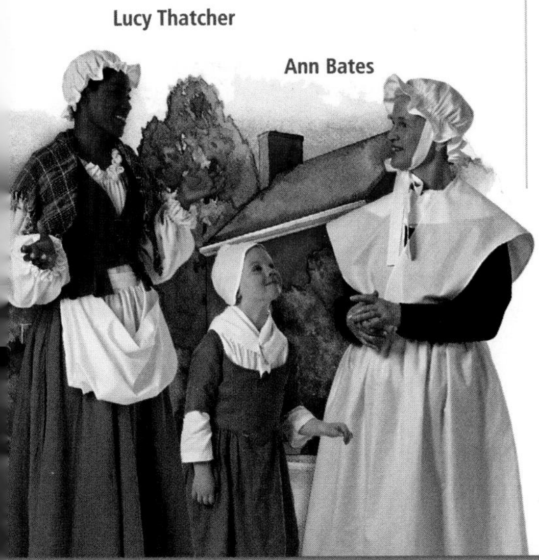

Lucy Thatcher (Patriot): We have to support the Patriots. Their Declaration of Independence says we are all born equal and have the right to be free. Maybe they will end slavery if they win.

Paul Salem (Loyalist): You are free already, but I am not. The Declaration doesn't say anything about ending slavery. I support the British. They have promised freedom if we fight for them.

Narrator: Did everyone have a chance to speak?

Everyone: Yes.

Narrator: Good! Thank you for sharing your views. Now, if you'll excuse me, I must say good-bye.

Lucy Thatcher (Patriot): Wait a minute, please! We all must live together, but we disagree. What do we do now?

Ann Bates (Patriot): Maybe we can agree to disagree. I respect that you have opinions and beliefs, just as I do.

Reverend David Whittle (Loyalist): Shall we respect each other's right to have an opinion?

Everyone: Yes! Thank you! Good-bye!

Activities

1. **THINK ABOUT IT** How did the characters show good citizenship in the Readers' Theater?
2. **WRITE ABOUT IT** Write a part for one more character. Your character should explain why he or she is a Patriot, a Loyalist, or neutral.

3 Leveled Activities

1 Think About It *For Extra Support*

The characters allowed each other to speak their minds and were polite even if they disagreed.

2 Write About It *For Challenge*

Writing Rubric

4	Character's position is clearly stated; reasons are supported by information from the text; spelling, grammar, and punctuation are correct.
3	Character's position is adequately stated; most reasons are supported by information from the text; few errors in spelling, grammar, and punctuation.
2	Character's position is stated, but reasons are confused or poorly supported by information from the text; some errors in spelling, grammar, and punctuation.
1	Character's position is stated, but reasons are confused or poorly supported by information from the text; some errors in spelling, grammar, and punctuation.

Music

Compare Lyrics

- Explain that Loyalists liked the song "God Save the King."
  God save our gracious King
  Long live our noble King
  God save the King!
  Send him victorious,
  Happy and glorious,
  Long to reign over us,
  God Save the King.
- Tell students that it has the same melody as "My Country 'Tis of Thee."
- Compare lyrics of both songs.

Musical-auditory

Graphic Organizer

Patriots	Loyalists	Neutrals
"We are tired of being pushed around" "High taxes hurt my business" "Maybe they will end slavery"	"I'd lose my job if the Patriots won" "The British have been good to us"	"I just want peace" "We Quakers are against the whole idea of war"

Graphic Organizer 2

Tested Objectives

U4-14 History Compare the strengths and weaknesses of the British and Continental Armies.

U4-15 History List and describe the outcomes of major battles of the Revolution fought in the North.

U4-16 History Explain how aid from France and other European powers affected the course of the Revolution.

Lesson Quick Look

Lesson 3 is about the challenges the Continental Army faced.

Teaching Option **Extend Lesson 3** allows students to examine a painting of Valley Forge and objects colonial soldiers used.

1 Get Set to Read

Preview Tell students to look at the map on page 280. Ask them what it depicts. What does it tell them about the lesson?

Reading Skill: Cause and Effect Students may include the effect of Washington's leadership.

Build on What You Know Talk with students about the importance of strategy. If the opposing team has more players, a good strategy can help you win. Explain that George Washington was very good at strategy.

Vocabulary

retreat *verb,* to move back when an enemy attacks

mercenary *noun,* a soldier who is paid to fight

victory *noun,* the defeat of an enemy

Core Lesson 3

The War in the North

1774	1776	1778	1780	1782	1784
	1776–1778				

Build on What You Know Think about what it is like to play a game or a sport against a stronger team. How can you win? In the War for Independence, George Washington and his soldiers had to fight Britain's powerful army. To win, they needed careful planning, courage, and help from other countries.

VOCABULARY

retreat
mercenary
victory

Vocabulary Strategy

retreat

The word **retreat** comes from a word that means to draw back. In battle, retreat means to move back when an enemy attacks.

READING SKILL

Cause and Effect As you read, take notes to show what caused the outcome of each battle of the war.

CAUSE	EFFECT

Washington's First Battles

Main Idea Washington's leadership helped the Continental Army continue to fight.

While many Americans were deciding which side to support in the war, battles had already begun. The two armies fighting each other were very different.

At the start of the war, the Continental Army was not as large or as strong as the British army. British soldiers had better training and better weapons. The Continental Army, however, did have some strengths. American soldiers were fighting on home ground, and they could use their knowledge of the land to plan attacks. They had a cause that they believed in and the support of other Patriots. They also had a great leader in **George Washington**. 1 2

In the spring of 1776, the soldiers of Washington's army forced the British out of Boston. The British did not give up, though. In August, they defeated the Continental Army in the Battle of Long Island, near New York City.

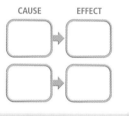

Signals Drum beats were used as signals for soldiers marching into battle.

Skill and Strategy

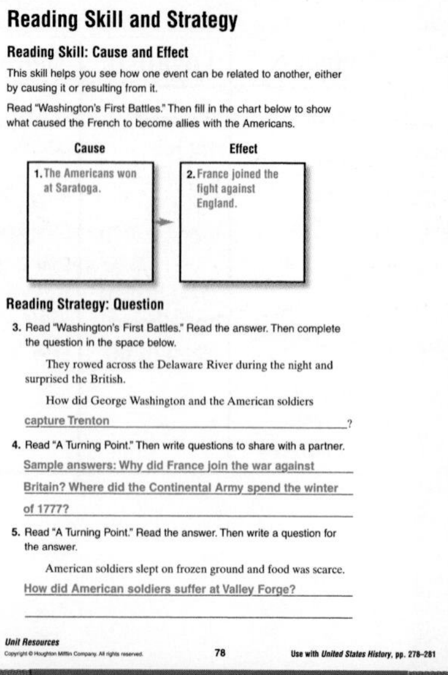

Reading Skill and Strategy

Reading Skill: Cause and Effect

This skill helps you see how one event can be related to another, either by causing it or resulting from it.

Read "Washington's First Battles." Then fill in the chart below to show what caused the French to become allies with the Americans.

Cause	Effect
1. The Americans won at Saratoga.	2. France joined the fight against England.

Reading Strategy: Question

3. Read "Washington's First Battles." Read the answer. Then complete the question in the space below.

They rowed across the Delaware River during the night and surprised the British.

How did George Washington and the American soldiers capture Trenton?

4. Read "A Turning Point." Then write questions to share with a partner.
Sample answers: Why did France join the war against Britain? Where did the Continental Army spend the winter of 1777?

5. Read "A Turning Point." Read the answer. Then write a question for the answer.

American soldiers slept on frozen ground and food was scarce.

How did American soldiers suffer at Valley Forge?

Unit Resources
Copyright © Houghton Mifflin Company. All rights reserved. 78 Use with *United States History*, pp. 278–281

Unit Resources, p. 78

Background

Battles

- One American wounded at the Battle of Trenton was James Monroe, who became the fifth President of the United States.
- Drums were used not only as soldiers marched into battle, but also to issue commands during the battle.

George Washington In this famous painting, George Washington and his army cross the Delaware River to attack Trenton. SKILL **Reading Visuals** How does the artist show Washington as a leader? by making him look strong and heroic

Washington's army had to retreat. **Retreat** means to move away from the enemy. As his army retreated, Washington needed spies to keep track of the British. Captain **Nathan Hale** of Connecticut volunteered. Hale was sent to spy behind enemy lines, but he was captured and hanged. His last words are now famous:

3 "I only regret that I have but one life to lose for my country."

Washington's army marched through New Jersey and into Pennsylvania. General Washington was worried. He only had about 3,000 soldiers left. Yet the British could not destroy the Continental Army. As long as Washington could keep his army together, he could prevent the British from winning the war.

Victory at Trenton

Washington wanted to win a battle so that his soldiers would not give up. He planned a surprise attack on an enemy camp in Trenton, New Jersey. The soldiers in Trenton were German mercenaries. A **mercenary** is a soldier who is paid to fight for a foreign country.

On the night of December 25, 1776, Washington and his soldiers rowed across the icy Delaware River to New Jersey. Just after dawn they attacked Trenton. The mercenaries were still sleepy after celebrating Christmas the night before. Washington's army caught them by surprise and took almost 1,000 prisoners. Patriots were overjoyed at the victory. A **victory** is the defeat of an enemy. 4

REVIEW Why did Washington decide to attack Trenton? so his soldiers would not give up

279

2 Teach

Washington's First Battles

Talk About It

1. **Q History** Which army was better prepared at the war's start?
   A the British
2. **Q Citizenship** Why do you think having "a cause that they believed in" was an advantage for the Americans?
   A People will try harder when they believe in what they are doing.
3. **Q Primary Source** What does Nathan Hale's famous quote say about how he felt about dying for his country?
   A He was proud to die for his country and would be willing to do it again.
4. **Q History** What was Washington's plan for attacking Trenton?
   A He wanted to surprise the enemy by attacking them when they least expected it, the morning after Christmas.

Vocabulary Strategy

retreat One meaning of the prefix *re-* is "backward" or "back." To *retreat* is to back away from a conflict.

mercenary Tell students that *mercenary* is from a Latin word meaning "wages."

victory A synonym for *victory* is "a win."

Reading Strategy: Question As students read, suggest that they keep in mind the question, "What made Washington a successful leader?"

REACHING ALL LEARNERS

Leveled Practice

Extra Support

As students read, have them list each battle they read about, the year it took place, and which side won. Bodily-kinesthetic

Challenge

Ask students to prepare a mock trial for Nathan Hale. The rest of the class can serve as the jury. Verbal-linguistic

REACHING ALL LEARNERS

ELL

Intermediate/Advanced

Discuss word use with students. Explain to students that *retreat* can be used as a verb and as a noun. Have them decide what it means in the text as a verb. Ask them what the word would mean if it were used as a noun. a movement back after an enemy attacks

Verbal-linguistic

A Turning Point

Talk About It

5 **Q Geography** Where did the British come from when they began a new attack in 1777?

A Canada

6 **Q History** How did Thaddeus Kosciuszko help the Americans at Saratoga?

A He set up a long wall of earth and logs on a hill so the Americans could fight from behind it.

7 **Q Geography** Which European countries helped the Americans during the Revolution?

A France, Spain, the Netherlands, Russia

8 **Q History** What difficulties did the Americans face at Valley Forge?

A At first they had to sleep on the frozen ground; food and shoes were scarce; diseases spread through the camp.

9 **Q History** How did von Steuben help the Continental Army?

A He taught the soldiers how to march together and use their weapons properly.

Critical Thinking

Analyze Why are allies important in winning a war?

A Turning Point

Main Idea After the Battle of Saratoga, France joined the war against Britain.

5 In June 1777, the British began a new attack from Canada. General **John Burgoyne** (bur GOIN) led an army south toward Albany, New York. An army of Americans prepared to stop the British near Saratoga, New York. A Polish
6 engineer named **Thaddeus Kosciuszko** (kahs ee US koh) helped them. He set up a long wall of earth and logs on a hill so that the Americans could fight from behind it.

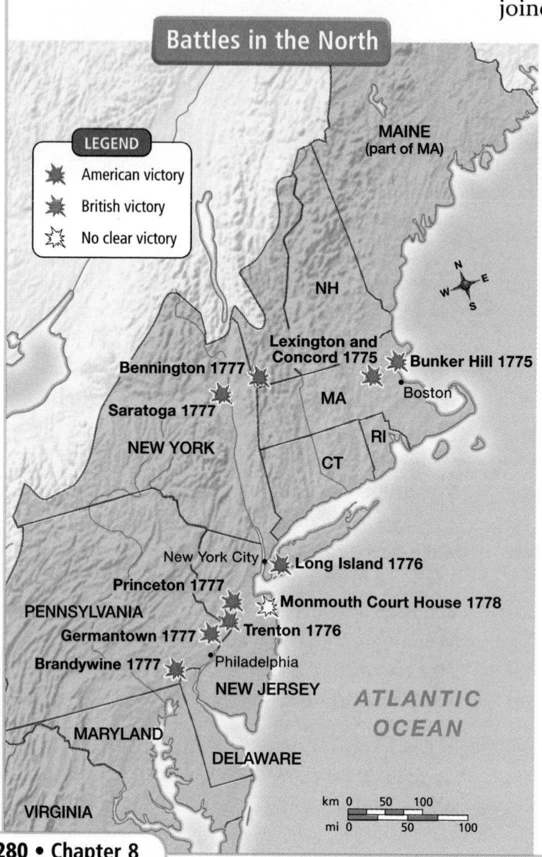

Victory Brings Help from France

When the two armies met, they fought two fierce battles. A brave officer named **Benedict Arnold** led many attacks against the British. The Americans won and forced Burgoyne and more than 5,000 of this soldiers to surrender.

Before the Battle of Saratoga, **Benjamin Franklin** had been trying to get help from France. After the American victory, the French were convinced that the Americans could win. They sent money, soldiers, and a powerful navy to help the Americans. As the war went on, 7
Spain, the Netherlands, and Russia also joined the fight against Britain.

One important French soldier came to America even before the Battle of Saratoga. In August 1777, the wealthy **Marquis de Lafayette** (mahr KEE duh laf ee ET) joined Washington's army. Lafayette was only 19 years old, but he led American soldiers in many battles.

Winter at Valley Forge

The victory at Saratoga was good news for Americans, but there was also troubling news. Washington's army lost two battles in Pennsylvania, and the British captured Philadelphia. The British settled into warm houses there for the winter of 1777. The Continental Army stayed about 20 miles away in Valley Forge, Pennsylvania.

Early Battles The ten battles shown were the major battles during the first years of the war.

SKILL **Reading Maps** Which battles took place in Pennsylvania?

Germantown and Brandywine

Math

Calculation: Multiplication

- Tell students the Continental Army's cook made up the recipe below.
- If it would feed four soldiers, how much of each ingredient would be needed to feed 640 soldiers?

Multiply each number by 160.

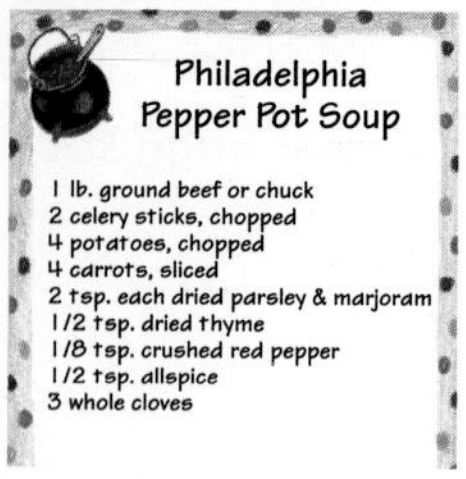

Logical-mathematical

Language Arts

Write a Speech

- Have students write a short speech for Benjamin Franklin to present to the French government to persuade it to join the American cause.
- Before they begin, have students suggest words or phrases that they think are persuasive.
- Ask several students to read their speeches to the class.

Verbal-linguistic

8 American soldiers suffered at Valley Forge. There were no huts at first, only tents, and men slept on the frozen ground. Food was scarce. Most of the soldiers went barefoot. Many soldiers died of disease.

Washington's leadership helped keep the army going during the difficult times at Valley Forge. He worked hard to get the supplies the army needed. By spring of 1778, his soldiers had more food and were wearing better uniforms.

A Stronger Continental Army

9 Washington's army was ready to fight when spring came. A German soldier named **Baron Friedrich von Steuben** (SHTOY ben) had joined the army at Valley Forge to train the soldiers.

Von Steuben taught the Americans to march together and use their weapons properly. The men of the Continental Army became good soldiers because of their training at Valley Forge. In their next battle, the Americans fought well against the British army.

With the help of France, and men such as Steuben and Lafayette, it looked as though the United States could win the war.

REVIEW What happened at Valley Forge to make the Continental Army better soldiers?
Baron von Steuben taught them to march together and use their weapons properly.

Lesson Summary

- **Summer 1776** Washington retreats
- **December 1776** Victory at Trenton
- **October 1777** Victory at Saratoga
- **1777–1778** Winter at Valley Forge

Why It Matters ...

The Continental soldiers fought hard during the difficult early years of the war. They kept alive the Patriots' hope of independence.

Lesson Review

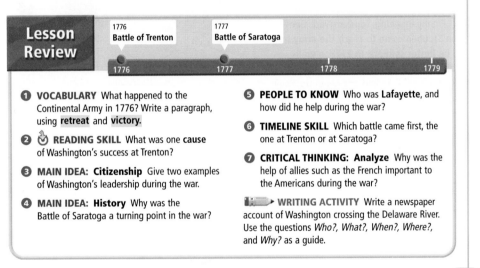

1776 Battle of Trenton — 1777 Battle of Saratoga

1776 — 1777 — 1778 — 1779

1. **VOCABULARY** What happened to the Continental Army in 1776? Write a paragraph, using **retreat** and **victory.**
2. **READING SKILL** What was one **cause** of Washington's success at Trenton?
3. **MAIN IDEA: Citizenship** Give two examples of Washington's leadership during the war.
4. **MAIN IDEA: History** Why was the Battle of Saratoga a turning point in the war?
5. **PEOPLE TO KNOW** Who was **Lafayette**, and how did he help during the war?
6. **TIMELINE SKILL** Which battle came first, the one at Trenton or at Saratoga?
7. **CRITICAL THINKING: Analyze** Why was the help of allies such as the French important to the Americans during the war?

WRITING ACTIVITY Write a newspaper account of Washington crossing the Delaware River. Use the questions *Who?*, *What?*, *When?*, *Where?*, and *Why?* as a guide.

3 Review/Assess

Review Tested Objectives

U4-14 British Army: bigger, stronger, better armed, better trained; Continental: knew the land, fighting for a cause, had a great leader

U4-15 Trenton: Americans won, took 1,000 prisoners; Saratoga: Americans won, thousands surrendered, including Burgoyne; Monmouth: Americans won, proving they could defeat the British.

U4-16 They gave the Americans the money, men, and naval support needed to win.

Lesson Review Answers

1. Paragraphs should show an understanding of events and the meanings of vocabulary.
2. They had the element of surprise on their side.
3. Washington worked hard to get his men the supplies they needed; he was aware of their morale.
4. It convinced the French that the Americans could win the war.
5. Lafayette was a French nobleman who led Americans in many battles.
6. Trenton
7. Allies such as the French lent the Americans experience and funds they needed to succeed.

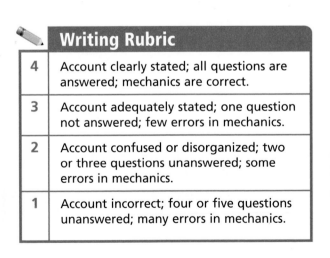

Writing Rubric

4	Account clearly stated; all questions are answered; mechanics are correct.
3	Account adequately stated; one question not answered; few errors in mechanics.
2	Account confused or disorganized; two or three questions unanswered; some errors in mechanics.
1	Account incorrect; four or five questions unanswered; many errors in mechanics.

Study Guide/Homework

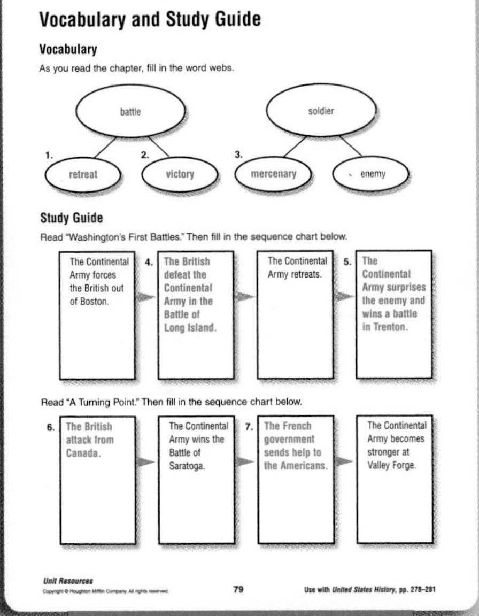
Vocabulary and Study Guide

Vocabulary

As you read the chapter, fill in the word webs.

battle: 1. retreat, 2. victory

soldier: 3. mercenary, enemy

Study Guide

Read "Washington's First Battles." Then fill in the sequence chart below.

The Continental Army forces the British out of Boston. → 4. The British defeat the Continental Army in the Battle of Long Island. → The Continental Army retreats. → 5. The Continental Army surprises the enemy and wins a battle in Trenton.

Read "A Turning Point." Then fill in the sequence chart below.

6. The British attack from Canada. → The Continental Army wins the Battle of Saratoga. → 7. The French government sends help to the Americans. → The Continental Army becomes stronger at Valley Forge.

Unit Resources 79 Use with *United States History*, pp. 278–281

Unit Resources, p. 79

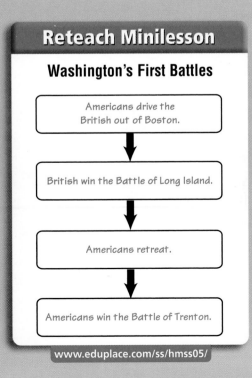

Reteach Minilesson

Washington's First Battles

Americans drive the British out of Boston.
↓
British win the Battle of Long Island.
↓
Americans retreat.
↓
Americans win the Battle of Trenton.

www.eduplace.com/ss/hmss05/

Extend Quick Look

Teaching Option: Connect to Core Lesson
This Extend provides an overview of the hardships Washington's soldiers experienced at Valley Forge, and of how they emerged from the desperate time as better soldiers.

2 Teach the Extend Lesson

Connect to Primary Sources

Through primary sources, we can gain a sense of what the past was like. As students examine the painting and the artifacts, they can see through the eyes of the soldiers and feel what they felt.

Connect to Prior Knowledge

Valley Forge was truly one of the revolution's classic stories to remember. The army overcame terrible suffering—many soldiers died—and still rallied to defeat the British.

Ask students what they think of the statement, "Valley Forge stands for an army's courage." What does courage mean to them?

Primary Sources

Valley Forge

Valley Forge stands for an army's courage. Why? The story of Valley Forge tells of terrible hardships. During the winter of 1777–1778, Washington's army suffered from cold and hunger. Supplies had run out. Soldiers should have had coats and warm uniforms, but some had only a shirt or a blanket, not enough against the fierce cold. They had little to eat. Instead of milk, meat, or vegetables, they ate "firecake," which was flour and water cooked over a campfire. Many soldiers got sick and died.

Finally in spring, food arrived. General von Steuben came to teach the army how to be better soldiers. In 1778, a well-trained army marched out of Valley Forge.

Those soldiers had not given up. They stayed loyal to Washington, and now they were ready for victory over the British.

This painting shows Washington and his troops on the way to Valley Forge. The artist painted it many years later and knew the story of their trial. The faces show courage. What else do you notice?

Canteens
Soldiers needed canteens for water. For meals at camp, soldiers had simple utensils like the ones below.

Reaching All Learners

Extra Support

Valley Forge Geography

- Have students research the location and climate of Valley Forge.
- Have them list ways that people in Washington's army coped with the cold.

Verbal-linguistic

On Level

Write a Skit

- Have students work in small groups to prepare a skit involving soldiers who want to leave Valley Forge and soldiers who want to stay.
- Students can perform the skits for the class.

Bodily-kinesthetic

Challenge

Journal Entries

- Have students write journal pages that could have been written by a soldier at Valley Forge. They might include sketches.
- Share and discuss journal entries.

Verbal-linguistic

"...Three or four days' bad weather would prove our destruction." —George Washington

PRIMARY SOURCES

Uniforms

Notice how ragged many uniforms are. Some soldiers are not even wearing boots. Hats were made of felt, but were not warm enough.

Equipment

Knapsacks held soldiers' belongings. Soldiers also carried up to 60 pounds of equipment. A musket could weigh nearly 10 pounds.

Activities

1. **TALK ABOUT IT** Look at the painting and discuss what it shows about Washington's army.
2. **WRITE ABOUT IT** A motto is a statement to express a goal or a belief. Create a motto for the Continental Army after Valley Forge. Explain why you chose it.

Technology Learn about other primary sources for this unit at Education Place. www.eduplace.com/kids/hmss05/

283

2 Leveled Activities

❶ **Talk About It** *For Extra Support*
snow; soldiers bend forward into wind; ragged uniforms; simple gear

❷ **Write About It** *For Challenge*

Writing Rubric

4	Motto is brief and inspiring; explanation is clear; mechanics are correct.
3	Motto is brief and inspiring; explanation is somewhat clear; few errors in mechanics.
2	Motto is sufficient; explanation is somewhat disorganized; some errors in mechanics.
1	Motto is poorly focused; explanation is disorganized; many errors in mechanics.

ELL

Intermediate/Advanced

- Ask students to reread the quote from Washington on the top of page 283. Discuss with them what Washington meant.
- Students may find his phrasing challenging; encourage them to express their ideas.

Verbal-linguistic

Literature

Historical Fiction

In *The Winter of Red Snow,* by Kristiana Gregory, eleven-year-old Abby Stewart keeps a journal as she watches the Continental Army encampment near her Valley Forge home.

Graphic Organizer

Winter	Spring
cold weather	warmer weather
lots of snow	less snow
supplies run low	new supplies arrive
soldiers feel discouraged	soldiers feel hopeful
army lacks training	General von Steuben helps train army

Graphic Organizer 1

Tested Objective

U4-16 Use a map to interpret the sequence of events during a battle.

1 Teach the Skill

Remind students of the many kinds of maps they have seen. Some maps depict information about the land (physical maps), and others depict information about people and their activities (thematic maps).

Battle maps are a special type of map that depict the events that took place during war. Like other maps students have used, battle maps include elements that help them understand the map: the legend, the compass rose, and the scale.

Ask students to find each of these elements on the map of the Battle of Long Island.

Map and Globe Skills

Skillbuilder

Read a Battle Map

▶ VOCABULARY
battle map

At the Battle of Long Island in 1776, the British army forced the Americans to retreat. Learn more about this important battle by reading a battle map. A battle map uses symbols to show how a battle was fought.

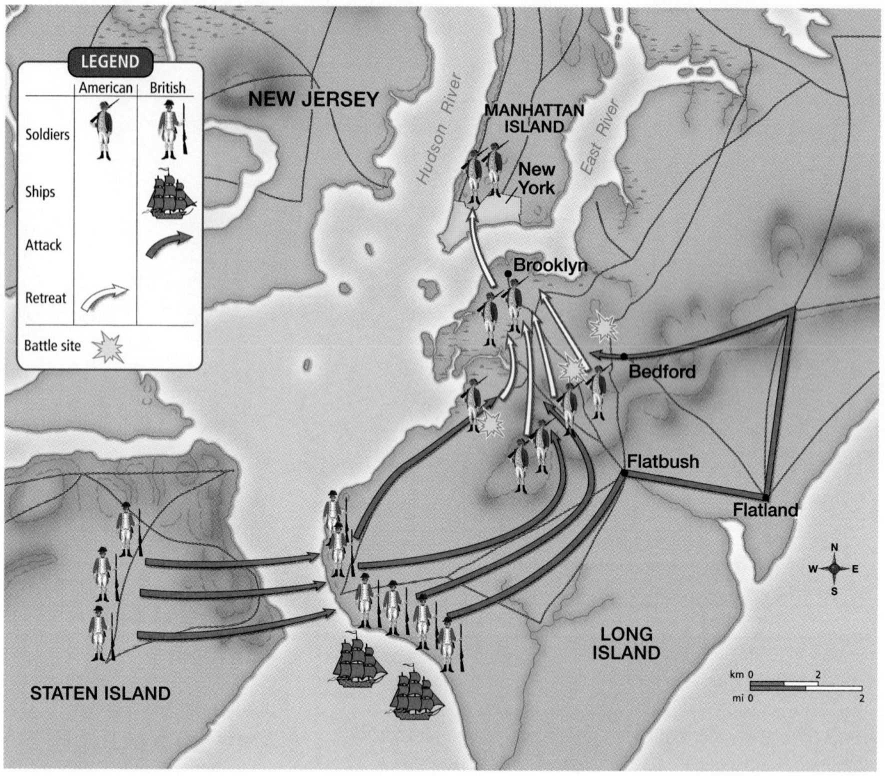

Reaching All Learners — Leveled Practice

Extra Support

Invite students to make a three-dimensional **model** of the battle map. Working in groups, they can draw the landscape on large sheets of paper, and use chess pieces or checkers to re-create the battle. Bodily-kinesthetic

Challenge

Invite students to consider how the **landforms** of the Yorktown area may have affected the outcome of the battle. Ask them to write a paragraph explaining their thoughts. Verbal-linguistic

Reaching All Learners — ELL

Intermediate/Advanced

Explain that *legend* has **multiple meanings** in English, including "a key to a map" and "a story." Both meanings can be traced back to the word's Latin root, which means "to read." Discuss with students comparable words that can be found in their own languages.

Verbal-linguistic

Learn the Skill

Step 1: Read the title and legend. On a battle map, different colors stand for different sides in the battle.

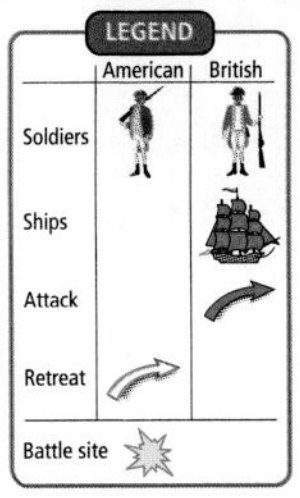

Step 2: Look for the symbols on the map. They show where the soldiers and ships were.

Step 3: Find the arrows on the map. The arrows show you which direction an army or navy moved. When soldiers or ships move towards their enemy, they are attacking. When soldiers move away from their enemy, they are retreating.

Practice the Skill

Study the map of the Battle of Long Island. Use the information on the map to answer the questions about the battle.

1. Which symbol shows the American army at Long Island?
2. Which three towns did British soldiers march through during their attack?
3. About how far, and in what direction, did American soldiers retreat from Bedford to New York?

Apply the Skill

Use the steps above to study the map of the Battle of Antietam on page 454. Then write a brief description of the battle.

285

2 Practice the Skill

1. the soldiers with their muskets on their shoulders
2. Flatbush, Flatland, and Bedford
3. about three miles; northwest

3 Apply the Skill

Ask students to turn to page 455 in their books and look at the map of the Battle of Antietam. Ask them to write a brief description of the battle. When evaluating students' descriptions, consider:

- Did the student correctly determine the parties involved in the conflict?
- Did the student correctly interpret the movement of the Union forces?
- Did the student correctly interpret the movement of the Confederate forces?
- Did the student identify the time at which the events occurred?

Skill Practice

Skillbuilder: Read a Battle Map

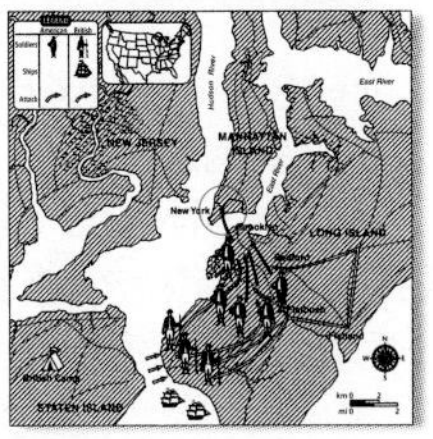

Practice

1. Who had ships in this battle? The British
2. Near what body of water is there a line of British soldiers? The Hudson River
3. Where did the American soldiers end up when they retreated? Circle the name of the place where the American soldiers retreated.
4. Did all of the British soldiers attack by moving in the same direction? What direction or directions did they travel? No. Some British soldiers moved north, some moved east, and some moved west.

Apply

Now you can use your map skills to show another version of this map. Show what might have happened if American soldiers standing on the coast of Long Island met the British ships. Using the same symbols as on this map, draw how the American soldiers and the British soldiers might have moved. Show which side might have retreated. Answers will vary.

Unit Resources

80

Use with *United States History*, pp. 284–285

Unit Resources, p. 80

Skill Transparency

MAP and GLOBE SKILLS

Skillbuilder Transparency 8

Read a Battle Map

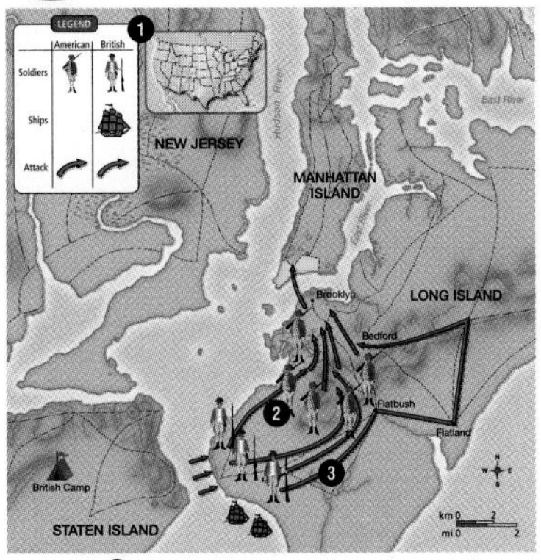

Step 1 Point out the legend. Describe the symbols. Identify the two armies by color of symbols.

Step 2 Circle the symbols for each country's symbols on the map.

Step 3 Follow the directions of the arrows to determine where the armies will meet.

Transparency 8

✔ Tested Objectives

U4-17 Describe the results of the major Revolutionary War battles that were fought in the South and the West.

U4-18 Explain how the Americans won the war.

Lesson Quick Look

This lesson describes important strategies and battles in the South and the West that led to victory and independence.

Teaching Option: Examine the map in the geography **Extend Lesson 4** to see what was going on in other nations at this time.

1 Get Set to Read

Preview Direct students to the map on page 285. What does it tell them about the lesson they are going to read?

Reading Skill: Sequence Students should check to be sure events are in chronological order.

Build on What You Know Discuss with students how they measure changes in their size and strength. Explain that Americans measured their increasing strength by the failure of the British to defeat them in the South and West.

Vocabulary

strategy *noun,* a plan of action for fighting a war

traitor *noun,* someone who is not loyal to his or her country; betrayer

surrender *verb,* to give up to another in a battle or war

Core Lesson 4

Winning the War

1774 | 1776 | 1778 | 1780 | 1782 | 1784

1778–1783

VOCABULARY

strategy
traitor
surrender

Vocabulary Strategy

surrender

Notice that **surrender** contains the smaller word **end**. At the end of a war, the losing army surrenders.

READING SKILL

Sequence As you read, list the main events in order.

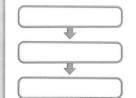

Build on What You Know Think about how much bigger and stronger you have grown in the past six years. After Valley Forge, it took six more years for the Americans to win the War for Independence. During that time, the Continental Army grew stronger and finally defeated the British army.

The War in the South and West

Main Idea The British invaded the South, but they could not defeat the Patriots there.

After over three years of war in the North, the British had not been able to win. They decided to change their strategy. A **strategy** is a plan of action. In 1779, they made a plan to invade the South with a small army. They thought that the South had more Loyalists than the North did. With support from these Loyalists, the British hoped to win the war. 1

At first, the new British strategy worked. They captured Savannah, Georgia, and Charleston, South Carolina. They defeated the Americans in every battle they fought. By the summer of 1780, the British controlled Georgia and South Carolina, and many Loyalists had come to help them.

The British also had the help of **Benedict Arnold.** Arnold had been the Patriot hero of the Battle of Saratoga. Later on, he secretly changed sides and became a British general. Patriots were shocked to hear that Arnold had changed sides. Today he is remembered as a traitor. A **traitor** is someone who is not loyal.

Benedict Arnold He betrayed the Patriot cause and fought for the British.

Skill and Strategy

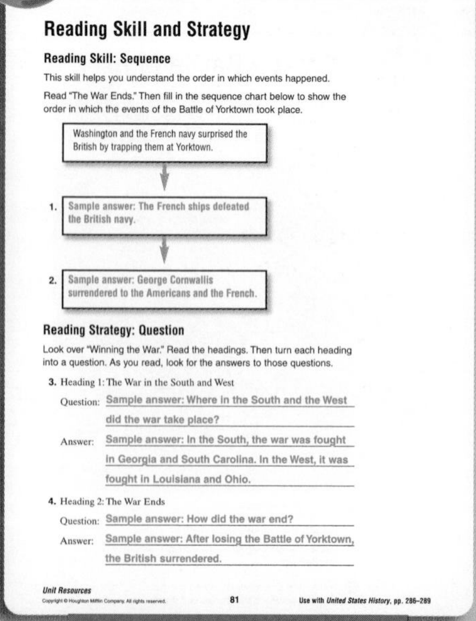

Reading Skill and Strategy

Reading Skill: Sequence

This skill helps you understand the order in which events happened.

Read "The War Ends." Then fill in the sequence chart below to show the order in which the events of the Battle of Yorktown took place.

Washington and the French navy surprised the British by trapping them at Yorktown.

1. Sample answer: The French ships defeated the British navy.

2. Sample answer: George Cornwallis surrendered to the Americans and the French.

Reading Strategy: Question

Look over "Winning the War." Read the headings. Then turn each heading into a question. As you read, look for the answers to those questions.

3. Heading 1: The War in the South and West
   Question: Sample answer: Where in the South and the West did the war take place?
   Answer: Sample answer: In the South, the war was fought in Georgia and South Carolina. In the West, it was fought in Louisiana and Ohio.

4. Heading 2: The War Ends
   Question: Sample answer: How did the war end?
   Answer: Sample answer: After losing the Battle of Yorktown, the British surrendered.

Unit Resources

81
Use with *United States History*, pp. 286–289

Unit Resources, p. 81

Background

Traitors and Spies

- For five years, Benedict Arnold was a Patriot. He switched sides when the British offered him the present-day equivalent of $1 million and an important position in their army.
- Ann Bates spied for the British by posing as a peddler. While selling thread and utensils to Patriot soldiers, she counted the soldiers and their weapons for the British.

Patriot Successes

Although the British won many battles in the South, southern Patriots fought back, often using surprise attacks. Groups of soldiers would sneak up on the British, attack, and retreat quickly. 2 Colonel **Francis Marion** was so good at attacking and retreating through swamps that he became known as the Swamp Fox.

The commander of the American army in the South, **Nathanael Greene,** made a plan to wear out the British army. His small army could move faster than the British. Greene forced the British army, led by General **Charles Cornwallis,** to chase him. This tired the British soldiers and used up their supplies of food and gunpowder. The British beat Greene in every major battle, but they could not destroy his army.

"We fight, get beat, rise and fight again," Greene said. In the spring of 1781, Cornwallis had to retreat. Greene's strategy to wear out the British had worked.

The British were losing the war in the West as well. **George Rogers Clark** and about 200 Patriots captured British forts in the Ohio River Valley. After Spain declared war on Britain in 1779, the governor of Louisiana, **Bernardo de Gálvez,** attacked British forts. His army captured forts at Baton Rouge, Natchez, Mobile, and Pensacola.

REVIEW What was Greene's strategy to defeat the British? He planned to make the British chase him until they wore out.

Battles in the South and West

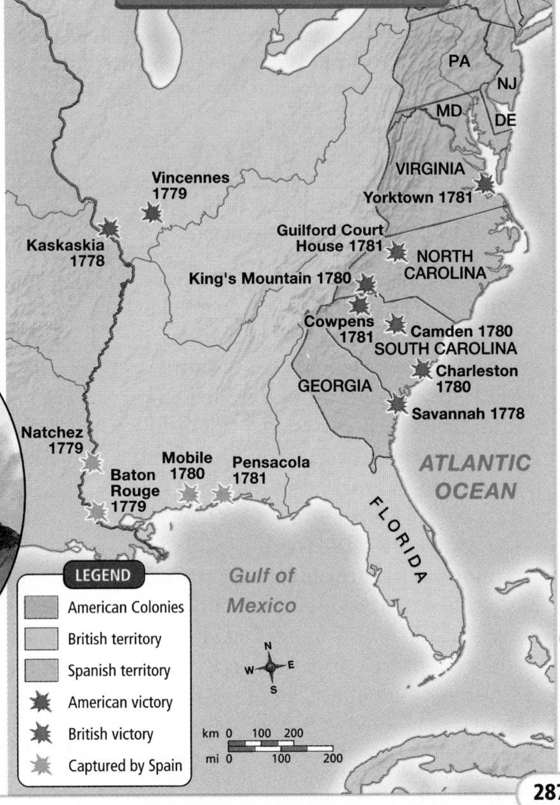

Later Battles This map shows the major battles during the last years of the American Revolution.

SKILL **Reading Maps** Which battles took place in 1781?
Yorktown, Cowpens, Guilford Court House, and Pensacola

Bernardo de Gálvez Spanish General de Gálvez captured British forts in cities near the Gulf of Mexico.

3

287

2 Teach

The War in the South and West

Talk About It

1 **Q History** Why did the British change their strategy and invade the South?

A The British thought that southern Loyalists would support them and help them win.

2 **Q Economics** What made Nathanael Greene's strategy successful?

A He forced the British army to chase him, which used up their supplies of food and gunpowder and led them to retreat.

3 **Q Visual Learning** Which battles did the Americans win in the South?

A Yorktown, Cowpens, Natchez, Baton Rouge, Mobile, and Pensacola

Vocabulary Strategy

strategy Tell students that *strategy* is often used to describe plans of action in war, but it is also used to describe plans of action in team sports, in politics, and in learning new skills or information.

traitor Explain to students that *traitor* comes from the Latin word for *betray* or *hand over.*

Reading Strategy: Question As students read, suggest they formulate their own questions and seek the answers. You may wish to use any unanswered questions as a jumping-off point for class discussion.

REACHING ALL LEARNERS

Leveled Practice

Extra Support

Have students make a "Who's Who in the War in the South and West" chart that lists each person's name, side taken in the War, and what he or she did during the war in the South and West. Verbal-linguistic; visual-spatial

Challenge

Tell students to suppose they are reporters assigned to cover one of the American military leaders mentioned in the lesson. Have them write a profile of the leader for their hometown newspaper. Verbal-linguistic

REACHING ALL LEARNERS

ELL

Intermediate/Advanced

- Model how to show dates and events in chronological order on a timeline.
- Have students work in pairs to make a timeline of important events in the lesson.

Verbal-linguistic; visual-spatial

The War Ends

Talk About It

4 Q Visual Learning Which army had the largest number of soldiers at the Battle of Yorktown?
A the American army

5 Q History What was the last big battle of the War for Independence?
A the Battle of Yorktown

6 Q History What two things did the Treaty of Paris give the United States?
A independence and land

7 Q History Who was Mercy Otis Warren?
A a writer

Vocabulary Strategy

surrender Tell students that *surrender* comes from a French word that means *to give back.*

Critical Thinking

Infer As part of the Treaty of Paris, the United States could have required the British to pay for the damage they caused to American property. The United States could also have taken British soldiers and commanders as prisoners and put them on trial. Why do you think the United States was satisfied with the Treaty as it was?

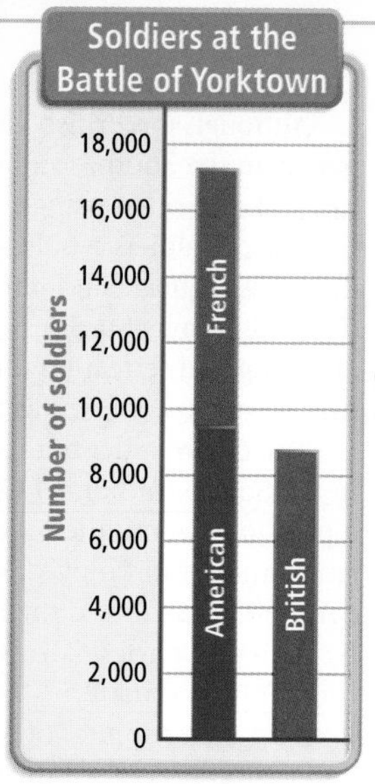

4

Attack on Yorktown American soldiers make a surprise attack on a British fort near Yorktown, Virginia. The graph to the right shows the number of soldiers who fought at Yorktown.

SKILL **Reading Graphs** About how many American and French soldiers fought together?
about 17,000

The War Ends

Main Idea By winning the Battle of Yorktown, the United States gained independence.

In the summer of 1781, the British army led by Cornwallis was camped at Yorktown, Virginia. When Washington learned of this, he marched his army south from New York to Virginia. Ships from the French navy sailed to meet him there. Cornwallis was taken by surprise. Washington's army and the French navy trapped the British army at Yorktown. The Americans and French fired their cannons at the British day and night.

At first, Cornwallis expected to be rescued. The British still had many soldiers and ships in New York City. However, the British navy could not defeat the French ships that blocked Yorktown.

After fighting for a week, Cornwallis realized he could not win the battle. He was surrounded by the Americans and the French, and no help was coming. On the morning of October 19, 1781, the British army surrendered at Yorktown. To **surrender** means to give up.

Over 7,000 British soldiers marched out of Yorktown, walking between long lines of French and American soldiers. The British laid down their weapons in a grassy field. The Battle of Yorktown was over.

Yorktown was the last big battle
of the War for Independence. The war 5
continued for two more years, but there was little fighting. The Americans had defeated one of the most powerful armies in the world. They had won the war and their independence.

288 • Chapter 8

Art

Design a Medal

- Tell students that George Washington designed the first Purple Heart; it was awarded to an American soldier for "singularly meritorious action." Today the Purple Heart is awarded to any soldier who is wounded or killed while serving in the armed forces.
- Have students design a medal that Revolutionary War soldiers would have been proud to wear.

Visual-spatial

Language Arts

Literature: Historical Fiction

Have students read a fictional account of the last battle of the Revolutionary War in Lynda Durrant's *Betsy Zane, The Rose of Fort Henry.* The events and heroine of the story are real. Betsy Zane was a 13-year-old girl who helped defend this West Virginia fort against more than 300 British and Native American forces in 1782.

Verbal-linguistic

The Treaty of Paris

On September 3, 1783, the United States and Britain signed the Treaty of Paris. The treaty gave Patriots the two things they wanted most. First, **King** ❻ **George III** agreed that the United States of America was an independent nation. Second, the Americans gained land. The United States now reached north to British Canada, west to the Mississippi River, and south to Spanish Florida.

The war was over, but Americans faced new challenges. One challenge was slavery. How could slavery exist in a country that believed in freedom and equality? African Americans began to demand their freedom in court, and some won. Several states passed laws against slavery.

Treaty of Paris 1783

Another challenge for Americans was how they would rule themselves. What kind of government would they create to replace King George III? Americans would have to decide. **Mercy Otis Warren**, a writer, called the new nation "a child just learning to walk." The new nation faced many questions as it took its place in the world. ❼

REVIEW What did the Treaty of Paris say? the U. S. was independent, and included more land than before

Lesson Summary

- The last part of the Revolution was fought in the West and the South.
- The United States won the war with the victory at Yorktown. With the Treaty of Paris in 1783, the United States gained its independence.

Why It Matters ...

By winning the Revolutionary War, Patriots achieved their dream of independence. Americans were free to set up their own government and rule themselves.

Lesson Review

1781 Battle of Yorktown — 1783 Treaty of Paris

1781 | 1782 | 1783 | 1784

1. **VOCABULARY** Write a sentence for each of the words below.
   traitor **surrender** **strategy**
2. **READING SKILL** What **sequence** of events led to the American victory at Yorktown?
3. **MAIN IDEA: Geography** Where was most of the fighting done in the last years of the War for Independence?
4. **MAIN IDEA: History** Why was Yorktown an important victory for the Americans?
5. **PEOPLE TO KNOW** Who was General **Cornwallis,** and what happened to him at Yorktown?
6. **TIMELINE SKILL** When was the Treaty of Paris signed?
7. **CRITICAL THINKING: Infer** Writer Mercy Otis Warren called the newly independent United States "a child just learning to walk." What do you think she meant?

WRITING ACTIVITY Write questions you would like to have asked the soldiers at Yorktown.

289

❸ Review/Assess

Review Tested Objectives

U4-17 Americans won important battles at Yorktown, Cowpens, Natchez, Baton Rouge, Mobile, and Pensacola.

U4-18 Americans won the war by using strategies and tactics that wore down their opponents.

Lesson Review Answers

1. Answers will vary.
2. Sequence chains should resemble the sequence chart shown below.
3. in the South and West
4. They gained independence with this victory.
5. He was the British general who surrendered to the Americans at Yorktown after being surprised and trapped there.
6. 1783
7. The newly independent country would face challenges as it learned how to govern itself.

HANDS ON Performance Task Rubric

4	Interview questions are clearly stated; responses are supported by information from the text; delivery is clear and easy to understand.
3	Interview questions are adequately stated; most responses are supported by information from the text; delivery is generally clear.
2	Interview questions are adequately stated, but responses are confused or poorly supported by information from the text; delivery is adequate.
1	Interview questions and responses are off topic; delivery is poor.

Study Guide/Homework

Vocabulary and Study Guide

Vocabulary

1. Draw a line connecting the vocabulary word to its meaning.

traitor	Someone who is not loyal
surrender	A plan of action
strategy	To give up

Study Guide

Read "Winning the War." Then fill in the compare and contrast chart below.

	What did the British do?	What did the Americans do?
The war in the South	2. Captured Savannah, Georgia, and Charleston, South Carolina	3. Fought back and defeated the British in 1781
The war in the West	Lost the war in the West	Won the war in the West
The Battle of Yorktown	4. Lost the Battle of Yorktown	5. Won the Battle of Yorktown

Unit Resources Copyright © Houghton Mifflin Company. All rights reserved. 82 Use with *United States History*, pp. 286–289

Unit Resources, p. 82

Reteach Minilesson

Use a sequence chart to reteach the American victory in the War for Independence.

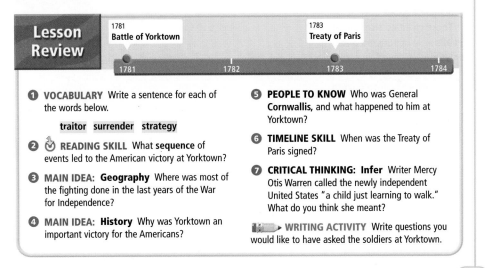

British invade the South and gain control of Georgia and South Carolina.

↓

Francis Marion leads successful surprise attacks against the British.

↓

Nathanael Greene wears out the British and forces them to retreat.

↓

British defeated at the Battle of Yorktown, the last big battle of the War for Independence.

www.eduplace.com/ss/hmss05/

Extend Quick Look

Teaching Option: Connect to the Core Lesson The time of America's birth was a time of dramatic changes throughout the world. This **Extend Lesson** helps students realize that the new nation was entering a world that was more global and less regional.

1 Teach the Extend Lesson

Connect to the Big Idea

Remind students that geography is about people, not just landforms and distance. As they look at this Extend Lesson, have them think about how economic developments and technological innovation changed the world in 1783.

A Changing World

Help students connect the text and the artwork with particular locations on the map.

Discuss with students events and persons depicted in this lesson that are familiar and unfamiliar. Encourage them to share what they know and ask questions.

Extend Lesson 4

Geography

A Global View, 1783

The American Revolution is over. What is happening in other lands? The American Revolution brought about a new nation in the late 1700s. Changes were taking place in other parts of the world as well.

Empires were expanding in the late 1700s. Trading around the world increased. Rulers sent explorers to search for new lands and resources. Trade and travel brought an exchange of goods and ideas.

These changes also meant that people were conquered and sometimes enslaved. In some places, people wanted liberty from their rulers. They wanted to govern themselves. Where were these places? Look on the map to find where revolutions were happening.

Canada
Britain has control of Canada, and traders explore the land. They are looking for furs and a route to the Pacific Ocean.

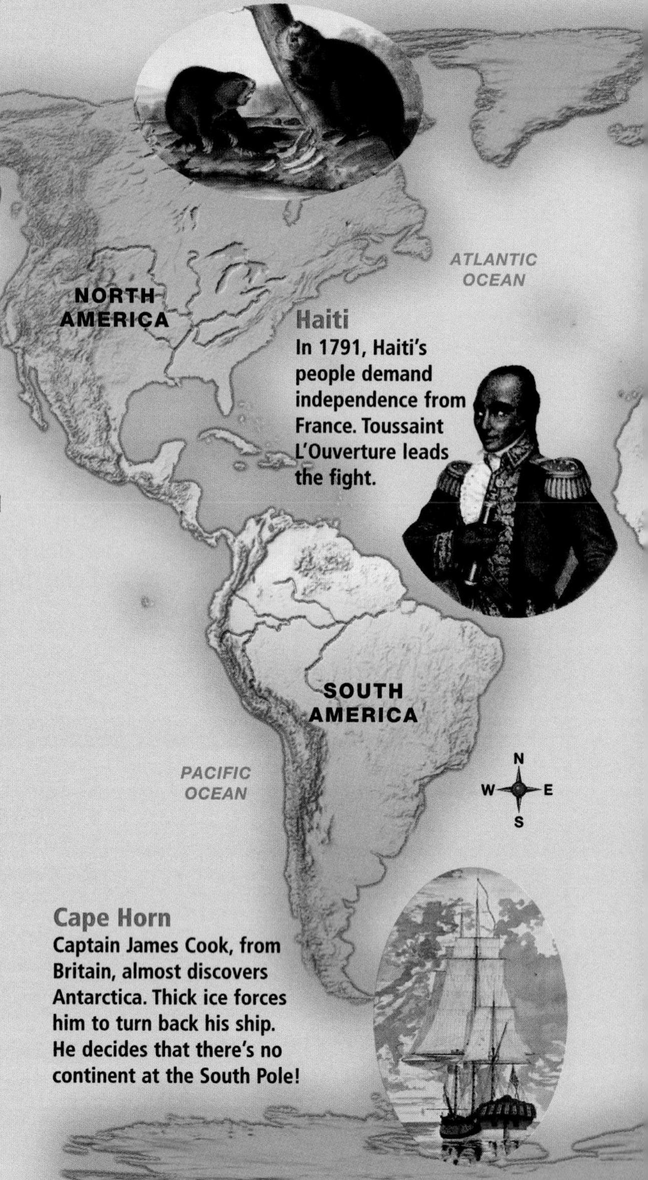

Haiti
In 1791, Haiti's people demand independence from France. Toussaint L'Ouverture leads the fight.

Cape Horn
Captain James Cook, from Britain, almost discovers Antarctica. Thick ice forces him to turn back his ship. He decides that there's no continent at the South Pole!

Reaching All Learners

Extra Support

Make Flash Cards

- To help students connect places and people, have them create flash cards.
- Each flash card can have the name of a person on the front. On the back, students should write the name of the part of the world with which he or she is associated.
- Pairs of students can quiz each other.

On Level

Travels with Captain Cook

- Point out to students that Captain James Cook is mentioned twice on the map. He visited Cape Horn and Australia.
- Have students research encyclopedias or other sources about Captain James Cook.
- Have them work in groups to compile a timeline of his life.

Challenge

A Bicentennial Map

- The United States celebrated its bicentennial on July 4, 1976.
- Have students find out about events that were going on in the world on that date.
- They can interview family members, use books, and read newspapers and magazines from the time.
- Ask them to work in groups to produce maps that depict "A Global View, 1976."

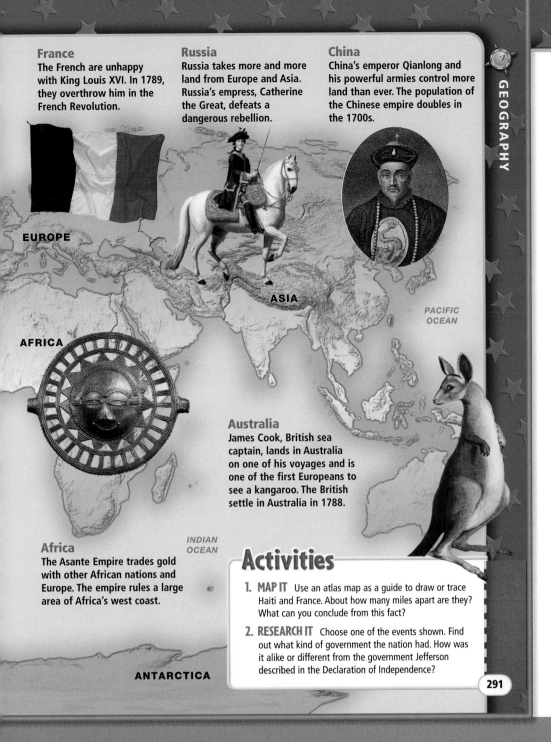

France
The French are unhappy with King Louis XVI. In 1789, they overthrow him in the French Revolution.

Russia
Russia takes more and more land from Europe and Asia. Russia's empress, Catherine the Great, defeats a dangerous rebellion.

China
China's emperor Qianlong and his powerful armies control more land than ever. The population of the Chinese empire doubles in the 1700s.

GEOGRAPHY

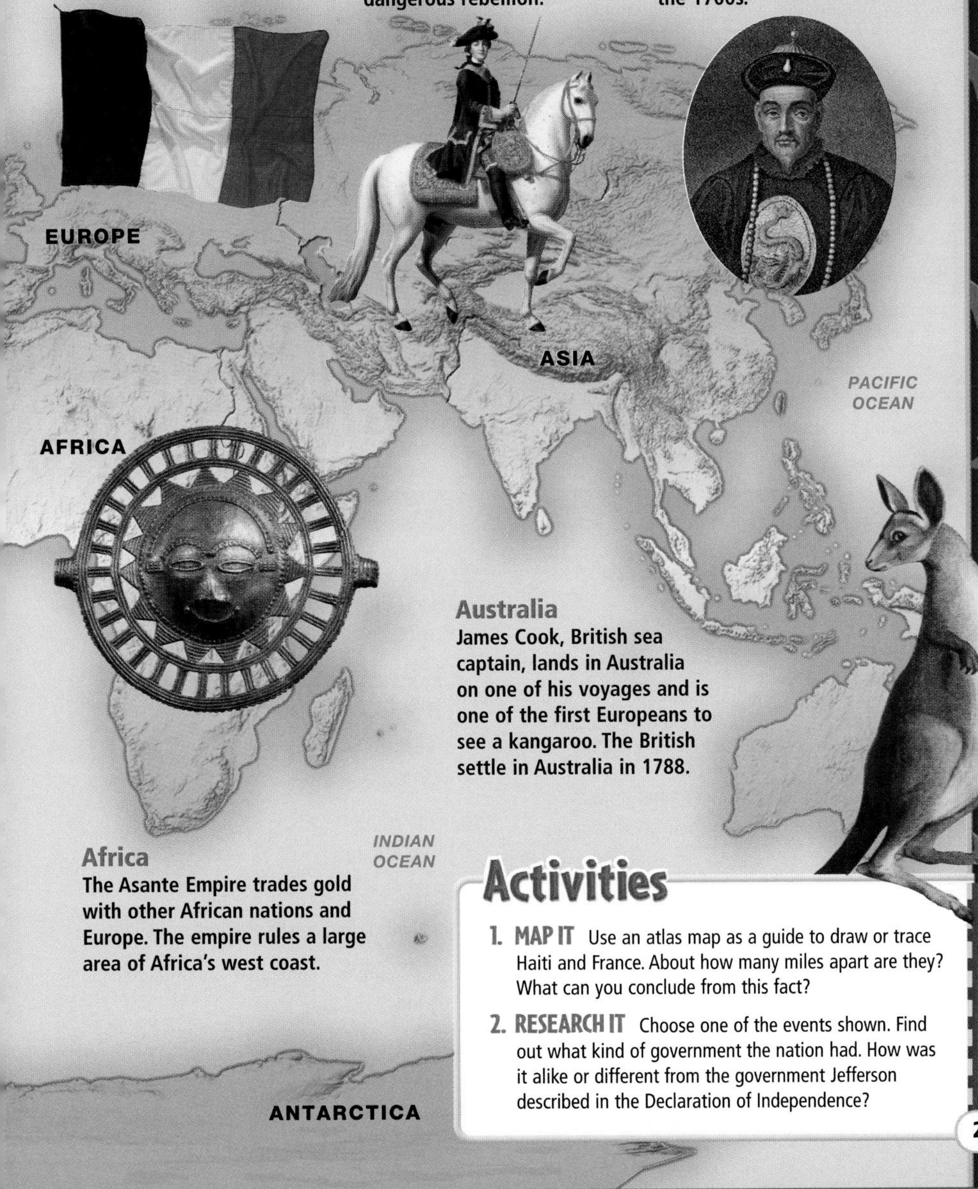

Australia
James Cook, British sea captain, lands in Australia on one of his voyages and is one of the first Europeans to see a kangaroo. The British settle in Australia in 1788.

Africa
The Asante Empire trades gold with other African nations and Europe. The empire rules a large area of Africa's west coast.

Activities

1. **MAP IT** Use an atlas map as a guide to draw or trace Haiti and France. About how many miles apart are they? What can you conclude from this fact?
2. **RESEARCH IT** Choose one of the events shown. Find out what kind of government the nation had. How was it alike or different from the government Jefferson described in the Declaration of Independence?

291

2 Leveled Activities

❶ **Map It** *For Extra Support*
To answer the question, students may need some review of how to use a map scale to determine distance.

❷ **Research It** *For Challenge* Students can present their findings as a written or oral report, or as a graphic presentation.

Pronunciation Help

Students may need help pronouncing the following names that are mentioned in the Extend Lesson:

Toussaint L'Ouverture (too SAN loo ver TYUR)

Qianlong (CHYAN LOONG)

ELL

REACHING ALL LEARNERS

Intermediate

- Help students connect the word *global* to the word *globe*.
- Explain that the suffix *-al* means "of."
- Have students contribute to a list of other words they may know that include this suffix, such as *local* or *regional*.

Science

Silk

- In China, Africa, and Europe, silk was prized above all other fibers for its beauty and strength, and was used in garments for royalty throughout the world.
- Provide students with a piece of silk cloth, as well as pieces of cotton and wool.
- Ask students to plan a way to test the strength of the three natural fibers.
- Have them carry out the test and present findings.

Graphic Organizer

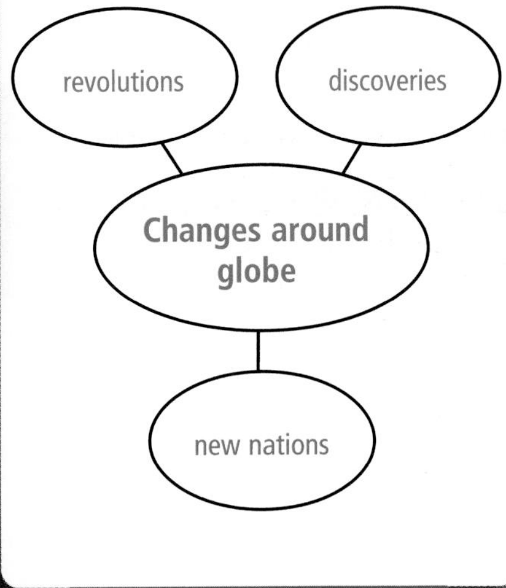

www.eduplace.com/ss/hmss05/

Chapter Review

✔ Tested Objectives

The lesson objective assessed by each question is shown in parentheses after the answer.

Visual Summary

1. Jefferson and Franklin presented the Declaration of Independence to the Second Continental Congress. *(Obj. U4-10)*
2. a turning point because it caused France to become America's ally *(Obj. U4-14)*
3. The British surrender ended the war *(Obj. U4-14)*
4. recognized America's independence and granted the new country land *(Obj. U4-18)*

Facts and Main Ideas

5. It convinced many colonists that separating from Britain was necessary. *(Obj. U4-10)*
6. Jefferson and four other delegates *(Obj. U4-10)*
7. If they waited they could sell their goods for more money. *(Obj. U4-13)*
8. The British surrender meant that the Americans gained their independence. *(Obj. U4-18)*
9. north to British Canada, west to the Mississippi River, and south to Spanish Florida *(Obj. U4-18)*

Vocabulary

10. **independence** *(Obj. U4-11)*
11. **neutral** *(Obj. U4-10)*
12. **rights** *(Obj. U4-10)*
13. **strategy** *(Obj. U4-18)*

Review and Test Prep

Visual Summary

1.–4. Write a description for each main event named below.

Declaration of Independence, 1776

Battle of Saratoga, 1777

Victory at Yorktown, 1781

Treaty of Paris, 1783

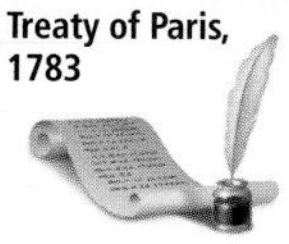

Facts and Main Ideas

✔ **TEST PREP** Answer each question below.

5. **History** Why was *Common Sense* an important document?
6. **Citizenship** Who wrote the Declaration of Independence?
7. **Economics** Why would some farmers and merchants not sell their goods during the war?
8. **History** Why was Yorktown an important victory for the Americans?
9. **Geography** What land did the United States gain in the Treaty of Paris?

Vocabulary

✔ **TEST PREP** Choose the correct word from the list below to complete each sentence.

independence, p. 262
rights, p. 264
neutral, p. 270
strategy, p. 286

10. In 1776, the colonies declared their _____ from Britain.
11. Some colonists chose to stay _____ instead of joining the Patriots or Loyalists.
12. _____ are freedoms that are protected by law.
13. The _____ of the British army was to invade the South.

Reading/Language Arts Wrap-Up

Reading Strategy: Question

Review with students the steps involved when they develop questions about a passage of text.

In pairs, have students take turns modeling the process of questioning as they read.

Individually, ask students to do a self-check: "How well did I practice questioning as I read?"

Writing Strategy

Explain to students that the process they use in questioning as they read can be used when they have to write questions. You may wish to review questions that students have written for Chapter 8. Guide students who want to revise their questions based on the discussion.

Apply Skills

TEST PREP **Map Skill** Study the battle map below. Then use your map skills to answer each question.

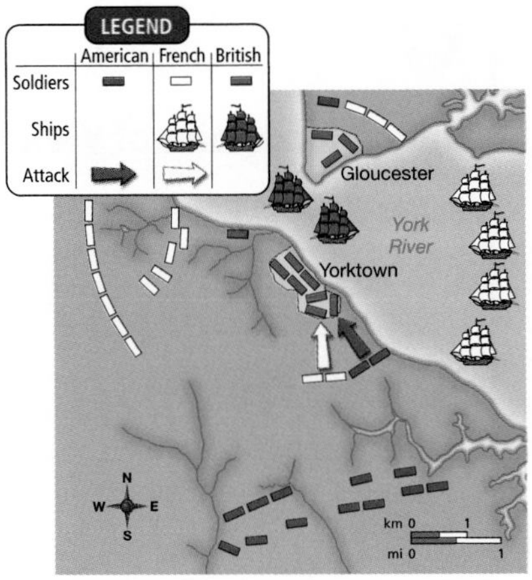

14. Where did the American and French armies attack the British?

A. Gloucester
B. York River
C. Yorktown
D. Richmond

15. Where were most of the French soldiers?

A. South of Yorktown
B. West of Yorktown
C. East of Yorktown
D. In Yorktown

Critical Thinking

TEST PREP Write a short paragraph to answer each question.

16. **Fact and Opinion** Were the ideas stated in the Declaration of Independence facts or opinions? Explain your answer.

17. **Cause and Effect** The British army had to fight many battles against Nathanael Greene's soldiers in the South. What effect did this have on the British army?

Timeline

Use the Chapter Summary Timeline above to answer the question.

18. In what year did the British and the Americans fight the last major battle of the War for Independence?

Activities

HANDS ON **Art Activity** Create a postage stamp that shows an important event that happened during the American Revolution.

Writing Activity Write a personal essay about a Patriot in this chapter. Describe what he or she did during the war and why you think this person's actions were important.

Technology
Writing Process Tips
Get help with your essay at
www.eduplace.com/kids/hmss05/

Technology

Test Generator

You can generate your own version of the chapter review by using the **Test Generator CD-ROM.**

Web Link

For more ideas, visit
www.eduplace.com/ss/hmss05/

Standards

National Standards

II b Identify key concepts such as conflict
II f Develop historical empathy
VI b Purpose of government
VI f Conditions that contribute to conflict
VII b Describe supply and demand
X a Origins of key ideals

Apply Skills

14. C *(Obj. U4-16)*
15. B *(Obj. U4-16)*

Critical Thinking

16. The Declaration of Independence announced America's desire to break with Britain and create its own government, as well as explained the reasons why the break was necessary. *(Obj. U4-11)*

17. Greene forced the British army to use up their precious supplies of food and gunpowder in chasing his forces, not in fighting a decisive battle. *(Obj. U4-17)*

Timeline

18. 1781 *(Obj. U4-18)*

Leveled Activities

HANDS ON Performance Task Rubric

4	Event shown is significant; picture is accurate; stamp details are all present.
3	Event shown is significant; picture is generally accurate; most stamp details are present.
2	Event shown is significant; picture contains some errors; few stamp details are present.
1	Event shown is not significant; picture is inaccurate; stamp details are absent.

Writing Rubric

4	Biographical information is accurate and supported by details; letter format is used correctly.
3	Biographical information is mostly accurate and supported by details; letter format is used.
2	Biographical information is somewhat accurate and supported by some details; letter format is attempted.
1	Biographical information is inaccurate; letter format not used.

Chapter Opener

Pages 294–295

30 minutes

Reading/Vocabulary

Chapter Reading Strategy:
Predict and Infer, p. 295

Resources

Grade Level Resources
- Vocabulary Cards, pp. 29–42

Reaching All Learners
- Challenge Activities, p. 87

Primary Sources Plus, p. 15

Big Idea Transparency 4

Interactive Transparency 4

Text & Music Audio CD

Lesson Planner & TR CD-ROM

eBook

eTE

Core Lesson 1

A New Nation

Pages 296–299

50 minutes

Tested Objectives

U4-18 Analyze the strengths and weaknesses of the Articles of Confederation.

U4-19 Identify problems facing the United States after the Revolutionary War.

Reading/Vocabulary

Reading Skill: Main Idea & Details

constitution	territory
citizen	ordinance

Cross-Curricular

Math, p. 298

Resources

Unit Resources:
- **Reading Skill/Strategy,** p. 83
- **Vocabulary/Study Guide,** p. 84

Reaching All Learners:
- **Lesson Summary,** p. 34
- **Support for Lang. Dev./ELL,** p. 131

Assessment Options:
- **Lesson Test,** p. 84

Extend Lesson 1

Economics

Chain of Debt

20–30 minutes

Pages 300–301

Focus: Why did some Massachusetts farmers owe so much money?

Core Lesson 2

Constitutional Convention

Pages 302–307

50 minutes

Tested Objectives

U4-20 Identify delegates to the Constitutional Convention.

U4-21 Explain compromises at the Constitutional Convention.

U4-22 Explain the Bill of Rights.

Reading/Vocabulary

Reading Skill: Problem & Solution

federal	compromise
republic	ratify

Cross-Curricular

Math, p. 305

Resources

Unit Resources:
- **Reading Skill/Strategy,** p. 85
- **Vocabulary/Study Guide,** p. 86

Reaching All Learners:
- **Lesson Summary,** p. 35
- **Support for Lang. Dev./ELL,** p. 132

Assessment Options:
- **Lesson Test,** p. 85

Extend Lesson 2

Citizenship

World Constitutions

20–30 minutes

Pages 308–309

Focus: Students see the influence of the U.S. Constitution around the world.

Skillbuilder

Citizenship Skill

Understand Point of View

Pages 310–311

20 minutes

Tested Objective

U4-23 Recognize and respect different points of view.

Reading/Vocabulary

point of view

Resources

Unit Resources:
- **Skill Practice,** p. 87

Skill Transparency 9

National Standards
I b How experiences may be interpreted differently **II e** People in different times and places view the world differently **VI b** Purpose of government **VI c** How government does /does not provide for needs and wants of people, establish order and security, and manage conflict **VI e** Local, state, and national government and representatives leaders **VI h** Tensions between the wants and needs and fairness, equity, and justice **IX b** Conflict, cooperation, and interdependence **X a** Key ideals of the United States' form of government **X b** Rights and responsibilities **X f** Actors that influence and shape public policy **X h** Policies and behaviors may or may not reflect ideals **X i** Public policies and public concerns

With the Program
CURRENT EVENTS from WEEKLY WR READER at www.eduplace.com

Core Lesson 3

The Constitution

Pages 312–317
50 minutes

Tested Objectives

U4-24 Describe the branches of the United States government and the ways that the powers of each are limited.

U4-25 Explain that the Constitution has changed.

Reading/Vocabulary

Reading Skill: Categorize

democracy, checks and balances, veto, unconstitutional, amendment

Cross-Curricular

Math, p. 315

Resources

Unit Resources:
- **Reading Skill/Strategy,** p. 88
- **Vocabulary/Study Guide,** p. 89

Reaching All Learners:
- **Lesson Summary,** p. 36
- **Support for Lang. Dev./ELL,** p. 133

Assessment Options:
- **Lesson Test,** p. 86

Extend Lesson 3

History
The Liberty Bell
20–30 minutes
Pages 318–319
Focus: How did one bell become an important symbol of freedom and liberty?

Core Lesson 4

President Washington

Pages 320–323
40 minutes

Tested Objectives

U4-26 Identify important policies established by President George Washington.

U4-27 Compare the views of Hamilton and Jefferson and describe their effect on American political parties.

Reading/Vocabulary

Reading Skill: Cause & Effect

inauguration, Cabinet, political party, interest, capital

Cross-Curricular

Math, p. 322

Resources

Unit Resources:
- **Reading Skill/Strategy,** p. 90
- **Vocabulary/Study Guide,** p. 91

Reaching All Learners:
- **Lesson Summary,** p. 37
- **Support for Lang. Dev./ELL,** p. 134

Assessment Options:
- **Lesson Test,** p. 87

Extend Lesson 4

Citizenship
Washington, D.C.
20–30 minutes
Pages 324–325
Focus: Meet some of the key people who helped plan and create our nation's capital.

Chapter Review

Pages 326–327
30 minutes

Resources

Assessment Options:
- Chapter 9 Test
- Test Generator

Chapter 9 Practice Options

Lesson 1 Skill and Strategy

TEST PREP

Reading Skill and Strategy

Reading Skill: Main Idea and Details

This skill helps you understand events by seeing how they are related.

Read "A New Nation." The large boxes contain the main idea for each section. Under each large box, write two details that support each main idea.

The Articles of Confederation gave Congress very little power.	The weak government could not solve the new nation's problems.
1. The states enjoyed more power than the national government.	3. Congress could not create taxes to pay off the nation's debts.
2. Congress could not set up an army or create taxes.	4. The government could not stop Shays's Rebellion because there was no army.

Reading Strategy: Predict and Infer

5. Look over "The Articles of Confederation." Then check the best prediction.
   - ✓ The Articles were the plan for creating a national government.
   - ___ The Articles acted as the state constitutions.
   - ___ The Articles made a strong national Congress.
6. Read "Problems for the New Nation." Then check the best inference.
   - ___ People had to pay expensive taxes to Congress.
   - ✓ The meeting in Philadelphia in 1787 led to the writing of the Constitution.
   - ___ Thomas Jefferson wanted to rewrite the Articles of Confederation.

Unit Resources 83 Use with *United States History*, pp. 296–299

Lesson 1 Vocabulary/Study Guide

TEST PREP

Vocabulary and Study Guide

Vocabulary

Write the definition of each vocabulary word below.

1. territory Land ruled by a national government that has no representatives in the government
2. constitution A written plan for government
3. ordinance A law
4. citizen An official member of a city, state, or nation
5. Use two of the words in a sentence.
   Sample answer: A constitution can give a citizen rights.

Study Guide

Read "The Articles of Confederation." Then fill in the cause and effects chart below.

Cause	Effects
The Articles of Confederation	Created a national government
	Could not make the states work together
	6. Gave Congress the power to declare war, make peace treaties, and print and borrow money
	7. Did not allow Congress to set up an army
	8. Did not allow Congress to tax or control trade

Unit Resources 84 Use with *United States History*, pp. 296–299

also in *Practice Book*, p. 50

Lesson 2 Skill and Strategy

TEST PREP

Reading Skill and Strategy

Reading Skill: Problem and Solution

This skill helps you see what problem some people faced and how they resolved it.

Read "Creating a New Government." Then fill in the problem and solution chart below. How did the Constitutional Convention solve each problem?

Problem	Solution
Small states disagreed with a Congress based on population.	1. Roger Sherman suggested the Great Compromise.
The delegates argued about slavery.	2. The delegates compromised and halted the slave trade after 1808.

Reading Strategy: Predict and Infer

3. Read "Leaders of the Convention." Then check the best inference.
   - ___ The delegates made the states stronger than the Articles did.
   - ✓ The convention established a new system of government.
   - ___ The Articles of Confederation were not changed during the convention.
4. Read "Creating a New Government." Then complete the prediction.
   The slavery issue was important to the delegates because Sample answer: Some states would not support the Constitution if slavery was illegal.

Unit Resources 85 Use with *United States History*, pp. 302–307

Lesson 2 Vocabulary/Study Guide

TEST PREP

Reading Skill and Strategy

Reading Skill: Categorize

This skill helps you understand and remember what you have read by organizing facts into groups, or categories.

Read "A Plan for Government." Then fill in the categorization chart below. What responsibilities does each branch of the government have?

Legislative	Executive	Judicial
1. Congress passes laws, raises money through taxes, and uses the money for the nation.	2. The President carries out the laws and is the commander of the military.	3. The courts interpret the laws, and the Supreme Court governs all other courts.

Reading Strategy: Predict and Infer

4. The following statements are based on "Changing the Constitution." Combine the information in the statements with what you already know. Then make an inference from the information given to complete the statement.

   Statement 1: A change to the Constitution is called an amendment.

   Statement 2: Two-thirds of Congress must approve an amendment.

   Statement 3: Three-fourths of the states must ratify an amendment.

   A great majority of Americans must agree with the change for it to be added to the Constitution
5. Read "The Growth of Democracy." Then make a prediction about how the rights of U.S. citizens might change in the future.
   Sample answer: Even more groups will be given equal protection of their rights.

Unit Resources 88 Use with *United States History*, pp. 312–317

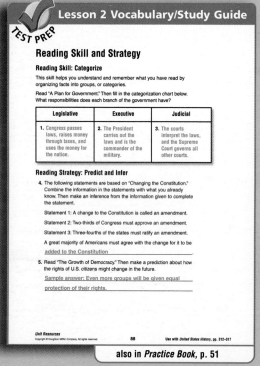

also in *Practice Book*, p. 51

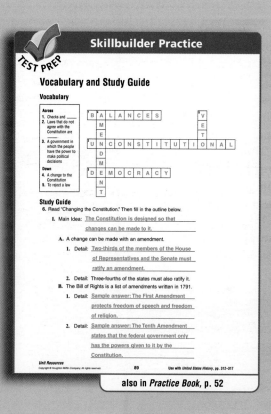

Skillbuilder Practice

TEST PREP

Vocabulary and Study Guide

Vocabulary

Across
1. Checks and ____
2. Laws that do not agree with the Constitution are ____
3. A government in which the people have the power to make political decisions

Down
4. A change to the Constitution
5. To reject a law

Crossword answers: 1. BALANCES; 2. UNCONSTITUTIONAL; 3. DEMOCRACY; 4. AMENDMENT; 5. VETO

Study Guide

6. Read "Changing the Constitution." Then fill in the outline below.
   - I. Main Idea: The Constitution is designed so that changes can be made to it.
     - A. A change can be made with an amendment.
       1. Detail: Two-thirds of the members of the House of Representatives and the Senate must ratify an amendment.
       2. Detail: Three-fourths of the states must also ratify it.
     - B. The Bill of Rights is a list of amendments written in 1791.
       1. Detail: Sample answer: The First Amendment protects freedom of speech and freedom of religion.
       2. Detail: Sample answer: The Tenth Amendment states that the federal government only has the powers given to it by the Constitution.

Unit Resources 89 Use with *United States History*, pp. 312–317

also in *Practice Book*, p. 52

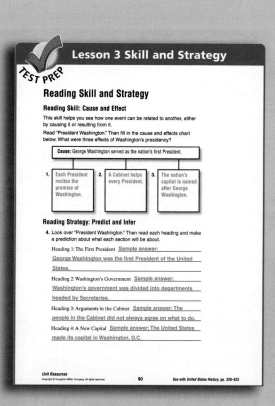

Lesson 3 Skill and Strategy

TEST PREP

Reading Skill and Strategy

Reading Skill: Cause and Effect

This skill helps you see how one event can be related to another, either by causing it or resulting from it.

Read "President Washington." Then fill in the cause and effects chart below. What were three effects of Washington's presidency?

Cause: George Washington served as the nation's first President.

1.	2.	3.
Each President recites the promise of Washington.	A Cabinet helps every President.	The nation's capital is named after George Washington.

Reading Strategy: Predict and Infer

4. Look over "President Washington." Then read each heading and make a prediction about what each section will be about.

   Heading 1: The First President Sample answer: George Washington was the first President of the United States.

   Heading 2: Washington's Government Sample answer: Washington's government was divided into departments headed by Secretaries.

   Heading 3: Arguments in the Cabinet Sample answer: The people in the Cabinet did not always agree on what to do.

   Heading 4: A New Capital Sample answer: The United States made its capital in Washington, D.C.

Unit Resources 90 Use with *United States History*, pp. 320–323

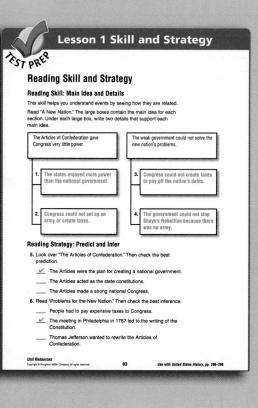

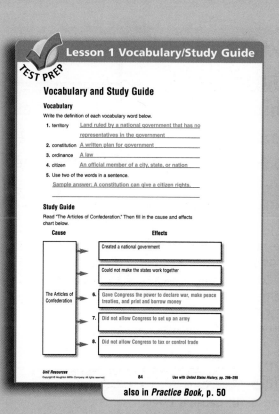

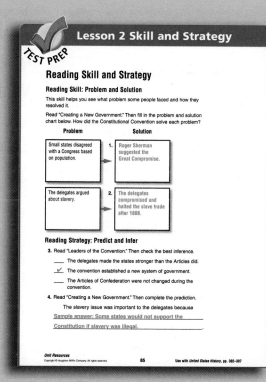

Lesson 3 Vocabulary/Study Guide

TEST PREP

Vocabulary and Study Guide

Vocabulary

Solve the clue and write the answer in the blank. Then find the word in the puzzle. Look up, down, forward, and backward. Look for a bonus word!

1.	An agreement reached in which each side gives up something that it wants compromise
2.	A government in which the citizens elect leaders to represent them republic
3.	A system in which the states share power with the central government federal
4.	To accept or officially approve ratify
	Bonus Word: freedom

C	O	X	B	C	N	R	M	E	A
W	J	S	K	O	L	T	I	H	U
V	X	L	D	M	Y	I	E	R	W
A	Q	R	E	P	U	B	L	I	C
F	E	D	E	R	A	L	S	P	E
A	K	G	F	O	F	Z	T	G	C
S	C	H	P	M	H	B	U	D	Q
M	R	A	T	I	F	Y	J	N	G
D	M	Y	K	S	L	V	O	I	J
N	F	R	E	E	D	O	M	Z	B

Study Guide

5. Read "Leaders of the Convention." Then fill in the blanks below.

Fifty-five delegates met in Philadelphia in 1787 for the Constitutional Convention. They wanted to create a republic, or a government in which citizens elect leaders. One delegate, James Madison, had a plan for a new system of government. Other important delegates were George Washington and Benjamin Franklin.

6. Read "Creating a New Government." Then fill in the blanks below.

The delegates wanted a federal system that allows states to share power. The Great Compromise divided Congress into two parts, the Senate and the House of Representatives. After the delegates made decisions, they had to ratify the Constitution.

Unit Resources

86

Use with *United States History*, pp. 302–307

also in *Practice Book*, p. 53

Lesson 4 Skill and Strategy

TEST PREP

Skillbuilder: Understand Point of View

"I have no fear but that the result of our experiment [new government] will be that men may be trusted to govern themselves without a master."

—Thomas Jefferson

"It has been observed that a pure democracy, it if were practicable [attainable], would be the most perfect government. Experience has proved that no position [opinion] is more false than this."

—Alexander Hamilton

Practice

1. From reading the chapter, what do you already know about Alexander Hamilton's experience and beliefs? Sample answer: He was a Federalist who wanted a strong central government.
2. What was Alexander Hamilton's point of view? People do not govern themselves well; strong central government is needed.
3. What was Thomas Jefferson's point of view? People are able to make good decisions and govern themselves.
4. Explain how knowing these two points of view can help you understand why Jefferson was against the national bank and why Hamilton was for the national bank. Sample answer: A national bank would give the federal government more control of money and make it stronger.

Apply

What experiences and beliefs affect your own point of view about the powers of the federal government? On a separate sheet of paper, write a paragraph expressing your point of view about government. Paragraphs should explain the students' points of view.

Unit Resources

87

Use with *United States History*, pp. 310–311

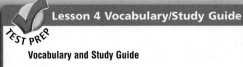

Lesson 4 Vocabulary/Study Guide

TEST PREP

Vocabulary and Study Guide

Vocabulary

Write the vocabulary word that matches each definition.

1. A group chosen by the President to help run the executive branch Cabinet
2. The city where the government meets capital
3. A group of people who share similar ideas about government political party
4. The official ceremony to make someone President inauguration
5. What people pay to borrow money interest
6. Use two of the vocabulary words in a sentence. Sample answer: The political party held a meeting in the nation's capital.

Study Guide

Read "Arguments in the Cabinet." Then fill in the Venn diagram below.

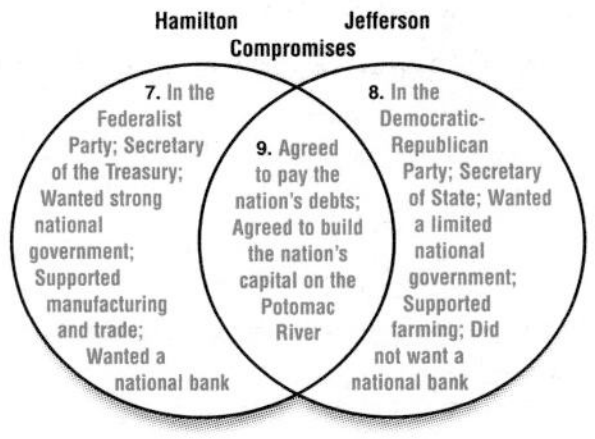

Unit Resources

91

Use with *United States History*, pp. 320–323

also in *Practice Book*, p. 54

Chapter 9 Assessment Options

Chapter 9 Test

TEST PREP

Chapter 9 Test

Test Your Knowledge

Match each word to its definition.

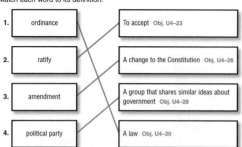

1. ordinance	To accept Obj. U4–23
2. ratify	A change to the Constitution Obj. U4–26
3. amendment	A group that shares similar ideas about government Obj. U4–28
4. political party	A law Obj. U4–20

Circle the letter of the best answer.

5. What was the Great Compromise? Obj. U4–22
   - (A.) a plan to divide Congress into two parts
   - B. a way to vote for the president of the national convention
   - C. an official ceremony for people to become U.S. citizens
   - D. an official ceremony to make someone U.S. President

6. In Alexander Hamilton's view, what was one role of the national government? Obj. U4–28
   - F. to support farming
   - G. to not take away states' rights
   - H to be limited
   - (J.) to support manufacturing and trade

7. What was one of George Washington's accomplishments as President of the United States? Obj. U4–27
   - A. He joined the Federalist Party.
   - (B.) He approved a law to create a national bank.
   - C. He signed the Northwest Ordinance.
   - D. He signed the Land Ordinance of 1785.

8. How are the powers of each branch of the national government limited? Obj. U4–25
   - F. through a process of voting
   - G. through a process of vetoing
   - (H.) through a process of checks and balances
   - J. through a process of debating

Chapter 9 Test

TEST PREP

Apply Your Knowledge

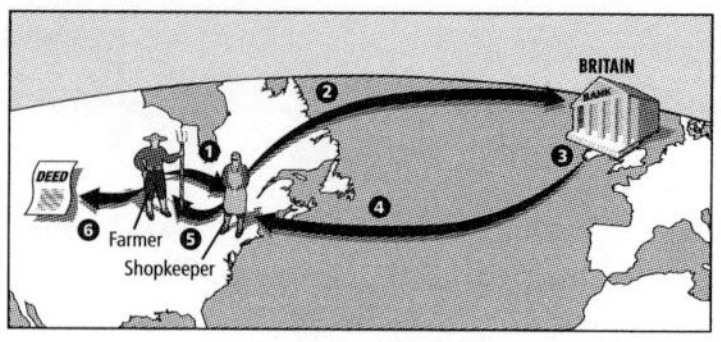

A chain of borrowing linked farmers in Massachusetts to bankers in London.

1. Farmers buy goods on credit from shopkeepers.
2. Shopkeepers borrow money from merchants.
3. Merchants (not shown on diagram) borrow money from British banks.
4. Merchants demand money from shopkeepers.
5. Shopkeepers demand money from farmers.
6. Farmers have to sell their land.

Use the diagram to answer the following questions.

9. What is the relationship between farmers and shopkeepers shown by arrow 1 in the diagram? Obj. U4–19
   - A. The shopkeepers buy goods from the bank.
   - B. The merchants borrow money from the farmers.
   - (C.) The farmers buy goods from the shopkeepers.
   - D. The banks demand money from the shopkeepers.

10. Why did the states seize, or take away, farmers' land? Obj. U4–19
    - F. The farmers had no crops to sell to the other states.
    - (G.) The farmers could not pay their debts and the states' high taxes.
    - H. The farmers did not approve the Articles of Confederation.
    - J. The farmers did not want to borrow money from the states.

Apply the Reading Skill: Categorize

Read the passage below. Then answer the question. Obj. U4–21

> James Madison created the Virginia Plan. This plan called for a national government with three parts. Delegates from small states did not like the way states would be represented in Congress. Roger Sherman suggested that Congress have two parts. This solution was called the Great Compromise.

11. Categorize the roles that James Madison and Roger Sherman had in the Great Compromise.
    Madison created a plan for a national government with three parts. Roger Sherman suggested that Congress have two parts.

Chapter 9 Test

TEST PREP

Test the Skill: Understand Point of View

> Like many Americans, George Washington felt an urgent need to create a new, stronger national government. He feared that a weak national government would not be able to stop fighting between states or against the national government. This would destroy the new country.
>
> Many Americans were afraid a strong national government could become as unfair as Great Britain's had been. Patrick Henry, for example, refused to be a delegate to the 1787 convention. When he was asked why, the famous speaker answered simply, "I smelt a rat."

12. Why did many Americans want a weak national government? Obj. U4–24
    They did not want a strong national government like Britain's.

Summarize in your own words both points of view from the passage. Obj. U4–24

13. George Washington: Sample answer: The country had to be preserved. A strong national government was the best way to preserve it.

14. Patrick Henry: Sample answer: He did not trust what was happening, and he did not attend the convention.

Apply the Skill

15. Thomas Jefferson and Alexander Hamilton had different points of view about how the government should act. With whom do you agree? Summarize that person's point of view, and explain why you agree with it. Obj. U4–24
    Sample answer: Thomas Jefferson: He thought that the central government should be limited and not take away states' rights; he thought government should support farmers; I agree because I think the rights of the states are important and should be protected.

Chapter 9 Test

TEST PREP

Think and Write

16. **Short Response:** Describe the role of each branch of the national government. Obj. U4–24
    - Legislative branch: To make laws
    - Executive branch: To carry out laws
    - Judicial branch: To decide the meaning of laws

17. **Critical Thinking: Draw Conclusions** How have amendments to the Constitution helped make the United States a better democracy? Obj. U4–26
    Sample answer: At first, the Constitution did not protect the rights of all Americans. It only protected the rights of white men. Over time, people realized that a true democracy gives everyone equal rights and that the Constitution should change to protect everyone's rights.

18. **Extended Response:** Write a speech from the point of view of one of the delegates that attended the Constitutional Convention. In your speech, persuade others to agree with this point of view. State the point of view clearly and offer strong reasons to support it. Write your speech on a separate sheet of paper. Obj. U4–21 Speeches may refer to different points of view about the Virginia Plan, the Great Compromise, and the issue of slavery.

Self-Assessment

Do I think replacing the Articles of Confederation with the Constitution was a good idea? Why or why not?

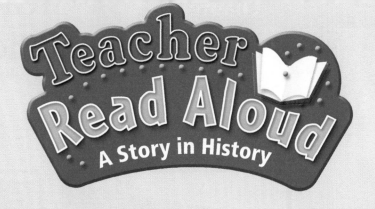

Teacher Read Aloud
A Story in History

You can read the following fiction selection to students before beginning the chapter.

Activate Prior Knowledge
Ask students to share what they know about the Constitutional Convention in 1787. Explain that the Read-Aloud selection presents what a delegate at the convention might have experienced.

Preview the Chapter
Have students skim the section Goals of the Convention on page 303 of their books. Ask them to find similarities and differences between the information in this section and the details mentioned in the Read Aloud.

Read-Aloud Vocabulary
Explain that a **constitution** is a written plan for government. A **federal** system shares power between the states and a central government.

Preview the Reading Strategy
Predict/Infer Explain to students that the reading strategy they will use in this chapter is predicting, or guessing what will happen next based on information they already have. You may wish to use the Read Aloud to model the strategy.

Think Aloud *The person in the first paragraph is a delegate at the Constitutional Convention. He describes how the delegates are arguing. The title "A Long Summer in Independence Hall" tells me that the convention will probably last all summer. I think I'm going to hear about one delegate's experience at this convention.*

A Long Summer in Independence Hall

Patience. That's the one thing a delegate at the Constitutional Convention can't afford to be without. I should know, because I've been sitting in this hot, stuffy hall in Philadelphia for days now, waiting for everyone to agree on a new **constitution** that will unite our country. Will there ever be an end to the bitter arguments?

One delegate, James Madison of Virginia, seems to keep calm despite the heat and the bickering. There he sits, taking notes in his journal again. Someday it should make amusing reading! Perhaps all that writing helps him think more clearly than the rest of us, because he's hit upon a brilliant plan for our new government. It will be a **federal** system, one that allows the states to keep some of their rights while giving others to the central government. Most delegates seem to like this plan.

I know Madison's idea suits me. Yet there has arisen a question about representation. How best to ensure that each state's interests are protected? Large states want one plan, small states want another—and for the arguing, there is no end in sight. What I would give to be outdoors, beneath the shade of an oak tree right now!

If we can get all the delegates to settle their disagreements, perhaps we'll escape from this hall by autumn. What a delight it would be to breathe fresh air again!

Begin the Chapter

Chapter Quick Look

Core Lesson 1 explores the government created by the Articles of Confederation.

Core Lesson 2 describes the Constitutional Convention.

Core Lesson 3 discusses the Constitution and Amendments.

Core Lesson 4 focuses on President Washington.

Vocabulary Preview

Use the vocabulary cards to preview the key vocabulary words before starting the lessons and to prepare students to understand the content of the chapter.

Vocabulary Strategy

Vocabulary strategies for this chapter:

- Mnemonic devices, p. 320
- Word origins, pp. 296, 302
- Word roots, pp. 302, 312

Vocabulary Help

Vocabulary card for constitution Ask students to notice part of the word "constitute" in *constitution*. To constitute means to make something out of various parts. The Constitution of the United States is a written document that explains the parts of the United States government.

Vocabulary card for amendment Tell students that the Constitution has many amendments, which are called by their numbers. Ask students if they can name any.

Chapter 9 Creating a Nation

Technology
e • glossary
e • word games
www.eduplace.com/kids/hmss05/

Vocabulary Preview

constitution

During the Revolutionary War, each state government had its own **constitution.** Many of these written plans of government became models for the U.S. Constitution. **page 296**

ratify

To **ratify** the Constitution, nine states had to accept it officially. New Hampshire became the ninth state in June 1788.
page 306

Chapter Timeline

1781 Articles of Confederation

1787 Constitutional Convention

1780 — 1783 — 1786

Background

Government Terms

Tell students that as they read this chapter, they will find more vocabulary words about government:

- *federal, republic,* p. 303
- *democracy,* p. 312
- *checks and balances, veto, unconstitutional,* p. 314
- *Cabinet,* p. 321
- *political party, capital,* p. 322

Explain that these terms are used by people to describe the United States government and its ways of functioning.

Vocabulary

Use the following graphic organizer to discuss the word "ratify."

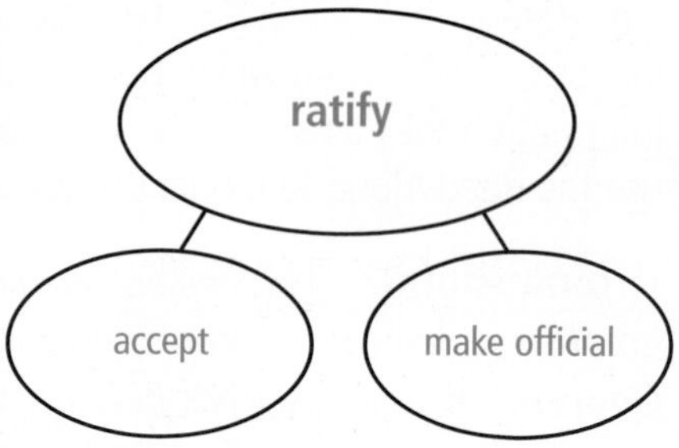

Reading Strategy

Predict and Infer Use this strategy as you read this chapter.

Quick Tip: Look at the pictures in a lesson to predict what it will be about.

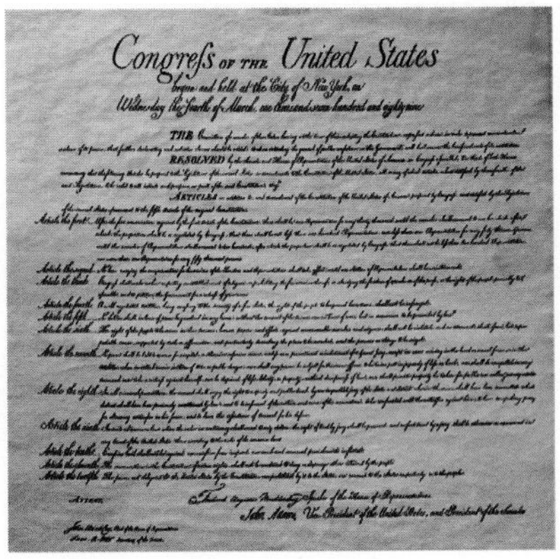

amendment

An **amendment** is a change to the Constitution. The first ten amendments, called the Bill of Rights, protect the rights of the people of the United States. page 316

inauguration

The ceremony making George Washington President was held in April 1789. This first **inauguration** was in New York City, the capital at the time. page 321

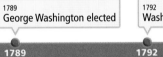

1789 George Washington elected

1792 Washington, D.C. founded

1789 — 1792 — 1795

Using the Timeline

- Direct students to look at the timeline on pages 294 and 295. Point out the segments of the timeline. Ask them how many years passed between the Constitutional Convention and the election of President Washington. 2
- Ask students who Washington, D.C. was named for. Do they know what the D.C. stands for? the District of Columbia, an area that is not governed by any of the states

Reading Strategy: Predict/Infer

To predict or infer, the reader uses information that he or she has. When predicting, the reader uses that information to make an informed guess about what will happen next. When inferring, the reader uses information to "read between the lines," and draw out information that the author has not explicitly stated. Explain to students that *predict* and *infer* are different, but related. Both are based on using knowledge at hand to determine what is not known.

To predict, a reader should ask the question, "What will happen next?"

To infer, a reader should ask the question, "Based on what I know, what can I figure out about this?"

Students can practice this reading strategy throughout this chapter, including on their Skill and Strategy pages.

Leveled Practice

Reaching All Learners

Extra Support

Ask students to match the words below with the vocabulary words they describe:

document approve ceremony addition

Verbal-linguistic

Challenge

Have students take the government words from the Background list on page 294 and find the definitions for them in the chapter. Ask students to write the words and their definitions in alphabetic order. Verbal-linguistic

ELL

Reaching All Learners

All Proficiency Levels

Ask students to think about what happens at an inauguration and what people are there. Have each student write a list of words that he or she thinks describes an inauguration and then write the antonym of each word. In pairs, each student should look at another's list and circle the correct words that describe an inauguration.

public	private
special	ordinary
silly	serious

Verbal-linguistic

Tested Objectives

U4-18 History Analyze the strengths and weaknesses of the Articles of Confederation.

U4-19 History Identify economic and political problems facing the United States after the Revolutionary War.

Lesson Quick Look

This lesson discusses the successes and weaknesses of the government created by the Articles of Confederation.

Teaching Option: Extend Lesson 1 explains how the farmers who took part in Shays's Rebellion got into debt.

1 Get Set to Read

Preview Ask students to describe the changes shown taking place in the United States by the map on page 297.

Reading Skill: Main Idea and Details Details might include problems, such as states printed their own money and people disagreed about what it was worth; Congress had problems paying war debts; Congress could not keep order or stop Shays's Rebellion.

Build on What You Know Ask students to describe what a leader does for a group. Explain that without a leader, the thirteen states accomplished very little.

Vocabulary

constitution *noun,* a written plan of how a country's government will work

citizen *noun,* an official member of a city, state, or nation

territory *noun,* an area of land that is ruled by a government; a frontier region before it became a U.S. state

ordinance *noun,* a law

Core Lesson 1

A New Nation

1780 1785 1790 1795 1800

1781–1787

VOCABULARY

constitution
citizen
territory
ordinance

Vocabulary Strategy

territory

Territory comes from a word that means earth. A territory is a section of land.

READING SKILL

Main Idea and Details

As you read, list details that support the second main idea in the lesson.

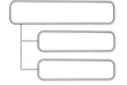

Build on What You Know Have you ever been part of a group whose members worked well together? After the War for Independence, the 13 states did not always work well together. Congress could not make them cooperate.

The Articles of Confederation

Main Idea The Articles of Confederation gave Congress very little power.

During the Revolutionary War, each American colony became a separate state. Each state had its own laws and constitution. A written plan for government is a **constitution**.

Americans did not want to give up power to a strong central government. They had fought the war for the right to self-government. State constitutions gave their citizens the right to make all the laws that would govern them. A **citizen** is an official member of a city, a state, or a nation.

Although the states did not want a strong central government, they needed to work together as one country. The Continental Congress created a plan for a national government. The plan was called the Articles of Confederation. The Articles created a weak national government that left most power with the states. The states accepted the Articles in 1781.

The Articles gave Congress the power to declare war, make peace treaties, and make treaties with other nations, including American Indian nations. It could print and borrow money. There were many powers, however, that Congress did not have. It could not set up an army, control trade, or create taxes. 1 2

Skill and Strategy

Reading Skill and Strategy

Reading Skill: Main Idea and Details

This skill helps you understand events by seeing how they are related.

Read "A New Nation." The large boxes contain the main idea for each section. Under each large box, write two details that support each main idea.

The Articles of Confederation gave Congress very little power.

1. The states enjoyed more power than the national government.
2. Congress could not set up an army or create taxes.

The weak government could not solve the new nation's problems.

3. Congress could not create taxes to pay off the nation's debts.
4. The government could not stop Shays's Rebellion because there was no army.

Reading Strategy: Predict and Infer

5. Look over "The Articles of Confederation." Then check the best prediction.
   - ✓ The Articles were the plan for creating a national government.
   - ___ The Articles acted as the state constitutions.
   - ___ The Articles made a strong national Congress.
6. Read "Problems for the New Nation." Then check the best inference.
   - ___ People had to pay expensive taxes to Congress.
   - ✓ The meeting in Philadelphia in 1787 led to the writing of the Constitution.
   - ___ Thomas Jefferson wanted to rewrite the Articles of Confederation.

Unit Resources

83
Use with *United States History*, pp. 296–299

Unit Resources, p. 83

Background

Early Government

- John Hanson of Maryland was the first person to preside over the Congress under the Articles of Confederation. He declared the fourth Thursday of November to be Thanksgiving.
- Congress made treaties with American Indian leaders. Many American Indians rejected the treaties because their leaders had not consulted them.

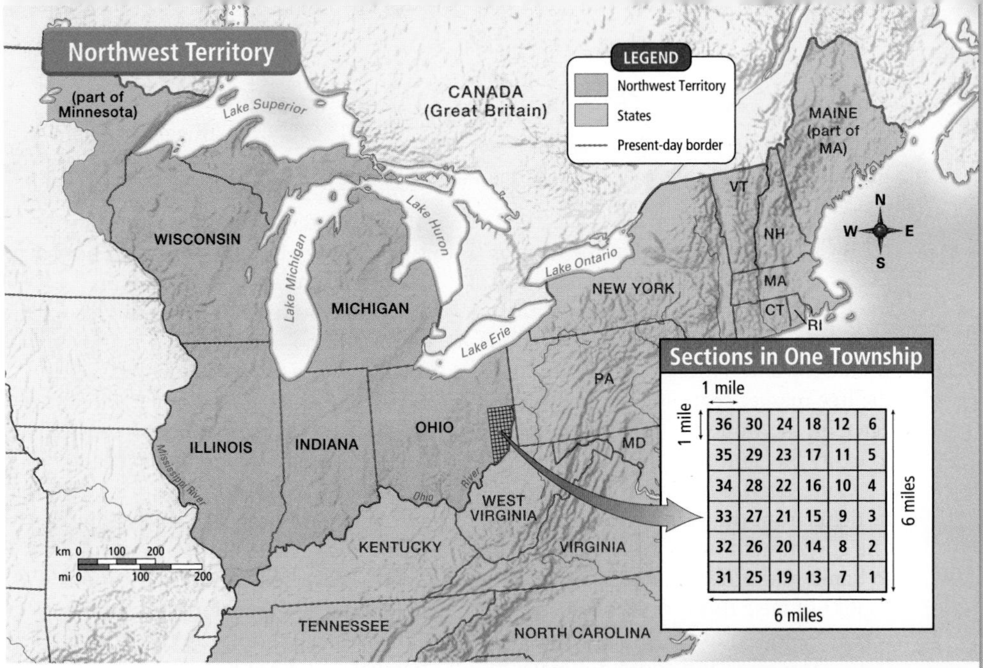

Townships Land in the Northwest Territory was measured and sold in square plots, as the grid on the map shows. These plots, which formed townships, created fields that looked like a patchwork quilt (right).

The Northwest Territory

Congress had to decide what to do with the land won in the Revolution. This western land was known as the Northwest Territory. A **territory** is land ruled by a national government but which has no representatives in the government.

As settlers moved to the Northwest Territory, Congress made treaties with American Indians to gain control of more land. Then Congress passed two ordinances to organize the Northwest Territory. An **ordinance** is a law.

The first law, the Land Ordinance of 1785, explained how the new land would be measured, divided, and sold.

The second law, the Northwest Ordinance of 1787, explained the government of the Northwest Territory. This law described how a territory could become a state. It also made slavery against the law in the Northwest Territory.

REVIEW What did Congress do to organize the Northwest Territory? passed the Land Ordinance of 1785 and the Northwest Ordinance of 1787

297

Leveled Practice

Extra Support

Have students **write a letter** to the editor of a 1781 newspaper. Their letter should express their view of the government created by the Articles of Confederation. Verbal-linguistic

Challenge

Have students **write a song** about the Articles of Confederation. If time allows, have them share their work with the class. Musical-auditory

ELL

Intermediate

- Have students **illustrate** one of the powers that Congress had under the Articles of Confederation.
- Below the picture, they should **write a sentence** describing the power they illustrated.

Visual-spatial; verbal-linguistic

2 Teach

The Articles of Confederation

Talk About It

1 **Q Citizenship** What powers did the Articles of Confederation give Congress?

A declare war, make treaties with other nations, and print and borrow money

2 **Q Citizenship** What powers did Congress lack?

A It could not set up an army, control trade, or tax.

Vocabulary Strategy

constitution When *constitution* is capitalized it refers to the written plan for the U.S. government.

citizen Tell students that *foreigner* and *alien* are antonyms of *citizen.*

territory Tell students that *territory* comes from the Latin word *terra,* which means *land.*

ordinance A mnemonic: An *ordinance* brings *order.*

Reading Strategy: Infer Ask students to think about what they have just read. Show them they can use this information to infer Congress's relationship with the states.

Think Aloud *Congress did not have the power to set up an army, create taxes, or control trade. These seem like important powers. I think this made working with the states very difficult.*

Problems for the New Nation

Talk About It

3 **Q Citizenship** What problems was the new government unable to resolve?

A The government could not resolve arguments between the states over trade and territory or pay its debts.

4 **Q History** What did Shays want?

A for farmers to have more time to pay their debts and for the state to stop taking farms

5 **Q History** What did Shays's Rebellion show about the new government?

A It was too weak to keep order.

Critical Thinking

Analyze George Washington said that under the Articles of Confederation the thirteen states behaved like thirteen separate countries. What did he mean?

Think Aloud *The thirteen states disagreed and argued with each other in order to protect their own citizens and businesses. They didn't see themselves as part of—or act like—one country.*

Problems for the New Nation

Main Idea The Articles of Confederation created a government that could not solve the problems facing the new nation.

3 By 1786, it was clear that the Articles of Confederation could not make the states work together. States printed their own money, and people disagreed about what each state's money was worth. In the free market economy of today, people agree on the value of money, and use it to easily buy and sell goods.

Congress was having trouble paying its debts from the War for Independence. The government owed millions of dollars to banks and other countries. Congress could not raise this money because it was not allowed to tax. It had to ask the states for money, but could not make them pay.

Shays's Rebellion

While Congress struggled, people grew frustrated. In western Massachusetts, farmers had to pay high state taxes. They also owed money to merchants for the supplies they bought. Many did not have money to pay their taxes or debts. Farmers who did not pay could lose their farms and go to jail.

In 1786, a farmer named **Daniel Shays** led a group of about 1,100 farmers in a protest. Shays had been a soldier during the War for Independence.

Shays and the other farmers wanted 4 the state government to stop taking their farms and give them time to pay their debts. They tried to capture weapons belonging to the national government. Congress could not stop the farmers because it did not have an army. State militia defeated the farmers.

Angry Farmers Standing on the courthouse steps, farmers keep the court from holding trials. One of their leaders, Daniel Shays, is shown below.

Daniel Shays

298 • Chapter 9

Math

Calculation: Multiplication

- Tell students that, under the terms of the Northwest Ordinance, a territory could become a state once its population reached 60,000.
- What would the total population of the Northwest Territory be if each territory had just enough people to become a state? 300,000

Logical-mathematical

Language Arts

Write to Persuade

- Have students write a persuasive paragraph in favor of or against the Articles of Confederation. Use information from the lesson to support their points of view.

Verbal-linguistic

Today, their protest is known as Shays's Rebellion. Shays's Rebellion showed that a
5 weak national government could not keep order. **George Washington** worried that the government was not strong enough to protect people's rights. He asked,

> "... what security has a man for life, liberty, or property?"

Many people agreed with Washington. In February 1787, Congress invited the states to send delegates to a meeting in Philadelphia to discuss how to change the Articles of Confederation.

REVIEW Why did farmers in western Massachusetts protest? They were losing their farms because they could not pay their taxes and debts.

George Mason He went to Philadelphia as a delegate from Virginia. Mason wanted a "wise and just government."

Lesson Summary

Articles of Confederation

Congress could	Congress could not
• declare war and peace • deal with other nations • print and borrow money • organize new territories	• regulate trade • set up army • raise money with taxes • force states to obey its laws

Why It Matters . . .

The failure of the Articles of Confederation caused many people to believe that they needed a stronger national government to solve the new nation's problems.

Lesson Review

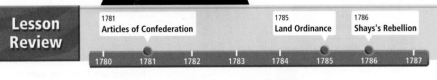

1781 Articles of Confederation — 1785 Land Ordinance — 1786 Shays's Rebellion

1780 · 1781 · 1782 · 1783 · 1784 · 1785 · 1786 · 1787

1. **VOCABULARY** Use **territory** and **ordinance** in a paragraph that shows what you know about the Northwest Ordinance.
2. **READING SKILL** Which **details** support the idea that Congress was too weak to stop Shays's Rebellion?
3. **MAIN IDEA: Government** Why did the states want a weak central government at first?
4. **MAIN IDEA: Economics** Why did Congress have trouble paying its debts?
5. **FACTS TO KNOW** What are the Articles of Confederation, and why are they important?
6. **TIMELINE SKILL** When was the Land Ordinance passed?
7. **CRITICAL THINKING: Analyze** Do you think the Articles of Confederation needed to be changed? Explain your answer.

WRITING ACTIVITY Write an invitation to the convention to change the Articles of Confederation. Be sure to explain what the Articles achieved, and why the Articles have to be changed.

Study Guide/Homework

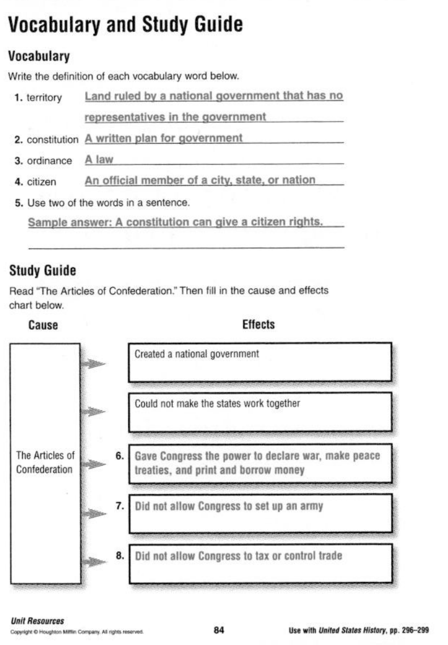
Vocabulary and Study Guide

Vocabulary

Write the definition of each vocabulary word below.

1. territory Land ruled by a national government that has no representatives in the government
2. constitution A written plan for government
3. ordinance A law
4. citizen An official member of a city, state, or nation
5. Use two of the words in a sentence. Sample answer: A constitution can give a citizen rights.

Study Guide

Read "The Articles of Confederation." Then fill in the cause and effects chart below.

Cause	Effects
The Articles of Confederation	Created a national government
	Could not make the states work together
	6. Gave Congress the power to declare war, make peace treaties, and print and borrow money
	7. Did not allow Congress to set up an army
	8. Did not allow Congress to tax or control trade

Unit Resources 84 Use with United States History, pp. 296–299

Unit Resources, p. 84

Reteach Minilesson

Use a two-column chart to reteach the strengths and weaknesses of the Articles of Confederation.

Accomplishments	Problems
• Land Ordinance of 1785 • Northwest Ordinance of 1787	• Government lacked power to make states work together • Government could not raise money through taxes and was unable to pay debts • Government had no army to keep order

Graphic Organizer 1

3 Review/Assess

Review Tested Objectives

U4-18 The Articles of Confederation gave Congress the power to declare war, make treaties, and print and borrow money. Congress did not have the power to set up an army, create taxes, or control trade.

U4-19 States did not work together. They took overseas trade away from each other and the new country could not raise taxes.

Lesson Review Answers

1. Answers should reflect an understanding of both *vocabulary* and *ordinance.*
2. Congress did not have any army that could keep order; it could not stop the states from arguing or printing their own money; it could not raise money to pay its debts.
3. They did not want to give up power to a strong central government such as Britain's.
4. It did not have the power to tax.
5. the first plan for a national government; they brought the states together under one government
6. 1785
7. Sample answer: They needed to be changed so Congress could solve the nation's problems.

Writing Rubric

4	Explanation is clear; invitation format is correct; reasons are well supported; mechanics are correct.
3	Explanation is adequate; invitation format is mostly correct; most reasons are supported; few errors in mechanics.
2	Explanation is stated; invitation format attempted; reasons poorly supported; some errors in mechanics.
1	Explanation not stated; invitation format not attempted; reasons not supported; many errors in mechanics.

Quick Look

Connect to the Core Lesson In Extend Lesson 1, students will learn more about the causes and effects of Shays's Rebellion and see how the debts of Massachusetts farmers were part of a chain of debts that also affected shopkeepers and merchants.

1 Teach the Extend Lesson

Connect to the Big Idea

Economic Performance By raising taxes to pay debts from the War for Independence, the government of Massachusetts was forcing farmers who couldn't pay their taxes off their land. This action hurt the income of farmers and the farm economy of the state.

Economics

Chain of Debt

Massachusetts farmers were in trouble. In 1786, many had lost their farms because they could not pay their debts. Farmers had borrowed money to buy goods. Many did not have enough money to repay these loans.

The state of Massachusetts was in trouble, too. To pay the costs of the Revolutionary War, it raised taxes. The taxes put farmers even more into debt. Farmers who could not pay their debts and taxes were brought to court. In western Massachusetts, where Daniel Shays and many other farmers struggled, these court cases, or debt cases, soared into the thousands. Follow the diagram on these pages to see how farmers got into debt and why getting out of debt seemed impossible.

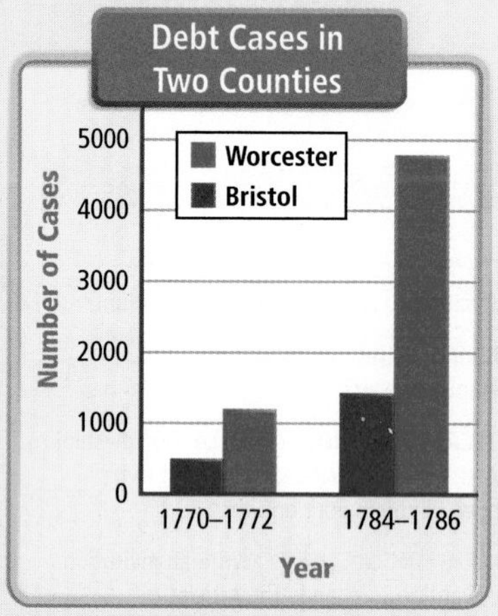

About how many more cases were there in Worcester County, Massachusetts, between 1784–1786 than between 1770–1772?

Between harvests, farmers borrowed money from shopkeepers to buy goods. The farmers would have to pay for the goods later, after they sold their next harvest.

FARMERS

Farmers often did not have enough money to pay their debts and their taxes. Those who did not pay could lose their farms or go to jail.

Reaching All Learners

Extra Support

Draw a Picture

- Have students draw pictures for one of the links in the chain of debt.
- Tell students to give their drawing a caption that explains which part of the chain they are illustrating.

Visual-spatial

On Level

Write a Letter

- Have students write a letter from the point of view of Daniel Shays to state leaders in Massachusetts. Letters should ask the leaders to stop taxing the state's citizens.
- Ask students to explain in their letters why the taxes hurt farmers, shopkeepers, and merchants.

Verbal-linguistic

Challenge

Debate Shays's Rebellion

- Divide students into two groups and have them debate whether the course of action taken by Daniel Shays and his followers was the right thing to do.
- Tell students to consider other courses of action the rebels could have taken and to compare the reasons for this rebellion with the reasons for the War for Independence.

Verbal-linguistic

Shopkeepers in western Massachusetts borrowed money from wealthy merchants in big cities such as Boston.

Boston merchants borrowed money from banks or wealthy merchant companies in Britain. The former colonies still needed British money to run their businesses.

To pay their debts to the merchants, shopkeepers demanded the money that the farmers owed them.

The debt went back down the chain. To pay what they owed the British banks, merchants demanded the money shopkeepers owed them.

ECONOMICS

Activities

1. **THINK ABOUT IT** Who suffered most in the chain of debt? Why?
2. **WRITE ABOUT IT** Write a short dialogue between a farmer and a shopkeeper or between a shopkeeper and a merchant.

2 Leveled Activities

❶ **Think About It** *For Extra Support*

The farmers suffered the most because they were left with nothing when the government took their farms.

❷ **Write About It** *For Challenge*

Writing Rubric

4	Dialogue states points of view clearly; conveys ideas effectively; facts are accurate.
3	Dialogue states points of view well; conveys ideas adequately; most facts cited are accurate.
2	Dialogue states points of view in a somewhat disorganized way; conveys ideas adequately; some errors.
1	Dialogue states no points of view or ones that are off topic; conveys ideas poorly; many errors.

ELL

REACHING ALL LEARNERS

Beginning

- Have students **design a sign** that farmers who were protesting might have carried around courthouses in Massachusetts.
- Explain that signs should show in words or pictures what the farmers were upset about.

Visual-spatial

Literature

Historical Fiction

The Winter Hero by James L. Collier and Christopher Collier is about a Massachusetts boy who is caught up in the farmers' rebellion against the government.

Place this book in your Reading Center for students who what to find out what Shays's Rebellion was like for young people.

Graphic Organizer

Chain of Debt

Farmers buy goods on credit from shopkeepers.

↓

Shopkeepers borrow money from merchants.

↓

Merchants borrow from British banks and merchant companies.

Graphic Organizer 5

✔ Tested Objectives

U4-20 History Identify important delegates and their roles in creating the Constitution of the United States.

U4-21 History Explain the major compromises reached during the creation of the Constitution.

U4-22 History Explain the process of ratification and the reasons for the creation of the Bill of Rights.

Lesson Quick Look

This lesson focuses on the Constitutional Convention delegates and the compromises they reached to create a new government.

Teaching Option: Extend Lesson 2 looks at passages from other nations' constitutions.

1 Get Set to Read

Preview After students look at the pictures, ask them what they think the lesson is about.

Reading Skill: Problem and Solution Students should consider the shortcomings of the Articles of Confederation discussed in Core Lesson 1.

Build on What You Know Discuss with students what they think the phrase "give-and-take" means. Explain that the delegates had to engage in give-and-take.

Vocabulary

federal *adjective*, describing a form of government in which states share power with the central government

republic *noun*, a government in which citizens elect leaders to represent them

compromise *noun*, an agreement in which each side of an argument gives up something it wants

ratify *verb*, officially accept

Core Lesson 2

Constitutional Convention

1780 1785 1790 1795 1800

1787–1789

VOCABULARY

federal
republic
compromise
ratify

Vocabulary Strategy

republic

Public comes from a word that means people. In a **republic**, the people choose leaders.

READING SKILL

Problem and Solution
Make notes on how delegates solved their disagreements about the Constitution.

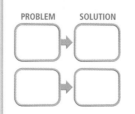

PROBLEM	SOLUTION

Build on What You Know Have you ever solved a problem by giving up one thing to get something else? Delegates who met to change the national government had to give up some things they wanted to solve their differences.

Leaders of the Convention

Main Idea Delegates gathered in Philadelphia to change the way the American government worked.

In the spring of 1787, 55 delegates traveled to Philadelphia. Remember that delegates are chosen to speak for others, or represent them. The delegates came from every state except Rhode Island. They met to discuss how to change the Articles of Confederation. Their meeting has become known as the Constitutional Convention. 1

The delegates were landowners, business people, and lawyers. Most were wealthy and educated. About 20 were slaveowners. About 30 had fought in the war against Britain. Eight had signed the Declaration of Independence. Many had served in Congress or state government.

Independence Hall Delegates met at Independence Hall in Philadelphia, the same place delegates met in 1776 to declare independence.

Skill and Strategy

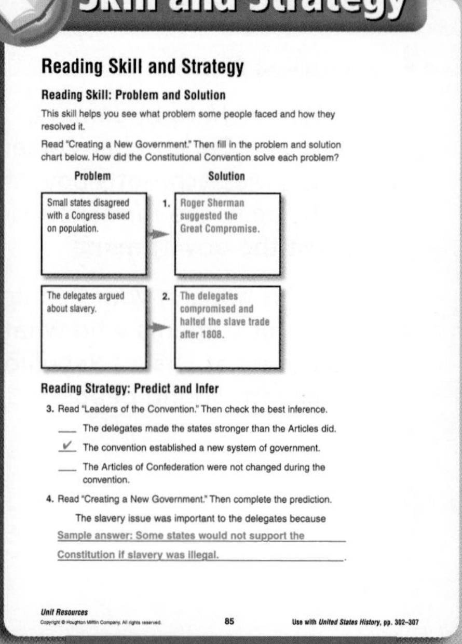

Reading Skill and Strategy

Reading Skill: Problem and Solution

This skill helps you see what problem some people faced and how they resolved it.

Read "Creating a New Government." Then fill in the problem and solution chart below. How did the Constitutional Convention solve each problem?

Problem	Solution
Small states disagreed with a Congress based on population.	1. Roger Sherman suggested the Great Compromise.
The delegates argued about slavery.	2. The delegates compromised and halted the slave trade after 1808.

Reading Strategy: Predict and Infer

3. Read "Leaders of the Convention." Then check the best inference.

___ The delegates made the states stronger than the Articles did.

✓ The convention established a new system of government.

___ The Articles of Confederation were not changed during the convention.

4. Read "Creating a New Government." Then complete the prediction.

The slavery issue was important to the delegates because Sample answer: Some states would not support the Constitution if slavery was illegal.

Unit Resources

85
Use with *United States History*, pp. 302–307

Unit Resources, p. 85

Background

Absent from the Convention

- Rhode Island refused to send delegates to the convention because the state viewed it as a gathering designed to overthrow the government.
- Several famous Americans did not attend the convention. Patrick Henry was suspicious of Madison's motives, saying he "smelt a rat." Thomas Jefferson and John Adams were serving as American ambassadors to France and Britain, respectively.

Delegates Statues of delegates at the National Constitution Center in Philadelphia include James Madison 1 (above), who read many books on law and government. Other famous delegates at the Convention were George Washington 2 and Alexander Hamilton 3.

Such a convention today would include Americans of many different backgrounds. In 1787, though, only white men who owned land were included. No women, African Americans, American Indians, or men who were not land-owners took part in the convention.

James Madison of Virginia arrived before the other delegates. He was a member of Congress. Madison wanted to do more than change the Articles. He had a plan for a new system of government. During the convention, Madison took notes. Thanks to these notes, we know much of what people said and did.

2 **George Washington**, the hero of the Revolution, came as another Virginia delegate. Ringing bells and cheering crowds greeted him in Philadelphia. **Benjamin Franklin**, representing Pennsylvania, was respected for his wisdom. He had served the United States for many years.

Goals of the Convention

The delegates knew that the Articles of Confederation had to change. As one said,

> **“If we do not establish a good government . . . we must either go to ruin, or have the work to do over again.”**

The Articles did not give Congress enough power. Some delegates, such as Madison and Washington, wanted a federal system. In a **federal** system, the states share power with the central government, but the central government has more power than the states. 3

Madison believed that a republic was the only type of government that could keep order and still protect rights. A **republic** is a government in which the citizens elect leaders to represent them. The power in a republic comes from the citizens themselves.

REVIEW What was the advantage of a federal system? It divided power between the states and the central government and gave the central government more control over the states.

303

2 Teach

Leaders of the Convention

Talk About It

1 **Q History** Why did delegates gather in Philadelphia in the spring of 1787?

A They met to discuss how to change the Articles of Confederation.

2 **Q Geography** Which state did Madison and Washington represent at the Convention?

A Virginia

3 **Q Citizenship** What is a federal system of government?

A It is a government in which states share power with a central government.

Vocabulary Strategy

federal Explain to students that *federal* comes from the Latin word for *league.*

republic The root word of *republic* comes from the Latin word *publica,* which means *of the people.*

Reading Strategy: Infer Have students read the first page of the lesson. Work with them to infer what they can about the convention.

REACHING ALL LEARNERS

Leveled Practice

Extra Support

Have students **make a two column chart**. The first column should list the problems with the Articles of Confederation. The second column should list how delegates at the Constitutional Convention hoped to solve the problems. Visual-spatial

Challenge

Have students use the information in the text to **write a newspaper article** about the convention. Articles should say who was there, when and where they met, what the issues were, and the results of the convention. Verbal-linguistic

REACHING ALL LEARNERS

ELL

Intermediate

- Have students write down the names of people who appear in this lesson. After each name, have students write a sentence explaining what each person did.

Verbal-linguistic

Creating a New Government

Talk About It

4 **Q Citizenship** What did the Virginia Plan propose?

A a federal government with three branches

5 **Q Citizenship** Why did small states create the New Jersey Plan?

A to get the same representation in Congress as large states

6 **Q History** What was Roger Sherman's solution called?

A the Great Compromise

7 **Q History** What was the Three-Fifths Compromise?

A It was a rule to count five slaves as three free people in slave states.

Vocabulary Strategy

compromise Explain to students that the prefix *com-* means *together, with,* or *jointly.*

Critical Thinking

Decision Making Why would slave states decide to count enslaved people for representation?

Creating a New Government

Main Idea The delegates all had to give up some of the things they wanted.

The Convention began on May 25, at the start of a very hot summer. The delegates elected George Washington as president of the convention. They also agreed to keep their debates secret. This allowed them to talk openly with each other without being influenced by people who were not part of the convention.

4 On May 29, **Edmund Randolph**, governor of Virginia, described Madison's plan for the new government. This plan, known as the Virginia Plan, called for a federal system in which the national government had three parts, or branches. Many state governments were already set up this way. One branch, the Congress, would make laws for the nation. Another branch would carry out the laws. Yet another branch, the courts, would settle legal arguments.

Representation

The delegates accepted most of the Virginia Plan, but many did not like one part of it. Madison had suggested that the number of each state's representatives in Congress be based on the state's population. Large states would get more votes in Congress than small states.

5 The small states did not like this plan. It gave more power to large states. Delegates from the small states created the New Jersey Plan. Like the Articles of Confederation, this plan gave each state one vote, so that small states would have as much power as large states. Delegates argued bitterly about these plans.

Roger Sherman of Connecticut came up with a solution. He suggested dividing Congress into two parts, or houses. Each state would have an equal number of representatives in one house, the Senate. The number of representatives each state sent to the other house, the House of Representatives, would depend on its population. Sherman's suggestion is called the Great Compromise. In a 6 **compromise**, both sides give up something to settle a disagreement. The delegates accepted this compromise, and moved on to other topics.

The Issue of Slavery

Another problem delegates argued about was slavery. Southern delegates wanted slaves to count as part of a state's population. Counting enslaved people would have given their states more representatives in Congress. Other delegates said this was unfair, because slaves were treated as property, not citizens.

Delegates also argued about whether to end the practice of bringing slaves into the United States. Delegates from the southern states said they would not accept the new government unless the slave trade continued.

Arguments over slavery led to another compromise, the Three-Fifths Rule. This 7 rule counted five slaves as three free people. The slave trade was also allowed to continue until 1808. Although some delegates disliked this compromise and wanted to end slavery, they agreed to let it continue so that all states would support the Constitution.

REVIEW Why did delegates argue over representation in Congress? States that had more representatives in Congress would have more votes, which would give them more power.

304 • Chapter 9

Math

Calculation: Division

- Have students use the graph on page 305 to determine how many people would equal three-fifths of South Carolina's slave population. approximately 64,256
- Have students add that number to the total white and free black population of South Carolina. 140,000 + 64,000 = 204,000
- Each state was given one representative for 30,000 people. How many representatives was South Carolina entitled to? 6

Language Arts

Write a Summary

- Have students write summaries methods of choosing representatives offered in the Virginia Plan, the New Jersey Plan, and the Great Compromise.

Visual-spatial

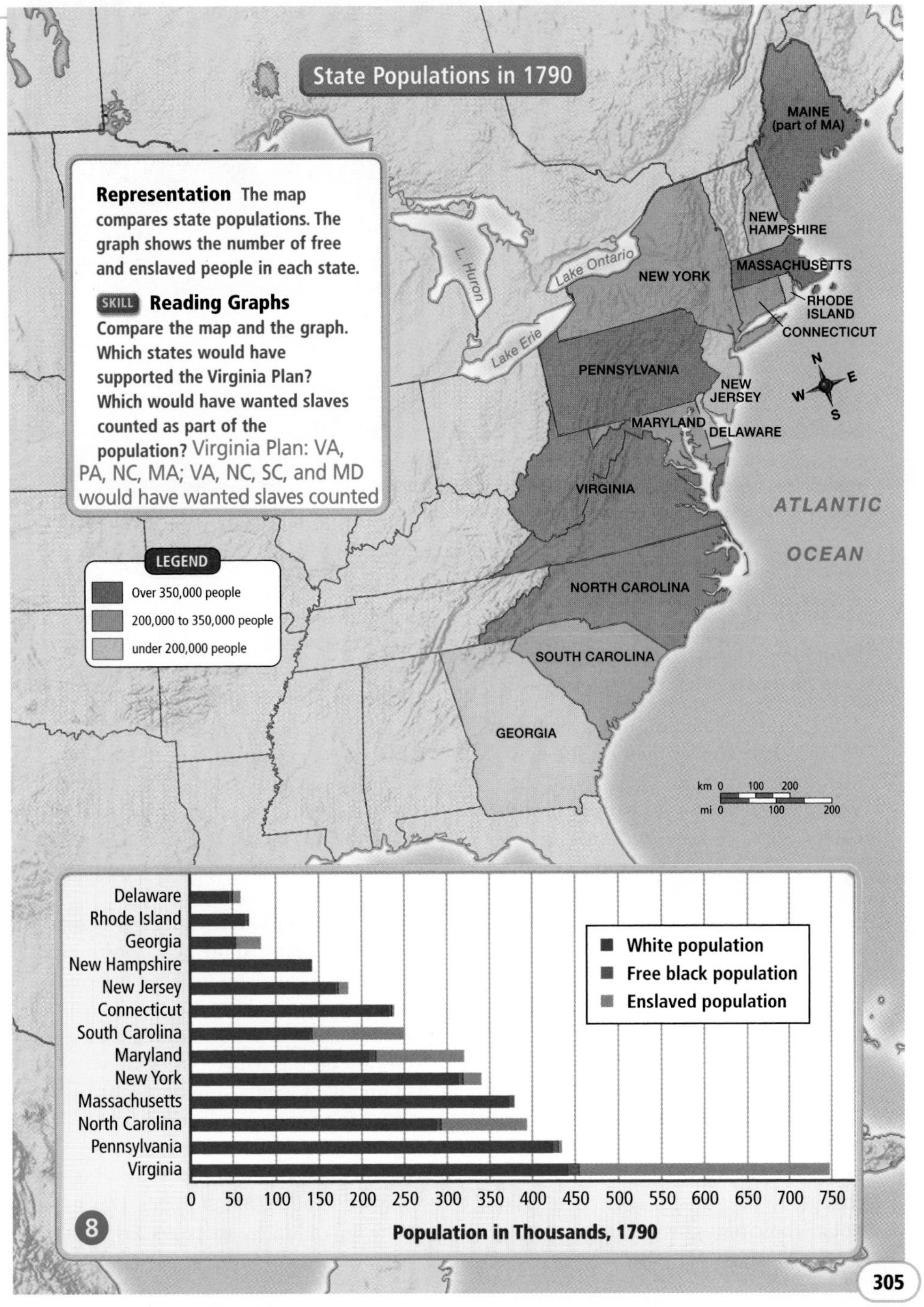

Creating a New Government *continued*

Talk About It

8 **Q Visual Learning** Which states had populations more than 350,000 people?

A Massachusetts, Pennsylvania, Virginia, and North Carolina

Reading Strategy: Infer Have students read about the compromises delegates made in creating the new government. Work with them to infer the reasons delegates were willing to compromise.

Map Help

Students may be confused by how Massachusetts and Virginia look on the map on page 305. Explain that Maine was part of Massachusetts until 1820, when it became a state as part of the Missouri Compromise. West Virginia split from Virginia around the time of the Civil War, and became a state in 1863.

Leveled Practice

Extra Support

Have students **make a diagram** of the two houses of Congress that were created by the Great Compromise. At the bottom of the diagram, ask students to explain what made this compromise "great." Visual-spatial

Challenge

Have students **brainstorm** different ways to represent states in Congress. Ask students to explain why their ideas might be better or worse than the Great Compromise. Verbal-linguistic

ELL

Intermediate/Advanced

- Have pairs of students **create a two-column chart**, with one column labeled "Virginia Plan," and the other column labeled "New Jersey Plan."
- Ask pairs to list three details about each plan in its column.
- Have pairs share their details with the class.

Visual-spatial

Ratifying the Constitution

Talk About It

9 **Q Citizenship** What had to happen before the Constitution could go into effect?

A Nine of the thirteen states had to ratify it.

10 **Q History** Why did Antifederalists think the Constitution was dangerous?

A They thought that the Constitution was a threat to liberty because it created a strong central government without a Bill of Rights.

11 **Q Citizenship** What did Federalists do to persuade the states to ratify the Constitution?

A They promised to add a Bill of Rights to the document.

Vocabulary Strategy

ratify Tell students that a synonym for *ratify* is *approve.*

Critical Thinking

Analyze Which side do you think Edmund Randolph supported on the slavery issue? Which side do you think Roger Sherman supported? Explain your answers.

Founders At the end of the Convention, Benjamin Franklin (center) said that the sun on the back of Washington's chair (right) was a rising and not a setting sun. The completion of the Constitution convinced him that the nation was beginning, not ending.

Ratifying the Constitution

Main Idea Americans argued over whether to accept the Constitution.

All through the hot, muggy summer of 1787, delegates worked on the new plan for government. They signed the final document, the Constitution of the United States of America, on September 17. It was based on Madison's Virginia Plan. Madison has been called the Father of the Constitution.

9 Before the Constitution could be used, at least nine states had to ratify it. To **ratify** means to accept. In each state, representatives from the towns met to decide whether or not to ratify.

Supporters of the Constitution, who were known as Federalists, faced a big challenge. Many people were shocked by the Constitution. They had expected changes to the Articles of Confederation, not a whole new government.

Federalists had to teach the public about the Constitution. To do this, Madison and two other Federalists, **Alexander Hamilton** and **John Jay**, wrote a series of essays called *The Federalist.* These essays explained how the federal system would work and why the new nation needed it to suceed. They said that the United States needed a strong central government like the one that would be created by the Constitution.

Not everyone wanted a federal system. People who opposed the new Constitution were called Antifederalists. They believed that a strong central government was a 10
threat to liberty. They also thought the Constitution was dangerous because it had no Bill of Rights. A Bill of Rights is a list of the rights of individuals, such as freedom of speech and freedom of religion. Madison and other Federalists promised to add a Bill of Rights. 11 (For more on the Bill of Rights, see pages 334–335.)

Art

Constitutional Portrait Gallery

- Have each student choose a delegate from the Constitutional Convention. Encourage students to research the background of the delegates and then draw a portrait of each delegate.
- Have them label the portrait with the person's name and a brief description of his background and contribution.

Visual-spatial; verbal-linguistic

Language Arts

Write a Persuasive Essay

- The Federalists wrote essays to explain the features and benefits of the Constitution to the public.
- Ask students to write a persuasive essay of three paragraphs about the features and benefits of the plan that they feel was best for the goverment.

Verbal-linguistic

Ratification

While Federalists and Antifederalists argued, state representatives met in their own conventions. Delaware was the first state to ratify the Constitution. In June 1788, New Hampshire became the ninth state to ratify. At that point, the Constitution became the country's law. In the end, all 13 states ratified. The United States had a new government.

REVIEW Why did Antifederalists demand a Bill of Rights?
to protect the rights of individuals

Lesson Summary

In 1787, delegates from the states met in Philadelphia to change the Articles of Confederation. Instead, they wrote a plan for a new government, the Constitution, based on James Madison's Virginia Plan. They made several compromises before agreeing on a final plan. After a long debate between Federalists and Antifederalists, the Constitution was ratified in June, 1788.

Why It Matters...

The Constitutional Convention created the government the United States still has today.

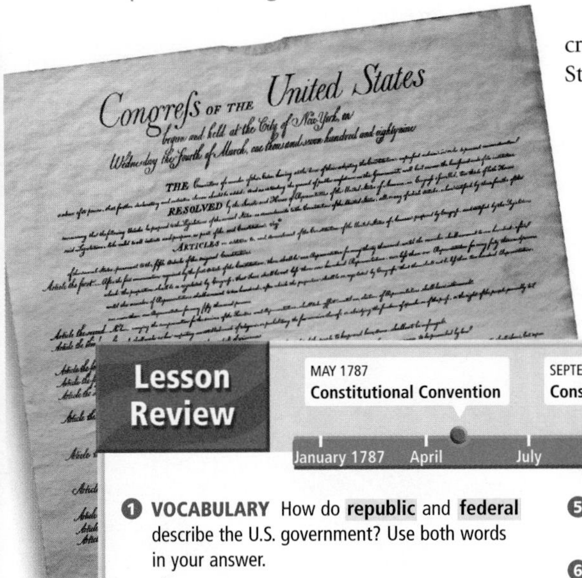

Congress of the United States

Bill of Rights This single page lists the 10 amendments written to protect many rights of the people of the United States.

Lesson Review

MAY 1787	SEPTEMBER 1787	JUNE 1788
Constitutional Convention	Constitution signed	Ninth state ratifies Constitution

January 1787 · April · July · October · January 1788 · April · July

1. **VOCABULARY** How do **republic** and **federal** describe the U.S. government? Use both words in your answer.
2. **READING SKILL** What did the delegates do to **solve** the **problem** of how many representatives each state could have?
3. **MAIN IDEA: Government** Which compromise did the delegates who wanted slavery agree to?
4. **MAIN IDEA: Citizenship** Why did Madison, Hamilton, and Jay write *The Federalist*?
5. **PEOPLE TO KNOW** Why is **James Madison** known as the Father of the Constitution?
6. **TIMELINE SKILL** How long after the convention did the Constitution become law?
7. **CRITICAL THINKING: Decision Making** What were some short-term effects of the delegates' decision to continue to allow slavery? What were some long-term effects?

HANDS ON **SPEAKING ACTIVITY** Federalists and Antifederalists made many speeches. In a small group, prepare a short speech to convince people to vote for or against the Constitution.

3 Review/Assess

Review Tested Objectives

U4-20 James Madison's Virginia Plan was ratified by Congress. Roger Sherman proposed the Great Compromise.

U4-21 The Great Compromise divided Congress into the Senate and the House of Representatives. The Three-Fifths Rule counted five slaves as three free people.

U4-22 At least nine states had to ratify the Constitution before it became law. Federalists promised to add a Bill of Rights to the Constitution.

Lesson Review Answers

1. Answer should indicate an understanding that the United States is a federal republic.
2. They compromised and divided Congress into two houses.
3. the Three-Fifths Rule
4. to explain how the federal system would work and why the nation needed it
5. The Constitution was based on Madison's Virginia Plan.
6. about 11 months
7. Short-term: States were able to compromise and support the Constitution; Long-term: slavery continued.

HANDS ON Performance Task Rubric

4	Speech states position clearly; conveys ideas effectively; facts are accurate.
3	Speech states position well; conveys ideas adequately; most facts cited are accurate.
2	Speech states position in a somewhat disorganized way; conveys ideas adequately; some errors.
1	Speech states no position or one that is off-topic; conveys ideas in a very general or incomprehensible way; many errors.

Study Guide/Homework

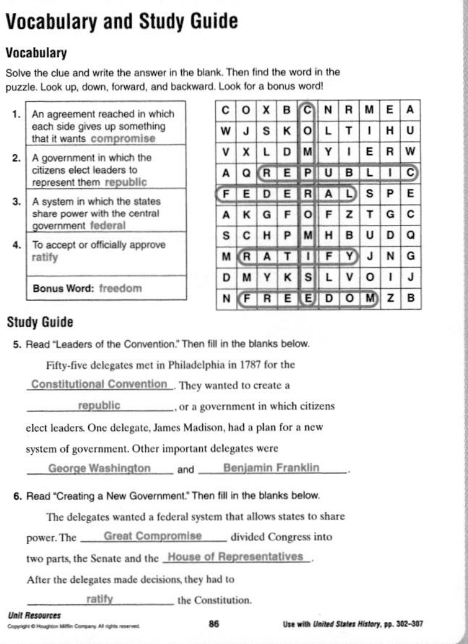
Vocabulary and Study Guide

Vocabulary

Solve the clue and write the answer in the blank. Then find the word in the puzzle. Look up, down, forward, and backward. Look for a bonus word!

1. An agreement reached in which each side gives up something that it wants compromise
2. A government in which the citizens elect leaders to represent them republic
3. A system in which the states share power with the central government federal
4. To accept or officially approve ratify

Bonus Word: freedom

C	O	X	B	C	N	R	M	E	A
W	J	S	K	O	L	T	I	H	U
V	X	L	D	M	Y	I	E	R	W
A	Q	R	E	P	U	B	L	I	C
F	E	D	E	R	A	L	S	P	E
A	K	G	F	O	F	Z	T	G	C
S	C	H	P	M	H	B	U	D	Q
M	R	A	T	I	F	Y	J	N	G
D	M	Y	K	S	L	V	O	I	J
N	F	R	E	E	D	O	M	Z	B

Study Guide

5. Read "Leaders of the Convention." Then fill in the blanks below.

Fifty-five delegates met in Philadelphia in 1787 for the Constitutional Convention. They wanted to create a republic, or a government in which citizens elect leaders. One delegate, James Madison, had a plan for a new system of government. Other important delegates were George Washington and Benjamin Franklin.

6. Read "Creating a New Government." Then fill in the blanks below.

The delegates wanted a federal system that allows states to share power. The Great Compromise divided Congress into two parts, the Senate and the House of Representatives. After the delegates made decisions, they had to ratify the Constitution.

Unit Resources 86 Use with *United States History*, pp. 302–307
Copyright © Houghton Mifflin Company. All rights reserved.

Unti Resources, p. 86

Reteach Minilesson

Use a Venn diagram to reteach the lesson.

Virginia Plan
Representatives to Congress should be based on a state's population
Great Compromise
New Jersey Plan
Each state should have the same number of representatives

Graphic Organizer 11

Extend Quick Look

Connect to the Core Lesson Students have learned about the Constitutional Convention in Lesson 2. In Extend Lesson 2, students will learn that all constitutions are not the same. They reflect the values and experiences of the country that creates them.

1 Teach the Extend Lesson

Connect to the Big Idea

Democratic Principles/International Relations The principles of American democracy are contained in the Constitution and were shaped by our nation's experiences with Britain. In the same way, the history of other countries has influenced the principles contained in their constitutions.

Connect to Prior Knowledge

Ask students whether they have noticed that different classrooms sometimes have different rules. Explain that nations also have different rules in their constitutions.

World Constitutions

What are the rules and ideas that guide a nation? In a written constitution, each country lists the rules its citizens are supposed to follow. The U.S. Constitution, ratified in 1788, is the oldest written constitution in the world. It has served as a model for many other countries. At the same time, each constitution is unique. These excerpts from constitutions show what each country values.

People visit the National Archives in Washington, D.C., where they can see the Constitution and the Declaration of Independence.

Reaching All Learners

Extra Support

Design Flags

- Have students select one of the countries in the lesson and design a flag to illustrate the ideas in that country's constitution that people regard as most important.
- Then have students design a flag for the United States.

Visual-spatial

On Level

Paraphrase the Excerpts

- Ask students to write down what each excerpt on page 309 means in their own words.
- Have students share their paraphrases with the class.
- Talk about similarities and differences between the excerpts and the values that they represent.

Verbal-linguistic

Challenge

Report on an Amendment

- Have students select one of the last four amendments to the U.S. Constitution and find out why Americans wanted to add it.
- Have students present their findings in a written report.

Verbal-linguistic

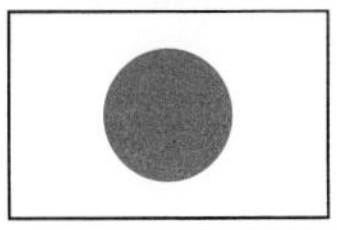		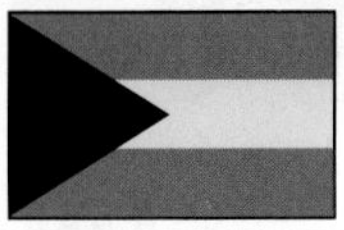
We, the Japanese people [resolve] that never again shall we be visited with the horrors of war through the action of government. – Preamble, Constitution of Japan, 1946	The Republic of China, founded on the Three Principles of the People, shall be a democratic republic of the people, by the people, and for the people. – Article 1, Constitution of Republic of China (Taiwan), 1947	(1) No person shall be held in slavery or servitude. (2) No person shall be required to perform forced labour. – Article 18, Constitution of the Bahamas, 1973
		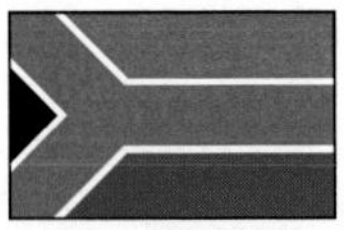
Activities tending and undertaken with the intent to disturb peaceful relations between nations, especially to prepare for aggressive war, are unconstitutional. – Article 26, Constitution of Germany, 1990	Every person has the right to a healthy and ecologically balanced environment. – Article 50, the Constitution of Costa Rica, 1994	We, the people of South Africa, recognise the injustices of our past; . . . and believe that South Africa belongs to all who live in it, united in our diversity. – Preamble, Constitution of South Africa, 1996

A nation's history can affect its constitution. For example, both Germany and Japan, which started wars in the 1940s, have constitutions that forbid going to war. In South Africa, the laws used to be very unfair to black people. Now its constitution protects all of its citizens.

Activities

1. **TALK ABOUT IT** Choose one of the excerpts shown here. Tell why you think it is important.
2. **WRITE ABOUT IT** Compare these excerpts to the U.S. Constitution. What similarities do you notice?

CITIZENSHIP

2 Leveled Activities

1 Talk About It *For Extra Support*

Answers will vary but should show that the excerpt expresses the values that are most important in that country.

2 Write About It *For Challenge*

Writing Rubric

4	Comparison is thorough; main ideas clearly stated and supported by details; mechanics are correct.
3	Comparison is made; main ideas adequately stated and supported by details; few errors in mechanics.
2	Comparison contains some factual errors; main ideas stated but supported by few details; some errors in mechanics.
1	Comparison is not made or contains many factual errors; main ideas are not stated or supported; many errors in mechanics.

ELL

REACHING ALL LEARNERS

Advanced

- Have students work in groups. Ask each group to choose one of the nations shown on page 309.
- Then have them **compare** that nation's excerpt to principles and rules contained in the U.S. Constitution. Are they similar or different?
- Ask them to share their findings with the class.

Verbal-linguistic

Music

Write a Song

- Play recordings of the national anthem, "My Country 'tis of Thee," and "America the Beautiful."
- Discuss the songs with the class. What do these songs celebrate about our country?
- Have students write a song that celebrates the Constitution.

Musical-auditory; verbal-linguistic

Graphic Organizer

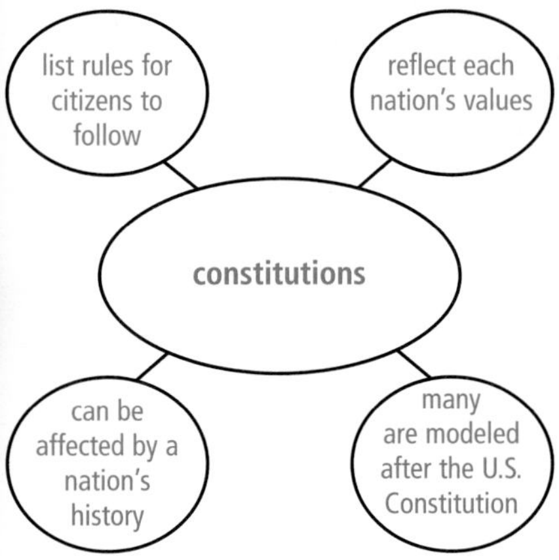

Graphic Organizer 13

Tested Objective

U4-24 Recognize and respect different points of view.

1 Teach the Skill

- Have students read aloud the introduction to the skill lesson on page 310. Discuss ways in which someone's point of view can influence the way that person thinks about an issue.
- Remind students that even sources like newspapers and television news programs show point of view.
- Point out that a person's point of view is influenced by his or her experiences and beliefs.
- Ask students to think of ways in which different points of view influenced the writing of the Constitution.

Citizenship Skills

Skillbuilder

Understand Point of View

VOCABULARY
point of view

Information can come from many different sources, including newspapers, books, and television. Each source of information has one or more points of view. A **point of view** is the way someone thinks about an issue, an event, or a person. A point of view is affected by a person's experiences and beliefs.

Understanding different points of view can help you understand the decisions and behavior of others. It can also help you form your own opinions. Part of being a good citizen is listening to and respecting different points of view.

"Who authorized them to speak the language of We, the People, instead of We, the States?... National Government... will destroy the state governments and swallow the liberties of the people without giving previous notice [warning]."

— Patrick Henry

"We have seen the necessity of the Union, as our bulwark [protection] against foreign danger, as the conservator of peace among ourselves, as the guardian of our commerce [trade]."

— James Madison

310 • Chapter 9

Reaching All Learners: Leveled Practice

Extra Support

Have students use their own words to explain Madison and Henry's points of view. Encourage students to think about why Madison and Henry might have felt the way they did. Verbal-linguistic

Challenge

Have students discuss ways in which point of view might influence news reporting. Have them create news headlines about the same event from several different points of view. Verbal-linguistic

Reaching All Learners: ELL

Advanced

- Discuss words or phrases from the quotations that show Madison's and Henry's points of view.
- Have partners write sentences about government that might have been said by Madison, by Henry, or by either person.
- Have students read their sentences aloud. For each sentence, ask classmates to identify who is speaking and explain how they know.

Verbal-linguistic

Apply Critical Thinking

Learn the Skill

Step 1: Identify the point of view. What is the subject, and what does the writer or speaker think about it?

Step 2: Identify the source of the information. Do you know of any experiences that may have influenced the writer or speaker?

Step 3: Summarize the writer or speaker's point of view in your own words. If you know about the person's experiences, explain how they might have influenced his or her point of view.

Practice the Skill

Read the passages on page 310 about the debate over whether the national government should have more power than the states. Then answer these questions.

1. What is Patrick Henry's point of view?
2. What is Madison's point of view?
3. How might Madison's experience at the Continental Congress have affected his point of view?

Apply the Skill

Choose a topic below or one of your own. Write a paragraph expressing your point of view on the subject. Describe any personal experiences that affect your point of view.

- Some towns have decided to start and end school later in the day. They are trying to give young people more time to sleep.
- A national helmet law has been suggested. Everyone who uses skates, bikes, and skateboards would need to wear a helmet.

311

2 Practice the Skill

1. A national government will take power away from the state governments and take away people's rights.
2. The Union will be good for the country. It will protect the people and their common interests.
3. Answers may discuss the problems Madison saw with the Articles of Confederation.

3 Apply the Skill

Ask students to write a paragraph expressing their point of view on a subject. When evaluating students' paragraphs, consider:

- Did the student express his or her point of view on the issue?
- Did the student give reasons supporting and explaining the point of view?
- Did the student use correct mechanics in the paragraph?

Skill Practice

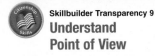

Skillbuilder: Understand Point of View

"I have no fear but that the result of our experiment [new government] will be that men may be trusted to govern themselves without a master."

—Thomas Jefferson

"It has been observed that a pure democracy, it if were practicable [attainable], would be the most perfect government. Experience has proved that no position [opinion] is more false than this."

—Alexander Hamilton

Practice

1. From reading the chapter, what do you already know about Alexander Hamilton's experience and beliefs? Sample answer: He was a Federalist who wanted a strong central government.
2. What was Alexander Hamilton's point of view? People do not govern themselves well; strong central government is needed.
3. What was Thomas Jefferson's point of view? People are able to make good decisions and govern themselves.
4. Explain how knowing these two points of view can help you understand why Jefferson was against the national bank and why Hamilton was for the national bank. Sample answer: A national bank would give the federal government more control of money and make it stronger.

Apply

What experiences and beliefs affect your own point of view about the powers of the federal government? On a separate sheet of paper, write a paragraph expressing your point of view about government. Paragraphs should explain the students' points of view.

Unit Resources

87
Use with *United States History*, pp. 310–311

Unit Resources, p. 87

Skill Transparency

Skillbuilder Transparency 9

Understand Point of View

❶ "Who authorized them to speak the language of We, the People, instead of We, the States?...National Government...will destroy the state governments and swallow the liberties of the people without giving previous notice [warning]."

— Patrick Henry ❷

❶ "We have seen the necessity of the Union, as our bulwark [protection] against foreign danger, as the conservator of peace among ourselves, as the guardian of our commerce [trade]."

— James Madison ❷

Step ❶ Identify the point of view. What is the subject, and what does the writer or speaker think about it?

Step ❷ Identify the source of the information. Do you know what might have influenced the writer or speaker?

Step ❸ Write a summary of the writer or speaker's point of view in your own words. If you know about the person's experiences, explain how they might have influenced his or her point of view.

Skillbuilder Transparency

Use with *United States History*, pp. 310–311

Transparency 9

Tested Objectives

U4-24 Citizenship Describe the three branches of the United States government and how the powers of each are limited.

U4-25 Citizenship Explain that the Constitution has changed, through amendment and interpretation, throughout United States history.

Lesson Quick Look

This lesson explains what is in our Constitution and how our government works.

Teaching Option: **Extend Lesson 3** tells the history of the Liberty Bell.

1 Get Set to Read

Preview Ask students what the diagrams on pages 314 and 315 tell them about the United States government.

Reading Skill: Categorize Students can use their charts as study aids.

Build on What You Know Discuss with students why people need plans. Explain that plans are guides.

Vocabulary

democracy *noun,* a government in which the people make political decisions by voting, and the majority rules

checks and balances *noun,* a system of separating government so each part keeps the others from taking too much power

veto *verb,* to refuse to approve

unconstitutional *adjective,* not in agreement with the Constitution

amendment *noun,* a change made to the Constitution

Core Lesson 3

The Constitution

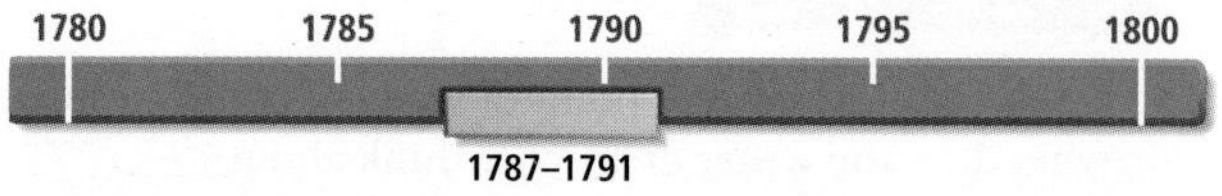

VOCABULARY

democracy
checks and balances
veto
unconstitutional
amendment

Vocabulary Strategy

amendment

Find **mend** in amendment. An **amendment** is a way to mend, or fix, a problem.

READING SKILL

Categorize As you read, list the jobs of each branch of the federal government.

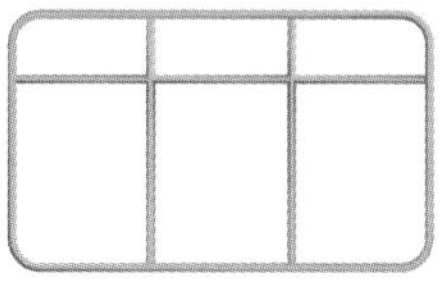

Build on What You Know Builders make a plan before they build a house. The founders of the United States made the Constitution as a plan for the nation's government.

A Plan for Government

Main Idea The Constitution describes how the United States government works.

> **"We the People of the United States . . ."**

These are the first words of the Constitution, and they have a special meaning. They tell us that our country is a democracy. A **democracy** is a government in which the people have the power to make political decisions. Citizens in a democracy take part in making laws and choosing leaders. In the United States, citizens usually make those decisions through representatives whom they elect.

The United States Constitution is the plan for our democracy. In the Preamble, or beginning, the authors listed their goals for the country. They hoped to create a country where people were safe, could live together in peace, and could have good lives. The rest of the Constitution describes how the government works. 1

The Constitution
This important document is on display at the National Archives in Washington, D.C.

Skill and Strategy

Reading Skill and Strategy

Reading Skill: Categorize

This skill helps you understand and remember what you have read by organizing facts into groups, or categories.

Read "A Plan for Government." Then fill in the categorization chart below. What responsibilities does each branch of the government have?

Legislative	Executive	Judicial
1. Congress passes laws, raises money through taxes, and uses the money for the nation.	2. The President carries out the laws and is the commander of the military.	3. The courts interpret the laws, and the Supreme Court governs all other courts.

Reading Strategy: Predict and Infer

4. The following statements are based on "Changing the Constitution." Combine the information in the statements with what you already know. Then make an inference from the information given to complete the statement.

Statement 1: A change to the Constitution is called an amendment.

Statement 2: Two-thirds of Congress must approve an amendment.

Statement 3: Three-fourths of the states must ratify an amendment.

A great majority of Americans must agree with the change for it to be added to the Constitution.

5. Read "The Growth of Democracy." Then make a prediction about how the rights of U.S. citizens might change in the future.

Sample answer: Even more groups will be given equal protection of their rights.

Unit Resources

88
Use with *United States History*, pp. 312–317

Unit Resources, p. 88

Background

The Branches of Government

- When the Supreme Court was first formed, it had only six judges. Today it has nine. While he served as President, George Washington appointed more Supreme Court justices than any other President, a total of 11.

State of the Union
Once a year, the President gives a speech called the State of the Union Address. The seal (above) is the symbol of the President.

Branches of Government

2 The Constitution divides the national government into three parts, or branches: the legislative branch, the executive branch, and the judicial branch. Each branch does a different job.

The legislative branch makes laws for the country. This branch is called Congress. Congress has two parts: the Senate and the House of Representatives. Each state elects two senators to the Senate. Each state also elects a certain number of representatives to the House. The number of representatives from each state depends on its population.

Congress has the power to raise money through taxes or by borrowing. It uses this money to pay for goods and services such as an army, roads, and national parks.

The executive branch can suggest laws. It also carries out the laws made by Congress. The head of this branch is the President. United States citizens elect a President every four years. The President is the commander of the United States military.

The judicial branch decides the meaning of laws and whether laws have been followed. Many courts across the nation make up the judicial branch. The highest court is the Supreme Court. 3

You remember that the Articles of Confederation created a weak federal government. The U.S. Constitution gives the federal government more power, but it does not give its leaders unlimited power. The Constitution is a plan for a limited government. Everyone must follow the law, including those who run the government.

REVIEW What are the jobs of each branch of the national government?
legislative makes laws and raises money; executive suggests and carries out laws; judicial decides the meaning of laws and whether laws are being followed

313

2 Teach

A Plan for Government

Talk About It

1 **Q Citizenship** What is in the Preamble to the Constitution?

A It lists the authors' goals for the country, which included creating a country where people could feel safe, live in peace with each other, and have good lives.

2 **Q Citizenship** What are the three branches of government?

A the legislative branch, the executive branch, and the judicial branch

3 **Q Citizenship** What is the highest court in the nation?

A the Supreme Court

Vocabulary Strategy

democracy Tell students that the root word of *democracy* is *demos,* a Greek word that means *people.*

Reading Strategy: Predict/Infer Have students read the headings in this lesson. Ask students to share their predictions.

Leveled Practice

Extra Support

Have students **draw** a three-branched tree. Ask them to label the branches after the branches of our government. Then have students write down each branch's powers and duties. **Visual-spatial**

Challenge

Have students **act out** the powers of a branch of government without speaking, as other students try to guess what they are portraying. **Bodily-kinesthetic**

ELL

Intermediate

- Have students **diagram** one of the powers of Congress, one of the powers of the President, and one of the powers of the judicial branch in a poster called *The Three Branches of Government.*
- When students are done, ask them to explain their posters to the class.

Visual-spatial

Limits on Government

Talk About It

4 **Q Citizenship** How does the division of powers help control the government?

A It prevents any one person or branch from having all the powers needed to run the government.

5 **Q Citizenship** What happens when the Supreme Court decides that a law is unconstitutional?

A The law is no longer in effect.

6 **Q Visual Learning** What can Congress do to pass a law that the President has vetoed?

A If two-thirds of the Senate and House agree, Congress can pass the law.

Vocabulary Strategy

checks and balances Tell students that a synonym for *checks* is *controls.*

veto *Veto* is Latin for *I forbid.*

unconstitutional Remind students that the prefix *un-* means *not.*

Critical Thinking

Conclude How would our government be different if the powers given to the states had been given to the national government?

Think Aloud *The national government would be much larger in order to take on all of these responsibilities.*

Limits on Government

Main Idea The Constitution puts limits on the power of the government.

4 **James Madison** and the other authors of the Constitution created a government with three branches to make sure that the government's powers were limited. No single person or branch has the power to run the United States government alone. Power is divided among the branches.

The delegates to the Constitutional Convention also worried that one branch might become stronger than the other two. They set up checks and balances to keep this from happening.

Checks and balances are a system that lets each branch limit the power of the other two.

The chart below shows examples of checks and balances. The President makes treaties and chooses judges. The President can also **veto,** or reject, laws made by Congress. Congress may reject judges selected by the President and treaties made by the President. Only Congress can declare war. The Supreme Court decides whether laws are unconstitutional. Laws that are **unconstitutional** do not follow rules laid out by the Constitution. If a law is unconstitutional, the law is no longer in effect. 5

Checks and Balances

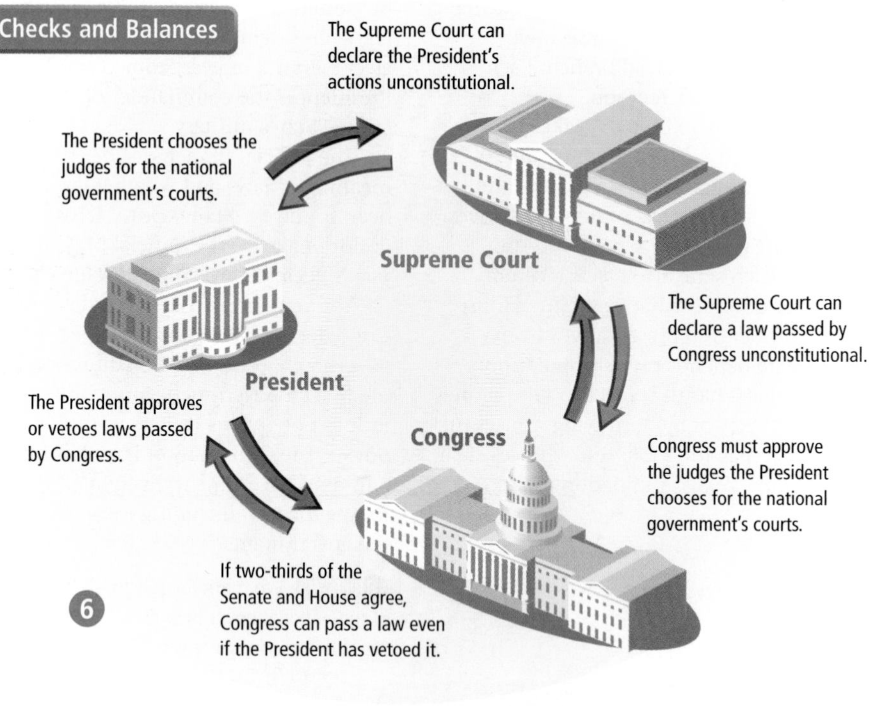

The Supreme Court can declare the President's actions unconstitutional.
The President chooses the judges for the national government's courts.
Supreme Court
The Supreme Court can declare a law passed by Congress unconstitutional.
President
The President approves or vetoes laws passed by Congress.
Congress
Congress must approve the judges the President chooses for the national government's courts.
6
If two-thirds of the Senate and House agree, Congress can pass a law even if the President has vetoed it.

Checks and Balances This diagram shows some of the ways that each branch of the national government can check the power of the other two branches.

314 • Chapter 9

Art

Illustrated Timeline

- Have students read a short biography of James Madison.
- Ask them to make an illustrated timeline of Madison's life.

Visual-spatial

Language Arts

Write a Speech

- Ask students to write a speech that begins with Thomas Jefferson's statement that the American people need a Bill of Rights "to guard the people against the federal government . . ."
- Have students make a list of rights they feel still need to be written into the Constitution, and why they think each right should be added.

Verbal linguistic

The Federal System

The Constitution created a federal system. Remember that under a federal system, the national government and the state governments each have certain powers. This system gives the national government more power than it had under the Articles of Confederation.

The federal government has power over issues that affect the whole country. Its jobs include defending the country, printing money, running the Post Office, and regulating trade between states.

States have more power over local issues. Public education and elections are two state responsibilities. The federal and state governments share certain powers as well. For example, federal and state governments both collect taxes and set (7) up court systems.

Even though the federal government's power is limited, the Constitution makes its laws stronger than state laws. When a state law and a federal law do not agree, the federal law must be obeyed. (8)

REVIEW Why did the authors of the Constitution create checks and balances and a federal system? to limit the power of the government and the branches of the government

Federal System of Government

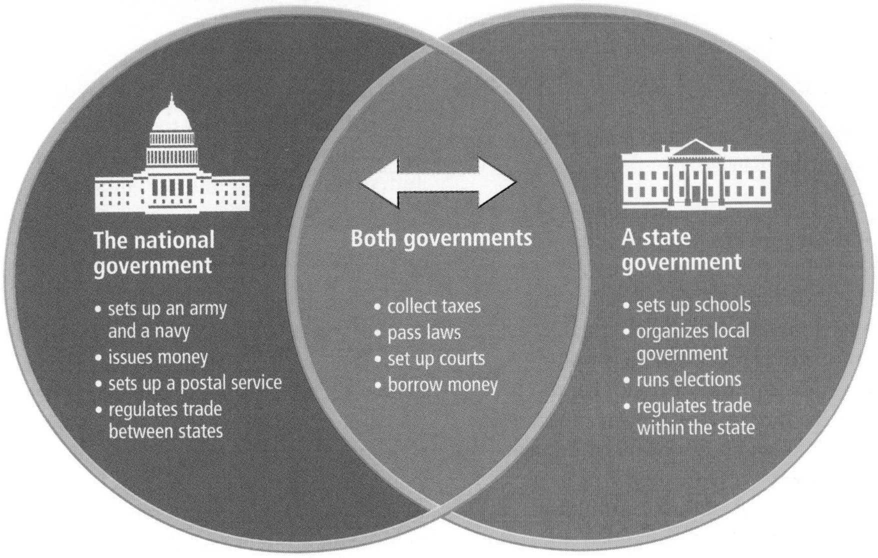

The national government
• sets up an army and a navy
• issues money
• sets up a postal service
• regulates trade between states
Both governments
• collect taxes
• pass laws
• set up courts
• borrow money
A state government
• sets up schools
• organizes local government
• runs elections
• regulates trade within the state

Federal System Some powers belong only to the national government, while others belong to state and local governments.

SKILL Reading Diagrams What are two powers that the state governments and the national government share?
Sample answer: collecting taxes and borrowing money.

Limits on Government *continued*

Talk About It

(7) **Q Economics** Who has the power to collect taxes?

A federal and state governments

(8) **Q Citizenship** When a state law and a federal law do not agree, which law must be obeyed?

A federal law

Reading Strategy: Infer Ask students to infer what would happen if our government did not have checks and balances. Have students share their inferences with the class.

Extra Support

Examples of the Federal System

- Distribute copies of newspapers to students and ask them to cut out articles that have to do with powers that belong to the states, to the national government, and powers that belong to both.
- Have students **highlight the sentences** in the article that have the information they are looking for, and ask them to share their findings with the class.

Verbal-linguistic

Challenge

Debate the Amendment Process

- Tell students they will debate whether the amendment process should be changed to make it easier to amend the Constitution.
- Divide students into two groups. Assign one group to make a list of arguments in favor of changing the amendment process and assign the other to think of arguments to support keeping the process the way it is.
- When students have finished their preparations, hold the debate.

Verbal-linguistic

Changing the Constitution

Talk About It

9 **Q Citizenship** How can an amendment be added to the Constitution?

A Usually, an amendment is proposed by two-thirds of both houses of Congress. Three-fourths of the states must ratify it.

10 **Q Citizenship** Why did people want a Bill of Rights?

A to make sure the federal government would recognize the rights of individuals

11 **Q Citizenship** What are some of the rights that are protected in the first amendment?

A freedom of speech and freedom of religion

Vocabulary Strategy

amendment The root word of *amendment* is the verb *amend.* It comes from the Latin word *emendare,* which means *to correct.*

Critical Thinking

Conclude Look at the Bill of Rights on pages 334–335. Which of these rights do you think is the most important? Why?

The Right to Vote Over time, amendments to the Constitution have protected the right to vote for more citizens. The chart on the right shows three amendments that have affected who can vote.

Voting Rights

1870
Fifteenth Amendment
Right of African American men to vote recognized.

1920
Nineteenth Amendment
Right of women to vote recognized.

1971
Twenty-sixth Amendment
Voting age lowered from 21 to 18.

Changing the Constitution

Main Idea The Constitution is designed so that it can be changed.

The authors of the Constitution knew that the nation would grow and change. They included a way to add amendments to the Constitution. An **amendment** is a change to the Constitution. Usually, an amendment is proposed by two-thirds of
9 the members of the House of Representatives and the Senate. Three-fourths of the states must ratify, or officially accept,
10 the amendment. Only then is the amendment part of the Constitution.

Many Americans demanded that a Bill of Rights be added to the Constitution. People wanted to be sure that the stronger federal government would recognize the rights of individuals.

State constitutions listed the rights of citizens and people wanted the U.S. Constitution to do so as well. **Thomas Jefferson** wanted a Bill of Rights

> "to guard the people against the federal government . . ."

James Madison agreed. He wrote amendments listing rights that were to be protected. In 1791, the 10 amendments known as the Bill of Rights were ratified.

Some of Madison's amendments are famous. The First Amendment protects
many important rights, such as freedom 11
of speech and freedom of religion. The Tenth Amendment says that the federal government only has the powers given to it by the Constitution. All other powers belong to the states or to the people.

316 • Chapter 9

Math

Calculation: Division

- Today, Congress has 100 Senators and 435 Representatives. How many members of each house would have to ratify an amendment before it could be sent to the states for approval? 67 Senators and 290 Representatives
- How many states would then have to ratify the amendment for it to become a part of the Constitution? 38

Logical-mathematical

Language Arts

Write a Personal Opinion Essay

Ask students to write a three or four paragraph essay to express their opinion about the importance of freedom of speech or freedom of religion.

Verbal-linguistic

Speaking Out Americans have often worked together to demand their rights. These women demanded the right to vote.

The Growth of Democracy

In 1790, the Constitution did not protect the rights of all Americans. Thousands of African Americans remained in slavery. Some states allowed only white men who had a certain amount of land or money to vote. The rights of women, African Americans, American Indians, and poor people were not recognized.

Ideas about democracy have changed since 1790, and the Constitution has changed with them. Different groups have fought for their rights and won.

Amendments have been added to the Constitution to protect the voting rights of men and women of all races. Today the equal protection promised by the Constitution is given to more citizens than ever before.

REVIEW Why does the Constitution include a way to make amendments? so that the Constitution can be changed

Lesson Summary

- The federal government is divided into the legislative, executive, and judicial branches.
- Checks and balances keep any one branch from becoming too powerful.
- The Constitution divides power between the federal government and the states.
- The Constitution can be changed by amendment.

Why It Matters . . .

The Constitution desribes the rules for the government under which you live today.

Lesson Review

1. **VOCABULARY** Use **democracy** and **amendment** in a paragraph about the Constitution.
2. **READING SKILL** Think about the **categories** of jobs the federal government does. What jobs can the legislative branch do that other branches cannot?
3. **MAIN IDEA: Government** Which powers do the states have that the federal government does not have?
4. **MAIN IDEA: Government** What must happen for an amendment to become part of the Constitution?
5. **CRITICAL THINKING: Conclude** Why did the authors of the Constitution want a limited government?
6. **CRITICAL THINKING: Summarize** How do the judicial and executive branches limit the power of the legislative branch?

RESEARCH ACTIVITY Find out who represents you in the Senate and the House of Representatives. The President is also your representative. List these people. Explain what each person's job is and how he or she represents you.

317

3 Review/Assess

Review Tested Objectives

U4-24 The legislative branch makes laws, the executive branch carries out laws, and the judicial branch decides the meaning of laws. A system of checks and balances limits the powers of each of the three branches.

U4-25 The Constitution has changed, through amendments and interpretation, throughout American history.

Lesson Review Answers

1. Answer should explain these terms in relation to the role of citizens in government and the power to change the Constitution.
2. Congress makes laws for the country. It raises money through taxes or by borrowing and uses the money to pay for goods and services.
3. setting up schools and running elections
4. Two-thirds of Congress must propose it and three-fourths of the states must agree to it.
5. to be sure no person or branch has the power to run the government alone
6. The judicial branch can decide a law is unconstitutional; the President can approve or veto laws Congress has passed.

Writing Rubric

4	List is accurate and complete; spelling is correct.
3	List is generally accurate and complete; spelling is mostly correct.
2	List is partly accurate and complete; some errors in spelling.
1	List is absent or incomplete; many errors in spelling.

Study Guide/Homework

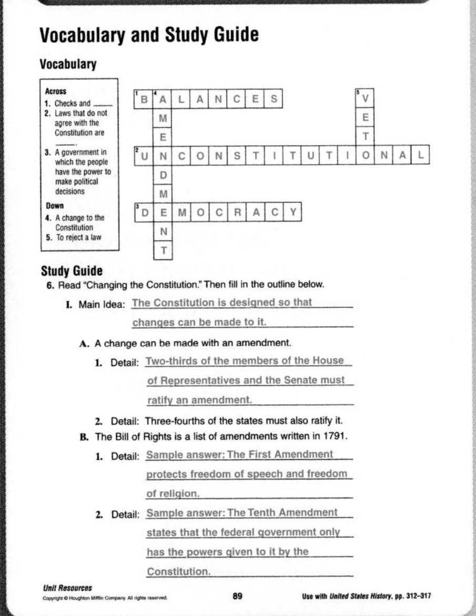

Vocabulary and Study Guide

Vocabulary

Across
1. Checks and ____ — BALANCES
2. Laws that do not agree with the Constitution are ____. — UNCONSTITUTIONAL
3. A government in which the people have the power to make political decisions — DEMOCRACY

Down
4. A change to the Constitution — AMENDMENT
5. To reject a law — VETO

Study Guide

6. Read "Changing the Constitution." Then fill in the outline below.
   - I. Main Idea: The Constitution is designed so that changes can be made to it.
     - A. A change can be made with an amendment.
       1. Detail: Two-thirds of the members of the House of Representatives and the Senate must ratify an amendment.
       2. Detail: Three-fourths of the states must also ratify it.
     - B. The Bill of Rights is a list of amendments written in 1791.
       1. Detail: Sample answer: The First Amendment protects freedom of speech and freedom of religion.
       2. Detail: Sample answer: The Tenth Amendment states that the federal government only has the powers given to it by the Constitution.

Unit Resources
Copyright © Houghton Mifflin Company. All rights reserved.
89
Use with *United States History*, pp. 312–317

Unit Resources, p. 89

Reteach Minilesson

Use a graphic organizer to reteach the functions of each branch of government.

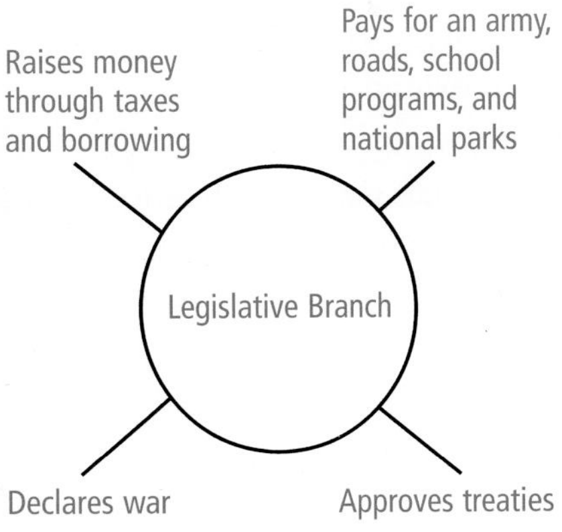

Raises money through taxes and borrowing
Pays for an army, roads, school programs, and national parks
Legislative Branch
Declares war
Approves treaties

Graphic Organizer 7

Extend Quick Look

Connect to the Core Lesson Core Lesson 3 discusses the writing and meaning of the United States Constitution. In Extend Lesson 3, students will learn more about the Liberty Bell, a symbol of the freedom that is protected by the Constitution.

1 Teach the Extend Lesson

Connect to the Big Idea

Democratic Values American democracy embraces certain values, including life, liberty, self-government, and patriotism. Throughout our history, Americans have adopted symbols that reflect their values. One of those symbols is the Liberty Bell.

Extend Lesson 3

History

The Liberty Bell

In 1751, Pennsylvania lawmakers had a bell made to celebrate freedom. That year was the 50th anniversary of Pennsylvania's charter. This charter, or official document, promised freedom to people in the colony.

Quakers founded Pennsylvania so they would be free to practice their religious beliefs. They gave people who practiced other beliefs the same freedom. They wrote a verse from the Bible on the bell: "Proclaim LIBERTY throughout the land unto all the inhabitants thereof."

The Bell rang to bring citizens together for important announcements and events. It rang on July 8, 1776 for the first public reading of the Declaration of Independence. It rang when the U.S. Constitution was ratified.

Independence
The Bell rang on July 8, 1776, to call the people of Philadelphia. They listened to Captain John Dixon read aloud the Declaration of Independence.

The Great Train Ride
In 1915, the Bell traveled from Philadelphia to San Francisco by train. In towns and cities along the way, flag-waving crowds greeted the Bell with brass bands.

318 • Chapter 9

Reaching All Learners

Extra Support

Illustrate a Fact

- Ask students to illustrate one fact that they have learned about the Liberty Bell.
- Have students include the fact as a caption on their illustrations.
- Display illustrations in class.

Visual-spatial; verbal-linguistic

On Level

Make a Timeline

- Have students make a timeline of the history of the Liberty Bell.
- Tell students that their timelines should extend from 1751 to today.

Visual-spatial; verbal-linguistic

Challenge

Write an Essay

- Ask students to suppose that they could ring the Liberty Bell at an important event.
- Have students write an essay about what event they would choose and why. What would it mean to ring the bell at this event?
- Ask students to share their essays with the class.

Verbal-linguistic

HISTORY

Liberty Bell Facts

★ ★ ★ ★

Circumference around the lip: 12 feet

Height from lip to crown: 3 feet

Weight: 2080 pounds

Length of clapper: 3 feet, 2 inches

Length of crack: 2 feet, 1/2 inch

Activities

1. **DRAW YOUR OWN** What object would you choose to celebrate freedom on a special anniversary? Draw the object. Explain why it is a symbol of freedom.
2. **ACT IT OUT** More than one million people visit the Liberty Bell each year. Prepare a talk that a tour guide might give visitors about the bell's history.

319

2 Leveled Activities

❶ **Draw Your Own** *For Extra Support*
Answers will vary but should clearly explain why it is a symbol of freedom.

❷ **Act It Out** *For Challenge*

HANDS ON Performance Task Rubric

4	Talk is engaging, creative, and clear; facts are thorough and accurate.
3	Talk is somewhat engaging and clear; most facts are accurate.
2	Talk is somewhat unclear and is not very engaging; some facts are inaccurate.
1	Talk is unclear and does not address or engage the audience; most facts are inaccurate.

REACHING ALL LEARNERS — ELL

Advanced

- Ask students to work in pairs to paraphrase the Liberty Bell's inscription: "Proclaim LIBERTY throughout the land unto all the inhabitants thereof."
- Have pairs share their paraphrases with the class.

Verbal-linguistic

Language Arts

Write a Poem

- Have students write a poem about the Liberty Bell.
- Poems should include history and facts from the Extend Lesson.
- Ask students to share their poems with the class.

Verbal-linguistic

Graphic Organizer

Liberty Bell

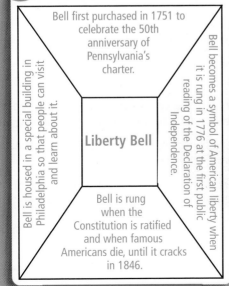

- Bell first purchased in 1751 to celebrate the 50th anniversary of Pennsylvania's charter.
- Bell becomes a symbol of American liberty when it is rung in 1776 at the first public reading of the Declaration of Independence.
- Bell is rung when the Constitution is ratified and when famous Americans die, until it cracks in 1846.
- Bell is housed in a special building in Philadelphia so that people can visit and learn about it.

Graphic Organizer 12

✓ Tested Objectives

U4-26 Citizenship Identify important policies established by President George Washington.

U4-27 Citizenship Compare the views of Hamilton and Jefferson and describe how they affected the development of American political parties.

Lesson Quick Look

This lesson describes the presidency of George Washington.

Teaching Option: Extend Lesson 4 presents some of the people who shaped Washington, D.C.

1 Get Set to Read

Preview Have students share what they already know about Washington.

Reading Skill: Cause and Effect Details may include Washington's interactions with Cabinet members.

Build on What You Know Discuss with students what can help them succeed at something new. Explain that having expert advice and learning as much as possible in advance helped George Washington succeed.

Vocabulary

inauguration *noun,* the ceremony at which a government official is sworn into office

Cabinet *noun,* a group appointed by a President to help govern the country

political party *noun,* a group that works together to gain power in government

interest *noun,* the fee that a borrower pays to a lender

capital *noun,* the city where a state or national government officially meets

Core Lesson 4

President Washington

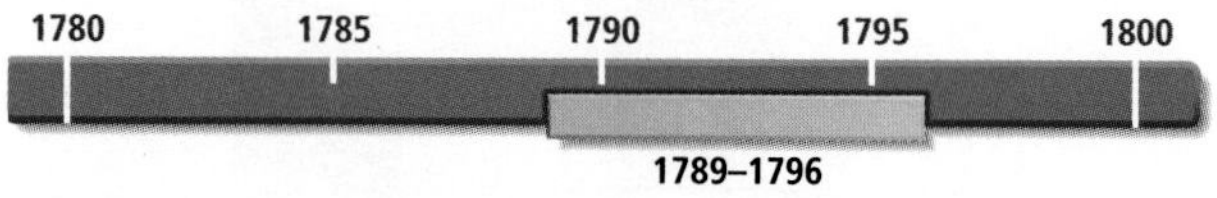

VOCABULARY

inauguration
Cabinet
political party
interest
capital

Vocabulary Strategy

Cabinet

The President's group of advisors is called the **Cabinet**. Such groups used to meet in small private rooms. Rooms like this were called cabinets.

READING SKILL

Cause and Effect As you read, note results of George Washington's presidency.

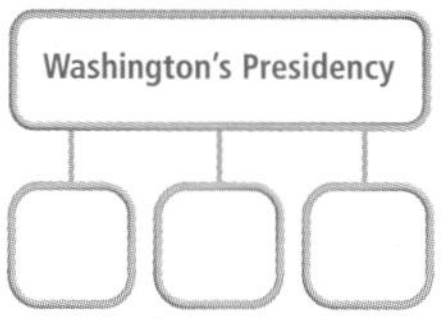

Build on What You Know Are you sometimes nervous when you start something new? Many people are. Even George Washington was not sure he would do a good job as the first President of the United States.

The First President

Main Idea George Washington became the first President under the Constitution.

The United States elected a President for the first time in 1789. The Constitution set up the system for elections. The states chose representatives for a group called the Electoral College. It was the job of the members of the Electoral College to vote for the President. Everyone in the first Electoral College agreed that **George Washington** was the only one for the job. Washington, however, was not sure he would succeed. He wrote,

> **"My Countrymen will expect too much from me,"**

Washington knew his actions would set an example for other Presidents to follow. He acted with thought and care. 1

Souvenirs These buttons celebrated the new Congress and President.

SKILL Primary Source What do you think the letters GW on the souvenir stand for?
George Washington

Skill and Strategy

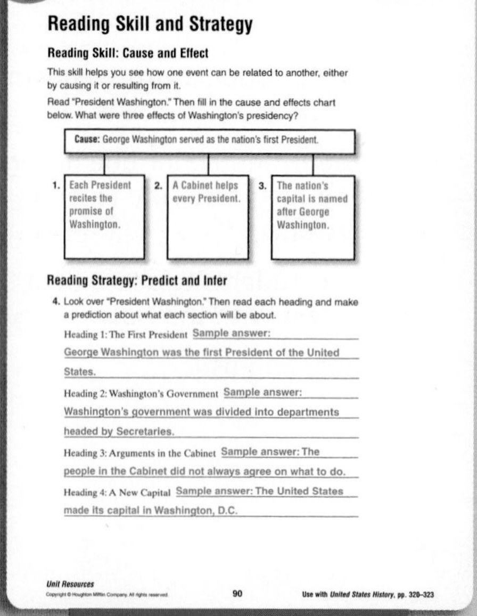

Reading Skill and Strategy

Reading Skill: Cause and Effect

This skill helps you see how one event can be related to another, either by causing it or resulting from it.

Read "President Washington." Then fill in the cause and effects chart below. What were three effects of Washington's presidency?

Cause: George Washington served as the nation's first President.

1. Each President recites the promise of Washington.
2. A Cabinet helps every President.
3. The nation's capital is named after George Washington.

Reading Strategy: Predict and Infer

4. Look over "President Washington." Then read each heading and make a prediction about what each section will be about.

Heading 1: The First President Sample answer: George Washington was the first President of the United States.

Heading 2: Washington's Government Sample answer: Washington's government was divided into departments headed by Secretaries.

Heading 3: Arguments in the Cabinet Sample answer: The people in the Cabinet did not always agree on what to do.

Heading 4: A New Capital Sample answer: The United States made its capital in Washington, D.C.

Unit Resources

90
Use with *United States History*, pp. 320–323

Unit Resources, p. 90

Background

New Traditions

- Congress debated how to properly address the President. John Adams proposed, "His Most Benign Highness." Others supported, "His Highness, the President of the United States, and Protector of the Rights of the Same." They finally agreed on a simpler title, "Mr. President."

Inauguration George Washington takes the oath of office at Federal Hall in New York City. Those behind him include Alexander Hamilton and Henry Knox.

Washington's Government

In April 1789, Washington traveled to New York City, where the government met. He was greeted as a hero. An excited crowd watched his inauguration (ihn aw gyur AY shun) in New York City. An **inauguration** is an official ceremony to make someone President. Washington promised to

> "preserve, protect, and defend the Constitution of the United States."

Every President since Washington has made the same promise.

Congress created three departments to help the President run the executive branch. Washington chose people he trusted to run the departments. They were called Secretaries. **Thomas Jefferson** became Washington's Secretary of State. He would decide how the United States acted toward other countries. Washington picked **Alexander Hamilton** to take care of the nation's finances as Secretary of the Treasury. General **Henry Knox**, who had been in the army with Washington, became Secretary of War. Knox would be in charge of protecting the nation. **Edmund Randolph** became Attorney General. He would see that federal laws were obeyed. 2 3

These men often met at Washington's house to advise him. Together, they became known as the President's Cabinet. The **Cabinet** is a group chosen by the President to help run the executive branch and give advice. Every President since Washington has had a Cabinet.

REVIEW What is the purpose of the Cabinet?
to give the President advice and help run the executive branch

2 Teach

The First President

Talk About It

1. **Q History** Why did George Washington act with care as President?
   A He was the nation's first President and knew his actions would set an example for other Presidents to follow.

2. **Q Citizenship** What is the job of the Secretary of State?
   A The Secretary of State decides how the United States should behave toward other countries.

3. **Q Economics** What is the job of the Attorney General?
   A to see that federal laws are obeyed

Vocabulary Strategy

inauguration Explain to students that the prefix *in-* in *inauguration* means *in, into,* or *within.* An *inauguration* is the ceremony at which a government official is sworn *into* office.

Cabinet Tell students that *cabinet* comes from a French word for *small room.*

Reading Strategy: Infer Ask students to infer some of the challenges Washington faced as the first President.

Reaching All Learners — Leveled Practice

Extra Support

Have students **make a chart** of the four Cabinet departments organized during Washington's presidency. Tell students to write down the duties of each department and the name of the first person Washington chose to run the department. Visual-spatial

Challenge

Have students research the Cabinet departments of today, listing each and briefly describing what it does. Verbal-linguistic

Reaching All Learners — ELL

Beginning

- Working in pairs, have students write down the names of the four Cabinet offices discussed in the text.
- Encourage students to **illustrate** what each Cabinet officer does for the government.

Visual-spatial

Arguments in the Cabinet

Talk About It

4 **Q History** Why did Jefferson and Hamilton often give the President opposite advice?

A Hamilton wanted a strong central government, while Jefferson felt it should be weak.

5 **Q History** Which side did Washington take on the national bank?

A He took Hamilton's advice and approved the law creating it.

6 **Q Geography** Where was the nation's new capital located?

A on the Potomac River, between Virginia and Maryland

Vocabulary Strategy

political party *Party* has several meanings, including *a gathering of people for pleasure* (birthday party), *for an activity* (search party), and *for promoting ideas about government* (political party).

Interest Mnemonic: People are interested in earning *interest.*

capital Homophonic mnemonic: Congress meets in the *Capitol* building in our nation's *capital* city, Washington, D.C.

Critical Thinking

Analyze George Washington opposed political parties because he felt they divided people instead of bringing them together. Do you agree or disagree?

Jefferson wanted the nation's economy to help the farmers who owned small plots of land. He felt the people should be as free of government control as possible.

Points of View

Thomas Jefferson and Alexander Hamilton were both in Washington's Cabinet. They argued about the role of the government in the United States.

Hamilton believed that the nation would be stronger if its economy helped large businesses and trade. He thought that a strong government was necessary to keep order and make rules about trade.

Arguments in the Cabinet

Main Idea Hamilton and Jefferson argued about how the government should act.

4 Two Cabinet members, Hamilton and Jefferson, often disagreed. Hamilton wanted a strong national government that supported trade and manufacturing. Jefferson felt that the government should be limited so that it could not take away states' rights. He said it should support farming instead of trade.

Jefferson and Hamilton both had followers who formed political parties. A **political party** is a group of people who share similar ideas about government. People supporting Jefferson formed the Democratic-Republican Party. Hamilton's party was known as the Federalist Party.

Hamilton and Jefferson often gave the President opposite advice. For example, Hamilton wanted to start a national bank. He believed it would make the nation wealthier and stronger.

Jefferson was against the idea. He said that the government did not have the power to create the bank. Washington took Hamilton's advice. He approved the law that created a national bank. 5

The national bank controlled the money of the United States. Customers could keep money in savings accounts there. Today, a savings account is a way to earn money. The bank borrows from savings accounts to make loans. It earns money on the loans by charging interest. **Interest** is what people pay to borrow money. The bank also pays interest for the use of the money to each person who has a savings account.

Hamilton and Jefferson compromised on some problems. Hamilton supported Jefferson's wish to build a new national capital on the Potomac River, between Virginia and Maryland. A **capital** is the city where the government meets. In return, Jefferson agreed to Hamilton's plan to pay the nation's war debts. 6

322 • Chapter 9

Math

Calculate Perimeter and Area

- Washington, D.C. today is the site of many national monuments, including the Washington Monument.
- Tell students that the base of the Washington Monument is square, and is about 55 feet long on each side.
- Have them calculate the perimeter and area of the monument.

Logical-mathematical

Language Arts

Write a Farewell Address

Ask students to **write a farewell address** that a member of Congress might have offered upon Washington's retirement. Tell students to describe Washington's accomplishments in the address.

Verbal-linguistic

President Washington chose the new capital's exact location. **Andrew Ellicott** and **Benjamin Banneker,** both astronomers, measured the land. A French engineer, **Pierre L'Enfant** (lahn FAHN), designed the city. Building began in 1792. The city was named Washington, to honor the President.

After eight years as President, Washington announced his retirement in a farewell address, or speech, to the nation. In his address, he advised people not to form political parties. He felt parties divided people. Washington also wanted the nation to stay out of wars between other countries. Britain and France were at war at this time. Washington refused to take sides. For many years after that, the nation did not take sides in any foreign wars.

George Washington is remembered as a great hero. One of Washington's friends said that he was

> **"first in war, first in peace, and first in the hearts of his countrymen."**

REVIEW Why did Hamilton and Jefferson disagree about creating a national bank? Jefferson believed the government did not have the power to start the national bank that Hamilton wanted.

Lesson Summary

- George Washington became the first President under the Constitution.
- Disagreements in the Cabinet led to the first political parties.
- Washington agreed to a plan for a national bank and chose the location of a capital city.

Why It Matters . . .

The presidency of George Washington set up traditions that have been followed by all American Presidents.

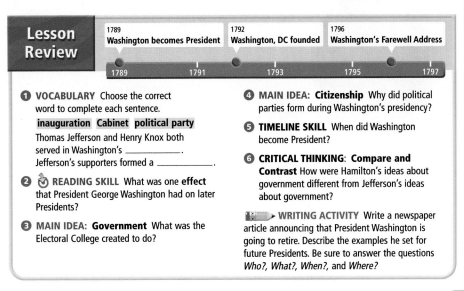

Lesson Review

1789 Washington becomes President
1792 Washington, DC founded
1796 Washington's Farewell Address

1789 — 1791 — 1793 — 1795 — 1797

1. **VOCABULARY** Choose the correct word to complete each sentence.
   inauguration **Cabinet** **political party**
   Thomas Jefferson and Henry Knox both served in Washington's __________.
   Jefferson's supporters formed a __________.
2. **READING SKILL** What was one **effect** that President George Washington had on later Presidents?
3. **MAIN IDEA: Government** What was the Electoral College created to do?
4. **MAIN IDEA: Citizenship** Why did political parties form during Washington's presidency?
5. **TIMELINE SKILL** When did Washington become President?
6. **CRITICAL THINKING: Compare and Contrast** How were Hamilton's ideas about government different from Jefferson's ideas about government?

WRITING ACTIVITY Write a newspaper article announcing that President Washington is going to retire. Describe the examples he set for future Presidents. Be sure to answer the questions *Who?, What?, When?,* and *Where?*

3 Review/Assess

Review Tested Objectives

U4-26 Washington created the national bank. He opposed political parties and taking sides in international wars.

U4-27 Hamilton wanted a strong national government while Jefferson thought that states' rights should be protected from a strong national government. Hamilton's followers formed the Federalist party, while Jefferson's followers formed the Democratic-Republican party.

Lesson Review Answers

1. Cabinet; political party
2. Washington set examples for other Presidents to follow by promising to defend the Constitution, setting up the first Cabinet, and retiring after two terms.
3. vote for the President
4. Jefferson and Hamilton argued about the role of government and their followers formed political parties.
5. 1789
6. Hamilton wanted a strong national government. Jefferson wanted a weaker one. Hamilton felt that the Constitution was flexible enough to let Congress create a national bank, but Jefferson did not.

Writing Rubric

4	Article is clearly written; all questions answered; mechanics correct.
3	Article is well written; one question not answered; few errors in mechanics.
2	Article is disorganized; some questions unanswered; some errors in mechanics.
1	Article is confusing; many questions unanswered; many errors in mechanics.

Study Guide/Homework

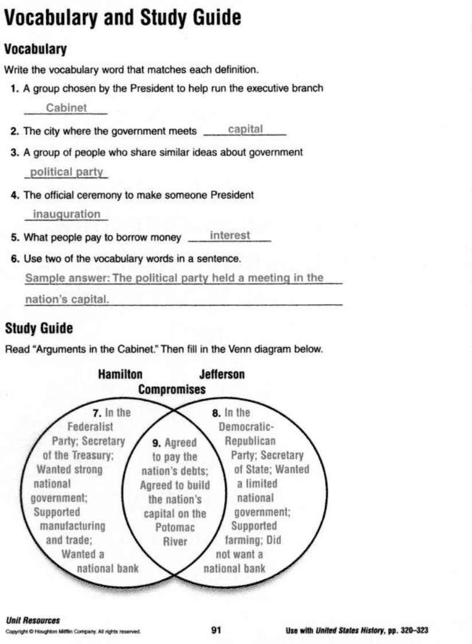
Vocabulary and Study Guide

Vocabulary

Write the vocabulary word that matches each definition.

1. A group chosen by the President to help run the executive branch Cabinet
2. The city where the government meets capital
3. A group of people who share similar ideas about government political party
4. The official ceremony to make someone President inauguration
5. What people pay to borrow money interest
6. Use two of the vocabulary words in a sentence. Sample answer: The political party held a meeting in the nation's capital.

Study Guide

Read "Arguments in the Cabinet." Then fill in the Venn diagram below.

Hamilton / Compromises / Jefferson

7. In the Federalist Party; Secretary of the Treasury; Wanted strong national government; Supported manufacturing and trade; Wanted a national bank

9. Agreed to pay the nation's debts; Agreed to build the nation's capital on the Potomac River

8. In the Democratic-Republican Party; Secretary of State; Wanted a limited national government; Supported farming; Did not want a national bank

Unit Resources
Copyright © Houghton Mifflin Company. All rights reserved.
91
Use with *United States History*, pp. 320–323

Unit Resources, p. 91

Reteach Minilesson

Use a graphic organizer to reteach the presidency of George Washington.

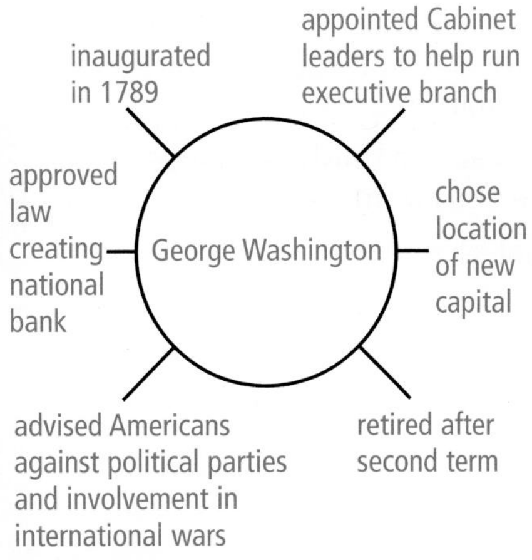
George Washington
inaugurated in 1789
appointed Cabinet leaders to help run executive branch
approved law creating national bank
chose location of new capital
advised Americans against political parties and involvement in international wars
retired after second term

Graphic Organizer 7

Quick Look

Connect to the Core Lesson Students have learned about President Washington in Lesson 4. In Extend Lesson 4, students will learn more about people who played important roles in the planning, design, and growth of our nation's capital.

1 Teach the Extend Lesson

Connect to the Big Idea

American Government Our government is made up of various branches, and each oversees parts of the government. To provide the government with a place to meet and do its work, George Washington selected a location on the Potomac River for the nation's new capital. Many people helped in its design and growth.

Citizenship

Washington, D.C.

Could Washington, D.C. be changed from a small, muddy town to a city as glorious as Paris? A French city planner thought so. Pierre L'Enfant [lahn-FAHN] imagined a great capital city for the United States. Located on the Potomac River, the city would have parks, tree-lined avenues, and grand public buildings. He created a plan for the city in 1791. By 1800, his plan became reality. Washington, D.C. became the capital of the United States. The city center is much as L'Enfant designed it.

Although L'Enfant planned the city, many other people helped make it what it is today. Three of them are shown here.

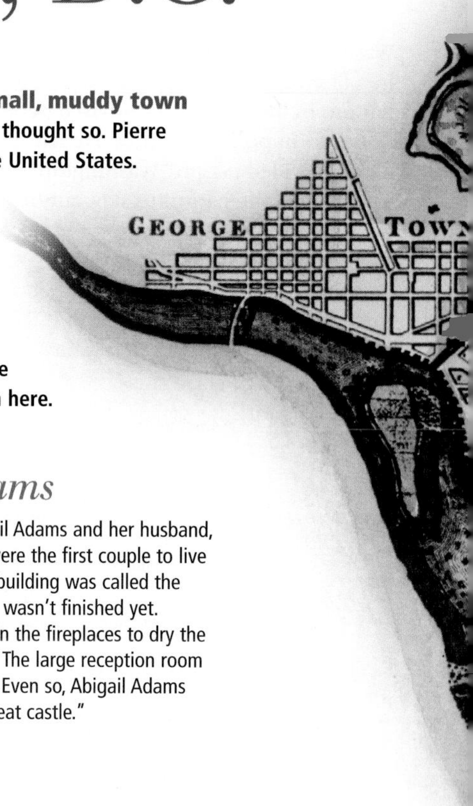

Abigail Adams

In 1800, First Lady Abigail Adams and her husband, President John Adams, were the first couple to live in the White House. The building was called the President's House, and it wasn't finished yet. Fires were kept burning in the fireplaces to dry the wet plaster on the walls. The large reception room was used to dry laundry. Even so, Abigail Adams called the building a "great castle."

Benjamin Banneker

Benjamin Banneker was a farmer who studied astronomy and other sciences. In 1791, Banneker helped survey, or measure, the land for the new capital city. As part of the job of surveying the land, Banneker set the boundaries for what would be the city. Today, many buildings and organizations are named for Banneker, including a high school in Washington, D.C.

Reaching All Learners

Extra Support

Write Descriptions

- Divide students into small groups. Ask each group to write a description of one of the people who helped make Washington, D.C. what it is today.
- Tell students that their descriptions should not include the person's name.
- When groups are finished, have a student from each group read the group's description to the class. Have the class try to figure out the identity of the person described.

Verbal-linguistic

On Level

Make a Stamp

- Have students design a postage stamp for Washington, D.C., using the information in the Extend Lesson for ideas and subject matter.
- Display the finished stamps in the classroom.

Visual-spatial

Challenge

Redesign D.C.

- Ask students to suppose that they could redesign Washington, D.C. Have them consider what they would change about the location, layout, architecture, name, and purpose of the nation's capital. What would they keep the same?
- Ask them to draw plans of the capital as they would redesign it, and have them present their plans to the class. If they think that the capital should not be changed, have them explain why.

Visual-spatial

William Thornton

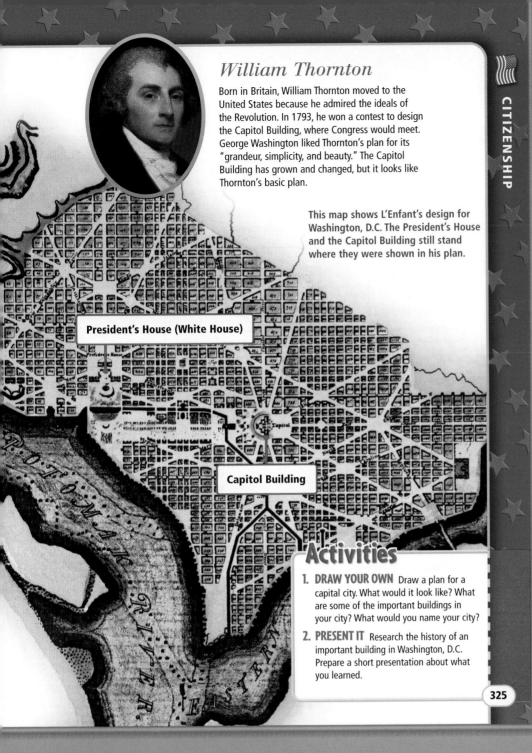

Born in Britain, William Thornton moved to the United States because he admired the ideals of the Revolution. In 1793, he won a contest to design the Capitol Building, where Congress would meet. George Washington liked Thornton's plan for its "grandeur, simplicity, and beauty." The Capitol Building has grown and changed, but it looks like Thornton's basic plan.

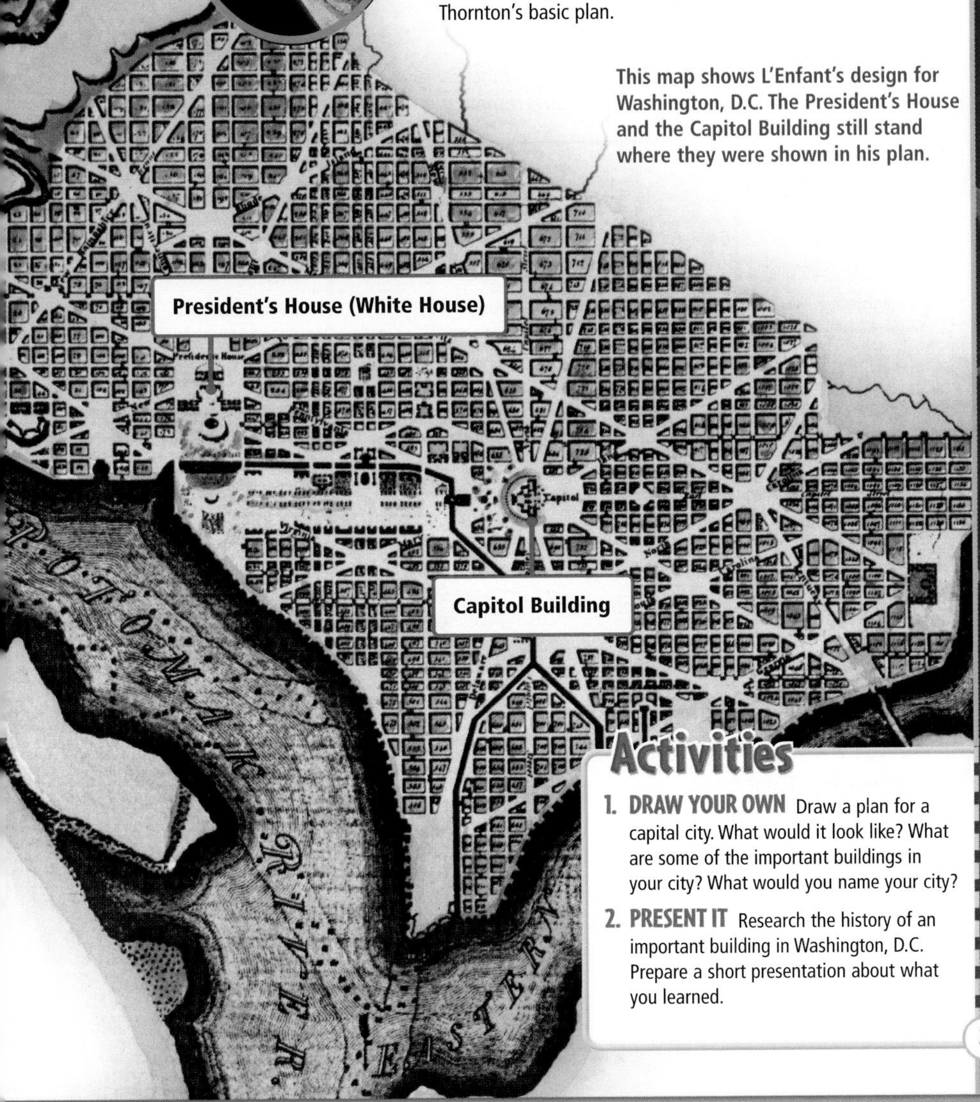

This map shows L'Enfant's design for Washington, D.C. The President's House and the Capitol Building still stand where they were shown in his plan.

CITIZENSHIP

Activities

1. **DRAW YOUR OWN** Draw a plan for a capital city. What would it look like? What are some of the important buildings in your city? What would you name your city?
2. **PRESENT IT** Research the history of an important building in Washington, D.C. Prepare a short presentation about what you learned.

325

2 Leveled Activities

❶ **Draw Your Own** *For Extra Support*
Drawings will vary, but students should include buildings for the branches of government they have learned about.

❷ **Present It** *For Challenge*

HANDS ON

	Performance Task Rubric
4	Presentation conveys information clearly; facts are accurate; mechanics are correct.
3	Presentation conveys information adequately; most facts cited are accurate; most mechanics are correct.
2	Presentation conveys ideas adequately; some errors in facts or mechanics.
1	Presentation conveys ideas in a very general or incomprehensible way; many errors in facts or mechanics.

REACHING ALL LEARNERS

ELL

Intermediate

- Have students work in small groups to **draw a cartoon strip** about the growth of Washington, D.C. as our nation's capital.
- Ask students to **write short captions** for their cartoons.

Visual-spatial

Math

Make a Bar Graph

- Have students make a bar graph of the heights of various government buildings and monuments in Washington, D.C. Tell students that one bar should represent each building. Have students label each bar.
- Washington Monument: 555 feet
- Capitol: 288 feet
- Jefferson Memorial: 129 feet
- Lincoln Memorial: 99 feet
- White House: 70 feet

Logical-mathematical

Graphic Organizer

1	1791—L'Enfant completes plan of capital; Benjamin Banneker surveys land.
2	1793—William Thornton wins contest to design the Capitol.
3	1800—Washington, D.C. becomes the nation's capital. John and Abigail Adams move into the President's House.
4	1935—Supreme Court gets its own building.

Graphic Organizer 15

Chapter Review

Tested Objectives

The lesson objective assessed by each question is shown in parentheses after the answer.

Visual Summary

1. makes laws for the United States *(Obj. U4-25)*
2. carries out the laws made by the Congress *(Obj. U4-25)*
3. decides the meaning of laws and whether they have been followed *(Obj. U4-25)*

Facts and Main Ideas

4. It was a protest by Daniel Shays and other farmers against Massachusetts government. *(Obj. U4-20)*
5. Roger Sherman suggested that Congress should be divided into the House of Representatives and the Senate. *(Obj. U4-22)*
6. He was a member of Congress and a delegate to the Convention. He wanted a strong federal government. *(Obj. U4-21)*
7. Sample answers: freedom of religion, freedom of speech *(Obj. U4-23)*
8. The Cabinet is a group of people that helps run the executive branch and gives advice to the President. *(Obj. U4-25)*

Vocabulary

9. **compromise** *(Obj. U4-22)*
10. **political party** *(Obj. U4-28)*
11. **Constitution** *(Obj. U4-21)*

Visual Summary

1–3. Write a description of each branch of government.

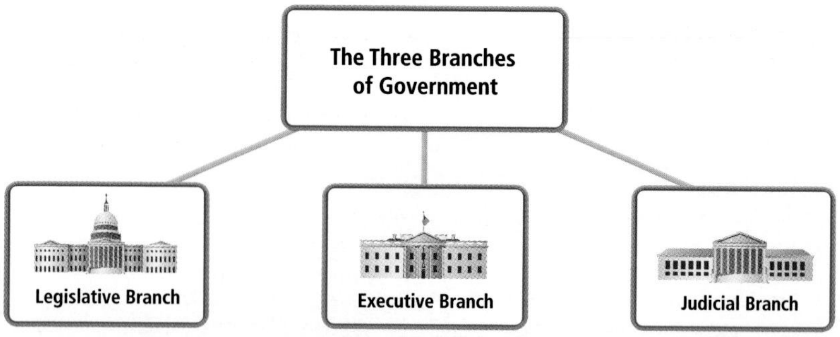

Facts and Main Ideas

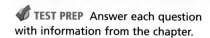

TEST PREP Answer each question with information from the chapter.

4. **History** What was Shays's Rebellion?
5. **Government** What was the Great Compromise?
6. **History** Who was James Madison and what did he do at the Constitutional Convention?
7. **Citizenship** Name two rights guaranteed by the Bill of Rights.
8. **Government** What is the purpose of the Cabinet?

Vocabulary

TEST PREP Choose the correct word from the list below to complete each sentence.

constitution, p. 296
compromise, p. 304
political party, p. 322

9. Two sides give up something they want in order to reach a _____.
10. The supporters of Alexander Hamilton formed a _____ and so did the supporters of Thomas Jefferson.
11. Delegates in Philadelphia wrote a new _____ for the United States in 1787.

Reading/Language Arts Wrap-Up

Reading Strategy: Predict/Infer

Review with students the process of evaluating information in order to make a prediction.

Based on what students have read in the chapter, you may wish to involve the class in making predictions about what they will read next.

Writing Strategy

As students write, they can apply what they know about predicting and inferring to how their readers will react to their text.

Have students review their written work and look for places where the reader has to infer or predict. Have students do a self-check: "Have I given the reader enough information to predict or infer correctly?"

CHAPTER SUMMARY TIMELINE

1781 Articles of Confederation — 1787 Constitutional Convention — 1789 Washington elected — 1792 Washington, D.C. founded

1780 | 1783 | 1786 | 1789 | 1792 | 1795

Apply Skills

TEST PREP Citizenship Skill Read the quotations below and use what you have learned about point of view to answer each question.

> "The local interests of a state ought, in every case, to give way to the interests of the Union."
> — Alexander Hamilton

> "...Some have weakly imagined that it is necessary to annihilate [destroy] the several states, and [give] Congress... government of the continent.... This however, would be impractical."
> — *Freeman's Journal* of Philadelphia

12. What was Hamilton's point of view?
    - **A.** States' interests are more important than the interests of the federal government.
    - **B.** The interests of the federal government are more important than states' interests.
    - **C.** The federal government is not important.
    - **D.** States are not important.
13. Describe the point of view expressed by the *Freeman's Journal* in your own words.

Critical Thinking

TEST PREP Write a short paragraph to answer each question.

14. **Infer** What effect did the Northwest Ordinance have on settlers?
15. **Problem and Solution** Name two problems caused by the Articles of Confederation. What solutions did delegates at the Constitutional Convention offer?

Timeline

Use the Chapter Summary Timeline above to answer the question.

16. When was the first President elected?

Activities

HANDS ON **Drama Activity** Prepare a scene of the debate that took place at the Constitutional Convention. Include delegates from both large and small states.

Writing Activity Write a personal essay that George Washington might have written in his autobiography. Describe how he might have felt about being the first President.

Technology
Writing Process Tips
Get help with your personal essay at **www.eduplace.com/kids/hmss05/**

327

Apply Skills

12. B *(Obj. U4-24)*
13. Some people think Congress should have more power than the states, but that would be a bad idea. *(Obj. U4-24)*

Critical Thinking

14. It affected how land was measured and sold to settlers and made slavery illegal in the Northwest Territory. *(Obj. U4-20)*
15. Congress could not tax so the government was not able to pay the debts owed from the war or set up an army. Delegates decided on a stronger federal government that could tax. *(Obj. U4-19)*

Timeline

16. 1789 *(Obj. U4-21)*

Leveled Activities

HANDS ON Performance Task Rubric

4	Positions clearly stated and supported; mechanics are correct.
3	Positions adequately stated and supported; few errors in mechanics.
2	Positions are stated; reasons confused or poorly supported by text information; some errors in mechanics.
1	Positions not stated; reasons not supported; many errors in mechanics.

Writing Rubric

4	Autobiography format is used correctly; main points are correct and supported; mechanics are correct.
3	Autobiography format is used; most main points are correct and supported; mechanics generally correct.
2	Autobiography format is attempted; main points contain errors or omissions; some errors in mechanics are present.
1	Autobiography format not used; main points contain errors; many errors in mechanics are present.

Technology

Test Generator

You can generate your own version of the chapter review by using the **Test Generator CD-ROM**.

Web Link

For more ideas, visit
www.eduplace.com/ss/hmss05/

Standards

National Standards

I b How experiences may be interpreted differently **II e** People view the world differently **VI b** Purpose of government **VI c** How government provides for needs and wants of people and establishes order and security **VI e** Local, state, and national government and representative leaders **VI h** Tensions between the wants and needs and fairness, equity, and justice **IX b** Conflict, cooperation, and interdependence **X a** Key ideals of the United States **X b** Rights and responsibilities **X f** Actors that influence and shape public policy **X h** Policies and behaviors may or may not reflect ideals **X i** Public policies and public concerns

Government

Unit Quick Look

This special section provides students with a succinct explanation of government, its levels, and its responsibilities.

1 Get Set to Read

Preview Ask students what they know about what government does and how it is structured.

Reading Skill: Main Idea and Details Students should look for the main idea and supporting details in each section, and take notes using a graphic organizer or an outline.

Special Section

The Government of the United States

Principles of Democracy

★★★

All nations have governments. A government is a group of people who make and enforce the laws of a political region, such as a country. Just as your school has rules, the nation has laws to govern its citizens.

Life in the United States would be difficult without government. The government sets up ways to choose leaders and makes laws to protect people at home and in the community. Governments run public schools and libraries and print stamps and money. When governments work well, they protect freedom and keep order.

Democratic Government

Governments take many forms. The United States is a democracy. A democracy is a government in which people govern themselves. In a democracy, citizens have the power to make political decisions.

The United States has a form of democracy called representative democracy. That means citizens elect representatives who speak or act for them in making laws.

Majority and Minority

In the United States, the majority of voters usually decides who will win an election. Majority means more than half. Many important decisions are made by majority rule. For example, the majority of lawmakers in Congress must agree on a law before it is passed.

Even though most decisions are made by majority rule, the rights of the minority are protected. Minority means fewer than half. The majority cannot take away the rights of small groups of people to express unpopular views or take part in the government. This limit on majority rule is sometimes called minority rights.

Reading/Language Arts Wrap-Up

Types of Government

The government of the United States is just one form of government. These other forms are also found around the world:

Monarchy: A system of government in which leadership is passed down through a family, from one generation to another.

Oligarchy: A government run by a few select persons or families.

Dictatorship: A system of government in which one person has absolute power and control.

The Rule of Law

The Constitution is the plan for the United States government. It is also the supreme, or highest, law of the United States. Everyone, including the President, must obey the country's laws. This is known as the rule of law. The rule of law is a system in which laws are made by elected representatives, not one or two individuals. The rule of law promises justice to all. In other words, it promises that laws will protect everyone equally.

Two Hundred Years Thousands of balloons were released to celebrate the 200th anniversary of the U.S. Constitution in 1987.

REVIEW What does the rule of law promise to everyone?

329

2 Teach

Principles of Democracy

Talk About It

1 **Q Citizenship** What are some of the roles of government?

A to run schools and libraries, and print stamps and money

2 **Q Citizenship** What is majority rule?

A a decision made by a majority, or more than half of the people involved

3 **Q Citizenship** What is the rule of law?

A Everyone must obey the nation's laws, even the President.

Leveled Practice

Extra Support

You may wish to have students use a main idea/details graphic organizer and take notes on the information on page 329.

Challenge

Have students investigate another form of government and present a brief oral report about it to the class.

ELL

Intermediate

Have students make a Constitution Timeline.

Provide them with the following, and ask them to construct a timeline with the information.

1776: Colonies declare independence.
1783: Revolutionary War ends.
1787: Constitution approved
1987: Constitution's 200th anniversary

Structure of the Government

Talk About It

4 Q Citizenship How does the system of checks and balances keep one branch of government from becoming too powerful?

A Each branch has powers that allow it to limit the actions of the other branches.

5 Q Citizenship What is the goal of the three branches of government?

A to work for the good of all people in the country

Vocabulary Strategies

Unconstitutional Help students find the word *constitution* in *unconstitutional*. Note that the prefix *un-* means "not," and the suffix *-al* means "of." So *unconstitutional* means not of the constitution—it describes a law or action that goes against the constitution.

Balance Explain to students that *balance* refers to the balance of power among the branches—by being balanced, power is never concentrated in one branch.

Structure *of the* Government

★★★

The federal government is our national government. The Constitution created a federal government with three branches. These branches, or parts, are the legislative, executive, and judicial branches.

The three branches of government work together, but each branch has its own powers. A system of checks and balances prevents any one branch from having too much power. In this system, each branch limits the power of the other two branches.

For example, the President can veto, or reject, laws passed by Congress. Congress can refuse to approve treaties made by the President. The courts of the judicial branch can rule that laws made by Congress or actions taken by the President are unconstitutional.

All three branches are supposed to work toward the common good of the country's citizens. The common good means what is best for the whole country, not just for a few individuals.

330 • Special Section

Background

The Structure of Congress

The two-house structure of Congress was based on the structure of England's Parliament. The important difference is that only persons who are born in noble families can be elected to one of the houses of Parliament, the House of Lords. The other house of Parliament is called the House of Commons, meaning that its members come from the common people.

White House

Executive Branch The head of the executive branch is the President. The Vice President and the heads of government departments give advice to the President.

- ★ proposes, approves, and enforces laws made by Congress
- ★ makes treaties with other countries
- ★ leads the military

Capitol

Legislative Branch The legislative branch is called Congress. Congress has two parts: the Senate and the House of Representatives.

- ★ makes laws
- ★ raises money by collecting taxes or borrowing money
- ★ approves the printing of money
- ★ can declare war

Supreme Court

Judicial Branch The Supreme Court and other courts make up the judicial branch. One Chief Justice and eight Associate Justices serve on the Supreme Court.

- ★ decides whether laws follow the guidelines of the Constitution
- ★ decides what laws mean
- ★ decides whether laws have been followed

REVIEW **Why is it important that a balance of power exist among the three branches of government?**

Structure of the Government

continued

Talk About It

6 **Q Citizenship** Of what branch is the vice president a part?

A the executive branch

7 **Q Citizenship** What does the Supreme Court do?

A It looks at laws and decides whether they follow the Constitution, what they mean, and whether they have been followed.

Vocabulary Strategies

Senate The word *senate* comes from Latin. Ancient Rome had a senate. The name comes from the same word as senior, meaning older, because the members of the Roman senate were supposed to be old and wise.

Justice A synonym for justice in this context is judge.

Technology

- You can find out more about your state and the federal government by doing research on the Internet.
- Each state has a website that gives information about its laws, history, and services.
- The departments of the federal government have useful and informative sites as well.

Sites can easily be found through a reliable search engine.

Levels of Government

Talk About It

8 **Q Citizenship** What units make up our state?

A Answers will vary. You can use the notes box at the bottom of this page to record the information about your state.

Critical Thinking

Infer What do you think would happen if states had the right to print their own money?

Levels of Government

★ ★ ★

The federal government is not the only government in the United States. Every state has a government, which is led by a governor. Some decisions are made by the federal government, while others are made by a state government.

Each state is broken into smaller units that have local governments. These units may include counties (parts of states made up of several towns), townships (small parts of counties), cities, and school districts. Local governments take many forms. Some are headed by a mayor. Others are run by a city manager or by a group of people such as a town council.

Federal, state, and local governments have their own powers, but they also share some powers. For example, both the federal and state governments collect taxes, set up courts, and make and enforce laws.

Federal Government

Main Powers

- ★ prints money
- ★ declares war
- ★ runs the postal system
- ★ makes treaties with other countries
- ★ collects income taxes

Background

Taxes

State and local governments, like the federal government, depend on taxes for their income. Many states have income taxes. Sales taxes, which are levied on goods sold, are also important to state and local governments. Most local governments earn their money from property taxes on houses, land, and vehicles.

Special Section
Government

State Government

Main Powers

- ★ issues licenses, such as marriage licenses and driver's licenses
- ★ runs elections
- ★ sets up local governments
- ★ collects income and sales taxes

Local Government

Main Powers

- ★ provides police and fire protection
- ★ runs public schools and public libraries (with help from the state)
- ★ provides public transportation, such as buses and subways
- ★ collects sales and property taxes

REVIEW Which level of government has the power to run elections?

333

Levels of Government

continued

Talk About It

9 **Q Citizenship** What powers do the levels of government have in common?

A Both federal and state governments collect taxes, set up courts, and enforce laws.

10 **Q Citizenship** Which level of government provides police and fire protection?

A local government

Math

Calculate Sales Tax

- After providing students with the sales tax rate in your state or city, have them calculate how much tax they would have to pay on each of the following items.
- (Note: In your state, some of these items may not be subject to tax.)

The Bill of Rights

Talk About It

11 Q Citizenship How do the 10 Amendments included in the Bill of Rights help protect individuals?

A They spell out in the government's basic document what people have the right to do and to not do, and the Ninth Amendment says that people have other rights that are not included in the Constitution.

Vocabulary Strategy

Amendment Have students find the word *amend* in amendment. Explain that to amend something means to change it.

Critical Thinking

Explain Which amendment in the Bill of Rights do you feel is the most important? Why?

The Bill *of* Rights

★ ★ ★

The first 10 amendments to the Constitution are called the Bill of Rights. An amendment is an official change or addition to a law. The Bill of Rights is like a promise to the people of the United States. It lists many of the individual rights the U.S. government promises to protect. This chart explains each amendment.

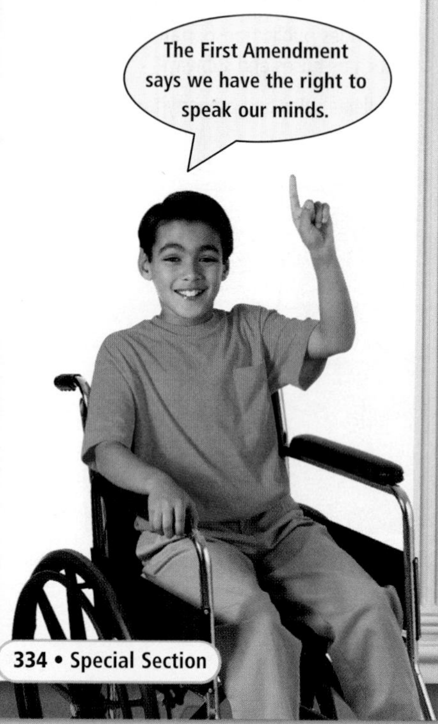

The First Amendment says we have the right to speak our minds.

1 First Amendment The government cannot support any religion above another. It may not prevent people from practicing whichever religion they wish. People have the right to say and write their opinions, and the press has the right to publish them. People can also meet together and ask the government to make changes.

2 Second Amendment Because people may have to fight to protect their country, they may own weapons.

3 Third Amendment People do not have to allow soldiers to live in their homes.

4 Fourth Amendment The police cannot search people or their homes without a good reason.

5 Fifth Amendment People accused of a crime have the right to a fair trial. They cannot be tried more than once for the same crime. Accused people do not have to speak against themselves at a trial.

334 • Special Section

Language Arts

Write a New Bill of Rights

- Have students work in pairs to develop their own versions of the Bill of Rights.
- What rights do they think should be protected by the Constitution that are not protected now?
- Display student Bills of Rights on the bulletin board.

Sixth Amendment People accused of a crime have the right to a speedy, public trial by a jury. A jury is a group of people who hear evidence and make a decision. Accused people also have the right to a lawyer, to be told what crime they are accused of, and to question witnesses.

Seventh Amendment People who have a disagreement about something worth more than $20 have the right to a trial by a jury.

Eighth Amendment In most cases, accused people can remain out of jail until their trial if they pay bail. Bail is a sum of money they will lose if they don't appear for their trial. Courts cannot demand bail that is too high or punish people in cruel ways.

Ninth Amendment People have other rights besides those stated in the Constitution.

Tenth Amendment Any powers the Constitution does not give to the federal government belong to the states or the people.

REVIEW List three rights that are protected by the Bill of Rights.

Review

★★★

Complete two of the following activities.

Art Activity Work with a group to create a poster titled, *What Democracy Means to Me.* Cut out pictures from newspapers and magazines that illustrate some part of government or something government does.

Writing Activity Choose one of the branches of government and write a short report about it. Give an example of how the branch provides for the common good of the American people.

Research Activity A state capital is a city in which a state's government is located. Make a list of every state's capital. Write a fact card for one capital on your list, including its population and the year it was founded.

Writing Activity Find out who your leaders are at each level of government. Write the names of the President and your senators, representatives, and local leaders. Write to a local leader. Ask questions about that person's job.

Speaking Activity The Bill of Rights still matters today. Prepare an oral report on one of the amendments, explaining how it has affected a current event.

335

Writing Activity

4	Questions are thoughtful; letter format is used; list is complete.
3	Questions show effort; letter format used; one name missing from list.
2	Question shows some effort; letter format is attempted; two or three names missing.
1	Questions poor or absent; letter format not used; four or more names missing.

Speaking Activity

HANDS ON

4	Explanation is clear and well organized; speech is easy to understand and clear.
3	Explanation is clear and fairly well organized; speech is somewhat easy to understand.
2	Explanation is some what confused; speech is hurried or overly slow.
1	Explanation is unclear and poorly organized; speech is extremely difficult to understand.

3 Activities

The following rubrics will help you evaluate student performance on the activities.

Hands-on Art Activity

HANDS ON

4	Poster shows considerable thought and creative effort; message is clear.
3	Poster shows thought and effort; message is somewhat clear.
2	Poster shows some effort, but message is unclear.
1	Lack of effort is apparent; message is absent altogether.

Writing Activity

4	Report is well organized and shows evidence of thorough research; example is excellent.
3	Report is fairly well organized and shows that research effort was made; example is good.
2	Report is somewhat confusing but shows that research effort was made; example is fair.
1	Report is poorly organized; lack of research is obvious; example is poor or absent.

Research Activity

4	List is complete; fact card focuses on one capital and includes population and founding date.
3	List is complete; fact card focuses on one capital and includes either population or founding date.
2	List missing one to five capitals; fact card focuses on one capital and includes either population or founding date.
1	List missing more than five capitals; fact card incomplete.

Unit Review

Vocabulary and Main Ideas

1. It kept them from settling west of the Appalachian Mountains and farming the Ohio Valley. *(Obj. U4-2)*
2. They had not agreed to the taxes and had no representatives in the British Parliament. *(Obj. U4-3)*
3. Patriots believed in independence for the American colonies; Loyalists supported the English government and king. *(Obj. U4-12)*
4. It convinced France to support the Americans in their war against Britain. *(Obj. U4-15)*
5. The delegates compromised—they all gave up something they wanted in order for the states to come to agreement. *(Obj. U4-22)*
6. The three branches of federal government are the legislative, the executive, and the judicial. *(Obj. U4-25)*

Critical Thinking

7. **Sample answer:** They believed in the importance of their cause; many were willing to die for what they believed in. *(Obj. U4-12)*
8. **Sample answer:** Students' answers should show understanding of the roles of the three branches of government and how they limit each other's power. *(Obj. U4-25)*

Apply Skills

9. A *(Obj. U4-7)*
10. C *(Obj. U4-7)*

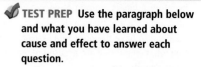

UNIT 4

Review and Test Prep

Vocabulary and Main Ideas

Write a sentence to answer each question below.

1. Why did American colonists object to the **Proclamation** of 1763?
2. Why were the Americans against paying **taxes** to the British?
3. What was the main difference between the **Patriots** and the **Loyalists?**
4. Why was the American **victory** at Saratoga a turning point of the Revolution?
5. How did the **delegates** to the Constitutional Convention settle their differences?
6. What are the three branches of the **federal** government?

Critical Thinking

TEST PREP Write a short paragraph to answer each question below.

7. **Drawing Conclusions** Why do you think the Patriots would continue to fight the British even when it seemed that they could not win?
8. **Synthesize** Write a short paragraph explaining how the system of checks and balances protects democracy. Use details from the unit to support your answer.

Apply Skills

TEST PREP Use the paragraph below and what you have learned about cause and effect to answer each question.

Nine states needed to ratify the new Constitution for it to become law. Some of the states, however, thought the Constitution did not protect people's rights. The Federalists agreed to add a Bill of Rights to the Constitution. Then, all 13 states ratified the Constitution.

9. What caused the Bill of Rights to be added to the Constitution?
   - **A.** Some states wanted to protect people's rights.
   - **B.** Some states did not want a Constitution.
   - **C.** Thirteen states needed to ratify the Constitution.
   - **D.** The Constitution was too short.
10. What was an effect of adding the Bill of Rights to the Constitution?
    - **A.** The government's rights were protected.
    - **B.** The people's rights were taken away.
    - **C.** Thirteen states ratified the Constitution.
    - **D.** Nine states refused to ratify the Constitution.

336 • Unit 4

Technology

Test Generator

Use the **Test Generator CD-ROM** to create tests customized to your class. Access hundreds of test questions and make lesson, chapter, and unit quizzes and tests.

Updates

To update your Unit Bibliography, visit www.eduplace.com/ss/hmss05 to learn about new titles related to the unit theme.

Extra Support

REACHING ALL LEARNERS

Flash Cards

Suggest that students use the vocabulary cards to quiz each other on vocabulary if they are having difficulty, or have them make their own vocabulary flash card game.

Unit Activity

The Big Idea

Create a Freedom Fighters Portrait Gallery

- Choose a person mentioned in this unit who fought for freedom.
- Research to find a picture of the person and facts about his or her life.
- Create a portrait, or picture, of the person. Write about his or her life underneath the picture.
- Post the portraits in your classroom.

At the Library

You may find these books at your school or public library.

The Boston Tea Party, by Steven Kroll
The events of December 16, 1773, changed the course of American history.

If You Lived at the Time of the American Revolution, by Kay Moore
What was life like for Patriots and Loyalists during the Revolution?

CURRENT EVENTS
WEEKLY WR READER

Connect to Today

Create a bulletin board about freedom and independence around the world today.

- Find articles that tell about nations of the world and ideals of freedom and independence.
- Write a summary of each article. Draw a picture or map to illustrate each summary.
- Post your illustrated summaries on a bulletin board.

Technology
Get your information for the bulletin board from the Weekly Reader at **www.eduplace.com/kids/hmss05/**

Read About It

Look for these Social Studies books in your classroom.

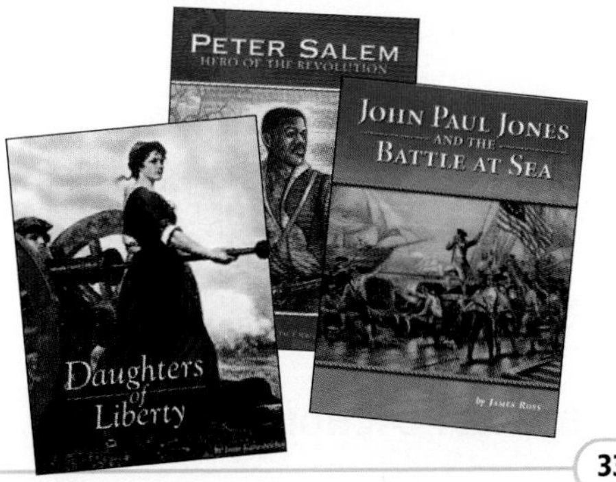

337

Math

Test Taking Tip

Tell students that when they have to read a graph on a test, they should use a straightedge to help them. Show them how to place a ruler or the edge of a piece of paper across the top of a bar and use it to read across to the y-axis of the graph.

Standards

National Standards

VI c How government does/does not provide for needs and wants of people, establish order and security, and manage conflict
VI e Local, state, and national government and representative leaders
VI h Tensions between wants and needs and fairness, equity, and justice
VII f Influence of incentives, values, traditions, and habits on economic decisions
IX b Conflict, cooperation, and interdependence
X a Key ideals of the United States' form of government

Unit Activity

HANDS ON Performance Task Rubric

4	Biographical information is accurate; portrait has visual appeal; mechanics are correct.
3	Biographical information is mostly accurate; portrait has visual appeal; mechanics are generally correct.
2	Biographical information is somewhat accurate; portrait has some visual appeal; some errors in mechanics are present.
1	Biographical information is inaccurate; portrait has little visual appeal; many errors in mechanics are present.

WEEKLY WR READER

Unit Project

- Students can wrap up the unit activity by sharing the bulletin board they have made with other classes or classroom visitors.
- You may want to ask volunteers to prepare an oral presentation about what the class discovered about independence and freedom around the world.

At the Library

Leveled Readers and Literature

- You may wish to wrap up the unit by reading aloud from one of these titles or from one of the Read-Aloud selections listed in the Unit Bibliography.

Read About It

- You may wish to provide students with the appropriate Leveled Book for this unit. Teaching options for these titles appear on page 221B.
- If students have written reviews or summaries of the Leveled Books or bibliography selections, you may wish to compile them into an anthology and place them in your classroom Reading Corner or school library.

References

Citizenship Handbook

Resources

R1

Pledge of Allegiance

I pledge allegiance to the flag
of the United States of America
and to the Republic for which it stands,
one Nation under God, indivisible,
with liberty and justice for all.

Spanish

Prometo lealtad a la bandera
de los Estados Unidos de América,
y a la república que representa,
una nación bajo Diós, indivisible,
con libertad y justicia para todos.

Russian

Я даю клятву верности флагу
Соединённых Штатов Америки
и стране, символом которой
он является, народу, единому
перед Богом, свободному
и равноправному.

Tagalog

Ako ay nanunumpa ng katapatan
sa bandila ng Estados Unidos
ng Amerika, at sa Republikang
kanyang kinakatawan, isang
Bansang pumapailalim sa isang
Maykapal hindi nahahati, may
kalayaan at katarungan para
sa lahat.

Arabic

ادين بالولاء لعلم الولايات المتحده الامريكيه و الى
الجمهوريه التي تمثلها و دولة واحدة تؤمن باللة و
متحدة تمنح الحرية و العدالة للجميع

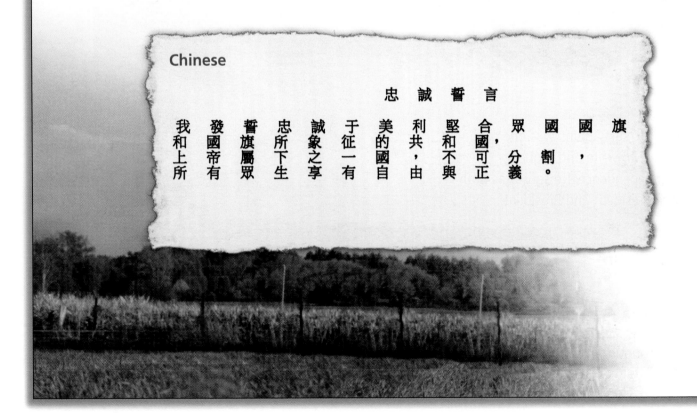

Chinese

忠誠誓言

我發誓忠誠于美利堅合眾國國旗
和國旗所象征的共和國，
上帝屬下之一國，不可分割，
所有眾生享有自由與正義。

R3

Character Traits

Character includes feelings, thoughts, and behaviors. A character trait is something people show by the way they act. To act bravely shows courage, and courage is one of several character traits.

Positive character traits, such as honesty, caring, and courage, lead to positive actions. Character traits are also called "life skills." Life skills can help you do your best, and doing your best leads to reaching your goals.

John Adams

Patriotism Adams was one of the first people to write and argue for the cause of independence. He served as both Vice President and President.

Martha Washington

Responsibility During the hard years of the war, Washington helped the army and General Washington. As First Lady, her sense of responsibility toward the nation set an example.

Courage means acting bravely. Doing what you believe to be good and right, and telling the truth, requires courage.

Patriotism means working for the goals of your country. When you show national pride, you are being patriotic.

Responsibility is taking care of work that needs to be done. Responsible people are reliable and trustworthy, which means they can be counted on.

Respect means paying attention to what other people want and believe. The "golden rule," or treating others as you would like to be treated, shows thoughtfulness and respect.

Fairness means working to make things fair, or right, for everyone. Often one needs to try again and again to achieve fairness. This requires diligence, or not giving up.

Civic virtue is good citizenship. It means doing things, such as cooperating and solving problems, to help communities live and work well together.

Caring means noticing what others need and helping them get what they need. Feeling concern or compassion is another way to define caring.

Historical Documents

The Mayflower Compact (1620)

Pilgrims are shown writing the Mayflower Compact while still aboard the ship.

". . . We whose names are underwritten, . . . Having undertaken, for the Glory of God, and Advancement of the Christian Faith, and Honor of our King and Country, a Voyage to plant the first Colony in the northern Parts of Virginia; Do by these Presents, solemnly and mutually, in the Presence of God and one of another, covenant and combine ourselves together into a civil Body Politick, for our better Ordering and Preservation, and Furtherance of the Ends aforesaid: And by Virtue hereof do enact, constitute, and frame such just and equal Laws, Ordinances, Acts, Constitutions, and Officers, from time to time, as shall be thought most meet and convenient for the general Good of the Colony; unto which we promise all due Submission and Obedience. . . ."

Mr. John Carver	Mr. Samuel Fuller	Edward Tilly
Mr. William Bradford	Mr. Christopher Martin	John Tilly
Mr. Edward Winslow	Mr. William Mullins	Francis Cooke
Mr. William Brewster	Mr. William White	Thomas Rogers
Isaac Allerton	Mr. Richard Warren	Thomas Tinker
Myles Standish	John Howland	John Ridgdale
John Alden	Mr. Steven Hopkins	Edward Fuller
John Turner	Digery Priest	Richard Clark
Francis Eaton	Thomas Williams	Richard Gardiner
James Chilton	Gilbert Winslow	Mr. John Allerton
John Craxton	Edmund Margesson	Thomas English
John Billington	Peter Brown	Edward Doten
Joses Fletcher	Richard Britteridge	Edward Liester
John Goodman	George Soule	

Historical Documents

Pitt's Speech to Parliament on the Stamp Act (1766)

"The Americans have not acted in all things with prudence and temper. They have been wronged. They have been driven to madness by injustice. Will you punish them for the madness you have occasioned? Rather let prudence and temper come first from this side. I will undertake for America, that she will follow the example. . . .

Upon the whole, I will beg leave to tell the House what is really my opinion. It is, that the Stamp-Act be repealed absolutely, totally, and immediately; that the reason for the repeal should be assigned, because it was founded on an erroneous principle."

William Pitt

Burke's Speech to Parliament on Conciliation with America (1775)

"The proposition is peace. Not peace through the medium of war; not peace to be hunted through the labyrinth of intricate and endless negotiations . . . It is simple peace, sought in its natural course and in its ordinary haunts. . . .

Let the colonies always keep the idea of their civil rights associated with your government — they will cling and grapple to you, and no force under heaven will be of power to tear them from their allegiance. But let it be once understood that your government may be one thing and their privileges another, that these two things may exist without any mutual relation — the cement is gone, the cohesion is loosened, and everything hastens to decay and dissolution. . . .

Magnanimity in politics is not seldom the truest wisdom; and a great empire and little minds go ill together."

Edmund Burke

Historical Documents

In the Declaration of Independence, the colonists explained why they were breaking away from Britain. They believed they had the right to form their own country.

The Declaration of Independence

In Congress, July 4, 1776

The unanimous declaration of the thirteen United States of America

Members of the Continental Congress are shown signing the Declaration of Independence.

Introduction*

When, in the course of human events, it becomes necessary for one people to dissolve the political bonds which have connected them with another, and to assume, among the powers of the earth, the separate and equal station to which the laws of nature and of nature's God entitle them, a decent respect to the opinions of mankind requires that they should declare the causes which impel them to the separation.

Basic Rights

WE hold these truths to be self-evident: That all men are created equal, that they are endowed by their Creator with certain unalienable rights; that among these are life, liberty, and the pursuit of happiness; that, to secure these rights, governments are instituted among men, deriving their just powers from the consent of the governed; that whenever any form of government becomes destructive of these ends, it is the right of the people to alter or to abolish it, and to institute new government, laying its foundation on such principles, and organizing its powers in such form, as to them shall seem most likely to effect their safety and happiness. Prudence, indeed, will dictate that governments long established should not be changed for light and transient causes; and accordingly all experience hath shown that mankind are more disposed to suffer, while evils are sufferable, than to right themselves by abolishing the forms to which they are accustomed. But when a long train of abuses and usurpations, pursuing invariably the same object, evinces a design to reduce them under absolute despotism, it is their right, it is their duty, to throw off such government, and to provide new guards for their future security. Such has been the patient sufferance of these colonies; and such is now the necessity which constrains them to alter their former systems of government. The history of the present King of Great Britain is a history of repeated injuries and usurpations, all having in direct object the establishment of an absolute tyranny over these states. To prove this, let facts be submitted to a candid world.

The opening part of the Declaration is very famous. It says that all people are created equal. Everyone has certain basic rights that are "unalienable." That means that these rights cannot be taken away. Governments are formed to protect these basic rights. If a government does not do this, then the people have a right to begin a new one.

Forming a new government meant ending the colonial ties to the king. The writers of the Declaration listed the wrongs of King George III to prove the need for their actions.

Charges Against the King

HE has refused his assent to laws, the most wholesome and necessary for the public good.

HE has forbidden his governors to pass laws of immediate and pressing importance, unless suspended in their operation till his assent should be obtained; and, when so suspended, he has utterly neglected to attend to them.

Colonists said the king had not let the colonies make their own laws. He had limited the people's representation in their assemblies.

HE has refused to pass other laws for the accommodation of large districts of people, unless those people would relinquish the right of representation in the legislature, a right inestimable to them, and formidable to tyrants only.

HE has called together legislative bodies at places unusual, uncomfortable, and distant from the depository of their public records, for the sole purpose of fatiguing them into compliance with his measures.

HE has dissolved representative houses repeatedly, for opposing, with manly firmness his invasions on the rights of the people.

*Titles have been added to the Declaration to make it easier to read. These titles are not in the original document.

Historical Documents

HE has refused for a long time, after such dissolutions, to cause others to be elected; whereby the legislative powers, incapable of annihilation, have returned to the people at large for their exercise; the state remaining in the mean time, exposed to all the dangers of invasions from without and convulsions within.

The king had made colonial assemblies meet at unusual times and places. This made going to assembly meetings hard for colonial representatives.

In some cases the king stopped the assembly from meeting at all.

HE has endeavored to prevent the population of these states; for that purpose obstructing the laws for the naturalization of foreigners; refusing to pass others to encourage their migration hither, and raising the conditions of new appropriations of lands.

The king tried to stop people from moving to the colonies and into new western lands.

HE has obstructed the administration of justice, by refusing his assent to laws for establishing judiciary powers.

HE has made judges dependent on his will alone, for the tenure of their offices, and the amount of payment of their salaries.

The king prevented the colonies from choosing their own judges. Instead, he sent over judges who depended on him for their jobs and pay.

HE has erected a multitude of new offices, and sent hither swarms of officers to harass our people and eat out their substance.

HE has kept among us, in times of peace, standing armies, without the consent of our legislatures.

The king kept British soldiers in the colonies, even though the colonists had not asked for them.

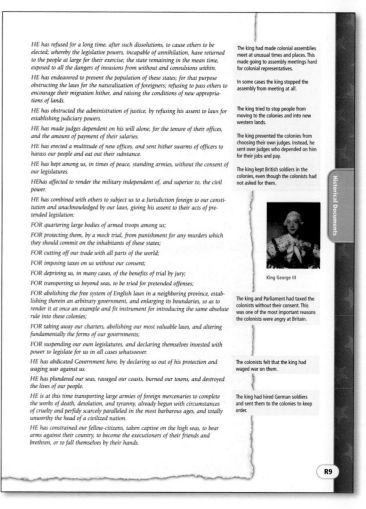

HEhas affected to render the military independent of, and superior to, the civil power.

HE has combined with others to subject us to a Jurisdiction foreign to our constitution and unacknowledged by our laws, giving his assent to their acts of pretended legislation:

FOR quartering large bodies of armed troops among us;

FOR protecting them, by a mock trial, from punishment for any murders which they should commit on the inhabitants of these states;

FOR cutting off our trade with all parts of the world;

FOR imposing taxes on us without our consent;

FOR depriving us, in many cases, of the benefits of trial by jury;

FOR transporting us beyond seas, to be tried for pretended offenses;

King George III

FOR abolishing the free system of English laws in a neighboring province, establishing therein an arbitrary government, and enlarging its boundaries, so as to render it at once an example and fit instrument for introducing the same absolute rule into these colonies;

The king and Parliament had taxed the colonists without their consent. This was one of the most important reasons the colonists were angry at Britain.

FOR taking away our charters, abolishing our most valuable laws, and altering fundamentally the forms of our governments;

FOR suspending our own legislatures, and declaring themselves invested with power to legislate for us in all cases whatsoever.

HE has abdicated Government here, by declaring us out of his protection and waging war against us.

The colonists felt that the king had waged war on them.

HE has plundered our seas, ravaged our coasts, burned our towns, and destroyed the lives of our people.

HE is at this time transporting large armies of foreign mercenaries to complete the works of death, desolation, and tyranny, already begun with circumstances of cruelty and perfidy scarcely paralleled in the most barbarous ages, and totally unworthy the head of a civilized nation.

The king had hired German soldiers and sent them to the colonies to keep order.

HE has constrained our fellow-citizens, taken captive on the high seas, to bear arms against their country, to become the executioners of their friends and brethren, or to fall themselves by their hands.

Historical Documents

British soldiers became a symbol of British misrule to many colonists.

HE has excited domestic insurrections amongst us, and has endeavored to bring on the inhabitants of our frontiers, the merciless Indian savages, whose known rule of warfare is an undistinguished destruction of all ages, sexes, and conditions.

Response to the King

The colonists said that they had asked the king to change his policies, but he had not listened to them.

IN every stage of these oppressions we have petitioned for redress in the most humble terms; Our repeated petitions have been answered only by repeated injury. A prince, whose character is thus marked by every act which may define a tyrant, is unfit to be the ruler of a free people.

NOR have we been wanting in our attentions to our British brethren. We have warned them from time to time, of attempts by their legislature to extend an unwarrantable jurisdiction over us. We have reminded them of the circumstances of our emigration and settlement here. We have appealed to their native justice and magnanimity; and we have conjured them, by the ties of our common kindred, to disavow these usurpations, which, would inevitably interrupt our connections and correspondence. They, too, have been deaf to the voice of justice and of consanguinity. We must, therefore, acquiesce in the necessity which denounces our separation, and hold them, as we hold the rest of mankind, enemies in war, in peace, friends.

Independence

The writers declared that the colonies were free and independent states, equal to the world's other states. They had the powers to make war and peace and to trade with other countries.

WE, therefore, the representatives of the United States of America, in General Congress Assembled, appealing to the Supreme Judge of the world for the rectitude of our intentions, do, in the name and by authority of the good people of these colonies, solemnly publish and declare, that these United Colonies are, and of right ought to be, FREE AND INDEPENDENT STATES; that they are absolved from all allegiance to the British crown, and that all political connection between them and the state of Great Britain is, and ought to be, totally dissolved; and that, as free and independent states, they have full power to levy war, conclude peace, contract alliances, establish commerce, and do all other acts and things which independent states may of right do. And for the support of this declaration, with a firm reliance on the protection of Divine Providence, we mutually pledge to each other our lives, our fortunes, and our sacred honor.

The signers pledged their lives to the support of this Declaration. The Continental Congress ordered copies of the Declaration of Independence to be sent to all the states and to the army.

Congress ordered copies of the Declaration of Independence to be sent to all the states and to the army.

NEW HAMPSHIRE
Josiah Bartlett
William Whipple
Matthew Thornton

MASSACHUSETTS
John Hancock
John Adams
Samuel Adams
Robert Treat Paine
Elbridge Gerry

NEW YORK
William Floyd
Philip Livingston
Francis Lewis
Lewis Morris

RHODE ISLAND
Stephen Hopkins
William Ellery

NEW JERSEY
Richard Stockton
John Witherspoon
Francis Hopkinson
John Hart
Abraham Clark

PENNSYLVANIA
Robert Morris
Benjamin Rush
Benjamin Franklin
John Morton
George Clymer
James Smith
George Taylor
James Wilson
George Ross

DELAWARE
Caesar Rodney
George Read
Thomas McKean

MARYLAND
Samuel Chase
William Paca
Thomas Stone
Charles Carroll of Carrollton

NORTH CAROLINA
Willam Hooper
Joseph Hewes
John Penn

VIRGINIA
George Wythe
Richard Henry Lee
Thomas Jefferson
Benjamin Harrison
Thomas Nelson, Jr.
Francis Lightfoot Lee
Carter Braxton

SOUTH CAROLINA
Edward Rutledge
Thomas Heyward, Jr.
Thomas Lynch, Jr.
Arthur Middleton

CONNECTICUT
Roger Sherman
Samuel Huntington
William Williams
Oliver Wolcott

GEORGIA
Button Gwinnett
Lyman Hall
George Walton

Historical Documents

The Constitution of the United States

Preamble*

Preamble The Preamble, or introduction, states the purposes of the Constitution. The writers wanted to strengthen the national government and give the nation a more solid foundation. The Preamble makes it clear that it is the people of the United States who have the power to establish or change a government.

We the people of the United States, in order to form a more perfect Union, establish justice, insure domestic tranquility, provide for the common defense, promote the general welfare, and secure the blessings of liberty to ourselves and our posterity, do ordain and establish this Constitution for the United States of America.

ARTICLE I
Legislative Branch

SECTION 1. CONGRESS

All legislative powers herein granted shall be vested in a Congress of the United States, which shall consist of a Senate and House of Representatives.

Congress Section 1 gives Congress the power to make laws. Congress has two parts, the House of Representatives and the Senate.

SECTION 2. HOUSE OF REPRESENTATIVES

1. ***Election and Term of Members*** *The House of Representatives shall be composed of members chosen every second year by the people of the several States, and the electors in each State shall have the qualifications requisite for electors of the most numerous branch of the State Legislature.*

2. ***Qualifications*** *No person shall be a representative who shall not have attained to the age of twenty-five years, and been seven years a citizen of the United States, and who shall not, when elected, be an inhabitant of that State in which he shall be chosen.*

3. ***Number of Representatives per State*** *Representatives ~~and direct taxes~~** shall be apportioned among the several States which may be included within this Union, according to their respective numbers, ~~which shall be determined by adding to the whole number of free persons, including those bound to service for a term of years, and excluding Indians not taxed, three fifths of all other persons.~~ The actual enumeration shall be made within three years after the first meeting of the Congress of the United States, and within every subsequent term of ten years, in such manner as they shall by law direct. The number of representatives shall not exceed one for every thirty thousand, but each State shall have at least one representative; ~~and until such enumeration shall be made, the State of New Hampshire shall be entitled to choose three, Massachusetts eight, Rhode Island and Providence Plantations one, Connecticut five, New York six, New Jersey four, Pennsylvania eight, Delaware one, Maryland six, Virginia ten, North Carolina five, South Carolina five, and Georgia three.~~*

4. ***Vacancies*** *When vacancies happen in the representation from any State, the executive authority thereof shall issue writs of election to fill such vacancies.*

5. ***Special Powers*** *The House of Representatives shall choose their speaker and other officers; and shall have the sole power of impeachment.*

Election and Team Members Citizens elect the members of the House of Representatives every two years.

Qualifications Representatives must be at least 25 years old. They must have been United States citizens for at least seven years. They also must live in the state they represent.

Number of Representatives per State The number of representatives each state has is based on its population. The biggest states have the most representatives. Each state must have at least one representative. An enumeration, or census, must be taken every 10 years to find out a state's population. The number of representatives in the House is now fixed at 435.

George Washington watches delegates sign the Constitution.

*The titles of the Preamble, and of each article, section, clause, and amendment have been added to make the Constitution easier to read. These titles are not in the original document.

**Parts of the Constitution have been crossed out to show that they are not in force any more. They have been changed by amendments or they no longer apply.

Historical Documents

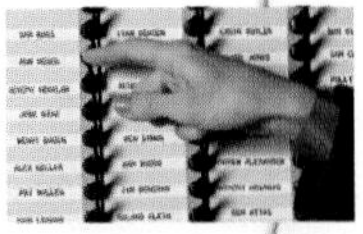

Americans often use voting machines on election day.

SECTION 3. SENATE

1. ***Number, Term, and Selection of Members*** *The Senate of the United States shall be composed of two senators from each State, chosen by the Legislature thereof, for six years; and each Senator shall have one vote.*

2. ***Overlapping Terms and Filling Vacancies*** *Immediately after they shall be assembled in consequence of the first election, they shall be divided as equally as may be into three classes. ~~The seats of the senators of the first class shall be vacated at the expiration of the second year, of the second class at the expiration of the fourth year, and of the third class at the expiration of the sixth year, so~~ that one-third may be chosen every second year; ~~and if vacancies happen by resignation, or otherwise, during the recess of the legislature of any State, the executive thereof may make temporary appointments until the next meeting of the legislature, which shall then fill such vacancies.~~*

3. ***Qualifications*** *No person shall be a senator who shall not have attained to the age of thirty years, and been nine years a citizen of the United States, and who shall not, when elected, be an inhabitant of that State for which he shall be chosen.*

4. ***President of the Senate*** *The Vice President of the United States shall be President of the Senate, but shall have no vote, unless they be equally divided.*

5. ***Other Officers*** *The Senate shall choose their other officers, and also a President pro tempore, in the absence of the Vice President, or when he shall exercise the office of the President of the United States.*

6. ***Impeachment Trials*** *The Senate shall have the sole power to try all impeachments. When sitting for that purpose, they shall be on oath or affirmation. When the President of the United States is tried, the Chief Justice shall preside: and no person shall be convicted without the concurrence of two-thirds of the members present.*

7. ***Penalties*** *Judgment in cases of impeachment shall not extend further than to removal from office, and disqualification to hold and enjoy any office of honor, trust, or profit under the United States: but the party convicted shall nevertheless be liable and subject to indictment, trial, judgement and punishment, according to law.*

Number, Term, and Selection of Members In each state, citizens elect two members of the Senate. This gives all states, whether big or small, equal power in the Senate. Senators serve six year terms. Originally, state legislatures chose the senators for their states. Today, however, people elect their senators directly. The Seventeenth Amendment made this change in 1913.

Qualifications Senators must be at least 30 years old and United States citizens for at least nine years. Like representatives, they must live in the state they represent.

President of the Senate The Vice President of the United States acts as the President, or chief officer, of the Senate. The Vice President votes only in cases of a tie.

Impeachment Trials If the House of Representatives impeaches, or charges, an official with a crime, the Senate holds a trial. If two-thirds of the senators find the official guilty, then the person is removed from office. The only President ever impeached was Andrew Johnson in 1868. He was found not guilty.

SECTION 4. ELECTIONS AND MEETINGS

1. ***Election of Congress*** *The times, places and manner of holding elections for senators and representatives, shall be prescribed in each State by the legislature thereof; but the Congress may at any time by law make or alter such regulations, except as to the places of choosing Senators.*

2. ***Annual Sessions*** *The Congress shall assemble at least once in every year, ~~and such meeting shall be on the first Monday in December,~~ unless they shall by law appoint a different day.*

SECTION 5. RULES OF PROCEDURE

1. ***Organization*** *Each house shall be the judge of the elections, returns and qualifications of its own members, and a majority of each shall constitute a quorum to do business; but a smaller number may adjourn from day to day, and may be authorized to compel the attendance of absent members, in such manner, and under such penalties as each house may provide.*

Election of Congress Each state decides where and when to hold elections. Today congressional elections are held in even-numbered years, on the Tuesday after the first Monday in November.

Annual Sessions The Constitution requires Congress to meet at least once a year. In 1933, the 20th Amendment made January 3rd the day for beginning a regular session of Congress.

Organization A quorum is the smallest number of members that must be present for an organization to hold a meeting. For each house of Congress, this number is the majority, or more than one-half, of its members.

Historical Documents

2. ***Rules*** *Each house may determine the rules of its proceedings, punish its members for disorderly behavior, and, with the concurrence of two-thirds, expel a member.*

3. ***Journal*** *Each house shall keep a journal of its proceedings, and from time to time publish the same, excepting such parts as may in their judgement require secrecy; and the yeas and nays of the members of either house on any question shall, at the desire of one-fifth of those present, be entered on the journal.*

4. ***Adjournment*** *Neither house, during the session of Congress, shall, without the consent of the other, adjourn for more than three days, nor to any other place than that in which the two houses shall be sitting.*

Rules Each house can make rules for its members and expel a member by a two-thirds vote.

Journal The Constitution requires each house to keep a record of its proceedings. *The Congressional Record* is published every day. It includes parts of speeches made in each house and allows any person to look up the votes of his or her representative.

SECTION 6. PRIVILEGES AND RESTRICTIONS

1. ***Pay and Protection*** *The senators and representatives shall receive a compensation for their services, to be ascertained by law, and paid out of the treasury of the United States. They shall in all cases, except treason, felony and breach of the peace, be privileged from arrest during their attendance at the session of their respective houses, and in going to and returning from the same; and for any speech or debate in either house, they shall not be questioned in any other place.*

2. ***Restrictions*** *No senator or representative shall, during the time for which he was elected, be appointed to any civil office under the authority of the United States, which shall have been created, or the emoluments whereof shall have been increased during such time; and no person holding any office under the United States, shall be a member of either house during his continuance in office.*

Pay and Protection Congress sets the salaries of its members, and they are paid by the federal government. No member can be arrested for anything he or she says while in office. This protection allows members to speak freely in Congress.

Restrictions Members of Congress cannot hold other federal offices during their terms. This rule strengthens the separation of powers and protects the checks and balances system set up by the Constitution.

SECTION 7. MAKING LAWS

1. ***Tax Bills*** *All bills for raising revenue shall originate in the House of Representatives; but the Senate may propose or concur with amendments as on other bills.*

2. ***Passing a Law*** *Every bill which shall have passed the House of Representatives and the Senate, shall, before it became a law, be presented to the President of the United States; if he approve, he shall sign it, but if not, he shall return it, with his objections, to that house in which it shall have originated, who shall enter the objections at large on their journal, and proceed to reconsider it. If after such reconsideration two-thirds of that house shall agree to pass the bill, it shall be sent, together with the objections, to the other house, by which it shall likewise be reconsidered, and if approved by two-thirds of that house, it shall become a law. But in all such cases the votes of both houses shall be determined by yeas and nays, and the names of the persons voting for and against the bill shall be entered on the journal of each house respectively. If any bill shall not be returned by the president within ten days (Sundays excepted) after it shall have been presented to him, the same shall be a law, in like manner as if he had signed it, unless the Congress by their adjournment prevent its return, in which case it shall not be a law.*

3. ***Orders and Resolutions*** *Every order, resolution, or vote to which the concurrence of the Senate and House of Representatives may be necessary (except on a question of adjournment) shall be presented to the President of the United States; and before the same shall take effect, shall be approved by him, or, being disapproved by him, shall be repassed by two-thirds of the Senate and House of Representatives, according to the rules and limitations prescribed in the case of a bill.*

Tax Bills A bill is a proposed law. Only the House of Representatives can introduce bills that tax the people.

Passing a Law A bill must be passed by the majority of members in each house of Congress. Then it is sent to the President. If the President signs it, the bill becomes a law. If the President refuses to sign a bill, and Congress is in session, the bill becomes law ten days after the President receives it.

The President can also veto, or reject, a bill. However, if each house of Congress repasses the bill by a two-thirds vote, it becomes a law. Passing a law after the President vetoed it is called overriding a veto. This process is an important part of the checks and balances system set up by the Constitution.

Orders and Resolutions Congress can also pass resolutions that have the same power as laws. Such acts are also subject to the President's veto.

Historical Documents

SECTION 8. POWERS DELEGATED TO CONGRESS

1. **Taxation** *The Congress shall have the power to lay and collect taxes, duties, imposts, and excises, to pay the debts and provide for the common defense and general welfare of the United States; but all duties, imposts and excises shall be uniform throughout the United States;*

Taxation Only Congress has the power to collect taxes. Federal taxes must be the same in all parts of the country.

2. **Borrowing** *To borrow money on the credit of the United States;*

3. **Commerce** *To regulate commerce with foreign nations, and among the several States, and with the Indian tribes;*

Commerce Congress controls both trade with foreign countries and trade among states.

4. **Naturalization and Bankruptcy** *To establish an uniform rule of naturalization, and uniform laws on the subject of bankruptcies throughout the United States;*

Naturalization and Bankruptcy Naturalization is the process by which a person from another country becomes a United States citizen. Congress decides the requirements for this procedure.

5. **Coins and Measures** *To coin money, regulate the value thereof, and of foreign coin, and fix the standard of weights and measures;*

Coins and Measures Congress has the power to coin money and set its value.

6. **Counterfeiting** *To provide for the punishment of counterfeiting the securities and current coin of the United States;*

7. **Post Offices** *To establish post offices and post roads;*

8. **Copyrights and Patents** *To promote the progress of science and useful arts by securing for limited times to authors and inventors the exclusive right to their respective writings and discoveries;*

Copyrights and Patents Copyrights protect authors. Patents allow inventors to profit from their work by keeping control over it for a certain number of years. Congress grants patents to encourage scientific research.

9. **Courts** *To constitute tribunals inferior to the Supreme Court;*

10. **Piracy** *To define and punish piracies and felonies committed on the high seas, and offenses against the law of nations;*

11. **Declaring War** *To declare war, ~~grant letters of marque and reprisal,~~ and make rules concerning captures on land and water;*

Declaring War Only Congress can declare war on another country.

12. **Army** *To raise and support armies, but no appropriation of money to that use shall be for a longer term than two years;*

13. **Navy** *To provide and maintain a navy;*

14. **Military Regulations** *To make rules for the government and regulation of the land and naval forces;*

15. **Militia** *To provide for calling forth the militia to execute the laws of the Union, suppress insurrections and repel invasions;*

Militia Today the Militia is called the National Guard. The National Guard often helps people after floods, tornadoes, and other disasters.

16. **Militia Regulations** *To provide for organizing, arming and disciplining the militia, and for governing such part of them as may be employed in the service of the United States, reserving to the States respectively the appointment of the officers, and the authority of training the militia according to the discipline prescribed by Congress;*

17. **National Capital** *To exercise exclusive legislation in all cases whatsoever, over such district (not exceeding ten miles square) as may, by cession of particular states, and the acceptance of Congress, become the seat of the government of the United States, and to exercise like authority over all places purchased by the consent of the legislature of the State in which the same shall be, for the erection of forts, magazines, arsenals, dock-yards, and other needful buildings;—and*

National Capital Congress makes the laws for the District of Columbia, the area where the nation's capital is located.

18. **Necessary Laws** *To make all laws which shall be necessary and proper for carrying into execution the foregoing powers, and all other powers vested by this Constitution in the government of the United States, or in any department or officer thereof.*

Necessary Laws This clause allows Congress to make laws on issues, such as television and radio, that are not mentioned in the Constitution.

SECTION 9. POWERS DENIED TO CONGRESS

1. **Slave Trade** *~~The migration or importation of such persons as any of the States now existing shall think proper to admit, shall not be prohibited by the Congress prior to the year 1808, but a tax or duty may be imposed on such importation, not exceeding ten dollars for each person.~~*

Slave Trade This clause was another compromise between the North and the South. It prevented Congress from regulating the slave trade for 20 years. Congress outlawed the slave trade in 1808.

2. **Habeas Corpus** *The privilege of the writ of habeas corpus shall not be suspended, unless when in cases of rebellion or invasion the public safety may require it.*

Habeas Corpus A writ of habeas corpus requires the government either to charge a person in jail with a particular crime or let the person go free. Except in emergencies, Congress cannot deny the right of a person to a writ.

3. **Special Laws** *No bill of attainder or ex post facto law shall be passed.*

4. **Direct Taxes** *~~No capitation or other direct tax shall be laid, unless in proportion to the census or enumeration herein before directed to be taken.~~*

5. **Export Taxes** *No tax or duty shall be laid on articles exported from any State.*

6. **Ports** *No preference shall be given by any regulation of commerce or revenue to the ports of one State over those of another; nor shall vessels bound to, or from, one State, be obliged to enter, clear, or pay duties in another.*

Ports When regulating trade, Congress must treat all states equally. Also, states cannot tax goods traveling between states.

7. **Regulations on Spending** *No money shall be drawn from the treasury, but in consequence of appropriations made by law; and a regular statement and account of the receipts and expenditures of all public money shall be published from time to time.*

Regulations on Spending Congress controls the spending of public money. This clause checks the President's power.

8. **Titles of Nobility and Gifts** *No title of nobility shall be granted by the United States: and no person holding any office or profit or trust under them, shall, without the consent of the Congress, accept of any present, emolument, office, or title, of any kind whatever, from any king, prince, or foreign state.*

SECTION 10. POWERS DENIED TO THE STATES

1. **Complete Restrictions** *No State shall enter into any treaty, alliance, or confederation; grant letters of marque and reprisal; coin money; emit bills of credit; make anything but gold and silver coin a tender in payment of debts; pass any bill of attainder, ex post facto law, or law impairing the obligation of contracts, or grant any title of nobility.*

Complete Restrictions The Constitution prevents the states from acting like individual countries. States cannot make treaties with foreign nations. They cannot issue their own money.

2. **Partial Restrictions** *No State shall, without the consent of the Congress, lay any imposts or duties on imports or exports, except what may be absolutely necessary for executing its inspection laws; and the net produce of all duties and imposts, laid by any State on imports or exports, shall be for the use of the treasury of the United States; and all such laws shall be subject to the revision and control of the Congress.*

Partial Restrictions States cannot tax imports and exports without approval from Congress.

3. **Other Restrictions** *No State shall, without the consent of Congress, lay any duty of tonnage, keep troops, or ships of war in time of peace, enter into any agreement or compact with another State, or with a foreign power, or engage in war, unless actually invaded, or in such imminent danger as will not admit of delay.*

Other Restrictions States cannot declare war. They cannot keep their own armies.

ARTICLE II
Executive Branch

SECTION 1. PRESIDENT AND VICE PRESIDENT

1. **Term of Office** *The executive power shall be vested in a President of the United States of America. He shall hold his office during the term of four years, and together with the Vice President, chosen for the same term, be elected as follows:*

Term of Office The President has the power to carry out the laws passed by Congress. The President and the Vice President serve four-year terms.

2. **Electoral College** *Each State shall appoint, in such manner as the legislature thereof may direct, a number of electors, equal to the whole number of senators and representatives to which the State may be entitled in the Congress; but no*

Electoral College A group of people called the Electoral College actually elects the President. The number of electors each state receives equals the total number of its representatives and senators.

senator or representative, or person holding an office of trust or profit under the United States, shall be appointed an elector.

3. **Election Process** *~~The electors shall meet in their respective States, and vote by ballot for two persons, of whom one at least shall not be an inhabitant of the same State with themselves. And they shall make a list of all the persons voted for, and of the number of votes for each; which list they shall sign and certify, and transmit sealed to the seat of the government of the United States, directed to the President of the Senate. The President of the Senate shall, in the presence of the Senate and House of Representatives, open all the certificates, and the votes shall then be counted. The person having the greatest number of votes shall be the President, if such number be a majority of the whole number of electors appointed, and if there be more than one who have such majority, and have an equal number of votes, then the House of Representatives shall immediately choose by ballot one of them for President; and if no person have a majority, then from the five highest on the list the said house shall in like manner choose the President. But in choosing the President, the votes shall be taken by States, the representation from each State having one vote; a quorum for this purpose shall consist of a member or members from two thirds of the States, and a majority of all the States shall be necessary to a choice. In every case, after the choice of the President, the person having the greatest number of votes of the electors shall be the Vice President. But if there should remain two or more who have equal votes, the Senate shall choose from them by ballot the Vice President.~~*

Election Process Originally, electors voted for two people. The candidate who received the majority of votes became President. The runner-up became Vice President. Problems with this system led to the 12th Amendment, which changed the electoral college system.

Today electors almost always vote for the candidate who won the popular vote in their states. In other words, the candidate who wins the popular vote in a state also wins its electoral votes.

4. **Time of Elections** *The Congress may determine the time of choosing the electors, and the day on which they shall give their votes; which day shall be the same throughout the United States.*

Time of Elections Today we elect our President on the Tuesday after the first Monday in November.

5. **Qualifications** *No person except a natural-born citizen, ~~or a citizen of the United States at the time of the adoption of this Constitution,~~ shall be eligible to the office of President; neither shall any person be eligible to that office who shall not have attained to the age of thirty-five years, and been fourteen years a resident within the United States.*

Qualifications A President must be at least 35 years old, a United States citizen by birth, and a resident of the United States for at least 14 years.

6. **Vacancies** *~~In case of the removal of the President from office, or of his death, resignation, or inability to discharge the powers and duties of the said office, the same shall devolve on the Vice President, and the Congress may by law provide for the case of removal, death, resignation, or inability, both of the President and Vice President, declaring what officer shall then act as President, and such officer shall act accordingly, until the disability be removed, or a President shall be elected.~~*

Vacancies If the President resigns, dies, or is impeached and found guilty, the Vice President becomes President. The 25th Amendment replaced this clause in 1967.

7. **Salary** *The President shall, at stated times, receive for his services a compensation, which shall neither be increased nor diminished during the period for which he shall have been elected, and he shall not receive within that period any other emolument from the United States, or any of them.*

Salary The President receives a yearly salary that cannot be increased or decreased during his or her term. The President cannot hold any other paid government positions while in office.

8. **Oath of Office** *Before he enter on the execution of his office, he shall take the following oath or affirmation:—"I do solemnly swear (or affirm) that I will faithfully execute the office of President of the United States, and will to the best of my ability, preserve, protect and defend the Constitution of the United States."*

Oath of Office Every President must promise to uphold the Constitution. The Chief Justice of the Supreme Court usually administers this oath.

SECTION 2. POWERS OF THE PRESIDENT

1. **Military Powers** *The President shall be commander in chief of the army and navy of the United States, and of the militia of the several States, when called into the actual service of the United States; he may require the opinion, in writing, of the principal officer in each of the executive departments, upon any subject relating to the duties of their respective offices, and he shall have power to*

Military Powers The President is the leader of the country's military forces.

grant reprieves and pardons for offenses against the United States, except in cases of impeachment.

2. **Treaties and Appointments** *He shall have power, by and with the advice and consent of the Senate, to make treaties, provided two-thirds of the Senators present concur; and he shall nominate, and by and with the advice and consent of the Senate, shall appoint ambassadors, other public ministers and consuls, judges of the Supreme Court, and all other officers of the United States, whose appointments are not herein otherwise provided for, and which shall be established by law: but the Congress may by law vest the appointment of such inferior officers, as they think proper, in the President alone, in the courts of law, or in the heads of departments.*

Treaties and Appointments The President can make treaties with other nations. However, treaties must be approved by a two-thirds vote of the Senate. The President also appoints Supreme Court Justices and ambassadors to foreign countries. The Senate must approve these appointments.

3. **Temporary Appointments** *The President shall have power to fill up all vacancies that may happen during the recess of the Senate, by granting commissions which shall expire at the end of their next session.*

SECTION 3. DUTIES

He shall from time to time give to the Congress information of the State of the Union, and recommend to their consideration such measures as he shall judge necessary and expedient; he may on extraordinary occasions, convene both houses, or either of them, and in case of disagreement between them with respect to the time of adjournment, he may adjourn them to such time as he shall think proper; he shall receive ambassadors and other public ministers; he shall take care that the laws be faithfully executed, and shall commission all the officers of the United States.

Duties The President must report to Congress at least once a year and make recommendations for laws. This report is known as the State of the Union address. The President delivers it each January.

SECTION 4. IMPEACHMENT

The President, Vice President, and all civil officers of the United States, shall be removed from office on impeachment for, and conviction of, treason, bribery, or other high crimes and misdemeanors.

Impeachment The President and other officials can be forced out of office only if found guilty of particular crimes. This clause protects government officials from being impeached for unimportant reasons.

ARTICLE III
Judicial Branch

SECTION 1. FEDERAL COURTS

The judicial power of the United States shall be vested in one Supreme Court, and in such inferior courts as the Congress may from time to time ordain and establish. The judges, both of the Supreme and inferior courts, shall hold their offices during good behaviour, and shall, at stated times, receive for their services, a compensation, which shall not be diminished during their continuance in office.

Federal Courts The Supreme Court is the highest court in the nation. It makes the final decisions in all of the cases it hears. Congress decides the size of the Supreme Court. Today it contains nine judges. Congress also has the power to set up a system of lower federal courts. All federal judges may hold their offices for as long as they live.

SECTION 2. AUTHORITY OF THE FEDERAL COURTS

1. **General Jurisdiction** *The judicial power shall extend to all cases, in law and equity, arising under this Constitution, the laws of the United States, and treaties made, or which shall be made, under their authority; to all cases affecting ambassadors, other public ministers and consuls; to all cases of admiralty and maritime jurisdiction; to controversies to which the United States shall be a party; to controversies between two or more States; between a State and citizens of another State; between citizens of different States; between citizens of the same State claiming lands under grants of different States, and between a State, or the citizens thereof, and foreign states, citizens or subjects.*

General Jurisdiction Jurisdiction means the right of a court to hear a case. Federal courts have jurisdiction over such cases as those involving the Constitution, federal laws, treaties, and disagreements between states.

The President delivers the State of the Union address each year.

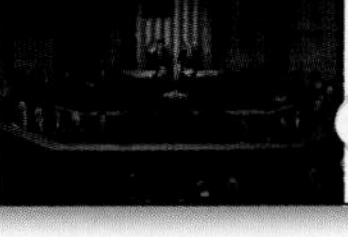

The Supreme Court One of the Supreme Court's most important jobs is to decide whether laws that pass are constitutional. This power is another example of the checks and balances system in the federal government.

Trial by Jury The Constitution guarantees everyone the right to a trial by jury. The only exception is in impeachment cases, which are tried in the Senate.

*2. **The Supreme Court** In all cases affecting ambassadors, other public ministers and consuls, and those in which a State shall be party, the Supreme Court shall have original jurisdiction. In all the other cases before mentioned, the Supreme Court shall have appellate jurisdiction, both as to law and fact, with such exceptions, and under such regulations as the Congress shall make.*

*3. **Trial by Jury** The trial of all crimes, except in cases of impeachment, shall be by jury; and such trial shall be held in the State where the said crimes shall have been committed; but when not committed within any state, the trial shall be at such place or places as the Congress may by law have directed.*

SECTION 3. TREASON

Definition People cannot be convicted of treason in the United States for what they think or say. To be guilty of treason, a person must rebel against the government by using violence or helping enemies of the country.

*1. **Definition** Treason against the United States shall consist only in levying war against them, or in adhering to their enemies, giving them aid and comfort. No person shall be convicted of treason unless on the testimony of two witnesses to the same overt act, or on confession in open court.*

*2. **Punishment** The Congress shall have power to declare the punishment of treason, but no attainder of treason shall work corruption of blood, or forfeiture except during the life of the person attainted.*

ARTICLE IV
Relations Among the States

SECTION 1. OFFICIAL RECORDS

Official Records Each state must accept the laws, acts, and legal decisions made by other states.

Full faith and credit shall be given in each state to the public acts, records and judicial proceedings of every other State. And the Congress may by general laws prescribe the manner in which such acts, records, and proceedings shall be proved, and the effect thereof.

SECTION 2. PRIVILEGES OF THE CITIZENS

Privileges States must give the same rights to citizens of other states that they give to ther own citizens.

Return of a Person Accused of a Crime If a person charged with a crime escapes to another state, he or she must be returned to the original state to go on trial. This act of returning someone from one state to another is called extradition.

*1. **Privileges** The citizens of each State shall be entitled to all privileges and immunities of citizens in the several states.*

*2. **Return of a Person Accused of a Crime** A person charged in any State with treason, felony, or other crime, who shall flee from justice, and be found in another State, shall on demand of the executive authority of the State from which he fled, be delivered up, to be removed to the State having jurisdiction of the crime.*

*3. **Return of Fugitive Slaves** ~~No person held to service or labor in one State, under the laws thereof, escaping into another, shall, in consequence of any law or regulation therein, be discharged from such service or labor, but shall be delivered up on claim of the party to whom such service or labor may be due.~~*

Every American has a right to a trial by jury. Jurors' chairs are shown below.

SECTION 3. NEW STATES AND TERRITORIES

*1. **New States** New states may be admitted by the Congress into this Union; but no new State shall be formed or erected within the jurisdiction of any other State, nor any State be formed by the junction of two or more States, or parts of States, without the consent of the legislatures of the States concerned, as well as of the Congress.*

*2. **Federal Lands** The Congress shall have power to dispose of and make all needful rules and regulations respecting the territory or other property belonging to the United States; and nothing in this Constitution shall be so construed as to prejudice any claims of the United States, or of any particular State.*

New States Congress has the power to create new states out of the nation's territories. All new states have the same rights as the old states. This clause made it clear that the United States would not make colonies out of its new lands.

SECTION 4. GUARANTEES TO THE STATES

The United States shall guarantee to every State in this Union a republican form of government, and shall protect each of them against invasion; and on application of the legislature, or of the executive (when the legislature cannot be convened) against domestic violence.

Guarantees to the State The federal government must defend the states from rebellions and from attacks by other countries.

ARTICLE V
Amending the Constitution

The Congress, whenever two-thirds of both houses shall deem it necessary, shall propose amendments to this Constitution, or, on the application of the legislatures of two-thirds of the several States, shall call a convention for proposing amendments, which, in either case, shall be valid to all intents and purposes, as part of this Constitution, when ratified by the legislatures of three-fourths of the several States, or by conventions in three-fourths thereof, as the one or the other mode of ratification may be proposed by the Congress; provided, ~~that no amendment which may be made prior to the year 1808, shall in any manner affect the first and fourth clauses in the ninth section of the first article;~~ and that no State, without its consent, shall be deprived of its equal suffrage in the Senate.

Amending the Constitution An amendment to the Constitution may be proposed either by a two-thirds vote of each house of Congress or by a national convention called by Congress at the request of two-thirds of the state legislatures. To be ratified, or approved, an amendment must be supported by three-fourths of the state legislatures or by three-fourths of special conventions held in each state.

Once an amendment is ratified, it becomes part of the Constitution. Only a new amendment can change it. Amendments have allowed people to change the Constitution to meet the changing needs of the nation.

ARTICLE VI
General Provisions

*1. **Public Debt** All debts contracted and engagements entered into, before the adoption of this Constitution, shall be as valid against the United States under this Constitution, as under the Confederation.*

*2. **Federal Supremacy** This Constitution, and the laws of the United States which shall be made in pursuance thereof; and all treaties made, or which shall be made, under the authority of the United States, shall be the supreme law of the land; and the judges in every State shall be bound thereby, anything in the Constitution or laws of any State to the contrary notwithstanding.*

*3. **Oaths of Office** The senators and representatives before mentioned, and the members of the several State legislatures, and all executive and judicial officers, both of the United States, and of the several States, shall be bound by oath or affirmation to support this Constitution; but no religious test shall ever be required as a qualification to any office or public trust under the United States.*

Federal Supremacy The Constitution is the highest law in the nation. Whenever a state law and a federal law are different, the federal law must be obeyed.

Oaths of Office All state and federal officials must take an oath promising to obey the Constitution.

ARTICLE VII
Ratification

Ratification The Constitution went into effect as soon as nine of the 13 states approved it.

Each state held a special convention to debate the Constitution. The ninth state to approve the Constitution, New Hampshire, voted for ratification on June 21, 1788.

The ratification of the conventions of nine States shall be sufficient for the establishment of this Constitution between the States so ratifying the same.

Done in Convention by the unanimous consent of the States present the seventeenth day of September in the year of our Lord one thousand seven hundred and eighty-seven and of the independence of the United States of America the twelfth. In witness whereof we have hereunto subscribed our names.

George Washington, President and deputy from Virginia

DELAWARE
George Read
Gunning Bedford, Junior
John Dickinson
Richard Bassett
Jacob Broom

MARYLAND
James McHenry
Daniel of St. Thomas Jenifer
Daniel Carroll

VIRGINIA
John Blair
James Madison, Junior

NORTH CAROLINA
William Blount
Richard Dobbs Spaight
Hugh Williamson

SOUTH CAROLINA
John Rutledge
Charles Cotesworth Pinckney
Charles Pinckney
Pierce Butler

GEORGIA
William Few
Abraham Baldwin

NEW HAMPSHIRE
John Langdon
Nicholas Gilman

MASSACHUSETTS
Nathaniel Gorham
Rufus King

CONNECTICUT
William Samuel Johnson
Roger Sherman

NEW YORK
Alexander Hamilton

NEW JERSEY
William Livingston
David Brearley
William Paterson
Jonathan Dayton

PENNSYLVANIA
Benjamin Franklin
Thomas Mifflin
Robert Morris
George Clymer
Thomas FitzSimons
Jared Ingersoll
James Wilson
Gouverneur Morris

Delegates wait for their turn to sign the new Constitution.

AMENDMENTS TO THE CONSTITUTION

Amendments to the Constitution

AMENDMENT I (1791)*
Basic Freedoms

Congress shall make no law respecting an establishment of religion, or prohibiting the free exercise thereof; or abridging the freedom of speech, or of the press; or the right of the people peaceably to assemble, and to petition the government for a redress of grievances.

Basic Freedoms The government cannot pass laws that favor one religion over another. Nor can it stop people from saying or writing whatever they want. The people have the right to gather openly and discuss problems they have with the government.

AMENDMENT II (1791)
Weapons and the Militia

A well-regulated militia, being necessary to the security of a free State, the right of the people to keep and bear arms, shall not be infringed.

Weapons and the Militia This amendment was included to prevent the federal government from taking away guns used by members of state militias.

AMENDMENT III (1791)
Housing Soldiers

No soldier shall, in time of peace, be quartered in any house, without the consent of the owner, nor in time of war, but in a manner to be prescribed by law.

Housing Soldiers The army cannot use people's homes to house soldiers unless it is approved by law. Before the American Revolution, the British housed soldiers in private homes without permission of the owners.

AMENDMENT IV (1791)
Search and Seizure

The right of the people to be secure in their persons, houses, papers, and effects, against unreasonable searches and seizures, shall not be violated, and no warrants shall issue, but upon probable cause, supported by oath or affirmation, and particularly describing the place to be searched, and the persons or things to be seized.

Search and Seizure This amendment protects people's privacy in their homes. The government cannot search or seize anyone's property without a warrant, or a written order, from a court. A warrant must list the people and the property to be searched and give reasons for the search.

AMENDMENT V (1791)
Rights of the Accused

No person shall be held to answer for a capital, or otherwise infamous crime, unless on a presentment or indictment of a grand jury, except in cases arising in the land or naval forces, or in the militia, when in actual service in time of war or public danger; nor shall any person be subject for the same offense to be twice put in jeopardy of life or limb; nor shall be compelled in any criminal case to be a witness against himself, nor be deprived of life, liberty, or property, without due process of law; nor shall private property be taken for public use without just compensation.

Rights of the Accused A person accused of a crime has the right to a fair trial. A person cannot be tried twice for the same crime. This amendment also protects a person from self-incrimination, or having to testify against himself or herself.

AMENDMENT VI (1791)
Right to a Fair Trial

In all criminal prosecutions, the accused shall enjoy the right to a speedy and public trial, by an impartial jury of the State and district wherein the crime shall have been committed, which district shall have been previously ascertained by law, and to be informed of the nature and cause of the accusation; to be confronted with the witnesses against him; to have compulsory process for obtaining witnesses in his favor, and to have the assistance of counsel for his defense.

Right to a Fair Trial Anyone accused of a crime is entitled to a quick and fair trial by jury. This right protects people from being kept in jail without being convicted of a crime. Also, the government must provide a lawyer for anyone accused of a crime who cannot afford to hire a lawyer.

AMENDMENT VII (1791)
Jury Trial in Civil Cases

In suits at common law, where the value in controversy shall exceed twenty dollars, the right of trial by jury shall be preserved, and no fact tried by a jury shall be otherwise reexamined in any court of the United States, than according to the rules of the common law.

Jury Trial in Civil Cases Civil cases usually involve two or more people suing each other over money, property, or personal injury. A jury trial is guaranteed in large lawsuits.

*The date after each amendment indicates the year the amendment was ratified.

Bail and Punishment Courts cannot treat people accused of crimes in ways that are unusually harsh.

Powers Reserved to the People The people keep all rights not listed in the Constitution.

Powers Reserved to the States Any rights not clearly given to the federal government by the Constitution belong to the states or the people.

Suits Against the States A citizen from one state cannot sue the government of another state in a federal court. Such cases are decided in state courts.

Election of the President and Vice President Under the original Constitution, each member of the Electoral College voted for two candidates for President. The candidate with the most votes became President. The one with the second highest total became Vice President.

The 12th Amendment changed this system. Members of the electoral college distinguish between their votes for the President and Vice President. This change was an important step in the development of the two party system. It allows each party to nominate its own team of candidates.

The Twelfth Amendment allowed parties to nominate teams of candidates, as this campaign poster shows.

AMENDMENT VIII (1791)
Bail and Punishment

Excessive bail shall not be required, nor excessive fines imposed, nor cruel and unusual punishments inflicted.

AMENDMENT IX (1791)
Powers Reserved to the People

The enumeration in the Constitution, of certain rights, shall not be construed to deny or disparage others retained by the people.

AMENDMENT X (1791)
Powers Reserved to the States

The powers not delegated to the United States by the Constitution, nor prohibited by it to the States, are reserved to the States respectively, or to the people.

AMENDMENT XI (1795)
Suits Against States

The judicial power of the United States shall not be construed to extend to any suit in law or equity, commenced or prosecuted against one of the United States by citizens of another State, or by citizens or subjects of any foreign State.

AMENDMENT XII (1804)
Election of the President and Vice President

The electors shall meet in their respective States and vote by ballot for President and Vice President, one of whom, at least, shall not be an inhabitant of the same State with themselves; they shall name in their ballots the person voted for as President, and in distinct ballots the person voted for as Vice President, and they shall make distinct lists of all persons voted for as President, and of all persons voted for as Vice President, and of the number of votes for each, which lists they shall sign and certify, and transmit sealed to the seat of the government of the United States, directed to the President of the Senate; the President of the Senate shall, in the presence of the Senate and House of Representatives, open all the certificates and the votes shall then be counted; the person having the greatest number of votes for President, shall be the President, if such number be a majority of the whole number of electors appointed; and if no person have such majority, then from the persons having the highest numbers not exceeding three on the list of those voted for as President, the House of Representatives shall choose immediately, by ballot, the President. But in choosing the President, the votes shall be taken by States, the representation from each State having one vote; a quorum for this purpose shall consist of a member or members from two-thirds of the States, and a majority of all the States shall be necessary to a choice. And if the House of Representatives shall not choose a President whenever the right of choice shall devolve upon them, before the fourth day of March next following, then the Vice President shall act as President, as in case of the death or other constitutional disability of the President. The person having the greatest number of votes as Vice President, shall be the Vice President, if such number be a majority of the whole number of electors appointed, and if no person have a majority, then from the two highest numbers on the list, the Senate shall choose the Vice President; a quorum for the purpose shall consist of two-thirds of the whole number of senators, and a majority of the whole number shall be necessary to a choice. But no person constitutionally ineligible to the office of President shall be eligible to that of Vice President of the United States.

This etching shows a group of former slaves celebrating their emancipation.

AMENDMENT XIII (1865)
End of Slavery

SECTION 1. ABOLITION

Neither slavery nor involuntary servitude, except as a punishment for crime whereof the party shall have been duly convicted, shall exist within the United States, or any place subject to their jurisdiction.

SECTION 2. ENFORCEMENT

Congress shall have power to enforce this article by appropriate legislation.

AMENDMENT XIV (1868)
Rights of Citizens

SECTION 1. CITIZENSHIP

All persons born or naturalized in the United States, and subject to the jurisdiction thereof, are citizens of the United States and of the State wherein they reside. No State shall make or enforce any law which shall abridge the privileges or immunities of citizens of the United States; nor shall any State deprive any person of life, liberty, or property, without due process of law; nor deny to any person within its jurisdiction the equal protection of the laws.

SECTION 2. NUMBER OF REPRESENTATIVES

Representatives shall be apportioned among the several States according to their respective numbers, counting the whole number of persons in each State, excluding Indians not taxed. But when the right to vote at any election for the choice of electors for President and Vice President of the United States, representatives in Congress, the executive and judicial officers of a State, or the members of the legislature thereof, is denied to any of the male inhabitants of such State, being twenty-one years of age, and citizens of the United States, or in any way abridged, except for participation in rebellion, or other crime, the basis of representation therein shall be reduced in the proportion which the number of such male citizens shall bear to the whole number of male citizens twenty-one years of age in such State.

SECTION 3. PENALTY FOR REBELLION

No person shall be a senator or representative in Congress, or elector of President and Vice President, or hold any office, civil or military, under the United States, or under any State, who, having previously taken an oath, as a member of Congress, or as an officer of the United States, or as a member of any State legislature, or as an executive or judicial officer of any State, to support the Constitution of the United States, shall have engaged in insurrection or rebellion against the same, or given aid or comfort to the enemies thereof. But Congress may by a vote of two-thirds of each house, remove such disability.

SECTION 4. GOVERNMENT DEBT

The validity of the public debt of the United States, authorized by law, including debts incurred for payment of pensions and bounties for services in suppressing insurrection or rebellion, shall not be questioned. But neither the United States nor any State shall assume or pay any debt or obligation incurred in aid of insurrection or rebellion against the United States, or any claim for the loss or emancipation of any slave; but all such debts, obligations and claims shall be held illegal and void.

Abolition This amendment ended slavery in the United States. It was ratified after the Civil War.

Citizenship This amendment defined citizenship in the United States. "Due process of law" means that no state can deny its citizens the rights and privileges they enjoy as United States citizens. The goal of this amendment was to protect the rights of the recently freed African Americans.

Number of Representatives This clause replaced the Three-Fifths Clause in Article 1. Each state's representation is based on its total population. Any state denying its male citizens over the age of 21 the right to vote will have its representation in Congress decreased.

Penalty of Rebellion Officials who fought against the Union in the Civil War could not hold public office in the United States. This clause tried to keep Confederate leaders out of power. In 1872, Congress removed this limit.

Government Debt The United States paid all of the Union's debts from the Civil War. However, it did not pay any of the Confederacy's debts. This clause prevented the southern states from using public money to pay for the rebellion or from compensating citizens who lost their enslaved persons.

Right to Vote No state can deny its citizens the right to vote because of their race. This amendment was designed to protect the voting rights of African Americans.

Income Tax Congress has the power to tax personal incomes.

Direct Election of Senators In the original Constitution, the state legislatures elected senators. This amendment gave citizens the power to elect their senators directly. It made senators more responsible to the people they represented.

The Prohibition movement used posters like this to reach the public.

Prohibition This amendment made it against the law to make or sell alcoholic beverages in the United States. This law was called prohibition. Fourteen years later, the 21st Amendment ended Prohibition.

SECTION 5. ENFORCEMENT

The Congress shall have power to enforce, by appropriate legislation, the provisions of this article.

AMENDMENT XV (1870)
Voting Rights

SECTION 1. RIGHT TO VOTE

The right of citizens of the United States to vote shall not be denied or abridged by the United States or by any State on account of race, color, or previous condition of servitude.

SECTION 2. ENFORCEMENT

The Congress shall have power to enforce this article by appropriate legislation.

AMENDMENT XVI (1913)
Income Tax

The Congress shall have power to lay and collect taxes on incomes, from whatever sources derived, without apportionment among the several States, and without regard to any census or enumeration.

AMENDMENT XVII (1913)
Direct Election of Senators

SECTION 1. METHOD OF ELECTION

The Senate of the United States shall be composed of two senators from each State, elected by the people thereof, for six years; and each senator shall have one vote. The electors in each State shall have the qualifications requisite for electors of the most numerous branch of the State legislatures.

SECTION 2. VACANCIES

When vacancies happen in the representation of any State in the Senate, the executive authority of such State shall issue writs of election to fill such vacancies: Provided, that the legislature of any State may empower the executive thereof to make temporary appointments until the people fill the vacancies by election as the legislature may direct.

SECTION 3. EXCEPTION

~~*This amendment shall not be so construed as to affect the election or term of any Senator chosen before it becomes valid as part of the Constitution.*~~

AMENDMENT XVIII (1919)
Ban on Alcoholic Drinks

SECTION 1. PROHIBITION

~~*After one year from the ratification of this article the manufacture, sale, or transportation of intoxicating liquors within, the importation thereof into, or the exportation thereof from the United States and all territory subject to the jurisdiction thereof for beverage purposes is hereby prohibited.*~~

SECTION 2. ENFORCEMENT

~~*The Congress and the several States shall have concurrent power to enforce this article by appropriate legislation.*~~

SECTION 3. RATIFICATION

~~*This article shall be inoperative unless it shall have been ratified as an amendment to the Constitution by the legislatures of the several States, as provided in the Constitution, within seven years from the date of the submission hereof to the States by Congress.*~~

AMENDMENT XIX (1920)
Women's Suffrage

SECTION 1. RIGHT TO VOTE

The right of citizens of the United States to vote shall not be denied or abridged by the United States or by any State on account of sex.

SECTION 2. ENFORCEMENT

The Congress shall have power to enforce this article by appropriate legislation.

AMENDMENT XX (1933)
Terms of Office

SECTION 1. BEGINNING OF TERMS

The terms of the President and Vice-President shall end at noon on the 20th day of January, and the terms of senators and representatives at noon on the 3rd day of January, of the years in which such terms would have ended if this article had not been ratified; and the terms of their successors shall then begin.

SECTION 2. SESSIONS OF CONGRESS

The Congress shall assemble at least once in every year, and such meeting shall begin at noon on the 3rd day of January, unless they shall by law appoint a different day.

SECTION 3. PRESIDENTIAL SUCCESSION

If, at the time fixed for the beginning of the term of the President, the President-elect shall have died, the Vice President-elect shall become President. If a President shall not have been chosen before the time fixed for the beginning of his term, or if the President-elect shall have failed to qualify, then the Vice President-elect shall act as President until a President shall have qualified; and the Congress may by law provide for the case wherein neither a President-elect nor a Vice President-elect shall have qualified, declaring who shall then act as President, or the manner in which one who is to act shall be selected, and such person shall act accordingly until a President or Vice President shall have qualified.

SECTION 4. ELECTIONS DECIDED BY CONGRESS

The Congress may by law provide for the case of the death of any of the persons from whom the House of Representatives may choose a President whenever the right of choice shall have devolved upon them, and for the case of the death of any of the persons from whom the Senate may choose a Vice President whenever the right of choice shall have devolved upon them.

SECTION 5. EFFECTIVE DATE

~~*Sections 1 and 2 shall take effect on the 15th day of October following the ratification of this article.*~~

Ratification The amendment for Prohibition was the first one to include a time limit for ratification. To go into effect, the amendment had to be approved by three-fourths of the states within seven years.

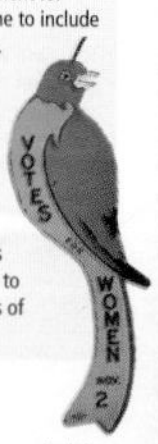

Women's Suffrage This amendment gave the right to vote to all women 21 years of age and older.

This 1915 banner pushed the cause of women's suffrage.

Beginning of Terms The President and Vice President's terms begin on January 20th of the year after their election. The terms for senators and representatives begin on January 3rd. Before this amendment, an official defeated in November stayed in office until March.

Presidential Succession A President who has been elected but has not yet taken office is called the President-elect. If the President-elect dies, then the Vice President-elect becomes President. If neither the President-elect nor the Vice President-elect can take office, then Congress decides who will act as President.

President Kennedy delivers his inaugural address in 1961.

SECTION 6. RATIFICATION

~~This article shall be inoperative unless it shall have been ratified as an amendment to the Constitution by the legislatures of three fourths of the several States within seven years from the date of its submission.~~

AMENDMENT XXI (1933)
End of Prohibition

End of Prohibition This amendment repealed, or ended, the 18th Amendment. It made alcoholic beverages legal once again in the United States. However, states can still control or stop the sale of alcohol within their borders.

SECTION 1. REPEAL OF EIGHTEENTH AMENDMENT

The eighteenth article of amendment to the Constitution of the United States is hereby repealed.

SECTION 2. STATE LAWS

The transportation or importation into any State, territory, or possession of the United States for delivery or use therein of intoxicating liquors, in violation of the laws thereof, is hereby prohibited.

SECTION 3. RATIFICATION

~~This article shall be inoperative unless it shall have been ratified as an amendment to the Constitution by conventions in the several States, as provided in the Constitution, within seven years from the date of the submission hereof to the States by the Congress.~~

AMENDMENT XXII (1951)
Limit on Presidential Terms

Two-Term Limit George Washington set a precedent that Presidents should not serve more than two terms in office. However, Franklin D. Roosevelt broke the precedent. He was elected President four times between 1932 and 1944. Some people feared that a President holding office for this long could become too powerful. This amendment limits Presidents to two terms in office.

SECTION 1. TWO-TERM LIMIT

No person shall be elected to the office of the President more than twice, and no person who has held the office of President, or acted as President, for more that two years of a term to which some other person was elected President shall be elected to the office of the President more than once. ~~But this article shall not apply to any person holding the office of President when this article was proposed by the Congress, and shall not prevent any person who may be holding the office of President, or acting as President, during the term within which this article becomes operative from holding the office of President or acting as President during the remainder of such term.~~

SECTION 2. RATIFICATION

~~This article shall be inoperative unless it shall have been ratified as an amendment to the Constitution by the legislatures of three fourths of the several States within seven years from the date of its submission to the States by the Congress.~~

AMENDMENT XXIII (1961)
Presidential Votes for Washington, D.C.

Presidential Votes for Washington, D.C. This amendment gives people who live in the nation's capital a vote for President. The electoral votes in Washington D.C., are based on its population. However, it cannot have more votes than the state with the smallest population. Today, Washington, D.C. has three electoral votes.

SECTION 1. NUMBER OF ELECTORS

The District constituting the seat of government of the United States shall appoint in such manner as the Congress may direct:

A number of electors of President and Vice President equal to the whole number of senators and representatives in Congress to which the District would be entitled if it were a State, but in no event more than the least populous State; they shall be in addition to those appointed by the States, but they shall be considered, for the purposes of the election of President and Vice President, to be elec-

tors appointed by a State; and they shall meet in the District and perform such duties as provided by the twelfth article of amendment.

SECTION 2. ENFORCEMENT

The Congress shall have power to enforce this article by appropriate legislation.

African Americans vote in Selma, Alabama, in 1966.

AMENDMENT XXIV (1964)
Ban on Poll Taxes

Ban on Poll Taxes A poll tax requires a person to pay a certain amount of money to register to vote. These taxes were used to stop poor African Americans from voting. This amendment made any such taxes illegal in federal elections.

SECTION 1. POLL TAXES ILLEGAL

The right of citizens of the United States to vote in any primary or other election for President or Vice President, for electors for President or Vice President, or for senator or representative in Congress, shall not be denied or abridged by the United States or any State by reason of failure to pay any poll tax or other tax.

SECTION 2. ENFORCEMENT

The Congress shall have power to enforce this article by appropriate legislation.

AMENDMENT XXV (1967)
Presidential Succession

SECTION 1. VACANCY IN THE PRESIDENCY

In case of the removal of the President from office or of his death or resignation, the Vice President shall become President.

SECTION 2. VACANCY IN THE VICE PRESIDENCY

Vacancy in the Vice Presidency If the Vice President becomes President, he or she may nominate a new Vice President. This nomination must be approved by both houses of Congress.

Whenever there is a vacancy in the office of the Vice President, the President shall nominate a Vice President who shall take office upon confirmation by a majority vote of both houses of Congress.

SECTION 3. DISABILITY OF THE PRESIDENT

Disability of the President This section tells what happens if the President suddenly becomes ill or is seriously injured. The Vice President takes over as Acting President. When the President is ready to take office again, he or she must tell Congress.

Whenever the President transmits to the President pro tempore of the Senate and the Speaker of the House of Representatives his written declaration that he is unable to discharge the powers and duties of his office, and until he transmits to them a written declaration to the contrary, such powers and duties shall be discharged by the Vice President as Acting President.

SECTION 4. DETERMINING PRESIDENTIAL DISABILITY

Whenever the Vice President and a majority of either the principal officers of the executive departments or of such other body as Congress may by law provide, transmit to the President pro tempore of the Senate and the Speaker of the House of Representatives their written declaration that the President is unable to discharge the powers and duties of his office, the Vice President shall immediately assume the powers and duties of the office as Acting President.

Thereafter, when the President transmits to the President pro tempore of the Senate and the Speaker of the House of Representatives his written declaration that no inability exists, he shall resume the powers and duties of his office unless the Vice President and a majority of either the principal officers of the executive departments or of such other body as Congress may by law provide, transmit within four days to the President pro tempore of the Senate and the Speaker of the House of Representatives their written declaration that the President is unable to discharge the powers and duties of his office. Thereupon Congress shall decide

the issue, assembling within 48 hours for that purpose if not in session. If the Congress, within 21 days after receipt of the latter written declaration, or, if Congress is not in session, within 21 days after Congress is required to assemble, determines by two-thirds vote of both houses that the President is unable to discharge the powers and duties of his office, the Vice President shall continue to discharge the same as Acting President; otherwise, the President shall resume the powers and duties of his office.

AMENDMENT XXVI (1971)
Voting Age

Right to Vote This amendment gave the vote to everyone 18 years of age and older.

SECTION 1. RIGHT TO VOTE

The right of citizens of the United States, who are 18 years of age or older, to vote shall not be denied or abridged by the United States or by any state on account of age.

SECTION 2. ENFORCEMENT

The Congress shall have power to enforce this article by appropriate legislation.

AMENDMENT XXVII (1992)
Congressional Pay

Limit on Pay Raises This amendment prohibits a Congressional pay raise from taking effect during the current term of the Congress that voted for the raise.

No law, varying the compensation for the services of the senators and representatives, shall take effect, until an election of representatives shall have intervened.

The voting age was lowered to 18 in 1971.

from *The Federalist* (No. 10) (1787)

The two great points of difference between a democracy and a republic are: first, the delegation of the government, in the latter, to a small number of citizens selected by the rest; secondly, the greater number of citizens and greater sphere of country, over which the latter may be extended.

The effect of the first difference is, on the one hand, to refine and enlarge the public views, by passing them through the medium of a chosen body of citizens, whose wisdom may best discern the true interest of their country and whose patriotism and love of justice will be least likely to sacrifice it to temporary or partial considerations. . . .

By enlarging too much the number of electors, you render the representative too little acquainted with all their local circumstances and lesser interests; as by reducing it too much, you render him unduly attached to these, and too little fit to comprehend and pursue great and national objects. . . .

Extend the sphere and you take in a greater variety of parties and interests; you make it less probable that a majority of the whole will have a common motive to invade the rights of other citizens.

The Star-Spangled Banner (1814)

O say, can you see, by the dawn's early light,
What so proudly we hailed at the twilight's last gleaming,
Whose broad stripes and bright stars, through the perilous fight,
O'er the ramparts we watched were so gallantly streaming?
And the rockets' red glare, the bombs bursting in air,
Gave proof through the night that our flag was still there.
O say, does that Star-Spangled Banner yet wave
O'er the land of the free and the home of the brave?

On the shore, dimly seen through the mists of the deep,
Where the foe's haughty host in dread silence reposes,
What is that which the breeze, o'er the towering steep,
As it fitfully blows, half conceals, half discloses?
Now it catches the gleam of the morning's first beam,
In full glory reflected now shines on the stream;
'Tis the Star-Spangled Banner, O long may it wave
O'er the land of the free and the home of the brave!

O thus be it ever when free men shall stand
Between their loved homes and the war's desolation!
Blest with vict'ry and peace, may the heav'n-rescued land
Praise the Power that hath made and preserved us a nation.
then conquer we must, for our cause it is just,
And this be our motto: 'In God is our trust.'
And the Star-Spangled Banner in triumph shall wave
O'er the land of the free and the home of the brave.

Francis Scott Key wrote "The Star-Spangled Banner" in 1814 while aboard ship during the battle of Fort McHenry. The gallantry and courage displayed by his fellow countrymen that night inspired Key to pen the lyrics to the song that officially became our national anthem in 1931.

John F. Kennedy was the 35th President of the United States.

President Kennedy gives a speech. Jackie Kennedy is at his left.

from President John F. Kennedy's Inaugural Address (1961)

"In your hands, my fellow citizens, more than mine, will rest the final success or failure of our course. Since this country was founded, each generation of Americans has been summoned to give testimony to its national loyalty. The graves of young Americans who answered the call to service surround the globe.

Now the trumpet summons us again—not as a call to bear arms, though arms we need—not as a call to battle, though embattled we are—but a call to bear the burden of a long twilight struggle, year in and year out, 'rejoicing in hope, patient in tribulation'—a struggle against the common enemies of man: tyranny, poverty, disease, and war itself.

Can we forge against these enemies a grand and global alliance, North and South, East and West, that can assure a more fruitful life for all mankind? Will you join in that historic effort? . . .

And so, my fellow Americans: ask not what your country can do for you—ask what you can do for your country.

My fellow citizens of the world: ask not what America will do for you, but what together we can do for the freedom of man."

from Martin Luther King Jr.'s "I Have a Dream" Speech (1963)

"I say to you today, my friends, that in spite of the difficulties and frustrations of the moment I still have a dream. It is a dream deeply rooted in the American dream.

I have a dream that one day this nation will rise up and live out the true meaning of its creed: 'We hold these truths to be self-evident; that all men are created equal.'

I have a dream that one day on the red hills of Georgia the sons of former slaves and the sons of former slaveowners will be able to sit down together at the table of brotherhood. . . .

I have a dream that my four little children will one day live in a nation where they will not be judged by the color of their skin but by the content of their character.

I have a dream today. . . .

. . . From every mountainside, let freedom ring.

When we let freedom ring, when we let it ring from every village and every hamlet, from every state and every city, we will be able to speed up that day when all of God's children, black men and white men, Jews and Gentiles, Protestants and Catholics, will be able to join hands and sing in the words of the old Negro spiritual, 'Free at last! Free at last! Thank God Almighty, we are free at last!'"

In August 1963, while Congress debated civil rights legislation, Martin Luther King Jr. led a quarter of a million demonstrators on a march on Washington. On the steps of the Lincoln Memorial he gave a stirring speech in which he told of his dream for America.

Presidents of the United States

U.S. Presidents

George Washington 1
(1732–1799)
President from: 1789–1797
Party: Federalist
Home state: Virginia
First Lady: Martha Dandridge Custis Washington

John Adams 2
(1735–1826)
President from: 1797–1801
Party: Federalist
Home state: Massachusetts
First Lady: Abigail Smith Adams

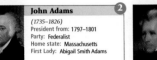

Thomas Jefferson 3
(1743–1826)
President from: 1801–1809
Party: Democratic-Republican
Home state: Virginia
First Lady: Martha Jefferson Randolph (daughter)

James Madison 4
(1751–1836)
President from: 1809–1817
Party: Democratic-Republican
Home state: Virginia
First Lady: Dolley Payne Todd Madison

James Monroe 5
(1758–1831)
President from: 1817–1825
Party: Democratic-Republican
Home state: Virginia
First Lady: Elizabeth Kortright Monroe

John Quincy Adams 6
(1767–1848)
President from: 1825–1829
Party: Democratic-Republican
Home state: Massachusetts
First Lady: Louisa Catherine Johnson Adams

Andrew Jackson 7
(1767–1845)
President from: 1829–1837
Party: Democratic
Home state: Tennessee
First Lady: Emily Donelson (late wife's niece)

Martin Van Buren 8
(1782–1862)
President from: 1837–1841
Party: Democratic
Home state: New York
First Lady: Angelica Singleton Van Buren (daughter-in-law)

William Henry Harrison 9
(1773–1841)
President: 1841
Party: Whig
Home state: Ohio
First Lady: Jane Irwin Harrison (daughter-in-law)

John Tyler 10
(1790–1862)
President from: 1841–1845
Party: Whig
Home state: Virginia
First Lady: Letitia Christian Tyler

James K. Polk 11
(1795–1849)
President from: 1845–1849
Party: Democratic
Home state: Tennessee
First Lady: Sarah Childress Polk

Zachary Taylor 12
(1784–1850)
President from: 1849–1850
Party: Whig
Home state: Louisiana
First Lady: Margaret Mackall Smith Taylor

Millard Fillmore 13
(1800–1874)
President from: 1850–1853
Party: Whig
Home state: New York
First Lady: Abigail Powers Fillmore

Franklin Pierce 14
(1804–1869)
President from: 1853–1857
Party: Democratic
Home state: New Hampshire
First Lady: Jane Means Appleton Pierce

James Buchanan 15
(1791–1868)
President from: 1857–1861
Party: Democratic
Home state: Pennsylvania
First Lady: Harriet Lane (niece)

Abraham Lincoln 16
(1809–1865)
President from: 1861–1865
Party: Republican
Home state: Illinois
First Lady: Mary Todd Lincoln

Andrew Johnson 17
(1808–1875)
President from: 1865–1869
Party: Democratic
Home state: Tennessee
First Lady: Eliza McCardle Johnson

Ulysses S. Grant 18
(1822–1885)
President from: 1869–1877
Party: Republican
Home state: Illinois
First Lady: Julia Dent Grant

Rutherford B. Hayes 19
(1822–1893)
President from: 1877–1881
Party: Republican
Home state: Ohio
First Lady: Lucy Ware Webb Hayes

James A. Garfield 20
(1831–1881)
President: 1881
Party: Republican
Home state: Ohio
First Lady: Lucretia Rudolph Garfield

Chester A. Arthur 21
(1830–1886)
President from: 1881–1885
Party: Republican
Home state: New York
First Lady: Mary Arthur McElroy (sister)

Grover Cleveland 22 24
(1837–1908)
President from: 1885–1889 and 1893–1897
Party: Democratic
Home state: New York
First Lady: Frances Folsom Cleveland

U.S. Presidents

Benjamin Harrison 23
(1833–1901)
President from: 1889–1893
Party: Republican
Home state: Indiana
First Lady: Caroline Lavina Scott Harrison

William McKinley 25
(1843–1901)
President from: 1897–1901
Party: Republican
Home state: Ohio
First Lady: Ida Saxton McKinley

Theodore Roosevelt 26
(1858–1919)
President from: 1901–1909
Party: Republican
Home state: New York
First Lady: Edith Kermit Carow Roosevelt

William Howard Taft 27
(1857–1930)
President from: 1909–1913
Party: Republican
Home state: Ohio
First Lady: Helen Herron Taft

Woodrow Wilson 28
(1856–1924)
President from: 1913–1921
Party: Democratic
Home state: New Jersey
First Lady: Edith Bolling Galt Wilson

Warren G. Harding 29
(1865–1923)
President from: 1921–1923
Party: Republican
Home state: Ohio
First Lady: Florence Kling Harding

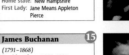

Calvin Coolidge 30
(1872–1933)
President from: 1923–1929
Party: Republican
Home state: Massachusetts
First Lady: Grace Anna Goodhue Coolidge

Herbert Hoover 31
(1874–1964)
President from: 1929–1933
Party: Republican
Home state: California
First Lady: Lou Henry Hoover

Franklin Delano Roosevelt 32
(1882–1945)
President from: 1933–1945
Party: Democratic
Home state: New York
First Lady: Anna Eleanor Roosevelt Roosevelt

Harry S. Truman 33
(1884–1972)
President from: 1945–1953
Party: Democratic
Home state: Missouri
First Lady: Elizabeth Virginia Wallace Truman

Dwight D. Eisenhower 34
(1890–1969)
President from: 1953–1961
Party: Republican
Home state: New York
First Lady: Mamie Geneva Doud Eisenhower

John F. Kennedy 35
(1917–1963)
President from: 1961–1963
Party: Democratic
Home state: Massachusetts
First Lady: Jacqueline Lee Bouvier Kennedy

U.S. Presidents

Lyndon Baines Johnson 36
(1908–1973)
President from: 1963–1969
Party: Democratic
Home state: Texas
First Lady: Claudia Alta (Lady Bird) Taylor Johnson

Richard M. Nixon 37
(1913–1994)
President from: 1969–1974
Party: Republican
Home state: New York
First Lady: Thelma Catherine (Pat) Ryan Nixon

Gerald R. Ford 38
(1913–)
President from: 1974–1977
Party: Republican
Home state: Michigan
First Lady: Elizabeth Bloomer Ford

Jimmy Carter 39
(1924–)
President from: 1977–1981
Party: Democratic
Home state: Georgia
First Lady: Rosalynn Smith Carter

Ronald Reagan 40
(1911–)
President from: 1981–1989
Party: Republican
Home state: California
First Lady: Nancy Davis Reagan

George Bush 41
(1924–)
President from: 1989–1993
Party: Republican
Home state: Texas
First Lady: Barbara Pierce Bush

William Clinton 42
(1946–)
President from: 1993–2001
Party: Democratic
Home state: Arkansas
First Lady: Hillary Rodham Clinton

George W. Bush 43
(1946–)
President from: 2001–
Party: Republican
Home state: Texas
First Lady: Laura Welch Bush

U.S. Presidents

Biographical Dictionary

The page number after each entry refers to the place where the person is first mentioned. For more complete references to people, see the Index.

A

Abigail Adams

Adams, Abigail 1744–1818, Patriot during the American Revolution (p. 266).

Adams, John 1735–1826, 2nd President of the United States, 1797–1801 (p. 241).

Adams, Samuel 1722–1803, helped inspire the American Revolution (p. 235).

Albright, Madeleine K. 1937–, first female Secretary of State for the United States (p. 513).

Anthony, Susan B. 1820–1906, reformer who fought for women's rights (p. 391).

Arnold, Benedict 1741–1801, general in American Revolution; committed treason (p. 280).

Attucks, Crispus 1723–1770, former slave; killed in the Boston Massacre (p. 240).

B

Balboa, Vasco Núñez de 1475–1519, Spanish explorer (p. 100).

Banneker, Benjamin 1731–1806, helped survey Washington, D.C. (p. 324).

Barton, Clara 1821–1912, nurse in Civil War; began American Red Cross (p. 461).

Boone, Daniel 1734–1820, frontiersman who cut trail into Kentucky (p. 345).

Bradford, William 1590–1657, governor of Plymouth Colony (p. 138).

Brant, Joseph 1742–1807, Mohawk chief who fought for the British (p. 271).

Brown, John 1800–1859, abolitionist who led rebellion at Harpers Ferry (p. 435).

Bruce, Blanche K. 1841–1898, African American planter and politician (p. 476).

C

Cabot, John 1450–1499, English explorer; reached Newfoundland (p. 123).

Calhoun, John C. 1782–1850, politician who supported slavery and states' rights (p. 419).

Carter, Jimmy 1924–, 39th President of the United States, 1977–1981 (p. 506).

Cartier, Jacques 1491–1557, French explorer; sailed up St. Lawrence River (p. 123).

Chavez, Cesar 1927–1993, labor leader; founded the United Farm Workers (p. 534).

Dennis Chavez

Chavez, Dennis 1888–1962, first Hispanic American elected to the U.S. Senate.

Clark, George Rogers 1752–1818, captured three British forts during Revolutionary War (p. 287).

Clark, William 1770–1838, explored Louisiana Purchase with Lewis (p. 355).

Clay, Henry 1777–1852, proposed the Missouri Compromise and the Compromise of 1850 (p. 432).

Clinton, William J. 1946–, 42nd President of the United States, 1993–2001; impeached, then acquitted (p. 513).

Columbus, Christopher 1451–1506, Italian navigator; reached the Americas (p. 96).

Cooper, James Fenimore 1789–1851, novelist and historian; wrote stories about the American frontier (p. 365).

Cornwallis, Charles 1738–1805, English general in Revolutionary War; surrendered to Americans in 1781 (p. 287).

Coronado, Francisco Vázquez de 1510–1554, Spanish conquistador (p. 106).

Cortés, Hernán 1485–1547, Spanish conquistador (p. 104).

Crockett, Davy 1786–1836, pioneer and member of Congress; died at the Alamo (p. 398).

D

Davis, Jefferson 1808–1889, president of Confederacy during Civil War (p. 444).

Dawes, William 1745–1799, patriot who rode with Paul Revere (p. 251).

de las Casas, Bartolomé 1474–1566, Spanish missionary opposed to slavery (p. 112).

de Soto, Hernando 1500?–1542, Spanish explorer (p. 106).

Dias, Bartholomeu 1450?–1500, Portuguese navigator (p. 93).

Dix, Dorothea 1802–1887, reformer who worked to improve care for the mentally ill (p. 393).

Douglass, Frederick 1817–1895, abolitionist and writer; escaped from slavery (p. 392).

Du Bois, W.E.B. 1868–1963, educator who helped create the NAACP (p. 526).

E

Edwards, Jonathan 1703–1758, preached American Puritanism (p. 178).

Elizabeth I 1533–1603, queen of England, 1558–1603; supported Walter Raleigh's colonization of Virginia (p. 124).

Equiano, Olaudah 1745–1797, West African taken into slavery; was freed and became abolitionist in England (p. 176).

F

Franklin, Benjamin 1706–1790, printer, writer, publisher, scientist, and inventor (p. 190).

Friedan, Betty 1921–, author of *The Feminine Mystique* and leader of women's rights movement (p. 529).

Fulton, Robert 1765–1815, civil engineer; built first profitable steamboat (p. 382).

G

Gálvez, Bernardo de 1746–1786, Spanish colonial administrator (p. 287).

Gama, Vasco da 1460–1524, Portuguese navigator (p. 93).

Garrison, William Lloyd 1805–1879, reformer and abolitionist (p. 425).

George III 1738–1820, king of England, 1760–1820; supported British policies that led to American Revolution (p. 204).

Goizueta, Roberto 1931–1998, immigrant from Cuba who became President of The Coca-Cola Company (p. 513).

Grant, Ulysses S. 1822–1885, 18th President of the United States, 1869–1877; Union general in Civil War (p. 454).

Greene, Nathanael 1742–1786, general in South during Revolutionary War (p. 287).

Grimke, Angelina 1805–1879, abolitionist and supporter of women's rights (p. 425).

Grimke, Sarah 1792–1873, abolitionist and supporter of women's rights (p. 425).

H

Hale, Nathan 1755–1776, patriot spy during Revolutionary War; hanged by British (p. 279).

Hamilton, Alexander 1755–1804, contributor to *The Federalist*; first Secretary of the Treasury (p. 306).

Hancock, John 1737–1793, first signer of Declaration of Independence (p. 265).

Henry, Patrick 1736–1799, Revolutionary leader and orator (p. 235).

Houston, Samuel 1793–1863, first president of Republic of Texas (p. 395).

Hudson, Henry ?–1611, English navigator; gave name to Hudson River (p. 124).

Huerta, Dolores 1930–, labor leader; founded United Farm Workers with Cesar Chavez (p. 534).

Hurston, Zora Neale 1891?–1960, writer during the Harlem Renaissance.

Zora Neale Hurston

I

Irving, Washington 1783–1859, writer of humorous tales, history, and biography (p. 365).

Isabella 1451–1504 queen of Spain, 1474–1504; supported and financed Columbus (p. 96).

Biographical Dictionary

R37

J

Jackson, Andrew 1767–1845, 7th President of the United States, 1829–1837; encouraged Western expansion (p. 364).

Jay, John 1745–1829, contributor to *The Federalist;* Chief Justice, U.S. Supreme Court (p. 306).

Jefferson, Thomas 1743–1826, 3rd President of the United States, 1801–1809; wrote Declaration of Independence (p. 264).

Johnson, Andrew 1808–1875, 17th President of the United States, 1865–1869; impeached, then acquitted (p. 474).

K

Key, Francis Scott 1779–1843, writer of *Star-Spangled Banner* (p. 363).

King, Martin Luther, Jr. 1929–1968, civil rights leader; assassinated (p. 531).

Knox, Henry 1750–1806, first U.S. Secretary of War (p. 255).

L

Lafayette, Marquis de 1757–1834, French; fought in American Revolution (p. 280).

Lee, Richard Henry 1732–1794, delegate to Continental Congress (p. 263).

Lee, Robert E. 1807–1870, commander of Confederacy (p. 452).

Lewis, Meriwether 1774–1809, explored Louisiana Purchase with Clark (p. 355).

Lincoln, Abraham 1809–1865, 16th President of the United States; issued Emancipation Proclamation; assassinated (p. 440).

Lowell, Francis Cabot 1775–1817, built first complete cotton spinning and weaving mill in the United States (p. 380).

M

Madison, Dolley 1768–1849, wife of James Madison; first lady during War of 1812 (p. 363).

Madison, James 1751–1836, 4th President of the United States (p. 303).

Magellan, Ferdinand 1480?–1521, Portuguese explorer (p. 100).

Malinche 1500?–1531, Aztec interpreter and guide for Cortés in 1519 (p. 105).

Mann, Horace 1796–1859, educator who reformed public schools (p. 393).

Marion, Francis 1732?–1795, commander in American Revolution (p. 287).

Marquette, Jacques 1637–1675, French explorer; sailed down Mississippi River (p. 147).

Marshall, John 1755–1835, Chief Justice of U.S. Supreme Court (p. 370).

Marshall, Thurgood 1908–1993, first African American appointed to U.S. Supreme Court.

Metacomet ?–1676, American Indian leader, known as King Philip to British (p. 168).

Mink, Patsy Takemoto 1927–2002, first Asian American woman elected to U.S. Congress.

Patsy Takemoto Mink

Moctezuma 1480?–1520, Aztec emperor during Spanish conquest of Mexico (p. 44).

Monroe, James 1758–1831, 5th President of the United States, 1817–1825 (p. 364).

O

O'Connor, Sandra Day 1930–, first woman appointed to U.S. Supreme Court (p. 529).

Oglethorpe, James 1696–1785, founder of Georgia (p. 204).

Oñate, Juan de 1549?–1624?, conquerer and colonizer of New Mexico (p. 111).

Osceola 1800?–1838, American Indian leader in Florida (p. 371).

P

Paine, Thomas 1737–1809, wrote *Common Sense,* urging a declaration of independence (p. 262).

Parks, Rosa 1913–, African American who refused to obey segregation laws in Alabama (p. 531).

Pei, I. M. 1917–, famous architect who emigrated from China (p. 513).

Penn, William 1644–1718, founder of Pennsylvania (p. 189).

Pinckney, Eliza Lucas 1722–1793, introduced growing of indigo (blue dye) in South (p. 211).
Pocahontas 1595?–1617, married colonist John Rolfe; converted to Christianity; American Indian name: Matoaka (p. 132).
Ponce de Léon, Juan 1460?–1521, Spanish explorer of Florida (p. 106).
Pontiac ?–1769, Ottowa chief; united several American Indian nations (p. 230).
Popé ?–1692, Pueblo leader who led a revolt against Spanish settlers in 1680 (p. 113).

R

Randolph, Edmund 1753–1813, U.S. Attorney General and Secretary of State (p. 304).
Rankin, Jeannette 1880–1973, first woman elected to U.S. Congress (p. 529).
Revels, Hiram R. 1822–1901, African American Senator during Reconstruction (p. 476).
Revere, Paul 1735–1818, rode from Boston to Lexington to warn Patriots that the British were coming (p. 241).
Rolfe, John 1585–1622, English colonist; married Pocahontas (p. 132).
Ross, Betsy 1752–1836, maker of flags during the American Revolution.

S

Sacagawea 1787?–1812, Shoshone interpreter for Lewis and Clark (p. 356).
Salem, Peter 1750–1816, patriot who fought at Battle of Bunker Hill in 1775 (p. 271).
Santa Anna, Antonio López de 1795–1876, Mexican general and president during Texas revolution (p. 395).
Scott, Dred 1795?–1858, enslaved African American who sued for his freedom (p. 434).
Sequoya 1770?–1843, Cherokee scholar (p. 370).
Shays, Daniel 1747?–1825, led a rebellion of Massachusetts farmers (p. 298).
Sherman, Roger 1721–1793, member of Constitutional Convention (p. 304).
Sherman, William Tecumseh 1820–1891, Union general in Civil War (p. 466).
Slater, Samuel 1768–1835, set up cotton mill in Rhode Island (p. 378).
Smith, John 1580–1631, leader of Jamestown colony (p. 131).
Stanton, Elizabeth Cady 1815–1902, organized first women's rights conference in Seneca Falls (p. 390).
Steuben, Baron Friedrich von 1730–1794, Prussian soldier; trained American soldiers for Revolution (p. 281).
Stowe, Harriet Beecher 1811–1896, author of *Uncle Tom's Cabin* (p. 434).

T

Tecumseh 1768?–1813, Shawnee chief (p. 361).
Truth, Sojourner 1797?–1883, abolitionist and supporter of women's rights (p. 392).
Tubman, Harriet 1821?–1913, helped enslaved African Americans to freedom (p. 427).
Turner, Nat 1800–1831, led rebellion of enslaved people; was captured and hanged (p. 417).

W

Warren, Mercy Otis 1728–1814, author of political works (p. 250).
Washington, George 1732–1799, commanded Continental armies during Revolution; first President of the United States, 1789–1797 (p. 228).
Webster, Noah 1758–1843, wrote first American dictionary (p. 365).
Wheatley, Phillis 1753?–1784, African American poet (p. 272).
Whitefield, George 1714–1770, popular Great Awakening minister (p. 178).
Whitman, Marcus 1802–1847, missionary and pioneer in Oregon territory (p. 400).
Whitney, Eli 1765–1825, inventor of the cotton gin (p. 379).
Wright, Orville 1871–1948, made first successful flight in motorized plane.
Wright, Wilbur 1867–1912, made first successful flight in motorized plane.

Orville Wright

Wilbur Wright

Y

Young, Brigham 1801–1877, Mormon leader; settled in Utah (p. 401).

Biographical Dictionary

FACTS TO KNOW

The 50 United States

ALABAMA

22nd
Heart of Dixie

Population: 4,500,752
Area: 52,423 square miles
Admitted: December 14, 1819

ALASKA

49th
The Last Frontier

Population: 648,818
Area: 656,424 square miles
Admitted: January 3, 1959

ARIZONA

48th
Grand Canyon State

Population: 5,580,811
Area: 114,006 square miles
Admitted: February 14, 1912

ARKANSAS

25th
The Natural State

Population: 2,725,714
Area: 53,182 square miles
Admitted: June 15, 1836

CALIFORNIA

31st
Golden State

Population: 35,484,453
Area: 163,707 square miles
Admitted: September 9, 1850

COLORADO

8th
Centennial State

Population: 4,550,688
Area: 104,100 square miles
Admitted: August 1, 1876

CONNECTICUT

5th
Constitution State

Population: 3,483,372
Area: 5,544 square miles
Admitted: January 9, 1788

DELAWARE

1st
First State

Population: 817,491
Area: 2,489 square miles
Admitted: December 7, 1787

FLORIDA

27th
Sunshine State

Population: 17,019,068
Area: 65,758 square miles
Admitted: March 3, 1845

GEORGIA

4th
Peach State

Population: 8,684,715
Area: 59,441 square miles
Admitted: January 2, 1788

HAWAII

50th
The Aloha State

Population: 1,257,608
Area: 10,932 square miles
Admitted: August 21, 1959

IDAHO

43rd
Gem State

Population: 1,366,332
Area: 83,574 square miles
Admitted: July 3, 1890

ILLINOIS

21st
The Prairie State

Population: 12,653,544
Area: 57,918 square miles
Admitted: December 3, 1818

INDIANA

19th
Hoosier State

Population: 6,195,643
Area: 36,420 square miles
Admitted: December 11, 1816

IOWA

29th
Hawkeye State

Population: 2,944,062
Area: 56,276 square miles
Admitted: December 28, 1846

KANSAS

34th
Sunflower State

Population: 2,723,507
Area: 82,282 square miles
Admitted: January 29, 1861

KENTUCKY

15th
Bluegrass State

Population: 4,117,827
Area: 40,411 square miles
Admitted: June 1, 1792

LOUISIANA

18th
Pelican State

Population: 4,496,334
Area: 51,843 square miles
Admitted: April 30, 1812

MAINE

23rd
Pine Tree State

Population: 1,305,728
Area: 35,387 square miles
Admitted: March 15, 1820

MARYLAND

7th
Old Line State

Population: 5,508,909
Area: 12,407 square miles
Admitted: April 28, 1788

MASSACHUSETTS

6th
Bay State

Population: 6,433,422
Area: 10,555 square miles
Admitted: February 6, 1788

MICHIGAN

26th
Great Lakes State

Population: 10,079,985
Area: 96,810 square miles
Admitted: January 26, 1837

MINNESOTA

32nd
North Star State

Population: 5,059,375
Area: 86,943 square miles
Admitted: May 11, 1858

MISSISSIPPI

20th
Magnolia State

Population: 2,881,281
Area: 48,434 square miles
Admitted: December 10, 1817

MISSOURI

24th
Show Me State
Population: 5,704,484
Area: 69,709 square miles
Admitted: August 10, 1821

MONTANA

41st
Treasure State
Population: 917,621
Area: 147,046 square miles
Admitted: November 8, 1889

NEBRASKA

37th
Cornhusker State
Population: 1,739,291
Area: 77,358 square miles
Admitted: March 1, 1867

NEVADA

36th
Sagebrush State
Population: 2,241,154
Area: 110,567 square miles
Admitted: October 31, 1864

NEW HAMPSHIRE

9th
Granite State
Population: 1,287,687
Area: 9,351 square miles
Admitted: June 21, 1788

NEW JERSEY

3rd
Garden State
Population: 8,638,396
Area: 8,722 square miles
Admitted: December 18, 1787

NEW MEXICO
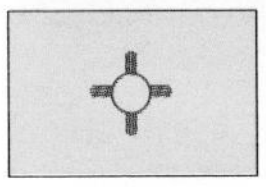
47th
Land of Enchantment
Population: 1,874,614
Area: 121,598 square miles
Admitted: January 6, 1912

NEW YORK

11th
Empire State
Population: 19,190,115
Area: 54,475 square miles
Admitted: July 26, 1788

NORTH CAROLINA

12th
Tarheel State
Population: 8,407,248
Area: 53,821 square miles
Admitted: November 21, 1789

NORTH DAKOTA

39th
Peace Garden State
Population: 633,837
Area: 70,704 square miles
Admitted: November 2, 1889

OHIO
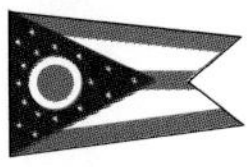
17th
Buckeye State
Population: 11,435,798
Area: 44,828 square miles
Admitted: March 1, 1803

OKLAHOMA

46th
Sooner State
Population: 3,511,532
Area: 69,903 square miles
Admitted: November 16, 1907

OREGON

33rd
Beaver State
Population: 3,559,596
Area: 98,386 square miles
Admitted: February 14, 1859

PENNSYLVANIA

2nd
Keystone State
Population: 12,365,455
Area: 46,058 square miles
Admitted: December 12, 1787

RHODE ISLAND

13th
Ocean State
Population: 1,076,164
Area: 1,545 square miles
Admitted: May 29, 1790

SOUTH CAROLINA

8th
Palmetto State
Population: 4,147,152
Area: 32,007 square miles
Admitted: May 23, 1788

SOUTH DAKOTA

40th
Coyote State
Population: 764,309
Area: 77,121 square miles
Admitted: November 2, 1889

TENNESSEE

16th
Volunteer State
Population: 5,841,748
Area: 42,146 square miles
Admitted: June 1, 1796

TEXAS

28th
Lone Star State
Population: 22,118,509
Area: 261,914 square miles
Admitted: December 29, 1845

UTAH

45th
Beehive State
Population: 2,351,467
Area: 84,904 square miles
Admitted: January 4, 1896

VERMONT

14th
Green Mountain State
Population: 619,107
Area: 9,615 square miles
Admitted: March 4, 1791

VIRGINIA

10th
Old Dominion
Population: 7,386,330
Area: 42,769 square miles
Admitted: June 25, 1788

WASHINGTON

42nd
Evergreen State
Population: 6,131,445
Area: 71,303 square miles
Admitted: November 11, 1889

WEST VIRGINIA

35th
Mountain State
Population: 1,810,354
Area: 24,231 square miles
Admitted: June 20, 1863

WISCONSIN

30th
Badger State
Population: 5,472,299
Area: 65,503 square miles
Admitted: May 29, 1848

WYOMING

44th
Equality State
Population: 501,242
Area: 97,818 square miles
Admitted: July 10, 1890

DISTRICT OF COLUMBIA

No nickname
Population: 563,384
Area: 68 square miles
Incorporated: 1802

Geographic Terms

basin
a round area of land surrounded by higher land

bay
part of a lake or ocean extending into the land

coast
the land next to an ocean

coastal plain
a flat, level area of land near an ocean

delta
a triangular area of land formed by deposits at the mouth of a river

desert
a dry area where few plants grow

▲ **glacier**
a large ice mass that moves slowly down a mountain or over land

gulf
a large body of sea water partly surrounded by land

harbor
a sheltered body of water where ships can safely dock

hill
a raised area of land, smaller than a mountain

island
a body of land surrounded by water

isthmus
a narrow strip of land connecting two larger bodies of land

lake
a body of water surrounded by land

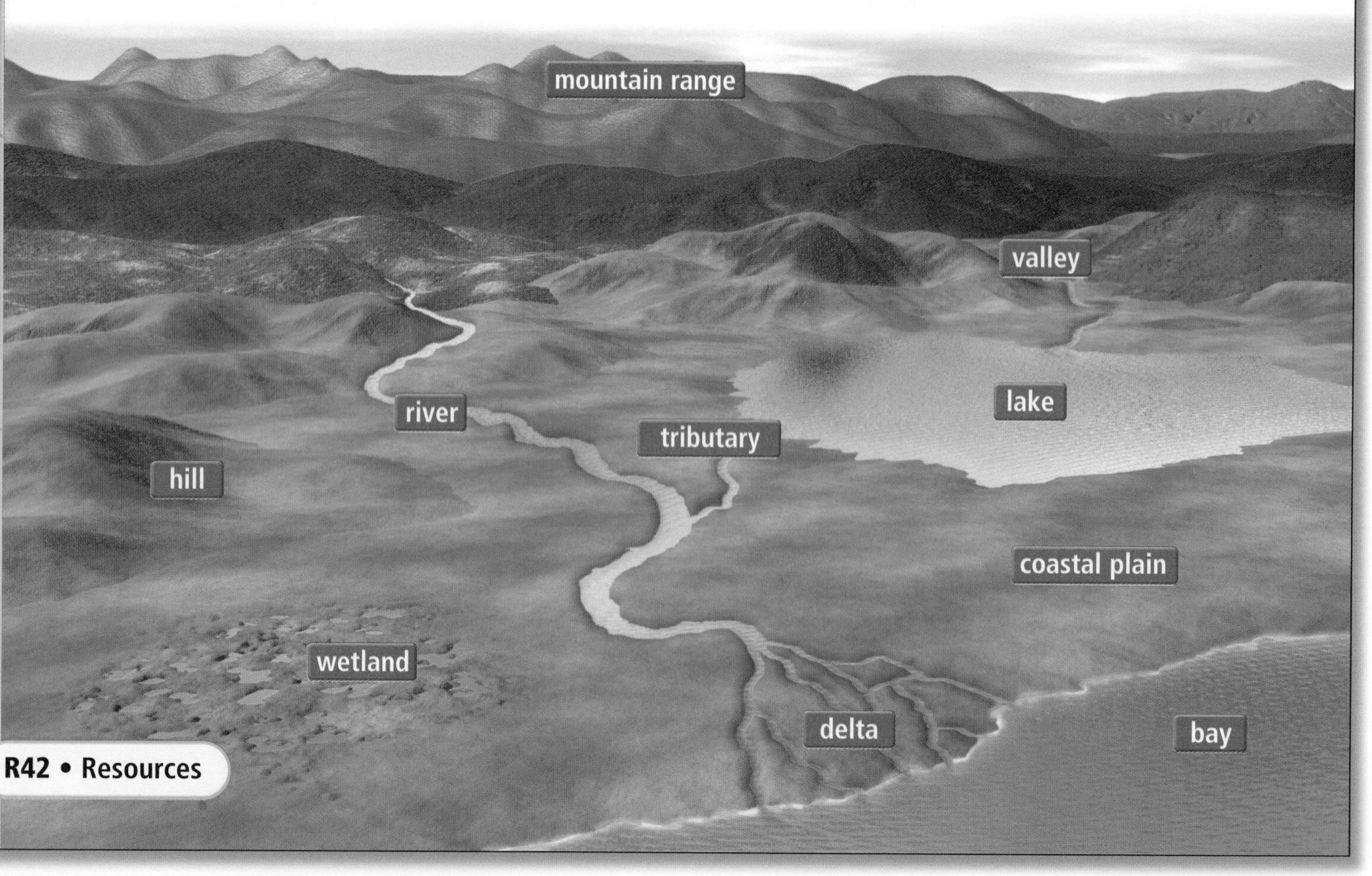

mesa
a wide flat-topped mountain with steep sides, found mostly in dry areas

mountain
a steeply raised mass of land, much higher than the surrounding country

mountain range
a row of mountains

ocean or sea
a salty body of water covering a large area of the earth

plain
a large area of flat or nearly flat land

plateau
a large area of flat land higher than the surrounding land

prairie
a large, level area of grassland with few or no trees

river
a large stream that runs into a lake, ocean, or another river

sea level
the level of the surface of the ocean

strait
a narrow channel of water connecting two larger bodies of water

tree line
the area on a mountain above which no trees grow

tributary
a river or stream that flows into a larger river

valley
low land between hills or mountains

volcano
an opening in the earth, through which lava and gases from the earth's interior escape

wetland
a low area saturated with water

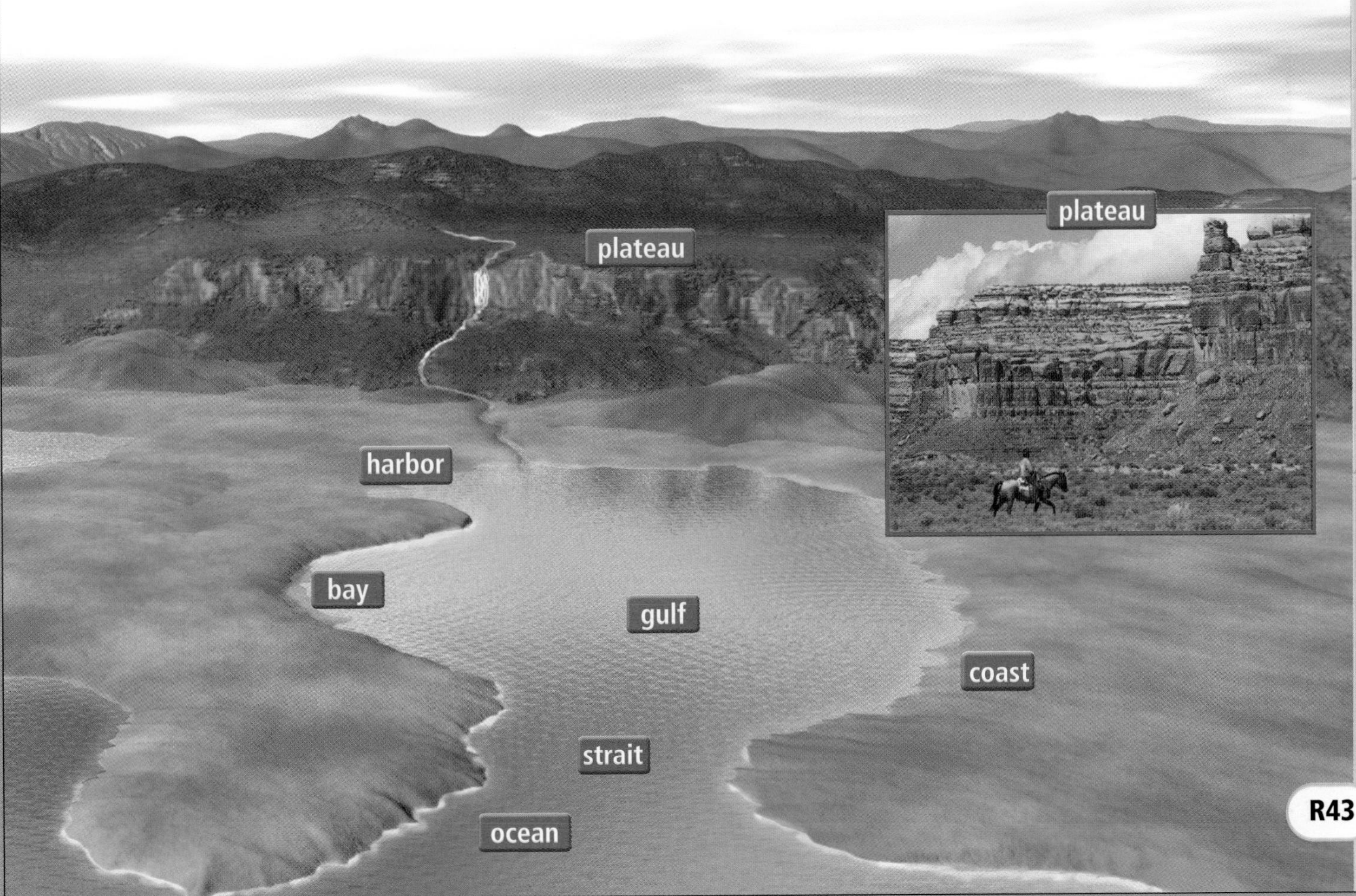

Atlas

The World: Political

ALB. —Albania
AZER. —Azerbaijan
BOS. & HERZ. —Boznia & Herzegovina
CEN. AFR. REP. —Central African Republic
DEM. REP. OF CONGO —Democratic Republic of Congo
FR. —France
IT. —Italy
LIECH. —Liechtenstein
LUX. —Luxembourg
NETH. —Netherlands
N.Z. —New Zealand
REP. OF CONGO —Republic of Congo
SERB. & MONT. —Serbia & Montenegro
SLOV. —Slovenia
SWITZ. —Switzerland
U.A.E. —United Arab Emirates
U.K. —United Kingdom
U.S. —United States

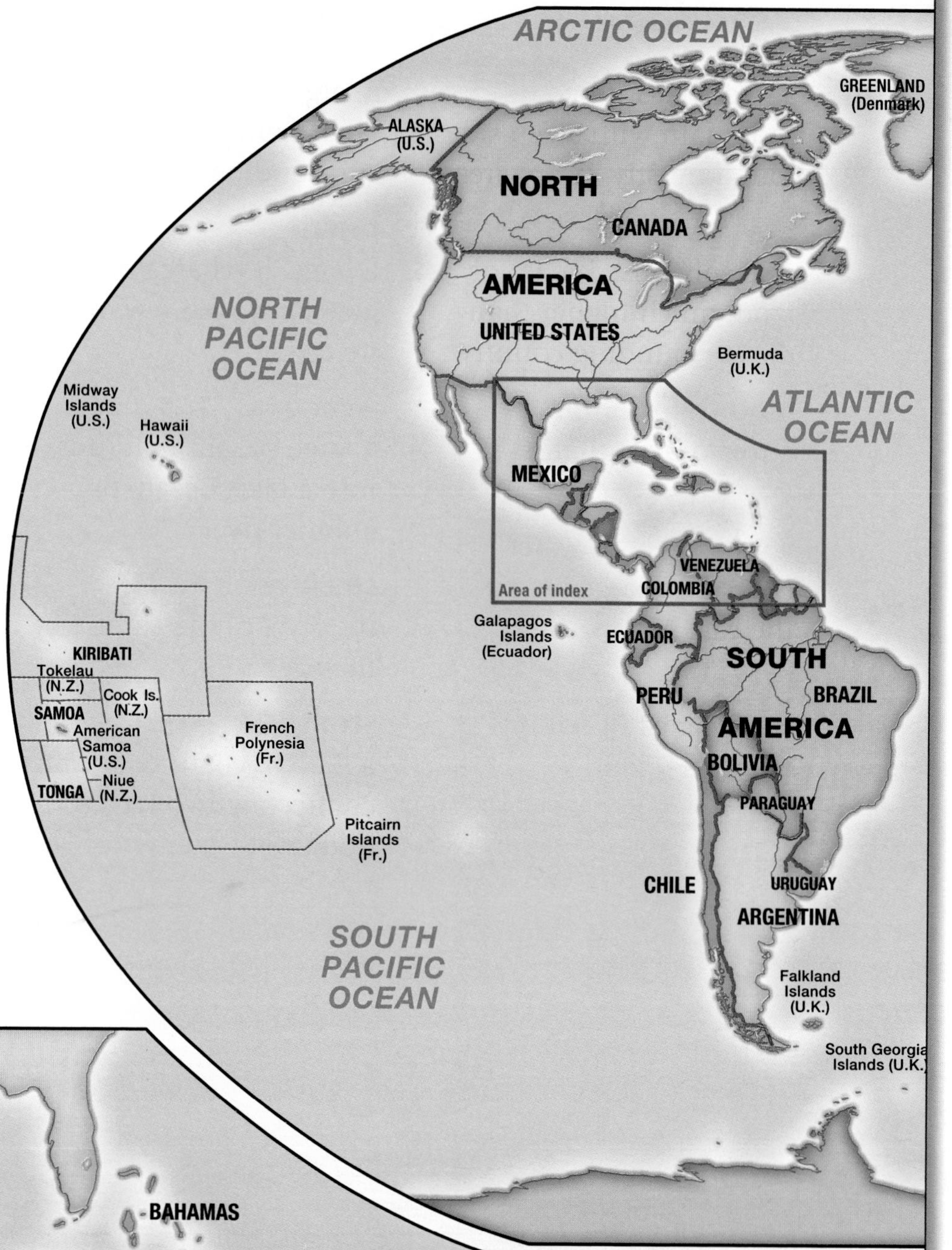

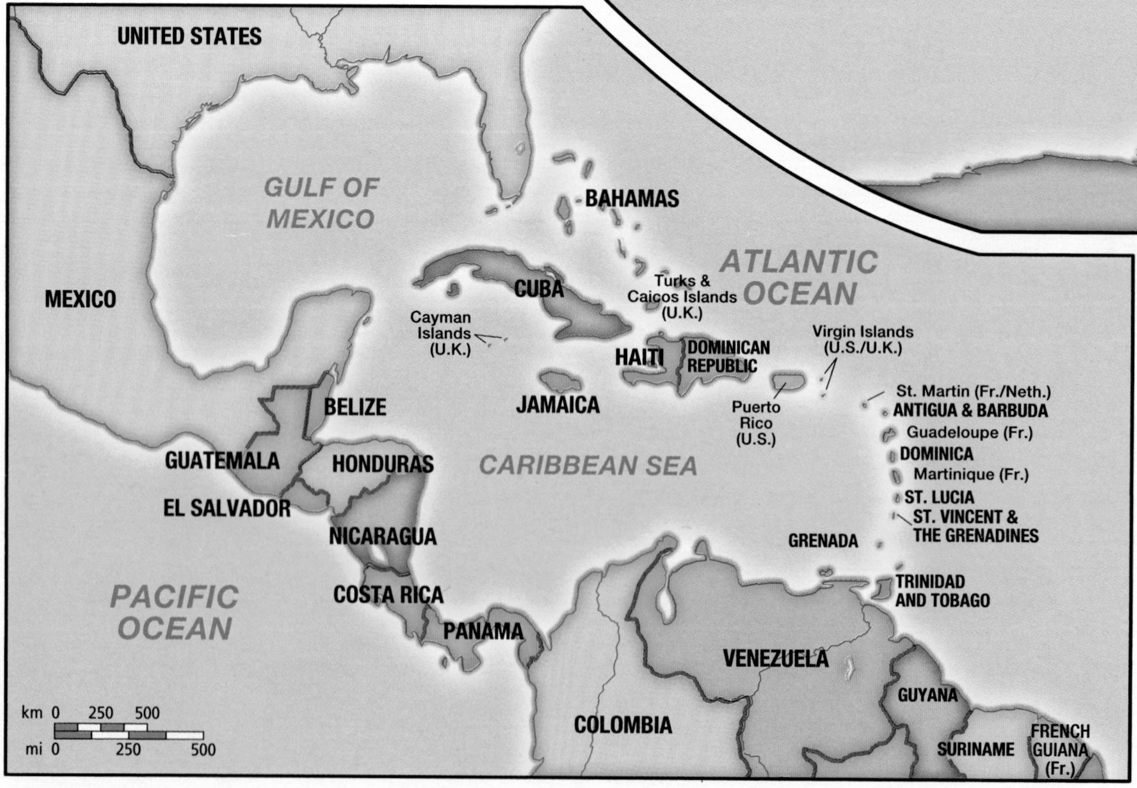

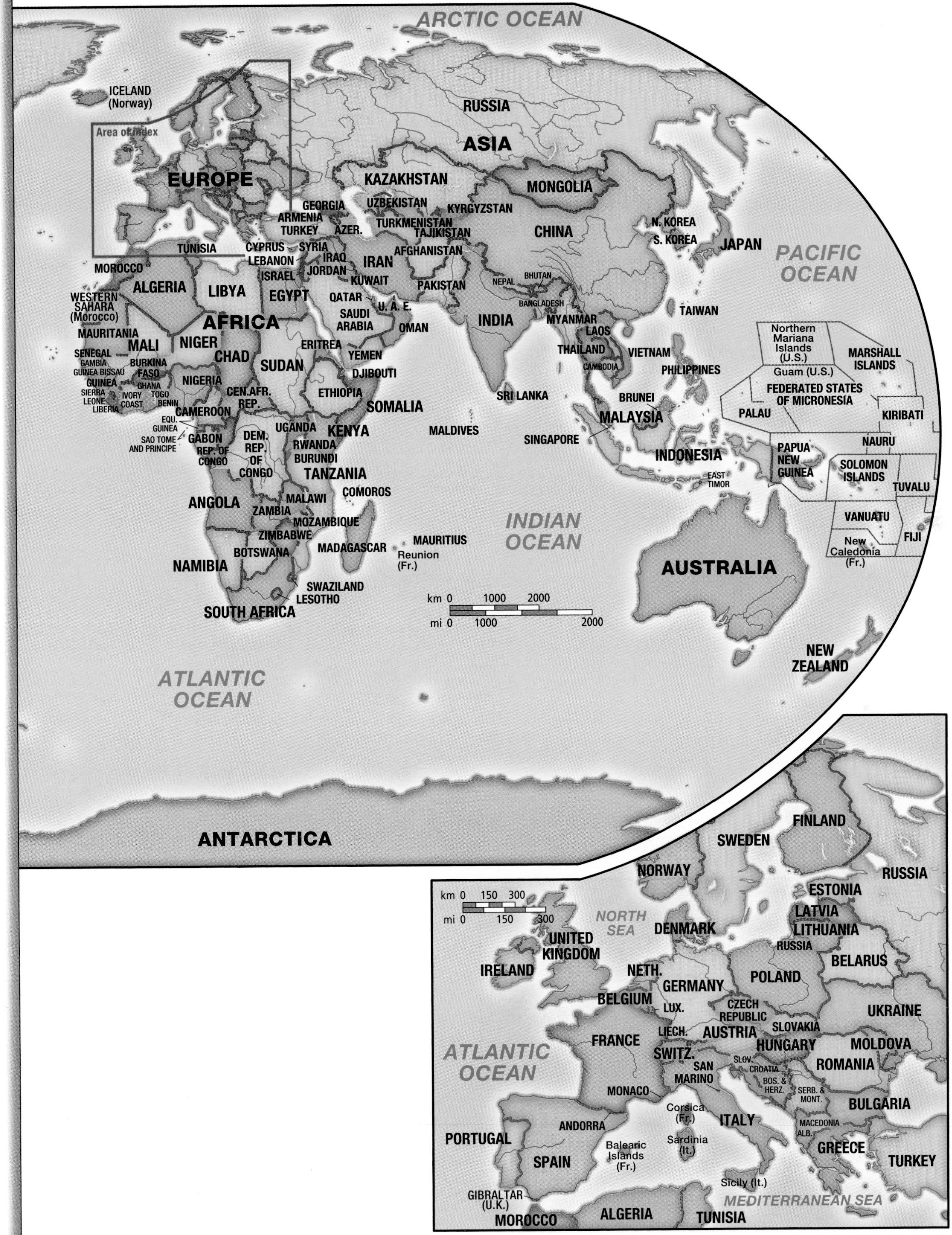
ARCTIC OCEAN
ICELAND (Norway)
Area of index
RUSSIA
ASIA
EUROPE
KAZAKHSTAN
MONGOLIA
GEORGIA
ARMENIA
TURKEY
AZER.
UZBEKISTAN
KYRGYZSTAN
TURKMENISTAN
TAJIKISTAN
CHINA
N. KOREA
S. KOREA
JAPAN
PACIFIC OCEAN
TUNISIA
CYPRUS
LEBANON
ISRAEL
SYRIA
IRAQ
JORDAN
IRAN
AFGHANISTAN
KUWAIT
MOROCCO
ALGERIA
LIBYA
EGYPT
QATAR
PAKISTAN
NEPAL
BHUTAN
BANGLADESH
TAIWAN
WESTERN SAHARA (Morocco)
AFRICA
SAUDI ARABIA
U. A. E.
OMAN
INDIA
MYANMAR
LAOS
MAURITANIA
MALI
NIGER
CHAD
ERITREA
YEMEN
THAILAND
VIETNAM
CAMBODIA
PHILIPPINES
Northern Mariana Islands (U.S.)
MARSHALL ISLANDS
Guam (U.S.)
FEDERATED STATES OF MICRONESIA
PALAU
KIRIBATI
SENEGAL
GAMBIA
GUINEA BISSAU
GUINEA
SIERRA LEONE
LIBERIA
BURKINA FASO
GHANA
IVORY COAST
TOGO
BENIN
NIGERIA
SUDAN
DJIBOUTI
ETHIOPIA
CEN.AFR. REP.
SOMALIA
SRI LANKA
BRUNEI
MALAYSIA
CAMEROON
EQU. GUINEA
SAO TOME AND PRINCIPE
GABON
REP. OF CONGO
DEM. REP. OF CONGO
UGANDA
KENYA
RWANDA
BURUNDI
TANZANIA
MALDIVES
SINGAPORE
INDONESIA
EAST TIMOR
PAPUA NEW GUINEA
NAURU
SOLOMON ISLANDS
TUVALU
ANGOLA
ZAMBIA
MALAWI
COMOROS
MOZAMBIQUE
ZIMBABWE
BOTSWANA
NAMIBIA
MADAGASCAR
MAURITIUS
Reunion (Fr.)
INDIAN OCEAN
VANUATU
New Caledonia (Fr.)
FIJI
AUSTRALIA
SWAZILAND
LESOTHO
SOUTH AFRICA
km 0 1000 2000
mi 0 1000 2000
NEW ZEALAND
ATLANTIC OCEAN
ANTARCTICA
FINLAND
SWEDEN
NORWAY
RUSSIA
ESTONIA
LATVIA
LITHUANIA
RUSSIA
km 0 150 300
mi 0 150 300
NORTH SEA
DENMARK
UNITED KINGDOM
IRELAND
NETH.
GERMANY
POLAND
BELARUS
BELGIUM
LUX.
CZECH REPUBLIC
UKRAINE
SLOVAKIA
LIECH.
AUSTRIA
FRANCE
SWITZ.
HUNGARY
MOLDOVA
ATLANTIC OCEAN
SLOV.
CROATIA
SAN MARINO
ROMANIA
BOS. & HERZ.
SERB. & MONT.
MONACO
BULGARIA
Corsica (Fr.)
ITALY
ANDORRA
MACEDONIA
ALB.
PORTUGAL
Balearic Islands (Fr.)
Sardinia (It.)
GREECE
SPAIN
TURKEY
Sicily (It.)
GIBRALTAR (U.K.)
MEDITERRANEAN SEA
MOROCCO
ALGERIA
TUNISIA

Atlas

R45

The World: Physical

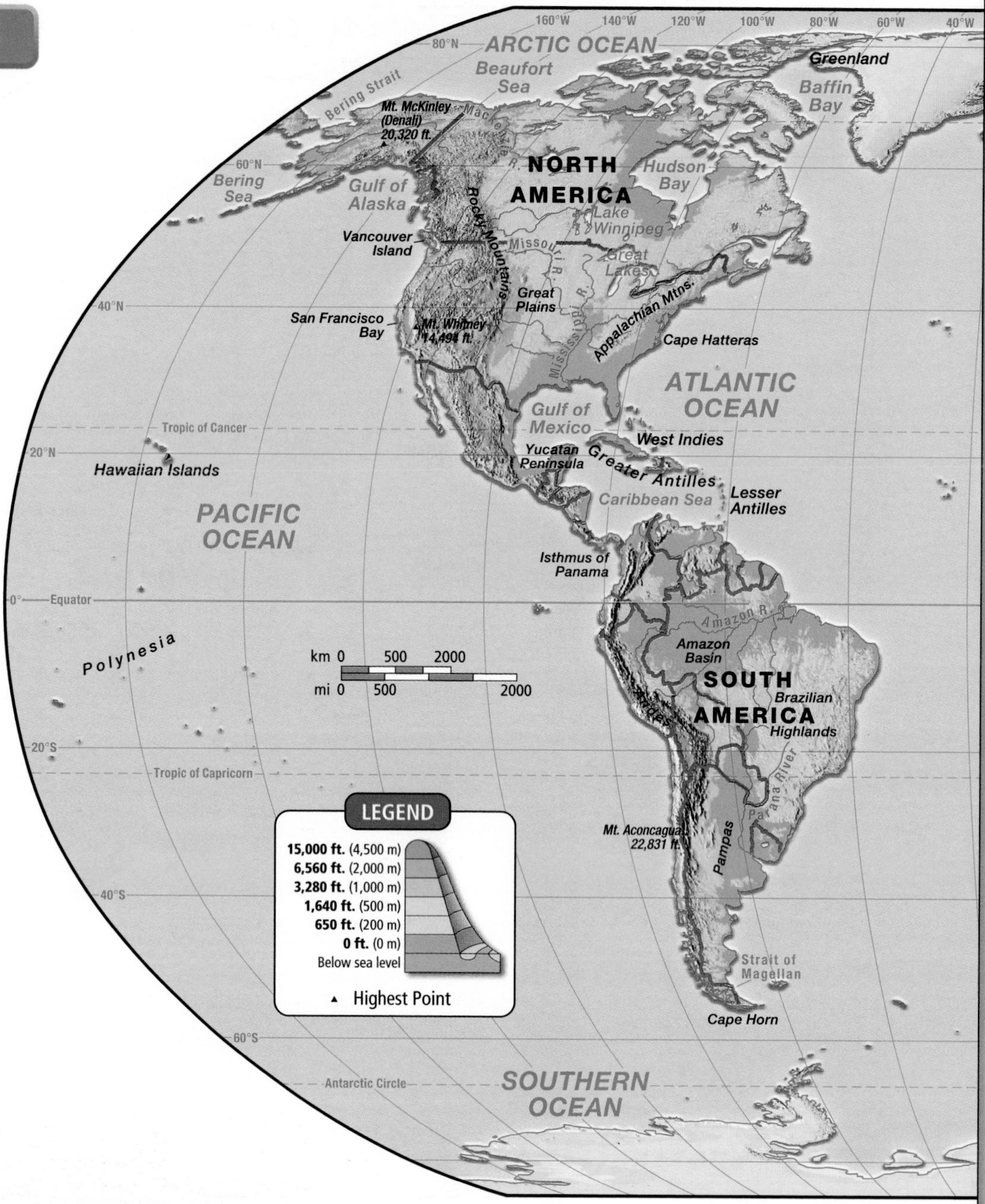

160°W
140°W
120°W
100°W
80°W
60°W
40°W
80°N
ARCTIC OCEAN
Greenland
Beaufort Sea
Baffin Bay
Bering Strait
Mt. McKinley (Denali) 20,320 ft.
60°N
Bering Sea
Gulf of Alaska
NORTH AMERICA
Hudson Bay
Rocky Mountains
Lake Winnipeg
Vancouver Island
Missouri R.
Great Lakes
Great Plains
Appalachian Mtns.
40°N
San Francisco Bay
Mt. Whitney 14,494 ft.
Mississippi R.
Cape Hatteras
ATLANTIC OCEAN
Gulf of Mexico
Tropic of Cancer
West Indies
20°N
Hawaiian Islands
Yucatan Peninsula
Greater Antilles
Lesser Antilles
Caribbean Sea
PACIFIC OCEAN
Isthmus of Panama
0°
Equator
Amazon R.
Amazon Basin
Polynesia
km 0 500 2000
mi 0 500 2000
SOUTH AMERICA
Brazilian Highlands
Andes
20°S
Tropic of Capricorn
Paraná River
LEGEND
15,000 ft. (4,500 m)
6,560 ft. (2,000 m)
3,280 ft. (1,000 m)
1,640 ft. (500 m)
650 ft. (200 m)
0 ft. (0 m)
Below sea level
Highest Point
Mt. Aconcagua 22,831 ft.
Pampas
40°S
Strait of Magellan
Cape Horn
60°S
Antarctic Circle
SOUTHERN OCEAN

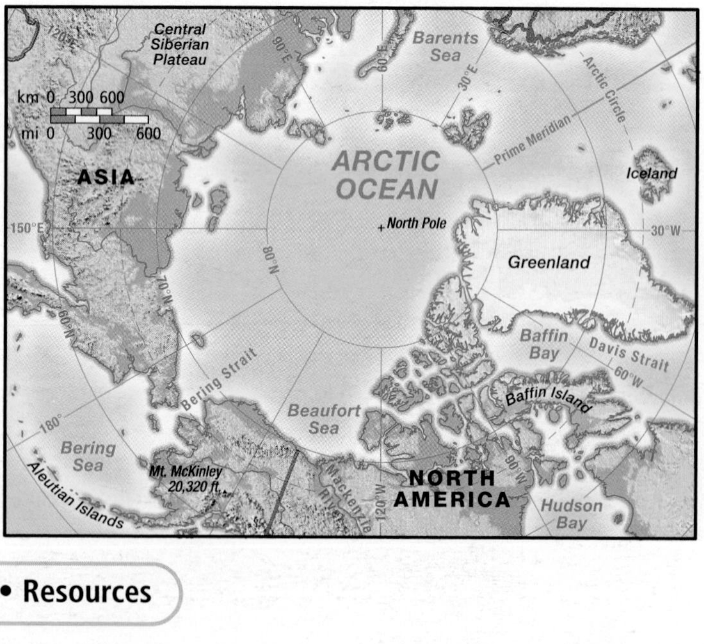

Central Siberian Plateau
Barents Sea
120°E
90°E
60°E
30°E
Arctic Circle
km 0 300 600
mi 0 300 600
Prime Meridian
ARCTIC OCEAN
ASIA
Iceland
150°E
North Pole
80°N
30°W
Greenland
70°N
60°N
Baffin Bay
Davis Strait
Bering Strait
60°W
Baffin Island
180°
Beaufort Sea
Bering Sea
Mt. McKinley 20,320 ft.
Mackenzie River
120°W
90°W
NORTH AMERICA
Hudson Bay
Aleutian Islands

ARCTIC OCEAN
Barents Sea
Arctic Circle
Iceland
EUROPE
North Sea
Northern European Plain
Ural Mountains
Ob River
Central Siberian Plateau
ASIA
Lake Baikal
Sea of Okhotsk
Kamchatka Peninsula
Volga River
Danube
Alps
Pyrenees
Mt. Elbrus 18,510 ft.
Black Sea
Caucasus Mountains
Caspian Sea
Aral Sea
Gobi Desert
Amur River
Sea of Japan
Plateau of Tibet
Himalaya Mountains
Mt. Everest 29,035 ft.
Ganges River
Atlas Mtns.
Mediterranean Sea
East China Sea
PACIFIC OCEAN
Tropic of Cancer
SAHARA
SAHEL
Niger River
Nile River
AFRICA
Congo River
Lake Victoria
Mt. Kilimanjaro 19,340 ft.
Great Rift Valley
Arabian Sea
Bay of Bengal
South China Sea
Philippine Islands
Micronesia
Borneo
Sumatra
Java
Strait of Sunda
Equator
New Guinea
Melanesia
INDIAN OCEAN
Prime Meridian
Madagascar
Kalahari Desert
Tropic of Capricorn
Great Sandy Desert
Coral Sea
AUSTRALIA
Darling River
Nullarbor Plain
Tasman Sea
Mt. Kosciusko 7,310 ft.
North Island
South Island
ATLANTIC OCEAN
Cape of Good Hope
Antarctic Circle
ANTARCTICA
20°W
0°
20°E
40°E
60°E
80°E
100°E
120°E
140°E
160°E
80°N
60°N
40°N
20°N
0°
20°S
60°S

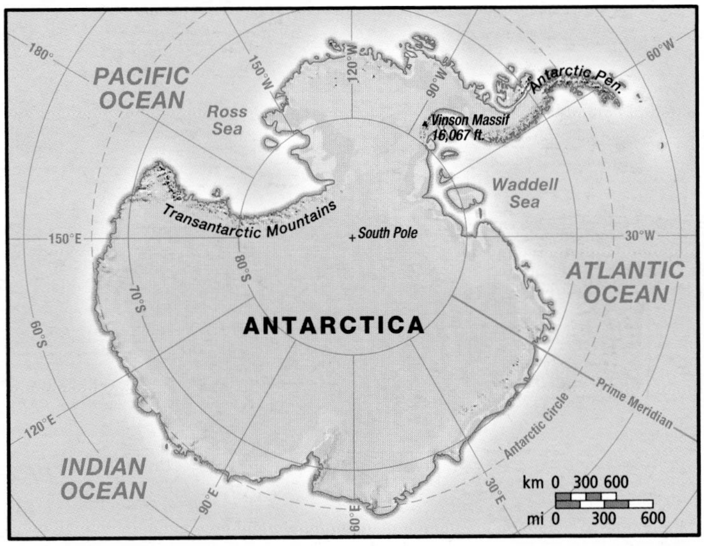
PACIFIC OCEAN
Ross Sea
Antarctic Pen.
Vinson Massif 16,067 ft.
Waddell Sea
Transantarctic Mountains
South Pole
ATLANTIC OCEAN
ANTARCTICA
Antarctic Circle
Prime Meridian
INDIAN OCEAN
180°
150°W
120°W
90°W
60°W
30°W
150°E
120°E
90°E
60°E
30°E
80°S
70°S
60°S
km 0 300 600
mi 0 300 600

R47

Eastern Hemisphere: Political
ARCTIC OCEAN
Beaufort Sea
GREENLAND (DENMARK)
Alaska (U.S.)
Hudson Bay
Labrador Sea
CANADA
Great Lakes
Ottawa
Great Salt Lake
UNITED STATES
Washington, D.C.
ATLANTIC OCEAN
Gulf of Mexico
BAHAMAS
Havana
CUBA
HAITI
DOMINICAN REPUBLIC
U.S. VIRGIN ISLANDS
ST. KITTS AND NEVIS
ST. LUCIA
BARBADOS
GRENADA
Tropic of Cancer
Hawaii (U.S.)
MEXICO
Mexico City
BELIZE
Belmopan
Kingston
JAMAICA
Santo Domingo
Port-Au-Prince
GUATEMALA
Guatemala City
Tegucigalpa
EL SALVADOR
San Salvador
Managua
San José
HONDURAS
NICARAGUA
COSTA RICA
PANAMA
Panama City
Caracas
VENEZUELA
Georgetown
Paramaribo
Cayenne
FRENCH GUIANA (FRANCE)
SURINAME
GUYANA
Bogotá
COLOMBIA
PACIFIC OCEAN
Equator
Galápagos Is. (Ecuador)
ECUADOR
Quito
Lima
PERU
BRAZIL
Brasilia
La Paz
BOLIVIA
Sucre
French Polynesia (France)
Tropic of Capricorn
PARAGUAY
Asunción
CHILE
Santiago
URUGUAY
Buenos Aires
Montevideo
ARGENTINA
Falkland Islands (U.K.)
South Georgia (U.K.)
N
W
E
S
LEGEND
National capital
National border
km 0 500 1000
mi 0 500 1000
140°W
120°W
100°W
80°W
60°W
40°W
60°N
40°N
20°N
0°
20°S
40°S
60°S
Atlas

Eastern Hemisphere: Physical
GREENLAND
ARCTIC OCEAN
Beaufort Sea
Baffin Bay
Bering Strait
Yukon R.
Mackenzie R.
Davis Strait
Mt. McKinley (Denali) 20,320 ft. (6,194 m)
Hudson Bay
Labrador Sea
Bering Sea
Gulf of Alaska
Coast Mountains
ROCKY MOUNTAINS
CANADIAN SHIELD
NORTH AMERICA
Great Lakes
Missouri R.
Mississippi R.
APPALACHIAN MOUNTAINS
Coast Ranges
Great Salt Lake
Range and Basin
GREAT PLAINS
Mt. Whitney 14,495 ft. (4,418 m)
Death Valley -282 ft. (-86 m)
Coastal Plain
ATLANTIC OCEAN
Rio Grande
Gulf of Mexico
Bahamas
Tropic of Cancer
Cuba
Hispaniola
Hawaiian Islands
Puerto Rico
Caribbean Sea
Lake Nicaragua
Lake Maracaibo
PACIFIC OCEAN
Line Islands
Equator
Amazon R.
Galápagos Islands
AMAZON BASIN
Marquesas
ANDES
SOUTH AMERICA
Society Islands
Cook Islands
Tropic of Capricorn
Atacama Desert
N
W
E
S
Mt. Aconcagua 22,834 ft. (6,960 m)
LEGEND
15,000 ft. (4,500 m)
6,560 ft. (2,000 m)
3,280 ft. (1,000 m)
1,640 ft. (500 m)
650 ft. (200 m)
0 ft. (0 m)
Below sea level
Highest Point
Rio de la Plata
Valdés Peninsula -131 ft. (-40 m)
Falkland Islands
South Georgia
Strait of Magellan
km 0 500 1000
mi 0 500 1000
160°W
140°W
120°W
100°W
80°W
60°W
40°W
80°N
60°N
40°N
20°N
0°
20°S
40°S
60°S
R49

Atlas

North America: Physical

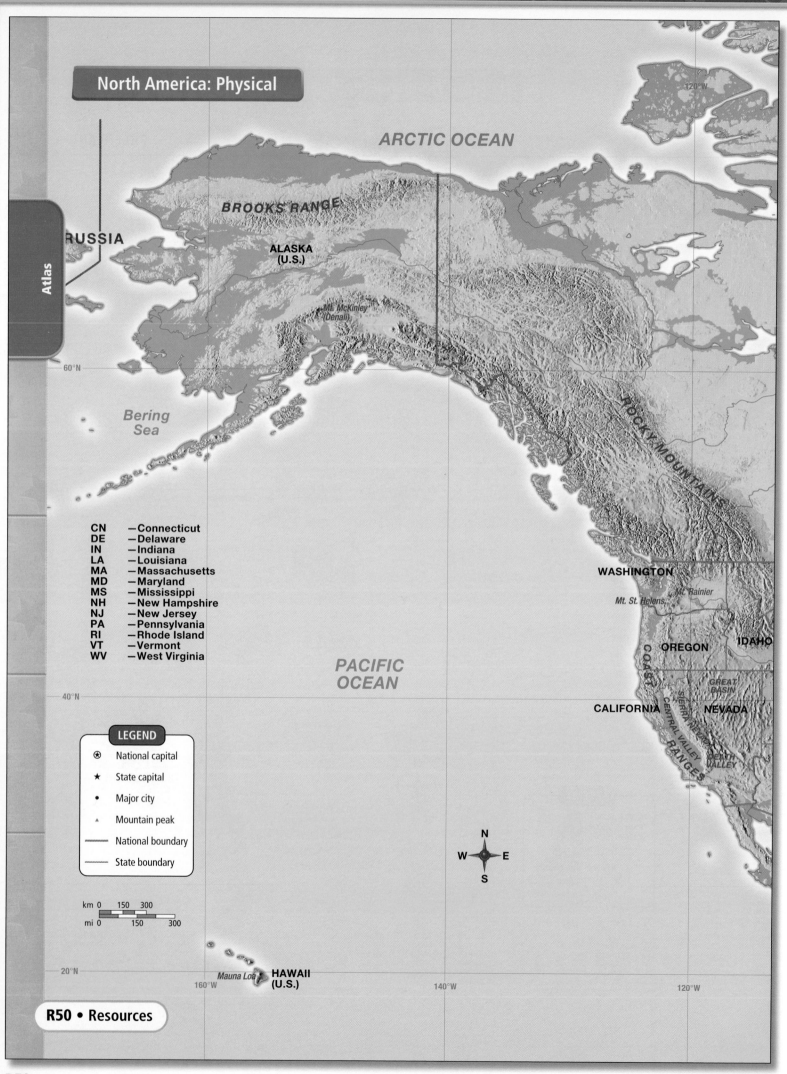

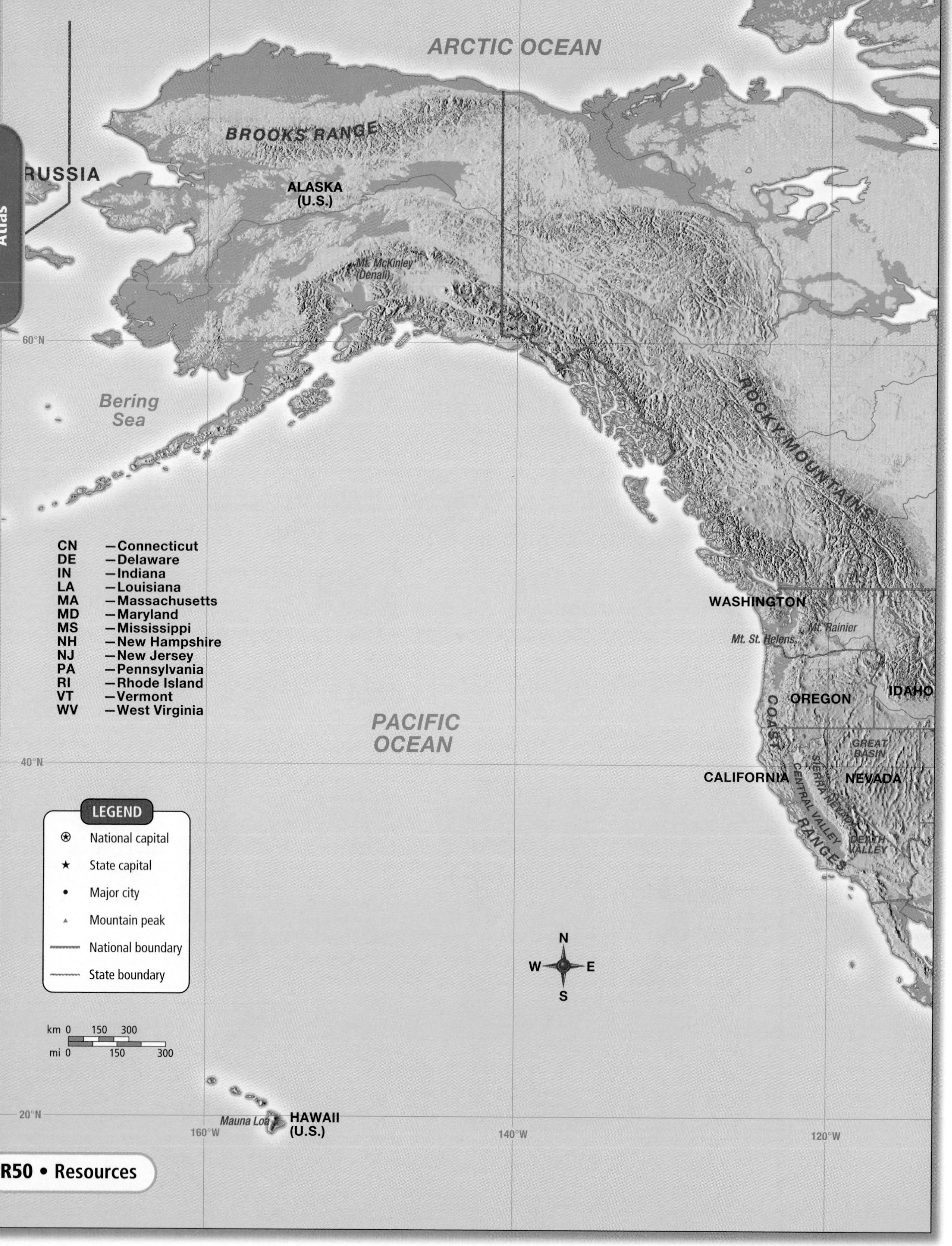

ARCTIC OCEAN
BROOKS RANGE
RUSSIA
ALASKA (U.S.)
Mt. McKinley (Denali)
Bering Sea
ROCKY MOUNTAINS
WASHINGTON
Mt. Rainier
Mt. St. Helens
OREGON
IDAHO
COAST RANGES
GREAT BASIN
SIERRA NEVADA
CENTRAL VALLEY
CALIFORNIA
NEVADA
DEATH VALLEY
PACIFIC OCEAN
HAWAII (U.S.)
Mauna Loa
60°N
40°N
20°N
160°W
140°W
120°W
N
W
E
S
CN —Connecticut
DE —Delaware
IN —Indiana
LA —Louisiana
MA —Massachusetts
MD —Maryland
MS —Mississippi
NH —New Hampshire
NJ —New Jersey
PA —Pennsylvania
RI —Rhode Island
VT —Vermont
WV —West Virginia
LEGEND
National capital
State capital
Major city
Mountain peak
National boundary
State boundary
km 0 150 300
mi 0 150 300

Atlas

R50 • Resources

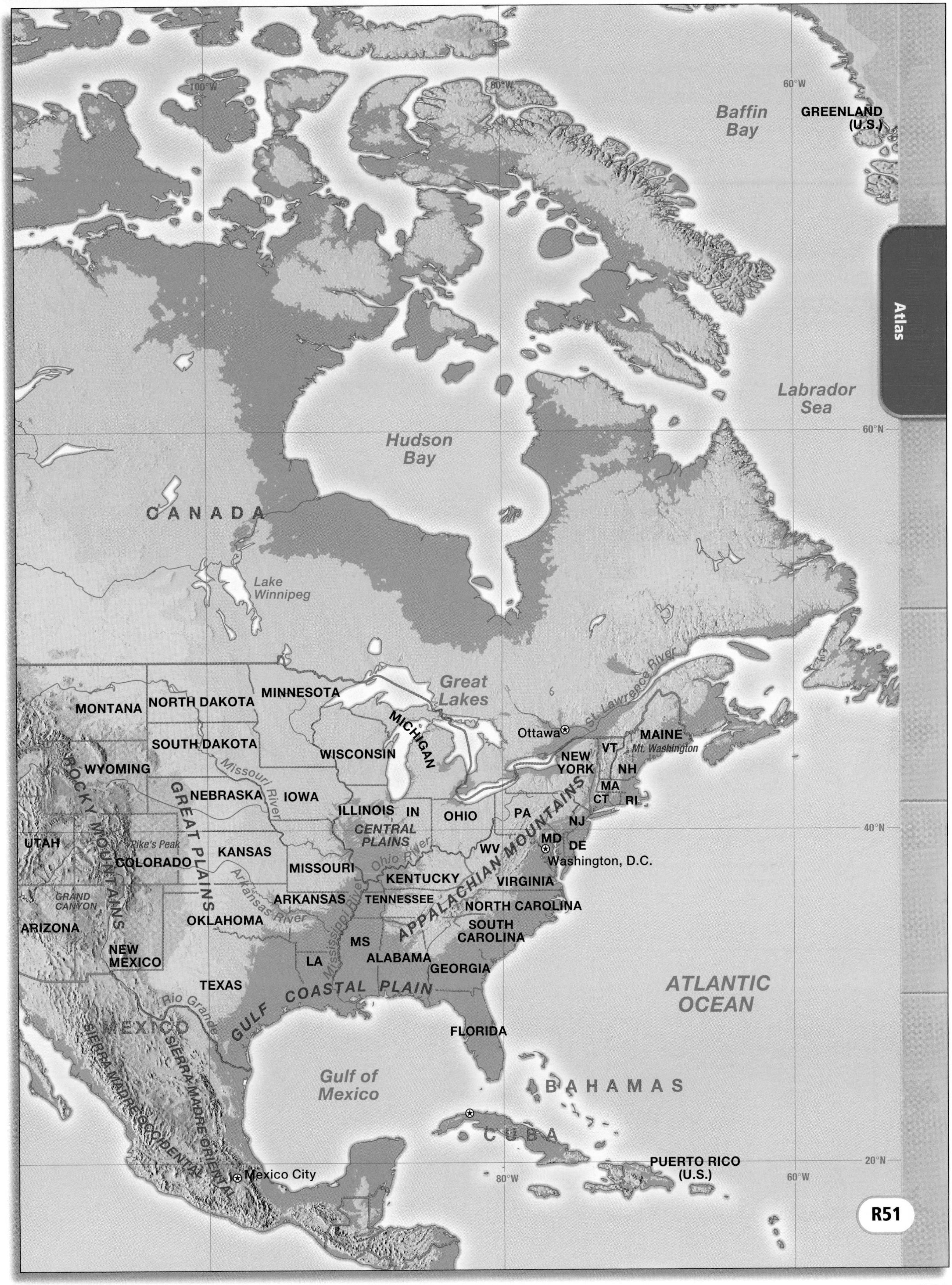

Baffin Bay
GREENLAND (U.S.)
Labrador Sea
Hudson Bay
CANADA
Lake Winnipeg
Great Lakes
St. Lawrence River
Ottawa
MONTANA
NORTH DAKOTA
MINNESOTA
SOUTH DAKOTA
WISCONSIN
MICHIGAN
MAINE
Mt. Washington
VT
NH
NEW YORK
MA
CT
RI
WYOMING
ROCKY MOUNTAINS
GREAT PLAINS
NEBRASKA
IOWA
Missouri River
ILLINOIS
IN
OHIO
PA
NJ
UTAH
Pike's Peak
COLORADO
KANSAS
CENTRAL PLAINS
Ohio River
MD
DE
Washington, D.C.
WV
APPALACHIAN MOUNTAINS
MISSOURI
KENTUCKY
VIRGINIA
GRAND CANYON
ARKANSAS
TENNESSEE
NORTH CAROLINA
Arkansas River
Mississippi River
ARIZONA
OKLAHOMA
SOUTH CAROLINA
MS
NEW MEXICO
LA
ALABAMA
GEORGIA
TEXAS
GULF COASTAL PLAIN
ATLANTIC OCEAN
Rio Grande
MEXICO
FLORIDA
SIERRA MADRE OCCIDENTAL
SIERRA MADRE ORIENTAL
Gulf of Mexico
BAHAMAS
CUBA
PUERTO RICO (U.S.)
Mexico City
100°W
80°W
60°W
60°N
40°N
20°N
R51
Atlas

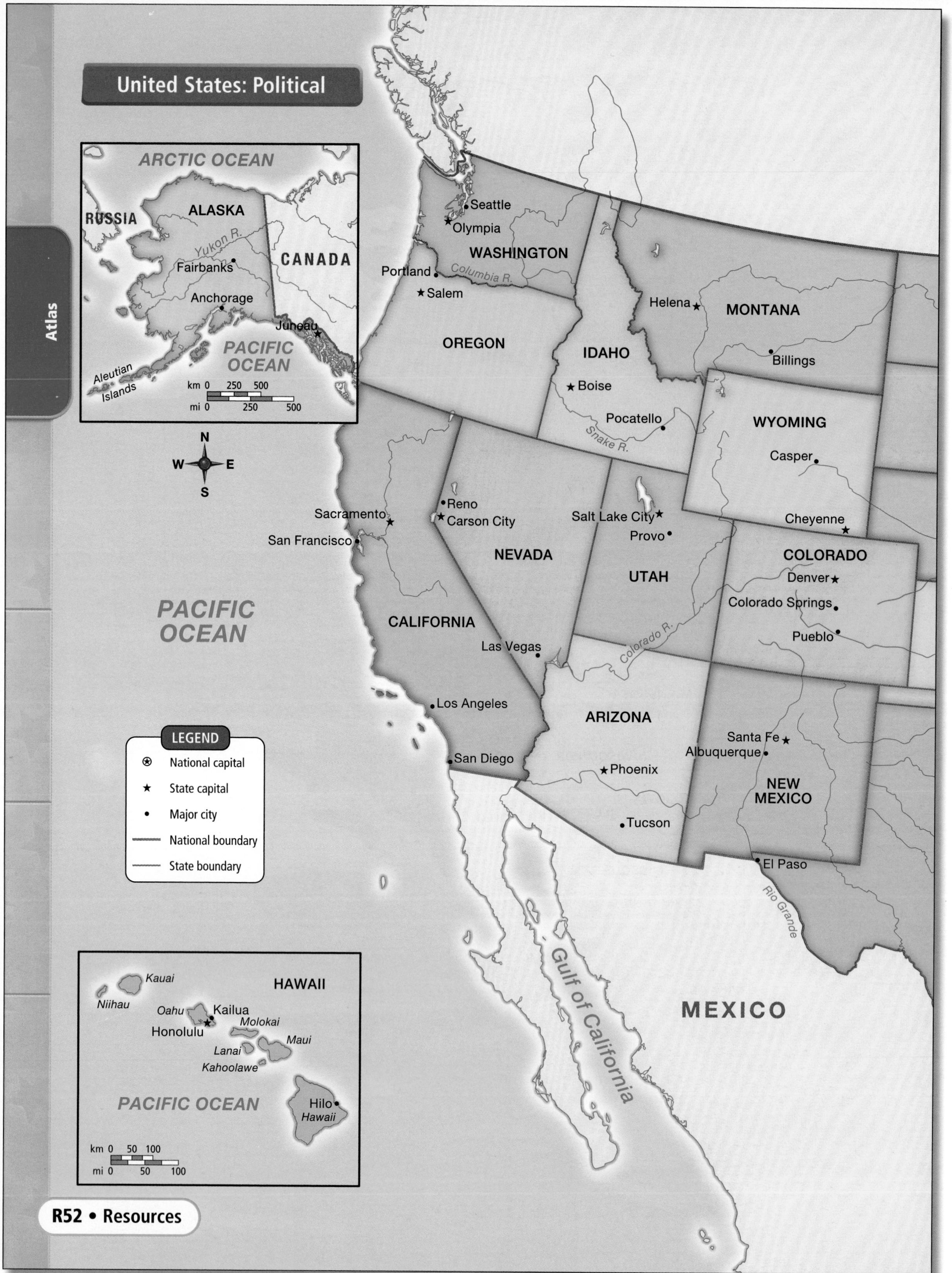
United States: Political
ARCTIC OCEAN
RUSSIA
ALASKA
CANADA
Yukon R.
Fairbanks
Anchorage
Juneau
PACIFIC OCEAN
Aleutian Islands
km 0 250 500
mi 0 250 500
N
W
E
S
Seattle
Olympia
WASHINGTON
Portland
Columbia R.
Salem
OREGON
IDAHO
Boise
Pocatello
Snake R.
Helena
MONTANA
Billings
WYOMING
Casper
Cheyenne
Reno
Carson City
Sacramento
San Francisco
NEVADA
Salt Lake City
Provo
UTAH
COLORADO
Denver
Colorado Springs
Pueblo
PACIFIC OCEAN
CALIFORNIA
Las Vegas
Colorado R.
Los Angeles
San Diego
ARIZONA
Phoenix
Tucson
Santa Fe
Albuquerque
NEW MEXICO
El Paso
Rio Grande
Gulf of California
MEXICO
LEGEND
National capital
State capital
Major city
National boundary
State boundary
HAWAII
Kauai
Niihau
Oahu
Kailua
Honolulu
Molokai
Maui
Lanai
Kahoolawe
Hilo
Hawaii
PACIFIC OCEAN
km 0 50 100
mi 0 50 100

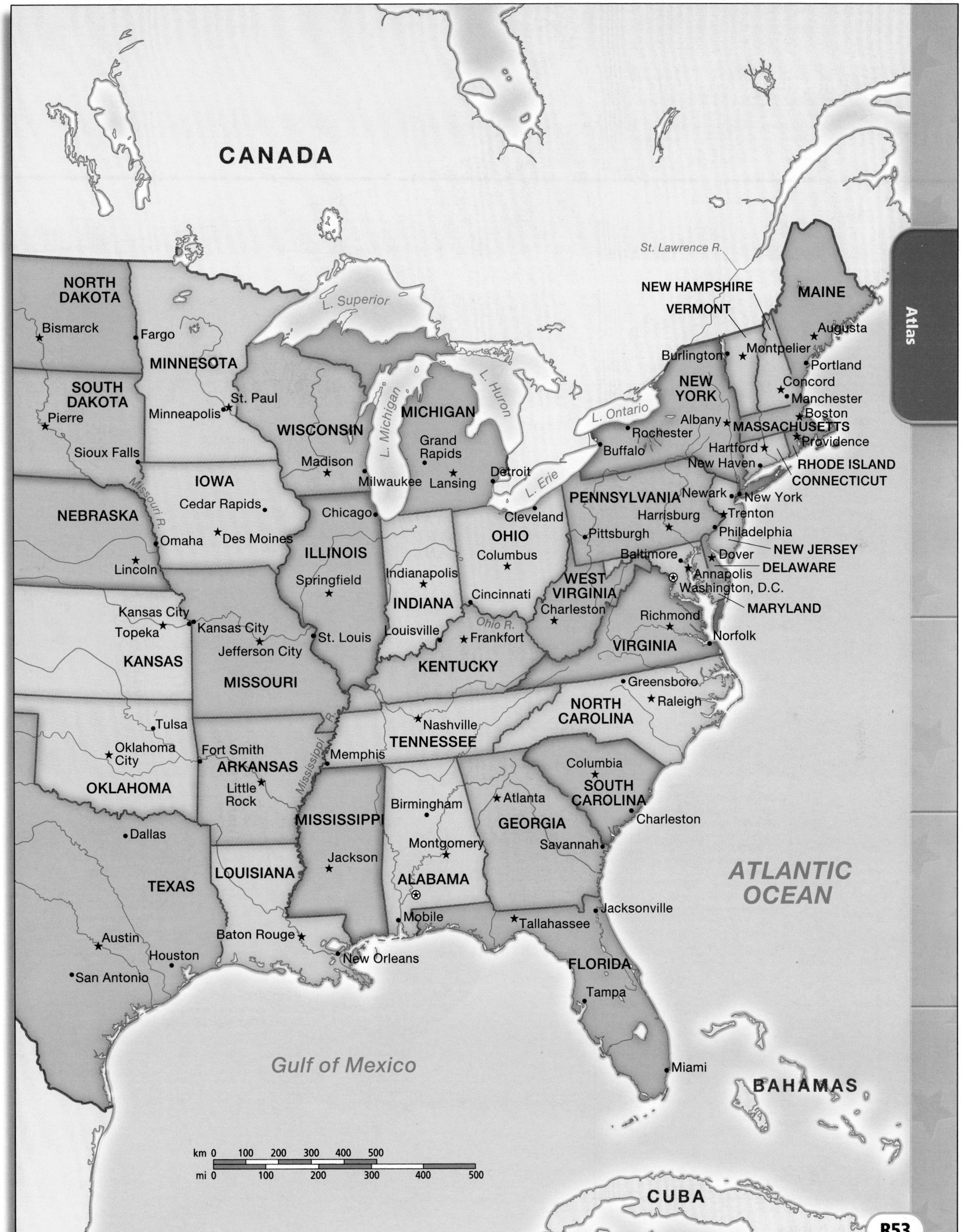
CANADA
St. Lawrence R.
L. Superior
L. Michigan
L. Huron
L. Ontario
L. Erie
NORTH DAKOTA
Bismarck
Fargo
MINNESOTA
St. Paul
Minneapolis
SOUTH DAKOTA
Pierre
Sioux Falls
WISCONSIN
Madison
Milwaukee
MICHIGAN
Grand Rapids
Lansing
Detroit
IOWA
Cedar Rapids
Des Moines
Missouri R.
NEBRASKA
Omaha
Lincoln
ILLINOIS
Chicago
Springfield
INDIANA
Indianapolis
OHIO
Cleveland
Columbus
Cincinnati
Ohio R.
NEW HAMPSHIRE
VERMONT
MAINE
Augusta
Montpelier
Burlington
Portland
Concord
Manchester
NEW YORK
Albany
Rochester
Buffalo
MASSACHUSETTS
Boston
Providence
Hartford
New Haven
RHODE ISLAND
CONNECTICUT
PENNSYLVANIA
Newark
New York
Harrisburg
Trenton
Pittsburgh
Philadelphia
NEW JERSEY
Baltimore
Dover
DELAWARE
Annapolis
Washington, D.C.
MARYLAND
WEST VIRGINIA
Charleston
Richmond
Norfolk
VIRGINIA
Kansas City
Topeka
Kansas City
St. Louis
Jefferson City
KANSAS
MISSOURI
Louisville
Frankfort
KENTUCKY
Greensboro
Raleigh
NORTH CAROLINA
Tulsa
Oklahoma City
OKLAHOMA
Fort Smith
ARKANSAS
Little Rock
Mississippi R.
Memphis
Nashville
TENNESSEE
Columbia
SOUTH CAROLINA
Charleston
Birmingham
Atlanta
GEORGIA
MISSISSIPPI
Jackson
Montgomery
Savannah
ALABAMA
Dallas
TEXAS
LOUISIANA
Austin
Houston
San Antonio
Baton Rouge
New Orleans
Mobile
Tallahassee
Jacksonville
FLORIDA
Tampa
Miami
ATLANTIC OCEAN
Gulf of Mexico
BAHAMAS
CUBA
km 0 100 200 300 400 500
mi 0 100 200 300 400 500

United States: Physical

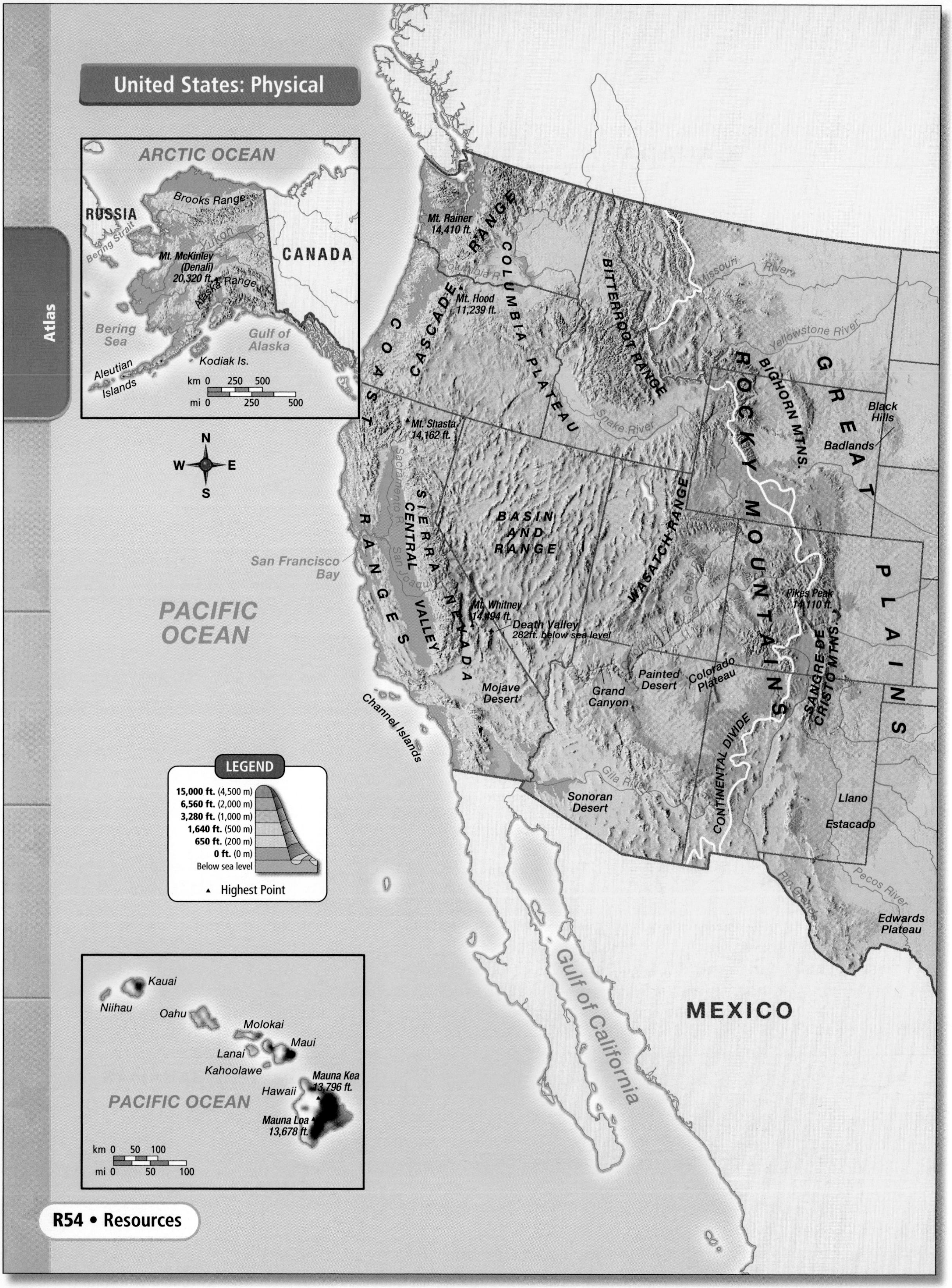
ARCTIC OCEAN
RUSSIA
Brooks Range
Bering Strait
Yukon R.
Mt. McKinley (Denali) 20,320 ft.
Alaska Range
CANADA
Bering Sea
Gulf of Alaska
Aleutian Islands
Kodiak Is.
km 0 250 500
mi 0 250 500
N
W
E
S
Mt. Rainier 14,410 ft.
CASCADE RANGE
COLUMBIA PLATEAU
Columbia R.
Mt. Hood 11,239 ft.
COAST RANGES
BITTERROOT RANGE
Missouri River
Yellowstone River
Snake River
BIGHORN MTNS.
GREAT PLAINS
Black Hills
Badlands
ROCKY MOUNTAINS
Mt. Shasta 14,162 ft.
Sacramento R.
SIERRA NEVADA
CENTRAL VALLEY
San Joaquin R.
BASIN AND RANGE
WASATCH RANGE
San Francisco Bay
PACIFIC OCEAN
Mt. Whitney 14,494 ft.
Death Valley 282 ft. below sea level
Pikes Peak 14,110 ft.
SANGRE DE CRISTO MTNS.
Mojave Desert
Grand Canyon
Painted Desert
Colorado Plateau
Channel Islands
CONTINENTAL DIVIDE
Gila River
Sonoran Desert
Llano Estacado
Rio Grande
Pecos River
Edwards Plateau
Gulf of California
MEXICO
LEGEND
15,000 ft. (4,500 m)
6,560 ft. (2,000 m)
3,280 ft. (1,000 m)
1,640 ft. (500 m)
650 ft. (200 m)
0 ft. (0 m)
Below sea level
Highest Point
Kauai
Niihau
Oahu
Molokai
Maui
Lanai
Kahoolawe
Hawaii
Mauna Kea 13,796 ft.
Mauna Loa 13,678 ft.
PACIFIC OCEAN
km 0 50 100
mi 0 50 100

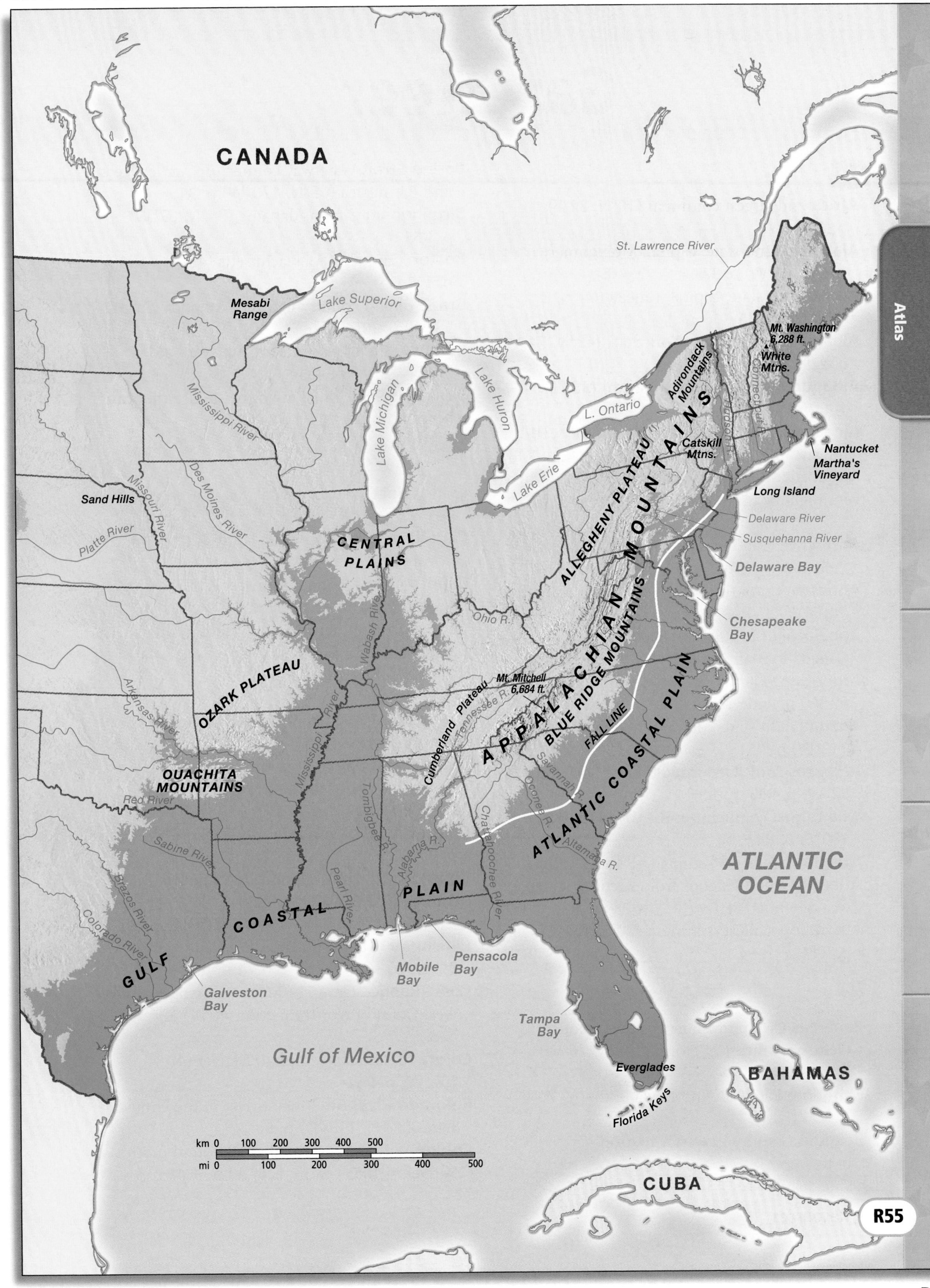

CANADA
St. Lawrence River
Lake Superior
Mesabi Range
Mississippi River
Lake Michigan
Lake Huron
L. Ontario
Lake Erie
Adirondack Mountains
Mt. Washington 6,288 ft.
White Mtns.
Connecticut R.
Hudson R.
Catskill Mtns.
Nantucket
Martha's Vineyard
Long Island
Delaware River
Susquehanna River
Delaware Bay
Chesapeake Bay
Sand Hills
Missouri River
Des Moines River
Platte River
CENTRAL PLAINS
ALLEGHENY PLATEAU
APPALACHIAN MOUNTAINS
BLUE RIDGE MOUNTAINS
Ohio R.
Wabash River
OZARK PLATEAU
Arkansas River
Mt. Mitchell 6,684 ft.
Cumberland Plateau
Tennessee R.
FALL LINE
ATLANTIC COASTAL PLAIN
OUACHITA MOUNTAINS
Red River
Mississippi River
Tombigbee R.
Savannah R.
Oconee R.
Altamaha R.
Chattahoochee River
Alabama R.
Sabine River
Pearl River
Brazos River
Colorado River
GULF COASTAL PLAIN
Galveston Bay
Mobile Bay
Pensacola Bay
Tampa Bay
Gulf of Mexico
ATLANTIC OCEAN
Everglades
Florida Keys
BAHAMAS
CUBA
km 0 100 200 300 400 500
mi 0 100 200 300 400 500

Gazetteer

A

Africa 2nd largest continent (10°N, 22°E) p. R47
Alabama 22nd state; capital: Montgomery (33°N, 88°W) p. 373
Alaska 49th state; capital: Juneau (64°N, 150°W) p. 533
Albany Capital of New York State (43°N, 74°W) p. 229
Albuquerque City in New Mexico (35°N, 106°W) p. 117
Amazon River 2nd longest river in the world; longest in South America (2°S, 53°W) p. R48
Angel Island Island in San Francisco Bay where immigrants to the United States arrived (38°N 122°W) p. 499
Antarctica Continent surrounding the South Pole, mostly covered in ice (90°S); p. R49
Antietam In Maryland; site of Civil War battle (39°N, 77°W) p. 454
Appalachian Mountains Range stretching from Canada to Alabama (37°N, 82°W) p. 164
Argentina Country in South America (36°S, 67°W) p. R46
Arizona 48th state; capital: Phoenix (34°N, 113°W) p. R54
Arkansas 25th state; capital: Little Rock (34°N, 92°W) p. R55, p. 108
Asia Largest continent in the world (50°N, 100°E) p. R47
Atlanta Capital of Georgia (34°N, 84°W) p. 467
Atlantic Ocean Extends from Arctic to Antarctic; east of United States (5°S, 25°W) p. R46
Australia Smallest continent (30°S, 151°E) p. R47

B

Bahamas Group of islands in the Atlantic Ocean; southeast of Florida (26°N, 76°W) p. 309
Baltimore Large city in Maryland (39°N, 77°W) p. R55
Belgium Country in western Europe (51°N, 3°E) p. R47
Bering Strait Waterway connecting Arctic Ocean and Bering Sea (65°N, 170°W) p. 39
Birmingham City in Alabama (34°N, 87°W) p. R55
Boston Capital of Massachusetts (42°N, 71°W) p. 190
Brazil Largest country in South America (9°S, 53°W) p. 101
Bull Run Site of two major Civil War battles (39°N, 78°W) p. 453
Bunker Hill Site of lst major battle of American Revolution (42°N, 71°W) p. 245

C

California 31st state; capital: Sacramento (38°N, 121°W) p. 499
Canada Country bordering United States on north (50°N, 100°W) p. R46
Cape of Good Hope Southwest extremity of Africa (34°S, 18°E) p. 93
Cape Horn Southernmost point of South America (55°S, 67°W) p. 290
Caribbean Sea North Atlantic sea (15°N, 76°W) p. 97
Charleston City in South Carolina (33°N, 80°W) p. 198
Chesapeake Bay Inlet of the Atlantic Ocean on the East Coast of the United States (37°N, 76°W) p. 134
Chicago Large city in Illinois (42°N, 88°W) p. R55
Chile Country on western coast of South America (35°S, 72°W) p. R50
China Country in East Asia (37°N, 93°E) p. R47
Cincinnati City in southwestern Ohio (39°N, 84°W) p. 348
Coast Ranges Group of mountain ranges along West Coast of North America (40°N, 123°W) p. 8
Colorado 38th state; capital: Denver (40°N, 107°W) p. R54
Colorado River 5th longest river in the United States (32°N, 115°W) p. 8
Columbia River Lewis and Clark found mouth of river in 1805 (46°N, 120°W) p. 356

Gazetteer

Concord Site in Massachusetts of early Revolutionary War battle (42°N, 71°W) p. 251
Connecticut 5th state; capital: Hartford (42°N, 73°W) p. 202
Cuba Island nation in Caribbean Sea, south of Florida (22°N, 79°W) p. 97
Cumberland Gap Pass through the Appalachian Mountains (36°N, 83°W) p. 345

D

Delaware 1st state; capital: Dover (39°N, 76°W) p. 144
Delaware River Flows from New York to Delaware Bay (42°N, 75°W) p. 144
Denver Capital of Colorado (40°N, 105°W) p. R54
Detroit City in eastern Michigan (42°N, 83°W) p. 23

E

Egypt Country in North Africa; capital: Cairo (30°N, 31°E) p. 471
El Paso City in west Texas, on Rio Grande (32°N, 106°W) p. R54
Ellis Island Island in New York Harbor where immigrants to United States arrived (41°N, 74°W) p. 499
England Country in western Europe; part of the United Kingdom (52°N, 2°W) p. 123
Europe 6th largest continent (50°N, 15°E) p. R47

F

Florida 27th state; capital: Tallahassee (31°N, 85°W) p. R55
France Country in western Europe (47°N, 1°E) p. 123

G

Georgia 4th state; capital: Atlanta (33°N, 84°W) p. 203
Germany Country in western Europe (51°N, 10°E) p. 309
Gettysburg Site in Pennsylvania of Civil War battle (40°N, 77°W) p. 456
Grand Canyon In Arizona, deep gorge formed by the Colorado River (36°N, 112°W) p. R56
Great Lakes Five freshwater lakes between the United States and Canada (45°N, 83°W) p. R57
Great Plains In central North America, high grassland region (45°N, 104°W) p. 6
Greensboro City in North Carolina (36°N, 80°W) p. R55
Guatemala Country in Central America (16°N, 92°W) p. R50
Gulf of Mexico Body of water along southern United States and Mexico (25°N, 94°W) p. R57

H

Haiti Nation in the West Indies on the island of Hispaniola; capital: Port-au-Prince (18°N, 72°W) p. 290
Havana Capital of Cuba (23°N, 82°W) p. R50
Hawaii 50th state; capital: Honolulu (20°N, 158°W) p. R54
Hispaniola Island in the West Indies (18°N, 73°W) p. 97
Honolulu Capital of Hawaii (21°N, 158°W) p. R54
Houston City in Texas (30°N, 95°W) p. 507
Hudson River In New York; named for explorer Henry Hudson (43°N, 74°W) p. 124

I

Idaho 43rd state; capital: Boise (44°N, 115°W) p. R54
Illinois 21st state; capital: Springfield (40°N, 91°W) p. 434
India Country in south Asia (23°N, 78°E) p. 93
Indiana 19th state; capital: Indianapolis (40°N, 87°W) p. R55
Iowa 29th state; capital: Des Moines (41°N, 93°W) p. R55
Ireland Island in North Atlantic Ocean, divided between Republic of Ireland and Northern Ireland (53°N, 6°W) p. 388
Italy Country in southern Europe (44°N, 11°E) p. 471

J

Jamestown, Virginia First permanent English settlement in Americas (37°N, 76°W) p. 131

R57

Japan Island country off east coast of Asia (37°N, 134°E) p. 309

K

Kansas 34th state; capital: Topeka (39°N, 100°W) p. 433

Kentucky 15th state; capital: Frankfort (38°N, 88°W) p. 452

L

Lexington Site in Massachusetts of lst shots fired in Revolutionary War (42°N, 71°W) p. 251

London Capital of United Kingdom (52°N, 0°W) p. 137

Los Angeles City in California (34°N, 118°W) p. 507

Louisiana 18th state; capital: Baton Rouge (31°N, 93°W) p. 444

M

Madrid Capital of Spain (40°N, 3°W) p. 126

Maine 23rd state; capital: Augusta (45°N, 70°W) p. 202

Mali Country in West Africa (16°N, 0°W) p. 86

Maryland 7th state; capital: Annapolis (39°N, 76°W) p. 203

Massachusetts 6th state; capital: Boston (42°N, 73°W) p. 137

Mecca Muslim holy city (21°N, 39°E) p. 87

Mexico Country bordering the United States to the south (24°N, 104°W) p. R50

Mexico City Capital of Mexico (19°N, 99°W) p. R50

Miami City in Florida (26°N, 80°W) p. R55

Michigan 26th state; capital: Lansing (46°N, 87°W) p. R55

Milwaukee City in Wisconsin (43°N, 88°W) p. 389

Minnesota 32nd state; capital: St. Paul (45°N, 93°W) p. R55

Mississippi 20th state; capital: Jackson (33°N, 90°W) p. 444

Mississippi River Principal river of United States and North America (32°N, 92°W) p. R57

Missouri 24th state; capital: Jefferson City (38°N, 94°W) p. 433

Missouri River A major river in United States (41°N, 96°W) p. 356

Montana 41st state; capital: Helena (47°N, 112°W) p. 525

Montgomery City in Alabama (32°N, 86°W) p. 531

Montreal City in Quebec, Canada (46°N, 74°W) p. 230

N

Natchez City in Mississippi (32°N, 91°W) p. 287

Nebraska 37th state; capital: Lincoln (42°N, 102°W) p. 433

Netherlands Country in northwestern Europe; also called Holland (52°N, 6°E) p. 124

Nevada 36th state; capital: Carson City (40°N, 117°W) p. R54

New Hampshire 9th state; capital: Concord (44°N, 72°W) p. 202

New Jersey 3rd state; capital: Trenton (41°N, 75°W) p. 188

New Mexico 47th state; capital: Santa Fe (35°N, 107°W) p. 533

New Netherland Dutch colony in North America (41°N, 74°W) p. 144

New Orleans City in Louisiana (30°N, 90°W) p. 355

New York 11th state; capital: Albany (43°N, 78°W) p. R55

New York City Large city in New York State (41°N, 74°W) p. R55

North America Northern continent of Western Hemisphere (45°N, 100°W) pp. R52–R53

North Carolina 12th state; capital: Raleigh (36°N, 82°W) p. 203

North Dakota 39th state; capital: Bismarck (46°N, 100°W) pp. R54–R55

North Korea Country in northeast Asia; capital: Pyongyang (39°N, 125°E) p. 512

Northwest Territory Land extending from Ohio and Mississippi rivers to Great Lakes (41°N, 85°W) p. 297

Gazetteer

O

Ohio 17th state; capital: Columbus (41°N, 83°W) p. R55

Ohio River Flows from Pennsylvania to the Mississippi River (37°N, 88°W) p. R57

Ohio River Valley Farming region west of the Appalachian Mountains (37°N, 88°W) p. 228

Oklahoma 46th state; capital: Oklahoma City (36°N, 98°W) p. 370

Omaha Large city in Nebraska (41°N, 96°W) pp. R54–R55

Oregon 33rd state; capital: Salem (44°N, 122°W) p. 400

Oregon Territory Area from Rocky Mountains to Pacific Ocean (45°N, 120°W) p. 401

P

Pacific Ocean Largest ocean; west of the United States (0°, 170°W) pp. R46–R47

Panama Country in Central America (9°N, 80°W) p. 100

Paris Capital of France (49°N, 2°E) p. 324

Pennsylvania 2nd state; capital: Harrisburg (41°N, 78°W) p. 189

Peru Country on the Pacific coast of South America (10°S, 75°W) p. R50

Philadelphia Large port city in Pennsylvania (40°N, 75°W) p. 190

Philippines Island country southeast of Asia (14°N, 125°E) p. R47

Phoenix Capital of Arizona (33°N, 112°W) p. 13

Pittsburgh Manufacturing city in Pennsylvania (40°N, 80°W) p. R55

Plymouth In Massachusetts; site of first Pilgrim settlement (42°N, 71°W) p. 137

Poland Country in eastern Europe; capital: Warsaw (52°N, 21°E) p. 498

Portugal Country in western Europe; capital: Lisbon (38°N, 8°W) p. 92

Potomac River Runs from western Maryland past Washington, D.C. (38°N, 77°W) p. 322

Puerto Rico A U.S. territory in the Caribbean; capital: San Juan (18°N, 67°W) p. R50

Q

Quebec Province of Canada; capital: Quebec City (47°N, 71°W) p. 123

R

Rhode Island 13th state; capital: Providence (42°N, 72°W) p. 201

Richmond Capital city of Virginia; also was Confederate capital (38°N, 78°W) p. 453

Rio Grande River forming part of the Texas–Mexico border (26°N, 97°W) p. R54

Roanoke Island Island off the coast of North Carolina; site of first English colony in the Americas (37°N, 80°W) p. 130

Rocky Mountains Mountain range in the western United States (50°N, 114°W) p. R56

Russia Formerly part of the Soviet Union; capital: Moscow (61°N, 60°E) p. 498

S

Sacramento Capital of California (39°N, 122°W) p. R54

St. Augustine, Florida Oldest European-founded city in U.S. (30°N, 81°W) p. 113

St. Lawrence River Links the Great Lakes to the Atlantic Ocean (49°N, 67°W) p. 123

St. Louis City in Missouri; on Mississippi River (39°N, 90°W) p. 356

Salem An early English settlement in Massachusetts (43°N, 71°W) p. 139

Salt Lake City Capital of Utah (40°N, 112°W) p. 13

San Antonio City in Texas (29°N, 98°W) p. 395

San Diego City in southern California (32°N, 117°W) p. 28

San Francisco A major port city in California (38°N, 122°W) p. 318

San Salvador Caribbean island where Columbus landed (24°N, 74°W) p. 97

Santa Fe Capital of New Mexico (35°N, 106°W) p. 13

Saratoga New York site of an important American victory against the British in 1777 (43°N, 75°W) p. 280

Savannah Oldest city in Georgia (32°N, 81°W) p. 286

R59

Seattle Large city in Washington State (48°N, 122°W) p. R54
Sierra Madre A system of mountain ranges in Mexico (27°N, 104°W) p. R53
Sierra Nevada Mountain range mainly in eastern California (39°N, 120°W) p. R56
Sonoran Desert Desert in southwestern United States (33°N, 112°W) p. 6
South Africa Nation of southern Africa; capitals: Cape Town, Pretoria, Bloemfontein (34°S, 18°E) p. 309
South America Southern continent of Western Hemisphere (10°S, 60°W) p. R50
South Carolina 8th state; capital: Columbia (34°N, 81°W) p. 203
South Dakota 40th state; capital: Pierre (44°N, 100°W) pp. R54–R55
South Korea Country in eastern Asia on Korean peninsula; capital: Seoul (37°N, 127°E) p. 512
Spain Country in Western Europe; capital: Madrid (40°N, 5°W) p. 96

T

Tennessee 16th state; capital: Nashville (36°N, 88°W) p. 368
Tenochtitlán Aztec city; present-day Mexico City (19°N, 99°W) p. 43
Texas 28th state; capital: Austin (31°N, 101°W) p. 394
Timbuktu City in Mali, W. Africa (17°N, 3°W) p. 86
Trenton Capital of New Jersey (40°N, 75°W) p. 279
Tucson City in Arizona (32°N, 111°W) p. R54

U

United Kingdom England, Scotland, and Wales (57°N, 2°W) p. R47
United States Country in central and northwest North America (38°N, 110°W) p. R46
Utah 45th state; capital: Salt Lake City (40°N, 112°W) p. 13

V

Valley Forge George Washington's winter camp in 1777; near Philadelphia (40°N, 75°W) p. 280
Venice City in Italy (45°N, 12°E) p. 84
Vermont 14th state; capital: Montpelier (44°N, 72°W) p. 29
Vicksburg, Mississippi Site of Civil War battle (32°N, 91°W) p. 454
Vietnam Country in southeast Asia (18°N, 107°E) p. 506
Virginia 10th state; capital: Richmond (37°N, 81°W) p. 131

W

Washington 42nd state; capital: Olympia (48°N, 121°W) p. 533
Washington, D.C. Capital of the U.S. (39°N, 77°W) p. R55
West Indies Islands separating the Caribbean Sea and the Atlantic (19°N, 79°W) p. 97
West Virginia 35th state; capital: Charleston (38N, 81°W) p. R55
Williamsburg Colonial capital of Virginia (37°N, 77°W) p. 206
Wisconsin 30th state; capital: Madison (40°N, 89°W) p. R55
Wyoming 44th state; capital: Cheyenne (43°N, 109°W) p. R54

Y

Yorktown In Virginia; site of last major battle of Revolutionary War (37°N, 77°W) p. 288

Glossary

A

abolitionist (ab uh LIH shuhn ist) someone who joined the movement to abolish, or end, slavery. (p. 424)

absolute location (AB suh loot loh KAY shuhn) the exact latitude and longitude of a place on the globe. (p. 116)

activist (AK tuh vihst) a person who takes action to change social conditions or unfair laws. (p. 526)

agriculture (AG rih kuhl chur) farming or growing plants. (p. 40)

ally (AL ly) a person or group that joins with another to work toward a goal. (p. 229)

amendment (uh MEND muhnt) a change to the Constitution. (p. 316)

annexation (uh nehks AY shuhn) the act of joining two countries or pieces of land together. (p. 395)

Antifederalist (an tee FEHD ur uh lihst) someone who opposed the new Constitution. (p. 306)

apprentice (uh PREHN tihs) someone who studies with a master to learn a skill or business. (p. 198)

armada (ahr MAH duh) the Spanish word for a large fleet of ships. (p. 125)

artisan (AR tih zuhn) someone who is skilled at making something by hand, such as silver spoons or wooden chairs. (p. 198)

assassination (uh SAS uh nay shuhn) the murder of an important leader. (p. 473)

astrolabe (AS truh layb) a tool that measures the height of the sun or a star above the horizon. (p. 91)

B

backcountry (BAK kuhn tree) the mountainous area west of where most colonists settled. (p. 163)

banish (BAN ihsh) to force someone to leave a place. (p. 167)

bar graph (bahr graf) a graph that compares amounts of things. (p. 422)

barter (BAHR tur) to exchange goods without using money. (p. 70)

benefit (BEHN uh fiht) a gain or an advantage. (p. 194)

Black Codes (blak kohds) laws that limited the rights of former enslaved people to travel, vote, and work in certain jobs. (p. 474)

boomtown (BOOM toun) a town whose population booms, or grows very quickly. (p. 402)

border state (BOHR dur stayt) a slave state that stayed in the Union. (p. 452)

boycott (BOI kaht) the refusal to buy, sell, or use certain goods. (p. 236)

braceros (brah SHE rohs) Mexicans invited to work in the United States as temporary workers. (p. 505)

C

Cabinet (KAB uh niht) a group chosen by the President to help run the executive branch and give advice. (p. 321)

campaign (kam PAYN) a series of actions taken toward a goal, such as winning a presidential election. (p. 369)

canal (kuh NAL) a waterway built for boat travel and shipping. (p. 346)

cape (kayp) a strip of land that stretches into a body of water. (p. 137)

capital (KAP ih tuhl) the city where the government meets. (p. 322)

capital resource (KAP ih tuhl REE sawrs) a tool, machine, or building that people use to produce goods and services. (p. 17)

caravan (KAR uh van) a group of people and animals who travel together. (p. 86)

cardinal directions (KAR dn uhl dih REHK shuhns) the main directions: north, south, east, and west. (p. 13)

cash crop (kash krahp) a crop that people grow and sell to earn money. (p. 132)

R61

casualties (KAHZ oo uhl teez) soldiers who are killed or wounded. (p. 454)

cause (kawz) an event or action that makes something else happen. (p. 248)

century (SEHN chuh ree) a period of 100 years. (p. 128)

ceremony (SEHR uh moh nee) a formal event at which people gather to express important beliefs. (p. 56)

cession (SEHSH uhn) something that is given up. (p. 397)

charter (CHAHR ter) a document giving permission to a person or group to do something. (p. 131)

checks and balances (chehks uhnd BAHL uhns ehz) a system that lets each branch of government limit the power of the other two. (p. 314)

circle graph (SUR kuhl graf) a graph that illustrates how a part compares with the whole. (p. 422)

circumnavigate (sur kuhm NAV i gayt) to sail completely around something. (p. 101)

citizen (SIHT ih zuhn) an official member of a city, state, or nation. (p. 296)

civil rights (SIHV uhl ryts) the rights that countries guarantee their citizens. (p. 530)

civil war (SIHV uhl wawr) a war between two groups or regions within a nation. (p. 445)

civilian (sih VIHL yuhn) a person who is not in the military. (p. 462)

civilization (sihv uh lih ZAY shuhn) a group of people living together who have systems of government, religion, and culture. (p. 40)

claim (klaym) something declared as one's own, especially a piece of land. (p. 124)

clan (klan) a group of related families. (p. 48)

climate (KLY miht) the type of weather a place has over a long period of time. (p. 9)

colony (KAHL uh nee) an area of land ruled by another country. (p. 110)

commander (kuh MAN dur) the officer in charge of an army. (p. 254)

compact (KAHM pakt) an agreement. (p. 137)

compass rose (KUHM puhs rohz) a part of a map that shows the cardinal and intermediate directions. (p. 13)

compromise (KAHM pruh myz) when both sides give up something they want to settle a disagreement. (p. 304)

Confederacy (kuhn FEHD ur uh see) the name for South Carolina, Mississippi, Florida, Alabama, Georgia, Louisiana, Texas, and later Arkansas, North Carolina, Tennessee, and Virginia. (p. 444)

confederation (kuhn fehd ur AY shuhn) a type of government in which separate groups of people join together, but local leaders still make many decisions for their group. (p. 70)

congress (KAHNG grihs) a group of representatives who meet to discuss a subject. (p. 229)

conquistador (kahn KEES tuh dawr) the Spanish word for conqueror. (p. 104)

conservation (kahn sur VAY shuhn) the protection and wise use of natural resources. (p. 18)

constitution (kahn stih TOO shuhn) a written plan for government. (p. 296)

consumer (kuhn SOO mur) someone who buys goods and services. (p. 25)

convert (kahn VURT) to change a religion or a belief. (p. 110)

corps (kawr) a team of people who work together. (p. 356)

correspondence (kawr ih SPAHN duhns) written communication. (p. 241)

cost (kawst) a loss or sacrifice. (p. 194)

D

debtor (DEHT ur) a person who owes money. (p. 204)

decade (DEHK ayd) a period of 10 years. (p. 128)

declaration (dehk luh RAY shuhn) a statement that declares, or announces, an idea. (p. 264)

delegate (DEHL ih giht) someone chosen to speak and act for others. (p. 243)

democracy (dih MAHK ruh see) a government in which the people have the power to make political decisions. (p. 312)

Glossary

desert (dih ZURT) to leave the army without permission. (p. 468)

discrimination (dih skrihm uh NAY shuhn) the unfair treatment of particular groups. (p. 425)

dissenter (dih SEHN tur) a person who does not agree with the beliefs of his or her leaders. (p. 167)

diversity (dih VUR sih tee) the variety of people in a group. (p. 145)

draft (draft) when the government chooses people who have to serve in the military. (p. 455)

E

economy (ih KAHN uh mee) the system people use to produce goods and services. (p. 24)

ecosystem (EH koh sihs tuhm) a community of plants and animals, along with the surrounding soil, air, and water. (p. 31)

effect (ih FEHKT) an event or action that is a result of a cause. (p. 248)

Electoral College (ih LEHK tur uhl KAH luhdj) representatives from each state who vote for the President. (p. 320)

emancipation (ih MAN suh pay shuhn) the freeing of enslaved people. (p. 456)

empire (EHM pyr) many nations or territories ruled by a single group or leader. (p. 104)

entrepreneur (ahn truh pruh NUR) a person who takes risks to start a business. (p. 380)

environment (ehn VY ruhn muhnt) the surroundings in which people, plants, and animals live. (p. 29)

epidemic (ehp ih DEHM ihk) an outbreak of disease that spreads quickly and affects many people. (p. 98)

equator (ih KWAY tur) the imaginary line around the middle of the Earth. (p. 9)

erosion (ih ROH zhuhn) the process by which water and wind wear away the land. (p. 30)

ethnic group (EHTH nihk groop) a group of people who share a language or culture. (p. 500)

executive branch (ihg ZEHK yuh tihv branch) the branch of government that suggests laws and carries out the laws made by Congress. (p. 313)

expedition (ehk spih DIHSH uhn) a journey to achieve a goal. (p. 104)

export (ihk SPAWRT) a product sent to another country and sold. (p. 175)

F

fall line (fahl lyn) the line where rivers from higher land flow to lower land and often form waterfalls. (p. 162)

famine (FAM ihn) a widespread shortage of food. (p. 389)

federal (FEHD ur uhl) a system in which the states share power with the central government. (p. 303)

Federalist (FEHD ur uh lihst) a supporter of the Constitution. (p. 306)

flatboat (FLAT boht) a large, rectangular boat partly covered by a roof. (p. 346)

flow lines (floh lyns) lines that show where people or objects come from and where they go. The thickness of the lines shows how many have moved. (p. 510)

foreign policy (FAWR ihn PAWL ih see) a government's actions toward other nations. (p. 364)

forty-niner (FAWR tee NY nur) a miner who went to California in 1849. (p. 402)

free enterprise (free EHN tuh pryz) the system in which people may start any business that they believe will succeed. (p. 198)

free market economy (free MAHR kiht ih KAHN uh mee) an economic system in which the people, not the government, decide what will be produced. (p. 198)

free state (free stayt) a state that did not have slavery. (p. 432)

Freedmen's Bureau (FREED mehnz BYOOR oh) an organization that provided food, clothing, medical care, and legal advice to poor blacks and whites. (p. 474)

front (fruhnt) where the fighting takes place in a war. (p. 396)

frontier (FRUHN teer) the edge of a country or settled region. (p. 345)

R63

fugitive (FYOO jih tihv) a person who is running away. (p. 434)

G

geography (jee AHG ruh fee) the study of the world and the people and things that live there. (p. 6)

glacier (GLAY shur) a huge, thick sheet of slowly moving ice. (p. 39)

gold rush (gohld ruhsh) when many people hurry to the same area to look for gold. (p. 402)

Great Compromise (grayt KAHM pruh myz) Roger Sherman's suggestion that the states with the largest populations send the most representatives to the House of Representatives but each state have the same number of representatives in the Senate. (p. 304)

growing season (GROH eeng SEE zuhn) the time of year when it is warm enough for plants to grow. (p. 161)

H

hacienda (hah see EHN duh) a large farm or ranch, often with its own village and church. (p. 112)

heritage (HEHR ih tihj) something that is passed down from one generation to the next. (p. 514)

home front (hohm fruhnt) all the people in a country who are not in the military during wartime. (p. 462)

human resources (HYOO muhn REE sohrs uhz) people and the skills and knowledge they bring to their work. (p. 17)

I

immigrant (IHM ih gruhnt) a person who moves to another country to live. (p. 388)

impeach (ihm PEECH) to charge a government official with a crime. (p. 475)

import (IHM pawrt) a good brought into one country from another. (p. 175)

inauguration (ihn AW gyuh ray shuhn) the official ceremony to make someone President. (p. 321)

indentured servant (ihn DEHN churd SUR vuhnt) someone who agreed to work for a number of years in exchange for the cost of a voyage to North America. (p. 132)

independence (ihn duh PEHN duhns) freedom from being ruled by someone else. (p. 262)

indigo (IHN duh goh) a plant that can be made into a dark blue dye. (p. 211)

Industrial Revolution (ihn DUHS tree uhl rehv uh LOO shuhn) a period of time marked by changes in manufacturing and transportation. (p. 378)

industry (IHN duh stree) all the businesses that make one kind of product or provide one kind of service. (p. 174)

inflation (ihn FLAY shuhn) a rise in the prices of goods. (p. 273)

injustice (ihn JUHS tihs) unfair treatment that abuses a person's rights. (p. 390)

inset map (IHN seht map) a small map within a larger one that may show a close-up of an area or provide other information about it. (p. 13)

interchangeable parts (ihn tur CHAYN juh buhl pahrts) parts made by a machine to be exactly the same in size and shape. (p. 379)

interest (IHN trihst) what people pay to borrow money. (p. 322)

intermediate directions (ihn tur MEE dee iht dih REHK shuhns) the in-between directions of northeast, southeast, southwest, and northwest. (p. 13)

interpreter (ihn TUR prih tur) someone who helps speakers of different languages understand each other. (p. 356)

invasion (ihn VAY zhuhn) an attack by an armed force to conquer another country. (p. 125)

invest (ihn VEHST) to put money into something to try to earn more money. (p. 131)

irrigation (ihr ih GAY shuhn) a way of supplying water to crops with streams, ditches, or pipes. (p. 55)

Glossary

J

Jim Crow (jihm kroh) laws that segregated African Americans from other Americans. (p. 484)

judicial branch (joo DISH uhl branch) the branch of government that decides the meaning of laws and whether the laws have been followed. (p. 313)

K

kingdom (KIHNG duhm) a place ruled by a king or queen. (p. 86)

L

laborer (LAY buhr ur) a person who does hard physical work. (p. 198)

landform (LAND fohrm) a feature on the surface of the land. (p. 8)

legislative branch (LEHJ ih slay tihv branch) the branch of government that makes laws for the country. (p. 313)

legislature (LEHJ ih slay chur) a group of people with the power to make and change laws. (p. 203)

liberty (LIHB uhr tee) freedom from being controlled by another government. (p. 235)

line graph (lyn graf) a graph that shows change over time. (p. 422)

lodge (lawj) a type of home that Plains Indians made using bark, earth, and grass. (p. 61)

longhouse (LAWNG hows) a large house made out of wood poles and covered with bark. (p. 69)

Loyalist (LOI uh lihst) someone who was still loyal to the king. (p. 270)

M

manifest destiny (MAN uh fehst DEHS tuh nee) the belief that the United States should spread across the entire North American continent, from the Atlantic Ocean to the Pacific Ocean. (p. 395)

manufacturer (man yuh FAK chuhr ur) someone who uses machines to make goods. (p. 354)

map legend (map LEHJ uhnd) a part of a map that explains any symbols or colors on a map. (p. 13)

map scale (map skayl) a part of a map that compares distance on a map to distance in the real world. (p. 13)

mass production (mas pruh DUHK shuhn) making many identical products at once. (p. 379)

massacre (MAS uh kur) the killing of many people. (p. 240)

mercenary (MUR suh nehr ee) a soldier who is paid to fight for a foreign country. (p. 279)

merchant (MUR chunt) someone who buys and sells goods to earn money. (p. 85)

meridian (muh RIHD ee uhn) a line of longitude. (p. 116)

Middle Passage (MIHD uhl PAHS ihj) the trip from Africa to the West Indies. (p. 176)

migrant worker (MY gruhnt WUR kuhr) a person who moves from place to place to find work, mostly on farms. (p. 534)

migration (MY gray shuhn) a movement from one region to another. (p. 39)

militia (muh LIHSH uh) a group of ordinary people who train for battle. (p. 250)

minutemen (MIHN iht mehn) militia with special training. They had to be ready for battle at a minute's notice. (p. 251)

mission (MIHSH uhn) a religious community where priests taught Christianity. (p. 110)

missionary (MIHSH uh nehr ee) a person who teaches his or her religion to others who have different beliefs. (p. 146)

motto (MAHT oh) a short statement that explains an ideal or a goal. (p. 515)

N

nationalism (NASH uh nuh lihz uhm) the belief that your country deserves more success than others. (p. 364)

natural resource (NACH ur uhl REE sawrs) a material from nature, such as soil or water. (p. 14)

naturalization (nach ur uh lihz AY shuhn) the process of becoming a citizen by learning the laws of the country and the rights and duties of its citizens. (p. 540)

navigation (nav ih GAY shuhn) the science of planning and controlling the direction of a ship. (p. 91)

R65

neutral (NOO truhl) not to take sides. (p. 270)

nomad (NOH mad) a person who moves around and does not live in one place. (p. 61)

nonrenewable resource (nahn rih NOO uh buhl REE sawrs) a natural resource that cannot be replaced once it is used, such as oil. (p. 15)

nonviolent protest (nahn VY uh luhnt PROH test) a way of bringing change without using violence. (p. 531)

Northwest Passage (nawrth WEHST PAS ihj) the water route that explorers were hoping to find. (p. 123)

O

opportunity cost (ahp ur TOO nih tee kahst) the thing you give up when you decide to do or have something else. (p. 18)

ordinance (AWR dn uhns) a law. (p. 297)

outline (OWT lyn) text that identifies the main ideas and supporting details of a topic. (p. 352)

overseer (OH vuhr see uhr) a person who watches and directs the work of other people. (p. 214)

P

parallel (PAR uh lehl) a line of latitude. (p. 116)

parallel timelines (PAR uh lehl TYM lynz) two or more timelines grouped together. (p. 128)

Patriot (PAY tree uht) a colonist who opposed British rule. (p. 250)

persecution (pur sih KYOO shuhn) unfair treatment that causes suffering. (p. 499)

petition (puh TIHSH uhn) a written request from a number of people. (p. 254)

physical map (FIHZ ih kuhl map) a map that shows the location of physical features, such as landforms, bodies of water, or resources. (p. 12)

pilgrim (PIHL gruhm) a person who makes a long journey for religious reasons. (p. 136)

pioneer (py uh NEER) one of the first of a group of people to enter or settle a region. (p. 345)

plantation (plan TAY shuhn) a large farm on which crops are raised by workers who live on the farm. (p. 202)

plateau (pla TOH) a high, steep-sided area rising above the surrounding land. (p. 8)

point of view (poynt uhv vyoo) the way someone thinks about an issue, an event, or a person. (p. 310)

political map (puh LIHT ih kuhl map) a map that shows cities, states, and countries. (p. 12)

political party (puh LIHT ih kuhl PAHR tee) an organized group of people who share similar ideas about government. (p. 322)

pollution (puh LOO shuhn) anything that makes the soil, air, or water dirty and unhealthy. (p. 30)

popular sovereignty (PAHP yuh luhr SAHV uhr ihn tee) an idea that the people who live in a place make decisions for themselves. (p. 433)

potlatch (PAHT lach) a large feast that could last for several days. (p. 47)

prejudice (PREHJ uh dihs) an unfair, negative opinion that can lead to unjust treatment. (p. 526)

presidio (prih SEE dee oh) a fort built by the Spanish to protect their claims and guard themselves against attack. (p. 111)

primary source (PRY mehr ee sawrs) firsthand information about an event, a place, or a time period. (p. 480)

prime meridian (prym muh RIHD ee uhn) the main line of longitude located at zero degrees. (p. 116)

proclamation (prahk luh MAY shuhn) an official public statement. (p. 230)

productivity (proh duhk TIHV ih tee) the amount of goods and services produced by workers in a certain amount of time. (p. 379)

profit (PRAHF iht) the money a business has left over after all expenses have been paid. (p. 92)

proprietor (pruh PRY ih tur) a person who owned and controlled all the land of a colony. (p. 188)

prosperity (prah SPEHR ih tee) economic success and security. (p. 364)

protest (PROH tehst) an event at which people speak out about an issue. (p. 235)

pueblo (PWEH bloh) the Spanish word for town. (p. 42)

Q

quarter (KWAWR tur) to give people food and shelter. (p. 242)

quota (KWOH tur) the maximum number of people allowed to enter a country. (p. 504)

R

ratify (RAT uh fy) to accept. (p. 306)

rebellion (rih BEHL yun) a fight against a government (p. 230)

Reconstruction (ree kuhn STRUHK shuhn) the period when the South rejoined the Union. (p. 472)

reform (rih FOWRM) an action that makes something better. (p. 390)

refuge (REHF yooj) a safe place. (p. 203)

refugee (REHF yoo jee) a person who escapes war or other danger and seeks safety in another country. (p. 506)

region (REE jehn) an area that has one or more features in common. (p. 22)

register (REHJ ih stur) to sign up to vote. (p. 541)

renewable resource (rih NOO uh buhl REE sawrs) a natural resource that can be replaced, such as wood. (p. 15)

repeal (rih PEEL) to cancel something, such as a law. (p. 236)

representative (rehp rih ZEHN tuh tihv) someone who is chosen to speak and act for others. (p. 189)

republic (rih PUHB lihk) a government in which the citizens elect leaders to represent them. (p. 303)

responsibility (rih sphahn suh BIHL ih tee) a duty that someone is expected to fulfill. (p. 541)

retreat (rih TREET) to move away from the enemy. (p. 279)

revolt (reh VUHLT) a violent uprising against a ruler. (p. 113)

rights (ryts) freedoms that are protected by a government's laws. (p. 264)

ruling (ROO lihng) an official decision. (p. 370)

S

scarcity (SKAIR sih tee) not having as much of something as people would like. (p. 18)

secession (sih SEHSH uhn) when a part of a country leaves or breaks off from the rest. (p. 440)

secondary source (SEHK uhn dehr ee sawrs) information from someone who did not witness an event. (p. 480)

sectionalism (SEHK shuh nuh lihz uhm) loyalty to one part of the country. (p. 419)

segregation (sehg rih GAY shuhn) the forced separation of the races. (p. 484)

self-government (sehlf GUHV urn muhnt) when the people who live in a place make laws for themselves. (p. 167)

settlement (SEHT uhl muhnt) a small community of people living in a new place. (p. 98)

sharecropping (SHAIR krahp ihng) when landowners let poor farmers use small areas of their land. In return, the sharecropper gave the landowner a share of the crop. (p. 483)

Silk Road (sihlk rohd) several trade routes connecting China and Europe. (p. 85)

slave state (slayv stayt) a state that permitted slavery. (p. 432)

slave trade (slayv trayd) the business of buying and selling human beings. (p. 176)

slavery (SLAY vuh ree) a cruel system in which people are bought and sold and made to work without pay. (p. 93)

smuggling (SMUHG lihng) to import goods illegally. (p. 235)

source (sawrs) the place where a river begins. (p. 357)

specialization (spehsh uh lih ZAY shuhn) when people make the goods they are best able to produce with the resources they have. (p. 24)

spiritual (SPIHR ih choo uhl) a religious song. (p. 215)

staple (STAY puhl) a main crop that is used for food. (p. 56)

R67

states' rights (stayts ryts) the idea that states, not the federal government, should make the final decisions about matters that affect them. (p. 419)

stock (stahk) a share of ownership in a company. (p. 131)

strategy (STRAT uh jee) a plan of action. (p. 286)

suffrage (SUHF rihj) the right to vote. (p. 368)

suffragist (SUHF ruh jihst) a woman who worked to gain the right to vote. (p. 525)

summary (SUHM uh ree) a short description of the main points in a piece of writing. (p. 66)

surplus (SUHR pluhs) extra. (p. 47)

surrender (suh REHN dur) to give up. (p. 288)

T

tariff (TAR ihf) a tax on imported goods. (p. 418)

tax (taks) money that people pay to their government in return for services. (p. 234)

technology (tehk NAHL uh jee) the use of scientific knowledge and tools to do things better and more rapidly. (p. 90)

telegraph (TEHL ih graf) a machine that sends electric signals over wires. (p. 467)

temperance (TEHM pur uhns) controlling or cutting back on the drinking of alcohol. (p. 390)

tenement (TEHN uh muhnt) a poorly built apartment building. (p. 500)

territory (TEHR ih tawr ee) land ruled by a national government but which has no representatives in the government. (p. 297)

textile (TEHKS tyl) cloth or fabric. (p. 378)

tidewater (TYD wah tur) where the water in rivers and streams rises and falls with the ocean's tides. (p. 162)

tolerance (TAHL ur uhns) the respect for beliefs that are different from one's own. (p. 145)

total war (TOHT uhl wawr) the strategy of destroying an enemy's resources. (p. 467)

town meeting (town MEET ihng) a gathering where colonists held elections and voted on the laws for their towns. (p. 166)

trade (trayd) the buying and selling of goods. (p. 25)

traitor (TRAY tur) someone who is not loyal. (p. 286)

travois (truh VOY) equipment similar to a sled that was made from two long poles and usually pulled by a dog. (p. 61)

treason (TREE zuhn) the crime of fighting against one's own government. (p. 266)

treaty (TREE tee) an official agreement between nations or groups. (p. 190)

U

unconstitutional (uhn kahn stih TOO shuh nuhl) when a law does not agree with the Constitution. (p. 314)

Underground Railroad (UHN dur ground RAYL rohd) a series of escape routes and hiding places to bring slaves out of the South. (p. 426)

Union (YOON yuhn) another name for the United States. (p. 433)

V

veto (VEE toh) to reject. (p. 314)

victory (VIHK tuh ree) success in battle against an enemy. (p. 279)

volunteer (vahl uhn TEER) someone who helps other people without being paid. (p. 543)

W

wagon train (WAG uhn trayn) a line of covered wagons that moved together. (p. 401)

wampum (WAHM puhm) pieces of carefully shaped and cut seashell. (p. 70)

Glossary

Index

Page numbers with *m* after them refer to maps. Page numbers that are in italics refer to pictures.

A

B

R69

Index

R71

K

L

M

N

Index

R73

Index

U

V

W

Y

Z

Index

Acknowledgments

Permissioned Literature Selections

Excerpt from *Ann's Story: 1747,* by Joan Lowery Nixon. Copyright © 2000 by Joan Lowery Nixon and The Colonial Williamsburg Foundation. Used by permission of Random House Children's Books, a division of Random House, Inc. and Daniel Weiss Associates, Inc. Excerpt from *"Chinook Wind Wrestles Cold Wind,"* from *They Dance in the Sky: Native American Star Myths,* by Jean Guard Monroe and Ray A. Williamson. Text copyright © 1987 by Jean Guard Monroe and Ray A. Williamson. Reprinted by permission of Houghton Mifflin Company. *"City of Bridges"/"Ciudad de pientes,"* from *Iguanas in the Snow and Other Poems / Iguanas en la nieve y otros poemas de invierno,* by Francisco X. Alarcon. Poem copyright © 2001 by Francisco X. Alarcon. Reprinted with the permission of the publisher, Children's Book Press, San Francisco, CA. *"Dream Variation,"* from *The Collected Poems of Langston Hughes,* by Langston Hughes. Copyright © 1994 by The Estate of Langston Hughes. Used by permission of Alfred A. Knopf, a division of Random House, Inc. and Harold Ober Associates Incorporated. Excerpt from *Emma's Journal: The Story Of A Colonial Girl,* by Marissa Moss. Copyright © 1999 by Marissa Moss. Reprinted by permission of Harcourt, Inc. and the author. Excerpt from *First In Peace: George Washington, the Constitution, and the Presidency,* by John Rosenburg. Copyright © 1998 by John Rosenburg. Reprinted by permission of The Millbrook Press, Inc. *"For Purple Mountains' Majesty,"* from *The Malibu and Other Poems,* by Myra Cohn Livingston. Copyright © 1972 by Myra Cohn Livingston. Reprinted by permission of Marian Reiner. *"Green Card Fever"* from *We The People,* by Bobbi Katz. Text copyright © 2000 by Bobbi Katz. Used by permission of HarperCollins Publishers. Excerpt from the Speech, *"I Have a Dream,"* by Dr. Martin Luther King Jr. Copyright © 1963 by Dr. Martin Luther King Jr., copyright renewed © 1991 by Coretta Scott King. Reprinted by arrangement with the Estate of Martin Luther King Jr., c/o Writers House as agent for the proprietor New York, NY. Excerpt from *In the Days of the Vaqueros: America's First True Cowboys,* by Russell Freedman. Text copyright © 2001 by Russell Freedman. Reprinted by permission of Houghton Mifflin Company. Excerpt from *"Juan Ponce de Leon,"* from *Around the World In A Hundred Years: From Henry The Navigator To Magellan,* by Jean Fritz. Text copyright © 1994 by Jean Frtiz. Used by permission of G.P. Putnam's Sons, a division of Penguin Young Readers Group, a member of Penguin Group (USA) Inc., 345 Hudson Street, New York, NY 10014. All rights reserved. Excerpt from *"Our Friend Squanto,"* from *This New Land,* by G. Clifton Wisler. Copyright © 1987 by G. Clifton Wisler. Published by arrangement with Walker & Co. Excerpt from *Remember Me,* by Irene N. Watts, published by Tundra Books of Northern New York. Copyright © 2000 by Irene N. Watts. Permission to reproduce work must be sought from originating publisher. Reprinted by permission. *"Speak Up,"* from *Good Luck Gold and Other Poems,* by Janet S. Wong. Copyright © 1994 by Janet S. Wong. Reprinted with the permission of Margaret K. McElderry Books, an imprint of Simon & Schuster Children's Publishing Division. All rights reserved. Excerpt from *Stealing Freedom,* by Elisa Carbone. Text copyright © 1998 by Elisa Carbone. Reprinted by arrangement with Random House Children's Boosk, a division of Random House, Inc., New York, New York. *"Torn Map,"* from *Come With Me: Poems For A Journey,* by Naomi Shihab Nye. Text copyright © 2000 by Naomi Shihab Nye, Reprinted by permission of HarperCollins Publishers.

Photography

COVER (Lincoln Memorial) © Dennis Brack. (Capitol) © Royalty Free/CORBIS. (map) © Granger Collection, New York. (compass) HMCo./Michael Indresano. (spine Lincoln memorial) © Peter Gridley/Getty Images. (back cover statue) © Connie Ricca/CORBIS. (back cover nickel) Courtesy of the United States Mint. **vi-vii** © Neil Rabinowitz/CORBIS **vii** (t) The Art Archive/ National Anthropological Museum Mexico/Dagli Orti. **viii** (t) Photodisc/Getty Images. (b) © National Portrait Gallery, Smithsonian Institution/Art Resource, NY. **ix** (t) Royal Albert Memorial Museum, Exeter, Devon, UK/ Bridgeman Art Library. (b) Colonial Williamsburg Foundation. **x** (t) Courtesy Bostonian Society/Old State House. **x-xi** © Private Collection/Art Resource, NY. **xi** (t) © Andrea Pistolesi/Getty Images. **xii** (t) The Granger Collection, New York. (b) © D. Robert & Lorri Franz/ CORBIS. **xiii** (t) Courtesy Don Troiani, Historical Military Image Bank. (b) © Bettmann/Corbis. **xiv** (t) Brown Brothers. (b) NASA. xv © Yann Arthus-Bertrand/CORBIS. **xx-xxi** The Granger Collection, New York. **1** Terry Donnelly/Getty Images **2** (l) © David Muench.(m) The Granger Collection, New York. (r) © Archivo Iconografico, S.A./CORBIS. **3** (r) Smithsonian American Art Museum, Washington, DC/Art Resource, NY. **4** (l) Bill Strode/ Woodfin Camp.(r) © E. R. Degginger. **5** (l) © Grant Heilman/Grant Heilman Photography, Inc. Alan Kearny/ Getty Images. **10** (b) © Warren Faidley/ Weatherstock. **10-11** Laboratory for Atmospheres at NASA Goddard Space Flight Center. **14-15** Grant Heilman/Grant Heilman Photography, Inc. **16** (l, m) Grant Heilman/Grant Heilman Photography, Inc. (r) Debra Ferguson/AgStockUSA. **17** (l, ml) Arthur C. Smith III/Grant Heilman Photography, Inc. **18** © Russell Curtis/Photo Researchers, Inc. **19** © Adamsmith/ SuperStock **20-21** Stefano Paltera/American Solar Challenge **22** Paul McCormick/Getty Images **24** (l) © Larry Lefever/Grant Heilman Photography, Inc. (r) © Grant Heilman/Grant Heilman Photography, Inc. **26** Courtesy Dawn Wright. **27** (l) Courtesy Mei-Po Kwan. (r) Courtesy Dr. William Wood, Photo: Ray Isawa. **28** D. Megna/Raw Talent Photo. **30** (l) David R. Frazier. (r) Mine-engineer.com, Long Beach, California. **32** Library Of Congress, LCZ62-114352. **36** (l) Art Archive/Museo Cuidad Mexico/Nicolas Sapieha. (r) Jeff Greenberg/Photo Researchers, Inc. **37** (l) Garry D. McMichael/Photo Researchers, Inc. (r) NativeStock **38** Bill Varie/CORBIS. **39** Jonathan Blair/CORBIS. **40-41** Cahokia Mounds State Historic Site, painting by Michael Hampshire. **41** (t) Richard A. Cooke/CORBIS. (b) Ohio Historical Society. **42** (t) © J.C. Leacock/Network Aspen. (b) © David Muench. **43** The Art Archive/National Anthropological Museum Mexico/Dagli Orti. **44-45** The Art Archive/Mireille Vautier. **46** © David Muench. **49** © 1997 Clark James Mishler. **54** © David Muench. **57** © Suzi Moore/Woodfin Camp & Associates, Inc. **58** Courtesy Victor Mesayesva Jr. **58-59** Courtesy Leslie Marmon Silko. **59** (t) Los Alamos National Laboratory, Public Affairs Office. Photo: Leroy Sanchez. **60** © Tom Bean. **62** Smithsonian American Art Museum, Washington, DC/Art Resource, NY. **63** © Marilyn Angel Wynn/Nativestock.com. **64** Cincinatti Art Museum, Gift of General M. F. Force, Photo: T. Walsh. **64-65** University of Pennsylvania Museum, T4-3061. **68** © E. R. Degginger/Photo Researchers, Inc. **70** (l) The Granger Collection, New York. (r) Hiawatha Wampum Belt, NYSM Ref. #E-37309; now curated at The Onondaga Nation. Photo courtesy of New York State Museum, used with permission of The Council of Chiefs, Onondaga Nation. **71** Ray Ellis/Photo Researchers, Inc. **78** (t) Musée National de la Renaissance, Ecouen, France/Bridgeman Art Library. (b) Archivo Iconografico, S.A./CORBIS. **79** (tl) National Museum of Fine Arts, Madrid. (tr) © SuperStock. (bl) Granada Cathedral Photo: Oronoz. (br) The Art Archive/ National Anthropological Museum Mexico/Dagli Orti. **80** (l) Metropolitan Museum of Art, New York/Bridgeman Art Library. (m) © Giraudon/Art Resource, NY. (r) © Schalkwijk/ Art Resource, NY. **81** (t) Higgins Amory Museum, Worcester, MA, (HAM #13), Photo: Don Eaton. (bl) North Wind Picture Archives. (br) Photodisc/Getty Images. **82** (l) Time Life Pictures/Getty Images. (r) Stockbyte/PictureQuest **83** (l) Private Collection/ Bridgeman Art Library. (r) Wood Ronsaville Harlin, Inc. **85** (t) British Library,London, UK/Bridgeman Art library. (b) © China Stock. **87** The Art Archive/John Webb. **89** AP Wide World Photo. **90** © SPL/ Photo Researchers, Inc. **91** Bibliothéque Nationale, Paris, France/Bridgeman Art Library **92** © Stapleton Collection/ CORBIS. **95** (t) © Giraudon/Art Resource, NY. (b) © Victoria & Albert Museum, London/Art Resource, NY. **96** Metropolitan Museum of Art, New York/Bridgeman Art Library. **98** (t) © Giraudon/Art Resource, NY. **98-99** Royalty-Free/CORBIS. **101** The Art Archive/General Archive of the Indies Seville/Dagli Orti. **102-3** Library Of Congress. **104** © Archivo Iconografico, S.A./CORBIS. **105** © Giraudon/ Art Resource, NY. **106** Higgins Amory Museum, Worcester, MA, (HAM #13), Photo: Don Eaton. **107** © Ron Watts/ CORBIS. **108** (l, m) The Granger Collection, New York. (r) © Bettmann/CORBIS. **109** (bkgd) © Library of Congress/ Geography and Map Division. (l, r) The Granger Collection, New York. **110** © Schalkwijk/Art Resource, NY. **111** The Granger Collection, New York. **112** (t) North Wind Picture Archives. (b) © A. Ramey/Photo Edit. **114** Mithra-Index/ Bridgeman Art Library. **115** © Nancy Carter/North Wind Picture Archives. **120** (l) Erich Lessing/Art Resource, NY. (r) Library Of Congress. **121** (l) Pilgrim Society, Plymouth, Massachusetts. (r) New York Public Library/Art Resource, NY. **122** Bristol City Museum and Art Gallery, UK/Bridgeman Art Library. **124** © Erich Lessing/Art Resource, NY. **126** The Granger Collection, New York. **127** Private Collection/Bridgeman Art Library. **128** © Jeffrey L. Rotman/CORBIS. **129** © Giraudon/Art Resource, NY. **130** The Granger Collection, New York. **131** © Susan M. Glascock. **132** (l) © Marilyn Angel Wynn/Nativestock.com. (r) Ashmolean Museum, Oxford, UK/Bridgeman Art Library. **133** © National Portrait Gallery, Smithsonian Institution/Art Resource, NY. **134** (t) © North Wind Picture Archives. **134-5** Sidney King, National Park Service, Colonial National Historic Park, Jamestown Collection. **136** Photodisc/Getty Images. **137** Pilgrim Society, Plymouth, Massachusetts. **139** The Granger Collection, New York. **141** © Dorothy Littell Greco/Stock, Boston Inc./PictureQuest. **143** © Joseph Sohm;ChromoSohm Inc./CORBIS. **144** © CORBIS. **145** The Granger Collection, New York. **147** The Granger Collection, New York. **154** (t) © Bettmann/CORBIS. (b) © Photodisc/Getty Images. **155** (tl) The Granger Collection, New York. (tr) The Granger Collection, New York. (bl) North Wind Picture Archives. (br) Photodisc/Getty Images. **156** (l) The Granger Collection, New York. (m) The Granger Collection, New York. (r) © Shelburne Museum, Shelburne, Vermont. **157** (l) The Granger Collection, New York. (r) Private Collection/ Bridgeman Art Library. **158** (l) David Parnes/Index Stock Imagery. (r) Private Collection/Bridgeman Art Library. **159** (l) The Granger Collection, New York. (r) Archives Charmet/ Bridgeman Art Library. **160-1** © Neil Rabinowitz/CORBIS **162** (l) © Robert Estall/CORBIS. (r) © Jason Hawkes/ CORBIS. **163** © Phil Degginger. **165** © Alex S. MacLean/ Landslides. **166** Private Collection/Bridgeman Art Library. **167** (l) The Granger Collection, New York. (r) © Kindra Clineff. **169** © Shelburne Museum, Shelburne, Vermont. **174** Archives Charmet/Bridgeman Art Library. **176** (l) Royal Albert Memorial Museum, Exeter, Devon, UK/ Bridgeman Art Library. **176-7** Addison Gallery of American Art, Phillips Academy, Andover, Massachusetts. All Rights Reserved. **178** (l) North Wind Picture Archives. (r) Stock Montage. **179** Private Collection/Bridgeman Art Library. **180-1** Dorset Museum, Dorchester, England. **180** (l) © Stapleton Collection/CORBIS. **186** (l) The Granger Collection, New York. (r) Colonial Williamsburg Foundation. **187** (l) © Andre Jenny/Focus Group/Picture

R77

Quest. (r) © Alan Detrick/Photo Researchers, Inc. **188** The Granger Collection, New York. **190** (t) © Bettmann/ CORBIS. (b) The Granger Collection, New York. **191** Courtesy, CIGNA Museum and Art Collection. **192** (t) © National Portrait Gallery, Smithsonian Institution/Art Resource, NY. (b) American Philosophical Society Library. **193** (t, m, mr) Franklin Institute. (ml) Digital Stock. (b) The Granger Collection, New York. **196** North Wind Picture Archives. **198** (l) New York Public Library/Art Resource, NY. (r) Colonial Williamsburg Foundation. **199** Colonial Williamsburg Foundation. **202-3** © Andre Jenny/Focus Group/Picture Quest. **203** (r) The Granger Collection, New York. **205** Corpus Christi College, Oxford, UK/Bridgeman Art Library. **210** Hulton/Archive/Getty Images. **211** (l) Glen Allison/Stone/Getty Images. (m) ©Photo Edit. (r) ©Alan Detrick/Photo Researchers, Inc. **212** (t) Kaminski House Museum. (b) © Joseph Sohm: Visions of America/CORBIS. **213** (l) North Carolina Museum of History. (r) Colonial Williamsburg Foundation. **214** "View of Mulberry, House and Street", 1805, by Thomas Coram (1756-1811), oil on paper, Gibbes Museum of Art/Carolina Art Association, 68.18.01. **215** (l) Abby Aldrich Rockefeller Folk Art Center, Williamsburg, Virigina 35.301.3. (r) Collection of the Blue Ridge Institute & Museums, Ferrum College. **216-7** Colonial Williamsburg Foundation. **217** © Farrell Grehan/CORBIS. **222** (t) Museum of Fine Arts, Boston: Gift of Joseph W. Revere, William B. Revere and Edward H. R. Revere 30.781. (b) Concord Museum. **223** (tl) Museum of Fine Arts, Boston: Bequest of Winslow Warren 31.212. (tr) © New-York Historical Society, New York, USA/Bridgeman Art Library. (bl) Photodisc/Getty Images (digital composite). (br) The Daughters of the American Revolution Museum, Washington, D.C. **224** (l) Courtesy Colonial Williamsburg Foundation. (m) © Kevin Fleming/CORBIS. (r) © Henryk Kaiser/Index Stock Imagery. **225** (bl) The Granger Collection, New York. (br) Lauros/Giraudon/Bridgeman Art Library. (tr) © Bettmann/CORBIS. (br) Antony Edwards/ Getty Images. **226** (l) Architect of the Capitol. (r) The Granger Collection, New York. **227** (l) Courtesy of the Trustees of the Boston Public Library: George Washington at Dorchester Heights, by Emmanuel Luetze. (r) Hulton Archive/Getty Images. **229** (t) The Granger Collection, New York. (b) © Stock Montage. **231** The Granger Collection, New York. **232** (l) © CORBIS. **233** (t) © Bettmann/CORBIS. (b) © New-York Historical Society, New York, USA/Bridgeman Art Library. **234** Giraudon/ Bridgeman Art Library. **235** (l) © Bettmann/CORBIS. (m) © North Wind Picture Archives. (r) The Granger Collection, New York. **236** © North Wind Picture Archives. **237** American Philosophical Society. **240** © Stock Montage. **241** The Granger Collection, New York. **242** The Granger Collection, New York. **250** © Lee Snider/CORBIS. **252** (l) Massachusetts State House Art Collection, Courtesy Mass. Art Commission. (m) Photo from the collection of the Lexington, Massachusetts Historical Society. (r) © Bettmann/CORBIS. **253** (l) Massachusetts State House Art Collection, Courtesy Mass. Art Commission. (r) Courtesy Don Troiani, Historical Military Image Bank. **254** (l) Courtesy of the Trustees of the Boston Public Library: George Washington at Dorchester Heights, by Emmanuel Luetze. (r) National Museum of American History by Shirley Abbott (Harry N. Abrams, Inc.), ©Smithsonian Institution. **255** Tom Lovell, "The Noble Train of Artillery", Fort Ticonderoga Museum. **260** (l) © Pete Saloutos/CORBIS. (r) The Granger Collection, New York. **261** (tl) Reproduced from the original held by the Department of Special Collections of the University Libraries of Notre Dame. (bl, mt, mb, r) The Granger Collection, New York. **262** The Granger Collection, New York. **263** (l) Lilly Library, Indiana University. (r) © Bettmann/CORBIS. **264** (t) SuperStock. (b) Rhode Island Historical Society. **265** (b) Photodisc/Getty Images (digital composite). **266** The Granger Collection, New York. **267** Michael Herron/Take Stock. **268** (t) Independence National Historical Park. (bl) © Royalty-Free/CORBIS. (bm) © Ted Spiegel/CORBIS. (br) Monticello/ Thomas Jefferson Foundation, Inc. **269** (t) Library of Congress. (b) National Museum of American History, Smithsonian Institution, Behring Center, Neg #83-4689. **270-1** (bkgd) © Christie's Images/CORBIS. **271** (t) The Granger Collection, New York. (b) Fenimore Art Museum, Cooperstown, New York. Photo: Richard Walker. **272** (t) The Fraunces Tavern Museum. (m) The Granger Collection, New York. (b) Library of Congress, LC-USZC4-5316DLC. **273** (t) The Granger Collection, New York. (bl) Reproduced from the original held by the Department of Special Collections of the University Libraries of Notre Dame. (br) The Granger Collection, New York. **274** (r) Photodisc/Getty Images. **278** Courtesy Bostonian Society/Old State House. **279** The Metropolitan Museum of Art, Gift of John Stewart Kennedy, 1897 (97.34) Photograph © 1992 the Metropolitan Museum of Art. **282** (ml, r) Courtesty National Park Service, Museum Management Program and Morristown National Historical Park. (mr) Courtesty National Park Service, Museum Management Program and Valley Forge National Historical Park. **282-3** SuperStock. **285** Comstock KLIPS. **286** The Granger Collection, New York. **287** The Granger Collection, New York. **288** The Senate of the Commonwealth of Virginia, Courtesy of the Library of Virginia. **289** National Archives. **290** (t) © Academy of Natural Sciences of Philadelphia/CORBIS. (m) The Granger Collection, New York. (b) The Granger Collection, New York. **291** (tm) © Erich Lessing/Art Resource, NY.(tr) © Bettmann/CORBIS. (bl) The Art Archive/ Dagli Orti. (br) The Granger Collection, New York. **294** (r) The Granger Collection, New York. **295** (r) New York Historical Society/Bridgeman Art Library. **297** © Alex S. MacLean/Landslides. 298 (l) © North Wind Picture Archives. (r) The Granger Collection, New York. **299** Virginia Historical Society, Richmond, Virginia. **302-3** Independence National Historical Park. **303** (l) Courtesy of National Constitution Center (Scott Frances, Ltd.). (r) © Reunion des Musées Nationaux/Art Resource, NY. **306** (t) © Art Resource. NY. (b) © Joseph Sohm; ChromoSohm Inc./CORBIS. **308** © Dennis Brack. **310** (t) The Granger Collection, New York. (b) © Reunion des Musées Nationaux/Art Resource, NY. **313** (l) © Reuters New Media Inc.CORBIS. (r) © Joseph Sohm/Visions of America, LLC/Picture Quest. **316** © Bob Daemmrich/The Image Works. **317** © Bettmann/CORBIS. **318** (l) © Bettmann/CORBIS. (r) Independence National Historical Park. **318-9** Independence National Historical Park. **320** National Museum of American History, Smithsonian Institution, Behring Center, Neg #s 97-7908 and 97-7917. **321** New York Historical Society/Bridgeman Art Library. **322** (l) White House Historical Association. (r) © National Portrait Gallery, Smithsonian Institution/Art Resource, NY. **324** (t) (detail) Abigail Smith Adams (Mrs. John Adams), by Gilbert Stuart Gift of Mrs. Robert Homans, Image © 2003 Boar of Trustees, National Gallery of Art, Washington. (b) The Granger Collection, New York. **324-5** The Granger Collection, New York. **325** (t) (detail) William Thornton, by Gilbert Stuart, Andrew Mellon Collection, Image © 2003 Board of Trustees, National Gallery of Art, Washington. **328-9** Photodisc/Getty Images. **331** (t) Peter Gridley/Getty Images. (m) Andrea Pistolesi/Getty Images. (b) Photodisc/ Getty Images. **332** (b) © Dennis Brack/Black Star Publishing/PictureQuest. **333** (bl) © SW Productions/Brand X Pictures/PictureQuest. (br)Photodisc/Getty Images. **338**(t) Independence National Historical Park. (b) National Museum of American History, Smithsonian Institution, Behring Center, Neg# 95-3550. **339** (tl) Stock Montage. (tr) The Granger Collection, New York. (bl) National Museum of American History, Smithsonian Institution, Print/Neg # 73-11287. (br) Artville. **341** © Steve Vidler/ SuperStock. **340** (l) National Museum of American History, Smithsonian Institution 89-6712. (m) Monticello/Thomas Jefferson Foundation, Inc. **342** (l) Albany Institute of History & Art. (r) Montana Historical Society. **343** (l, r) The Granger Collection, New York. **344** George Caleb Bingham, Daniel Boone Escorting Settlers through the Cumberland Gap, 1851-52. Oil on canvas, 36 1/2 X 50 1/4". Washington University Gallery of Art, St. Louis. Gift of Nathaniel Phillips, 1890. **346** The Granger Collection, New York. **347** (detail) Robert Griffing, "Logan's Revenge" **354** © Burstein Collection/ CORBIS. (frame) Image Farm. **356** John Ford Clymer, "Up the Jerfferson", Courtesy Mrs. John F. Clymer and The Clymer Museum. **358** (l) © John Warden/SuperStock. (r) Jack Olson. **359** (l) © Shan Cunningham. (r) Jack Olson. **360** © Bettman/CORBIS. **361** (t) The Granger Collection, New York. (b) Library of Congress. **363** New York Historical Society/Bridgeman Art Library. (frame)Image Farm. **365** The Granger Collection, New York. **367** © Bettmann/CORBIS. **368** Architect of the Capitol. **370** (l) © National Portrait Gallery, Smithsonian Institution/Art Resource, NY. (r) Library of Congress. **371** Private Collection/Bridgeman Art Library. (frame) Image Farm. **376** (l) The Granger Collection, New York. (r) © Bettmann/ CORBIS. **377** (l) Star of the Republic Museum. (r) North Wind Picture Archives. **379** National Museum of American History, Smithsonian Institution Neg # 89-6712. **380** (t) The Granger Collection, New York. (b) American Textile History Museum, Lowell, Massachusetts. **381** (l) The Granger Collection, New York. (r) Courtesy of PictureHistory. **383** The Granger Collection, New York. **389** © CORBIS. **390** © Bettmann/CORBIS. **391** The Granger Collection, New York. **393** (t) The Granger Collection, New York. (ml, mr) © Bettmann/CORBIS. (bl) © National Portrait Gallery, Smithsonian Institution/Art Resource, NY. (br) Library of Congress - May Wright Sewall Collection, LC-USZ61-790DLC. **394** Yale University, Beinecke Rare Book & Manuscript Library, WAMSS S498 Box 1/File 13. **395** © Steve Vidler/SuperStock. **396** Star of the Republic Museum. **398** (t) State Preservation Board (Austin, Texas). (b) The San Jacinto Museum of History, Houston (detail). **399** (t) The Daughters of the Republic of Texas Library at the Alamo. (b) Texas State Library and Archives Commission. **400** Whitman Mission National Historic Site. **401** Culver Pictures. **403** California State Library. **404** Rick Egan. **410** (t) © CORBIS. **411** (tl) Library of Congress, LCUSZ62-984. (tr) Library of Congress.(bl) National Museum of American History, Smithsonian Institution, Behring Center, Neg # 95-5528. (br) Photodisc/Getty Images. **412** (l) The Granger Collection, New York. (m) © National Portrait Gallery, Smithsonian Institution/Art Resource, NY. (r) © Scala/Art Resource, NY. **413** (l) © Bettman/CORBIS. **414** (l) © National Portrait Gallery, Smithsonian Institution/Art Resource, NY. (r) © Bettman/CORBIS. **415** (l) Picture Research Consultants, Inc. (r) The Granger Collection, New York. **416-7** Private Collection/Bridgeman Art Library. **418** The Granger Collection, New York. **419** (frame) Image Farm. **419** © National Portrait Gallery, Smithsonian Institution/Art Resource, NY. **421** © Burke/Triolo/Brand X Pictures/PictureQuest. **424** South Carolina Confederate Relic Room and Museum. **425** (l) © National Portrait Gallery, Smithsonian Institution/Art Resource, NY. (m) © National Portrait Gallery, Smithsonian Institution/Art Resource, NY. (r) © Bettman/CORBIS. **427** © Bettman/ CORBIS. **432** The Granger Collection, New York. **434** (tl) Picture Research Consultants Archives.(tr) Schlesinger Library, Radcliffe Institute, Harvard University. (b) The Granger Collection, New York. **435** The Granger Collection, New York. **440** © Bettman/CORBIS. **441** (t) Robertstock. (b) Library of Congress. **442-3** State Historical Society of Illinois, Chicago, IL, USA/Bridgeman Art Library. **443** (t) Courtesy PictureHistory (digital composite). (b) Stanley King Collection. **444** National Archives. **445** © Scala/Art Resource, NY. **450** (l) Library of Congress, USZCN4-49, G01231. (r) © Medford Historical Society Collection/CORBIS . **451** Electricity Collection, NMAH, Smithsonian Institution, Neg # 74-2491. (r) Brown Brothers. **452** Cook Collection, Valentine Museum. **456** Library of Congress, USZCN4- 49, G01231. **457** Gettysburg National Military Park. **458** The Granger Collection, New York. **460** The Granger Collection, New York. **461** (l) Library of Congress. (r) Paragon Light, Inc. **462** The Granger Collection, New York. **463** Larry Kolvoord/The Image Works. **464** National Archives. **465** (t) The Granger Collection, New York. (b) © Private Collection/Art Resource, NY. **466** Library of Congress. **467** National Archives, 77-F-194-6-56. **468** (l) Tom Lovell/ National Geographic. (r) National Museum of American History, Smithsonian Institution Neg #95-5515-7. **470** (l) Fort Loreto Museum, Puebla. (r) Electricity Collection, NMAH, Smithsonian Institution, Neg # 74-2491. **471** (tl)

The Granger Collection, New York. (tr) Hulton Archive/Getty Images. (bl) The Granger Collection, New York. (br) © Polak Matthew/CORBIS SYGMA. **472** The Meserve Collection. **473** (l) Courtesy of the New York Historical Society, NYC, Neg#21185. (r) New York Historical Society/Bridgeman Art Library. **477** © CORBIS. (frame) Image Farm. **478** (t) © Medford Historical Society Collection/CORBIS. **478-9** Charleston Museum. **482-3** Brown Brothers. **484** (l) The Granger Collection, New York. (r) © Dhimitri/Folio Inc. **485** Brown Brothers. **486** © CORBIS. **486-7** © CORBIS **492** (t) AP Wide World Photos. (b) Photodisc/Getty Images. **493** (tl) Mario Tama/Getty Images. (tr) © 1976 George Balthis/ Take Stock. (bl) Courtesy State Department. (br) Hulton Archive/Getty Images. **494** (l) © Bettmann/CORBIS. (m) Hulton/Archive/ Getty Images. (r) Carl Iwasaki/Time Life Pictures/Getty Images. **495** (l) Robert E. Daemmrich/Getty Images. (r) AP Wide World Photos. **496** (l) © Laurie Platt Winfrey Inc. (r) New York Public Library. **497** (r) (detail) Independence National Historical Park. **498** Photographs taken by MetaForm Incorporated/Karen Yamauchi of artifacts in the National Park Service Collection, Statue of Liberty National Monument, Ellis Island Immigration Museum. **499** California State Museum. **501** © Laurie Platt Winfrey Inc. **502-3** The Granger Collection, New York. **503** (l) Brown Brothers. (r) © Yoshio Tomii/SuperStock. **504** Library of Congress. **505** Brown Brothers. **506** Robert E. Daemmrich/Getty Images. **507** © Tony Freeman/ PhotoEdit. **509** Brown Brothers. **512** © Lawrence Midgale/Photo Researchers, Inc. **513** (l) Carl Mydans/Time Life Pictures/Getty Images. (m) © AFP/CORBIS. (r) © Maroon/FOLIO, Inc. **514** © Richard T. Nowitz/Photo Researchers, Inc. **516-7** Bill Losh/Getty Images. **518-9** David Lawrence/Panoramic Images. **522** (l) © Bettmann/CORBIS. (r) Michael Herron/Take Stock. **523** (l) © Wally McNamee/CORBIS. (r) © Tony Freeman/ PhotoEdit. **524** © Bettmann/CORBIS. **525** Hulton Archive/Getty Images. **526** © Bettmann/CORBIS. **527** © Bettmann/CORBIS. **531** Robert W. Kelley/Time Life Pictures/Getty Images. **532** (l) © Charles Gatewood/The Image Works. (r) NASA. **533** (l) © Wally McNamee/ CORBIS. (r) AP Wide World Photos. **534** © Bob Fitch/Take Stock. **535** AP Wide World Photos. **536** Arthur Schatz/Time Life Pictures/Getty Images. **537** Arthur Schatz/Time Life Pictures/Getty Images. **538** AP Wide World Photos. **539** © Syracuse Newspapers/The Image Works. **540** © Jim West/The Image Works. **544** © Myrleen Ferguson Cate/PhotoEdit. **545** (t) © Ellen Senisi/The Image Works. (b) © Michael Newman/ PhotoEdit.

Assignment Photography

All Photography © HMCo./Angela Coppola. 539 © HMCo./Allan Landau.

Illustration

21 (t) Joel Dubin. **32-33** Matthew Pippin. **72-73** Karen Minot. **48** Will Williams. **50-53** David Diaz. **56** Wood Ronsaville Harlin, Inc ©. **148-149** Wood Ronsaville Harlin, Inc. **149** (t) Joel Dubin. **200-201** Inklink. **207-209** David Soman. **238-239** Wood Ronsaville Harlin, Inc. **274-277** Steve Patricia. **300-301** Will Williams. **348-351** Steve Patricia. **372-373** Wood Ronsaville Harlin, Inc. **404-405** Wood Ronsaville Harlin, Inc ©. **420-421** Inklink. **429-430** Beth Peck. **436-439** Will Williams. **474-475** Barbara Higgins Bond. **512-513** Pat Rossi Calkin. **585** William Brinkley. **668** Matthew Pippin. **702-705** Dave Klug.

Charts and Graphs by Pronk&Associates

R79

Overview

Videotapes on social studies topics are an excellent way to enhance, extend, and reinforce social studies concepts and content. They provide students an opportunity to hear and see the people, places, and events they read about in their texts. Students and teachers have few chances to travel outside the classroom to different places and time periods; videos can provide the "field trip" experience without permission slips and bus rentals.

As with real field trips, however, videos are most useful when they are integrated into the curriculum. Houghton Mifflin Social Studies provides the opportunity to use a video that is correlated to the unit. They have been specifically chosen to interest students in the contents of the unit. These videos can be used to

- Provide an alternate instructional mode to meet individual needs
- Generate interest in the unit
- Supplement existing classroom teaching
- Review and wrap up the unit
- Offer opportunities for extending activities and collaborative learning

Using the Unit Video

Videos can be shown as an introduction to the unit; as a means of reinforcing a concept taught in the unit; and/or as a way to wrap-up the unit. You may wish to choose one of the following models throughout the year or vary your approach unit by unit.

Introducing the Unit

Begin by having students look at the Unit Opener and discuss the Big Idea presented there. You may enhance the discussion through the use of the Big Idea Transparency.

Once students have begun to explore their ideas about what they will be learning in the unit, show them the Unit Video.

- Practice listening and viewing skills by having them jot down notes as they watch. Suggest that they write only the most important ideas and information that they have learned.
- After viewing, ask students to write one sentence that describes the main idea of the video. You may wish to ask volunteers to read aloud their sentences as a starting point for class discussion: do other students agree? Would they modify the sentence at all?
- You may wish to discuss point of view with your class. What feelings were expressed in the video and who expressed them? How did the students themselves feel after they watched it?
- Next, talk about the unit in the text. Ask students to predict what they think it will be about.

Before teaching a specific lesson that is connected to the content of the Unit Video, build background by showing the video to the class.

- Create a KWL chart: ask students what they know about the topic and what they want to learn about the topic. Use the video as a springboard to their brainstorming. After teaching the lesson, complete the chart with what students have learned about the topic.
- If students seem unsure about the concepts or people covered in the lesson, reshow the video to review.

After completing the unit, give students a chance to review what they remember. Ask them to suggest ideas, people, and events from the unit that they think are important and to explain why. Before assessing their understanding, show the class the unit video.

- Encourage students to be active listeners by taking notes while viewing the video.
- Discuss what ideas, people, and/or events the video focused on and how that compares with their list of important ideas, people, and events.
- Use the video as a jumping off point for a unit activity, by having students create a screenplay for a unit video that they would like to show. If your school has the equipment, you may encourage one or more groups to produce and film their unit videos.

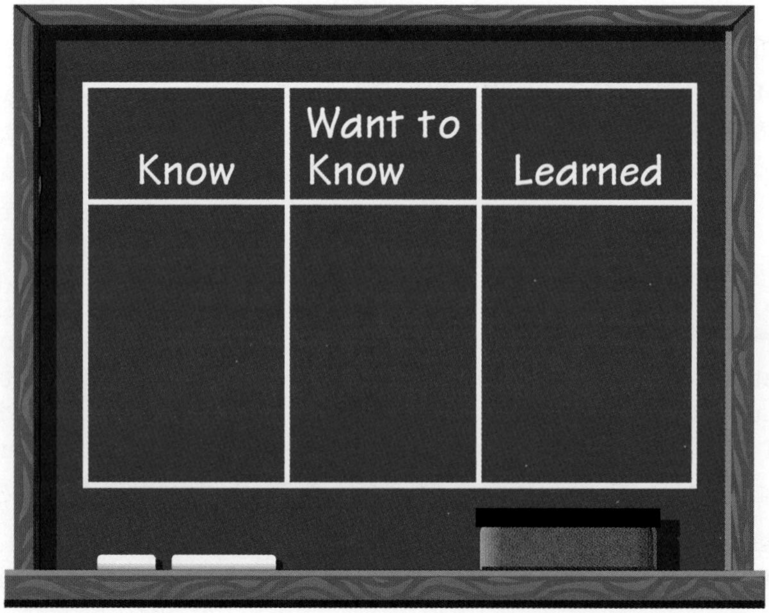

SOCIAL STUDIES at Home

Family Newsletter for Unit 1

Our Land and Its First People

Learn About It

In this unit, your child will learn:

- the location, features, and natural resources of the United States
- about the first Americans and how the geography of the Americas influenced their lives

Here are some ways that you can help your child learn:

Read to Learn More About It

Ahyoka and the Talking Leaves, by Peter and Connie Roop. Ahyoka helps her father Sequoyah create the Cherokee alphabet.

The Aztecs, by Tim Wood. Colorful illustrations and see-through cut-away diagrams illustrate and explain all aspects of Aztec culture and history.

The Earliest Americans, by Helen Roney Sattler. A description of the most widely accepted theories on who the first Americans were.

Talk About It

Chapter 1: America's Land

Scarce food When something is scarce, people may need to use or take less than they want. For example, six people would like to each have a full glass of orange juice. However, there are only enough oranges for three people to have a full glass. Talk with your child about how the scarcity of fruit affects the amount of juice each person gets.

Chapter 2: The First Americans

Water in the right place There is a lack of rain in the southwestern United States, so American Indians had to find ways to get water to their crops. What are some ways water can be moved without electricity? How do these ways compare with what the American Indians did?

Make It

Build a home American Indians in different parts of North America used different materials to build their homes. Think about the natural resources in your community, such as rocks, trees, dirt, or clay, that you could use to build a place to live. Then design a home you could build using one or all of these materials.

Technology
Check out **www.eduplace.com/parents/hmss05/** for more information.

ESTUDIOS SOCIALES en casa

Carta a la familia: Unidad 1

Nuestra tierra y sus primeros habitantes

Investíguenlo

En esta unidad, su niño aprenderá:

- la ubicación, características y recursos naturales de los Estados Unidos
- acerca de los primeros americanos y de cómo la geografía del continente influenció sus vidas

Aquí tiene algunas formas de ayudar a que su niño aprenda:

Lean para aprender más

El poni de barro: Un cuento tradicional Skidi Pawnee por Caron Lee Cohen Leyenda indígena americana de un niño y su poni maravilloso.

Los navajo (The Navajo) por Susan Stan La autora presenta una perspectiva histórica sobre estos indígenas norteamericanos.

Coméntenlo

Capítulo 1: La tierra de América

La escasez de alimentos Cuando hay escasez de algo, es necesario que las personas usen menos de lo que desean. Por ejemplo, a seis personas les gustaría tomar un vaso de jugo de naranja; sin embargo sólo hay suficientes naranjas para que tres personas tomen vasos llenos de jugo. Hablen con su niño acerca de cómo, en este caso, la escasez de fruta afecta la cantidad de jugo que puede tomar cada persona.

Capítulo 2: Los primeros norteamericanos

Dónde debe haber agua La lluvia es escasa en el suroeste de los Estados Unidos, así que los grupos indígenas tuvieron que hallar maneras de regar sus cultivos. ¿Cuáles son algunas maneras en que el agua se puede transportar sin electricidad? Comparen lo que ustedes pensaron con lo que hicieron los grupos indígenas.

Háganlo

La construcción de una vivienda Los grupos indígenas usaron diferentes materiales en diferentes lugares para construir sus viviendas. Piensen en los distintos recursos naturales en su comunidad, como rocas, árboles o barro, que usarían para construir una vivienda. Luego diseñen una vivienda con los materiales que escogieron.

Tecnología
Para obtener más información, visite **www.eduplace.com/parents/hmss05/**

SOCIAL STUDIES at Home

Family Newsletter for Unit 2

Exploring and Settling the Americas

Learn About It

In this unit, your child will learn:

- how trade and exploration led to the conquest and settlement of the Americas
- how the first settlements were founded

Here are some ways that you can help your child learn:

Read to Learn More About It

Exploration and Conquest, by Betsy and Giulio Maestro. Illustrated account of European exploration and conquest of the Americas.

A Journey to the New World: The Diary of Remember Patience Whipple, Mayflower 1620, by Kathryn Lasky. Patience writes in her diary about her mother's fatal illness aboard the Mayflower and about her new friends and later contacts with Native Americans at Plimoth Plantation.

Who Really Discovered America? by Stephen Krensky. Examines the many sides of the controversy over who really "discovered" America.

Talk About It

Chapter 3: Age of Exploration

Taking the land The Europeans arrived in the Americas and believed the land they found belonged to them. Discuss with your child a time when someone took something that belonged to him or her. How did that make your child feel? How was the situation resolved?

Chapter 4: Europeans Settle North America

Religious freedom The Pilgrims and Puritans settled in North America to pursue religious freedom. Talk with your child about a time when he or she was not allowed to do something. How did your child react? What did he or she do to solve the situation?

Make It

A list for a journey Columbus sailed from Europe to what he thought was Asia. Journeys across the oceans often took many months and were difficult. Food became scarce and people often got sick. Plan a long trip. How many days will your trip last? Make a list of what you would bring and why.

Technology
Check out **www.eduplace.com/parents/hmss05/** for more information.

ESTUDIOS SOCIALES en casa

Carta a la familia: Unidad 2

Exploración y asentamiento

Investíguenlo

En esta unidad, su niño aprenderá:

- acerca de cómo el intercambio comercial y la exploración resultaron en la conquista y el asentamiento del continente americano
- acerca de cómo fueron fundados los primeros asentamientos

Aquí tiene algunas formas de ayudar a que su niño aprenda:

Lean para aprender más

El nuevo mundo: desde el descubrimiento hasta la independencia por Mónica Dambrosio y Roberto Barbieri Una mirada al desarrollo del Nuevo Mundo desde el descubrimiento hasta la independencia.

El diario de Pedro (Pedro's Journey) por Pam Conrad Pedro, un joven marinero en la *Santa María*, relata en su diario sus aventuras navegando con Colón hacia el Nuevo Mundo.

Coméntenlo

Capítulo 3: Una era de exploración

Apropiándose de las tierras Los europeos llegaron a América y creyeron que las tierras que encontraron les pertenecían. Hablen de una ocasión en que alguien haya tomado algo que le pertenecía a su niño. ¿Cómo se sintió? ¿Cómo se resolvió la situación?

Capítulo 4: Colonias europeas

Libertad religiosa Los peregrinos y los puritanos se asentaron en Norteamérica en busca de libertad religiosa. Hablen acerca de una ocasión en que a su niño no se le haya permitido hacer algo. ¿Cómo reaccionó? ¿Qué hizo para resolver la situación?

Háganlo

Una lista para un viaje Colón navegó desde Europa hasta donde él creyó que era Asia. Los viajes a través de los oceános con frecuencia se demoraban muchos meses y eran muy difíciles. Los alimentos eran escasos y la gente se enfermaba con frecuencia. Hagan planes para un viaje largo. ¿Cuántos días durará? Hagan una lista de lo que llevarán al viaje y por qué lo llevarán.

Tecnología
Para obtener más información, visite **www.eduplace.com/parents/hmss05/**

SOCIAL STUDIES at Home

Family Newsletter for Unit 3

The English Colonies

Learn About It

In this unit, your child will learn:

- how the thirteen colonies were established and what life was like there
- how the Middle and Southern colonies were founded and what life was like there

Here are some ways that you can help your child learn:

Read to Learn More About It

African-Americans in the Thirteen Colonies, by Deborah Kent. The author presents an overview of social conditions and achievements of both free and enslaved African Americans.

. . . If You Lived in Colonial Times, by Ann McGovern. Text and pictures tell what it was like to live in colonial New England.

William Penn: Quaker Colonist, by Kieran Doherty. The author offers an in-depth look at the life of William Penn, the English Quaker who founded Pennsylvania.

Talk About It

Chapter 5: The Thirteen Colonies Grow

Farming and fishing Many colonists in New England made a living by farming or fishing. What types of jobs do people in your community have? Do you know any people who farm or fish? Discuss how the work that people do now is different from that done in colonial times.

Chapter 6: The Middle and Southern Colonies

Growing cities The cities of New York and Philadelphia became very important to the Middle Colonies. What are the important cities in your area? Talk about how large cities serve as the centers of information for the areas around them, such as the center for newspapers and TV and radio stations.

Make It

Words of wisdom Benjamin Franklin wrote many wise sayings about ways to live. Working with your child, write some words of wisdom, such as "A penny saved is a penny earned." Discuss these wise sayings with your child and then put them together in a small pamphlet or binder.

Technology
Check out
www.eduplace.com/parents/hmss05/
for more information.

ESTUDIOS SOCIALES
en casa

Carta a la familia: Unidad 3

Las colonias inglesas

Investíguenlo

En esta unidad, su niño aprenderá:

- cómo fueron establecidas las trece colonias y cómo era la vida en ellas
- cómo fueron fundadas las colonias centrales y del Sur y cómo era la vida en ellas

Aquí tiene algunas formas de ayudar a que su niño aprenda:

Lean para aprender más

La cabalgata de Paul Revere (Paul Revere's Ride) por Henry Wadsworth Longfellow El famoso poema de Longfellow, ilustrado por Ted Rand.

El valor de Sarah Noble (The Courage of Sarah Noble) por Alice Dalgliesh Sarah acompaña a su papá a Connecticut en 1707 para construir allí su nuevo hogar.

Coméntenlo

Capítulo 5: Colonias de Nueva Inglaterra

La siembra y la pesca Muchos colonos de Nueva Inglaterra vivían de la agricultura y la pesca. ¿Qué tipos de trabajos tiene la gente de su comunidad? ¿Conocen a alguien que viva de la agricultura o de la pesca? Hablen de cómo el trabajo que hace la gente hoy en día es diferente del trabajo que se hacía en la época de los colonos.

Capítulo 6: Colonias del centro y del Sur

El crecimiento de las ciudades Las ciudades de Nueva York y Filadelfia se volvieron muy importantes para las colonias centrales. ¿Cuáles son las ciudades más importantes de la región donde viven? Hablen acerca de cómo las ciudades grandes sirven como centros de información para las regiones cercanas, ya que muchas veces de ahí se generan los diarios, la televisión y las estaciones de radio.

Háganlo

Palabras de sabiduría Benjamín Franklin escribió muchos dichos sabios acerca del diario vivir. Escriban con su niño palabras de sabiduría como, por ejemplo: "Un centavo ahorrado es un centavo ganado". Hablen de los dichos que se inventen y luego pónganlos en forma de panfleto o cuaderno.

Tecnología
Para obtener más información, visite **www.eduplace.com/parents/hmss05/**

SOCIAL STUDIES at Home

Family Newsletter for Unit 4

Revolution and Independence

Learn About It

In this unit, your child will learn:

- the factors that led the American colonies to decide to become independent of Britain
- how and where the American Revolution was fought
- the Declaration of Independence and the Constitution of the United States

Here are some ways that you can help your child learn:

Read to Learn More About It

The Many Lives of Benjamin Franklin, by Mary Pope Osborne. Engagingly captures the multiple dimensions of Franklin's character and accomplishments, and highlights his goals and beliefs.

Those Remarkable Women of the American Revolution, by Karen Zeinert. During the Revolution, women contributed to the war effort on the home front and on the battlefield.

A Young Patriot: The American Revolution as Experienced by One Boy, by Jim Murphy. Fifteen-year-old Joseph Plumb Martin enlists in the Revolutionary Army and fights alongside Washington, Lafayette, and Steuben.

Talk About It

Chapter 7: Causes of the American Revolution

Resolving conflicts Discuss what to do when two people want to watch different television programs. Discuss how the colonies tried to resolve their conflict with Britain.

Chapter 8: The War for Independence

Heroes George Washington was and still is a hero to many people. Talk with your child about your personal heroes. Ask your child about his or her heroes. Discuss what qualities in a hero are important to each of you.

Chapter 9: The Constitution of the United States

Rules and rights Together, read the Bill of Rights and discuss the meaning of some or all of the amendments. How have these rights affected your life and the lives of others?

Make It

National symbols Benjamin Franklin thought the wild turkey should be the symbol of the United States. Working together, design a new national symbol. Draw or make a postage stamp or coin that shows your new symbol.

Technology
Check out **www.eduplace.com/parents/hmss05/** for more information.

ESTUDIOS SOCIALES en casa

Carta a la familia: Unidad 4

La Revolución Norteamericana

Investíguenlo

En esta unidad, su niño aprenderá:

- acerca de la decisión de las colonias norteamericanas de independizarse de Inglaterra
- cómo y dónde se peleó la Revolución Norteamericana
- acerca de la Declaración de Independencia y la Constitución de los Estados Unidos

Aquí tiene algunas formas de ayudar a que su niño aprenda:

Lean para aprender más

La independencia americana por Nelson Martínez Díaz y Eduardo L. Moyano Bozzani Una mirada histórica a las guerras que se libraron en las Américas para ganar la independencia.

Una unión más perfecta (A More Perfect Union) por Betsy Maestro La autora ofrece detalles acerca de la planificación, redacción y firma de la Constitución de los Estados Unidos.

Coméntenlo

Capítulo 7: Causas de la Revolución

Resolver conflictos Hablen de qué hacer cuando dos personas quieren ver dos programas distintos de televisión. Luego hablen de cómo las colonias trataron de resolver su conflicto con Inglaterra.

Capítulo 8: La Guerra de Independencia

Los héroes George Washington fue y aún es un héroe para mucha gente. Hable con su niño acerca de los héroes de cada uno. Hablen de las cualidades de un héroe que son importantes para ustedes.

Capítulo 9: Formar una nación

Las reglas y los derechos Lean juntos el *Bill of Rights* (Enmiendas sobre Derechos Civiles) y hablen del significado de algunas o de todas las enmiendas. ¿Cómo han afectado esos derechos sus vidas y las de otros?

Háganlo

Símbolos nacionales Benjamin Franklin pensó que el pavo salvaje debió haber sido el símbolo del país. Diseñen juntos un nuevo símbolo nacional. Luego dibujen o hagan un sello postal o moneda que tenga ese símbolo.

Tecnología
Para obtener más información, visite
www.eduplace.com/parents/hmss05/

Name ______________________________ Date ________________

Two-Column Chart

Name ________________________ Date ________________

Three-Column Chart

Name ______________________ Date ______________

Two-Step Flow Chart

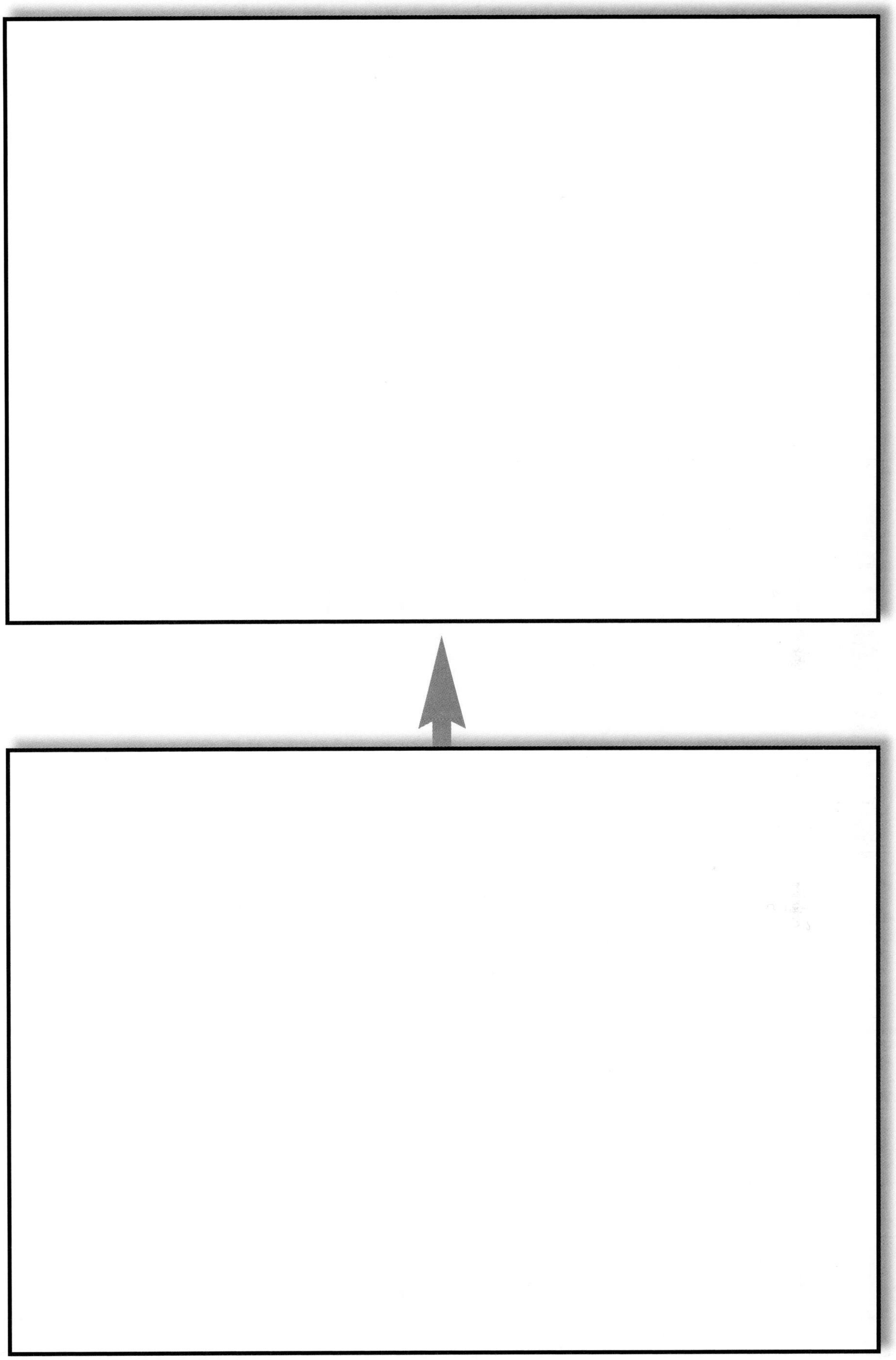

Name ______________________ Date ______________

Two-Part Flow Chart

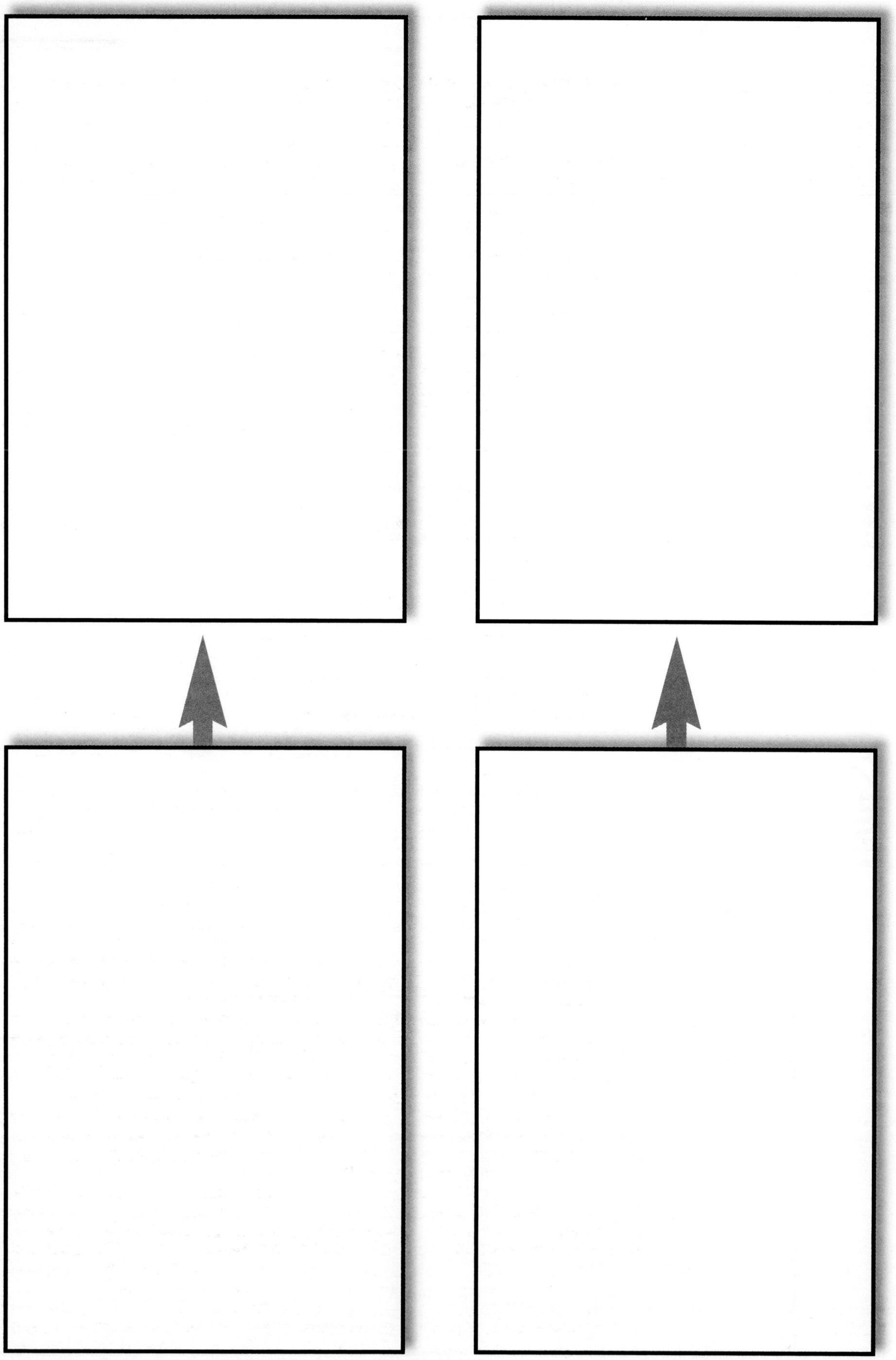

Name ____________________ Date ____________________

Three-Step Flow Chart

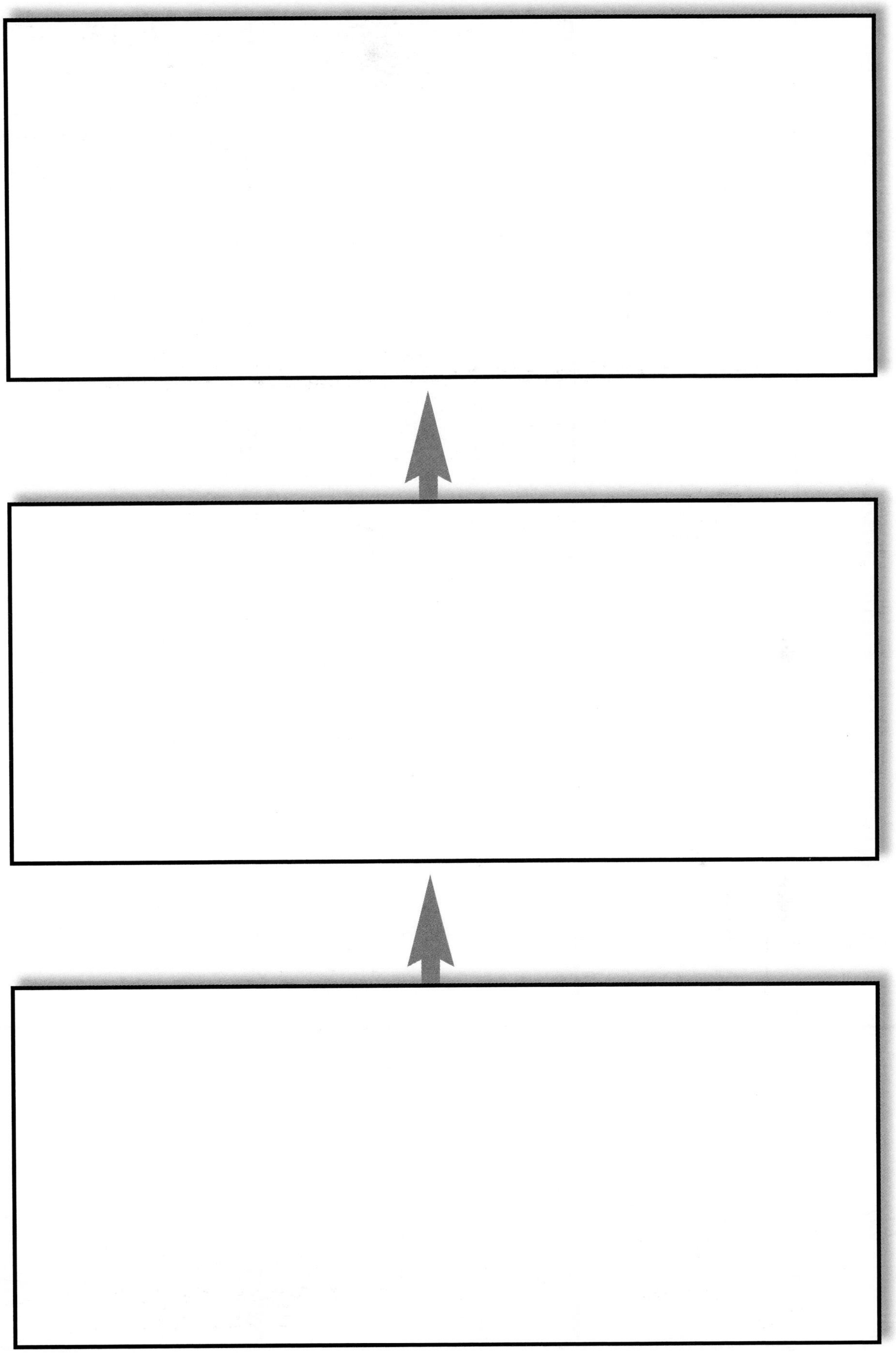

Name ______________________________ Date ____________________

Three-Level Flow Chart

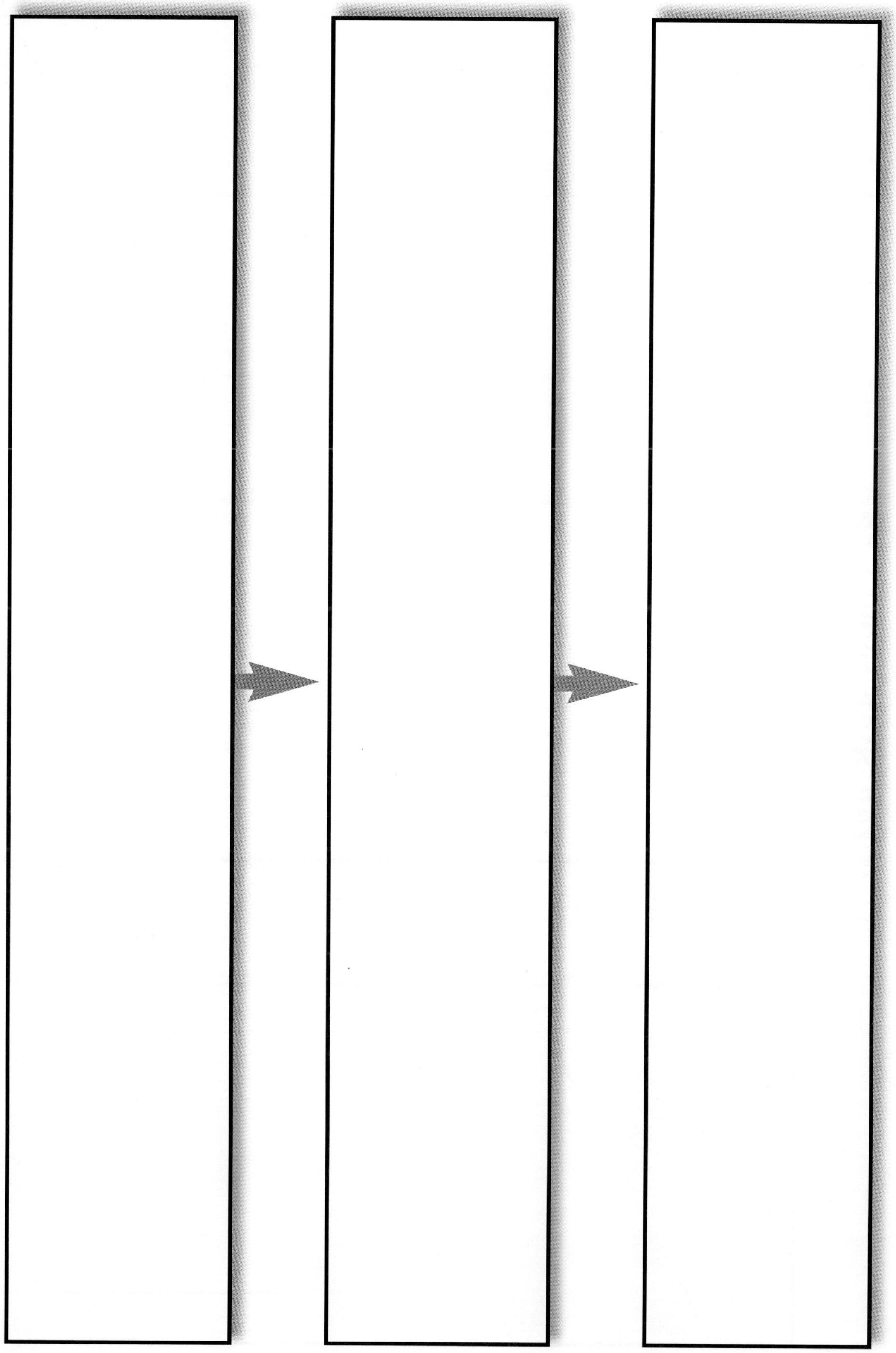

Name ______________________________ Date ____________________

Idea Web

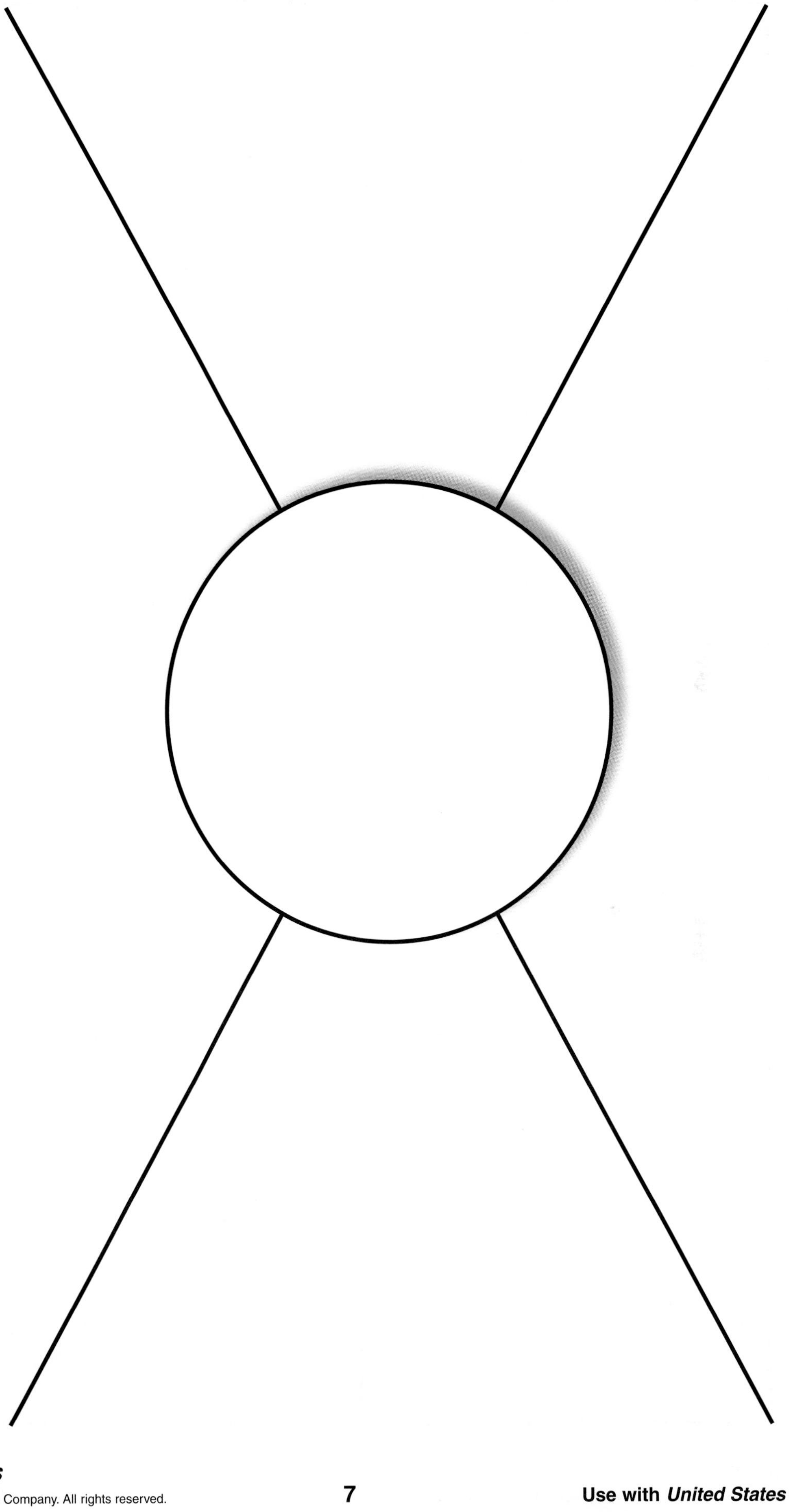

Name ______________________ Date ______________

Organizer 1

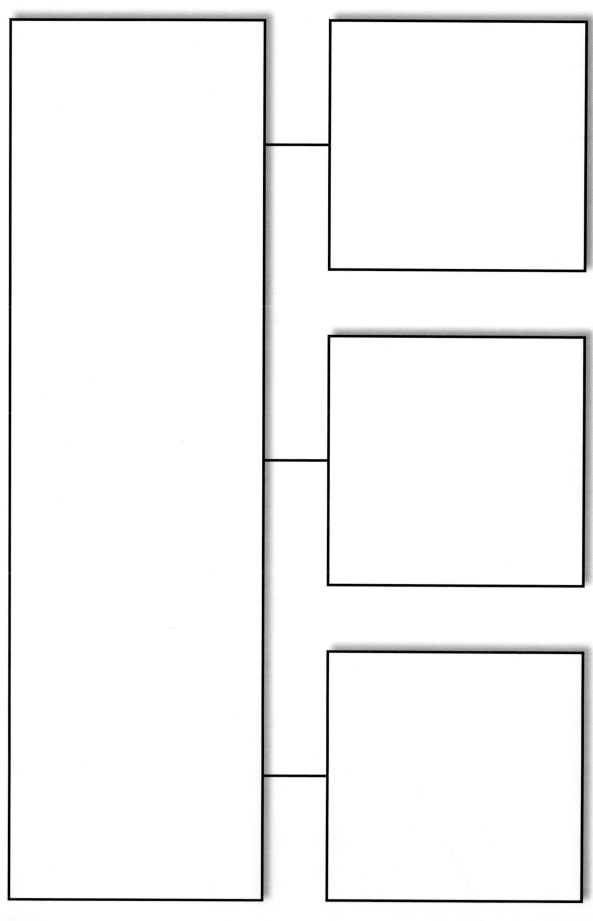

Name ______________________ Date ______________

Organizer 2

Name ______________________ Date ______________

Organizer 3

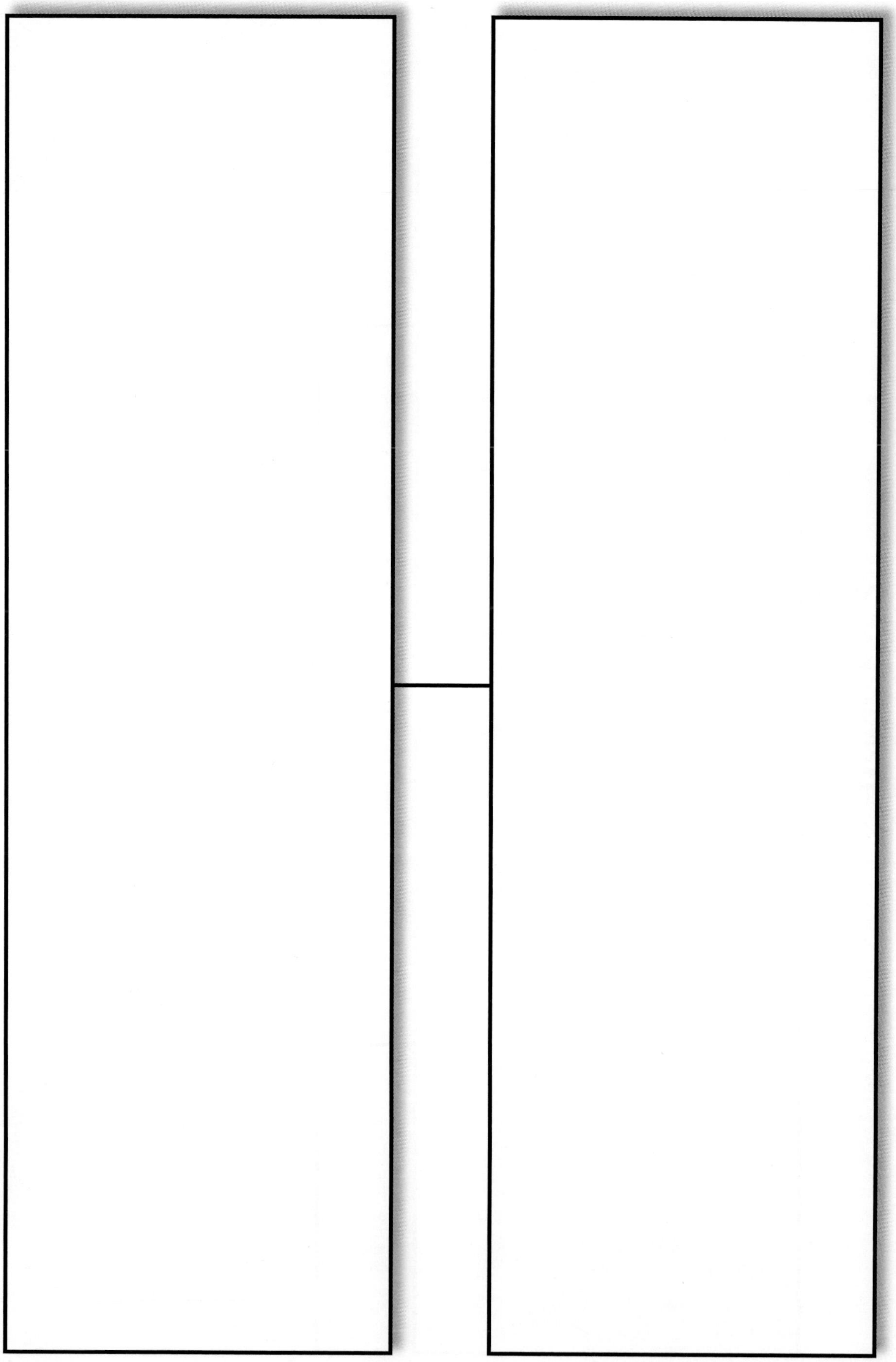

Name ______________________________ Date ____________________

Venn Diagram

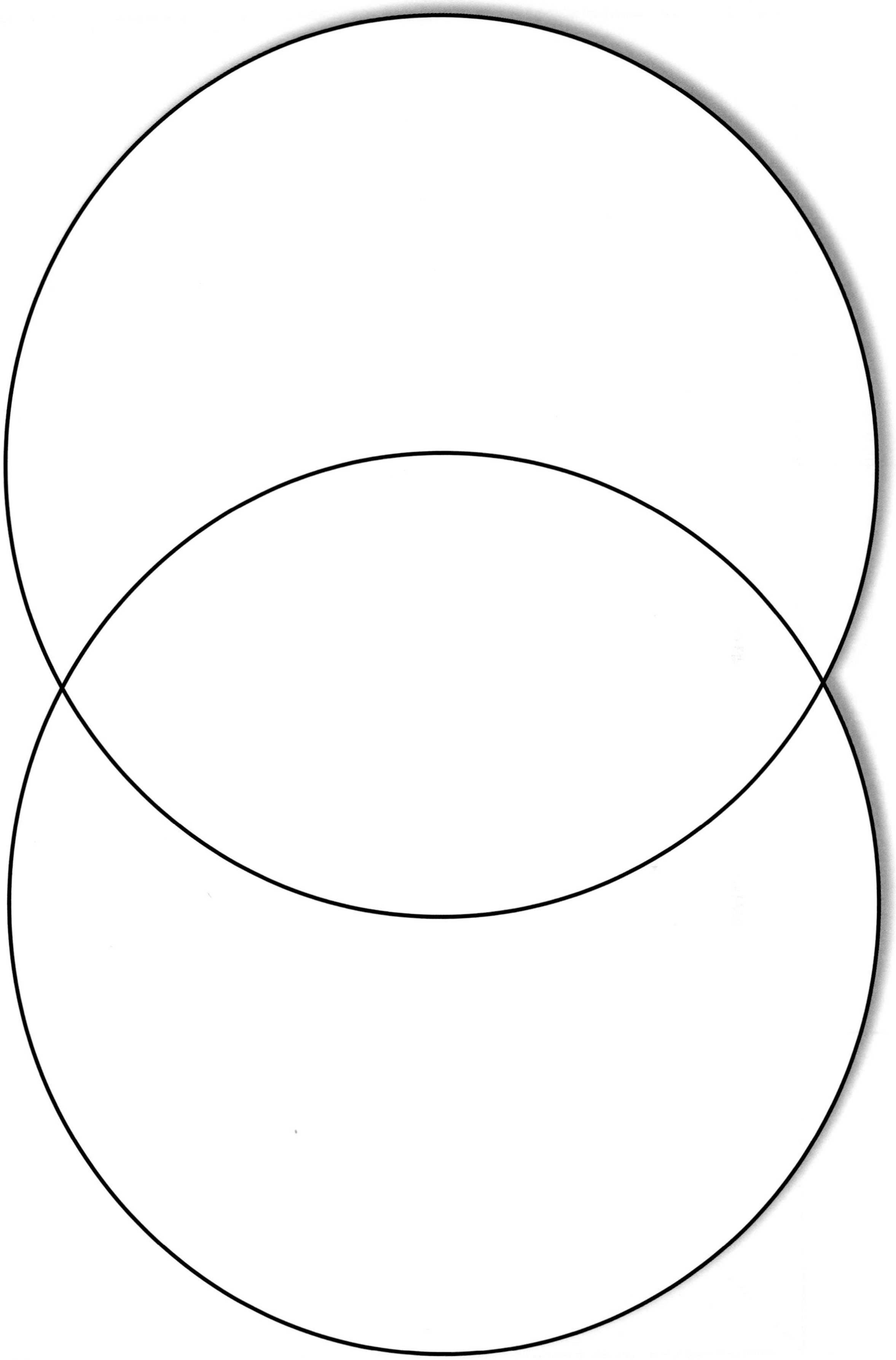

Name ______________________________ Date ____________________

Frame Game

Name ______________________ Date ______________

Word Web

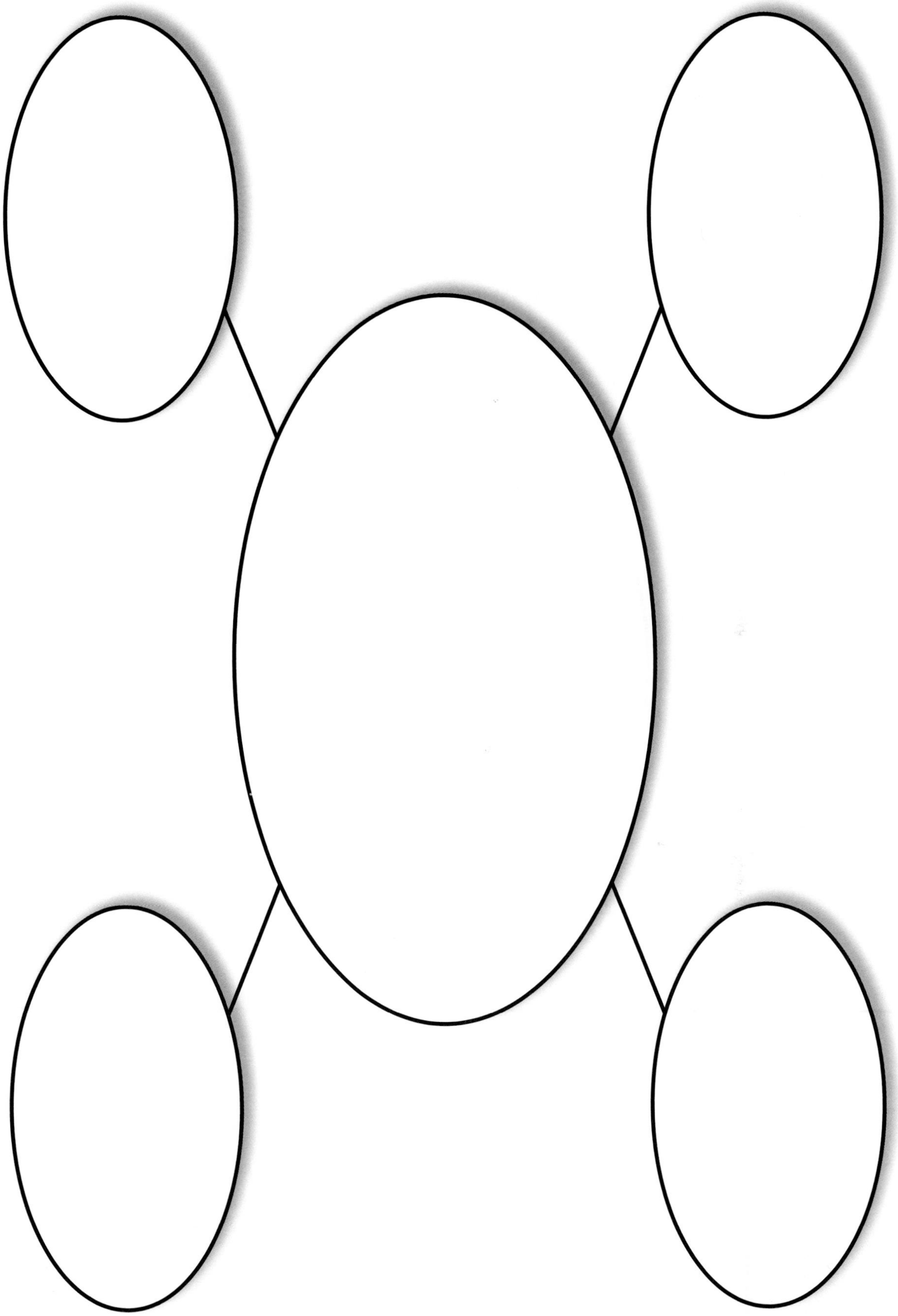

Name ______________________ Date ______________

Spider Map

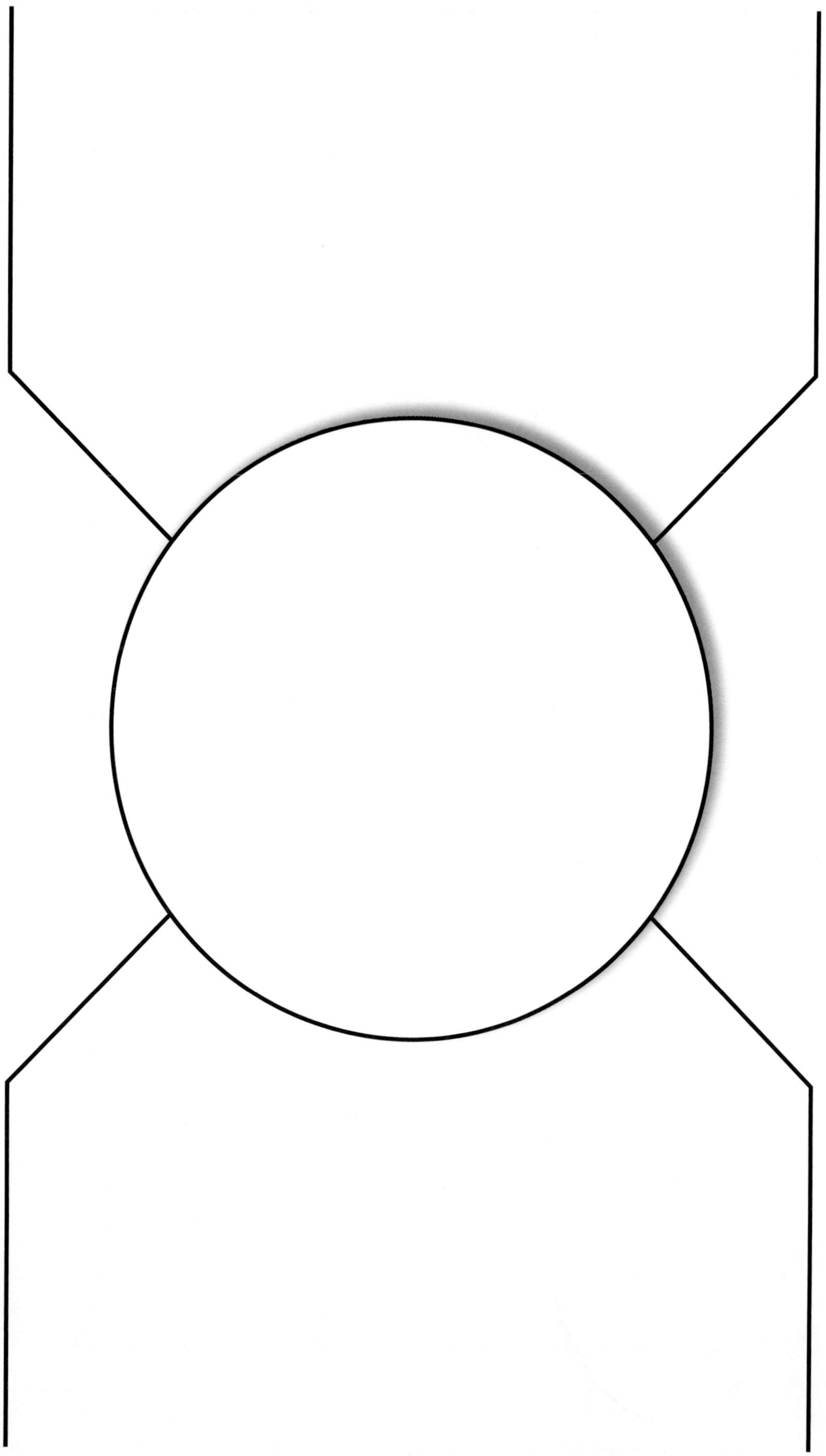

Name ______________________________ Date ____________________

Sequence Chart

1	
2	
3	
4	

Name ______________________________ Date ____________________

United States Overview

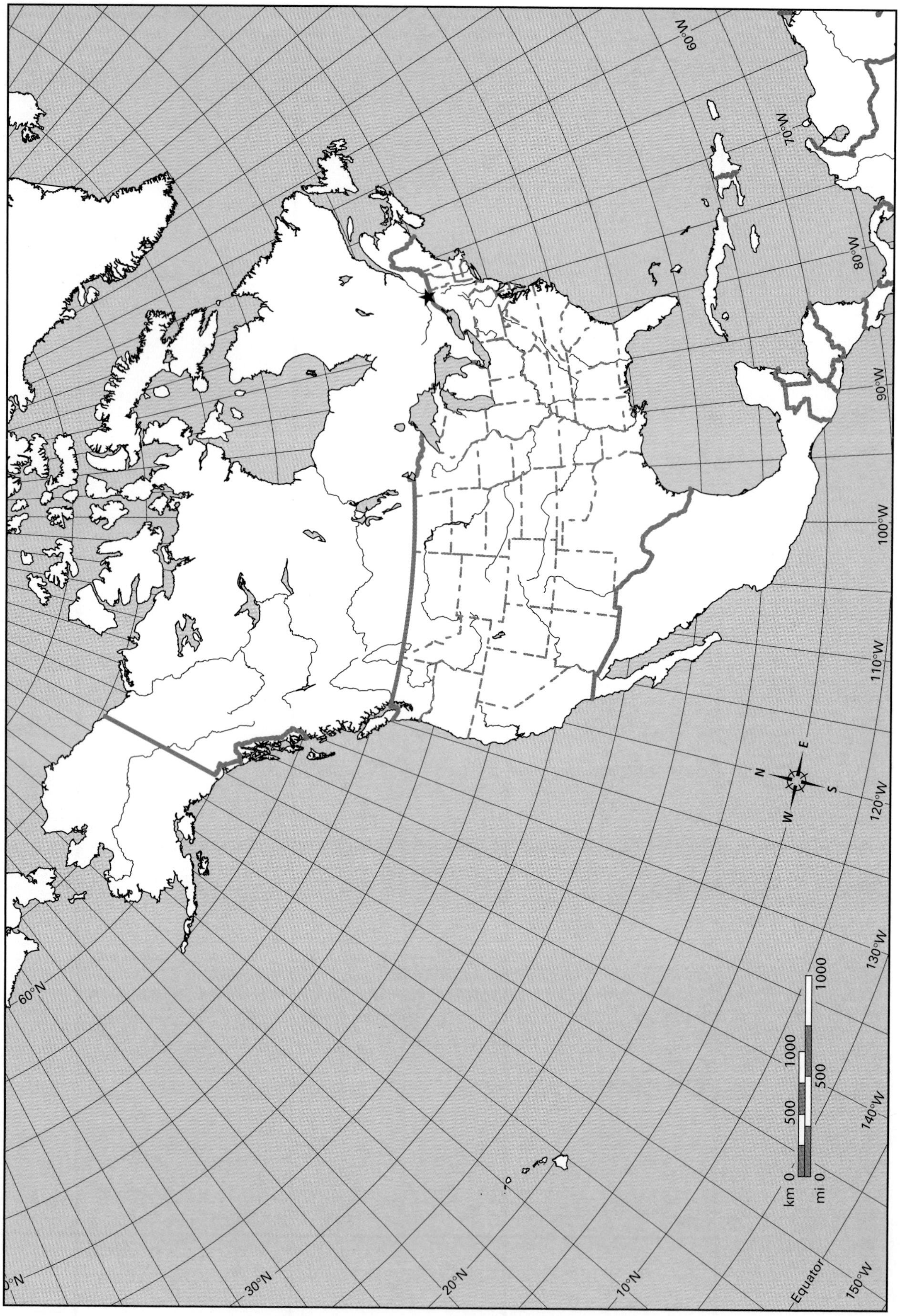

Name ______________________________ Date ____________________

United States

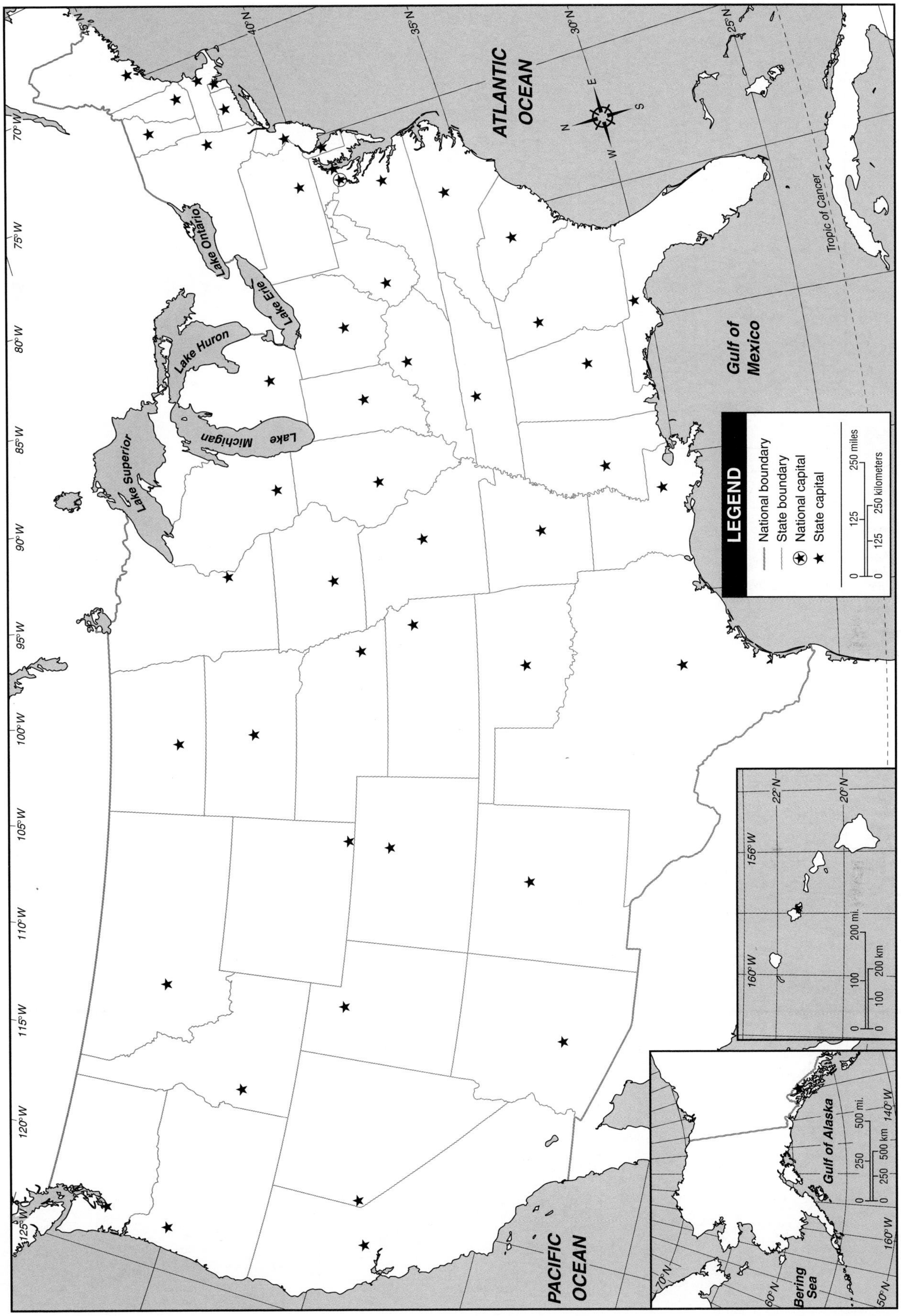

ATLANTIC OCEAN
Gulf of Mexico
PACIFIC OCEAN
Lake Ontario
Lake Erie
Lake Huron
Lake Michigan
Lake Superior
Tropic of Cancer
LEGEND
National boundary
State boundary
National capital
State capital
0 125 250 miles
0 125 250 kilometers
N
E
S
W
40° N
35° N
30° N
25° N
70° W
75° W
80° W
85° W
90° W
95° W
100° W
105° W
110° W
115° W
120° W
125° W
22° N
20° N
156° W
160° W
0 100 200 mi.
0 100 200 km
Gulf of Alaska
Bering Sea
0 250 500 mi.
0 250 500 km
70° N
60° N
50° N
140° W
160° W

Name ______________________ Date ______________

States and Major Cities

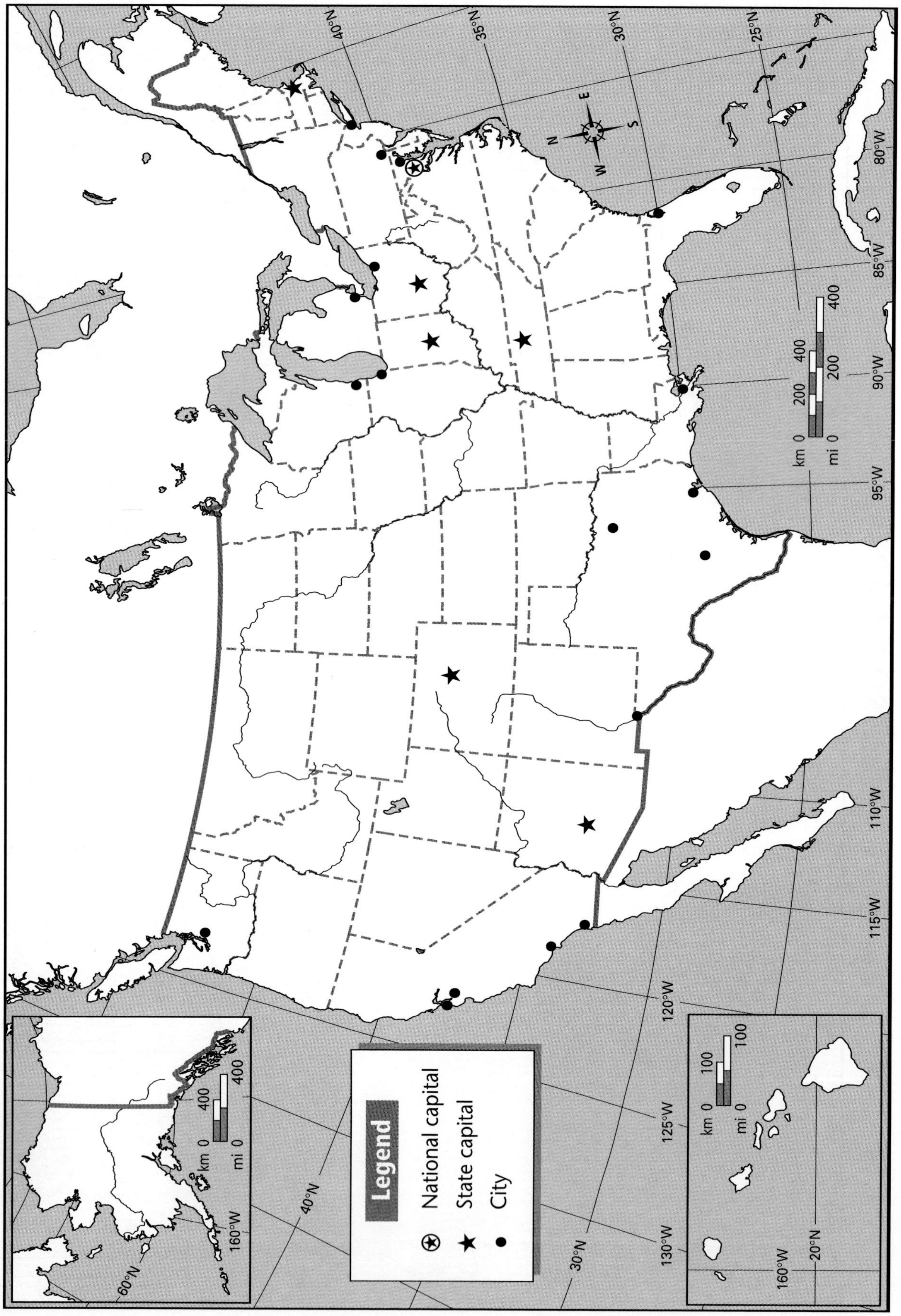

Name ______________________ Date ______________

United States Landforms

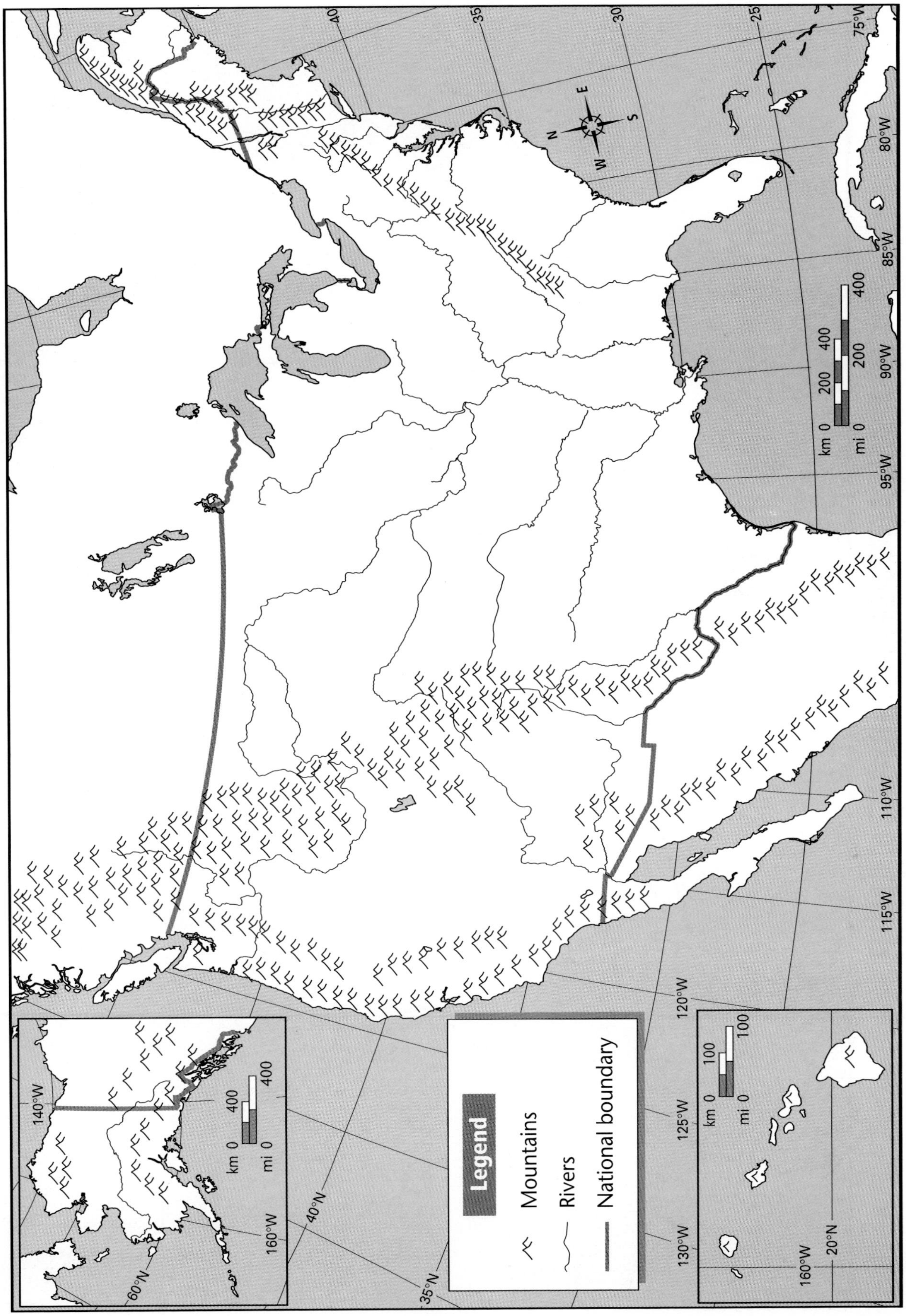

Name ______________________ Date ______________________

United States Political/Physical

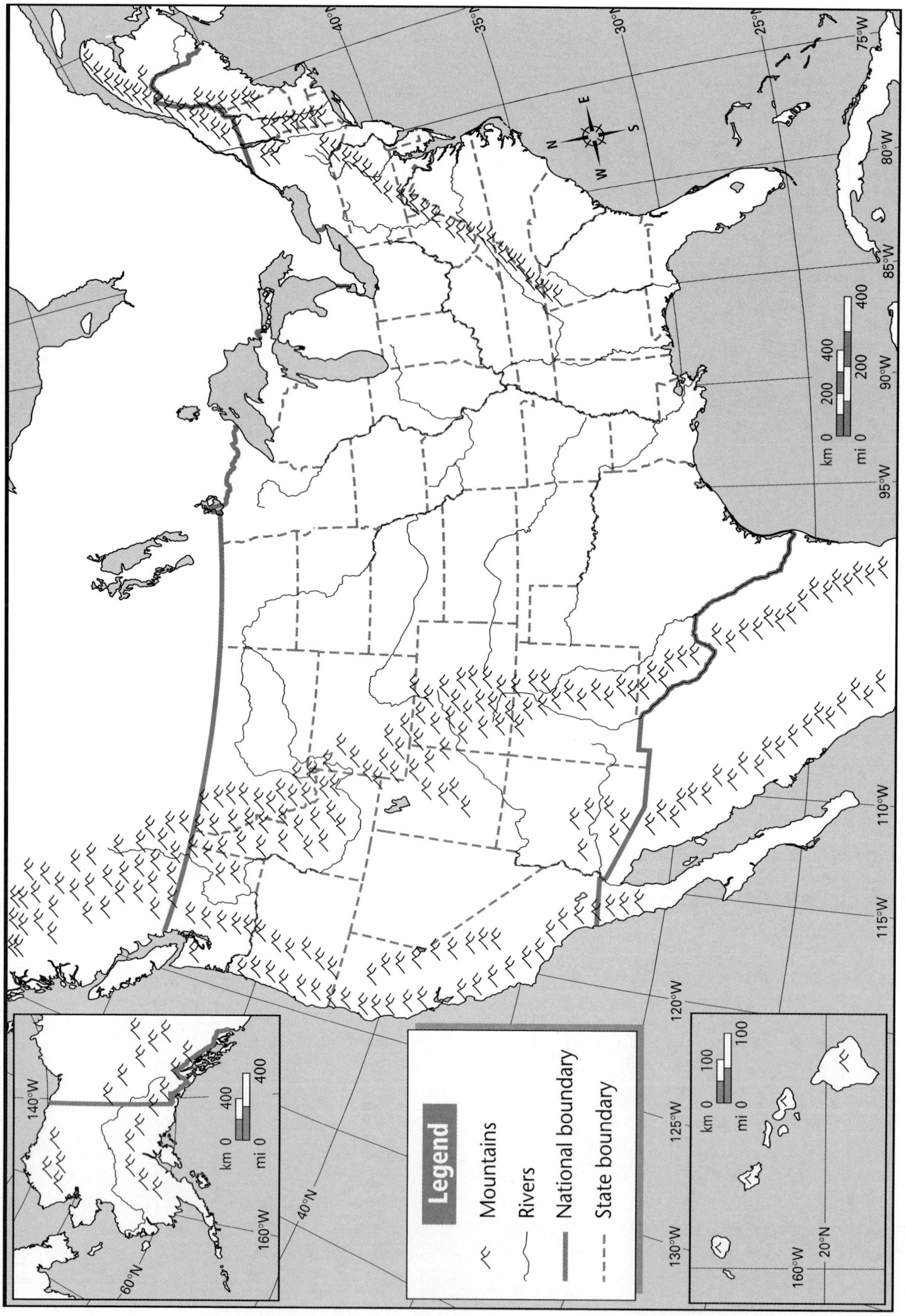

Name ______________________________ Date ____________________

United States Regions

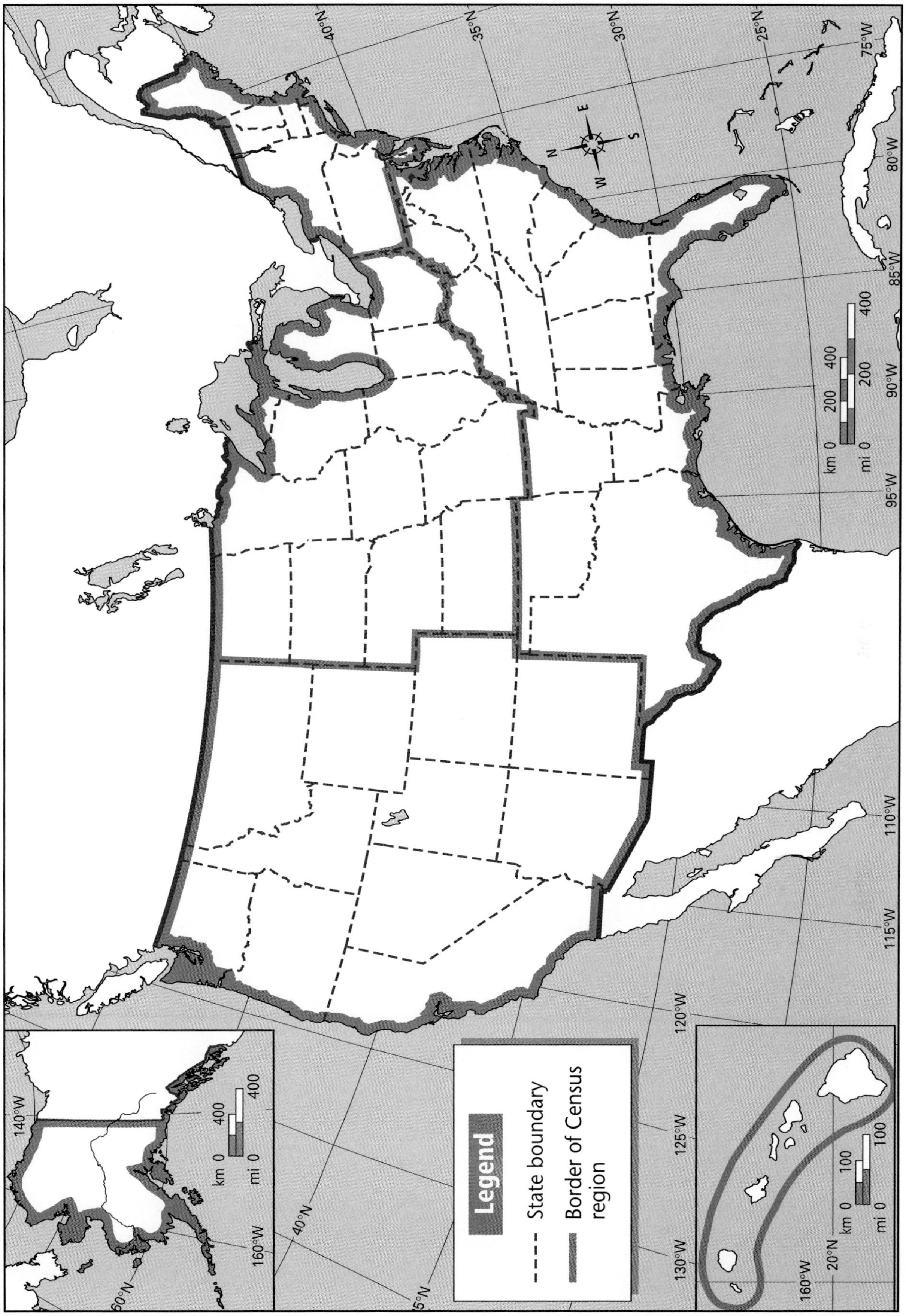

Name ______________________ Date ______________

Western Hemisphere: Countries

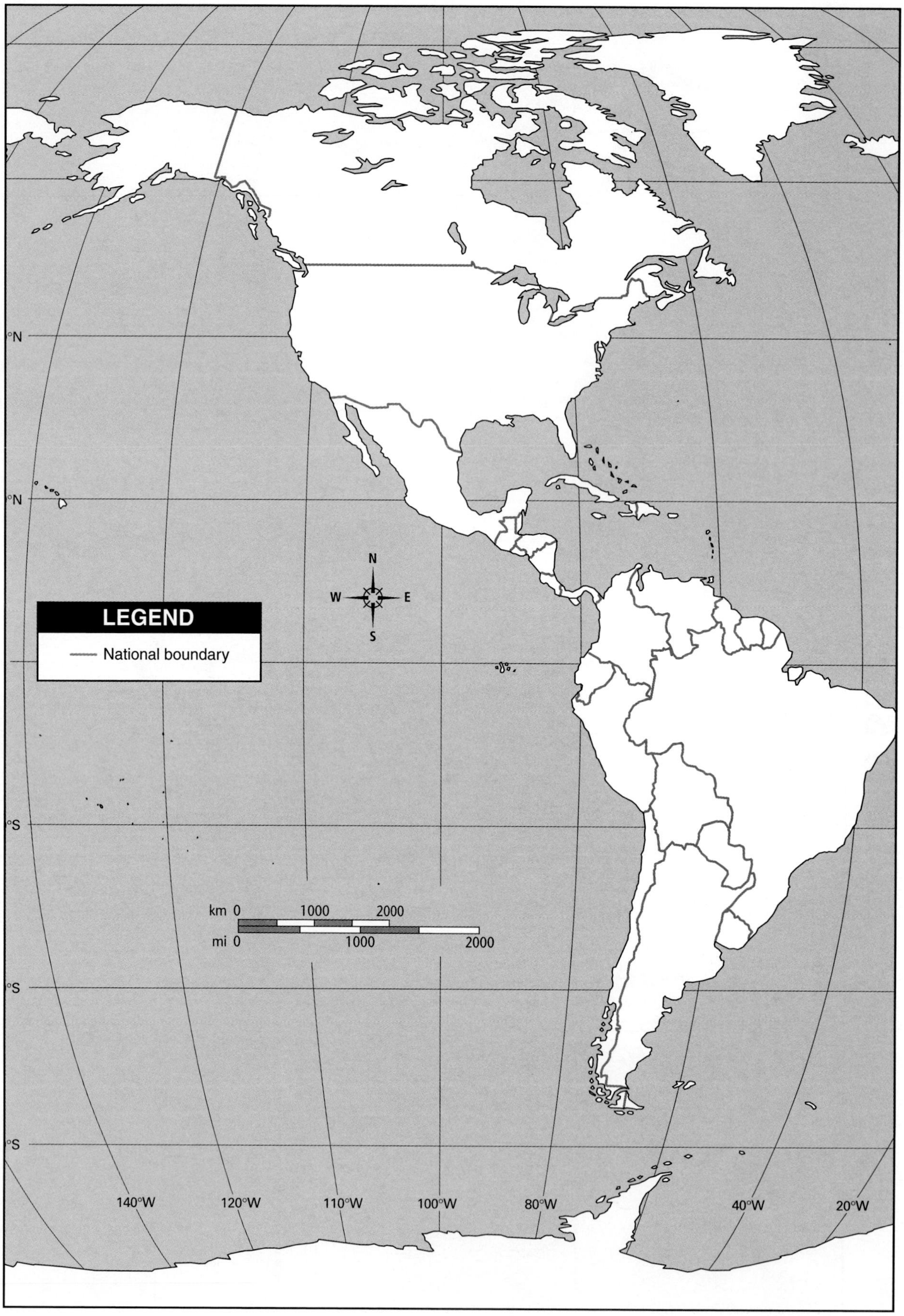

Name ______________________ Date ______________

World Continents

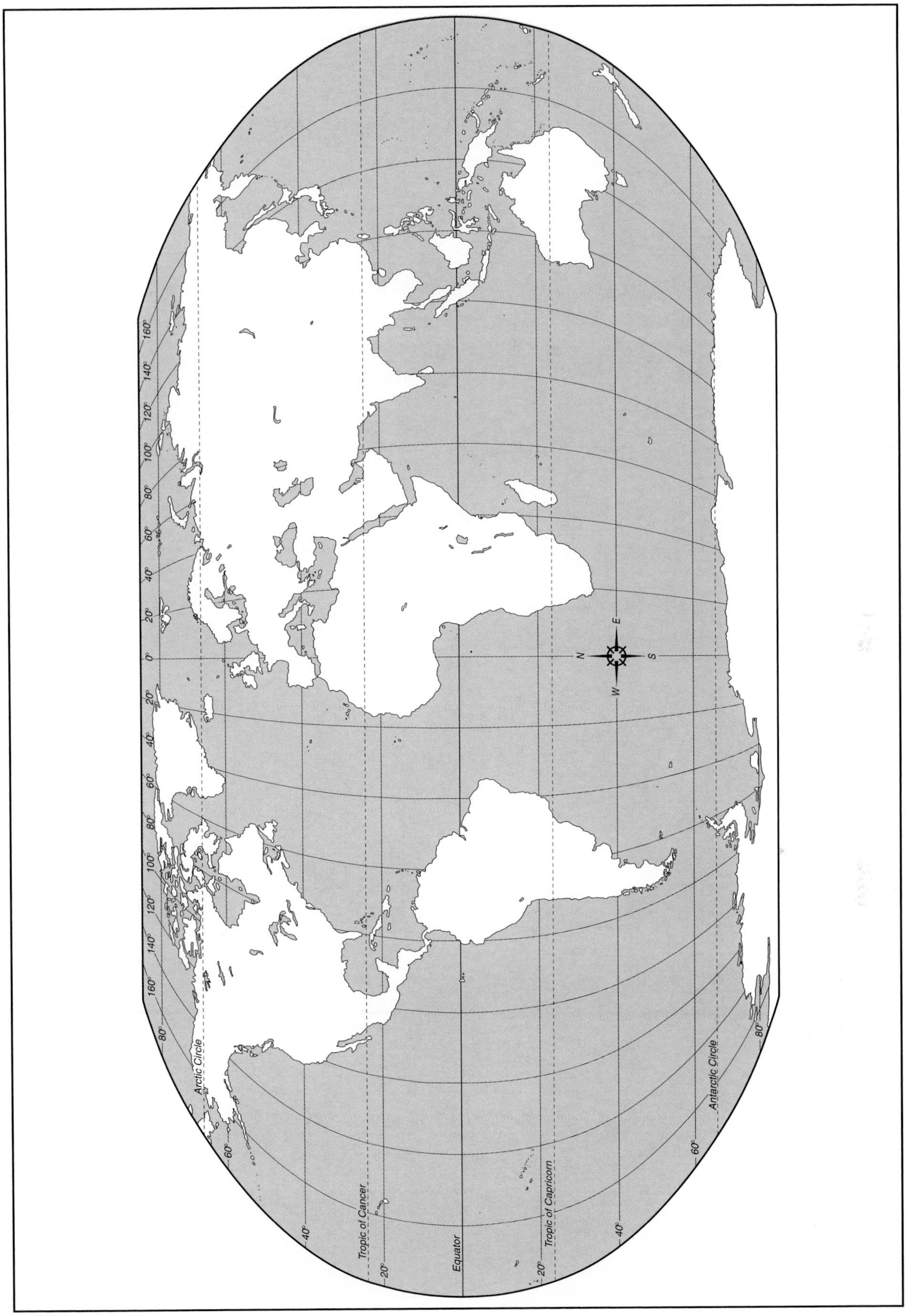

Name ______________________ Date ______________

World Countries

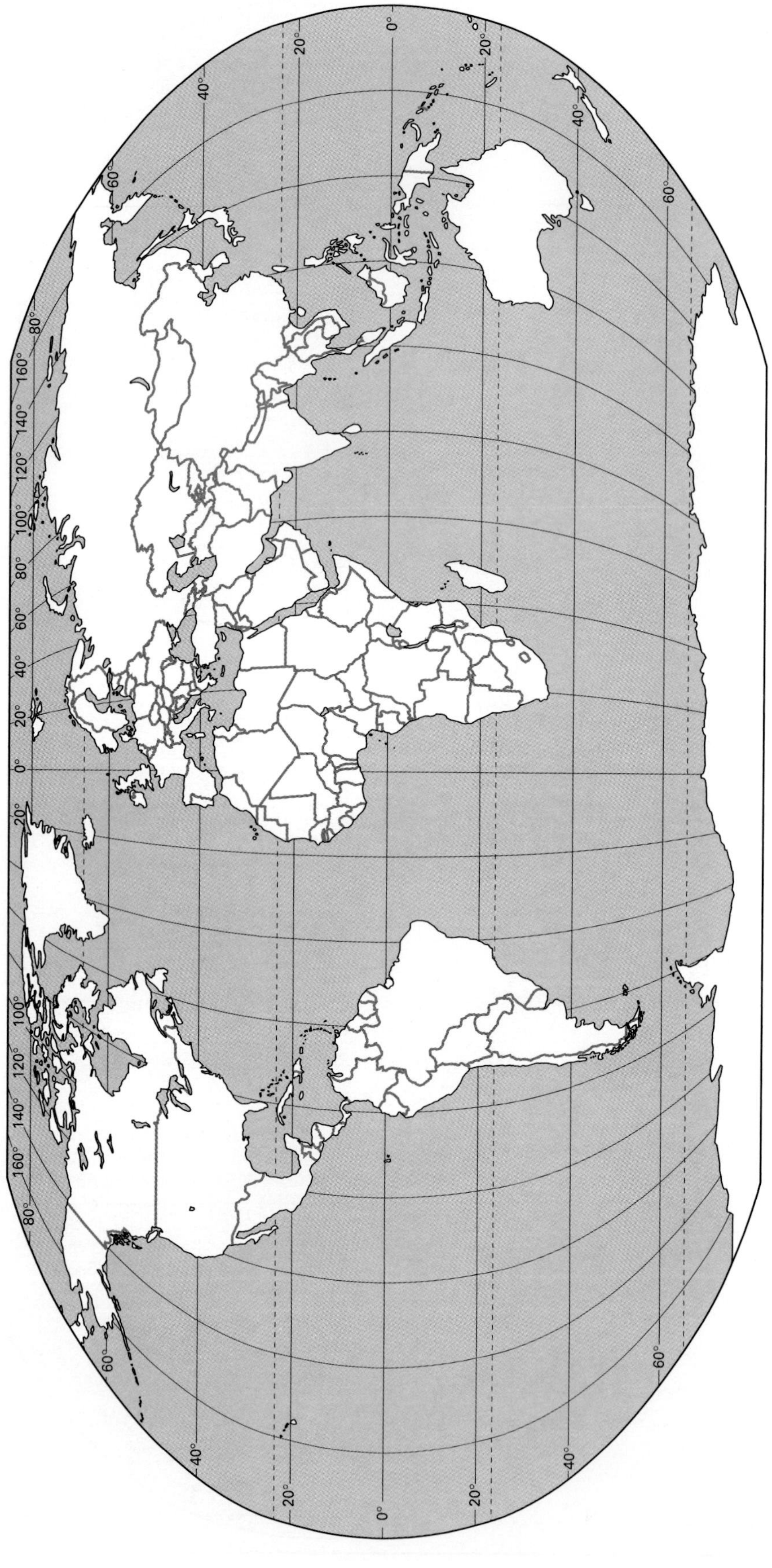

Name ______________________________ Date ____________________

World Landforms

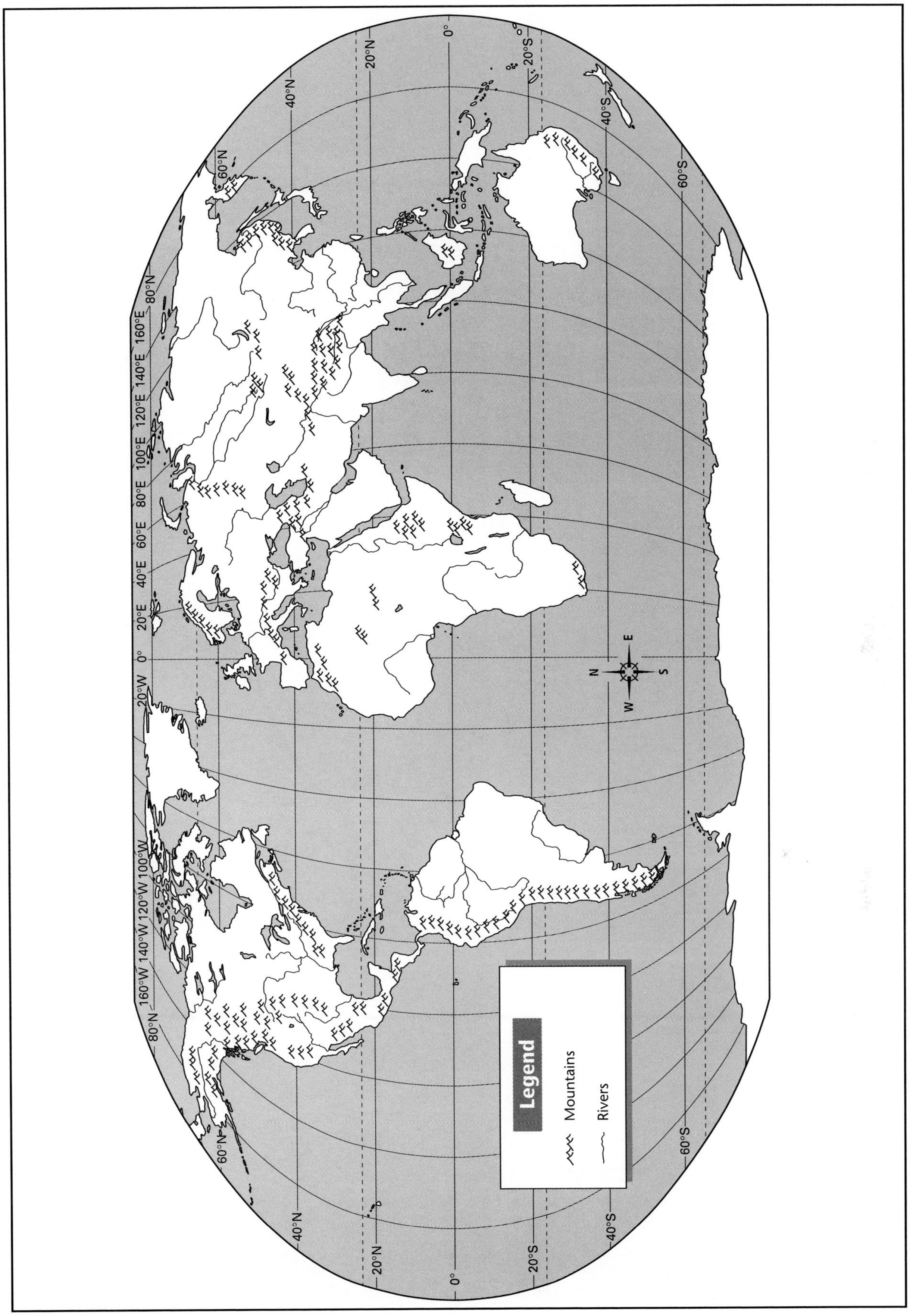

Name ______________________ Date ______________________

Colonial America 1776

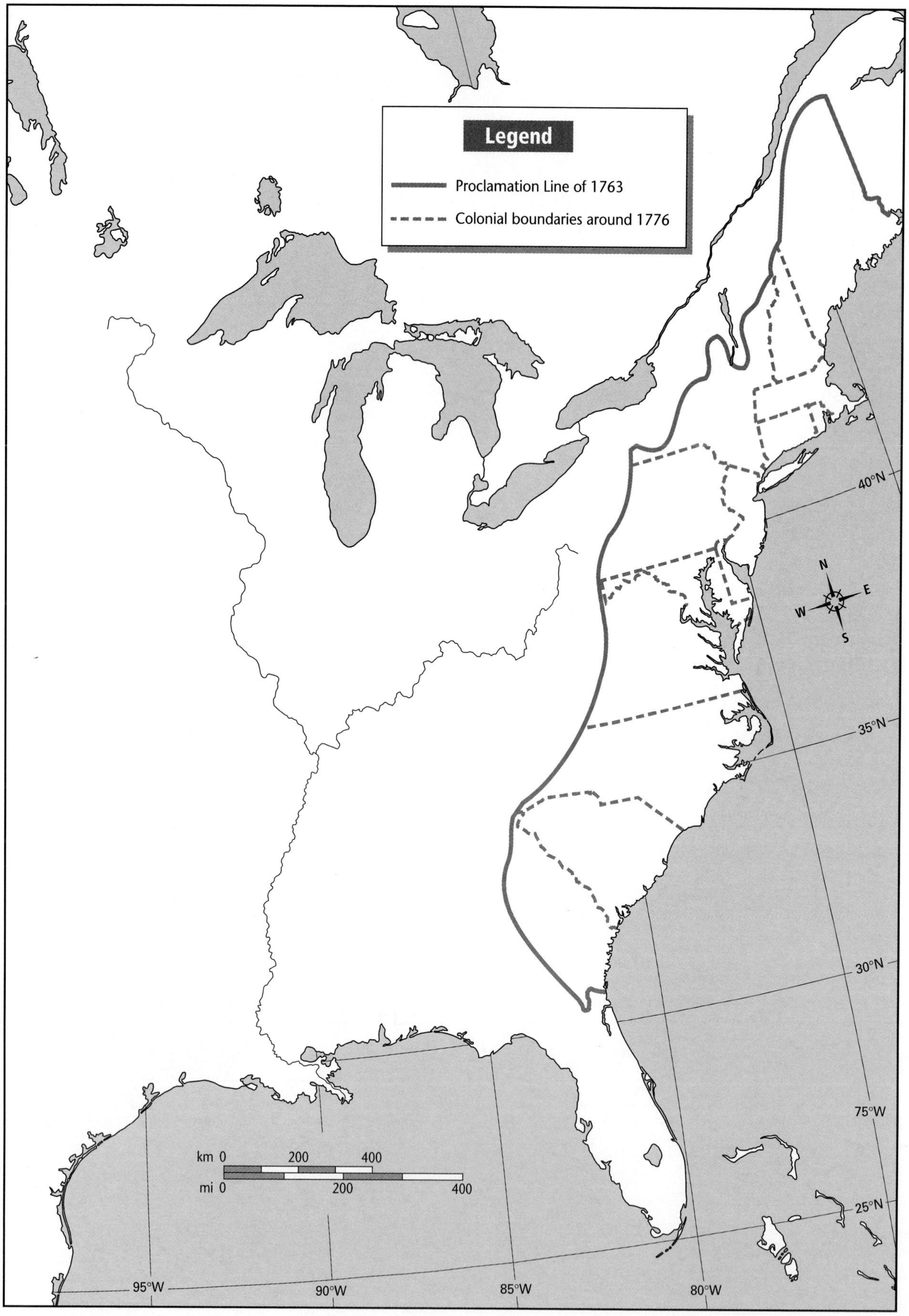

Name ______________________ Date ______________

United States 1790

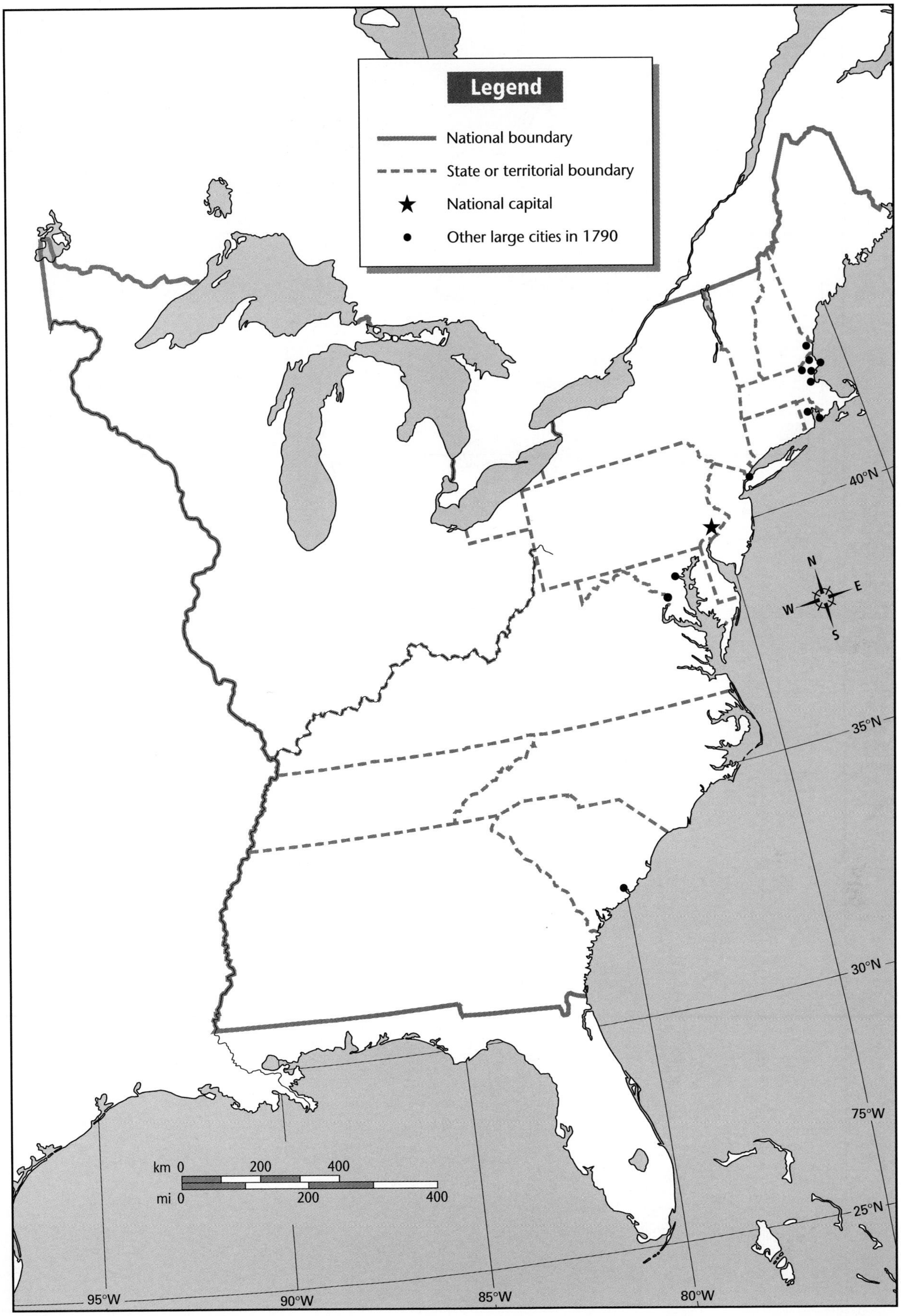

Name ______________________ Date ______________

United States 1820

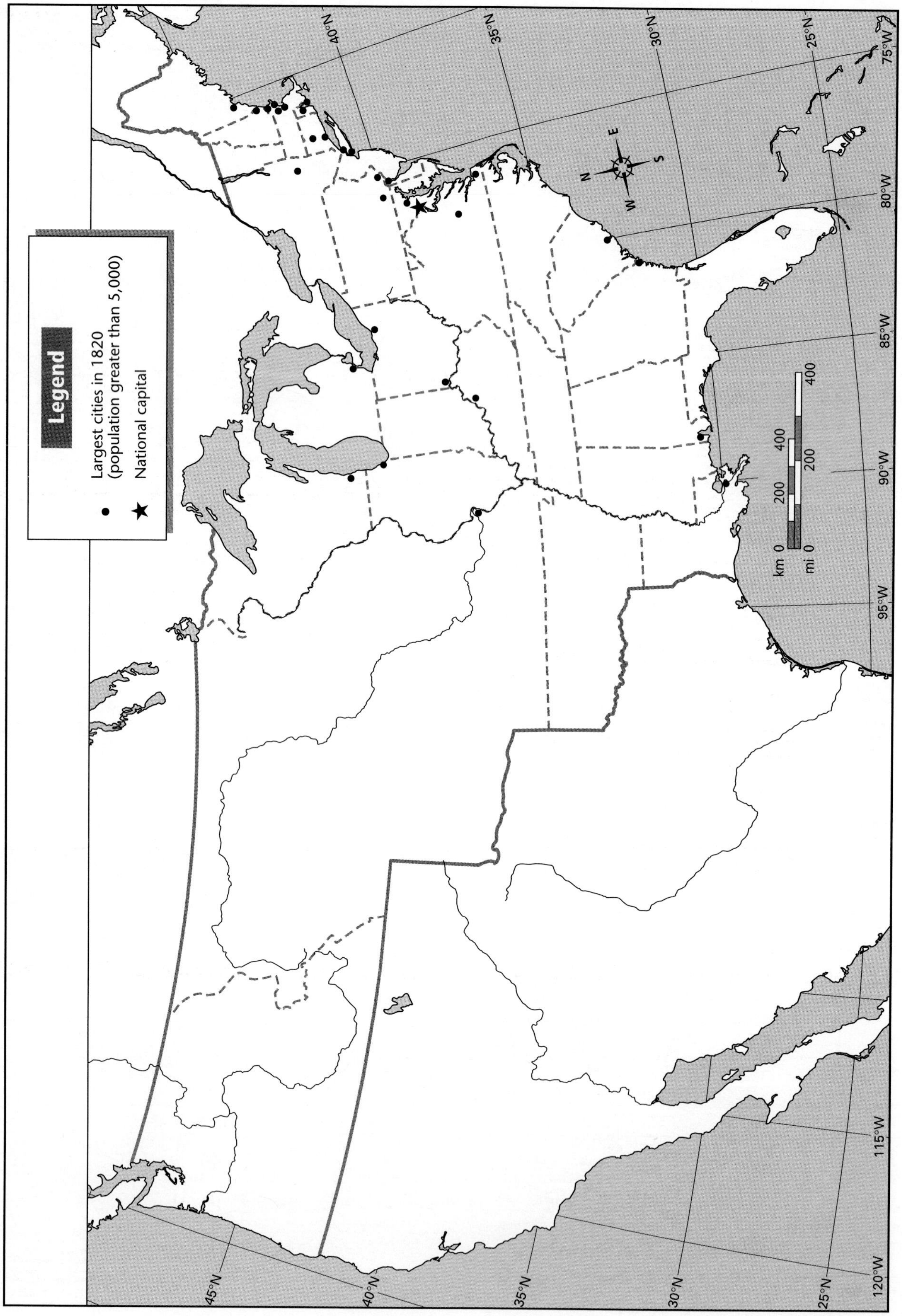

Name ______________________ Date ______________

United States 1860

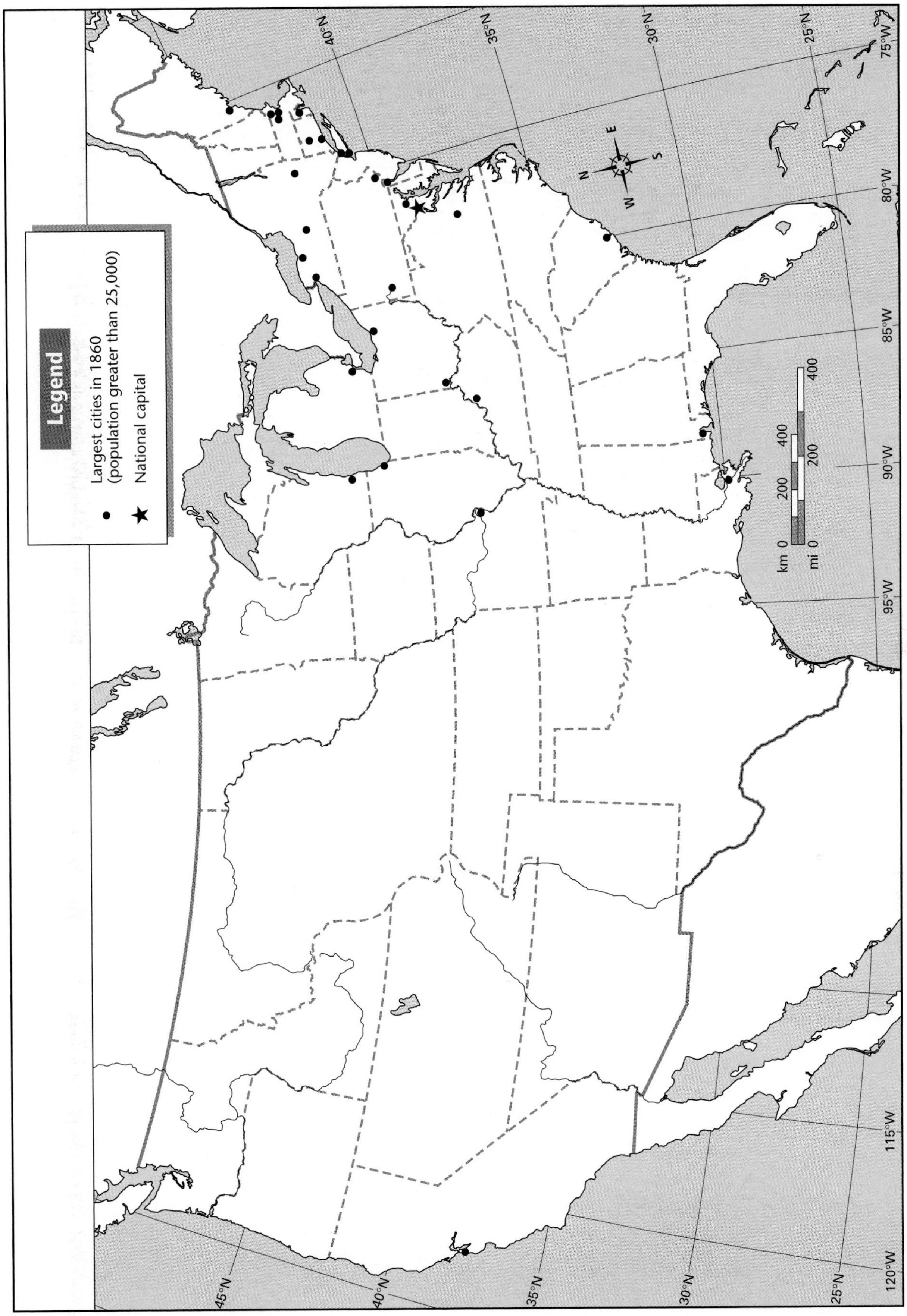

Name ______________________ Date ______________

United States 1900

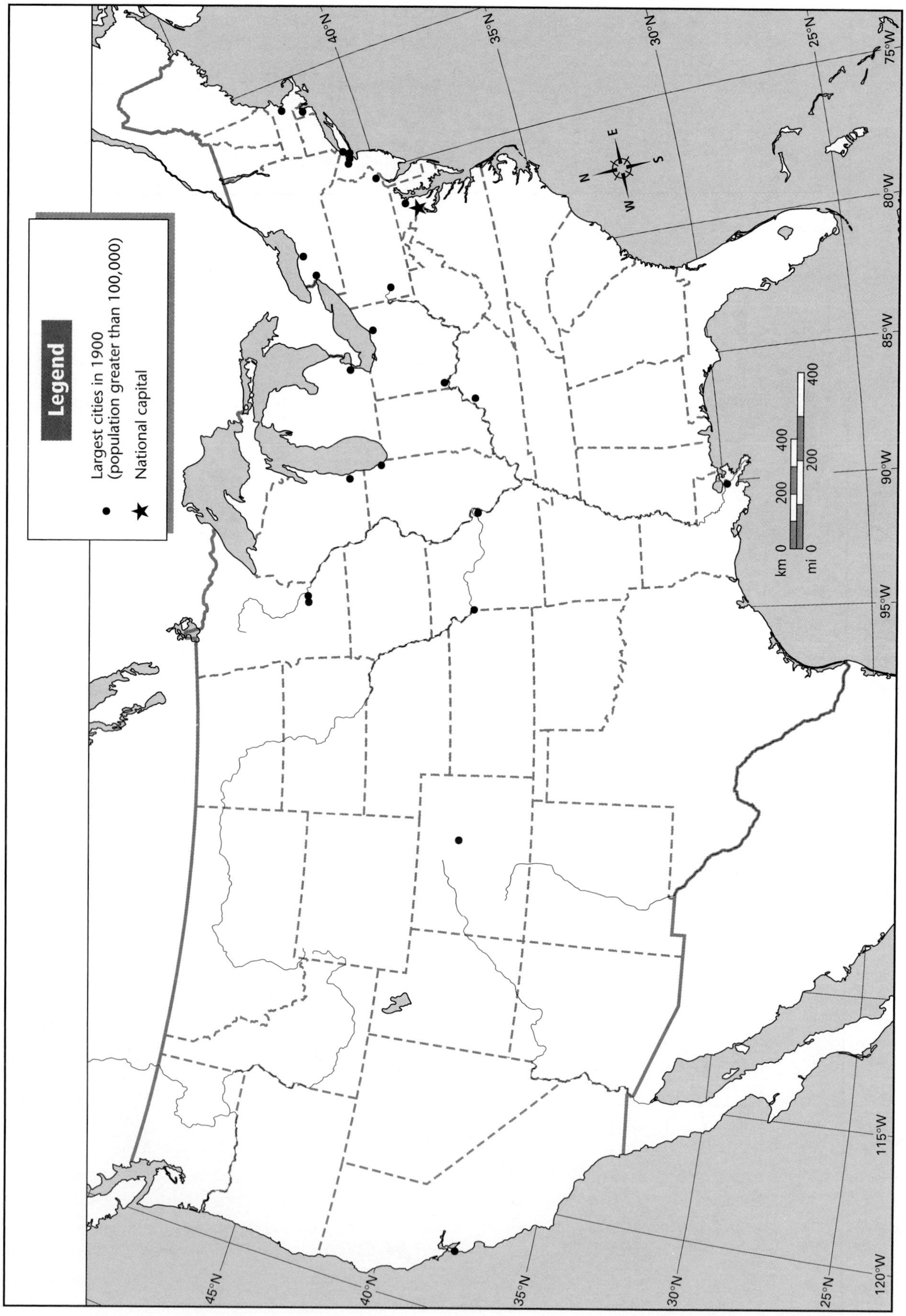

Name ______________________ Date ______________

North America: Countries

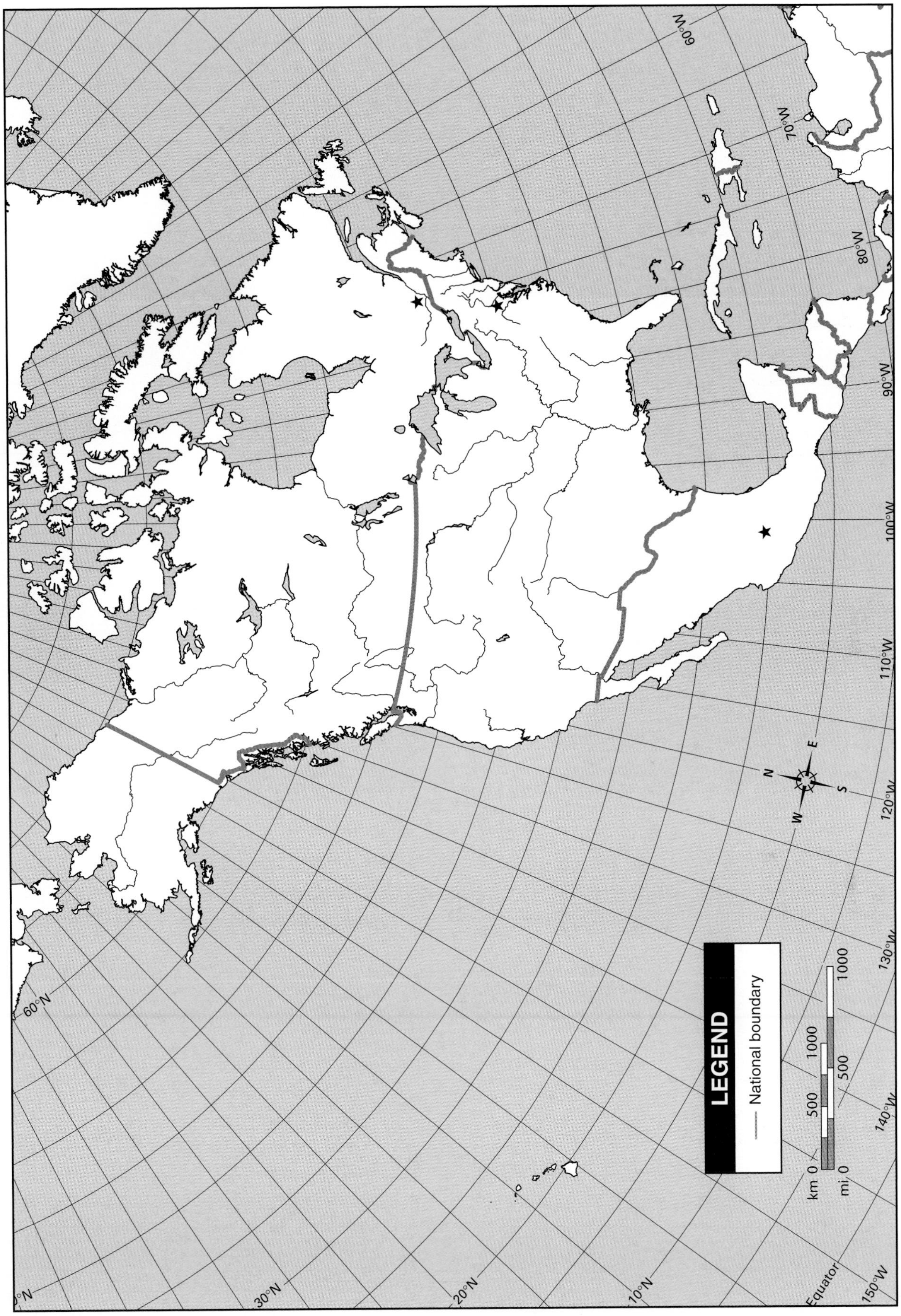

Name ______________________ Date ______________

South America: Countries

Name ______________________ Date ______________

Africa: Countries

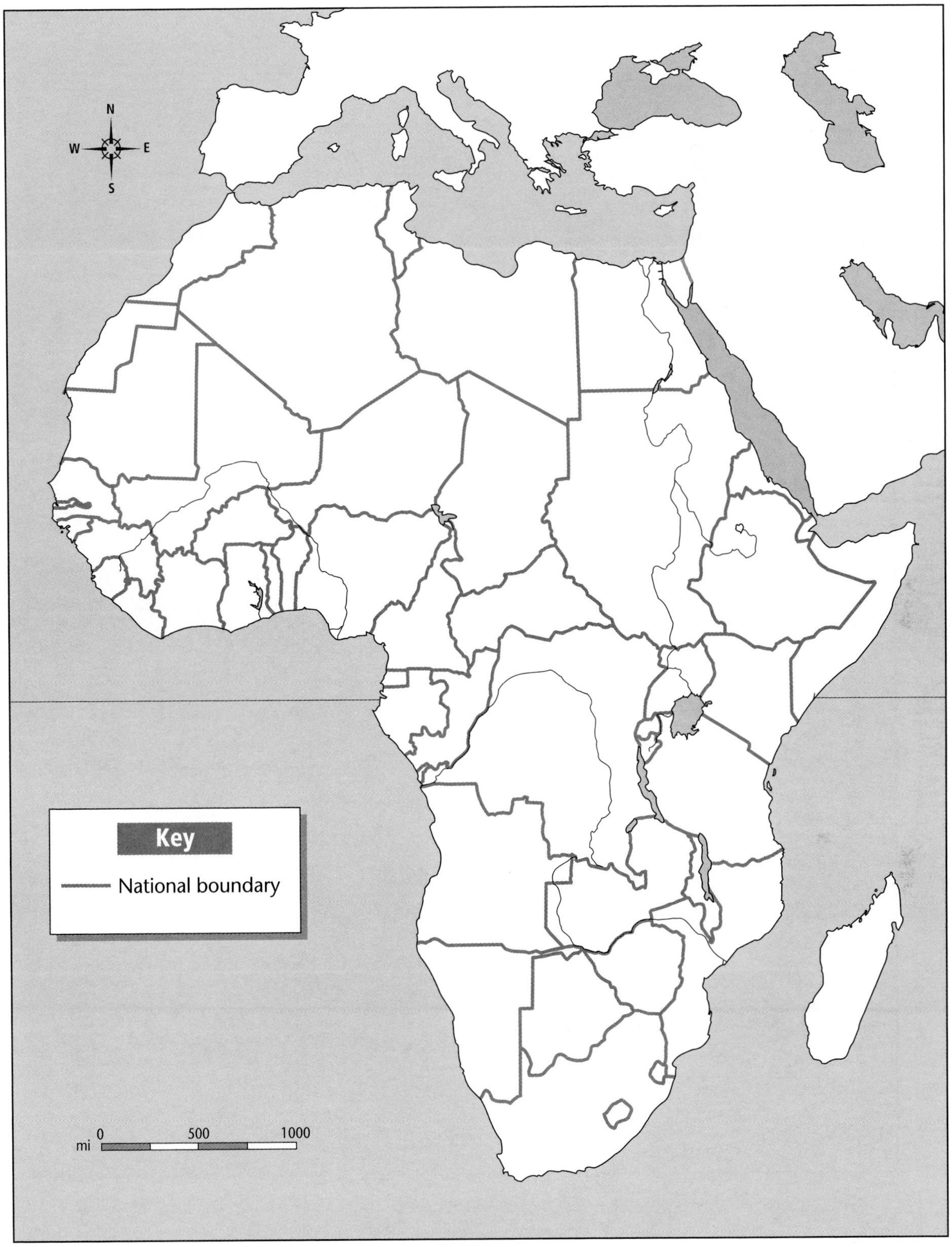

Name ______________________________ Date ____________________

Europe: Countries

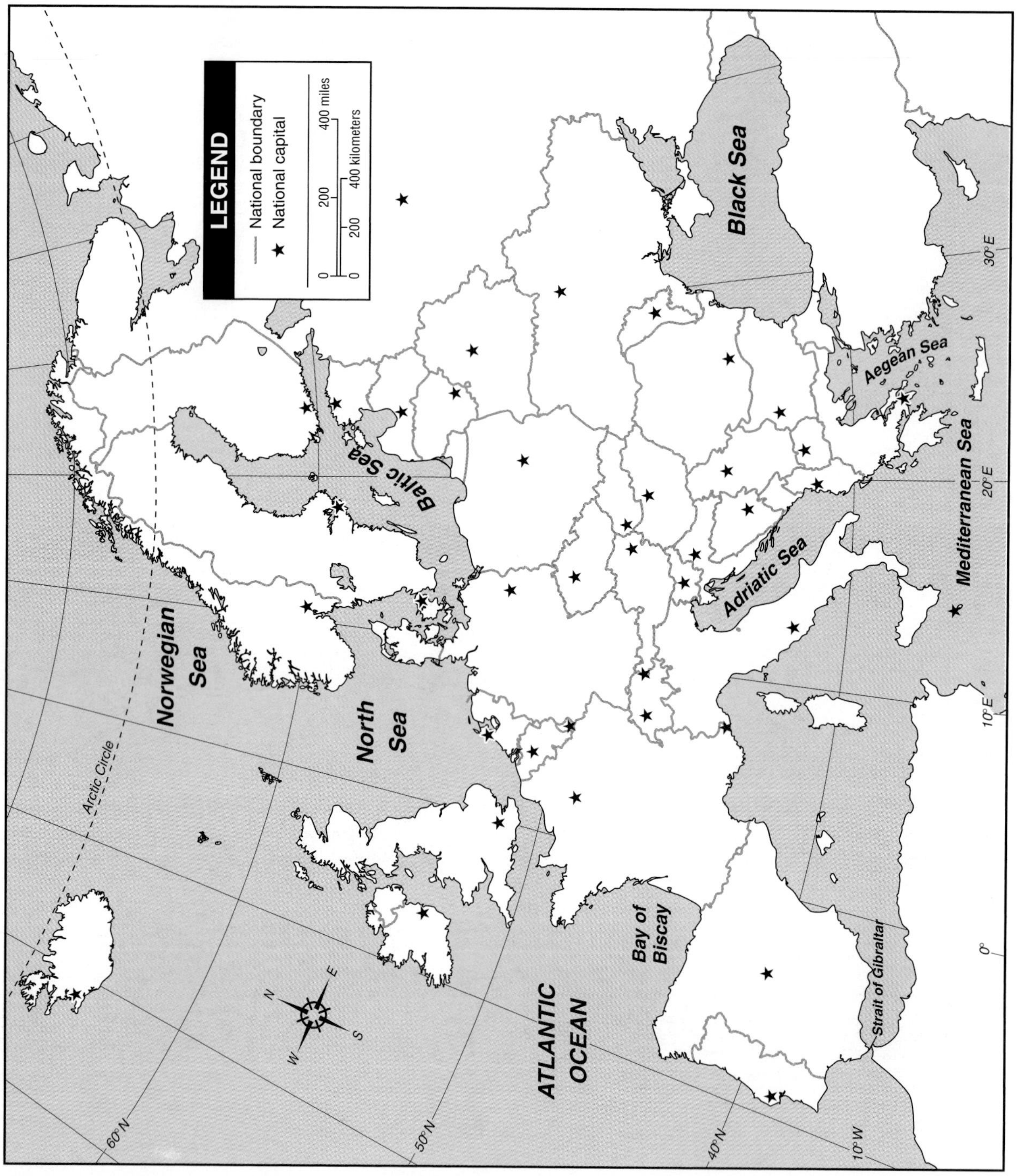
LEGEND
National boundary
National capital
0 200 400 miles
0 200 400 kilometers
Black Sea
Aegean Sea
Mediterranean Sea
Baltic Sea
Adriatic Sea
Norwegian Sea
North Sea
Bay of Biscay
Strait of Gibraltar
ATLANTIC OCEAN
Arctic Circle
N
E
S
W
60°N
50°N
40°N
10°W
0°
10°E
20°E
30°E

Name ______________________ Date ______________

Asia and the South Pacific: Countries

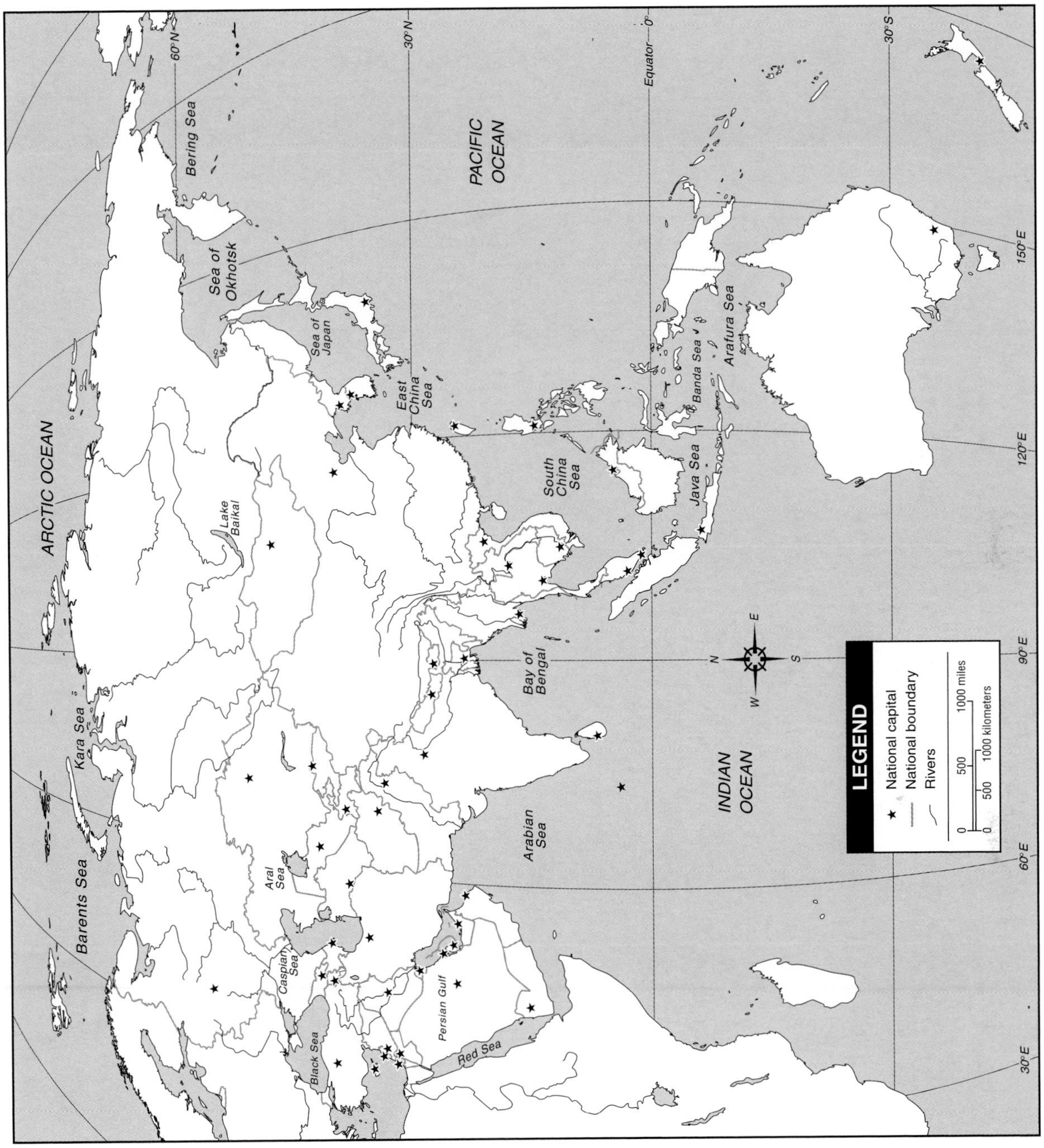

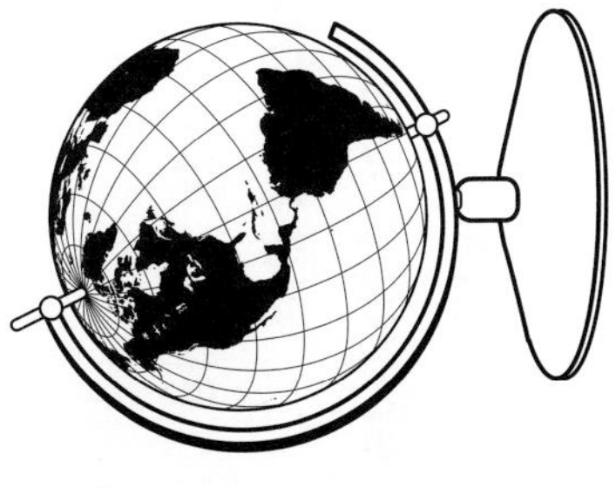

geography

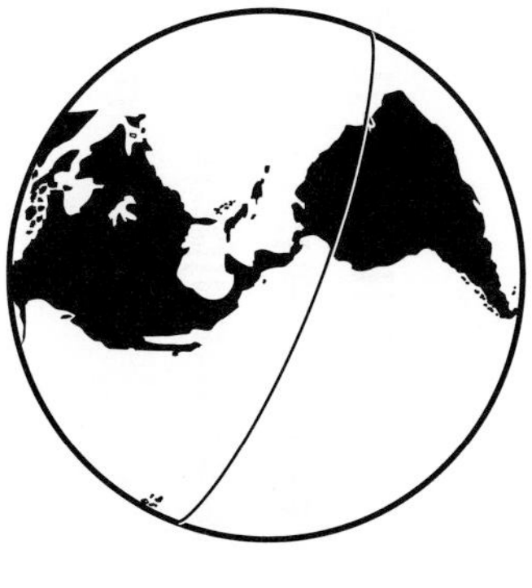

equator

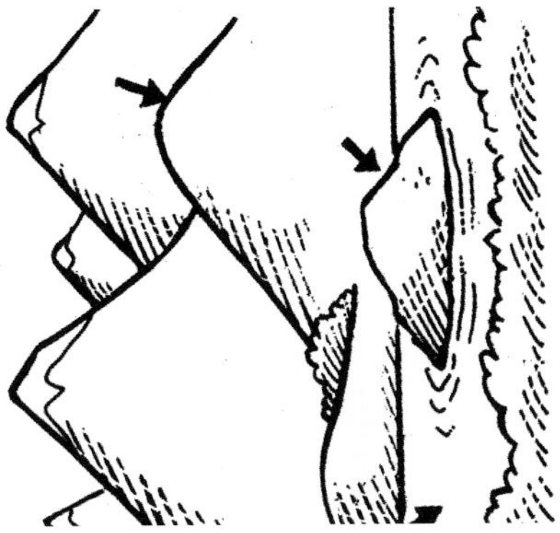

landform

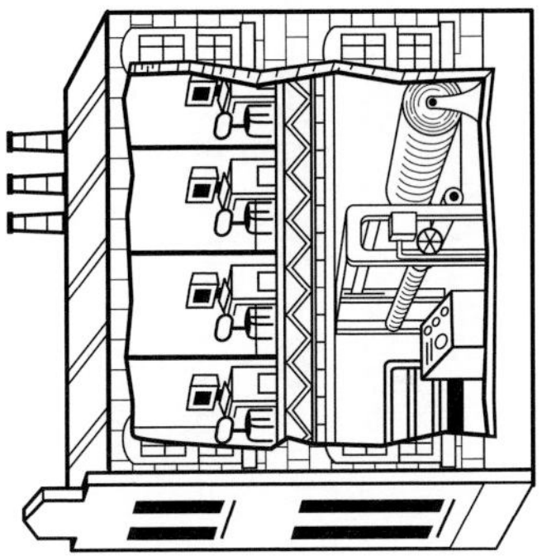

capital resource

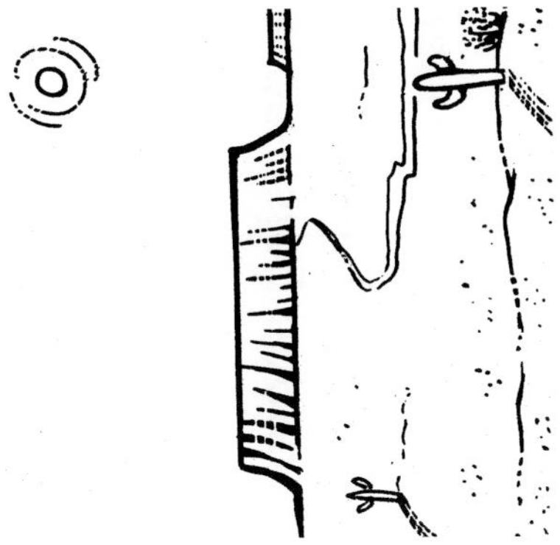

plateau

human resources

climate

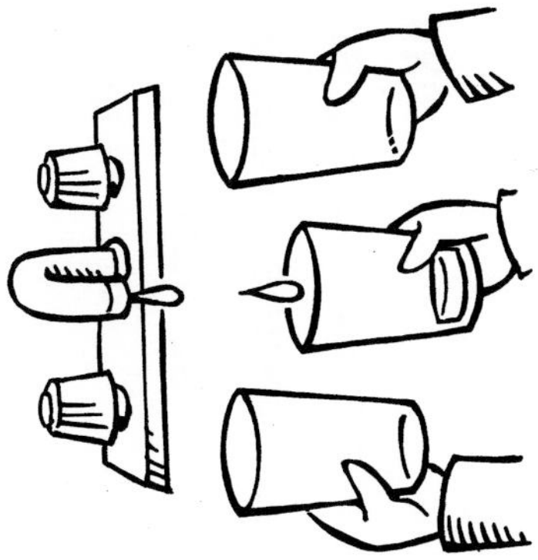

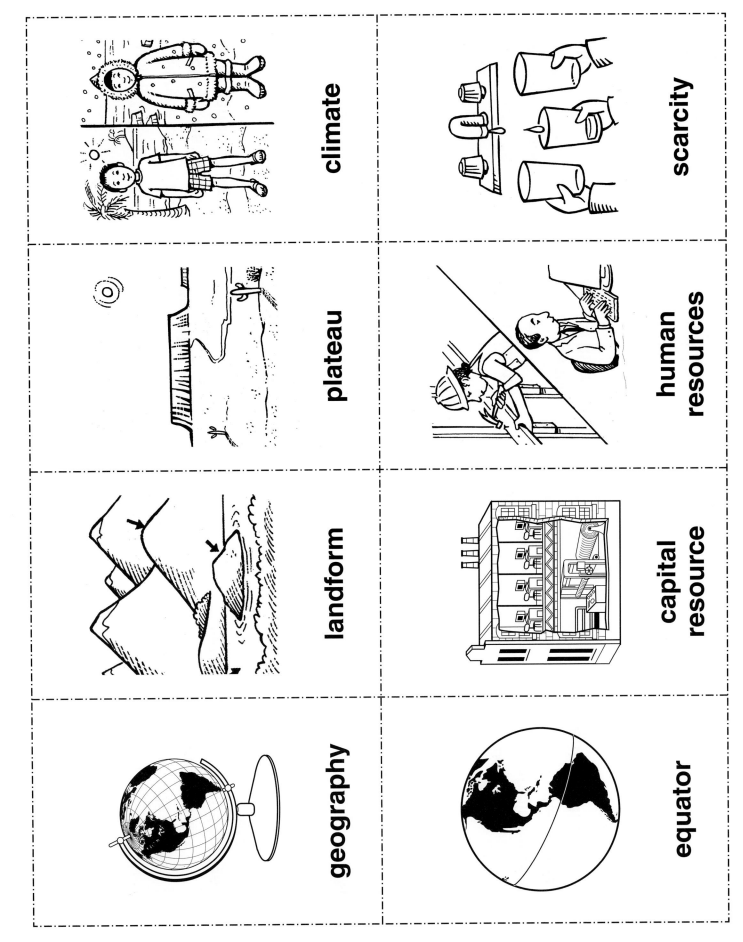

scarcity

Noun **The type of weather a place has over a long period of time.** (Chapter 1, Lesson 1)	*Noun* **A high, steep-sided area rising above the surrounding land.** (Chapter 1, Lesson 1)	*Noun* **A feature on the surface of the land.** (Chapter 1, Lesson 1)	*Noun* **The study of the world and the people and things that live there.** (Chapter 1, Lesson 1)
Noun **Not having as much of something as people would like.** (Chapter 1, Lesson 2)	*Noun* **People and the skills and knowledge they bring to their work.** (Chapter 1, Lesson 2)	*Noun* **A tool, machine, or building that people use to produce goods and services.** (Chapter 1, Lesson 2)	*Noun* **The imaginary line around the middle of the earth.** (Chapter 1, Lesson 1)

opportunity cost

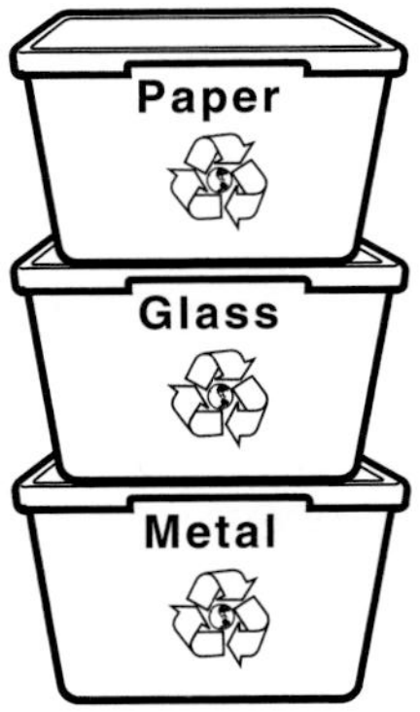

conservation

region

economy

specialization

consumer

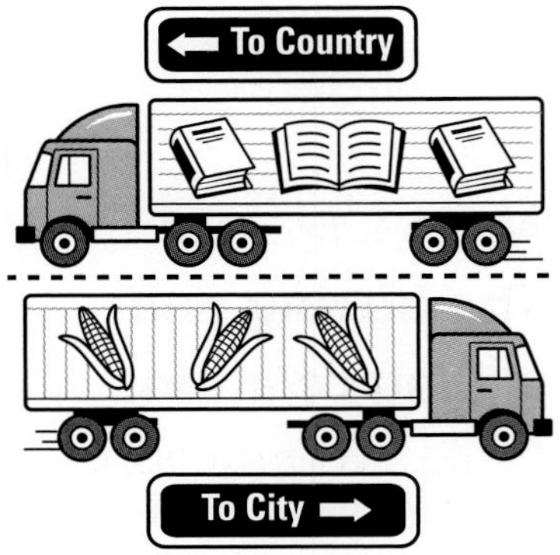

trade

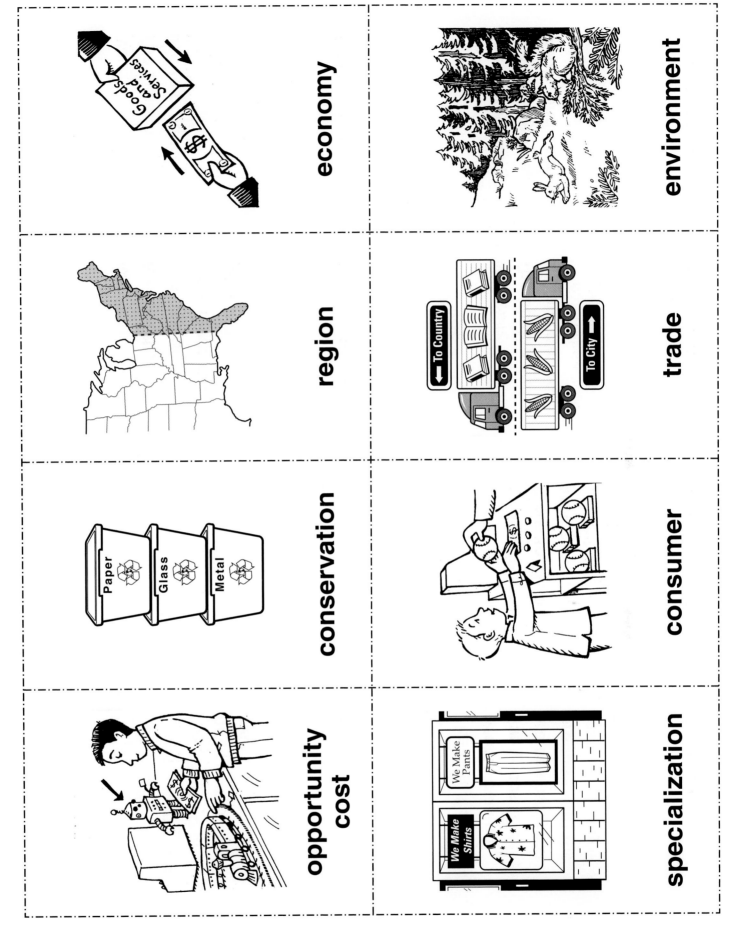

environment

Noun **The system people use to produce goods and services.** (Chapter 1, Lesson 3)	*Noun* **An area that has one or more features in common.** (Chapter 1, Lesson 3)	*Noun* **The protection and wise use of natural resources.** (Chapter 1, Lesson 2)	*Noun* **The thing you give up when you decide to do or have something else.** (Chapter 1, Lesson 2)
Noun **The surroundings in which people, plants, and animals live.** (Chapter 1, Lesson 3)	*Noun* **The buying and selling of goods.** (Chapter 1, Lesson 3)	*Noun* **Someone who buys goods and services.** (Chapter 1, Lesson 3)	*Noun* **The result of people making the goods they are best able to produce with the resources they have.** (Chapter 1, Lesson 3)

glacier

pueblo

ecosystem

civilization

pollution

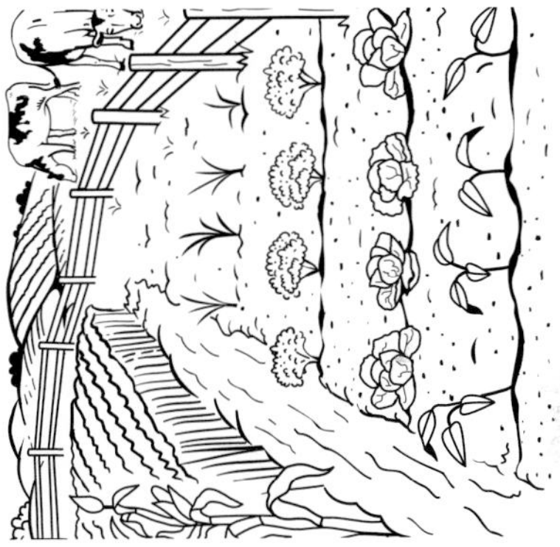

agriculture

erosion

migration

Noun **A huge, thick sheet of slowly moving ice.** (Chapter 2, Lesson 1)	*Noun* **A community of plants and animals, along with the surrounding soil, air, and water.** (Chapter 1, Lesson 4)	*Noun* **Anything that makes the soil, air, or water dirty and unhealthy.** (Chapter 1, Lesson 4)	*Noun* **The process by which water and wind wear away the land.** (Chapter 1, Lesson 4)
Noun **The Spanish word for town.** (Chapter 2, Lesson 1)	*Noun* **A group of people living together with organized systems of government, religion, and culture.** (Chapter 2, Lesson 1)	*Noun* **Farming or growing plants.** (Chapter 2, Lesson 1)	*Noun* **A movement from one place to another.** (Chapter 2, Lesson 1)

irrigation

nomad

clan

lodge

potlatch

ceremony

surplus

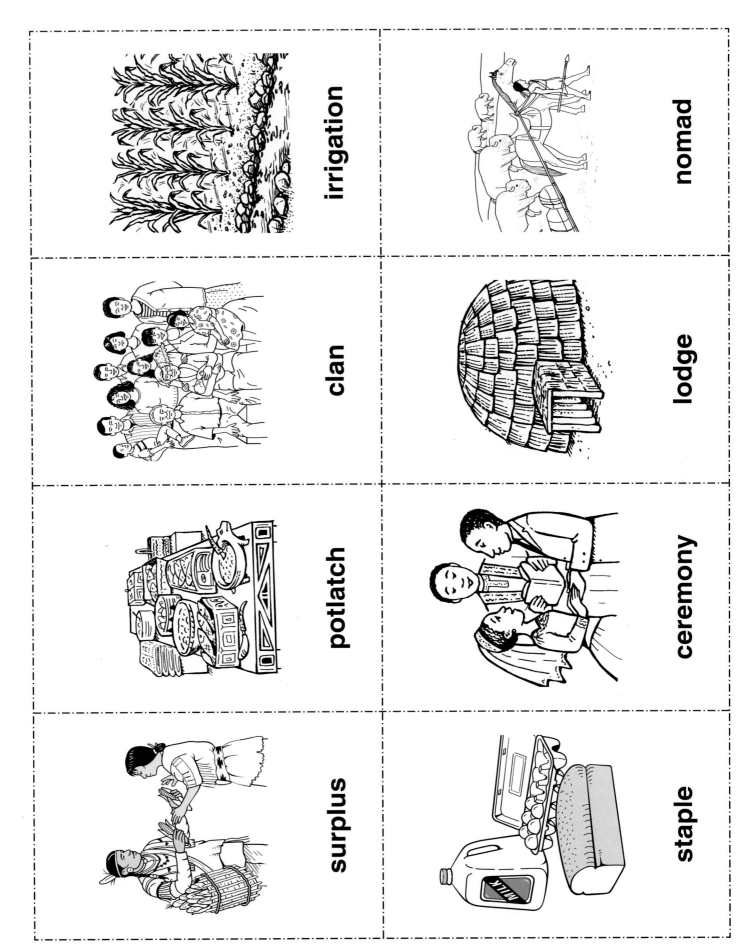

staple

Noun
A way of supplying water with streams, ditches, or pipes.

(Chapter 2, Lesson 3)

Noun
A group of related families.

(Chapter 2, Lesson 2)

Noun
A large feast that may last for several days.

(Chapter 2, Lesson 2)

Noun
Extra.

(Chapter 2, Lesson 2)

Noun
A person who moves around and does not live in one place.

(Chapter 2, Lesson 4)

Noun
A type of home that Plains Indians made using bark, earth, and grass.

(Chapter 2, Lesson 4)

Noun
An event at which people gather to express important beliefs.

(Chapter 2, Lesson 3)

Noun
A main crop.

(Chapter 2, Lesson 3)

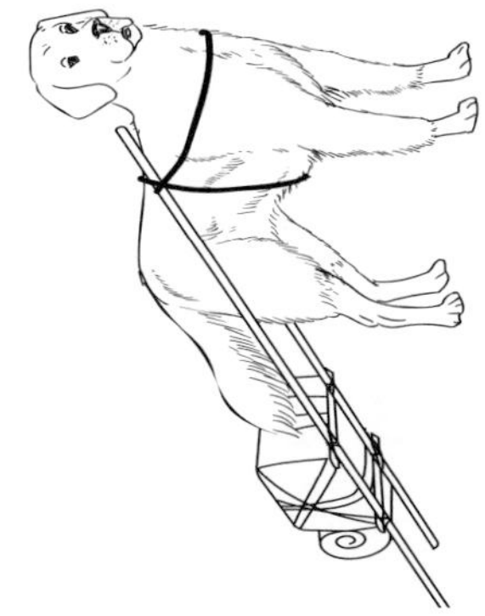

travois

longhouse

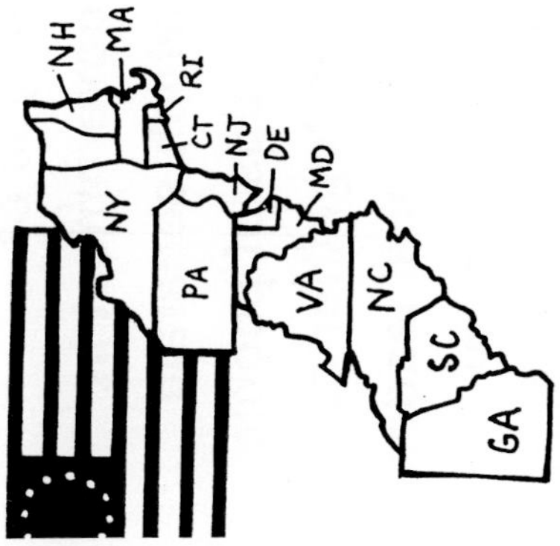

confederation

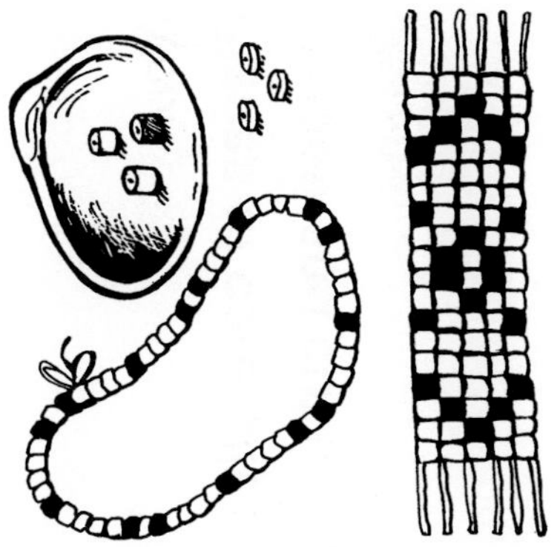

wampum

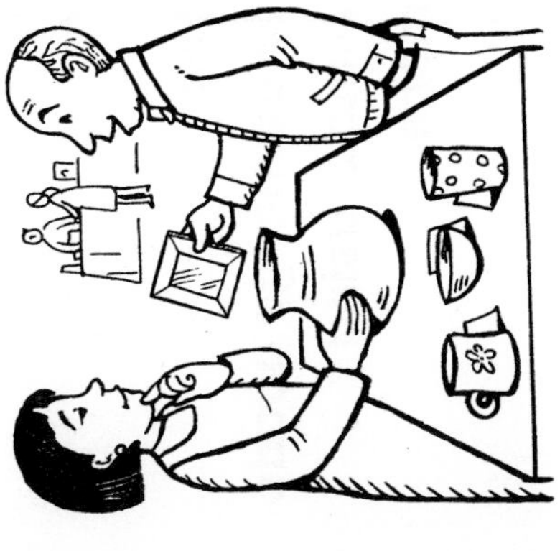

barter

merchant

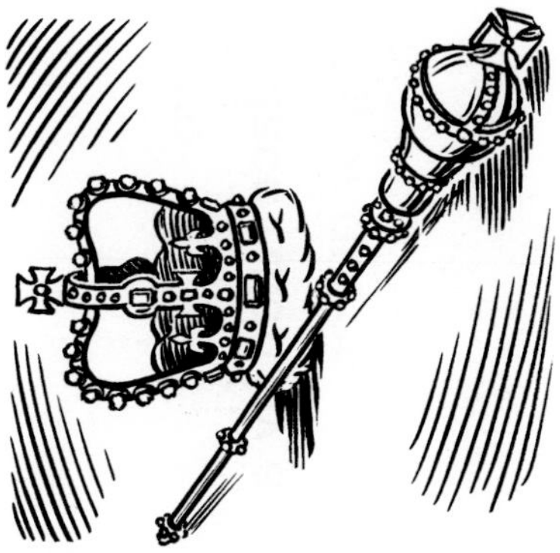

kingdom

caravan

Noun **Pieces of carefully shaped and cut seashell.** (Chapter 2, Lesson 5)	*Noun* **A type of government in which separate groups of people join together but allow local leaders to make many decisions for their group.** (Chapter 2, Lesson 5)	*Noun* **A large house made out of wooden poles and covered with bark.** (Chapter 2, Lesson 5)	*Noun* **Equipment similar to a sled that was made from two long poles and usually pulled by a dog.** (Chapter 2, Lesson 4)
Noun **A group of people and animals that travel together.** (Chapter 3, Lesson 1)	*Noun* **A place ruled by a king or queen.** (Chapter 3, Lesson 1)	*Noun* **Someone who buys and sells goods to earn money.** (Chapter 3, Lesson 1)	*Verb* **To exchange goods without using money.** (Chapter 2, Lesson 5)

technology

navigation

astrolabe

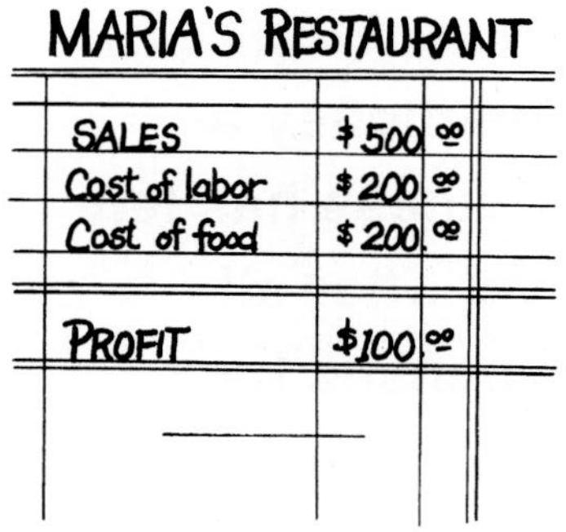
MARIA'S RESTAURANT
SALES $500.00
Cost of labor $200.00
Cost of food $200.00
PROFIT $100.00

profit

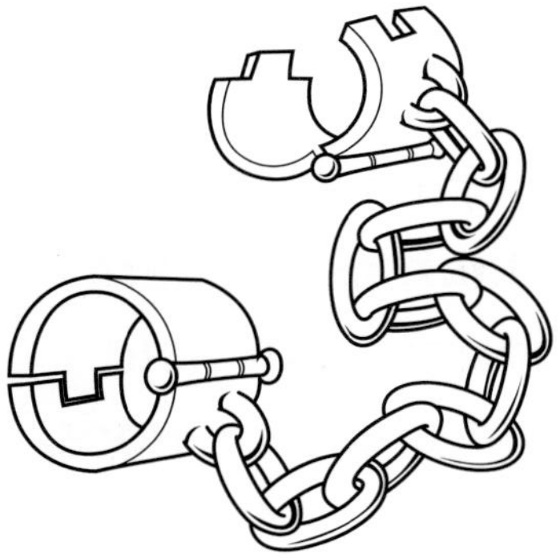

slavery

settlement

epidemic

circumnavigate

Noun
The money a business has left over after all expenses have been paid.

(Chapter 3, Lesson 2)

Noun
A tool that measures the height of the sun or a star above the horizon.

(Chapter 3, Lesson 2)

Noun
The science of planning and controlling the direction of a ship.

(Chapter 3, Lesson 2)

Noun
The use of scientific knowledge and tools to do things better and more rapidly.

(Chapter 3, Lesson 2)

Verb
To sail completely around something.

(Chapter 3, Lesson 3)

Noun
An outbreak of disease that spreads quickly and affects many people.

(Chapter 3, Lesson 3)

Noun
A small community of people living in a new place.

(Chapter 3, Lesson 3)

Noun
A cruel system in which people are bought and sold and made to work without pay.

(Chapter 3, Lesson 2)

expedition

conquistador

empire

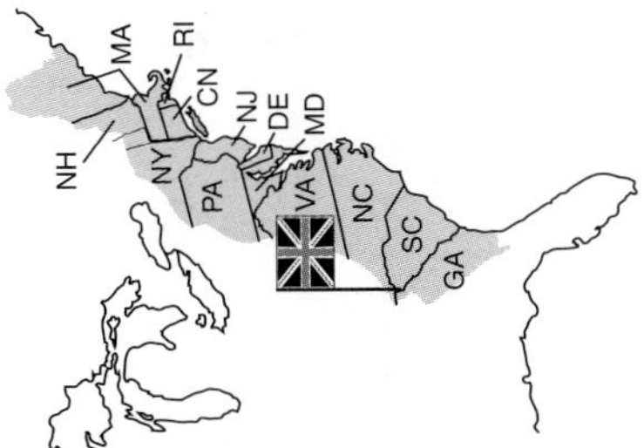

colony

mission

convert

hacienda

revolt

Noun **A territory ruled by another country.** (Chapter 3, Lesson 5)	*Noun* **Many nations or territories ruled by a single group or leader.** (Chapter 3, Lesson 4)	*Noun* **The Spanish word for conqueror.** (Chapter 3, Lesson 4)	*Noun* **A journey to achieve a goal.** (Chapter 3, Lesson 4)
Noun **A violent uprising.** (Chapter 3, Lesson 5)	*Noun* **A large farm or ranch, often with its own village and church.** (Chapter 3, Lesson 5)	*Verb* **To change a religion or a belief.** (Chapter 3, Lesson 5)	*Noun* **A religious community where priests taught Christianity.** (Chapter 3, Lesson 5)

claim

armada

invasion

charter

invest

stock

cash crop

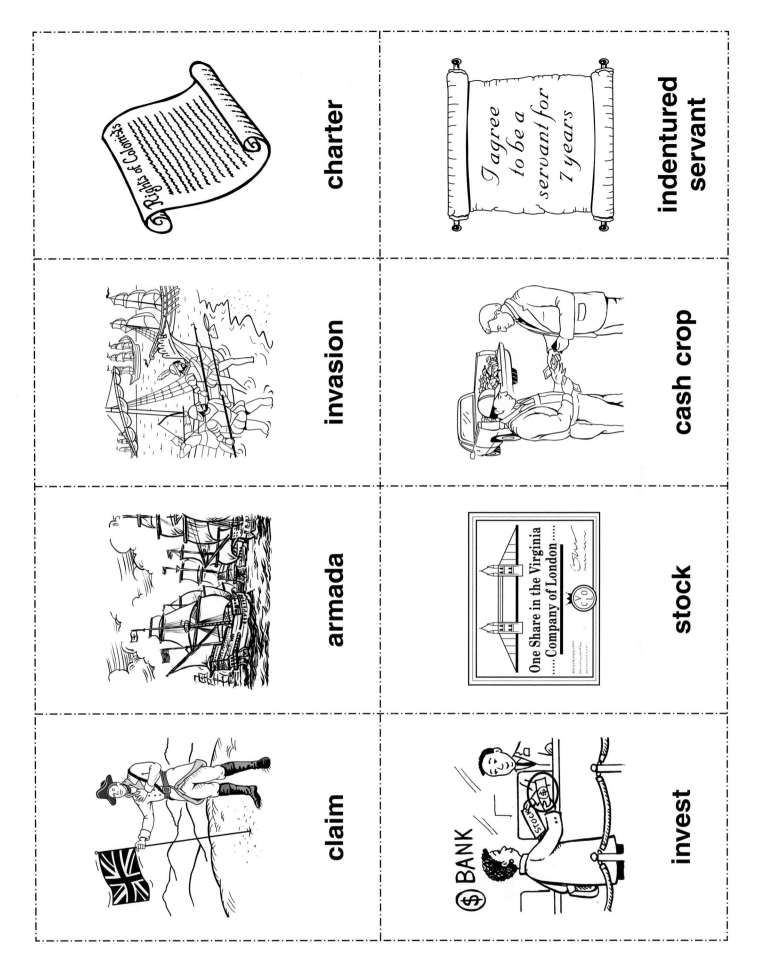

indentured servant

Noun **A document that gives certain freedoms to a person or group.** (Chapter 4, Lesson 2)	*Noun* **An attack by an armed force to conquer another country.** (Chapter 4, Lesson 1)	*Noun* **The Spanish word for a large fleet of ships.** (Chapter 4, Lesson 1)	*Noun* **Something declared as one's own, especially a piece of land.** (Chapter 4, Lesson 1)
Noun **Someone who agreed to work for a number of years in exchange for a trip to America.** (Chapter 4, Lesson 2)	*Noun* **A crop that people grow and sell to earn money.** (Chapter 4, Lesson 2)	*Noun* **A piece of ownership in a company.** (Chapter 4, Lesson 2)	*Verb* **To put money into something to try to make more money.** (Chapter 4, Lesson 2)

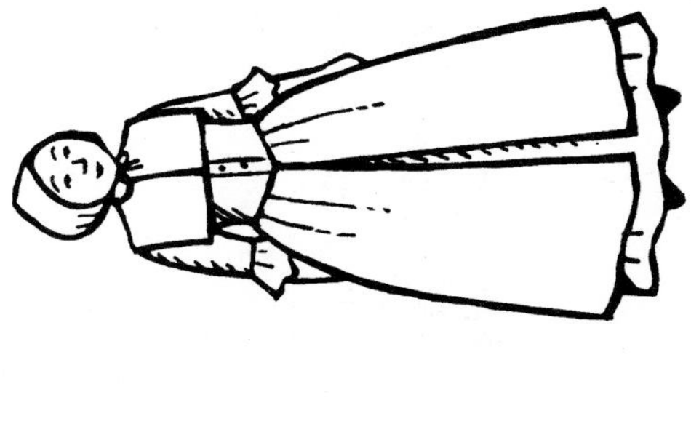

pilgrim

compact

cape

diversity

tolerance

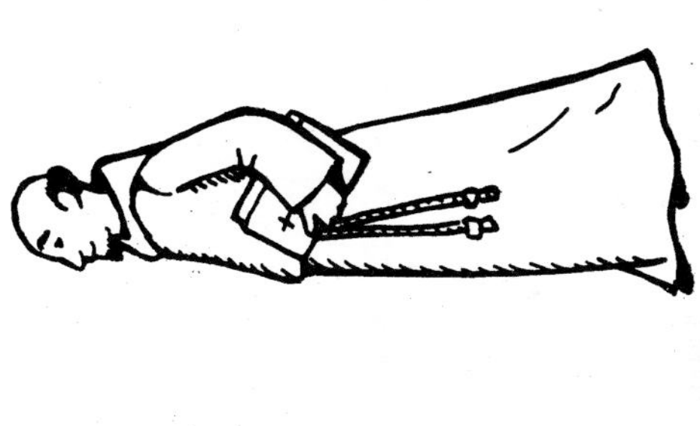

missionary

growing season

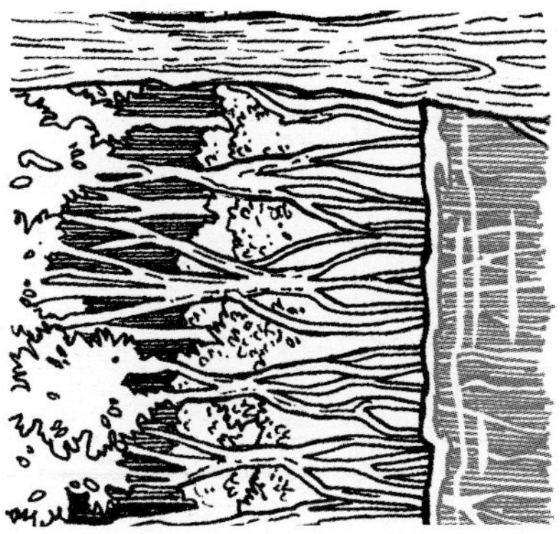

tidewater

Noun
The variety of people in a group.

(Chapter 4, Lesson 4)

Noun
A strip of land that stretches into a body of water.

(Chapter 4, Lesson 3)

Noun
An agreement.

(Chapter 4, Lesson 3)

Noun
A person who makes a long journey for religious reasons.

(Chapter 4, Lesson 3)

Noun
Where the water in rivers and streams rises and falls with the ocean's tides.

(Chapter 5, Lesson 1)

Noun
The time of year when it is warm enough for plants to grow.

(Chapter 5, Lesson 1)

Noun
A person who teaches his or her religion to others who have different beliefs.

(Chapter 4, Lesson 4)

Noun
The respect for beliefs that are different from one's own.

(Chapter 4, Lesson 4)

fall line

backcountry

town meeting

self-government

dissenter

banish

industry

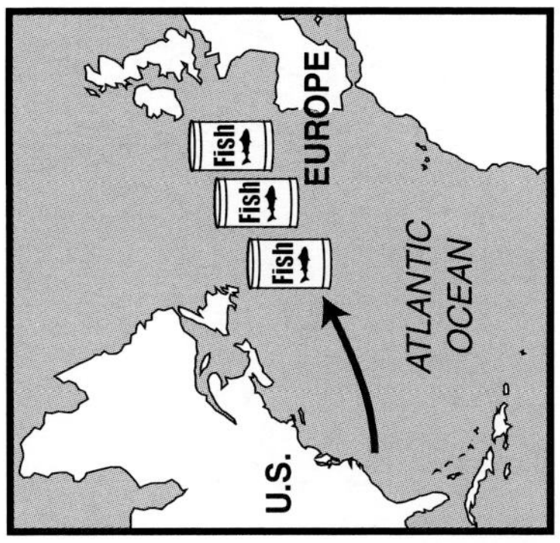

export

Noun

A form of government in which people who live in a place make laws for themselves.

(Chapter 5, Lesson 2)

Noun

A gathering at which colonists held elections and voted on the laws for their towns.

(Chapter 5, Lesson 2)

Noun

The land "in back of" the area where most colonists settled.

(Chapter 5, Lesson 1)

Noun

The line where rivers from higher land flow to lower land and often form waterfalls.

(Chapter 5, Lesson 1)

Noun

A product sent to another country and sold.

(Chapter 5, Lesson 3)

Noun

All the businesses that make one kind of product or provide one kind of service.

(Chapter 5, Lesson 3)

Verb

To force someone to leave a place.

(Chapter 5, Lesson 2)

Noun

A person who does not agree with the beliefs of his or her leaders.

(Chapter 5, Lesson 2)

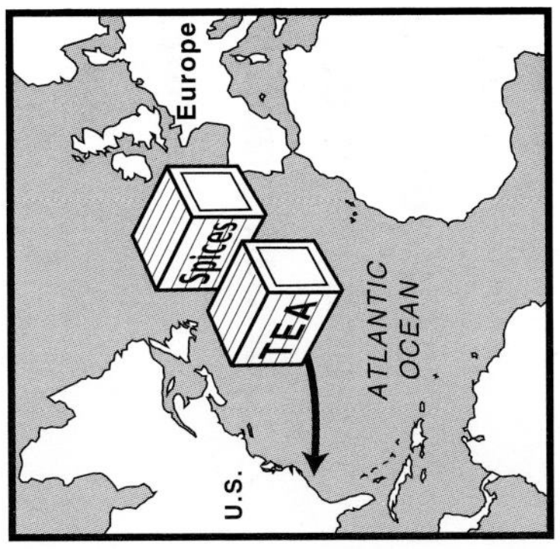

import

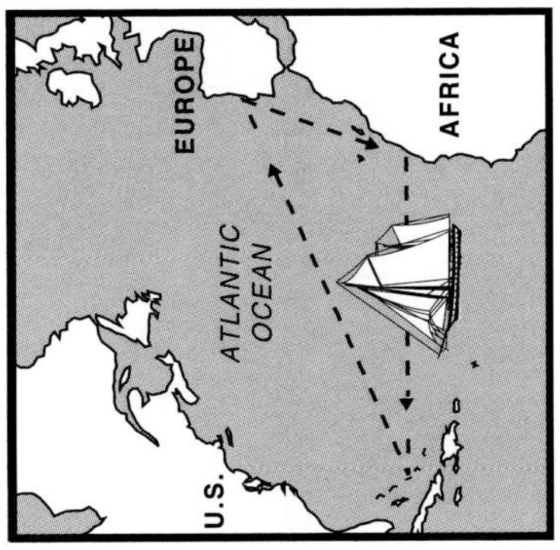

Middle Passage

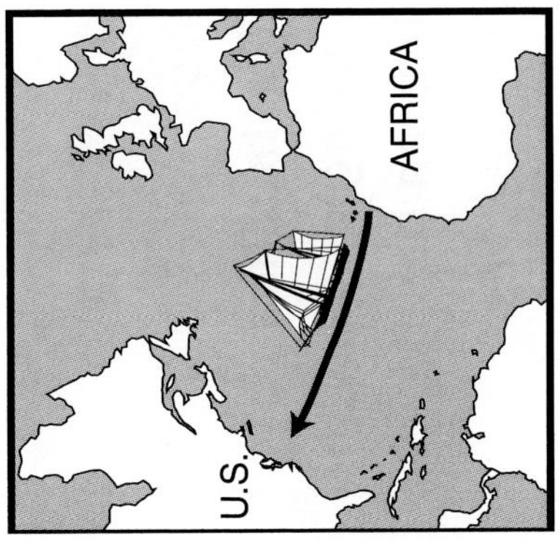

slave trade

proprietor

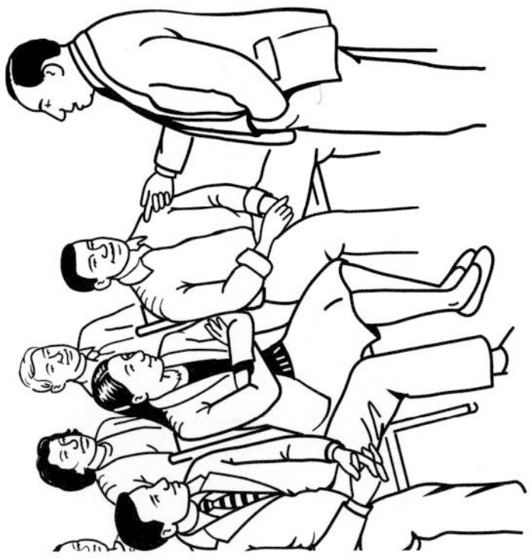

representative

treaty

free market economy

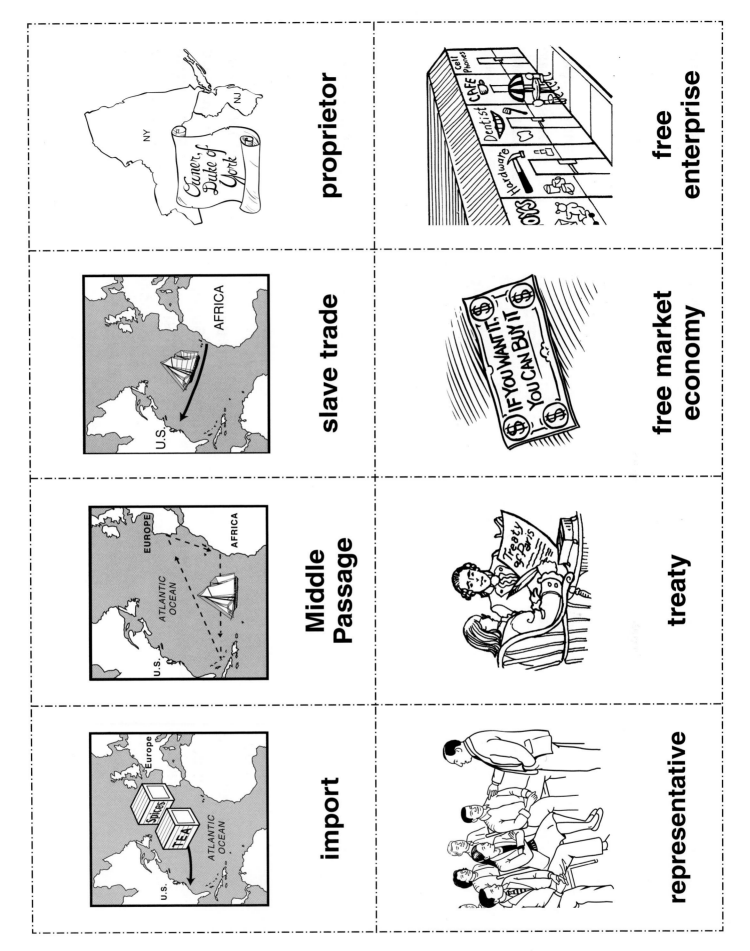

free enterprise

Noun
A person who owned and controlled all the land of a colony.
(Chapter 6, Lesson 1)

Noun
The business of buying and selling human beings.
(Chapter 5, Lesson 3)

Noun
The trip from Africa to the West Indies.
(Chapter 5, Lesson 3)

Noun
A good brought into one country from another.
(Chapter 5, Lesson 3)

Noun
A system in which people may start any business that they believe will succeed.
(Chapter 6, Lesson 2)

Noun
An economic system in which the people, not the government, decide what will be produced.
(Chapter 6, Lesson 2)

Noun
An official agreement between nations or groups.
(Chapter 6, Lesson 1)

Noun
Someone who is chosen to speak and act for others.
(Chapter 6, Lesson 1)

plantation

indigo

apprentice

debtor

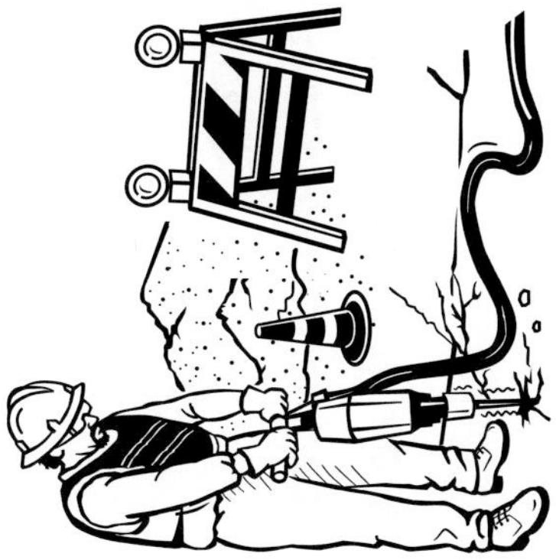

laborer

refuge

artisan

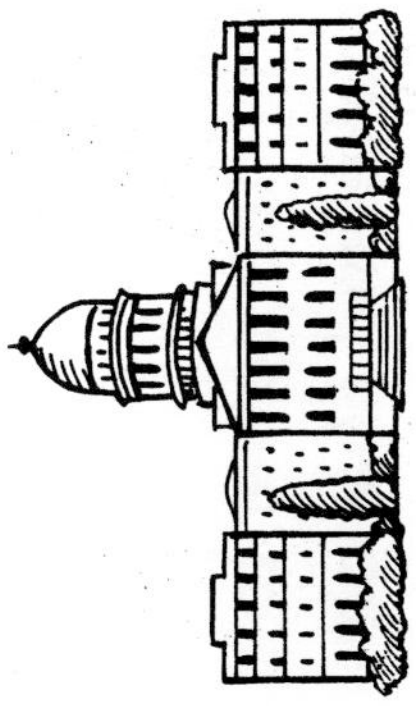

legislature

Noun
A large farm on which crops are raised by workers who live on the farm.

(Chapter 6, Lesson 3)

Noun
Someone who studies with a master to learn a skill or business.

(Chapter 6, Lesson 2)

Noun
A person who does hard physical work.

(Chapter 6, Lesson 2)

Noun
Someone who is skilled at making something by hand, such as silver spoons or wooden chairs.

(Chapter 6, Lesson 2)

Noun
A plant that can be made into a dark blue dye.

(Chapter 6, Lesson 4)

Noun
A person who owes money.

(Chapter 6, Lesson 3)

Noun
A safe place.

(Chapter 6, Lesson 3)

Noun
A group of people with the power to make and change laws.

(Chapter 6, Lesson 3)

overseer

spiritual

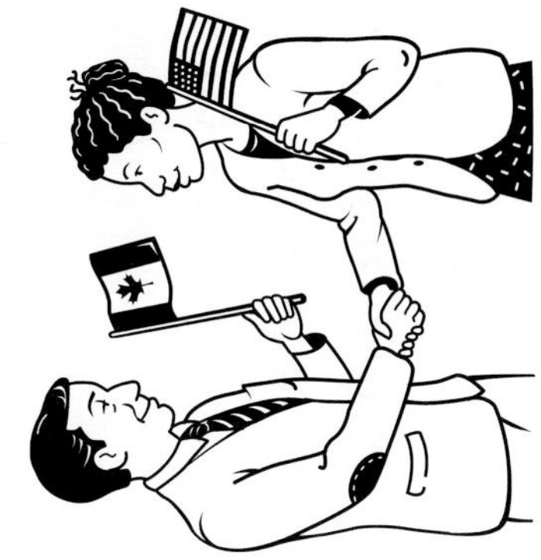

ally

congress

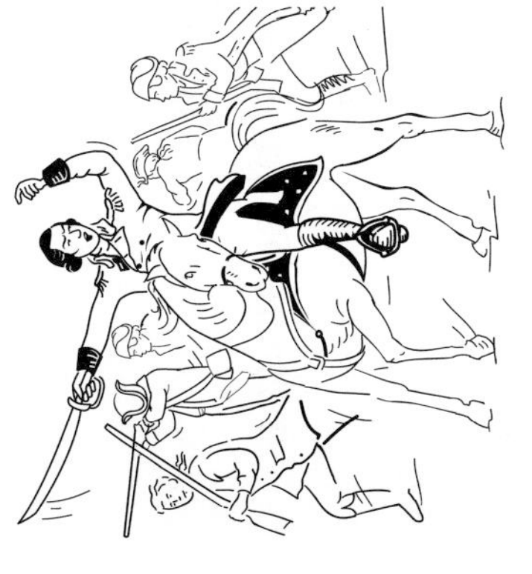

rebellion

proclamation

tax

smuggling

Noun
A group of representatives who meet to discuss a subject.
(Chapter 7, Lesson 1)

Noun
A person or group that joins with another to work toward a goal.
(Chapter 7, Lesson 1)

Noun
A religious song.
(Chapter 6, Lesson 4)

Noun
A person who watches and directs the work of other people.
(Chapter 6, Lesson 4)

Verb
Importing goods illegally.
(Chapter 7, Lesson 2)

Noun
Money that people pay to their government in return for services.
(Chapter 7, Lesson 2)

Noun
An official public statement.
(Chapter 7, Lesson 1)

Noun
A fight against a government.
(Chapter 7, Lesson 1)

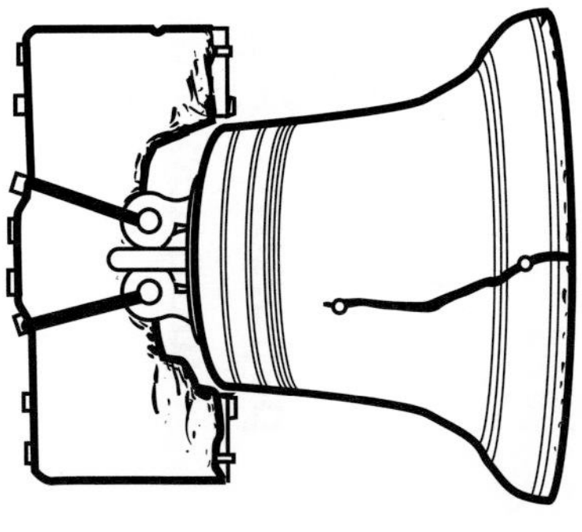

liberty

protest

boycott

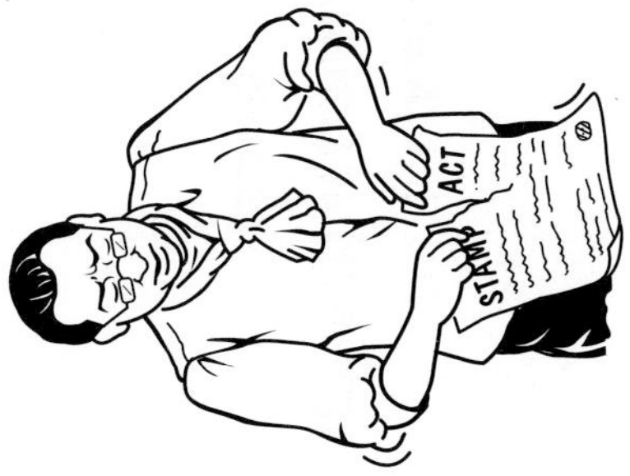

repeal

massacre

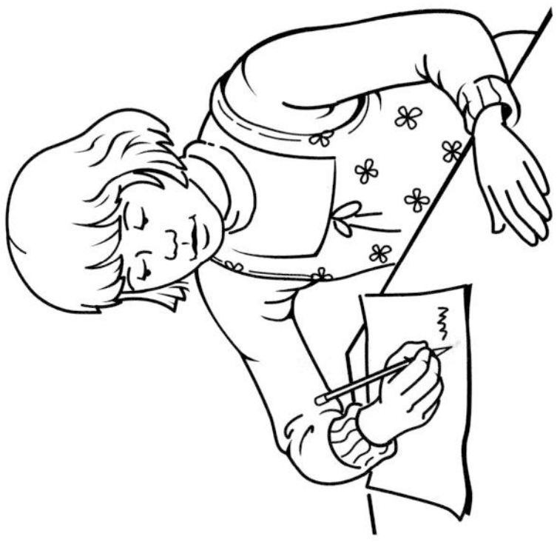

correspondence

quarter

delegate

Verb **To cancel something, such as a law.** (Chapter 7, Lesson 2)	*Noun* **The refusal to buy, sell, or use certain goods.** (Chapter 7, Lesson 2)	*Noun* **An event at which people complain about some issue.** (Chapter 7, Lesson 2)	*Noun* **Freedom from being controlled by another government.** (Chapter 7, Lesson 2)
Noun **Someone chosen to speak and act for others.** (Chapter 7, Lesson 3)	*Verb* **To give people food and shelter.** (Chapter 7, Lesson 3)	*Noun* **Written communication.** (Chapter 7, Lesson 3)	*Noun* **The killing of many people.** (Chapter 7, Lesson 3)

Patriot

militia

minutemen

commander

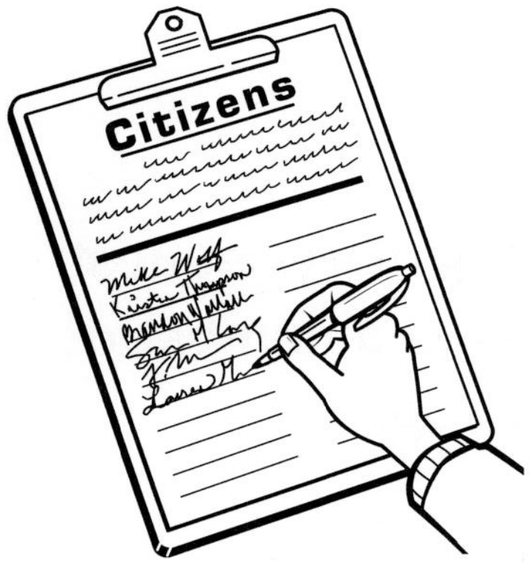

petition

independence

declaration

rights

Noun **The officer in charge of an army.** (Chapter 7, Lesson 4)	*Noun* **Militia with special training who had to be ready for battle at a minute's notice.** (Chapter 7, Lesson 4)	*Noun* **A group of ordinary people who train for battle.** (Chapter 7, Lesson 4)	*Noun* **A colonist who opposed British rule.** (Chapter 7, Lesson 4)
Noun **Freedoms that are protected by a government's laws.** (Chapter 8, Lesson 1)	*Noun* **A statement that declares, or announces, an idea.** (Chapter 8, Lesson 1)	*Noun* **Freedom from being ruled by someone else.** (Chapter 8, Lesson 1)	*Noun* **A written request from a number of people.** (Chapter 7, Lesson 4)

treason

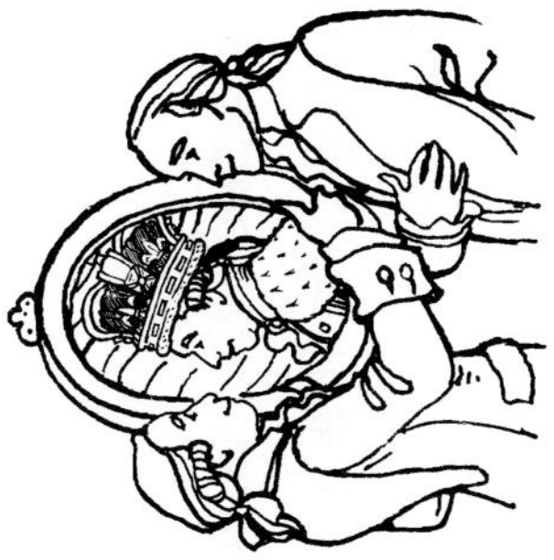

Loyalist

neutral

inflation

retreat

mercenary

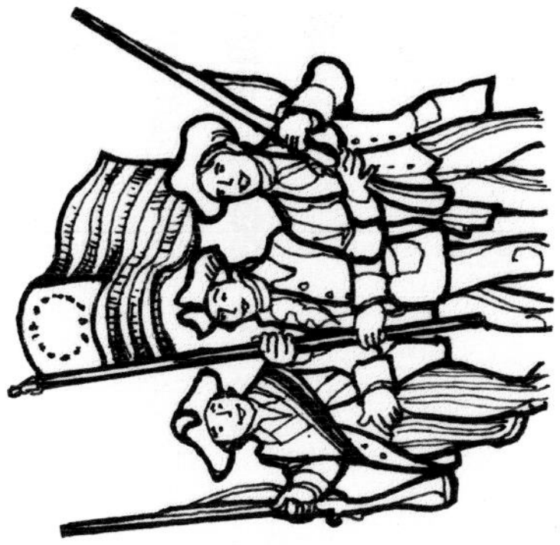

victory

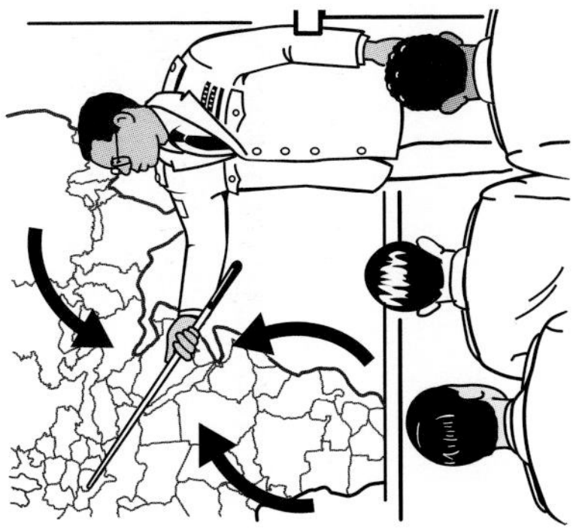

strategy

Noun
A rise in the price of goods.
(Chapter 8, Lesson 2)

Adjective
Not taking sides.
(Chapter 8, Lesson 2)

Noun
Someone who was still loyal to the king.
(Chapter 8, Lesson 2)

Noun
The crime of fighting against one's own government.
(Chapter 8, Lesson 1)

Noun
A plan of action.
(Chapter 8, Lesson 4)

Noun
The defeat of an enemy.
(Chapter 8, Lesson 3)

Noun
A soldier who is paid to fight for a foreign country.
(Chapter 8, Lesson 3)

Verb
To move away from the enemy.
(Chapter 8, Lesson 3)

traitor

surrender

constitution

citizen

territory

ordinance

federal

republic

Noun **An official member of a city, state, or nation.** (Chapter 9, Lesson 1)	*Noun* **A written plan for government.** (Chapter 9, Lesson 1)	*Verb* **To give up.** (Chapter 8, Lesson 4)	*Noun* **Someone who is not loyal.** (Chapter 8, Lesson 4)
Noun **A government in which the citizens elect leaders to represent them.** (Chapter 9, Lesson 2)	*Adjective* **A type of system in which the states share power with the central government.** (Chapter 9, Lesson 2)	*Noun* **A law.** (Chapter 9, Lesson 1)	*Noun* **Land that is ruled by a national government but has no representatives in the government.** (Chapter 9, Lesson 1)

compromise

ratify

democracy

checks and balances

veto

unconstitutional

amendment

inauguration

Noun **A system that lets each branch of government limit the power of the other two.** (Chapter 9, Lesson 3)	*Noun* **A government in which the people have the power to make political decisions.** (Chapter 9, Lesson 3)	*Verb* **To accept.** (Chapter 9, Lesson 2)	*Noun* **A way of settling a disagreement, in which both sides give up something they want.** (Chapter 9, Lesson 2)
Noun **The official ceremony to make someone President.** (Chapter 9, Lesson 4)	*Noun* **A change to the Constitution.** (Chapter 9, Lesson 3)	*Adjective* **When a law is not in agreement with the Constitution.** (Chapter 9, Lesson 3)	*Verb* **To reject.** (Chapter 9, Lesson 3)

Cabinet

political party

interest

capital

pioneer

frontier

flatboat

canal

Noun
A city where the government meets.

(Chapter 9, Lesson 4)

Noun
What people pay to borrow money.

(Chapter 9, Lesson 4)

Noun
A group of people who share similar ideas about government.

(Chapter 9, Lesson 4)

Noun
A group chosen by the President to help run the executive branch and give advice.

(Chapter 9, Lesson 4)

Noun
A waterway built for boat travel and shipping.

(Chapter 10, Lesson 1)

Noun
A large, rectangular boat partly covered by a roof.

(Chapter 10, Lesson 1)

Noun
The edge of a country or settled region.

(Chapter 10, Lesson 1)

Noun
One of the first of a group of people to enter or settle a region.

(Chapter 10, Lesson 1)